INSTRUCTOR'S ANNOTATED EDITION

SECOND EDITION

ESPACES

Rendez-vous avec le monde francophone

Cherie Mitschke

Cheryl Tano

VISTA
HIGHER LEARNING
Boston, Massachusetts

Publisher: José A. Blanco
Managing Editor: Rafael Ríos
Project Manager: Isabelle Alouane
Editors: Armando Brito, Mónica González, Aliza Krefetz
Technology Managing Editor: Paola Ríos Schaaf
Technology Editor: Christian Biagetti
Production and Design Director: Marta Kimball
Design Manager: Susan Prentiss
Design and Production Team: Manuela Arango, Sarah Cole, Oscar Díez, Natalia González, Mauricio Henao, Jhoany Jimenez, Sónia Teixeira, Nick Ventullo

Student Text ISBN: 978-1-60576-090-2
Instructor's Annotated Edition ISBN: 978-1-60576-094-0

1 2 3 4 5 6 7 8 9 RJ 14 13 12 11 10 09

Instructor's Annotated Edition

Table of Contents

The Vista Higher Learning Story

Your Specialized Foreign Language Publisher

Independent, specialized, and privately owned, Vista Higher Learning was founded in 2000 with one mission: to raise the teaching and learning of world languages to a higher level. This mission is based on the following beliefs:

- It is essential to prepare students for a world in which learning another language is a necessity, not a luxury.
- Language learning should be fun and rewarding, and all students should have the tools necessary for achieving success.
- Students who experience success learning a language will be more likely to continue their language studies both inside and outside the classroom.

With this in mind, we decided to take a fresh look at all aspects of language instructional materials. Because we are specialized, we dedicate 100 percent of our resources to this goal and base every decision on how well it supports language learning.

That is where you come in. Since our founding in 2000, we have relied on the continuous and invaluable feedback from language instructors and students nationwide. This partnership has proved to be the cornerstone of our success by allowing us to constantly improve our programs to meet your instructional needs.

The result? Programs that make language learning exciting, relevant, and effective through:

- an unprecedented access to resources
- a wide variety of contemporary, authentic materials
- the integration of text, technology, and media, and
- a bold and engaging textbook design

By focusing on our singular passion, we let you focus on yours.

The Vista Higher Learning Team

VISTA
HIGHER LEARNING

31 St. James Avenue Boston, MA 02116-4104 TOLLFREE: 800-618-7375
TELEPHONE: 617-426-4910 FAX: 617-426-5209 **www.vistahigherlearning.com**

Getting to Know the Second Edition of ESPACES

The Second Edition of **ESPACES** retains the highly successful underpinnings of the first edition. It takes a fresh, student-friendly approach to introductory French aimed at making students' learning and instructors' teaching easier, more enjoyable, and more successful. At the same time, **ESPACES** takes a communicative approach to language learning. It develops students' speaking, listening, reading, and writing skills so that they will be able to express their own ideas and interact with others meaningfully. It emphasizes frequently used vocabulary, and it presents grammar as a tool for effective communication. Finally, because cultural knowledge is an integral part of both language learning and successful communication, **ESPACES** introduces students to the everyday lives of French speakers, in France as well as in many areas and countries of the French-speaking world.

Whereas other introductory college French programs are based on many of these same pedagogical principles, **ESPACES** offers several additional features that make it truly different.

- **ESPACES** uses the interior design—page layout, colors, typefaces, and other graphic elements—as an integral part of the learning process. To enhance learning and make navigation easy, lesson sections are color-coded and appear either completely on one page or on spreads of two facing pages. The textbook pages themselves are also visually engaging, with an array of photos, drawings, realia, charts, graphs, diagrams, and word lists, all designed for both instructional impact and visual appeal.
- **ESPACES** integrates video with the student textbook in a distinct, more cohesive way up-front in each lesson's **Espace roman-photo** section, in one of the unit's **Espace culture** sections, and in the **Espace synthèse** section of the first lesson of every unit.
- **ESPACES** uses **Coup de main** boxes with on-the-spot linguistic, cultural, and language-learning information to help students get a fuller understanding of the point at hand, and it includes **ressources** boxes for every section with correlations to student supplements for additional practice.
- **ESPACES** integrates the grammar presentation and the practice activities in a more supportive way to facilitate learning. It provides students with immediate access to information essential for completing the practice by having each grammar explanation and its activities appear on one self-contained spread of two facing pages.
- **ESPACES** provides a unique four-part practice sequence for every grammar point. It moves from form-focused **Essayez!** activities to directed yet meaningful **Mise en pratique** activities to communicative, interactive **Communication** activities, and lastly to open-ended, re-entering activities in the **Espace synthèse** section.
- **ESPACES** incorporates groundbreaking technology to aid students' learning and to broaden instructors' teaching options. The **ESPACES** Supersite, powered by MAESTRO®, is where you and your students can access all of the textbook's multimedia (audio, video, TV commercials, and short films), plus a wealth of practice and Internet activities.

To get the most out of pages IAE-6 – IAE-16 in your Instructor's Annotated Edition, you should familiarize yourself with the following pages of the Student Text front matter: page iii (To the Student), pages xii–xxv (**ESPACES** At-A-Glance), pages xxvi–xxvii (Video Program), and pages xxviii–xxx (Icons, Integrated Technology, and Ancillaries).

Learning to Use Your Instructor's Annotated Edition

The Second Edition of **ESPACES** offers you a comprehensive, thoroughly developed Instructor's Annotated Edition (IAE). It features the student text pages slightly reduced and overprinted with answers to all activities with discrete responses. It also includes surrounding side and bottom panels that place a wealth of teaching resources at your fingertips. The panel annotations were written to complement and support varied teaching styles, to extend the already rich contents of the student textbook, and to save you time in class preparation and course management.

Because the **ESPACES** IAE is different from instructor's editions available with other French programs, this section is designed as a quick orientation to the principal types of instructor annotations it contains. As you familiarize yourself with them, it is important to know that the annotations are only suggestions. Any French questions, sentences, models, or simulated instructor-student exchanges are not meant to be prescriptive or limiting. You are encouraged to view these suggested "scripts" as flexible points of departure that will help you achieve your instructional goals.

On the Unit Opening Page

- **Unit Goals** A list of the lexical, grammatical, and socio-cultural goals of each unit, including language-learning strategies and skill-building techniques
- **Pour commencer** The answers to the **Pour commencer** activity in the student text
- **Instructional Resources** A correlation to all student and instructor supplements available to reinforce the unit

In the Side Panels

- **Section Goals** A list of the lexical, grammatical, and/or socio-cultural goals of the corresponding section
- **Instructional Resources** A correlation to all ancillaries
- **Suggestion** Teaching suggestions for leading into the corresponding section, working with on-page materials, and carrying out specific activities, as well as quick ways for starting classes or activities by recycling language or ideas
- **Expansion** Expansions and variations on activities
- **Script** Printed transcripts of the Textbook MP3 recordings for the **Mise en pratique** audio activity in each **Contextes** section and the **Stratégie** and **À vous d'écouter** features in each **À l'écoute** section
- **Video Recap** Questions or a true/false activity to help students recall the events of the previous lesson's **Roman-photo** episode
- **Video Synopsis** Summaries of the **Roman-photo** sections that recap that lesson's video module
- **Expressions utiles** Suggestions for introducing upcoming **Structures** grammar points incorporated into the **Roman-photo** episode

- **Stratégie** Suggestions for working with the listening, reading, and writing strategies presented in the **À l'écoute, Lecture,** and **Écriture** sections, respectively
- **Thème** Ideas for presenting and expanding the writing assignment topic in **Écriture**
- **Map-related Annotations** Suggestions for working with the maps in the **Panorama** sections
- **Le pays, la région, la province, l'archipel en chiffres** Additional information expanding on the data presented for each French-speaking area or country featured in the **Panorama** sections
- **Incroyable mais vrai!** Curious facts about a lesser-known aspect of the area or country featured in the **Panorama** sections
- **Section-specific Annotations** Suggestions for presenting, expanding, varying, and reinforcing individual instructional elements
- **Successful Language Learning** Tips and strategies to enhance students' language-learning experience

In the Options Boxes

- **Content-based Annotations With French Titles** More detailed information about an interesting aspect of the history, geography, culture, or peoples of the French-speaking world
- **Extra Practice, Pairs, and Small Groups** Activities in addition to those already in the student textbook
- **Game** Games that practice the language of the section and/or re-enter previously learned language
- **TPR** Total Physical Response activities that engage students physically in learning French
- **Cultural Comparison** Suggestions to help students compare the culture they are learning with their own culture
- **Avant de regarder la vidéo/Regarder la vidéo** Techniques and activities that can be used to prepare the students to view and work with the dramatic episodes of the **ESPACES** Video in the **Roman-photo** sections
- **Video** Suggestions for using the dramatic episodes of the **ESPACES** Video in the **Structures** sections
- **Proofreading Activity** Activities exclusive to the **Écriture** sections that guide students in the development of good proofreading skills. Each item contains errors related to a structure taught in the unit's **Structures** sections and/or a spelling rule taught in its **Les sons et les lettres** sections
- **Evaluation** Suggested rubrics in **Écriture** for grading students' writing efforts

Please check the **ESPACES** Supersite at **espaces.vhlcentral.com** for additional teaching support.

General Teaching Considerations

Orienting Students to the Student Textbook

Because the Second Edition of **ESPACES** treats interior and graphic design as an integral part of students' language-learning experience, you may want to take a few minutes to orient students to the student textbook. Have them flip through one unit, and point out that they are all organized exactly the same way with two short lessons and a concluding **Savoir-faire** section. Also point out how the major sections of each lesson are color-coded for easy navigation: blue for **Espace contextes**, green for **Espace roman-photo**, purple for **Espace culture**, orange for **Espace structures**, teal for **Espace synthèse**, red for **Savoir-faire**, and dark blue for **Vocabulaire**. Let them know that, because of these design elements, they can be confident that they will always know "where they are" in their textbook.

Emphasize that sections are self-contained, occupying either a full page or a spread of two facing pages, thereby eliminating "bad breaks" and the need to flip back and forth to do activities or to work with explanatory material. Finally, call students' attention to the use of color to highlight key information in elements such as charts, diagrams, word lists, activity models, titles, and help boxes such as **Attention!**, **Coup de main**, and **Boîte à outils**.

Flexible Lesson Organization

ESPACES uses a flexible lesson organization designed to meet the needs of diverse teaching styles, instructional goals, and institutional requirements. For example, you can begin with the unit opening page and progress sequentially through a unit. If you do not want to devote class time to grammar, you can assign the **Structures** explanations for outside study, freeing up class time for other purposes like developing oral communication skills; increasing awareness of Francophone television broadcasts; building listening, reading, or writing skills; learning more about the French-speaking world; or working with the video program. You might decide to work extensively with the **Savoir-faire** section in order to focus on students' reading and writing skills and their knowledge of the French-speaking world. On the other hand, you might prefer to skip these sections entirely, exploiting them periodically in response to your students' interests as the opportunity arises. If you plan on using the **ESPACES** Testing Program, however, be aware that, like the first edition, its tests and exams check language presented in **Contextes**, **Structures**, and the **Expressions utiles** boxes of **Roman-photo**.

Identifying Active Vocabulary

All words and expressions taught in the illustrations, **Vocabulaire** lists, and **Attention!** boxes in **Contextes** are considered active, testable vocabulary. The words and expressions in the **Expressions utiles** boxes in **Roman-photo**, as well as words in charts, word lists, and sample sentences in **Structures** are also part of the active vocabulary load. At the end of each unit, **Vocabulaire** provides a convenient one-page summary of the items students should know and that may appear on tests and exams. You will want to point this out to students. You might also tell them that an easy way to study from **Vocabulaire** is to cover up the French half of each section, leaving only the English equivalents exposed. They can then quiz themselves on the French items. To focus on the English equivalents of the French entries, they simply reverse this process.

Taking into Account the Affective Dimension

While many factors contribute to the quality and success rate of learning experiences, two factors are particularly germane to language learning. One is students' beliefs about how language is learned; the other is language-learning anxiety.

As studies show and experienced instructors know, students often come to modern languages courses either with a lack of knowledge about how to approach language learning or with mistaken notions about how to do so. For example, many students believe that making mistakes when speaking the target language must be avoided because doing so will lead to permanent errors. Others are convinced that learning another language is like learning any other academic subject. In other words, they believe that success is guaranteed, provided they attend class regularly, learn the assigned vocabulary words and grammar rules, and study for exams. In fact, in a study of college-level beginning language learners in the United States, over one-third of the participants thought that they could become fluent if they studied the language for only one hour a day for two years or less. Mistaken and unrealistic beliefs such as these can cause frustration and ultimately demotivation, thereby significantly undermining students' ability to achieve a successful language-learning experience.

Another factor that can negatively impact students' language-learning experiences is language-learning anxiety. As Professor Elaine K. Horwitz of The University of Texas at Austin and Senior Consulting Editor of **VISTAS**, First Edition, wrote, "Surveys indicate that up to one-third of American foreign language students feel moderately to highly anxious about studying another language. Physical symptoms of foreign language anxiety can include heart-pounding or palpitations, sweating, trembling, fast breathing, and general feelings of unease." The late Dr. Philip Redwine Donley, **VISTAS** co-author and author of articles on language-learning anxiety, spoke with many students who reported feeling nervous or apprehensive in their classes. They mentioned freezing when called on by their instructors or going inexplicably blank when taking tests. Some so dreaded their classes that they skipped them or dropped the course.

Based on what Vista Higher Learning learned from instructors and students using **VISTAS**, **AVENTURAS**, and its other successful introductory Spanish programs, **ESPACES** contains several features aimed at reducing students' language anxiety and supporting their successful language learning. First of all, the highly structured, visually dramatic interior design of the **ESPACES** student text was conceived as a learning tool to make students feel comfortable with the content and confident about navigating the lessons. The Instructor's Annotated Edition also includes *Successful Language Learning* annotations with suggestions for managing and/or reducing language-learning anxieties and for enhancing students' learning experiences. In addition, the student text provides on-the-spot **Attention!**, **Coup de main**, and **Boîte à outils** boxes that assist students by making immediately relevant connections with new information or reminding them of previously learned concepts.

ESPACES and *the Standards for Foreign Language Learning*

Since 1982, when the *ACTFL Proficiency Guidelines* were first published, that seminal document and its subsequent revisions have influenced the teaching of modern languages in the United States. **ESPACES** was written with the concerns and philosophy of the *ACTFL Proficiency Guidelines* in mind, incorporating a proficiency-oriented approach from its planning stages.

ESPACES' pedagogy was also informed from its inception by the *Standards for Foreign Language Learning in the 21st Century.* First published in 1996 under the auspices of the National Standards in Foreign Language Education Project, the Standards are organized into five goal areas, often called the Five Cs: Communication, Cultures, Connections, Comparisons, and Communities.

Since **ESPACES** takes a communicative approach to the teaching and learning of French, the Communication goal is central to the student text. For example, the diverse formats used in the **Communication** and **Révision** activities in each lesson—pair work, small group work, class circulation, information gap, task-based, and so forth—engage students in communicative exchanges, providing and obtaining information, and expressing feelings and emotions. The **À l'écoute** and **Écriture** sections also develop students' communication skills using listening prompts and writing tasks.

The Cultures goal is most overtly evident on four pages of each lesson: the **Espace roman-photo** and the **Espace culture** sections. It is also covered in the **Panorama** section at the end of each unit. However, **ESPACES** also weaves culture into virtually every page, exposing students to the multiple facets of practices, products, and perspectives of the French-speaking world. In keeping with the Connections goal, students can connect with other disciplines such as communications, business, geography, history, fine arts, and science in the **Le zapping** and **Panorama** sections; they can acquire information and recognize distinctive cultural viewpoints in the non-literary and literary texts of the **Lecture** sections. Moreover, **Sur Internet** boxes in **Espace culture** and **Panorama** support the Connections and Communities goals as students work through those sections and complete the related activities on the **ESPACES** Supersite. As for the Comparisons goal, it is reflected in **Les sons et les lettres** pronunciation and spelling sections and the **Structures** sections.

Special Standards icons also appear on the student text pages of your Instructor's Annotated Edition to call out sections that have a particularly strong relationship with the Standards. These are a few examples of how **ESPACES** was written with the Standards firmly in mind, but you will find many more as you work with the student textbook and its ancillaries.

General Suggestions for Using the ESPACES *Roman-photo* Video Episodes

The **Roman-photo** section in each of the student textbook's lessons and the **ESPACES** Video were created as interlocking pieces. All photos in **Roman-photo** are actual video stills from the corresponding video episode, while the printed conversations are abbreviated versions of the dramatic segment. Both the **Roman-photo** conversations and their expanded video versions represent comprehensible input at the discourse level; they were purposefully written to use language from the corresponding lesson's **Contextes** and **Structures** sections. Thus, as of **Leçon 1A**, they re-enter known language, preview grammar points students will study later in the lesson, and, in keeping with Krashen's concept of "i + 1," contain a small amount of unknown language.

Because the **Roman-photo** textbook sections and the dramatic episodes of the **ESPACES** Video are so closely connected, you may use them in many different ways. For instance, you can use **Roman-photo** as an advance organizer, presenting it before showing the video episode. You can also show the video episode first and follow up with **Roman-photo**. You can even use **Roman-photo** as a stand-alone, video-independent section.

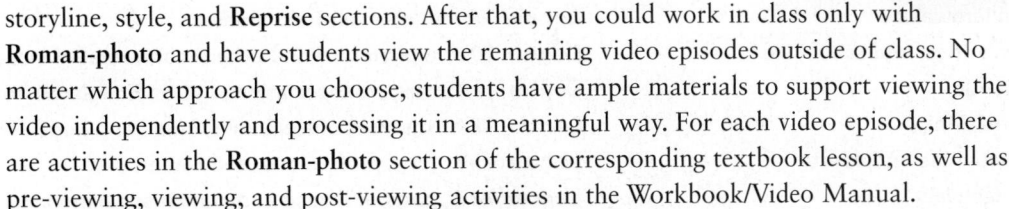

Depending on your teaching preferences and campus facilities, you might decide to show all video episodes in class or to assign them solely for viewing outside of the classroom. You could begin by showing the first one or two episodes in class to familiarize yourself and students with the characters, storyline, style, and **Reprise** sections. After that, you could work in class only with **Roman-photo** and have students view the remaining video episodes outside of class. No matter which approach you choose, students have ample materials to support viewing the video independently and processing it in a meaningful way. For each video episode, there are activities in the **Roman-photo** section of the corresponding textbook lesson, as well as pre-viewing, viewing, and post-viewing activities in the Workbook/Video Manual.

You might also want to use the **ESPACES** Video in class when working with the **Structures** sections. You could show selected scenes and ask students to identify certain grammar points.

You could also focus on the **Reprise** sections that appear at the end of each lesson's dramatic episode to summarize the key language functions and grammar points used. In class, you could play the parts of the **Reprise** section that exemplify individual grammar points as you progress through each **Structures** section. You could also wait until you complete a **Structures** section and review it and the lesson's **Contextes** section by showing the corresponding **Reprise** section in its entirety.

General Suggestions for Using the ESPACES *Flash culture* Video Episodes

The **Flash culture** video segments were specially planned and shot for **ESPACES** to bring France and the French-speaking world "alive" within the context of the themes in the textbook's units. The footage was selected for visual appeal and information of interest that both reinforces content presented in the textbook's lessons and goes beyond it. The segments are hosted by the **ESPACES** narrators, Csilla and Benjamin who alternate between odd-numbered and even-numbered segments, respectively. Csilla and Benjamin introduce each segment, provide transitions between topics, and, as appropriate, hold micro-interviews with French speakers whom they encounter as they visit parks, public squares, schools, stores, cafés, markets, and more.

Like the conversations in the **Roman-photo** dramatic episodes, the **Flash culture** narrations represent comprehensible input. Each was written to make the most of the vocabulary and grammar students learned in the corresponding and previous units while still providing a small amount of unknown language and/or cognates. In Units 1–7, the narrators begin the segments in English, but, as much as possible, use French that will be comprehensible to students to explain and describe the images shown. As of Unit 8, the **Flash culture** segments are entirely in French.

Each segment is approximately two-to-three minutes long and is correlated in the TOC of the **ESPACES** student text to the appropriate **Espace culture** section of each unit.

Flash culture Video Segments Table of Contents

Leçon 1A: greetings and farewells
Leçon 2A: colleges, universities, and school life
Leçon 3A: family and friends
Leçon 4B: cafés, food, and drink
Leçon 5A: leisure-time activities and sports
Leçon 6A: holidays and festivals
Leçon 7A: travel and vacation-related activities
Leçon 8A: apartments, homes, and other types of housing
Leçon 9A: an open-air food market
Leçon 10B: a pharmacy and other health-related locations
Leçon 11B: cars, transportation, and traffic-related items
Leçon 12A: the post office, banks, small and large stores
Leçon 13B: jobs, professions, and careers
Leçon 14B: parts of France and French-speaking countries
Leçon 15A: films, documentaries, books, magazines, and newspapers

Activities for the **Flash culture** video are located in the Video Manual section of the **ESPACES** Workbook/Video Manual. They follow a process approach of pre-viewing, viewing, and post-viewing and use a variety of formats to prepare students for watching the video segments, to focus them while watching, and to check comprehension after they have watched the footage.

When showing the **Flash culture** video segments in your classes, you might also want to implement a process approach. You could start with an activity that prepares students for the video segment by taking advantage of what they learned in the lesson. This could be followed by an activity that students do while you play parts of or the entire video segment.

The final activity, done in the same class period or in the next one as warm-up, could recap what students saw and heard and move beyond the video segment's topic. The following suggestions for working with the **Flash culture** video segments in class, which are in addition to those on the individual pages of the Instructor's Annotated Edition, can be carried out as described or expanded upon in any number of ways.

Before viewing

- Ask students to guess what the segment might be about based on what they've learned about the lesson's theme, especially in the **Contextes**, **Roman-photo**, and **Culture** sections.
- Have pairs make a list of the unit vocabulary they expect to hear in the video segment.
- Read a list of true-false or multiple-choice questions about the video to the class. Students must use what they learned over the lesson to guess the answers. Confirm their guesses after watching the segment.

While viewing

- Show the video segment with the audio turned off and ask students to use unit vocabulary and structures to describe what they see. Have them confirm their guesses by showing the segment again with the audio on.
- Have students refer to the list of words they brainstormed before viewing the video and put a check in front of any words they actually hear or see in the segment.
- First, have students simply watch the video. Then, show it again and ask students to take notes on what they see and hear. Finally, have them compare their notes in pairs or groups for confirmation.
- Download and print the segment's videoscript from the Instructor's Resource Manual found on the Supersite and white out words and expressions related to the lesson theme. Distribute the scripts for pairs or groups to complete as cloze paragraphs.
- Show the video segment before moving on to **Contextes** to jump-start the lesson's vocabulary, grammar, and cultural focus. Have students tell you what vocabulary and grammar they recognize from previous lessons.

After viewing

- Have students say what aspects of the information presented in the corresponding textbook lesson are observable in the video segment.
- Ask groups to write a brief summary of the content of the video segment. Have them exchange papers with another group for peer editing.
- Have students pick one new aspect of the corresponding textbook lesson's cultural theme that they learned about from watching the video segment. Have them research more about that topic and write a list or paragraph to expand on it.

About Le zapping and À l'écoute

One of two features appears at the end of each textbook lesson: **Le zapping** or **À l'écoute**. **Le zapping** features TV commercials, presentations of various aspects of the city of Rennes, France, and short films, so your students can experience the language and culture contained in authentic television pieces. **À l'écoute** is a listening skill-building feature. It contains a strategy with its own audio track and activity to practice the particular suggestion. The feature takes a process approach to listening. It focuses on how the students work by dividing the activity sequence into three parts: pre-listening (**Préparation**), listening (**À vous d'écouter**), and post-listening (**Compréhension**) activities. The following convenient lists of commercials, short films, and listening topics are organized by unit and lesson for your reference.

Le zapping TV Clips and Short Films

Unité 1	**Leçon 1A**	(23 seconds) *Moulinex*
Unité 2	**Leçon 2A**	(25 seconds) *Clairefontaine*
Unité 3	**Leçon 3A**	(31 seconds) *Pages d'Or*
Unité 4	**Leçon 4A**	(1' 02 seconds) *SWISS*
Unité 5	**Leçon 5A**	(34 seconds) *SwissLife*
Unité 6	**Leçon 6A**	(31 seconds) *La Poste belge*
Unité 7	**Leçon 7A**	(30 seconds) *TER*
Unité 8	**Leçon 8A**	(30 seconds) *Century 21 France*
Unité 9	**Leçon 9A**	(1' 45 seconds) *Le far breton*
Unité 10	**Leçon 10A**	(24 seconds) *Diadermine*
Unité 11	**Leçon 11A**	(32 seconds) *KellyMobile*
Unité 12	**Leçon 12A**	(4' 40 seconds) *Rennes*
Unité 13	**Leçon 13A**	(16' 51 seconds) *Mi-Temps*
Unité 14	**Leçon 14A**	(1' 20 seconds) *BMCE*
Unité 15	**Leçon 15A**	(8' 21 seconds) *La tartine*

À l'écoute Sections

Unité 1	**Leçon 1B**	*Listen to some students greet each other.*
Unité 2	**Leçon 2B**	*Listen to some students talk about their schedules.*
Unité 3	**Leçon 3B**	*Listen to a conversation between friends.*
Unité 4	**Leçon 4B**	*Listen to customers order in a café.*
Unité 5	**Leçon 5B**	*Listen to a weather broadcast.*
Unité 6	**Leçon 6B**	*Listen to a conversation in a boutique.*
Unité 7	**Leçon 7B**	*Listen to a travel ad.*
Unité 8	**Leçon 8B**	*Listen to a real estate consultation.*
Unité 9	**Leçon 9B**	*Listen to a cooking show.*
Unité 10	**Leçon 10B**	*Listen to how two friends stay healthy.*
Unité 11	**Leçon 11B**	*Listen to a police officer enforce traffic laws.*
Unité 12	**Leçon 12B**	*Listen to friends giving directions.*
Unité 13	**Leçon 13B**	*Listen to a job interview.*
Unité 14	**Leçon 14B**	*Listen to a speech about the environment.*
Unité 15	**Leçon 15B**	*Listen to the review of a play.*

About strategies in À l'écoute, Lecture, and Écriture

The Second Edition of **ESPACES** takes a process approach to the development of listening, reading, and writing skills. These are lists of the different strategies taught in each unit so that you may refer to them in one convenient place.

À l'écoute

Unité 1	**Leçon 1B**	Listening for words you know
Unité 2	**Leçon 2B**	Listening for cognates
Unité 3	**Leçon 3B**	Asking for repetition / Replaying the recording
Unité 4	**Leçon 4B**	Listening for the gist
Unité 5	**Leçon 5B**	Listening for key words
Unité 6	**Leçon 6B**	Listening for linguistic cues
Unité 7	**Leçon 7B**	Recognizing the genre of spoken discourse
Unité 8	**Leçon 8B**	Using visual cues
Unité 9	**Leçon 9B**	Jotting down notes as you listen
Unité 10	**Leçon 10B**	Listening for specific information
Unité 11	**Leçon 11B**	Guessing the meaning of words through context
Unité 12	**Leçon 12B**	Using background information
Unité 13	**Leçon 13B**	Using background knowledge / Listening for specific information
Unité 14	**Leçon 14B**	Listening for the gist / Listening for cognates
Unité 15	**Leçon 15B**	Listening for key words / Using the context

Lecture

Unité 1	Recognizing cognates
Unité 2	Predicting content through formats
Unité 3	Predicting content from visuals
Unité 4	Scanning
Unité 5	Skimming
Unité 6	Recognizing word families
Unité 7	Predicting content from the title
Unité 8	Guessing meaning from context
Unité 9	Reading for the main idea
Unité 10	Activating background knowledge
Unité 11	Recognizing the purpose of a text
Unité 12	Identifying point of view
Unité 13	Summarizing a text in your own words
Unité 14	Recognizing chronological order
Unité 15	Making inferences and recognizing metaphors

Écriture

Unité 1	Writing in French
Unité 2	Brainstorming
Unité 3	Using idea maps
Unité 4	Adding details
Unité 5	Using a dictionary
Unité 6	How to report an interview
Unité 7	Making an outline
Unité 8	Mastering the simple past tenses
Unité 9	Expressing and supporting opinions
Unité 10	Sequencing events
Unité 11	Listing key words
Unité 12	Using linking words
Unité 13	Using note cards
Unité 14	Considering audience and purpose
Unité 15	Writing strong introductions and conclusions

COURSE PLANNING

The entire **ESPACES** program was developed with an eye to flexibility and ease of use in a wide variety of course configurations. Likewise, the Second Edition of **ESPACES** can be used in courses taught on semester or quarter systems, and in courses that complete the book in two or three semesters. Here are some sample course plans that illustrate how the Second Edition of **ESPACES** can be used in different academic situations. You should, of course, feel free to organize your courses in the way that best suits your students' needs and your instructional objectives.

Two-Semester System

The following chart illustrates how **ESPACES** can be completed in a two-semester course. This division of material allows the present tense, the near future, the **passé composé** with **avoir** and **être**, and the imperfect to be presented in the first semester; the second semester focuses on the **passé composé** vs. the imperfect, the conditional, the future, and the present subjunctive.

Semester 1	Semester 2
Units 1–7	Units 8–15

Three-Semester or Quarter System

This chart shows how **ESPACES** can be used in a three-semester or quarter course. The units are equally divided over each semester/quarter, allowing students to absorb the material at a steady pace.

Semester/Quarter 1	Semester/Quarter 2	Semester/Quarter 3
Units 1–5	Units 6–10	Units 11–15

Lesson Plans

Lesson plans for each unit of the Second Edition of **ESPACES** are available on the instructor's part of the **ESPACES** Supersite at **espaces.vhlcentral.com**. You will find plans for the two lessons in each unit, as well as each end-of-unit **Savoir-faire** section. The lesson plans are not prescriptive. You should feel free to present lesson materials as you see fit, tailoring them to your own teaching preferences and to your students' learning styles. You may, for example, want to allow extra time for concepts students find challenging. You may want to allot less time to topics they comprehend without difficulty or to group topics together when making assignments. Based on your students' needs and the contact hours of your course, you may want to omit certain topics or activities altogether. It is our hope that you will find the **ESPACES** program very flexible: simply pick and choose from its array of instructional resources and sequence them in the way that makes the most sense for your course.

SECOND EDITION

ESPACES

Rendez-vous avec le monde francophone

Cherie Mitschke

Cheryl Tano

VISTA HIGHER LEARNING

Boston, Massachusetts

Publisher: José A. Blanco
Managing Editor: Rafael Ríos
Project Manager: Isabelle Alouane
Editors: Armando Brito, Mónica González, Aliza Krefetz
Technology Managing Editor: Paola Ríos Schaaf
Technology Editor: Christian Biagetti
Production and Design Director: Marta Kimball
Design Manager: Susan Prentiss
Design and Production Team: Manuela Arango, Sarah Cole, Oscar Díez, Natalia González, Mauricio Henao, Jhoany Jimenez, Sónia Teixeira, Nick Ventullo

Student Text ISBN: 978-1-60576-090-2
Instructor's Annotated Edition ISBN: 978-1-60576-094-0

1 2 3 4 5 6 7 8 9 RJ 14 13 12 11 10 09

TO THE STUDENT

Welcome to the **Second Edition** of **ESPACES**, an introductory French program from Vista Higher Learning. In French, the word **espaces** means *spaces* in the sense of spaces reserved for a particular purpose. The spaces in **ESPACES** are its major sections, and they are reserved for helping you learn French and explore the cultures of the French-speaking world in the most user-friendly way possible. In light of this goal, here are some of the features you will encounter in **ESPACES**.

- A unique, easy-to-navigate design built around color-coded sections that appear either completely on one page or on two facing pages
- Abundant illustrations, photos, charts, graphs, diagrams, and other graphic elements, all created or chosen to help you learn
- Integration of a specially shot video in each lesson of the student text
- Clear, concise grammar explanations in an innovative format, which support you as you work through the practice activities
- Practical, high-frequency vocabulary for use in real-life situations
- Abundant guided vocabulary and grammar exercises to give you a solid foundation for communicating in French
- An emphasis on communicative interactions with a classmate, small groups, the whole class, and your instructor
- Systematic development of reading, writing, and listening skills, incorporating learning strategies and a process approach
- A rich, contemporary cultural presentation of the everyday life of French speakers and the diverse cultures of the countries and areas of the entire French-speaking world
- Exciting integration of culture and multimedia, through TV commercials and short films thematically linked to each unit
- A full set of completely integrated print and technology ancillaries to make learning French easier
- Built-in correlation of all ancillaries, right down to the page numbers

ESPACES has fifteen units with two lessons in each unit, followed by an end-of-unit **Savoir-faire** section and a list of active vocabulary. To familiarize yourself with the textbook's organization, features, and ancillary package, turn to page xii and take the **ESPACES**-at-a-glance tour.

TABLE OF CONTENTS

(Flash culture) means that there is a ***Flash culture*** video on the Supersite for that lesson.

espace structures

espace synthèse

savoir-faire

TABLE OF CONTENTS

TABLE OF CONTENTS

UNITÉ 9

La nourriture

UNITÉ 10

La santé

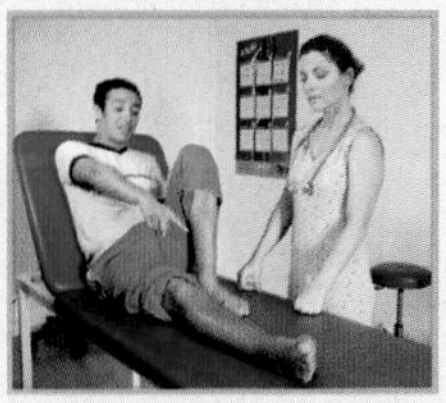

UNITÉ 11

La technologie

UNITÉ 12

En ville

TABLE OF CONTENTS

Appendices

espace structures	espace synthèse	savoir-faire

UNIT OPENERS

outline the content and features of each unit.

La famille et les copains

UNITÉ **3**

Pour commencer

- Combien de personnes y a-t-il?
- Où sont ces personnes?
- Que font-elles?
- Ont-elles l'air agréables ou désagréables?

Pour commencer activities jump-start the units, allowing you to use the French you know to talk about the photos.

Content thumbnails break down each unit into its two lessons and one **Savoir-faire** section, giving you an at-a-glance summary of the vocabulary, grammar, cultural topics, and language skills on which you will focus.

ESPACE CONTEXTES

presents and practices vocabulary in meaningful contexts.

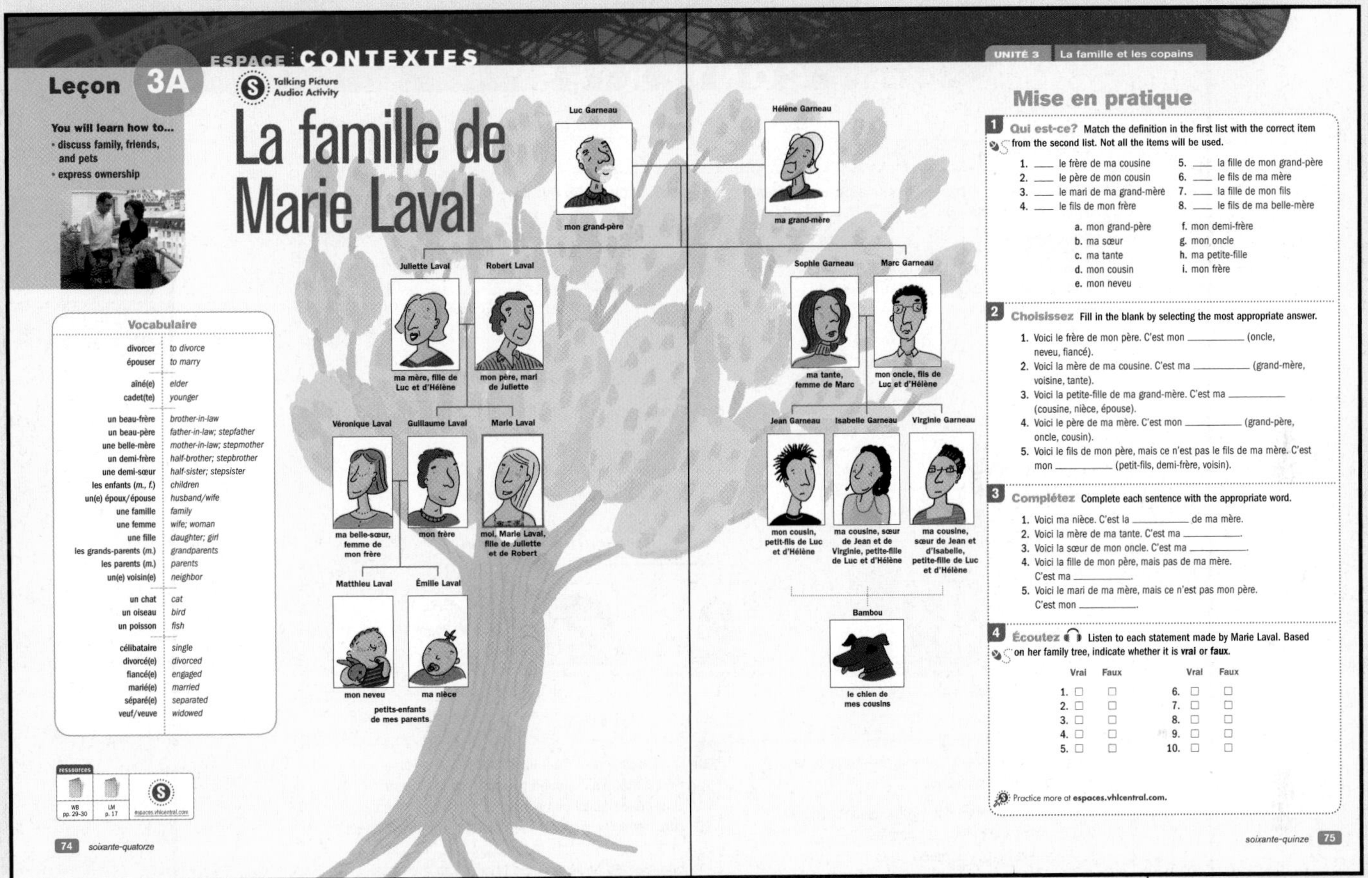

You will learn how to elements highlight the communicative goals and real-life tasks you will be able to carry out in French by the end of each lesson.

Illustrations High-frequency vocabulary is introduced through full-color illustrations that contextualize the words and concepts.

Vocabulaire boxes call out other important theme-related vocabulary in easy-to-reference French-English lists.

Ressources boxes let you know exactly what ancillaries you can use to reinforce and expand on every section of every lesson in your textbook.

Mise en pratique activities always practice the new vocabulary in meaningful contexts, and there is always one listening activity among them.

Mouse icons identify activities from the book that are on the Supersite with auto-grading.
Supersite icons show when additional activities or materials are available for you to use.

ESPACE CONTEXTES

practices vocabulary in a variety of formats.

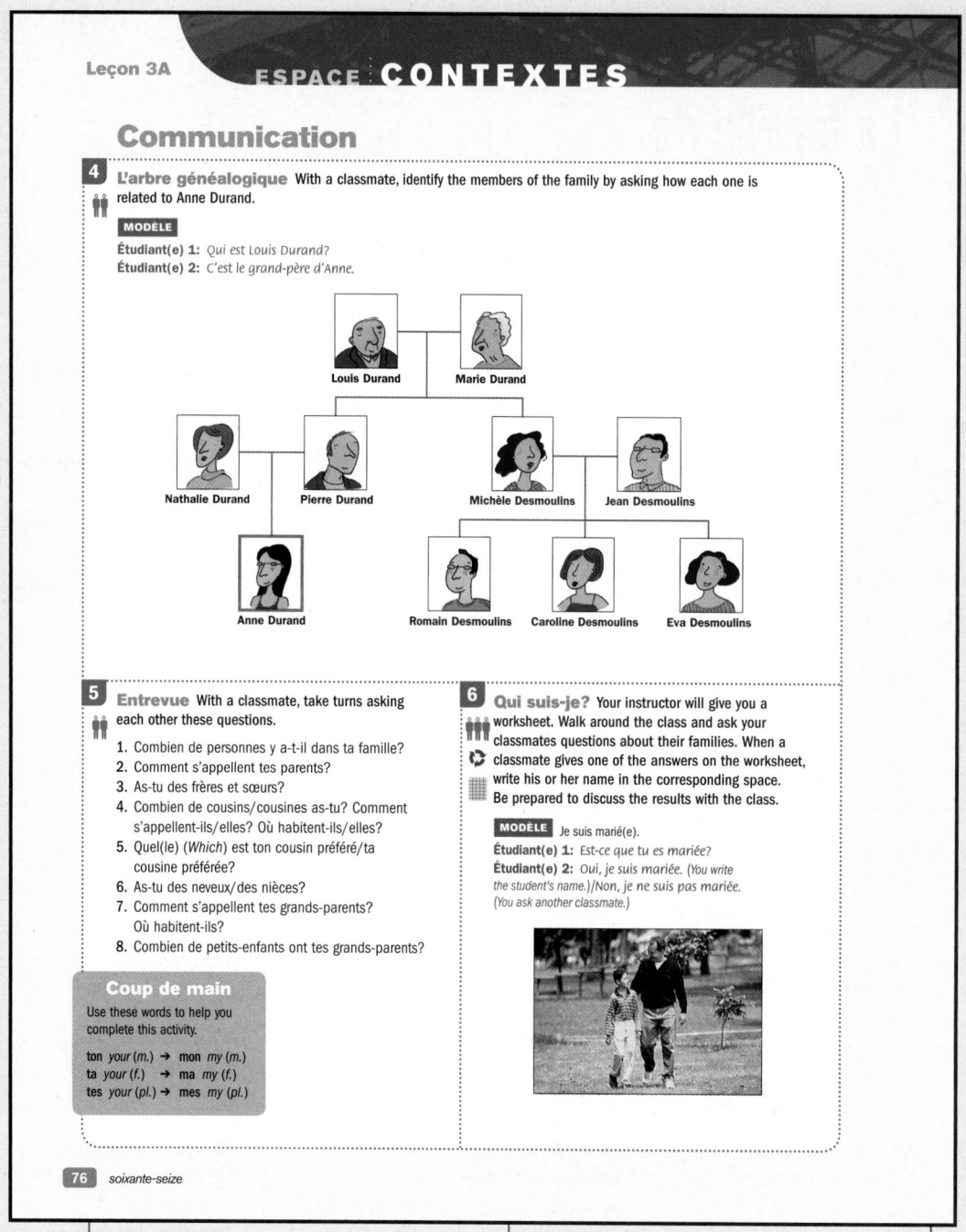

Leçon 3A — ESPACE CONTEXTES

Communication

4 L'arbre généalogique With a classmate, identify the members of the family by asking how each one is related to Anne Durand.

MODÈLE

Étudiant(e) 1: *Qui est Louis Durand?*
Étudiant(e) 2: *C'est le grand-père d'Anne.*

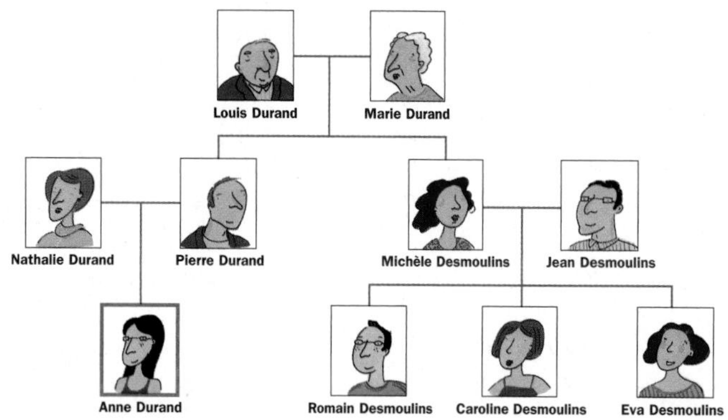

5 Entrevue With a classmate, take turns asking each other these questions.

1. Combien de personnes y a-t-il dans ta famille?
2. Comment s'appellent tes parents?
3. As-tu des frères et sœurs?
4. Combien de cousins/cousines as-tu? Comment s'appellent-ils/elles? Où habitent-ils/elles?
5. Quel(le) (*Which*) est ton cousin préféré/ta cousine préférée?
6. As-tu des neveux/des nièces?
7. Comment s'appellent tes grands-parents? Où habitent-ils?
8. Combien de petits-enfants ont tes grands-parents?

Coup de main

Use these words to help you complete this activity.

ton *your (m.)* → **mon** *my (m.)*
ta *your (f.)* → **ma** *my (f.)*
tes *your (pl.)* → **mes** *my (pl.)*

6 Qui suis-je? Your instructor will give you a worksheet. Walk around the class and ask your classmates questions about their families. When a classmate gives one of the answers on the worksheet, write his or her name in the corresponding space. Be prepared to discuss the results with the class.

MODÈLE Je suis marié(e).

Étudiant(e) 1: *Est-ce que tu es mariée?*
Étudiant(e) 2: *Oui, je suis mariée.* (*You write the student's name.*)/*Non, je ne suis pas mariée.* (*You ask another classmate.*)

76 *soixante-seize*

Coup de main boxes provide handy, on-the-spot, language, or grammar information that helps you complete the activities.

Communication activities allow you to use the vocabulary creatively in interactions with a partner, a small group, or the entire class.

Icons provide on-the-spot visual cues for various types of activities: pair, small group, re-entering, listening-based, video-related, handout-based, and information gap. For a legend explaining all icons used in the student text, see page xxviii.

ESPACE CONTEXTES

Les sons et les lettres presents the rules of French pronunciation and spelling.

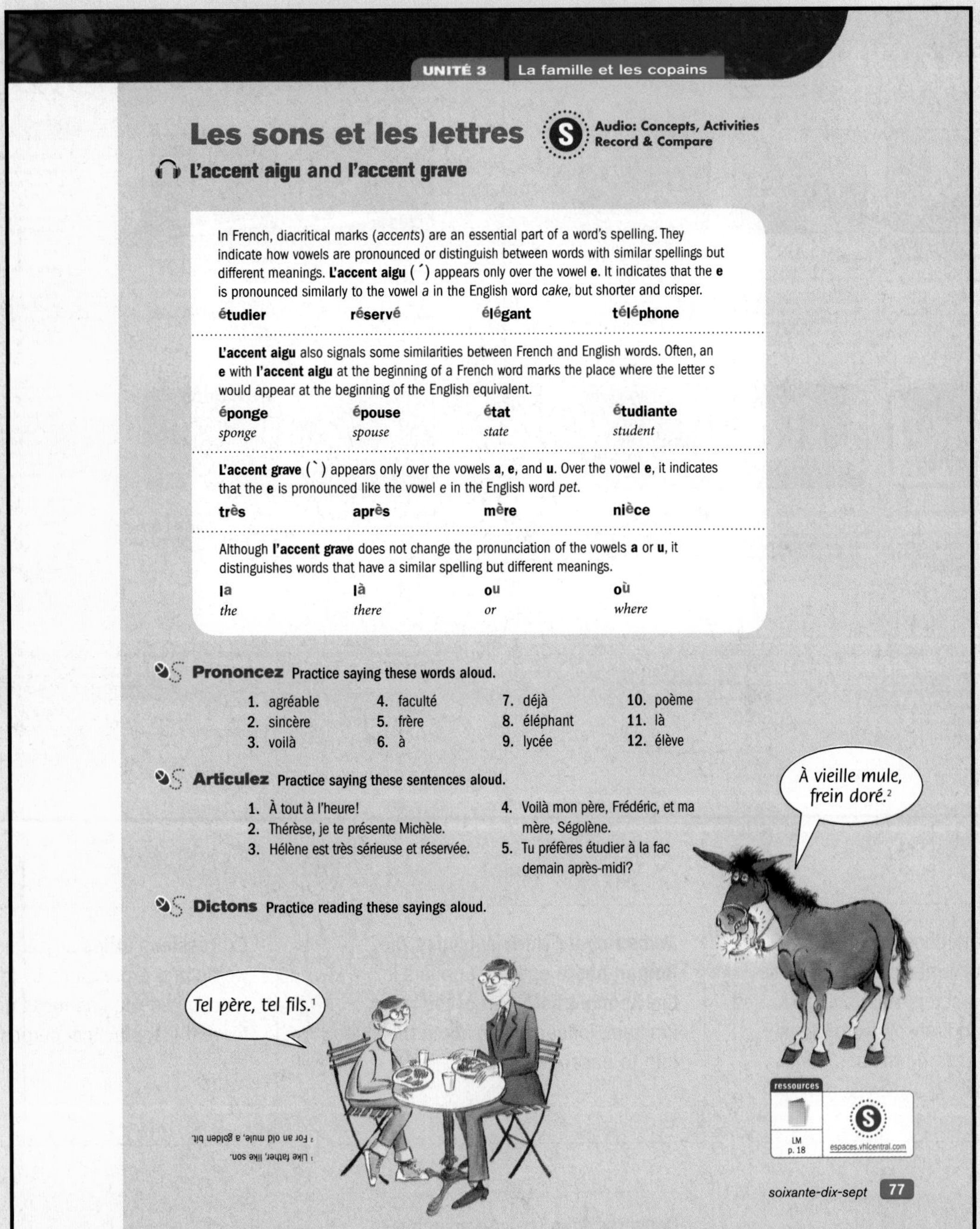

UNITÉ 3 La famille et les copains

Les sons et les lettres

Audio: Concepts, Activities
Record & Compare

L'accent aigu and l'accent grave

In French, diacritical marks (*accents*) are an essential part of a word's spelling. They indicate how vowels are pronounced or distinguish between words with similar spellings but different meanings. **L'accent aigu** (´) appears only over the vowel **e**. It indicates that the **e** is pronounced similarly to the vowel *a* in the English word *cake*, but shorter and crisper.

étudier **réservé** **élégant** **téléphone**

L'accent aigu also signals some similarities between French and English words. Often, an **e** with **l'accent aigu** at the beginning of a French word marks the place where the letter *s* would appear at the beginning of the English equivalent.

éponge	**épouse**	**état**	**étudiante**
sponge	*spouse*	*state*	*student*

L'accent grave (`) appears only over the vowels **a**, **e**, and **u**. Over the vowel **e**, it indicates that the **e** is pronounced like the vowel *e* in the English word *pet*.

très **après** **mère** **nièce**

Although **l'accent grave** does not change the pronunciation of the vowels **a** or **u**, it distinguishes words that have a similar spelling but different meanings.

la	**là**	**ou**	**où**
the	*there*	*or*	*where*

Prononcez Practice saying these words aloud.

1. agréable
2. sincère
3. voilà
4. faculté
5. frère
6. à
7. déjà
8. éléphant
9. lycée
10. poème
11. là
12. élève

Articulez Practice saying these sentences aloud.

1. À tout à l'heure!
2. Thérèse, je te présente Michèle.
3. Hélène est très sérieuse et réservée.
4. Voilà mon père, Frédéric, et ma mère, Ségolène.
5. Tu préfères étudier à la fac demain après-midi?

Dictons Practice reading these sayings aloud.

Tel père, tel fils.[1]

À vieille mule, frein doré.[2]

[1] Like father, like son.
[2] For an old mule, a golden bit.

ressources
LM p. 18
espaces.vhlcentral.com

soixante-dix-sept 77

Explanation Rules and tips to help you learn French pronunciation and spelling are presented clearly with abundant model words and phrases.

Practice Pronunciation and spelling practice is provided at the word- and sentence-levels. The final activity features illustrated sayings and proverbs so you can practice the pronunciation or spelling point in an entertaining cultural context.

The headset icon at the top of the page indicates when an explanation and activities are recorded for convenient use in or outside of class.

ESPACE ROMAN-PHOTO

tells the story of a group of students living in Aix-en-Provence, France.

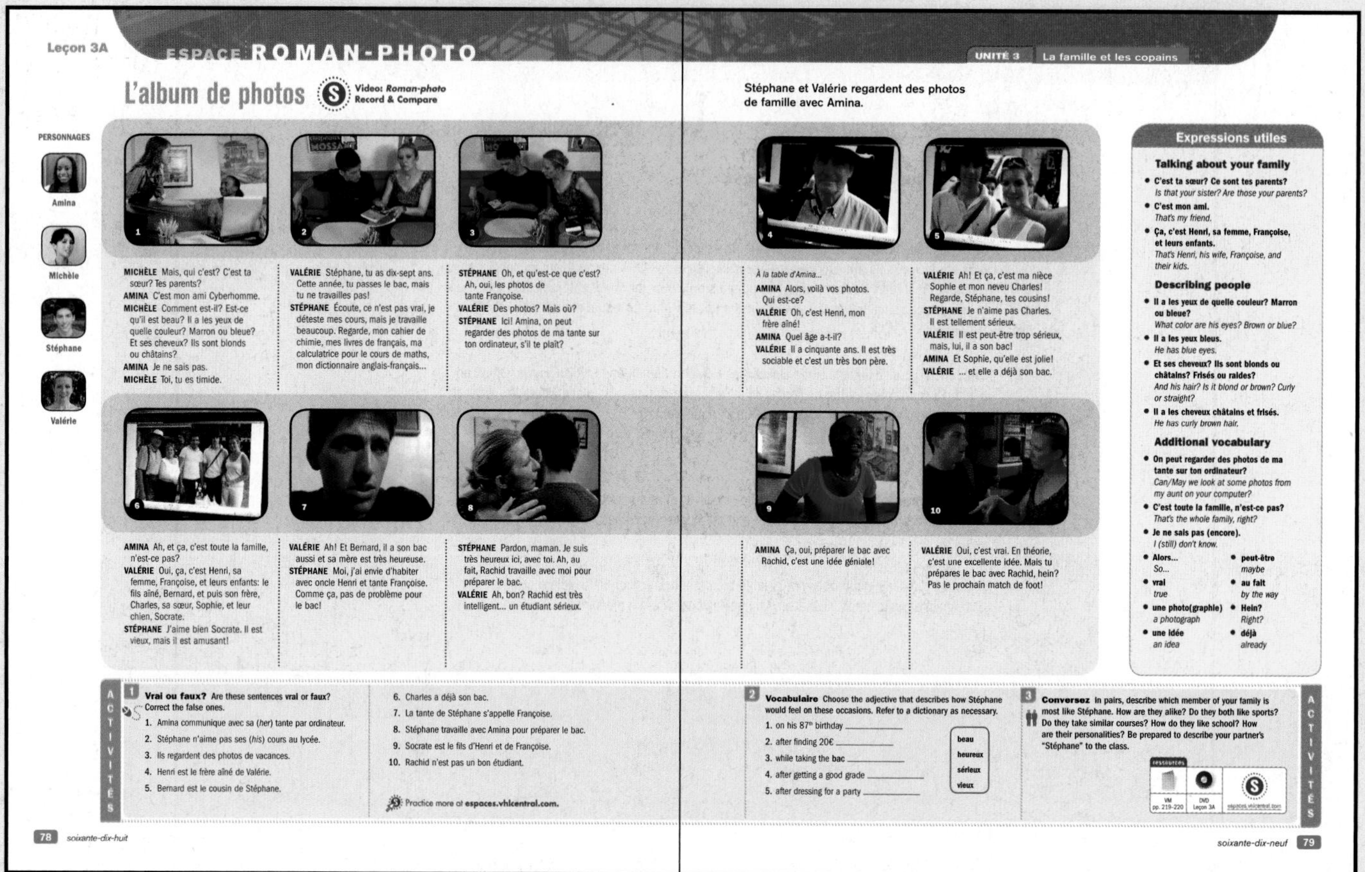

Leçon 3A

ESPACE ROMAN-PHOTO

UNITÉ 3 La famille et les copains

L'album de photos Video: *Roman-photo* Record & Compare

Stéphane et Valérie regardent des photos de famille avec Amina.

PERSONNAGES: Amina, Michèle, Stéphane, Valérie

MICHÈLE Mais, qui c'est? C'est ta sœur? Tes parents?
AMINA C'est mon ami Cyberhomme.
MICHÈLE Comment est-il? Est-ce qu'il est beau? Il a les yeux de quelle couleur? Marron ou bleue? Et ses cheveux? Ils sont blonds ou châtains?
AMINA Je ne sais pas.
MICHÈLE Toi, tu es timide.

VALÉRIE Stéphane, tu as dix-sept ans. Cette année, tu passes le bac, mais tu ne travailles pas!
STÉPHANE Écoute, ce n'est pas vrai, je déteste mes cours, mais je travaille beaucoup. Regarde, mon cahier de chimie, mes livres de français, ma calculatrice pour le cours de maths, mon dictionnaire anglais-français...

STÉPHANE Oh, et qu'est-ce que c'est? Ah, oui, les photos de tante Françoise.
VALÉRIE Des photos? Mais où?
STÉPHANE Ici! Amina, on peut regarder des photos de ma tante sur ton ordinateur, s'il te plaît?

À la table d'Amina...
AMINA Alors, voilà vos photos. Qui est-ce?
VALÉRIE Oh, c'est Henri, mon frère aîné!
AMINA Quel âge a-t-il?
VALÉRIE Il a cinquante ans. Il est très sociable et c'est un très bon père.

VALÉRIE Ah! Et ça, c'est ma nièce Sophie et mon neveu Charles! Regarde, Stéphane, tes cousins!
STÉPHANE Je n'aime pas Charles. Il est tellement sérieux.
VALÉRIE Il est peut-être trop sérieux, mais, lui, il a son bac!
AMINA Et Sophie, qu'elle est jolie!
VALÉRIE ... et elle a déjà son bac.

AMINA Ah, et ça, c'est toute la famille, n'est-ce pas?
VALÉRIE Oui, ça, c'est Henri, sa femme, Françoise, et leurs enfants: le fils aîné, Bernard, et puis son frère, Charles, sa sœur, Sophie, et leur chien, Socrate.
STÉPHANE J'aime bien Socrate. Il est vieux, mais il est amusant!

VALÉRIE Ah! Et Bernard, il a son bac aussi et sa mère est très heureuse.
STÉPHANE Moi, j'ai envie d'habiter avec oncle Henri et tante Françoise. Comme ça, pas de problème pour le bac!

STÉPHANE Pardon, maman. Je suis très heureux ici, avec toi. Ah, au fait, Rachid travaille avec moi pour préparer le bac.
VALÉRIE Ah, bon? Rachid est très intelligent... un étudiant sérieux.

AMINA Ça, oui, préparer le bac avec Rachid, c'est une idée géniale!

VALÉRIE Oui, c'est vrai. En théorie, c'est une excellente idée. Mais tu prépares le bac avec Rachid, hein? Pas le prochain match de foot!

Expressions utiles

Talking about your family
- **C'est ta sœur? Ce sont tes parents?** *Is that your sister? Are those your parents?*
- **C'est mon ami.** *That's my friend.*
- **Ça, c'est Henri, sa femme, Françoise, et leurs enfants.** *That's Henri, his wife, Françoise, and their kids.*

Describing people
- **Il a les yeux de quelle couleur? Marron ou bleue?** *What color are his eyes? Brown or blue?*
- **Il a les yeux bleus.** *He has blue eyes.*
- **Et ses cheveux? Ils sont blonds ou châtains? Frisés ou raides?** *And his hair? Is it blond or brown? Curly or straight?*
- **Il a les cheveux châtains et frisés.** *He has curly brown hair.*

Additional vocabulary
- **On peut regarder des photos de ma tante sur ton ordinateur?** *Can/May we look at some photos from my aunt on your computer?*
- **C'est toute la famille, n'est-ce pas?** *That's the whole family, right?*
- **Je ne sais pas (encore).** *I (still) don't know.*
- **Alors...** *So...*
- **peut-être** *maybe*
- **vrai** *true*
- **au fait** *by the way*
- **une photo(graphie)** *a photograph*
- **Hein?** *Right?*
- **une idée** *an idea*
- **déjà** *already*

ACTIVITÉS

1 Vrai ou faux? Are these sentences **vrai** or **faux**? Correct the false ones.
1. Amina communique avec sa (*her*) tante par ordinateur.
2. Stéphane n'aime pas ses (*his*) cours au lycée.
3. Ils regardent des photos de vacances.
4. Henri est le frère aîné de Valérie.
5. Bernard est le cousin de Stéphane.
6. Charles a déjà son bac.
7. La tante de Stéphane s'appelle Françoise.
8. Stéphane travaille avec Amina pour préparer le bac.
9. Socrate est le fils d'Henri et de Françoise.
10. Rachid n'est pas un bon étudiant.

Practice more at **espaces.vhlcentral.com.**

2 Vocabulaire Choose the adjective that describes how Stéphane would feel on these occasions. Refer to a dictionary as necessary.
1. on his 87th birthday ____
2. after finding 20€ ____
3. while taking the **bac** ____
4. after getting a good grade ____
5. after dressing for a party ____

beau / heureux / sérieux / vieux

3 Conversez In pairs, describe which member of your family is most like Stéphane. How are they alike? Do they both like sports? Do they take similar courses? How do they like school? How are their personalities? Be prepared to describe your partner's "Stéphane" to the class.

ressources: VM pp. 219–220; DVD Leçon 3A; espaces.vhlcentral.com

78 soixante-dix-huit — soixante-dix-neuf 79

Personnages The photo-based conversations take place among a cast of recurring characters—four college students, the landlady of two of them (who owns the café downstairs), and her teenage son.

***Roman-photo* video episodes** The **Roman-photo** episode appears in the **Roman-photo** part of the Video Program. To learn more about the video, turn to page xxvi.

Expressions utiles organizes new, active words and expressions by language function so you can focus on using them for real-life, practical purposes.

Conversations The conversations reinforce vocabulary from **Espace contextes**. They also preview structures from the upcoming **Espace structures** section in context and in a comprehensible way.

ESPACE CULTURE

explores cultural themes introduced in **ESPACE CONTEXTES** and **ESPACE ROMAN-PHOTO**.

Leçon 3A ESPACE CULTURE

Video: *Flash culture*

CULTURE À LA LOUPE

La famille en France

Comment est la famille française? Est-elle différente de la famille américaine? La majorité des Français sont-ils mariés, divorcés ou célibataires?

Il n'y a pas de réponse simple à ces questions. Les familles françaises sont très diverses. Le mariage est toujours° très populaire: la majorité des hommes et des femmes sont mariés. Mais attention! Les nombres° de personnes divorcées et de personnes célibataires augmentent chaque° année.

La structure familiale traditionnelle existe toujours en France, mais il y a des structures moins traditionnelles, comme les familles monoparentales, où° l'unique parent est divorcé, séparé ou veuf. Il y a aussi des familles recomposées, c'est-à-dire qui combinent deux familles, avec un beau-père, une belle-mère, des demi-frères et des demi-sœurs. Certains couples choisissent° le Pacte Civil de Solidarité (PACS), qui offre certains droits° et protections aux couples non-mariés.

Géographiquement, les membres d'une famille d'immigrés peuvent° habiter près ou loin° les uns des autres°. Mais en général, ils préfèrent habiter les uns près des autres parce que l'intégration est parfois° difficile. Il existe aussi des familles d'immigrés séparées entre° la France et le pays d'origine.

Alors, oubliez les stéréotypes des familles en France. Elles sont grandes et petites, traditionnelles et non-conventionnelles; elles changent et sont toujours les mêmes°.

toujours *still* **nombres** *numbers* **chaque** *each* **où** *where* **choisissent** *choose* **droits** *rights* **peuvent** *can* **près ou loin** *near or far from* **les uns des autres** *one another* **parfois** *sometimes* **entre** *between* **mêmes** *same* **tranche** *bracket*

Coup de main

Remember to read decimal places in **French** using the French word **virgule** (*comma*) where you would normally say *point* in English. To say *percent*, use **pour cent**.

64,3% soixante-quatre virgule trois pour cent

sixty-four point three percent

La situation familiale des Français
(par tranche° d'âge)

ÂGE	CÉLIBATAIRE	EN COUPLE SANS ENFANTS	EN COUPLE AVEC ENFANTS	PARENT D'UNE FAMILLE MONOPARENTALE
< 25 ans	3,6%	2,8%	1%	0,3%
25–29 ans	16,7%	26,5%	26,2%	2,6%
30–44 ans	10,9%	9,8%	64,3%	6,2%
45–59 ans	11,7%	29,9%	47,2%	5,9%
> 60 ans	20,3%	59,2%	11,7%	2,9%

SOURCE: INSEE

ACTIVITÉS

1 Complétez Provide logical answers, based on the reading.

1. Si on regarde la population française d'aujourd'hui, on observe que les familles françaises sont très ________
2. Le ________ est toujours très populaire en France.
3. La majorité des hommes et des femmes sont ________
4. Le nombre de Français qui sont ________ augmente.
5. Dans les familles ________, l'unique parent est divorcé, séparé ou veuf.
6. Il y a des familles qui combinent ________ familles.
7. Le ________ offre certains droits et protections aux couples qui ne sont pas mariés.
8. Les immigrés aiment ________ les uns près des autres.
9. Oubliez les ________ des familles en France.
10. Les familles changent et sont toujours ________.

Practice more at **espaces.vhlcentral.com.**

UNITÉ 3 La famille et les copains

LE FRANÇAIS QUOTIDIEN

La famille

un frangin	*brother*
une frangine	*sister*
maman	*Mom*
mamie	*Nana, Grandma*
un minou	*kitty*
papa	*Dad*
papi	*Grandpa*
tata	*Auntie*
tonton	*Uncle*
un toutou	*doggy*

LE MONDE FRANCOPHONE

Les fêtes et la famille

Les États-Unis ont quelques fêtes° en commun avec le monde francophone, mais les dates et les traditions de ces fêtes diffèrent d'un pays° à l'autre°. Voici deux fêtes associées à la famille.

La Fête des mères
En France le dernier° dimanche de mai ou le premier° dimanche de juin
En Belgique le deuxième° dimanche de mai
À l'île Maurice le dernier dimanche de mai
Au Canada le deuxième dimanche de mai

La Fête des pères
En France le troisième° dimanche de juin
En Belgique le deuxième dimanche de juin
Au Canada le troisième dimanche de juin

quelques fêtes *some holidays* **pays** *country* **autre** *other* **dernier** *last* **premier** *first* **deuxième** *second* **troisième** *third*

PORTRAIT

Les Noah

Dans° la famille Noah, le sport est héréditaire. À chacun son° sport: pour° Yannick, né° en France, c'est le tennis; pour son père, Zacharie, né à Yaoundé, au Cameroun, c'est le football°; pour son fils, Joakim, né aux États-Unis, c'est le basket-ball. Yannick est champion junior à Wimbledon en 1977 et participe aux championnats° du Grand Chelem° dans les années 1980. Son fils, Joakim, est un joueur° de basket-ball aux États-Unis. Il gagne° la finale du *Final Four NCAA* en 2006 et en 2007 avec les Florida Gators. Il est aujourd'hui joueur professionnel avec les Chicago Bulls. Le sport est dans le sang° chez les Noah!

Dans *In* **À chacun son** *To everybody his* **pour** *for* **né** *born* **football** *soccer* **championnats** *championships* **Chelem** *Slam* **joueur** *player* **gagne** *wins* **sang** *blood*

SUR INTERNET

Yannick Noah: célébrité du tennis et… de la chanson?°

Tennis star and singing sensation?

Go to [illegible] to find more information related to this **ESPACE CULTURE**. Then watch the corresponding **Flash culture**.

2 Vrai ou faux? Indicate if these statements are **vrai** or **faux**.

1. Le tennis est héréditaire chez les Noah.
2. Zacharie Noah est né au Cameroun.
3. Zacharie Noah était (*was*) un joueur de basket-ball.
4. Yannick gagne à l'US Open.
5. Joakim joue (*plays*) pour les Lakers.
6. Le deuxième dimanche de mai, c'est la Fête des mères en Belgique et au Canada.

3 À vous… With a partner, write six sentences describing another celebrity family whose members all share a common field or profession. Be prepared to share your sentences with the class.

ressources
VM pp. 275-276
espaces.vhlcentral.com

ACTIVITÉS

Culture à la loupe presents a main, in-depth reading about the lesson's cultural theme. Full-color photos bring to life important aspects of the topic, while charts with statistics and/or intriguing facts support and extend the information.

Le français quotidien exposes you to current, contemporary language by presenting familiar words and phrases related to the lesson's theme that are used in everyday spoken French.

Portrait profiles people, places, and events throughout the French-speaking world, highlighting their importance, accomplishments, and/or contributions to the cultures of the French-speaking people and the global community.

Supersite video icons in one of the **Espace culture** sections of each unit mean that an episode of **Flash culture**, a cultural video related to the lesson's theme, is available for viewing. To learn more about the video, see page xxvii.

Le monde francophone puts the spotlight on the people, places, and traditions of the countries and areas of the French-speaking world.

Sur Internet boxes, with their provocative questions and photos, direct you to the **ESPACES** Supersite where you can continue to learn more about the topics of **Espace culture**, **Flash culture**, and the lesson's theme.

ESPACE STRUCTURES

uses innovative design to support the learning of French.

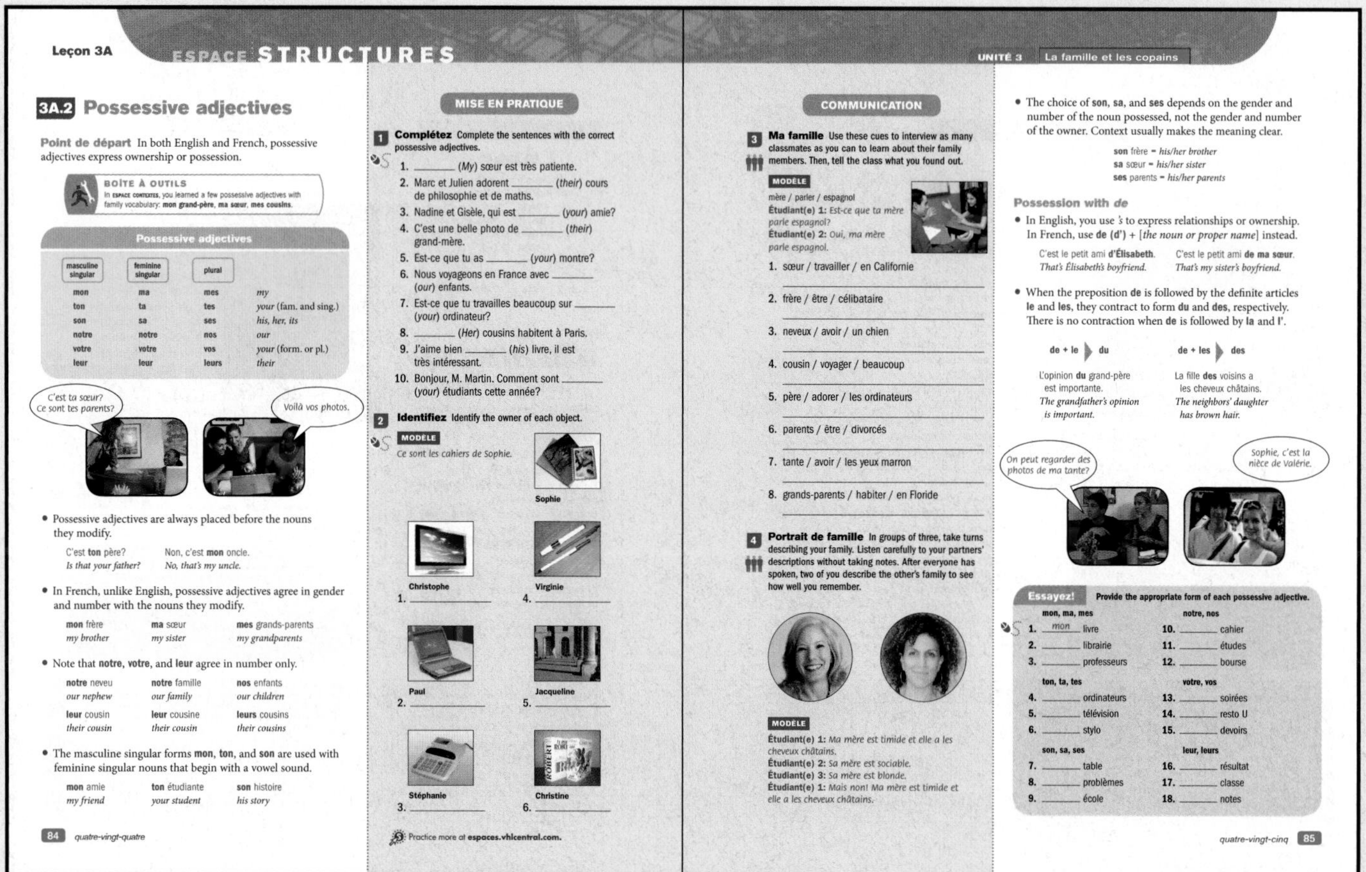

Leçon 3A ESPACE STRUCTURES

3A.2 Possessive adjectives

Point de départ In both English and French, possessive adjectives express ownership or possession.

BOÎTE À OUTILS
In ESPACE CONTEXTES, you learned a few possessive adjectives with family vocabulary: **mon grand-père, ma sœur, mes cousins.**

Possessive adjectives

masculine singular	feminine singular	plural	
mon	ma	mes	*my*
ton	ta	tes	*your* (fam. and sing.)
son	sa	ses	*his, her, its*
notre	notre	nos	*our*
votre	votre	vos	*your* (form. or pl.)
leur	leur	leurs	*their*

- Possessive adjectives are always placed before the nouns they modify.

C'est **ton** père? *Is that your father?* Non, c'est **mon** oncle. *No, that's my uncle.*

- In French, unlike English, possessive adjectives agree in gender and number with the nouns they modify.

mon frère *my brother* **ma** sœur *my sister* **mes** grands-parents *my grandparents*

- Note that **notre, votre,** and **leur** agree in number only.

notre neveu *our nephew* **notre** famille *our family* **nos** enfants *our children*
leur cousin *their cousin* **leur** cousine *their cousin* **leurs** cousins *their cousins*

- The masculine singular forms **mon, ton,** and **son** are used with feminine singular nouns that begin with a vowel sound.

mon amie *my friend* **ton** étudiante *your student* **son** histoire *his story*

84 quatre-vingt-quatre

MISE EN PRATIQUE

1 Complétez Complete the sentences with the correct possessive adjectives.

1. _______ (*My*) sœur est très patiente.
2. Marc et Julien adorent _______ (*their*) cours de philosophie et de maths.
3. Nadine et Gisèle, qui est _______ (*your*) amie?
4. C'est une belle photo de _______ (*their*) grand-mère.
5. Est-ce que tu as _______ (*your*) montre?
6. Nous voyageons en France avec _______ (*our*) enfants.
7. Est-ce que tu travailles beaucoup sur _______ (*your*) ordinateur?
8. _______ (*Her*) cousins habitent à Paris.
9. J'aime bien _______ (*his*) livre, il est très intéressant.
10. Bonjour, M. Martin. Comment sont _______ (*your*) étudiants cette année?

2 Identifiez Identify the owner of each object.

MODÈLE
Ce sont les cahiers de Sophie.

Sophie

Christophe 1. _______
Virginie 4. _______
Paul 2. _______
Jacqueline 5. _______
Stéphanie 3. _______
Christine 6. _______

Practice more at **espaces.vhlcentral.com.**

UNITÉ 3 La famille et les copains

COMMUNICATION

3 Ma famille Use these cues to interview as many classmates as you can to learn about their family members. Then, tell the class what you found out.

MODÈLE
mère / parler / espagnol
Étudiant(e) 1: *Est-ce que ta mère parle espagnol?*
Étudiant(e) 2: *Oui, ma mère parle espagnol.*

1. sœur / travailler / en Californie
2. frère / être / célibataire
3. neveux / avoir / un chien
4. cousin / voyager / beaucoup
5. père / adorer / les ordinateurs
6. parents / être / divorcés
7. tante / avoir / les yeux marron
8. grands-parents / habiter / en Floride

4 Portrait de famille In groups of three, take turns describing your family. Listen carefully to your partners' descriptions without taking notes. After everyone has spoken, two of you describe the other's family to see how well you remember.

MODÈLE
Étudiant(e) 1: *Ma mère est timide et elle a les cheveux châtains.*
Étudiant(e) 2: *Sa mère est sociable.*
Étudiant(e) 3: *Sa mère est blonde.*
Étudiant(e) 1: *Mais non! Ma mère est timide et elle a les cheveux châtains.*

- The choice of **son, sa,** and **ses** depends on the gender and number of the noun possessed, not the gender and number of the owner. Context usually makes the meaning clear.

son frère = *his/her brother*
sa sœur = *his/her sister*
ses parents = *his/her parents*

Possession with *de*

- In English, you use *'s* to express relationships or ownership. In French, use **de (d')** + [*the noun or proper name*] instead.

C'est le petit ami **d'Élisabeth.** *That's Élisabeth's boyfriend.* C'est le petit ami **de ma sœur.** *That's my sister's boyfriend.*

- When the preposition **de** is followed by the definite articles **le** and **les,** they contract to form **du** and **des,** respectively. There is no contraction when **de** is followed by **la** and **l'**.

de + le ▶ **du** L'opinion **du** grand-père est importante. *The grandfather's opinion is important.*
de + les ▶ **des** La fille **des** voisins a les cheveux châtains. *The neighbors' daughter has brown hair.*

Essayez! Provide the appropriate form of each possessive adjective.

mon, ma, mes
1. mon livre
2. _______ librairie
3. _______ professeurs

ton, ta, tes
4. _______ ordinateurs
5. _______ télévision
6. _______ stylo

son, sa, ses
7. _______ table
8. _______ problèmes
9. _______ école

notre, nos
10. _______ cahier
11. _______ études
12. _______ bourse

votre, vos
13. _______ soirées
14. _______ resto U
15. _______ devoirs

leur, leurs
16. _______ résultat
17. _______ classe
18. _______ notes

quatre-vingt-cinq 85

Text format For each grammar point, the explanation and practice activities appear on two facing pages. Grammar explanations in the outside panels offer handy on-page support for the activities in the central panels, providing you with immediate access to information essential to communication.

Charts and diagrams Within the clear, easy-to-grasp grammar explanations, colorful, carefully designed charts and diagrams call out key grammatical structures and forms, as well as important related vocabulary.

Graphics-intensive design Photos from the **ESPACES** Video Program consistently integrate the lesson's video episode and **Espace roman-photo** section with the grammar explanations. Additional photos, drawings, and graphic devices liven up activities and heighten visual interest.

ESPACE STRUCTURES

provides varied types of directed and communicative practice.

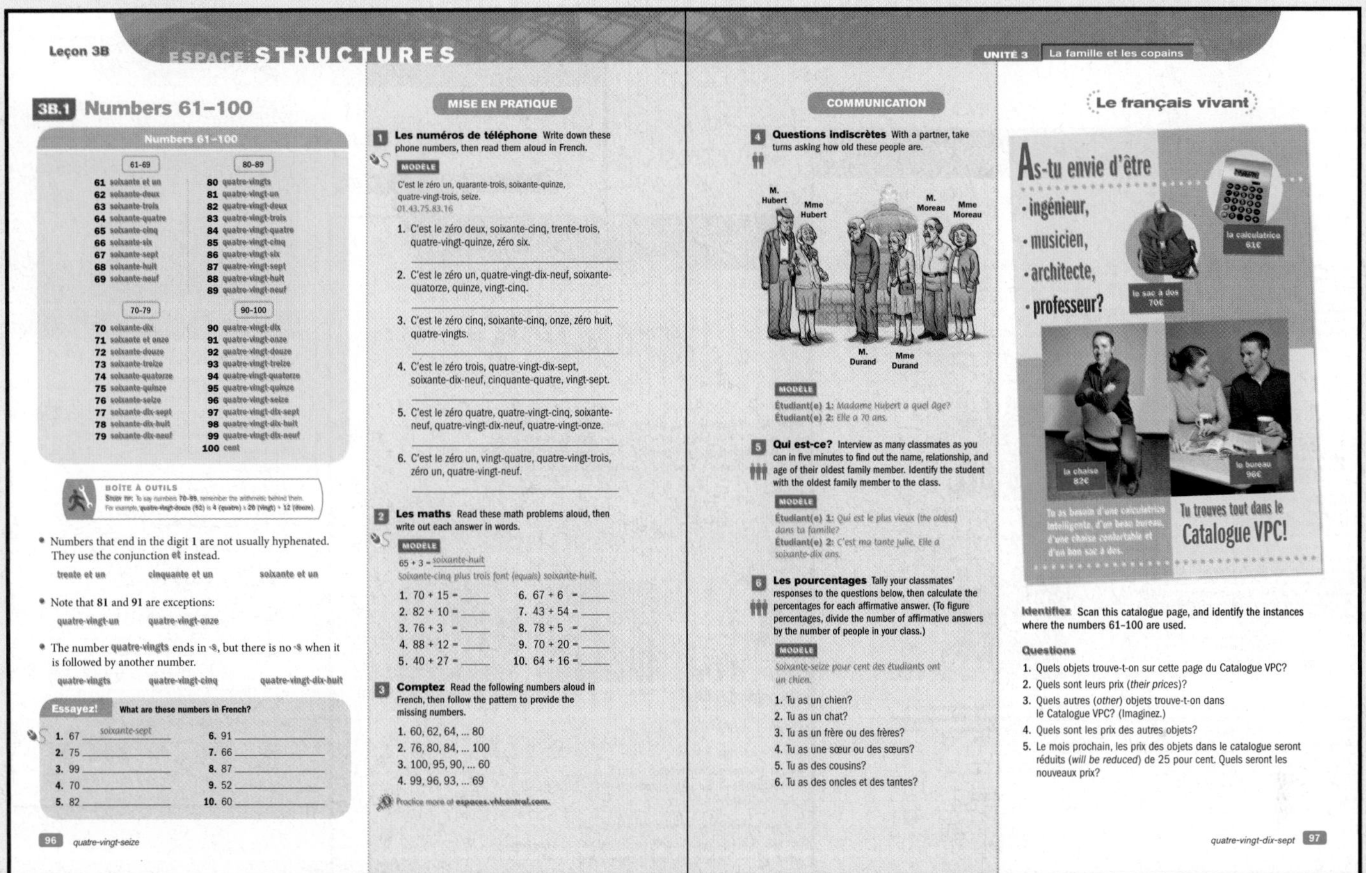

Essayez! offers you your first practice of each new grammar point. The **Essayez!** activities get you working with the grammar point right away in simple, easy-to-understand formats.

Mise en pratique activities provide a wide range of guided exercises in contexts that combine current and previously learned vocabulary with the current grammar point.

Le français vivant activities incorporate documents, like advertisements and posters, into the grammar practice, highlighting the new grammar point in a real-life context.

Communication activities offer opportunities for creative expression using the lesson's grammar and vocabulary. You should do these activities with a partner, in small groups, or with the whole class.

ESPACE SYNTHÈSE

pulls the lesson together with cumulative practice in **Révision**. The second page of the section alternates between **Le zapping** and **À l'écoute**.

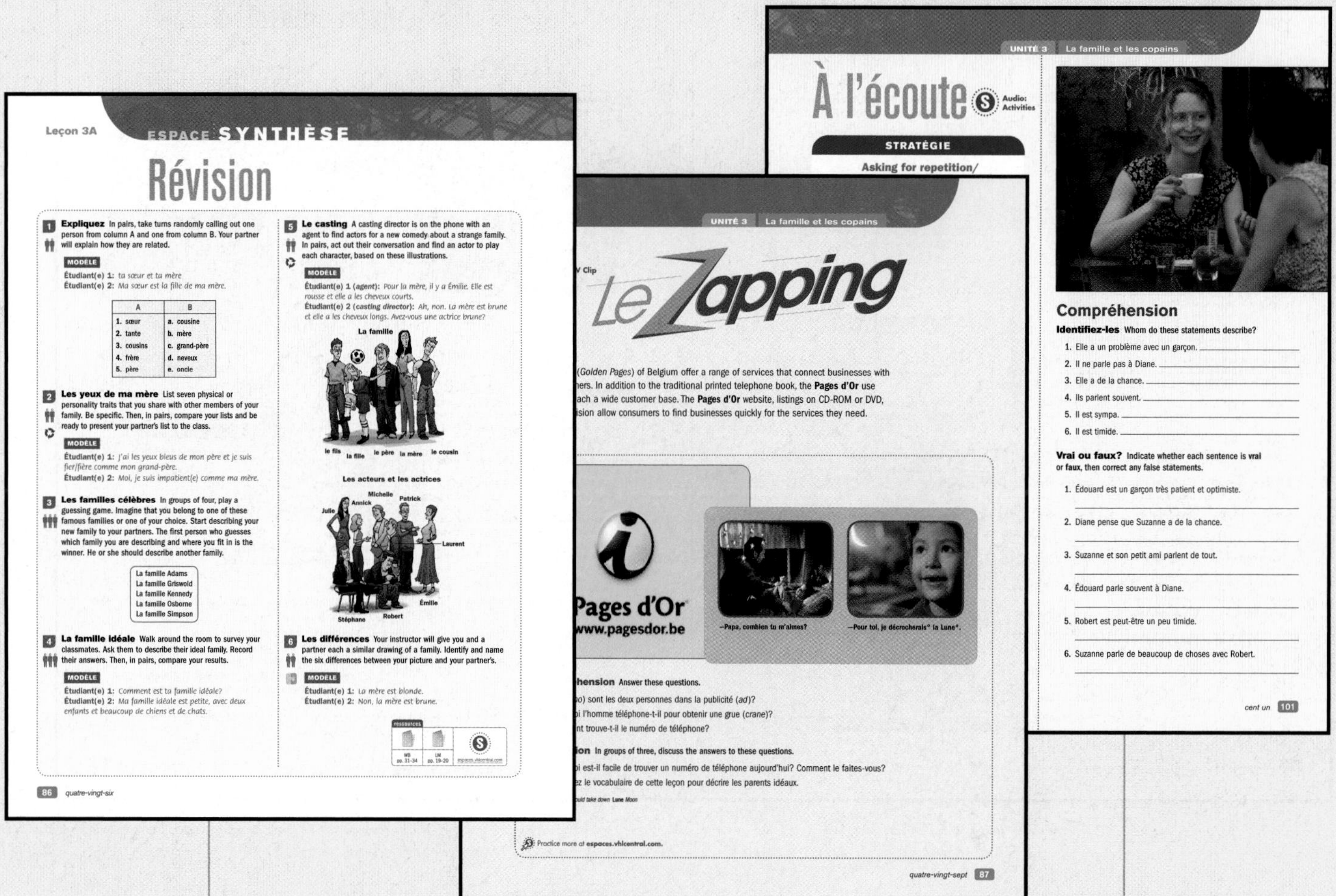

Révision activities integrate the lesson's two grammar points with previously learned vocabulary and structures, providing consistent, built-in review and re-entering as you progress through the text.

Pair and group icons call out the communicative nature of the activities. Situations, role-plays, games, personal questions, interviews, and surveys are just some of the types of activities that you will experience.

Information gap activities, identified by the interlocking puzzle pieces, engage you and a partner in problem-solving situations. You and your partner each have only half of the information you need, so you must work together to accomplish the task at hand.

Le zapping features television clips in French—commercials, a recipe, a tourism notice for Rennes, and short films—supported by background information, images from the videos and activities to help you understand and to check your comprehension of what you see.

À l'écoute presents a recorded conversation or narration to develop your listening skills in French. **Stratégie** and **Préparation** prepare you for listening to the recorded passage.

À vous d'écouter tracks you through the recorded passage, and **Compréhension** checks your understanding of what you heard.

ESPACE SYNTHÈSE

Le zapping court métrage

Units 13 and 15 feature short-subject dramatic films by contemporary French filmmakers.

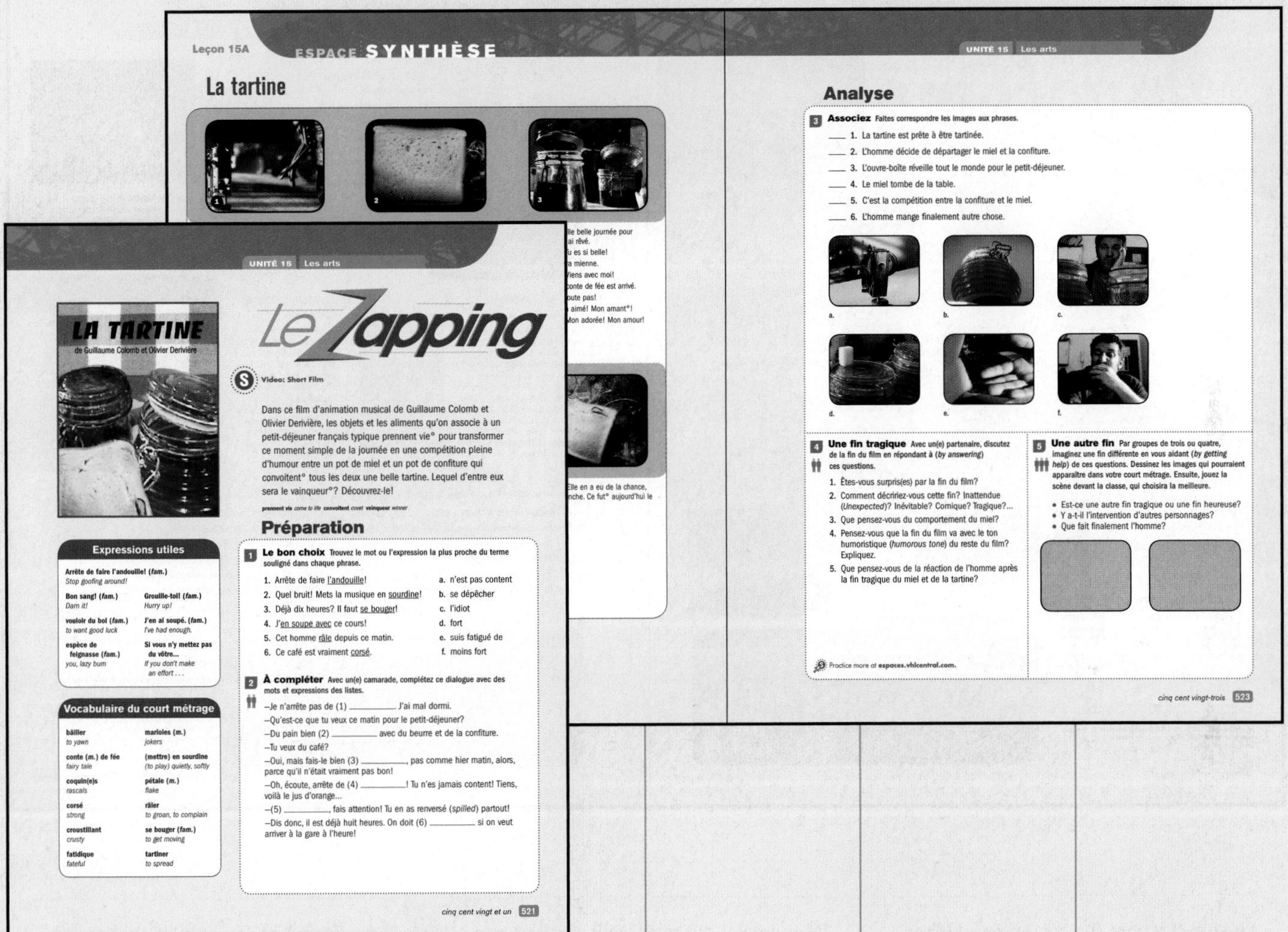

Leçon 15A
ESPACE SYNTHÈSE
La tartine
UNITÉ 15 Les arts
Analyse
3 Associez Faites correspondre les images aux phrases.
___ 1. La tartine est prête à être tartinée.
___ 2. L'homme décide de départager le miel et la confiture.
___ 3. L'ouvre-boîte réveille tout le monde pour le petit-déjeuner.
___ 4. Le miel tombe de la table.
___ 5. C'est la compétition entre la confiture et le miel.
___ 6. L'homme mange finalement autre chose.
4 Une fin tragique Avec un(e) partenaire, discutez de la fin du film en répondant à (by answering) ces questions.
1. Êtes-vous surpris(es) par la fin du film?
2. Comment décririez-vous cette fin? Inattendue (Unexpected)? Inévitable? Comique? Tragique?...
3. Que pensez-vous du comportement du miel?
4. Pensez-vous que la fin du film va avec le ton humoristique (humorous tone) du reste du film? Expliquez.
5. Que pensez-vous de la réaction de l'homme après la fin tragique du miel et de la tartine?
5 Une autre fin Par groupes de trois ou quatre, imaginez une fin différente en vous aidant (by getting help) de ces questions. Dessinez les images qui pourraient apparaître dans votre court métrage. Ensuite, jouez la scène devant la classe, qui choisira la meilleure.
• Est-ce une autre fin tragique ou une fin heureuse?
• Y a-t-il l'intervention d'autres personnages?
• Que fait finalement l'homme?
Practice more at espaces.vhlcentral.com.
cinq cent vingt-trois 523
UNITÉ 15 Les arts
LA TARTINE
de Guillaume Colomb et Olivier Derivière
Le Zapping
Video: Short Film
Dans ce film d'animation musical de Guillaume Colomb et Olivier Derivière, les objets et les aliments qu'on associe à un petit-déjeuner français typique prennent vie° pour transformer ce moment simple de la journée en une compétition pleine d'humour entre un pot de miel et un pot de confiture qui convoitent° tous les deux une belle tartine. Lequel d'entre eux sera le vainqueur°? Découvrez-le!
prennent vie come to life convoitent covet vainqueur winner
Expressions utiles
Arrête de faire l'andouille! (fam.) Stop goofing around!
Bon sang! (fam.) Darn it!
Grouille-toi! (fam.) Hurry up!
vouloir du bol (fam.) to want good luck
J'en ai soupé. (fam.) I've had enough.
espèce de feignasse (fam.) you, lazy bum
Si vous n'y mettez pas du vôtre... If you don't make an effort . . .
Vocabulaire du court métrage
bâiller to yawn
marioles (m.) jokers
conte (m.) de fée fairy tale
(mettre) en sourdine (to play) quietly, softly
coquin(e)s rascals
pétale (m.) flake
corsé strong
râler to groan, to complain
croustillant crusty
se bouger (fam.) to get moving
fatidique fateful
tartiner to spread
Préparation
1 Le bon choix Trouvez le mot ou l'expression la plus proche du terme souligné dans chaque phrase.
1. Arrête de faire l'andouille!
2. Quel bruit! Mets la musique en sourdine!
3. Déjà dix heures? Il faut se bouger!
4. J'en soupe avec ce cours!
5. Cet homme râle depuis ce matin.
6. Ce café est vraiment corsé.
a. n'est pas content
b. se dépêcher
c. l'idiot
d. fort
e. suis fatigué de
f. moins fort
2 À compléter Avec un(e) camarade, complétez ce dialogue avec des mots et expressions des listes.
—Je n'arrête pas de (1) ________. J'ai mal dormi.
—Qu'est-ce que tu veux ce matin pour le petit-déjeuner?
—Du pain bien (2) ________ avec du beurre et de la confiture.
—Tu veux du café?
—Oui, mais fais-le bien (3) ________, pas comme hier matin, alors, parce qu'il n'était vraiment pas bon!
—Oh, écoute, arrête de (4) ________! Tu n'es jamais content! Tiens, voilà le jus d'orange...
—(5) ________, fais attention! Tu en as renversé (spilled) partout!
—Dis donc, il est déjà huit heures. On doit (6) ________ si on veut arriver à la gare à l'heure!
cinq cent vingt et un 521

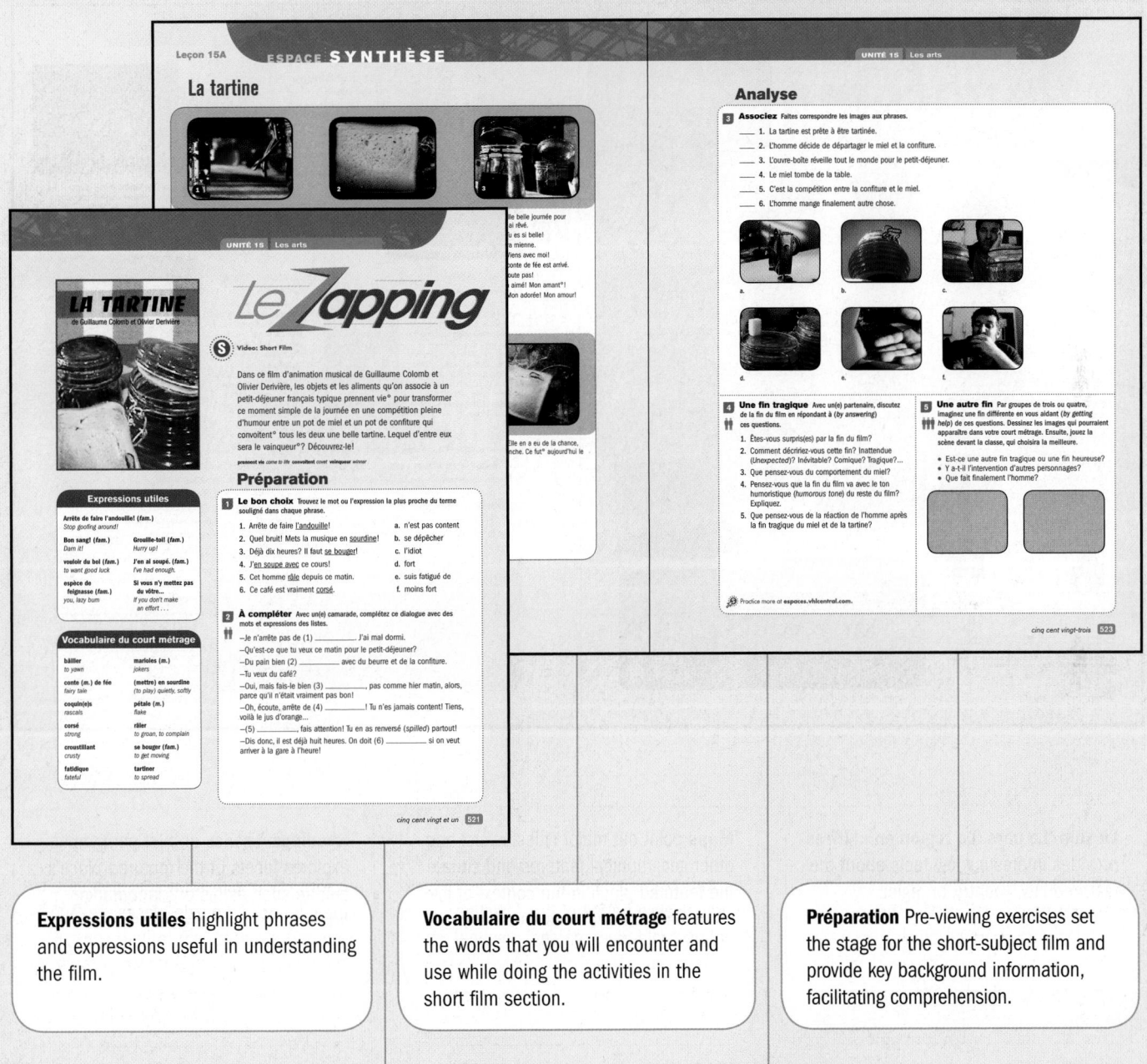

Expressions utiles highlight phrases and expressions useful in understanding the film.

Vocabulaire du court métrage features the words that you will encounter and use while doing the activities in the short film section.

Préparation Pre-viewing exercises set the stage for the short-subject film and provide key background information, facilitating comprehension.

Scène A synopsis of the film's plot with captioned video stills prepares you visually for the film.

Analyse Post-viewing activities go beyond checking comprehension, allowing you to discover broader themes.

SAVOIR-FAIRE

Panorama presents the French-speaking world.

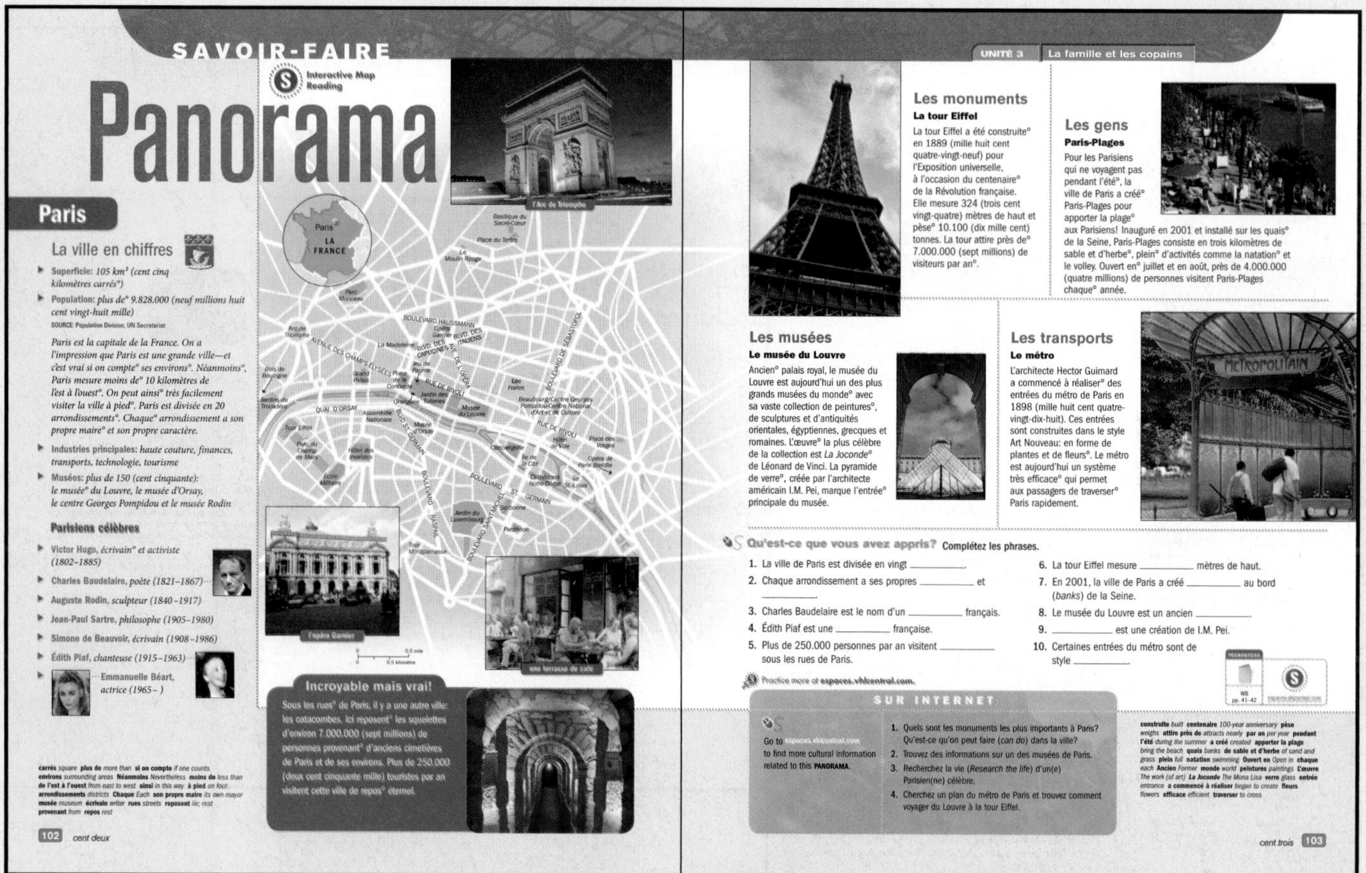
SAVOIR-FAIRE

Panorama

Interactive Map Reading

Paris

La ville en chiffres

- Superficie: 105 km² (cent cinq kilomètres carrés°)
- Population: plus de° 9.828.000 (neuf millions huit cent vingt-huit mille)

Paris est la capitale de la France. On a l'impression que Paris est une grande ville—et c'est vrai si on compte° ses environs°. Néanmoins°, Paris mesure moins de° 10 kilomètres de l'est à l'ouest°. On peut ainsi° très facilement visiter la ville à pied°. Paris est divisée en 20 arrondissements°. Chaque° arrondissement a son propre maire° et son propre caractère.

- Industries principales: haute couture, finances, transports, technologie, tourisme
- Musées: plus de 150 (cent cinquante): le musée° du Louvre, le musée d'Orsay, le centre Georges Pompidou et le musée Rodin

Parisiens célèbres

- Victor Hugo, écrivain° et activiste (1802–1885)
- Charles Baudelaire, poète (1821–1867)
- Auguste Rodin, sculpteur (1840–1917)
- Jean-Paul Sartre, philosophe (1905–1980)
- Simone de Beauvoir, écrivain (1908–1986)
- Édith Piaf, chanteuse (1915–1963)
- Emmanuelle Béart, actrice (1965–)

L'Arc de Triomphe

L'opéra Garnier

une terrasse de café

Incroyable mais vrai!

Sous les rues° de Paris, il y a une autre ville: les catacombes. Ici reposent° les squelettes d'environ 7.000.000 (sept millions) de personnes provenant° d'anciens cimetières de Paris et de ses environs. Plus de 250.000 (deux cent cinquante mille) touristes par an visitent cette ville de repos° éternel.

102 cent deux

UNITÉ 3 La famille et les copains

Les monuments

La tour Eiffel

La tour Eiffel a été construite° en 1889 (mille huit cent quatre-vingt-neuf) pour l'Exposition universelle, à l'occasion du centenaire° de la Révolution française. Elle mesure 324 (trois cent vingt-quatre) mètres de haut et pèse° 10.100 (dix mille cent) tonnes. La tour attire près de° 7.000.000 (sept millions) de visiteurs par an°.

Les gens

Paris-Plages

Pour les Parisiens qui ne voyagent pas pendant l'été°, la ville de Paris a créé° Paris-Plages pour apporter la plage° aux Parisiens! Inauguré en 2001 et installé sur les quais° de la Seine, Paris-Plages consiste en trois kilomètres de sable et d'herbe°, plein° d'activités comme la natation° et le volley. Ouvert en° juillet et en août, près de 4.000.000 (quatre millions) de personnes visitent Paris-Plages chaque° année.

Les musées

Le musée du Louvre

Ancien° palais royal, le musée du Louvre est aujourd'hui un des plus grands musées du monde° avec sa vaste collection de peintures°, de sculptures et d'antiquités orientales, égyptiennes, grecques et romaines. L'œuvre° la plus célèbre de la collection est *La Joconde*° de Léonard de Vinci. La pyramide de verre°, créée par l'architecte américain I.M. Pei, marque l'entrée° principale du musée.

Les transports

Le métro

L'architecte Hector Guimard a commencé à réaliser° des entrées du métro de Paris en 1898 (mille huit cent quatre-vingt-dix-huit). Ces entrées sont construites dans le style Art Nouveau: en forme de plantes et de fleurs°. Le métro est aujourd'hui un système très efficace° qui permet aux passagers de traverser° Paris rapidement.

Qu'est-ce que vous avez appris? Complétez les phrases.

1. La ville de Paris est divisée en vingt ________.
2. Chaque arrondissement a ses propres ________ et ________.
3. Charles Baudelaire est le nom d'un ________ français.
4. Édith Piaf est une ________ française.
5. Plus de 250.000 personnes par an visitent ________ sous les rues de Paris.
6. La tour Eiffel mesure ________ mètres de haut.
7. En 2001, la ville de Paris a créé ________ au bord (*banks*) de la Seine.
8. Le musée du Louvre est un ancien ________.
9. ________ est une création de I.M. Pei.
10. Certaines entrées du métro sont de style ________.

SUR INTERNET

1. Quels sont les monuments les plus importants à Paris? Qu'est-ce qu'on peut faire (*can do*) dans la ville?
2. Trouvez des informations sur un des musées de Paris.
3. Recherchez la vie (*Research the life*) d'un(e) Parisien(ne) célèbre.
4. Cherchez un plan du métro de Paris et trouvez comment voyager du Louvre à la tour Eiffel.

cent trois 103

La ville/Le pays/La région en chiffres provides interesting key facts about the featured city, country, or region.

Maps point out major cities, rivers, and other geographical features and situate the featured place in the context of its immediate surroundings and the world.

Readings A series of brief paragraphs explores facets of the featured place's culture such as history, landmarks, fine art, literature, and aspects of everyday life.

Incroyable mais vrai! highlights an intriguing fact about the featured place or its people.

Qu'est-ce que vous avez appris? exercises check your understanding of key ideas, and **ressources** boxes reference the two pages of additional activities in the **ESPACES** Workbook.

Sur Internet offers Internet activities on the **ESPACES** Supersite for additional avenues of discovery.

SAVOIR-FAIRE

Lecture develops reading skills in the context of the unit's theme.

SAVOIR-FAIRE

UNITÉ 3 La famille et les copains

Lecture

Reading

Avant la lecture

STRATÉGIE

Predicting content from visuals

When you are reading in French, be sure to look for visual clues that will orient you as to the content and purpose of what you are reading. Photos and illustrations, for example, will often give you a good idea of the main points that the reading covers. You may also encounter helpful visuals that summarize large amounts of data in a way that is easy to comprehend; these visuals include bar graphs, pie charts, flow charts, lists of percentages, and other diagrams.

Le Top 10 des chiens de race°
% DE FOYERS° POSSESSEURS
les caniches° **9,3%**
les labradors **7,8%**
les yorkshires **5,6%**
les épagneuls bretons° **4,6%**
les bergers allemands° **4,1%**
les autres bergers **3,3%**
les bichons **2,7%**
les cockers/fox-terriers **2,2%**
les boxers **2%**
les colleys **1,6%**

Examinez le texte

Take a quick look at the visual elements of the article in order to generate a list of ideas about its content. Then, compare your list with a classmate's. Are your lists the same or are they different? Discuss your lists and make any changes needed to produce a final list of ideas.

race *breed* **foyers** *households* **caniches** *poodles* **épagneuls bretons** *Brittany Spaniels* **bergers allemands** *German Shepherds*

104 *cent quatre*

Fido en famille

Les Français adorent les animaux. Plus de la moitié° des foyers en France ont un chien, un chat ou un autre animal de compagnie°. Les chiens sont particulièrement appréciés et intégrés dans la famille et la société françaises.

Qui possède un chien en France et pourquoi? Souvent°, la présence d'un chien en famille suit l'arrivée° d'enfants, parce que les parents pensent qu'un chien contribue positivement à leur développement. Il est aussi commun de trouver deux chiens ou plus dans le même° foyer.

Les chiens sont d'excellents compagnons. Leurs maîtres° sont moins seuls° et déclarent avoir moins de stress. Certaines personnes possèdent un chien pour avoir plus d'exercice physique. Et il y a aussi des personnes qui possèdent un chien parce qu'elles en ont toujours eu un° et n'imaginent pas une vie° sans° chien.

Les chiens ont parfois° les mêmes droits° que les autres membres de la famille, et parfois des droits spéciaux. Bien sûr, ils accompagnent leurs maîtres pour les courses en ville° et les promenades dans le parc, et ils entrent même dans certains magasins°. Ne trouvez-vous pas parfois un caniche ou un labrador, les deux races les plus° populaires en France, avec son maître dans un restaurant?

En France, il n'est pas difficile d'observer que les chiens ont une place privilégiée au sein de° la famille.

Pourquoi avoir un animal de compagnie?

RAISON	CHIENS	CHATS	OISEAUX	POISSONS
Pour l'amour des animaux	61,4%	60,5%	61%	33%
Pour avoir de la compagnie	43,5%	38,2%	37%	10%
Pour s'occuper°	40,4%	37,7%	0%	0%
Parce que j'en ai toujours eu un°	31,8%	28,9%	0%	0%
Pour le bien-être° personnel	29,2%	26,2%	0%	0%
Pour les enfants	23,7%	21,3%	30%	48%

Plus de la moitié *More than half* **animal de compagnie** *pet* **Souvent** *Often* **suit l'arrivée** *follows the arrival* **même** *same* **maîtres** *owners* **moins seuls** *less lonely* **en ont toujours eu un** *have always had one* **vie** *life* **sans** *without* **parfois** *sometimes* **droits** *rights* **courses en ville** *errands in town* **magasins** *stores* **les plus** *the most* **au sein de** *in the heart of* **s'occuper** *keep busy* **Parce que j'en ai toujours eu un** *Because I've always had one* **bien-être** *well-being*

Après la lecture

Vrai ou faux? Indicate whether these items are **vrai** or **faux**, based on the reading. Correct the false ones.

	Vrai	Faux
1. Les chiens accompagnent leurs maîtres pour les promenades dans le parc.	☐	☐
2. Parfois, les chiens accompagnent leurs maîtres dans les restaurants.	☐	☐
3. Le chat n'est pas un animal apprécié en France.	☐	☐
4. Certaines personnes déclarent posséder un chien pour avoir plus d'exercice physique.	☐	☐
5. Certaines personnes déclarent posséder un chien pour avoir plus de stress.	☐	☐
6. En France, les familles avec enfants n'ont pas de chien.	☐	☐

Fido en famille Choose the correct response according to the article.

1. Combien de foyers en France ont au moins (*at least*) un animal de compagnie?
   a. 20%-25%
   b. 40%-45%
   c. 50%-55%
2. Pourquoi est-ce une bonne idée d'avoir un chien?
   a. pour plus de compagnie et plus de stress
   b. pour l'exercice physique et être seul
   c. pour la compagnie et le développement des enfants
3. Que pensent les familles françaises de leurs chiens?
   a. Les chiens sont plus importants que les enfants.
   b. Les chiens font partie (*are part*) de la famille et participent aux activités quotidiennes (*daily*).
   c. Le rôle des chiens est limité aux promenades.
4. Quelles races de chien les Français préfèrent-ils?
   a. les caniches et les oiseaux
   b. les labradors et les bergers allemands
   c. les caniches et les labradors
5. Y a-t-il des familles avec plus d'un chien?
   a. non
   b. oui
   c. les caniches et les labradors

Mes animaux In groups of three, say why you own or someone you know owns a pet. Give one of the reasons listed in the table on the left or a different one. Use the verb **avoir** and possessive adjectives.

MODÈLE

Mon grand-père a un chien pour son bien-être personnel.

cent cinq 105

Avant la lecture presents valuable reading strategies and pre-reading activities that strengthen your reading abilities in French.

Readings are directly tied to the unit theme and recycle vocabulary and grammar you have learned. The selections in Units 1–11 are cultural texts, while those in Units 12–15 are literary pieces.

Après la lecture includes post-reading activities that check your comprehension of the reading.

SAVOIR-FAIRE

Écriture develops writing skills in the context of the unit's theme.

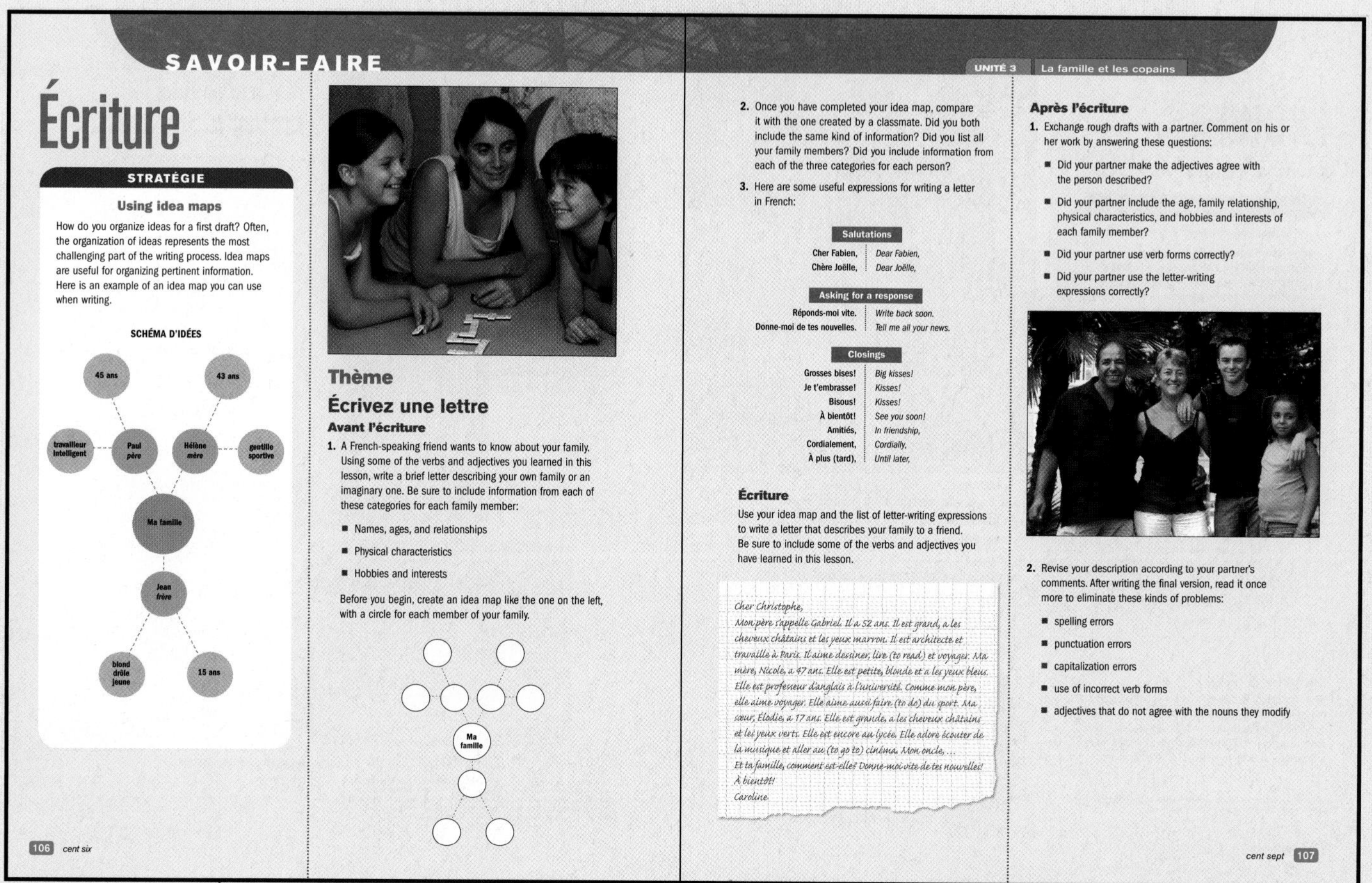

SAVOIR-FAIRE

UNITÉ 3 La famille et les copains

Écriture

STRATÉGIE

Using idea maps

How do you organize ideas for a first draft? Often, the organization of ideas represents the most challenging part of the writing process. Idea maps are useful for organizing pertinent information. Here is an example of an idea map you can use when writing.

SCHÉMA D'IDÉES

Thème

Écrivez une lettre

Avant l'écriture

1. A French-speaking friend wants to know about your family. Using some of the verbs and adjectives you learned in this lesson, write a brief letter describing your own family or an imaginary one. Be sure to include information from each of these categories for each family member:
   - Names, ages, and relationships
   - Physical characteristics
   - Hobbies and interests

   Before you begin, create an idea map like the one on the left, with a circle for each member of your family.

2. Once you have completed your idea map, compare it with the one created by a classmate. Did you both include the same kind of information? Did you list all your family members? Did you include information from each of the three categories for each person?
3. Here are some useful expressions for writing a letter in French:

Salutations	
Cher Fabien,	*Dear Fabien,*
Chère Joëlle,	*Dear Joëlle,*

Asking for a response	
Réponds-moi vite.	*Write back soon.*
Donne-moi de tes nouvelles.	*Tell me all your news.*

Closings	
Grosses bises!	*Big kisses!*
Je t'embrasse!	*Kisses!*
Bisous!	*Kisses!*
À bientôt!	*See you soon!*
Amitiés,	*In friendship,*
Cordialement,	*Cordially,*
À plus (tard),	*Until later,*

Écriture

Use your idea map and the list of letter-writing expressions to write a letter that describes your family to a friend. Be sure to include some of the verbs and adjectives you have learned in this lesson.

Cher Christophe,
Mon père s'appelle Gabriel. Il a 52 ans. Il est grand, a les cheveux châtains et les yeux marron. Il est architecte et travaille à Paris. Il aime dessiner, lire (to read) et voyager. Ma mère, Nicole, a 47 ans. Elle est petite, blonde et a les yeux bleus. Elle est professeur d'anglais à l'université. Comme mon père, elle aime voyager. Elle aime aussi faire (to do) du sport. Ma sœur, Élodie, a 17 ans. Elle est grande, a les cheveux châtains et les yeux verts. Elle est encore au lycée. Elle adore écouter de la musique et aller au (to go to) cinéma. Mon oncle, ...
Et ta famille, comment est-elle? Donne-moi vite de tes nouvelles!
À bientôt!
Caroline

Après l'écriture

1. Exchange rough drafts with a partner. Comment on his or her work by answering these questions:
   - Did your partner make the adjectives agree with the person described?
   - Did your partner include the age, family relationship, physical characteristics, and hobbies and interests of each family member?
   - Did your partner use verb forms correctly?
   - Did your partner use the letter-writing expressions correctly?
2. Revise your description according to your partner's comments. After writing the final version, read it once more to eliminate these kinds of problems:
   - spelling errors
   - punctuation errors
   - capitalization errors
   - use of incorrect verb forms
   - adjectives that do not agree with the nouns they modify

106 cent six

cent sept 107

Process approach Like **À l'écoute** and **Lecture**, **Écriture** is a skill building feature. It was developed using a process approach in order to guide your efforts better. It has pre-writing tasks (**Avant l'écriture**), a task to use during writing (**Écriture**), and post-writing tasks (**Après l'écriture**).

Stratégie provides useful strategies that prepare you for the writing task presented in **Thème**.

Thème describes the writing topic and includes suggestions for approaching it.

Vocabulaire

summarizes all the active vocabulary of the unit.

Flashcards
Audio: Vocabulary

VOCABULAIRE UNITÉ 3

La famille

aîné(e)	*elder*
cadet(te)	*younger*
un beau-frère	*brother-in-law*
un beau-père	*father-in-law; stepfather*
une belle-mère	*mother-in-law; stepmother*
une belle-sœur	*sister-in-law*
un(e) cousin(e)	*cousin*
un demi-frère	*half-brother; stepbrother*
une demi-sœur	*half-sister; stepsister*
les enfants (*m., f.*)	*children*
un époux/une épouse	*spouse*
une famille	*family*
une femme	*wife; woman*
une fille	*daughter; girl*
un fils	*son*
un frère	*brother*
une grand-mère	*grandmother*
un grand-père	*grandfather*
les grands-parents (*m.*)	*grandparents*
un mari	*husband*
une mère	*mother*
un neveu	*nephew*
une nièce	*niece*
un oncle	*uncle*
les parents (*m.*)	*parents*
un père	*father*
une petite-fille	*granddaughter*
un petit-fils	*grandson*
les petits-enfants (*m.*)	*grandchildren*
une sœur	*sister*
une tante	*aunt*
un chat	*cat*
un chien	*dog*
un oiseau	*bird*
un poisson	*fish*

Adjectifs descriptifs

antipathique	*unpleasant*
bleu(e)	*blue*
blond(e)	*blond*
brun(e)	*dark (hair)*
court(e)	*short*
drôle	*funny*
faible	*weak*
fatigué(e)	*tired*
fort(e)	*strong*
frisé(e)	*curly*
génial(e) (géniaux *pl.*)	*great*
grand(e)	*big; tall*
jeune	*young*
joli(e)	*pretty*
laid(e)	*ugly*
lent(e)	*slow*
mauvais(e)	*bad*
méchant(e)	*mean*
modeste	*modest, humble*
noir(e)	*black*
pauvre	*poor, unfortunate*
pénible	*tiresome*
petit(e)	*small, short (stature)*
prêt(e)	*ready*
raide	*straight*
rapide	*fast*
triste	*sad*
vert(e)	*green*
vrai(e)	*true; real*

Vocabulaire supplémentaire

divorcer	*to divorce*
épouser	*to marry*
célibataire	*single*
divorcé(e)	*divorced*
fiancé(e)	*engaged*
marié(e)	*married*
séparé(e)	*separated*
veuf/veuve	*widowed*
un(e) voisin(e)	*neighbor*

Expressions utiles	*See pp. 79 and 93.*
Possessive adjectives	*See p. 84.*
Numbers 61-100	*See p. 96.*
Prepositions of location	*See p. 98.*

Professions et occupations

un(e) architecte	*architect*
un(e) artiste	*artist*
un(e) athlète	*athlete*
un(e) avocat(e)	*lawyer*
un coiffeur/une coiffeuse	*hairdresser*
un(e) dentiste	*dentist*
un homme/une femme d'affaires	*businessman/woman*
un ingénieur	*engineer*
un(e) journaliste	*journalist*
un médecin	*doctor*
un(e) musicien(ne)	*musician*

Adjectifs irréguliers

actif/active	*active*
beau/belle	*beautiful; handsome*
bon(ne)	*kind; good*
châtain	*brown (hair)*
courageux/courageuse	*courageous, brave*
cruel(le)	*cruel*
curieux/curieuse	*curious*
discret/discrète	*discreet; unassuming*
doux/douce	*sweet; soft*
ennuyeux/ennuyeuse	*boring*
étranger/étrangère	*foreign*
favori(te)	*favorite*
fier/fière	*proud*
fou/folle	*crazy*
généreux/généreuse	*generous*
gentil(le)	*nice*
gros(se)	*fat*
inquiet/inquiète	*worried*
intellectuel(le)	*intellectual*
jaloux/jalouse	*jealous*
long(ue)	*long*
(mal)heureux/(mal)heureuse	*(un)happy*
marron	*brown*
naïf/naïve	*naïve*
nerveux/nerveuse	*nervous*
nouveau/nouvelle	*new*
paresseux/paresseuse	*lazy*
roux/rousse	*red-haired*
sérieux/sérieuse	*serious*
sportif/sportive	*athletic*
travailleur/travailleuse	*hard-working*
vieux/vieille	*old*

ressources
espaces.vhlcentral.com

108 *cent huit*

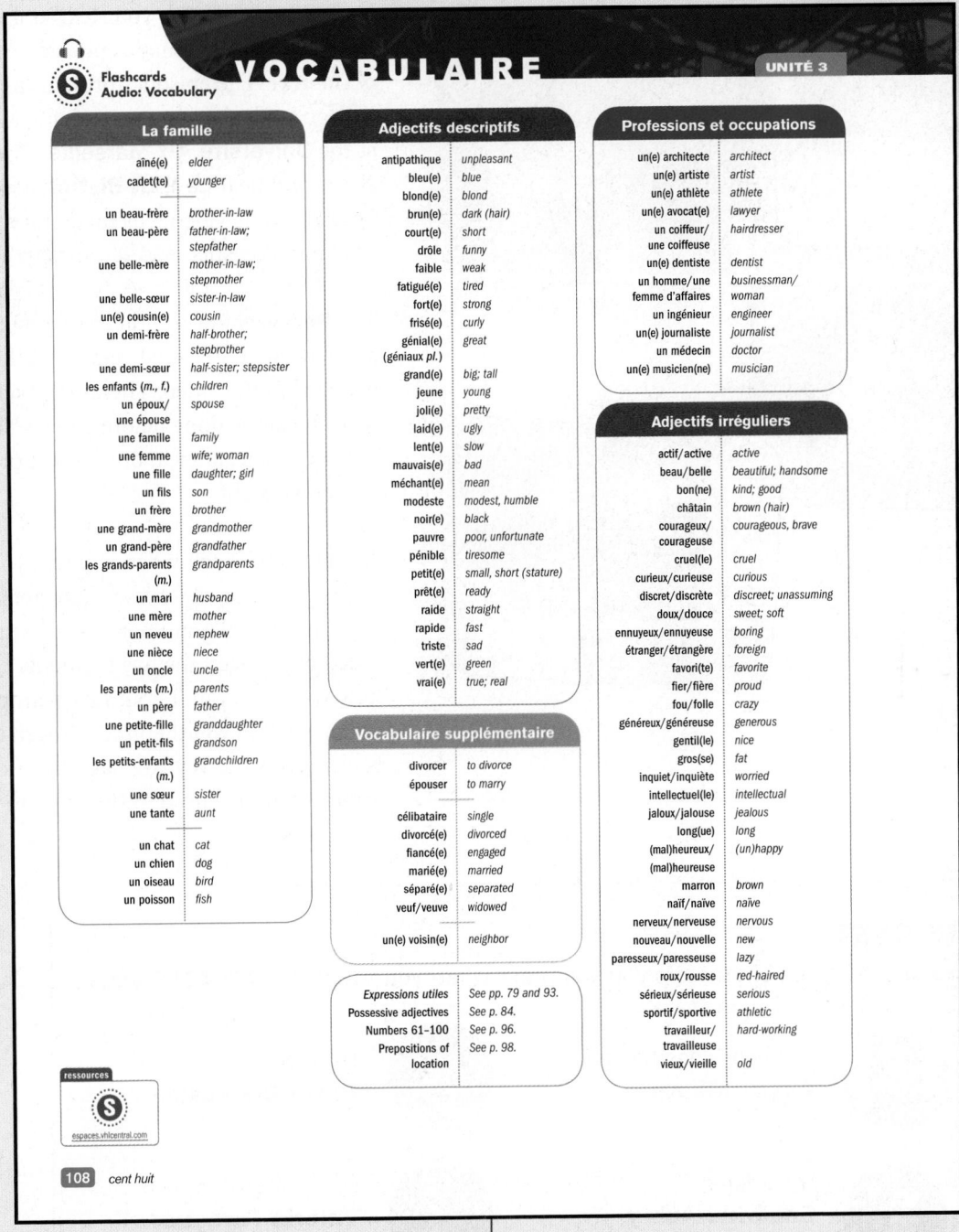

Recorded vocabulary The headset icon at the top of the page and the **ressources** box at the bottom of the page highlight that the active lesson vocabulary is recorded for convenient study and practice on the **ESPACES** Supersite.

VIDEO PROGRAM

THE *ROMAN-PHOTO* EPISODES

Fully integrated with your textbook, the **ESPACES** Video contains thirty dramatic episodes, one for each lesson of the text. The episodes present the adventures of four college students who are studying in the south of France at the **Université Aix-Marseille**. They live in apartments above and near **Le P'tit Bistrot**, a café owned by Valérie Forestier. The video tells their story and the story of Madame Forestier and her teenage son, Stéphane.

The **Roman-photo** section in each textbook lesson is actually an abbreviated version of the dramatic episode featured in the video. Therefore, each **Roman-photo** section can be done before you see the corresponding video episode, after it, or as a section that stands alone in its own right.

As you watch each video episode, you will first see a live segment in which the characters interact using vocabulary and grammar you are studying. As the video progresses, the live segments carefully combine new vocabulary and grammar with previously taught language. You will then see a **Reprise** segment that summarizes the key language functions and/or grammar points used in the dramatic episode.

THE CAST

Here are the main characters you will meet when you watch the ESPACES Video:

Of Senegalese heritage
Amina Mbaye

From Paris
Sandrine Aubry

Of Algerian heritage
Rachid Kahlid

From Washington, D.C.
David Duchesne

From Aix-en-Provence
Valérie Forestier

And, also from
Aix-en-Provence
Stéphane Forestier

THE *FLASH CULTURE* SEGMENTS

In one lesson of each unit, a **Flash culture** segment allows you to experience the sights and sounds of France, the French-speaking world, and the daily life of French speakers. Each segment is from two-to-three minutes long and is correlated to your textbook in the **Sur Internet** box in **Espace culture**.

Hosted by the **ESPACES** narrators, Csilla and Benjamin, these segments of specially shot footage transport you to a variety of venues: schools, parks, public squares, cafés, stores, cinemas, outdoor markets, city streets, festivals, and more. They also incorporate mini-interviews with French speakers in various walks of life, for example, family members, friends, students, and people in different professions.

The footage was filmed taking special care to capture rich, vibrant images that will expand your cultural perspectives with information directly related to the content of your textbook. In addition, the narrations were carefully written to reflect the vocabulary and grammar covered in the Second Edition of **ESPACES**.

ICONS AND *RESSOURCES* BOXES

Icons

These icons in the Second Edition of **ESPACES** alert you to the type of activity or section involved.

Icons legend	
Listening activity/section	Additional content found on the Supersite: audio, video, and presentations
Activity also on the Supersite	Additional practice on the Supersite.
Pair activity	Information Gap activity
Group activity	Feuilles d'activités
Re-entering activity	

- The Information Gap activities and those involving **Feuilles d'activités** (*activity sheets*) require handouts that your instructor will give you.
- The listening icon appears in **Contextes**, **Les sons et les lettres**, **À l'écoute**, and **Vocabulaire** sections.
- The video icon appears in **Roman-photo**, either one of the **Culture** sections, and **Le zapping**.
- The re-entering icon tells you that to finish a specific activity you will need to use vocabulary and/or grammar learned in previous lessons.

Ressources Boxes

Ressources boxes let you know exactly which print and technology ancillaries you can use to reinforce and expand on every section of every lesson in your textbook. They even include page numbers when applicable. See the next page for a description of the ancillaries.

Ressources boxes legend	
WB pp. 29–30 — Workbook	DVD Leçon 3A — DVD
LM p. 17 — Lab Manual	espaces.vhlcentral.com — ESPACES Supersite
VM pp. 219–220 — Video Manual	

Powered by MAESTRO®

Free with the purchase of a new textbook, the **ESPACES** Supersite provides a wealth of learning tools for students.

- Interactive practice activities with auto-grading and real-time feedback
  - directed practice from the textbook, including audio activities
  - additional practice for each and every textbook section
- Audio practice
  - record-and-compare audio activities
  - all audio material related to the **ESPACES** program
- Complete **Roman-photo** and **Flash culture** video programs

Plus MP3 files for the complete audio program

STUDENT ANCILLARIES

- **Workbook/Video Manual**
  The Workbook activities provide additional practice of the vocabulary and grammar in each textbook lesson and the cultural information in each unit's **Panorama** section. The Video Manual includes pre-viewing, viewing, and post-viewing activities for the **ESPACES** Video.
- **Lab Manual**
  The Lab Manual contains activities for each textbook lesson that build listening comprehension, speaking, and pronunciation skills in French.
- **Lab Program MP3s and HiFis***
  The Lab Program MP3s and HiFis provide the recordings to be used in conjunction with the activities in the Lab Manual.
- **Textbook MP3s***
  The Textbook MP3s contain the recordings for the listening activities in **Espace contextes**, **Les sons et les lettres**, **À l'écoute**, and **Vocabulaire** sections.
- **VIDEO* DVDs**
  The Video DVD, available for purchase, provides the **Roman-photo** and **Flash culture** Videos with French and English subtitles.
- **Online Workbook/Video Manual/Lab Manual**
  Incorporating the **ESPACES** Video, as well as the complete Lab Program, this component delivers the Workbook, Video Manual, and Lab Manual online with automatic scoring. Instructors have access to the powerful Maestro® classroom management and gradebook tools that allow in-depth tracking of students' scores.
- **ESPACES Supersite****
  Your passcode to the Supersite (**espaces.vhlcentral.com**) gives you access to a wide variety of interactive activities for each section of every lesson of the student text; auto-graded exercises for extra practice of vocabulary, grammar, video, and cultural content; reference tools; the **Le zapping** TV commercials and short films; the complete Video Program; the Textbook MP3s, and the Lab Program MP3s.

**Available on the Supersite*
***Included with the purchase of a new Student Text*
****Included in the Instructor's DVD Set*

INSTRUCTOR ANCILLARIES

- **Instructor's Annotated Edition (IAE)**
  The unique format of the IAE provides comprehensive support for classroom teaching: expansions, variations, teaching tips, cultural information, additional activities, scripts, and the answer key to the textbook activities.
- **Workbook/Video Manual/Lab Manual Answer Key***
- **ESPACES Video Program on DVDs*****
  These DVDs contain the complete **ESPACES** Video Program, both the **Roman-photo** episodes and the **Flash culture** segments, with French and English subtitles.
- **Instructor's DVD Set**
  This set contains the **Roman-photo** and **Flash culture** DVDs, the Test Generator, and the Testing Program MP3 files.
- **Overhead Transparencies (OHTs)***
  The OHTs consist of maps of the French-speaking world and the **Espace contextes** illustrations.
- **Instructor's Resource Manual (IRM)***
  The IRM contains the Textbook and Lab Audioscripts, the videoscript, English translations of the **Roman-photo** conversations, Supplementary Vocabulary lists, Information Gap activities, **Feuilles d'activités** handouts, answers to **Mise en pratique** and **Essayez!** exercises, French transcriptions and English translations of **Le zapping** TV Clips and Short Films.
- **Testing Program***
  This contains two versions of tests for each textbook lesson, semester exams and quarter exams, listening scripts, answer keys, and optional reading, cultural, and video test items. It is provided in ready-to-print PDFs and in RTF Word processing files for ease of editing.
- **Testing Program MP3s* *****
  These audio files provide the recordings of the Testing Program's listening sections.
- **Test Generator*****
  The Introductory French Test Generator provides a test bank of quizzes and exams from our introductory French programs. Instructors can modify existing tests, create their own tests, and randomly generate new tests.
- **Online Testing Program**
  It consists of all quizzes and exams from the printed Testing Program. Test items with discrete answers are automatically scored, and all grades are easily exported to Blackboard and WebCT.
- **ESPACES Supersite**
  The Supersite allows instructors access to student site and offers a robust course management system to assign and track student progress. It also contains the full contents of the instructor's resources.

ACKNOWLEDGMENTS

On behalf of its authors and editors, Vista Higher Learning expresses its sincere appreciation to the many college professors nationwide who reviewed materials from **ESPACES**. Their input and suggestions were vitally helpful in forming and shaping the program in its final, published form.

We also extend a special thank you to the contributing writer whose hard work was central to bringing **ESPACES** to fruition: Nora Portillo.

In-depth reviewers

Dorothy E. Diehl
Saint Mary's University of Minnesota

Lynne Wettig
Park University, Kansas

Reviewers

Ellen Abrams
New England Community College, MA

Norma Alvarez
College of Southern Nevada

Eileen M. Angelini
Canisius College, NY

Christine Armstrong
Denison University, OH

Michael Armstrong
Florida Atlantic University

Kathleen Attwood
Owens Community College, OH

Marty Bandini
Southwestern College, CA

Samira Belaoun
Bunker Hill Community College, MA

Maria Benson
Virginia Commonwealth University

Juan A. Bernabeu
Laramie County Community College, WY

Marie Bertola
West Valley College, CA

Kaye Bletso
Jefferson Community College, KY

Julia Bordeaux
Mansfield University, PA

Christine Boudin-Stoa
Saint Mary's University of Minnesota

Cavella Bullard
Wake Technical Community College, NC

Thomas Buresi
Southern Polytechnic State University, GA

Allegra Clement-Bayard
John Burroughs School, MO

Helene Coignet
Canisius College, NY

Margaret Colvin
Otterbein College, OH

Mary Beth Crane
College of Southern Idaho

LaVerne Dalka
Hanover College, IN

Nathalie Davaut
Rowan Cabarrus Community College, NC

David de Posada
Macon State College, GA

Linda Downing
Diablo Valley College, CA

Beth Droppleman
Columbia College, SC

Kamila Dudley
University of Hawaii

Vicki Earnest
Calhoun College, AL

Paula Egan-Wright
Laramie County Community College, WY

Natasha Engering-Ward
Justin-Siena High School, CA

Lisa C. Franks
Cabrini College, PA

Kerwin Friebel
Muskegon Community College, MI

Barbara I. Friedman
Florida Atlantic University

Trisha Frye
Salem Academy and College, NC

Maria Gardeta-Healey
Mesa Community College, AZ

Sophie Gelaw
University of the Virgin Islands

Virginie Gindoff
Plymouth State University, NH

Martha Grant
Falmouth High School, ME

Stella Greenbaum
The Hun School of Princeton, NJ

Sue Grove
Riverland Community College, MN

Luc Guglielmi
Kennesaw State University, GA

Nathan Guss
Clemson University, SC

Kwaku A. Gyasi
University of Alabama in Huntsville

B. Sabastian Hobson
Northern Virginia Community College

Jessica Hoy
Illinois State University

Rejane Jehanno
Pacific Union College, CA

Zhen Ji
Our Lady of the Lake University, TX

E. Joe Johnson
Clayton State University, GA

Nikki L. Kaltenbach
Indiana University Northwest

Ann Kirkland
Hanover College, IN

Ute S. Lahaie
Gardner-Webb University, NC

Stanley F. Levine
University of South Carolina Aiken

Leanne Lindelof
San Jose State University, CA

Oksana Lutsyshyna
University of South Florida

Olivia Marancy-Ferrer
North Broward Preparatory School, FL

Jackie Mauldin
Gainsville State College, GA

Kitzie McKinney
Bentley College, MA

Mireille McNabb
West Valley College, CA

Sylvie Merlier-Rowen
Shoshana S. Cardin School, MD

Cedric Michel
University of South Florida

Isabelle Miller
Bellevue Community College, WA

Doug Mrazek
Clark College, WA

Martine Motard-Noar
McDaniel College, MD

Shonu Nangia
Louisiana State University at Alexandria

Justin Niati
Houghton College, NY

Eva Norling
Bellevue Community College, WA

Leslie Norman
Gonzaga University, WA

Marie-Noelle Olivier
University of Nevada, Las Vegas

Scooter Pegram
Indiana University Northwest

Christiane E. Reese
Florida Atlantic University, FL

Anna K. Sandstrom
University of New Hampshire

Amy Sawyer
Clemson University, SC

Lisa F. Signori
Erskine College, SC

Virginia Stamanis
The Meadows School, NV

Janis Tansey
Pine Crest School, FL

Maria-Elena Torales
Imperial Valley College, CA

Michael Vermy
Fullerton College, CA

Nirva Vernet
Virginia Commonwealth University

Terri Woellner
University of Denver, CO

Lisa Yigit
North Broward Preparatory, FL

Samuel Zadi
Wheaton College, IL

Elizabeth Zwanziger
Wartburg College, IA

Salut!

UNITÉ **1**

Pour commencer
- What are these young women saying?
  a. Excusez-moi. b. Bonjour! c. Merci.
- How many women are there in the photo?
  a. une b. deux c. trois
- What do you think is an appropriate title for either of these women?
  a. Monsieur b. Madame c. Mademoiselle

Unit Goals

Leçon 1A
In this lesson, students will learn:
- terms for greetings, farewells, and introductions
- expressions of courtesy
- the French alphabet and the names of accent marks
- about shaking hands and **bises**
- more about greetings and farewells through specially shot video footage
- gender of nouns
- articles (definite and indefinite)
- the numbers 0–60
- the expression **il y a**
- about the company Moulinex

Leçon 1B
In this lesson, students will learn:
- terms to identify people
- terms for objects in the classroom
- rules for silent letters
- about France's multicultural society
- subject pronouns
- the present tense of **être**
- **c'est** and **il/elle est**
- adjective agreement
- some descriptive adjectives and adjectives of nationality
- to listen for familiar words

Savoir-faire
In this section, students will learn:
- cultural, linguistic, and historical information about the francophone world
- to recognize cognates
- strategies for writing in French
- to write a telephone/address book

Pour commencer
- **b. Bonjour!**
- **b. deux**
- **c. Mademoiselle**

RESOURCES

Workbook/Video Manual: WB Activities, pp. 1–14
Laboratory Manual: Lab Activities, pp. 1–8
Workbook/Video Manual: Video Activities, pp. 211–214; pp. 271–272
WB/VM/LM Answer Key

espaces.vhlcentral.com: Textbook MP3s; Lab MP3s; Instructor's Resource Manual [IRM] (Textbook Audioscript; Lab Audioscript; Videoscript; **Roman-photo** Translations; **Vocabulaire supplémentaire**; **Feuilles d'activités**; Info Gap Activities; **Le zapping** TV clip transcription; **Essayez!** and **Mise en pratique** answers); Transparencies #13, #14, #15, #16; Testing Program, pp. 1–8; Test Files; Testing Program MP3s
Test Generator
Video on DVD

Section Goals

In this section, students will learn and practice vocabulary related to:

- basic greetings and farewells
- introductions
- courtesy expressions

Instructional Resources
*espaces.vhlcentral.com: Transparencies #13, #14; IRM (**Vocabulaire supplémentaire**; **Mise en pratique** answers; Textbook Audioscript; Lab Audioscript); Textbook MP3s; Lab MP3s; WB/VM/LM Answer Key; activities; downloads; reference tools*

Suggestions

- To familiarize students with the meanings of headings used in the lessons and important vocabulary for classroom interactions, pass out **Vocabulaire supplémentaire: vocabulaire pour la classe de français** from the Supersite.
- For complete lesson plans, go to **espaces.vhlcentral.com** to access the instructor's part of the **ESPACES** companion Supersite.
- With books closed, write a few greetings, farewells, and courtesy expressions on the board, explain their meaning, and model their pronunciation. Circulate around the room, greeting students, making introductions, and encouraging responses. Then, have students open their books to pages 2–3. Ask them to identify which conversations are exchanges between friends and which seem more formal. Then point out the use of **vous** vs. **tu** in each conversation. Give examples of different situations in which each form would be appropriate.

Successful Language Learning Encourage students to make flash cards to help them memorize or review vocabulary.

Leçon 1A

You will learn how to...

- **greet people in French**
- **say good-bye**

Talking Picture
Audio: Activity

Ça va?

GEORGES Ça va, Julien?
JULIEN Oui, ça va très bien, merci. Et vous, comment allez-vous?
GEORGES Je vais bien, merci.
VINCENT Merci!
QUENTIN Il n'y a pas de quoi.
MARIE À plus tard, Guillaume!
GUILLAUME À tout à l'heure, Marie!
JACQUES Bonjour, Monsieur Boniface. Je vous présente Inès Lemaire.
M. BONIFACE Bonjour, Mademoiselle.
INÈS Enchantée.

Vocabulaire

Bonsoir.	*Good evening.; Hello.*
À bientôt.	*See you soon.*
À demain.	*See you tomorrow.*
Bonne journée!	*Have a good day!*
Au revoir.	*Good-bye.*
Comme ci, comme ça.	*So-so.*
Je vais bien/mal.	*I am doing well/badly.*
Moi aussi.	*Me too.*
Comment t'appelles-tu? (fam.)	*What is your name?*
Je vous/te présente... (form./fam.)	*I would like to introduce (name) to you.*
De rien.	*You're welcome.*
Excusez-moi. (form.)	*Excuse me.*
Excuse-moi. (fam.)	*Excuse me.*
Merci beaucoup.	*Thanks a lot.*
Pardon.	*Pardon (me).*
S'il vous plaît. (form.)	*Please.*
S'il te plaît. (fam.)	*Please.*
Je vous/t'en prie. (form./fam.)	*You're welcome.; It's nothing.*
Monsieur (M.)	*Sir (Mr.)*
Madame (Mme)	*Ma'am (Mrs.)*
Mademoiselle (Mlle)	*Miss*
ici	*here*
là	*there*
là-bas	*over there*

ressources

WB pp. 1–2 | LM p. 1 | espaces.vhlcentral.com

OPTIONS

Language Notes Point out that **Salut** and **À plus**, the shortened form of **À plus tard**, are familiar expressions. Explain that the translation of **Je vais bien/mal** is not literal. **Je vais** means *I go*, but **je vais bien** means *I am doing well.*

Game Divide the class into two teams. Create sentences and questions based on the **Vocabulaire** and the illustrated conversations. Choose one person at a time, alternating between teams. Tell students to respond logically to your statement or question. Award a point for each correct response. The team with the most points at the end of the game wins.

Attention!

In French, people can be addressed formally or informally. Use the **tu/toi** forms with close friends, family, or children. Use the **vous** forms with groups, a boss, someone older than you, or someone you do not know, unless they ask you to use **tu**.

MARC Bonjour, je m'appelle Marc, et vous, comment vous appelez-vous?
CHLOÉ Je m'appelle Chloé.
MARC Enchanté.
SOPHIE Bonjour, Léa!
LÉA Salut, Sophie!
SOPHIE Ça va?
LÉA Oui, ça va bien, merci. Et toi, comment vas-tu?
SOPHIE Pas mal.

Mise en pratique

1 Chassez l'intrus Circle the word or expression that does not belong.

1. a. Bonjour.
   b. Bonsoir.
   c. Salut.
   (d.) Pardon.
2. a. Bien.
   b. Très bien.
   (c.) De rien.
   d. Comme ci, comme ça.
3. a. À bientôt.
   b. À demain.
   c. À tout à l'heure.
   (d.) Enchanté.
4. a. Comment allez-vous?
   (b.) Comment vous appelez-vous?
   c. Ça va?
   d. Comment vas-tu?
5. **(a.) Pas mal.**
   b. Excuse-moi.
   c. Je vous en prie.
   d. Il n'y a pas de quoi.
6. a. Comment vous appelez-vous?
   b. Je vous présente Dominique.
   c. Enchanté.
   (d.) Comment allez-vous?
7. a. Pas mal.
   b. Très bien.
   c. Mal.
   (d.) Et vous?
8. a. Comment allez-vous?
   b. Comment vous appelez-vous?
   (c.) Et toi?
   d. Je vous en prie.

2 Écoutez Listen to each of these questions or statements and select the most appropriate response.

1.	Enchanté.	☐	Je m'appelle Thérèse.	☑
2.	Merci beaucoup.	☐	Je vous en prie.	☑
3.	Comme ci, comme ça.	☑	De rien.	☐
4.	Bonsoir, Monsieur.	☑	Moi aussi.	☐
5.	Enchanté.	☑	Et toi?	☐
6.	Bonjour.	☐	À demain.	☑
7.	Pas mal.	☑	Pardon.	☐
8.	Il n'y a pas de quoi.	☑	Moi aussi.	☐
9.	Enchanté.	☐	Très bien. Et vous?	☑
10.	À bientôt.	☑	Mal.	☐

3 Conversez Madeleine is introducing her classmate Khaled to Libby, an American exchange student. Complete their conversation, using a different expression from **ESPACE CONTEXTES** in each blank. Answers will vary.

MADELEINE (1) ______________!
KHALED Salut, Madeleine. (2) ______________?
MADELEINE Pas mal. (3) ______________?
KHALED (4) ______________, merci.
MADELEINE (5) ______________ Libby. Elle est de (*She is from*) Boston.
KHALED (6) ______________ Libby. (7) ______________ Khaled.
(8) ______________?
LIBBY (9) ______________, merci.
KHALED Oh, là, là. Je vais rater (*I am going to miss*) le bus. À bientôt.
MADELEINE (10) ______________.
LIBBY (11) ______________.

Practice more at **espaces.vhlcentral.com.**

1 Suggestion Go over the answers with the class and have students explain why each expression does not belong.

2 Tapescript
1. Comment vous appelez-vous?
2. Excusez-moi.
3. Comment allez-vous?
4. Bonsoir, Mademoiselle.
5. Je te présente Thérèse.
6. À bientôt.
7. Comment vas-tu?
8. Merci.
9. Bonjour, comment allez-vous?
10. Au revoir.
(On Textbook MP3s)

2 Suggestion Before students listen, tell them to read the possible responses provided and write down the questions or statements that they think would elicit each response. After completing the listening activity, go over the answers to check whether students' predictions were accurate.

3 Suggestion Have students work in groups of three on the activity. Tell them to choose a role and complete the conversation. Then ask groups to act out their conversation for the class.

OPTIONS

Pairs Have students work in pairs. Tell them to write an original conversation with six to eight lines. After completing this task, they should rewrite the conversation and scramble the order of the sentences. Have pairs exchange their scrambled conversations and put them in a logical order. Remind students that they should verify the answers.

Small Groups Have small groups role-play a conversation in which other adults, children, and college-age people interact. Remind students to use formal and informal expressions in the appropriate situations. Give them time to prepare, and then have a few groups present their conversations to the class.

4 Suggestions
- Before beginning the activity, encourage students to use as many different words and expressions as they can from the **Vocabulaire** on page 2 rather than repeating the same expressions in each conversation.
- Have a few volunteers write their conversations on the board. Ask the class to identify, correct, and explain any errors.

4 Expansions
- Have students look at the photo, identify the conversation it most likely corresponds to (**Conversation 3**), and explain their reasoning. Point out that nearly all formal greetings are accompanied by a handshake. Tell the class that they will learn more about gestures used in greetings in the **Espace culture** section of this lesson.
- Have students rewrite **Conversation 1** in the formal register, and **Conversations 2** and **3** in the informal register.

5 Suggestions
- Before beginning this activity, ask students if they would use **tu** or **vous** in each situation.
- If class time is limited, assign a specific situation to each pair.
- Call on volunteers to act out their conversations for the class.

6 Suggestion Have two volunteers read the **modèle** aloud. Remind students to use **vous** when addressing more than one classmate at a time.

Communication

4 Discutez With a partner, complete these conversations. Then act them out. Answers will vary.

Conversation 1 Salut! Je m'appelle François. Et toi, comment t'appelles-tu?

____

Ça va?

____

Conversation 2 ________________

Comme ci, comme ça. Et vous?

____

Bon (*Well*), à demain.

____

Conversation 3 Bonsoir, je vous présente Mademoiselle Barnard.

____

Enchanté(e).

____

Très bien, merci. Et vous?

____

5 C'est à vous! How would you greet these people, ask them for their names, and ask them how they are doing? With a partner, write a short dialogue for each item and act it out. Pay attention to the use of **tu** and **vous.** Answers will vary.

1. Madame Colombier

2. Mademoiselle Estèves

3. Monsieur Marchand

4. Marie, Guillaume et Geneviève

6 Présentations Form groups of three. Introduce yourself, and ask your partners their names and how they are doing. Then, join another group and take turns introducing your partners. Answers will vary.

MODÈLE

Étudiant(e) 1: *Bonjour. Je m'appelle Fatima. Et vous?*
Étudiant(e) 2: *Je m'appelle Fabienne.*
Étudiant(e) 3: *Et moi, je m'appelle Antoine. Ça va?*
Étudiant(e) 1: *Ça va bien, merci. Et toi?*
Étudiant(e) 3: *Comme ci, comme ça.*

OPTIONS

Extra Practice Read some sentences to the class and ask if they would use them with another student of the same age or an older person. Examples: **1. Je te présente Guillaume.** (student) **2. Merci beaucoup, Monsieur.** (older person) **3. Comment vas-tu?** (student) **4. Bonjour, professeur ____.** (older person) **5. Comment vous appelez-vous?** (older person)

Extra Practice Have students circulate around the classroom and conduct mini-conversations in French with other students, using the words and expressions they learned on pages 2–3. As students are carrying out the activity, move around the room, monitoring their work and offering assistance if requested.

Les sons et les lettres

Audio: Concepts, Activities
Record & Compare

comparisons — NATIONAL STANDARDS

The French alphabet

The French alphabet is made up of the same 26 letters as the English alphabet. While they look the same, some letters are pronounced differently. They also sound different when you spell.

lettre	exemple	lettre	exemple	lettre	exemple
a (a)	**a**dresse	**j** (ji)	**j**ustice	**s** (esse)	**s**pécial
b (bé)	**b**anane	**k** (ka)	**k**ilomètre	**t** (té)	**t**able
c (cé)	**c**arotte	**l** (elle)	**l**ion	**u** (u)	**u**nique
d (dé)	**d**essert	**m** (emme)	**m**ariage	**v** (vé)	**v**idéo
e (e)	r**e**belle	**n** (enne)	**n**ature	**w** (double vé)	**w**agon
f (effe)	**f**ragile	**o** (o)	**o**live	**x** (iks)	**x**ylophone
g (gé)	**g**enre	**p** (pé)	**p**ersonne	**y** (i grec)	**y**oga
h (hache)	**h**éritage	**q** (ku)	**q**uiche	**z** (zède)	**z**éro
i (i)	**i**nnocent	**r** (erre)	**r**adio		

Notice that some letters in French words have accents. You'll learn how they influence pronunciation in later lessons. Whenever you spell a word in French, include the name of the accent after the letter. For double letters, use **deux**: **ss = deux s.**

accent	nom	exemple	orthographe
´	*accent aigu*	**identité**	*I-D-E-N-T-I-T-E-accent aigu*
`	*accent grave*	**problème**	*P-R-O-B-L-E-accent grave-M-E*
ˆ	*accent circonflexe*	**hôpital**	*H-O-accent circonflexe-P-I-T-A-L*
¨	*tréma*	**naïve**	*N-A-I-tréma-V-E*
¸	*cédille*	**ça**	*C-cédille-A*

Tout est bien qui finit bien.²
Lundi
Mardi

L'alphabet Practice saying the French alphabet and example words aloud.

Ça s'écrit comment? Spell these words aloud in French.

1. judo
2. yacht
3. forêt
4. zèbre
5. existe
6. clown
7. numéro
8. français
9. musique
10. favorite
11. kangourou
12. parachute
13. différence
14. intelligent
15. dictionnaire
16. alphabet

Dictons Practice reading these sayings aloud.

Grande invitation, petites portions.¹

¹ Great boast, small roast.
² All's well that ends well.

ressources
LM p. 2
espaces.vhlcentral.com

Section Goals

In this section, students will learn about:

- the French alphabet and how it contrasts with the English alphabet
- the names of the letters
- the names of the accent marks

Instructional Resources
espaces.vhlcentral.com: Textbook MP3s; Lab MP3s; WB/VM/LM Answer Key; IRM (Textbook Audioscript; Lab Audioscript); activities; downloads; reference tools

Suggestions

- Model the pronunciation of the French alphabet and the example words. Have students repeat.
- Point out that vowel sounds can have many different pronunciations when combined with other vowels or when spelled with accents, particularly the **e**.
- Point out the different diacritical marks and model their pronunciation. For a detailed explanation of **l'accent aigu** and **l'accent grave**, see **Leçon 3A**, page 77. For an explanation of **l'accent circonflexe, le tréma,** and **la cédille**, see **Leçon 3B**, page 91.
- Draw attention to any posters, signs, or maps in the classroom. Point out individual letters, and ask the class to identify them in French.
- Write on the board the French abbreviations of several famous organizations (Examples: **ONU**, **OPEP**), and have students spell them in French. Explain what each abbreviation represents: **ONU = l'Organisation des Nations Unies** (*United Nations, UN*); **OPEP = l'Organisation des pays exportateurs de pétrole** (*Organization of Petroleum-Exporting Countries, OPEC*).
- Have students work on the **Ça s'écrit comment?** activity in pairs.
- The explanation and exercises are available on the **ESPACES** Supersite. You may want to play them in class so students hear French speakers other than yourself.

OPTIONS

Extra Practice Do a dictation activity in which you spell out a list of words in French to the class. Spell each word twice to allow students sufficient time to write. After you have finished, write your list on the board or project it on a transparency and have students check their work.

Extra Practice Tell students to greet two classmates that they haven't met yet, ask each person his or her name, and ask the person to spell the last name as they write it down. Tell them to verify the spelling with the person to make sure it is correct. Before beginning the activity, write this question on the board and model the pronunciation: **Comment s'écrit** *last name*?

Section Goals

In this section, students will learn functional phrases for making introductions and speaking on the telephone through comprehensible input.

Instructional Resources
*espaces.vhlcentral.com: WB/VM/LM Answer Key; IRM (Videoscript; **Roman-photo** Translations); activities; downloads; reference tools*
Video on DVD

Video Synopsis Sandrine buys a magazine at Monsieur Hulot's newsstand. At **Le P'tit Bistrot**, Rachid introduces David, his American friend, to Sandrine and Amina. Madame Forestier (Valérie), who owns the café, gets a phone call from her son's high school French teacher because he didn't do well on his French exam. Stéphane tells Rachid to introduce David to his mother so he can avoid talking to her.

Suggestions
- Have students cover the French captions and guess the plot based only on the video stills. Write their predictions on the board.
- Have students volunteer to read the characters' parts in the **Roman-photo** aloud. Then have them get together in groups of eight to act out the episode.
- After students have read the **Roman-photo**, quickly review their predictions, and ask them which ones were correct.
- Point out that 100 centimes = 1 euro, the monetary unit of the European Union, which includes France.

Au café

Video: *Roman-photo*
Record & Compare

PERSONNAGES

Amina

David

Monsieur Hulot

Michèle

Rachid

Sandrine

Stéphane

Valérie

Au kiosque...
SANDRINE Bonjour, Monsieur Hulot!
M. HULOT Bonjour, Mademoiselle Aubry! Comment allez-vous?
SANDRINE Très bien, merci! Et vous?
M. HULOT Euh, ça va. Voici 45 (quarante-cinq) centimes. Bonne journée!
SANDRINE Merci, au revoir!

À la terrasse du café...
AMINA Salut!
SANDRINE Bonjour, Amina. Ça va?
AMINA Ben... ça va. Et toi?
SANDRINE Oui, je vais bien, merci.
AMINA Regarde! Voilà Rachid et... un ami?

RACHID Bonjour!
AMINA ET SANDRINE Salut!
RACHID Je vous présente un ami, David Duchesne.
SANDRINE Je m'appelle Sandrine.
DAVID Enchanté.

STÉPHANE Oh, non! Madame Richard! Le professeur de français!
DAVID Il y a un problème?

STÉPHANE Oui! L'examen de français! Présentez-vous, je vous en prie!

VALÉRIE Oh... l'examen de français! Oui, merci, merci Madame Richard, merci beaucoup! De rien, au revoir!

ACTIVITÉS

1 Vrai ou faux? Decide whether each statement is **vrai** or **faux**. Correct the false statements. Answers may vary.

1. Sandrine va (*is doing*) bien. Vrai.
2. Sandrine et Amina sont (*are*) amies. Vrai.
3. David est français. Faux. David est américain.
4. David est de Washington. Vrai.
5. Rachid présente son frère (*his brother*) David à Sandrine et Amina. Faux. Rachid présente son ami David à Sandrine et à Amina.
6. Stéphane est étudiant à l'université. Faux. Stéphane est au lycée.
7. Il y a un problème avec l'examen de sciences politiques. Faux. Il y a un problème avec l'examen de français.
8. Amina, Rachid et Sandrine sont (*are*) à Paris. Faux. Amina, Rachid et Sandrine sont à Aix-en-Provence.
9. Michèle est au P'tit Bistrot. Vrai.
10. Madame Richard est le professeur de Stéphane. Vrai.
11. Valérie va mal. Vrai.
12. Rachid a (*has*) cours de français dans 30 minutes. Faux. Rachid a cours de sciences politiques dans 30 minutes.

Practice more at **espaces.vhlcentral.com.**

6 *six*

OPTIONS

Video Tips General suggestions for using video clips in the classroom can be found on page IAE-11 of this Instructor's Annotated Edition.

Avant de regarder la vidéo Before showing the video episode, have students brainstorm some greetings and some other expressions that they might hear in an episode in which some of the characters meet each other for the first time.

Regarder la vidéo Play the episode once and tell the class to listen for basic greetings. After the video is over, have students recall the greetings they heard and write them on the board. Show the episode again and ask the class to write down all of the courtesy expressions that they hear, including ways to say *pleased to meet you.*

Les étudiants se retrouvent (*meet*) au café.

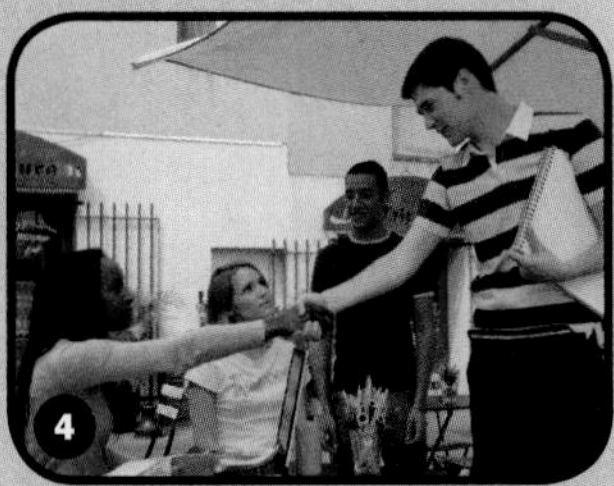
4

DAVID Et toi..., comment t'appelles-tu?
AMINA Je m'appelle Amina.
RACHID David est un étudiant américain. Il est de Washington, la capitale des États-Unis.
AMINA Ah, oui! Bienvenue à Aix-en-Provence.
RACHID Bon..., à tout à l'heure.
SANDRINE À bientôt, David.

5

À l'intérieur (inside) du café...
MICHÈLE Allô. Le P'tit Bistrot. Oui, un moment, s'il vous plaît. Madame Forestier! Le lycée de Stéphane.
VALÉRIE Allô. Oui. Bonjour, Madame Richard. Oui. Oui. Stéphane? Il y a un problème au lycée?

9

RACHID Bonjour, Madame Forestier. Comment allez-vous?
VALÉRIE Ah, ça va mal.
RACHID Oui? Moi, je vais bien. Je vous présente David Duchesne, étudiant américain de Washington.

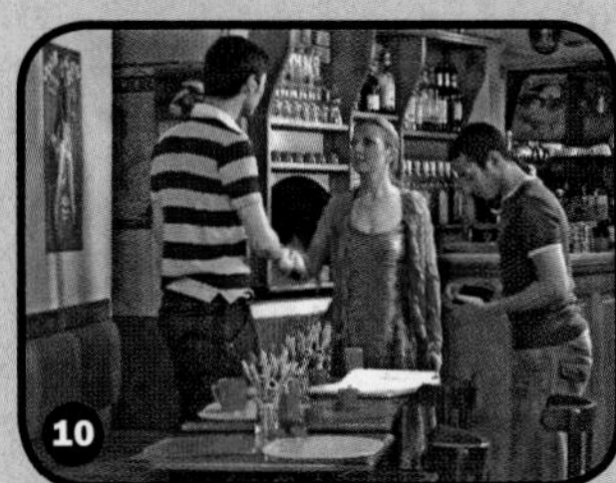
10

DAVID Bonjour, Madame. Enchanté!
RACHID Ah, j'ai cours de sciences politiques dans 30 (trente) minutes. Au revoir, Madame Forestier. À tout à l'heure, David.

Expressions utiles

Introductions

- **David est un étudiant américain. Il est de Washington.**
  David is an American student. He's from Washington.
- **Présentez-vous, je vous en prie!**
  Introduce yourselves, please!
- **Il/Elle s'appelle...**
  His/Her name is...
- **Bienvenue à Aix-en-Provence.**
  Welcome to Aix-en-Provence.

Speaking on the telephone

- **Allô.**
  Hello.
- **Un moment, s'il vous plaît.**
  One moment, please.

Additional vocabulary

- **Regarde! Voilà Rachid et... un ami?**
  Look! There's Rachid and... a friend?
- **J'ai cours de sciences politiques dans 30 (trente) minutes.**
  I have political science class in thirty minutes.
- **Il y a un problème au lycée?**
  Is there a problem at the high school?
- **Il y a...**
  There is/are...
- **Il/Elle est**
  He/She is...
- **Voici...**
  Here's...
- **Voilà...**
  There's...
- **euh**
  um
- **bon**
  well; good
- **centimes**
  cents

2 Complétez Fill in the blanks with the words from the list. Refer to the video scenes as necessary.

ai	est
bienvenue	voici
capitale	

1. ___Bienvenue___ à Aix-en-Provence.
2. Il est de Washington, la ___capitale___ des États-Unis.
3. ___Voici___ 45 (quarante-cinq) centimes. Bonne journée!
4. J'___ai___ cours de sciences politiques.
5. David ___est___ un étudiant américain.

3 Conversez In groups of three, write a conversation where you introduce an exchange student to a friend. Be prepared to present your conversation to the class.

ressources
VM pp. 211-212 | DVD Leçon 1A | espaces.vhlcentral.com

ACTIVITÉS

Successful Language Learning Tell your students that their conversational skills will grow more quickly as they learn each lesson's **Expressions utiles**. This feature is designed to teach phrases that will be useful in conversation, and it will also help students understand key phrases in each **Roman-photo**.

Expressions utiles
- Tell students that all the items in **Expressions utiles** are active vocabulary for which they are responsible. Model the pronunciation of the words and expressions and have the class repeat.
- As you work through the list, point out examples of nouns with indefinite articles (**un étudiant, un moment, un ami, un problème**). Tell students that nouns and articles will be formally presented in the **Espace structures** section.

1 Suggestion Have students correct the false statements.

2 Expansion Tell students to write three additional fill-in-the-blank statements based on the **Roman-photo**. Then have them exchange papers with a classmate and complete the sentences.

3 Suggestion Have volunteers act out their conversations for the class or another group.

OPTIONS

Extra Practice Choose four or five lines of the **Roman-photo** to use as a dictation. Read each line twice, pausing after each line so that students have time to write. Have students check their own work by comparing it with the **Roman-photo** text.

Cultural Comparison Have students make observations about the places and people that they saw in the video. Ask what was surprising or different about any of the scenes or the characters' mannerisms. Did they notice anything different about the way that the American student, David, introduced himself compared to the others?

Point out that greeting friends, family members, and loved ones with a kiss on both cheeks is not unique to the French-speaking world. This custom is common throughout Europe and in other parts of the world.

Section Goals

In this section, students will:
- learn about gestures used with greetings
- learn some familiar greetings and farewells
- learn some tips about good manners in different francophone countries
- read about Aix-en-Provence
- view authentic cultural footage

Instructional Resources
espaces.vhlcentral.com: Video; WB/VM/LM Answer Key; IRM (Videoscript); activities; downloads; reference tools
Video on DVD

Culture à la loupe

Avant la lecture Ask students how they greet their friends, family members, fellow students, co-workers, and people they meet for the first time. Ask them for some examples of regional variations in greetings in the United States (e.g., Howdy, Hiya, Yo).

Lecture
- Ask students what information the map on this page shows. (It shows the number of kisses traditionally given by region.)
- Explain that **faire la bise** does not actually mean to kiss another's cheek, but rather to kiss parallel to the other person's face, so that physical contact is limited to a grazing of cheeks.

Après la lecture Have students compare French and American greetings or any other method of greeting with which they are familiar.

1 Expansion Have students work in pairs. Tell them to role-play the situations in items 1–6. Example: 1. Students give each other four kisses because they are in northwestern France.

connections cultures (National Standards)

Video: *Flash culture*

CULTURE À LA LOUPE

La poignée de main ou la bise?

French friends and relatives usually exchange a kiss (la bise) on alternating cheeks whenever they meet and again when they say good-bye. Friends of friends may also kiss when introduced, even though they have just met. This is particularly true among students and young adults. It is normal for men of the same family to exchange **la bise**; otherwise, men generally greet one another with a handshake (**la poignée de main**). As the map shows, the number of kisses varies from place to place in France. In some regions, two kisses (one on each cheek) is the standard while in others, people may exchange as many as four kisses. Whatever the number, each kiss is accompanied by a slight kissing sound.

Unless they are also friends, business acquaintances and coworkers usually shake hands each time they meet and do so again upon leaving. A French handshake is brief and firm, with a single downward motion.

Coup de main

If you are not sure whether you should shake hands or kiss someone, or if you don't know which side to start on, you can always follow the other person's lead.

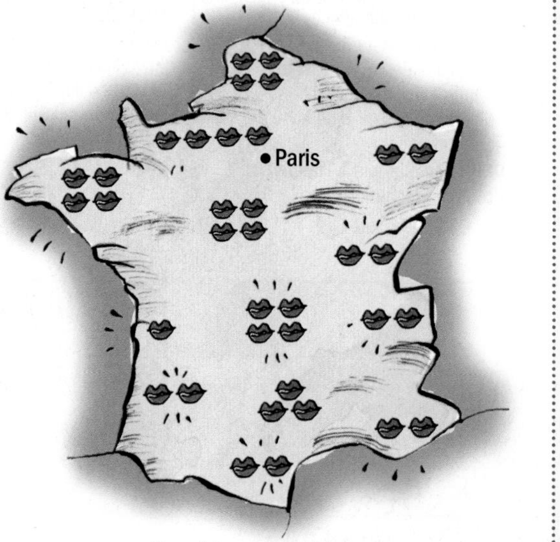

Combien de° bises?

Combien de *How many*

ACTIVITÉS

1 Vrai ou faux? Indicate whether each statement is **vrai** or **faux**. Correct any false statements.

1. In northwestern France, giving four kisses is common. Vrai.
2. Business acquaintances usually kiss one another on the cheek. Faux. They usually shake hands.
3. French people may give someone they've just met **la bise**. Vrai.
4. **Bises** exchanged between French men at a family gathering are common. Vrai.
5. In a business setting, French people often shake hands when they meet each day and again when they leave. Vrai.
6. When shaking hands, French people prefer a long and soft handshake. Faux. A French handshake is brief and firm.
7. The number of kisses given can vary from one region to another. Vrai.
8. It is customary for kisses to be given silently. Faux. Each kiss is accompanied by a slight kissing sound.

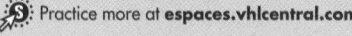

Practice more at **espaces.vhlcentral.com.**

OPTIONS

La bise Tell students that, although people in some social circles in the United States commonly kiss each other on the cheek once, this is not common practice in France. It could be considered impolite to give only one **bise** since the other person would be waiting for the second kiss. In some regions of France and Switzerland, people may even give three **bises**, but just one is rare.

Game Divide the class into two teams. Indicate one team member at a time, alternating between teams. Give situations in which people are greeting each other. Students should say if the people should greet each other with **la poignée de main** or **la bise**. Examples: female friends (**la bise**); male and female business associates (**la poignée de main**). Give a point for each correct answer. The team with the most points at the end of the game wins.

LE FRANÇAIS QUOTIDIEN

Les salutations

À la prochaine!	*Until next time!*
À plus!	*See you later!*
Ciao!	*Bye!*
Coucou!	*Hi there!/Hey!*
Pas grand-chose.	*Nothing much.*
Quoi de neuf?	*What's new?*
Rien de nouveau.	*Nothing new.*

LE MONDE FRANCOPHONE

Les bonnes manières

In any country, an effort to speak the native language is appreciated. Using titles of respect and a few polite expressions, such as excusez-moi, merci, and s'il vous plaît, can take you a long way when conversing with native Francophones.

Dos and don'ts in the francophone world:

France Always greet shopkeepers upon entering a store and say good-bye upon leaving.

Northern Africa Use your right hand when handing items to others.

Quebec Province Make eye contact when shaking hands.

Sub-Saharan Africa Do not show the soles of your feet when sitting.

Switzerland Do not litter or jaywalk.

PORTRAIT

Aix-en-Provence: ville d'eau, ville d'art°

Aix-en-Provence is a vibrant university town that welcomes international students. Its main boulevard, **le cours Mirabeau**, is great for people-watching or just relaxing in a sidewalk café. One can see many beautiful fountains, traditional and ethnic restaurants, and the daily vegetable and flower market among the winding, narrow streets of **la vieille ville** (*old town*).

Aix is also renowned for its dedication to the arts, hosting numerous cultural festivals every year such as **le Festival International d'Art Lyrique**, and **Aix en Musique**. For centuries, artists have been drawn to Provence for its natural beauty and its unique quality of light. Paul Cézanne, artist and native son of Provence, spent his days painting the surrounding countryside.

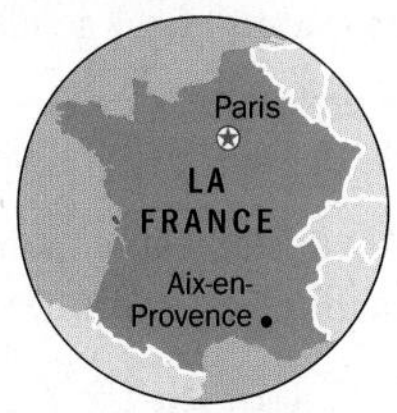

ville d'eau, ville d'art *city of water, city of art*

SUR INTERNET

What behaviors are socially unacceptable in French-speaking countries?

Go to **espaces.vhlcentral.com** to find more information related to this **ESPACE CULTURE**. Then watch the corresponding **Flash culture.**

ACTIVITÉS

2 **Les bonnes manières** In which places might these behaviors be particularly offensive?

1. littering
   Switzerland
2. offering a business card with your left hand
   Northern Africa
3. sitting with the bottom of your foot facing your host
   Sub-Saharan Africa
4. failing to greet a salesperson
   France
5. looking away when shaking hands
   Quebec Province

3 **À vous** With a partner, practice meeting and greeting people in French in various social situations.

1. Your good friend from Provence introduces you to her close friend.
2. You walk into your neighborhood bakery.
3. You arrive for an interview with a prospective employer.

ressources
VM pp. 271-272
espaces.vhlcentral.com

Le français quotidien
- Model the pronunciation of each expression and have students repeat.
- Tell students to list all the situations they can think of in which they could use these expressions. Then have them compare their lists in pairs or small groups.

Portrait Mention that Aix-en-Provence is often referred to simply as Aix. Ask students why they think Aix is called **ville d'eau, ville d'art** in the title. Tell them that the Romans made Aix famous for its thermal baths. Then ask if they would like to visit Aix, and which aspects of the town attract them the most.

Le monde francophone Ask students which dos and don'ts in the francophone world should be followed in the anglophone world, too. Have the class think of logical reasons for following each custom or social convention, especially for North Africa and Sub-Saharan Africa. Example: In North Africa, the left hand is reserved for using the toilets.

Sur Internet Point out to students that they will find supporting activities and information at **espaces.vhlcentral.com.**

2 Suggestion Have students check their answers with a partner.

3 Suggestion Before beginning this activity, ask students if they would use **tu** or **vous** in each situation. Remind them to use appropriate gestures and manners.

Flash culture Tell students that they will learn more about greetings and farewells in French by watching a variety of real-life images narrated by Csilla. Show the video segment, then have students jot down in French at least three examples of situations or things they saw. You can also use the activities in the video manual in class to reinforce this **Flash culture** or assign them as homework.

OPTIONS

Cultural Activity Have students choose one of these topics to research on the Internet: **Aix-en-Provence, le Festival International d'Art Lyrique, Aix en Musique,** or **Paul Cézanne.** Tell them to come to the next class with printouts of two photos illustrating their topic and a sentence or two in French, if possible, about each photo. Divide the class into groups of three or four students so that they can present the material to one another while looking at the images.

Small Groups Have students work in groups of three or four. Tell them to create an informal conversation using the expressions in **Le français quotidien** and appropriate gestures. Have a few groups act out their conversations for the class.

Section Goals

In this section, students will learn:

- gender and number of nouns
- definite and indefinite articles

Instructional Resources

*espaces.vhlcentral.com: Lab MP3s; WB/VM/LM Answer Key; IRM (**Essayez!** and **Mise en pratique** answers; Lab Audioscript); activities; downloads; reference tools*

Suggestions

- Explain what a noun is by giving examples of people (**professeur**), places (**café**), things (**examen**), and ideas (**problème**). Then write these nouns on the board: **ami, amie, cours, télévision**. Point out the gender of each noun. Explain that nouns for male beings are usually masculine, and nouns for female beings are usually feminine. All other nouns can be either masculine or feminine. Tell students that they should memorize the gender of a noun along with the word.
- Write these nouns on the board: **professeur, professeurs, étudiante, étudiantes**. Ask students to point out the singular and plural nouns and to explain why. Then have students pronounce the words. Point out that the **-s** is not pronounced in French.
- Write **bureau** and **bureaux** on the board. Explain that words ending in **-eau** add **-x** to form the plural.
- Write these words on the board: **le café, les cafés, l'ami, les amis, la personne, les personnes**. Explain the use of the definite article. Point out that singular nouns beginning with a vowel or silent **h** use **l'**.
- Follow the same procedure for indefinite articles using these words: **un café, des cafés, un ami, des amis, une personne, des personnes**. Point out that the **-n** of **un** is pronounced before a vowel.
- Model how to pronounce **les** and **des** before words beginning with a consonant and a vowel.

1A.1 Nouns and articles

NATIONAL STANDARDS comparisons

Point de départ A noun designates a person, place, or thing. As in English, nouns in French have number (singular or plural). However, French nouns also have gender (masculine or feminine).

masculine singular	masculine plural	feminine singular	feminine plural
le café *the café*	**les cafés** *the cafés*	**la bibliothèque** *the library*	**les bibliothèques** *the libraries*

- Nouns that designate a male are usually masculine. Nouns that designate a female are usually feminine.

masculine		feminine	
l'acteur	*the actor*	**l'actrice**	*the actress*
l'ami	*the (male) friend*	**l'amie**	*the (female) friend*
le chanteur	*the (male) singer*	**la chanteuse**	*the (female) singer*
l'étudiant	*the (male) student*	**l'étudiante**	*the (female) student*
le petit ami	*the boyfriend*	**la petite amie**	*the girlfriend*

- Some nouns can designate either a male or a female regardless of their grammatical gender.

le professeur *the (male or female) professor*	**la personne** *the (male or female) person*

- Nouns for objects that have no natural gender can be either masculine or feminine.

masculine		feminine	
le bureau	*the office; desk*	**la chose**	*the thing*
le lycée	*the high school*	**la différence**	*the difference*
l'examen	*the test, exam*	**la faculté**	*the university; faculty*
l'objet	*the object*	**la littérature**	*literature*
l'ordinateur	*the computer*	**la sociologie**	*sociology*
le problème	*the problem*	**l'université**	*the university*

- You can usually form the plural of a noun by adding **-s**, regardless of gender. However, in the case of words that end in **-eau** in the singular, add **-x** to the end to form the plural. For most nouns ending in **-al**, drop the **-al** and add **-aux**.

	singular		plural	
typical masculine noun	**l'objet**	*the object*	**les objets**	*the objects*
typical feminine noun	**la télévision**	*the television*	**les télévisions**	*the televisions*
noun ending in -eau	**le bureau**	*the office*	**les bureaux**	*the offices*
noun ending in -al	**l'animal**	*the animal*	**les animaux**	*the animals*

MISE EN PRATIQUE

1 Les singuliers et les pluriels Make the singular nouns plural, and vice versa.

1. l'actrice les actrices
2. les lycées le lycée
3. les différences la différence
4. la chose les choses
5. le bureau les bureaux
6. le café les cafés
7. les librairies la librairie
8. la faculté les facultés
9. les acteurs l'acteur
10. l'ami les amis
11. l'université les universités
12. les tableaux le tableau
13. le problème les problèmes
14. les bibliothèques la bibliothèque

2 L'université Complete the sentences with an appropriate word from the list. Don't forget to provide the missing articles. Answers may vary slightly. Suggested answers below.

bibliothèque	examen	ordinateurs	sociologie
bureau	faculté	petit ami	

1. À la faculté, les tableaux et les ordinateurs sont (*are*) modernes.
2. Marc, c'est le petit ami de (*of*) Marie. Marc étudie (*studies*) la littérature.
3. Marie étudie la sociologie. Elle (*She*) est dans la bibliothèque de l'université.

3 Les mots Find ten words (**mots**) hidden in this word jumble. Then, provide the corresponding indefinite articles. une amie; des bureaux; un café; une chose; une faculté; un lycée; des objets; des ordinateurs; une librairie; un tableau

G	N	I	O	R	Z	Y	M	I	P	X	L	R	W
E	B	U	R	E	A	U	X	U	J	V	C	B	N
C	A	F	B	S	M	V	B	G	H	M	N	I	P
A	N	R	Y	E	I	H	K	B	E	F	K	V	F
J	G	O	S	T	E	J	B	O	B	E	G	D	D
E	K	E	L	H	N	U	Q	R	V	F	D	B	M
G	W	F	G	E	R	E	S	D	C	N	U	H	E
P	S	V	B	C	H	O	S	I	U	K	H	S	C
U	Q	K	S	I	Y	M	F	N	A	D	O	X	R
A	B	V	Z	R	I	V	V	A	J	H	W	I	J
E	I	W	Q	L	P	W	J	T	C	P	Y	E	Y
L	I	B	R	A	I	R	I	E	D	U	E	K	L
B	D	O	I	B	S	S	E	U	C	H	L	D	Y
A	Y	P	E	P	J	C	N	R	L	S	G	T	C
T	D	G	A	E	S	Y	L	S	V	C	A	F	E
S	I	J	E	M	X	K	P	Z	A	A	S	O	E
R	I	A	R	B	I	L	A	D	S	F	H	C	W

Practice more at **espaces.vhlcentral.com.**

OPTIONS

Extra Practice Write ten singular nouns on the board. In a rapid-response drill, call on students to give the appropriate gender. Examples: **bureau** (masculine), **étudiante** (feminine). You may also do this activity without writing the words on the board.

Game Divide the class into groups of three to four students. Bring in photos or magazine pictures, point to various objects or people, and say the French word without saying the article. Call on groups to indicate the person's or object's gender. Give a point for each correct answer. Deduct a point for each wrong answer. The group with the most points at the end wins.

COMMUNICATION

4 Qu'est-ce que c'est? In pairs, take turns identifying each image.

MODÈLE

Étudiant(e) 1: *Qu'est-ce que c'est?*
Étudiant(e) 2: *C'est un ordinateur.*

1. Ce sont des tables.

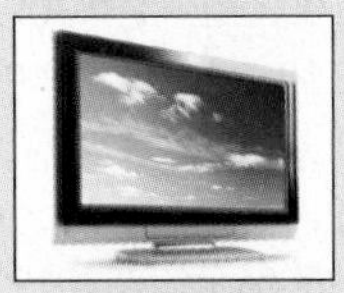

4. C'est une télévision.

2. Ce sont des étudiants.

5. C'est une bibliothèque/un étudiant.

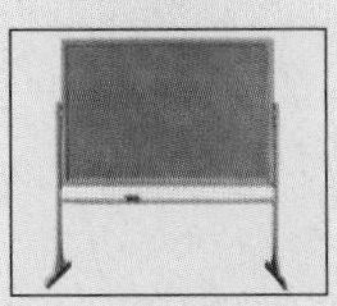

3. C'est un tableau.

6. Ce sont des cafés.

5 Identifiez In pairs, take turns providing a category for each item.

MODÈLE

Michigan, UCLA, Rutgers, Duke
Ce sont des universités.

1. saxophone C'est un instrument.
2. Ross, Rachel, Joey, Monica, Chandler, Phoebe Ce sont des amis.
3. SAT C'est un examen.
4. Library of Congress C'est une bibliothèque.
5. Angelina Jolie, Halle Berry, Juliette Binoche Ce sont des actrices.
6. Céline Dion, Bruce Springsteen Ce sont des chanteurs.

6 Pictogrammes In groups of four, someone draws a person, object, or concept for the others to guess. Whoever guesses correctly draws next. Continue until everyone has drawn at least once. Answers will vary.

- Refer to a group composed of males and females with a masculine plural noun.

les amis	**les étudiants**
the (male and female) friends	the (male and female) students

- The English definite article *the* never varies for number or gender. However, the French definite article takes different forms according to the gender and number of the noun that it accompanies.

	singular noun beginning with a consonant	singular noun beginning with a vowel sound	plural noun
masculine	**le tableau** *the picture/ blackboard*	**l'ami** *the (male) friend*	**les cafés** *the cafés*
feminine	**la librairie** *the bookstore*	**l'université** *the university*	**les télévisions** *the televisions*

- In English, the singular indefinite article is *a/an*, and the plural indefinite article is *some*. Although *some* is often omitted in English, the plural indefinite article cannot be omitted in French.

	singular		plural	
masculine	**un instrument**	*an instrument*	**des instruments**	*(some) instruments*
feminine	**une table**	*a table*	**des tables**	*(some) tables*

Il y a **un ordinateur** ici.
There's a computer here.

Il y a **des ordinateurs** ici.
There are (some) computers here.

Il y a **une université** ici.
There's a university here.

Il y a **des universités** ici.
There are (some) universities here.

- Use **c'est** followed by a singular article and noun or **ce sont** followed by a plural article and noun to identify people and objects.

Qu'est-ce que c'est?	**C'est une librairie.**	**Ce sont des bureaux.**
What is that?	*It's a bookstore.*	*They're offices.*

Essayez! Select the correct article for each noun.

le, la, l' ou les?	un, une ou des?
1. le café	1. un bureau
2. la bibliothèque	2. une différence
3. l' acteur	3. un objet
4. l' amie	4. des amis
5. les problèmes	5. des amies
6. le lycée	6. une université
7. les examens	7. un ordinateur
8. la littérature	8. des tableaux

Essayez! Have students change the singular nouns and articles to the plural and vice versa.

1 Suggestion To check students' answers, have volunteers write them on the board or spell out the nouns orally.

1 Expansion Have students close their books. Tell them to change the plural nouns they hear to the singular and vice versa. Then randomly give them the answers to the items in the activity.

2 Suggestion Have volunteers read the words in the list aloud. Tell students to read all three items before attempting to start filling in blanks.

3 Suggestion This activity can also be done in pairs or groups.

4 Suggestion Before beginning this activity, have students identify the objects in the photos. Then read the **modèle** aloud with a volunteer. Remind them that **Ce sont** is used with plural nouns.

5 Expansion Have students work in pairs. Tell them to write two more items for the activity. Example: GRE, GMAT, LSAT **(Ce sont des examens.)** Then have volunteers read their items aloud, while the rest of the class guesses the category.

6 Suggestions
- Before beginning the activity, remind students that they must choose something the class knows how to say in French, and that to guess what the picture is, they should say: **C'est un(e) ___?** or **Ce sont des ___?**
- Tell students they will learn more about **c'est/ce sont** on p. 25.

OPTIONS

TPR Distribute cards preprinted with articles and nouns to each of four students. Then line up ten students, each of whom is assigned a noun. Include a mix of masculine, feminine, singular, and plural nouns. Say one of the nouns (without the article), and that student must step forward. The student assigned the corresponding article has five seconds to join the student with the noun.

Video Show the video episode again to offer more input on singular and plural nouns and their articles. With their books closed, have students write down every noun and article that they hear. After viewing the video, ask volunteers to list the nouns and articles they heard.

Section Goals

In this section, students will learn:

- numbers 0–60
- the expression **il y a**

Instructional Resources
*espaces.vhlcentral.com: Lab MP3s; WB/VM/LM Answer Key; IRM (**Essayez!** and **Mise en pratique** answers; Lab Audioscript); activities; downloads; reference tools*

Suggestions

- Introduce numbers by asking students how many of them can count to ten in French. Hold up varying numbers of fingers and ask students to shout out the corresponding number in French.
- Go through the numbers, modeling the pronunciation of each. Write individual numbers on the board and call on students at random to say each number as you point to it.
- Assign each student a number at random that they must remember. When finished, have the student assigned **un** say his or her number aloud, then **deux**, **trois**, etc. Help anyone who struggles with his or her number.
- Emphasize the variable forms of **un** and **une**, **vingt et un**, and **vingt et une**, giving examples of each. Examples: **vingt et un étudiants, vingt et une personnes.**
- Ask questions like the following: **Il y a combien d'étudiants dans la classe? (Il y a seize étudiants dans la classe.)**

1A.2 Numbers 0–60

NATIONAL comparisons STANDARDS

Point de départ Numbers in French follow patterns, as they do in English. First, learn the numbers **0–30**. The patterns they follow will help you learn the numbers **31–60**.

Numbers 0–30

0-10	11-20	21-30
0 zéro		
1 un	**11** onze	**21** vingt et un
2 deux	**12** douze	**22** vingt-deux
3 trois	**13** treize	**23** vingt-trois
4 quatre	**14** quatorze	**24** vingt-quatre
5 cinq	**15** quinze	**25** vingt-cinq
6 six	**16** seize	**26** vingt-six
7 sept	**17** dix-sept	**27** vingt-sept
8 huit	**18** dix-huit	**28** vingt-huit
9 neuf	**19** dix-neuf	**29** vingt-neuf
10 dix	**20** vingt	**30** trente

- When counting, use **un** for *one*. Use **une** before a feminine noun.

un objet — *an/one object*
une télévision — *a/one television*

- Note that the number **21** (**vingt et un**) follows a different pattern than the numbers **22–30**. When **vingt et un** precedes a feminine noun, add **-e** to the end of it: **vingt et une**.

vingt et un objets — *twenty-one objects*
vingt et une choses — *twenty-one things*

- Notice that the numbers **31–39**, **41–49**, and **51–59** follow the same pattern as the numbers **21–29**.

Numbers 31–60

31-34	35-38	39, 40, 50, 60
31 trente et un	**35** trente-cinq	**39** trente-neuf
32 trente-deux	**36** trente-six	**40** quarante
33 trente-trois	**37** trente-sept	**50** cinquante
34 trente-quatre	**38** trente-huit	**60** soixante

- To indicate a count of **31**, **41**, or **51** for a feminine noun, change the **un** to **une**.

trente et un objets — *thirty-one objects*
trente et une choses — *thirty-one things*

cinquante et un objets — *fifty-one objects*
cinquante et une choses — *fifty-one things*

MISE EN PRATIQUE

1 Logique Provide the number that completes each series. Then, write out the number in French.

MODÈLE
2, 4, __6__, 8, 10; __six__

1. 9, 12, __15__, 18, 21; __quinze__
2. 15, 20, __25__, 30, 35; __vingt-cinq__
3. 2, 9, __16__, 23, 30; __seize__
4. 0, 10, 20, __30__, 40; __trente__
5. 15, __17__, 19, 21, 23; __dix-sept__
6. 29, 26, __23__, 20, 17; __vingt-trois__
7. 2, 5, 9, __14__, 20, 27; __quatorze__
8. 30, 22, 16, 12, __10__; __dix__

2 Il y a combien de...? Provide the number that you associate with these pairs of words.

MODÈLE
lettres: l'alphabet *vingt-six*

1. mois (*months*): année (*year*) douze
2. états (*states*): USA cinquante
3. semaines (*weeks*): année cinquante-deux
4. jours (*days*): octobre trente et un
5. âge: le vote dix-huit
6. Noël: décembre vingt-cinq

3 Numéros de téléphone Your roommate left behind a list of phone numbers to call today. Now he or she calls you and asks you to read them off. Be sure to add the correct definite article. (Note that French phone numbers are read as double, not single, digits.)

MODÈLE
Le bureau, c'est le zéro un, vingt-trois, quarante-cinq, vingt-six, dix-neuf.

1. *bureau: 01.23.45.26.19*
2. *bibliothèque: 01.47.15.54.17* La bibliothèque, c'est le zéro un, quarante-sept, quinze, cinquante-quatre, dix-sept.
3. *café: 01.41.38.16.29* Le café, c'est le zéro un, quarante et un, trente-huit, seize, vingt-neuf.
4. *librairie: 01.10.13.60.23* La librairie, c'est le zéro un, dix, treize, soixante, vingt-trois.
5. *faculté: 01.58.36.14.12* La faculté, c'est le zéro un, cinquante-huit, trente-six, quatorze, douze.

Practice more at **espaces.vhlcentral.com.**

OPTIONS

TPR Assign ten students a number from 0–60 and line them up in front of the class. Call out one of the numbers at random and have the student assigned to that number take a step forward. When two students have stepped forward, ask them to repeat their numbers. Then ask individuals to add (say: **plus**) or subtract (say: **moins**) the two numbers.

Game Hand out Bingo cards with B-I-N-G-O across the top of five columns. The 25 squares underneath will contain random numbers. From a hat, draw letters and numbers and call them out in French. The first student that can fill in a number in each one of the lettered columns yells "Bingo!" and wins.

COMMUNICATION

4 Sur le campus Nathalie's inquisitive best friend wants to know everything about her new campus. In pairs, take turns acting out the roles.

MODÈLE

bibliothèques: 3
Étudiant(e) 1: *Il y a combien de bibliothèques?*
Étudiant(e) 2: *Il y a trois bibliothèques.*

1. professeurs de littérature: 22
   Il y a vingt-deux professeurs de littérature.
2. étudiants dans (*in*) la classe de français: 15
   Il y a quinze étudiants dans la classe de français.
3. télévision dans la classe de sociologie: 0
   Il n'y a pas de télévision dans la classe de sociologie.
4. ordinateurs dans le café: 8
   Il y a huit ordinateurs dans le café.
5. employés dans la librairie: 51
   Il y a cinquante et un employés dans la librairie.
6. tables dans le café: 21
   Il y a vingt et une tables dans le café.

5 Contradiction Thierry is describing the new Internet café in the neighborhood, but Paul is in a bad mood and contradicts everything he says. In pairs, act out the roles using words from the list. Answers will vary.

MODÈLE

Étudiant(e) 1: *Dans (In) le café, il y a des tables.*
Étudiant(e) 2: *Non, il n'y a pas de tables.*

actrices	professeurs
bureau	tableau
étudiants	tables
ordinateur	télévision

6 Choses et personnes In groups of three, make a list of ten things or people that you see or don't see in the classroom. Use **il y a** and **il n'y a pas de**, and specify the number of items you can find. Then, compare your list with that of another pair. Answers will vary.

MODÈLE

Étudiant(e) 1: *Il y a un étudiant français.*
Étudiant(e) 2: *Il n'y a pas de télévision.*

- Use **il y a** to say *there is* or *there are* in French. This expression doesn't change, even if the noun that follows it is plural.

Il y a un ordinateur dans le bureau. There is a computer in the office.	**Il y a des tables** dans le café. There are tables in the café.

Il y a deux amies.

Il y a trois étudiants.

- In most cases, the indefinite article (**un**, **une**, or **des**) is used with **il y a**, rather than the definite article (**le**, **la**, **l'**, or **les**).

Il y a un professeur de biologie américain. *There's an American biology professor.*	**Il y a des** étudiants français et anglais. *There are French and English students.*

- Use the expression **il n'y a pas de/d'** followed by a noun to express *there isn't a...* or *there aren't any...* Note that no article (definite or indefinite) is used in this case. Use **de** before a consonant sound and **d'** before a vowel sound.

before a consonant

Il n'y a pas de tables dans le café.
There aren't any tables in the café.

before a vowel sound

Il n'y a pas d'ordinateur dans le bureau.
There isn't a computer in the office.

- Use **combien de/d'** to ask how many of something there are.

Il y a **combien de tables**? *How many tables are there?*	Il y a **combien d'ordinateurs**? *How many computers are there?*

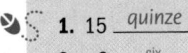

Essayez! Write out or say the French word for each number below.

1. 15 quinze	6. 8 huit	11. 44 quarante-quatre
2. 6 six	7. 30 trente	12. 14 quatorze
3. 22 vingt-deux	8. 21 vingt et un	13. 38 trente-huit
4. 5 cinq	9. 1 un	14. 56 cinquante-six
5. 12 douze	10. 17 dix-sept	15. 19 dix-neuf

Essayez! Have students write four more numbers from 0–60. Tell them to exchange papers with a classmate and write the numbers as words.

1 Expansion Ask the class to list the prime numbers (**les nombres premiers**) up to 30. Explain that a prime number is any number that can only be divided by itself and 1. Prime numbers to 30 are: 1, 2, 3, 5, 7, 11, 13, 17, 19, 23, 29.

2 Suggestion Have students form complete sentences using **Il y a** when answering. Example: **Il y a douze mois dans une année.**

2 Expansion For additional practice, give students these items. **7. jours: semaine (sept) 8. jours: novembre (trente) 9. minutes: heure** (*hour*) **(soixante) 10. saisons** (*seasons*)**: année (quatre)**

3 Expansion Write on the board three more telephone numbers for real places on campus or in town with their area codes, using double digits as in the activity. Call on volunteers to read the numbers aloud. Permit students to say the digits one by one if the numbers exceed 60.

4 Suggestion Have two volunteers read the **modèle** aloud. Remind students to use **combien d'** before a noun that begins with a vowel sound.

5 Suggestion Have two volunteers read the **modèle** aloud. Remind students that they shouldn't use any article (definite or indefinite) after **Il n'y a pas de/d'**.

6 Expansion After groups have compared their answers, convert the statements into questions. Example: **Il y a combien d'étudiants?**

OPTIONS

TPR Give ten students a card with a number from 0–60. (You may want to assign numbers in fives to simplify the activity.) The card must be visible to the other students. Then call out simple math problems (addition or subtraction) involving the assigned numbers. When the first two numbers are called, each student steps forward. The student whose assigned number completes the math problem has five seconds to join them.

Extra Practice Ask questions about the university and the town or city in which it is located. Examples: **Il y a combien de professeurs dans le département de français? Il y a combien de bibliothèques sur le campus? Il y a combien d'universités à ____?** Encourage students to guess the number if they don't know it.

Suggestion Tell students that this section reviews and recycles the lesson vocabulary and grammar points.

Instructional Resources
espaces.vhlcentral.com: IRM (Info Gap Activities); Testing Program, pp. 1–4; Test Files; Testing Program MP3s; activities; downloads; reference tools
Test Generator

1 Suggestion Before beginning this activity, you may wish to review the alphabet and how to say the accent marks.

2 Suggestion Tell students not to accept a guess if the letter is not pronounced correctly in French.

3 Suggestion Before beginning the activity, have two volunteers read the **modèle** aloud.

4 Suggestion Remind students to use appropriate gestures and encourage them to add information to the introduction, such as the person's hometown.

5 Suggestions
- Before beginning this activity, quickly review the numbers 0–60. Hold up cards with various numbers, and have the class or individuals say them in French.
- Read the **modèle** aloud with a volunteer.

6 Suggestion Divide the class into pairs and distribute the Info Gap Handouts on the Supersite for this activity. Give students ten minutes to complete the activity.

Révision

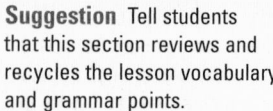

1 Des lettres In pairs, take turns choosing nouns. One partner chooses only masculine nouns, while the other chooses only feminine. Slowly spell each noun for your partner, who will guess the word. Find out who can give the quickest answers. Answers will vary.

2 Le pendu In groups of four, play hangman (**le pendu**). Form two teams of two partners each. Take turns choosing a French word or expression you learned in this lesson for the other team to guess. Continue to play until your team guesses at least one word or expression from each category. Answers will vary.

1. un nom féminin
2. un nom masculin
3. un nombre entre (*number between*) 0 et 30
4. un nombre entre 31 et 60
5. une expression

3 C'est... Ce sont... Doug is spending a week in Paris with his French e-mail pal, Marc. As Doug points out what he sees, Marc corrects him sometimes. In pairs, act out the roles. Doug should be right half the time. Answers will vary.

MODÈLE

Étudiant(e) 1: *C'est une bibliothèque?*
Étudiant(e) 2: *Non, c'est une librairie.*

1. C'est une bibliothèque./ Ce sont des étudiants.

2. C'est un café.

3. C'est une actrice.

4. Ce sont des acteurs.

5. C'est un professeur. / Ce sont des étudiants.

6. Ce sont des amies.

4 Les présentations In pairs, introduce yourselves. Together, meet another pair. One person per pair should introduce him or herself and his or her partner. Use the items from the list in your conversations. Switch roles until you have met all of the other pairs in the class. Answers will vary.

ami	étudiant
c'est	petit(e) ami(e)
ce sont	professeur

5 S'il te plaît You are new on campus and ask another student for help finding these places. He or she gives you the building (**le bâtiment**) and room (**la salle**) number and you thank him or her. Then, switch roles and repeat with another place from the list. Answers will vary.

MODÈLE

Étudiant(e) 1: *Pardon... l'examen de sociologie, s'il te plaît?*
Étudiant(e) 2: *Ah oui... bâtiment E, salle dix-sept.*
Étudiant(e) 1: *Merci beaucoup!*
Étudiant(e) 2: *De rien.*

Bibliothèque d'anglais	Bâtiment C Salle 11
Bureau de Mme Girard	Bâtiment A Salle 35
Bureau de M. Brachet	Bâtiment J Salle 42
Café	Bâtiment H Salle 59
Littérature française	Bâtiment B Salle 46
Examen de littérature	Bâtiment E Salle 24
Examen de sociologie	Bâtiment E Salle 17
Salle de télévision	Bâtiment F Salle 33
Salle des ordinateurs	Bâtiment D Salle 40

6 Mots mélangés You and a partner each have half the words of a wordsearch (**des mots mélangés**). Pick a number and a letter and say them to your partner, who must tell you if he or she has a letter in the corresponding space. Do not look at each other's worksheet. Answers will vary.

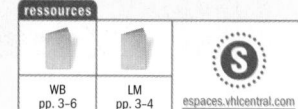

ressources: WB pp. 3–6; LM pp. 3–4; espaces.vhlcentral.com

OPTIONS

Extra Practice Bring in pictures from newspapers, magazines, or the Internet of nouns that students have learned, and ask them to identify the people or objects. Examples: **C'est un(e) ____? Ce sont des ____? Qu'est-ce que c'est?** You might also ask how many people or objects are in the picture if there are more than one. Example: **Il y a combien de(d') ____?**

Small Groups Bring in family photos or magazine pictures showing people greeting or introducing each other in different situations. Assign a photo to each group or allow them to choose one. Tell students to write a brief conversation based on the photo. Remind the class to use formal and informal expressions as appropriate.

Video: TV Clip

Le Zapping

La Triplette de Moulinex... un, deux, trois!

The story of Moulinex started with an invention. In 1932, Jean Mantelet invented the electric potato masher to help his wife. Later, he invented an electric coffee grinder called **Moulin° X**, which went on to become the company brand. After World War II, Moulinex came up with the famous slogan, **Moulinex libère la femme** (*Moulinex liberates women*). In the 1980s, Moulinex started facing tough competition and in 2001 was bought out by Groupe SEB, another French company specializing in small appliances and kitchen equipment.

Coup de main

Moulin X is a play on words. **Moulin** means *grinder* and you need to pronounce the x the English way, not the French way. That's how you obtain Moulinex.

—Un, deux, trois, elle fait° la raclette°.

—Un, deux, trois, elle fait des crêpes.

Compréhension Answer these questions. Some answers will vary.

1. What numbers and articles did you recognize? un, deux, trois, la, des
2. What is special about this device?

Discussion In groups of four, discuss the answers to these questions. Use as much French as you can. Answers will vary.

1. Have you ever eaten **raclette** or **crêpes** before? Where?
2. When would one use **la Triplette**?
3. What other appliance can you think of that performs more than one job?
4. If you could invent an appliance with several functions, what would it do? What would you name it?

Moulin *grinder* **elle fait** *it makes* **raclette** *dish made from melted cheese scraped onto bread or boiled potatoes*

Practice more at **espaces.vhlcentral.com.**

OPTIONS

Les appareils ménagers There are more than 280 million small appliances in French households. The three most common appliances are irons, vacuum cleaners, and hair dryers. In the kitchen, the three main types of appliances are coffee makers, toasters, and food processors. Seventy-five percent of households buy one or more small household appliances per year. These new products represent an increasing part of the market: steam irons and espresso makers. Twenty-five percent of all appliances are offered as gifts.

Section Goals

In this section, students will:

- read about Moulinex, a company that makes small household appliances
- watch the commercial for one of its devices, the **Triplette**
- answer questions about the device and Moulinex

Instructional Resources
*espaces.vhlcentral.com: TV commercial; IRM (**Le zapping** TV clip transcription); activities; downloads; reference tools*

Introduction
To check comprehension, ask these questions.
1. What did Jean Mantelet invent? (He invented an electric potato masher and an electric coffee grinder.)
2. What was Moulinex's slogan after World War II? (**«Moulinex libère la femme»**)
3. Who bought Moulinex in 2001? (Seb, another French company specializing in small appliances and kitchen equipment)

Avant de regarder la vidéo

- Have students look at the video stills, read the captions, and describe the device and what it is used for. (It's an electric cooking device that you can use to prepare **raclette** and **crêpes**.)
- Before showing the video, explain to students that they do not need to understand every word they hear. Tell them to listen for numbers, articles, and cognates.

Compréhension Have students work in pairs or groups for this activity. Tell them to write their answers. Then show the video again so that they can check their answers and add any missing information.

Discussion

- Have volunteers report their answers to the class.
- Take a quick class survey to find out who likes or would like to try either **raclette** or **crêpes**.

Section Goals

In this section, students will learn and practice vocabulary related to:

- objects in the classroom
- identifying people

Instructional Resources
*espaces.vhlcentral.com: Transparency #15; IRM (**Vocabulaire supplémentaire**; **Mise en pratique** answers; Textbook Audioscript; Lab Audioscript; Info Gap Activities); Textbook MP3s; Lab MP3s; WB/VM/LM Answer Key; activities; downloads; reference tools*

Suggestions

- Introduce vocabulary for classroom objects, such as **un cahier, une carte, un dictionnaire, un stylo**. Hold up or point to an object and say: **C'est un stylo.**
- Hold up or point to an object and ask either/or questions. Examples: **C'est un crayon ou un stylo? C'est une porte ou une fenêtre?**
- Using either objects in the classroom or **Transparency #15**, point to items or people and ask questions, such as **Qu'est-ce que c'est? Qui est-ce? C'est un stylo? C'est un professeur?**
- Have students pick up or point out objects you name. You might want to teach them the expression **Montrez-moi un/une ____.**
- Additional vocabulary for this lesson can be found in the **Vocabulaire supplémentaire** on the Supersite.

Leçon 1B

You will learn how to...

- identify yourself and others
- ask yes/no questions

Talking Picture
Audio: Activity

En classe

Vocabulaire

Qui est-ce?	*Who is it?*
Quoi?	*What?*
une calculatrice	*calculator*
une montre	*watch*
une porte	*door*
un résultat	*result*
une salle de classe	*classroom*
un(e) camarade de chambre	*roommate*
un(e) camarade de classe	*classmate*
une classe	*class (group of students)*
un copain/ une copine (*fam.*)	*friend*
un(e) élève	*pupil, student*
une femme	*woman*
une fille	*girl*
un garçon	*boy*
un homme	*man*

ressources
WB pp. 7-8 | LM p. 5 | espaces.vhlcentral.com

OPTIONS

Pairs Have students work in pairs and take an inventory of all the people and items in the classroom. Tell them to write their list in French using the expression **Il y a ____**. After students have finished, tell them to compare their lists with another pair to see if they are the same.

Game Divide the class into teams. Then, in English, say the name of a classroom object and ask one of the teams to provide the French equivalent. If the team provides the correct term, it gets a point. If not, the second team gets a chance to give the correct term. Alternate giving items to the two teams. The team with the most points at the end of the game wins.

Mise en pratique

1 Chassez l'intrus Circle the word that does not belong.

1. étudiants, élèves, (professeur)
2. un stylo, un crayon, (un cahier)
3. un livre, un dictionnaire, (un stylo)
4. un homme, (un crayon), un garçon
5. une copine, (une carte), une femme
6. une porte, une fenêtre, (une chaise)
7. une chaise, (un professeur), une fenêtre
8. (un crayon), une feuille de papier, un cahier
9. une calculatrice, une montre, (une copine)
10. une fille, (un sac à dos), un garçon

2 Écoutez Listen to Madame Arnaud as she describes her French classroom, then check the items she mentions.

1. une porte	☑	6. vingt-quatre cahiers	☐
2. un professeur	☐	7. une calculatrice	☐
3. une feuille de papier	☐	8. vingt-sept chaises	☑
4. un dictionnaire	☑	9. une corbeille à papier	☑
5. une carte	☑	10. un stylo	☑

3 C'est... Work with a partner to identify the items you see in the image.

MODÈLE

Étudiant(e) 1: *Qu'est-ce que c'est?*
Étudiant(e) 2: *C'est un tableau.*

1.	un tableau	7.	une feuille (de papier)
2.	une porte	8.	un bureau
3.	un crayon/stylo	9.	un dictionnaire
4.	un livre	10.	une corbeille à papier
5.	une calculatrice	11.	une chaise
6.	un stylo/crayon	12.	un professeur

Practice more at **espaces.vhlcentral.com.**

1 Suggestion Have students compare their answers in pairs or small groups. Tell them to explain why a word does not belong if they don't have the same answer.

1 Expansion For additional practice, read these items aloud or write them on the board.
11. une calculatrice, un étudiant, un professeur (une calculatrice)
12. une femme, un garçon, une fille (un garçon)
13. un cahier, un copain, un camarade de chambre (un cahier)

2 Tapescript Bonjour! Dans la salle de classe, il y a beaucoup de choses! Il y a trois fenêtres, une porte, une carte, un tableau, vingt-sept chaises et une corbeille à papier. Il y a aussi vingt-quatre étudiants et vingt-quatre sacs à dos. Dans les sacs à dos, il y a généralement un cahier, un crayon ou un stylo, un livre et un dictionnaire pour le cours de français.
(On Textbook MP3s)

2 Suggestion Have students check their answers by going over **Activité 2** with the whole class. Repeat any sections of the recording that the students missed or did not understand.

3 Suggestion Remind students to use the appropriate form of the indefinite article when doing this activity.

3 Expansion In pairs, tell students to take turns pointing to the items in the drawing and asking: **C'est un(e) ____?** If it's correct, the other person says: **Oui, c'est un(e) ____.** If it is not correct, the persons says: **Non, c'est un(e) ____.**

OPTIONS

Extra Practice Review numbers and practice vocabulary for classroom objects using printouts of advertisements in French from stores that sell school supplies, such as Monoprix. Make sure the ads include prices. As you show the pictures, ask students about the prices. Examples: **La corbeille à papier est à 15 euros ou à 20 euros? C'est combien, la calculatrice?**

Game Have the class do a chain activity in which the first student says a word in French, for example, **chaise**. The next student has to think of a word that begins with the last letter of the first person's word, such as **étudiant**. If a student can't think of a word, he or she is out of the game, and it's the next person's turn. The last student left in the game is the winner.

4 Expansion For additional practice, point to different students' desks that have objects on them and ask: **Qu'est ce qu'il y a sur le bureau de ____?** You might also ask: **Qu'est-ce qu'il y a sur mon bureau?**

5 Suggestion Before beginning the activity, have a few volunteers demonstrate what students should do using the **modèle**.

6 Suggestions
- Divide the class into pairs and distribute the Info Gap Handouts on the Supersite for this activity. Give students ten minutes to complete the activity.
- Have two volunteers read the **modèle** aloud.

6 Suggestion Before beginning the activity, remind students that to guess what the drawing represents they should say: **C'est un(e) ____?** or **Ce sont des ____?**

7 Expansion Have students describe the people and objects in the photo using **Il y a.**

Successful Language Learning Remind the class that errors are a natural part of language learning. Point out that it is impossible to speak "perfectly" in any language. Emphasize that their spoken and written French will improve if they make an effort to practice.

Communication

4 **Qu'est-ce qu'il y a dans mon sac à dos?** Make a list of six different items that you have in your backpack, then work with a partner to compare your answers. Answers will vary.

Dans mon (*my*) sac à dos, il y a...	Dans le sac à dos de ___*nom*___, il y a...
1. ________	1. ________
2. ________	2. ________
3. ________	3. ________
4. ________	4. ________
5. ________	5. ________
6. ________	6. ________

5 **Qu'est-ce que c'est?** Point at eight different items around the classroom and ask a classmate to identify them. Write your partner's responses on the spaces provided below. Answers will vary.

MODÈLE

Étudiant(e) 1: *Qu'est-ce que c'est?*
Étudiant(e) 2: *C'est un stylo.*

1. ________	5. ________
2. ________	6. ________
3. ________	7. ________
4. ________	8. ________

6 **Pictogrammes** Play pictionary as a class. Answers will vary.

- Take turns going to the board and drawing words you learned on pp. 16–17.
- The person drawing may not speak and may not write any letters or numbers.
- The person who guesses correctly in French what the **grand artiste** is drawing will go next.
- Your instructor will time each turn and tell you if your time runs out.

7 **Sept différences** Your instructor will give you and a partner two different drawings of a classroom. Do not look at each other's worksheet. Find seven differences between your picture and your partner's by asking each other questions and describing what you see.

MODÈLE

Étudiant(e) 1: *Il y a une fenêtre dans ma (my) salle de classe.*
Étudiant(e) 2: *Oh! Il n'y a pas de fenêtre dans ma salle de classe.*

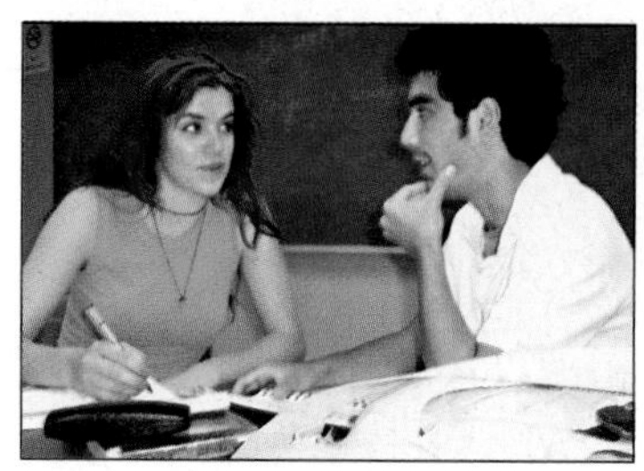

OPTIONS

Game Divide the class into two teams. Put labels of classroom vocabulary in a box. Alternating between teams, one person picks a label out of the box without showing it to anyone. This person must place the label on the correct person or object in the classroom and say the word aloud. Each player is allowed only 15 seconds and one guess per turn. Award a point for a correct response. If a player is incorrect, the next player on the opposing team may "steal" the point by placing the label on the correct person or object. The team with the most points at the end of the game wins.

Les sons et les lettres

Audio: Concepts, Activities
Record & Compare

NATIONAL STANDARDS comparisons

Silent letters

Final consonants of French words are usually silent.

françai~~s~~ **spor~~t~~** **vou~~s~~** **salu~~t~~**

An unaccented **-e** (or **-es**) at the end of a word is silent, but the preceding consonant is pronounced.

français~~e~~ **américain~~e~~** **orang~~es~~** **japonais~~es~~**

The consonants **-c**, **-r**, **-f**, and **-l** are usually pronounced at the ends of words. To remember these exceptions, think of the consonants in the word **car**e**ful**.

parc	**bonjour**	**actif**	**animal**
lac	**professeur**	**naïf**	**mal**

Prononcez Practice saying these words aloud.

1. traditionnel	6. Monsieur	11. timide
2. étudiante	7. journalistes	12. sénégalais
3. généreuse	8. hôtel	13. objet
4. téléphones	9. sac	14. normal
5. chocolat	10. concert	15. importante

Articulez Practice saying these sentences aloud.

1. Au revoir, Paul. À plus tard!
2. Je vais très bien. Et vous, Monsieur Dubois?
3. Qu'est-ce que c'est? C'est une calculatrice.
4. Il y a un ordinateur, une table et une chaise.
5. Frédéric et Chantal, je vous présente Michel et Éric.
6. Voici un sac à dos, des crayons et des feuilles de papier.

Dictons Practice reading these sayings aloud.

Mieux vaut tard que jamais.[1]

Aussitôt dit, aussitôt fait.[2]

ressources
LM p. 6
espaces.vhlcentral.com

[1] Better late than never.
[2] No sooner said than done.

Section Goals

In this section, students will learn about:
- silent letters
- a strategy for remembering which consonants are pronounced at the end of words

Instructional Resources
espaces.vhlcentral.com: Textbook MP3s; Lab MP3s; WB/VM/LM Answer Key; IRM (Textbook Audioscript; Lab Audioscript); activities; downloads; reference tools

Suggestions

- Write the sentences below on the board or a transparency. Then say each sentence and ask students which letters are silent. Draw a slash through the silent letters as students say them.
  Qui est-ce? C'est Gilbert. Il est français.
  Qu'est-ce que c'est? C'est un éléphant.
- Work through the example words. Model the pronunciation of each word and have students repeat after you.
- Tell students that the final consonants of a few words that end in **c**, **r**, **f**, or **l** are silent. Examples: **porc** (*pork*), **blanc** (*white*), **nerf** (*nerve*), and **gentil** (*nice*).
- Point out that the letters **-er** at the end of a word are pronounced like the vowel sound in the English word *say*. Examples: **cahier** and **papier**.
- Explain that numbers are exceptions to pronunciation rules. When counting, some final consonants are pronounced. Have students compare the pronunciation of the following: **six**, **sept**, **huit**; **six cahiers**, **sept stylos**, **huit crayons**.
- Tell students that the final consonants of words borrowed from other languages are often pronounced. Examples: **snob**, **autobus**, and **club**. This topic will be presented in **Leçon 11A**.
- The explanations and exercises are recorded on the Textbook MP3s CD-ROM and are available on the **ESPACES** Supersite. You may want to play them in class so students hear French speakers other than yourself.

OPTIONS

Extra Practice Write on the board or an overhead transparency a list of words that have silent letters. Call on volunteers to spell each word in French and then pronounce it. Examples: **art**, **comment**, **sont**, **est**, **intelligent**, **sac à dos**, and **résultat**.

Small Groups Working in groups of three or four, have students practice pronunciation by reading the vocabulary words aloud on pages 16–17. Circulate among the groups and model correct pronunciation as needed. When they have finished, ask them if they discovered any exceptions to the pronunciation rules. (**cahier, papier**)

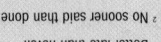

Section Goals

In this section, students will learn functional phrases for describing people's character traits and talking about their nationalities through comprehensible input.

Instructional Resources
espaces.vhlcentral.com: WB/VM/LM Answer Key; IRM (Videoscript; ***Roman-photo*** *Translations); activities; downloads; reference tools Video on DVD*

Video Recap: Leçon 1A Before doing this **Roman-photo**, review the previous one. Write the names of the main characters on the board and ask students with whom they associate the following people, places, or objects.

1. un étudiant américain (David)
2. Le P'tit Bistrot (Valérie et Stéphane)
3. un magazine (Sandrine)
4. un examen de français (Stéphane)
5. un cours de sciences politiques (Rachid)
6. le lycée (Stéphane)

Video Synopsis At the café, Valérie waits on some tourists. Valérie argues with Stéphane about his failed math test. While Michèle and Valérie prepare the tourists' orders, Michèle advises Valérie to be patient with her son. At another table, David asks Amina about herself, Rachid, and Sandrine. David repeats his questions about the others to Valérie, who warns him not to get involved with Sandrine because she is seeing Pascal.

Suggestions

- Have students scan the captions and find six adjectives of nationality plus five phrases that describe people's personality or character. Call on volunteers to read the adjectives or phrases they found aloud.
- Have students volunteer to read the characters' parts in the **Roman-photo** aloud.

NATIONAL STANDARDS communication cultures

Les copains

Video: *Roman-photo*
Record & Compare

PERSONNAGES

Amina

David

Michèle

Stéphane

Touriste

Valérie

À la terrasse du café...
VALÉRIE Alors, un croissant, une crêpe et trois cafés.
TOURISTE Merci, Madame.
VALÉRIE Ah, vous êtes... américain?
TOURISTE Um, non, je suis anglais. Il est canadien et elle est italienne.
VALÉRIE Moi, je suis française.

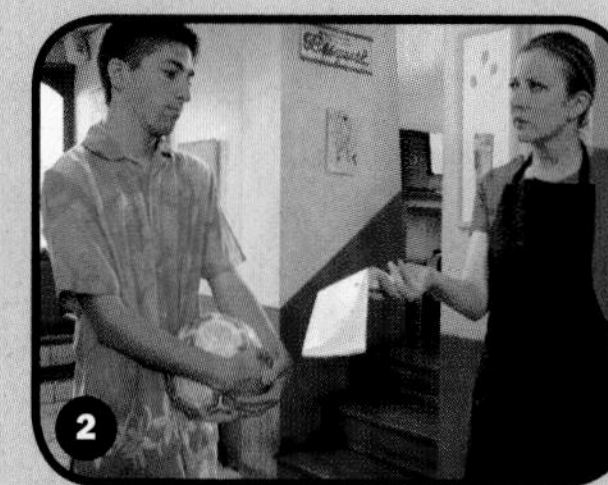

À l'intérieur du café...
VALÉRIE Stéphane!!!
STÉPHANE Quoi?! Qu'est-ce que c'est?
VALÉRIE Qu'est-ce que c'est! Qu'est-ce que c'est! Une feuille de papier! C'est l'examen de maths! Qu'est-ce que c'est?
STÉPHANE Oui, euh, les maths, c'est difficile.

VALÉRIE Stéphane, tu es intelligent, mais tu n'es pas brillant! En classe, on fait attention au professeur, au cahier et au livre! Pas aux fenêtres. Et pas aux filles!
STÉPHANE Oh, oh, ça va!!

À la table d'Amina et de David...
DAVID Et Rachid, mon colocataire? Comment est-il?
AMINA Il est agréable et très poli... plutôt réservé mais c'est un étudiant brillant. Il est d'origine algérienne.

DAVID Et toi, Amina. Tu es de quelle origine?
AMINA D'origine sénégalaise.
DAVID Et Sandrine?

AMINA Sandrine? Elle est française.
DAVID Mais non... Comment est-elle?
AMINA Bon, elle est chanteuse, alors elle est un peu égoïste. Mais elle est très sociable. Et charmante. Mais attention! Elle est avec Pascal.
DAVID Pfft, Pascal, Pascal...

ACTIVITÉS

1 Identifiez Indicate which character would make each statement: Amina (**A**), David (**D**), Michèle (**M**), Sandrine (**S**), Stéphane (**St**), or Valérie (**V**).

1. Les maths, c'est difficile. St
2. En classe, on fait attention au professeur! V
3. Michèle, les trois cafés sont pour les trois touristes. V
4. Ah, Madame, du calme! M
5. Ma mère est très impatiente! St
6. J'ai (*I have*) de la famille au Sénégal. A
7. Je suis une grande chanteuse! S
8. Mon colocataire est très poli et intelligent. D
9. Pfft, Pascal, Pascal... D
10. Attention, David! Sandrine est avec Pascal. A/V

Practice more at **espaces.vhlcentral.com.**

OPTIONS

Video Tips General suggestions for using video clips in the classroom can be found on page IAE-11 of the Instructor's Annotated Edition.

Avant de regarder la vidéo Before showing the video episode, have students brainstorm the type of information they might give when describing people.

Regarder la vidéo Show the video episode and have students give you a play-by-play description of the action. Write their descriptions on the board. Then show the episode a second time so students can add details if necessary, or simply consolidate information. Finally, discuss the material on the board and call attention to any incorrect information. Help students prepare a brief plot summary.

Amina, David et Stéphane passent la matinée (*spend the morning*) au café.

Au bar...
VALÉRIE Le croissant, c'est pour l'Anglais, et la crêpe, c'est pour l'Italienne.
MICHÈLE Mais, Madame. Ça va? Qu'est-ce qu'il y a?
VALÉRIE Ben, c'est Stéphane. Des résultats d'examens, des professeurs... des problèmes!

MICHÈLE Ah, Madame, du calme! Je suis optimiste. C'est un garçon intelligent. Et vous, êtes-vous une femme patiente?
VALÉRIE Oui... oui, je suis patiente. Mais le Canadien, l'Anglais et l'Italienne sont impatients. Allez! Vite!

VALÉRIE Alors, ça va bien?
AMINA Ah, oui, merci.
DAVID Amina est une fille élégante et sincère.
VALÉRIE Oui! Elle est charmante.
DAVID Et Rachid, comment est-il?
VALÉRIE Oh! Rachid! C'est un ange! Il est intelligent, poli et modeste. Un excellent camarade de chambre.

DAVID Et Sandrine? Comment est-elle?
VALÉRIE Sandrine?! Oh, là, là. Non, non, non. Elle est avec Pascal.

Expressions utiles

Describing people

- **Vous êtes/Tu es américain?**
  You're American?
- **Je suis anglais. Il est canadien et elle est italienne.**
  I'm English. He's Canadian, and she's Italian.
- **Et Rachid, mon colocataire? Comment est-il?**
  And Rachid, my roommate (in an apartment)? What's he like?
- **Il est agréable et très poli... plutôt réservé mais c'est un étudiant brillant.**
  He's nice and polite... rather reserved, but a brilliant student.
- **Tu es de quelle origine?**
  What's your heritage?
- **Je suis d'origine algérienne/sénégalaise.**
  I'm of Algerian/Senegalese heritage.
- **Elle est avec Pascal.**
  She's with (dating) Pascal.
- **Rachid! C'est un ange!**
  Rachid! He's an angel!

Asking questions

- **Ça va? Qu'est-ce qu'il y a?**
  Are you OK? What is it?/What's wrong?

Additional vocabulary

- **Ah, Madame, du calme!**
  Oh, ma'am, calm down!
- **On fait attention à...**
  One pays attention to...
- **Mais attention!**
  But watch out!
- **Allez! Vite!**
  Go! Quickly!
- **Mais non...**
  Of course not...
- **alors**
  so
- **mais**
  but
- **un peu**
  a little

ACTIVITÉS

2 Complétez Use words from the list to describe these people in French. Refer to the video scenes and a dictionary as necessary.

1. Michèle always looks on the bright side. optimiste
2. Rachid gets great grades. intelligent
3. Amina is very honest. sincère
4. Sandrine thinks about herself a lot. égoïste
5. Sandrine has a lot of friends. sociable

égoïste
intelligent
optimiste
sincère
sociable

3 Conversez In pairs, choose the words from this list you would use to describe yourselves. What personality traits do you have in common? Be prepared to share your answers with the class.

brillant	modeste
charmant	optimiste
égoïste	patient
élégant	sincère
intelligent	sociable

ressources
VM pp. 213-214
DVD Leçon 1B
espaces.vhlcentral.com

Expressions utiles
- Model the pronunciation of the **Expressions utiles** and have students repeat after you.
- Point out forms of the verb **être** and adjective agreement in the captions and in the **Expressions utiles**. Tell students that this material will be formally presented in the **Structures** section.
- Ask a few questions based on the **Expressions utiles**. Examples: **Et ____, vous êtes américain(e) [canadien(ne)/ italien(ne)]? Ça va? Qu'est-ce qu'il y a?**

1 Expansion For additional practice, read these items aloud or write them on the board.
11. Je suis optimiste. (Michèle)
12. Je suis anglais. (le touriste)
13. Rachid! C'est un ange! (Valérie)

2 Expansion Write the following adjectives on the board and ask students which video character they describe.
1. sénégalais(e) (Amina)
2. algérien(ne) (Rachid)
3. français(e) (Sandrine, Stéphane, Valérie, Michèle)
4. charmant(e) (Sandrine)
5. réservé (Rachid)

3 Expansion After the students complete the activity, tell them to write a brief description of themselves using **Je suis ____**. Read some of the descriptions aloud and have the class guess who wrote them.

OPTIONS

Extra Practice Choose four or five lines of the **Roman-photo** to use as a dictation. Read each line twice, pausing after each line so that students have time to write. Have students check their own work by comparing it with the **Roman-photo** text.

Pairs Have students work in pairs. Tell them to look at video stills 2–3 and 6–8, and choose a situation to ad-lib. Assure them that it is not necessary to follow or memorize the **Roman-photo** word for word. Students should be creative while getting the general meaning across with the vocabulary and expressions they know.

NATIONAL STANDARDS connections cultures

Section Goals

In this section, students will:
- learn about France's multicultural society
- learn some familiar terms for identifying people
- read the mottos of some francophone countries
- read about ***Superdupont***, a popular comic-strip character

Instructional Resources
espaces.vhlcentral.com: activities; downloads; reference tools

Culture à la loupe

Avant la lecture Have students discuss what their idea of a typical French person is.

Lecture
- Point out the regions where Provençal **(Provence)**, Breton **(Bretagne)**, and Basque **(Le Pays basque)** are spoken on the map of France in **Appendix A.**
- Explain that there are other regional languages not mentioned in the text: Alsatian, Caribbean Creole, Catalan, Corsican, Dutch, Gascon, Lorraine German dialect, and Occitan.

Après la lecture Ask students what facts in this reading are interesting or surprising to them.

1 Expansion For additional practice, give students these items. 11. There are several official languages in France. (**Faux.** French is the only official language.) 12. South Africans represent a significant immigrant population in France. (**Faux.** North and West Africans represent significant immigrant populations.) 13. There are more immigrants in France from both Italy and Spain than from Tunisia. (**Vrai.**) 14. There aren't many Asians in France. (**Faux.** There are significant Indo-Chinese populations.)

CULTURE À LA LOUPE

Qu'est-ce qu'un Français typique?

What is your idea of a typical Frenchman? Do you picture a man wearing a **béret**? How about French women? Are they all fashionable and stylish? Do you picture what is shown in these photos? While real French people fitting one aspect or another of these cultural stereotypes do exist, rarely do you find individuals who fit all aspects.

France is a multicultural society with no single, national ethnicity. While the majority of French people are of Celtic or Latin descent, France has significant North and West African (e.g., Algeria, Morocco, Senegal) and Asian (e.g., Vietnam, Laos, Cambodia) populations as well. Long a **terre d'accueil**°, France today has over four million foreigners and immigrants. Even as France has maintained a strong concept of its culture through the preservation of its language, history, and traditions, French culture has been ultimately enriched by the contributions of its immigrant populations. Each region of the country also has its own traditions, folklore, and, often, its own language. Regional languages, such as Provençal, Breton, and Basque, are still spoken in some areas, but the official language is, of course, French.

Immigrants in France, by country of birth

COUNTRY NAME	NUMBER OF PEOPLE
Algeria	574,200
Portugal	571,900
Other European countries	568,800
Morocco	522,500
Italy	378,700
Spain	316,200
Tunisia	201,600
Turkey	174,200
Cambodia, Laos, Vietnam	159,800
Poland	98,600

SOURCE: INSEE

terre d'accueil *a land welcoming of newcomers*

ACTIVITÉS

1 Vrai ou faux? Indicate whether each statement is **vrai** or **faux.** Correct the false statements.

1. Cultural stereotypes are generally true for most people in France. Faux. Rarely do you find individuals who fit all aspects of a stereotype.
2. People in France no longer speak regional languages. Faux. Regional languages are still spoken in some areas.
3. Many immigrants from North Africa live in France. Vrai.
4. More immigrants in France come from Portugal than from Morocco. Vrai.
5. Algerians and Moroccans represent the largest immigrant populations in France. Faux. Algerians and Portuguese are the largest immigrant populations.
6. Immigrant cultures have little impact on French culture. Faux. French culture has been enriched by immigrant cultures.
7. Because of immigration, France is losing its cultural identity. Faux. France has maintained its culture.
8. French culture differs from region to region. Vrai.
9. Most French people are of Anglo-Saxon heritage. Faux. The majority of French people are of Celtic or Latin descent.
10. For many years, France has received immigrants from many countries. Vrai.

Practice more at **espaces.vhlcentral.com.**

OPTIONS

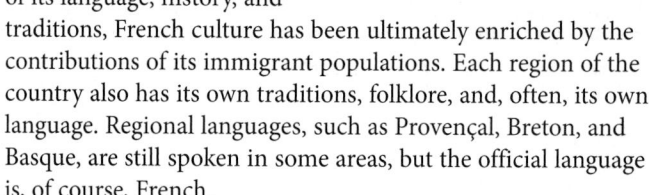

Cultural Activity Ask students what stereotypical ideas a French person might have of Americans. If students have difficulty answering, then give them a few examples of American stereotypes and ask them if they are true or valid. Examples: Americans are loud and obnoxious. Americans only speak English. Americans are overweight.

Small Groups Divide the class into groups of three or four. Give groups five minutes to brainstorm names of cities, states, lakes, rivers, mountain ranges, and so forth in the United States that have French origins. One member of each group should write down the names. Then have groups share their lists with the class.

LE FRANÇAIS QUOTIDIEN

Les gens

ado (*m./f.*)	*adolescent, teen*
bonhomme (*m.*)	*fellow*
gars (*m.*)	*guy*
mec (*m.*)	*guy*
minette (*f.*)	*young woman, sweetie*
nana (*f.*)	*young woman, girl*
pote (*m.*)	*buddy*
type (*m.*)	*guy*

LE MONDE FRANCOPHONE

Les devises

Here are the **devises** (*national mottos*) of some francophone countries.

Belgium L'union fait la force (*Unity is strength*)
Ivory Coast Union, Discipline, Travail (*Unity, Discipline, Work*)
France Liberté, Égalité, Fraternité (*Liberty, Equality, Fraternity*)
Monaco Avec l'aide de Dieu (*With the help of God*)
Morocco Dieu, la Patrie, le Roi (*God, Country, King*)
Senegal Un Peuple, un But, une Foi (*One People, one Goal, one Faith*)
Switzerland Un pour tous, tous pour un (*One for all, all for one*)
Tunisia Liberté, Ordre, Justice (*Liberty, Order, Justice*)

PORTRAIT

Superdupont

Superdupont is an ultra-French superhero in a popular comic strip parodying French nationalism. The protector of all things French, he battles the secret enemy organization **Anti-France**, whose agents speak **anti-français**, a mixture of English, Spanish, Italian, Russian, and German. ***Superdupont*** embodies just about every French stereotype imaginable. For example, the name Dupont, much like Smith in the United States, is extremely common in France. In addition to his **béret** and moustache, he wears a blue, white, and red belt around his waist representing **le drapeau français** (*the French flag*). Physically, he is overweight and has a red nose—signs that he appreciates rich French food and wine. Finally, on his arm is **un coq** (*a rooster*), the national symbol of France. The Latin word for rooster (*gallus*) also means "inhabitant of Gaul," as France used to be called.

SUR INTERNET

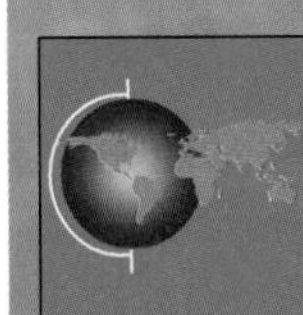

What countries are former French colonies?

Go to **espaces.vhlcentral.com** to find more information related to this **ESPACE CULTURE.**

ACTIVITÉS

2 Complétez Provide responses to these questions.

1. France is often symbolized by this bird: ___the rooster___.
2. ___Blue, white, and red___ are the colors of the French flag.
3. France was once named ___Gaul___.
4. The French term ___ado___ refers to a person aged 15 or 16.
5. ___Liberty, equality, and fraternity___ are three basic principles of French society.

3 Et les Américains? What might a comic-book character based on a "typical American" be like? With a partner, brainstorm a list of stereotypes to create a profile for such a character. Compare the profile you create with your classmates'. Do they fairly represent Americans? Why or why not?

ressources
espaces.vhlcentral.com

OPTIONS

Cultural Comparison Have students compare ***Superdupont*** to American comic-book superheroes, such as Superman, Batman, and Wonder Woman. Bring in pictures of these comic-book characters, if possible, to facilitate the discussion. Have students discuss the following aspects: their clothing and general appearance, the reason for their existence or purpose, what they represent, and why they are so popular.

Les devises Tell students to take out a coin and find mottos of the United States. ("In God We Trust" and "*E Pluribus Unum*") Point out that "*E Pluribus Unum*" means "*One Out of Many*". Then ask students which countries in the francophone world have mottos that express similar ideas. "In God We Trust" is the official national motto according to a law passed in 1956.

Le français quotidien
- Point out that this vocabulary is very familiar. These words are usually used in informal conversations among young people.
- Model the pronunciation of each term and have students repeat.

Portrait
- Explain that this political comic strip is not unique and that **la bande dessinée (B.D.)** represents serious reading for young and old alike in France. An international comic-book festival takes place every year in the small town of Angoulême, France.
- Ask students why they think ***Superdupont*** is so popular in France.

Le monde francophone
- Have students locate the countries listed here on the world map in **Appendice A.**
- To check comprehension, ask these questions. 1. Which countries' mottos include the word *union*? (Belgium and Ivory Coast) 2. How do other mottos express this same idea? (Senegal: **Un Peuple, un But, une Foi** and Switzerland: **Un pour tous, tous pour un**) 3. Whose motto mentions freedom? (France and Tunisia) 4. Whose motto mentions God? (Monaco and Morocco) 5. What other country considers religion important? (Senegal: **une Foi**) 6. What does Morocco's motto tell you about the country's political structure? (It's a monarchy.)

Sur Internet Point out to students that they will find supporting activities and information at **espaces.vhlcentral.com**.

2 Expansion Have students write four more fill-in-the-blank statements based on the information on this page. Then tell them to exchange papers with a classmate and complete the activity.

3 Expansion Have students draw a picture of their comic-book character or find a photo in a newspaper or magazine to illustrate the character's profile.

Section Goals

In this section, students will learn:
- subject pronouns
- the verb **être**
- **c'est** and **il/elle est**

Instructional Resources
*espaces.vhlcentral.com: Lab MP3s; WB/VM/LM Answer Key; IRM (**Essayez!** and **Mise en pratique** answers; Lab Audioscript); activities; downloads; reference tools*

Suggestions
- Point to yourself and say: **Je suis professeur**. Then walk up to a student and say: **Tu es...**The student should say: **étudiant(e)**. Once the pattern has been established, include other subject pronouns and forms of **être** while pointing to other students. Examples: **Il est étudiant. Elle est étudiante. Elles sont étudiantes.**
- Ask students a few simple questions and tell them to respond **Oui** or **Non**. Examples: **Brad Pitt est acteur? Jennifer Aniston est chanteuse?**
- Point out that in French you do not use an article before a profession after **il/elle est** and **ils/elles sont.** You say: **Il est acteur,** not **Il est un acteur.**
- Ask students to give examples of situations in which they would use the **tu** and **vous** forms of **être**.
- Give examples of how **on** can mean *we* in casual conversation: **On est copains.** Explain that **On est copains** is in the plural because it means *We are friends.*
- Point out the liaison in **vous êtes**. Also point out that the **-n** in **on est** is pronounced. Have students pronounce these phrases.
- When teaching the difference between **c'est/ce sont** and **il(s)/elle(s) est/sont**, explain that **c'est/ce sont** is most often followed by a noun and **il(s)/elle(s) est/sont** is most often followed by an adjective. Point out the exceptions: **C'est très bien. Elle est chanteuse.**
- Tell students that the term **la photo**, which appears in the example **Ce sont des photos**, comes from the word **la photographie.**

1B.1 The verb *être*

NATIONAL comparisons STANDARDS

Point de départ In French, as in English, the subject of a verb is the person or thing that carries out the action. The verb expresses the action itself.

SUBJECT ⟷	VERB
Le professeur	parle français.
The professor	*speaks French.*

Subject pronouns

- Subject pronouns replace a noun that is the subject of a verb.

SUBJECT PRONOUN ⟷	VERB
Il	parle français.
He	*speaks French.*

French subject pronouns

	singular		plural	
first person	je	*I*	nous	*we*
second person	tu	*you*	vous	*you*
third person	il	*he/it* (masc.)	ils	*they* (masc.)
	elle	*she/it* (fem.)	elles	*they* (fem.)
	on	*one*		

- Subject pronouns in French show number (singular vs. plural) and gender (masculine vs. feminine). When a subject consists of both genders, use the masculine form.

Ils dansent très bien.
They dance very well.

Ils sont de Dakar.
They are from Dakar.

- Use **tu** for informal address and **vous** for formal. **Vous** is also the plural form of *you*, both informal and formal.

Comment vas-**tu**?	Comment allez-**vous**?
How's it going?	*How are you?*

- The subject pronoun **on** refers to people in general, just as the English subject pronouns *one, they,* or *you* sometimes do. **On** can also mean *we* in a casual style. **On** always takes the same verb form as **il** and **elle**.

En France, **on** parle français.	**On** est au café.
In France, they speak French.	*We are at the coffee shop.*

MISE EN PRATIQUE

1 Pascal répète Pascal repeats everything his older sister Odile says. Give his response after each statement, using subject pronouns.

MODÈLE Chantal est étudiante. *Elle est étudiante.*

1. Les professeurs sont en Tunisie. Ils sont en Tunisie.
2. Mon (*My*) petit ami Charles n'est pas ici. Il n'est pas ici.
3. Moi, je suis chanteuse. Tu es chanteuse.
4. Nadège et moi, nous sommes à l'université. Vous êtes à l'université.
5. Tu es un ami. Je suis un ami.
6. L'ordinateur est dans (*in*) la chambre. Il est dans la chambre.
7. Claude et Charles sont là. Ils sont là.
8. Lucien et toi, vous êtes copains. Nous sommes copains.

2 Où sont-ils? Thérèse wants to know where all her friends are. Tell her by completing the sentences with the appropriate subject pronouns and the correct forms of **être**.

MODÈLE Sylvie / au café *Elle est au café.*

1. Georges / à la faculté de médecine Il est à la faculté de médecine.
2. Marie et moi / dans (*in*) la salle de classe Nous sommes dans la salle de classe.
3. Christine et Anne / à la bibliothèque Elles sont à la bibliothèque.
4. Richard et Vincent / là-bas Ils sont là-bas.
5. Véronique, Marc et Anne / à la librairie Ils sont à la librairie.
6. Jeanne / au bureau Elle est au bureau.

3 Identifiez Describe these photos using **c'est, ce sont, il/elle est,** or **ils/elles sont.**

1. C'est un acteur.

4. Elle est chanteuse.

2. Il est ici.

5. Elle est là.

3. Elles sont copines.

6. Ce sont des montres.

Practice more at **espaces.vhlcentral.com.**

OPTIONS

Extra Practice As a rapid-response drill, call out subject pronouns and have students respond with the correct form of **être**. Examples: **tu (es)** and **vous (êtes)**. Then reverse the drill; say the forms of **être** and have students give the subject pronouns. Accept multiple answers for **est** and **sont**.

Extra Practice Ask students to indicate whether the following people would be addressed as **vous** or **tu**. Examples: a roommate, a friend's grandmother, a doctor, and a neighbor's child.

Extra Practice Bring in pictures of people and objects and ask students to describe them using **c'est, ce sont, il/elle est,** or **ils/elles sont.**

COMMUNICATION

4 **Assemblez** In pairs, take turns using the verb **être** to combine elements from both columns. Talk about yourselves and people you know. Answers will vary.

A	B
Singulier:	
Je	agréable
Tu	d'origine française
Mon (*My*, masc.) prof	difficile
Mon/Ma (*My*, fem.) camarade de chambre	étudiant(e)
Mon cours	sincère
	sociable
______	______
Pluriel:	
Nous	agréables
Mes (*My*) profs	copains/copines
Mes camarades de chambre	difficiles
Mes cours	étudiant(e)s
	sincères
______	______

5 **Qui est-ce?** In pairs, identify who or what is in each picture. If possible, use **il/elle est** or **ils/elles sont** to add something else about each person or place. Answers will vary.

MODÈLE

C'est Céline Dion. Elle est chanteuse.

1.

4.

2.

5.

3.

6.

6 **Enchanté** You and your roommate are in a campus bookstore. You run into one of his or her classmates, whom you've never met. In a brief conversation, introduce yourselves, ask how you are, and say something about yourselves using a form of **être**. Answers will vary.

The verb *être*

- **Être** (*to be*) is an irregular verb; its conjugation (set of forms for different subjects) does not follow a pattern. The form **être** is called the infinitive; it does not correspond to any particular subject.

Être			
je suis	*I am*	nous sommes	*we are*
tu es	*you are*	vous êtes	*you are*
il/elle est	*he/she/it is*	ils/elles sont	*they are*
on est	*one is*		

- Note that the **-s** of the subject pronoun **vous** is pronounced as an English *z* in the phrase **vous êtes**.

Vous êtes à Paris.
You are in Paris.

Vous êtes M. Leclerc? Enchantée.
Are you Mr. Leclerc? Pleased to meet you.

C'est and *il/elle est*

- Use **c'est** or its plural form **ce sont** plus a noun to identify who or what someone or something is. Except with proper names, an article must always precede the noun.

C'est un téléphone.
That's a phone.

Ce sont des photos.
Those are pictures.

C'est Amina.
That's Amina.

- Use the phrases **il/elle est** and **ils/elles sont** to refer to someone or something previously mentioned. Any noun that follows directly must not be accompanied by an article or adjective.

La bibliothèque?
Elle est moderne.
The library?
It's modern.

Voilà M. Richard.
Il est professeur.
There's Mr. Richard.
He's a professor.

BOÎTE À OUTILS
Note that in French, unlike English, you cannot use an article before a profession after **il/elle est** and **ils/elles sont**: **il est chanteur** (*he is a singer*); **elles sont actrices** (*they are actresses*).

Essayez! Fill in the blanks with the correct forms of the verb **être**.

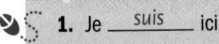

1. Je ___suis___ ici.
2. Ils ___sont___ intelligents.
3. Tu ___es___ étudiante.
4. Nous ___sommes___ à Québec.
5. Vous ___êtes___ Mme Lacroix?
6. Marie ___est___ chanteuse.

Essayez! Have students create additional simple sentences using the verb **être**.

1 Suggestion Have students work on this activity in pairs. Tell them to switch roles for items 5–8.

2 Suggestion To check students' answers, call on volunteers to read the sentences aloud or write them on the board.

3 Suggestion Before beginning the activity, have students quickly identify the items or people in the photos.

4 Suggestion Tell students to add two questions of their own to the list and to jot down notes during their interviews.

5 Suggestion Tell students to write down their descriptions. After they have completed the activity, call on volunteers to read their descriptions.

6 Suggestion Have volunteers act out their conversations for the class.

OPTIONS

Video Replay the video episode, having students focus on subject pronouns and the verb **être**. Ask them to write down as many examples of sentences that use forms of **être** as they can. Stop the video where appropriate to ask comprehension questions about what the characters said.

Small Groups Working in small groups, have students invent a story about the people in the photo of **Activité 5**. Tell them to include who the people are, where they are from, and what they do in their story. Circulate around the room and assist with unfamiliar vocabulary as necessary, but encourage students to use terms they already know.

Section Goals

In this section, students will learn:
- forms, agreement, and position of adjectives
- some descriptive adjectives
- adjectives of nationality

Instructional Resources
*espaces.vhlcentral.com: Lab MP3s; WB/VM/LM Answer Key; IRM (**Essayez!** and **Mise en pratique** answers; Lab Audioscript); activities; downloads; reference tools*

Suggestions
- Write these adjectives on the board: **impatient, impatiente, impatients, impatientes.** Model each adjective in a sentence and ask volunteers to tell you whether it is masculine or feminine and singular or plural.
- Model the pronunciation of adjectives of nationality and have students repeat them. Point out that the feminine forms ending in **-ienne**.
- Go around the room asking **Quelle est votre nationalité?** Also have a few students ask each other their nationalities.
- Use pictures and the names of celebrities to practice other adjectives of nationality. Examples: **Le prince William est-il canadien? (Non, il est anglais.) Julia Roberts est-elle française? (Non, elle est américaine.)**
- Explain that adjectives of nationality can be used as nouns as well. Examples: **La femme anglaise est réservée. L'Anglaise est réservée.**
- Point out that in English most adjectives are placed before the noun, but in French they are placed after the noun. Write the following example on the board, circle the adjective, and draw an arrow pointing to the noun. Example: **C'est un examen difficile.**
- At this point you may want to present the adjectives in the **Vocabulaire supplémentaire** on the Supersite.

1B.2 Adjective agreement

NATIONAL comparisons STANDARDS

Point de départ Adjectives are words that describe people, places, and things. In French, adjectives are often used with the verb **être** to point out the qualities of nouns or pronouns.

- Many adjectives in French are cognates; that is, they have the same or similar spellings and meanings in French and English.

Cognate descriptive adjectives

agréable	*pleasant*	**intelligent(e)**	*intelligent*
amusant(e)	*fun*	**intéressant(e)**	*interesting*
brillant(e)	*bright*	**occupé(e)**	*busy*
charmant(e)	*charming*	**optimiste**	*optimistic*
désagréable	*unpleasant*	**patient(e)**	*patient*
différent(e)	*different*	**pessimiste**	*pessimistic*
difficile	*difficult*	**poli(e)**	*polite*
égoïste	*selfish*	**réservé(e)**	*reserved*
élégant(e)	*elegant*	**sincère**	*sincere*
impatient(e)	*impatient*	**sociable**	*sociable*
important(e)	*important*	**sympathique (sympa)**	*nice*
indépendant(e)	*independent*	**timide**	*shy*

- In French, most adjectives agree in number and gender with the nouns they describe. Most adjectives form the feminine by adding a silent **-e** (no accent) to the end of the masculine form, unless one is already there. Adding a silent **-s** to the end of masculine and feminine forms gives you the plural forms of both.

MASCULINE SINGULAR — MASCULINE SINGULAR
Henri est **élégant**.
Henri is elegant.

FEMININE SINGULAR — FEMININE SINGULAR
Patricia est **élégante**.
Patricia is elegant.

MASCULINE PLURAL — MASCULINE PLURAL
Henri et Jérôme sont **élégants**.
Henri and Jérôme are elegant.

FEMININE PLURAL — FEMININE PLURAL
Patricia et Marie sont **élégantes**.
Patricia and Marie are elegant.

BOÎTE À OUTILS
Use the masculine plural form of an adjective to describe a group composed of masculine and feminine nouns: **Henri et Patricia sont élégants.**

MISE EN PRATIQUE

1 Nous aussi! Olivier is bragging about himself, but his younger sisters Stéphanie and Estelle believe they possess the same attributes. Tell what they say.

MODÈLE
Je suis amusant. Nous aussi, nous sommes *amusantes.*

1. Je suis intelligent. Nous aussi, nous sommes... intelligentes.
2. Je suis sincère. Nous aussi, nous sommes... sincères.
3. Je suis élégant. Nous aussi, nous sommes... élégantes.
4. Je suis patient. Nous aussi, nous sommes... patientes.
5. Je suis sociable. Nous aussi, nous sommes... sociables.
6. Je suis poli. Nous aussi, nous sommes... polies.

2 Les nationalités You are with a group of students from all over the world. Indicate their nationalities according to the cities from which they come.

MODÈLE
Monique est de (*from*) Paris. *Elle est française.*

1. Les amies Fumiko et Keiko sont de Tokyo. Elles sont japonaises.
2. Hans est de Berlin. Il est allemand.
3. Juan et Pablo sont de Guadalajara. Ils sont mexicains.
4. Wendy est de Londres. Elle est anglaise.
5. Jared est de San Francisco. Il est américain.
6. Francesca est de Rome. Elle est italienne.
7. Salim et Mehdi sont de Casablanca. Ils sont marocains.
8. Jean-Pierre et Mario sont de Québec. Ils sont québécois/canadiens.

3 Voilà Mme... Your parents are having a party and you point out different people to your friend. Use words and expressions from this grammar point. Answers will vary.

MODÈLE
Voilà M. Duval. Il est sénégalais.
C'est un ami.

Practice more at **espaces.vhlcentral.com.**

OPTIONS

Extra Practice As a rapid-response drill, say the name of a country and have students respond with the appropriate adjective of nationality. For variation, have students write the adjective on the board or tell them to spell the adjective after they say it.

Extra Practice Write each descriptive adjective on two cards or slips of paper and put them in two separate piles in random order. Hand out one card to each student. Tell students they have to find the person who has the same adjective as they do. Example: **Étudiant(e) 1: Tu es optimiste? Étudiant(e) 2: Oui, je suis optimiste./Non, je suis sociable.** For variation, this activity can also be used to practice adjectives of nationality.

COMMUNICATION

4 Ils sont comment? In pairs, take turns describing each item below. Tell your partner whether you agree (**C'est vrai.**) or disagree (**C'est faux.**) with the descriptions. Answers will vary.

MODÈLE

Johnny Depp
Étudiant(e) 1: *C'est un acteur désagréable.*
Étudiant(e) 2: *C'est faux. Il est charmant.*

1. Beyoncé et Céline Dion
2. les étudiants de Harvard
3. Bono
4. la classe de français
5. le président des États-Unis (*United States*)
6. Tom Hanks et Gérard Depardieu
7. le prof de français
8. Steven Spielberg
9. notre (*our*) université
10. Tina Fey et Angelina Jolie

5 Interview You are looking for a roommate and interview someone to see what he or she is like. In pairs, play both roles. Are you compatible? Answers will vary.

MODÈLE

pessimiste
Étudiant(e) 1: *Tu es pessimiste?*
Étudiant(e) 2: *Non, je suis optimiste.*

1. impatient
2. modeste
3. timide
4. sincère
5. égoïste
6. sociable
7. indépendant
8. amusant

6 Au café You and two classmates are talking about your new bosses (**patrons**), each of whom is very different from the other two. In groups of three, create a dialogue in which you greet one another and describe your bosses. Answers will vary.

- French adjectives are usually placed after the noun they modify when they don't directly follow a form of **être**.

Ce sont des **étudiantes brillantes**. *They're brilliant students.*	Bernard est un homme **agréable et poli**. *Bernard is a pleasant and polite man.*

- Here are some adjectives of nationality. Note that the **-n** of adjectives that end in **-ien** doubles before the final **-e** of the feminine form: **algérienne, canadienne, italienne, vietnamienne.**

Adjectives of nationality

algérien(ne)	*Algerian*	**japonais(e)**	*Japanese*
allemand(e)	*German*	**marocain(e)**	*Moroccan*
anglais(e)	*English*	**martiniquais(e)**	*from Martinique*
américain(e)	*American*	**mexicain(e)**	*Mexican*
canadien(ne)	*Canadian*	**québécois(e)**	*from Quebec*
espagnol(e)	*Spanish*	**sénégalais(e)**	*Senegalese*
français(e)	*French*	**suisse**	*Swiss*
italien(ne)	*Italian*	**vietnamien(ne)**	*Vietnamese*

- The first letter of adjectives of nationality is not capitalized.

Il est américain.

Elle est française.

- An adjective whose masculine singular form already ends in **-s** keeps the identical form in the masculine plural.

Pierre est **un ami sénégalais**. *Pierre is a Senegalese friend.*	Pierre et Yves sont **des amis sénégalais**. *Pierre and Yves are Senegalese friends.*

- To ask someone's nationality or heritage, use **Quelle est ta/votre nationalité?** or **Tu es/Vous êtes de quelle origine?**

Quelle est votre nationalité? *What is your nationality?*	**Je suis de nationalité canadienne.** *I'm of Canadian nationality.*
Tu es de quelle origine? *What is your heritage?*	**Je suis d'origine italienne.** *I'm of Italian heritage.*

Essayez! Write in the correct forms of the adjectives.

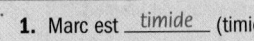

1. Marc est __timide__ (timide).
2. Ils sont __anglais__ (anglais).
3. Elle adore la littérature __française__ (français).
4. Ce sont des actrices __suisses__ (suisse).
5. Elles sont __réservées__ (réservé).
6. Il y a des universités __importantes__ (important).
7. Christelle est __amusante__ (amusant).
8. Les étudiants sont __polis__ (poli) en cours.

1 Suggestion Before beginning the activity, make sure students understand that they should use feminine plural forms of the adjectives. For each item, call on one student to read the sentence in the book and another student to respond.

2 Expansion For additional practice, change the subject of the sentence and have students restate or write the sentences. Examples: **1. Kazumi est de Tokyo. (Il est japonais.) 2. Gerta et Katarina sont de Berlin. (Elles sont allemandes.) 3. Carmen est de Guadalajara. (Elle est mexicaine.) 4. Tom et Susan sont de Londres. (Ils sont anglais.) 5. Linda est de San Francisco. (Elle est américaine.) 6. Luciano et Gino sont de Rome. (Ils sont italiens.) 7. Fatima est de Casablanca. (Elle est marocaine.) 8. Denise et Monique sont de Québec. (Elles sont canadiennes/québécoises.)**

3 Expansion Have students say what each person in the drawing is not. Example: **Madame Malbon n'est pas sociable.**

4 Suggestion Have two volunteers read the **modèle** aloud.

4 Expansion Have small groups brainstorm names of famous people, places, and things not found in the activity and write them in a list. Tell them to include some plural items. Then ask the groups to exchange lists and describe the people, places, and things on that list.

5 Suggestions
- Have students add two more qualities to the list that are important to them.
- After students have completed the activity, ask them if they are compatible roommates and to explain why or why not.

6 Suggestion Tell students to give their bosses a name so that it is obvious if they are male or female. Also encourage students to ask each other questions about their bosses during the conversation.

OPTIONS

Extra Practice Do a quick class survey to find out how many nationalities are represented in your class. As students respond, write the nationality and number of students on the board. Ask: **Combien d'étudiants sont d'origine américaine? Mexicaine? Vietnamienne?** If students ask, clarify that the gender of the adjective of nationality agrees with the word **origine**, which is feminine.

Extra Practice Have students collect several interesting pictures of people from magazines or newspapers. Have them prepare a description of one of the pictures ahead of time. Invite them to show the pictures to the class and then give their descriptions orally without indicating which picture they are talking about. The class will guess which of the pictures is being described.

Instructional Resources
espaces.vhlcentral.com:
*IRM (**Feuilles d'activités**; Info Gap Activities); Testing Program, pp. 5–8; Test Files; Testing Program MP3s; activities; downloads; reference tools*
Test Generator

1 Suggestion Have pairs act out their conversations for the rest of the class.

2 Suggestion Before students begin to make corrections on their classmates' papers, tell them to check the following: correct use of articles and subject pronouns, subject-verb agreement, and adjective agreement.

3 Expansion Have students repeat the activity and describe their differences this time.

4 Suggestion Because this is the first activity in which the **Feuilles d'activités** (found on the Supersite) are used, tell students that they use the **feuilles** to complete the corresponding activity. Explain that they must approach their classmates with their paper in hand and ask questions following the **modèle**. When they find someone who answers affirmatively, that student signs his or her name.

5 Expansion Have a few volunteers read their descriptions to the class. Then ask the class to point out the differences between the various descriptions.

6 Suggestions
- Divide the class into pairs and distribute the Info Gap Handouts on the Supersite for this activity. Give students ten minutes to complete the activity.
- Have two volunteers read the **modèle** aloud.

Révision

1 Festival francophone With a partner, choose two characters from the list and act out a conversation between them. The people are meeting for the first time at a Francophone festival. Then, change characters and repeat. Answers will vary.

Angélique, Sénégal

Abdel, Algérie

Laurent, Martinique

Sylvain, Suisse

Hélène, Canada

Daniel, France

Mai, Viêt-Nam

Nora, Maroc

2 Tu ou vous? How would the conversations between the characters in **Activité 1** differ if they were all 19-year-old students at a university orientation? Write out what you would have said differently. Then, exchange papers with a new partner and make corrections. Return the paper to your partner and act out the conversation using a new character. Answers will vary.

3 En commun In pairs, tell your partner the name of a friend. Use adjectives to say what you both **(tous les deux)** have in common. Then, share with the class what you learned about your partner and his or her friend. Answers will vary.

MODÈLE

Charles est un ami. Nous sommes tous les deux amusants. Nous sommes patients aussi.

4 Comment es-tu? Your instructor will give you a worksheet. Survey as many classmates as possible to ask if they would use the adjectives listed to describe themselves. Then, decide which two students in the class are most similar. Answers will vary.

MODÈLE

Étudiant(e) 1: *Tu es timide?*
Étudiant(e) 2: *Non. Je suis sociable.*

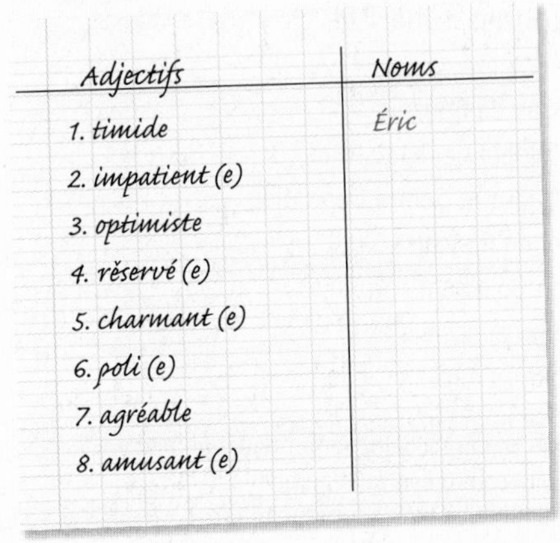

Adjectifs
Noms
1. timide
Éric
2. impatient (e)
3. optimiste
4. réservé (e)
5. charmant (e)
6. poli (e)
7. agréable
8. amusant (e)

5 Mes camarades de classe Write a brief description of the students in your French class. What are their names? What are their personalities like? What is their heritage? Use all the French you have learned so far. Your paragraph should be at least eight sentences long. Remember, be complimentary! Answers will vary.

6 Les descriptions Your instructor will give you one set of drawings of eight people and a different set to your partner. Each person in your drawings has something in common with a person in your partner's drawings. Find out what it is without looking at your partner's sheet. Answers will vary.

MODÈLE

Étudiant(e) 1: *Jean est à la bibliothèque.*
Étudiant(e) 2: *Gina est à la bibliothèque.*
Étudiant(e) 1: *Jean et Gina sont à la bibliothèque.*

ressources: WB pp. 9-12; LM pp. 7-8; espaces.vhlcentral.com

OPTIONS

Small Groups Have students work in groups of three or four. Tell them to prepare a skit on any situation they wish, provided that they use material presented in this lesson. Possible situations can include meeting at a café (as in **Roman-photo**), meeting in between classes, and introducing friends to professors. Remind them to use as many adjectives as possible. Encourage students to have fun with the skit and be creative.

Extra Practice To practice **vous**, have students ask you yes/no questions. First, have them guess your nationality. Example: **Vous êtes français(e)?** Then have them ask you about your personality. Example: **Vous êtes impatient(e)?**

À l'écoute

NATIONAL communication STANDARDS

Audio: Activities

STRATÉGIE

Listening for words you know

You can get the gist of a conversation by listening for words and phrases you already know.

To help you practice this strategy, listen to this sentence and make a list of the words you have already learned.

________ ________
________ ________

Préparation

Look at the photograph. Where are these people? What are they doing? In your opinion, do they know one another? Why or why not? What do you think they're talking about?

À vous d'écouter

As you listen, circle the items you associate with Hervé and those you associate with Laure and Lucas.

HERVÉ	LAURE ET LUCAS
(la littérature)	(le café)
(l'examen)	la littérature
le bureau	la sociologie
le café	la librairie
la bibliothèque	le lycée
(la librairie)	l'examen
le tableau	(l'université)

Practice more at **espaces.vhlcentral.com.**

Compréhension

Vrai ou faux? Based on the conversation you heard, indicate whether each of the following statements is **vrai** or **faux**.

	Vrai	Faux
1. Lucas and Hervé are good friends.	☐	☑
2. Hervé is preparing for an exam.	☑	☐
3. Laure and Lucas know each other from school.	☑	☐
4. Hervé is on his way to the library.	☐	☑
5. Lucas and Laure are going to a café.	☑	☐
6. Lucas studies literature.	☐	☑
7. Laure is in high school.	☐	☑
8. Laure is not feeling well today.	☐	☑

Présentations It's your turn to get to know your classmates. Using the conversation you heard as a model, select a partner you do not know and introduce yourself to him or her in French. Follow the steps below.

- Greet your partner.
- Find out his or her name.
- Ask how he or she is doing.
- Introduce your partner to another student.
- Say good-bye.

Section Goals

In this section, students will:
- learn to listen for known vocabulary
- listen to sentences containing familiar and unfamiliar vocabulary
- listen to a conversation and complete several activities

Instructional Resources
espaces.vhlcentral.com: Textbook MP3s; IRM (Textbook Audioscript); downloads; reference tools

Stratégie
Script Je vous présente une amie, Juliette Lenormand. Elle étudie la sociologie à la faculté.

Successful Language Learning Tell your students that many people feel nervous about their ability to comprehend what they learn in a foreign language. Tell them that they will probably feel less anxious if they follow the advice for increasing listening comprehension in the **Stratégie** sections.

Préparation Have students look at the photo and describe what they see. Ask them to justify their responses based on the visual clues.

À vous d'écouter
Script
HERVÉ: Salut, Laure! Ça va?
LAURE: Bonjour, Hervé. Ça va bien. Et toi?
HERVÉ: Pas mal, merci.
LAURE: Je te présente un copain de l'université. Lucas, Hervé. Hervé, Lucas.
LUCAS: Enchanté.
H: Bonjour, Lucas. Comment vas-tu?
LU: Très bien, merci.
LA: Qu'est-ce que tu fais, Hervé?
H: Je vais à la librairie pour acheter un livre sur la littérature.
LA: Pour un examen?
H: Oui, pour un examen. Et vous?
LA: Nous, on va au café.
H: Alors, à plus tard.
LA: Oui, salut.
LU: Au revoir, Hervé.
H: À bientôt.

Section Goals
In this section, students will:
- read statistics and cultural information about the French language and the francophone world
- learn historical and cultural information about Québec, Louisiana, and Algeria

Instructional Resources
espaces.vhlcentral.com; Transparency #16; WB/VM/LM Answer Key; activities; downloads; reference tools

Carte du monde francophone
Have students look at the map or use **Transparency #16**. Ask them to identify the continents where French is spoken. Then ask them to make inferences about why French is spoken in these regions.

Les pays en chiffres
- Call on volunteers to read the sections. Point out cognates and clarify unfamiliar words.
- Have students locate the capitals of the countries listed in **Villes capitales** on the maps in **Appendice A.**
- After reading **Francophones célèbres**, ask students if they know any additional information about these people.

Francophones célèbres
Ask students if they know of other Francophone celebrities, e.g. Édith Piaf, Chopin, Jacques Brel.

Incroyable mais vrai!
French is one of the official languages of UNESCO, which is the United Nations Educational Scientific and Cultural Organization. UNESCO not only builds classrooms in impoverished countries, but it also brings nations together on social issues.

SAVOIR-FAIRE

NATIONAL STANDARDS connections cultures

Interactive Map Reading

Panorama

Heiva°, Papeete, Tahiti

Le monde francophone

Les pays en chiffres°

Organisation internationale de la Francophonie

- **Nombre de pays° où le français est langue° officielle:** *28*
- **Nombre de pays où le français est parlé°:** *plus de° 60*
- **Nombre de francophones dans le monde°:** *200.000.000 (deux cents millions)*

SOURCE: Organisation internationale de la Francophonie

Villes capitales

- **Algérie:** *Alger*
- **Cameroun:** *Yaoundé*
- **France:** *Paris*
- **Guinée:** *Conakry*
- **Haïti:** *Port-au-Prince*
- **Laos:** *Vientiane*
- **Mali:** *Bamako*
- **Rwanda:** *Kigali*
- **Seychelles:** *Victoria*
- **Suisse:** *Berne*

Francophones célèbres

- **Marie Curie,** *Pologne, scientifique, prix Nobel en chimie et physique (1867–1934)*
- **René Magritte,** *Belgique, peintre° (1898–1967)*

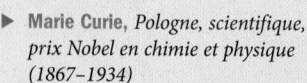

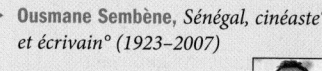

- **Ousmane Sembène,** *Sénégal, cinéaste° et écrivain° (1923–2007)*

- **Jean Reno,** *France, acteur (1948–)*
- **Céline Dion,** *Québec, chanteuse° (1968–)*

- **Marie-José Pérec,** *Guadeloupe (France), athlète (1968–)*

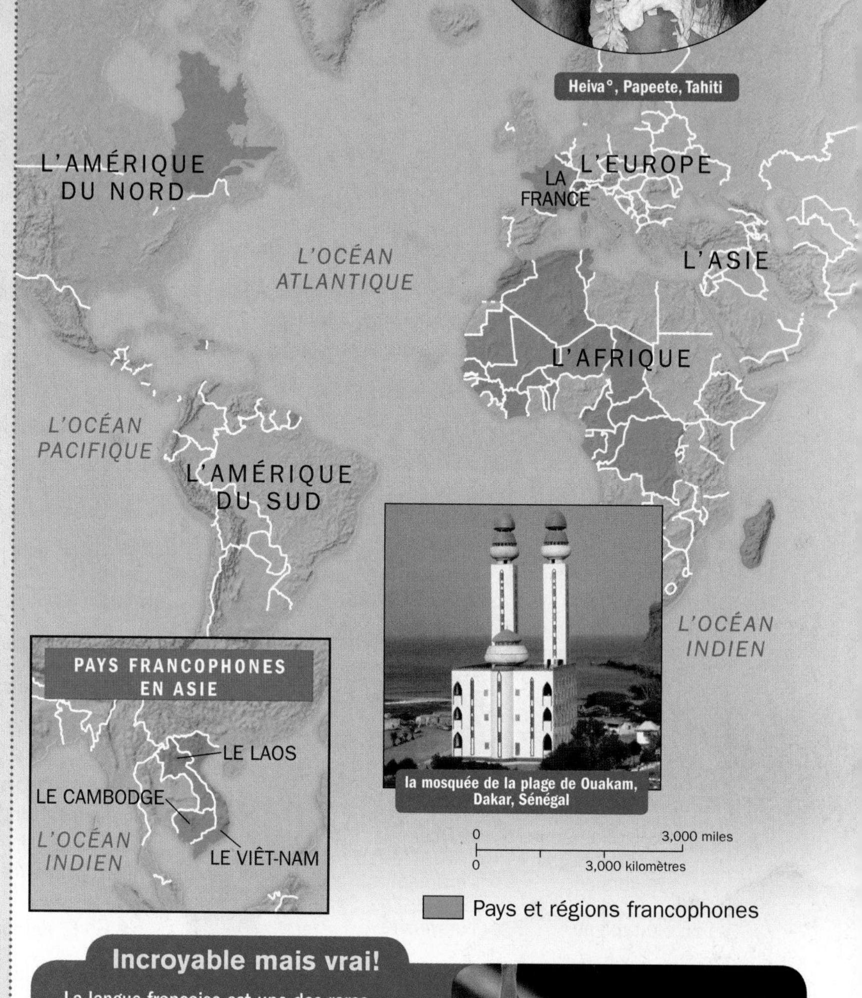

la mosquée de la plage de Ouakam, Dakar, Sénégal

Incroyable mais vrai!

La langue française est une des rares langues à être parlées sur° cinq continents. C'est aussi la langue officielle de beaucoup d'organisations internationales comme° l'OTAN°, les Nations unies, l'Union européenne, et aussi les Jeux° Olympiques! Le français est la deuxième° langue enseignée° dans le monde, après l'anglais.

chiffres *numbers* **pays** *countries* **langue** *language* **parlé** *spoken* **plus de** *more than* **monde** *world* **peintre** *painter* **cinéaste** *filmmaker* **écrivain** *writer* **chanteuse** *singer* **sur** *on* **comme** *such as* **l'OTAN** *NATO* **Jeux** *Games* **deuxième** *second* **enseignée** *taught* **Heiva** *an annual Tahitian festival*

OPTIONS

Francophones célèbres Marie Curie received Nobel Prizes for the discovery of radioactivity and the isolation of radium. **René Magritte** was one of the most prominent surrealist painters. For more information on **Magritte**, see **Unité 11, Panorama**, page 391. **Ousmane Sembène** is considered one of the founders of the African realist tradition and the first African to produce a film.

Jean Reno has played a variety of roles in French and American films. **Céline Dion** has received Grammy awards in the U.S., Juno and Felix awards in Canada, and World Music Awards in Europe for her vocal talents. **Marie-José Pérec** is the first sprinter to win consecutive gold medals in the 400-meter dash.

La société

Le français au Québec

Au Québec, province du Canada, le français est la langue officielle, parlée par° 80% (quatre-vingts pour cent) de la population. Les Québécois, pour° préserver l'usage de la langue, ont° une loi° qui oblige l'affichage° en français dans les lieux° publics. Le français est aussi la langue co-officielle du Canada: les employés du gouvernement doivent° être bilingues.

Les gens

Les francophones d'Algérie

Depuis° 1830 (mille huit cent trente), date de l'acquisition de l'Algérie par la France, l'influence culturelle française y° est très importante. À présent ancienne° colonie, l'Algérie est un des plus grands° pays francophones au monde. L'arabe est la langue officielle, mais le français est la deuxième langue parlée et est compris° par la majorité de la population algérienne.

Les destinations

La Louisiane

Ce territoire au sud° des États-Unis a été nommé° «Louisiane» en l'honneur du Roi° de France Louis XIV. En 1803 (mille huit cent trois), Napoléon Bonaparte vend° la colonie aux États-Unis pour 15 millions de dollars, pour empêcher° son acquisition par les Britanniques. Aujourd'hui° en Louisiane, 200.000 (deux cent mille) personnes parlent° le français cajun. La Louisiane est connue° pour sa° cuisine cajun, comme° le jambalaya, ici sur° la photo avec le chef Paul Prudhomme.

Les traditions

La Journée internationale de la Francophonie

Chaque année°, l'Organisation internationale de la Francophonie (O.I.F.) coordonne la Journée internationale de la Francophonie. Dans plus de° 100 (cent) pays et sur cinq continents, on célèbre la langue française et la diversité culturelle francophone avec des festivals de musique, de gastronomie, de théâtre, de danse et de cinéma. Le rôle principal de l'O.I.F. est la promotion de la langue française et la défense de la diversité culturelle et linguistique du monde francophone.

Qu'est-ce que vous avez appris? Complete the sentences.

1. Ousmane Sembène est un cinéaste africain.
2. 200 millions de personnes parlent français dans le monde.
3. L'Organisation internationale de la Francophonie est responsable de la promotion de la diversité culturelle francophone.
4. Les employés du gouvernement du Canada parlent anglais et français.
5. En Algérie, la langue officielle est l'arabe.
6. Une majorité d'Algériens comprend (*understands*) le français.
7. Le nom «Louisiane» vient du (*comes from the*) nom de Louis XIV.
8. Plus de 100 pays célèbrent la Journée internationale de la Francophonie.
9. Le français est parlé sur cinq continents.
10. En 1803, Napoléon Bonaparte vend la Louisiane aux États-Unis.

ressources: WB pp. 13–14 | espaces.vhlcentral.com

Practice more at **espaces.vhlcentral.com.**

SUR INTERNET

Go to espaces.vhlcentral.com to find more cultural information related to this **PANORAMA**.

1. Les États-Unis célèbrent la Journée internationale de la Francophonie. Faites (*Make*) une liste de trois événements (*events*) et dites (*say*) où ils ont lieu (*take place*).
2. Trouvez des informations sur un(e) chanteur/chanteuse francophone célèbre aux États-Unis. Citez (*Cite*) trois titres de chanson (*song titles*).

parlée par *spoken by* **pour** *in order to* **ont** *have* **loi** *law* **affichage** *posting* **lieux** *places* **doivent** *must* **Depuis** *Since* **y** *there* **ancienne** *former* **un des plus grands** *one of the largest* **compris** *understood* **au sud** *in the South* **a été nommé** *was named* **Roi** *King* **vend** *sells* **empêcher** *to prevent* **Aujourd'hui** *Today* **parlent** *speak* **connue** *known* **sa** *its* **comme** *such as* **sur** *in* **Chaque année** *Each year* **dans plus de** *in more than*

Le français au Québec Since Jacques Cartier first arrived in the Gaspé and claimed the land for the French king in 1534, the people of Quebec have maintained their language and culture, despite being outnumbered and surrounded by English speakers. French became an official language of Canada in 1867. Ask students if they know of any places in the United States where people speak two languages or they can see bilingual signs.

Les francophones d'Algérie Algeria gained its independence from France in 1962, but French is still taught from primary school through high school. French is principally used in business relations, some social situations, and in the information industries. Some newspapers, as well as several television and radio broadcasts, are produced in French.

La Louisiane The early settlers of Louisiana came from France and Acadia (now Nova Scotia and adjacent areas) during the seventeenth and eighteenth centuries. The Acadian settlers were descendents of French Canadians who were exiled from Acadia by the English and eventually settled in the bayou region. Cajun French evolved over time borrowing terms from American Indian, German, English, African, and Spanish speakers.

La Journée internationale de la Francophonie
- The members of **l'Organisation internationale de la Francophonie** comprise 63 states and governments. The celebrations in the various Francophone regions take place throughout the month of March. The name **20 mars** was chosen to commemorate the signature of a treaty which created **l'Agence intergouvernementale de la Francophonie.**
- Point out the symbol of **l'Organisation internationale de la Francophonie** on page 30 next to the heading **Les pays en chiffres.**

OPTIONS

Pairs Have students work in pairs. Tell them to look at the maps in **Appendice A** and make a list of the Francophone countries and capitals that do not appear in the section **Villes capitales**. Point out that they need to find eighteen countries.

Cultural Comparison In groups of three, have students compare **la Journée internationale de la Francophonie** to a cultural celebration held in their town, city, or country. Tell them to discuss the purpose of each celebration, the reasons why people attend them, and the types of events or activities that are part of the celebration.

Section Goals

In this section, students will:

- learn to recognize cognates
- use context to guess the meaning of new words
- read some pages from an address book in French

Stratégie Tell students that cognates are words in one language that have identical or similar counterparts in another language. True cognates are close in meaning, so recognizing French words that are cognates of English words can help them read French. To help students recognize cognates, write these common correspondences between French and English on the board: **-ie** = *-y* (**sociologie**); **-ique** = *-ic* (**fantastique**); **-if(-ive)** = *-ive* (**active**).

Successful Language Learning Tell students that reading in French will be less anxiety provoking if they follow the advice in the **Stratégie** sections, which are designed to reinforce and improve reading comprehension skills.

Examinez le texte Ask students to tell you what type of text this is and how they can tell. (It's an excerpt from an address book. You can tell because it contains names and telephone numbers.)

Mots apparentés

- Check to see if students found all of the cognates from the **Stratégie** box in the reading: **pharmacie, dentiste, télévision, médecin, banque,** and **restaurant**.
- If students are having trouble finding other cognates in the reading, point out a few to get them started: **route** (*route*), **avenue** (*avenue*), **boulevard** (*boulevard*), **théâtre** (*theater*), **comédie** (*comedy*), **dîner** (*dinner*), and **municipale** (*municipal*).
- Let students know there are also false cognates like **librairie** (bookstore).

Devinez Ask volunteers to share their responses with the class. Find out how many were able to guess the meanings correctly: **horaires** (*schedule [hours open]*), **lundi** (*Monday*), **ouvert** (*open*), **soirs** (*evenings; nights*), and **tous** (*all; every*).

Lecture

NATIONAL STANDARDS communication cultures

S Reading

Avant la lecture

STRATÉGIE

Recognizing cognates

Cognates are words that share similar meanings and spellings in two or more languages. When reading in French, it's helpful to look for cognates and use them to guess the meaning of what you're reading. However, watch out for false cognates. For example, **librairie** means *bookstore*, not *library*, and **coin** means *corner*, not *coin*. Look at this list of French words. Can you guess the meaning of each word?

important	**banque**
pharmacie	**culture**
intelligent	**actif**
dentiste	**sociologie**
décision	**fantastique**
télévision	**restaurant**
médecine	**police**

Examinez le texte

Briefly look at the document. What kind of information is listed? In what order is it listed? Where do you usually find such information? Can you guess what this document is?

Mots apparentés

Read the list of cognates in the **Stratégie** box again. How many cognates can you find in the reading selection? Are there additional cognates in the reading? Which ones? Can you guess their English equivalents?

Devinez

In addition to using cognates and words you already know, you can also use context to guess the meaning of words you do not know. Find the following words in the reading selection and try to guess what they mean. Compare your answers with those of a classmate.

horaires **lundi** **ouvert** **soirs** **tous**

Carnet d'adresses

Carnet d'adresses

Recherche

A B C D E F G H I J K L

DAMERY Jean-Claude
dentiste
18, rue des Lilas — 02 38 23 45 46
45000 Orléans

Café de la Poste
Ouvert° tous les jours°, de 7h00° à 22h00
25, place de la Poste — 02 38 27 18 00
45000 Orléans

Librairie Balzac
Horaires: 9h00–12h00 et 14h00–18h00
18, route de Lorient — 02 38 18 60 36
45000 Orléans

DANTEC Pierre-Henri
médecin généraliste
23, rue du Lac — 02 38 47 34 20
45000 Orléans

Banque du Centre
Ouvert de 9h00 à 17h00 du lundi° au vendredi°
17, boulevard Giroud — 02 38 58 35 00
45000 Orléans

Dîner vendredi 8h00
Restaurant du Chat qui dort

OPTIONS

Extra Practice Write these words on the board and have students guess the English meaning: **un agent** (*agent*), **un concert** (*concert*), **la géographie** (*geography*), **une guitare** (*guitar*), **la musique** (*music*), **un réfrigérateur** (*refrigerator*), **confortable** (*comfortable*), **courageux** (*courageous*), **riche** (*rich*), and **typique** (*typical*). Then have them look at the **Vocabulaire** on page 36 and identify all the cognates they have learned.

Small Groups Have students work in groups of three or four. Assign four letters of the alphabet to each group. (Adjust the number of letters according to your class size so that the entire alphabet is covered.) Tell students to use a French-English dictionary and make a list of all the cognates they find beginning with their assigned letters. Have groups read their list of cognates to the rest of the class.

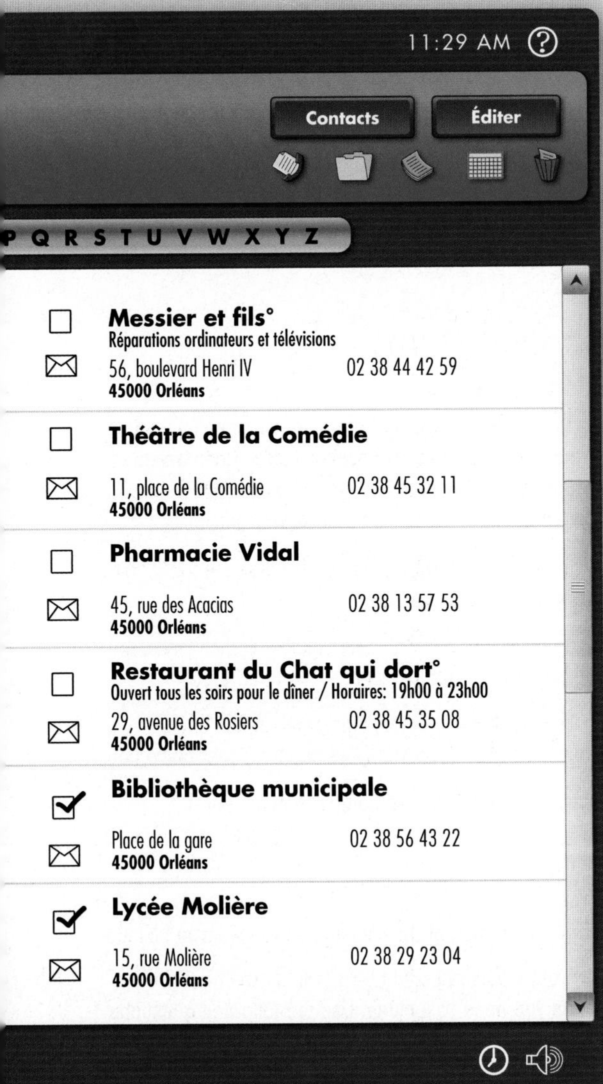

11:29 AM ?
Contacts
Éditer
P Q R S T U V W X Y Z
Messier et fils°
Réparations ordinateurs et télévisions
56, boulevard Henri IV 02 38 44 42 59
45000 Orléans
Théâtre de la Comédie
11, place de la Comédie 02 38 45 32 11
45000 Orléans
Pharmacie Vidal
45, rue des Acacias 02 38 13 57 53
45000 Orléans
Restaurant du Chat qui dort°
Ouvert tous les soirs pour le dîner / Horaires: 19h00 à 23h00
29, avenue des Rosiers 02 38 45 35 08
45000 Orléans
Bibliothèque municipale
Place de la gare 02 38 56 43 22
45000 Orléans
Lycée Molière
15, rue Molière 02 38 29 23 04
45000 Orléans

Ouvert *Open* **tous les jours** *every day* **7h00 (sept heures)** *7:00* **lundi** *Monday* **vendredi** *Friday* **fils** *son(s)* **Chat qui dort** *Sleeping cat*

Après la lecture

Où aller? **Tell where each of these people should go based on what they need or want to do.**

MODÈLE

Camille's daughter is starting high school.
Lycée Molière

1. Mrs. Leroy needs to deposit her paycheck.
   Banque du Centre
2. Laurent would like to take his girlfriend out for a special dinner.
   Restaurant du Chat qui dort
3. Marc has a toothache.
   DAMERY Jean-Claude, dentiste
4. Céleste would like to go see a play tonight.
   Théâtre de la Comédie
5. Pauline's computer is broken.
   Messier et fils, Réparations ordinateurs et télévisions
6. Mr. Duchemin needs to buy some aspirin for his son.
   Pharmacie Vidal
7. Jean-Marie needs a book on French history but he doesn't want to buy one.
   Bibliothèque municipale
8. Noémie thinks she has the flu.
   DANTEC Pierre-Henri, médecin généraliste
9. Mr. and Mrs. Prudhomme want to go out for breakfast this morning.
   Café de la Poste
10. Jonathan wants to buy a new book for his sister's birthday.
    Librairie Balzac

Notre annuaire **With a classmate, select three of the listings from the reading and use them as models to create similar listings in French advertising places or services in your area.**

MODÈLE

Restaurant du Chat qui dort
Ouvert tous les soirs pour le dîner
Horaires: 19h00 à 23h00
29, avenue des Rosiers
45000 Orléans
02 38 45 35 08

Always Good Eats Restaurant
Ouvert tous les jours
Horaires: 6h00 à 19h00
1250 9th Avenue
San Diego, CA 92108
224-0932

Où aller? Go over the activity with the class. If students have trouble inferring the answer to any question, help them identify the cognate or provide additional context clues.

Notre annuaire

- Before beginning the activity, have students brainstorm places and services in the area, and write a list on the board. You might also want to bring in a few local telephone books for students to use as references for addresses and phone numbers.
- You may wish to have students include e-mail addresses (**les adresses e-mail**) in their lists.

OPTIONS

Pairs To review numbers 0–60, have students work in pairs and take turns asking each other the phone numbers and addresses of the people and places listed in the reading. Example: **Étudiant(e) 1: Le numéro de téléphone du dentiste Jean-Claude DAMERY? Étudiant(e) 2: C'est le zéro deux, trente-huit, vingt-trois, quarante-cinq, quarante-six. Étudiant(e) 1: Et l'adresse? Étudiant(e) 2: Dix-huit, rue des Lilas, Orléans.**

Extra Practice Have several students select one of the three listings they created for the **Notre annuaire** activity to read aloud. Instruct the rest of the class to write down the information they hear. To check students' work, have the students who read the listings write the information on the board.

Section Goals
In this section, students will:
- learn strategies for writing in French
- learn to write a telephone/ address book in French
- integrate vocabulary and structures taught in **Leçons 1A–1B**

Stratégie Have students focus on the final point under the "Do" section. Ask them to think about the types of writing that most interests them as readers. Why? Is it that the writer supplies vivid detail? Interesting anecdotes? An easy-to-read style? Is it simply that the subject is important to them? This shows the value of putting themselves in their reader's place.

Thème Introduce students to standard headings used in a telephone/address list: **Nom**, **Adresse**, **Numéro de téléphone**, **Numéro de portable**, and **Adresse e-mail**. Students may wish to add notes pertaining to home (**Numéro de domicile**) or office (**Numéro de bureau**) telephone numbers, fax numbers (**Numéro de fax**), or office hours (**Horaires de bureau**).

Écriture

NATIONAL STANDARDS communication cultures

STRATÉGIE

Writing in French

Why do we write? All writing has a purpose. For example, we may write a poem to reveal our innermost feelings, a letter to impart information, or an essay to persuade others to accept a point of view. Proficient writers are not born, however. Writing requires time, thought, effort, and a lot of practice. Here are some tips to help you write more effectively in French.

DO

- **Write your ideas in French.**
- **Make an outline of your ideas.**
- **Decide what the purpose of your writing will be.**
- **Use the grammar and vocabulary that you know.**
- **Use your textbook for examples of style, format, and expressions in French.**
- **Use your imagination and creativity to make your writing more interesting.**
- **Put yourself in your reader's place to determine if your writing is interesting.**

DON'T

- **Translate your ideas from English to French.**
- **Repeat what is in the textbook or on a web page.**
- **Use a bilingual dictionary until you have learned how to use one effectively.**

Thème

Faites une liste!

Avant l'écriture

1. Imagine that several students from a French-speaking country will be spending a year at your school. You've been asked to put together a list of people and places that might be useful and of interest to them. Your list should include:
   - Your name, address, phone number(s) (home and/or cell), and e-mail address
   - The names of four other students in your French class, their addresses, phone numbers, and e-mail addresses
   - Your French teacher's name, office and/or cell phone number(s), e-mail address, as well as his or her office hours
   - Your school library's phone number and hours
   - The names, addresses, and phone numbers of three places near your school where students like to go
2. Write down the names of the classmates you want to include.
3. Interview your classmates and your teacher to find out the information you need to include. Use the following questions and write down their responses.

Informal	Formal
Comment t'appelles-tu?	Comment vous appelez-vous?
Quel est ton numéro de téléphone?	Quel est votre numéro de téléphone?
Quelle est ton adresse e-mail?	Quelle est votre adresse e-mail?

OPTIONS

Stratégie Review the **Do** list with students. Ask them if they have tried any of these tips. Tell them that they should refer back to this list as they complete the **Écriture** tasks in each lesson. Students may also find it helpful to keep track of which tips work best for them.

Avant l'écriture Before students begin writing, brainstorm a list of popular places where students frequently go. Group them by name in different categories, such as **bibliothèques, cafés, restaurants, magasins, théâtres, parcs, librairies**, and so on. Encourage students to incorporate these category headings into their lists, along with the specific names of different businesses that fall into the categories.

4. Think of three places in your community that a group of students from a French-speaking country would enjoy visiting. They could be a library, a bookstore, a coffee shop, a restaurant, a theater, or a park. Find out their e-mail addresses, telephone numbers, and URLs and write them down.
5. Go online and do a search for two websites that promote your town or area's history, culture, and attractions. Write down their URLs.

Écriture

Write your complete list, making sure it includes all the relevant information. It should include at least five people (with their phone numbers and e-mail addresses), four places (with phone numbers and e-mail addresses), and two websites (with URLs). Avoid using a dictionary and just write what you can in French.

Après l'écriture

1. Exchange your list with a partner's. Comment on his or her work by answering these questions.
   - Did your partner include the correct number of people, places, and websites?
   - Did your partner include the pertinent information for each?

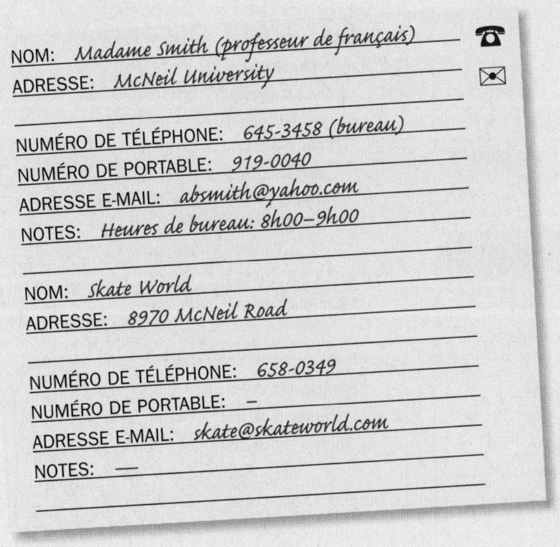

NOM: *Madame Smith (professeur de français)*
ADRESSE: *McNeil University*

NUMÉRO DE TÉLÉPHONE: *645-3458 (bureau)*
NUMÉRO DE PORTABLE: *919-0040*
ADRESSE E-MAIL: *absmith@yahoo.com*
NOTES: *Heures de bureau: 8h00–9h00*

NOM: *Skate World*
ADRESSE: *8970 McNeil Road*

NUMÉRO DE TÉLÉPHONE: *658-0349*
NUMÉRO DE PORTABLE: –
ADRESSE E-MAIL: *skate@skateworld.com*
NOTES: —

2. Edit your partner's work, pointing out any spelling or content errors. Notice the use of these editing symbols:

   - ℊ delete
   - ^ insert letter or word(s) written in margin
   - | replace letter or word(s) with one(s) in margin
   - ≡ change to uppercase
   - / change to lowercase
   - ∽ transpose indicated letters or words

   Now look at this model of what an edited draft looks like:

o *Nm: Sally Wagner*
é *Telephone: 655-8888*
Adresse e-mail: sally@uru.edu

Nom: Madame Nancy smith
Téléphone: *655-8090*
Adresse e-mail: nsmith@uru.edu

3. Revise your list according to your partner's comments and corrections. After writing the final version, read it one more time to eliminate these kinds of problems:
   - spelling errors
   - punctuation errors
   - capitalization errors
   - use of incorrect verb forms
   - use of incorrect adjective agreement
   - use of incorrect definite and indefinite articles

EVALUATION

Criteria

Content Includes all the information mentioned in the five parts of the task description.
Scale: 1 2 3 4 5

Organization Organizes the list similarly to the model provided.
Scale: 1 2 3 4 5

Accuracy Spells the French words used to designate the list categories correctly, including correct accentuation.
Scale: 1 2 3 4 5

Creativity Includes extra information (such as home, office, and fax numbers), more than three students, more than three places.
Scale: 1 2 3 4 5

Scoring

Excellent	18-20 points
Good	14-17 points
Satisfactory	10-13 points
Unsatisfactory	< 10 points

OPTIONS

Après l'écriture Share the evaluation rubric with students before they begin writing. Tell them that you will use these criteria to evaluate their work. Be sure you do this for each **Écriture** task in subsequent units so students will have a clear understanding of your expectations for their work before they undertake the writing task.

Extra practice Ask the class to come up with other categories, such as **postes, banques, docteurs, pharmacies**. Then have them complete their address book list with new items falling into these categories.

Instructional Resources
espaces.vhlcentral.com: Textbook MP3s; IRM (Textbook Audioscript); downloads; reference tools

Suggestions
- Tell students that this is active vocabulary for which they are responsible and that it will appear on tests and exams.
- Tell them that an easy way to study from **Vocabulaire** is to cover up the French half of each section, leaving only the English equivalents exposed. They can then quiz themselves on the French items. To focus on the English equivalents of the French entries, they simply reverse this process.

Le campus

une bibliothèque	*library*
un café	*café*
une faculté	*university; faculty*
une librairie	*bookstore*
un lycée	*high school*
une salle de classe	*classroom*
une université	*university*
un dictionnaire	*dictionary*
une différence	*difference*
un examen	*exam, test*
la littérature	*literature*
un livre	*book*
un problème	*problem*
un résultat	*result*
la sociologie	*sociology*
un bureau	*desk; office*
une carte	*map*
une chaise	*chair*
une fenêtre	*window*
une horloge	*clock*
un ordinateur	*computer*
une porte	*door*
une table	*table*
un tableau	*blackboard; picture*
la télévision	*television*
un cahier	*notebook*
une calculatrice	*calculator*
une chose	*thing*
une corbeille (à papier)	*wastebasket*
un crayon	*pencil*
une feuille (de papier)	*sheet of paper*
un instrument	*instrument*
une montre	*watch*
un objet	*object*
un sac à dos	*backpack*
un stylo	*pen*

Les personnes

un(e) ami(e)	*friend*
un(e) camarade de chambre	*roommate*
un(e) camarade de classe	*classmate*
une classe	*class (group of students)*
un copain/une copine (*fam.*)	*friend*
un(e) élève	*pupil, student*
un(e) étudiant(e)	*student*
un(e) petit(e) ami(e)	*boyfriend/girlfriend*
une femme	*woman*
une fille	*girl*
un garçon	*boy*
un homme	*man*
une personne	*person*
un acteur/une actrice	*actor*
un chanteur/une chanteuse	*singer*
un professeur	*teacher, professor*

Les présentations

Comment vous appelez-vous? (*form.*)	*What is your name?*
Comment t'appelles-tu? (*fam.*)	*What is your name?*
Enchanté(e).	*Delighted.*
Et vous/toi? (*form./fam.*)	*And you?*
Je m'appelle...	*My name is...*
Je vous/te présente... (*form./fam.*)	*I would like to introduce (name) to you.*

Identifier

c'est/ce sont	*it's/they are*
Combien...?	*How much/many...?*
ici	*here*
Il y a...	*There is/are...*
là	*there*
là-bas	*over there*
Qu'est-ce que c'est?	*What is it?*
Qui est-ce?	*Who is it?*
Quoi?	*What?*
voici	*here is/are*
voilà	*there is/are*

Bonjour et au revoir

À bientôt.	*See you soon.*
À demain.	*See you tomorrow.*
À plus tard.	*See you later.*
À tout à l'heure.	*See you later.*
Au revoir.	*Good-bye.*
Bonne journée!	*Have a good day!*
Bonjour.	*Good morning.; Hello.*
Bonsoir.	*Good evening.; Hello.*
Salut!	*Hi!; Bye!*

Comment ça va?

Ça va?	*What's up?; How are things?*
Comment allez-vous? (*form.*)	*How are you?*
Comment vas-tu? (*fam.*)	*How are you?*
Comme ci, comme ça.	*So-so.*
Je vais bien/mal.	*I am doing well/badly.*
Moi aussi.	*Me too.*
Pas mal.	*Not badly.*
Très bien.	*Very well.*

Expressions de politesse

De rien.	*You're welcome.*
Excusez-moi. (*form.*)	*Excuse me.*
Excuse-moi. (*fam.*)	*Excuse me.*
Il n'y a pas de quoi.	*You're welcome.*
Je vous/t'en prie. (*form./fam.*)	*You're welcome.; It's nothing.*
Merci beaucoup.	*Thank you very much.*
Monsieur (M.)	*Sir (Mr.)*
Madame (Mme)	*Ma'am (Mrs.)*
Mademoiselle (Mlle)	*Miss*
Pardon.	*Pardon (me).*
S'il vous plaît. (*form.*)	*Please.*
S'il te plaît. (*fam.*)	*Please.*

Expressions utiles	*See pp. 7 and 21.*
Numbers 0–60	*See p. 12.*
Subject pronouns	*See p. 24.*
être	*See p. 25.*
Descriptive adjectives	*See p. 26.*
Adjectives of nationality	*See p. 27.*

ressources
espaces.vhlcentral.com

À la fac

UNITÉ **2**

Pour commencer
- What object is on the table?
  a. une montre b. un stylo c. un tableau
- What is Rachid looking at?
  a. un cahier b. un ordinateur c. un livre
- How does Rachid look in this photo?
  a. intelligent b. sociable c. égoïste
- Which word describes what he is doing?
  a. arriver b. voyager c. étudier

Unit Goals
Leçon 2A
In this lesson, students will learn:
- terms for courses and places at the university
- to express likes and dislikes
- about liaisons
- about the French university system and **l'Université Laval**
- more about university life through specially shot video footage
- the present tense of regular **-er** verbs
- about spelling changes in **-cer** and **-ger** verbs
- to ask questions and express negation
- about the French company Clairefontaine

Leçon 2B
In this lesson, students will learn:
- terms for talking about schedules and when things happen
- to pronounce the French **r**
- about university courses and **le bac** in France
- the present tense of **avoir**
- some expressions with **avoir**
- to tell time
- to listen for cognates

Savoir-faire
In this section, students will learn:
- cultural, economic, geographical, and historical information about France
- to use text formats to predict content
- to brainstorm before writing
- to write a personal description

Pour commencer
- **b. un stylo**
- **b. un ordinateur**
- **a. intelligent**
- **c. étudier**

RESOURCES

Workbook/Video Manual: WB Activities, pp. 15–28
Laboratory Manual: Lab Activities, pp. 9–16
Workbook/Video Manual: Video Activities, pp. 215–218; pp. 273–274
WB/VM/LM Answer Key
espaces.vhlcentral.com: Textbook MP3s; Lab MP3s; Instructor's Resource Manual [IRM] (Textbook Audioscript; Lab Audioscript; Videoscript; **Roman-photo** Translations; **Vocabulaire supplémentaire**; **Feuilles d'activités**; Info Gap Activities; **Le zapping** TV clip transcription; **Essayez!** and **Mise en pratique** answers); Transparencies #17, #18, #19, #20; Testing Program, pp. 9–16; Test Files; Testing Program MP3s
Test Generator
Video on DVD

Section Goals

In this section, students will learn and practice vocabulary related to:

- courses and fields of study
- places at the university
- expressing likes and dislikes

Instructional Resources
*espaces.vhlcentral.com: Transparency #17; IRM (**Vocabulaire supplémentaire; Mise en pratique** answers, Textbook Audioscript; Lab Audioscript; **Feuilles d'activités**); Textbook MP3s; Lab MP3s; WB/VM/LM Answer Key; activities; downloads; reference tools*

Suggestions

- Have students look at the new vocabulary and identify cognates. Say the words and have students guess the meaning. Point out that the words **lettres** and **note** are **faux amis** in this context.
- Call students' attention to the pronunciation of **ps** in **psychologie**.
- Point out that abbreviations, such as **sciences po** and **resto U**, are common. For more examples, see **Le français quotidien** on page 45.
- To review classroom objects and practice new vocabulary, show items and ask what courses they might be used for. Example: **Un dictionnaire, c'est pour quel cours?**
- Explain that many of the adjectives they learned for nationalities in **Leçon 1B** are also used for languages and language classes. Examples: **le cours de français (d'anglais, d'italien, d'espagnol)**
- Introduce vocabulary for expressing likes and dislikes by talking about your own. Use facial and hand gestures to convey meaning. Examples: **J'adore la littérature française. J'aime bien l'histoire. Je n'aime pas tellement la biologie. Je déteste l'informatique.**
- Additional vocabulary for this lesson can be found in the **Vocabulaire supplémentaire** on the Supersite.

Leçon 2A

You will learn how to...

- **talk about your classes**
- **ask questions and express negation**

Talking Picture Audio: Activity

Les cours

Vocabulaire

J'aime bien...	*I like...*
Je n'aime pas tellement...	*I don't like... very much*
être reçu(e) à un examen	*to pass an exam*
l'art (*m.*)	*art*
la chimie	*chemistry*
le droit	*law*
l'éducation physique (*f.*)	*physical education*
la géographie	*geography*
la gestion	*business administration*
les lettres (*f.*)	*humanities*
la philosophie	*philosophy*
les sciences (politiques / po) (*f.*)	*(political) science*
une bourse	*scholarship, grant*
un cours	*class, course*
un devoir	*homework*
un diplôme	*diploma, degree*
l'école (*f.*)	*school*
les études (supérieures) (*f.*)	*(higher) education; studies*
le gymnase	*gymnasium*
une note	*grade*
un restaurant universitaire (un resto U)	*university cafeteria*
difficile	*difficult*
facile	*easy*
inutile	*useless*
utile	*useful*
surtout	*especially; above all*

ressources
WB pp. 15-16 | LM p. 9 | espaces.vhlcentral.com

OPTIONS

Extra Practice Ask students questions using the new vocabulary words. Examples: **La physique, c'est facile ou difficile? Une bourse, c'est utile ou inutile?**

Extra Practice Have them brainstorm adjectives that can describe their courses and write them: **facile, difficile, utile, inutile, intéressant, amusant, agréable, différent,** and **important**. Ask students to describe various courses. Example: **Le cours de philosophie est difficile.**

Game Divide the class into teams. Say the name of a course in English and ask one team to say it in French. If the team is correct, it gets a point. If not, the other team gets a chance to say it and "steal" the point. Alternate giving words to the two teams.

Attention!

The French system of grading is based on a scale of 0–20. A score below 10 is not a passing grade. It is rare to earn a grade between 18–20. Most students are happy to earn a grade between 12–14.

Mise en pratique

1 Associez Which classes, activities, or places do you associate with these words? Not all items in the second column will be used.

d 1. manger	a. les mathématiques
e 2. un ordinateur	b. la physique
i 3. le français	c. l'histoire
a 4. une calculatrice	d. un restaurant universitaire
f 5. le sport	e. l'informatique
h 6. Socrate	f. l'éducation physique
b 7. E=MC^2	g. la biologie
c 8. Napoléon	h. la philosophie
	i. les langues étrangères
	j. l'art

2 Écoutez On their first day back to school, Aurélie and Hassim are discussing their classes, likes, and dislikes. Indicate who is most likely to use the books listed: Aurélie (A), Hassim (H), both (A & H), or neither (X). Not all items will be used.

1. Informatique et statistiques A & H
2. L'économie de la France A
3. L'architecture japonaise X
4. Histoire de France H
5. Études Freudiennes H
6. La géographie de l'Europe H
7. L'italien, c'est facile! A & H
8. Le droit international A

3 Qu'est-ce que j'aime? Read each statement and indicate whether you think it is **vrai** or **faux**. Compare your answers with a classmate's. Do you agree? Why? Answers will vary.

	Vrai	Faux
1. C'est facile d'être reçu à l'examen de mathématiques.	☐	☐
2. Je déteste manger au restaurant universitaire.	☐	☐
3. Je vais recevoir (*receive*) une bourse; c'est très utile.	☐	☐
4. La mode, c'est inutile.	☐	☐
5. Avoir un diplôme de l'université, c'est facile.	☐	☐
6. La chimie, c'est un cours difficile.	☐	☐
7. Je déteste les lettres.	☐	☐
8. 18 est une très bonne note.	☐	☐
9. Je n'aime pas tellement les études.	☐	☐
10. J'adore les langues étrangères.	☐	☐

Practice more at **espaces.vhlcentral.com.**

1 Expansions
- Items g. and j. were not used. Ask the class what words they associate with **la biologie** and **l'art**.
- Have students brainstorm a list of famous people that they associate with the following fields: **le stylisme** (Ralph Lauren, Vera Wang); **l'informatique** (Bill Gates, Michael Dell); and **la gestion** (Donald Trump, Lee Iacocca). Then have the class guess the field associated with each of the following people: Louis Pasteur **(la biologie)**, Alan Greenspan **(l'économie)**, and Maya Angelou **(les lettres)**.

2 Tapescript AURÉLIE: Bonjour, Hassim. Comment ça va?
HASSIM: Bien. Et toi?
A: Pas mal, merci.
H: Tu aimes le cours d'informatique?
A: Oui, j'adore et j'aime bien l'économie et le droit aussi.
H: Moi, je n'aime pas tellement l'informatique, c'est difficile. J'aime l'histoire, la géographie et la psychologie. C'est très intéressant.
A: Tu aimes la gestion?
H: Ah non, je déteste!
A: Mais c'est très utile!
H: Mais non! Les langues, oui, sont utiles. J'aime bien l'italien.
A: Oui, j'adore l'italien, moi aussi!
H: Bon, à tout à l'heure, Aurélie!
A: Oui, à bientôt!
(On Textbook MP3s)

2 Expansion Play the recording again and ask students these true/false statements or write them on the board. **1. Aurélie n'aime pas le cours d'économie. (Faux.) 2. Hassim déteste le cours de gestion. (Vrai.) 3. Pour Hassim, le cours d'informatique est facile. (Faux.) 4. Hassim aime la psychologie et la géographie. (Vrai.) 5. Aurélie et Hassim aiment bien l'italien. (Vrai.)**

3 Expansion Take a class survey of students' responses to each question and tally the results on the board. Ask students which questions are most controversial. Then ask them on which questions they agree. You might want to introduce the expression **être d'accord**, which will be presented later in **Leçon 2A**.

OPTIONS

Small Groups Write the names of different fields of study across the board (for example, **les langues, les sciences naturelles, les sciences humaines, les cours techniques**). Working in groups of three or four, have students list the courses under the appropriate category.

Extra Practice Using **Transparency #17**, point to various people in the drawing and ask general questions about them. Examples: **Les étudiants sont au resto U? Il aime la physique?**

4 Suggestion Before doing this activity, complete a similar exchange; scramble the order of the sentences and write them on the board or on a transparency. Tell students to put the sentences in order to make a logical conversation.

5 Suggestion Have several volunteers write their captions on the board.

6 Suggestion For more practice, come up with other names.

7 Suggestions
- Read the **modèle** aloud with a volunteer. Then distribute the **Feuilles d'activités** from the Supersite.
- Have volunteers share their findings with the class.

Communication

4 Conversez In pairs, fill in the blanks according to your own situations. Then, act out the conversation for the class. Answers will vary.

Étudiant(e) A: ______________, comment ça va?
Étudiant(e) B: ______________. Et toi?
Étudiant(e) A: ______________ merci.
Étudiant(e) B: Est-ce que tu aimes le cours de ______________?
Étudiant(e) A: J'adore le cours de ______________.
Étudiant(e) B: Moi aussi. Tu aimes ______________?
Étudiant(e) A: Non, j'aime mieux (*better*) ______________.
Étudiant(e) B: Bon, à bientôt.
Étudiant(e) A: À ______________.

5 Qu'est-ce que c'est? Write a caption for each image, stating where the students are and how they feel about the classes they are attending. Then, in pairs, take turns reading your captions for your partner to guess about whom you are talking. Answers will vary. Suggested answers.

MODÈLE

C'est le cours de français.
Le français, c'est facile.

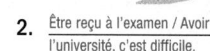

1. C'est le cours d'informatique. Je déteste l'informatique.

2. Être reçu à l'examen / Avoir le diplôme de l'université, c'est difficile.

Nietzsche, philosophe allemand...

3. C'est la philosophie. J'adore la philosophie.

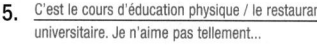

4. C'est le cours de chimie. La chimie, c'est facile.

5. C'est le cours d'éducation physique / le restaurant universitaire. Je n'aime pas tellement...

6. C'est un devoir d'architecture / de stylisme. J'aime bien...

6 Vous êtes... Imagine what subjects these celebrities liked and disliked as students. In pairs, take turns playing the role of each one and guessing the answer. Answers will vary.

MODÈLE

Étudiant(e) 1: *J'aime la physique et la chimie, mais je n'aime pas tellement les cours d'économie.*
Étudiant(e) 2: *Vous êtes Albert Einstein!*

- Albert Einstein
- Louis Pasteur
- Donald Trump
- Bill Clinton
- Christian Dior
- Le docteur Phil
- Bill Gates
- Frank Lloyd Wright

7 Sondage Your instructor will give you a worksheet to conduct a survey (**un sondage**). Go around the room to find people that study the subjects listed. Ask what your classmates think about their subjects. Keep a record of their answers to discuss with the class. Answers will vary.

MODÈLE

Étudiant(e) 1: *Jean, est-ce que tu étudies (do you study) le droit?*
Étudiant(e) 2: *Oui. J'aime bien le droit. C'est un cours utile.*

OPTIONS

Game Divide the class into two teams. Write names of courses or people on index cards and tape them face down on the board. Play a game of Concentration in which students match courses with an expert in the field. Examples: **le stylisme**/Jean-Paul Gaultier, **l'art/** Claude Monet, and **la philosophie**/Jean-Paul Sartre. As students turn over a card, they must read it aloud. If a player has a match, that player's team collects those cards. When all the cards have been matched, the team with the most cards wins.

Extra Practice To practice expressing likes and dislikes, ask students yes/no and either/or questions. Examples: **Vous aimez bien la psychologie? Vous détestez la géographie? Vous adorez les lettres ou les sciences?**

Les sons et les lettres

Audio: Concepts, Activities
Record & Compare

NATIONAL STANDARDS comparisons

Liaisons

Consonants at the end of French words are generally silent but are usually pronounced when the word that follows begins with a vowel sound. This linking of sounds is called a liaison.

À tout à l'heure! **Comment allez-vous?**

An **s** or an **x** in a liaison sounds like the letter **z**.

les étudiants **trois élèves** **six élèves** **deux hommes**

Always make a liaison between a subject pronoun and a verb that begins with a vowel sound; always make a liaison between an article and a noun that begins with a vowel sound.

nous aimons **ils ont** **un étudiant** **les ordinateurs**

Always make a liaison between **est** (a form of **être**) and a word that begins with a vowel or a vowel sound. Never make a liaison with the final consonant of a proper name.

Robert est anglais. **Paris est exceptionnelle.**

Never make a liaison with the conjunction **et** (*and*).

Carole et Hélène **Jacques et Antoinette**

Never make a liaison between a singular noun and an adjective that follows it.

un cours horrible **un instrument élégant**

Prononcez Practice saying these words and expressions aloud.

1. un examen
2. des étudiants
3. les hôtels
4. dix acteurs
5. Paul et Yvette
6. cours important
7. des informations
8. les études
9. deux hommes
10. Bernard aime
11. chocolat italien
12. Louis est

Articulez Practice saying these sentences aloud.

1. Nous aimons les arts.
2. Albert habite à Paris.
3. C'est un objet intéressant.
4. Sylvie est avec Anne.
5. Ils adorent les deux universités.

Dictons Practice reading these sayings aloud.

Les amis de nos amis sont nos amis.1

1 Friends of our friends are our friends.
2 An uninvited guest must bring his own chair.

ressources
LM p. 10
espaces.vhlcentral.com

Section Goals

In this section, students will learn about liaisons.

Instructional Resources
espaces.vhlcentral.com: Textbook MP3s; Lab MP3s; WB/VM/LM Answer Key; IRM (Textbook Audioscript; Lab Audioscript); activities; downloads; reference tools

Suggestions

- Model the pronunciation of each phrase and have students repeat. Explain the liaison for each case.
- Point out expressions with liaison in **Espace contextes** or ask students to find them. Have them repeat after you. Example: **les études.**
- Ask students to provide expressions from **Leçons 1A–1B** that contain a liaison. Examples: **les États-Unis** and **Comment allez-vous?**
- Write the sentences in **Articulez** on the board or a transparency. Have students listen to the recording and tell you where they hear liaisons. Alternately, have students write the sentences on a sheet of paper, draw lines linking letters that form liaisons, and cross out silent final consonants.
- **Liaisons obligatoires** and **liaisons interdites** will be formally presented in **Leçon 15A.**
- The explanation and exercises are available on the **ESPACES** Supersite. You may want to play them in class so students practice listening to French speakers other than yourself.

Dictons Tell students to pronounce the liaison between **n** and **in** in **non invité**. Have students compare the saying **«Un hôte non invité doit apporter son siège»** with its literal translation. Ask what they think it means figuratively. (Possible answer: People who show up unexpectedly have no right to complain about the service.) Ask: What do the two sayings in this section reveal about French culture?

OPTIONS

Extra Practice Dictate the following phrases with liaisons, saying each one at least two times. Then write them on the board or on a transparency and have students check what they wrote. **1. dix-huit étudiants 2. les mathématiques 3. un cours utile 4. la chimie et l'architecture 5. les langues étrangères**

Extra Practice Here are additional sentences with liaisons to use for oral practice or dictation. **1. Robert et Alex sont anglais. 2. C'est un film très intéressant. 3. Il y a trois enfants. 4. C'est un restaurant italien.**

Section Goals

In this section, students will learn functional phrases for talking about their courses.

Instructional Resources
*espaces.vhlcentral.com: WB/VM/LM Answer Key; IRM (Videoscript; **Roman-photo** Translations); activities; downloads; reference tools*
Video on DVD

Video Recap: Leçon 1B Before doing this **Roman-photo**, review the previous one.

1. Le cours d'histoire est difficile pour Stéphane, n'est-ce pas? (Non, les maths et le français sont difficiles pour Stéphane.)
2. Comment est Sandrine? (égoïste, sociable et charmante)
3. De quelle origine est Amina? (sénégalaise) Et Rachid? (algérienne)
4. Comment est Amina? (charmante, sincère et élégante)
5. Comment est Rachid? (intelligent, poli, modeste, réservé et brillant)

Video Synopsis Rachid and Antoine discuss their political science class. As they are walking, David joins them, and Rachid introduces him. Then Antoine leaves. When the two roommates get to Rachid's car, Sandrine and Amina are waiting for them. The girls ask David about school and his classes. Later, at **Le P'tit Bistrot**, Stéphane joins the four friends and they continue their discussion about classes. Stéphane hates all of his courses.

Suggestions

- Have students predict what they think the episode will be about. Record predictions on the board.
- Have students work in groups of six. Tell them to choose a role and read the **Roman-photo** conversation aloud. Ask one or two groups to act out the conversation for the class.
- After students read the **Roman-photo**, review their predictions and ask which ones were correct. Then ask a few questions to guide them in summarizing this episode.

NATIONAL STANDARDS communication cultures

Trop de devoirs!

Video: *Roman-photo*
Record & Compare

PERSONNAGES

Amina

Antoine

David

Rachid

Sandrine

Stéphane

1

ANTOINE Je déteste le cours de sciences po.
RACHID Oh? Mais pourquoi? Je n'aime pas tellement le prof, Monsieur Dupré, mais c'est un cours intéressant et utile!
ANTOINE Tu crois? Moi, je pense que c'est très difficile, et il y a beaucoup de devoirs. Avec Dupré, je travaille, mais je n'ai pas de bons résultats.

2

RACHID Si on est optimiste et si on travaille, on est reçu à l'examen.
ANTOINE Toi, oui, mais pas moi! Toi, tu es un étudiant brillant! Mais moi, les études, oh là là.
DAVID Eh! Rachid! Oh! Est-ce que tu oublies ton coloc?

3

RACHID Pas du tout, pas du tout. Antoine, voilà, je te présente David, mon colocataire américain.
DAVID Nous partageons un des appartements du P'tit Bistrot.
ANTOINE Le P'tit Bistrot? Sympa!

6

SANDRINE Salut! Alors, ça va l'université française?
DAVID Bien, oui. C'est différent de l'université américaine, mais c'est intéressant.
AMINA Tu aimes les cours?
DAVID J'aime bien les cours de littérature et d'histoire françaises. Demain, on étudie *les Trois Mousquetaires* d'Alexandre Dumas.

7

SANDRINE J'adore Dumas. Mon livre préféré, c'est *le Comte de Monte-Cristo*.
RACHID Sandrine! S'il te plaît! *Le Comte de Monte-Cristo*?
SANDRINE Pourquoi pas? Je suis chanteuse, mais j'adore les classiques de la littérature.
DAVID Donne-moi le sac à dos, Sandrine.

8

Au P'tit Bistrot...
RACHID Moi, j'aime le cours de sciences po, mais Antoine n'aime pas Dupré. Il pense qu'il donne trop de devoirs.

ACTIVITÉS

1 Vrai ou faux? Choose whether each statement is **vrai** or **faux**. Correct the false statements.
Answers may vary slightly.

1. Rachid et Antoine n'aiment pas le professeur Dupré. Vrai.
2. Antoine aime bien le cours de sciences po. Faux. Antoine déteste le cours de sciences po.
3. Rachid et Antoine partagent (*share*) un appartement. Faux. Rachid et David partagent un appartement.
4. David et Rachid cherchent (*look for*) Amina et Sandrine après (*after*) les cours. Vrai.
5. Le livre préféré de Sandrine est le *Comte de Monte-Cristo*. Vrai.
6. L'université française est très différente de l'université américaine. Vrai.
7. Stéphane aime la chimie. Faux. Stéphane n'aime pas la chimie.
8. Monsieur Dupré est professeur de maths. Faux. Monsieur Dupré est professeur de sciences po.
9. Antoine a (*has*) beaucoup de devoirs. Vrai.
10. Stéphane adore l'anglais. Faux. Stéphane déteste l'anglais.

Practice more at **espaces.vhlcentral.com.**

OPTIONS

Avant de regarder la vidéo Before showing the video episode, have students brainstorm some expressions people might use when talking about their classes and professors.

Regarder la vidéo Download and print the videoscript and white out ten words or expressions in order to create a master for a cloze activity. Hand out the photocopies and tell students to fill in the missing words as they watch the video episode. You may want to show the episode twice if students have difficulty with the activity. Then have students compare their answers in small groups.

Antoine, David, Rachid et Stéphane parlent (*talk*) de leurs (*their*) cours.

RACHID Ah... on a rendez-vous avec Amina et Sandrine. On y va?
DAVID Ah, oui, bon, ben, salut, Antoine!
ANTOINE Salut, David. À demain, Rachid!

SANDRINE Bon, Pascal, au revoir, chéri.
RACHID Bonjour, chérie. Comme j'adore parler avec toi au téléphone! Comme j'adore penser à toi!

STÉPHANE Dupré? Ha! C'est Madame Richard, mon prof de français. Elle, elle donne trop de devoirs.
AMINA Bonjour, comment ça va?
STÉPHANE Plutôt mal. Je n'aime pas Madame Richard. Je déteste les maths. La chimie n'est pas intéressante. L'histoire-géo, c'est l'horreur. Les études, c'est le désastre!

DAVID Le français, les maths, la chimie, l'histoire-géo... mais on n'étudie pas les langues étrangères au lycée en France?
STÉPHANE Si, malheureusement! Moi, j'étudie l'anglais. C'est une langue très désagréable! Oh, non, non, ha, ha, c'est une blague, ha, ha. L'anglais, j'adore l'anglais. C'est une langue charmante....

Expressions utiles

Talking about classes

- **Tu aimes les cours?**
  Do you like the classes?
- **Antoine n'aime pas Dupré.**
  Antoine doesn't like Dupré.
- **Il pense qu'il donne trop de devoirs.**
  He thinks he gives too much homework.
- **Tu crois? Mais pourquoi?**
  You think? But why?
- **Avec Dupré, je travaille, mais je n'ai pas de bons résultats.**
  With Dupré, I work, but I don't get good results (grades).
- **Demain, on étudie *les Trois Mousquetaires*.**
  Tomorrow we're studying The Three Musketeers.
- **C'est mon livre préféré.**
  It's my favorite book.

Additional vocabulary

- **On a rendez-vous.**
  We have a meeting.
- **Comme j'adore...**
  How I love...
- **parler au téléphone**
  to talk on the phone
- **C'est une blague.**
  It's a joke.
- **Si, malheureusement!**
  Yes, unfortunately!
- **On y va? / On y va.**
  Are you ready? / Let's go.
- **Eh!**
  Hey!
- **pas du tout**
  not at all
- **chéri(e)**
  darling

2 Complétez Match the people in the second column with the verbs in the first. Refer to a dictionary, the dialogue, and the video stills as necessary. Use each option once.

b/e 1. travailler	a. Sandrine is very forgetful.
c 2. partager	b. Rachid is very studious.
a 3. oublier	c. David can't afford his own apartment.
b/e 4. étudier	d. Amina is very generous.
d 5. donner	e. Stéphane needs to get good grades.

3 Conversez In this episode, Rachid, Antoine, David, and Stéphane talk about the subjects they are studying. Get together with a partner. Do any of the characters' complaints or preferences remind you of your own? Whose opinions do you agree with? Whom do you disagree with?

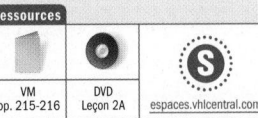

ressources: VM pp. 215-216 | DVD Leçon 2A | espaces.vhlcentral.com

ACTIVITÉS

Expressions utiles
- Model the pronunciation of the **Expressions utiles** and have students repeat after you.
- As you work through the list, point out forms of **-er** verbs. Also identify examples of negation. Tell students that **-er** verbs and negation will be formally presented in **Espace structures.**
- Ask students a few questions about their classes and professors. Examples: **Vous aimez le cours de sciences po? Comment s'appelle le prof de sciences po? Est-ce que ____ donne trop de devoirs?**
- Point out that **si** is used instead of **oui** to contradict a negative statement or question. Example: **Si, malheureusement!**

1 Suggestion Have students correct the false statements.

1 Expansion For additional practice, give students these items. **11. Rachid pense que le cours de sciences po est inutile. (Faux.) 12. Madame Richard est prof de français. (Vrai.) 13. Pour Stéphane, les études, c'est le désastre. (Vrai.)**

2 Expansion Write these verbs on the board: **aimer**, **détester**, **adorer**, and **penser**. Have students create additional statements about the video characters that relate to each verb.

3 Suggestion Encourage students to express their opinions in simple French. Write a few sentence starters on the board. Example: **Comme Stéphane, je n'aime pas...**

OPTIONS

Alexandre Dumas Alexandre Dumas (**père**) (1802–1870) was a prolific French novelist and dramatist. With the assistance of a group of collaborators, he wrote almost 300 works. *The Three Musketeers (**Les Trois Mousquetaires**), The Count of Monte Cristo (**le Comte de Monte-Cristo**),* and *The Black Tulip (**La Tulipe noire**)* are among his most famous and popular novels. These historical romances feature swashbuckling characters. Ask students if they have read any of these books or seen any movies based on them.

Small Groups Working in groups of four, have students create a short skit similar to the scenes in video stills 6–10 in which some students are talking about their classes and professors. Give students about ten minutes to prepare, and then call on groups to perform their skits for the class.

NATIONAL STANDARDS connections cultures

Video: *Flash culture*

Section Goals

In this section, students will:

- learn about French universities and **les grandes écoles**
- learn some familiar terms for talking about academic courses
- learn the names of some well-known universities in the francophone world
- read about **l'Université Laval**
- view authentic video footage

Instructional Resources
espaces.vhlcentral.com: Video; WB/VM/LM Answer Key; IRM (Videoscript); activities; downloads; reference tools
Video on DVD

Culture à la loupe

Avant la lecture Have the class brainstorm and make a list of the different types of educational institutions that exist in the United States.

Lecture

- Point out the chart **Les étudiants en France**. Ask students what information the chart shows. (The percentages of students enrolled at different types of educational institutions in France.) Then ask them to name the types of institutions that exist.
- Tell students that an urban university system may have many individual campuses that operate autonomously. The **Université de Paris**, for example, comprises 13 campuses that are located within the city and in its suburbs.

Après la lecture Have small groups compare French and American universities. Tell them to make a list of the similarities and differences. Then ask several groups to read their lists to the class.

1 Expansion For additional practice, give students these items. 11. Students need to pass an exam in order to advance to a university. (**Vrai.**) 12. France changed its university system in 1998. (**Faux.** France changed its university system in 2005.) 13. A **Master** is the highest degree awarded at a French university. (**Faux.** A **Doctorat** is the highest degree awarded.)

CULTURE À LA LOUPE

À l'université

French students who pass le bac° may continue on to study in a university. By American standards, university tuition is low. In 1999, 29 European countries, including France, decided to reform their university systems in order to create a more uniform European system. France began implementing these reforms in 2005. As a result, French students' degrees (**diplômes**) are now accepted in most European countries. It is also easier for French students to study in other European countries for a semester, and for other European students to study in France, because studies are now organized by semesters. Students are awarded a **Licence°** after six semesters (usually three years). If they continue their studies, they can earn a **Master°** after the fifth year and then proceed to a **Doctorat°**. If students choose technical studies, they receive a **BTS (Brevet de Technicien Supérieur)** after two years.

In addition to universities, France has an extremely competitive, elite branch of higher education called **les grandes écoles°**. These schools train most of the high-level administrators, scientists, businesspeople, and engineers in the country. There are about 300 of them, including **ENA** (**École Nationale d'Administration**), **HEC** (**Hautes° Études Commerciales**), and **IEP** (**Institut d'Études Politiques, «Sciences Po»**).

Some French universities are city-based, lacking campuses and offering few extra-curricular activities like organized sports. Others boast both a more defined campus and a great number of student **associations**. Many students live with their families, in a **résidence universitaire,** or in an apartment.

Les étudiants en France

Universités	62,1%
Sections de Techniciens Supérieurs	11,7%
Autres Écoles ou Formations	6,3%
Écoles Paramédicales et Sociales	5,8%
Instituts Universitaires de Technologie	5,1%
Formation d'Ingénieurs	4,8%
Classes Préparatoires aux grandes écoles	3,5%
Instituts Universitaires de Formation de Maîtres°	3,3%
Écoles de Commerce°	2,3%

SOURCE: Ministère de l'Éducation nationale

bac *exit exam taken after high school* **Licence** *the equivalent of a Bachelor's degree* **Master** *Master's degree* **Doctorat** *Ph.D.* **grandes écoles** *competitive, prestigious university-level schools* **Hautes** *High* **Formation de Maîtres** *teacher training* **Écoles de Commerce** *business schools*

ACTIVITÉS

1 Vrai ou faux? Indicate whether each statement is **vrai** or **faux**. Correct the false statements. Answers may vary slightly.

1. French university students can earn a **Licence** after only three years of study.
   Vrai.
2. It takes five years to earn a **BTS**.
   Faux. It takes two years to earn a BTS.
3. Entry into the **grandes écoles** is not competitive.
   Faux. Entry into the grandes écoles is extremely competitive.
4. The **grandes écoles** train high-level engineers.
   Vrai.
5. Some French universities lack campuses.
   Vrai.
6. Extra-curricular activities are uncommon in some French universities.
   Vrai.
7. All French students live at home with their families.
   Faux. Some students also live in résidences universitaires or in an apartment.
8. Most French students choose not to attend university.
   Faux. Most French students choose to attend university.
9. More French students study business than engineering.
   Faux. More French students study engineering.
10. Some French students are studying for a teaching degree.
   Vrai.

Practice more at **espaces.vhlcentral.com.**

OPTIONS

Pairs Explain how to read percentages so students can quiz each other in pairs about the information in the chart **Les étudiants en France**. Model how to say percentages. Example: 62,1% (**soixante-deux virgule un pour cent**). To help students, write some sample questions on the board. Examples: **Il y a plus** (*more*) **d'étudiants dans les universités ou dans les écoles de commerce? Il y a moins** (*less*) **d'étudiants dans les instituts de technologie ou dans les écoles vétérinaires?**

À l'université Despite France's longstanding low fees for a university education, tuition has increased rapidly. France has only recently needed seriously to consider a federal program of low-interest student loans to offset rising tuition costs since it is unusual for students to work while studying.

LE FRANÇAIS QUOTIDIEN

Les études

être fort(e) en...	*to be good at...*
être nul(le) en...	*to be bad at...*
bio	*biology*
éco	*economics*
géo	*geography*
maths	*math*
philo	*philosophy*
psycho	*psychology*

LE MONDE FRANCOPHONE

Des universités francophones

Voici quelques-unes° des universités du monde francophone où vous pouvez étudier°.

En Belgique Université Libre de Bruxelles

En Côte d'Ivoire Université d'Adobo-Adjamé

En France Université de Paris

Au Maroc Université Mohammed V Souissi à Rabat

En Polynésie française Université de la Polynésie française, à Faa'a, à Tahiti

Au Québec Université de Montréal

Au Sénégal Université Cheikh Anta Diop de Dakar

En Suisse Université de Genève

En Tunisie Université Libre de Tunis

quelques-unes *some* **où vous pouvez étudier** *where you can study*

PORTRAIT

L'Université Laval

Un cours de français au Québec, ça vous dit?° Avec le programme «Français pour non-francophones», les étudiants étrangers peuvent apprendre° le français. Fondée° au XVIIe (dix-septième) siècle° à Québec, l'Université Laval est l'université francophone la plus ancienne° du continent américain. Les études offertes sont diverses et d'excellente qualité: les sciences humaines, la littérature, la musique, la foresterie, les technologies, les sciences. Laval est célèbre° pour être un grand centre universitaire canadien pour la recherche° scientifique. Il existe même° un astéroïde dans le système solaire qui porte le nom de° l'université!

ça vous dit? *what do you think?* **peuvent apprendre** *can learn* **Fondée** *Founded* **siècle** *century* **la plus ancienne** *the oldest* **célèbre** *famous* **recherche** *research* **même** *even* **porte le nom de** *is named after*

Coup de main

In French, a superscript $^{-e}$ following a numeral tells you that it is an ordinal number. It is the equivalent of a $^{-th}$ after a numeral in English: 4e (quatrième) = 4th.

SUR INTERNET

Quelles (*What*) sont les caractéristiques d'un campus universitaire en France?

Go to espaces.vhlcentral.com to find more information related to this **ESPACE CULTURE.** Then watch the corresponding **Flash culture.**

ACTIVITÉS

2 Vrai ou faux? Indicate whether each statement is **vrai** or **faux**. Correct the false statements. Answers may vary.

1. Les étudiants étrangers peuvent étudier le français à l'Université Laval. Vrai.
2. L'Université Laval est l'université francophone la plus ancienne du monde (*world*). Faux. Elle est l'université francophone la plus ancienne du continent américain.
3. Laval offre une grande diversité de cours. Vrai.
4. Laval est un grand centre universitaire de recherche artistique. Faux. Laval est un grand centre universitaire de recherche scientifique.

3 Les cours Research two of the universities mentioned in **Le monde francophone** and make a list in French of at least five courses taught at each. You may search in your library or online.

ressources
VM pp. 273-274
espaces.vhlcentral.com

Le français quotidien Have students work in pairs. Tell them to take turns describing the courses they are good and bad at using the vocabulary in this section. Examples: **Je suis nul(le) en maths. Je suis fort(e) en géo.**

Portrait

- Show the class a photo of **l'Université Laval**. Ask: **Qu'est-ce que c'est? (une université) Comment s'appelle-t-elle?** Then ask students if they know why it is well known.
- Point out the **Coup de main** box. Say the ordinal numbers in French and have volunteers write them on the board using a superscript.

Le monde francophone Have students read the list. Ask: What do you notice about the names of these schools? (All include the name of the city in which they are located, except for two. **L'Université Mohammed V Souissi** in Rabat is named after the king of Morocco from 1957–1961, and **l'Université d'Adobo-Adjamé** is named after two of the ten municipalities in the city of Abidjan.)

2 Suggestion Have students compare their answers with a classmate.

3 Expansion Have students find out the following information as part of their research: when the universities were founded, how many languages are taught, and whether or not they have programs for foreign students and study abroad programs.

Flash culture Tell students that they will learn more about classes and university life by watching a variety of real-life images narrated by Benjamin. Show the video segment, then have students jot down in French at least three examples of people or things they saw. You can also use the activities in the video manual in class to reinforce this **Flash culture** or assign them as homework.

OPTIONS

Cultural Comparison Have students compare their university to **l'Université Laval**. Begin by having students look at the photo and discuss the architecture and campus. Then have them compare other aspects mentioned in the reading, such as fields of study, number of campuses or universities, and courses for foreign students.

Des universités francophones Tell students to imagine that they have the opportunity to go on a study abroad program at one of the universities listed in **Le monde francophone**. Have them choose a location and explain why they would like to attend that particular school.

Section Goals

In this section, students will learn:

- the present tense of regular **-er** verbs
- spelling changes in **-cer** and **-ger** verbs

Instructional Resources
*espaces.vhlcentral.com: Lab MP3s; WB/VM/LM Answer Key; IRM (**Mise en pratique** answers; Lab Audioscript); activities; downloads; reference tools*

Suggestions

- Point out that students have been using verbs from the start: **Comment t'appelles-tu?**, **il y a**, forms of **être**, etc. Ask the class: **Quels cours aimez-vous?** Model the response **J'aime….** Ask a student: ____ **aime quels cours?** Model **Il/Elle aime….** Give other subjects.
- Introduce the idea of a "boot verb." Write the conjugation of a common **-er** verb on the board with the singular forms in the first column and the plural forms in the second column. Draw a line around **je**, **tu**, **il/elle**, and **ils/elles**, forming the shape of a boot. The four verb forms inside the "boot" are pronounced alike.
- Model the pronunciation of each infinitive, having students repeat. Create sentences with **j'aime…** and **j'adore…** followed by infinitives. Stress that **je** changes to **j'** before verbs starting with a vowel and most verbs starting with **h**. Ask if students like some of the activities. Example: **Vous aimez voyager?**
- Explain that the French present tense equals four English present tenses. Ask volunteers to translate examples like these: **À l'université, je mange bien.** (*At college, I eat well.*) **Excusez-moi, je mange.** (*Excuse me, I'm eating.*)
- Point out that verbs ending in **-cer** and **-ger** have a spelling change in the **nous** form. Write **commençons** and **mangeons** on the board, and circle the change.
- Tell students they can find the complete explanation of the **impératif** in **Appendice B**, on p. 552.
- Model the pronunciation of adverbs in **Boîte à outils.** Have students repeat. Ask volunteers for sentences using each word.

2A.1 Present tense of regular *-er* verbs

NATIONAL comparisons STANDARDS

Point de départ The infinitives of most French verbs end in **-er**. To form the present tense of regular **-er** verbs, drop the **-er** from the infinitive and add the corresponding endings for the different subject pronouns. This chart demonstrates how to conjugate regular **-er** verbs.

Parler **(to speak)**			
je parle	*I speak*	**nous parlons**	*we speak*
tu parles	*you speak*	**vous parlez**	*you speak*
il/elle parle	*he/she/it speaks*	**ils/elles parlent**	*they speak*

- Here are some other verbs that are conjugated the same way as **parler**.

Common *-er* verbs			
adorer	*to love*	**habiter (à/en)**	*to live in*
aimer	*to like; to love*	**manger**	*to eat*
aimer mieux	*to prefer (to like better)*	**oublier**	*to forget*
		partager	*to share*
arriver	*to arrive*	**penser (que/qu'...)**	*to think (that...)*
chercher	*to look for*	**regarder**	*to look (at)*
commencer	*to begin, to start*	**rencontrer**	*to meet*
dessiner	*to draw*	**retrouver**	*to meet up with; to find (again)*
détester	*to hate*		
donner	*to give*	**travailler**	*to work*
étudier	*to study*	**voyager**	*to travel*

- Note that **je** becomes **j'** when it appears before a verb that begins with a vowel sound.

J'habite à Bruxelles. — *I live in Brussels.*
J'étudie la psychologie. — *I study psychology.*

- With the verbs **adorer**, **aimer**, and **détester**, use the definite article before a noun to tell what someone loves, likes, prefers, or hates.

J'aime mieux **l'**art. — *I prefer art.*
Marine déteste **les** devoirs. — *Marine hates homework.*

- Use infinitive forms after the verbs **adorer**, **aimer**, and **détester** to say that you like (or hate, etc.) to do something. Only the first verb should be conjugated.

Ils **adorent travailler** ici. — *They love to work here.*
Ils **détestent étudier** ensemble. — *They hate to study together.*

MISE EN PRATIQUE

1 Complétez Complete the conversation with the correct forms of the verbs.

ARTHUR Tu (1) _parles_ (parler) bien français!

OLIVIER Mon colocataire Marc et moi, nous (2) _retrouvons_ (retrouver) un professeur de français et nous (3) _étudions_ (étudier) ensemble. Et toi, tu (4) _travailles_ (travailler)?

ARTHUR Non, j' (5) _étudie_ (étudier) l'art et l'économie. Je (6) _dessine_ (dessiner) bien et j' (7) _aime_ (aimer) beaucoup l'art moderne. Marc et toi, vous (8) _habitez_ (habiter) à Paris?

2 Phrases Form sentences using the words provided. Conjugate the verbs and add any necessary words.

1. je / oublier / devoir de littérature
   J'oublie le devoir de littérature.
2. nous / commencer / études supérieures
   Nous commençons des études supérieures.
3. vous / rencontrer / amis / à / fac
   Vous rencontrez des amis à la fac.
4. Hélène / détester / travailler
   Hélène déteste travailler.
5. tu / chercher / cours / facile
   Tu cherches un cours facile.
6. élèves / arriver / avec / dictionnaires
   Les élèves arrivent avec des dictionnaires.

3 Après l'école Say what Stéphanie and her friends are doing after (**après**) school.
Answers may vary.

MODÈLE

Nathalie cherche un livre.

1. André _travaille_ à la bibliothèque.

4. Julien et Audrey _parlent_ avec Simon.

2. Maxime _retrouve_ Caroline au café.

5. Alexis et toi, vous _voyagez_ avec la classe.

3. Jérôme et moi, nous _dessinons_.

6. Je _mange_ au resto U.

Practice more at **espaces.vhlcentral.com.**

OPTIONS

Extra Practice Do a rapid-response drill. Write an infinitive from the list of **-er** verbs on the board. Call out subject pronouns and/or names, and have students respond with the correct verb form. Then reverse the drill; write a verb form on the board and have students say the subject pronouns.

Game Divide the class into two teams. Choose one team member at a time to go to the board, alternating between teams. Say an infinitive and a subject pronoun. The person at the board must write and say the correct present tense form. Example: **parler: vous (vous parlez).** Give a point for each correct answer. The team with the most points at the end of the game wins.

COMMUNICATION

4 **Activités** In pairs, say which of these activities you and your roommate both do. Be prepared to share your partner's answers with the class. Then, get together with another partner and report to the class again. Answers will vary.

MODÈLE

To your partner: *Nous parlons au téléphone, nous…*
To the class: *Ils/Elles travaillent, ils/elles…*

manger au resto U	étudier une langue étrangère
partager un appartement	regarder la télévision
retrouver des amis au café	aimer les cours
travailler	voyager

5 **Les études** In pairs, take turns asking your partner if he or she likes one academic subject or another. If you don't like a subject, mention one you do like. Then, use **tous les deux** (*both of us*) to tell the class what subjects both of you like or hate. Answers will vary.

MODÈLE

Étudiant(e) 1: *Tu aimes la chimie?*
Étudiant(e) 2: *Non, je déteste la chimie. J'aime mieux les langues. Et toi?*
Étudiant(e) 1: *Moi aussi... Nous adorons tous les deux les langues.*

6 **Adorer, aimer, détester** In groups of four, ask each other if you like to do these activities. Then, use an adjective to tell why you like them or not and say whether you do them often (**souvent**), sometimes (**parfois**), or rarely (**rarement**). Answers will vary.

MODÈLE

Étudiant(e) 1: *Tu aimes voyager?*
Étudiant(e) 2: *Oui, j'adore voyager. C'est amusant! Je voyage souvent.*
Étudiant(e) 3: *Moi, je n'aime pas tellement voyager. C'est désagréable! Je voyage rarement.*

dessiner	partager un appartement
étudier le week-end	retrouver des amis
manger au restaurant	travailler à la bibliothèque
oublier les devoirs	voyager
parler avec les professeurs	

- The present tense in French can be translated in different ways in English. The English equivalent depends on the context.

Ils **étudient** le droit.	Nous **travaillons** ici demain.
They study law.	*We work here tomorrow.*
They are studying law.	*We are working here tomorrow.*
They do study law.	*We will work here tomorrow.*

- Verbs ending in **-ger** (**manger**, **partager**, **voyager**) and **-cer** (**commencer**) have a spelling change in the **nous** form.

manger ▸ **nous mangeons**	**commencer** ▸ **nous commençons**
Nous **voyageons** avec une amie.	Nous **commençons** les devoirs.
We are traveling with a friend.	*We are starting the homework.*

- Unlike the English *to look for,* the French **chercher** requires no preposition before the noun that follows it.

Nous **cherchons les stylos**.	Vous **cherchez la montre**?
We are looking for the pens.	*Are you looking for the watch?*

- Use present tense verb forms to give commands. The **nous** and **vous** command forms are identical to those of the present tense. The **tu** command form of **-er** verbs drops the **-s** from the present tense form. The command forms of **être** are irregular: **sois**, **soyons**, **soyez**.

Regarde!	**Travaillons.**	**Parlez** français.	**Sois** patiente!
Look!	*Let's work.*	*Speak French.*	*Be patient!*

Est-ce que tu oublies ton coloc?

Nous partageons un des appartements du P'tit Bistrot.

BOÎTE À OUTILS

To express yourself with greater accuracy, use these adverbs: **assez** (*enough*), **d'habitude** (*usually*), **de temps en temps** (*from time to time*), **parfois** (*sometimes*), **rarement** (*rarely*), **souvent** (*often*), **toujours** (*always*).

Essayez! **Complete the sentences with the correct present tense forms of the verbs in parentheses.**

1. Je __parle__ (parler) français en classe.
2. Nous __habitons__ (habiter) près de (*near*) l'université.
3. Ils __aiment__ (aimer) le cours de sciences politiques.
4. Élodie! __Regarde__ (regarder) le professeur!
5. Le cours __commence__ (commencer) à huit heures (*at eight o'clock*).
6. Claire et Sylvain, __partagez__ (partager) le livre.

Essayez! Have students create new sentences orally or in writing by changing the subject of the sentence.

1 Suggestion Go over the answers quickly in class, then ask several pairs of students to act out the conversation and add at least two lines of their own at the end.

2 Suggestion To check students' answers, have volunteers write the sentences on the board and read them aloud.

2 Expansion For additional practice, change the subjects of the sentences and have students restate or write the sentences. Examples: **1. Tu (Tu oublies le devoir de littérature.) 2. Chantal (Chantal commence des études supérieures.) 3. Je (Je rencontre des amis à la fac.) 4. Les étudiants (Les étudiants détestent travailler.) 5. Nous (Nous cherchons un cours facile.) 6. Pascale (Pascale arrive avec des dictionnaires.)**

3 Expansion Have students add additional sentences to the captions below the drawings. Example: **1. Il étudie l'histoire. Il y a un examen.**

4 Suggestion Encourage students to personalize the information and to add additional information. Examples: **étudier** *a different subject* , **travailler dans** *a place* , and **regarder la télé.**

5 Suggestion Before beginning the activity, tell students to jot down a list of academic subjects that they can ask their partner about and to note their partner's responses. Examples: **Il/Elle aime** or **Il/Elle déteste**.

6 Suggestion Before beginning the activity, have students brainstorm adjectives they can use and write them on the board.

OPTIONS

Video Show the video episode again to give students additional input on verbs. Pause the video where appropriate to discuss how certain verbs were used and to ask comprehension questions.

Game Have students play a game of pantomime in groups of four or five. Tell students to pick a verb from the list on page 46 and act out the word. The other members of the group have to guess what the person is doing. Example: **Tu travailles?** The first person to guess correctly acts out the next pantomime.

Section Goals

In this section, students will learn:

- to form questions
- to express negation
- expressions for agreeing and disagreeing

Instructional Resources
*espaces.vhlcentral.com: Lab MP3s; WB/VM/LM Answer Key; IRM (**Mise en pratique** answers; Lab Audioscript); activities; downloads; reference tools*

Suggestions

- Model the pronunciation and intonation of the different types of example questions. Point out that the questions on page 48 signal yes-no responses.
- Explain how to form inverted questions. Point out that inversion is usually used in written and formal language. Inversion with **je** is rare in spoken French, but seen in literary language, especially questions. Examples: **Ai-je le droit? Qui suis-je?**
- Point out that any question word can go before **est-ce que.** Example: **Que** as in **Qu'est-ce que c'est?**
- Explain the positions of **ne (n')** and **pas** in negative phrases and in inverted questions. If an infinitive follows a conjugated verb, **ne (n')** and **pas** surround the conjugated verb. Example: **Tu n'aimes pas regarder la vidéo?**
- Tell students that **ne (n')** in negative sentences is sometimes dropped in informal speech.
- Model the expressions indicating agreement and disagreement. Show how **mais** can precede **oui** as well as **non** if you want to say yes or no more emphatically.
- Make sure students grasp when to say **si** instead of **oui** by asking questions like these: **Tu n'étudies pas le français? (Si, j'étudie le français.) Je ne suis pas le professeur? (Si, vous êtes le professeur.)** Choose two students that are friends and ask: ____ **et** ____ **ne sont pas copains/copines? (Si, nous sommes copains/copines.)** Tell students to say, **Mais si!** if they want to contradict a negative question more forcefully.

2A.2 Forming questions and expressing negation

NATIONAL STANDARDS comparisons

Point de départ You have learned how to make affirmative and declarative statements in French. Now you will learn how to form questions and make negative statements.

Forming questions

- There are several ways to ask a question in French. The simplest way is to use the same wording as for a statement but with rising intonation (when speaking) or setting a question mark at the end (when writing). This method is considered informal.

Vous habitez à Bordeaux?	**Tu aimes le cours de français?**
You live in Bordeaux?	*You like French class?*

- A second way is to place the phrase **Est-ce que...** directly before a statement. If the next word begins with a vowel sound, use **Est-ce qu'**. Questions with **est-ce que** are somewhat formal.

Est-ce que vous parlez français?	**Est-ce qu'**il aime dessiner?
Do you speak French?	*Does he like to draw?*

- A third way is to place a tag question at the end of a statement. This method can be formal or informal.

On commence à deux heures, **d'accord**?	Nous mangeons à midi, **n'est-ce pas**?
We're starting at two o'clock, OK?	*We eat at noon, don't we?*

- A fourth way is to invert the order of the subject pronoun and the verb and hyphenate them. If the verb ends in a vowel and the subject pronoun is **il** or **elle**, **-t-** is inserted between the verb and the pronoun. Inversion is considered more formal.

Parlez-vous français?	**Mange-t-il** à midi?	**Est-elle** étudiante?
Do you speak French?	*Does he eat at noon?*	*Is she a student?*

- If the subject is a noun rather than a pronoun, invert the pronoun and the verb, and place the noun before them.

Le professeur parle-t-il français?	**Nina arrive-t-elle** demain?
Does the professor speak French?	*Does Nina arrive tomorrow?*

- The inverted form of **il y a** is **y a-t-il**. **C'est** becomes **est-ce**.

Y a-t-il une horloge dans la classe?	**Est-ce** le professeur de lettres?
Is there a clock in the class?	*Is he the humanities professor?*

- Use **pourquoi** to ask *why?* Use **parce que** (**parce qu'** before a vowel sound) in the answer to express *because.*

Pourquoi retrouves-tu Sophie ici?	**Parce qu'**elle habite près d'ici.
Why are you meeting Sophie here?	*Because she lives near here.*

MISE EN PRATIQUE

1 L'inversion Restate the questions using inversion.

1. Est-ce que vous parlez espagnol? Parlez-vous espagnol?
2. Est-ce qu'il étudie à Paris? Étudie-t-il à Paris?
3. Est-ce qu'ils voyagent avec des amis? Voyagent-ils avec des amis?
4. Est-ce que tu aimes les cours de langues? Aimes-tu les cours de langues?
5. Est-ce que le professeur parle anglais? Le professeur parle-t-il anglais?
6. Est-ce que les étudiants aiment dessiner? Les étudiants aiment-ils dessiner?

2 Les questions Ask the questions that correspond to the answers. Use **est-ce que/qu'** and inversion for each item.

MODÈLE

Nous habitons sur le campus.
Est-ce que vous habitez sur le campus? / Habitez-vous sur le campus?

1. Il mange au resto U. Est-ce qu'il mange au resto U? / Mange-t-il au resto U?
2. J'oublie les examens. Est-ce que tu oublies les examens? / Oublies-tu les examens?
3. François déteste les maths. Est-ce que François déteste les maths? / François déteste-t-il les maths?
4. Nous adorons voyager. Est-ce que vous adorez voyager? / Adorez-vous voyager?
5. Les cours ne commencent pas demain. Est-ce que les cours ne commencent pas demain? / Les cours ne commencent-ils pas demain?
6. Les étudiantes arrivent en classe. Est-ce que les étudiantes arrivent en classe? / Les étudiantes arrivent-elles en classe?

3 Complétez Complete the conversation with the correct questions for the answers given. Act it out with a partner. Suggested answers

MYLÈNE Salut, Arnaud. Ça va?
ARNAUD Oui, ça va. Alors (*So*)... (1) Tu aimes les cours?
MYLÈNE J'adore le cours de sciences po, mais je déteste l'informatique.
ARNAUD (2) Pourquoi est-ce que tu détestes l'informatique?
MYLÈNE Parce que le prof est très strict.
ARNAUD (3) Il y a des étudiants sympathiques, n'est-ce pas?
MYLÈNE Oui, il y a des étudiants sympathiques... Et demain? (4) Tu retrouves Béatrice?
ARNAUD Peut-être, mais demain je retrouve aussi Dominique.
MYLÈNE (5) Tu cherches une petite amie?
ARNAUD Pas du tout!

Practice more at **espaces.vhlcentral.com.**

OPTIONS

Pairs Write ten statements on the board or a transparency. Have students work in pairs. Tell them to convert the statements into questions by inverting the subject and verb. When they have finished writing the questions, call on volunteers to read their questions aloud. This activity can also be done orally with the class.

Extra Practice Using the same ten statements from the previous activity, ask students to form tag questions. Encourage them to use both **d'accord?** and **n'est-ce pas?** Have students answer some of the questions. Then add a few negative statements so that students will have to respond with **si**.

COMMUNICATION

4 Au café In pairs, take turns asking each other questions about the drawing. Use verbs from the list. Answers will vary.

MODÈLE

Étudiant(e) 1: *Monsieur Laurent parle à Madame Martin, n'est-ce pas?*
Étudiant(e) 2: *Mais non. Il déteste parler!*

arriver	dessiner	manger	partager
chercher	étudier	oublier	rencontrer

5 Questions You and your partner want to know each other better. Take turns asking each other questions. Modify or add elements as needed. Some answers will vary.

MODÈLE aimer / l'art

Étudiant(e) 1: *Est-ce que tu aimes l'art?*
Étudiant(e) 2: *Oui, j'adore l'art.*

1. habiter / à l'université
   Est-ce que tu habites à l'université?
2. étudier / avec / amis
   Est-ce que tu étudies avec des amis?
3. penser qu'il y a / cours / intéressant / à la fac
   Est-ce que tu penses qu'il y a des cours intéressants à la fac?
4. cours de sciences / être / facile
   Est-ce que les cours de sciences sont faciles?
5. aimer mieux / biologie / ou / physique
   Est-ce que tu aimes mieux la biologie ou la physique?
6. retrouver / copains / au resto U
   Est-ce que tu retrouves des copains au resto U?

6 Confirmez In groups of three, confirm whether the statements are true of your school. Correct any untrue statements by making them negative. Answers will vary.

MODÈLE

Les profs sont désagréables.
Pas du tout. Les profs ne sont pas désagréables.

1. Les cours d'informatique sont inutiles.
2. Il y a des étudiants de nationalité allemande.
3. Nous mangeons une cuisine excellente au resto U.
4. Tous (*All*) les étudiants habitent sur le campus.
5. Les cours de chimie sont faciles.
6. Nous travaillons pour obtenir un diplôme.

Expressing negation

- To make a sentence negative in French, place **ne** (**n'** before a vowel sound) before the conjugated verb and **pas** after it.

Je **ne dessine pas** bien. *I don't draw well.*	**Ne parlez pas** en cours. *Don't talk in class.*

- In the construction [*conjugated verb + infinitive*], **ne** (**n'**) comes before the conjugated verb and **pas** after it.

Abdel **n'aime pas étudier**. *Abdel doesn't like to study.*	Vous **ne détestez pas travailler**? *You don't hate to work?*

- In questions with inversion, place **ne** before the inversion and **pas** after it.

Abdel **n'aime-t-il pas** étudier? *Doesn't Abdel like to study?*	**Ne détestez-vous pas** travailler? *Don't you hate to work?*

- Use these expressions to respond to a statement or a question that requires a *yes* or *no* answer.

Expressions of agreement and disagreement

oui	*yes*	(mais) non	*no (but of course not)*
bien sûr	*of course*	pas du tout	*not at all*
moi/toi non plus	*me/you neither*	peut-être	*maybe, perhaps*

Vous mangez souvent au resto U? *Do you eat often in the cafeteria?*	**Non, pas du tout.** *No, not at all.*

- Use **si** instead of **oui** to contradict a negative question.

Il **ne cherche pas** le sac à dos? *Isn't he looking for the backpack?*	**Si**. Il cherche aussi les crayons. *Yes. He's looking for the pencils too.*

Essayez! Make questions out of these statements. Use **est-ce que/qu'** in items 1–6 and inversion in 7–12.

Statement	Question
1. Vous mangez au resto U.	*Est-ce que vous mangez au resto U?*
2. Ils adorent les devoirs.	Est-ce qu'ils adorent les devoirs?
3. La biologie est difficile.	Est-ce que la biologie est difficile?
4. Tu travailles.	Est-ce que tu travailles?
5. Elles cherchent le prof.	Est-ce qu'elles cherchent le prof?
6. Aude voyage beaucoup.	Est-ce qu'Aude voyage beaucoup?
7. Vous arrivez demain.	*Arrivez-vous demain?*
8. L'étudiante oublie le livre.	L'étudiante oublie-t-elle le livre?
9. La physique est utile.	La physique est-elle utile?
10. Il y a deux salles de classe.	Y a-t-il deux salles de classe?
11. Ils n'habitent pas à Québec.	N'habitent-ils pas à Québec?
12. C'est le professeur de gestion.	Est-ce le professeur de gestion?

Essayez! Have students repeat using inversion for items 1–6 and **est-ce que/qu'** in 7–12.

1 Expansion Have students work in pairs, and take turns asking and answering the questions in the negative.

2 Expansion Have students write two additional statements. Tell them to exchange papers with a partner who will ask the questions that would elicit those statements.

3 Expansion Have pairs of students create a similar conversation, replacing the answers and some of the questions with information that is true for them. Then have volunteers act out their conversations for the class.

4 Suggestion Tell students to vary the method of asking questions instead of always using a tag question as in the **modèle**.

5 Suggestions
- Have two volunteers read the **modèle** aloud.
- After students have completed the activity, ask volunteers to report what they learned about their partner.

6 Suggestion Encourage students to use as many expressions indicating agreement or disagreement as they can.

6 Expansion Have groups write three additional true/false statements about their school. Ask several groups to read their statements and have the class respond to them. Encourage students to respond with **Mais oui!** or **Mais non!** where appropriate.

OPTIONS

Video Replay the video episode, having students focus on the different forms of questions used. Tell them to write down each question they hear. Stop the video where suitable to give students time to write and to discuss what was heard.

Extra Practice Prepare eight questions. Write their answers on the board in random order. Then read your questions aloud, having students match the question to the appropriate answer. Make sure that only one of the possible answers corresponds logically to the questions you ask. Example: **Pourquoi ____ déteste-t-il les maths? (Il n'aime pas le prof.)**

Instructional Resources
espaces.vhlcentral.com: IRM (Info Gap Activities); Testing Program, pp. 9–12; Test Files; Testing Program MP3s; activities; downloads; reference tools
Test Generator

1 Expansion Have students compare two of their own classes that are very different, such as a large lecture and a small class, and explain which one they prefer. This activity can be done orally or in writing.

2 Suggestion Have two volunteers read the **modèle** aloud. Tell students to add at least two more items to the list, one that applies to both of them and one that does not.

3 Suggestion As students share their responses with the class, make a list of their likes and dislikes on the board under the headings **Nous aimons** and **Nous n'aimons pas.**

4 Suggestion Tell students they may use adjectives that are not in the list.

5 Suggestion Before beginning the activity, have the class decide on names for the people in the drawings. Also have them brainstorm possible relationships between the people, for example, strangers meeting for the first time or classmates.

6 Suggestion Divide the class into pairs and distribute the Info Gap Handouts on the Supersite for this activity. Give students ten minutes to complete the activity.

6 Expansion Have pairs compare their answers with another pair to confirm the people's likes and dislikes. Then ask a few groups to share some of their sentences with the class.

Révision

1 Des styles différents In pairs, compare these two very different classes. Then, tell your partner which class you prefer and why. Answers will vary.

2 Les activités In pairs, discuss whether these expressions apply to both of you. React to every answer you hear. Answers will vary.

MODÈLE

Étudiant(e) 1: *Est-ce que tu étudies le week-end?*
Étudiant(e) 2: *Non! Je n'aime pas étudier le week-end.*
Étudiant(e) 1: *Moi non plus. J'aime mieux étudier le soir.*

1. adorer le resto U
2. retrouver des amis au café
3. étudier à la bibliothèque
4. manger souvent (*often*) des sushis
5. oublier les devoirs
6. parler espagnol
7. travailler le soir
8. voyager souvent

3 Le campus In pairs, prepare ten questions inspired by the list and what you know about your campus. Together, survey as many classmates as possible to find out what they like and dislike on campus. Answers will vary.

MODÈLE

Étudiant(e) 1: *Est-ce que tu aimes étudier à la bibliothèque?*
Étudiant(e) 2: *Non, pas trop. J'étudie plutôt au café.*

bibliothèque	étudiant	resto U
bureau	gymnase	salle de classe
cours	librairie	salle d'ordinateurs

4 Pourquoi? Survey as many classmates as possible to find out if they like these subjects and why. Ask what adjective they would pick to describe them. Tally the most popular answers for each subject. Answers will vary.

MODÈLE

Étudiant(e) 1: *Est-ce que tu aimes la philosophie?*
Étudiant(e) 2: *Pas tellement.*
Étudiant(e) 1: *Pourquoi?*
Étudiant(e) 2: *Parce que c'est trop difficile.*

1. la biologie	a. agréable
2. la chimie	b. amusant
3. l'histoire de l'art	c. désagréable
4. l'économie	d. difficile
5. la gestion	e. facile
6. les langues	f. important
7. les mathématiques	g. inutile
8. la psychologie	h. utile

5 Les conversations In pairs, act out a short conversation between the people shown in each drawing. They should greet each other, describe what they are doing, and discuss their likes or dislikes. Choose your favorite skit and role-play it for another pair. Answers will vary.

MODÈLE

Étudiant(e) 1: *Bonjour, Aurélie.*
Étudiant(e) 2: *Salut! Tu travailles, n'est-ce pas?*

6 Les portraits Your instructor will give you and a partner a set of drawings showing the likes and dislikes of eight people. Discuss each person's tastes. Do not look at each other's worksheet. Answers will vary.

MODÈLE

Étudiant(e) 1: *Sarah n'aime pas travailler.*
Étudiant(e) 2: *Mais elle adore manger.*

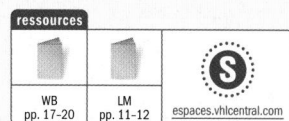

ressources
WB pp. 17–20 | LM pp. 11–12 | espaces.vhlcentral.com

OPTIONS

Extra Practice Have students write a brief paragraph describing the activities they like or don't like to do. Collect the descriptions and read a few of them to the class. Have the class guess who wrote each description by asking: **Est-ce que c'est...?**

Small Groups Tell students to turn to the **Roman-photo** on pages 42–43 and write five comprehension questions based on the dialogue. Then have them get together in groups of three or four, and take turns asking and answering each other's questions.

Video: TV Clip

Le Zapping

communication cultures NATIONAL STANDARDS

connections communities NATIONAL STANDARDS

Clairefontaine: l'écrit du cœur

In 1858, Jean-Baptiste Bichelberger founded a paper factory in eastern France. Soon the company became Clairefontaine and started making envelopes and notebooks. In 1950, Charles Nusse took over the company, offering schoolchildren notebooks made of high-quality paper. He was the creator of the Clairefontaine logo, which became famous. Today, the company has branches all over Europe and even in the United States. It manufactures school supplies, accounting ledgers, and stationery.

—C'est pas vrai°...!

—Je suis votre° nouveau prof d'histoire.

Compréhension Answer these questions. Answers will vary.

1. What school-related vocabulary did you understand?
2. Why did one of the girls throw the notebook on the ground?

Discussion In pairs, discuss the answers to these questions. Answers will vary.

1. If the commercial were to continue, what would the characters say next?
2. Do you know of any TV commercials advertising stationery?

vrai *true* **votre** *your*

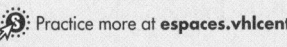

Practice more at **espaces.vhlcentral.com.**

cinquante et un 51

Section Goals

In this section, students will:
- read about the company Clairefontaine
- watch a commercial for Clairefontaine notebooks
- answer questions about the commercial and Clairefontaine

Instructional Resources
*espaces.vhlcentral.com: TV commercial; IRM (**Le zapping** TV clip transcription); activities; downloads; reference tools*

Introduction
To check students' comprehension, ask these questions.
1. What was the origin of the Clairefontaine company? (It was a paper factory founded in 1858 in eastern France.)
2. What product did Clairefontaine start making after Charles Nusse took over? (It started to make notebooks with high-quality paper.)
3. Is Clairefontaine a successful brand? (Yes. It has a famous logo, and the company has branches in Europe and the United States.)

Avant de regarder la vidéo
- Have students look at the video stills, read the captions, and predict what is happening in the commercial for each visual. (1. Two teenage girls are chatting at school. 2. They meet their new teacher.)
- Before showing the video, explain to students that they do not need to understand every word they hear. Tell them to listen for cognates, school-related vocabulary, and the slogan.

Compréhension Have students work in pairs or groups for this activity. Tell them to write their answers. Then show the video again so that they can check their work and add any missing information.

Discussion After discussing the questions, ask volunteers to report their comments and ideas to the class.

OPTIONS

Le papier Clairefontaine People love Clairefontaine notebooks for the quality of their paper. The company uses ultra-smooth, brushed vellum paper that it manufactures itself. This paper weighs 90 grams per square meter. It is also very white and anti-glare. Clairefontaine is currently the only manufacturer making its own paper for its stationery products. This helps the company maintain consistent paper quality and also controls the environmental impact of the paper manufacturing process. The company uses pulp exclusively from trees grown in certified sustainable forests.

Section Goals

In this section, students will learn and practice vocabulary related to:
- talking about schedules
- the days of the week
- sequencing events

Instructional Resources
*espaces.vhlcentral.com: Transparency #18; IRM (**Vocabulaire supplémentaire; Mise en pratique** answers; Textbook Audioscript; Lab Audioscript; **Feuilles d'activités**); Textbook MP3s; Lab MP3s; WB/VM/LM Answer Key; activities; downloads; reference tools*

Suggestions

- Write days of the week across the board and present them like this: **Aujourd'hui, c'est ____. Demain, c'est ____. Après-demain, c'est ____?**
- Write the following questions and answers on the board, explaining their meaning:
  —Quel jour sommes-nous?
  —Nous sommes ____.
  —C'est quel jour demain?
  —Demain, c'est ____.
  —C'est quand l'examen?
  —L'examen est ____.

Ask students the questions.
- Tell students Monday is the first day of the week in France.
- Point out that days of the week are masculine and lowercase.
- Explain the differences between **le matin/la matinée, le soir/la soirée,** and **le jour/ la journée.**
- Introduce new vocabulary using **Transparency #18.** Give the student a name, for example, Henri. Ask students picture-based questions. Examples: **Quel jour Henri assiste-t-il au cours d'économie? Il assiste au cours d'économie le matin ou le soir? Quels jours visite-t-il Paris avec Annette?**
- Point out that **visiter** is used with places, not people.
- Additional vocabulary for this lesson can be found in the **Vocabulaire supplémentaire** on the Supersite.

Leçon 2B

You will learn how to...
- say when things happen
- discuss your schedule

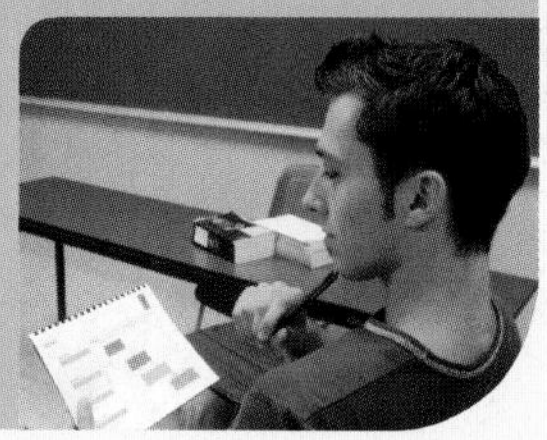

Talking Picture
Audio: Activity

Une semaine à la fac

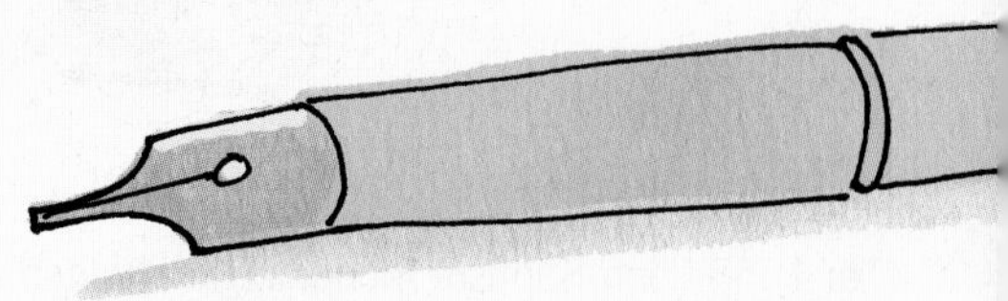

Vocabulaire

demander	*to ask*
échouer	*to fail*
écouter	*to listen (to)*
enseigner	*to teach*
expliquer	*to explain*
trouver	*to find; to think*
Quel jour sommes-nous?	*What day is it?*
un an	*year*
une/cette année	*one/this year*
après	*after*
après-demain	*day after tomorrow*
un/cet après-midi	*an/this afternoon*
aujourd'hui	*today*
demain (matin/après-midi/soir)	*tomorrow (morning/afternoon/evening)*
un jour	*day*
une journée	*day*
un/ce matin	*a/this morning*
la matinée	*morning*
un mois/ce mois-ci	*month/this month*
une/cette nuit	*a/this night*
une/cette semaine	*a/this week*
un/ce soir	*an/this evening*
une soirée	*evening*
un/le/ce week-end	*a/the/this weekend*
dernier/dernière	*last*
premier/première	*first*
prochain(e)	*next*

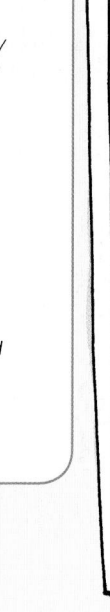

ressources
WB pp. 21-22
LM p. 13
espaces.vhlcentral.com

OPTIONS

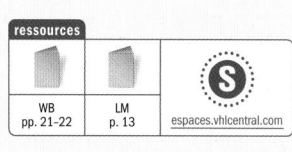

Extra Practice Write **le matin, l'après-midi,** and **le soir** on the board or a transparency. Have your students tell when they do various activities, such as **préparer les cours, assister aux cours, téléphoner à des amis, écouter de la musique, regarder la télévision, rentrer à la maison,** and **dîner.**

Pairs Have the class brainstorm a list of nouns associated with verbs from **Espace contextes.** For example, for the verb **regarder,** students might think of **télévision** or **vidéo.** Write the verbs and nouns on the board as students say them. Then have students work in pairs. Give them five minutes to write original sentences using these words. Ask volunteers to write their sentences on the board.

Attention!

Use the masculine definite article **le** + [*day of the week*] when an activity is done on a weekly basis. Omit **le** when it is done on a specific day.

Le prof enseigne le lundi.
The professor teaches on Mondays.

Je passe un examen lundi.
I'm taking a test on Monday.

Mise en pratique

1 Écoutez You will hear Lorraine describing her schedule. Listen carefully and indicate whether the statements are **vrai** or **faux.**

	Vrai	Faux
1. Lorraine étudie à l'université le soir.	☐	☑
2. Elle trouve le cours de mathématiques facile.	☐	☑
3. Elle étudie le week-end.	☐	☑
4. Lorraine étudie la chimie le mardi et le jeudi matin.	☐	☑
5. Le professeur de mathématiques explique bien.	☐	☑
6. Lorraine regarde la télévision, écoute de la musique ou téléphone à Claire et Anne le soir.	☑	☐
7. Lorraine travaille dans (*in*) une librairie.	☐	☑
8. Elle étudie l'histoire le mardi et le jeudi matin.	☑	☐
9. Lorraine adore dîner avec sa famille le week-end.	☑	☐
10. Lorraine rentre à la maison le soir.	☐	☑

2 La classe de Mme Arnaud Complete this paragraph by selecting the correct verb from the list below. Make sure to conjugate the verb. Some verbs will not be used.

demander	expliquer	rentrer
écouter	passer un examen	travailler
enseigner	préparer	trouver
étudier	regarder	visiter

Madame Arnaud (1) ___travaille___ à l'université. Elle (2) ___enseigne___ le français. Elle (3) ___explique___ les verbes et la grammaire aux étudiants. Le vendredi, en classe, les étudiants (4) ___regardent___ une vidéo en français ou (*or*) (5) ___écoutent___ de la musique française. Ce week-end, ils (6) ___étudient/travaillent___ pour (*for*) (7) ___préparer___ l'examen très difficile de lundi matin. Je/J' (8) ___travaille/étudie___ beaucoup pour ce cours, mais mes (*my*) amis et moi, nous (9) ___trouvons___ la classe sympa.

3 Quel jour sommes-nous? Complete each statement with the correct day of the week.

1. Aujourd'hui, c'est ___Answers will vary.___.
2. Demain, c'est ___Answers will vary.___.
3. Après-demain, c'est ___Answers will vary.___.
4. Le week-end, c'est ___le samedi et le dimanche___.
5. Le premier jour de la semaine en France, c'est ___le lundi___.
6. Les jours du cours de français sont ___Answers will vary.___.
7. Mon (*My*) jour préféré de la semaine, c'est ___Answers will vary.___.
8. Je travaille à la bibliothèque ___Answers will vary.___.

Practice more at **espaces.vhlcentral.com.**

1 Tapescript Cette année à l'université j'étudie: la chimie, le lundi et le mercredi matin; l'histoire, le mardi et le jeudi matin; l'art, le vendredi matin et les mathématiques, le lundi et le mercredi après-midi. Je déteste les mathématiques; le professeur n'explique pas bien et je trouve le cours difficile. J'étudie l'après-midi quand je rentre à la maison. Le soir, je ne travaille pas, alors je regarde la télévision, j'écoute de la musique ou je téléphone à mes amies, Claire et Anne. Le week-end, j'adore rendre visite à ma famille pour dîner! *(On Textbook MP3s)*

1 Suggestions

- Before playing the recording, have students read the statements and identify the expressions that describe when things occur. Examples: **le soir, le week-end**, and **le jeudi matin.**
- Go over the answers with the class. If students have difficulty, replay the recording.

2 Expansion Have pairs write original sentences about Madame Arnaud and her class using the verbs that weren't in this paragraph. Ask volunteers to read their sentences aloud.

3 Expansions

- Give these items for more practice. **9. Le jour après lundi, c'est ____. 10. Il n'y a pas de cours de français le ____.**
- Have students repeat items 1–5 from the perspective of a different day of the week.

OPTIONS

TPR Create a schedule for an imaginary student using the whole class. Assign each day of the week to a different student and assign each of the remaining students a different activity. As you describe the schedule, students arrange themselves as a page in a weekly day-planner, starting with the day of the week and then each activity you mention. Example: **Le lundi matin, j'assiste au cours. L'après-midi, je passe un examen de français. Le soir, je dîne au resto U.**

Extra Practice Have students write a paragraph similar to the one in **Activité 2** describing your French class or a different class. They should use as many verbs from the list as possible. Ask volunteers to read their paragraph aloud.

4 Suggestion Before doing this activity, you may want to write a short list of musical genres on the board for item 5. Also tell students that **quand** means *when*.

4 Expansions
- Have volunteers report what they learned about their classmate.
- To practice the **nous** forms, ask students what they have in common with their partner.

5 Suggestion Tell students to switch roles after completing the conversation so that both students have the opportunity to ask and answer questions.

6 Suggestions
- Have two volunteers read the **modèle** aloud. Make sure students understand the directions. Then distribute the **Feuilles d'activités** from the Supersite.
- Have students repeat the activity with a different partner.

7 Suggestion To save time in class, assign the written part of this activity the day before as homework.

Communication

NATIONAL communication STANDARDS

4 Conversez Interview a classmate. Answers will vary.

1. Quel jour sommes-nous?
2. Quand (*When*) est le prochain cours de français?
3. Quand rentres-tu à la maison? Demain soir? Après-demain?
4. Est-ce que tu prépares un examen cette année?
5. Est-ce que tu écoutes la radio? Quel genre de musique aimes-tu?
6. Quand téléphones-tu à des amis?
7. Est-ce que tu regardes la télévision le matin, l'après-midi ou (or) le soir?
8. Est-ce que tu dînes dans un restaurant ce mois-ci?

5 Le premier jour à la fac You make a new friend in your French class and want to know what his or her class schedule is like this semester. With a partner, prepare a conversation to perform for the class where you: Answers will vary.

- ask his or her name
- ask what classes he or she is taking
- ask on which days of the week he or she has class
- ask at which times of day (morning or afternoon) he or she has class

6 Bataille navale Your instructor will give you a worksheet. Choose four spaces on your chart and mark them with a battleship. In pairs, formulate questions by using the subjects in the first column and the verbs in the first row to find out where your partner has placed his or her battleships. Whoever "sinks" the most battleships wins. Answers will vary.

MODÈLE

Étudiant(e) 1: *Est-ce que Luc et Sabine travaillent le week-end?*
Étudiant(e) 2: *Oui, ils travaillent le week-end.*
(if you marked that square)
Non, ils ne travaillent pas le week-end.
(if you didn't mark that square)

	enseigner	travailler
Marie		
Luc et Sabine		

7 Le week-end Write a schedule to show what you do during a typical weekend. Use the verbs you know. Compare your schedule with a classmate's, and talk about the different activities that you do and when. Be prepared to discuss your results with the class. Answers will vary.

	Moi	Nom
Le vendredi soir		
Le samedi matin		
Le samedi après-midi		
Le samedi soir		
Le dimanche matin		
Le dimanche après-midi		
Le dimanche soir		

OPTIONS

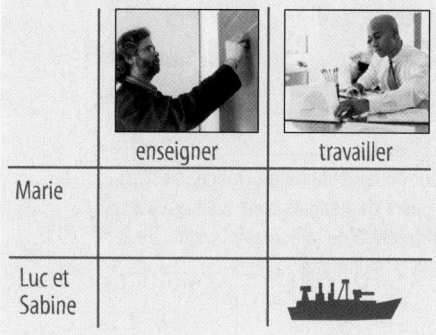

Game Play a memory game in which the first player says one activity he or she does on a particular day of the week. The next player repeats what the first person said, then adds what he or she does on the following day. The third player must remember what the first two people said before saying what he or she does on the next day. Continue until the end of a week. If someone makes a mistake, then choose another student to continue.

Small Groups Have students work in groups of three. Tell them to take turns asking what days of the week TV shows are on and answering. Example: **Quel(s) jour(s) est la série *CSI*?**

Les sons et les lettres

Audio: Concepts, Activities
Record & Compare

NATIONAL comparisons STANDARDS

The letter r

The French **r** is very different from the English *r*. The English *r* is pronounced by placing the tongue in the middle and toward the front of the mouth. The French **r** is pronounced in the throat. You have seen that an **-er** at the end of a word is usually pronounced **-ay**, as in the English word *way*, but without the glide sound.

chanter **manger** **expliquer** **aimer**

In most other cases, the French **r** has a very different sound. Pronunciation of the French **r** varies according to its position in a word. Note the different ways the **r** is pronounced in these words.

rivière **littérature** **ordinateur** **devoir**

If an **r** falls between two vowels or before a vowel, it is pronounced with slightly more friction.

rare **garage** **Europe** **rose**

An **r** sound before a consonant or at the end of a word is pronounced with slightly less friction.

porte **bourse** **adore** **jour**

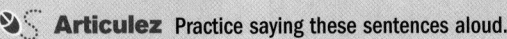

Prononcez Practice saying these words aloud.

1. crayon
2. professeur
3. plaisir
4. différent
5. terrible
6. architecture
7. trouver
8. restaurant
9. rentrer
10. regarder
11. lettres
12. réservé
13. être
14. dernière
15. arriver
16. après

Quand le renard prêche, gare aux oies.²

Articulez Practice saying these sentences aloud.

1. Au revoir, Professeur Colbert!
2. Rose arrive en retard mardi.
3. Mercredi, c'est le dernier jour des cours.
4. Robert et Roger adorent écouter la radio.
5. La corbeille à papier, c'est quarante-quatre euros!
6. Les parents de Richard sont brillants et très agréables.

Dictons Practice reading these sayings aloud.

Qui ne risque rien n'a rien.¹

¹ Nothing ventured, nothing gained.
² When the fox preaches, watch your geese.

ressources
LM p. 14
espaces.vhlcentral.com

Section Goals

In this section, students will learn about the letter **r**.

Instructional Resources
espaces.vhlcentral.com: Textbook MP3s; Lab MP3s; WB/VM/LM Answer Key; IRM (Textbook Audioscript; Lab Audioscript); activities; downloads; reference tools

Suggestions

- Model the pronunciation of words and expressions with **r** from **Espace contextes**. Then have students repeat. Examples: **regarder, préparer un examen**, etc.
- Explain that the French **r** has more in common with a **k** sound than it does with the English *r*. The **k** sound is velar, produced when the back of the tongue touches the soft palate. The French **r** is uvular, produced a bit farther back in the mouth with the back of the tongue and the uvula.
- Model the pronunciation of each example word and have students repeat.
- Ask students to provide words or expressions from previous lessons that contain the letter **r**. Examples: **au revoir, très bien, professeur**, and **merci**.
- The explanation and exercises are available on the **ESPACES** Supersite. You may want to play them in class so students hear French speakers other than yourself.

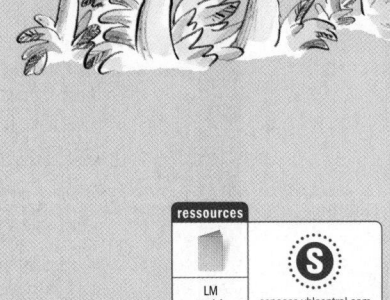

Dictons Ask students if they can think of an English saying that is similar to **«Quand le renard prêche, gare aux oies.»** (*Don't let a fox guard the hen house.*)

OPTIONS

Extra Practice Dictate five familiar words with the **r** in different places, saying each one at least two times. Examples: **librairie, résultat, jour, chercher**, and **montre**. Then write them on the board or a transparency and have students check their spelling.

Extra Practice Use these sentences with the letter **r** for additional oral practice or dictation. **1. Renée regarde un garçon américain. 2. Le colocataire de Grégoire est réservé. 3. Je travaille le mercredi après-midi et le vendredi soir. 4. Nous trouvons le cours d'histoire très intéressant.**

Section Goals

In this section, students will learn functional phrases for talking about their schedules and classes and telling time.

Instructional Resources
*espaces.vhlcentral.com: WB/VM/LM Answer Key; IRM (Videoscript; **Roman-photo** Translations); activities; downloads; reference tools*
Video on DVD

Video Recap: Leçon 2A
Before doing this **Roman-photo**, review the previous one with this activity.
1. Comment est-ce que Rachid trouve le cours de sciences po? (intéressant et utile)
2. Comment s'appelle le colocataire de Rachid? (David)
3. Comment est-ce que David trouve l'université française? (C'est différent de l'université américaine, mais c'est intéressant.)
4. Quels cours est-ce que David aime? (littérature et histoire françaises)
5. Stéphane a des problèmes dans quels cours? (français, maths, chimie et histoire-géo)

Video Synopsis At **Le P'tit Bistrot**, Rachid, Sandrine, Amina and David discuss their schedules. Astrid arrives; she is supposed to study with Stéphane. While she waits, Astrid talks about **le bac** and how Stéphane never does his homework. Rachid and Astrid decide to go to the park because they think Stéphane is there. At the park, Astrid and Stéphane argue. When Stéphane complains about his problems at school, Rachid offers to help him study.

Suggestions
- Have volunteers play the roles of Rachid, Sandrine, Amina, David, and Astrid in the scenes that match video stills 1–5.
- Have the class predict what will happen in scenes 6–10. Write predictions on the board.
- Read remaining scenes correcting the predictions. Ask questions to help students summarize this episode.

NATIONAL STANDARDS communication cultures

On trouve une solution.

S Video: *Roman-photo* Record & Compare

PERSONNAGES

Amina

Astrid

David

Rachid

Sandrine

Stéphane

À la terrasse du café...
RACHID Alors, on a rendez-vous avec David demain à cinq heures moins le quart pour rentrer chez nous.
SANDRINE Aujourd'hui, c'est mercredi. Demain... jeudi. Le mardi et le jeudi, j'ai cours de chant de trois heures vingt à quatre heures et demie. C'est parfait!
AMINA Pas de problème. J'ai cours de stylisme...

AMINA Salut, Astrid!
ASTRID Bonjour.
RACHID Astrid, je te présente David, mon (*my*) coloc américain.
DAVID Alors, cette année, tu as des cours très difficiles, n'est-ce pas?

ASTRID Oui? Pourquoi?
DAVID Ben, Stéphane pense que les cours sont très difficiles.
ASTRID Ouais, Stéphane, il assiste au cours, mais... il ne fait pas ses (*his*) devoirs et il n'écoute pas les profs. Cette année est très importante, parce que nous avons le bac...
DAVID Ah, le bac...

Au parc...
ASTRID Stéphane! Quelle heure est-il? Tu n'as pas de montre?
STÉPHANE Oh, Astrid, excuse-moi! Le mercredi, je travaille avec Astrid au café sur le cours de maths...
ASTRID Et le mercredi après-midi, il oublie! Tu n'as pas peur du bac, toi!

STÉPHANE Tu as tort, j'ai très peur du bac! Mais je n'ai pas envie de passer mes (*my*) journées, mes soirées et mes week-ends avec des livres!
ASTRID Je suis d'accord avec toi, Stéphane! J'ai envie de passer les week-ends avec mes copains... des copains qui n'oublient pas les rendez-vous!

RACHID Écoute, Stéphane, tu as des problèmes avec ta (*your*) mère, avec Astrid aussi.
STÉPHANE Oui, et j'ai d'énormes problèmes au lycée. Je déteste le bac.
RACHID Il n'est pas tard pour commencer à travailler pour être reçu au bac.
STÉPHANE Tu crois, Rachid?

ACTIVITÉS

1 Vrai ou faux? **Choose whether each statement is vrai or faux. Correct the false statements.**
Answers may vary slightly.

1. Le mardi et le mercredi, Sandrine a (*has*) cours de chant. Faux. Sandrine a cours de chant le mardi et le jeudi.
2. Le jeudi, Amina a cours de stylisme. Vrai.
3. Astrid pense qu'il est impossible de réussir (*pass*) le bac. Faux. Astrid pense que ce n'est pas impossible.
4. La famille de David est allemande. Faux. La famille de David est française.
5. Le mercredi, Stéphane travaille avec Astrid au café sur le cours de maths. Vrai.
6. Stéphane a beaucoup de problèmes. Vrai.
7. Rachid est optimiste. Vrai.
8. Stéphane dîne chez Rachid samedi. Faux. Stéphane dîne chez Rachid dimanche.
9. Le sport est très important pour Stéphane. Vrai.
10. Astrid est fâchée (*angry*) contre Stéphane. Vrai.

Practice more at **espaces.vhlcentral.com.**

OPTIONS

Avant de regarder la vidéo Write the title **On trouve une solution** on the board. Ask the class: Who has a problem in the video? What is it? Then ask the class to predict how the problem will be solved.

Regarder la vidéo Show the video episode and have students give you a play-by-play description of the action. Write their descriptions on the board. Then show the episode again so students can add more details to the description.

Les amis organisent des rendez-vous.

4

5

RACHID C'est un examen très important que les élèves français passent la dernière année de lycée pour continuer en études supérieures.
DAVID Euh, n'oublie pas, je suis de famille française.
ASTRID Oui, et c'est difficile, mais ce n'est pas impossible. Stéphane trouve que les études ne sont pas intéressantes. Le sport, oui, mais pas les études.

RACHID Le sport? Tu cherches Stéphane, n'est-ce pas? On trouve Stéphane au parc! Allons-y, Astrid.
ASTRID D'accord. À demain!

9

10

RACHID Oui. Mais le sport, c'est la dernière des priorités. Écoute, dimanche prochain, tu dînes chez moi et on trouve une solution.
STÉPHANE Rachid, tu n'as pas envie de donner des cours à un lycéen nul comme moi!
RACHID Mais si, j'ai très envie d'enseigner les maths...

STÉPHANE Bon, j'accepte. Merci, Rachid. C'est sympa.
RACHID De rien. À plus tard!

Expressions utiles

Talking about your schedule

- **Alors, on a rendez-vous demain à cinq heures moins le quart pour rentrer chez nous.**
  So, we're meeting tomorrow at quarter to five to go home (our home).
- **J'ai cours de chant de trois heures vingt à quatre heures et demie.**
  I have voice (singing) class from three-twenty to four-thirty.
- **J'ai cours de stylisme de deux heures à quatre heures vingt.**
  I have fashion design class from two o'clock to four-twenty.
- **Quelle heure est-il?**
  What time is it?
- **Tu n'as pas de montre?**
  You don't have a watch?

Talking about school

- **Nous avons le bac.**
  We have the **bac**.
- **Il ne fait pas ses devoirs.**
  He doesn't do his homework.
- **Tu n'as pas peur du bac!**
  You're not afraid of the **bac**!
- **Tu as tort, j'ai très peur du bac!**
  You're wrong, I'm very afraid of the **bac**!
- **Je suis d'accord avec toi.**
  I agree with you.
- **J'ai d'énormes problèmes.**
  I have big/enormous problems.
- **Tu n'as pas envie de donner des cours à un(e) lycéen(ne) nul(le) comme moi.**
  You don't want to teach a high school student as bad as myself.

Useful expressions

- **C'est parfait!**
  That's perfect!
- **Allons-y!**
  Let's go!
- **D'accord.**
  OK./All right.
- **Ouais.**
  Yeah.
- **C'est sympa.**
  That's nice/fun.

ACTIVITÉS

2 Répondez Answer these questions. Refer to the video scenes and use a dictionary as necessary. You do not have to answer in complete sentences. Answers will vary.

1. Où est-ce que tu as envie de voyager?
2. Est-ce que tu as peur de quelque chose? De quoi?
3. Qu'est-ce que tu dis (*say*) quand tu as tort?

3 À vous! With a partner, describe someone you know whose personality, likes, or dislikes resemble those of Rachid or Stéphane.

MODÈLE

Paul est comme (like) Rachid... il est sérieux.

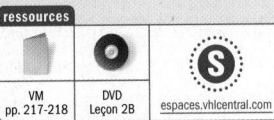

ressources
VM pp. 217-218 | DVD Leçon 2B | espaces.vhlcentral.com

Expressions utiles

- Model the pronunciation of the **Expressions utiles** and have students repeat after you.
- As you work through the list, point out forms of **avoir**, idiomatic expressions with **avoir**, and expressions for telling time. Tell students that these concepts will be formally presented in **Espace structures**.
- Respond briefly to questions about **avoir** and reinforce correct forms, but do not expect students to produce them consistently at this time.
- Ask students a few questions based on the **Expressions utiles**. Examples: **Tu as cours de chant aujourd'hui? Tu as cours de stylisme?**
- Have students scan the video-still captions for phrases or sentences that show a sequence of time or events. Examples: **Aujourd'hui, c'est mercredi. Demain jeudi, ...**

1 Suggestion Have students correct the false statements.

2 Expansion For additional practice, ask these questions. **4. Où est-ce que tu as envie de dîner? 5. À qui est-ce que tu as envie de téléphoner? 6. Est-ce que tu as peur de regarder les films d'horreur?**

3 Suggestion Before beginning the activity, tell pairs to brainstorm and write a list of adjectives or phrases that describe Rachid and Stéphane.

OPTIONS

Small Groups Working in groups of three, have students create a short skit similar to the scenes in video stills 6–10 in which one of the students forgets to show up for a study session or a meeting. Give students ten minutes to prepare, then call on groups to perform their skits for the class.

Pairs Have students work in pairs. Tell them to create two-line conversations using as many of the **Expressions utiles** as they can. Example:
—Alors, on a rendez-vous à cinq heures?
—Ouais! C'est parfait!

connections cultures — NATIONAL STANDARDS

Section Goals

In this section, students will:
- learn about university courses in France
- learn familiar terms for talking about classes and exams
- learn the names of some universities with French programs for foreigners
- read about **le bac**

Instructional Resources
espaces.vhlcentral.com: activities; downloads; reference tools

Culture à la loupe

Avant la lecture Ask students: What would you want to know about classes at a French university of your choice if you were going there to study for a year?

Lecture
- Tell students that the word **amphi** is often used instead of **amphithéâtre**. Similarly, the word **fac** (for **faculté**) is used more often than **université**. The start of the school year is also known as the **rentrée scolaire.**
- Point out the **Coup de main**. Explain that commas are used instead of periods in percentages.
- Explain that French students rarely get praise from teachers. While American teachers are trained to encourage students for effort, the French typically reserve approbation for only truly excellent work.

Après la lecture Ask students if they prefer the French or American university system and have them explain why.

1 Expansion For extra practice, give students these items. 11. Lecture courses are rare in France. (**Faux.** They are common.) 12. The French discourage open debate. (**Faux.**) 13. The French university system relies heavily on exams for assessment. (**Vrai.**) 14. After studying abroad in France, a student needs to make sure that the overseas university provides information about grade conversion to the home institution. (**Vrai.**)

CULTURE À LA LOUPE

Les cours universitaires

French university courses often consist of lectures in large halls called amphithéâtres. Some also include discussion-based sessions with fewer students. Other than in the **grandes écoles** and specialized schools, class attendance is not mandatory in most universities. Students are motivated to attend by their desire to pass. Course grades are often based upon only one or two exams or term papers, so students generally take their studies seriously. They often form study groups to discuss the lectures and share class notes. This practice encourages open exchange of ideas and debate, a tradition that continues well past university life in France.

The start of classes each year is known as the **rentrée universitaire** and takes place at the beginning of October. The academic year is divided into two semesters. Four to six classes each semester is typical.

Students in some classes take exams throughout the semester, a practice known as **contrôle continu**°. At final exams in May or June, they can retake other exams they might have failed during that year or the preceding year. French grades range from 0–20, rather than from 0–100. Scores over 17 or 18 are rare and even the best students do not expect to score consistently in the near-perfect range. A grade of 10 is a passing grade, and is therefore not the equivalent of a 50 in the American system. If you plan to study abroad for credit, ask the foreign institution to provide your school with grade equivalents.

contrôle continu *continuous assessment*

Système français de notation

NOTE FRANÇAISE	NOTE AMÉRICAINE	%	NOTE FRANÇAISE	NOTE AMÉRICAINE	%
0	F	0	11	B-	82
2	F	3	12	B+	88
3	F	8	13	A-	93
4	F	18	14	A	95
5	F	28	15	A	96
6	F	38	16	A+	98
7	D-	60	17	A+	98
8	D-	65	18	A+	99
9	D+	68	19	A+	99
10	C	75	20	A+	100

Coup de main

To read decimal places in French, use the French word **virgule** (*comma*) where you would normally say *point* in English. To say *percent*, use **pour cent**.

60,4% soixante virgule quatre pour cent
sixty point four percent

ACTIVITÉS

1 Vrai ou faux? Indicate whether each statement is **vrai** or **faux**. Correct the false statements.

1. Class attendance is optional in some French universities.
   Vrai.
2. Final course grades are usually based on several exam grades and class participation.
   Faux. Grades may be based upon only one or two exams or papers.
3. The French university system discourages note sharing.
   Faux. Note sharing is completely normal.
4. The French grading system is similar to the American system.
   Faux. The French and American grading systems are very different.
5. The **rentrée universitaire** happens each year in August.
   Faux. The rentrée happens in October.
6. A grade of 11 is not a passing grade.
   Faux. A grade of 11 is equal to an A- in the United States.
7. The academic year in France is typically divided into trimesters.
   Faux. The academic year is divided into two semesters.
8. Scores of 18 or 19 are very rare.
   Vrai.
9. French students typically take three classes each semester.
   Faux. They typically take four to six classes.
10. The final exams in May or June are called the **contrôle continu.**
    Faux. The exams given throughout the semester are called the contrôle continu.

Practice more at **espaces.vhlcentral.com.**

OPTIONS

Pairs To review numbers and the alphabet, have students take turns making true/false statements about the French and American grading systems based on the information in the chart. Write on the board: a plus sign = **plus**; a minus sign = **moins**. Example: **Un vingt en France est un A plus plus plus plus plus plus aux États-Unis. (Vrai.)**

Small Groups Working in groups of three, have students describe the photos on this page. Tell them to create as many sentences in French as they can about the people, what they are doing, and why they are there. Then have volunteers read their descriptions to the class.

LE FRANÇAIS QUOTIDIEN

Les cours et les examens

cours (*m.*) magistral	*lecture*
cours (*m.*) de rattrapage	*remedial class*
bosser	*to work hard*
cartonner à un examen	*to ace an exam*
potasser	*to cram*
rater (un examen)	*to fail (an exam)*
sécher un cours	*to skip a class*

LE MONDE FRANCOPHONE

Le français langue étrangère

Voici quelques° écoles du monde francophone où vous pouvez étudier° le français.

En Belgique Université de Liège

En France Université de Franche-Comté–Centre de linguistique appliquée, Université de Grenoble, Université de Paris IV-Sorbonne

À la Martinique Institut Supérieur d'Études Francophones, à Schoelcher

En Nouvelle-Calédonie Centre de Rencontres et d'Échanges Internationaux du Pacifique, à Nouméa

Au Québec Université Laval, Université de Montréal

Aux îles Saint-Pierre et Miquelon Le FrancoForum, à Saint-Pierre

En Suisse Université Populaire de Lausanne, Université de Neuchâtel

quelques-unes *some* **où vous pouvez étudier** *where you can study*

PORTRAIT

Le bac

Au lycée, les élèves ont des cours communs, comme le français, l'histoire et les maths, et aussi un choix° de spécialisation. À la fin° du lycée, à l'âge de dix-sept ou dix-huit ans, les jeunes Français passent un examen très important: le baccalauréat. Le bac est nécessaire pour faire° des études supérieures.

Les lycéens° passent des bacs différents: le bac L (littéraire), le bac ES (économique et social) et le bac S (scientifique) sont des bacs généraux. Il y a aussi des bacs techniques et des bacs technologiques, comme° le bac STI (sciences et technologies industrielles) ou le bac ST2S (sciences et technologies de la santé et du social). Il y a même° un bac techniques de la musique et de la danse (TMD) et un bac hôtellerie°! Entre 70 (soixante-dix) et 80 (quatre-vingts) pour cent des élèves passent le bac avec succès.

choix *choice* **À la fin** *At the end* **faire** *do* **lycéens** *high school students* **comme** *such as* **même** *even* **hôtellerie** *hotel trade*

SUR INTERNET

Où avez-vous envie d'étudier?

Go to **espaces.vhlcentral.com** to find more information related to this **ESPACE CULTURE.**

ACTIVITÉS

2 Quel bac? Which bac best fits the following interests?

1. le ballet le bac techniques de la musique et de la danse
2. la littérature le bac littéraire
3. la médecine le bac scientifique
4. le tourisme le bac hôtellerie
5. la technologie le bac sciences et technologies industrielles
6. le piano et la flûte le bac technique de la musique et de la danse

3 Et les cours? In French, name two courses you might take in preparation for each of these baccalauréat exams. Answers will vary. Possible answers shown.

1. un bac L
   la français et la philosophie
2. un bac SMS
   la biologie et la psychologie
3. un bac ES
   l'économie et la sociologie
4. un bac STI
   la physique et les maths

ressources
espaces.vhlcentral.com

Le français quotidien Model the pronunciation of each term and have students repeat it. You might also add these words to this list: **une dissert(ation)** (*writing assignment*), **réussir à un examen** (*to pass an exam*), **recaler** (*to fail*), and **les travaux pratiques (TP)** (*labs*).

Portrait Explain that, if a student fails the **bac**, he or she must pass an **examen de rattrapage** or repeat **terminale** and retake the exam the next year in order to pursue further study.

Le monde francophone Have students read the list. Use this as an opportunity to explain the importance of language immersion in a French-speaking country and to encourage students to start thinking about study abroad. If possible, bring in brochures or refer students to websites for study abroad programs.

2 Expansion For additional practice, give students these items. **7. l'histoire (le bac littéraire) 8. la biologie (le bac scientifique) 9. l'informatique (le bac sciences et technologies industrielles) 10. les sciences po (le bac économique et social)**

3 Expansion Tell students to imagine that they are in high school. Given their interests or major, ask them which **bac** they are preparing for. Example: **Quel bac est-ce que vous préparez? (Je prépare le bac S parce que j'étudie la chimie et la physique.)**

OPTIONS

Cultural Comparison Have students compare the French **lycée** to an American high school. Have them discuss the differences between the two educational systems. Then ask them what determines a student's ability to enroll in a university in France versus in the United States.

Pairs Have students work in pairs. Tell them to take turns asking and answering questions using the expressions in **Le français quotidien**. Examples: **Tu bosses pour le cours de français? Tu aimes les cours magistraux?**

Section Goals

In this section, students will learn:

- the verb **avoir**
- some common expressions with **avoir**

Instructional Resources
*espaces.vhlcentral.com: Lab MP3s; WB/VM/LM Answer Key; IRM (**Mise en pratique** answers; Lab Audioscript; **Feuilles d'activités**); activities; downloads; reference tools*

Suggestions

- Model **avoir** by asking questions such as: **Avez-vous un examen cette semaine? Avez-vous une calculatrice? ____ a-t-il/elle une calculatrice?** Point out that forms of **avoir** were in the **Roman-photo.**
- Explain that **avoir** is irregular and must be memorized. Begin a paradigm for **avoir** by writing **j'ai** on the board and asking volunteers questions that elicit **j'ai**. Examples: **J'ai un stylo. Qui a un crayon?**
- Add **tu as** and **il/elle a** to the paradigm on the board. Point out that **as** and **a** are pronounced alike. Tell students that **avoir** has no real stem apart from the letter **a**.
- Write **nous avons** and **vous avez**. Point out that **-ons** and **-ez** are the same endings as in **-er** verbs. Add **ils/elles ont**.
- Remind students of liaisons in the plural forms of **avoir** and have them pronounce these forms again.
- Tell the class that many French expressions use **avoir** + *noun* instead of **être** to say *to be* + *adjective* in English. Also point out that, to ask people if they feel like doing something, use **avoir envie de** + *infinitive*.
- Model the use of the expressions by talking about yourself while gesturing and asking students questions about themselves. Examples: **J'ai froid ce matin/cet après-midi. Vous avez froid aussi ou vous avez chaud? J'ai besoin d'un dictionnaire. Avez-vous un dictionnaire?**

2B.1 Present tense of *avoir*

Point de départ The verb **avoir** (*to have*) is used frequently. You will have to memorize each of its present tense forms because they are irregular.

Present tense of *avoir*

j'ai	*I have*	**nous avons**	*we have*
tu as	*you have*	**vous avez**	*you have*
il/elle a	*he/she/it has*	**ils/elles ont**	*they have*

On a rendez-vous avec David demain.

Cette année, nous avons le bac.

- Liaison is required between the final consonants of **on, nous, vous, ils,** and **elles** and the forms of **avoir** that follow them. When the final consonant is an **-s**, pronounce it as a *z* before the verb forms.

On a un prof sympa.
We have a nice professor.

Nous avons un cours d'art.
We have an art class.

- Keep in mind that an indefinite article, whether singular or plural, usually becomes **de/d'** after a negation.

J'ai **un** cours difficile.
I have a difficult class.

Je n'ai pas **de** cours difficile.
I do not have a difficult class.

Il a **des** examens.
He has exams.

Il n'a pas **d'**examens.
He does not have exams.

MISE EN PRATIQUE

1 On a... Use the correct forms of **avoir** to form questions from these elements. Use inversion and provide an affirmative or negative answer as cued.

MODÈLE
tu / bourse (oui)
As-tu une bourse? Oui, j'ai une bourse.

1. nous / dictionnaire (oui)
   Avons-nous un dictionnaire? Oui, nous avons un dictionnaire.
2. Luc / diplôme (non)
   Luc a-t-il un diplôme? Non, il n'a pas de diplôme.
3. elles / montre (non)
   Ont-elles une montre? Non, elles n'ont pas de montre.
4. vous / copains (oui)
   Avez-vous des copains? Oui, j'ai/nous avons des copains.
5. Thérèse / téléphone (oui)
   Thérèse a-t-elle un téléphone? Oui, elle a un téléphone.
6. Charles et Jacques / calculatrice (non)
   Charles et Jacques ont-ils une calculatrice? Non, ils n'ont pas de calculatrice.

2 C'est évident Describe these people using expressions with **avoir**. Answers may vary.

1. J' ai besoin d' étudier.

2. Tu as honte.

3. Vous avez froid.

4. Elles ont sommeil.

3 Assemblez Use the verb **avoir** and combine elements from the two columns to create sentences about yourself, your class, and your school. Make any necessary changes or additions. Answers will vary.

A	B
Je	cours utiles
L'université	bourses importantes
Les profs	professeurs brillants
Mon (*My*) petit ami	ami(e) mexicain(e) / anglais(e) / canadien(ne) / vietnamien(ne)
Ma (*My*) petite amie	étudiants intéressants
Nous	resto U agréable
	école de droit

Practice more at **espaces.vhlcentral.com.**

OPTIONS

Extra Practice Do a quick substitution drill with **avoir**. Write a sentence on the board and have students read it aloud. Then say a new subject and have students repeat the sentence, substituting the new subject. Examples: **1. J'ai des problèmes. (Éric et moi, tu, Stéphane, vous, les hommes) 2. Pierre a cours de chimie le mardi et le jeudi. (Pierre et Julie, nous, je, vous, tu)**

Game Divide the class into two teams. Choose one team member at a time to go to the board, alternating between teams. Say a subject pronoun. The person at the board must write and say the correct form of **avoir**. Example: **elle (elle a)**. Give a point for each correct answer. The team with the most points at the end of the game wins.

COMMUNICATION

4 Besoins Your instructor will give you a worksheet. Ask different classmates if they need to do these activities. Find at least one person to answer **Oui** and at least one to answer **Non** for each item. Answers will vary.

MODÈLE regarder la télé

Étudiant(e) 1: *Tu as besoin de regarder la télé?*
Étudiant(e) 2: *Oui, j'ai besoin de regarder la télé.*
Étudiant(e) 3: *Non, je n'ai pas besoin de regarder la télé.*

Activités	Oui	Non
1. regarder la télé	Anne	Louis
2. étudier ce soir		
3. passer un examen cette semaine		
4. trouver un cours d'informatique		
5. travailler à la bibliothèque		
6. commencer un devoir important		
7. téléphoner à un(e) copain/copine ce week-end		
8. parler avec le professeur		

5 C'est vrai? Interview a classmate by transforming each of these statements into a question. Be prepared to report the results of your interview to the class. Answers will vary.

MODÈLE J'ai deux ordinateurs.

Étudiant(e) 1: *Tu as deux ordinateurs?*
Étudiant(e) 2: *Non, je n'ai pas deux ordinateurs.*

1. J'ai peur des examens.
2. J'ai vingt et un ans.
3. J'ai envie de visiter Montréal.
4. J'ai un cours de biologie.
5. J'ai sommeil le lundi matin.
6. J'ai un(e) petit(e) ami(e) égoïste.

6 Interview You are talking to the campus housing advisor. Answer his or her questions. In pairs, practice the scene and role-play it for the class. Answers will vary.

1. Qu'est-ce que (*What*) vous étudiez?
2. Est-ce que vous avez d'excellentes notes?
3. Est-ce que vous avez envie de partager la chambre?
4. Est-ce que vous mangez au resto U?
5. Est-ce que vous avez un ordinateur?
6. Est-ce que vous retrouvez des amis à la fac?
7. Est-ce que vous écoutez de la musique?
8. Est-ce que vous avez des cours le matin?

- The verb **avoir** is used in certain idiomatic or set expressions where English generally uses *to be* or *to feel*.

Expressions with *avoir*

avoir... ans	*to be... years old*	**avoir froid**	*to be cold*
avoir besoin (de)	*to need*	**avoir honte (de)**	*to be ashamed (of)*
avoir de la chance	*to be lucky*	**avoir l'air**	*to look like*
avoir chaud	*to be hot*	**avoir peur (de)**	*to be afraid (of)*
avoir envie (de)	*to feel like*	**avoir raison**	*to be right*
		avoir sommeil	*to be sleepy*
		avoir tort	*to be wrong*

Il a chaud.

Ils ont froid.

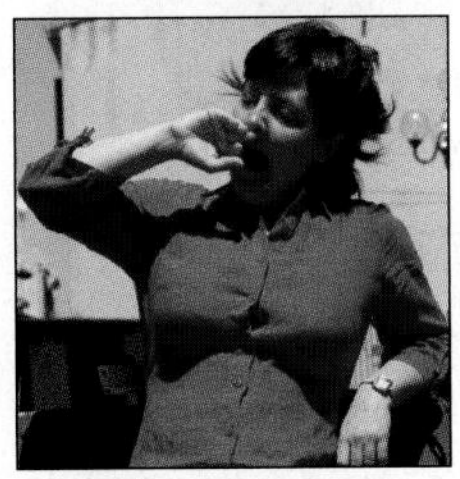
Elle a sommeil.

Il a de la chance.

- The command forms of **avoir** are irregular: **aie, ayons, ayez.**

Aie un peu de patience.
Be a little patient.

N'**ayez** pas peur.
Don't be afraid.

Essayez! Complete the sentences with the correct forms of **avoir.**

1. La température est de 35 degrés Celsius. Nous <u>avons</u> chaud.
2. En Alaska, en décembre, vous <u>avez</u> froid.
3. Martine écoute la radio et elle <u>a</u> envie de danser.
4. Ils <u>ont</u> besoin d'une calculatrice pour le devoir.
5. N'<u>aie/ayez</u> pas peur des insectes.
6. Sébastien pense que je travaille aujourd'hui. Il <u>a</u> raison.
7. J'<u>ai</u> cours d'économie le lundi et le mercredi.
8. Mes amis voyagent beaucoup. Ils <u>ont</u> de la chance.
9. Mohammed <u>a</u> deux cousins à Marseille.
10. Vous <u>avez</u> un grand appartement.

Essayez! Ask students to identify the idiomatic expressions in the sentences. (All are idiomatic expressions, except items 7, 9, and 10.)

1 Suggestion This activity can be done in pairs. Tell students to alternate asking and answering the questions.

2 Expansion For each drawing, ask students how many people there are, their names, and their ages. Example: **Combien de personnes y a-t-il sur le dessin numéro 1? Comment s'appellent-elles? Quel âge a ___?**

3 Suggestion This activity can be done orally or in writing in pairs or groups.

4 Suggestions
- Have three volunteers read the **modèle** aloud. Then distribute the **Feuilles d'activités** from the Supersite.
- Have students add at least two activities of their own.

5 Suggestion Have two volunteers read the **modèle** aloud. Remind students that an indefinite article becomes **de (d')** if it follows **avoir** in the negative.

6 Suggestions
- Remind students to do the interview twice so each person asks and answers the questions.
- Ask volunteers to summarize their partners' responses. Record the responses on the board as a survey (**un sondage**) about the class' characteristics. Then ask questions like this: **Combien d'étudiants dans la classe étudient l'économie?**

OPTIONS

TPR Assign gestures to expressions with **avoir**. Examples: **avoir chaud**: *wipe brow*, **avoir froid**: *wrap arms around oneself and shiver*, **avoir peur**: *hold one's hand over mouth in fear*, **avoir faim:** *rub stomach*; **avoir sommeil**: *yawn and stretch.* Have students stand. Say an expression at random as you point to a student who performs the appropriate gesture. Vary by indicating more than one student at a time.

Small Groups Have students work in groups of three. Tell them to write nine sentences, each of which uses a different expression with **avoir**. Call on volunteers to write some of their group's best sentences on the board. Have the class read the sentences aloud and correct any errors.

Section Goals

In this section, students will learn:
- to tell time
- some time expressions
- the 24-hour system of telling time

Instructional Resources
*espaces.vhlcentral.com: Lab MP3s; WB/VM/LM Answer Key; Transparency #19; IRM (**Essayez!** and **Mise en pratique** answers; Lab Audioscript); activities; downloads; reference tools*

Suggestions

- To prepare for telling time, review the meanings of **il est** and numbers 0–60.
- Introduce: **Il est sept heures (huit heures, neuf heures…).**
- Explain to students that **heures** refers to *hours* when telling time, but can also mean *o'clock*.
- Introduce: **Il est ____ heure(s) cinq, dix, et quart,** and **et demie.**
- Using a paper plate clock, display various times on the hour. Ask: **Quelle heure est-il?**
- Introduce and explain: **Il est ____ heure(s) moins cinq, moins dix, moins le quart,** and **moins vingt.** Repeat the procedure above using your movable-hands clock.
- Explain that the French view times of day differently from Americans. In France, they say **«bonjour»** until about 4:00 or 5:00 p.m. After that, they use the greeting **«bonsoir»**. They say **«bonne nuit»** only when going to sleep.
- Explain the use of the 24-hour clock. Have students practice saying times this way by adding 12.
- Model the pronunciation of the time expressions in the box and have students repeat. Point out that a.m. and p.m. are not used in France or most francophone regions. Instead, they use **du matin, de l'après midi**, and **du soir.**
- Tell students that **et demi(e)** agrees in gender with the noun it follows, but not in number. After **midi** and **minuit**, both **et demi** and **et demie** are accepted.

2B.2 Telling time

NATIONAL STANDARDS comparisons

Point de départ Use the verb **être** with numbers to tell time.

- There are two ways to ask what time it is.

Quelle heure est-il?	**Est-ce que vous avez l'heure?**
What time is it?	*Do you have the time?*

- Use **heures** by itself to express time on the hour. Use **heure** for one o'clock.

Il est **six heures**.

Il est **une heure**.

- Express time from the hour to the half-hour by adding minutes.

Il est quatre heures **cinq**.

Il est onze heures **vingt**.

- Use **et quart** to say that it is fifteen minutes past the hour. Use **et demie** to say that it is thirty minutes past the hour.

Il est une heure **et quart**.

Il est sept heures **et demie**.

- To express time from the half hour to the hour, subtract minutes or a portion of an hour from the next hour.

Il est trois heures **moins dix**.

Il est une heure **moins le quart**.

- To express at what time something happens, use the preposition **à**.

Céline travaille **à sept heures moins vingt**.	On passe un examen **à une heure**.
Céline works at 6:40.	*We take a test at one o'clock.*

MISE EN PRATIQUE

1 Quelle heure est-il? Give the time shown on each clock or watch. Some answers may vary.

MODÈLE
Il est quatre heures et quart de l'après-midi.

1. Il est midi/minuit et demi.
2. Il est une heure du matin.
3. Il est huit heures dix.
4. Il est onze heures moins le quart.

5. Il est deux heures douze.
6. Il est sept heures cinq.
7. Il est quatre heures moins cinq.
8. Il est minuit moins vingt-cinq.

2 À quelle heure? Find out when you and your friends are going to do certain things.

MODÈLE
À quelle heure est-ce qu'on étudie? (about 8 p.m.)
On étudie vers huit heures du soir.

À quelle heure...
1. ... est-ce qu'on arrive au café? (at 10:30 a.m.) On arrive au café à dix heures et demie du matin.
2. ... est-ce que vous parlez avec le professeur? (at noon) Nous parlons avec le professeur à midi.
3. ... est-ce que tu rentres? (late, at 11:15 p.m.) Je rentre tard, à onze heures et quart du soir.
4. ... est-ce qu'on regarde la télé? (at 9:00 p.m.) On regarde la télé à neuf heures du soir.
5. ... est-ce que Marlène et Nadine mangent? (around 1:45 p.m.) Elles mangent vers deux heures moins le quart de l'après-midi.
6. ... est-ce que le cours commence? (very early, at 8:20 a.m.) Il commence très tôt, à huit heures vingt du matin.

3 Départ à… Tell what each of these times would be on a 24-hour clock.

MODÈLE
Il est trois heures vingt de l'après-midi.
Il est quinze heures vingt.

1. Il est dix heures et demie du soir. Il est vingt-deux heures trente.
2. Il est deux heures de l'après-midi. Il est quatorze heures.
3. Il est huit heures et quart du soir. Il est vingt heures quinze.
4. Il est minuit moins le quart. Il est vingt-trois heures quarante-cinq.
5. Il est six heures vingt-cinq du soir. Il est dix-huit heures vingt-cinq.
6. Il est trois heures moins cinq du matin. Il est deux heures cinquante-cinq.

Practice more at **espaces.vhlcentral.com.**

OPTIONS

Extra Practice Draw a large clock face on the board with its numbers but without the hands. Say a time and ask a volunteer to come up and draw the hands to indicate that time. The rest of the class verifies whether or not the person has written the correct time, saying: **Il/Elle a raison/tort.** Repeat this procedure a number of times.

Pairs Have pairs take turns telling each other what time their classes are this semester/trimester/term. Example: **J'ai un cours à ____ heures....** For each time given, the other student draws a clock face with the corresponding time. The first student verifies if the clock is correct.

NATIONAL communication STANDARDS

COMMUNICATION

4 **Télémonde** Look at this French TV guide. In pairs, ask questions about program start times. Answers will vary.

MODÈLE

Étudiant(e) 1: *À quelle heure commence Télé-ciné?*
Étudiant(e) 2: *Télé-ciné commence à dix heures dix du soir.*

dessins animés	*cartoons*
feuilleton télévisé	*soap opera*
film policier	*detective film*
informations	*news*
jeu télévisé	*game show*

VENDREDI

Antenne 2	Antenne 4	Antenne 5
15h30 Pomme d'Api (dessins animés) **17h35** Reportage spécial: le sport dans les lycées **20h15** La famille Menet (feuilleton télévisé) **21h35** Télé-ciné: L'inspecteur Duval (film policier)	**14h00** Football: match France-Italie **19h45** Les informations **20h30** Concert: Orchestre de Nice **22h10** Télé-ciné: Une chose difficile (comédie dramatique)	**18h25** Montréal: une ville à visiter **19h30** Des chiffres et des lettres (jeu télévisé) **21h05** Reportage spécial: les Sénégalais **22h05** Les informations

5 **Où es-tu?** In pairs, take turns asking where (**où**) your partner usually is on these days at these times. Choose from the places listed. Answers will vary.

au lit (*bed*)	chez mes (*at my*) parents
au resto U	chez mes copains
à la bibliothèque	chez mon (*my*) petit ami
en ville (*town*)	chez ma (*my*) petite amie
au parc	
en cours	

1. Le samedi: à 8h00 du matin; à midi; à minuit
2. En semaine: à 9h00 du matin; à 3h00 de l'après-midi; à 7h00 du soir
3. Le dimanche: à 4h00 de l'après-midi; à 6h30 du soir; à 10h00 du soir
4. Le vendredi: à 11h00 du matin; à 5h00 de l'après-midi; à 11h00 du soir

6 **Le suspect** A student on campus is a suspect in a crime. You and a partner are detectives. Keeping a log of the student's activities, use the 24-hour clock to say what he or she is doing when. Answers will vary.

MODÈLE

À vingt-deux heures trente-trois, il parle au téléphone.

- **Liaison** occurs between numbers and the word **heure(s)**. Final **-s** and **-x** in **deux**, **trois**, **six**, and **dix** are pronounced like a *z*. The final **-f** of **neuf** is pronounced like a *v*.

Il est **deux heures**. *It's two o'clock.*	Il est **neuf heures** et quart. *It's 9:15.*

- You do not usually make a **liaison** between the verb form **est** and a following number that starts with a vowel sound.

Il est **onze** heures. *It's eleven o'clock.*	Il est **une** heure vingt. *It's 1:20.*	Il est **huit** heures et demie. *It's 8:30.*

Expressions for telling time

À quelle heure?	*(At) what time/ when?*	**midi**	*noon*
		minuit	*midnight*
de l'après-midi	*in the afternoon*	**pile**	*on the dot*
du matin	*in the morning*	**presque**	*almost*
du soir	*in the evening*	**tard**	*late*
en avance	*early*	**tôt**	*early*
en retard	*late*	**vers**	*about*

Il est **minuit** à Paris. *It's midnight in Paris.*	Il est six heures **du soir** à New York. *It's six o'clock in the evening in New York.*

- The 24-hour clock is often used to express official time. Departure times, movie times, and store hours are expressed in this fashion. Only numbers are used to tell time this way. Expressions like **et demie, moins le quart**, etc. are not used.

Le train arrive à **dix-sept heures six**. *The train arrives at 5:06 p.m.*	Le film est à **vingt-deux heures trente sept**. *The film is at 10:37 p.m.*

J'ai cours de trois heures vingt à quatre heures et demie.

Stéphane! Quelle heure est-il?

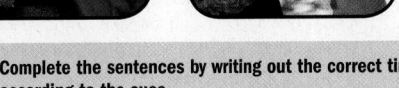

Essayez! **Complete the sentences by writing out the correct times according to the cues.**

1. (1:00 a.m.) Il est <u>une heure</u> du matin.
2. (2:50 a.m.) Il est <u>trois heures moins dix</u> du matin.
3. (8:30 p.m.) Il est <u>huit heures et demie</u> du soir.
4. (12:00 p.m.) Il est <u>midi</u>.
5. (4:05 p.m.) Il est <u>quatre heures cinq</u> de l'après-midi.
6. (4:45 a.m.) Il est <u>cinq heures moins le quart</u> du matin.

Essayez! For additional practice, give students these items.
7. 6:20 p.m. 8. 9:10 a.m.
9. 2:15 p.m. 10. 10:35 a.m.
11. 12:00 a.m. 12. 9:55 p.m.

1 Expansion At random, say the times shown and have students say the number of the clock or watch described. Example: **Il est sept heures cinq. (C'est le numéro six.)**

2 Suggestion Read the **modèle** aloud with a volunteer. Working in pairs, have students take turns asking and answering the questions.

3 Expansion Create a train schedule and write it on the board or use photocopies of a real one. Ask students questions based on the schedule. Example: **À quelle heure est le train Paris-Bordeaux le vendredi soir?**

4 Suggestion Before starting this activity, have students read the TV guide, point out cognates, and predict their meaning. Provide examples for non-cognate categories so students can guess their meaning. Examples: **dessins animés, feuilleton télévisé**, and **jeu télévisé**.

4 Expansion Have pairs ask each other additional questions based on the TV guide. Examples: **Est-ce qu'il y a un reportage à vingt heures dix? (Non, les reportages sont à dix-sept heures trente-cinq et à vingt et une heures cinq.) J'ai envie de regarder le film policier. À quelle heure est-il? (Le film policier est à vingt et une heures trente-cinq.)**

5 Suggestion Before beginning the activity, provide students with a model. Example: **Étudiant(e) 1: Où es-tu le samedi à midi? Étudiant(e) 2: Le samedi à midi, je suis au resto U.**

6 Expansion After completing the activity, ask students if the suspect has an alibi at certain times. Tell them to respond using the information on their logs. Example: **Le suspect a-t-il un alibi à vingt-trois heures? (Oui, à vingt-trois heures il étudie avec un ami.)**

OPTIONS

Video Play the video episode again to give students additional input on telling time and the verb **avoir**. Pause the video where appropriate to discuss how time or **avoir** were used and to ask comprehension questions. Example: **Est-ce que Stéphane a peur de parler à Astrid? (Mais non, il a peur du bac.)**

Small Groups Have students work in groups of three. Tell them to take turns asking what time various TV shows start and answering. Example: **À quelle heure est *60 Minutes*? (C'est à dix-neuf heures.)** Remind students to use the 24-hour system when talking about TV shows.

Révision

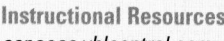

Instructional Resources
espaces.vhlcentral.com:
IRM (Info Gap Activities);
Testing Program, pp. 13–16;
Test Files; Testing Program
MP3s; activities; downloads;
reference tools
Test Generator

1 Suggestion Have two volunteers read the **modèle** aloud. Encourage students to add other items to the list.

2 Suggestion Before beginning the activity, tell students to choose two language classes, a science class, and an elective in the list. Then read the **modèle** aloud with a volunteer.

3 Expansion Have volunteers report their findings to the class. Then do a quick class survey to find out how many students are taking the same courses. Example: **Combien d'étudiants ont sciences politiques ce semestre?**

4 Suggestion Before doing the activity, point out the use of the construction **avoir envie de** + *infinitive.* Encourage students to add activities to the list. Examples: **regarder un film, manger/partager une pizza, parler au téléphone,** and **voyager en France/Europe.**

5 Suggestion Ask what expressions express likes and dislikes, and write them on the board before assigning this activity.

6 Suggestions
- Divide the class into pairs and distribute the Info Gap Handouts on the Supersite for this activity. Have two volunteers read the **modèle**. Give students ten minutes to complete the activity.
- After completing the activity, ask students what activities Patrick would like to do this weekend.

1 J'ai besoin de... In pairs, take turns saying which items you need. Your partner will guess why you need them. How many times did each of you guess correctly? Answers will vary.

MODÈLE

Étudiant(e) 1: *J'ai besoin d'un cahier et d'un dictionnaire pour demain.*
Étudiant(e) 2: *Est-ce que tu as un cours de français?*
Étudiant(e) 1: *Non. J'ai un examen d'anglais.*

un cahier	un livre de physique
une calculatrice	une montre
une carte	un ordinateur
un dictionnaire	un stylo
une feuille de papier	un téléphone

2 À l'université française To complete your degree, you need two language classes, a science class, and an elective of your choice. Take turns deciding what classes you need or want to take. Your partner will tell you the days and times so you can set up your schedule. Answers will vary.

MODÈLE

Étudiant(e) 1: *J'ai besoin d'un cours de maths, peut-être «Initiation aux maths».*
Étudiant(e) 2: *C'est le mardi et le jeudi après-midi, de deux heures à trois heures et demie.*
Étudiant(e) 1: *J'ai aussi besoin d'un cours de langue...*

Les cours	Jours et heures
Allemand	mardi, jeudi; 14h00-15h30
Biologie II	mardi, jeudi; 9h00-10h30
Chimie générale	lundi, mercredi; 11h00-12h30
Espagnol	lundi, mercredi; 11h00-12h30
Gestion	mercredi; 13h00-14h30
Histoire des États-Unis	jeudi; 12h15-14h15
Initiation à la physique	lundi, mercredi; 12h00-13h30
Initiation aux maths	mardi, jeudi; 14h00-15h30
Italien	lundi, mercredi; 12h00-13h30
Japonais	mardi, jeudi; 9h00-10h30
Les philosophes grecs	lundi; 15h15-16h45
Littérature moderne	mardi; 10h15-11h15

3 Les cours Your partner will tell you what classes he or she is currently taking. Make a list, including the times and days of the week. Then, talk to as many classmates as you can, and find at least two students who take at least two of the same classes as your partner. Answers will vary.

4 On y va? Walk around the room and find at least one classmate who feels like doing each of these activities with you. For every affirmative answer, record the name of your classmate and agree on a time and date. Do not speak to the same classmate twice. Answers will vary.

MODÈLE

Étudiant(e) 1: *Tu as envie de retrouver des amis avec moi?*
Étudiant(e) 2: *Oui, pourquoi pas? Samedi, à huit heures du soir, peut-être?*
Étudiant(e) 1: *D'accord!*

chercher un café sympa	regarder la télé française
dîner au resto U	retrouver des amis
écouter des CD	travailler à la bibliothèque
étudier le français cette semaine	visiter un musée

5 Au téléphone Two high school friends are attending different universities. In pairs, imagine a conversation where they discuss the time, their classes, and likes or dislikes about campus life. Then, role-play the conversation for the class and vote for the best skit. Answers will vary.

MODÈLE

Étudiant(e) 1: *J'ai cours de chimie à dix heures et demie.*
Étudiant(e) 2: *Je n'ai pas de cours de chimie cette année.*
Étudiant(e) 1: *N'aimes-tu pas les sciences?*
Étudiant(e) 2: *Si, mais...*

6 La semaine de Patrick Your instructor will give you and a partner different incomplete pages from Patrick's day planner. Do not look at each other's worksheet while you complete your own. Answers will vary.

MODÈLE

Étudiant(e) 1: *Lundi matin, Patrick a cours de géographie à dix heures et demie.*
Étudiant(e) 2: *Lundi, il a cours de sciences po à deux heures de l'après-midi.*

ressources
WB pp. 23-26 | LM pp. 15-16 | espaces.vhlcentral.com

OPTIONS

Small Groups Working in groups of three or four, have students create a short skit similar to the scene in video still 1 of the **Roman-photo**. Tell them that they have to decide on a day, time, and place to meet for a study session in order to prepare for the next French test. Have groups perform their skits for the class.

Extra Practice Have students make a list of six items that students normally carry in their backpacks to class. Then tell them to circulate around the room asking their classmates if they have those items in their backpacks. Also tell them to ask how many they have. Example: **As-tu un cahier dans le sac à dos? Combien de cahiers as-tu?**

À l'écoute

NATIONAL communication STANDARDS

Audio: Activities

STRATÉGIE

Listening for cognates

You already know that cognates are words that have similar spellings and meanings in two or more languages: for example *group* and **groupe** or *activity* and **activité**. Listen for cognates to increase your comprehension of spoken French.

To help you practice this strategy, you will listen to two sentences. Make a list of all the cognates you hear.

Préparation

Based on the photograph, who and where do you think Marie-France and Dominique are? Do you think they know each other well? Where are they probably going this morning? What do you think they are talking about?

À vous d'écouter

Listen to the conversation and list any cognates you hear. Listen again and complete the highlighted portions of Marie-France's schedule.

28 OCTOBRE lundi

8H00	*jogging*	14H00	psychologie
8H30		14H30	
9H00		15H00	
9H30	biologie	15H30	physique
10H00		16H00	
10H30		16H30	
11H00	chimie	17H00	
11H30		17H30	*étudier*
12H00	resto U	18H00	
12H30		18H30	
13H00	*bibliothèque*	19H00	*téléphoner à papa*
13H30		19H30	*Sophie:* restaurant vietnamien

Practice more at **espaces.vhlcentral.com.**

Compréhension

Vrai ou faux? Indicate whether each statement is **vrai** or **faux**. Then correct the false statements.

1. D'après Marie-France, la biologie est facile.
   Vrai.
2. Marie-France adore la chimie.
   Faux. Marie-France déteste la chimie.
3. Marie-France et Dominique mangent au restaurant vietnamien à midi.
   Faux. Marie-France et Dominique mangent au restaurant vietnamien à sept heures et demie du soir.
4. Dominique aime son cours de sciences politiques.
   Faux. Dominique aime son cours d'informatique.
5. Monsieur Meyer est professeur de physique.
   Vrai.
6. Monsieur Meyer donne des devoirs faciles.
   Faux. Monsieur Meyer donne des devoirs très difficiles.
7. Le lundi après-midi, Marie-France a psychologie et physique.
   Vrai.
8. Aujourd'hui, Dominique mange au resto U.
   Faux. Aujourd'hui, Marie-France mange au resto U.

Votre emploi du temps With a partner, discuss the classes you're taking this semester. Be sure to say when you have each one, and give your opinion of at least three courses.

Section Goals

In this section, students will:
- learn to listen for cognates
- listen to sentences containing familiar and unfamiliar vocabulary
- listen to a conversation, complete a schedule, and answer true/false questions

Instructional Resources
espaces.vhlcentral.com: Textbook MP3s; IRM (Textbook Audioscript); downloads; reference tools

Stratégie
Script 1. Dans certaines institutions d'études supérieures, les étudiants reçoivent un salaire. 2. Ma cousine étudie la médecine vétérinaire. C'est sa passion!

Préparation Have students describe the photo. Ask them to justify their descriptions based on the visual clues.

Suggestion To check answers for the **À vous d'écouter** activity, have students work in pairs and take turns asking questions about Marie-France's schedule. Example: **Est-ce que Marie-France a cours de biologie à 14h00? (Non, elle a cours de biologie à 9h30.)**

À vous d'écouter
Script DOMINIQUE: Tiens, bonjour, Marie-France. Comment ça va?
MARIE-FRANCE: Salut, Dominique. Ça va bien. Et toi?
D: Très bien, merci. Tu vas en cours?
M: Oui, j'ai cours toute la journée, le lundi. Ce matin, j'ai biologie à neuf heures et demie.
D: Tu aimes la biologie?
M: Oui, j'aime bien. C'est facile. Après, à onze heures, j'ai chimie. Ça, je déteste! C'est difficile! À midi, je mange au resto U avec des copains.
D: Et cet après-midi?
M: Alors, à deux heures, j'ai psychologie et à trois heures et demie, j'ai physique.
D: Est-ce que tu aimes ça, la physique?
M: Oui, mais cette année, le prof n'est pas très intéressant.
D: Ah bon? Qui est-ce?
M: Monsieur Meyer.
D: Ah oui! Tu as raison. Il n'est pas très intéressant. Et il donne des devoirs et des examens très difficiles.
M: C'est vrai. Et toi, tu aimes tes cours cette année?
D: Oui, beaucoup. J'adore l'informatique. Le prof est amusant et il explique bien.
M: Tu as de la chance! Dis, est-ce que tu as envie de dîner au restaurant avec Sophie et moi ce soir? On va au restaurant vietnamien près de l'université.
D: Oui, avec plaisir. À quelle heure?
M: À sept heures et demie.
D: Bon, d'accord. À ce soir.
M: Salut.

Section Goals

In this section, students will learn historical, cultural, and geographical information about France.

Instructional Resources
espaces.vhlcentral.com: Transparency #20; WB/VM/LM Answer Key; activities; downloads; reference tools

Carte de la France
- Have students look at the map of France or use **Transparency #20**. Ask volunteers to read the cities' names aloud.
- Have students identify the location of the place or object in each photo.

Le pays en chiffres
- Have students read the section headings. Point out the type of information contained in each section and clarify unfamiliar words.
- Have volunteers read the sections aloud. After each section, ask questions about the content.
- Ask students to share any additional information they might know about the people in **Français célèbres**.

Incroyable mais vrai!
L'Académie française was founded by Cardinal Richelieu during the reign of Louis XIII. In the beginning, the Academy's primary role was to standardize the language for French-speaking people by establishing rules to make it pure, eloquent, and capable of dealing with the arts and sciences.

NATIONAL STANDARDS connections cultures

Interactive Map Reading

Panorama

La France

un bateau-mouche sur la Seine

le château de Chenonceau

le pont° du Gard

Le pays en chiffres

- **Superficie:** *549.000 km²* *(cinq cent quarante-neuf mille kilomètres carrés°)*
- **Population:** *62.106.000 (soixante-deux millions cent six mille)*
  SOURCE: INSEE
- **Industries principales:** *agro-alimentaires°, assurance°, banques, énergie, produits pharmaceutiques, produits de luxe, télécommunications, tourisme, transports*

  La France est le pays° le plus° visité du monde° avec plus de° 60 millions de touristes chaque° année. Son histoire, sa culture et ses monuments–plus de 12.000 (douze mille)–et musées–plus de 1.200 (mille deux cents)–attirent° des touristes d'Europe et de partout° dans le monde.
- **Villes principales:** *Paris, Lille, Lyon, Marseille, Toulouse*
- **Monnaie°:** *l'euro*
  La France est un pays membre de l'Union européenne et, en 2002, l'euro a remplacé° le franc français comme° monnaie nationale.

Français célèbres

- **Jeanne d'Arc,** *héroïne française (1412–1431)*
- **Émile Zola,** *écrivain° (1840–1902)*

- **Auguste Renoir,** *peintre° (1841–1919)*
- **Claude Debussy,** *compositeur et musicien (1862–1918)*
- **Camille Claudel,** *femme sculpteur (1864–1943)*
- **Claudie André-Deshays,** *médecin, première astronaute française (1957–)*

carrés *square* **agro-alimentaires** *food processing* **assurance** *insurance* **pays** *country* **le plus** *the most* **monde** *world* **plus de** *more than* **chaque** *each* **attirent** *attract* **partout** *everywhere* **Monnaie** *Currency* **a remplacé** *replaced* **comme** *as* **écrivain** *writer* **peintre** *painter* **élus à vie** *elected for life* **Depuis** *Since* **mots** *words* **courrier** *mail* **pont** *bridge*

Incroyable mais vrai!

Être «immortel», c'est réguler et défendre le bon usage du français! Les académiciens de l'Académie française sont élus à vie° et s'appellent les «Immortels». Depuis° 1635 (mille six cent trente-cinq), ils décident de l'orthographe correcte des mots° et publient un dictionnaire. Attention, c'est «courrier° électronique», pas «e-mail»!

OPTIONS

Le pays en chiffres France is the third largest country in Europe. It is divided into 22 **régions** (*regions*), which include **la Corse** (*Corsica*). The **régions** are divided into 95 **départements** (*departments*). France also has four overseas **Départements et régions d'outre-mer (DROM): la Guadeloupe, la Guyane française, la Réunion,** and **la Martinique**. Using the map of France in **Appendice A** that shows the **régions** and **départements**, have students locate various cities as you say the names. Example: **Marseille (C'est dans le département des Bouches-du-Rhône.)**

Oral Presentation If a student has visited France (preferably outside Paris), ask him or her to prepare a short presentation about his or her experiences there. Encourage the student to bring in photos and souvenirs of France.

La géographie

L'Hexagone

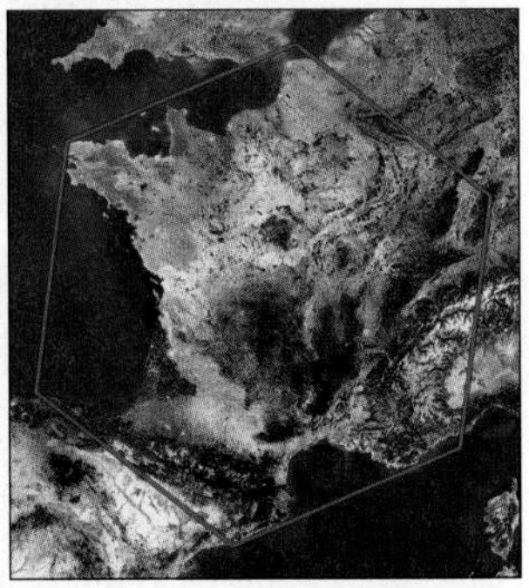

Surnommé° l'Hexagone à cause de° sa forme géométrique, le territoire français a trois fronts maritimes: l'océan Atlantique, la mer° Méditerranée et la Manche°; et trois frontières° naturelles: les Pyrénées, les Ardennes, les Alpes et le Jura. À l'intérieur du pays°, le Massif central et les Vosges ponctuent° un relief composé de vastes plaines et de forêts. La Loire, la Seine, la Garonne, le Rhin et le Rhône sont les fleuves° principaux de l'Hexagone.

La technologie

Le Train à Grande Vitesse

Le chemin de fer° existe en France depuis° 1827 (mille huit cent vingt-sept). Aujourd'hui, la SNCF (Société nationale des chemins de fer français) offre la possibilité aux voyageurs de se déplacer° dans tout° le pays et propose des tarifs° avantageux aux étudiants et aux moins de 25 ans°. Le TGV (Train à Grande Vitesse°) roule° à plus de 300 (trois cent) km/h (kilomètres/heure) et emmène° les voyageurs jusqu'à° Londres et Bruxelles.

Les arts

Le cinéma, le 7e art!

L'invention du cinématographe par les frères° Lumière en 1895 (mille huit cent quatre-vingt-quinze) marque le début° du «7e (septième) art». Le cinéma français donne naissance° aux prestigieux César° en 1976 (mille neuf cent soixante-seize), à des cinéastes talentueux comme° Jean Renoir, François Truffaut et Luc Besson, et à des acteurs mémorables comme Brigitte Bardot, Catherine Deneuve, Olivier Martinez et Audrey Tautou (*Amélie, The Da Vinci Code*).

L'économie

L'industrie

Avec la richesse de la culture française, il est facile d'oublier que l'économie en France n'est pas limitée à l'artisanat°, à la gastronomie ou à la haute couture°. En fait°, la France est une véritable puissance° industrielle et se classe° parmi° les économies les plus° importantes du monde. Ses° activités dans des secteurs comme la construction automobile (Peugeot, Citroën, Renault), l'industrie aérospatiale (Airbus) et l'énergie nucléaire (Électricité de France) sont considérables.

Qu'est-ce que vous avez appris? Complete these sentences.

1. ___Camille Claudel___ est une femme sculpteur française.
2. Les Académiciens sont élus ___à vie___.
3. Pour «e-mail», on utilise aussi l'expression ___courrier électronique___.
4. À cause de sa forme, la France s'appelle aussi ___«l'Hexagone»___.
5. La ___SNCF___ offre la possibilité de voyager dans tout le pays.
6. Avec le ___TGV___, on voyage de Paris à Londres.
7. Les ___frères Lumière___ sont les inventeurs du cinéma.
8. ___Answers will vary. Possible answer: Jean Renoir___ est un grand cinéaste français.
9. La France est une grande puissance ___industrielle___.
10. Électricité de France produit (*produces*) ___l'énergie nucléaire___.

ressources
WB pp. 27-28 | espaces.vhlcentral.com

Practice more at **espaces.vhlcentral.com.**

SUR INTERNET

Go to **espaces.vhlcentral.com** to find more cultural information related to this **PANORAMA**.

1. Cherchez des informations sur l'Académie française. Faites (*Make*) une liste de mots ajoutés à la dernière édition du dictionnaire de l'Académie française.
2. Cherchez des informations sur l'actrice Catherine Deneuve. Quand a-t-elle commencé (*did she begin*) sa (*her*) carrière? Trouvez ses (*her*) trois derniers films.

Surnommé *Nicknamed* **à cause de** *because of* **mer** *sea* **Manche** *English Channel* **frontières** *borders* **pays** *country* **ponctuent** *punctuate* **fleuves** *rivers* **chemin de fer** *railroad* **depuis** *since* **se déplacer** *travel* **dans tout** *throughout* **tarifs** *fares* **moins de 25 ans** *people under 25* **Train à Grande Vitesse** *high speed train* **roule** *rolls, travels* **emmène** *takes* **jusqu'à** *all the way to* **frères** *brothers* **début** *beginning* **donne naissance** *gives birth* **César** *equivalent of the Oscars in France* **comme** *such as* **artisanat** *craft industry* **haute couture** *high fashion* **En fait** *In fact* **puissance** *power* **se classe** *ranks* **parmi** *among* **les plus** *the most* **Ses** *Its*

L'Hexagone Have students locate the geographical features mentioned on the map or use **Transparency #20**.

Le Train à Grande Vitesse
- The first **TGV** service was from Paris to Lyon in 1981. Since then, its service has expanded. Presently, the high-speed network has over 30,000 kilometers of track that connect over 150 cities and towns in France.
- Have students look at the photo and compare the **TGV** to the trains they have traveled on or seen in the United States. Then have them figure out the speed of the **TGV** in miles per hour (1 km = 0.62 mile). (300 km/h = 186 mph)

Le cinéma, le 7e art!
- Each year the members of **l'Académie des Arts et Techniques du Cinéma** choose the actors, actresses, directors, and others involved in film-making to receive the **César** awards for their outstanding achievements. The ceremony was named after the artist who designed the award trophies.
- The six traditional arts are **architecture**, **sculpture**, **peinture** (painting), **littérature**, **musique**, and **danse**.

L'industrie
- The craft industry, **l'Artisanat**, can be found throughout France. Using traditional methods that are centuries old, French artisans craft products, such as pottery and figurines, but also work as bakers, carpenters, confectioners, butchers, or masons. Each region's products reflect the history and culture of that particular area.
- Bring in some French craft items or magazine photos of items to show the class.

OPTIONS

Game Create categories for the newly learned information on France: **Géographie, Français célèbres, Technologie,** etc. Make index cards with a question on one side and category on the other. Tape cards to the board under the appropriate categories with questions face down. Teams take turns picking a card and answering the question. Give a point for each right answer. The team with the most points at the end wins.

Cultural Comparison Distribute a list in French of the award categories for the **César** from the website of **l'Académie des Arts et Techniques du Cinéma** (**www.lescesarducinema.com**). Ask if the same categories exist for the Oscars. Show them pictures of a **César** and an Oscar. Have students compare the trophies. Ask what other film festivals occur in France. (Cannes Film Festival and the American Film Festival)

Section Goals

In this section, students will:

- learn to use text formats to predict content
- read a brochure for a French language school

Stratégie
Tell students that many documents have easily identifiable formats that can help them predict the content. Have them look at the document in the **Stratégie** box and ask them to identify the recognizable elements:

- days of the week
- times
- classes

Ask what kind of document it is. (a student's weekly schedule)

Examinez le texte Have students look at the headings and ask them what type of information is contained in **École de français (pour étrangers) de Lille**. (lists of courses by level and specialization, a list of supplementary activities, and a list of types of housing available) Then ask students what types of documents contain these elements. (brochures)

Mots apparentés

- In pairs, have students scan the brochure, identify cognates, and guess their meanings.
- Ask students what this document is and its purpose. (It's a brochure. It's advertising a French language and culture immersion program. Its purpose is to attract students.)

Lecture

Reading

NATIONAL STANDARDS communication cultures

Avant la lecture

STRATÉGIE

Predicting content through formats

Recognizing the format of a document can help you to predict its content. For instance, invitations, greeting cards, and classified ads follow an easily identifiable format, which usually gives you a general idea of the information they contain. Look at the text and identify it based on its format.

	lundi	mardi	mercredi	jeudi	vendredi
8h30	*biologie*		*biologie*		*biologie*
9h00		*histoire*		*histoire*	
9h30	*anglais*		*anglais*		*anglais*
10h00					
10h30					
11h00					
11h30					
12h00					
12h30					
1h00	*art*		*art*		*art*

If you guessed that this is a page from a student's schedule, you are correct. You can now infer that the document contains information about a student's weekly schedule, including days, times, and activities.

Examinez le texte

Briefly look at the document. What is its format? What kind of information is given? How is it organized? Are there any visuals? What kind? What type(s) of documents usually contain these elements?

Mots apparentés

As you have already learned, in addition to format, you can use cognates to help you predict the content of a document. With a classmate, make a list of all the cognates you find in the reading selection. Based on these cognates and the format of the document, can you guess what this document is and what it's for?

ÉCOLE DE FRANÇAIS

(pour étrangers°) DE LILLE

COURS DE FRANÇAIS POUR TOUS°	COURS DE SPÉCIALISATION
Niveau° débutant°	Français pour enfants°
Niveau élémentaire	Français des affaires°
Niveau intermédiaire	Droit° français
Niveau avancé	Français pour le tourisme
Conversation	Culture et civilisation
Grammaire française	Histoire de France
	Art et littérature
	Arts culinaires

26, place d'Arsonval • 59000 Lille
Tél. 03.20.52.48.17 • Fax. 03.20.52.48.18 • www.efpelille.fr

OPTIONS

Extra Practice Have students write a friend's or family member's weekly schedule as homework. Tell them to label the days of the week in French and add notes for that person's appointments and activities. In class, ask students questions about the schedules they wrote. Examples: **Quel cours est-ce que ____ a aujourd'hui? Combien de jours est-ce que ____ travaille cette semaine?**

Cultural Activity Ask students what aspects of this school they find appealing or interesting: **Qu'est-ce que vous trouvez intéressant à l'école?** Jot down their responses on the board. Then do a quick class survey to find out which aspect is the most appealing.

Programmes de 2 à 8 semaines,
4 à 8 heures par jour
Immersion totale
Professeurs diplômés

le Musée des Beaux-Arts, Lille

GRAND CHOIX° D'ACTIVITÉS SUPPLÉMENTAIRES

- Excursions à la journée dans la région
- Visites de monuments et autres sites touristiques
- Sorties° culturelles (théâtre, concert, opéra et autres spectacles°)
- Sports et autres activités de loisir°

HÉBERGEMENT°

- En cité universitaire°
- Dans° une famille française
- À l'hôtel

pour étrangers *for foreigners* **tous** *all* **Niveau** *Level* **débutant** *beginner* **enfants** *children* **affaires** *business* **Droit** *Law* **choix** *choice* **Sorties** *Outings* **spectacles** *shows* **loisir** *leisure* **hébergement** *lodging* **cité universitaire** *university dormitories (on campus)* **Dans** *In*

Après la lecture

Répondez Select the correct response or completion to each question or statement, based on the reading selection.

1. C'est une brochure pour...
   a. des cours de français pour étrangers.
   b. une université française.
   c. des études supérieures en Belgique.
2. «Histoire de France» est...
   a. un cours pour les professeurs diplômés.
   b. un cours de spécialisation.
   c. un cours pour les enfants.
3. Le cours de «Français pour le tourisme» est utile pour...
   a. une étudiante qui (*who*) étudie les sciences po.
   b. une femme qui travaille dans un hôtel de luxe.
   c. un professeur d'administration des affaires.
4. Un étudiant étranger qui commence le français assiste probablement à quel (*which*) cours?
   a. Cours de français pour tous, Niveau avancé
   b. Cours de spécialisation, Art et littérature
   c. Cours de français pour tous, Niveau débutant
5. Quel cours est utile pour un homme qui parle assez bien français et qui travaille dans l'économie?
   a. Cours de spécialisation, Français des affaires
   b. Cours de spécialisation, Arts culinaires
   c. Cours de spécialisation, Culture et civilisation
6. Le week-end, les étudiants...
   a. passent des examens.
   b. travaillent dans des hôtels.
   c. visitent la ville et la région.
7. Les étudiants qui habitent dans une famille...
   a. ont envie de rencontrer des Français.
   b. ont des bourses.
   c. ne sont pas reçus aux examens.
8. Un étudiant en architecture va aimer...
   a. le cours de droit français.
   b. les visites de monuments et de sites touristiques.
   c. les activités sportives.

Complétez Complete these sentences.

1. Le numéro de téléphone est le 03.20.52.48.17.
2. Le numéro de fax est le 03.20.52.48.18.
3. L'adresse de l'école est 26, place d'Arsonval, 59000 Lille.
4. L'école offre des programmes de Français de 2 à 8 semaines et de 4 à 8 heures par jour.

Répondez Go over the answers with the whole class or have students check their answers in pairs.

Complétez For additional practice, give students these items. **5. L'école est à ____. (Lille) 6. L'adresse Internet de l'école est ____. (www.efpelille.fr) 7. «Grammaire française» est un cours de ____. (français pour tous) 8. Les professeurs de l'école sont ____. (diplômés) 9. On habite en cité universitaire, ____ ou à l'hôtel. (dans une famille française)**

Suggestion Encourage students to record unfamiliar words and phrases that they learn in **Lecture** in their notebooks.

OPTIONS

Small Groups Provide students with magazines and newspapers in French. Have groups of three or four students work together to look for documents in French with easily recognizable formats, such as classified ads or other advertisements. Ask them to use cognates and other context clues to predict the content. Then have groups present their examples and findings to the class.

Oral Presentation Invite a student who has studied abroad to come and speak to the class about the school he or she attended, the classes, and any interesting experiences he or she had there. Encourage the class to ask questions.

Section Goals

In this section, students will:

- learn to brainstorm and organize their ideas for writing
- learn to write a description of themselves
- integrate vocabulary and structures taught in **Leçon 2B** and previous lessons

Stratégie Discuss information students might want to include in a self-description, recording their suggestions on the board in French. Quickly review structures students will include in their writing, such as **j'aime** and **je n'aime pas** as well as the first person singular of several verbs. Examples: **je m'appelle, je suis, j'étudie, j'ai cours de…,** and **je travaille**.

Thème Copy on the board the brief chat room description for Xavier Dupré, leaving blanks where his name, nationality, course of study, and university name appear. At the end, add the sentences **J'aime ____.** and **Je n'aime pas ____.** Model completing the description orally with your own information and then ask volunteers to complete it with their own information.

Écriture

NATIONAL STANDARDS communication cultures

STRATÉGIE

Brainstorming

How do you find ideas to write about? In the early stages of writing, brainstorming can help you generate ideas on a specific topic. You should spend ten to fifteen minutes brainstorming and jotting down any ideas about the topic that occur to you. Whenever possible, try to write down your ideas in French. Express your ideas in single words or phrases, and jot them down in any order. While brainstorming, do not worry about whether your ideas are good or bad. Selecting and organizing ideas should be the second stage of your writing. Remember that the more ideas you write down while brainstorming, the more options you will have to choose from later when you start to organize your ideas.

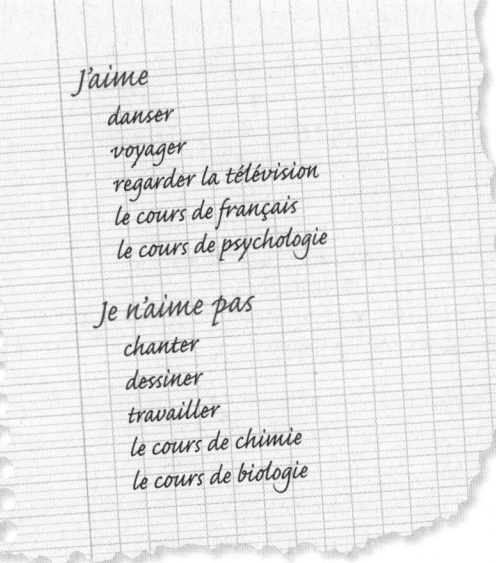

J'aime
danser
voyager
regarder la télévision
le cours de français
le cours de psychologie

Je n'aime pas
chanter
dessiner
travailler
le cours de chimie
le cours de biologie

Thème

Une description personnelle

Avant l'écriture

1. Write a description of yourself to post on a website in order to find a francophone e-pal. Your description should include:

   - your name and where you are from
   - the name of your school and where it is located
   - the courses you are currently taking and your opinion of each one
   - some of your likes and dislikes
   - where you work if you have a job
   - any other information you would like to include

   Use a chart like this one to brainstorm information about your likes and dislikes.

J'aime	Je n'aime pas

OPTIONS

Avant l'écriture Demonstrate how to brainstorm ideas about a topic. Choose a celebrity everyone knows and use a word web to brainstorm ideas about what that person likes and dislikes. Once you have generated 10-12 ideas, choose one of them and brainstorm words related to it.

Have pairs ask each other questions about their likes and dislikes using **j'aime** and **je n'aime pas**. Each student writes down the other's answers, then they exchange their lists in order to use them as a basis for the writing task. Before students begin writing, help them personalize their lists by supplying any unknown vocabulary they may need.

2. Now take the information about your likes and dislikes and fill out this new chart to help you organize the content of your description.

Je m'appelle...	(name).
Je suis de...	(where you are from).
J'étudie...	(names of classes) à/au/à la (name of school).
Je ne travaille pas./ Je travaille à/au/ à la/chez...	(place where you work).
J'aime...	(activities you like).
Je n'aime pas...	(activities you dislike).

Écriture

Use the information from the second chart to write a paragraph describing yourself. Make sure you include all the information from the chart in your paragraph. Use the structures provided for each topic.

Bonjour!

Je m'appelle Michael Adams. Je suis américain. J'étudie le droit à l'Université de Chicago. Je travaille au restaurant Students' Corner. J'aime parler avec des amis, lire (*read*), écouter de la musique et voyager, parce que j'aime rencontrer des gens. Par contre, je n'aime pas le sport...

Après l'écriture

1. Exchange a rough draft of your description with a partner. Comment on his or her work by answering these questions:

- Did your partner include all the necessary information (at least six facts)?
- Did your partner use the structures provided in the chart?
- Did your partner use the vocabulary of the unit?
- Did your partner use the grammar of the unit?

2. Revise your description according to your partner's comments. After writing the final version, read it one more time to eliminate these kinds of problems:

- spelling errors
- punctuation errors
- capitalization errors
- use of incorrect verb forms
- use of incorrect adjective agreement
- use of incorrect definite and indefinite articles

EVALUATION

Criteria

Content Includes all the information mentioned in the six bulleted items in the description of the task.
Scale: 1 2 3 4 5

Organization Organizes the description similarly to the model provided.
Scale: 1 2 3 4 5

Accuracy Uses **j'aime/je n'aime pas**, regular **-er** verbs, and negation patterns correctly. Words are spelled correctly and adjectives agree with the nouns they modify.
Scale: 1 2 3 4 5

Creativity Includes additional information that is not specified in the task and makes an effort to create longer sentences with a number of items.
Scale: 1 2 3 4 5

Scoring

Excellent	18–20 points
Good	14–17 points
Satisfactory	10–13 points
Unsatisfactory	< 10 points

OPTIONS

Écriture Before students begin writing, give them some transition words they may want to incorporate into their descriptions. Words and expressions such as **mais**, **parce que**, **alors**, **pourtant**, **par contre**, **ou**, and **et** can be used to make sentences longer and to make transitions between them.

Après l'écriture Once students have written their descriptions, choose several among those and ask the authors for their permission to read them aloud. As you read each one, see if the class can guess whom it is describing, based on the likes, dislikes, and other information included.

Instructional Resources
espaces.vhlcentral.com: Textbook MP3s; IRM (Textbook Audioscript); downloads; reference tools

Suggestion Tell students that an easy way to study from **Vocabulaire** is to cover up the French half of each section, leaving only the English equivalents exposed. They can then quiz themselves on the French items. To focus on the English equivalents of the French entries, they simply reverse this process.

Verbes

adorer	*to love*
aimer	*to like; to love*
aimer mieux	*to prefer*
arriver	*to arrive*
chercher	*to look for*
commencer	*to begin, to start*
dessiner	*to draw*
détester	*to hate*
donner	*to give*
étudier	*to study*
habiter (à/en)	*to live in*
manger	*to eat*
oublier	*to forget*
parler (au téléphone)	*to speak (on the phone)*
partager	*to share*
penser (que/qu')	*to think (that)*
regarder	*to look (at), to watch*
rencontrer	*to meet*
retrouver	*to meet up with; to find (again)*
travailler	*to work*
voyager	*to travel*

Vocabulaire supplémentaire

J'adore...	*I love...*
J'aime bien...	*I like...*
Je n'aime pas tellement...	*I don't like... very much.*
Je déteste...	*I hate...*
être reçu(e) à un examen	*to pass an exam*

Des questions et des opinions

bien sûr	*of course*
d'accord	*OK, all right*
Est-ce que/qu'...?	*question phrase*
(mais) non	*no (but of course not)*
moi/toi non plus	*me/you neither*
ne... pas	*no, not*
n'est-ce pas?	*isn't that right?*
oui/si	*yes*
parce que	*because*
pas du tout	*not at all*
peut-être	*maybe, perhaps*
pourquoi?	*why?*

ressources
espaces.vhlcentral.com

L'université

assister	*to attend*
demander	*to ask*
dîner	*to have dinner*
échouer	*to fail*
écouter	*to listen (to)*
enseigner	*to teach*
expliquer	*to explain*
passer un examen	*to take an exam*
préparer	*to prepare (for)*
rentrer (à la maison)	*to return (home)*
téléphoner à	*to telephone*
trouver	*to find; to think*
visiter	*to visit (a place)*
l'architecture (*f.*)	*architecture*
l'art (*m.*)	*art*
la biologie	*biology*
la chimie	*chemistry*
le droit	*law*
l'économie (*f.*)	*economics*
l'éducation physique (*f.*)	*physical education*
la géographie	*geography*
la gestion	*business administration*
l'histoire (*f.*)	*history*
l'informatique (*f.*)	*computer science*
les langues (étrangères) (*f.*)	*(foreign) languages*
les lettres (*f.*)	*humanities*
les mathématiques (maths) (*f.*)	*mathematics*
la philosophie	*philosophy*
la physique	*physics*
la psychologie	*psychology*
les sciences (politiques/po) (*f.*)	*(political) science*
le stylisme	*fashion design*
une bourse	*scholarship, grant*
un cours	*class, course*
un devoir	*homework*
un diplôme	*diploma, degree*
l'école (*f.*)	*school*
les études (supérieures) (*f.*)	*(higher) education; studies*
le gymnase	*gymnasium*
une note	*grade*
un restaurant universitaire (un resto U)	*university cafeteria*

Expressions utiles	*See pp. 43 and 57.*
Telling time	*See pp. 62–63.*

Expressions de temps

Quel jour sommes-nous?	*What day is it?*
un an	*year*
une/cette année	*one/this year*
après	*after*
après-demain	*day after tomorrow*
un/cet après-midi	*an/this afternoon*
aujourd'hui	*today*
demain (matin/après-midi/soir)	*tomorrow (morning/afternoon/evening)*
un jour	*day*
une journée	*day*
(le) lundi, mardi, mercredi, jeudi, vendredi, samedi, dimanche	*(on) Monday(s), Tuesday(s), Wednesday(s), Thursday(s), Friday(s), Saturday(s), Sunday(s)*
un/ce matin	*a/this morning*
la matinée	*morning*
un mois/ce mois-ci	*a month/this month*
une/cette nuit	*a/this night*
une/cette semaine	*a/this week*
un/ce soir	*an/this evening*
une soirée	*evening*
un/le/ce week-end	*a/the/this weekend*
dernier/dernière	*last*
premier/première	*first*
prochain(e)	*next*

Adjectifs et adverbes

difficile	*difficult*
facile	*easy*
inutile	*useless*
utile	*useful*
surtout	*especially; above all*

Expressions avec avoir

avoir	*to have*
avoir... ans	*to be... years old*
avoir besoin (de)	*to need*
avoir chaud	*to be hot*
avoir de la chance	*to be lucky*
avoir envie (de)	*to feel like*
avoir froid	*to be cold*
avoir honte (de)	*to be ashamed (of)*
avoir l'air	*to look like*
avoir peur (de)	*to be afraid (of)*
avoir raison	*to be right*
avoir sommeil	*to be sleepy*
avoir tort	*to be wrong*

La famille et les copains

UNITÉ 3

Leçon 3A

ESPACE CONTEXTES
pages 74–77
- Family, friends, and pets
- **L'accent aigu** and **l'accent grave**

ESPACE ROMAN-PHOTO
pages 78–79
- **L'album de photos**

ESPACE CULTURE
pages 80–81
- The family in France
- **Flash culture**

ESPACE STRUCTURES
pages 82–85
- Descriptive adjectives
- Possessive adjectives

ESPACE SYNTHÈSE
pages 86–87
- **Révision**
- **Le zapping**

Leçon 3B

ESPACE CONTEXTES
pages 88–91
- More descriptive adjectives
- Professions and occupations
- **L'accent circonflexe**, **la cédille**, and **le tréma**

ESPACE ROMAN-PHOTO
pages 92–93
- **On travaille chez moi!**

ESPACE CULTURE
pages 94–95
- Relationships

ESPACE STRUCTURES
pages 96–99
- Numbers 61–100
- Prepositions of location

ESPACE SYNTHÈSE
pages 100–101
- **Révision**
- **À l'écoute**

Pour commencer
- Combien de personnes y a-t-il?
- Où sont ces personnes?
- Que font-elles?
- Ont-elles l'air agréables ou désagréables?

Savoir-faire
pages 102–107
Panorama: Paris
Lecture: Read a short article about pets.
Écriture: Write a letter to a friend.

Unit Goals

Leçon 3A
In this lesson, students will learn:
- words for family members and marital status
- some words for pets
- usage of **l'accent aigu** and **l'accent grave**
- about the French family
- more about families and friends through specially shot video footage
- descriptive adjectives
- possessive adjectives
- about the Belgian company **Pages d'Or**

Leçon 3B
In this lesson, students will learn:
- words for some professions and occupations
- more descriptive adjectives
- usage of **l'accent circonflexe, la cédille**, and **le tréma**
- about different types of friendships and relationships
- the numbers 61–100
- some prepositions of location
- disjunctive pronouns
- to ask for repetition in oral communication

Savoir-faire
In this section, students will learn:
- historical and cultural information about Paris
- to use visuals and graphic elements to predict content
- to use idea maps to organize information
- to write an informal letter

Pour commencer
- **Il y a trois personnes.**
- **Elles sont dans un café.**
- **Elles ne mangent pas. Elles parlent.**
- **Elles ont l'air agréables.**

RESOURCES

Workbook/Video Manual: WB Activities, pp. 29–42
Laboratory Manual: Lab Activities, pp. 17–24
Workbook/Video Manual: Video Activities, pp. 219–222; pp. 275–276
WB/VM/LM Answer Key
espaces.vhlcentral.com: Textbook MP3s; Lab MP3s; Instructor's Resource Manual [IRM] (Textbook Audioscript; Lab Audioscript; Videoscript; **Roman-photo** Translations; **Vocabulaire supplémentaire**; **Feuilles d'activités**; Info Gap Activities; **Essayez!** and **Mise en pratique** answers; Transparencies #21, #22, #23, #24; Testing Program, pp. 17–24, pp. 121–128; Test Files; Testing Program MP3s
Test Generator
Video on DVD

Section Goals

In this section, students will learn and practice vocabulary related to:

- family members
- some pets
- marital status

Instructional Resources
*espaces.vhlcentral.com: Transparencies #21, #22; IRM (**Vocabulaire supplémentaire**; **Mise en pratique** answers; Textbook Audioscript; Lab Audioscript; **Feuilles d'activités**); Textbook MP3s; Lab MP3s; WB/VM/LM Answer Key; activities; downloads; reference tools*

Suggestions

- Introduce active lesson vocabulary with questions and gestures. Ask: **Comment s'appelle ton frère?** Ask a different student: **Comment s'appelle le frère de ____?** Work your way through various family relationships.
- Point out the meanings of plural family terms so students understand that the masculine plural forms can refer to mixed groups of males and females: **les enfants** *male children; male and female children* **les cousins** *male cousins; male and female cousins* **les petits-enfants** *male grandchildren; male and female grandchildren*
- Point out the difference in meaning between the noun **mari** (*husband*) and the adjective **marié(e)** (*married*).
- Use **Transparency #21.** Point out that the family tree is drawn from the point of view of Marie Laval. Have students refer to the family tree to answer your questions about it. Example: **Comment s'appelle la mère de Marie?**
- Additional vocabulary for this lesson can be found in the **Vocabulaire supplémentaire** on the Supersite.

Leçon 3A

Talking Picture
Audio: Activity

You will learn how to...

- discuss family, friends, and pets
- express ownership

La famille de Marie Laval

Vocabulaire

divorcer	*to divorce*
épouser	*to marry*
aîné(e)	*elder*
cadet(te)	*younger*
un beau-frère	*brother-in-law*
un beau-père	*father-in-law; stepfather*
une belle-mère	*mother-in-law; stepmother*
un demi-frère	*half-brother; stepbrother*
une demi-sœur	*half-sister; stepsister*
les enfants (*m., f.*)	*children*
un(e) époux/épouse	*husband/wife*
une famille	*family*
une femme	*wife; woman*
une fille	*daughter; girl*
les grands-parents (*m.*)	*grandparents*
les parents (*m.*)	*parents*
un(e) voisin(e)	*neighbor*
un chat	*cat*
un oiseau	*bird*
un poisson	*fish*
célibataire	*single*
divorcé(e)	*divorced*
fiancé(e)	*engaged*
marié(e)	*married*
séparé(e)	*separated*
veuf/veuve	*widowed*

ressources
WB pp. 29–30 | LM p. 17 | espaces.vhlcentral.com

OPTIONS

Extra Practice Draw your own family tree on a transparency or the board and label it with names. Ask students questions about it. Examples: **Est-ce que ____ est ma sœur ou ma tante? Comment s'appelle ma grand-mère? ____ est le neveu ou le frère de ____? Qui est le grand-père de ____?** Help them identify the relationships between members. Then invite them to ask you questions.

Les noms de famille français Ask for a show of hands to see if any students' last names are French in origin. Examples: names that begin with **Le____** or **La____** such as **Leblanc** or **Larose**, or even names such as **Fitzgerald** or **Fitzpatrick** (**Fitz-** = **fils de**). Ask these students what they know about their French heritage or family history.

Mise en pratique

1 Qui est-ce? Match the definition in the first list with the correct item from the second list. Not all the items will be used.

1. _d_ le frère de ma cousine
2. _g_ le père de mon cousin
3. _a_ le mari de ma grand-mère
4. _e_ le fils de mon frère
5. _c_ la fille de mon grand-père
6. _i_ le fils de ma mère
7. _h_ la fille de mon fils
8. _f_ le fils de ma belle-mère

a. mon grand-père
b. ma sœur
c. ma tante
d. mon cousin
e. mon neveu
f. mon demi-frère
g. mon oncle
h. ma petite-fille
i. mon frère

2 Choisissez Fill in the blank by selecting the most appropriate answer.

1. Voici le frère de mon père. C'est mon _oncle_ (oncle, neveu, fiancé).
2. Voici la mère de ma cousine. C'est ma _tante_ (grand-mère, voisine, tante).
3. Voici la petite-fille de ma grand-mère. C'est ma _cousine_ (cousine, nièce, épouse).
4. Voici le père de ma mère. C'est mon _grand-père_ (grand-père, oncle, cousin).
5. Voici le fils de mon père, mais ce n'est pas le fils de ma mère. C'est mon _demi-frère_ (petit-fils, demi-frère, voisin).

3 Complétez Complete each sentence with the appropriate word.

1. Voici ma nièce. C'est la _petite-fille_ de ma mère.
2. Voici la mère de ma tante. C'est ma _grand-mère_.
3. Voici la sœur de mon oncle. C'est ma _tante_.
4. Voici la fille de mon père, mais pas de ma mère. C'est ma _demi-sœur_.
5. Voici le mari de ma mère, mais ce n'est pas mon père. C'est mon _beau-père_.

4 Écoutez Listen to each statement made by Marie Laval. Based on her family tree, indicate whether it is **vrai** or **faux**.

	Vrai	Faux
1.	☑	☐
2.	☐	☑
3.	☑	☐
4.	☐	☑
5.	☐	☑
6.	☐	☑
7.	☐	☑
8.	☑	☐
9.	☑	☐
10.	☑	☐

Practice more at **espaces.vhlcentral.com.**

Successful Language Learning Tell students that it isn't necessary to understand every word they hear in French. They will feel less anxious if they listen for general meaning.

1 Suggestion Mention that adjectives such as **beau** and **petit** in hyphenated family terms must agree in gender. Exceptions: **la grand-mère, la demi-sœur.**

2 & 3 Expansion Have students provide additional examples for the class to identify.

4 Tapescript
1. Marc est mon oncle.
2. Émilie est la nièce de Véronique.
3. Jean est le petit-fils d'Hélène.
4. Robert est mon grand-père.
5. Luc est le père de Sophie.
6. Isabelle est ma tante.
7. Matthieu est le fils de Jean.
8. Émilie est la fille de Guillaume.
9. Juliette est ma mère.
10. Virginie est ma cousine.
(On Textbook MP3s)

4 Expansion Play Marie's statements again, stopping at the end of each. Where the statements are true, have students repeat. Where the statements are false, have students correct them by referring to Marie Laval's family tree.

OPTIONS

Game As a class or group activity, have students state the relationship between people on Marie Laval's family tree. Their classmates will guess which person on the family tree they are describing. Example: **C'est la sœur de Jean et la fille de Sophie. (Isabelle ou Véronique)** Take turns until each member of the class or group has had a chance to state a relationship.

Extra Practice Have students draw their own family tree as homework. Tell them to label each position on the tree with the appropriate French term and the person's name. Also tell them to write five fill-in-the-blank statements based on their family tree. Examples: **Je suis la fille de ____. Mon frère s'appelle ____.** In the next class, have students exchange papers with a classmate and complete the activity.

5 Suggestion Use **Transparency #22** for this activity.

6 Suggestion Tell students to jot down their partner's responses.

6 Expansion After they have finished the interview, ask students questions about their partner's answers. Examples: **Combien de personnes y a-t-il dans la famille de ____? Comment s'appellent les parents de ____?**

7 Suggestion Have two volunteers read the **modèle**. Then distribute the **Feuilles d'activités** from the Supersite.

7 Expansion After students have finished, ask true/false questions. Example: **Est-ce que ____ est marié(e)?**

Communication

5 **L'arbre généalogique** With a classmate, identify the members of the family by asking how each one is related to Anne Durand. Answers will vary.

MODÈLE

Étudiant(e) 1: *Qui est Louis Durand?*
Étudiant(e) 2: *C'est le grand-père d'Anne.*

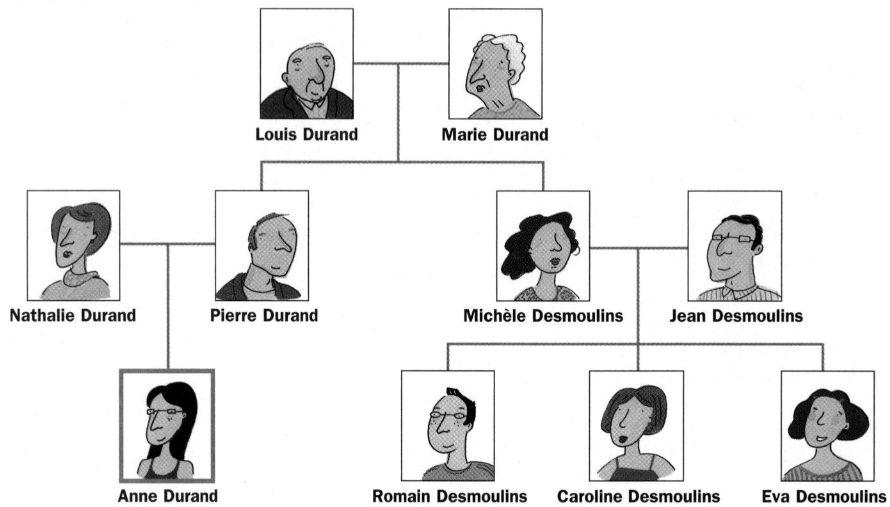

6 **Entrevue** With a classmate, take turns asking each other these questions. Answers will vary.

1. Combien de personnes y a-t-il dans ta famille?
2. Comment s'appellent tes parents?
3. As-tu des frères et sœurs?
4. Combien de cousins/cousines as-tu? Comment s'appellent-ils/elles? Où habitent-ils/elles?
5. Quel(le) (*Which*) est ton cousin préféré/ta cousine préférée?
6. As-tu des neveux/des nièces?
7. Comment s'appellent tes grands-parents? Où habitent-ils?
8. Combien de petits-enfants ont tes grands-parents?

Coup de main

Use these words to help you complete this activity.

ton *your (m.)* → **mon** *my (m.)*
ta *your (f.)* → **ma** *my (f.)*
tes *your (pl.)* → **mes** *my (pl.)*

7 **Qui suis-je?** Your instructor will give you a worksheet. Walk around the class and ask your classmates questions about their families. When a classmate gives one of the answers on the worksheet, write his or her name in the corresponding space. Be prepared to discuss the results with the class. Answers will vary.

MODÈLE Je suis marié(e).

Étudiant(e) 1: *Est-ce que tu es mariée?*
Étudiant(e) 2: *Oui, je suis mariée.* (*You write the student's name.*)/*Non, je ne suis pas mariée.* (*You ask another classmate.*)

OPTIONS

Extra Practice Have students bring in some family photos. In pairs, tell them to take turns pointing to people in their partner's photo and asking who it is. Example: **Qui est-ce? (C'est mon/ma ____.)** Model a few examples. If necessary, write the question and a sample response on the board.

TPR Make a family tree using the whole class. Have each student write down the family designation you assign him or her on a note card or sheet of paper, then arrange students as in a family tree with each one displaying the note card. Then, ask questions about relationships. Examples: **Qui est la mère de ____? Comment s'appelle l'oncle de ____?** Give students the opportunity to ask questions by switching roles with them.

Les sons et les lettres

Audio: Concepts, Activities
Record & Compare

NATIONAL comparisons STANDARDS

L'accent aigu and l'accent grave

In French, diacritical marks (*accents*) are an essential part of a word's spelling. They indicate how vowels are pronounced or distinguish between words with similar spellings but different meanings. **L'accent aigu** (´) appears only over the vowel **e**. It indicates that the **e** is pronounced similarly to the vowel *a* in the English word *cake*, but shorter and crisper.

étudier **réservé** **élégant** **téléphone**

L'accent aigu also signals some similarities between French and English words. Often, an **e** with **l'accent aigu** at the beginning of a French word marks the place where the letter *s* would appear at the beginning of the English equivalent.

éponge	**épouse**	**état**	**étudiante**
sponge	*spouse*	*state*	*student*

L'accent grave (`) appears only over the vowels **a**, **e**, and **u**. Over the vowel **e**, it indicates that the **e** is pronounced like the vowel *e* in the English word *pet*.

très **après** **mère** **nièce**

Although **l'accent grave** does not change the pronunciation of the vowels **a** or **u**, it distinguishes words that have a similar spelling but different meanings.

la	**là**	**ou**	**où**
the	*there*	*or*	*where*

Prononcez Practice saying these words aloud.

1. agréable
2. sincère
3. voilà
4. faculté
5. frère
6. à
7. déjà
8. éléphant
9. lycée
10. poème
11. là
12. élève

Articulez Practice saying these sentences aloud.

1. À tout à l'heure!
2. Thérèse, je te présente Michèle.
3. Hélène est très sérieuse et réservée.
4. Voilà mon père, Frédéric, et ma mère, Ségolène.
5. Tu préfères étudier à la fac demain après-midi?

Dictons Practice reading these sayings aloud.

1 Like father, like son.
2 For an old mule, a golden bit.

ressources
LM p. 18
espaces.vhlcentral.com

Section Goals

In this section, students will learn about:
- **l'accent aigu**
- **l'accent grave**
- a strategy for recognizing cognates

Instructional Resources
espaces.vhlcentral.com: Textbook MP3s; Lab MP3s; WB/VM/LM Answer Key; IRM (Textbook Audioscript; Lab Audioscript); activities; downloads; reference tools

Suggestions
- Write **é** on the board. Tell students to watch your mouth as you pronounce the sound. Explain that when **é** appears at the beginning of a word, the corners of your mouth are slightly turned up and your tongue is low behind your bottom teeth. Have students repeat **é** after you several times.
- Write words and/or French names from the Laval family with **l'accent aigu** on the board. Pronounce each word as you point to it and have students repeat it after you. Examples: **époux**, **célibataire**, **fiancé**, **séparé**, **Émilie**, and **Véronique**.
- Give students some sample sentences with **la**, **là**, **ou**, or **où** and ask them what the words mean to demonstrate how context clarifies meaning. Examples: **1. Où est la fille? 2. La fille est là. 3. Est-ce que Sophie est la tante ou la grand-mère de Marie Laval?**
- Ask students to provide more examples of words they know with these accents.
- The explanation and exercises are available on the **ESPACES** Supersite. You may want to play them in class so students hear French speakers besides yourself.

Dictons Explain to students that the saying **«À vieille mule, frein doré»** applies to a situation in which someone tries to sell something old by dressing it up or decorating it. For example, to have a better chance at selling an old car, give it a new paint job.

OPTIONS

Extra Practice Here are additional sentences to use for extra practice with **l'accent aigu** and **l'accent grave**. **1. Étienne est mon frère préféré. 2. Ma sœur aînée est très occupée avec les études. 3. André et Geneviève sont séparés. 4. Vous êtes marié ou célibataire? 5. Éric et Sabine sont fiancés.**

Game Have a spelling bee using words with **l'accent aigu** and/or **l'accent grave** from **Leçon 3A** or previous lessons. Divide the class into two teams. Call on one team member at a time, alternating between teams. Give a point for each correct answer. The team with the most points at the end of the game wins. Before students begin, remind them that they must indicate the accent marks in the words. Give them an example: **très T-R-E accent grave-S**.

Section Goals

In this section, students will learn functional phrases for talking about their families and describing people through comprehensible input.

Instructional Resources
espaces.vhlcentral.com: WB/VM/LM Answer Key; IRM (Videoscript; ***Roman-photo*** *Translations); activities; downloads; reference tools*
Video on DVD

Video Recap: Leçon 2B

Before doing this **Roman-photo**, review the previous one with this activity.

1. Comment s'appelle la copine de Stéphane? (Astrid)
2. Qu'est-ce qu'elle pense de Stéphane? (Answers will vary. **Elle pense qu'il n'est pas sérieux, qu'il ne fait pas ses devoirs et qu'il n'écoute pas en classe.)**
3. Qui téléphone à Sandrine? (Pascal)
4. Comment Stéphane prépare-t-il le bac? (Il étudie les maths avec Rachid.)

Video Synopsis

Michèle wants to know what Amina's friend, Cyberhomme, looks like. Valérie describes her brother's family as she, Stéphane, and Amina look at their photos. Valérie keeps pointing out all the people who have their **bac** because she thinks Stéphane is not studying enough to pass his **bac**. To ease his mother's mind, Stéphane finally tells her that Rachid is helping him study.

Suggestions

- Ask students to read the title, glance at the video stills, and predict what they think the episode will be about. Record their predictions.
- Have students work in groups of four. Tell them to choose a role and read the **Roman-photo** conversation aloud.
- After students have read the **Roman-photo**, quickly review their predictions and ask them which ones were correct. Then ask a few questions to help guide students in summarizing this episode.

NATIONAL STANDARDS communication cultures

L'album de photos

Video: *Roman-photo*
Record & Compare

PERSONNAGES

Amina

Michèle

Stéphane

Valérie

MICHÈLE Mais, qui c'est? C'est ta sœur? Tes parents?
AMINA C'est mon ami Cyberhomme.
MICHÈLE Comment est-il? Est-ce qu'il est beau? Il a les yeux de quelle couleur? Marron ou bleue? Et ses cheveux? Ils sont blonds ou châtains?
AMINA Je ne sais pas.
MICHÈLE Toi, tu es timide.

VALÉRIE Stéphane, tu as dix-sept ans. Cette année, tu passes le bac, mais tu ne travailles pas!
STÉPHANE Écoute, ce n'est pas vrai, je déteste mes cours, mais je travaille beaucoup. Regarde, mon cahier de chimie, mes livres de français, ma calculatrice pour le cours de maths, mon dictionnaire anglais-français...

STÉPHANE Oh, et qu'est-ce que c'est? Ah, oui, les photos de tante Françoise.
VALÉRIE Des photos? Mais où?
STÉPHANE Ici! Amina, on peut regarder des photos de ma tante sur ton ordinateur, s'il te plaît?

AMINA Ah, et ça, c'est toute la famille, n'est-ce pas?
VALÉRIE Oui, ça, c'est Henri, sa femme, Françoise, et leurs enfants: le fils aîné, Bernard, et puis son frère, Charles, sa sœur, Sophie, et leur chien, Socrate.
STÉPHANE J'aime bien Socrate. Il est vieux, mais il est amusant!

VALÉRIE Ah! Et Bernard, il a son bac aussi et sa mère est très heureuse.
STÉPHANE Moi, j'ai envie d'habiter avec oncle Henri et tante Françoise. Comme ça, pas de problème pour le bac!

STÉPHANE Pardon, maman. Je suis très heureux ici, avec toi. Ah, au fait, Rachid travaille avec moi pour préparer le bac.
VALÉRIE Ah, bon? Rachid est très intelligent... un étudiant sérieux.

ACTIVITÉS

1 Vrai ou faux? Are these sentences **vrai** or **faux**? Correct the false ones.

1. Amina communique avec sa (*her*) tante par ordinateur. Faux. Elle communique avec Cyberhomme.
2. Stéphane n'aime pas ses (*his*) cours au lycée. Vrai.
3. Ils regardent des photos de vacances. Faux. Ils regardent les photos de tante Françoise.
4. Henri est le frère aîné de Valérie. Vrai.
5. Bernard est le cousin de Stéphane. Vrai.
6. Charles a déjà son bac. Vrai.
7. La tante de Stéphane s'appelle Françoise. Vrai.
8. Stéphane travaille avec Amina pour préparer le bac. Faux. Il travaille avec Rachid.
9. Socrate est le fils d'Henri et de Françoise. Faux. C'est le chien d'Henri et de Françoise.
10. Rachid n'est pas un bon étudiant. Faux. C'est un étudiant sérieux.

Practice more at **espaces.vhlcentral.com.**

OPTIONS

Avant de regarder la vidéo Before students view the video episode **L'album de photos**, ask them to brainstorm a list of things someone might say when describing his or her family photos.

Regarder la vidéo Play the first half of the video episode and have students describe what happened. Write their observations on the board. Then ask them to guess what will happen in the second half of the episode. Write their ideas on the board. Play the entire video episode; then help the class summarize the plot.

Stéphane et Valérie regardent des photos de famille avec Amina.

4

À la table d'Amina...

AMINA Alors, voilà vos photos. Qui est-ce?

VALÉRIE Oh, c'est Henri, mon frère aîné!

AMINA Quel âge a-t-il?

VALÉRIE Il a cinquante ans. Il est très sociable et c'est un très bon père.

5

VALÉRIE Ah! Et ça, c'est ma nièce Sophie et mon neveu Charles! Regarde, Stéphane, tes cousins!

STÉPHANE Je n'aime pas Charles. Il est tellement sérieux.

VALÉRIE Il est peut-être trop sérieux, mais, lui, il a son bac!

AMINA Et Sophie, qu'elle est jolie!

VALÉRIE ... et elle a déjà son bac.

9

AMINA Ça, oui, préparer le bac avec Rachid, c'est une idée géniale!

10

VALÉRIE Oui, c'est vrai. En théorie, c'est une excellente idée. Mais tu prépares le bac avec Rachid, hein? Pas le prochain match de foot!

Expressions utiles

Talking about your family

- **C'est ta sœur? Ce sont tes parents?**
  Is that your sister? Are those your parents?
- **C'est mon ami.**
  That's my friend.
- **Ça, c'est Henri, sa femme, Françoise, et leurs enfants.**
  That's Henri, his wife, Françoise, and their kids.

Describing people

- **Il a les yeux de quelle couleur? Marron ou bleue?**
  What color are his eyes? Brown or blue?
- **Il a les yeux bleus.**
  He has blue eyes.
- **Et ses cheveux? Ils sont blonds ou châtains? Frisés ou raides?**
  And his hair? Is it blond or brown? Curly or straight?
- **Il a les cheveux châtains et frisés.**
  He has curly brown hair.

Additional vocabulary

- **On peut regarder des photos de ma tante sur ton ordinateur?**
  Can/May we look at some photos from my aunt on your computer?
- **C'est toute la famille, n'est-ce pas?**
  That's the whole family, right?
- **Je ne sais pas (encore).**
  I (still) don't know.
- **Alors...** *So...*
- **vrai** *true*
- **une photo(graphie)** *a photograph*
- **une idée** *an idea*
- **peut-être** *maybe*
- **au fait** *by the way*
- **Hein?** *Right?*
- **déjà** *already*

ACTIVITÉS

2 Vocabulaire Choose the adjective that describes how Stéphane would feel on these occasions. Refer to a dictionary as necessary.

1. on his 87th birthday vieux
2. after finding 20€ heureux
3. while taking the bac sérieux
4. after getting a good grade heureux
5. after dressing for a party beau

beau
heureux
sérieux
vieux

3 Conversez In pairs, describe which member of your family is most like Stéphane. How are they alike? Do they both like sports? Do they take similar courses? How do they like school? How are their personalities? Be prepared to describe your partner's "Stéphane" to the class.

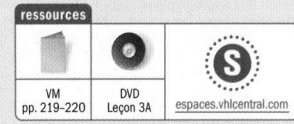

ressources
VM pp. 219-220 | DVD Leçon 3A | espaces.vhlcentral.com

OPTIONS

Pairs Working in pairs, have students draw a family tree based on Valérie's description of her brother's family. Tell them to use the family tree on page 74 as a model. Remind them to include Valérie and Stéphane. Then have them get together with another pair of students and compare their drawings.

Small Groups Have students write four questions about Henri's family based on the conversation and video still #6. Then have them get together in groups of three and take turns asking and answering each other's questions. Examples: **Combien de personnes y a-t-il dans la famille d'Henri? Comment s'appelle le fils aîné? Combien de frères a Sophie?**

Expressions utiles

- Point out the various forms of possessive adjectives and descriptive adjectives in the captions and the **Expressions utiles.** Tell students that this material will be formally presented in the **Structures** section. Do not expect students to produce the forms correctly at this time.
- Model the pronunciation of the **Expressions utiles** and have students repeat them.
- To practice new vocabulary, ask students to describe their classmates' eyes and hair. Examples: ____ **a les yeux de quelle couleur? Marron ou bleue? Avez-vous les yeux bleus?** ____ **a-t-il/elle les cheveux blonds ou châtains? Qui a les cheveux blonds/châtains dans la classe? Est-ce que les cheveux de** ____ **sont frisés ou raides?**

1 Suggestion Have students correct the false statements.

1 Expansion For additional practice, give students these items. **11. Valérie n'aime pas son frère, Henri. (Faux.) 12. Stéphane aime les gens très sérieux. (Faux.) 13. Socrate est un chien. (Vrai.) 14. Stéphane et Rachid préparent le prochain match de foot. (Faux.)**

2 Suggestion Before students begin the activity, you might want to introduce the adjectives in the word list using pictures or people in the video stills, rather than having students look them up in the dictionary.

2 Expansion Have students describe Rachid, Charles, and Henri using the adjectives in the word list. At this point, avoid asking students to describe people that would require a feminine or plural form of these adjectives.

3 Suggestion If time is limited, this activity may be assigned as a written composition for homework.

connections cultures NATIONAL STANDARDS

Video: *Flash culture*

Section Goals

In this section, students will:
- learn about different types of families in France
- learn some informal terms for family members
- find out when Mother's Day and Father's Day are celebrated in various French-speaking regions
- read about Yannick Noah and his family
- view authentic video footage

Instructional Resources
espaces.vhlcentral.com: Video; WB/VM/LM Answer Key; IRM (Videoscript); activities; downloads; reference tools
Video on DVD

Culture à la loupe
Avant la lecture
- Have students look at the photo and describe the family there. Ask: **La famille est-elle traditionnelle ou non-conventionnelle? (Elle est traditionnelle.)**
- Tell students to scan the reading, identify the cognates, and guess their meanings.

Lecture Point out the statistics chart. Tell students that this data refers to Metropolitan France. Ask them what information this chart shows. (The percentages of different types of French families by age group.) Ask students to name the types of families. **(Célibataires, couples sans enfants, couples avec enfants,** and **familles monoparentales)**

Après la lecture
- Ask students what facts about families in France are new or surprising to them.
- Have students compare French and American families. Ask: **Est-ce qu'il y a des similitudes** (*similarities*) **entre la famille française et la famille américaine? Et des différences?**

1 Suggestion If students have difficulty filling in the blanks, provide them with a word bank.

1 Expansion Have pairs write four more fill-in-the-blank statements. Tell them to exchange papers with another pair and complete the sentences.

CULTURE À LA LOUPE

La famille en France

Comment est la famille française? Est-elle différente de la famille américaine? La majorité des Français sont-ils mariés, divorcés ou célibataires?

Il n'y a pas de réponse simple à ces questions. Les familles françaises sont très diverses. Le mariage est toujours° très populaire: la majorité des hommes et des femmes sont mariés. Mais attention! Les nombres° de personnes divorcées et de personnes célibataires augmentent chaque° année.

La structure familiale traditionnelle existe toujours en France, mais il y a des structures moins traditionnelles, comme les familles monoparentales, où° l'unique parent est divorcé, séparé ou veuf. Il y a aussi des familles recomposées, c'est-à-dire qui combinent deux familles, avec un beau-père, une belle-mère, des demi-frères et des demi-sœurs. Certains couples choisissent° le Pacte Civil de Solidarité (PACS), qui offre certains droits° et protections aux couples non-mariés.

Géographiquement, les membres d'une famille d'immigrés peuvent° habiter près ou loin° les uns des autres°. Mais en général, ils préfèrent habiter les uns près des autres parce que l'intégration est parfois° difficile. Il existe aussi des familles d'immigrés séparées entre° la France et le pays d'origine.

Alors, oubliez les stéréotypes des familles en France. Elles sont grandes et petites, traditionnelles et non-conventionnelles; elles changent et sont toujours les mêmes°.

toujours *still* **nombres** *numbers* **chaque** *each* **où** *where* **choisissent** *choose* **droits** *rights* **peuvent** *can* **près ou loin** *near or far from* **les uns des autres** *one another* **parfois** *sometimes* **entre** *between* **mêmes** *same* **tranche** *bracket*

Coup de main

Remember to read decimal places in **French** using the French word **virgule** (*comma*) where you would normally say *point* in English. To say *percent*, use **pour cent.**

64,3% soixante-quatre virgule trois pour cent

sixty-four point three percent

La situation familiale des Français
(par tranche° d'âge)

ÂGE	CÉLIBATAIRE	EN COUPLE SANS ENFANTS	EN COUPLE AVEC ENFANTS	PARENT D'UNE FAMILLE MONOPARENTALE
< 25 ans	3,6%	2,8%	1%	0,3%
25–29 ans	16,7%	26,5%	26,2%	2,6%
30–44 ans	10,9%	9,8%	64,3%	6,2%
45–59 ans	11,7%	29,9%	47,2%	5,9%
> 60 ans	20,3%	59,2%	11,7%	2,9%

SOURCE: INSEE

ACTIVITÉS

1 Complétez Provide logical answers, based on the reading.

1. Si on regarde la population française d'aujourd'hui, on observe que les familles françaises sont très ___diverses___.
2. Le ___mariage___ est toujours très populaire en France.
3. La majorité des hommes et des femmes sont ___mariés___.
4. Le nombre de Français qui sont ___célibataires___ augmente.
5. Dans les familles ___monoparentales___, l'unique parent est divorcé, séparé ou veuf.
6. Il y a des familles qui combinent ___deux___ familles.
7. Le ___PACS___ offre certains droits et protections aux couples qui ne sont pas mariés.
8. Les immigrés aiment ___habiter___ les uns près des autres.
9. Oubliez les ___stéréotypes___ des familles en France.
10. Les familles changent et sont toujours ___les mêmes___.

Practice more at **espaces.vhlcentral.com.**

OPTIONS

La famille française Explain to students that the concept of family is changing in France. In the past, extended families (grandparents, parents, and children) often lived in the same dwelling. Today fewer grandparents live with their children, and the number of traditional nuclear families (mother, father, and children) as well as non-traditional families is increasing.

In spite of these changes, family life is still an important social institution in French culture. When people say **la famille**, the majority of them are referring to their extended family. Most holidays are spent with family, and students often choose a university near their home so that they can spend the weekends with their family.

LE FRANÇAIS QUOTIDIEN

La famille

un frangin	*brother*
une frangine	*sister*
maman	*Mom*
mamie	*Nana, Grandma*
un minou	*kitty*
papa	*Dad*
papi	*Grandpa*
tata	*Auntie*
tonton	*Uncle*
un toutou	*doggy*

LE MONDE FRANCOPHONE

Les fêtes et la famille

Les États-Unis ont quelques fêtes° en commun avec le monde francophone, mais les dates et les traditions de ces fêtes diffèrent d'un pays° à l'autre°. Voici deux fêtes associées à la famille.

La Fête des mères
En France le dernier° dimanche de mai ou le premier° dimanche de juin
En Belgique le deuxième° dimanche de mai
À l'île Maurice le dernier dimanche de mai
Au Canada le deuxième dimanche de mai

La Fête des pères
En France le troisième° dimanche de juin
En Belgique le deuxième dimanche de juin
Au Canada le troisième dimanche de juin

quelques fêtes *some holidays* **pays** *country* **autre** *other* **dernier** *last* **premier** *first* **deuxième** *second* **troisième** *third*

PORTRAIT

Les Noah

Dans° la famille Noah, le sport est héréditaire. À chacun son° sport: pour° Yannick, né° en France, c'est le tennis; pour son père, Zacharie, né à Yaoundé, au Cameroun, c'est le football°; pour son fils, Joakim, né aux États-Unis, c'est le basket-ball. Yannick est champion junior à Wimbledon en 1977 et participe aux championnats° du Grand Chelem° dans les années 1980. Son fils, Joakim, est un joueur° de basket-ball aux États-Unis. Il gagne° la finale du *Final Four NCAA* en 2006 et en 2007 avec les Florida Gators. Il est aujourd'hui joueur professionnel avec les Chicago Bulls. Le sport est dans le sang° chez les Noah!

Dans *In* **À chacun son** *To everybody his* **pour** *for* **né** *born* **football** *soccer* **championnats** *championships* **Chelem** *Slam* **joueur** *player* **gagne** *wins* **sang** *blood*

SUR INTERNET

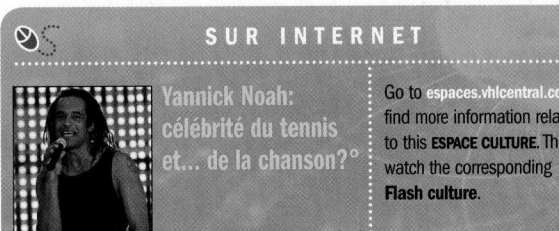

Yannick Noah: célébrité du tennis et... de la chanson?

Tennis star and singing sensation?

Go to **espaces.vhlcentral.com** to find more information related to this **ESPACE CULTURE**. Then watch the corresponding **Flash culture**.

2 Vrai ou faux? Indicate if these statements are **vrai** or **faux**.

1. Le tennis est héréditaire chez les Noah. Faux. Le sport est héréditaire chez les Noah.
2. Zacharie Noah est né au Cameroun. Vrai.
3. Zacharie Noah était (*was*) un joueur de basket-ball. Faux. Zacharie Noah était un joueur de football.
4. Yannick gagne à l'US Open. Faux. Yannick gagne à Wimbledon.
5. Joakim joue (*plays*) pour les Lakers. Faux. Joakim joue pour les Chicago Bulls.
6. Le deuxième dimanche de mai, c'est la Fête des mères en Belgique et au Canada. Vrai.

3 À vous... With a partner, write six sentences describing another celebrity family whose members all share a common field or profession. Be prepared to share your sentences with the class.

ressources: VM pp. 275-276 | espaces.vhlcentral.com

ACTIVITÉS

Le français quotidien Point out that this vocabulary, while quite common in day-to-day language, is very familiar. These words are usually used in informal conversations with family members, children, and close friends.

Portrait Show the class a photo of Yannick Noah. Ask: **Qui est-ce? Comment s'appelle-t-il?** Ask students what they know about him. Explain that thanks to his active involvement in charity work, Noah is often referred to as **Tonton Yannick**.

Le monde francophone Explain that Mother's Day and Father's Day did not originate in France. The first **Journée des mères** took place in France in 1926; it became an official holiday, **La Fête des mères,** in 1950.

2 Suggestion Have students correct the false statements.

2 Expansion Have students write three more true/false statements based on **Portrait** and **Le monde francophone**. Then have them work in groups of three and take turns reading their statements while the other group members respond **vrai** or **faux**.

3 Expansion Have students work in pairs. Tell them to create a brief conversation in which they talk about their families and pets, using vocabulary in **Le français quotidien**. Example: **Est-ce que tu as un minou? Non, mais ma tata, elle a des minous.** Remind students that this level of language is only appropriate when talking to small children.

Flash culture Tell students that they will learn more about family and friends by watching a variety of real-life images narrated by Csilla. Show the video segment, then have students jot down in French at least three examples of people or things they saw. You can also use the activities in the video manual in class to reinforce this **Flash culture** or assign them as homework.

OPTIONS

Les fêtes de la famille Explain to students that many countries around the world have a special day to honor mothers. **La Fête des mères** and **La Fête des pères** are celebrated somewhat similarly in France, Belgium, and Canada to the way Mother's Day and Father's Day are celebrated in the United States. Children create cards, write poems, and make handicrafts in school to give to their parents on these holidays. Older sons and daughters often give a small gift. On **l'île Maurice**, they do not officially celebrate Father's Day. In other francophone regions, such as North and West Africa, there is no official holiday for either Mother's or Father's Day.

Section Goals

In this section, students will learn:

- forms, agreement, and position of adjectives
- high-frequency descriptive adjectives and some irregular adjectives

Instructional Resources
*espaces.vhlcentral.com: Lab MP3s; WB/VM/LM Answer Key; IRM (**Essayez!** and **Mise en pratique** answers; Lab Audioscript); activities; downloads; reference tools*

Suggestions

- Write these adjectives on the board: **américain, amusant, intelligent, timide, aînée**. Say each word and ask students if it is masculine or feminine. Model one of the adjectives in a sentence and ask volunteers to use the others in sentences.
- Work through the discussion of adjective forms point by point, writing examples on the board. Remind students that grammatical gender doesn't necessarily reflect the actual gender. Example: **Charles est une personne nerveuse.**
- Use magazine pictures and the names of celebrities to teach or practice descriptive adjectives in semantic pairs. Use either/or questions, yes/no questions, or a combination. Examples: **Tiger Woods est-il grand ou petit? (Il est grand.) Jessica Simpson est-elle brune? (Non, elle est blonde.)**
- Point out the adjectives that have the same masculine and feminine form.
- Teach students the mnemonic device **BAGS** to help them remember the adjectives placed before a noun: **B** as in beauty for **joli, beau**; **A** as in age for **jeune, vieux, nouveau**; **G** as in goodness for **bon, mauvais, pauvre**; and **S** as in size for **grand, petit, long,** and **gros**.
- Point out that the endings of adjectives patterned after **beau, bon, heureux, intellectuel**, and **naïf** are predictable. Students can apply these patterns when learning new adjectives.
  Ex: **affreux, affreuse, affreux, affreuses; professionnel, professionnelle, professionnels, professionnelles; actif, active, actifs, actives.**

3A.1 Descriptive adjectives

NATIONAL STANDARDS comparisons

Point de départ As you learned in **Leçon 1B**, adjectives describe people, places, and things. In French, most adjectives agree in gender and number with the nouns or pronouns they modify.

SINGULAR MASCULINE NOUN ⟷ SINGULAR MASCULINE ADJECTIVE

Le **père** est **américain**.
The father is American.

PLURAL MASCULINE NOUN ⟷ PLURAL MASCULINE ADJECTIVE

As-tu des **cours faciles**?
Do you have easy classes?

- You've already learned several adjectives of nationality and some adjectives to describe your classes. Here are some adjectives used to describe physical characteristics.

Adjectives of physical description

bleu(e)	*blue*	**joli(e)**	*pretty*
blond(e)	*blond*	**laid(e)**	*ugly*
brun(e)	*dark (hair)*	**marron**	*brown (not for hair)*
châtain	*brown (hair)*	**noir(e)**	*black*
court(e)	*short*	**petit(e)**	*small, short (stature)*
grand(e)	*tall, big*	**raide**	*straight*
jeune	*young*	**vert(e)**	*green*

- Notice that, in the examples below, the adjectives agree in gender and number with the subjects.

Elles sont **blondes** et **petites**.
They are blond and short.

L'examen est **long**.
The exam is long.

- Use the expression **de taille moyenne** to describe someone or something of medium size.

Victor est un homme **de taille moyenne**.
Victor is a man of medium height.

C'est une université **de taille moyenne**.
It's a medium-sized university.

- The adjective **marron** is invariable; that is, it does not agree in gender and number with the noun it modifies. The adjective **châtain** is almost exclusively used to describe hair color.

Mon neveu a les **yeux marron**.
My nephew has brown eyes.

Ma nièce a les **cheveux châtains**.
My niece has brown hair.

MISE EN PRATIQUE

1 Ressemblances Family members often look and behave alike. Describe these family members.

MODÈLE
Caroline est intelligente. Elle a un frère.
Il est intelligent aussi.

1. Jean est curieux. Il a une sœur. Elle est curieuse aussi.
2. Carole est blonde. Elle a un cousin. Il est blond aussi.
3. Albert est gros. Il a trois tantes. Elles sont grosses aussi.
4. Sylvie est fière et heureuse. Elle a un fils. Il est fier et heureux aussi.
5. Christophe est vieux. Il a une demi-sœur. Elle est vieille aussi.
6. Martin est laid. Il a une petite-fille. Elle est laide aussi.
7. Sophie est intellectuelle. Elle a deux grands-pères. Ils sont intellectuels aussi.
8. Céline est naïve. Elle a deux frères. Ils sont naïfs aussi.
9. Anne est belle. Elle a cinq neveux. Ils sont beaux aussi.
10. Anissa est rousse. Elle a un oncle. Il est roux aussi.

2 Une femme heureuse Christine has a happy life. To know why, complete these sentences. Make any necessary changes.

MODÈLE
Christine / avoir / trois enfants (beau)
Christine a trois beaux enfants.

1. Elle / avoir / des amis (sympathique)
   Elle a des amis sympathiques.
2. Elle / habiter / dans un appartement (nouveau)
   Elle habite dans un nouvel appartement.
3. Son (*Her*) mari / avoir / un travail (bon)
   Son mari a un bon travail.
4. Ses (*Her*) filles / être / des étudiantes (sérieux)
   Ses filles sont des étudiantes sérieuses.
5. Christine / être (fier) / de son succès
   Christine est fière de son succès.
6. Son mari / être / un homme (beau)
   Son mari est un bel homme.
7. Elle / avoir / des collègues (amusant)
   Elle a des collègues amusants.
8. Sa (*Her*) secrétaire / être / une fille (jeune/intellectuel)
   Sa secrétaire est une jeune fille intellectuelle.
9. Elle / avoir / des chiens (bon)
   Elle a de bons chiens.
10. Ses voisins / être (poli)
    Ses voisins sont polis.

Practice more at **espaces.vhlcentral.com.**

OPTIONS

Extra Practice Have pairs of students write sentences using adjectives such as **jeune, grand, joli,** and **petit**. When they have finished, ask volunteers to dictate their sentences to you to write on the board. After you have written a sentence and corrected any errors, ask volunteers to suggest a sentence that uses the antonym of the adjective.

Game Divide the class into two teams. Call on one team member at a time, alternating between teams. Give a certain form of an adjective and name another form that the person must say and write on the board. Example: **beau**; feminine plural (**belles**). Give a point for each correct answer. The team with the most points at the end of the game wins.

COMMUNICATION

3 Comparaisons In pairs, take turns comparing these brothers and their sister. Make as many comparisons as possible, then share them with the class. Answers will vary.

Jean-Paul Tristan Géraldine

MODÈLE

Géraldine et Jean-Paul sont grands, mais Tristan est petit.

4 Qui est-ce? Choose a classmate. Your partner must guess the person's name by asking up to 10 **oui** or **non** questions. Then, switch roles. Answers will vary.

MODÈLE

Étudiant(e) 1: *C'est un homme?*
Étudiant(e) 2: *Oui.*
Étudiant(e) 1: *Il est de taille moyenne?*
Étudiant(e) 2: *Non.*

5 Les bons copains Interview two classmates to learn about one of their friends, using these questions and descriptive adjectives. Be prepared to report to the class what you learned. Answers will vary.

- Est-ce que tu as un(e) bon(ne) copain/copine?
- Comment est-ce qu'il/elle s'appelle?
- Quel âge a-t-il/elle?
- Comment est-il/elle?
- Il/Elle est de quelle origine?
- Quels cours est-ce qu'il/elle aime?
- Quels cours est-ce qu'il/elle déteste?

Some irregular adjectives

masculine singular	feminine singular	masculine plural	feminine plural	
beau	**belle**	**beaux**	**belles**	*beautiful; handsome*
bon	**bonne**	**bons**	**bonnes**	*good; kind*
fier	**fière**	**fiers**	**fières**	*proud*
gros	**grosse**	**gros**	**grosses**	*fat*
heureux	**heureuse**	**heureux**	**heureuses**	*happy*
intellectuel	**intellectuelle**	**intellectuels**	**intellectuelles**	*intellectual*
long	**longue**	**longs**	**longues**	*long*
naïf	**naïve**	**naïfs**	**naïves**	*naïve*
roux	**rousse**	**roux**	**rousses**	*red-haired*
vieux	**vieille**	**vieux**	**vieilles**	*old*

- The forms of the adjective **nouveau** (*new*) follow the same pattern as those of **beau**.
- Other adjectives that follow the pattern of **heureux** are **curieux** (*curious*), **malheureux** (*unhappy*), **nerveux** (*nervous*), and **sérieux** (*serious*).

Position of adjectives

- These adjectives are usually placed before the noun they modify: **beau**, **bon**, **grand**, **gros**, **jeune**, **joli**, **long**, **nouveau**, **petit**, and **vieux**.

J'aime bien les **grandes familles**.
I like large families.

Joël est un **vieux copain**.
Joël is an old friend.

- These forms are used before masculine singular nouns that begin with a vowel sound.

beau →	**bel** →	un **bel** appartement
nouveau →	**nouvel** →	un **nouvel** ami
vieux →	**vieil** →	un **vieil** homme

- These adjectives are also generally placed before a noun: **mauvais(e)** (*bad*), **pauvre** (*poor, unfortunate*), **vrai(e)** (*true, real*).
- The plural indefinite article **des** changes to **de** before an adjective followed by a noun.

J'habite avec **des amis sympathiques**.
I live with nice friends.

J'habite avec **de bons amis**.
I live with good friends.

Essayez! Provide all four forms of these adjectives.

1. grand *grand, grande, grands, grandes*
2. nerveux nerveux, nerveuse, nerveux, nerveuses
3. roux roux, rousse, roux, rousses
4. bleu bleu, bleue, bleus, bleues
5. naïf naïf, naïve, naïfs, naïves
6. gros gros, grosse, gros, grosses
7. long long, longue, longs, longues
8. fier fier, fière, fiers, fières

Language Note Point out that the adjective **châtain** comes from the noun **une châtaigne**, which is a type of sweet chestnut. The adjective **marron** is also a noun; **un marron** means horse chestnut.

Essayez! Have students create sentences using these adjectives. Examples: **La tour Eiffel est grande. Les étudiants ne sont pas naïfs.**

1 Expansion Have students restate the answers, except #3, #7, #8 and #9, using the phrase **les deux** to practice plural forms. Example: **1. Les deux sont curieux.**

2 Suggestion To check students' work, have volunteers write their sentences on the board and read them aloud.

2 Expansion For additional practice, change the adjective(s) and have students restate or write the sentences. Examples: **1. bon (Elle a de bons amis.) 2. beau (Elle habite dans un bel appartement.) 3. agréable (Son mari a un travail agréable.) 4. bon (Ses filles sont de bonnes étudiantes.) 5. indépendant/élégant (Christine est indépendante et élégante.) 6. fier (Son mari est un homme fier.) 7. poli (Elle a des collègues polis.) 8. joli/intelligent (Sa secrétaire est une jolie fille intelligente.)**

3 Expansion To practice negation, have students say what the people in the drawings are not. Example: **Géraldine et Jean-Paul ne sont pas petits.**

4 Suggestion This activity can also be done in small groups or with the whole class.

5 Suggestions
- To model this activity, have students look at the photo and respond as you ask the interview questions. Tell them to invent answers, where necessary.
- Tell students to add two questions of their own to the list and to jot down notes during their interviews.
- If time is limited, have students write a description of one of their classmates' friends as written homework.

OPTIONS

Extra Practice Have students brainstorm and make a list of adjectives in French that describe their ideal friend **(Mon copain idéal/Ma copine idéale)**. Tell them to rank each adjective in terms of its importance to them. Then take a quick class survey to find out what the most important and least important qualities are in the ideal friend. Tally the results on the board.

Extra Practice Prepare short descriptions of five easily recognizable people. Write their names on the board in random order. Tell students to write your descriptions as you dictate them. Then have them match the description to the appropriate name. Example: **Elle est jeune, brune, athlétique et intellectuelle. (Serena Williams)**

Section Goals

In this section, students will learn:
- possessive adjectives
- to express possession and relationships with **de**

Instructional Resources
*espaces.vhlcentral.com: Lab MP3s; WB/VM/LM Answer Key; IRM (**Essayez!** and **Mise en pratique** answers; Lab Audioscript); activities; downloads; reference tools*

Suggestions
- Introduce the concept of possessive adjectives. Ask volunteers questions, such as: **Est-ce que votre mère est heureuse? Comment est votre oncle préféré?** Point out the possessive adjectives in questions and responses.
- List the possessive adjectives on the board. Use each with a noun to illustrate agreement. Point out that all possessive adjectives agree in number with the noun they modify, but that all singular possessives must agree in gender and number. Examples: **son cousin, sa cousine, ses cousin(e)s; leur cousin, leur cousine, leurs cousin(e)s.** Also point out that **mon**, **ton**, and **son** are used before feminine singular nouns beginning with a vowel sound or silent **h**. Examples: **mon épouse, ton idée, son université.**
- Have students give the plural or singular of possessive adjectives with nouns. Say: **Donnez le pluriel: mon étudiant, ton examen, notre cours.** Say: **Donnez le singulier: mes sœurs, nos frères, leurs chiens, ses enfants.**
- To introduce possession with **de**, write the following phrases in a list on the board: **l'ordinateur de Monique, l'ordinateur d'Alain, l'ordinateur du professeur, les ordinateurs des professeurs.** Explain the use of the contractions **d'**, **du (de + le)**, and **des (de + les)**.
- Ask students these questions. **C'est mon stylo? C'est votre amie? Ce sont leurs devoirs? C'est sa feuille de papier? Ce sont nos livres de français? C'est l'ordinateur de ____? C'est le sac à dos de ____?**

3A.2 Possessive adjectives

NATIONAL STANDARDS comparisons

Point de départ In both English and French, possessive adjectives express ownership or possession.

BOÎTE À OUTILS
In ESPACE CONTEXTES, you learned a few possessive adjectives with family vocabulary: **mon grand-père, ma sœur, mes cousins.**

Possessive adjectives

masculine singular	feminine singular	plural	
mon	ma	mes	*my*
ton	ta	tes	*your* (fam. and sing.)
son	sa	ses	*his, her, its*
notre	notre	nos	*our*
votre	votre	vos	*your* (form. or pl.)
leur	leur	leurs	*their*

- Possessive adjectives are always placed before the nouns they modify.

C'est **ton** père?	Non, c'est **mon** oncle.
Is that your father?	*No, that's my uncle.*

- In French, unlike English, possessive adjectives agree in gender and number with the nouns they modify.

mon frère	**ma** sœur	**mes** grands-parents
my brother	*my sister*	*my grandparents*

- Note that **notre**, **votre**, and **leur** agree in number only.

notre neveu	**notre** famille	**nos** enfants
our nephew	*our family*	*our children*
leur cousin	**leur** cousine	**leurs** cousins
their cousin	*their cousin*	*their cousins*

- The masculine singular forms **mon**, **ton**, and **son** are used with feminine singular nouns that begin with a vowel sound.

mon amie	**ton** étudiante	**son** histoire
my friend	*your student*	*his story*

MISE EN PRATIQUE

1 Complétez Complete the sentences with the correct possessive adjectives.

1. ___Ma___ (*My*) sœur est très patiente.
2. Marc et Julien adorent ___leurs___ (*their*) cours de philosophie et de maths.
3. Nadine et Gisèle, qui est ___votre___ (*your*) amie?
4. C'est une belle photo de ___leur___ (*their*) grand-mère.
5. Est-ce que tu as ___ta___ (*your*) montre?
6. Nous voyageons en France avec ___nos___ (*our*) enfants.
7. Est-ce que tu travailles beaucoup sur ___ton___ (*your*) ordinateur?
8. ___Ses___ (*Her*) cousins habitent à Paris.
9. J'aime bien ___son___ (*his*) livre, il est très intéressant.
10. Bonjour, M. Martin. Comment sont ___vos___ (*your*) étudiants cette année?

2 Identifiez Identify the owner of each object.

MODÈLE
Ce sont les cahiers de Sophie.

Sophie

Christophe
1. C'est la télévision de Christophe.

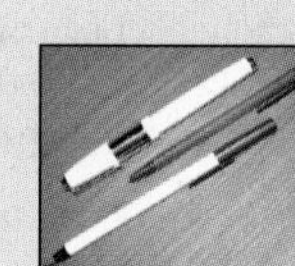
Virginie
4. Ce sont les stylos de Virginie.

Paul
2. C'est l'ordinateur de Paul.

Jacqueline
5. C'est l'université de Jacqueline.

Stéphanie
3. C'est la calculatrice de Stéphanie.

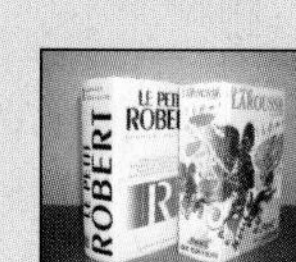

Christine
6. Ce sont les dictionnaires de Christine.

Practice more at **espaces.vhlcentral.com.**

OPTIONS

Video Replay the video episode, having students focus on possessive adjectives. Tell them to write down each one they hear with the noun it modifies. Afterward, ask the class to describe Valérie and Stéphane's family. Remind them to use definite articles and **de** if necessary.

Small Groups Give small groups three minutes to brainstorm how many words they can associate with the phrases **notre université** and **notre cours de français**. Have them model their responses on **Dans notre cours, nous avons un(e), des ____** and **Notre université est ____**. Have the groups share their associations with the rest of the class.

COMMUNICATION

3 Ma famille Use these cues to interview as many classmates as you can to learn about their family members. Then, tell the class what you found out. Answers will vary.

MODÈLE

mère / parler / espagnol
Étudiant(e) 1: *Est-ce que ta mère parle espagnol?*
Étudiant(e) 2: *Oui, ma mère parle espagnol.*

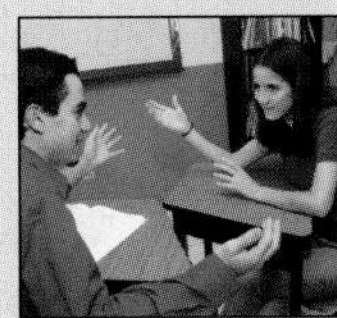

1. sœur / travailler / en Californie
____
2. frère / être / célibataire
____
3. neveux / avoir / un chien
____
4. cousin / voyager / beaucoup
____
5. père / adorer / les ordinateurs
____
6. parents / être / divorcés
____
7. tante / avoir / les yeux marron
____
8. grands-parents / habiter / en Floride
____

4 Portrait de famille In groups of three, take turns describing your family. Listen carefully to your partners' descriptions without taking notes. After everyone has spoken, two of you describe the other's family to see how well you remember. Answers will vary.

MODÈLE

Étudiant(e) 1: *Ma mère est timide et elle a les cheveux châtains.*
Étudiant(e) 2: *Sa mère est sociable.*
Étudiant(e) 3: *Sa mère est blonde.*
Étudiant(e) 1: *Mais non! Ma mère est timide et elle a les cheveux châtains.*

- The choice of **son**, **sa**, and **ses** depends on the gender and number of the noun possessed, not the gender and number of the owner. Context usually makes the meaning clear.

son frère = *his/her brother*
sa sœur = *his/her sister*
ses parents = *his/her parents*

Possession with *de*

- In English, you use *'s* to express relationships or ownership. In French, use **de (d')** + [*the noun or proper name*] instead.

C'est le petit ami **d'Élisabeth**.	C'est le petit ami **de ma sœur**.
That's Élisabeth's boyfriend.	*That's my sister's boyfriend.*

- When the preposition **de** is followed by the definite articles **le** and **les**, they contract to form **du** and **des**, respectively. There is no contraction when **de** is followed by **la** and **l'**.

de + le ▶ du	**de + les ▶ des**
L'opinion **du** grand-père est importante.	La fille **des** voisins a les cheveux châtains.
The grandfather's opinion is important.	*The neighbors' daughter has brown hair.*

On peut regarder des photos de ma tante?

Sophie, c'est la nièce de Valérie.

Essayez! Provide the appropriate form of each possessive adjective.

mon, ma, mes
1. <u>mon</u> livre
2. <u>ma</u> librairie
3. <u>mes</u> professeurs

ton, ta, tes
4. <u>tes</u> ordinateurs
5. <u>ta</u> télévision
6. <u>ton</u> stylo

son, sa, ses
7. <u>sa</u> table
8. <u>ses</u> problèmes
9. <u>son</u> école

notre, nos
10. <u>notre</u> cahier
11. <u>nos</u> études
12. <u>notre</u> bourse

votre, vos
13. <u>vos</u> soirées
14. <u>votre</u> resto U
15. <u>vos</u> devoirs

leur, leurs
16. <u>leur</u> résultat
17. <u>leur</u> classe
18. <u>leurs</u> notes

Essayez! Have students create sentences using these phrases. Examples: **C'est mon livre. Mes professeurs sont patients.**

1 Suggestion To check answers, call on volunteers to read the completed sentences aloud.

1 Expansion For additional practice, give students these items. **11. Est-ce que ____ (*your, form.*) famille est française? (votre) 12. ____ (*My*) femme est italienne. (Ma) 13. ____ (*Our*) professeur est américain. (Notre) 14. Est-ce que ____ (*her*) cousins sont espagnols? (ses) 15. ____ (*Their*) parents sont canadiens. (Leurs) 16. ____ (*Your, fam.*) amis sont anglais? (Tes)**

2 Suggestion Have students work in pairs. Tell them to take turns identifying the owners of the items.

2 Expansion To reinforce the relationship between possessive adjectives and possession with **de**, have students restate the answers using **son**, **sa**, or **ses**. Example: **C'est sa télévision.**

3 Suggestion Have two volunteers read the **modèle**. Explain to students that they use the cues to create the questions.

3 Expansion To practice asking questions with the formal *you* forms, tell students that they are going to interview the head of the French Department about his or her family. Then have students restate the questions.

4 Suggestion Before students begin the activity, tell them to make a list of the family members they plan to describe. Call on three volunteers to read the **modèle**. Explain that one student will describe his or her own family (using **mon, ma, mes**) and then the other two will describe the first student's family (using **son, sa, ses**).

OPTIONS

Pairs To practice plural possessive adjectives, have pairs describe the family on pages 74–75 from the point of view of Luc and Hélène Garneau. Encourage them to include descriptive adjectives and be creative in their sentences. You might want to introduce the term **les arrière-petits-enfants** (*great-grandchildren*) for this activity. Examples: **Juliette et Marc sont nos enfants. Juliette est blonde, mais Marc est brun. Juliette et son époux, Robert, ont trois enfants. Leurs enfants s'appellent Véronique, Guillaume et Marie.**

Extra Practice To practice **votre** and **vos**, have students ask you questions about your family. Examples: **Comment s'appellent vos parents? Est-ce que vous avez des enfants? Comment s'appellent-ils? Est-ce que vous avez des neveux ou des nièces? Comment s'appellent-ils?**

Révision

1 Expliquez In pairs, take turns randomly calling out one person from column A and one from column B. Your partner will explain how they are related. Answers will vary.

MODÈLE

Étudiant(e) 1: *ta sœur et ta mère*
Étudiant(e) 2: *Ma sœur est la fille de ma mère.*

A	B
1. sœur	a. cousine
2. tante	b. mère
3. cousins	c. grand-père
4. frère	d. neveux
5. père	e. oncle

2 Les yeux de ma mère List seven physical or personality traits that you share with other members of your family. Be specific. Then, in pairs, compare your lists and be ready to present your partner's list to the class. Answers will vary.

MODÈLE

Étudiant(e) 1: *J'ai les yeux bleus de mon père et je suis fier/fière comme mon grand-père.*
Étudiant(e) 2: *Moi, je suis impatient(e) comme ma mère.*

3 Les familles célèbres In groups of four, play a guessing game. Imagine that you belong to one of these famous families or one of your choice. Start describing your new family to your partners. The first person who guesses which family you are describing and where you fit in is the winner. He or she should describe another family. Answers will vary.

La famille Adams
La famille Griswold
La famille Kennedy
La famille Osborne
La famille Simpson

4 La famille idéale Walk around the room to survey your classmates. Ask them to describe their ideal family. Record their answers. Then, in pairs, compare your results. Answers will vary.

MODÈLE

Étudiant(e) 1: *Comment est ta famille idéale?*
Étudiant(e) 2: *Ma famille idéale est petite, avec deux enfants et beaucoup de chiens et de chats.*

5 Le casting A casting director is on the phone with an agent to find actors for a new comedy about a strange family. In pairs, act out their conversation and find an actor to play each character, based on these illustrations. Answers will vary.

MODÈLE

Étudiant(e) 1 (*agent*): *Pour la mère, il y a Émilie. Elle est rousse et elle a les cheveux courts.*
Étudiant(e) 2 (*casting director*): *Ah, non. La mère est brune et elle a les cheveux longs. Avez-vous une actrice brune?*

6 Les différences Your instructor will give you and a partner each a similar drawing of a family. Identify and name the six differences between your picture and your partner's.

MODÈLE

Étudiant(e) 1: *La mère est blonde.*
Étudiant(e) 2: *Non, la mère est brune.*

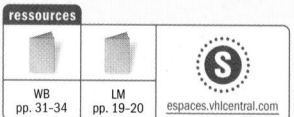

ressources
WB pp. 31–34 | LM pp. 19–20 | espaces.vhlcentral.com

Instructional Resources
espaces.vhlcentral.com: IRM (Info Gap Activities); Testing Program, pp. 17–20; Test Files; Testing Program MP3s; activities; downloads; reference tools
Test Generator

1 Suggestion You may also do this activity with the whole class using **Transparency #21**. Have two students do the **modèle**. The first student will read **Étudiant(e) 1**. The second student [**Étudiant(e) 2**] will point to the people on the transparency as he or she states the relationship. Continue calling on different students to name the family members and other students to state the relationship.

2 Suggestion Have students brainstorm a list of adjectives that describe personality traits and write them on the board.

3 Suggestion Before students begin the activity, show them pictures of the families listed for identification purposes. You might also wish to add a few names. Examples: **la famille Noah, la famille Bush, la famille Clinton, la famille Soprano, la famille Skywalker**, or **la famille Barone.**

4 Expansion Do a class survey to find out how many students think a large or small family is ideal and the ideal number of children. Ask: **La famille idéale est grande? Petite? Combien d'enfants a la famille idéale? Un? Deux? Trois? Plus?** Tally the results.

5 Suggestion Before students begin the activity, have two volunteers read the **modèle**. Make sure students understand that **Étudiant(e) 1** is the agent and **Étudiant(e) 2** is the casting director. Then ask students to describe the family in the comedy. Example: **Comment est le fils? (Il est brun et grand.)**

6 Suggestion Divide the class into pairs and distribute the Info Gap Handouts on the Supersite for this activity.

6 Expansion Ask students questions based on the artwork. Examples: **Le grand-père est-il grand? Les filles sont-elles heureuses?**

OPTIONS

Extra Practice Use this paragraph as a dictation. Read each sentence twice, pausing to give students time to write. **Ma famille est très grande. Mes parents sont divorcés. Mon beau-père a une fille. La mère de mon demi-frère cadet est française. Leur père est américain. Leurs enfants sont franco-américains. Ma demi-sœur et son frère sont blonds, grands et beaux. Il y a aussi ma sœur aînée. Elle est jolie et de taille moyenne. Notre mère est très fière.**

Call on volunteers to write the sentences on the board. Then ask students to draw a family tree based on this description. You can also ask a few comprehension questions. Examples: **Combien de filles a son beau-père? (Il a une fille.) Qui est franco-américain? (la demi-sœur et le demi-frère)**

Video: TV Clip

Le Zapping

NATIONAL communication cultures STANDARDS

NATIONAL connections communities STANDARDS

Pages d'Or

The **Pages d'Or** (*Golden Pages*) of Belgium offer a range of services that connect businesses with potential customers. In addition to the traditional printed telephone book, the **Pages d'Or** use technology to reach a wide customer base. The **Pages d'Or** website, listings on CD-ROM or DVD, and digital television allow consumers to find businesses quickly for the services they need.

Pages d'Or
www.pagesdor.be

—Papa, combien tu m'aimes?

—Pour toi, je décrocherais° la Lune°.

Compréhension Answer these questions. Some answers will vary.

1. Qui (*Who*) sont les deux personnes dans la publicité (*ad*)? C'est un père et son fils.
2. Pourquoi l'homme téléphone-t-il pour obtenir une grue (*crane*)? Il aime beaucoup son fils.
3. Comment trouve-t-il le numéro de téléphone? Il cherche dans les Pages d'Or.

Discussion In groups of three, discuss the answers to these questions. Answers will vary.

1. Pourquoi est-il facile de trouver un numéro de téléphone aujourd'hui? Comment le faites-vous?
2. Employez le vocabulaire de cette leçon pour décrire les parents idéaux.

décrocherais *would take down* **Lune** *Moon*

Practice more at **espaces.vhlcentral.com.**

Section Goals

In this section, students will:
- read about the **Pages d'Or** of Belgium
- watch a commercial for their information services
- answer questions about the commercial and the **Pages d'Or**

Instructional Resources
*espaces.vhlcentral.com: TV commercial; IRM (**Le zapping** TV clip transcription); activities; downloads; reference tools*

Introduction
Have students compare and contrast the **Pages d'Or** to the Yellow Pages. Have them visit each company's website and ask them to compare the range of services each offers.

Avant de regarder la vidéo
- Have students look at the video stills, read the captions, and predict what is happening in the commercial for each visual. **(1. Le petit garçon parle à son père. Le père écoute son fils. 2. Le garçon regarde la Lune. Il est heureux.)**
- Before showing the video, explain to students that they do not need to understand every word they hear. Tell them to listen for the text in the captions and for cognates or any familiar words from this lesson.

Compréhension Have students work in pairs or groups for this activity. Tell them to write their answers. Then show the video again so that they can check their answers and add any missing information.

Discussion
- Ask volunteers to share their group's answers to the first item with the class.
- Write on the board the students' descriptions of the ideal parents. Determine the three most common answers and discuss why it is so important for a good parent to have these particular skills.

OPTIONS

Les Pages d'Or Obtaining a business telephone listing has come a long way since the printed phone book. The **Pages d'Or** website offers customers an attractive and user-friendly interface for finding a specific number, of course. However, its services go a great deal beyond that. Depending on the time of year, for instance, the site might provide lists of seasonal tasks that people typically need to accomplish around that time. A selection of categories not only reminds the user that it is spring and time to plant a new garden, but also provides links to business throughout Belgium for starting the job.

Section Goals

In this section, students will learn and practice vocabulary related to:

- professions and occupations
- character traits and some emotional states

Instructional Resources
*espaces.vhlcentral.com: Transparency #23; IRM (**Vocabulaire supplémentaire**; **Mise en pratique** answers; Textbook Audioscript; Lab Audioscript); Textbook MP3s; Lab MP3s; WB/VM/LM Answer Key; activities; downloads; reference tools*

Suggestions

- Use magazine pictures to introduce occupations. As you show each picture identify the occupation and write it on the board. Example: **Il/Elle est architecte.**
- To introduce the adjectives, pantomime the emotions or character traits using facial expressions and/or body language. Example: **Je suis triste.** (Make a sad face.) Then ask a few students if they feel or are the same way. Example: ____, **êtes-vous triste aujourd'hui?**
- Point out that **paresseux** and **travailleur** follow the patterns of **généreux** and **coiffeur**, respectively, to form the feminine **paresseuse** and **travailleuse**.
- Point out that the masculine noun **médecin** is also used to refer to a female doctor. The expression **une femme médecin** is also common.
- Project **Transparency #23**. Ask students yes/no or either/or questions using the new vocabulary. Examples: **Est-ce que la petite fille est drôle? (Non, elle n'est pas drôle.) Le petit garçon est-il heureux ou triste? (Il est triste.)**
- Additional vocabulary for this lesson can be found in the **Vocabulaire supplémentaire** on the Supersite.

Leçon 3B

You will learn how to...
- describe people
- talk about occupations

Talking Picture
Audio: Activity

Comment sont-ils?

Vocabulaire

actif/active	*active*
antipathique	*unpleasant*
courageux/courageuse	*courageous, brave*
cruel(le)	*cruel*
doux/douce	*sweet; soft*
ennuyeux/ennuyeuse	*boring*
étranger/étrangère	*foreign*
faible	*weak*
favori(te)	*favorite*
fou/folle	*crazy*
généreux/généreuse	*generous*
génial(e) (géniaux *pl.*)	*great*
gentil(le)	*nice*
lent(e)	*slow*
méchant(e)	*mean*
modeste	*modest, humble*
pénible	*tiresome*
prêt(e)	*ready*
sportif/sportive	*athletic*
un(e) architecte	*architect*
un(e) artiste	*artist*
un(e) athlète	*athlete*
un(e) avocat(e)	*lawyer*
un(e) dentiste	*dentist*
un homme/une femme d'affaires	*businessman/woman*
un ingénieur	*engineer*
un(e) journaliste	*journalist*
un médecin	*doctor*

ressources
WB pp. 35-36 | LM p. 21 | espaces.vhlcentral.com

OPTIONS

Game Have students play a miming game in groups of four or five. Tell them that each person should think of an adjective presented in this lesson and act out the word. The first person to guess correctly acts out the next one. Example: **Es-tu fatigué(e)?** Then have each group pick out the best mime. Ask students to act out their mimes while the class guesses what they are doing.

Extra Practice Say the French term for a profession, for example, **un médecin**. Tell students to write down as many words as possible, especially the new adjectives, that they associate with this job. Then call on volunteers to read their lists as you write the words on the board, or have students compare their lists in pairs.

Mise en pratique

1 Les célébrités Match these famous people with their professions. Not all of the professions will be used.

h	1. Donald Trump	a.	médecin
e	2. Claude Monet	b.	journaliste
d	3. Paul Mitchell	c.	musicien(ne)
a	4. Dr. Phil C. McGraw	d.	coiffeur/coiffeuse
i	5. Serena Williams	e.	artiste
b	6. Katie Couric	f.	architecte
c	7. Beethoven	g.	avocat(e)
g	8. Johnny Cochran	h.	homme/femme d'affaires
		i.	athlète
		j.	dentiste

2 Les contraires Complete each sentence with the opposite adjective.

1. Ma grand-mère n'est pas cruelle, elle est douce/gentille.
2. Mon frère n'est pas travailleur, il est paresseux.
3. Mes cousines ne sont pas faibles, elles sont fortes.
4. Ma tante n'est pas drôle, elle est ennuyeuse.
5. Mon oncle est un bon athlète. Il n'est pas lent, il est rapide.
6. Ma famille et moi, nous ne sommes pas antipathiques, nous sommes sympathiques.
7. Mes parents ne sont pas méchants, ils sont gentils/doux.
8. Mon oncle n'est pas heureux, il est triste.

3 Écoutez You will hear descriptions of three people. Listen carefully and indicate whether the statements about them are **vrai** or **faux**.

Nora

Ahmed

Françoise

	Vrai	Faux
1. L'architecte aime le sport.	☐	☑
2. L'artiste est paresseuse.	☐	☑
3. L'artiste aime son travail.	☑	☐
4. Ahmed est médecin.	☐	☑
5. Françoise est gentille.	☑	☐
6. Nora est avocate.	☐	☑
7. Nora habite au Québec.	☐	☑
8. Ahmed est travailleur.	☑	☐
9. Françoise est mère de famille.	☑	☐
10. Ahmed habite avec sa femme.	☐	☑

Practice more at **espaces.vhlcentral.com**.

1 Suggestion To check students' answers, tell them to form complete sentences using the verb **être**. Example: **Donald Trump est un homme d'affaires.** You might also have them include the person's nationality. Example: **Claude Monet est un artiste français.**

1 Expansion Have students provide additional names of famous people for each profession listed. Example: **Henri Matisse est un artiste.**

2 Expansion Ask students to write two more fill-in-the-blank statements modeled on the activity. Then have them exchange papers with a classmate and complete the sentences.

3 Tapescript NORA: Moi, c'est Nora. J'ai 27 ans. Je suis artiste. Je suis mexicaine et j'habite à Paris. Je ne suis pas paresseuse. Je suis active, sportive et sympa. J'adore les animaux et l'art, bien sûr!
AHMED: Moi, je m'appelle Ahmed. J'ai 30 ans. Je suis architecte. Je suis discret, travailleur et un peu jaloux. Je ne suis pas sportif; je trouve le sport ennuyeux. J'habite avec mes parents au Québec.
FRANÇOISE: Moi, c'est Françoise. J'ai 51 ans. Je suis médecin. Je suis généreuse et gentille. Je travaille dans un hôpital. J'ai deux enfants, une fille et un fils. Les deux sont étudiants à l'université.
(On Textbook MP3s)

3 Suggestions
- Before students begin the activity, have them describe the people in the photos.
- To check students' answers, call on volunteers to read the sentences and answers.

OPTIONS

Game Divide the class into two teams. Indicate one team member at a time, alternating between teams. Give a certain form of an adjective and name another form which the team member should say. Example: **fou**; feminine singular (**folle**). Give a point for each correct answer. Deduct a point for each wrong answer. The team with the most points at the end of the game wins.

Small Groups Have students work in groups of three. Tell them to decide which of the character traits presented in **Contextes** are positive qualities and which ones are negative or undesirable qualities. Have groups list the adjectives under the headings **Qualités** and **Défauts**.

4 Expansion Ask the class questions about the photos. Examples: **Qui est artiste? (Édouard est artiste.) Qui travaille avec un ordinateur? (Charles travaille avec un ordinateur.) Qui est coiffeur? (Jean est coiffeur.) Est-il un bon coiffeur? (Oui, il est un bon coiffeur./Non, il est un mauvais coiffeur.) Qui est actif? (Jacques et Brigitte sont actifs.)**

5 Suggestions
- Tell students to add at least two more questions to the list and to jot down their partner's responses.
- After completing the interviews, have volunteers report to the class what their partner said.

6 Suggestions
- Provide students with a few models by passing out copies of authentic French personal ads or using transparencies of personal ads.
- Have students divide a sheet of paper into two columns, labeling one **Moi** and the other **Mon petit ami idéal/Ma petite amie idéale.** Have them brainstorm French adjectives for each column. Ask them to rank each adjective in the second column in terms of its importance to them.

7 Suggestions
- Give pairs a few minutes to decide which role they are going to play and to plan what they are going to say. Have them role-play their conversation and then change partners and repeat.
- Ask a few pairs to present their conversations to the class.

Communication

NATIONAL communication STANDARDS

4 Les professions In pairs, say what the real professions of these people are. Alternate reading and answering the questions.

MODÈLE

Étudiant(e) 1: *Est-ce que Sabine et Sarah sont femmes d'affaires?*
Étudiant(e) 2: *Non, elles sont avocates.*

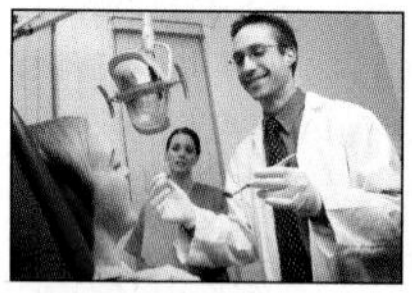

1. Est-ce que Louis est architecte? Non, il est dentiste.

2. Est-ce que Jean est professeur? Non, il est coiffeur.

3. Est-ce que Juliette est ingénieur? Non, elle est journaliste.

4. Est-ce que Charles est médecin? Non, il est homme d'affaires.

5. Est-ce que Pauline est musicienne? Non, elle est architecte.

6. Est-ce que Jacques et Brigitte sont avocats? Non, ils sont athlètes.

7. Est-ce qu'Édouard est dentiste? Non, il est artiste.

8. Est-ce que Martine et Sophie sont dentistes? Non, elles sont musiciennes.

5 Conversez Interview a classmate. Your partner should answer **pourquoi** questions with **parce que** (*because*). Answers will vary.

1. Quel âge ont tes parents? Comment sont-ils?
2. Quelle est la profession de tes parents?
3. Qui est ton/ta cousin(e) préféré(e)? Pourquoi?
4. Qui n'est pas ton/ta cousin(e) préféré(e)? Pourquoi?
5. As-tu des animaux de compagnie (*pets*)? Quel est ton animal de compagnie favori? Pourquoi?
6. Qui est ton professeur préféré? Pourquoi?
7. Qui est gentil dans la classe?
8. Quelles professions aimes-tu?

6 Les petites annonces Write a **petite annonce** (*personal ad*) where you describe yourself and your ideal significant other. Include details such as profession, age, physical characteristics, and personality, both for yourself and for the person you hope reads the ad. Your instructor will post the ads. In groups, take turns reading them and then vote for the most interesting one. Answers will vary.

7 Quelle surprise! You run into your best friend from high school ten years after you graduated and want to know what his or her life is like today. With a partner, prepare a conversation where you: Answers will vary.

- greet each other
- ask each other's ages
- ask what each other's professions are
- ask about marital status and for a description of your significant others
- ask if either of you have children, and if so, for a description of them

OPTIONS

Extra Practice For homework, have students write a short composition about a person they admire. Tell them to include the reasons why they admire that person. Provide them with the opening statement: **J'admire ____ parce que...** On the following day, ask a few volunteers to read their compositions aloud to the class.

Game Play a game of **Dix questions**. Have a volunteer think of a profession and have the class take turns asking yes/no questions until someone guesses the profession. Limit attempts to ten questions per item instead of twenty.

Les sons et les lettres

Audio: Concepts, Activities
Record & Compare

L'accent circonflexe, la cédille, and le tréma

L'accent circonflexe (^) can appear over any vowel.

pâté **prêt** **aîné** **drôle** **croûton**

L'accent circonflexe is also used to distinguish between words with similar spellings but different meanings.

mûr	**mur**	**sûr**	**sur**
ripe	*wall*	*sure*	*on*

L'accent circonflexe indicates that a letter, frequently an **s**, has been dropped from an older spelling. For this reason, **l'accent circonflexe** can be used to identify French cognates of English words.

***hospital* → hôpital** ***forest* → forêt**

La cédille (¸) is only used with the letter **c**. A **c** with a **cédille** is pronounced with a soft **c** sound, like the s in the English word *yes*. Use a **cédille** to retain the soft **c** sound before an **a**, **o**, or **u**. Before an **e** or an **i**, the letter **c** is always soft, so a **cédille** is not necessary.

garçon **français** **ça** **leçon**

Le tréma (¨) is used to indicate that two vowel sounds are pronounced separately. It is always placed over the second vowel.

égoïste **naïve** **Noël** **Haïti**

Prononcez Practice saying these words aloud.

1. naïf
2. reçu
3. châtain
4. âge
5. français
6. fenêtre
7. théâtre
8. garçon
9. égoïste
10. château

Articulez Practice saying these sentences aloud.

1. Comment ça va?
2. Comme ci, comme ça.
3. Vous êtes française, Madame?
4. C'est un garçon cruel et égoïste.
5. J'ai besoin d'être reçu à l'examen.
6. Caroline, ma sœur aînée, est très drôle.

Dictons Practice reading these sayings aloud.

Plus ça change, plus c'est la même chose.[2]

1 There's no such thing as "can't." (lit. Impossible is not French.)
2 The more things change, the more they stay the same.

ressources
LM p. 22
espaces.vhlcentral.com

Section Goals

In this section, students will learn about:

- **l'accent circonflexe**
- **la cédille**
- **le tréma**
- a strategy for recognizing cognates

Instructional Resources
espaces.vhlcentral.com: Textbook MP3s; Lab MP3s; WB/VM/LM Answer Key; IRM (Textbook Audioscript; Lab Audioscript); activities; downloads; reference tools

Suggestions

- Write the words **pâté, prêt, aîné, drôle,** and **croûton** on the board. Model the pronunciations and have students repeat. Explain that **l'accent circonflexe** can appear over any vowel. Repeat using examples with **la cédille** and **le tréma**.
- Have volunteers write **hôpital** and **forêt** on the board. Ask students what each means in English. As they respond, insert an **s** in the appropriate place above the French word. Then write these words and have students guess their meaning: **arrêter** (*to arrest*), **bête** (*beast*), **coûte** (*cost*), **île** (*isle, island*), and **Côte d'Ivoire** (*Ivory Coast*).
- Model the pronunciation of **mûr, mur,** and **sûr, sur.** Give students sentences with **mûr, mur, sûr,** or **sur** and ask them what the words mean based on the context. Examples: **1. Une grande carte est sur le mur. 2. J'ai raison; je suis sûr. 3. Les tomates ne sont pas mûres.**
- Write **comme ça** on the board and have students pronounce the words. Ask why **ça** needs **la cédille** and **comme** does not.
- The explanation and exercises are available on the **ESPACES** Supersite. You may want to play them in class so students hear French speakers besides yourself.

Dictons «Impossible n'est pas français» is a quote from Napoléon Bonaparte (1769–1821).

OPTIONS

Extra Practice Write on the board the names of French personalities. Pronounce them and have the class repeat after you. Then show students each celebrity's photo and say his or her name. Show the photos a second time and ask the class to call out each name. Examples: **François Mitterrand (ancien président), Marie Laforêt (chanteuse), Jérôme Rothen (footballeur), Loïc Herbreteau (cycliste)**

Pairs Have students work in pairs. Tell them to write three sentences using as many words as possible on this page with **l'accent circonflexe, la cédille,** and **le tréma**. Encourage students to be creative and even humorous. Then ask volunteers to share their sentences with the class.

Section Goals

In this section, students will learn through comprehensible input functional phrases for making complaints, expressing location, and reading numbers.

Instructional Resources
*espaces.vhlcentral.com: WB/VM/LM Answer Key; IRM (Videoscript; **Roman-photo** Translations); activities; downloads; reference tools*
Video on DVD

Video Recap: Leçon 3A
Before doing this **Roman-photo**, review the previous one with this activity.

1. Qui a un ami Cyberhomme sur Internet? (Amina)
2. Pourquoi est-ce que Valérie est très inquiète? (Parce que Stéphane ne travaille pas pour le bac.)
3. Qu'est-ce que Stéphane, Valérie et Amina regardent sur l'ordinateur portable? (les photos de la famille de Valérie et de Stéphane)
4. Qui travaille avec Stéphane pour préparer le bac? (Rachid)

Video Synopsis In the café, Sandrine searches frantically for her ringing cell phone, only to find that Stéphane is playing a joke on her. Rachid and Stéphane leave to go study. At Rachid's and David's apartment, Stéphane and Rachid complain about how tiresome it is to hear David constantly talk about Sandrine. They also look at photos of Rachid's parents. Finally, they start studying math. Stéphane says he wants to be an architect.

Suggestions
- Have students scan the captions under the video stills and find four phrases with descriptive adjectives and two that mention professions.
- Have the class read through the scenes that correspond to video stills 1–4 with volunteers playing character roles. Then have small groups read scenes 5–10.
- Have students locate **Algérie** on the world map in **Appendix A**.

NATIONAL STANDARDS communication cultures

On travaille chez moi!

Video: ***Roman-photo***
Record & Compare

PERSONNAGES

Amina

David

Rachid

Sandrine

Stéphane

Valérie

1

SANDRINE Alors, Rachid, où est David?
Un portable sonne (a cell phone rings)...
VALÉRIE Allô.
RACHID Allô.
AMINA Allô.

2

SANDRINE C'est Pascal! Je ne trouve pas mon téléphone!
AMINA Il n'est pas dans ton sac à dos?
SANDRINE Non!
RACHID Ben, il est sous tes cahiers.
SANDRINE Non plus!
AMINA Il est peut-être derrière ton livre... ou à gauche.

3

SANDRINE Mais non! Pas derrière! Pas à gauche! Pas à droite! Et pas devant!
RACHID Non! Il est là... sur la table. Mais non! La table à côté de la porte.
SANDRINE Ce n'est pas vrai! Ce n'est pas Pascal! Numéro de téléphone 06.62.70.94.87. Mais qui est-ce?

6

DAVID Sandrine? Elle est au café?
RACHID Oui... pourquoi?
DAVID Ben, j'ai besoin d'un bon café, oui, d'un café très fort. D'un espresso! À plus tard!
RACHID Tu sais, David, lui aussi, est pénible. Il parle de Sandrine. Sandrine, Sandrine, Sandrine.
RACHID ET STÉPHANE C'est barbant!

7

STÉPHANE C'est ta famille? C'est où?
RACHID En Algérie, l'année dernière chez mes grands-parents. Le reste de ma famille – mes parents, mes sœurs et mon frère, habitent à Marseille.
STÉPHANE C'est ton père, là?
RACHID Oui. Il est médecin. Il travaille beaucoup.

8

RACHID Et là, c'est ma mère. Elle, elle est avocate. Elle est très active... et très travailleuse aussi.

ACTIVITÉS

1 Identifiez Indicate which character would make each statement. The names may be used more than once. Write D for David, R for Rachid, S for Sandrine, and St for Stéphane.

1. J'ai envie d'être architecte. __St__
2. Numéro de téléphone 06.62.70.94.87. __S__
3. David est un colocataire pénible. __R__
4. Stéphane! Tu n'es pas drôle! __S__
5. Que c'est ennuyeux! __St__
6. On travaille chez moi! __R__
7. Sandrine, elle est tellement pénible. __St__
8. Sandrine? Elle est au café? __D__
9. J'ai besoin d'un café très fort. __D__
10. C'est pour ça qu'on prépare le bac. __R__

Practice more at **espaces.vhlcentral.com.**

OPTIONS

Avant de regarder la vidéo Write the episode title **On travaille chez moi!** on the board and have students guess its meaning. Then ask them to predict who might say this phrase in the video and to explain their reasons. Also ask them to guess in what context or situation the person might say this phrase.

Regarder la vidéo Show the video episode and have students give you a play-by-play description of the action. Write their descriptions on the board. Then show the episode again so students can add more details to the description.

Sandrine perd (*loses*) son téléphone.
Rachid aide Stéphane à préparer le bac.

4

STÉPHANE Qui est-ce? C'est moi!
SANDRINE Stéphane! Tu n'es pas drôle!
AMINA Oui, Stéphane. C'est cruel.
STÉPHANE C'est génial...
RACHID Bon, tu es prêt? On travaille chez moi!

5

À l'appartement de Rachid et de David...
STÉPHANE Sandrine, elle est tellement pénible. Elle parle de Pascal, elle téléphone à Pascal... Pascal, Pascal, Pascal! Que c'est ennuyeux!
RACHID Moi aussi, j'en ai marre.

9

STÉPHANE Avocate? Moi, j'ai envie d'être architecte.
RACHID Architecte? Alors, c'est pour ça qu'on prépare le bac.

10

Rachid et Stéphane au travail...
RACHID Allez, si *x* égale 83 et *y* égale 90, la réponse, c'est...
STÉPHANE Euh... 100?
RACHID Oui! Bravo!

Expressions utiles

Making complaints

- **Sandrine, elle est tellement pénible.**
  Sandrine is so tiresome.
- **J'en ai marre.**
  I'm fed up.
- **Tu sais, David, lui aussi, est pénible.**
  You know, David, he's tiresome, too.
- **C'est barbant!/C'est la barbe!**
  What a drag!

Reading numbers

- **Numéro de téléphone 06.62.70.94.87 (zéro six, soixante-deux, soixante-dix, quatre-vingt-quatorze, quatre-vingt-sept).**
  Phone number 06.62.70.94.87.
- **Si *x* égale 83 (quatre-vingt-trois) et *y* égale 90 (quatre-vingt-dix)...**
  If x equals 83 and y equals 90...
- **La réponse, c'est 100 (cent).**
  The answer is 100.

Expressing location

- **Où est le téléphone de Sandrine?**
  Where is Sandrine's telephone?
- **Il n'est pas dans son sac à dos.**
  It's not in her backpack.
- **Il est sous ses cahiers.**
  It's under her notebooks.
- **Il est derrière son livre, pas devant.**
  It's behind her book, not in front.
- **Il est à droite ou à gauche?**
  Is it to the right or to the left?
- **Il est sur la table à côté de la porte.**
  It's on the table next to the door.

2 Vocabulaire Refer to the video stills and dialogues to match these people and objects with their locations.

a/c/e	1. sur la table	a.	le téléphone de Sandrine
a	2. pas sous les cahiers	b.	Sandrine
b/c/e	3. devant Rachid	c.	l'ordinateur de Rachid
b	4. au café	d.	la famille de Rachid
a/f	5. à côté de la porte	e.	le café de Rachid
d	6. en Algérie	f.	la table

3 Écrivez In pairs, write a brief description in French of one of the video characters. Do not mention the character's name. Describe his or her personality traits, physical characteristics, and career path. Be prepared to read your description aloud to your classmates, who will guess the identity of the character.

ressources
VM pp. 221–222 | DVD Leçon 3B | espaces.vhlcentral.com

ACTIVITÉS

Expressions utiles

- Point out any numbers between 61–100 and prepositions of location in the captions in the **Expressions utiles**. Tell students that this material will be formally presented in the **Structures** section.
- Model the pronunciation of the **Expressions utiles** and have students repeat after you. If available, use a cell phone to model the phrases that express location.
- To practice expressing location, point to different objects in the room and ask students where they are located. Examples: **Le livre de ____ est-il sur ou sous le bureau? Où est le sac à dos de ____?**

1 Expansion Give students these additional items: **11. Ce n'est pas Pascal! (Sandrine) 12. Elle est avocate. (Rachid) 13. Si *x* égale 83 et *y* égale 90, la réponse, c'est... (Rachid)**

2 Suggestion To check students' answers, have them form complete sentences using **être**. Examples: **Le téléphone de Sandrine est sur la table. L'ordinateur de Rachid est sur la table.**

3 Suggestions

- Tell pairs to choose a video character and brainstorm a list of adjectives that describe the person before they begin to write their descriptions. Remind them that they can include information from previous episodes.
- Have volunteers read their descriptions and ask the class to guess who it is. Alternatively, you can have students read their descriptions in small groups.

OPTIONS

Extra Practice To practice the terms **à droite** and **à gauche**, ask students to describe the people's positions in reference to each other in the video stills of the **Roman-photo**. Example: **1. Amina est à droite de Sandrine.**

Small Groups Have groups create a short skit similar to the scenes in video stills 1–4 in which someone is searching for a lost object. Provide suggestions for objects. Examples: a notebook (**un cahier**), their homework (**leurs devoirs**), a calculator (**une calculatrice**), a dictionary (**un dictionnaire**), a pen (**un stylo**), and a pencil (**un crayon**). Give students ten minutes to prepare, then call on groups to act out their skits for the class.

Section Goals

In this section, students will:

- learn to distinguish between different types of friendships
- learn some commonly used adjectives to describe people
- learn about some marriage traditions in the francophone world
- read about the Depardieu family

Instructional Resources
espaces.vhlcentral.com: activities; downloads; reference tools

Culture à la loupe

Avant la lecture

- Introduce the reading topic by asking: **Avez-vous beaucoup de copains? Combien d'amis avez-vous? De quoi parlez-vous avec vos copains? Et avec vos amis? Avez-vous un(e) petit(e) ami(e)?**
- Have students look at the photos and describe the people.
- Tell students to scan the reading, identify the cognates, and guess their meanings.

Lecture

- Point out that **un(e) petit(e) ami(e)** is the main term for boyfriend and girlfriend, but **mon ami(e)** or **mon copain/ma copine** alone without **petit(e)** can also imply a romantic relationship. Context determines the meaning.
- Tell students that it is not uncommon to hear people describe their significant others as **fiancé(e)** even if they are not officially engaged.

Après la lecture

- Have students classify the following people as **copains, amis, petits amis,** or **fiancés**.
  1. two classmates (**copains**) 2. an engaged couple (**fiancés**)
  3. two coworkers (**copains**) 4. you and your best friend (**ami[e]s**)
  5. a boyfriend and girlfriend in junior high (**petits amis**)
- Have students identify some differences in French and American dating customs. Ask: **Quelles sont les différences entre les coutumes françaises et américaines des jeunes couples?**

1 Expansion Have students write two more true/false statements. Then tell them to exchange their papers with a classmate and complete the activity.

National Standards: connections, cultures

CULTURE À LA LOUPE

L'amitié

Quelle est la différence entre un copain et un ami? Un petit ami, qu'est-ce que c'est? Avoir plus de copains que° d'amis, c'est normal. Des copains sont des personnes qu'on voit assez souvent°, comme° des gens de l'université ou du travail°, et avec qui on parle de sujets ordinaires. L'amitié° entre copains est souvent éphémère et n'est pas très profonde. D'habitude°, ils ne parlent pas de problèmes très personnels.

Par contre°, des amis parlent de choses plus importantes et plus intimes. L'amitié est plus profonde, solide et stable, même si° on ne voit pas ses amis très souvent. Un ami, c'est une personne très proche° qui vous écoute quand vous avez un problème.

Un(e) petit(e) ami(e) est une personne avec qui on a une relation très intime et établie°, basée sur l'amour. Les jeunes couples français sortent° souvent en groupe avec d'autres° couples plutôt que° seuls; même si un jeune homme et une jeune femme sortent ensemble°, normalement chaque personne paie sa part.

plus de... que *more... than* **voit assez souvent** *sees rather often* **comme** *such as* **du travail** *from work* **L'amitié** *Friendship* **D'habitude** *Usually* **Par contre** *On the other hand* **même si** *even if* **proche** *close* **établie** *established* **sortent** *go out* **d'autres** *other* **plutôt que** *rather than* **ensemble** *together*

Coup de main

To ask *what is* or *what are*, you can use **quel** and a form of the verb **être**. The different forms of **quel** agree in gender and number with the nouns to which they refer:

Quel/Quelle est...?
What is...?

Quels/Quelles sont...?
What are...?

ACTIVITÉS

1 Vrai ou faux? Are these statements **vrai** or **faux**? Correct the false statements.

1. D'habitude, on a plus d'amis que de copains. Faux. On a plus de copains que d'amis.
2. Un copain est une personne qu'on ne voit pas souvent. Faux. C'est une personne qu'on voit souvent.
3. On parle de sujets intimes avec un copain. Faux. On parle de sujets ordinaires.
4. Un ami est une personne avec qui on a une relation très solide. Vrai.
5. Normalement, on ne parle pas de ses problèmes personnels avec ses copains. Vrai.
6. Un ami vous écoute quand vous avez un problème. Vrai.
7. L'amitié entre amis est plus profonde que l'amitié entre copains. Vrai.
8. En général, les jeunes couples français vont au café ou au cinéma en groupe. Vrai.
9. Un petit ami est comme un copain. Faux. Un petit ami est une personne avec qui on a une relation intime.
10. En France, les femmes ne paient pas quand elles sortent. Faux. Chaque personne paie sa part.

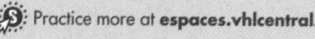

Practice more at **espaces.vhlcentral.com.**

OPTIONS

Extra Practice In small groups, have students draw a chart with three columns. Tell them to label the columns with the three main types of relationships between people: fellow students or coworkers (**les copains, les collègues**); intimate, platonic friends (**les amis**); and people that are boyfriend and girlfriend (**un[e] petit[e] ami[e]**). Then have students list at least five adjectives in each column in French that apply to the people in that type of relationship. Tell them that they can use adjectives from the reading or others that they know. Examples: **normal, ordinaire, intime, personnel, établi, profond, stable, solide,** and **éphémère**. When students have finished, ask different groups to read their lists of adjectives and compile the results on the board.

LE FRANÇAIS QUOTIDIEN

Pour décrire les gens

bête	*stupid*
borné(e)	*narrow-minded*
canon	*good-looking*
coincé(e)	*inhibited*
cool	*relaxed*
dingue	*crazy*
malin/maligne	*clever*
marrant(e)	*funny*
mignon(ne)	*cute*
zarbi	*weird*

PORTRAIT

Les Depardieu

Gérard

Les Depardieu sont une famille d'acteurs français. Gérard, le père, est l'acteur le plus célèbre° de France. Lauréat° de deux César°, un pour *Le Dernier Métro*° et l'autre° pour *Cyrano de Bergerac*, et d'un Golden Globe pour le film américain *Green Card*, il joue depuis plus de trente ans° et a tourné dans° plus de 120 (cent vingt) films. Sa fille, Julie, a aussi du succès dans la profession: elle a déjà° deux César et a joué° dans *Un long dimanche de fiançailles*°. Son fils, Guillaume (1971–2008), a joué dans beaucoup de films dont° *Tous les matins du monde*° avec son père. Les deux enfants ont joué avec leur père dans *Le Comte de Monte-Cristo*.

Guillaume

Julie

le plus célèbre *most famous* **Lauréat** *Winner* **César** *César awards (the equivalent of the Oscars in France)* **Le Dernier Métro** *The Last Metro* **l'autre** *the other* **il joue depuis plus de trente ans** *he has been acting for more than thirty years* **a tourné dans** *has been in* **déjà** *already* **a joué** *has acted* **Un long dimanche de fiançailles** *A Very Long Engagement* **dont** *including* **Tous les matins du monde** *All the Mornings of the World*

LE MONDE FRANCOPHONE

Le mariage et les traditions

Voici des objets et traditions associés au mariage dans le monde francophone.

En France Les jeunes mariés boivent° dans une coupe de mariage°, un objet de famille°.

En Belgique Une femme, à l'occasion de son mariage, porte° le mouchoir° familial où son nom et le nom de toutes les femmes mariées de sa famille sont brodés°.

Au Maroc Les amies de la mariée lui appliquent° du henné sur les mains°.

Au Québec Les jeunes mariés et leurs invités boivent le caribou°.

boivent *drink* **dans une coupe de mariage** *from an engraved, double-handled wedding goblet* **objet de famille** *family heirloom* **porte** *carries* **mouchoir** *handkerchief* **brodés** *embroidered* **lui appliquent** *apply* **henné sur les mains** *henna to the hands* **caribou** *red wine with whisky*

SUR INTERNET

Quand ils sortent (*go out*), où vont (*go*) les jeunes couples français?

Go to **espaces.vhlcentral.com** to find more information related to this **ESPACE CULTURE.**

ACTIVITÉS

2 Les Depardieu Complete these statements with the correct information.

1. Gérard Depardieu a joué dans plus de ___120___ films.
2. Guillaume était (*was*) ___le fils___ de Gérard Depardieu.
3. Julie est ___la fille___ de Gérard Depardieu.
4. Julie joue avec Gérard dans ___*Le Comte de Monte-Cristo*___.
5. Guillaume a joué avec Gérard dans ___*Tous les matins du monde/ Le Comte de Monte-Cristo.*___.
6. Julie a déjà ___deux___ César.

3 Comment sont-ils? Look at the photos of the Depardieu family. With a partner, take turns describing each person in detail in French. How old do you think they are? What do you think their personalities are like? Do you see any family resemblances?

ressources

espaces.vhlcentral.com

Le français quotidien Have students work in pairs. Tell them to take turns describing their friends or classmates using these words.

Portrait Show the class a photo of Gérard Depardieu. Ask: **Qui est-ce? Comment s'appelle-t-il? Quelle est sa profession?** Repeat the questions with a photo of his son and/or daughter. Then ask students to name any movies starring one or more of the Depardieus that they have seen, for example, *Jean de Florette* (1986), *The Man in the Iron Mask* (1998), *Last Holiday* (2006), or one of the *Astérix* movies.

Le monde francophone Ask students which tradition they find most interesting. Then explain that not everyone in these countries follows these customs. As in the United States, the wedding traditions a couple chooses to follow often depend upon their religion. For example, a Jewish couple might observe Jewish traditions at their wedding, and an Algerian or Moroccan couple might follow Islamic traditions.

2 Expansion To check students' answers, have them work in pairs. Tell students to take turns asking the questions that would elicit each statement and responding with the completed sentence.

3 Expansions

- Give students these dates of birth and have them calculate each person's age: Gérard (1948), Julie (1973)
- You might want to tell students that Gérard was born in Châteauroux, France, and that Depardieu is a typical name from the center of France.
- In October 2008, Guillaume Depardieu passed away in France at the age of 37. He had contracted severe pneumonia in Romania on the set of a new film.

OPTIONS

Le mariage et les traditions Here are some other wedding customs or traditions.

- In France, most couples have two wedding ceremonies on the same day. By law, there must be a civil ceremony, and it has to take place before the religious ceremony.
- A traditional Moroccan wedding ceremony lasts from four to seven days. After the couple exchanges vows, the bride walks around the exterior of her new home three times.
- In Belgium, wedding invitations are traditionally printed on two sheets of paper—one sheet is from the bride's family and the other sheet is from the groom's family. The two sheets of paper symbolize the union of two families.

Section Goals

In this section, students will learn numbers 61–100.

Instructional Resources
*espaces.vhlcentral.com: Lab MP3s; WB/VM/LM Answer Key; IRM (**Essayez!** and **Mise en pratique** answers; Lab Audioscript); activities; downloads; reference tools*

Suggestions
- Review numbers 0–20 by having the class count with you. Then have them count by tens to 60.
- Model the pronunciation of numbers 61–100 and have students repeat them.
- Explain that the numbers 70–99 follow a slightly different pattern than the numbers 21–69. Point out that 61 and 71 use the conjunction **et**, while 81 and 91 need hyphens.
- Write a few numbers on the board, such as 68, 72, 85, and 99. Have students say each number in French as you point to it. Then have students count by fives from 60–100.
- Numbers 101 and greater are presented in **Leçon 5B**.

Essayez! Have students write five more numbers between 61–100. Then tell them to get together with a classmate and take turns dictating their numbers to each other and writing them down. Remind students to check each other's answers.

3B.1 Numbers 61–100

NATIONAL STANDARDS comparisons

Numbers 61–100

61–69		80–89	
61	soixante et un	**80**	quatre-vingts
62	soixante-deux	**81**	quatre-vingt-un
63	soixante-trois	**82**	quatre-vingt-deux
64	soixante-quatre	**83**	quatre-vingt-trois
65	soixante-cinq	**84**	quatre-vingt-quatre
66	soixante-six	**85**	quatre-vingt-cinq
67	soixante-sept	**86**	quatre-vingt-six
68	soixante-huit	**87**	quatre-vingt-sept
69	soixante-neuf	**88**	quatre-vingt-huit
		89	quatre-vingt-neuf

70–79		90–100	
70	soixante-dix	**90**	quatre-vingt-dix
71	soixante et onze	**91**	quatre-vingt-onze
72	soixante-douze	**92**	quatre-vingt-douze
73	soixante-treize	**93**	quatre-vingt-treize
74	soixante-quatorze	**94**	quatre-vingt-quatorze
75	soixante-quinze	**95**	quatre-vingt-quinze
76	soixante-seize	**96**	quatre-vingt-seize
77	soixante-dix-sept	**97**	quatre-vingt-dix-sept
78	soixante-dix-huit	**98**	quatre-vingt-dix-huit
79	soixante-dix-neuf	**99**	quatre-vingt-dix-neuf
		100	cent

BOÎTE À OUTILS
Study tip: To say numbers **70–99**, remember the arithmetic behind them. For example, **quatre-vingt-douze (92)** is **4 (quatre)** x **20 (vingt)** + **12 (douze)**.

- Numbers that end in the digit **1** are not usually hyphenated. They use the conjunction **et** instead.

  trente et un **cinquante et un** **soixante et un**

- Note that **81** and **91** are exceptions:

  quatre-vingt-un **quatre-vingt-onze**

- The number **quatre-vingts** ends in **-s**, but there is no **-s** when it is followed by another number.

  quatre-vingts **quatre-vingt-cinq** **quatre-vingt-dix-huit**

Essayez! What are these numbers in French?

1. 67 *soixante-sept*
2. 75 soixante-quinze
3. 99 quatre-vingt-dix-neuf
4. 70 soixante-dix
5. 82 quatre-vingt-deux
6. 91 quatre-vingt-onze
7. 66 soixante-six
8. 87 quatre-vingt-sept
9. 52 cinquante-deux
10. 60 soixante

MISE EN PRATIQUE

1 Les numéros de téléphone Write down these phone numbers, then read them aloud in French.

MODÈLE

C'est le zéro un, quarante-trois, soixante-quinze, quatre-vingt-trois, seize.
01.43.75.83.16

1. C'est le zéro deux, soixante-cinq, trente-trois, quatre-vingt-quinze, zéro six. 02.65.33.95.06
2. C'est le zéro un, quatre-vingt-dix-neuf, soixante-quatorze, quinze, vingt-cinq. 01.99.74.15.25
3. C'est le zéro cinq, soixante-cinq, onze, zéro huit, quatre-vingts. 05.65.11.08.80
4. C'est le zéro trois, quatre-vingt-dix-sept, soixante-dix-neuf, cinquante-quatre, vingt-sept. 03.97.79.54.27
5. C'est le zéro quatre, quatre-vingt-cinq, soixante-neuf, quatre-vingt-dix-neuf, quatre-vingt-onze. 04.85.69.99.91
6. C'est le zéro un, vingt-quatre, quatre-vingt-trois, zéro un, quatre-vingt-neuf. 01.24.83.01.89

2 Les maths Read these math problems aloud, then write out each answer in words.

MODÈLE

65 + 3 = *soixante-huit*
Soixante-cinq plus trois font (equals) soixante-huit.

1. 70 + 15 = quatre-vingt-cinq
2. 82 + 10 = quatre-vingt-douze
3. 76 + 3 = soixante-dix-neuf
4. 88 + 12 = cent
5. 40 + 27 = soixante-sept
6. 67 + 6 = soixante-treize
7. 43 + 54 = quatre-vingt-dix-sept
8. 78 + 5 = quatre-vingt-trois
9. 70 + 20 = quatre-vingt-dix
10. 64 + 16 = quatre-vingts

3 Comptez Read the following numbers aloud in French, then follow the pattern to provide the missing numbers.

1. 60, 62, 64, ... 80 66, 68, 70, 72, 74, 76, 78
2. 76, 80, 84, ... 100 88, 92, 96
3. 100, 95, 90, ... 60 85, 80, 75, 70, 65
4. 99, 96, 93, ... 69 90, 87, 84, 81, 78, 75, 72

Practice more at **espaces.vhlcentral.com.**

OPTIONS

Game Play a game of Bingo. Have students draw a square on a sheet of paper with three horizontal and three vertical rows. Tell them to write nine different numbers between 61–100 in the boxes. Explain that they should cross out the numbers as they hear them and that they should say "Bingo!" if they have three numbers in a horizontal, vertical, or diagonal row. Then call out numbers at random and write them down to verify.

TPR Assign ten students a number from 0–100 and line them up in front of the class. As you call out a number at random, that student should take a step forward. When two students have stepped forward, ask them to repeat their numbers. Then ask volunteers to add or subtract the two numbers given. Make sure the resulting sum is not greater than 100.

communication NATIONAL STANDARDS

COMMUNICATION

4 **Questions indiscrètes** With a partner, take turns asking how old these people are. Answers will vary.

MODÈLE

Étudiant(e) 1: *Madame Hubert a quel âge?*
Étudiant(e) 2: *Elle a 70 ans.*

5 **Qui est-ce?** Interview as many classmates as you can in five minutes to find out the name, relationship, and age of their oldest family member. Identify the student with the oldest family member to the class. Answers will vary.

MODÈLE

Étudiant(e) 1: *Qui est le plus vieux (the oldest) dans ta famille?*
Étudiant(e) 2: *C'est ma tante Julie. Elle a soixante-dix ans.*

6 **Les pourcentages** Tally your classmates' responses to the questions below, then calculate the percentages for each affirmative answer. (To figure percentages, divide the number of affirmative answers by the number of people in your class.) Answers will vary.

MODÈLE

Soixante-seize pour cent des étudiants ont un chien.

1. Tu as un chien?
2. Tu as un chat?
3. Tu as un frère ou des frères?
4. Tu as une sœur ou des sœurs?
5. Tu as des cousins?
6. Tu as des oncles et des tantes?

Le français vivant

As-tu envie d'être
• ingénieur,
• musicien,
• architecte,
• professeur?
la calculatrice
61€
le sac à dos
70€
la chaise
82€
le bureau
96€
Tu as besoin d'une calculatrice intelligente, d'un beau bureau, d'une chaise confortable et d'un bon sac à dos.
Tu trouves tout dans le
Catalogue VPC!

Identifiez Scan this catalogue page, and identify the instances where the numbers 61–100 are used. Answers will vary.

Questions Answers will vary.

1. Quels objets trouve-t-on sur cette page du Catalogue VPC?
2. Quels sont leurs prix (*their prices*)?
3. Quels autres (*other*) objets trouve-t-on dans le Catalogue VPC? (Imaginez.)
4. Quels sont les prix des autres objets?
5. Le mois prochain, les prix des objets dans le catalogue seront réduits (*will be reduced*) de 25 pour cent. Quels seront les nouveaux prix?

1 Expansions
- Model the question: **Quel est ton numéro de téléphone?** Then have students circulate around the room asking each other their phone numbers. Tell them to write the person's number next to his or her name and have the person verify it.
- Dictate actual phone numbers to the class and tell them to write the numerals. Examples: your office number, the department's number, etc.

2 Expansion Have each student write five more addition or subtraction problems. Then have students work in pairs and take turns reading their problems aloud while the other person says the answer.

3 Expansion Tell students to write three additional series of numbers. Then have them exchange papers with a classmate and take turns reading the series and filling in the numbers.

4 Expansion To review descriptive adjectives, have students describe the people in the drawing.

5 Suggestions
- Have two volunteers read the **modèle**.
- You may wish to provide a few supplementary terms for family members, such as **l'arrière-grand-mère** and **l'arrière-grand-père**.
- Ask various students to identify the person who has the oldest family member from their interviews. Continue this until students identify the oldest person among all the families.

6 Expansion Have students make a pie chart or bar graph that shows the percentages of affirmative answers to each question. Call on volunteers to present their graphs to the class and to explain them in French.

Le français vivant
- Call on a volunteer to read the catalogue page aloud. Point out the prices in euros.
- Ask students: **Combien d'objets y a-t-il sur la photo?**

OPTIONS

Game Ask for two volunteers and station them at opposite ends of the board so neither one can see what the other is writing. Say a number from 0–100 and tell them to write it on the board. If both students are correct, continue to give numbers until one writes an incorrect number. The winner continues on to play against another student.

Extra Practice Ask students to write down their university mailbox numbers on a slip of paper. Collect the papers. Tell students to say **«C'est ma boîte aux lettres!»** when they hear their mailbox number. Then proceed to read the numbers aloud at random.

Section Goals

In this section, students will learn:
- prepositions of location
- disjunctive pronouns

Instructional Resources
*espaces.vhlcentral.com: Lab MP3s; WB/VM/LM Answer Key; IRM (**Essayez!** and **Mise en pratique** answers; Lab Audioscript); activities; downloads; reference tools*

Suggestions
- Explain that prepositions typically indicate where one thing or person is in relation to another: *near, far, on, between, under.* Model the pronunciation of the prepositions and have students repeat.
- Remind students that they may need to use the contractions **du** and **des**.
- Take a book or other object and place it in various locations in relation to your desk or a student's desk as you ask individual students about its location. Examples: **Où est le livre? Est-ce qu'il est derrière le bureau? Quel objet est à côté du livre?** Work through various locations, eliciting all prepositions of location.
- Ask where different students are in relation to one another. Example: ____**, où est** ____**? (Il/Elle est à côté de [à droite de, à gauche de, derrière]** ____**.)**
- Model the pronunciation of the disjunctive pronouns and have students repeat them. Explain that these pronouns are used in prepositional phrases. Examples: **1. Ma famille vient** (*comes*) **souvent chez moi. 2. Je suis en face de toi.** Then ask volunteers for examples.
- Write the following in a column on the board and explain each usage of **chez**: **chez** + *person's name or person* (**chez Rachid, chez des amis**); **chez** + *professional's office or business* (**chez le docteur**); and **chez** + *disjunctive pronoun* (**chez toi**).

NATIONAL comparisons STANDARDS

3B.2 Prepositions of location and disjunctive pronouns

Point de départ You have already learned expressions in French containing prepositions like **à**, **de**, and **en**. Prepositions of location describe the location of something or someone in relation to something or someone else.

Prepositions of location

à côté de	*next to*	**en face de**	*facing, across from*
à droite de	*to the right of*	**entre**	*between*
à gauche de	*to the left of*	**loin de**	*far from*
dans	*in*	**par**	*by*
derrière	*behind*	**près de**	*close to, near*
devant	*in front of*	**sous**	*under*
en	*in*	**sur**	*on*

La librairie est **derrière** l'université.
The bookstore is behind the university.

Ma maison est **loin de** la ville.
My house is far from the city.

- Use the preposition **à** before the name of any city to express *in* or *to*. The preposition that accompanies the name of a country varies, but you can use **en** in many cases. In **Leçon 7A**, you will learn more names of countries and their corresponding prepositions.

Il étudie **à Nice**.
He studies in Nice.

Je voyage **en France** et **en Belgique**.
I'm traveling in France and Belgium.

- Use the contractions **du** and **des** in prepositional expressions when they are appropriate.

Le resto U est **à côté du** gymnase.
The cafeteria is next to the gym.

Notre chien aime manger **près des** enfants.
Our dog likes to eat close to the children.

- You can further modify prepositions of location by using intensifiers such as **tout** (*very, really*) and **juste** (*just, right*).

Ma sœur habite **juste à côté de** l'université.
My sister lives right next to the university.

Jules et Alain travaillent **tout près de** la fac.
Jules and Alain work really close to campus.

- You may use prepositions without the word **de** when they are not followed by a noun.

Ma sœur habite **juste à côté**.
My sister lives right next door.

Elle travaille **tout près**.
She works really close by.

MISE EN PRATIQUE

1 Où est ma montre? Claude has lost her watch. Choose the appropriate prepositions to complete her friend Pauline's questions.

1. Elle est (sur / entre) le bureau? sur
2. Elle est (par / derrière) la télévision? derrière
3. Elle est (entre / dans) le lit et la table? entre
4. Elle est (en / sous) la chaise? sous
5. Elle est (sur / à côté de) la fenêtre? à côté de
6. Elle est (près du / entre le) sac à dos? près du
7. Elle est (devant / sur) la porte? devant
8. Elle est (dans / sous) la corbeille? dans

2 Complétez Complete these sentences with the appropriate prepositions, based on what you see in the illustration. Suggested answers

MODÈLE

Nous sommes _chez_ nos cousins.

1. Nous sommes _devant_ la maison de notre tante.
2. Michel est _loin de_ Béatrice.
3. _Entre_ Jasmine et Laure, il y a le petit cousin, Adrien.
4. Béatrice est juste _à côté de_ Jasmine.
5. Jasmine est tout _près de_ Béatrice.
6. Michel est _derrière_ Laure.
7. Un oiseau est _sur_ la maison.
8. Laure est _à droite d'_ Adrien.

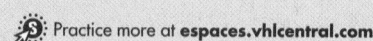

Practice more at **espaces.vhlcentral.com.**

OPTIONS

Video Show the video episode again to give students more input containing prepositions and disjunctive pronouns. Stop the video where appropriate to discuss how the prepositions of location and disjunctive pronouns were used. Ask comprehension questions.

TPR Have one student start with a small beanbag or rubber ball. You call out another student identified only by his or her location with reference to other students. Example: **C'est la personne derrière** ____**.** The student with the beanbag or ball has to throw it to the student identified. The latter student must then throw the object to the next person you identify.

COMMUNICATION

3 Où est l'objet? In pairs, take turns asking where these items are in the classroom. Use prepositions of location. Answers will vary.

MODÈLE la carte
Étudiant(e) 1: *Où est la carte?*
Étudiant(e) 2: *Elle est devant la classe.*

1. l'horloge
2. l'ordinateur
3. le tableau
4. la fenêtre
5. le bureau du professeur
6. ton livre de français
7. la corbeille
8. la porte

4 Qui est-ce? Choose someone in the room. The class will guess whom you chose by asking yes/no questions that use prepositions of location. Answers will vary.

MODÈLE
Est-ce qu'il/elle est derrière Dominique?
Est-ce qu'il/elle est entre Jean-Pierre et Suzanne?

5 S'il vous plaît...? A tourist stops someone on the street to ask where certain places are located. In pairs, play these roles using the map to locate the places. Answers will vary.

MODÈLE la banque
Étudiant(e) 1: *La banque, s'il vous plaît?*
Étudiant(e) 2: *Elle est en face de l'hôpital.*

1. le cinéma Ambassadeur
2. le restaurant Chez Marlène
3. la librairie Antoine
4. le lycée Camus
5. l'hôtel Royal
6. le café de la Place

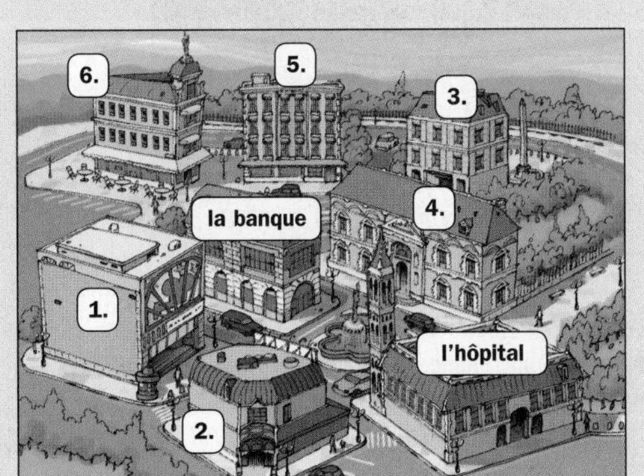

- The preposition **chez** has no exact English equivalent. It expresses the idea of *at* or *to someone's house* or *place*.

  Louise n'aime pas étudier **chez** Arnaud parce qu'il parle beaucoup.
  Louise doesn't like studying at Arnaud's because he talks a lot.

  Ce matin, elle n'étudie pas parce qu'elle est **chez** sa cousine.
  This morning she's not studying because she's at her cousin's.

- The preposition **chez** is also used to express the idea of *at* or *to a professional's office* or *business*.

  chez le docteur — *at the doctor's*
  chez la coiffeuse — *to the hairdresser's*

On travaille chez moi!
Stéphane est chez Rachid.

Disjunctive pronouns

- Use disjunctive pronouns after prepositions instead of subject pronouns:

singular		plural	
je	moi	nous	nous
tu	toi	vous	vous
il	lui	ils	eux
elle	elle	elles	elles

Maryse travaille **à côté de moi.**
Maryse is working next to me.

J'aime mieux dîner **chez eux.**
I prefer to dine at their house.

Nous pensons **à lui.**
We're thinking about him.

Essayez! Provide the preposition indicated in parentheses.

1. La librairie est <u>derrière</u> (*behind*) le resto U.
2. J'habite <u>près de</u> (*close to*) leur lycée.
3. Le laboratoire est <u>à côté de</u> (*next to*) ma résidence.
4. Tu retournes <u>chez</u> (*to the house of*) tes parents ce week-end?
5. La fenêtre est <u>en face de</u> (*across from*) la porte.
6. Mon sac à dos est <u>sous</u> (*under*) la chaise.
7. Ses crayons sont <u>sur</u> (*on*) la table.
8. Votre ordinateur est <u>dans</u> (*in*) la corbeille!

Essayez! Have students write three more fill-in-the-blank sentences describing where certain objects are located in their dorm room or apartment. Then tell them to exchange papers with a classmate and complete the sentences.

1 Suggestion To check students' answers, have them work in pairs and take turns asking the completed questions and answering them in the affirmative or negative.

2 Suggestion Before students begin the activity, have them identify the people, places, and other objects in the drawing. Example: **Il y a un oiseau.**

2 Expansion Have students create additional sentences about the location of the people or objects in the drawing. To practice negation, have students describe where the people and other objects are not located. Example: **La famille n'est pas devant la bibliothèque.**

3 Suggestion Have two volunteers read the **modèle** aloud. Remind students to pay attention to the gender of the nouns when responding.

3 Expansion For additional practice, give students these items if they are present in the classroom. **9. le dictionnaire de français 10. la calculatrice 11. les examens**

4 Suggestion To continue this activity, allow the student who guessed the correct person to choose another person and have the class ask the student yes/no questions.

5 Suggestion Before students begin this activity, make sure they understand that the numbers on the illustration correspond to the places on the list. Have two volunteers read the **modèle** aloud.

OPTIONS

Extra Practice Have students look at the world map in **Appendice A** or use **Transparencies #1** and **#2**. Make true/false statements about the locations of various countries. Examples: **1. La Chine est près des États-Unis. (Faux.) 2. Le Luxembourg est entre la France et l'Allemagne. (Vrai.)** For variation, you can make statements or ask true/false questions about the location of various cities in France.

Small Groups In groups of three or four, have students think of a city or town within a 100-mile radius of your university city or town. They need to figure out how many miles away it is and what other cities or towns are nearby (**La ville est près de...**). Then have them get together with another group and read their descriptions. The other group has to guess which city or town is being described.

Instructional Resources
espaces.vhlcentral.com: IRM (Info Gap Activities); Testing Program, pp. 21–24; Test Files; Testing Program MP3s; activities; downloads; reference tools
Test Generator

1 Suggestion Point out that in France and most francophone countries (except Canada) it is not common for universities to have sports teams. If they do, their fans are usually limited to university students. The general public doesn't usually follow college sports.

2 Expansion To review descriptive adjectives, ask students to give physical descriptions of the people.

3 Suggestion You might want to make photocopies of your university's campus map and distribute them to the class for this activity since some students might not know the campus well.

4 Suggestion To practice listening skills, tell students to cover the phone numbers with one hand and write the phone numbers down as their partner says them.

5 Suggestion Encourage students to ask questions when they are playing the role of the customer. For example, they can ask if the store has certain brands of an item, backpacks and notebooks in certain colors, or a specific type of dictionary.

6 Suggestion Divide the class into pairs and distribute the Info Gap Handouts on the Supersite for this activity. Give students ten minutes to complete the activity.

6 Expansion Ask students questions based on the artwork. Example: **Est-ce que le neveu est à côté de la mère?**

National Standards: communication

Révision

1 Le basket These basketball rivals are competing for the title. In pairs, predict the missing playoff scores. Then, compare your predictions with those of another pair. Be prepared to share your predictions with the class. Answers will vary.

1. Ohio State 76, Michigan ________
2. Florida ________, Florida State 84
3. Stanford ________, UCLA 79
4. Purdue 81, Indiana ________
5. Duke 100, Virginia ________
6. Kansas 95, Colorado ________
7. Texas ________, Oklahoma 88
8. Kentucky 98, Tennessee ________

2 La famille d'Édouard In pairs, take turns guessing how the members of Édouard's family are related to him and to each other by describing their locations in the photo. Compare your answers with those of another pair. Answers will vary.

MODÈLE

Son père est derrière sa mère.

Édouard

3 À la fac In pairs, take turns describing the location of a building (**un bâtiment**) on your campus. Your partner must guess which building you are describing in three tries. Keep score to determine the winner after several rounds. Answers will vary.

MODÈLE

Étudiant(e) 1: *C'est un bâtiment entre la bibliothèque et Sherman Hall.*
Étudiant(e) 2: *C'est le resto U?*
Étudiant(e) 1: *C'est ça!*

4 C'est quel numéro? What courses would you take if you were studying at a French university? Take turns deciding and having your partner give you the phone number for enrollment information. Answers will vary.

MODÈLE

Étudiant(e) 1: *Je cherche un cours de philosophie.*
Étudiant(e) 2: *C'est le zéro quatre...*

Département	Numéro de téléphone
Architecture	04.76.65.74.92
Biologie	04.76.72.63.85
Chimie	04.76.84.79.64
Littérature anglaise	04.76.99.90.82
Mathématiques	04.76.86.66.93
Philosophie	04.76.75.99.80
Psychologie	04.76.61.88.91
Sciences politiques	04.76.68.96.81
Sociologie	04.76.70.83.97

5 À la librairie In pairs, role-play a customer at a campus bookstore and a clerk who points out where supplies are located. Then, switch roles. Each turn, the customer picks four items from the list. Use the drawing to find the supplies. Answers will vary.

MODÈLE

Étudiant(e) 1: *Je cherche des stylos.*
Étudiant(e) 2: *Ils sont à côté des cahiers.*

des cahiers	un dictionnaire
une calculatrice	un iPhone®
une carte	du papier
des crayons	un sac à dos

6 Trouvez Your instructor will give you and your partner each a drawing of a family picnic. Ask each other questions to find out where all of the family members are located. Answers will vary.

MODÈLE

Étudiant(e) 1: *Qui est à côté du père?*
Étudiant(e) 2: *Le neveu est à côté du père.*

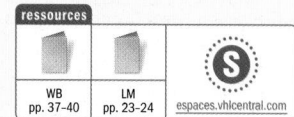

ressources: WB pp. 37–40 | LM pp. 23–24 | espaces.vhlcentral.com

OPTIONS

Game Divide the class into two teams. Select a student from the first team to choose an item in the classroom and to write it down. Call on five students from the other team one at a time to ask questions in French about where this item is. The first student can respond only with **oui**, **non**, **chaud** (*hot*), or **froid** (*cold*). If a team guesses the item within five tries, give them a point. The team with the most points wins.

Extra Practice Have students work in pairs. Tell them to take turns reading phone numbers at random from the list in **Activité 4** without mentioning the department. The person who responds should say the name of the department. Example: **Étudiant(e) 1: 04.76.65.74.92 Étudiant(e) 2: C'est le département d'architecture.**

À l'écoute

communication STANDARDS

S Audio: Activities

STRATÉGIE

Asking for repetition/ Replaying the recording

Sometimes it is difficult to understand what people say, especially in a noisy environment. During a conversation, you can ask someone to repeat by asking **Comment?** (*What?*) or **Pardon?** (*Pardon me?*). In class, you can ask your instructor to repeat by saying, **Répétez, s'il vous plaît** (*Repeat, please*). If you don't understand a recorded activity, you can simply replay it.

To help you practice this strategy, you will listen to a short paragraph. Ask your instructor to repeat it or replay the recording, and then summarize what you heard.

Préparation

Based on the photograph, where do you think Suzanne and Diane are? What do you think they are talking about?

À vous d'écouter

Now you are going to hear Suzanne and Diane's conversation. Use **R** to indicate adjectives that describe Suzanne's boyfriend, Robert. Use **E** for adjectives that describe Diane's boyfriend, Édouard. Some adjectives will not be used.

E brun	R optimiste
___ laid	E intelligent
E grand	___ blond
E intéressant	E beau
E gentil	R sympathique
R drôle	R patient

Practice more at **espaces.vhlcentral.com.**

Compréhension

Identifiez-les Whom do these statements describe?

1. Elle a un problème avec un garçon. Diane
2. Il ne parle pas à Diane. Édouard
3. Elle a de la chance. Suzanne
4. Ils parlent souvent. Suzanne et Robert
5. Il est sympa. Robert
6. Il est timide. Édouard

Vrai ou faux? Indicate whether each sentence is **vrai** or **faux**, then correct any false statements.

1. Édouard est un garçon très patient et optimiste.
   Faux. Robert est très patient et optimiste.
2. Diane pense que Suzanne a de la chance.
   Vrai.
3. Suzanne et son petit ami parlent de tout.
   Vrai.
4. Édouard parle souvent à Diane.
   Faux. Édouard ne parle pas à Diane.
5. Robert est peut-être un peu timide.
   Faux. Édouard est peut-être un peu timide.
6. Suzanne parle de beaucoup de choses avec Robert.
   Vrai.

Section Goals

In this section, students will:
- learn to ask for repetition in oral communication
- listen to and summarize a short paragraph
- listen to a conversation and complete several activities

Instructional Resources
espaces.vhlcentral.com: Textbook MP3s; IRM (Textbook Audioscript); downloads; reference tools

Stratégie
Script Bonjour, je m'appelle Christine Dupont. Je suis médecin et mère de famille. Mon mari, Richard, est ingénieur. Il est intelligent et très drôle aussi. Nous avons trois enfants charmants: deux fils et une fille. Les garçons sont roux et notre fille est blonde. Notre fils aîné, Marc, a 17 ans. Le cadet, Pascal, a 15 ans. Leur petite sœur, Véronique, a 12 ans.

Préparation Before students do the activity, tell them to look at the photo and describe what they see. Ask students to justify their responses based on visual clues in the photo.

Suggestion To check students' answers for the **À vous d'écouter** activity, have them work in pairs and take turns asking and answering questions using the adjectives listed. Example: **Est-ce que Robert est brun? Non, Édouard est brun.**

À vous d'écouter
Script
SUZANNE: Salut, Diane. Est-ce que ça va?
DIANE: Oh, comme ci, comme ça. J'ai un petit problème. Ce n'est pas grand-chose, mais...
S: Quel genre de problème?
D: Tu sais que j'aime bien Édouard.
S: Oui.
D: Le problème, c'est qu'il ne me parle pas!
S: Il t'aime bien aussi. Il est peut-être un peu timide?
D: Tu crois? ...Il est si beau! Grand, brun... Et puis, il est gentil, très intelligent et aussi très intéressant. Et Robert et toi, comment ça va?
S: Euh... plutôt bien. Robert est sympa. Je l'aime beaucoup. Il est patient, optimiste et très drôle.
D: Vous parlez souvent?
S: Oui. Nous parlons deux à trois heures par jour. Nous parlons de beaucoup de choses! De nos cours, de nos amis, de nos familles... de tout.
D: C'est super! Tu as de la chance.

SAVOIR-FAIRE

Section Goals

In this section, students will learn historical and cultural information about the city of Paris.

Instructional Resources
espaces.vhlcentral.com: Transparency #24; WB/VM/LM Answer Key; activities; downloads; reference tools

Plan de Paris

- Have students look at the map of Paris or use **Transparency #24**. Point out that **Paris** and its surrounding areas (**la banlieue**) are called **l'Île-de-France**. This area is also known as **la Région parisienne.** Ask students to locate places mentioned in the **Panorama** on the map. Examples: **le musée du Louvre, le musée d'Orsay, le centre Georges Pompidou, l'Arc de Triomphe,** and **la tour Eiffel.**
- Point out that the Seine River (**la Seine**) divides Paris into two parts: the left bank (**la rive gauche**) and the right bank (**la rive droite**).

La ville en chiffres

- Point out the city's coat of arms.
- Call on volunteers to read the sections. After each section, ask questions about content.
- Point out that the population figure for Paris includes the city and the surrounding areas.
- Tell students that there is a Rodin Museum in Paris and one in Philadelphia. If possible, show students pictures of two of Rodin's most famous sculptures: *The Kiss* (**le Baiser**) and *The Thinker* (**le Penseur**).

Incroyable mais vrai! The miles of tunnels and catacombs under Paris used to be quarries; the city was built with much of the stone dug from them. Some of these quarries date back to Roman times. The skeletons in the catacombs are Parisians who were moved from overcrowded cemeteries in the late 1700s.

NATIONAL STANDARDS connections cultures

Interactive Map Reading

Panorama

Paris

La ville en chiffres

- **Superficie:** *105 km² (cent cinq kilomètres carrés°)*
- **Population:** *plus de° 9.828.000 (neuf millions huit cent vingt-huit mille)*
  SOURCE: Population Division, UN Secretariat

Paris est la capitale de la France. On a l'impression que Paris est une grande ville—et c'est vrai si on compte° ses environs°. Néanmoins°, Paris mesure moins de° 10 kilomètres de l'est à l'ouest°. On peut ainsi° très facilement visiter la ville à pied°. Paris est divisée en 20 arrondissements°. Chaque° arrondissement a son propre maire° et son propre caractère.

- **Industries principales:** *haute couture, finances, transports, technologie, tourisme*
- **Musées:** *plus de 150 (cent cinquante): le musée° du Louvre, le musée d'Orsay, le centre Georges Pompidou et le musée Rodin*

Parisiens célèbres

- **Victor Hugo,** *écrivain° et activiste (1802–1885)*
- **Charles Baudelaire,** *poète (1821–1867)*

- **Auguste Rodin,** *sculpteur (1840–1917)*
- **Jean-Paul Sartre,** *philosophe (1905–1980)*
- **Simone de Beauvoir,** *écrivain (1908–1986)*
- **Édith Piaf,** *chanteuse (1915–1963)*

- **Emmanuelle Béart,** *actrice (1965–)*

carrés *square* **plus de** *more than* **si on compte** *if one counts* **environs** *surrounding areas* **Néanmoins** *Nevertheless* **moins de** *less than* **de l'est à l'ouest** *from east to west* **ainsi** *in this way* **à pied** *on foot* **arrondissements** *districts* **Chaque** *Each* **son propre maire** *its own mayor* **musée** *museum* **écrivain** *writer* **rues** *streets* **reposent** *lie; rest* **provenant** *from* **repos** *rest*

l'Arc de Triomphe

l'opéra Garnier

une terrasse de café

Incroyable mais vrai!

Sous les rues° de Paris, il y a une autre ville: les catacombes. Ici reposent° les squelettes d'environ 7.000.000 (sept millions) de personnes provenant° d'anciens cimetières de Paris et de ses environs. Plus de 250.000 (deux cent cinquante mille) touristes par an visitent cette ville de repos° éternel.

OPTIONS

Oral Presentation If a student has visited Paris, ask the person to prepare a short presentation about his or her experiences there. Encourage the student to bring in photos and souvenirs. If no students have been to Paris, then invite a French graduate student who has been there to speak to the class. Tell the presenter to include what his or her favorite place or activity is in Paris and to explain why.

Parisiens célèbres **Jean-Paul Sartre** and **Simone de Beauvoir** had a personal and professional relationship. Sartre became famous as the leader of a group of intellectuals who used to gather regularly at the **Café de Flore**. This group included Simone de Beauvoir and **Albert Camus**. Ask students to name some works they may have read or heard of by Sartre, de Beauvoir, or Camus.

Les monuments

La tour Eiffel

La tour Eiffel a été construite° en 1889 (mille huit cent quatre-vingt-neuf) pour l'Exposition universelle, à l'occasion du centenaire° de la Révolution française. Elle mesure 324 (trois cent vingt-quatre) mètres de haut et pèse° 10.100 (dix mille cent) tonnes. La tour attire près de° 7.000.000 (sept millions) de visiteurs par an°.

Les gens

Paris-Plages

Pour les Parisiens qui ne voyagent pas pendant l'été°, la ville de Paris a créé° Paris-Plages pour apporter la plage° aux Parisiens! Inauguré en 2001 et installé sur les quais° de la Seine, Paris-Plages consiste en trois kilomètres de sable et d'herbe°, plein° d'activités comme la natation° et le volley. Ouvert en° juillet et en août, près de 4.000.000 (quatre millions) de personnes visitent Paris-Plages chaque° année.

Les musées

Le musée du Louvre

Ancien° palais royal, le musée du Louvre est aujourd'hui un des plus grands musées du monde° avec sa vaste collection de peintures°, de sculptures et d'antiquités orientales, égyptiennes, grecques et romaines. L'œuvre° la plus célèbre de la collection est *La Joconde*° de Léonard de Vinci. La pyramide de verre°, créée par l'architecte américain I.M. Pei, marque l'entrée° principale du musée.

Les transports

Le métro

L'architecte Hector Guimard a commencé à réaliser° des entrées du métro de Paris en 1898 (mille huit cent quatre-vingt-dix-huit). Ces entrées sont construites dans le style Art Nouveau: en forme de plantes et de fleurs°. Le métro est aujourd'hui un système très efficace° qui permet aux passagers de traverser° Paris rapidement.

Qu'est-ce que vous avez appris? Complétez les phrases.

1. La ville de Paris est divisée en vingt ___arrondissements___.
2. Chaque arrondissement a ses propres ___maire___ et ___caractère___.
3. Charles Baudelaire est le nom d'un ___poète___ français.
4. Édith Piaf est une ___chanteuse___ française.
5. Plus de 250.000 personnes par an visitent ___les catacombes___ sous les rues de Paris.
6. La tour Eiffel mesure ___324___ mètres de haut.
7. En 2001, la ville de Paris a créé ___Paris-Plages___ au bord (*banks*) de la Seine.
8. Le musée du Louvre est un ancien ___palais___.
9. ___La pyramide de verre___ est une création de I.M. Pei.
10. Certaines entrées du métro sont de style ___Art Nouveau___.

ressources
WB pp. 41–42 | espaces.vhlcentral.com

Practice more at **espaces.vhlcentral.com.**

SUR INTERNET

Go to **espaces.vhlcentral.com** to find more cultural information related to this **PANORAMA**.

1. Quels sont les monuments les plus importants à Paris? Qu'est-ce qu'on peut faire (*can do*) dans la ville?
2. Trouvez des informations sur un des musées de Paris.
3. Recherchez la vie (*Research the life*) d'un(e) Parisien(ne) célèbre.
4. Cherchez un plan du métro de Paris et trouvez comment voyager du Louvre à la tour Eiffel.

construite *built* **centenaire** *100-year anniversary* **pèse** *weighs* **attire près de** *attracts nearly* **par an** *per year* **pendant l'été** *during the summer* **a créé** *created* **apporter la plage** *bring the beach* **quais** *banks* **de sable et d'herbe** *of sand and grass* **plein** *full* **natation** *swimming* **Ouvert en** *Open in* **chaque** *each* **Ancien** *Former* **monde** *world* **peintures** *paintings* **L'œuvre** *The work (of art)* **La Joconde** *The Mona Lisa* **verre** *glass* **entrée** *entrance* **a commencé à réaliser** *began to create* **fleurs** *flowers* **efficace** *efficient* **traverser** *to cross*

La tour Eiffel Constructed of wrought iron, the architectural design of the Eiffel Tower was an engineering masterpiece for its time. Critics of Gustave Eiffel's design said it couldn't be built, but he proved them wrong. Later, some of the engineering techniques employed would be used to build the first steel skyscrapers. The Eiffel Tower remained the world's tallest building until 1930.

Paris-Plages To create this manmade beach, each year about 2,000 tons of sand are spread over what is a busy highway the rest of the year. In 2007, it cost more than two million euros to create the beach. A swimming pool was added in 2004 because the Seine is too dirty to swim in. When it is open, **Paris-Plages** is a popular center for relaxation and fun, with numerous organized sports activities and concerts. Ask students if they think that **Paris-Plages** is worth the money.

Le musée du Louvre Bring in photos or slides of the **Louvre** and some of the most famous artwork in its collection, such as the *Mona Lisa*, the *Venus de Milo*, the *Winged Victory of Samothrace*, *Vermeer's Lacemaker*, and *Delacroix's Liberty Leading the People* (***La Liberté guidant le peuple***). Ask students to describe the woman in the *Mona Lisa*. Point out that only a fraction of the 300,000 works owned by the museum are on display.

Le métro The Paris public transportation system, **le métro** (short for **le Métropolitain**), has 14 lines. It is the most convenient and popular means of transportation in the city since every building in Paris is within 500 meters of a **métro** station. Ask students what cities in the United States have metro or subway systems.

OPTIONS

Cultural Activity Assign each student a famous site in Paris. Examples: **l'Île de la Cité, la Sainte-Chapelle, le quartier latin**, etc. Tell students to research the site and write a brief description. Encourage them to include photos from the Internet or magazines. Ask a few volunteers to share their descriptions with the class.

Pairs Have students work in pairs. Tell them that they have three days in Paris, and they have to make a list of places they want to see or visit each day so that they can make the most of their time there. Remind students that many famous sights, other than those mentioned in the text, appear on the map. Example: **Jour 1: visiter le musée du Louvre.** Ask volunteers to share their lists with the class.

Section Goals

In this section, students will:
- learn to use visuals and graphic elements to predict content
- read an article about pets in France

Stratégie Tell students that they can infer a great deal of information about the content of an article or text by examining the visual and graphic elements. Some items they should look at are:
- titles and headings
- photos
- photo captions
- graphs, tables, and diagrams

To practice this strategy, have students read the headings in the chart **Le Top 10 des chiens de race.** Ask: What information does this chart contain? (It lists the top ten dog breeds and the percentage of households that owns each breed.)

Examinez le texte After students have finished the activity, tell them to look at the visual elements in the article again. Then ask them the following questions and have them explain their answers.
1. What is the article about? (It is about dogs as family pets. The title of the article and the photos of dogs indicate the main topic.)
2. What information does the table on page 105 contain? (It lists the reasons why people have pets and shows the percentages of people who own dogs, cats, birds, and fish for each reason.)
3. What can you learn from the photo on page 105? (Answers will vary.)

Lecture

Reading

Avant la lecture

STRATÉGIE

Predicting content from visuals

When you are reading in French, be sure to look for visual clues that will orient you as to the content and purpose of what you are reading. Photos and illustrations, for example, will often give you a good idea of the main points that the reading covers. You may also encounter helpful visuals that summarize large amounts of data in a way that is easy to comprehend; these visuals include bar graphs, pie charts, flow charts, lists of percentages, and other diagrams.

Le Top 10 des chiens de race°
% DE FOYERS° POSSESSEURS
les caniches° **9,3%**
les labradors **7,8%**
les yorkshires **5,6%**
les épagneuls bretons° **4,6%**
les bergers allemands° **4,1%**
les autres bergers **3,3%**
les bichons **2,7%**
les cockers/fox-terriers **2,2%**
les boxers **2%**
les colleys **1,6%**

Examinez le texte

Take a quick look at the visual elements of the article in order to generate a list of ideas about its content. Then, compare your list with a classmate's. Are your lists the same or are they different? Discuss your lists and make any changes needed to produce a final list of ideas.

race *breed* **foyers** *households* **caniches** *poodles* **épagneuls bretons** *Brittany Spaniels* **bergers allemands** *German Shepherds*

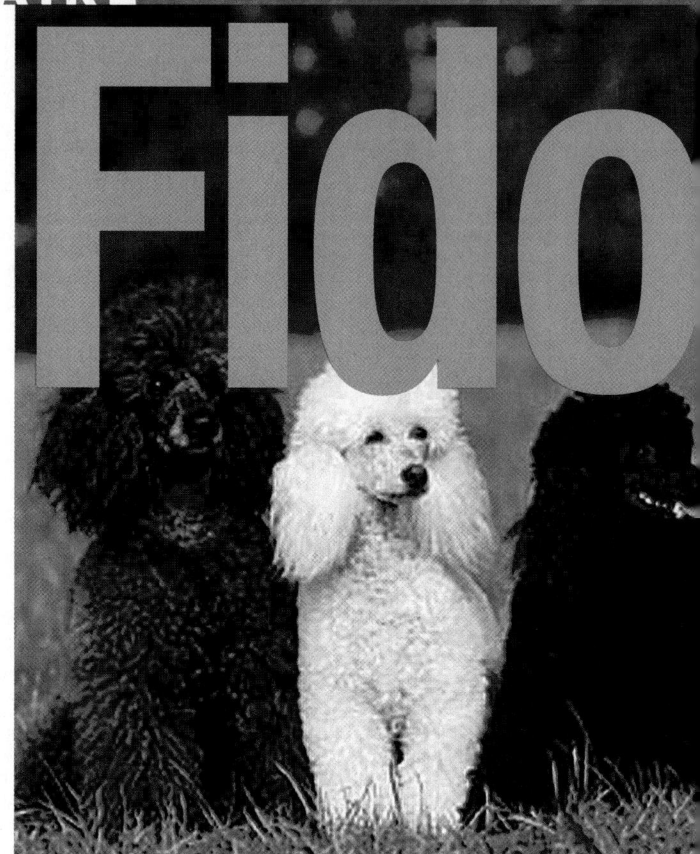

Fido

Les Français adorent les animaux. Plus de la moitié° des foyers en France ont un chien, un chat ou un autre animal de compagnie°. Les chiens sont particulièrement appréciés et intégrés dans la famille et la société françaises.

Qui possède un chien en France et pourquoi? Souvent°, la présence d'un chien en famille suit l'arrivée° d'enfants, parce que les parents pensent qu'un chien contribue positivement à leur développement. Il est aussi commun de trouver deux chiens ou plus dans le même° foyer.

Les chiens sont d'excellents compagnons. Leurs maîtres° sont moins seuls° et déclarent avoir moins de stress. Certaines personnes possèdent un chien pour avoir plus d'exercice

OPTIONS

Pairs Working in pairs, students should read the article aloud and write four questions about it. After they have finished, tell them to exchange their papers with another pair and answer the questions.

Extra Practice Tell students to read the chart **Le Top 10 des chiens de race**. Then pronounce the name of each dog breed and have students repeat it after you. To check comprehension, give students these true/false statements. **1. Le caniche est la race de chien la plus populaire. (Vrai.) 2. Les boxers n'existent pas en France. (Faux.) 3. Les labradors sont moins populaires que les épagneuls. (Faux.) 4. Les Français aiment mieux les yorkshires que les bergers. (Faux.) 5. Les colleys sont le numéro dix sur la liste. (Vrai.)**

en famille

physique. Et il y a aussi des personnes qui possèdent un chien parce qu'elles en ont toujours eu un° et n'imaginent pas une vie° sans° chien.

Les chiens ont parfois° les mêmes droits° que les autres membres de la famille, et parfois des droits spéciaux. Bien sûr, ils accompagnent leurs maîtres pour les courses en ville° et les promenades dans le parc, et ils entrent même dans certains magasins°. Ne trouvez-vous pas parfois un caniche ou un labrador, les deux races les plus° populaires en France, avec son maître dans un restaurant?

En France, il n'est pas difficile d'observer que les chiens ont une place privilégiée au sein de° la famille.

Pourquoi avoir un animal de compagnie?

RAISON	CHIENS	CHATS	OISEAUX	POISSONS
Pour l'amour des animaux	61,4%	60,5%	61%	33%
Pour avoir de la compagnie	43,5%	38,2%	37%	10%
Pour s'occuper°	40,4%	37,7%	0%	0%
Parce que j'en ai toujours eu un°	31,8%	28,9%	0%	0%
Pour le bien-être° personnel	29,2%	26,2%	0%	0%
Pour les enfants	23,7%	21,3%	30%	48%

Plus de la moitié *More than half* **animal de compagnie** *pet* **Souvent** *Often* **suit l'arrivée** *follows the arrival* **même** *same* **maîtres** *owners* **moins seuls** *less lonely* **en ont toujours eu un** *have always had one* **vie** *life* **sans** *without* **parfois** *sometimes* **droits** *rights* **courses en ville** *errands in town* **magasins** *stores* **les plus** *the most* **au sein de** *in the heart of* **s'occuper** *keep busy* **Parce que j'en ai toujours eu un** *Because I've always had one* **bien-être** *well-being*

Après la lecture

Vrai ou faux? Indicate whether these items are **vrai** or **faux**, based on the reading. Correct the false ones.

	Vrai	Faux
1. Les chiens accompagnent leurs maîtres pour les promenades dans le parc.	☑	☐
2. Parfois, les chiens accompagnent leurs maîtres dans les restaurants.	☑	☐
3. Le chat n'est pas un animal apprécié en France. En France, plus de la moitié des foyers ont un chien, un chat ou un autre animal de compagnie.	☐	☑
4. Certaines personnes déclarent posséder un chien pour avoir plus d'exercice physique.	☑	☐
5. Certaines personnes déclarent posséder un chien pour avoir plus de stress. Certaines personnes déclarent avoir moins de stress avec un chien.	☐	☑
6. En France, les familles avec enfants n'ont pas de chien. Souvent, la présence d'un chien dans une famille suit l'arrivée d'enfants.	☐	☑

Fido en famille Choose the correct response according to the article.

1. Combien de foyers en France ont au moins (*at least*) un animal de compagnie?
   a. 20%–25%
   b. 40%–45%
   (c.) 50%–55%
2. Pourquoi est-ce une bonne idée d'avoir un chien?
   a. pour plus de compagnie et plus de stress
   b. pour l'exercice physique et être seul
   (c.) pour la compagnie et le développement des enfants
3. Que pensent les familles françaises de leurs chiens?
   a. Les chiens sont plus importants que les enfants.
   (b.) Les chiens font partie (*are part*) de la famille et participent aux activités quotidiennes (*daily*).
   c. Le rôle des chiens est limité aux promenades.
4. Quelles races de chien les Français préfèrent-ils?
   a. les caniches et les oiseaux
   b. les labradors et les bergers allemands
   (c.) les caniches et les labradors
5. Y a-t-il des familles avec plus d'un chien?
   a. non
   (b.) oui
   c. les caniches et les labradors

Mes animaux In groups of three, say why you own or someone you know owns a pet. Give one of the reasons listed in the table on the left or a different one. Use the verb **avoir** and possessive adjectives.

MODÈLE

Mon grand-père a un chien pour son bien-être personnel.

Vrai ou faux? Have students correct the false statements and check their answers with a partner.

Fido en famille Go over the answers with the class. Ask students to read the corresponding line(s) of the text that contain the answer to each question.

Suggestion Encourage students to record unfamiliar words and phrases that they learn in **Lecture** in their notebooks.

Expansions
- Ask students to describe their pets. If they don't own a pet, then tell them to describe someone else's pet. Example: **Mon chat s'appelle Tyler. Il est très gentil avec tout le monde. Il est noir et c'est un bon copain.**
- Write these headings on the board: **animaux de compagnie, chiens, chats, oiseaux, poissons**, and **autres animaux**. Do a quick class survey to find out how many have pets in general and how many have dogs, cats, birds, fish, and other animals. Record the results on the board. Then ask them why they have a pet. If students need help expressing their reasons, tell them to look at the reasons in the chart on this page.

Mes animaux Ask students to report their partners' answers to the class.

OPTIONS

Cultural Comparison Have students work in pairs or groups of three. Tell them to draw a two-column chart and write the headings **Similitudes** (*Similarities*) and **Différences** (*Differences*). Then, tell them to list the similarities and differences between the French and American attitudes toward dogs based on the facts in the reading and what they know about Americans and their pets. Allow students to use their books for this activity. After pairs have completed their charts, call on volunteers to read their lists. Ask the class if they agree or disagree with the similarities.

Section Goals

In this section, students will:

- learn to use idea maps to organize information
- learn to write an informal letter in French

Stratégie Tell students that they might find it helpful to use note cards to create idea maps. Writing each detail on a separate card will allow them to rearrange ideas and experiment with organization. Remind students to write their ideas in French, since they may not have the vocabulary or structures for some English terms they generate.

Thème Introduce the common salutations and closings used in informal letters in French. Point out the difference between **cher** (masculine) and **chère** (feminine). Model the pronunciation to show students that the two words sound the same. Explain that the closings **Grosses bises!** and **Bisous!** are often used with close friends. If the relationship is informal but the person is not a close friend, then **À plus** is an appropriate choice. **Amitiés** and **Cordialement** are less familiar than the other options.

Écriture

NATIONAL STANDARDS communication cultures

STRATÉGIE

Using idea maps

How do you organize ideas for a first draft? Often, the organization of ideas represents the most challenging part of the writing process. Idea maps are useful for organizing pertinent information. Here is an example of an idea map you can use when writing.

SCHÉMA D'IDÉES

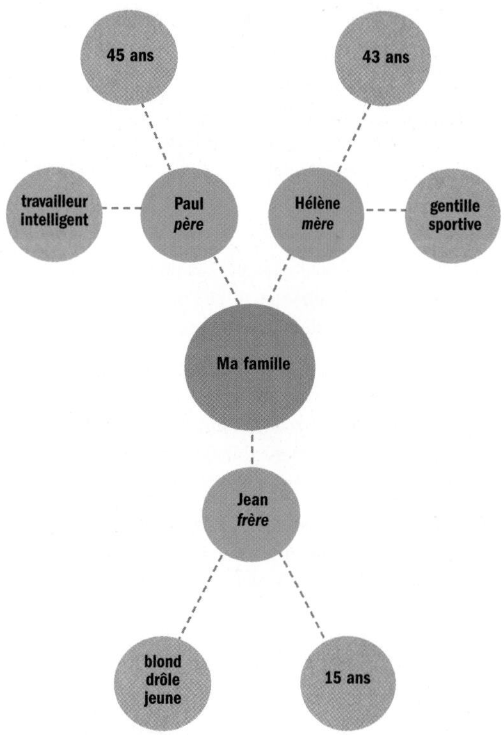

Thème

Écrivez une lettre

Avant l'écriture

1. A French-speaking friend wants to know about your family. Using some of the verbs and adjectives you learned in this lesson, write a brief letter describing your own family or an imaginary one. Be sure to include information from each of these categories for each family member:

   - Names, ages, and relationships
   - Physical characteristics
   - Hobbies and interests

   Before you begin, create an idea map like the one on the left, with a circle for each member of your family.

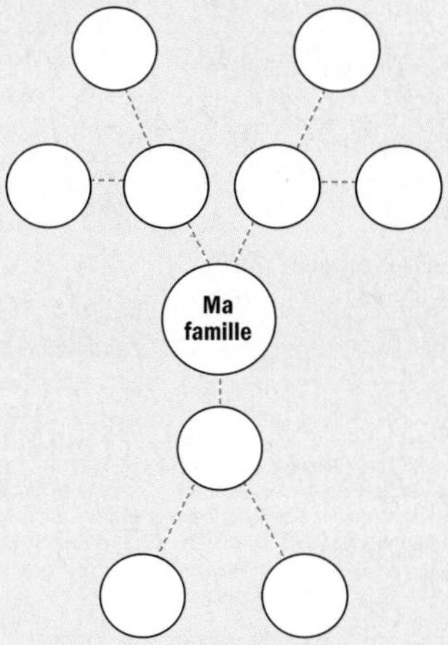

OPTIONS

Avant l'écriture Remind students that they used a word web to brainstorm ideas in Unit 2. Tell them that an idea map is similar, but that it links various ideas to a central topic and breaks those ideas down into smaller categories. Point out the colors used in the idea map on page 106 and how they are used to group similar levels of information.

Help students create an outline for a typical letter: a salutation, an introductory paragraph with greetings, a second paragraph with the family description, a third paragraph with a request for a response, a closing, and a signature. Tell them their first paragraph should include an inquiry into how the person is doing, along with a similar comment about themselves.

2. Once you have completed your idea map, compare it with the one created by a classmate. Did you both include the same kind of information? Did you list all your family members? Did you include information from each of the three categories for each person?
3. Here are some useful expressions for writing a letter in French:

Salutations

Cher Fabien,	*Dear Fabien,*
Chère Joëlle,	*Dear Joëlle,*

Asking for a response

Réponds-moi vite.	*Write back soon.*
Donne-moi de tes nouvelles.	*Tell me all your news.*

Closings

Grosses bises!	*Big kisses!*
Je t'embrasse!	*Kisses!*
Bisous!	*Kisses!*
À bientôt!	*See you soon!*
Amitiés,	*In friendship,*
Cordialement,	*Cordially,*
À plus (tard),	*Until later,*

Écriture

Use your idea map and the list of letter-writing expressions to write a letter that describes your family to a friend. Be sure to include some of the verbs and adjectives you have learned in this lesson.

Cher Christophe,
Mon père s'appelle Gabriel. Il a 52 ans. Il est grand, a les cheveux châtains et les yeux marron. Il est architecte et travaille à Paris. Il aime dessiner, lire (to read) et voyager. Ma mère, Nicole, a 47 ans. Elle est petite, blonde et a les yeux bleus. Elle est professeur d'anglais à l'université. Comme mon père, elle aime voyager. Elle aime aussi faire (to do) du sport. Ma sœur, Élodie, a 17 ans. Elle est grande, a les cheveux châtains et les yeux verts. Elle est encore au lycée. Elle adore écouter de la musique et aller au (to go to) cinéma. Mon oncle, ...
Et ta famille, comment est-elle? Donne-moi vite de tes nouvelles!
À bientôt!
Caroline

Après l'écriture

1. Exchange rough drafts with a partner. Comment on his or her work by answering these questions:
   - Did your partner make the adjectives agree with the person described?
   - Did your partner include the age, family relationship, physical characteristics, and hobbies and interests of each family member?
   - Did your partner use verb forms correctly?
   - Did your partner use the letter-writing expressions correctly?

2. Revise your description according to your partner's comments. After writing the final version, read it once more to eliminate these kinds of problems:
   - spelling errors
   - punctuation errors
   - capitalization errors
   - use of incorrect verb forms
   - adjectives that do not agree with the nouns they modify

EVALUATION

Criteria

Content Includes all the information mentioned in the three bulleted items in the task description as well as some of the expressions in the list of salutations, requests for response, and closings.
Scale: 1 2 3 4 5

Organization Organizes the letter into a salutation, a family description, a request for a response, and a closing.
Scale: 1 2 3 4 5

Accuracy Uses possessive and descriptive adjectives and modifies them accordingly. Spells words and conjugates verbs correctly throughout.
Scale: 1 2 3 4 5

Creativity The student includes additional information that is not included in the task and/or provides detailed information about numerous family members.
Scale: 1 2 3 4 5

Scoring

Excellent	18–20 points
Good	14–17 points
Satisfactory	10–13 points
Unsatisfactory	< 10 points

OPTIONS

Écriture Remind students of the **–er** verbs that they can use to talk about family members' hobbies and interests: **adorer**, **aimer**, and **détester**. Encourage them to go beyond the task to talk about what their family members dislike as well. Brainstorm a list of possible interests and hobbies that students can draw upon as they write.

Clarify the cultural differences among the closing expressions shown. **Grosses bises**, **Bisous**, and **À plus** are used with close friends. Where the relationship is informal but the person is not a close friend, **À plus tard** is a better choice. **Amitiés** and **Cordialement** are more formal and often used when addressing an older person or a business associate.

Instructional Resources
espaces.vhlcentral.com: Textbook MP3s; IRM (Textbook Audioscript); downloads; reference tools

Suggestion Tell students that an easy way to study from **Vocabulaire** is to cover up the French half of each section, leaving only the English equivalents exposed. They can then quiz themselves on the French items. To focus on the English equivalents of the French entries, they simply reverse this process.

Flashcards
Audio: Vocabulary

VOCABULAIRE

La famille

aîné(e)	*elder*
cadet(te)	*younger*
un beau-frère	*brother-in-law*
un beau-père	*father-in-law; stepfather*
une belle-mère	*mother-in-law; stepmother*
une belle-sœur	*sister-in-law*
un(e) cousin(e)	*cousin*
un demi-frère	*half-brother; stepbrother*
une demi-sœur	*half-sister; stepsister*
les enfants (*m., f.*)	*children*
un époux/une épouse	*spouse*
une famille	*family*
une femme	*wife; woman*
une fille	*daughter; girl*
un fils	*son*
un frère	*brother*
une grand-mère	*grandmother*
un grand-père	*grandfather*
les grands-parents (*m.*)	*grandparents*
un mari	*husband*
une mère	*mother*
un neveu	*nephew*
une nièce	*niece*
un oncle	*uncle*
les parents (*m.*)	*parents*
un père	*father*
une petite-fille	*granddaughter*
un petit-fils	*grandson*
les petits-enfants (*m.*)	*grandchildren*
une sœur	*sister*
une tante	*aunt*
un chat	*cat*
un chien	*dog*
un oiseau	*bird*
un poisson	*fish*

Adjectifs descriptifs

antipathique	*unpleasant*
bleu(e)	*blue*
blond(e)	*blond*
brun(e)	*dark (hair)*
court(e)	*short*
drôle	*funny*
faible	*weak*
fatigué(e)	*tired*
fort(e)	*strong*
frisé(e)	*curly*
génial(e) (géniaux *pl.*)	*great*
grand(e)	*big; tall*
jeune	*young*
joli(e)	*pretty*
laid(e)	*ugly*
lent(e)	*slow*
mauvais(e)	*bad*
méchant(e)	*mean*
modeste	*modest, humble*
noir(e)	*black*
pauvre	*poor, unfortunate*
pénible	*tiresome*
petit(e)	*small, short (stature)*
prêt(e)	*ready*
raide	*straight*
rapide	*fast*
triste	*sad*
vert(e)	*green*
vrai(e)	*true; real*

Vocabulaire supplémentaire

divorcer	*to divorce*
épouser	*to marry*
célibataire	*single*
divorcé(e)	*divorced*
fiancé(e)	*engaged*
marié(e)	*married*
séparé(e)	*separated*
veuf/veuve	*widowed*
un(e) voisin(e)	*neighbor*

Expressions utiles	*See pp. 79 and 93.*
Possessive adjectives	*See p. 84.*
Numbers 61–100	*See p. 96.*
Prepositions of location	*See p. 98.*

Professions et occupations

un(e) architecte	*architect*
un(e) artiste	*artist*
un(e) athlète	*athlete*
un(e) avocat(e)	*lawyer*
un coiffeur/une coiffeuse	*hairdresser*
un(e) dentiste	*dentist*
un homme/une femme d'affaires	*businessman/woman*
un ingénieur	*engineer*
un(e) journaliste	*journalist*
un médecin	*doctor*
un(e) musicien(ne)	*musician*

Adjectifs irréguliers

actif/active	*active*
beau/belle	*beautiful; handsome*
bon(ne)	*kind; good*
châtain	*brown (hair)*
courageux/courageuse	*courageous, brave*
cruel(le)	*cruel*
curieux/curieuse	*curious*
discret/discrète	*discreet; unassuming*
doux/douce	*sweet; soft*
ennuyeux/ennuyeuse	*boring*
étranger/étrangère	*foreign*
favori(te)	*favorite*
fier/fière	*proud*
fou/folle	*crazy*
généreux/généreuse	*generous*
gentil(le)	*nice*
gros(se)	*fat*
inquiet/inquiète	*worried*
intellectuel(le)	*intellectual*
jaloux/jalouse	*jealous*
long(ue)	*long*
(mal)heureux/(mal)heureuse	*(un)happy*
marron	*brown*
naïf/naïve	*naïve*
nerveux/nerveuse	*nervous*
nouveau/nouvelle	*new*
paresseux/paresseuse	*lazy*
roux/rousse	*red-haired*
sérieux/sérieuse	*serious*
sportif/sportive	*athletic*
travailleur/travailleuse	*hard-working*
vieux/vieille	*old*

ressources
espaces.vhlcentral.com

Au café

UNITÉ

4

Pour commencer

- Quelle heure est-il?
  a. 6h00 du matin b. midi c. minuit
- Qu'est-ce que Sandrine et Amina ont envie de faire (*do*)?
  a. manger b. partager c. échouer
- Que vont-elles (*are going to*) manger?
  a. un café b. une limonade
  c. des sandwichs

Unit Goals

Leçon 4A

In this lesson, students will learn:
- names for places around town
- terms for activities around town
- to pronounce oral vowels
- about pastimes of young French people and **le verlan**
- the verb **aller** and to express future actions with it
- the preposition **à** and contractions with it
- interrogative words
- about the Swiss national airline

Leçon 4B

In this lesson, students will learn:
- terms for food items at a café
- expressions of quantity
- to pronounce nasal vowels
- about the role of the café in France and the cafés of North Africa
- more about cafés and food items through specially shot video footage
- the present tense of **prendre** and **boire**
- the formation and use of partitive articles
- regular **-ir** verbs
- to listen for the gist in oral communication

Savoir-faire

In this section, students will learn:
- cultural and historical information about the French regions of **Normandie** and **Bretagne**
- to scan a text to improve comprehension
- to add details in French to make writing more interesting

Pour commencer

- **b. midi**
- **a. manger**
- **c. des sandwichs**

RESOURCES

Workbook/Video Manual: WB Activities, pp. 43–56
Laboratory Manual: Lab Activities, pp. 25–32
Workbook/Video Manual: Video Activities, pp. 223–226; pp. 277–278
WB/VM/LM Answer Key
espaces.vhlcentral.com: Textbook MP3s; Lab MP3s; Instructor's Resource Manual [IRM] (Textbook Audioscript; Lab Audioscript; Videoscript; **Roman-photo** Translations; **Vocabulaire supplémentaire**; **Feuilles d'activités**; Info Gap Activities; **Le zapping** TV clip transcription; **Essayez!** and **Mise en pratique** answers); Transparencies #25, #26, #27; Testing Program, pp. 25–32; Test Files; Testing Program MP3s
Test Generator
Video on DVD

Section Goals

In this section, students will learn and practice vocabulary related to:
- places in a city
- pastimes

Instructional Resources
*espaces.vhlcentral.com: Transparency #25; IRM (**Vocabulaire supplémentaire**; **Mise en pratique** answers; Textbook Audioscript; Lab Audioscript; Info Gap Activities); Textbook MP3s; Lab MP3s; WB/VM/LM Answer Key; activities; downloads; reference tools*

Suggestions

- Have students look at the new vocabulary and identify the cognates.
- Use **Transparency #25**. As you point to different people, describe where they are and what they are doing. Examples: **Ils sont à la terrasse d'un café. Elles bavardent.** Follow up with simple questions based on your narrative.
- Ask students yes/no and either/or questions about their preferences using the new vocabulary. Examples: **Aimez-vous nager? Préférez-vous regarder un film au cinéma ou à la maison?**
- Tell students that proper names of places, like adjectives, usually follow generic nouns. Examples: **le cinéma Rex** and **le parc Monceau.**
- Point out that the term **une boîte de nuit** is familiar and usually used among young people. **Une discothèque** is the more formal word for *nightclub*.
- Point out that **un gymnase** in France generally has a track, exercise equipment, basketball or tennis courts, showers, but no pool.
- Additional vocabulary for this lesson can be found in the **Vocabulaire supplémentaire** on the Supersite.

Leçon 4A

You will learn how to...
- say where you are going
- say what you are going to do

Talking Picture
Audio: Activity

Où allons-nous?

Vocabulaire

danser	*to dance*
explorer	*to explore*
fréquenter	*to frequent; to visit*
inviter	*to invite*
nager	*to swim*
patiner	*to skate*
une banlieue	*suburbs*
une boîte (de nuit)	*nightclub*
un bureau	*office; desk*
un centre commercial	*shopping center, mall*
un centre-ville	*city/town center, downtown*
un cinéma (ciné)	*movie theater, movies*
un endroit	*place*
un grand magasin	*department store*
un gymnase	*gym*
un hôpital	*hospital*
un lieu	*place*
un magasin	*store*
un marché	*market*
un musée	*museum*
un parc	*park*
une piscine	*pool*
un restaurant	*restaurant*
une ville	*city, town*

ressources
WB pp. 43–44 | LM p. 25 | espaces.vhlcentral.com

OPTIONS

Game Divide the class into two teams. Put objects related to different places in a box (for example, movie ticket stubs, sunglasses, and a coffee cup). Without looking, have a student reach into the box and pick out an object. The next player on that person's team has five seconds to name a place associated with the object. If the person cannot do so within the time limit, the other team may "steal" the point by giving a correct response. When the box is empty, the team with the most points wins.

Extra Practice Use magazine photos or clip art from the Internet to make flash cards representing places in and around town. As you show each image, students should say the name of the place and as many activities associated with it as they can think of.

Attention!

Remember that nouns that end in **-al** have an irregular plural. Replace **-al** with **-aux**.
un hôpital → deux hôpitaux

À (*to, at*) before **le** or **les** makes these contractions:
à + le = au   **à + les = aux**
le musée → au musée
les endroits → aux endroits
À does NOT contract with **l'** or **la**.

Mise en pratique

1 Associez **Quels lieux associez-vous à ces activités?**

1. nager ___une piscine___
2. danser ___une boîte (de nuit)___
3. dîner ___un restaurant___
4. travailler ___un bureau___
5. habiter ___une maison___
6. épouser ___une église___
7. voir (*to see*) un film ___un cinéma___
8. acheter (*to buy*) des fruits ___un marché, une épicerie___

2 Écoutez **Djamila parle de sa journée à son amie Samira. Écoutez la conversation et mettez (*put*) les lieux de la liste dans l'ordre chronologique. Il y a deux lieux en trop (*extra*).**

___3___ a. à l'hôpital
___8___ b. à la maison
___1___ c. à la piscine
___5___ d. au centre commercial
___6___ e. au cinéma
___NA___ f. à l'église
___2___ g. au musée
___7___ h. au bureau
___NA___ i. au parc
___4___ j. au restaurant

Coup de main

Note that the French **Je vais à...** is the equivalent of the English *I am going to...*

3 Logique ou illogique **Lisez chaque phrase et déterminez si l'action est logique ou illogique. Corrigez si nécessaire.** Suggested answers

	logique	illogique
1. Maxime invite Delphine à une épicerie. Maxime invite Delphine au musée.	☐	☑
2. Caroline et Aurélie bavardent au marché.	☑	☐
3. Nous déjeunons à l'épicerie. Nous déjeunons au restaurant.	☐	☑
4. Ils dépensent beaucoup d'argent au centre commercial.	☑	☐
5. Vous explorez une ville.	☑	☐
6. Vous escaladez (*climb*) une montagne.	☑	☐
7. J'habite en banlieue.	☑	☐
8. Tu danses dans un marché. Tu danses dans une boîte (de nuit).	☐	☑

Practice more at **espaces.vhlcentral.com.**

1 Expansions
- For additional practice, give students these items. **9. chanter (une église) 10. manger (un restaurant/un café) 11. dessiner (un musée)**
- Do this activity in reverse. Name places and have students say what activities can be done there.

2 Tapescript DJAMILA: Allô, Samira. Comment ça va?
SAMIRA: Très bien, et toi?
D: Aujourd'hui, très bien, mais alors demain, quelle journée!
S: Comment ça?
D: Eh bien… demain matin, je vais à la piscine avec mon frère, Hassan, à 8h00. À 10h00, je vais au musée Rodin avec ma classe. À 11h00, je passe un moment avec grand-mère à l'hôpital. À midi, je vais au restaurant Chez Benoît, près de la place Carnot. L'après-midi, je vais au centre commercial et au cinéma voir le dernier film de Jean Reno. Pour terminer, à 17h00, je vais au bureau de maman pour travailler un peu et nous rentrons à la maison ensemble.
S: Quel programme! Bon, courage Jamila et à bientôt.
D: Merci, bonne soirée.
(On Textbook MP3s)

2 Suggestion Before beginning the activity, have students read the list of places and the **Coup de main**.

3 Suggestion Tell students to write their corrections. Then have volunteers write their sentences on the board.

3 Expansion For additional practice, give students these items. **9. Vous dansez au magasin. (illogique) 10. Je nage au musée. (illogique) 11. Madame Ducharme habite dans une maison. (logique)**

OPTIONS

TPR Have students represent various stores and places in town by giving them signs to hold. Ask them where one does various activities. Examples: **Où est-ce qu'on regarde un film/mange/nage?** The student with the appropriate sign should step forward and answer. Examples: **On regarde un film au cinéma. On mange au restaurant. On nage à la piscine.**

Extra Practice Ask students about their favorite places. Tell them to use generic place names in front of proper nouns, such as **le parc Zilker** and **le musée du Louvre**. Ask: **Quel(le) est votre restaurant/musée/épicerie préféré(e)?**

4 Suggestion Have two volunteers read the **modèle** aloud.

4 Expansion After completing the activity, have students share their partner's opinions with the rest of the class.

5 Suggestion Divide the class into pairs and distribute the Info Gap Handouts found on the Supersite for this activity. Give students ten minutes to complete the activity.

6 Suggestion Tell students that they should use the salutation **chère** if they are writing to a female. Remind them to include expressions of time, such as **le lundi après-midi** and **le samedi soir** in their letters.

Successful Language Learning Remind students that it's important to proofread their work. Have them brainstorm a checklist of potential errors, for example, accents, adjective agreement, and subject-verb agreement. Tell students to add grammar points to their checklists as they learn new structures and make mistakes.

Communication

4 Conversez Avec un(e) partenaire, échangez vos opinions sur ces activités. Utilisez un élément de chaque colonne dans vos réponses. Answers will vary.

MODÈLE

Étudiant(e) 1: *Moi, j'adore bavarder au restaurant, mais je déteste parler au musée.*
Étudiant(e) 2: *Moi aussi, j'adore bavarder au restaurant. Je ne déteste pas parler au musée, mais j'aime mieux bavarder au parc.*

Opinion	Activité	Lieu
adorer	bavarder	au bureau
aimer (mieux)	danser	au centre commercial
ne pas tellement aimer	déjeuner	au centre-ville
détester	dépenser de l'argent	au cinéma
	étudier	au gymnase
	inviter	au musée
	nager	au parc
	parler	à la piscine
	patiner	au restaurant

5 La journée d'Anne Votre professeur va vous donner, à vous et à votre partenaire, une feuille d'activités partiellement illustrée. À tour de rôle, posez-vous des questions pour compléter vos feuilles respectives. Utilisez le vocabulaire de la leçon. Attention! Ne regardez pas la feuille de votre partenaire. Answers will vary.

MODÈLE

Étudiant(e) 1: *À 7h30, Anne quitte la maison. Qu'est-ce qu'elle fait ensuite (do next)?*
Étudiant(e) 2: *À 8h00, elle...*

Anne

6 Une lettre Écrivez une lettre à un(e) ami(e) dans laquelle (*in which*) vous décrivez vos activités de la semaine. Utilisez les expressions de la liste. Answers will vary.

bavarder	passer chez quelqu'un
déjeuner	travailler
dépenser de l'argent	quitter la maison
étudier	un centre commercial
manger au restaurant	une boîte de nuit

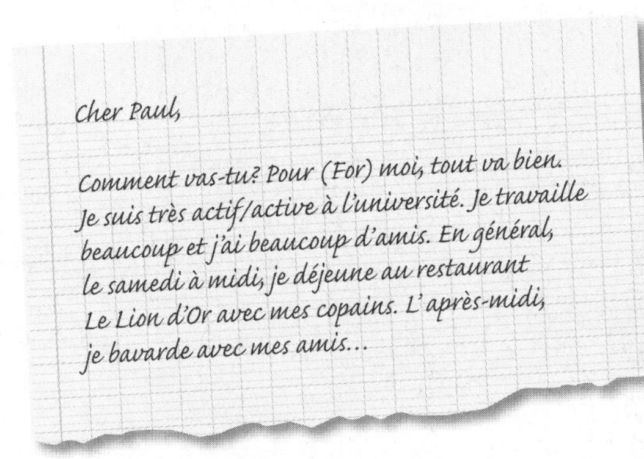

Cher Paul,

Comment vas-tu? Pour (For) moi, tout va bien. Je suis très actif/active à l'université. Je travaille beaucoup et j'ai beaucoup d'amis. En général, le samedi à midi, je déjeune au restaurant Le Lion d'Or avec mes copains. L'après-midi, je bavarde avec mes amis...

OPTIONS

Extra Practice On a sheet of paper, have students write down six places they like to go and what they like to do there. Tell them to circulate around the room trying to find other students who also like to go to those places or do those things. Remind them to jot down the names of people who share something in common with them. Then have them report what they have in common with their classmates.

Small Groups Have small groups plan and design an ideal town or neighborhood. Have them draw the plan, label each place, and list fun activities to do at each one. One person from each group should present the plan to the class. Hold a secret vote and give prizes for the best plan in various categories, such as **le plus amusant**, **le plus créateur**, and **le plus réaliste**.

Les sons et les lettres

Audio: Concepts, Activities
Record & Compare

NATIONAL comparisons STANDARDS

Oral vowels

French has two basic kinds of vowel sounds: oral vowels, the subject of this discussion, and nasal vowels, presented in **Leçon 4B**. Oral vowels are produced by releasing air through the mouth. The pronunciation of French vowels is consistent and predictable.

In short words (usually two-letter words), **e** is pronounced similarly to the *a* in the English word *about*.

le **que** **ce** **de**

The letter **a** alone is pronounced like the *a* in *father*.

la **ça** **ma** **ta**

The letter **i** by itself and the letter **y** are pronounced like the vowel sound in the word *bee*.

ici **livre** **stylo** **lycée**

The letter combination **ou** sounds like the vowel sound in the English word *who*.

vous **nous** **oublier** **écouter**

The French **u** sound does not exist in English. To produce this sound, say *ee* with your lips rounded.

tu **du** **une** **étudier**

Prononcez Répétez les mots suivants à voix haute.

1. je
2. chat
3. fou
4. ville
5. utile
6. place
7. jour
8. triste
9. mari
10. active
11. Sylvie
12. rapide
13. gymnase
14. antipathique
15. calculatrice
16. piscine

Articulez Répétez les phrases suivantes à voix haute.

1. Salut, Luc. Ça va?
2. La philosophie est difficile.
3. Brigitte est une actrice fantastique.
4. Suzanne va à son cours de physique.
5. Tu trouves le cours de maths facile?
6. Viviane a une bourse universitaire.

Dictons Répétez les dictons à voix haute.

Plus on est de fous, plus on rit.[2]

[1] He who steps out of line loses his place.
[2] The more the merrier.

ressources
LM p. 26
espaces.vhlcentral.com

Section Goals

In this section, students will learn about oral vowels.

Instructional Resources
espaces.vhlcentral.com: Textbook MP3s; Lab MP3s; WB/VM/LM Answer Key; IRM (Textbook Audioscript; Lab Audioscript); activities; downloads; reference tools

Suggestions

- Point out that although the pronunciation of the French **e caduc** and that of the *a* in the English word *about* are close, they are not identical. There is a difference in vowel quality and articulation.
- Model the pronunciation of each vowel sound. Have students watch the shape of your mouth, then repeat the sound after you. Pronounce each of the example words and have students repeat them.
- Tell students that an unaccented **e** at the end of a word is silent, but will cause a consonant that precedes it to be pronounced. Example: **petit/petite**.
- Contrast the pronunciation of words containing **u** and **ou**. Examples: **vous/vu** and **tous/tu**.
- Point out that this lesson primarily addresses the pronunciation of single oral vowels. Tell them that like **ou**, various vowel pairs create different sounds when combined. They will learn about these letter combinations in other lessons.
- Dictate five familiar words containing oral vowels to the class, repeating each one at least two times. Then write them on the board or on a transparency and have students check their spelling.

Dictons Ask students if they can think of a saying in English that is similar to **«Qui va à la chasse perd sa place.»** (*You snooze, you lose.*)

OPTIONS

Game Have a spelling bee using vocabulary words from **Leçons 1–7** that contain oral vowel sounds. Pronounce each word, use it in a sentence, and then say the individual word again. Tell students that they must spell the words in French and include the diacritical marks.

Extra Practice Use these sentences with oral vowels for additional practice or dictation. **1. Madame Duclos et son mari sont séparés. 2. Marianne prépare le bac. 3. Tu aimes mieux le parc ou le gymnase? 4. Coralie nage à la piscine.**

Section Goals

In this section, students will learn functional phrases for talking about their plans through comprehensible input.

Instructional Resources
*espaces.vhlcentral.com: Video; WB/VM/LM Answer Key; IRM (Videoscript; **Roman-photo** Translations); activities; downloads; reference tools*
Video on DVD

Video Recap: Leçon 3B Before doing this **Roman-photo**, review the previous one with this activity.

1. De qui Sandrine parle-t-elle souvent? (de Pascal)
2. Où Rachid et Stéphane travaillent-ils? (chez Rachid)
3. Quelle est la profession du père de Rachid? (médecin)
4. Quelle est la profession de la mère de Rachid? (avocate)
5. Qui a envie d'être architecte? (Stéphane)

Video Synopsis David thinks he sees the actress Juliette Binoche in a grocery store. He runs to tell Sandrine. At the café, Sandrine is on the phone with Pascal; he wants to know her weekend plans. David arrives with his news. He, Sandrine, and Amina rush off to try to catch a glimpse of the actress, but have difficulty locating the correct store. At the store, they discover that David saw a store clerk, not Juliette Binoche.

Suggestions
- Ask students to read the title, glance at the video stills, and predict what they think the episode will be about. Record their predictions.
- Have students work in groups and read the **Roman-photo** conversation aloud.
- After students have read the **Roman-photo**, review their predictions and ask them which ones were correct. Then ask a few questions to help them summarize this episode.

Star du cinéma

Video: *Roman-photo*
Record & Compare

PERSONNAGES

Amina

David

Pascal

Sandrine

1

À l'épicerie...
DAVID Juliette Binoche? Pas possible! Je vais chercher Sandrine!

2

Au café...
PASCAL Alors, chérie, tu vas faire quoi de ton week-end?
SANDRINE Euh, demain je vais déjeuner au centre-ville.
PASCAL Bon... et quand est-ce que tu vas rentrer?
SANDRINE Euh, je ne sais pas. Pourquoi?

3

PASCAL Pour rien. Et demain soir, tu vas danser?
SANDRINE Ça dépend. Je vais passer chez Amina pour bavarder avec elle.
PASCAL Combien d'amis as-tu à Aix-en-Provence?
SANDRINE Oh, Pascal...
PASCAL Bon, moi, je vais continuer à penser à toi jour et nuit.

6

DAVID Mais l'actrice! Juliette Binoche!
SANDRINE Allons-y! Vite! C'est une de mes actrices préférées! J'adore le film *Chocolat*!
AMINA Et comme elle est chic! C'est une vraie star!
DAVID Elle est à l'épicerie! Ce n'est pas loin d'ici!

7

Dans la rue...
AMINA Mais elle est où, cette épicerie? Nous allons explorer toute la ville pour rencontrer Juliette Binoche?
SANDRINE C'est là, l'épicerie Pierre Dubois, à côté du cinéma?
DAVID Mais non, elle n'est pas à l'épicerie Pierre Dubois, elle est à l'épicerie près de l'église, en face du parc.

8

AMINA Et combien d'églises est-ce qu'il y a à Aix?
SANDRINE Il n'y a pas d'église en face du parc!
DAVID Bon, hum, l'église sur la place.
AMINA D'accord, et ton église sur la place, elle est ici au centre-ville ou en banlieue?

ACTIVITÉS

1 Vrai ou faux? **Indiquez pour chaque phrase si l'affirmation est vraie ou fausse et corrigez si nécessaire.**

1. David va chercher Pascal. Faux. David va chercher Sandrine.
2. Sandrine va déjeuner au centre-ville. Vrai.
3. Pascal va passer chez Amina. Faux. Sandrine va passer chez Amina.
4. Pascal va continuer à penser à Sandrine jour et nuit. Vrai.
5. Pascal va bien. Vrai.
6. Juliette Binoche est l'actrice préférée de Sandrine. Vrai.
7. L'épicerie est loin du café. Faux. L'épicerie n'est pas loin.
8. L'épicerie Pierre Dubois est à côté de l'église. Faux. L'épicerie Pierre Dubois est à côté du cinéma.
9. Il n'y a pas d'église en face du parc. Vrai.
10. Juliette Binoche fréquente le P'tit Bistrot. Faux. Juliette Binoche ne fréquente pas le P'tit Bistrot.

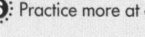

Practice more at **espaces.vhlcentral.com.**

OPTIONS

Avant de regarder la vidéo Before viewing the video, have students brainstorm possible activities that Sandrine might include in her weekend plans. Write their predictions on the board.

Regarder la vidéo Photocopy the videoscript and opaque out ten key words or phrases with white correction fluid in order to create a master for a cloze activity. Hand out photocopies and tell students to fill in the missing words as they watch the video episode. You may want to show the episode twice if students have difficulty with the activity. Then have students compare their answers in small groups.

David et les filles à la recherche de (*in search of*) leur actrice préférée

SANDRINE Oui. Génial. Au revoir, Pascal.
AMINA Salut, Sandrine. Comment va Pascal?
SANDRINE Il va bien, mais il adore bavarder.

DAVID Elle est là, elle est là!
SANDRINE Mais, qui est là?
AMINA Et c'est où, «là»?
DAVID Juliette Binoche! Mais non, pas ici!
SANDRINE ET AMINA Quoi? Qui? Où?

Devant l'épicerie...
DAVID C'est elle, là! Hé, JULIETTE!
AMINA Oh, elle est belle!
SANDRINE Elle est jolie, élégante!
AMINA Elle est... petite?
DAVID Elle, elle... est... vieille?!?

AMINA Ce n'est pas du tout Juliette Binoche!
SANDRINE David, tu es complètement fou! Juliette Binoche, au centre-ville d'Aix?
AMINA Pourquoi est-ce qu'elle ne fréquente pas le P'tit Bistrot?

Expressions utiles

Talking about your plans

- **Tu vas faire quoi de ton week-end?**
  What are you doing this weekend?
- **Je vais déjeuner au centre-ville.**
  I'm going to have lunch downtown.
- **Quand est-ce que tu vas rentrer?**
  When are you coming back?
- **Je ne sais pas.**
  I don't know.
- **Je vais passer chez Amina.**
  I am going to Amina's (house).
- **Nous allons explorer toute la ville.**
  We're going to explore the whole city.

Additional vocabulary

- **C'est une de mes actrices préférées.**
  She's one of my favorite actresses.
- **Comme elle est chic!**
  She is so chic!
- **Ce n'est pas loin d'ici!**
  It's not far from here!
- **Ce n'est pas du tout...**
  It's not... at all.
- **Ça dépend.**
  It depends.
- **Pour rien.**
  No reason.
- **Vite!**
  Quick!, Hurry!

ACTIVITÉS

2 Questions À l'aide (*the help*) d'un dictionnaire, choisissez le bon mot pour chaque question.

1. (Avec qui, Quoi) Sandrine parle-t-elle au téléphone?
2. (Où, Parce que) Sandrine va-t-elle déjeuner?
3. (Qui, Pourquoi) Pascal demande-t-il à Sandrine quand elle va rentrer?
4. (Combien, Comment) d'amis Sandrine a-t-elle?
5. (Combien, À qui) Amina demande-t-elle comment va Pascal?
6. (Quand, Où) est Juliette Binoche?

3 Écrivez Pensez à votre acteur ou actrice préféré(e) et préparez un paragraphe où vous décrivez son apparence, sa personnalité et sa carrière. Comment est-il/elle? Dans quel(s) (*which*) film(s) joue-t-il/elle? Si un jour vous rencontrez cet acteur/cette actrice, qu'est-ce que vous allez lui dire (*say to him or her*)?

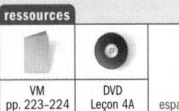

ressources
VM pp. 223-224	DVD Leçon 4A	espaces.vhlcentral.com

Expressions utiles

- Model the pronunciation of the **Expressions utiles** and have students repeat after you.
- As you work through the list, point out forms of **aller** and the interrogative words. Tell students that these concepts will be formally presented in **Espace structures**.
- Point out that, like the English verb *to go*, the verb **aller** is used to express future actions.
- Write **je vais** and **tu vas** on the board. Ask students the questions in the **Expressions utiles** and have them respond. Examples: **Tu vas faire quoi de ton week-end? Quand est-ce que tu vas rentrer?**
- Have students scan the video-still captions for interrogative words that are not in the list and read the sentences. Examples: **combien de, comment, qui, où,** and **pourquoi**.

1 Suggestion Have students write the correct answers to the false statements on the board.

1 Expansion For additional practice, give students these items. **11. Juliette Binoche est vieille. (Faux. Elle n'est pas vieille.) 12. Amina pense que Juliette Binoche est chic. (Vrai.)**

2 Expansion

- For additional practice, give students these items. **7. (Qui, Comment) est-ce que David voit (*see*) à l'épicerie? (Qui) 8. (Pourquoi, Comment) est Juliette Binoche? (Comment) 9. (Quand, Où) est-ce que Pascal va penser à Sandrine? (Quand)**
- Have students answer the questions.

3 Suggestion Have students exchange papers for peer editing. Remind them to pay particular attention to adjective agreement and subject-verb agreement.

OPTIONS

Juliette Binoche Juliette Binoche (1964–), often referred to by the French press simply as "La Binoche", was born in Paris. In addition to being an actress, she is a poster designer and avid painter. Her first film was *Liberty Belle* (1983). She has now acted in more that 30 films. She won a César for "Best actress" in *Bleu* (1983) and an Oscar for "Best Supporting Actress" in *The English Patient* (1996). *Chocolat* (2000) is the film version of the novel *Chocolat* by Joanne Harris.

Small Groups Working in groups of three, have students create a short skit similar to the scenes in video stills 5–10 in which someone thinks they have seen a famous person. Give students ten minutes to prepare, then call on groups to perform their skits for the class.

Section Goals

In this section, students will:
- learn about popular French pastimes
- learn about **le verlan**
- learn about **le maquis** and **le tangana** in Africa
- read about **le parc Astérix**

Instructional Resources
espaces.vhlcentral.com: activities; downloads; reference tools

Culture à la loupe

Avant la lecture Have students read the title and look at the photos. Ask: **À votre avis** (*In your opinion*), **quelles sont les activités préférées des jeunes Français?** Write a list on the board.

Lecture
- Point out the chart **Les activités culturelles des Français**. Ask students what information the chart shows. (The percentages of French people 15 years and older who participate in various cultural activities.)
- Have students verify their predictions and add any missing activities to the list.

Après la lecture Working in small groups, have students compare French and American pastimes. Tell them to make a list of the similarities and differences in French. Then ask several groups to read their lists to the class.

1 Expansion For additional practice, give students these items. **11. Les jeunes Français ne regardent pas souvent la télévision. (Faux. Ils regardent la télévision environ 12 heures par semaine.) 12. Les jeux vidéo ne sont pas très populaires en France. (Faux. Les jeux vidéo sont très populaires en France.) 13. Les jeunes Français aiment passer du temps avec leurs amis. (Vrai.) 14. Le piano est plus** (*more*) **populaire que la guitare en France. (Vrai.)**

NATIONAL STANDARDS connections cultures

CULTURE À LA LOUPE

Les passe-temps des jeunes Français

Comment est-ce que les jeunes occupent leur temps libre° en France? Les jeunes de 15 à 25 ans passent beaucoup de temps à regarder la télévision: environ° 12 heures par° semaine. Ils écoutent aussi beaucoup de musique: environ 16 heures par semaine, et surfent souvent° sur Internet (11 heures). Environ 25% des jeunes Français ont même° déjà° un blog sur Internet. Les jeux° vidéo sont aussi très populaires: les jeunes jouent° en moyenne° 15 heures par semaine.

En France, les jeunes aiment également° les activités culturelles, en particulier le cinéma: en moyenne, ils y° vont une fois° par semaine. Ils aiment aussi la littérature et l'art: presque° 50% (pour cent) visitent des musées ou des monuments historiques chaque année et plus de° 40% vont au théâtre ou à des concerts. Un jeune sur cinq° joue d'un instrument de musique ou chante°, et environ 20% d'entre eux° pratiquent une activité artistique, comme la danse, le théâtre, la sculpture, le dessin° ou la peinture°. La photographie et la vidéo sont aussi très appréciées.

Il ne faut pas° oublier de mentionner que les jeunes Français sont aussi très sportifs. Bien sûr, comme tous les jeunes, ils préfèrent parfois° simplement se détendre° et bavarder avec des amis.

Finalement, les passe-temps des jeunes Français sont similaires aux activités des jeunes Américains!

Les activités culturelles des Français
(% des Français qui les° pratiquent)

le dessin	7%
la peinture	4%
le piano	3%
autre instrument de musique	3%
la danse	2%
la guitare	2%
la sculpture	1%
le théâtre	1%

SOURCE: Francoscopie

temps libre *free time* **environ** *around* **par** *per* **souvent** *often* **même** *even* **déjà** *already* **jeux** *games* **jouent** *play* **en moyenne** *on average* **également** *also* **y** *there* **fois** *time* **presque** *almost* **plus de** *more than* **un... sur cinq** *one... in five* **chante** *sings* **d'entre eux** *of them* **dessin** *drawing* **peinture** *painting* **Il ne faut pas** *One must not* **parfois** *sometimes* **se détendre** *relax* **les** *them*

ACTIVITÉS

1 Vrai ou faux? Indiquez si les phrases sont vraies ou fausses. Corrigez les phrases fausses. Some answers may vary.

1. Les jeunes Français n'écoutent pas de musique. Faux. Les jeunes Français écoutent de la musique environ 16 heures par semaine.
2. Ils n'utilisent pas Internet. Faux. Ils utilisent Internet 11 heures par semaine.
3. Ils aiment aller au musée. Vrai.
4. Ils n'aiment pas beaucoup les livres. Faux. Ils aiment la littérature.
5. Ils n'aiment pas pratiquer d'activités artistiques. Faux. Possible answer: Ils aiment la danse, le théâtre et le dessin.
6. Les Français entre 15 et 25 ans ne font pas de sport. Faux. Les jeunes Français sont très sportifs.
7. Les passe-temps des jeunes Américains sont similaires aux passetemps des jeunes Français. Vrai.
8. L'instrument de musique le plus (*the most*) populaire en France est le piano. Vrai.
9. Plus de (*More*) gens pratiquent la peinture que la sculpture. Vrai.
10. Environ 10% des jeunes Français pratiquent la sculpture. Faux. 1% des jeunes Français pratiquent la sculpture.

Practice more at **espaces.vhlcentral.com.**

OPTIONS

Pairs Have students work in pairs and ask each other about the information in the chart **Les activités culturelles des jeunes Français**. To help them, write a model on the board. Example: **Étudiant(e) 1: Est-ce que le dessin est un passe-temps populaire en France? Étudiant(e) 2: Oui, sept pour cent des jeunes Français dessinent.**

Cultural Activity Distribute photocopies of the cinematic and cultural activities in the weekly ***Pariscope*** or ***Officiel des spectacles***. Tell students to make a list of the ones they would like to attend. Then have them compare their lists in small groups.

LE FRANÇAIS QUOTIDIEN

Le verlan

En France, on entend parfois° des jeunes parler en **verlan**. En verlan, les syllabes des mots sont inversées°:

l'envers° → vers-l'en → verlan.

Voici quelques exemples:

français	verlan	anglais
louche	chelou	*shady*
café	féca	*café*
mec	keum	*guy*
femme	meuf	*woman*

parfois *sometimes* **inversées** *inverted* **l'envers** *the reverse*

PORTRAIT

Le parc Astérix

Situé° à 30 kilomètres de Paris, en Picardie, le parc Astérix est le premier parc à thème français. Le parc d'attractions°, ouvert° en 1989, est basé sur la bande dessinée° française, *Astérix le Gaulois*. Création de René Goscinny et d'Albert Uderzo, Astérix est un guerrier gaulois° qui lutte° contre l'invasion des Romains. Au parc Astérix, il y a des montagnes russes°, des petits trains et des spectacles, tous° basés sur les aventures d'Astérix et de son meilleur ami, Obélix. Une des attractions, *le Tonnerre° de Zeus*, est la plus grande° montagne russe en bois° d'Europe.

Situé *Located* **parc d'attractions** *amusement park* **ouvert** *opened* **bande dessinée** *comic strip* **guerrier gaulois** *Gallic warrior* **lutte** *fights* **montagnes russes** *roller coasters* **tous** *all* **Tonnerre** *Thunder* **la plus grande** *the largest* **en bois** *wooden*

LE MONDE FRANCOPHONE

Où passer le temps

Voici quelques endroits typiques où les jeunes francophones aiment se restaurer° et passer du temps.

En Afrique de l'Ouest

Le maquis Commun dans beaucoup de pays° d'Afrique de l'Ouest°, le maquis est un restaurant où on peut manger à bas prix°. Situé en ville ou en bord de route°, le maquis est typiquement en plein air°.

Au Sénégal

Le tangana Le terme «tang» signifie «chaud» en wolof, une des langues nationales du Sénégal. Le tangana est un lieu populaire pour se restaurer. On trouve souvent les tanganas au coin de la rue°, en plein air, avec des tables et des bancs°.

se restaurer *have something to eat* **pays** *countries* **ouest** *west* **à bas prix** *inexpensively* **en bord de route** *on the side of the road* **en plein air** *outdoors* **coin de la rue** *street corner* **bancs** *benches*

SUR INTERNET

Comment sont les parcs d'attractions dans les autres pays francophones?

Go to espaces.vhlcentral.com to find more information related to this **ESPACE CULTURE**.

ACTIVITÉS

2 Compréhension Complétez les phrases.

1. Le parc Astérix est basé sur Astérix le Gaulois, une ___bande dessinée___.
2. Astérix le Gaulois est une ___création___ de René Goscinny et d'Albert Uderzo.
3. Le parc Astérix est près de la ville de ___Paris___.
4. Astérix est un ___guerrier___ gaulois.
5. En verlan, on peut passer du temps avec ses copains au ___féca___.
6. Au Sénégal, on parle aussi le ___wolof___.

3 Vos activités préférées Posez des questions à trois ou quatre de vos camarades de classe à propos de leurs activités favorites. Comparez vos résultats avec ceux (*those*) d'un autre groupe.

ressources
espaces.vhlcentral.com

Le français quotidien Model the pronunciation of each term and have students repeat it. Ask students what language or jargon in English is similar to **verlan**. (pig latin)

Portrait Point out Astérix and Obélix in the photo. If possible, bring in an Astérix comic strip to show the students.

Le monde francophone Have students read the text. Then ask a few comprehension questions. Examples: **1. Pourquoi les jeunes fréquentent-ils les maquis et les tanganas? (pour manger et passer le temps) 2. On trouve les maquis en ville ou en bord de route? (les deux) Et les tanganas? (Ils sont souvent au coin d'une rue.) 3. On mange à l'intérieur ou en plein air dans le maquis et le tangana? (en plein air)**

2 Expansion For additional practice, give students these items. **7. Le parc Astérix est le premier ____ à thème français. (parc) 8. Astérix lutte (*fights*) contre les ____. (Romains) 9. Au parc Astérix, il y a des montagnes ____. (russes) 10. L'ami d'Astérix s'appelle ____. (Obélix)**

3 Expansion Do a quick class survey to find out how many students like each activity and which one is the most popular. Tally the results on the board. Example: **Combien d'étudiants surfent sur Internet?**

OPTIONS

Le verlan Write on the board: **1. une bande 2. la musique 3. le métro 4. manger 5. bonjour 6. fou** Have students work in pairs. Tell them to copy the words and write the equivalents in **verlan**. Answers: **1. une deban 2. la siquemu/sicmu 3. le tromé 4. géman 5. jourbon 6. ouf**

Le parc Astérix Some other popular attractions at the park are **La Galère** (a giant swinging ship), **Les Chaises Volantes** (flying chairs), **Le Cheval de Troie** (the Trojan horse), and **Transdemonium** (a ghost train through a castle dungeon). Have students take a virtual tour of the park by going to **www.parcasterix.com**.

Section Goals

In this section, students will learn:
- the verb **aller**
- the **futur proche** with **aller**
- the preposition **à**

Instructional Resources
*espaces.vhlcentral.com: Lab MP3s; WB/VM/LM Answer Key; IRM (**Essayez!** and **Mise en pratique** answers; Lab Audioscript; Info Gap Activities); activities; downloads; reference tools*

Suggestions
- Write the paradigm of **aller** on the board and model the pronunciation. Ask students what forms of **aller** are irregular.
- Write your next day's schedule on the board using infinitives and nouns. Examples: **8h00: bibliothèque; 10h00: cours de français; 12h00: déjeuner** Explain what you are going to do using the verb **aller**. Examples: **Je vais (aller) à la bibliothèque à huit heures. Je vais déjeuner à midi**. Ask students questions about their schedules using forms of **aller**.
- Ask individuals questions about their future plans using **aller**. Examples: **Allez-vous chez vos parents ce week-end? Allez-vous manger avec des copains vendredi soir?**
- Bring in pictures of people dressed for different activities. Describe them to the class using the verb **aller**. Example: Showing a picture of a swimmer, say: **Il/Elle va à la piscine.** Then explain the contractions **à** + **le** = **au** and **à** + **les** = **aux**.
- Tell students that, when followed by another verb (in the infinitive), **penser** doesn't take a preposition. Example: **Je pense aller au café après les cours.**
- Model the pronunciation of the list of prepositions with places. Tell students that they should memorize these phrases.

4A.1 The verb *aller*

NATIONAL comparisons STANDARDS

Point de départ In **Leçon 1A**, you saw a form of the verb **aller** (*to go*) in the expression **ça va**. Now you will use this verb to talk about going places and to express actions that take place in the immediate future.

Aller

je vais	*I go*	nous allons	*we go*
tu vas	*you go*	vous allez	*you go*
il/elle va	*he/she/it goes*	ils/elles vont	*they go*

- Note that **aller** is irregular. Only the **nous** and **vous** forms resemble the infinitive.

Tu **vas** souvent au cinéma?
Do you go often to the movies?

Nous **allons** au marché le samedi.
We go to the market on Saturdays.

Je **vais** à la piscine.
I'm going to the pool.

Vous **allez** au parc aussi?
Are you going to the park too?

- **Aller** can also be used with another verb to tell what is going to happen. This construction is called **le futur proche** (*immediate future*). Conjugate **aller** in the present tense and place the other verb's infinitive form directly after it.

Nous **allons déjeuner** sur la terrasse.
We're going to eat lunch on the terrace.

Marc et Julie **vont explorer** le centre-ville.
Marc and Julie are going to explore downtown.

Demain, je vais déjeuner au centre-ville.
Et quand est-ce que tu vas rentrer?

- To negate an expression in **le futur proche**, place **ne/n'** before the conjugated form of **aller** and **pas** after it.

Je **ne vais pas** faire mes devoirs.
I'm not going to do my homework.

Nous **n'allons pas** quitter la maison.
We're not going to leave the house.

- Note that this construction can be used with the infinitive of **aller** to mean *going to go (somewhere)*.

Elle **va aller** à la piscine.
She's going to go to the pool.

Vous **allez aller** au gymnase ce soir?
You're going to go to the gym tonight?

MISE EN PRATIQUE

1 Questions parentales Votre père est très curieux. Trouvez les questions qu'il pose.

MODÈLE

tes frères / piscine *Tes frères vont à la piscine?*

1. tu / cinéma / ce soir
   Tu vas au cinéma ce soir?
2. tes amis et toi, vous / boîte
   Tes amis et toi, vous allez en boîte?
3. ta mère et moi, nous / ville / vendredi
   Ta mère et moi, nous allons en ville vendredi?
4. ta petite amie / souvent / marché
   Ta petite amie va souvent au marché?
5. je / musée / avec toi / demain
   Je vais au musée avec toi demain?
6. tes amis / parc
   Tes amis vont au parc?

2 Samedi prochain Voici ce que (*what*) vous et vos amis faites (*are doing*) aujourd'hui. Indiquez que vous allez faire les mêmes (*same*) choses samedi prochain.

MODÈLE

Je nage. *Samedi prochain aussi, je vais nager.*

1. Paul bavarde avec ses copains.
   Samedi prochain aussi, Paul va bavarder avec ses copains.
2. Nous dansons.
   ... nous allons danser.
3. Je dépense de l'argent dans un magasin.
   ... je vais dépenser de l'argent dans un magasin.
4. Luc et Sylvie déjeunent au restaurant.
   ... Luc et Sylvie vont déjeuner au restaurant.
5. Vous explorez le centre-ville.
   ... vous allez explorer le centre-ville.
6. Tu patines.
   ... tu vas patiner.

3 Où vont-ils? Avec un(e) partenaire, regardez les images et indiquez où vont les personnages. Answers will vary.

MODÈLE

Henri va au cinéma.

Henri

1. je

3. Paul et Luc

2. nous

4. vous

Practice more at **espaces.vhlcentral.com.**

OPTIONS

TPR Invent gestures to pantomime some activities taught in **Leçon 2B**. Examples: **nager:** *move arms as if swimming;* **bavarder:** *make talking gestures with hands;* **dépenser de l'argent:** *turn pockets inside out.* Signal individuals to gesture appropriately as you cue activities by saying: **Nous allons…** or **On va….**

Extra Practice Do a quick substitution drill to practice **aller**. Write a sentence on the board and have students read it aloud. Then say a new subject and have students repeat the sentence, substituting the new subject. Examples: **1. Tu vas à l'hôpital. (nous, mon frère, vous, mes parents, je) 2. Il va aller au kiosque. (je, Claudine, nous, tu, les enfants, vous)**

national communication standards

COMMUNICATION

4 Activités du week-end Avec un(e) partenaire, assemblez les éléments des colonnes pour poser des questions. Rajoutez (*Add*) d'autres éléments utiles. Answers will vary.

MODÈLE

Étudiant(e) 1: *Est-ce que tu vas déjeuner avec tes copains?*
Étudiant(e) 2: *Oui, je vais déjeuner avec mes copains.*

A	B	C	D
ta sœur	aller	voyager	professeur
vous		aller	cinéma
tes copains		déjeuner	boîte de nuit
nous		bavarder	piscine
tu		nager	centre commercial
ton petit ami		danser	café
ta petite amie		parler	parents
tes grands-parents			copains
			petit(e) ami(e)

5 À Deauville Votre professeur va vous donner, à vous et à votre partenaire, un plan (*map*) de Deauville. Attention! Ne regardez pas la feuille de votre partenaire. Answers will vary.

MODÈLE

Étudiant(e) 1: *Où va Simon?*
Étudiant(e) 2: *Il va au kiosque.*

6 Le grand voyage Vous avez gagné (*have won*) un voyage dans un lieu de votre choix. Par groupes de trois, expliquez à vos camarades ce que vous allez faire pendant (*during*) le voyage. Vos camarades vont deviner (*to guess*) où vous allez. Answers will vary.

MODÈLE

Étudiant(e) 1: *Je vais visiter le musée du Louvre.*
Étudiant(e) 2: *Est-ce que tu vas aller à Paris?*

The preposition *à*

- The preposition **à** contracts with the definite articles **le** and **les**. It does not contract with **la** or **l'**.

à + le ▶ au	à + les ▶ aux
Nous allons **au** magasin. *We're going to the store.*	Ils parlent **aux** profs. *They speak to the professors.*
Je rentre **à la** maison. *I'm going back home.*	Il va **à l'**épicerie. *He's going to the grocery store.*

- The preposition **à** can be translated in various ways in English: *to, in, at*. It often indicates a physical location, as with **aller à** and **habiter à**. However, it can have other meanings depending on the verb used.

Verbs with the preposition *à*

commencer à [+ infinitive]	*to start (doing something)*	penser à	*to think about*
parler à	*to talk to*	téléphoner à	*to phone (someone)*

Elle va **parler au** professeur.
She's going to talk to the professor.

Il **commence à travailler** demain.
He starts working tomorrow.

- In general, **à** is used to mean *at* or *in*, whereas **dans** is used to mean *inside*. When learning a place name in French, learn the preposition that accompanies it.

Prepositions with place names

à la maison	*at home*	dans la maison	*inside the house*
à Paris	*in Paris*	dans Paris	*inside Paris*
en ville	*in town*	dans la ville	*inside the town*
sur la place	*in the square*	à la/sur la/en terrasse	*on the terrace*

Tu travailles **à la maison**?
Are you working at home?

On mange **dans la maison**.
We'll eat inside the house.

Essayez! Utilisez la forme correcte du verbe **aller**.

1. Comment ça _va_?
2. Tu _vas_ à la piscine pour nager.
3. Ils _vont_ au centre-ville.
4. Nous _allons_ bavarder au café.
5. Vous _allez_ aller au restaurant ce soir?
6. Elle _va_ aller à l'église dimanche matin.
7. Ce soir, je _vais_ danser en boîte.
8. On ne _va_ pas passer par l'épicerie cet après-midi.

Essayez! Have students create a few additional sentences using the verb **aller**.

1 Suggestion To check students' answers, have a volunteer say the question, then call on another student to answer it.

2 Expansion For additional practice, give students these items. **7. Nous passons chez Martine. (Samedi prochain aussi, nous allons passer chez Martine.) 8. André travaille le matin. (... André va travailler le matin.) 9. Je dîne avec un ami. (... je vais dîner avec un ami.)**

3 Suggestion Have students take turns asking where the people in the drawings are going and answering the questions. Example: **Où va Henri? (Henri va au cinéma.)**

4 Suggestion Have two volunteers read the **modèle**. Remind students that they can answer in the negative. Encourage them to expand on their answers. Examples: **Oui, je vais déjeuner avec mes copains au Petit Croissant./Non, je ne vais pas déjeuner avec mes copains, mais je vais aller au centre commercial avec ma mère.**

5 Suggestions
- Tell students that Deauville is a fashionable seaside resort in Normandy frequented by the rich and famous.
- Divide the class into pairs and distribute the Info Gap Handouts found on the Supersite for this activity. Give students ten minutes to complete the activity.

6 Suggestion Have two volunteers read the **modèle**. Encourage students to choose famous places in the francophone world.

OPTIONS

Game Divide the class into four-member teams. Using the immediate future, each team will write a description of tomorrow's events for a well-known fictional character. Teams take turns reading and/or writing the description on the board without giving the character's name. The other teams will guess the identity. Each correct guess earns a point. If a team fools the others, it earns two points. The team with the most points wins.

Video Show the video episode again to give students additional input on the verb **aller**. Pause the video where appropriate to discuss how **aller** was used and to ask comprehension questions.

Section Goals

In this section, students will learn interrogative words.

Instructional Resources
*espaces.vhlcentral.com: Lab MP3s; WB/VM/LM Answer Key; IRM (**Essayez!** and **Mise en pratique** answers; Lab Audioscript); activities; downloads; reference tools*

Suggestions

- Write the interrogative words on the board. Have students identify the words they know. Examples: **comment?**, **combien?**, **pourquoi?**, **qui?**, and **quel(s)/quelle(s)?** Model the pronunciation of the new words and have students repeat.
- Point out that in informal conversation interrogative words can be placed after the verb. Examples: **Tu vas où? Il s'appelle comment?**
- Explain that **que/qu'...?**, **quel(le)(s)?**, and **quoi?** cannot be used interchangeably. **Que?** is often used in more formal questions or with **est-ce que**. Examples: **Que cherchez-vous? Qu'est-ce que vous cherchez?**
- Point out that **que?** and **quoi?** are used to ask about things. A preposition usually precedes **quoi?** or the word appears at the end of an informal question. Examples: **De quoi parlez-vous? Tu manges quoi?**
- Point out that **qui?** is used to ask about people. **Qui?** takes the third person singular verb form. You may also wish to introduce the expression **Qui est-ce qui...?**

4A.2 Interrogative words

NATIONAL comparisons STANDARDS

Point de départ In **Leçon 2A**, you learned four ways to formulate yes or no questions in French. However, many questions seek information that can't be provided by a simple yes or no answer.

- Use these words with **est-ce que** or inversion.

Interrogative words

à quelle heure?	*at what time?*	**quand?**	*when?*
combien (de)?	*how many?; how much?*	**que/qu'...?**	*what?*
comment?	*how?; what?*	**quel(le)(s)?**	*which?; what?*
où?	*where?*	**(à/avec/pour) qui?**	*(to/with/for) who(m)?*
pourquoi?	*why?*	**quoi?**	*what?*

À qui le professeur parle-t-il ce matin?
Whom is the professor talking to this morning?

Combien de villes **y a-t-il** en Suisse?
How many cities are there in Switzerland?

Pourquoi est-ce que tu danses?
Why are you dancing?

Que vas-tu manger?
What are you going to eat?

- Although **quand?** and **à quelle heure?** can be translated as *when?* in English, they are not interchangeable. Use **quand** to talk about a day or date, and **à quelle heure** to talk about a particular time of day.

Quand est-ce que le cours commence?
When does the class start?

À quelle heure est-ce qu'il commence?
At what time does it begin?

Il commence **le lundi 28 août**.
It starts Monday, August 28.

Il commence **à dix heures et demie**.
It starts at 10:30.

- Another way to formulate questions with most interrogative words is by placing them after a verb. This kind of formulation is very informal but very common.

Tu t'appelles **comment**?
What's your name?

Tu habites **où**?
Where do you live?

- Note that **quoi?** (*what?*) must immediately follow a preposition in order to be used with **est-ce que** or inversion. If no preposition is necessary, place **quoi** after the verb.

À quoi pensez-vous?
What are you thinking about?

Elle étudie **quoi**?
What does she study?

De quoi est-ce qu'il parle?
What is he talking about?

Tu regardes **quoi**?
What are you looking at?

MISE EN PRATIQUE

1 Le français familier Utilisez l'inversion pour refaire les questions.

MODÈLE
Tu t'appelles comment?
Comment t'appelles-tu?

1. Tu habites où? Où habites-tu?
2. Le film commence à quelle heure? À quelle heure le film commence-t-il?
3. Il est quelle heure? Quelle heure est-il?
4. Tu as combien de frères? Combien de frères as-tu?
5. Le prof parle quand? Quand le prof parle-t-il?
6. Vous aimez quoi? Qu'aimez-vous?
7. Elle téléphone à qui? À qui téléphone-t-elle?
8. Il étudie comment? Comment étudie-t-il?

2 La paire Trouvez la paire et formez des phrases complètes. Utilisez chaque (*each*) phrase une fois (*once*). Answers may vary.

1. À quelle heure d	a. est-ce que tu regardes?
2. Comment f	b. habitent-ils?
3. Combien de g	c. est-ce que tu habites dans le centre-ville?
4. Avec qui h	d. est-ce que le cours commence?
5. Où b	e. heure est-il?
6. Pourquoi c	f. vous appelez-vous?
7. Qu' a	g. villes est-ce qu'il y a aux États-Unis?
8. Quelle e	h. parlez-vous?

3 La question Vous avez les réponses. Quelles sont les questions? Some answers will vary.

MODÈLE
Il est midi.
Quelle heure est-il?

1. Les cours commencent à huit heures. À quelle heure est-ce que les cours commencent?
2. Stéphanie habite à Paris. Où est-ce que Stéphanie habite?
3. Julien danse avec Caroline. Avec qui est-ce que Julien danse?
4. Elle s'appelle Julie. Comment s'appelle-t-elle?
5. Laëtitia a deux chiens. Combien de chiens Laëtitia a-t-elle?
6. Elle déjeune dans ce restaurant parce qu'il est à côté de son bureau. Pourquoi déjeune-t-elle dans ce restaurant?
7. Nous allons bien, merci. Comment allez-vous?
8. Je vais au marché mardi. Quand est-ce que tu vas au marché?

Practice more at **espaces.vhlcentral.com.**

OPTIONS

Extra Practice Divide the class in two. Give a strip of paper with a question on it to each member of one group. Example: **Où va-t-on pour dépenser de l'argent?** Give an answer to each member of the other group. Example: **On va au centre commercial.** Have students circulate around the room asking their questions until they find the person with the appropriate response. Write only one possible answer for each question.

Extra Practice Have students turn to the **Roman-photo** on pages 114–115. Tell them to write as many questions as they can based on the photos. Example: **Où est David? (Il est à l'épicerie.)** Ask volunteers to read their questions aloud and then call other students to answer them. You may also have students ask their questions in pairs.

NATIONAL communication STANDARDS

COMMUNICATION

4 Questions et réponses À tour de rôle, posez une question à un(e) partenaire au sujet de chaque (*each*) thème de la liste. Posez une deuxième (*second*) question basée sur sa réponse. Answers will vary.

MODÈLE

Étudiant(e) 1: Où est-ce que tu habites?
Étudiant(e) 2: J'habite chez mes parents.
Étudiant(e) 1: Pourquoi est-ce que tu habites chez tes parents?

Thèmes

- où vous habitez
- ce que vous faites (*do*) le week-end
- à qui vous téléphonez
- combien de frères et sœurs vous avez
- les endroits que vous fréquentez avec vos copains

5 La montagne Par groupes de quatre, lisez (*read*) avec attention la lettre de Céline. Fermez votre livre. Une personne du groupe va poser une question basée sur l'information donnée. La personne qui répond pose une autre question au groupe, etc. Answers will vary.

Bonjour. Je m'appelle Céline. J'ai 20 ans. Je suis grande, mince et sportive. J'habite à Grenoble dans une maison agréable. Je suis étudiante à l'université. J'adore la montagne.

Tous les week-ends, je vais skier à Chamrousse avec mes trois amis Théo, Catherine et Pascal. Nous skions de midi à cinq heures. À six heures, nous prenons un chocolat chaud à la terrasse d'un café ou nous allons manger des crêpes dans un restaurant. Nous rencontrons souvent d'autres étudiants et nous allons en boîte tous ensemble.

- To answer a question formulated with **pourquoi**, use **parce que/qu'** (*because*).

Pourquoi habites-tu en banlieue?	**Parce que** je n'aime pas le centre-ville.
Why do you live in the suburbs?	*Because I don't like downtown.*

- It's impolite to use **Quoi?** to indicate that you don't understand what's being said. Use **Comment?** or **Pardon?** instead.

Vous allez voyager cette année?	**Comment?**
Are you going to travel this year?	*I beg your pardon?*

- Note that when **qui** is used as a subject, the verb that follows is always singular.

Qui fréquente le café?	Nora et Angélique fréquentent le café.
Who goes to the café?	*Nora and Angélique go to the café.*

- **Quel(le)(s)** agrees in gender and number with the noun it modifies.

The interrogative adjective *quel(le)(s)*

	singular		plural	
masculine	**quel hôpital?**	*which hospital?*	**quels restaurants?**	*which restaurants?*
feminine	**quelle place?**	*which public square?*	**quelles montagnes?**	*which mountains?*

- **Quel(le)(s)** can be placed before a form of the verb **être**.

Quels problèmes as-tu?	*but*	**Quels sont** tes problèmes?
What problems do you have?		*What are your problems?*

Tu es de quelle origine?

Quel jour sommes-nous?

Essayez! **Donnez les mots (*words*) interrogatifs.**

1. Comment allez-vous? Moi, je vais très bien, merci.
2. Qu' est-ce que vous allez faire (*do*) après le cours?
3. Le cours de français commence à quelle heure?
4. Pourquoi est-ce que tu ne travailles pas aujourd'hui?
5. Avec qui est-ce qu'on va au cinéma ce soir?
6. Combien d'étudiants y a-t-il dans la salle de classe?

Essayez! Have one student read the question aloud, then call on another student to respond.

1 Suggestion Have students compare their answers with a classmate.

2 Suggestion Have one student say the question and call on another student to answer it.

3 Suggestion Before beginning the activity, point out that there is more than one way to form some of the questions. Have students work in pairs. Tell them to take turns asking and answering the questions.

4 Suggestion Have two volunteers read the **modèle** aloud. Tell students to jot down their partner's responses.

5 Suggestion Circulate among the groups, lending help where necessary. You might want to have one person in each group keep the book open to verify answers.

OPTIONS

Extra Practice Bring in pictures or magazine photos of people doing various activities. Have students, as a class, create as many questions as they can about the pictures. Also, call on individuals to answer each question.

Extra Practice Tell students to write a simple statement about something they like, love, or hate. Have the first student say the statement. The next student asks **Pourquoi?** and the first student answers. Then the second student says his or her statement, and a third student asks why. Examples: **Étudiant(e) 1: Je déteste étudier le samedi soir. Étudiant(e) 2: Pourquoi? Étudiant(e) 1: Parce que c'est la barbe/barbant!**

Instructional Resources
espaces.vhlcentral.com: IRM (Info Gap Activities); Testing Program, pp. 25–28; Test Files; Testing Program MP3s; activities; downloads; reference tools
Test Generator

1 Suggestion Model the activity with a volunteer by asking questions about **le café**. Tell students to jot down notes during the interviews. Encourage them to add other places to the list.

2 Suggestion Photocopy and distribute a page from a French day planner so that students can make a note of the activities in the appropriate place. To review telling time, tell students to say the time at which they do the activities as well as the day.

3 Suggestion Before beginning the activity, have students make a list of possible activities for the weekend.

4 Suggestion Before beginning the activity, give students a few minutes to make a list of possible activities in their hometown to discuss.

5 Suggestion Have two volunteers to read the **modèle** aloud. Then have students brainstorm places they could go and things they could do in each city. Write their suggestions on the board.

6 Suggestion Divide the class into pairs and distribute the Info Gap Handouts for this activity. Give students ten minutes to complete the activity.

6 Expansion Call on volunteers to read their descriptions aloud and have the class compare them.

Révision

1 En ville Par groupes de trois, interviewez vos camarades. Où allez-vous en ville? Quand ils mentionnent un endroit de la liste, demandez des détails (quand? avec qui? pourquoi? etc.). Présentez les réponses à la classe. Answers will vary.

le café	le musée
le centre commercial	le parc
le cinéma	la piscine
le marché	le restaurant

2 La semaine prochaine Voici votre agenda (*day planner*). Parlez de votre semaine avec un(e) partenaire. Mentionnez trois activités associées au travail et trois activités d'un autre type. Deux des activités doivent (*must*) être des activités de groupe. Answers will vary.

MODÈLE

Lundi, je vais préparer un examen, mais samedi, je vais danser en boîte.

	L	M	M	J	V	S	D
8h30							
9h00							
9h30							
10h00							
10h30							
11h00							
11h30							
12h00							
12h30							

3 Le week-end Par groupes de trois, posez-vous des questions sur vos projets (*plans*) pour le week-end prochain. Donnez des détails. Mentionnez aussi des activités faites (*made*) pour deux personnes. Answers will vary.

MODÈLE

Étudiant(e) 1: *Quels projets avez-vous pour ce week-end?*
Étudiant(e) 2: *Nous allons au marché samedi.*
Étudiant(e) 3: *Et nous allons au café dimanche.*

4 Ma ville À tour de rôle, vous invitez votre partenaire dans votre ville d'origine pour une visite d'une semaine. Préparez une liste d'activités variées et proposez-les (*them*) à votre partenaire. Ensuite (*Then*), comparez vos villes et vos projets (*plans*) avec ceux (*those*) d'un autre groupe. Answers will vary.

MODÈLE

Étudiant(e) 1: *Samedi, on va au centre-ville.*
Étudiant(e) 2: *Nous allons dépenser de l'argent!*

5 Où passer un long week-end? Vous et votre partenaire avez la possibilité de passer un long week-end à Montréal ou à La Nouvelle-Orléans, mais vous préférez chacun(e) (*each one*) une ville différente. Jouez la conversation pour la classe. Answers will vary.

MODÈLE

Étudiant(e) 1: *À Montréal, on va aller dans les librairies!*
Étudiant(e) 2: *Oui, mais à La Nouvelle-Orléans, je vais aller à des concerts de musique cajun!*

Montréal
- le jardin (*garden*) botanique
- le musée des Beaux-Arts
- le parc du Mont-Royal
- le Vieux-Montréal

La Nouvelle-Orléans
- le Café du Monde
- la cathédrale Saint-Louis
- la route des plantations
- le vieux carré, quartier (*neighborhood*) français

6 La semaine de Martine Votre professeur va vous donner, à vous et à votre partenaire, des informations sur la semaine de Martine. Attention! Ne regardez pas la feuille de votre partenaire. Answers will vary.

MODÈLE

Lundi matin, Martine va dessiner au parc.

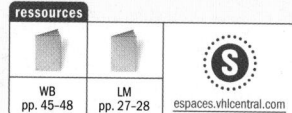

ressources
WB pp. 45-48
LM pp. 27-28
espaces.vhlcentral.com

OPTIONS

Cultural Activity Invite a native French speaker to class. Before the person arrives, have students prepare a list of questions that they would like to ask this person. For example, they could ask about the person's job, family, leisure-time activities, weekend plans, and the places he or she frequents. Have students use their questions to interview the person.

Pairs Give pairs three minutes to write as many questions as they can using interrogative words. Then have them get together with another pair and take turns asking and answering the questions.

Video: TV Clip

Le Zapping

National Standards: communication, cultures; connections, communities

SWISS made

La compagnie Swiss International Air Lines offre à ses passagers une alternative aux compagnies aériennes° contemporaines. En général, le public a une mauvaise opinion des compagnies: les gens° se plaignent° constamment du mauvais service et de la mauvaise cuisine. Voilà pourquoi Swiss International Air Lines propose à ses clients l'élégance et le confort. Sa stratégie de marketing bénéficie de l'excellente réputation des produits et des services suisses, dont° la qualité supérieure est reconnue° dans le monde entier.

—Le ventilateur doucement° murmure...

—Au micro° parle le copilote...

Compréhension Répondez aux questions.

1. Quels endroits d'une ville trouve-t-on dans la publicité (*ad*)? Dans la publicité, on trouve un parc, un bureau, un restaurant et une piscine.
2. Quels types de personnes y a-t-il dans la publicité? Pourquoi est-ce important? Answers will vary.

Discussion Par groupes de quatre, répondez aux questions. Answers will vary.

1. Avez-vous un produit fabriqué en Suisse? Si oui, quel produit? Décrivez sa qualité. Si non, quel produit suisse avez-vous envie de posséder? Pourquoi?
2. Vous allez fonder une compagnie aérienne différente des autres (*from the others*). Comment est-elle différente? Quelles destinations va-t-elle proposer?

compagnies aériennes *airlines* **les gens** *people* **se plaignent** *complain* **dont** *whose*
reconnue *recognized* **avion** *plane* **Le ventilateur doucement** *The fan gently* **micro** *microphone*

Practice more at **espaces.vhlcentral.com.**

Section Goals

In this section, students will:
- read about Swiss International Airlines
- watch a commercial for a Swiss airline
- answer questions about the commercial and Swiss International Airlines

Instructional Resources
*espaces.vhlcentral.com: TV commercial; IRM (**Le zapping** TV clip transcription); activities; downloads; reference tools*

Introduction
To check comprehension, ask these questions. **1. Que propose Swiss International Airlines à ses passagers? (Elle propose une alternative aux compagnies aériennes contemporaines.) 2. Quelle opinion le public a-t-il des compagnies aériennes? (Le public a une mauvaise opinion des compagnies aériennes.) 3. Pourquoi la stratégie de marketing bénéficie-t-elle de l'excellente réputation des produits suisses? (La qualité supérieure des produits suisses est reconnue dans le monde entier.)**

Avant de regarder la vidéo
- Have students look at the video stills, read the captions, and predict what is happening in the commercial for each visual. **(1. La femme joue avec des enfants dans un parc. Elle pense à un vol en avion. 2. L'étudiante est au resto U. Elle pense à un vol agréable.)**
- Tell students to listen for the sentences in the video still captions, and then try to understand the rest of the song.

Compréhension Have students work in pairs or groups for this activity. Tell them to write their answers. Then show the video again so that they can check their answers and add any missing information.

Discussion Have volunteers explain how their airline would be different. Have them name the airline's destinations and say how their group came to choose them.

OPTIONS

Swiss International Airlines Also known as SWISS, the airline was founded in 2001, after Swissair, the former Swiss national airline, filed for bankruptcy. During its first few years, SWISS struggled financially until 2005, when it made a profit after several consecutive years of losses. This coincided with the airline's takeover by the German Lufthansa. SWISS, however, maintains a high degree of autonomy from its parent company and retains its headquarters in Switzerland. Although the vast majority of the airline's destinations are in Europe, SWISS also flies to destinations all around the world. This includes service to Boston, Chicago, Los Angeles, Miami, and New York City in the United States, and to Montreal in Canada.

Section Goals

In this section, students will learn and practice vocabulary related to:

- foods and beverages
- eating at a café or restaurant

Instructional Resources
*espaces.vhlcentral.com: Transparency #26; IRM (**Vocabulaire supplémentaire**; **Mise en pratique** answers; Textbook Audioscript; Lab Audioscript; Info Gap Activities); Textbook MP3s; Lab MP3s; WB/VM/LM Answer Key; activities; downloads; reference tools*

Suggestions

- Use **Transparency #26**. Ask students to describe where the scene takes place and what people are doing. Have students identify items they know.
- Have students look at the new vocabulary and identify the cognates.
- Model the pronunciation of the words and have students repeat after you. Then ask students a few questions about the people in the drawing. Examples: **Qui a faim? Que mange l'homme? Qui a soif?**
- Point out the menu in the illustration. Explain the difference between **un menu** and **une carte**. Ask students what **soupe du jour** and **plat du jour** mean. Then ask: **Combien coûte le plat du jour? Et la soupe du jour?**
- Tell students that a 15% tip is usually included in the price of a meal in a café or restaurant. If the service is particularly good, it is customary to leave a little bit extra.
- Additional vocabulary for this lesson can be found in the **Vocabulaire supplémentaire** on the Supersite.

Leçon 4B

You will learn how to...

- order food and beverages
- ask for your check

Talking Picture
Audio: Activity

J'ai faim!

Vocabulaire

apporter	*to bring, to carry*
coûter	*to cost*
Combien coûte(nt)...?	*How much is/are...?*
une baguette	*baguette (long, thin loaf of bread)*
le beurre	*butter*
des frites (*f.*)	*French fries*
un fromage	*cheese*
le jambon	*ham*
un pain (de campagne)	*(country-style) bread*
un sandwich	*sandwich*
une boisson (gazeuse)	*(soft) (carbonated) drink/ beverage*
un chocolat (chaud)	*(hot) chocolate*
une eau (minérale)	*(mineral) water*
un jus (d'orange, de pomme, etc.)	*(orange, apple, etc.) juice*
le lait	*milk*
une limonade	*lemon soda*
un thé (glacé)	*(iced) tea*
(pas) assez (de)	*(not) enough (of)*
beaucoup (de)	*a lot (of)*
d'autres	*others*
un morceau (de)	*piece, bit (of)*
un peu (plus/moins) (de)	*a little (more/less) (of)*
plusieurs	*several*
quelque chose	*something; anything*
quelques	*some*
tous (*m. pl.*)	*all*
tout (*m. sing.*)	*all*
tout le/tous les (*m.*)	*all the*
toute la/toutes les (*f.*)	*all the*
trop (de)	*too many/much (of)*
un verre (de)	*glass (of)*

ressources
WB pp. 49–50 | LM p. 29 | espaces.vhlcentral.com

OPTIONS

Extra Practice Write **le matin**, **à midi**, and **le soir** on the board or on a transparency. Then ask students when they prefer to have various foods and beverages. Example: **Préférez-vous manger des frites le matin ou à midi?** Other items you can mention are **un éclair**, **un sandwich**, **une soupe**, and **un croissant**.

Pairs Have students work in pairs. Tell them to classify the foods and drinks under the headings **Manger** and **Boire** (*To drink*). After pairs have completed the activity, tell them to compare their lists with another pair and to resolve any differences.

Attention!

To read prices in French, say the number of euros (**euros**) followed by the number of cents (**centimes**). French decimals are marked with a comma, not a period.
8,10€ = huit euros dix (centimes)

Mise en pratique

1 Chassez l'intrus

Trouvez le mot qui ne va pas avec les autres.

1. un croissant, le pain, (le fromage), une baguette
2. une limonade, un jus de pomme, un jus d'orange, (le beurre)
3. des frites, un sandwich, (le sucre), le jambon
4. (le jambon), un éclair, un croissant, une baguette
5. l'eau, la boisson, l'eau minérale, (la soupe)
6. l'addition, (un chocolat), le pourboire, coûter
7. (apporter), d'autres, plusieurs, quelques
8. (un morceau), une bouteille, un verre, une tasse

2 Reliez

Choisissez les expressions de quantité qui correspondent le mieux (*the best*) aux produits.

MODÈLE

un morceau de baguette

une bouteille de	une tasse de
un morceau de	un verre de

1. un verre d'/une bouteille d' eau
2. un morceau de sandwich
3. un morceau de fromage
4. une tasse de chocolat
5. une tasse de café
6. un verre de/une bouteille de jus de pomme
7. une tasse de thé
8. un verre de limonade

3 Écoutez

Écoutez la conversation entre André et le serveur du café Gide, et décidez si les phrases sont vraies ou fausses.

	Vrai	Faux
1. André n'a pas très soif.	☑	☐
2. André n'a pas faim.	☐	☑
3. Au café, on peut commander (*one may order*) un jus d'orange, une limonade, un café ou une boisson gazeuse.	☑	☐
4. André commande un sandwich au jambon avec du fromage.	☐	☑
5. André commande une tasse de chocolat.	☐	☑
6. André déteste le lait et le sucre.	☐	☑
7. André n'a pas beaucoup d'argent.	☑	☐
8. André ne laisse pas de pourboire.	☑	☐

Practice more at **espaces.vhlcentral.com.**

1 Expansion For additional practice, give students these items. **9. beaucoup de, un verre de, assez de, un peu de (un verre de) 10. le café, le jus, le thé, le chocolat chaud (le jus) 11. l'addition, le prix, le serveur, le pourboire (le serveur)**

2 Suggestion You may wish to introduce words for other types of containers, such as **une assiette, un bol,** and **un paquet.**

2 Expansion For additional practice, give students these items. **9. lait (une bouteille de, un verre de) 10. beurre (un morceau de)**

3 Tapescript SERVEUR: Bonjour, Monsieur! Vous désirez?
ANDRÉ: Bonjour! Combien coûtent les sandwichs?
S: Ça dépend. Un sandwich au jambon coûte 3€, mais un sandwich au jambon avec du fromage et des frites coûtent 5,50€.
A: Et combien coûte le café?
S: Une tasse de café coûte 3€ et avec du lait 3,50€.
A: Y a-t-il d'autres boissons?
S: Bien sûr, il y a du jus d'orange, des boissons gazeuses, de la limonade et de l'eau.
A: Je n'ai pas beaucoup d'argent sur moi, mais j'ai très faim. J'ai envie d'un sandwich au jambon. Je n'ai pas très soif, alors une tasse de café au lait avec un peu de sucre, s'il vous plaît.
S: Très bien, Monsieur.
A: Excusez-moi, c'est combien?
S: C'est 6,50€.
A: Voici. Merci et bonne journée!
S: Merci, Monsieur, au revoir. Oh là là! Pas de pourboire!
(On Textbook MP3s)

3 Suggestion Have students correct the false items.

OPTIONS

Game Write these categories on the board: **Boissons froides / chaudes** and **Nourriture froide / chaude**. Toss a beanbag to a student at random and call out a category. The student has four seconds to name a food or beverage that fits the category. He or she then tosses the beanbag to another student and calls out a category. Players who cannot think of an item in time or repeat an item are eliminated. The last person standing wins.

Extra Practice For additional practice, ask students questions about their food and drink preferences. Examples: **Préférez-vous le thé ou le chocolat? Le lait ou l'eau minérale? Le jus d'orange ou le jus de pomme? Le jambon ou le fromage? Les sandwichs ou les éclairs? La soupe ou les frites? Les baguettes ou les croissants?**

4 Suggestion Tell students that in conversation, the word **euro** is often omitted when giving prices that contain whole euros and cents. Example: **10,50€ = dix, cinquante.**

5 Suggestion Tell students to jot down notes during their interviews. Then have volunteers report their findings to the class.

6 Suggestion Distribute photocopies of actual café menus for students to use or have students base their conversation on the menu in **Activité 4.**

7 Suggestion Divide the class into pairs and distribute the Info Gap Handouts found on the Supersite.

NATIONAL communication STANDARDS

Communication

4 Combien coûte...? Regardez la carte et, à tour de rôle, demandez à votre partenaire combien coûte chaque élément. Répondez par des phrases complètes.

MODÈLE

Étudiant(e) 1: *Combien coûte un sandwich?*
Étudiant(e) 2: *Un sandwich coûte 3,50€.*

1. Combien coûtent les frites? Les frites coûtent 2€.
2. Combien coûte une boisson gazeuse? Une boisson gazeuse coûte 2€.
3. Combien coûte une limonade? Une limonade coûte 1,75€.
4. Combien coûte une bouteille d'eau? Une bouteille d'eau coûte 2€.
5. Combien coûte une tasse de café? Une tasse de café coûte 3€.
6. Combien coûte une tasse de thé? Une tasse de thé coûte 2,50€.
7. Combien coûte un croissant? Un croissant coûte 1€.
8. Combien coûte un éclair? Un éclair coûte 1,95€.

5 Conversez Interviewez un(e) camarade de classe. Answers will vary.

1. Qu'est-ce que tu aimes boire (*drink*) quand tu as soif? Quand tu as froid? Quand tu as chaud?
2. Quand tu as faim, est-ce que tu manges au resto U? Qu'est-ce que tu aimes manger?
3. Est-ce que tu aimes le café ou le thé? Combien de tasses est-ce que tu aimes boire par jour?
4. Comment est-ce que tu aimes le café? Avec du lait? Avec du sucre? Noir (*Black*)?
5. Comment est-ce que tu aimes le thé? Avec du lait? Avec du sucre? Nature (*Black*)?
6. Dans ta famille, qui aime le thé? Et le café?
7. Quand tu manges dans un restaurant, est-ce que tu laisses un pourboire au serveur/à la serveuse?
8. Quand tu manges avec ta famille ou avec tes amis dans un restaurant, qui paie (*pays*) l'addition?

6 Au café Choisissez deux partenaires et écrivez une conversation entre deux client(e)s de café et leur serveur/serveuse. Préparez-vous à jouer (*perform*) la scène devant la classe. Answers will vary.

Client(e)s

- Demandez des détails sur le menu et les prix.
- Choisissez des boissons et des plats (*dishes*).
- Demandez l'addition.

Serveur/Serveuse

- Parlez du menu et répondez aux questions.
- Apportez les plats et l'addition.

Coup de main

Vous désirez?
What can I get you?

Je voudrais...
I would like...

C'est combien?
How much is it/this/that?

7 Sept différences Votre professeur va vous donner, à vous et à votre partenaire, deux feuilles d'activités différentes. Attention! Ne regardez pas la feuille de votre partenaire.

MODÈLE

Étudiant(e) 1: *J'ai deux tasses de café.*
Étudiant(e) 2: *Oh, j'ai une tasse de thé!*

OPTIONS

Game Divide the class into two teams. At the same time, give one person on each team a set of scrambled words that form a sentence about foods and/or beverages. The first person to unscramble the words and write the sentence on the board correctly scores a point for his or her team. The team with the most points at the end of the game wins.

Extra Practice To review vocabulary, bring in pictures or magazine photos of the foods and drinks listed. Ask students to identify the items. Example: **Qu'est-ce que c'est? (C'est ____.)** Or you can make false statements about the pictures and have students correct them. Example: **C'est un(e) ____, n'est-ce pas? (Non, c'est ____.)** When plural, remind students to say **Ce sont ____.**

Les sons et les lettres

Audio: Concepts, Activities
Record & Compare

Nasal vowels

In French, when vowels are followed by an **m** or an **n** in a single syllable, they usually become nasal vowels. Nasal vowels are produced by pushing air through both the mouth and the nose.

The nasal vowel sound you hear in **français** is usually spelled **an** or **en**.

an **français** **enchanté** **enfant**

The nasal vowel sound you hear in **bien** may be spelled **en**, **in**, **im**, **ain**, or **aim**. The nasal vowel sound you hear in **brun** may be spelled **un** or **um**.

examen **américain** **lundi** **parfum**

The nasal vowel sound you hear in **bon** is spelled **on** or **om**.

ton **allons** **combien** **oncle**

When **m** or **n** is followed by a vowel sound, the preceding vowel is not nasal.

image **inutile** **ami** **amour**

Prononcez Répétez les mots suivants à voix haute.

1. blond
2. dans
3. faim
4. entre
5. garçon
6. avant
7. maison
8. cinéma
9. quelqu'un
10. différent
11. amusant
12. télévision
13. impatient
14. rencontrer
15. informatique
16. comment

Articulez Répétez les phrases suivantes à voix haute.

1. Mes parents ont cinquante ans.
2. Tu prends une limonade, Martin?
3. Le Printemps est un grand magasin.
4. Lucien va prendre le train à Montauban.
5. Pardon, Monsieur, l'addition s'il vous plaît!
6. Jean-François a les cheveux bruns et les yeux marron.

Dictons Répétez les dictons à voix haute.

N'allonge pas ton bras au-delà de ta manche.[2]

1 Appetite comes from eating.
2 Don't bite off more than you can chew. (lit. Don't stretch your arm out farther than your sleeve.)

ressources
LM p. 30
espaces.vhlcentral.com

Section Goals

In this section, students will learn about nasal vowels.

Instructional Resources
espaces.vhlcentral.com: Textbook MP3s; Lab MP3s; WB/VM/LM Answer Key; IRM (Textbook Audioscript; Lab Audioscript); activities; downloads; reference tools

Suggestions

- Model the pronunciation of each nasal vowel sound and have students repeat after you. Then pronounce each of the example words and have students repeat them.
- Tell students that when an **m** or an **n** is followed by an unaccented **e** at the end of a word, the preceding vowel is not nasalized. Have them compare these words: **un/une**, **brun/brune**, and **faim/femme**.
- Ask students to provide more examples of words they know with nasal vowels. Examples: **croissant**, **boisson**, **jambon**, **inviter**, **quand**, **dépenser**, and **danser**.
- Dictate five simple sentences with words containing nasal vowels to the class, repeating each one at least two times. Then write them on the board or on a transparency and have students check their spelling.

Dictons Ask students if they can think of a saying in English that is similar to **«L'appétit vient en mangeant.»** (*The more one has, the more one wants.*)

OPTIONS

Extra Practice Teach students these French tongue-twisters that contain nasal vowel sounds. **1. Son chat chante sa chanson. 2. Un chasseur sachant chasser sait chasser sans son chien de chasse. 3. Dans la gendarmerie, quand un gendarme rit, tous les gendarmes rient dans la gendarmerie.**

Extra Practice Use these sentences with nasal vowels for additional practice or dictation. **1. Raymond mange un sandwich au jambon. 2. Martin invite ses cousins au restaurant. 3. Tante Blanche a soixante-cinq ans. 4. Mon oncle Quentin a envie de danser.**

Section Goals

In this section, students will learn functional phrases for ordering foods and drinks and talking about food through comprehensible input.

Instructional Resources
*espaces.vhlcentral.com: Video; WB/VM/LM Answer Key; IRM (Videoscript; **Roman-photo** Translations); activities; downloads; reference tools*
Video on DVD

Video Recap: Leçon 4A Before doing this **Roman-photo**, review the previous one with this activity.

1. David pense qu'il y a une femme célèbre à l'épicerie. Qui est-ce? (Juliette Binoche)
2. À qui Sandrine parle-t-elle au téléphone? (à Pascal)
3. Les jeunes trouvent-ils facilement l'épicerie? (non)
4. Comment est la femme à l'épicerie? (belle, jolie, élégante, petite et vieille)
5. En réalité, qui est la femme? (quelqu'un qui travaille à l'épicerie)

Video Synopsis As the four friends approach **Le P'tit Bistrot**, Amina and Sandrine are hungry and want to go eat. Rachid and David decide to go back to their apartment. Valérie tells Amina and Sandrine what she is serving for lunch that day, and they place their order. Michèle makes a mistake on a customer's check, and Valérie serves the wrong food and drinks to Amina and Sandrine.

Suggestions
- Ask students to read the title, glance at the video stills, and predict what the episode will be about. Record their predictions.
- Have students volunteer to read the characters' parts in the **Roman-photo** aloud.
- After reading the **Roman-photo**, review students' predictions and ask them which ones are correct. Then help them summarize this episode.

L'heure du déjeuner

Video: *Roman-photo*
Record & Compare

PERSONNAGES

Amina

David

Michèle

Rachid

Sandrine

Valérie

Près du café...
AMINA J'ai très faim. J'ai envie de manger un sandwich.
SANDRINE Moi aussi, j'ai faim, et puis j'ai soif. J'ai envie d'une bonne boisson. Eh, les garçons, on va au café?

RACHID Moi, je rentre à l'appartement étudier pour un examen de sciences po. David, tu vas au café avec les filles?
DAVID Non, je rentre avec toi. J'ai envie de dessiner un peu.
AMINA Bon, alors, à tout à l'heure.

Au café...
VALÉRIE Bonjour, les filles! Alors, ça va, les études?
AMINA Bof, ça va. Qu'est-ce qu'il y a de bon à manger, aujourd'hui?
VALÉRIE Eh bien, j'ai une soupe de poisson maison délicieuse! Il y a aussi des sandwichs jambon-fromage, des frites... Et, comme d'habitude, j'ai des éclairs, euh...

VALÉRIE Et pour toi, Amina?
AMINA Hmm... Pour moi, un sandwich jambon-fromage avec des frites.
VALÉRIE Très bien, et je vous apporte du pain tout de suite.
SANDRINE ET AMINA Merci!

Au bar...
VALÉRIE Alors, pour la table d'Amina et Sandrine, une soupe du jour, un sandwich au fromage... Pour la table sept, une limonade, un café, un jus d'orange et trois croissants.
MICHÈLE D'accord! Je prépare ça tout de suite. Mais Madame Forestier, j'ai un problème avec l'addition de la table huit.

VALÉRIE Ah, bon?
MICHÈLE Le monsieur ne comprend pas pourquoi ça coûte onze euros cinquante. Je ne comprends pas non plus. Regardez.
VALÉRIE Ah, non! Avec tout le travail que nous avons cet après-midi, des problèmes d'addition aussi?!

ACTIVITÉS

1 Identifiez Trouvez à qui correspond chacune (*each*) des phrases. Écrivez **A** pour Amina, **D** pour David, **M** pour Michèle, **R** pour Rachid, **S** pour Sandrine et **V** pour Valérie.

__M__ 1. Je ne comprends pas non plus.
__V__ 2. Vous prenez du jus d'orange uniquement le matin.
__S__ 3. Tu bois de l'eau aussi?
__M__ 4. Je prépare ça tout de suite.
__A__ 5. Je ne bois pas de limonade.
__S__ 6. Je vais apprendre à préparer des éclairs.
__D__ 7. J'ai envie de dessiner un peu.
__V__ 8. Je vous apporte du pain tout de suite.
__R__ 9. Moi, je rentre à l'appartement étudier pour un examen de sciences po.
__A__ 10. Qu'est-ce qu'il y a de bon à manger, aujourd'hui?

Practice more at **espaces.vhlcentral.com.**

OPTIONS

Avant de regarder la vidéo Before viewing the video, have students work in pairs and write a list of words and expressions that they might hear in a video episode entitled **L'heure du déjeuner**.

Regarder la vidéo Show the video episode and tell students to check off the words or expressions they hear on their lists. Then show the episode again and have students give you a play-by-play description of the action. Write their descriptions on the board.

Amina et Sandrine déjeunent au café.

SANDRINE Oh, Madame Forestier, j'adore! Un jour, je vais apprendre à préparer des éclairs. Et une bonne soupe maison. Et beaucoup d'autres choses.
AMINA Mais pas aujourd'hui. J'ai trop faim!
SANDRINE Alors, je choisis la soupe et un sandwich au fromage.

VALÉRIE Et comme boisson?
SANDRINE Une bouteille d'eau minérale, s'il vous plaît. Tu bois de l'eau aussi? Avec deux verres, alors.

VALÉRIE Ah, ça y est! Je comprends! La boisson gazeuse coûte un euro vingt-cinq, pas un euro soixante-quinze. C'est noté, Michèle?
MICHÈLE Merci, Madame Forestier. Excusez-moi. Je vais expliquer ça au monsieur. Et voilà, tout est prêt pour la table d'Amina et Sandrine.
VALÉRIE Merci, Michèle.

À la table des filles...
VALÉRIE Voilà, une limonade, un café, un jus d'orange et trois croissants.
AMINA Oh? Mais Madame Forestier, je ne bois pas de limonade!
VALÉRIE Et vous prenez du jus d'orange uniquement le matin, n'est-ce pas? Ah! Excusez-moi, les filles!

Expressions utiles

Talking about food

- **Moi aussi, j'ai faim, et puis j'ai soif.**
  Me too, I am hungry, and I am thirsty as well.
- **J'ai envie d'une bonne boisson.**
  I feel like having a nice drink.
- **Qu'est-ce qu'il y a de bon à manger, aujourd'hui?**
  What looks good on the menu today?
- **Une soupe de poisson maison délicieuse.**
  A delicious homemade fish soup.
- **Je vais apprendre à préparer des éclairs.**
  I am going to learn (how) to prepare éclairs.
- **Je choisis la soupe.**
  I choose the soup.
- **Tu bois de l'eau aussi?**
  Are you drinking water too?
- **Vous prenez du jus d'orange uniquement le matin.**
  You only have orange juice in the morning.

Additional vocabulary

- **On va au café?**
  Shall we go to the café?
- **Bof, ça va.**
  So-so.
- **comme d'habitude**
  as usual
- **Le monsieur ne comprend pas pourquoi ça coûte onze euros cinquante.**
  The gentleman doesn't understand why this costs 11,50€.
- **Je ne comprends pas non plus.**
  I don't understand either.
- **Je prépare ça tout de suite.**
  I am going to prepare this right away.
- **Ça y est! Je comprends!**
  That's it! I get it!
- **C'est noté?**
  Understood?/Got it?
- **Tout est prêt.**
  Everything is ready.

ACTIVITÉS

2 Mettez dans l'ordre Numérotez les phrases suivantes dans l'ordre correspondant à l'histoire.

5 a. Michèle a un problème avec l'addition.
3 b. Amina prend (*gets*) un sandwich jambon-fromage.
1 c. Sandrine dit qu'elle (*says that she*) a soif.
2 d. Rachid rentre à l'appartement.
4 e. Valérie va chercher du pain.
6 f. Tout est prêt pour la table d'Amina et Sandrine.

3 Conversez Au moment où Valérie apporte le plateau (*tray*) de la table sept à Sandrine et Amina, Michèle apporte le plateau de Sandrine et Amina à la table sept. Avec trois partenaires, écrivez la conversation entre Michèle et les client(e)s et jouez-la devant la classe.

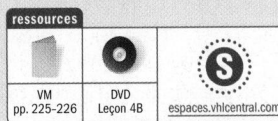

ressources: VM pp. 225-226 | DVD Leçon 4B | espaces.vhlcentral.com

Expressions utiles
- Model the pronunciation of the **Expressions utiles** and have students repeat after you.
- As you work through the list, point out the forms of the verbs **prendre** and **boire** and the partitive articles. Tell students that these verbs and the partitive articles will be formally presented in the **Structures** section.
- Ask students questions about foods and beverages using the vocabulary in the **Expressions utiles**. Examples: **Vous prenez du jus d'orange uniquement le matin? Quand est-ce que vous avez envie de boire de l'eau?**

1 Expansions
- For additional practice, give students these items. **11. Le monsieur ne comprend pas pourquoi ça coûte 11,50€. (M) 12. J'ai faim et puis j'ai soif. (S) 13. Mais pas aujourd'hui. J'ai trop faim! (A) 14. Non, je rentre avec toi. (D)**
- Write these adverbial expressions on the board: **non plus, aussi**, and **tout de suite**. Have students create sentences with them.

2 Suggestion Have students work in groups of six. Write each sentence on a strip of paper. Make a set of sentences for each group, then distribute them to students. Tell them to read their sentences aloud and arrange them in the proper order.

2 Expansion Have students create sentences to fill in the missing parts of the story.

3 Suggestion Before doing this activity, have the class brainstorm vocabulary and expressions they might use in this activity and write their ideas on the board.

OPTIONS

Pairs Have students work in pairs. Tell them to combine sentences in **Expressions utiles** with other words and expressions they know to create mini-dialogues. Example:
—Qu'est-ce qu'il y a de bon aujourd'hui?
—Il y a une soupe de poisson maison délicieuse.

Extra Practice Ask volunteers to ad-lib the **Roman-photo** episode for the class. Tell them that it is not necessary to memorize the episode or to stick strictly to its content. They should try to get the general meaning across with the vocabulary and expressions they know, and they should also feel free to be creative. Give them time to prepare.

Section Goals

In this section, students will:
- learn about the role of the café in French life
- learn some terms for describing how people eat and drink
- learn about some common snacks in different francophone countries
- read about the cafés of **North Africa**
- view authentic cultural footage

Instructional Resources
espaces.vhlcentral.com: Video; WB/VM/LM Answer Key; IRM (Videoscript); activities; downloads; reference tools

Culture à la loupe

Avant la lecture Have students look at the photos and describe what they see. Then ask: **Allez-vous au café? Où? Quand?**

Lecture Point out that you can order a drink or food at the bar (**le bar**) and pay less than sitting at a table. Sitting on the **terrasse** is even more expensive. The menu posted outside a café usually indicates the different **tarifs**.

Après la lecture Ask students what aspects of French cafés they find interesting or appealing.

1 Expansion For additional practice, give students these items. **11. Aller au café est une tradition récente en France. (Faux.) 12. Les étudiants et les adultes fréquentent les cafés en France. (Vrai.)**

Video: *Flash culture*

CULTURE À LA LOUPE

Le café français

Les Deux Magots
À Toute Heure
Quiches ....3,50€
Pâtisseries.................3,50€
Omelettes ....5,25€
Thé ....1,50€
Glaces ....5,50€
Café ....1,50€
Cappuccino ....2,00€
Chocolat chaud.......2,30€

Le premier café français, le Procope, a ouvert° ses portes à Paris en 1686. Depuis°, passer du temps° au café est une tradition. C'est un lieu de rendez-vous pour beaucoup de personnes: le matin, on y° va pour un café et un croissant; à midi, on y déjeune pour le plaisir ou pour des rendez-vous d'affaires, parce que c'est moins cher° et plus rapide qu'°au restaurant. Après le travail, les gens° y vont pour prendre l'apéritif°. Les étudiants ont souvent «leur» café où ils vont déjeuner, étudier ou se détendre° avec des amis.

Les cafés servent une grande variété de boissons: café, thé, chocolat chaud, eau minérale, sodas, jus de fruit, etc. En général, les cafés proposent aussi un menu: sandwichs, omelettes, quiches, soupes, salades, hot-dogs et, pour le dessert, des pâtisseries° et des glaces°. La terrasse d'un café est l'endroit° idéal pour se détendre, lire° ou pour observer la vie° de tous les jours et regarder passer les gens. Benjamin Franklin et Napoléon Bonaparte fréquentaient° le Procope. Alors, qui sait° sur qui vous allez tomber°!

a ouvert *opened* **Depuis** *Since* **passer du temps** *spending time* **gens** *people* **y** *there* **moins cher** *less expensive* **plus rapide qu'** *faster than* **les gens** *people* **apéritif** *before-dinner drink* **se détendre** *relax* **pâtisseries** *pastries* **glaces** *ice cream* **endroit** *place* **lire** *read* **vie** *life* **fréquentaient** *used to frequent* **sait** *knows* **allez tomber** *are going to run into*

ACTIVITÉS

1 Vrai ou faux? Indiquez si les phrases sont vraies ou fausses. Corrigez les phrases fausses. Some answers may vary.

1. Le premier café parisien date des années 1600. Vrai.
2. Les Français vont au café uniquement aux grandes occasions. Faux. Les Français vont aussi au café après le travail.
3. Le matin, les Français prennent du jambon et du fromage. Faux. Les Français prennent un café et un croissant.
4. En général, les cafés en France sont plus chers que les restaurants. Faux. Les cafés sont moins chers que les restaurants.
5. Les étudiants ont souvent un café où ils vont tous les jours (*every day*). Vrai.
6. Au café, on trouve des sandwichs et des salades, mais pas de desserts. Faux. On trouve aussi des desserts.
7. En France, on mange rarement (*rarely*) dans les cafés. Faux. Dans les cafés, on déjeune pour le plaisir ou pour des rendez-vous d'affaires.
8. Les cafés ont une grande variété de boissons. Vrai.
9. On peut se détendre au café et observer la vie de tous les jours. Vrai.
10. Napoléon Bonaparte et Benjamin Franklin sont d'anciens clients du Procope. Vrai.

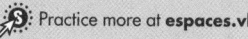

Practice more at **espaces.vhlcentral.com.**

OPTIONS

Cultural Comparison Have students work in groups of three and compare French cafés to the cafés they frequent. Tell them to list the similarities and differences in a two-column chart under the headings **Similitudes** and **Différences**. After completing their charts, have two groups get together and compare their lists.

Extra Practice Have students look at the **À Toute Heure** menu. Ask them what they are having and how much it costs. Examples: **Qu'est-ce que vous prenez? Combien coûte le chocolat chaud?** Alternatively, this activity can be done in pairs.

LE FRANÇAIS QUOTIDIEN

J'ai faim!

avoir les crocs	*to be hungry*
avoir un petit creux	*to be slightly hungry*
boire à petites gorgées	*to sip*
bouffer	*to eat*
dévorer	*to devour*
grignoter	*to snack on*
mourir de faim	*to be starving*
siroter	*to sip (with pleasure)*

PORTRAIT

Les cafés nord-africains

Comme en France, les cafés ont une grande importance culturelle en Afrique du Nord. C'est le lieu où les amis se rencontrent pour discuter° ou pour jouer aux cartes° ou aux dominos. Les cafés ont une variété de boissons, mais ils n'offrent° pas d'alcool. La boisson typique, au café comme à la maison, est le thé à la menthe°. Il a peu de caféine, mais il a des vertus énergisantes et il favorise la digestion. En général, ce sont les hommes qui le° préparent. C'est la boisson qu'on vous sert° quand vous êtes invité, et ce n'est pas poli de refuser!

pour discuter *to chat* **jouer aux cartes** *play cards* **offrent** *offer* **menthe** *mint* **le** *it* **on vous sert** *you are served*

LE MONDE FRANCOPHONE

Des spécialités à grignoter

Voici quelques spécialités à grignoter dans les pays et régions francophones.

En Afrique du Nord la merguez (saucisse épicée°) et le makroud (pâtisserie° au miel° et aux dattes)

En Côte d'Ivoire l'aloco (bananes plantains frites°)

En France le pan-bagnat (sandwich avec de la salade, des tomates, des oeufs durs° et du thon°) et les crêpes (pâte° cuite° composée de farine°, d'œufs et de lait, de forme ronde)

À la Martinique les accras de morue° (beignets° à la morue)

Au Québec la poutine (frites avec du fromage fondu° et de la sauce)

Au Sénégal le chawarma (de la viande°, des oignons et des tomates dans du pain pita)

saucisse épicée *spicy sausage* **pâtisserie** *pastry* **miel** *honey* **frites** *fried* **oeufs durs** *hard-boiled eggs* **thon** *tuna* **pâte** *batter* **cuite** *cooked* **farine** *flour* **morue** *cod* **beignets** *fritters* **fondu** *melted* **viande** *meat*

SUR INTERNET

Comment prépare-t-on le thé à la menthe au Maghreb?

Go to **espaces.vhlcentral.com** to find more information related to this **ESPACE CULTURE**. Then watch the corresponding **Flash culture.**

ACTIVITÉS

2 Compréhension Complétez les phrases.

1. Quand on a un peu soif, on a tendance à (*tends to*) boire à petites gorgées.
2. On ne peut pas y boire de/d' alcool.
3. Les hommes préparent le thé à la menthe dans les pays d'Afrique du Nord.
4. Il n'est pas poli de refuser une tasse de thé en Afrique du Nord.
5. Si vous aimez les frites, vous allez aimer la poutine au Québec.

3 Un café francophone Un(e) ami(e) a envie de créer un café francophone. Par groupes de quatre, préparez une liste de suggestions pour aider votre ami(e): noms pour le café, idées (*ideas*) pour le menu, prix, heures, etc. Indiquez où le café va être situé et qui va fréquenter ce café.

ressources
VM pp. 277-278
espaces.vhlcentral.com

Le français quotidien Model the pronunciation of each term and have students repeat it. Then ask questions based on the vocabulary. Examples: **Avez-vous les crocs? Vous mangez quoi quand vous avez les crocs? Vous dévorez votre déjeuner?**

Portrait Coffee was first consumed in Ethiopia in the ninth century, and it became controversial in the Islamic world during the beverage's early history. Many regarded it with suspicion and blamed its stimulating properties for inviting subversive thought and tempting drinkers away from religious observance.

Le monde francophone Have students read the text. Tell them to choose a specialty they would like to eat from the list. Then ask: **Quelle spécialité préférez-vous manger? Pourquoi?**

2 Expansion Have students write three more fill-in-the-blank statements based on **Portrait** and **Le monde francophone**. Then have them work in groups of three and take turns reading their statements while the other group members respond.

3 Expansion Have groups present their suggestions to the class. Then have the class discuss the role that the country's culture played in forming their ideas. For example, did it affect the name, the hours of operation, the menu, or the prices?

Flash culture Tell students that they will learn more about French cafés by watching a variety of real-life images narrated by Benjamin. Show the video segment, then have students jot down at least three examples of things they see. You can also use the activities in the video manual in class to reinforce this **Flash culture** or assign them as homework.

OPTIONS

Pairs Have students work in pairs. Tell them to take turns stating that they like one of the specialties in the list **Des spécialités à grignoter** at their house. The other person should guess where they live based on the snack named. Example: **Étudiant(e) 1: Chez moi, on aime les accras de morue. Étudiant(e) 2: Alors tu habites à la Martinique, n'est-ce pas?**

Extra Practice Have students write five true/false statements based on the information in the **J'ai faim!** and **Des spécialités à grignoter** sections. Then tell them to exchange papers with a classmate and complete the activity. Remind them to verify their answers.

Section Goals

In this section, students will learn:

- the verbs **prendre**, **apprendre**, and **comprendre**
- the verb **boire**
- partitive articles

Instructional Resources
*espaces.vhlcentral.com: Lab MP3s; WB/VM/LM Answer Key; IRM (**Essayez!** and **Mise en pratique** answers; Lab Audioscript; **Feuilles d'activités**); activities; downloads; reference tools*

Suggestions

- Point out that **prendre** means *to have* when saying what one is having to eat or drink, but it cannot be used to express possession. For possession, **avoir** must be used.
- Work through the forms of **boire**, asking students what they drink most often or rarely. Model a response by first saying what you drink: **Je bois souvent ____. Qu'est-ce que vous buvez?**
- Write the conjugation of **boire** on the board with the singular forms in one column and the plural forms in another column. Draw a line around the forms that have **oi**. Tell students that **boire** is a "boot verb."
- Write a summary chart of the articles on the board with these headings: Definite Articles, Indefinite Articles, and Partitive Articles. Briefly review definite and indefinite articles.
- Make sure students understand the idea of count nouns and non-count nouns. Have students classify vocabulary from **Espace contextes**.
- Point out that the use of partitives differs whether you are at home or in a café/restaurant. It is preferable to use **de** + [definite article] when at home or at someone's house, and indefinite articles when in a restaurant. Examples: **Bois-tu du café?** (at home) **Je prends un café.** (in a restaurant)

NATIONAL STANDARDS comparisons

4B.1 The verbs *prendre* and *boire*; Partitives

Point de départ The verbs **prendre** (*to take, to have*) and **boire** (*to drink*), like **être**, **avoir**, and **aller**, are irregular.

Prendre

je prends	*I take*	**nous prenons**	*we take*
tu prends	*you take*	**vous prenez**	*you take*
il/elle prend	*he/she/it takes*	**ils/elles prennent**	*they take*

Brigitte **prend** le métro le soir.
Brigitte takes the subway in the evening.

Nous **prenons** un café chez moi.
We are having a coffee at my house.

- The forms of the verbs **apprendre** (*to learn*) and **comprendre** (*to understand*) follow the same pattern as that of **prendre**.

Tu ne **comprends** pas l'espagnol?
Don't you understand Spanish?

Elles **apprennent** beaucoup en classe.
They're learning a lot in class.

Je ne comprends pas non plus.

Je ne bois pas de limonade.

Boire

je bois	*I drink*	**nous buvons**	*we drink*
tu bois	*you drink*	**vous buvez**	*you drink*
il/elle boit	*he/she/it drinks*	**ils/elles boivent**	*they drink*

Ton père **boit** un jus d'orange.
Your father is drinking an orange juice.

Vous **buvez** un chocolat, M. Dion?
Are you drinking hot chocolate, Mr. Dion?

Nous ne **buvons** pas pendant le repas.
We don't drink during the meal.

Je **bois** toujours du lait froid au petit-déjeuner.
I always drink cold milk for breakfast.

MISE EN PRATIQUE

1 Au restaurant Alain est au restaurant avec toute sa famille. Il note les préférences de tout le monde. Utilisez le verbe indiqué.

MODÈLE
Oncle Lucien aime bien le café. (prendre) *Il prend un café.*

1. Marie-Hélène et papa adorent le thé. (prendre) Ils prennent un thé.
2. Tu adores le chocolat chaud. (boire) Tu bois un chocolat chaud.
3. Vous aimez bien le jus de pomme. (prendre) Vous prenez un jus de pomme.
4. Mes nièces aiment la limonade. (boire) Elles boivent une limonade.
5. Tu aimes les boissons gazeuses. (prendre) Tu prends une boisson gazeuse.
6. Vous adorez le café. (boire) Vous buvez un café.

2 Au café Indiquez l'article correct.

MODÈLE
Prenez-vous __*du*__ thé glacé?

1. Avez-vous __du__ lait froid?
2. Je voudrais __une__ baguette, s'il vous plaît.
3. Elle prend __un__ croissant.
4. Nous ne prenons pas __de__ sucre avec le café.
5. Thérèse ne laisse pas __de__ pourboire.
6. Vous mangez __des__ frites.
7. Zeina boit __une__ boisson gazeuse.
8. Voici __de l'__ eau minérale.
9. Nous mangeons __du__ pain.
10. Je ne prends pas __de__ fromage.

3 Des suggestions Laurent est au café avec des amis et il fait (*makes*) des suggestions. Que suggère-t-il?

MODÈLE
On prend du jus d'orange?

1. __On prend de la limonade?__

3. __On prend du thé?__

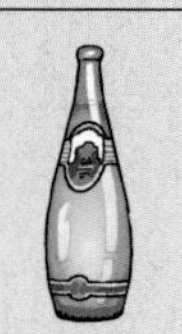

2. __On prend de l'eau minérale?__

4. __On prend des sandwichs?__

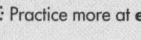

Practice more at **espaces.vhlcentral.com.**

OPTIONS

Extra Practice Distribute empty food and drink containers with labels or pictures of items to groups of three students. Call out the items saying: **du lait**, **des frites**, etc. The group with the item should hold up the package or photo and say: **Voici/Nous avons du lait!** To practice negative partitives, have them say: **Il n'y a pas de ____.**

Extra Practice Bring in pictures or magazine photos of people consuming food, drink, or taking various things. Have students describe what the people in the pictures are doing using **boire**, **prendre**, and partitive articles.

COMMUNICATION

4 Échanges Posez les questions à un(e) partenaire.

1. Qu'est-ce que tu bois quand tu as très soif?
2. Qu'est-ce que tu apprends à la fac?
3. Quelles langues est-ce que tes parents comprennent?
4. Est-ce que tu bois beaucoup de café? Pourquoi?
5. Qu'est-ce que tu prends à manger à midi?
6. Quelle langue est-ce que ton/ta camarade de chambre apprend?
7. Où est-ce que tu prends tes repas (*meals*)?
8. Qu'est-ce que tu bois le matin? À midi? Le soir?

5 Je bois, je prends Votre professeur va vous donner une feuille d'activités. Circulez dans la classe pour demander à vos camarades s'ils prennent rarement, une fois (*once*) par semaine ou tous les jours la boisson ou le plat (*dish*) indiqués. Écrivez (*Write*) les noms sur la feuille, puis présentez vos réponses à la classe.
Answers will vary.

MODÈLE

Étudiant(e) 1: *Est-ce que tu bois du café?*
Étudiant(e) 2: *Oui, je bois du café une fois par semaine. Et toi?*

boisson ou plat	*rarement*	*une fois par semaine*	*tous les jours*
1. café		*Didier*	
2. fromage			
3. thé			
4. soupe			
5. chocolat chaud			
6. jambon			

6 Après les cours Vous retrouvez des amis au café. Par groupes de quatre, jouez (*play*) les rôles d'un(e) serveur/serveuse et de trois clients. Utilisez les mots de la liste et présentez la scène à la classe.
Answers will vary.

addition	chocolat chaud	frites
avoir faim	coûter	prix
avoir soif	croissant	sandwich
boisson	eau minérale	soupe

Partitives

- Use partitive articles in French to express *some* or *any*. To form the partitive, use the preposition **de** followed by a definite article. Although the words *some* and *any* are often omitted in English, the partitive must always be used in French.

Je bois **du** thé chaud. *I drink (some) hot tea.*	Elle prend **de l'**eau? *Is she having (some) water?*

- Note that partitive articles are only used with non-count nouns (nouns whose quantity cannot be expressed by a number).

PARTITIVE ARTICLE / NON-COUNT NOUN	INDEFINITE ARTICLE / COUNT NOUN
Tu prends **de la** soupe tous les jours. *You have (some) soup every day.*	Tu prends **une** banane, aussi. *You have a banana, too.*

- The article **des** also means *some*, but it is the plural form of the indefinite article, not the partitive.

PARTITIVE ARTICLE	INDEFINITE ARTICLE
Vous prenez **de la** limonade. *You're having (some) lemon soda.*	Nous prenons **des** croissants. *We're having (some) croissants.*

- To give a negative response to a question asked using the partitive structure, as with indefinite articles, always use **ne... pas de**.

Est-ce qu'il y a **du** lait? *Is there (any) milk?*	Non, il **n'**y a **pas de** lait. *No, there isn't (any) milk.*
Prends-tu **de la** soupe? *Will you have (some) soup?*	Non, je **ne** prends **pas de** soupe. *No, I'm not having (any) soup.*

Essayez! Complétez les phrases. Utilisez la forme correcte du verbe entre parenthèses et l'article qui convient.

1. Ma sœur *prend* (prendre) *des* éclairs.
2. Tes parents boivent (boire) du café?
3. Louise ne boit (boire) pas de thé.
4. Est-ce qu'il y a (avoir) du sucre?
5. Nous buvons (boire) de la limonade.
6. Non, merci. Je ne prends (prendre) pas de frites.
7. Vous prenez (prendre) un taxi?
8. Nous apprenons (apprendre) le français.

Essayez! Have students create new sentences orally or in writing by changing the subjects of the sentences.

1 Suggestion This activity can also be done in pairs. One person should say the sentence and the other person responds. Remind students to switch roles after items 1–3.

2 Expansion Have students write two more fill-in-the-blank sentences. Tell them to exchange papers with a partner and complete the sentences.

3 Suggestion Have students say the questions, then call on other individuals to answer them. Examples: **Oui, on prend ____. Non, on ne prend pas de/d' ____.**

4 Suggestion Have students create two additional questions with **boire, apprendre, prendre,** or **comprendre** to ask their partner.

5 Suggestion Have two volunteers read the **modèle** aloud. Then distribute the **Feuilles d'activités** found on the Supersite.

6 Suggestions
- Bring in a few props, such as cups, bottles, and plates, for students to use in their role-plays.
- Have volunteers perform their role-plays for the class, then vote on the best one.

OPTIONS

Extra Practice Arrange students in rows of six. The first person in each row has a piece of paper. Call out the infinitive of **boire, prendre, apprendre,** or **comprendre**. Silently, the first student writes the **je** form and passes the paper to the student behind him or her. That student writes the **tu** form and passes the paper on. The last person holds up the completed paper. Have students rotate places before the next verb.

Extra Practice Write this activity on the board. Tell students to add the missing words and form complete sentences.
1. Marc / boire / eau / et / prendre / sandwich / jambon
2. Solange / prendre / soupe / et / boire / boisson gazeuse
3. Nous / boire / café / lait / et / prendre / éclairs
4. Henri et Paul / prendre / hot-dogs / et / frites
5. Anne / prendre / soupe / poisson / et / verre / thé glacé

Section Goals

In this section, students will learn regular **-ir** verbs.

Instructional Resources
*espaces.vhlcentral.com: Lab MP3s; WB/VM/LM Answer Key; IRM (**Essayez!** and **Mise en pratique** answers; Lab Audioscript); activities; downloads; reference tools*

Suggestions

- Model the pronunciation of **-ir** verbs and have students repeat them.
- Introduce the verbs by saying what time you finish teaching today and asking students what time they finish classes. Examples: **Aujourd'hui, je finis d'enseigner à cinq heures. Et vous, à quelle heure finissez-vous les cours?** Then ask students to ask a classmate: **Et toi, à quelle heure finis-tu, aujourd'hui?**
- Point out that the singular forms of **-ir** verbs all sound the same.
- Call students' attention to the **-iss-** in the plural forms of **-ir** verbs.
- Remind students that **-ss-** sounds like an *s*, but a single **s** between vowels is pronounced like a *z*.
- Tell students that many **-ir** verbs are derived from adjectives, such as **grand**, **rouge**, **gros**, or **vieux**.
- Ask students questions using **-ir** verbs in the present and also with the **futur proche**. Examples: **Quand allez-vous finir vos études? Réussissez-vous vos examens?**

Essayez! For additional practice, give students these items. **9. Comment ______ (réagir)-vous quand vous avez peur? (réagissez) 10. Vos grands-parents ______ (vieillir) ensemble. (vieillissent)**

4B.2 Regular *-ir* verbs

NATIONAL comparisons STANDARDS

Point de départ In **Leçon 2A**, you learned the pattern of **-er** verbs. Verbs that end in **-ir** follow a different pattern.

***Finir* (to finish)**

je finis	nous finissons
tu finis	vous finissez
il/elle finit	ils/elles finissent

Je **finis** mon sandwich avant tout le monde.
I am finishing my sandwich before everyone else.

Alain et Chloé **finissent** leur déjeuner.
Alain and Chloé are finishing their lunch.

- Here are some other verbs that follow the same pattern as **finir**.

Other regular *-ir* verbs

choisir	to choose	réfléchir (à)	to think (about), to reflect (on)
grandir	to grow	réussir (à)	to succeed (in doing something)
grossir	to gain weight	rougir	to blush
maigrir	to lose weight	vieillir	to grow old
obéir (à)	to obey		
réagir	to react		

Nous **grossissons** quand nous mangeons beaucoup d'éclairs.
We gain weight when we eat a lot of eclairs.

Je **choisis** un croissant avec du chocolat chaud.
I choose a croissant with hot chocolate.

- Like for **-er** verbs, use present tense verb forms to give commands.

Réagis vite! *React quickly!*
Obéissez-moi. *Obey me.*
Réfléchissons bien. *Let's think well.*
Ne **rougis** pas. *Don't blush.*

Essayez! **Complétez les phrases.**

1. Quand je mange de la salade, je _maigris_ (maigrir).
2. Il _réussit_ (réussir) son examen.
3. Nous _finissons_ (finir) notre déjeuner.
4. Quand les enfants mangent beaucoup de frites, ils _grossissent_ (grossir)!
5. Tu _choisis_ (choisir) le fromage ou le dessert?
6. _Réfléchis/Réfléchissez_ (réfléchir) au problème.
7. Mes enfants _grandissent_ (grandir) très vite (*fast*).
8. Vous ne m' _obéissez_ (obéir) jamais (*never*)!

MISE EN PRATIQUE

1 Au restaurant Complétez le dialogue avec la forme correcte du verbe entre parenthèses.

SERVEUR Vous désirez?
LISE Nous (1) _réfléchissons_ (réfléchir) encore.
FANNY Je pense savoir ce que je veux (*know what I want*).
SERVEUR Que (2) _choisissez_ (choisir)-vous, Mademoiselle?
FANNY Je (3) _choisis_ (choisir) un hamburger avec des frites. Et toi?
LISE Euh... je (4) _réfléchis_ (réfléchir). La soupe ou la salade, je pense... Oui, je prends la salade.
SERVEUR Très bien, Mesdemoiselles. Je vous apporte ça tout de suite (*right away*).
FANNY Tu n'as pas très faim?
LISE Non, pas trop. Et je suis au régime (*on a diet*). J'ai besoin de (5) _maigrir_ (maigrir) un peu.
FANNY Tu (6) _réussis_ (réussir) déjà. Ton jean est trop grand. Tu n'as pas envie de partager mon éclair?
LISE Mais non! Je vais (7) _grossir_ (grossir)!
FANNY Alors, je (8) _finis_ (finir) l'éclair.

2 Complétez Complétez les phrases avec la forme correcte des verbes de la liste. N'utilisez les verbes qu'une seule fois.

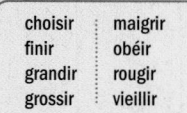

choisir	maigrir
finir	obéir
grandir	rougir
grossir	vieillir

1. Nous _choisissons_ l'endroit où nous allons déjeuner.
2. Corinne _rougit_ quand elle a honte.
3. Mes frères cadets _grandissent_ encore. Ils sont déjà (*already*) très grands!
4. Vous ne mangez pas assez et vous _maigrissez_. Attention!
5. Nous _obéissons_ aux profs.
6. Sylvie _finit_ ses études cette année.
7. Mes grands-parents _vieillissent_. Mais c'est la vie (*life*).
8. Quand on mange beaucoup de chocolat, on _grossit_.

Practice more at **espaces.vhlcentral.com.**

OPTIONS

Game Divide the class into two teams. Choose one team member at a time to go to the board, alternating between teams. Say a subject pronoun and an infinitive. The person at the board must write and say the correct verb form. Example: **tu: choisir (tu choisis)**. Give a point for each correct answer. The team with the most points at the end of the game wins.

Extra Practice Have students write fill-in-the-blank or dehydrated sentences for each of the **-ir** verbs. Then tell them to exchange papers with a partner and complete the activity. Remind students to verify their answers.

COMMUNICATION

3 **Réactions** Avec un(e) partenaire, dites ce que ces (*Say what these*) personnes font (*do*) dans ces situations. Utilisez un verbe en **-ir** dans vos réponses.
Answers may vary. Possible answers suggested

1. Il fait 35°C et Paul a très soif. Il est dans un café. Il choisit une boisson froide.
2. Nous sommes en classe. Le prof nous donne un problème de maths. Nous réfléchissons à la solution du problème.
3. Tes parents te demandent d'aller chercher ta sœur à l'école. Tu obéis à tes parents.
4. M. Lepic va avoir 84 ans. Il vieillit.
5. Florent mange deux sandwichs et boit un soda tous les midis. Il grossit beaucoup.

4 **Assemblez** Avec un(e) partenaire, assemblez les éléments des trois colonnes pour créer des phrases logiques. Answers will vary.

A	B	C
je	choisir	aujourd'hui
tu	finir	beaucoup
notre prof	grandir	cette (*this*) année
mes parents	grossir	cours
mon frère	maigrir	devoirs
ma sœur	réfléchir	diplôme
mon/ma petit(e) ami(e)	réussir	encore
mon/ma camarade de chambre	rougir	problème
mes camarades de classe	vieillir	vite
?		?

5 **Qui...?** Posez (*Ask*) des questions pour trouvez une personne dans la classe qui fait ces (*does these*) choses.

MODÈLE

Étudiant(e) 1: *Est-ce que tu rougis facilement?*
Étudiant(e) 2: *Non, je ne rougis pas facilement.*

1. rougir facilement (*easily*)
2. réagir vite
3. obéir à ses parents
4. finir toujours ses devoirs
5. choisir bien sa nourriture (*food*)
6. grossir ou maigrir cette année

Le français vivant

au choix *your choice of*

Répondez Avec un(e) partenaire, discutez de la carte et de ces (*these*) situations. Utilisez des verbes en **-ir**. Answers may vary.

1. Je prends quatre croissants. Tu grossis.
2. J'ai très faim. Tu choisis le petit-déjeuner complet.
3. Je ne mange pas beaucoup. Tu maigris./Tu choisis le petit-déjeuner simple.
4. Je ne commande pas encore. Tu réfléchis.
5. Je bois toute la bouteille d'eau minérale. Tu finis la bouteille d'eau.

1 Suggestion Go over the correct answers with the class. Then ask two volunteers to act out the conversation.

2 Expansion Have students create additional sentences using these verbs with different subjects.

3 Expansion Have students imagine themselves in these situations and tell what they do using **-ir** verbs.

4 Suggestion Give students five minutes to write as many sentences as they can using **–ir** verbs. Then have volunteers read some of their sentences aloud or write them on the board.

5 Suggestion Remind students to ask and answer using complete sentences. Have them write the name of the person they find for each question. Follow up with questions about what they found out. Example: **Qui finit toujours ses devoirs?**

Le français vivant

- Ask volunteers to share their responses with the class.
- Have students act out a scene in which they order from the café menu. Encourage them to use as many **-ir** verbs as possible. Ask volunteers to perform their scene for the class.

OPTIONS

Pairs List various categories of things on the board, such as classes, foods, and beverages, and have students discuss their preferences using the verb **choisir**. Example: **Boissons: je choisis un jus d'orange**. Then have them guess other people's preferences in the same categories.

Extra Practice Have students restate these sentences using **-ir** verbs. **1. Mes tantes sont moins jeunes qu'avant** (*than before*). **2. Cédric est moins gros qu'avant. 3. Nous sommes plus grands qu'avant. 4. Vous pensez beaucoup. 5. Je termine mes études.**

Instructional Resources
espaces.vhlcentral.com:
IRM (Info Gap Activities);
Testing Program, pp. 29–32;
Test Files; Testing Program
MP3s; activities; downloads;
reference tools
Test Generator

1 Suggestion Have two volunteers read the **modèle** aloud.

1 Expansion Have students write three things they are learning to do. Then have them exchange papers with a partner and ask each other why they are learning to do those things.

2 Suggestions
- Tell students to jot down notes during their interviews.
- Have students report some of their findings to the rest of the class.

3 Suggestion Tell students that a few **centimes** are almost always added to the price of each item if the people sit on the **terrasse**.

4 Suggestion After completing the activity, call on volunteers to state one difference until all options are exhausted.

5 Suggestion Give students five minutes to work with a partner. Then ask volunteers to share their responses with the class.

6 Suggestion Divide the class into pairs and distribute the Info Gap Handouts found on the Supersite for this activity. Give students ten minutes to complete the activity.

NATIONAL communication STANDARDS

Révision

1 Ils aiment apprendre Vous demandez à Sylvie et à Jérôme pourquoi ils aiment apprendre. Un(e) partenaire va poser des questions et l'autre partenaire va jouer les rôles de Jérôme et de Sylvie. Answers will vary.

MODÈLE

Étudiant(e) 1: *Pourquoi est-ce que tu apprends à travailler sur l'ordinateur?*
Étudiant(e) 2: *J'apprends parce que j'aime les ordinateurs.*

1.

4.

2.

5.

3.

6.

2 Quelle boisson? Interviewez une personne de votre classe. Que boit-on dans ces circonstances? Ensuite (*Then*), posez les questions à une personne différente. Utilisez des articles partitifs dans vos réponses. Answers will vary.

1. au café
2. au cinéma
3. en classe
4. le dimanche matin
5. le matin très tôt
6. quand il/elle passe des examens
7. quand il/elle a très soif
8. quand il/elle étudie toute la nuit

3 Notre café Vous et votre partenaire allez créer un café français. Choisissez le nom du café et huit boissons. Pour chaque (*each*) boisson, inventez deux prix, un pour le comptoir (*bar*) et un pour la terrasse. Comparez votre café au café d'un autre groupe. Answers will vary.

4 La terrasse du café Avec un(e) partenaire, observez les deux dessins et trouvez au minimum quatre différences. Comparez votre liste à la liste d'un autre groupe. Ensuite, écrivez (*write*) un paragraphe sur ces trois personnages en utilisant (*by using*) des verbes en **-ir**. Answers will vary.

MODÈLE

Étudiant(e) 1: *Mylène prend une limonade.*
Étudiant(e) 2: *Mylène prend de la soupe.*

5 Dialogue Avec un(e) partenaire, créez un dialogue avec les éléments de la liste. Answers will vary.

choisir	du chocolat
grossir	de l'eau minérale
maigrir	un sandwich au jambon
réagir	des frites
réfléchir (à)	de la soupe
réussir (à)	du jus de pomme

6 La famille Arnal au café Votre professeur va vous donner, à vous et à votre partenaire, des photos de la famille Arnal. Attention! Ne regardez pas la feuille de votre partenaire. Answers will vary.

MODÈLE

Étudiant(e) 1: *Qui prend un sandwich?*
Étudiant(e) 2: *La grand-mère prend un sandwich.*

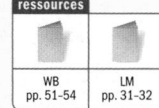

ressources
WB pp. 51-54 | LM pp. 31-32 | espaces.vhlcentral.com

OPTIONS

Extra Practice Have students write a brief story about inviting some friends or a date to go to a café and what happens when they are at the café. Tell students that the story can be real or imaginary. Encourage them to be creative.

Extra Practice Have students write five questions that they would like to ask you using the verbs **apprendre**, **comprendre**, **boire**, **prendre**, and **-ir** verbs. Then allow each student the opportunity to ask you one question.

À l'écoute

Audio: Activities

STRATÉGIE

Listening for the gist

Listening for the general idea, or gist, can help you follow what someone is saying even if you can't hear or understand some of the words. When you listen for the gist, you try to capture the essence of what you hear without focusing on individual words.

To help you practice this strategy, you will listen to three sentences. Jot down a brief summary of what you hear.

Préparation

Regardez la photo. Combien de personnes y a-t-il? Où sont Charles et Gina? Qu'est-ce qu'ils vont manger? Boire? Quelle heure est-il? Qu'est-ce qu'ils vont faire (*to do*) cet après-midi?

À vous d'écouter

Écoutez la conversation entre Charles, Gina et leur serveur. Écoutez une deuxième fois (*a second time*) et indiquez quelles activités ils vont faire.

✓ 1. acheter un livre
✓ 2. aller à la librairie
___ 3. aller à l'église
✓ 4. aller chez des grands-parents
___ 5. boire un coca
✓ 6. danser
✓ 7. dépenser de l'argent
___ 8. étudier
✓ 9. manger au restaurant
✓ 10. manger un sandwich

Practice more at **espaces.vhlcentral.com.**

Compréhension

Un résumé Complétez ce résumé (*summary*) de la conversation entre Charles et Gina avec des mots et expressions de la liste.

aller au cinéma	une eau minérale
aller au gymnase	en boîte de nuit
avec son frère	faim
café	un jus d'orange
chez ses grands-parents	manger au restaurant
des copains	du pain
un croissant	soif

Charles et Gina sont au (1) café. Charles va boire (2) une eau minérale. Gina n'a pas très (3) faim. Elle va manger (4) un croissant. Cet après-midi, Charles va (5) aller au gymnase. Ce soir, il va (6) manger au restaurant avec (7) des copains. Cet après-midi, Gina va peut-être (8) aller au cinéma. Ce soir, elle va manger (9) chez ses grands-parents. À onze heures, elle va aller (10) en boîte de nuit avec Charles.

Et vous? Avec un(e) camarade, discutez de vos projets (*plans*) pour ce week-end. Où est-ce que vous allez aller? Qu'est-ce que vous allez faire (*to do*)?

Section Goals
In this section, students will:
- learn to listen for the gist
- listen to and summarize a short paragraph
- listen to a conversation and complete several activities

Instructional Resources
espaces.vhlcentral.com: IRM (Textbook Audioscript); Textbook MP3s; downloads; reference tools

Stratégie
Script Aujourd'hui, c'est dimanche. Ce matin, Marie va aller au café avec une copine. Cet après-midi, elle va aller au centre commercial et ce soir, elle va aller danser.

Préparation Have students look at the photo and describe what they see. Ask them to justify their responses based on visual clues. Then have them guess what they might order at the café and what they might do this afternoon.

À vous d'écouter
Script CHARLES: Alors, Gina, où est-ce que tu vas cet après-midi? Au centre-ville pour du shopping?
GINA: Eh bien, oui. Je cherche un livre pour mon frère. Je vais aller à la librairie Monet, près de l'hôpital. Il y a beaucoup de livres intéressants là-bas.
C: Et après, où vas-tu?
G: Euh... Je vais peut-être aller au cinéma...
SERVEUR: Bonjour. Vous désirez?
C: Pour moi, un sandwich au jambon et une eau minérale, s'il vous plaît.
S: Pour le sandwich, de la baguette ou du pain de campagne?
C: De la baguette, s'il vous plaît.
S: Très bien. Et pour vous, Mademoiselle?
G: Euh... Je ne sais pas... euh... un café, s'il vous plaît. Et un croissant. Je n'ai pas très faim ce midi.
S: D'accord. Merci.
G: Et toi, tu vas où cet après-midi?
C: Je vais aller au gymnase avec Pierre. Et ce soir, je vais manger au restaurant avec des copains et après, on va aller danser.
G: Ah oui? Où ça? En banlieue, près du centre commercial?
C: Non, à la nouvelle boîte de nuit, au centre-ville, près du parc. Tu as envie d'y aller?
G: Au restaurant, non. Je vais manger chez mes grands-parents ce soir, mais en boîte de nuit, oui, pourquoi pas. À quelle heure?
C: Ben, je passe chez toi après le restaurant, vers onze heures, d'accord?
G: D'accord.
C: Excusez-moi, Monsieur, l'addition, s'il vous plaît.
S: Voilà.
G: C'est combien, pour mon croissant et mon café?
C: Alors, c'est 2,50 pour le croissant et pour le café, c'est... Oh, allez, je t'invite.
G: Merci. C'est gentil.

Section Goals

In this section, students will learn historical and cultural information about Normandy and Brittany.

Instructional Resources
espaces.vhlcentral.com: Transparency #27; WB/VM/LM Answer Key; activities; downloads; reference tools

Carte de la Normandie et de la Bretagne

- Have students look at the map of Normandy and Brittany or use **Transparency #27**. Ask volunteers to read the cities' names aloud.
- Have students read the photo captions and locate the places on the map.

La région en chiffres

- Have volunteers read the sections aloud. After each section, ask questions about the content.
- Have students compare the industries of these two regions.
- Ask students to share any information they might know about the **Personnes célèbres**.

Incroyable mais vrai! The Abbey of Mont-Saint-Michel was a small chapel in the eighth century. In 966 it became a Benedictine monastery. After the French Revolution, the abbey was a political prison. In 1874, it was declared a national monument, and it presently houses a small monastic community.

NATIONAL STANDARDS connections cultures

Interactive Map Reading

Panorama

La Normandie

La région en chiffres

- **Superficie:** *29.906 km² (vingt-neuf mille neuf cent six kilomètres carrés°)*
- **Population:** *3.248.000 (trois millions deux cent quarante-huit mille)*
  SOURCE: Institut National de la Statistique et des Études Économiques (INSEE)
- **Industries principales:** *élevage bovin°, énergie nucléaire, raffinage° du pétrole*
- **Villes principales:** *Alençon, Caen, Évreux, Le Havre, Rouen*

Personnes célèbres

- **la comtesse de Ségur,** *femme écrivain° (1799–1874)*
- **Guy de Maupassant,** *écrivain (1850–1893)*
- **Christian Dior,** *couturier° (1905–1957)*

La Bretagne

La région en chiffres

- **Superficie:** *27.208 km² (vingt-sept mille deux cent huit kilomètres carrés)*
- **Population:** *3.011.000 (trois millions onze mille)*
- **Industries principales:** *agriculture, élevage°, pêche°, tourisme*
- **Villes principales:** *Brest, Quimper, Rennes, Saint-Brieuc, Vannes*

Personnes célèbres

- **Anne de Bretagne,** *reine° de France (1477–1514)*
- **Jacques Cartier,** *explorateur (1491–1557)*
- **Bernard Hinault,** *cycliste (1954–)*

carrés *squared* **élevage bovin** *cattle raising* **raffinage** *refining* **femme écrivain** *writer* **couturier** *fashion designer* **élevage** *livestock raising* **pêche** *fishing* **reine** *queen* **les plus grandes marées** *the highest tides* **presqu'île** *peninsula* **entourée de sables mouvants** *surrounded by quicksand* **basse** *low* **île** *island* **haute** *high* **chaque** *each* **onzième siècle** *11th century* **pèlerinage** *pilgrimage* **falaises** *cliffs* **faire** *make* **moulin** *mill*

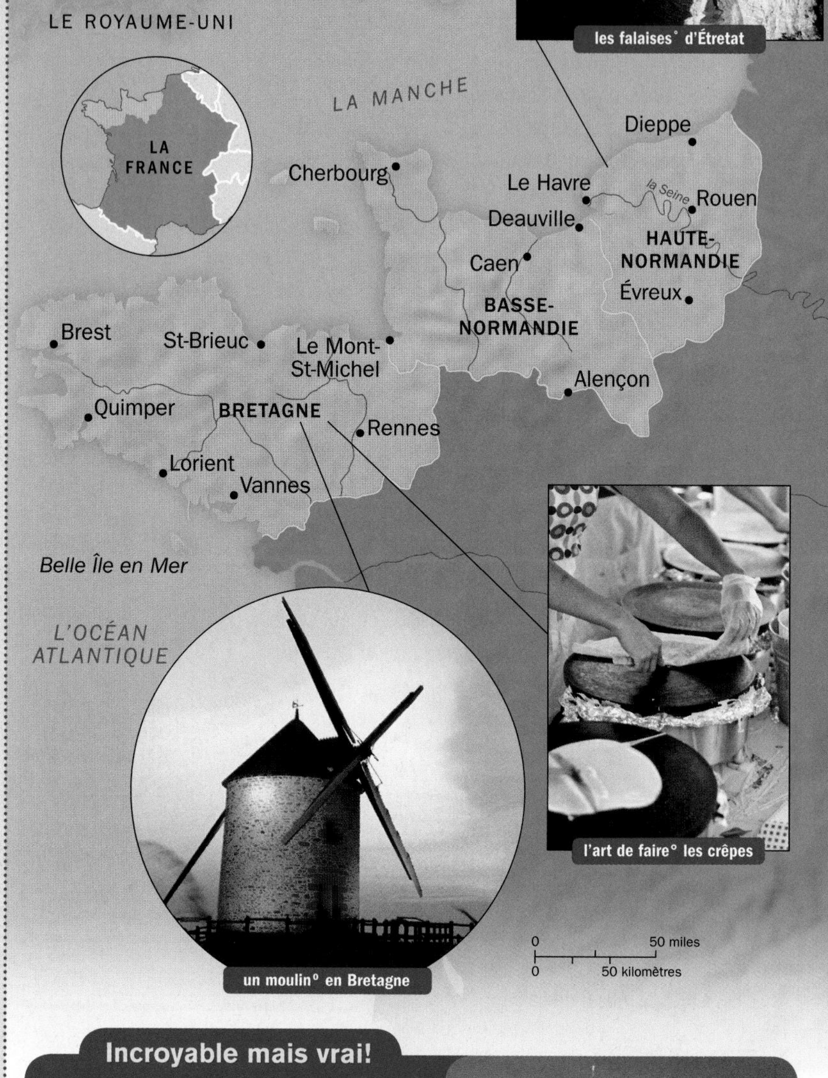

les falaises° d'Étretat

l'art de faire° les crêpes

un moulin° en Bretagne

Incroyable mais vrai!

C'est au Mont-Saint-Michel qu'il y a les plus grandes marées° d'Europe. Le Mont-Saint-Michel, presqu'île° entourée de sables mouvants° à marée basse°, est transformé en île° à marée haute°. Trois millions de touristes visitent chaque° année l'église du onzième siècle°, centre de pèlerinage° depuis 1000 (mille) ans.

OPTIONS

Personnes célèbres **La comtesse de Ségur** wrote 25 novels, notably ***les Malheurs de Sophie***. **Guy de Maupassant** published some 300 short stories and 6 novels. His stories present a picture of French life from 1870–1890. **Christian Dior** dominated post-World War II fashion. Today Christian Dior S.A. runs 160 boutiques worldwide. The company also markets lingerie, cosmetics, perfumes, handbags, watches, and accessories under the Dior name. **Anne de Bretagne** was Queen of France twice by marriage. She married Charles VIII in 1491 and Louis XII in 1499. **Jacques Cartier** explored the St. Lawrence River region during his three voyages to North America (1534, 1535, and 1541–1542). France based its claims to that area on Cartier's discoveries. **Bernard Hinault** won the **Tour de France** five times and dominated international cycling from 1977–1987.

La gastronomie

Les crêpes et galettes bretonnes et le camembert normand

Les crêpes et les galettes sont une des spécialités culinaires de Bretagne; en Normandie, c'est le camembert. Les crêpes sont appréciées sucrées, salées°, flambées... Dans les crêperies°, le menu est complètement composé de galettes et de crêpes! Le camembert normand est un des grands symboles gastronomiques de la France. Il est vendu° dans la fameuse boîte en bois ronde° pour une bonne conservation.

Les arts

Giverny et les impressionnistes

La maison° de Claude Monet, maître du mouvement impressionniste, est à Giverny, en Normandie. Après des rénovations, la résidence et les deux jardins° ont aujourd'hui leur ancienne° splendeur. Le légendaire jardin d'eau est la source d'inspiration pour les célèbres peintures° «Les Nymphéas°» et «Le pont japonais°». Depuis la fin° du dix-neuvième siècle°, beaucoup d'artistes américains, influencés par les techniques impressionnistes, font de la peinture à Giverny.

Les monuments

Les menhirs et les dolmens

À Carnac, en Bretagne, il y a 3.000 (trois mille) menhirs et dolmens. Les menhirs sont d'énormes pierres° verticales. Alignés ou en cercle, ils ont une fonction rituelle associée au culte de la fécondité ou à des cérémonies en l'honneur du soleil°. Les plus anciens° datent de 4.500 (quatre mille cinq cents) ans avant J.-C.° Les dolmens servent de° sépultures° collectives et ont une fonction culturelle comme° le rite funéraire du passage de la vie° à la mort°.

Les destinations

Deauville: station balnéaire de réputation internationale

Deauville, en Normandie, est une station balnéaire° de luxe et un centre de thalassothérapie°. La ville est célèbre pour sa marina, ses courses hippiques°, son casino, ses grands hôtels et son festival du film américain. La clientèle internationale apprécie beaucoup la plage°, le polo et le golf. L'hôtel le Royal Barrière est un palace° du début° du vingtième° siècle.

Compréhension Complétez ces phrases.

1. __Jacques Cartier__ est un explorateur breton.
2. Le Mont-Saint-Michel est une __île__ à marée haute.
3. __Les crêpes__ sont une spécialité bretonne.
4. Dans __les crêperies__, on mange uniquement des crêpes.
5. __Le camembert__ est vendu dans une boîte en bois ronde.
6. Le __jardin d'eau__ de Monet est la source d'inspiration de beaucoup de peintures.
7. Beaucoup d'artistes __américains__ font de la peinture à Giverny.
8. Les menhirs ont une fonction __rituelle__.
9. Les dolmens servent de __sépultures__.
10. Deauville est une __station balnéaire__ de luxe.

Practice more at **espaces.vhlcentral.com.**

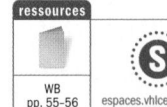

ressources
WB pp. 55-56
espaces.vhlcentral.com

SUR INTERNET

Go to **espaces.vhlcentral.com** to find more cultural information related to this **PANORAMA**.

1. Cherchez des informations sur les marées du Mont-Saint-Michel. À quelle heure est la marée haute aujourd'hui?
2. Cherchez des informations sur deux autres impressionnistes. Trouvez deux peintures que vous aimez et dites (*say*) pourquoi.

salées *salty* **crêperies** *crêpes restaurants* **vendu** *sold* **boîte en bois ronde** *round, wooden box* **maison** *house* **jardins** *gardens* **ancienne** *former* **peintures** *paintings* **Nymphéas** *Waterlilies* **pont japonais** *Japanese Bridge* **Depuis la fin** *Since the end* **dix-neuvième siècle** *19th century* **pierres** *stones* **soleil** *sun* **Les plus anciens** *The oldest* **avant J.-C.** *B.C.* **servent de** *serve as* **sépultures** *graves* **comme** *such as* **vie** *life* **mort** *death* **station balnéaire** *seaside resort* **thalassothérapie** *seawater therapy* **courses hippiques** *horse races* **plage** *beach* **palace** *luxury hotel* **début** *beginning* **vingtième** *twentieth*

Les crêpes bretonnes et le camembert normand

- There are various types of crêpes. In Brittany, the **galettes de blé noir** (buckwheat crêpes) are filled with foods such as egg, ham and cheese, or mushrooms. The **crêpes de froment** (wheat flour crêpes) frequently have sweet fillings such as honey, sugar, jam, or chocolate. Normandy has been known for its cheeses since the sixteenth century. Created in 1890, the wooden container permitted Camembert to be exported worldwide.
- Ask students if they have eaten crêpes or Camembert and if they like them. Or bring in some Camembert and a baguette for students to sample.

Giverny et les impressionnistes Considered one of the greatest landscape painters, Claude Monet lived in the village of Giverny from 1883 until his death in 1926. Bring in photos of ***les Nymphéas*** or ***Le pont japonais*** and briefly comment on the style and colors.

Les menhirs et les dolmens The megaliths, which are ancient granite blocks, can be found all over Brittany. The **menhir** is the most common form of megalith. The **dolmen** has two upright stones with a flat stone on top, like a table. The words **menhir** and **dolmen** come from Breton; **men** means *stone*, **hir** means *long*, and **dol** means *table*.

Deauville: station balnéaire de réputation internationale Founded by the Duke of Normandy in the 1860s, Deauville is famous for its **Promenade des Planches**, the wooden boardwalk alongside the beach, which was created so women wouldn't have to walk in the sand. Ask students: **Avez-vous envie de visiter Deauville? Pourquoi?**

OPTIONS

Cultural Comparison Working in small groups, have students compare Deauville to a famous American seaside resort. Tell them to list the similarities and differences in a two-column chart under the headings **Similitudes** and **Différences**. After completing their charts, call on volunteers to read their lists.

La Chandeleur On February 2, friends and family gather to celebrate the holiday **la Chandeleur** by cooking and eating crêpes and hoping for a prosperous year. Originally a religious celebration, **la Chandeleur** attracted pilgrims to Rome, and according to legend, the pope gave the pilgrims crêpes. Since then, crêpes have been associated with the holiday.

Section Goals

In this section, students will:
- learn to scan a text for specific information
- read an advertisement for a cybercafé

Stratégie Tell students that a good way to get an idea of what an article or other text is about is to scan it before reading. Scanning means running one's eyes over a text in search of specific information that can be used to infer the text's content. Explain that scanning a text before reading it is a good way to improve reading comprehension.

Examinez le texte Call on volunteers to identify the cognates. Then ask the class what the text is about. (a cybercafé)

Trouvez Have students give details about the information they found in the document. Examples: **une adresse (24 place Joliet 69006 LYON), les noms des propriétaires (Bernard et Marie-Claude Fouchier), les heures d'ouverture (7h à 20h), and le numéro de téléphone (04.72.45.87.90)**.

Décrivez Tell students to proofread each other's descriptions for spelling, verb agreement, and accuracy of information.

Lecture

NATIONAL STANDARDS communication cultures

Reading

Avant la lecture

STRATÉGIE

Scanning

Scanning involves glancing over a document in search of specific information. For example, you can scan a document to identify its format, to find cognates, to locate visual clues about the document's content, or to find specific facts. Scanning allows you to learn a great deal about a text without having to read it word-for-word.

Examinez le texte

Regardez le texte et indiquez huit mots apparentés (*cognates*) que vous trouvez. Answers may vary.

1. Chocolat
2. Cybercafé
3. Accès Internet
4. Omelette
5. Salade
6. Tarte
7. Soupe
8. Snack

Trouvez

Regardez le document. Indiquez si les informations suivantes sont présentes dans le texte.

- ✓ 1. une adresse
- ___ 2. le nombre d'ordinateurs
- ___ 3. un plat du jour (*daily special*)
- ✓ 4. une terrasse
- ✓ 5. les noms des propriétaires
- ___ 6. des prix réduits pour étudiants
- ___ 7. de la musique *live*
- ✓ 8. les heures d'ouverture (*business hours*)
- ✓ 9. un numéro de téléphone
- ___ 10. une librairie à l'intérieur

Décrivez

Regardez les photos. Écrivez un paragraphe succinct pour décrire (*describe*) le cybercafé. Comparez votre paragraphe avec le paragraphe d'un(e) camarade.

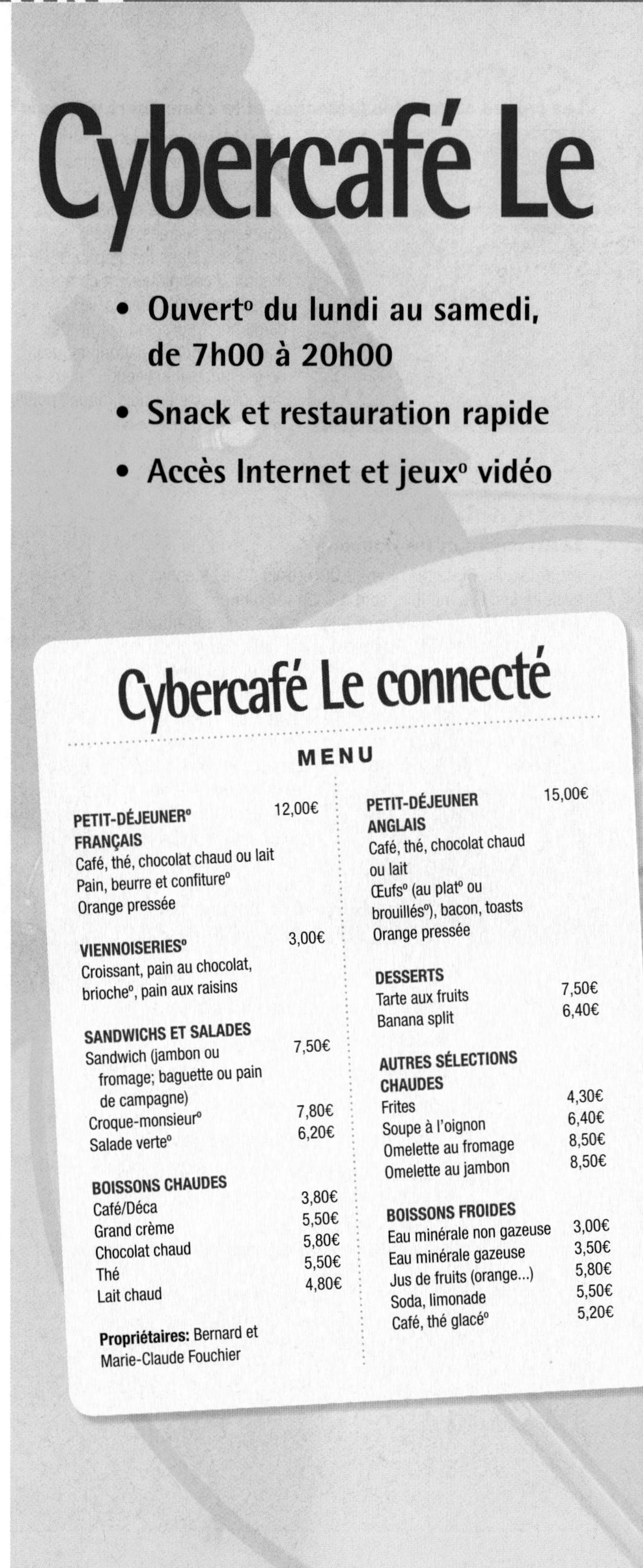

Cybercafé Le

- Ouvert° du lundi au samedi, de 7h00 à 20h00
- Snack et restauration rapide
- Accès Internet et jeux° vidéo

Cybercafé Le connecté

MENU

PETIT-DÉJEUNER° FRANÇAIS 12,00€
Café, thé, chocolat chaud ou lait
Pain, beurre et confiture°
Orange pressée

VIENNOISERIES° 3,00€
Croissant, pain au chocolat, brioche°, pain aux raisins

SANDWICHS ET SALADES
Sandwich (jambon ou fromage; baguette ou pain de campagne) 7,50€
Croque-monsieur° 7,80€
Salade verte° 6,20€

BOISSONS CHAUDES
Café/Déca 3,80€
Grand crème 5,50€
Chocolat chaud 5,80€
Thé 5,50€
Lait chaud 4,80€

Propriétaires: Bernard et Marie-Claude Fouchier

PETIT-DÉJEUNER ANGLAIS 15,00€
Café, thé, chocolat chaud ou lait
Œufs° (au plat° ou brouillés°), bacon, toasts
Orange pressée

DESSERTS
Tarte aux fruits 7,50€
Banana split 6,40€

AUTRES SÉLECTIONS CHAUDES
Frites 4,30€
Soupe à l'oignon 6,40€
Omelette au fromage 8,50€
Omelette au jambon 8,50€

BOISSONS FROIDES
Eau minérale non gazeuse 3,00€
Eau minérale gazeuse 3,50€
Jus de fruits (orange...) 5,80€
Soda, limonade 5,50€
Café, thé glacé° 5,20€

OPTIONS

Game Have students work in pairs and play a game of **Dix questions**. The first person thinks of a food or beverage listed in the **Cybercafé Le connecté** menu. The second person must guess the item by asking yes/no questions. Remind students that they may only ask ten questions.

Small Groups Have students work in groups of three or four. Tell them that they are going to open up a new cybercafé and they need to create a "must-have" list of services and foods for their establishment. After groups have completed their lists, have them describe their café to the class. Then have the class vote on the cybercafé with the best features.

connecté

- **Le connecté, le cybercafé préféré des étudiants**
- **Ordinateurs disponibles° de 10h00 à 18h00, 1,50€ les 10 minutes**

24, place des Terreaux
69001 LYON
Tél. 04.72.45.87.90
www.leconnecte.fr

Situé en face du musée des Beaux-Arts

Ouvert *Open* **jeux** *games* **Petit-déjeuner** *Breakfast* **confiture** *jam* **Viennoiseries** *Breakfast pastries* **brioche** *a light, slightly-sweet bread* **Croque-monsieur** *Grilled sandwich with cheese and ham* **verte** *green* **Œufs** *Eggs* **au plat** *fried* **brouillés** *scrambled* **glacé** *iced* **disponibles** *available*

Après la lecture

Répondez **Répondez aux questions par des phrases complètes.**

1. Combien coûte un sandwich?
   Un sandwich coûte 7,50€.
2. Quand est-ce qu'on peut (*can*) surfer sur Internet?
   On peut surfer sur Internet de 10h00 à 18h00.
3. Qui adore ce cybercafé?
   Les étudiants adorent ce cybercafé.
4. Quelles sont les deux boissons gazeuses? Combien coûtent-elles?
   L'eau minérale gazeuse coûte 3,50€. Un soda coûte 5,50€.
5. Combien de desserts sont proposés?
   Deux desserts sont proposés.
6. Vous aimez le sucre. Qu'est-ce que vous allez manger? (2 sélections) Answers may vary. Je vais manger… Any two of the following: un croissant, un pain au chocolat, une brioche, un pain aux raisins, une tarte aux fruits, un banana split.

Choisissez **Indiquez qui va prendre quoi. Écrivez des phrases complètes.** Answers may vary. Possible answers provided.

MODÈLE

Julie a soif. Elle n'aime pas les boissons gazeuses. Elle a 6 euros.
Julie va prendre un jus d'orange.

1. Lise a froid. Elle a besoin d'une boisson chaude. Elle a 4 euros et 90 centimes.
   Lise va prendre un café.
2. Nathan a faim et soif. Il a 14 euros.
   Nathan va prendre un croque-monsieur et un soda.
3. Julien va prendre un plat chaud. Il a 8 euros et 80 centimes.
   Julien va prendre une omelette au jambon.
4. Annie a chaud et a très soif. Elle a 5 euros et 75 centimes.
   Annie va prendre un thé glacé.
5. Martine va prendre une boisson gazeuse. Elle a 4 euros et 20 centimes.
   Martine va prendre une eau minérale gazeuse.
6. Ève va prendre un dessert. Elle n'aime pas les bananes. Elle a 8 euros.
   Ève va prendre une tarte aux fruits.

L'invitation **Avec un(e) camarade, jouez (*play*) cette scène: vous invitez un ami à déjeuner au cybercafé Le connecté. Parlez de ce que vous allez manger et boire. Puis (*Then*), bavardez de vos activités de l'après-midi et du soir.**

Répondez Go over the answers with the class. Take a quick class poll to find out what is the most popular food chosen for question 6.

Choisissez Have students write two more situations similar to those in the activity. Then tell them to exchange papers with a partner, write the answers, and verify the answers.

L'invitation Before beginning the activity, tell students that they only have 20€ to spend at the **Cybercafé Le connecté.**

OPTIONS

Cultural Comparison Working in groups of three, have students compare the **Cybercafé Le connecté** menu to a typical menu found at an American Internet café. Tell them to list the similarities and differences in a two-column chart under the headings **Similitudes** and **Différences**. After completing their charts, call on volunteers to read their lists.

Extra Practice To practice scanning written material, bring in short, simple French-language magazine or newspaper articles you have read. Have pairs or small groups scan the articles to determine what they are about. Have them write down all the clues that help them. When each group has come to a decision, ask it to present its findings to the class. Confirm the accuracy of their inferences.

Section Goals
In this section, students will:
- learn to add informative details
- learn to write an informative note

Stratégie Discuss the importance of being informative when writing a note and answering the "W" questions. For example, someone calls while you are out, and your roommate answers the phone. If your note has enough information, your roommate can answer the person's questions about where you are or when you will return.

Thème Have students read the model note and identify the details. (**aujourd'hui; avec Xavier et Laurent, deux étudiants belges de l'université**)

Proofreading Activity Have the class correct these sentences. **1. Ou est-ce que tu va après le cours? 2. Il vont à le magasin cet après-midi. 3. Est-ce que tu prend de le sucre dans le café? 4. Dominique bois de la thé avec le petit-déjeuner.**

Écriture

STRATÉGIE

Adding details

How can you make your writing more informative or more interesting? You can add details by answering the "W" questions: Who? What? When? Where? Why? The answers to these questions will provide useful and interesting details that can be incorporated into your writing. You can use the same strategy when writing in French. Here are some useful question words that you have already learned:

(À/Avec) Qui?	À quelle heure?
Quoi?	Où?
Quand?	Pourquoi?

Compare these two sentences.

Je vais aller nager.

Aujourd'hui, à quatre heures, je vais aller nager à la piscine du parc avec mon ami Paul, parce que nous avons chaud.

While both sentences give the same basic information (the writer is going to go swimming), the second, with its detail, is much more informative.

Thème

Un petit mot

Avant l'écriture

1. Vous passez un an en France et vous vivez (*are living*) dans une famille d'accueil (*host family*). C'est samedi, et vous allez passer la journée en ville avec des amis. Écrivez un petit mot (*note*) pour informer votre famille de vos projets (*plans*) pour la journée.
2. D'abord (*First*), choisissez (*choose*) cinq activités que vous allez faire (*to do*) avec vos amis aujourd'hui.

Activité 1:

Activité 2:

Activité 3:

Activité 4:

Activité 5:

OPTIONS

Avant l'écriture Discuss the importance of facts when writing a note and answering the "W" questions. Encourage students to identify a note's purpose (to provide specific information and instructions). Point out that if a note is not complete enough, it fails to serve its purpose. Redundancies can also detract from the message.

Demonstrate how the question strategy works by choosing a general topic and then, as a class, asking and answering the questions in the box. Put students in pairs and have them try it out on their own, using the questions provided to narrow their topic and add details while avoiding redundancies.

3. Ensuite (*Then*), complétez ce tableau (*this chart*) pour organiser vos idées. Répondez à (*Answer*) tous les pronoms interrogatifs.

	Activité 1	*Activité 2*	*Activité 3*	*Activité 4*	*Activité 5*
Qui?					
Quoi?					
Quand?					
Où?					
Comment?					
Pourquoi?					

4. Maintenant (*Now*), comparez votre tableau à celui (*to the one*) d'un(e) partenaire. Avez-vous tous les deux (*both of you*) cinq activités? Avez-vous des informations dans toutes les colonnes? Avez-vous répondu à tous les pronoms interrogatifs?

Écriture

Écrivez la note à votre famille d'accueil. Référez-vous au tableau que vous avez créé (*have created*) et incluez toutes les informations. Utilisez les verbes aller, boire et prendre, et le vocabulaire de l'unité. Organisez vos idées de manière logique.

> *Chère famille,*
> *Aujourd'hui, je vais visiter la ville avec Xavier et Laurent, deux étudiants belges de l'université...*

Après l'écriture

1. Échangez votre tableau et votre note avec ceux (*the ones*) d'un(e) partenaire. Faites des commentaires sur son travail (*work*) d'après (*according to*) ces questions:
   - Votre partenaire a-t-il/elle inclus dans la note toutes les informations du tableau?
   - A-t-il/elle correctement (*correctly*) utilisé le vocabulaire de l'unité?
   - A-t-il/elle utilisé la forme correcte des verbes aller, boire et prendre?
   - A-t-il/elle présenté ses informations de manière logique?

2. Corrigez (*Correct*) votre note d'après les commentaires de votre partenaire. Relisez votre travail pour éliminer ces (*these*) problèmes:
   - des fautes (*errors*) d'orthographe
   - des fautes de ponctuation
   - des fautes de conjugaison
   - des fautes d'accord (*agreement*) des adjectifs

EVALUATION

Criteria

Content Contains a greeting, describes the five planned activities, answers the questions: **qui? quoi? quand? où? pourquoi?**, and includes supporting detail without redundancy.
Scale: 1 2 3 4 5

Organization Organizes the note into a salutation, a description, and a signature.
Scale: 1 2 3 4 5

Accuracy Uses forms of **aller** and places in town correctly. Spells words, conjugates verbs, and modifies adjectives correctly throughout. Avoids redundant language.
Scale: 1 2 3 4 5

Creativity The student includes additional information that is not included in the task, mentions more than five activities and/or includes a closing (not shown in the model).
Scale: 1 2 3 4 5

Scoring

Excellent	18–20 points
Good	14–17 points
Satisfactory	10–13 points
Unsatisfactory	< 10 points

OPTIONS

Écriture Ask for other details that could be added, such as departure and return times, activities in the town, its name and the students' ages. Finally, have them analyze these extra details to see which are useful for the note's message and which are extraneous or redundant.

Show students how to avoid redundancies by combining similar sentences. Compare **Je vais en ville. Je vais avec mes amis. Je vais lundi matin.** with **Je vais en ville avec mes amis lundi matin.** Tell them to look for ways to condense language when they edit their work.

Flashcards
Audio: Vocabulary

VOCABULAIRE

Instructional Resources
espaces.vhlcentral.com: Textbook MP3s; IRM (Textbook Audioscript); downloads; reference tools

Suggestion Tell students that an easy way to study from **Vocabulaire** is to cover up the French half of each section, leaving only the English equivalents exposed. They can then quiz themselves on the French items. To focus on the English equivalents of the French entries, they simply reverse this process.

Dans la ville

une boîte (de nuit)	*nightclub*
un bureau	*office; desk*
un centre commercial	*shopping center, mall*
un cinéma (ciné)	*movie theater, movies*
une église	*church*
une épicerie	*grocery store*
un grand magasin	*department store*
un gymnase	*gym*
un hôpital	*hospital*
un kiosque	*kiosk*
un magasin	*store*
une maison	*house*
un marché	*market*
un musée	*museum*
un parc	*park*
une piscine	*pool*
une place	*square; place*
un restaurant	*restaurant*
une terrasse de café	*café terrace*
une banlieue	*suburbs*
un centre-ville	*city/town center, downtown*
un endroit	*place*
un lieu	*place*
une montagne	*mountain*
une ville	*city, town*

Les questions

à quelle heure?	*at what time?*
à qui?	*to whom?*
avec qui?	*with whom?*
combien (de)?	*how many?; how much?*
comment?	*how?; what?*
où?	*where?*
parce que	*because*
pour qui?	*for whom?*
pourquoi?	*why?*
quand?	*when?*
quel(le)(s)?	*which?; what?*
que/qu'...?	*what?*
qui?	*who?; whom?*
quoi?	*what?*

À table

avoir faim	*to be hungry*
avoir soif	*to be thirsty*
manger quelque chose	*to eat something*
une baguette	*baguette (long, thin loaf of bread)*
le beurre	*butter*
un croissant	*croissant (flaky, crescent-shaped roll)*
un éclair	*éclair (pastry filled with cream)*
des frites (*f.*)	*French fries*
un fromage	*cheese*
le jambon	*ham*
un pain (de campagne)	*(country-style) bread*
un sandwich	*sandwich*
une soupe	*soup*
le sucre	*sugar*
une boisson (gazeuse)	*(soft) (carbonated) drink/beverage*
un café	*coffee*
un chocolat (chaud)	*(hot) chocolate*
une eau (minérale)	*(mineral) water*
un jus (d'orange, de pomme, etc.)	*(orange, apple, etc.) juice*
le lait	*milk*
une limonade	*lemon soda*
un thé (glacé)	*(iced) tea*

Activités

bavarder	*to chat*
danser	*to dance*
déjeuner	*to eat lunch*
dépenser de l'argent (*m.*)	*to spend money*
explorer	*to explore*
fréquenter	*to frequent; to visit*
inviter	*to invite*
nager	*to swim*
passer chez quelqu'un	*to stop by someone's house*
patiner	*to skate*
quitter la maison	*to leave the house*

Expressions utiles	*See pp. 115 and 129.*
Prepositions	*See p. 119.*
Partitives	*See p. 133.*

Expressions de quantité

(pas) assez (de)	*(not) enough (of)*
beaucoup (de)	*a lot (of)*
d'autres	*others*
une bouteille (de)	*bottle (of)*
un morceau (de)	*piece, bit (of)*
un peu (plus/moins) (de)	*little (more/less) (of)*
plusieurs	*several*
quelque chose	*something; anything*
quelques	*some*
une tasse (de)	*cup (of)*
tous (*m. pl.*)	*all*
tout (*m. sing.*)	*all*
tout le/tous les (*m.*)	*all the*
toute la/toutes les (*f.*)	*all the*
trop (de)	*too many/much (of)*
un verre (de)	*glass (of)*

Au café

apporter	*to bring, to carry*
coûter	*to cost*
laisser un pourboire	*to leave a tip*
l'addition (*f.*)	*check, bill*
Combien coûte(nt)...?	*How much is/are...?*
un prix	*price*
un serveur/une serveuse	*server*

Verbes

aller	*to go*
apprendre	*to learn*
boire	*to drink*
comprendre	*to understand*
prendre	*to take; to have*

Verbes réguliers en -ir

choisir	*to choose*
finir	*to finish*
grandir	*to grow*
grossir	*to gain weight*
maigrir	*to lose weight*
obéir (à)	*to obey*
réagir	*to react*
réfléchir (à)	*to think (about), to reflect (on)*
réussir (à)	*to succeed (in doing something)*
rougir	*to blush*
vieillir	*to grow old*

ressources
espaces.vhlcentral.com

Les loisirs

UNITÉ

5

Pour commencer

- Où est Stéphane?
- A-t-il froid?
- Pensez-vous qu'il aime le sport?
- Quel sport pratique-t-il? Le football ou le basket-ball?
- Quel mois sommes-nous? En septembre ou en décembre?

Leçon 5A

Leçon 5B

Savoir-faire

Unit Goals

Leçon 5A

In this lesson, students will learn:
- terms for sports and leisure activities
- adverbs of frequency
- about intonation
- about **le football**
- more about sports and leisure activities through specially shot video footage
- the verb **faire**
- expressions with **faire**
- the expression **il faut**
- irregular **-ir** verbs
- about the insurance company SwissLife

Leçon 5B

In this lesson, students will learn:
- terms for seasons and months
- weather expressions
- to tell the date
- differences between open and closed vowels
- about public gardens and parks in the francophone world
- the numbers 101 and higher
- **-er** verbs with spelling changes
- to listen for key words in oral communication

Savoir-faire

In this section, students will learn:
- cultural and historical information about the French regions of **Pays de la Loire** and **Centre**
- to skim a text
- to use a French-English dictionary

Pour commencer

- **Il est dans le parc.**
- **Non, il n'a pas froid.**
- **Oui, je pense qu'il aime le sport.**
- **Il pratique le football.**
- **Nous sommes en septembre.**

RESOURCES

Workbook/Video Manual: WB Activities, pp. 57–70
Laboratory Manual: Lab Activities, pp. 33–40
Workbook/Video Manual: Video Activities, pp. 227–230; pp. 279–280
WB/VM/LM Answer Key
espaces.vhlcentral.com: Textbook MP3s; Lab MP3s; Instructor's Resource Manual [IRM] (Textbook Audioscript; Lab Audioscript; Videoscript; **Roman-photo** Translations; **Vocabulaire supplémentaire**; **Feuilles d'activités**; Info Gap Activities; **Le zapping** TV clip transcription; **Essayez!** and **Mise en pratique** answers); Transparencies #28, #29, #30;
Testing Program, pp. 33–40, pp. 185–196; Test Files; Testing Program MP3s
Test Generator
Video on DVD

Section Goals

In this section, students will learn and practice vocabulary related to:

- sports and leisure activities
- adverbs of frequency

Instructional Resources
*espaces.vhlcentral.com: Transparency #28; IRM (**Vocabulaire supplémentaire**; **Mise en pratique** answers; Textbook Audioscript; Lab Audioscript; **Feuilles d'activités**); Textbook MP3s; Lab MP3s; WB/VM/LM Answer Key; activities; downloads; reference tools*

Suggestions

- Have students look over the new vocabulary, covering the translations. Guide them to notice the numerous cognates for sports terms. See how many words students know without looking at the English.
- Use **Transparency #28** to describe what people are doing. Examples: **Ils jouent au football. Elles jouent au tennis.** Encourage students to add their remarks.
- Teach students the expression **aider quelqu'un à... (étudier, bricoler, travailler)**. Pointing to the person toward the right helping his injured friend, say: **Il aide son copain à marcher.**
- Point out the differences between the words **un jeu**, **jouer**, **un joueur**, and **une joueuse**.
- Ask students closed-ended questions about their favorite activities: **Tu préfères jouer au tennis ou aller à la pêche? Aller à un spectacle ou jouer au golf?**
- Call out sports and other activities from this section and have students classify them as either **un sport** or **un loisir**. List them on the board in two columns.
- Additional vocabulary for this lesson can be found in the **Vocabulaire supplémentaire** on the Supersite.

Leçon 5A

Talking Picture
Audio: Activity

You will learn how to...

- talk about activities
- tell how often and how well you do things

Le temps libre

Vocabulaire

aller à la pêche	*to go fishing*
bricoler	*to tinker; to do odd jobs*
désirer	*to want*
jouer (à/de)	*to play*
pratiquer	*to play regularly, to practice*
skier	*to ski*
le baseball	*baseball*
le cinéma	*movies*
le foot(ball)	*soccer*
le football américain	*football*
le golf	*golf*
un jeu	*game*
un loisir	*leisure activity*
un passe-temps	*pastime, hobby*
un spectacle	*show*
un stade	*stadium*
le temps libre	*free time*
le volley(-ball)	*volleyball*
une/deux fois	*one/two time(s)*
par jour, semaine, mois, an, etc.	*per day, week, month, year, etc.*
déjà	*already*
encore	*again, still*
jamais	*never*
longtemps	*long time*
maintenant	*now*
parfois	*sometimes*
rarement	*rarely*
souvent	*often*

ressources
WB pp. 57-58 | LM p. 33 | espaces.vhlcentral.com

OPTIONS

Extra Practice Have students give their opinions about activities in **Espace contextes**. Brainstorm pairs of adjectives that apply to activities and write them on the board or on a transparency. Examples: **agréable/désagréable, intéressant/ennuyeux, utile/inutile, génial/nul, facile/difficile**. Then ask questions like these: **Le football, c'est intéressant ou c'est ennuyeux? Les échecs, c'est facile ou difficile?**

Game Play a game of **Jacques a dit** (*Simon says*) using the activities in this section. Tell students to mime each activity only if they hear the words **Jacques a dit**. If a student mimes an activity not preceded by **Jacques a dit**, he or she is eliminated from the game. The last person standing wins. You might want students to take turns calling out activities.

Attention!

Use **jouer à** with games and sports.

Elle joue aux cartes/au baseball.
She plays cards/baseball.

Use **jouer de** with musical instruments.

Vous jouez de la guitare/du piano.
You play the guitar/piano.

Mise en pratique

1 Remplissez Choisissez dans la liste le mot qui convient (*the word that fits*) pour compléter les phrases. N'oubliez pas de conjuguer les verbes.

aider	jeu	pratiquer
bande dessinée	jouer	skier
bricoler	marcher	sport
équipe		

1. Notre __équipe__ joue un match cet après-midi.
2. Le tarot est un __jeu__ de cartes.
3. Mon livre préféré, c'est une __bande dessinée__ de Tintin, *Le sceptre d'Ottokar.*
4. J'aime __jouer__ aux cartes avec ma grand-mère.
5. Pour devenir (*To become*) champion de volley, je __pratique__ tous les jours.
6. Le dimanche, nous __marchons__ beaucoup, environ (*about*) cinq kilomètres.
7. Mon __sport__ préféré, c'est le foot.
8. Mon père __aide__ mon frère à préparer son match de tennis.
9. J'aime mieux __skier__ dans les Alpes que dans le Colorado.
10. Il faut réparer la table, mais je n'aime pas __bricoler__.

2 Écoutez Écoutez Sabine et Marc parler de leurs passe-temps préférés. Dans le tableau suivant, écrivez un **S** pour Sabine et un **M** pour Marc pour indiquer s'ils pratiquent ces activités **souvent**, **parfois**, **rarement** ou **jamais**. Attention, toutes les activités ne sont pas utilisées.

Activités	Souvent	Parfois	Rarement	Jamais
1. chanter	S			
2. le basket	S	M		
3. les cartes				
4. le tennis	M	S		
5. aller à la pêche			M	S
6. le golf				M
7. le cinéma	M, S			
8. le spectacle	M		S	

3 Les loisirs Utilisez un élément de chaque colonne pour former huit phrases au sujet des loisirs de ces personnes. N'oubliez pas les accords (*agreements*). Answers will vary.

Personnes	Activités	Fréquence
Je	jouer aux échecs	maintenant
Ma sœur	chanter	parfois
Mes parents	jouer au tennis	rarement
Christian	gagner le match	souvent
Sandrine et Cédric	skier	déjà
Les étudiants	regarder un spectacle	une fois par semaine
Élise	jouer au basket	une fois par mois
Mon ami(e)	aller à la pêche	encore

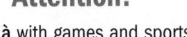

Practice more at **espaces.vhlcentral.com.**

1 Suggestions
- To review **-er** verb forms, conjugate on the board one of the verbs from the list.
- Tell students to use each item in the word box only once.

2 Tapescript SABINE: Bonjour, Marc, comment ça va?
MARC: Pas mal. Et toi?
S: Très bien, merci. Est-ce que tu joues au golf?
M: Non, jamais. Je n'aime pas ce sport. Je préfère jouer au tennis. En général, je joue au tennis trois fois par semaine. Et toi?
S: Moi? Jouer au tennis? Oui, parfois, mais j'aime mieux le basket. C'est un sport que je pratique souvent.
M: Ah le basket, je n'aime pas tellement. Je joue parfois avec des amis, mais ce n'est pas mon sport préféré. Le soir, j'aime bien aller au spectacle ou au cinéma. Et toi, qu'est-ce que tu aimes faire le soir?
S: Oh, je vais rarement au spectacle mais j'adore aller au cinéma. J'y vais très souvent.
M: C'est quoi, ton passe-temps préféré?
S: Mon passe-temps préféré, c'est le chant. J'aime chanter tous les jours.
M: Moi, j'adore aller à la pêche quand j'ai du temps libre, mais ce n'est que très rarement.
S: La pêche? Oh, moi, jamais. Je trouve ça ennuyeux.
M: Et est-ce que tu aimes le baseball?
S: Je ne sais pas; je n'ai jamais regardé un match de baseball.
M: Il y a un match toutes les semaines. C'est très intéressant.
(On Textbook MP3s)

2 Expansion Have students tell a partner how often they, themselves, do these activities.

3 Suggestion Ask volunteers to write one of their sentences on the board, making sure to have one example sentence for each of the verbs listed in this activity.

3 Expansion Ask students how frequently they do each of the activities listed. Encourage them to use as many different adverbial expressions as possible.

OPTIONS

Extra Practice Call out names of famous athletes and have students say: **Ils jouent au** __*sport*__. Examples: Tiger Woods, Arnold Palmer (**golf**), David Beckham, Zinédine Zidane (**football**), Serena Williams, André Agassi (**tennis**), Donovan McNabb, Troy Aikman (**football américain**), Shaquille O'Neal, Larry Bird (**basket-ball**), and Babe Ruth, Mark McGwire (**baseball**).

Game Write each of the words or expressions in **Activité 3** on an index card. Label three boxes **Personnes, Activités**, and **Fréquence**. Then place the cards in their respective boxes. Divide the class into two teams. Students take turns drawing one card from each box. Each player has five seconds to form a sentence using all of the words on the three cards. If they do not make a mistake, they score a point for their team.

4 Suggestion Follow up this activity by asking students about their partners' favorite sports and activities. Examples: **Est-ce que ____ est sportif/sportive? Quel sport pratique-t-il/elle? Combien de fois par mois est-ce que ____ va au cinéma?**

4 Expansion Have students conduct an informal survey by circulating around the room and asking these questions to five other students. Tell them to write down all of the responses for each question. As a class, share and compare students' findings.

5 Suggestions
- Have two volunteers read the **modèle** aloud to make sure students understand the directions. Then distribute the **Feuilles d'activités** found on the Supersite.
- Combine pairs of students to form groups of four. Have students share with the other pair what they learned about their partner.

5 Expansion Tally the results of the survey to determine the most and least popular activities among your students.

6 Suggestion Call on two students to read the **modèle** before assigning this activity.

7 Suggestion Have students exchange letters with a classmate. Remind them to begin the letter with **chère** if they are writing to a woman.

Successful Language Learning Suggest that students use mnemonics devices to memorize vocabulary. Examples: Use alliteration for interrogative words like **qui**, **quand**, and **quoi**. Group words in categories, such as team sports (**football, basket-ball, volley-ball**) versus those that are usually played one-on-one (**échecs, cartes, tennis**). Learn word "families," such as **un jeu, jouer, un joueur**, and **une joueuse**.

Communication

4 Répondez Avec un(e) partenaire, posez-vous (*ask each other*) ces (*these*) questions et répondez (*answer*) à tour de rôle. Answers will vary.

1. Quel est votre loisir préféré?
2. Quel est votre sport préféré à la télévision?
3. Êtes-vous sportif/sportive? Si oui, quel sport pratiquez-vous?
4. Qu'est-ce que vous désirez faire (*to do*) ce week-end?
5. Combien de fois par mois allez-vous au cinéma?
6. Que faites-vous (*do you do*) quand vous avez du temps libre?
7. Est-ce que vous aidez quelqu'un? Qui? À faire quoi? Comment?
8. Quel est votre jeu de société (*board game*) préféré? Pourquoi?

5 Sondage Avec la feuille d'activités que votre professeur va vous donner, circulez dans la classe et demandez à vos camarades s'ils pratiquent ces activités et si oui (*if so*), à quelle fréquence. Quelle est l'activité la plus pratiquée (*the most practiced*) de la classe? Answers will vary.

MODÈLE

aller à la pêche
Étudiant(e) 1: *Est-ce que tu vas à la pêche?*
Étudiant(e) 2: *Oui, je vais parfois à la pêche.*

Activités	*Noms*	*Fréquence*
1. aller à la pêche	*François*	*parfois*
2. jouer au tennis	____	____
3. jouer au foot	____	____
4. skier	____	____

6 Conversez Avec un(e) partenaire, utilisez les expressions de la liste et les mots d'**ESPACE CONTEXTES** et écrivez une conversation au sujet de vos loisirs. Présentez votre travail au reste de la classe. Answers will vary.

MODÈLE

Étudiant(e) 1: *Que fais-tu (do you do) comme sport?*
Étudiant(e) 2: *Je joue au volley.*
Étudiant(e) 1: *Tu joues souvent?*
Étudiant(e) 2: *Oui, trois fois par semaine, avec mon amie Julie. C'est un sport que j'adore. Et toi, quel est ton passe-temps préféré?*

Avec qui?	Pourquoi?
Combien de fois par...?	Quand?
Comment?	Quel(le)(s)?
Où?	Quoi?

7 La lettre Écrivez une lettre à un(e) ami(e). Dites ce que vous faites (do) pendant vos loisirs, quand, avec qui et à quelle fréquence.

Cher Marc,

Pendant (During) mon temps libre, j'aime bien jouer au basket et au tennis. J'aime gagner, mais ça n'arrive pas souvent! Je joue au tennis avec mes amis deux fois par semaine, le mardi et le vendredi, et au basket le samedi. J'adore les films et je vais souvent au cinéma avec ma sœur ou mes amis. Le soir...

OPTIONS

Extra Practice Give students five minutes to jot down a description of their typical weekend, including what they do, where they go, and with whom they spend time. Circulate among the class to help with unfamiliar vocabulary. Then have volunteers share their information with the rest of the class. The class decides whether or not each volunteer represents a "typical" student.

Game Play a game of **Dix questions**. Ask a volunteer to think of a sport, activity, person, or place from the vocabulary drawing or list. Other students get one chance to ask a yes/no question and make a guess until someone guesses the word. Limit attempts to 10 questions per word. You may want to write some phrases on the board to cue students' questions.

Les sons et les lettres

Audio: Concepts, Activities
Record & Compare

National Standards: comparisons

Intonation

In short, declarative sentences, the pitch of your voice, or intonation, falls on the final word or syllable.

Nathalie est française. **Hector joue au football.**

In longer, declarative sentences, intonation rises, then falls.

À trois heures et demie, j'ai sciences politiques.

In sentences containing lists, intonation rises for each item in the list and falls on the last syllable of the last one.

Martine est jeune, blonde et jolie.

In long, declarative sentences, such as those containing clauses, intonation may rise several times, falling on the final syllable.

Le samedi, à dix heures du matin, je vais au centre commercial.

Questions that require a yes or no answer have rising intonation. Information questions have falling intonation.

C'est ta mère? **Est-ce qu'elle joue au tennis?**

Quelle heure est-il? **Quand est-ce que tu arrives?**

Prononcez Répétez les phrases suivantes à voix haute.

1. J'ai dix-neuf ans.
2. Tu fais du sport?
3. Quel jour sommes-nous?
4. Sandrine n'habite pas à Paris.
5. Quand est-ce que Marc arrive?
6. Charlotte est sérieuse et intellectuelle.

Articulez Répétez les dialogues à voix haute.

1. –Qu'est-ce que c'est?
   –C'est un ordinateur.
2. –Tu es américaine?
   –Non, je suis canadienne.
3. –Qu'est-ce que Christine étudie?
   –Elle étudie l'anglais et l'espagnol.
4. –Où est le musée?
   –Il est en face de l'église.

Dictons Répétez les dictons à voix haute.

Petit à petit, l'oiseau fait son nid.[2]

Si le renard court, le poulet a des ailes.[1]

[1] Though the fox runs, the chicken has wings.
[2] Little by little, a bird builds its nest.

ressources
LM p. 34
espaces.vhlcentral.com

Section Goals

In this section, students will learn about using intonation.

Instructional Resources
espaces.vhlcentral.com: Textbook MP3s; Lab MP3s; WB/VM/LM Answer Key; IRM (Textbook Audioscript; Lab Audioscript); activities; downloads; reference tools

Suggestions

- Model the intonation of each of the example sentences and have students repeat them after you.
- Make sure students can recognize an information question. Tell them that information questions contain question words: **qui, qu'est-ce que, quand, comment, pourquoi**, etc. Remind students that the question word is not always the first word of the sentence. Examples: **À qui parles-tu? Ils arrivent quand?**
- Contrast the intonation of various types of declarative sentences (short, long, and those containing lists).
- Point out that the sentences without question words in the **Prononcez** activity (all except items 3 and 5) can be changed from a question to a statement and vice-versa simply by changing the intonation.

Dictons

- Ask students if they can think of sayings in English that are similar to **«Petit à petit, l'oiseau fait son nid.»** (*Slow and steady wins the race.*)
- Have students discuss the meaning of **«Si le renard court, le poulet a des ailes.»**

OPTIONS

Extra Practice Here are some sentences to use for additional practice with intonation: **1. Il a deux frères? 2. Il a deux frères. 3. Combien de frères est-ce qu'il a? 4. Vous jouez au tennis? 5. Vous jouez au tennis. 6. Avec qui est-ce que vous jouez au tennis?** Make sure students hear the difference between declarative and interrogative statements.

Game Divide the class into small groups. Pronounce ten phrases based on those in the examples and in **Prononcez**. Have students silently pass one piece of paper, numbered 1–10, around their group. Members of each group take turns recording whether the statements are declarative or interrogative. Collect the papers, one per group, when you finish saying the phrases. The group with the most correct answers wins.

Section Goals

In this section, students will learn functional phrases for talking about leisure activities through comprehensible input.

Instructional Resources
*espaces.vhlcentral.com: Video; WB/VM/LM Answer Key; IRM (Videoscript; **Roman-photo** Translations); activities; downloads; reference tools*
Video on DVD

Video Recap: Leçon 4B
Before doing this **Roman-photo**, review the previous episode.
1. Amina et Sandrine vont au café, mais David et Rachid... (rentrent à l'appartement/chez eux)
2. Rachid va étudier et David a envie de... (dessiner un peu)
3. Sandrine a envie d'apprendre à... (préparer des éclairs)
4. Amina commande... (un sandwich jambon-fromage et des frites)

Video Synopsis In a park, Rachid, David, and Sandrine talk about their favorite pastimes. David likes to draw; Rachid plays soccer. They run into Stéphane. He and Rachid talk about Stéphane's studies. Stéphane doesn't like his classes; he prefers sports. Sandrine tells David she doesn't like sports, but prefers movies and concerts. She also wants to be singer.

Suggestions
- Ask students to predict what the episode will be about.
- Have pairs of students list words they expect to hear in a video about sports and activities. As they watch, have them mark the words and expressions they hear.
- Have students scan the captions to find phrases used to talk about sports and activities. Examples: **Rachid, lui, c'est un grand sportif. Je fais du ski, de la planche à voile, du vélo... et j'adore nager.**
- Ask students to read the **Roman-photo** in groups of four. Ask groups to present their dramatic readings to the class.
- Review the predictions and confirm the correct ones. Have students summarize this episode.

NATIONAL STANDARDS communication cultures

Au parc

Video: *Roman-photo*
Record & Compare

PERSONNAGES

David

Rachid

Sandrine

Stéphane

DAVID Oh là là... On fait du sport aujourd'hui!
RACHID C'est normal! On est dimanche. Tous les week-ends à Aix, on fait du vélo, on joue au foot...
SANDRINE Oh, quelle belle journée! Faisons une promenade!
DAVID D'accord.

DAVID Moi, le week-end, je sors souvent. Mon passe-temps favori, c'est de dessiner la nature et les belles femmes. Mais Rachid, lui, c'est un grand sportif.
RACHID Oui, je joue au foot très souvent et j'adore.

RACHID Tiens, Stéphane! Déjà? Il est en avance.
SANDRINE Salut.
STÉPHANE Salut. Ça va?
DAVID Ça va.
STÉPHANE Salut.
RACHID Salut.

STÉPHANE Pfft! Je n'aime pas l'histoire-géo.
RACHID Mais, qu'est-ce que tu aimes alors, à part le foot?
STÉPHANE Moi? J'aime presque tous les sports. Je fais du ski, de la planche à voile, du vélo... et j'adore nager.
RACHID Oui, mais tu sais, le sport ne joue pas un grand rôle au bac.

RACHID Et puis, les études, c'est comme le sport. Pour être bon, il faut travailler!
STÉPHANE Ouais, ouais.
RACHID Allez, commençons. En quelle année Napoléon a-t-il...

SANDRINE Dis-moi David, c'est comment chez toi, aux États-Unis? Quels sont les sports favoris des Américains?
DAVID Euh... chez moi? Beaucoup pratiquent le baseball ou le basket et surtout, on adore regarder le football américain. Mais toi, Sandrine, qu'est-ce que tu fais de tes loisirs? Tu aimes le sport? Tu sors?

ACTIVITÉS

1 Les événements Mettez ces (*these*) événements dans l'ordre chronologique.

__10__ a. David dessine un portrait de Sandrine.
__6__ b. Stéphane se plaint (*complains*) de ses cours.
__4__ c. Rachid parle du match de foot.
__9__ d. David complimente Sandrine.
__2__ e. David mentionne une activité que Rachid aime faire.
__7__ f. Sandrine est curieuse de savoir (*to know*) quels sont les sports favoris des Américains.
__5__ g. Stéphane dit (*says*) qu'il ne sait (*knows*) pas s'il va gagner son prochain match.
__3__ h. Stéphane arrive.
__1__ i. David parle de son passe-temps favori.
__8__ j. Sandrine parle de sa passion.

Practice more at **espaces.vhlcentral.com.**

OPTIONS

Avant de regarder la vidéo Before viewing the **Au parc** episode, ask students to consider both the title and video still 1. Then brainstorm what David, Sandrine, and Rachid might talk about in an episode set in a park. Examples: sports and activities: **On fait du sport aujourd'hui!** or the weather: **Quelle belle journée!**

Regarder la vidéo Play the video episode once without sound and have the class create a plot summary based on the visual cues. Afterward, show the video with sound and have the class correct any mistaken guesses and fill in any gaps in the plot summary they created.

Les amis parlent de leurs loisirs.

4

RACHID Alors, Stéphane, tu crois que tu vas gagner ton prochain match?
STÉPHANE Hmm, ce n'est pas garanti! L'équipe de Marseille est très forte.
RACHID C'est vrai, mais tu es très motivé, n'est-ce pas?
STÉPHANE Bien sûr.

5

RACHID Et, pour les études, tu es motivé? Qu'est-ce que vous faites en histoire-géo en ce moment?
STÉPHANE Oh, on étudie Napoléon.
RACHID C'est intéressant! Les cent jours, la bataille de Waterloo...

9

SANDRINE Bof, je n'aime pas tellement le sport, mais j'aime bien sortir le week-end. Je vais au cinéma ou à des concerts avec mes amis. Ma vraie passion, c'est la musique. Je désire être chanteuse professionnelle.

10

DAVID Mais tu es déjà une chanteuse extraordinaire! Eh! J'ai une idée. Je peux faire un portrait de toi?
SANDRINE De moi? Vraiment? Oui, si tu insistes!

Expressions utiles

Talking about your activities

- **Qu'est-ce que tu fais de tes loisirs? Tu sors?**
  What do you do in your free time? Do you go out?
- **Le week-end, je sors souvent.**
  On weekends I often go out.
- **J'aime bien sortir.**
  I like to go out.
- **Tous les week-ends, on/tout le monde fait du sport.**
  Every weekend, people play/everyone plays sports.
- **Qu'est-ce que tu aimes alors, à part le foot?**
  What else do you like then, besides soccer?
- **J'aime presque tous les sports.**
  I like almost all sports.
- **Je peux faire un portrait de toi?**
  Can/May I do a portrait of you?
- **Qu'est-ce que vous faites en histoire-géo en ce moment?**
  What are you doing in history-geography at this moment?
- **Les études, c'est comme le sport. Pour être bon, il faut travailler!**
  Studies are like sports. To be good, you have to work!
- **Faisons une promenade!**
  Let's take a walk!

Additional vocabulary

- **Dis-moi.**
  Tell me.
- **Bien sûr.**
  Of course.
- **Tu sais.**
  You know.
- **Tiens.**
  Hey, look./Here you are.
- **Ce n'est pas garanti!**
  It's not guaranteed!
- **Vraiment?**
  Really?

ACTIVITÉS

2 Questions Choisissez la traduction (*translation*) qui convient pour chaque activité. Essayez de ne pas utiliser de dictionnaire. Combien de traductions y a-t-il pour le verbe **faire**?

c	1. faire du ski	a.	to play sports
d	2. faire une promenade	b.	to go biking
b	3. faire du vélo	c.	to ski
a	4. faire du sport	d.	to take a walk

3 À vous! David et Rachid parlent de faire des projets (*plans*) pour le week-end, mais les loisirs qu'ils aiment sont très différents. Ils discutent de leurs préférences et finalement choisissent (*choose*) une activité qu'ils vont pratiquer ensemble (*together*). Avec un(e) partenaire, écrivez la conversation et jouez la scène devant la classe.

ressources
VM pp. 227-228 | DVD Leçon 5A | espaces.vhlcentral.com

Expressions utiles
- Draw attention to the forms of the verb **faire** and irregular **-ir** verbs in the captions, in the **Expressions utiles** box, and as they occur in your conversation with students. Tell students that this material will be presented in **Structures**.
- Respond briefly to questions about **faire** and irregular **-ir** verbs. Reinforce correct forms, but do not expect students to produce them consistently at this time.
- Work through the **Expressions utiles** by asking students about their activities. As you do, respond to the content of their responses and ask other students questions about their classmates' answers. Example: **Qu'est-ce que tu fais de tes loisirs? Tu sors?**
- Remind students that the **nous** form of a verb can be used to say *Let's...* Example: **Faisons une promenade!** = *Let's take a walk!*

1 Suggestion Form several groups of eight students. Write each of these sentences on individual strips of paper and distribute them among the students in each group. Make a set of sentences for each group. Have students read their sentences aloud in the correct order.

1 Expansion Have students make sentences to fill in parts of the story not mentioned in this activity.

2 Suggestion Remind students that **faire** has several English translations.

3 Suggestion Remind students of expressions like **On...?** for suggesting activities and **D'accord** and **Non, je préfère...** for accepting or rejecting suggestions. As students write their scenes, circulate around the room to help with unfamiliar vocabulary and expressions.

OPTIONS

Pairs Have pairs of students create two-line mini-conversations using as many **Expressions utiles** as they can. Example:
—**Qu'est-ce que tu aimes alors, à part le foot?**
—**J'aime presque tous les sports.**
Then have them use the vocabulary in this section to talk about their own activities and those of their friends and family.

Extra Practice Ask volunteers to ad-lib the **Roman-photo** episode for the class. Assure them that it is not necessary to memorize the episode or to stick strictly to its content. They should try to get the general meaning across with the vocabulary and expressions they know. Encourage creativity. Give them time to prepare. You may want to assign this as homework and do it the next class period as a review activity.

Section Goals

In this section, students will:

- learn about a popular sport
- learn sports terms
- learn names of champions from French-speaking regions
- read about two celebrated French athletes
- view authentic video footage

Instructional Resources
espaces.vhlcentral.com: Video; WB/VM/LM Answer Key; IRM (Videoscript); activities; downloads; reference tools

Culture à la loupe

Avant la lecture Before opening their books, ask students to call out as many sports-related words as they can remember in French. Ask them to name the most popular sports in the United States and those that they associate with the French.

Lecture

- Point out the chart **Nombre de membres des fédérations sportives en France**. Ask students what information the chart shows. (The number of members of athletic federations in France for each sport listed.)
- Point out that the term **le foot** is a common abbreviation for **le football**. Make sure your class understands that **le football américain** is *football* and **le foot** is *soccer*.

Après la lecture Have students prepare a list of questions with **jouer** and frequency expressions to ask a classmate. Have them present the other person's preferences to the class. Example: **Étudiant(e) 1: Est-ce que tu joues parfois au volley-ball? Étudiant(e) 2: Non, je joue rarement au volley-ball.**

1 Expansion Continue the activity with these true/false statements.
11. En France, le basket-ball est plus populaire que la natation. (Vrai.) 12. On fait moins de rugby que de vélo en France. (Faux.) 13. L'équipe de foot de Marseille est très populaire. (Vrai.)

connections cultures — NATIONAL STANDARDS

Video: *Flash culture*

CULTURE À LA LOUPE

Le football

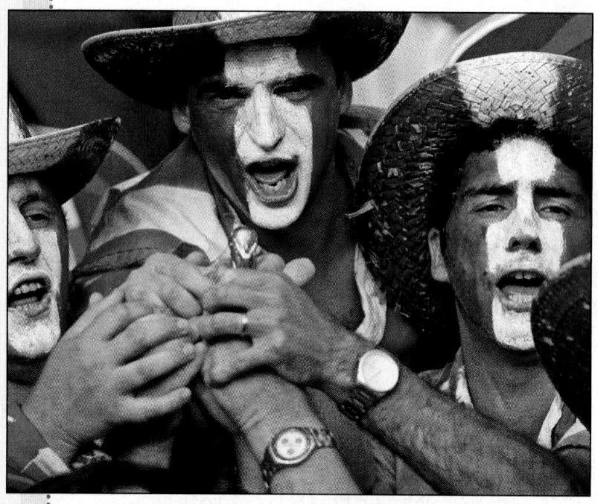

Le football est le sport le plus° populaire dans la majorité des pays° francophones. Tous les quatre ans°, des centaines de milliers de° fans, ou «supporters», regardent la Coupe du Monde°: le championnat de foot(ball) le plus important du monde. En 1998 (mille neuf cent quatre-vingt-dix-huit), l'équipe de France gagne la Coupe du Monde et en 2000 (deux mille), elle gagne la Coupe d'Europe, autre championnat important.

Le Cameroun a aussi une grande équipe de football. «Les Lions Indomptables°» gagnent la médaille d'or° aux Jeux Olympiques de Sydney en 2000. En 2007, l'équipe camerounaise est la première équipe africaine à être dans le classement mondial° de la FIFA (Fédération Internationale de Football Association). Certains «Lions» jouent dans les clubs français et européens.

les Lions Indomptables

En France, il y a deux ligues professionnelles de vingt équipes chacune°. Ça fait° quarante équipes professionnelles de football pour un pays plus petit que° le Texas! Certaines équipes, comme le Paris Saint-Germain («le PSG») ou l'Olympique de Marseille («l'OM»), ont beaucoup de supporters.

Les Français, comme les Camerounais, adorent regarder le football, mais ils sont aussi des joueurs très sérieux: aujourd'hui en France, il y a plus de 19.000 (dix-neuf mille) clubs amateurs de football et plus de deux millions de joueurs.

Nombre° de membres des fédérations sportives en France

Football	2.066.000
Tennis	1.068.000
Judo-jujitsu	577.000
Basket-ball	427.000
Hand-ball	334.000
Golf	325.000
Voile°	279.000
Rugby	253.000
Natation°	214.000
Ski	152.000

SOURCE: Ministère de la Jeunesse et des Sports

le plus *the most* **pays** *countries* **Tous les quatre ans** *Every four years* **centaines de milliers de** *hundreds of thousands of* **Coupe du Monde** *World Cup* **Indomptables** *Untamable* **or** *gold* **classement mondial** *world ranking* **chacune** *each* **Ça fait** *That makes* **un pays plus petit que** *a country smaller than* **Nombre** *Number* **Voile** *Sailing* **Natation** *Swimming*

ACTIVITÉS

1 Vrai ou faux? Indiquez si ces phrases sont **vraies** ou **fausses**. Corrigez les phrases fausses.

1. Le football est le sport le plus populaire en France. Vrai.
2. La Coupe du Monde a lieu (*takes place*) tous les deux ans. Faux. Elle a lieu tous les quatre ans.
3. En 2000, l'équipe de France gagne la Coupe du Monde. Faux. En 2000, elle gagne la Coupe d'Europe.
4. Le Cameroun gagne le tournoi de football aux Jeux Olympiques de Sydney. Vrai.
5. L'équipe du Cameroun est la première équipe africaine à être au classement mondial de la FIFA. Vrai.
6. Certains «Tigres Indomptables» jouent dans des clubs français et européens. Faux. Certains «Lions Indomptables» jouent dans des clubs français et européens.
7. En France, il y a vingt équipes professionnelles de football. Faux. Il y a quarante équipes professionnelles de football.
8. La France est plus petite que le Texas. Vrai.
9. L'Olympique de Marseille est un célèbre stade de football. Faux. L'OM est une célèbre équipe de football.
10. Les Français aiment jouer au football. Vrai.

Practice more at **espaces.vhlcentral.com.**

OPTIONS

Extra Practice Provide groups of three students with a list of words that are relevant to **Le football** like **gagner, longtemps, courir** from the **Leçon 5A** vocabulary list. Ask them to work together to create sentences about the reading by incorporating the lexical items you have prompted. Example: **gagner (En 1998, la France gagne la Coupe du Monde.)** Answers will vary in an open-ended activity like this, but remind the class to stick to learned material. Follow up by creating a column on the board for each word that you prompted so students can share sentences they consider successful. After at least one student has written a response for each word, correct the sentences as a class.

LE FRANÇAIS QUOTIDIEN

Le sport

arbitre (*m./f.*)	*referee*
ballon (*m.*)	*ball*
coup de sifflet (*m.*)	*whistle*
entraîneur	*coach*
maillot (*m.*)	*jersey*
terrain (*m.*)	*playing field*
hors-jeu	*off-side*
marquer	*to score*

PORTRAIT

Zinédine Zidane et Laura Flessel

Zinédine Zidane, ou «Zizou», est un footballeur français. Né° à Marseille de parents algériens, il joue dans différentes équipes françaises. Nommé trois fois «Joueur de l'année» par la FIFA (la Fédération Internationale de Football Association), il gagne la Coupe du Monde avec l'équipe de France en 1998 (mille neuf cent quatre-vingt-dix-huit). Pendant° sa carrière, il joue aussi pour une équipe italienne et pour le Real Madrid, en Espagne°.

Née à la Guadeloupe, **Laura Flessel** commence l'escrime à l'âge de sept ans. Après plusieurs titres° de championne de Guadeloupe, elle va en France pour continuer sa carrière. En 1991 (mille neuf cent quatre-vingt-onze), à 20 ans, elle est championne de France et cinq ans plus tard, elle est double championne olympique à Atlanta en 1996.

Né *Born* **Pendant** *During* **Espagne** *Spain* **plusieurs titres** *several titles*

LE MONDE FRANCOPHONE

Des champions

Voici quelques champions olympiques récents.

Algérie Nouria Merah-Benida, athlétisme°, or°, Sydney, 2000
Burundi Venuste Niyongabo, athlétisme, or, Atlanta, 1996
Cameroun Françoise Mbango-Etone, athlétisme, or, Pékin, 2008
Canada Éric Lamaze, équitation°, or, Pékin, 2008
France Alain Bernard, natation, or, Pékin, 2008
Maroc Hicham El Guerrouj, athlétisme, or, Athènes, 2004
Suisse Stéphane Lambiel, patinage artistique°, argent°, Turin, 2006
Tunisie Oussama Mellouli, natation, or, Pékin, 2008

athlétisme *track and field* **or** *gold* **équitation** *horseback riding* **patinage artistique** *figure skating* **argent** *silver*

SUR INTERNET

Qu'est-ce que le «free-running»?

Go to **espaces.vhlcentral.com** to find more information related to this **ESPACE CULTURE**. Then watch the corresponding **Flash culture.**

ACTIVITÉS

2 Zinédine ou Laura? Indiquez de qui on parle.

1. Zinédine est de France métropolitaine.
2. Laura est née à la Guadeloupe.
3. Zinédine gagne la Coupe du Monde pour la France en 1998.
4. Laura est championne de Guadeloupe en 1991.
5. Laura est double championne olympique en 1996.
6. Zinédine a été trois fois joueur de l'année.

3 Une interview Avec un(e) partenaire, préparez une interview entre un(e) journaliste et un(e) athlète que vous aimez. Jouez la scène devant la classe. Est-ce que vos camarades peuvent deviner (*can guess*) le nom de l'athlète?

ressources: VM pp. 279-280; espaces.vhlcentral.com

Le français quotidien You might extend this list to include **le poteau de but** (*goalpost*), **le coup d'envoi** (*kickoff*), **un penalty** (*penalty kick*), and **une faute** (*foul*).

Portrait Zinédine Zidane became the most expensive player in the history of soccer when Real Madrid acquired him for the equivalent of about $66 million American dollars. «Zizou» also made history as Christian Dior's first male model. Laura Flessel is a left-handed fencer called **«la Guêpe»** (*Wasp*) because of her competitive and dangerous attack.

Le monde francophone Model the pronunciation of names and places in this box. Then ask students if they know of any other athletes from the francophone world.

2 Expansion Continue the activity with additional fill-in-the-blank statements such as these.
7. ____ joue aussi pour une équipe espagnole. (Zinédine)
8. ____ est championne aux Jeux Olympiques de 1996. (Laura)

3 Expansion Have students prepare five sentences in the first person for homework, describing themselves as a well-known athlete. Ask students to introduce themselves to the class. The class tries to guess the presenter's identity.

Flash culture Tell students that they will learn more about sports and leisure activities by watching a variety of real-life images narrated by Csilla. Show the video, and then have students close their eyes and describe from memory what they saw. Write their descriptions on the board. You can also use the activities in the video manual in class to reinforce this **Flash culture** or assign them as homework.

OPTIONS

Des champions Look at the map of the world in **Appendice A** to remind students where francophone countries featured in **Le monde francophone** are located. Ask students to pick one of the athletes from this list to research for homework. They should come to the next class with five French sentences about that athlete's life and career. You may want to have students bring an image from the Internet of the athlete they chose to research. Collect the photos and gather different images of the same athlete. Have students who researched the same champion work together as a group to present that athlete while the rest of the class looks at the images they found.

Section Goals

In this section, students will learn:

- the verb **faire**
- expressions with **faire**
- the expression **il faut**

Instructional Resources
*espaces.vhlcentral.com: Lab MP3s; WB/VM/LM Answer Key; Transparency #28; IRM (**Essayez!** and **Mise en pratique** answers; Lab Audioscript; **Feuilles d'activités**); activities; downloads; reference tools*

Suggestions

- Point out that students have seen **faire** in previous lessons. Example: **faire ses devoirs** in **Leçon 2B Roman-photo.**
- Model **faire** with the whole class by asking: **Qu'est-ce que vous faites? Je fais...** Then, using **Transparency #28**, ask what people in the image are doing.
- Write the forms of **faire** on the board as students hear them in your questions. If **tu** and **nous** forms are missing, complete the conjugation by asking a student: **Tu fais attention?** Then ask: **Qu'est-ce que nous faisons? (Nous apprenons/faisons attention.)**
- Point out that **fai-** in **nous faisons** is pronounced differently than **fai-** in all other forms. Underline the first syllable of the **nous** form and have students repeat.
- Ask students where they have seen the **-s, -s, -t** pattern. (**boire: je bois, tu bois, il/elle boit**)
- To facilitate memorization, have students compare **faire** with **aller**, **avoir**, and **être**, noting similarities in the forms. Examples: **tu fais, vas, as, es**; **nous faisons, avons, allons**; **vous êtes, faites**; etc.
- Explain that **il faut** is a very common expression in French even though its English translations are not as widely used in everyday language.

5A.1 The verb *faire*

Point de départ Like other commonly used verbs, the verb **faire** (*to do, to make*) is irregular in the present tense.

Faire	
je fais	**nous faisons**
tu fais	**vous faites**
il/elle fait	**ils/elles font**

Il ne **fait** pas ses devoirs.
He's not doing his homework.

Qu'est-ce que vous **faites** ce soir?
What are you doing this evening?

On fait du sport aujourd'hui!

Qu'est-ce que vous faites en histoire-géo?

- Use the verb **faire** in these idiomatic expressions. Note that it is not always translated into English as *to do* or *to make*.

Expressions with *faire*			
faire de l'aérobic	*to do aerobics*	**faire de la planche à voile**	*to go wind-surfing*
faire attention (à)	*to pay attention (to)*	**faire une promenade**	*to go for a walk*
faire du camping	*to go camping*	**faire une randonnée**	*to go for a hike*
faire du cheval	*to go horseback riding*	**faire du ski**	*to go skiing*
faire la connaissance de...	*to meet (someone)*	**faire du sport**	*to do sports*
faire la cuisine	*to cook*	**faire un tour (en voiture)**	*to go for a walk (drive)*
faire de la gym	*to work out*	**faire du vélo**	*to go bike riding*
faire du jogging	*to go jogging*		

Tu **fais** souvent **du sport**?
Do you do sports often?

Nous **faisons attention** en classe.
We pay attention in class.

Elles **font du camping**.
They go camping.

Yves **fait la cuisine**.
Yves is cooking.

Je **fais de la gym**.
I'm working out.

Faites-vous **une promenade**?
Are you going for a walk?

MISE EN PRATIQUE

1 Chassez l'intrus Quelle activité ne fait pas partie du groupe?

1. a. faire du jogging b. faire une randonnée (c.) faire de la planche à voile
2. a. faire du vélo (b.) faire du camping c. faire du jogging
3. a. faire une promenade (b.) faire la cuisine c. faire un tour
4. a. faire du sport b. faire du vélo (c.) faire la connaissance de quelqu'un
5. (a.) faire ses devoirs b. faire du ski c. faire du camping
6. (a.) faire la cuisine b. faire du sport c. faire de la planche à voile

2 La paire Reliez (*Link*) les éléments des deux colonnes et ajoutez (*add*) la forme correcte du verbe **faire**.

1. Elle aime courir (*to run*), alors elle... e. fait du jogging.	a. du golf.
2. Ils adorent les animaux. Ils... d. font du cheval.	b. la cuisine.
3. Quand j'ai faim, je... b. fais la cuisine.	c. les devoirs.
4. L'hiver, vous... g. faites du ski.	d. du cheval.
5. Pour marcher, nous... f. faisons une promenade.	e. du jogging.
6. Tiger Woods... a. fait du golf.	f. une promenade.
	g. du ski.
	h. de l'aérobic.

3 Que font-ils? Regardez les dessins. Que font les personnages?

MODÈLE
Julien fait du jogging.

Julien

1. je Je fais du cheval.

3. Anne Anne fait de l'aérobic.

2. tu Tu fais de la planche à voile.

4. Louis et Paul Louis et Paul font du camping.

Practice more at **espaces.vhlcentral.com.**

OPTIONS

TPR Assign gestures to pantomime some of the expressions with **faire**. Examples: **faire de l'aérobic, la connaissance de..., du jogging, du ski**. Signal to individuals or pairs to gesture appropriately as you cue activities by saying: **Vous faites... ____ fait...** Then ask for a few volunteers to take your place calling out the activities.

Extra Practice Write on the board two headings: **Il faut...** and **Il ne faut pas...** Have students think of as many general pieces of advice (**les conseils**) as possible. Tell them to use **être**, any **-er** verbs, **avoir** and expressions with **avoir, aller, prendre, boire,** and **faire** to formulate the sentences. Examples: **Il faut souvent boire de l'eau. Il ne faut pas manger trop de sucre.** See how many sentences the class can write.

Essayez! Have students check each other's answers.

1 Suggestion Have pairs of students drill each other on the meanings of expressions with **faire** (that are not cognates). Then tell them to cover that half of the page with paper or a book before doing this activity.

2 Suggestion Have students check their answers with a partner. If partners disagree, have them say: **Mais non, il ne fait pas...** Remind students that any expression with the partitive must use **pas de** when negative.

3 Suggestion Bring in images of people doing other activities with **faire** expressions. Ask: **Que fait-il/elle?**

4 Expansion Have students come up with four more activities using expressions with **faire** that they would like to ask their partner about. Encourage students to include adverbs or other logical additions in their answers.

5 Expansion Write **Qu'est-ce qu'il faut faire pour...** on the board followed by a few of the most talked about expressions from the box. Have volunteers write their ideas under each expression, forming columns of categories. Accept several answers for each. Ask: **Êtes-vous d'accord? Pourquoi?**

6 Suggestions
- Read the **modèle** aloud with a volunteer. Then distribute the **Feuilles d'activités** found on the Supersite.
- Have students say how popular these activities are among classmates. Tell them to be prepared to justify their statements by citing how many students participate in each. Example: **Faire du jogging, c'est très populaire. Quinze étudiants de notre classe font du jogging.**

NATIONAL communication STANDARDS

COMMUNICATION

4 Ce week-end Que faites-vous ce week-end? Avec un(e) partenaire, posez les questions à tour de rôle. Some answers will vary.

MODÈLE

tu / jogging
Étudiant(e) 1: *Est-ce que tu fais du jogging ce week-end?*
Étudiant(e) 2: *Non, je ne fais pas de jogging. Je fais un tour en voiture.*

1. tu / le vélo
   Est-ce que tu fais du vélo ce week-end?
2. tes amis / la cuisine
   Est-ce que tes amis font la cuisine ce week-end?
3. ton/ta petit(e) ami(e) et toi, vous / le jogging
   Est-ce que ton/ta petit(e) ami(e) et toi, vous faites du jogging ce week-end?
4. toi et moi, nous / une randonnée
   Est-ce que toi et moi, nous faisons une randonnée ce week-end?
5. tu / la gym
   Est-ce que tu fais de la gym ce week-end?
6. ton/ta camarade de chambre / le sport
   Est-ce que ton/ta camarade de chambre fait du sport ce week-end?

5 De bons conseils Avec un(e) partenaire, donnez de bons conseils (*advice*). À tour de rôle, posez des questions et utilisez les éléments de la liste. Présentez vos idées à la classe. Answers will vary.

MODÈLE

Étudiant(e) 1: *Qu'est-ce qu'il faut faire pour avoir de bonnes notes?*
Étudiant(e) 2: *Il faut étudier jour et nuit.*

être en pleine forme (*great shape*)	avoir de bonnes notes
avoir de l'argent	gagner une course (*race*)
avoir beaucoup d'amis	bien manger
être champion de ski	réussir (*succeed*) aux examens

6 Les activités Votre professeur va vous donner une feuille d'activités. Faites une enquête sur le nombre d'étudiants qui pratiquent certaines activités dans votre classe. Présentez les résultats à la classe. Answers will vary.

MODÈLE

Étudiant(e) 1: *Est-ce que tu fais du jogging?*
Étudiant(e) 2: *Oui, je fais du jogging.*

Activités	Noms
1. jogging	Carole
2. vélo	
3. planche à voile	
4. cuisine	
5. camping	
6. cheval	

- Make sure to learn the correct article with each **faire** expression that calls for one. For **faire** expressions requiring a partitive or indefinite article, the article is replaced with **de** when the expression is negated.

Elles font **de la** gym trois fois par semaine.	Elles ne font pas **de** gym le dimanche.
They work out three times a week.	*They don't work out on Sundays.*

- Use **faire la connaissance de** before someone's name or another noun that identifies a person.

Je vais **faire la connaissance de Martin**.	Je vais **faire la connaissance des joueurs**.
I'm going to meet Martin.	*I'm going to meet the players.*

The expression *il faut*

Pour être bon, il faut travailler!
Il ne faut pas regarder la télé.
72
72

- When followed by a verb in the infinitive, the expression **il faut...** means *it is necessary to...* or *one must...*

Il faut faire attention en cours de maths.	**Il ne faut pas manger** après dix heures.
It is necessary to pay attention in math class.	*One must not eat after 10 o'clock.*
Faut-il laisser un pourboire?	**Il faut gagner** le match!
Is it necessary to leave a tip?	*We must win the game!*

Essayez! Complétez chaque phrase avec la forme correcte du verbe **faire** au présent.

1. Tu ___fais___ tes devoirs le samedi?
2. Vous ne ___faites___ pas attention au professeur.
3. Nous ___faisons___ du camping.
4. Ils ___font___ du jogging.
5. On ___fait___ une promenade au parc.
6. Il ___fait___ du ski en montagne.
7. Je ___fais___ de l'aérobic.
8. Elles ___font___ un tour en voiture.
9. Est-ce que vous ___faites___ la cuisine?
10. Nous ne ___faisons___ pas de sport.

OPTIONS

Game Divide the class into two teams. Pick one team member at a time to go to the board, alternating between teams. Give a subject pronoun that the team member must write and say aloud with the correct form of **faire**. Example: **vous (vous faites)**. Give a point for each correct answer. The game ends when all students have had a chance to go to the board. The team with the most points at the end of the game wins.

Extra Practice Have students study the captions from **Roman-photo**. In small groups, tell them to think of additional phrases containing **faire** expressions and **il faut** that the characters would likely say. Write the main characters' names on the board in a row and have volunteers put their ideas underneath. Ask what can be concluded about each character. Example: **Rachid donne beaucoup de conseils.**

Section Goals

In this section, students will learn:

- the verbs **sortir** and **partir**
- other irregular **-ir** verbs

Instructional Resources

*espaces.vhlcentral.com: Lab MP3s; WB/VM/LM Answer Key; IRM (**Essayez!** and **Mise en pratique** answers; Lab Audioscript); activities; downloads; reference tools*

Suggestions

- Ask students where they have heard irregular **-ir** verbs before. (They heard **sortir** in this lesson's **Roman-photo**. If students have been to French-speaking places, they may have noticed the noun derived from **sortir, la sortie,** on **SORTIE** signs.)
- Model the pronunciation of forms for **sortir** and **partir**. Ask students simple questions. Example: **Je sors d'habitude le vendredi soir. Quand sortez-vous? (Je sors le samedi soir.)** As you elicit responses, write the present-tense forms of **sortir** on the board until the conjugation is complete. Underline the endings.
- Point out the recurrence of the **-s, -s, -t** pattern in singular forms.
- Reiterate that **sortir** is used as *to go out* or *to exit* while **partir** means *to leave*. Ask students to think of more examples comparing the two verbs. Then remind them of the note about **quitter** in the **Boîte à outils**. Using ideas from students, write on the board a short paragraph (two to three sentences) that contains at least one form of each of the three verbs mentioned above. Make sure the context defines the meanings well.
- Go over other irregular **-ir** verbs, pointing out that they are all in the same grammatical "verb family" as **sortir** and **partir**. Note that all verbs of this type have two stems: **sortir:** singular stem **sor-** and plural stem **sort-**.

5A.2 Irregular *-ir* verbs

NATIONAL comparisons STANDARDS

Point de départ You are familiar with the class of French verbs whose infinitives end in **-er**. The infinitives of a second class of French verbs end in **-ir**. Some of the most commonly used verbs in this class are irregular.

- **Sortir** is used to express leaving a room or a building. It also expresses the idea of going out, as with friends or on a date. The preposition **de** is used after **sortir** when the place someone is leaving is expressed.

Sortir

je sors	nous sortons
tu sors	vous sortez
il/elle sort	ils/elles sortent

Tu **sors** souvent avec tes copains?
Do you go out often with your friends?

Pierre et moi **sortons de** la salle de classe.
Pierre and I leave the classroom.

Le week-end, je sors souvent.

Ils partent pour la fac.

- **Partir** is generally used to say someone is leaving a large place such as a city, country, or region. Often, a form of **partir** is accompanied by the preposition **pour** and a destination name to say *to leave for (a place).*

Partir

je pars	nous partons
tu pars	vous partez
il/elle part	ils/elles partent

Je **pars pour** l'Algérie.
I'm leaving for Algeria.

Ils **partent pour** Genève demain.
They're leaving for Geneva tomorrow.

BOÎTE À OUTILS

As you learned in **Leçon 4A**, **quitter** is used to say that someone leaves a place or another person: **Tu quittes la maison?** (*Are you leaving the house?*)

MISE EN PRATIQUE

1 Choisissez Monique et ses amis aiment bien sortir. Choisissez la forme correcte des verbes **partir** ou **sortir** pour compléter la description de leurs activités.

1. Samedi soir, je ____sors____ avec mes copains.
2. Mes copines Magali et Anissa ____partent____ pour New York.
3. Nous ____sortons____ du cinéma.
4. Nicolas ____part____ pour Dakar vers 10 heures du soir.
5. À minuit, vous ____partez____ pour la boîte.
6. Je ____pars____ pour le Maroc dans une semaine.
7. Tu ____sors____ avec ton petit ami ce week-end.
8. Olivier et Bernard ____sortent____ tard du bureau.

2 Vos habitudes Utilisez les éléments des colonnes pour décrire (*describe*) les habitudes de votre famille et de vos amis. Answers will vary.

A	B	C
je	(ne pas) courir	jusqu'à (*until*) midi
mon frère	(ne pas) dormir	tous les week-ends
ma sœur	(ne pas) partir	tous les jours
mes parents	(ne pas) sortir	souvent
mes cousins		rarement
mon petit ami		jamais
ma petite amie		une (deux, etc.) fois par jour/semaine
mes copains		?
?		

3 La question Vincent parle au téléphone avec sa mère. Vous entendez (*hear*) ses réponses, mais pas les questions. Avec un(e) partenaire, reconstruisez la conversation. Answers will vary.

MODÈLE

Comment vas-tu? Ça va bien, merci.

1. __________ Oui, je sors avec mes amis ce soir.
2. __________ Nous partons à six heures.
3. __________ Oui, nous allons jouer au tennis.
4. __________ Après, nous allons au restaurant.
5. __________ Nous sortons du restaurant à neuf heures.
6. __________ Marc et Audrey partent pour Nice le week-end prochain.

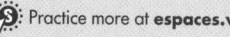

Practice more at **espaces.vhlcentral.com.**

OPTIONS

TPR Tell students that they will act out the appropriate gestures when you say what certain people in the class are doing. Examples: ____ **dort.** (The student gestures sleeping.) ____ **et** ____ **courent.** (The two students indicated run in place briefly.) Repeat verbs and vary forms as much as possible.

Extra Practice Dictate sentences like these to the class, saying each one twice and pausing between. **1. Je pars pour la France la semaine prochaine. 2. Mon copain et moi, nous sortons ce soir. 3. Les étudiants ne dorment jamais en classe. 4. Le café sent bon. 5. Tu cours vite. 6. Que servez-vous au restaurant?** Advise students to pay attention to the verbs.

National Standards communication

COMMUNICATION

4 Descriptions Avec un(e) partenaire, complétez les phrases avec la forme correcte d'un verbe de la liste.

courir dormir partir sentir servir sortir

1. Véronique /  / tard
Véronique dort tard.

2. je /  / sandwichs
Je sers des sandwichs.

3. les enfants /  / le chocolat chaud
Les enfants sentent le chocolat chaud.

4. nous /  / souvent
Nous courons souvent.

5. tu /  / de l'hôpital
Tu sors de l'hôpital.

6. vous /  / pour la France demain
Vous partez pour la France demain.

5 Indiscrétions Votre partenaire est curieux/curieuse et désire savoir (*to know*) ce que vous faites chez vous. Répondez à ses questions. Answers will vary.

1. Jusqu'à (*Until*) quelle heure dors-tu le week-end?
2. Dors-tu pendant (*during*) les cours à la fac? Pendant quels cours? Pourquoi?
3. À quelle heure sors-tu le samedi soir?
4. Avec qui sors-tu le samedi soir?
5. Que sers-tu quand tu as des invités à la maison?
6. Pars-tu bientôt en vacances (*vacation*)? Où?

6 Dispute Laëtitia est très active. Son petit ami Bertrand ne sort pas beaucoup, alors ils ont souvent des disputes. Avec un(e) partenaire, jouez les deux rôles. Utilisez les mots et les expressions de la liste. Answers will vary.

dormir	partir
faire des promenades	un passe-temps
faire un tour (en voiture)	sentir
par semaine	sortir
	rarement
	souvent

- Here is a list of verbs that are conjugated like **sortir** and **partir**.

Other irregular *-ir* verbs

	dormir (*to sleep*)	**servir** (*to serve*)	**sentir** (*to feel*)	**courir** (*to run*)
je	dors	sers	sens	cours
tu	dors	sers	sens	cours
il/elle	dort	sert	sent	court
nous	dormons	servons	sentons	courons
vous	dormez	servez	sentez	courez
ils/elles	dorment	servent	sentent	courent

Nous **servons** du thé glacé aux enfants.
We are serving iced tea to the children.

Je **sers** du fromage aux invités.
I'm serving cheese to the guests.

Vous **courez** vite!
You run fast!

Elles **dorment** jusqu'à midi.
They sleep until noon.

- **Sentir** can mean *to feel, to smell,* or *to sense.*

Je **sens** qu'il va arriver dans quelques minutes.
I sense that he's going to arrive in a few minutes.

Vous **sentez** l'odeur de ce bouquet de fleurs?
Do you smell the scent of these flowers?

Ça **sent** bon!
That smells good!

Ils **sentent** sa présence.
They feel his presence.

Essayez! Complétez les phrases avec la forme correcte du verbe.

1. Nous __sortons__ (sortir) vers neuf heures.
2. Je __sers__ (servir) des boissons gazeuses aux invités.
3. Tu __pars__ (partir) quand pour le Canada?
4. Nous ne __dormons__ (dormir) pas en cours.
5. Ils __courent__ (courir) pour attraper (*to catch*) le bus.
6. Tu manges des oignons? Ça __sent__ (sentir) mauvais.
7. Vous __sortez__ (sortir) avec des copains ce soir.
8. Elle __part__ (partir) pour Dijon ce week-end.

Essayez! Give these items for additional practice, having students choose which **-ir** verb(s) to use. **1. J'adore ____. Je ____ vingt à trente kilomètres par semaine. (courir, cours) 2. Les enfants ne ____ pas parce qu'ils ne sont pas fatigués. (dorment) 3. Qu'est-ce qu'on ____ au café en face de chez toi? (sert) 4. Merci pour les fleurs. Elles ____ très bon. (sentent)**

1 Suggestion Give a tip on how to choose between **sortir** and **partir**. Remind students that **partir** is often followed by the preposition **pour**.

2 Suggestions
- Have students write at least five sentences describing their family's and friends' habits.
- In pairs, have students compare the information. Example: **Étudiant(e) 1: Est-ce que tu dors jusqu'à midi? Étudiant(e) 2: Oui, mais rarement. Étudiant(e) 1: Moi, jamais!**
- Ask for volunteers to share some of their sentences with the class.

3 Expansion Ask students to imagine they are on the telephone and a classmate can overhear them. Have students write three answers to say in front of a partner who will guess the questions. Example: **Non, maman, on ne sort pas trop souvent. Je fais mes devoirs tous les soirs. (Tu ne sors pas trop souvent avec tes copains?)**

4 Suggestion Find a photo to use for a **modèle**. Example: Put on the board **Les chiens** / image of dogs sleeping / **beaucoup**. Have students ask **Que fait Véronique? Qu'est-ce que je fais?** etc. before partners answer.

5 Suggestion Remind students to answer in complete sentences.

6 Suggestion Have a couple of volunteer pairs act out their conversations for the class.

OPTIONS

Game Divide the class into two teams. Announce an infinitive and a subject pronoun. Example: **dormir**; **elle**. At the board, have the first member of Team A say and write down the given subject and the conjugated form of the verb. If the team member answers correctly, Team A gets one point. If not, give the first member of Team B the same example. The team with the most points at the end of the game wins.

Small Groups Have small groups of students create a short story in the present tense or a conversation in which they logically mention as many verb forms as possible of **sortir**, **partir**, **dormir**, **servir**, **sentir**, and **courir**. If the class is advanced, add **mentir**. Call on groups to tell their story to the class or act out their conversation. Have students vote on the best story or conversation.

Instructional Resources
espaces.vhlcentral.com: IRM (Info Gap Activities); Testing Program pp. 33–36; Test Files; Testing Program MP3s; activities; downloads; reference tools
Test Generator

1 Suggestion After collaborating on their efforts, ask groups how many activities they described. Have the group with most sentences share them with the class.

2 Suggestion Remind students that adverbs like **rarement**, **souvent**, and **toujours** should be placed immediately after the verb, not at the end of a sentence or anywhere else as one can say in English. Example: **Je fais rarement du cheval.** They should never say: **je fais du cheval rarement** or **je rarement fais du cheval**.

3 Suggestion Have students say what their partners are going to do on vacation, when, where, and with whom.

4 Suggestion Call on two volunteers to do the **modèle**.

4 Expansion Have students continue the activity with additional places, such as **à la faculté, au resto U, au centre-ville**, etc.

5 Suggestion Tell students to use as many irregular **-ir** verbs and **faire** expressions as possible.

6 Suggestion Divide the class into pairs and distribute the Info Gap Handouts found on the Supersite for this activity. Give students ten minutes to complete the activity.

NATIONAL communication STANDARDS

Révision

1 Au parc C'est dimanche. Avec un(e) partenaire, décrivez les activités de tous les personnages. Comparez vos observations avec les observations d'un autre groupe pour compléter votre description. Answers will vary.

2 Mes habitudes Avec un(e) partenaire, parlez de vos habitudes de la semaine. Que faites-vous régulièrement? Utilisez tous les mots de la liste. Answers will vary.

MODÈLE

Étudiant(e) 1: *Je fais parfois de la gym le lundi. Et toi?*
Étudiant(e) 2: *Moi, je fais parfois la cuisine le lundi.*

parfois le lundi	souvent à midi
le mercredi à midi	toujours le vendredi
le jeudi soir	tous les jours
le vendredi matin	trois fois par semaine
rarement le matin	une fois par semaine

3 Mes vacances Parlez de vos prochaines vacances (*vacation*) avec un(e) partenaire. Mentionnez cinq de vos passe-temps habituels en vacances et cinq nouvelles activités que vous allez essayer (*to try*). Comparez votre liste avec la liste de votre partenaire, puis présentez les réponses à la classe. Answers will vary.

4 Que faire ici? Avec un(e) partenaire, trouvez au minimum quatre choses à faire dans chaque (*each*) endroit. Quel endroit préférez-vous et pourquoi? Comparez votre liste avec un autre groupe et parlez de vos préférences avec la classe. Answers will vary.

MODÈLE

Étudiant(e) 1: *À la campagne, on fait des randonnées à cheval.*
Étudiant(e) 2: *Oui, et il faut marcher.*

1. à la campagne

3. au parc

2. à la plage

4. au gymnase

5 Le conseiller Un(e) conseiller/conseillère à la fac suggère des stratégies à un(e) étudiant(e) pour l'aider (*help him or her*) à préparer les examens. Avec un(e) partenaire, jouez les deux rôles. Vos camarades vont sélectionner les meilleurs conseils (*best advice*). Answers will vary.

MODÈLE

Il faut faire tous ses devoirs.

6 Quelles activités? Votre professeur va vous donner, à vous et à votre partenaire, deux feuilles d'activités différentes pour le week-end. Attention! Ne regardez pas la feuille de votre partenaire. Answers will vary.

MODÈLE

Étudiant(e) 1: *Est-ce que tu fais une randonnée dimanche après-midi?*
Étudiant(e) 2: *Oui, je fais une randonnée dimanche après-midi.*

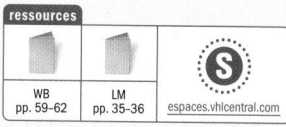

ressources
WB pp. 59-62 | LM pp. 35-36 | espaces.vhlcentral.com

OPTIONS

Extra Practice Ask students to write five sentences individually, at least two with **faire**, at least one with **il faut**, and at least three with different irregular **-ir** verbs. Tell them to try to include more than one requirement in each sentence. Have students dictate their sentences to their partner. After both students in each pair have finished dictating their sentences, have them exchange papers for correction.

Pairs Have students take turns telling their partners about a memorable vacation experience, who they were with, what they did, etc. Encourage students to express themselves using as much variety as possible in terms of vocabulary and grammar structures. Have students take notes as their partner narrates to reveal to the class later what was said.

Video: TV Clip

Le Zapping

NATIONAL STANDARDS communication cultures

NATIONAL STANDARDS connections communities

Sponsors de demain

Fondée en 1857, SwissLife est la plus grande° compagnie d'assurance vie° de Suisse, avec des filiales° aussi dans d'autres pays européens. C'est une entreprise° consciente de l'importance de la vie culturelle et sportive des communautés. SwissLife sponsorise des associations et des programmes aux niveaux° national et communautaire parce qu'elle reconnaît° qu'ils ont un effet positif sur les générations futures. En 2004, SwissLife commence à soutenir° l'équipe nationale suisse de football et, en 2007, le Kids Festival, tournois de football pour les enfants de six à dix ans.

—Gagner la Ligue des Champions...

—Jouer en finale de la Coupe du Monde...

Compréhension Répondez aux questions. Some answers will vary.

1. Qui sont les personnes dans la publicité (*ad*)? Ce sont des joueurs de football.
2. Quel âge le narrateur a-t-il à peu près (*approximately*)? Il a entre six et dix ans.
3. Qu'est-ce que le narrateur a envie de faire un jour? Some answers will vary. Suggested answers: Il a envie de gagner la Ligue des Champions et de jouer en finale de la Coupe du Monde.

Discussion Par groupes de trois, répondez aux questions. Answers will vary.

1. Pourquoi est-ce un enfant qui parle dans la pub, et non un adulte? Quel est le rôle des adultes?
2. Quelle personne est un modèle pour vous? Que fait-elle?

la plus grande *the largest* **assurance vie** *life insurance* **filiales** *branches* **entreprise** *company* **niveaux** *levels* **reconnaît** *recognizes* **soutenir** *to support*

Practice more at **espaces.vhlcentral.com.**

Section Goals

In this section, students will:

- read about the insurance company SwissLife
- watch a commercial for the company
- answer questions about the commercial and SwissLife

Instructional Resources
*espaces.vhlcentral.com: TV commercial; IRM (**Le zapping** TV clip transcription); activities; downloads; reference tools*

Introduction
To check comprehension, ask these questions:
1. En quelle année SwissLife est-elle fondée? (SwissLife est fondée en 1857.)
2. De quoi la compagnie est-elle consciente? (Elle est consciente de l'importance de la vie culturelle et sportive des communautés.)
3. Que commence à faire SwissLife en 2007? (Elle commence à soutenir le Kids Festival.)

Avant de regarder la vidéo

- Have students look at the video stills, read the captions, and predict what is happening in the commercial for each visual. **(1. L'homme joue au football. 2. Le garçon désire être joueur de foot professionnel.)**
- Before showing the video, explain to students that they do not need to understand every word they hear. Tell them to listen for vocabulary from this lesson as well as cognates that indicate the boy's wish to become a soccer hero.

Compréhension Have students work in pairs or groups for this activity. Tell them to write their answers. Then show the video again so that they can check their answers and add any missing information.

Discussion Ask students if they believe that a large company that sponsors cultural activities genuinely does so for the community's sake. Have them explain their answers.

OPTIONS

SwissLife As Switzerland's largest life insurance company and one of Europe's largest, SwissLife also operates in France, Belgium, Germany, the Netherlands, and other European countries. It also partners with other insurance companies around the world, thereby extending its market on a global scale. It takes community sponsorship seriously and practices it actively. In addition to the Swiss national soccer team and the Kids Festival tournaments, SwissLife also sponsors the Zurich Chamber Orchestra, the Swiss National Circus, running marathons, and the Swiss film festival, among others.

Section Goals

In this section, students will learn and practice vocabulary related to:
- the weather
- seasons and dates

Instructional Resources
*espaces.vhlcentral.com: Transparency #29; IRM (**Vocabulaire supplémentaire**; **Mise en pratique** answers; Textbook Audioscript; Lab Audioscript; Info Gap Activities); Textbook MP3s; Lab MP3s; WB/VM/LM Answer Key; activities; downloads; reference tools*

Suggestions
- Introduce weather-related vocabulary by describing the weather in your area today. Example: **Aujourd'hui, il pleut et il fait du vent.**
- Before going over the **Vocabulaire**, ask students to brainstorm the kinds of expressions they use to talk about the weather.
- Use **Transparency #29** to present new vocabulary. See how many of the words and expressions your students can understand without looking at their translations.
- Tell students that most weather expressions use the verb **faire**, but **neiger** and **pleuvoir** stand alone. Point out that they are only used in the third person singular.
- Point out that the expressions **avoir froid** and **avoir chaud** refer to people, but **faire froid** and **faire chaud** describe weather. Bring in photos that include people to illustrate this distinction.
- Mention to students that **temps** in this context means *weather*, not *time*.
- Using magazine photos of weather conditions and seasons, describe each image. Show photos again one at a time. Then ask: **En quelle saison sommes-nous? Quel temps fait-il?**
- Additional terms for this lesson can be found in the **Vocabulaire supplémentaire** on the Supersite.

Leçon 5B

You will learn how to...
- talk about seasons and the date
- discuss the weather

Talking Picture
Audio: Activity

Quel temps fait-il?

Il neige.
(neiger)
Il fait froid.

L'hiver (*m.*): décembre, janvier, février

Il fait (du) soleil.
Bal du 14 juillet
29°C
Il fait chaud.
Quelle est la date d'aujourd'hui?
C'est le 14 juillet.

L'été (*m.*): juin, juillet, août

Vocabulaire

Il fait 18 degrés.	*It is 18 degrees.*
Il fait beau.	*The weather is nice.*
Il fait bon.	*The weather is good/warm.*
Il fait mauvais.	*The weather is bad.*
Il fait un temps épouvantable.	*The weather is dreadful.*
Le temps est orageux.	*It is stormy.*
Quel temps fait-il?	*What is the weather like?*
Quelle température fait-il?	*What is the temperature?*
une saison	*season*
en automne	*in the fall*
en été	*in the summer*
en hiver	*in the winter*
au printemps	*in the spring*
Quelle est la date?	*What's the date?*
C'est le 1er (premier) octobre.	*It's the first of October.*
C'est quand votre/ton anniversaire?	*When is your birthday?*
C'est le 2 mai.	*It's the second of May.*
C'est quand l'anniversaire de Paul?	*When is Paul's birthday?*
C'est le 15 mars.	*It's March 15th.*
un anniversaire	*birthday*

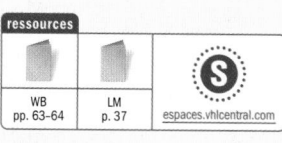

ressources
WB pp. 63–64 | LM p. 37 | espaces.vhlcentral.com

OPTIONS

Pairs Distribute a set of illustrations of various weather conditions to pairs of students. Choose images with variety and have students write detailed descriptions of each one. They should describe the weather, the season, and any activities represented.

Extra Practice Distribute a calendar that shows **les fêtes**. First, call out dates and have students give the corresponding name on the calendar. Then call out names on the calendar and have students provide the date. Example: **la Saint-Valentin (le 14 février)**.

Attention!

In France and in most of the francophone world, temperature is given in Celsius. Convert from Celsius to Fahrenheit with this formula: F = (C x 1.8) + 32. Convert from Fahrenheit to Celsius with this formula: C = (F – 32) x 0.56.
11°C = 52°F 78°F = 26°C

Le printemps (*m.*): mars, avril, mai

L'automne (*m.*): septembre, octobre, novembre

Mise en pratique

1 Les fêtes et les jours fériés Indiquez la date et la saison de chaque fête et jour férié (*holidays*).

	Date	Saison
1. la fête nationale française	le 14 juillet	l'été
2. l'indépendance des États-Unis	le 4 juillet	l'été
3. Poisson d'avril (*April Fool's Day*)	le 1er avril	le printemps
4. Noël	le 25 décembre	l'hiver
5. la Saint-Valentin	le 14 février	l'hiver
6. le Nouvel An	le 1er janvier	l'hiver
7. Halloween	le 31 octobre	l'automne
8. l'anniversaire de Washington	le 22 février	l'hiver

2 Quel temps fait-il? Répondez aux questions par des phrases complètes. Answers will vary.

1. Quel temps fait-il en été?
2. Quel temps fait-il en automne?
3. Quel temps fait-il au printemps?
4. Quel temps fait-il en hiver?
5. Où est-ce qu'il neige?
6. Quel est votre mois préféré de l'année? Pourquoi?
7. Quand est-ce qu'il pleut où vous habitez?
8. Quand est-ce que le temps est orageux où vous habitez?

3 Écoutez Écoutez le bulletin météorologique et répondez aux questions suivantes.

	Vrai	Faux
1. C'est l'été.	☐	☑
2. Le printemps commence le 21 mars.	☑	☐
3. Il fait 11 degrés vendredi.	☑	☐
4. Il fait du vent vendredi.	☐	☑
5. Il va faire soleil samedi.	☐	☑
6. Il faut utiliser le parapluie et l'imperméable vendredi.	☐	☑
7. Il va faire un temps épouvantable dimanche.	☑	☐
8. Il ne va pas faire chaud samedi.	☑	☐

Practice more at **espaces.vhlcentral.com.**

1 Suggestions
- Remind students to give the date in the correct order (day before month) and to include **le** before the day.
- Point out that the day always precedes the month in French when the date is written with numbers. Examples: **14 avril 2011, 14/04/2011**

1 Expansion Using this year's calendar, have students find the dates of these holidays. **9. la fête du travail aux États-Unis 10.** *Thanksgiving* **11.** *Easter* **(Pâques) 12.** *Memorial Day* You may ask students to look up dates of other secular celebrations or religious holidays from various faiths. Answers will vary from year to year.

2 Suggestions
- Have students work in pairs or small groups to answer these questions.
- Tell students they may also encounter the phrase **à l'automne**, meaning *this fall.* For other seasons, make sure they know to use **en** before those starting with a vowel sound and **au** with **printemps**, as it starts with a consonant.

3 Tapescript Aujourd'hui, vendredi 21 mars, nous commençons le printemps avec une température de 11 degrés; il n'y a pas de vent, mais il y a quelques nuages.
Votre météo du week-end: samedi, il ne va pas faire soleil; il va faire frais avec une température de 13 degrés; dimanche, encore 13 degrés, mais il va faire un temps épouvantable; il va pleuvoir toute la journée, alors, n'oubliez pas votre parapluie et votre imperméable!
(On Textbook MP3s)

3 Suggestion Have students correct the false items.

OPTIONS

Le calendrier républicain During the French Revolution, the official calendar was changed. The New Year began on September 22 (the autumnal equinox), and the year was divided into 30-day months named as follows: **Vendémiaire** (*Vintage*), **Brumaire** (*Mist*), **Frimaire** (*Frost*), **Nivôse** (*Snow*), **Pluviôse** (*Rain*), **Ventôse** (*Wind*), **Germinal** (*Seed time*), **Floréal** (*Flower*), **Prairial** (*Meadow*), **Messidor** (*Harvest*), **Thermidor** (*Heat*), and **Fructidor** (*Fruits*).

Game Have students take turns guessing another student's birthday. He or she responds by saying **avant** or **après** until someone guesses correctly. The class then tries to guess the winning student's birthday. Play several rounds of this game to give all students as many opportunities as possible to guess.

Communication

4 Conversez **Interviewez un(e) camarade de classe.** Answers will vary.

1. C'est quand ton anniversaire? C'est quand l'anniversaire de ton père? Et de ta mère?
2. En quelle saison est ton anniversaire? Quel temps fait-il?
3. Quelle est ta saison préférée? Pourquoi? Quelles activités aimes-tu pratiquer?
4. En quelles saisons utilises-tu un parapluie et un imperméable? Pourquoi?
5. À quel moment de l'année es-tu en vacances? Précise les mois. Pendant (*During*) quels mois de l'année préfères-tu voyager? Pourquoi?
6. À quelle période de l'année étudies-tu? Précise les mois.
7. Quelle saison détestes-tu le plus (*the most*)? Pourquoi?
8. Quand est l'anniversaire de mariage de tes parents?

5 Une lettre **Vous avez un(e) correspondant(e) (*pen pal*) en France qui veut (*wants*) vous rendre visite (*to visit you*). Écrivez (*Write*) une lettre à votre ami(e) où vous décrivez (*describe*) le temps qu'il fait à chaque saison et les activités que vous pouvez (*can*) pratiquer ensemble (*together*). Comparez votre lettre avec la lettre d'un(e) camarade de classe.** Answers will vary.

Cher Thomas,

Ici à Boston, il fait très froid en hiver et il neige souvent. Est-ce que tu aimes la neige? Moi, j'adore parce que je fais du ski tous les week-ends. Et toi, tu fais du ski? ...

6 Quel temps fait-il en France? **Votre professeur va vous donner, à vous et à votre partenaire, deux feuilles d'activités différentes. Attention! Ne regardez pas la feuille de votre partenaire.**

MODÈLE

Étudiant(e) 1: *Quel temps fait-il à Paris?*
Étudiant(e) 2: *À Paris, le temps est nuageux et la température est de dix degrés.*

7 La météo **Préparez avec un(e) camarade de classe une présentation où vous:** Answers will vary.

- mentionnez le jour, la date et la saison.
- présentez la météo d'une ville francophone.
- présentez les prévisions météo (*weather forecasts*) pour le reste de la semaine.
- préparez une affiche pour illustrer votre présentation.

La météo d'Haïti en juillet – Port-au-Prince

samedi 23	dimanche 24	lundi 25
27°C	35°C	37°C
soleil	nuageux	orageux

Aujourd'hui samedi, c'est le 23 juillet. C'est l'été. Il va faire soleil...

4 Suggestion Have students share what they've learned about their partners with another pair of students or with the rest of the class.

5 Suggestion Encourage students to use a wide variety of expressions for seasons and activities. Have them exchange papers for peer editing.

6 Suggestions
- Divide the class into pairs and distribute the Info Gap Handouts found on the Supersite for this activity. Give students ten minutes to complete the activity.
- Have two volunteers read the **modèle**.

7 Expansion Assign a different francophone location to each pair of students and have them research its weather forecast on the Internet. Hold a vote without revealing names of students, and give prizes for the best presentation in various categories (**le plus amusant, créateur, utile,** and so on).

Successful Language Learning Tell students that when looking at materials intended for native speakers like weather forecasts, they should pay attention to visual cues and use their background knowledge about the subject to help them understand. They should try to anticipate vocabulary they might hear, listen for familiar sounding words, and make intelligent guesses.

OPTIONS

TPR Write **C'est quand ton anniversaire?** on the board or on a transparency. Make a "human calendar" using students to represent various days. Have them form 12 rows (one for each month) and put themselves in order according to their birthdays by asking and answering the question. Give the person with the first birthday in each month a sign for that month. Call out each month and have students give their birthdays in order.

Small Groups Have students form groups of two to four. Hand out cards with the name of a holiday or other annual event. Instruct each group to hide their card from other groups. Groups come up with three sentences to describe the holiday or occasion without mentioning its name. They can mention the season. The other groups must first guess the month and day on which the event takes place, then name the event itself.

Les sons et les lettres

Audio: Concepts, Activities
Record & Compare

NATIONAL comparisons STANDARDS

Open vs. closed vowels: Part 1

You have already learned that **é** is pronounced like the vowel *a* in the English word *cake*. This is a closed **e** sound.

étudiant **agréable** **nationalité** **enchanté**

The letter combinations **-er** and **-ez** at the end of a word are pronounced the same way, as is the vowel sound in single-syllable words ending in **-es**.

travailler **avez** **mes** **les**

The vowels spelled **è** and **ê** are pronounced like the vowel in the English word *pet*, as is an **e** followed by a double consonant. These are open **e** sounds.

répète **première** **pêche** **italienne**

The vowel sound in *pet* may also be spelled **et**, **ai**, or **ei**.

secret **français** **fait** **seize**

Compare these pairs of words. To make the vowel sound in *cake*, your mouth should be slightly more closed than when you make the vowel sound in *pet*.

mes **mais** **ces** **cette** **théâtre** **thème**

Prononcez Répétez les mots suivants à voix haute.

1. thé
2. lait
3. belle
4. été
5. neige
6. aider
7. degrés
8. anglais
9. cassette
10. discret
11. treize
12. mauvais

Articulez Répétez les phrases suivantes à voix haute.

1. Hélène est très discrète.
2. Céleste achète un vélo laid.
3. Il neige souvent en février et en décembre.
4. Désirée est canadienne; elle n'est pas française.

Dictons Répétez les dictons à voix haute.

Qui sème le vent récolte la tempête.[2]

Péché avoué est à demi pardonné.[1]

1 An offense admitted is half pardoned.
2 You reap what you sow. (lit. He who sows the wind reaps a storm.)

ressources
LM p. 38
espaces.vhlcentral.com

Section Goals

In this section, students will learn about open and closed vowels.

Instructional Resources
espaces.vhlcentral.com: Textbook MP3s; Lab MP3s; WB/VM/LM Answer Key; IRM (Textbook Audioscript; Lab Audioscript); activities; downloads; reference tools

Suggestions

- Model the pronunciation of these open and closed vowel sounds and have students watch the shape of your mouth, then repeat each sound after you. Then pronounce each of the example words and have students repeat them.
- Mention words and expressions from the **Vocabulaire** on page 160 that contain the open and closed vowels presented on this page. Alternately, ask students to recall such vocabulary. Then have them repeat after you. Examples: **février**, **Il fait frais**, etc. See if a volunteer is able to recall any expression from previous lessons. Examples: **seize**, **vélo**, **aérobic**.
- Dictate five familiar words containing the open and closed vowels presented on this page, repeating each one at least two times. Then write them on the board or on a transparency and have students check and correct their spelling.
- Remind students that **ai** and **ei** are nasalized when followed by **m** or **n**. Compare the following words: **français** / **faim**, **seize** / **hein**.
- Point out that, unlike English, there is no diphthong or glide in these vowel sounds. To illustrate this, contrast the pronunciation of the English word *may* with that of the French word **mai**.

OPTIONS

Extra Practice Here are some sentences to use for additional practice with these open and closed vowel sounds. **1. Il fait soleil. 2. En janvier, il neige et il fait mauvais. 3. Toute la journée, j'aide ma mère. 4. Didier est français, mais Hélène est belge.**

Game Have a spelling bee using vocabulary words from **Leçons 1A–5B** that contain the two open and closed vowel sounds featured on this page. Pronounce each word, use it in a sentence, and then say the individual word again. Tell students that they must spell the words in French and include all diacritical marks.

Section Goals

In this section, students will learn functional phrases for talking about seasons, the weather, and birthdays through comprehensible input.

Instructional Resources
espaces.vhlcentral.com: Video; WB/VM/LM Answer Key; IRM (Videoscript; ***Roman-photo*** *Translations); activities; downloads; reference tools*
Video on DVD

Video Recap: Leçon 5A Before doing this **Roman-photo**, review the previous one with this activity.

1. Où sont les jeunes dans cet épisode? (Ils sont au parc.)
2. Que font Rachid et Stéphane? (Ils jouent au football.)
3. Qu'est-ce que Stéphane étudie? (de l'histoire-géo, Napoléon)
4. Qu'est-ce que Sandrine aime faire de ses loisirs? (aller au cinéma ou à des concerts)

Video Synopsis Rachid and Stéphane are in the park playing soccer. They talk about the weather. Meanwhile, David is sketching Sandrine at his apartment. They talk about the weather in Washington and things they like to do. Sandrine tells David that Stéphane's 18th birthday is next Saturday and invites him to the surprise party. Rachid arrives home and admires the portrait. Sandrine offers to make them all dinner.

Suggestions

- Ask students to predict what the episode will be about.
- Have students make a list of vocabulary they expect to see in an episode about weather and seasons.
- Ask students to read the **Roman-photo** conversation in groups of four. Ask one or two groups to present their dramatic readings to the class.
- Quickly review the predictions and confirm the correct ones.

NATIONAL STANDARDS: communication, cultures

Quel temps!

Video: *Roman-photo*
Record & Compare

PERSONNAGES

David

Rachid

Sandrine

Stéphane

Au parc...

RACHID Napoléon établit le Premier Empire en quelle année?
STÉPHANE Euh... mille huit cent quatre?
RACHID Exact! On est au mois de novembre et il fait toujours chaud.
STÉPHANE Oui, il fait bon!... dix-neuf, dix-huit degrés!

RACHID Et on a chaud aussi parce qu'on court.
STÉPHANE Bon, allez, je rentre faire mes devoirs d'histoire-géo.
RACHID Et moi, je rentre boire une grande bouteille d'eau.

RACHID À demain, Stéph! Et n'oublie pas: le cours du jeudi avec ton professeur, Monsieur Rachid Kahlid, commence à dix-huit heures, pas à dix-huit heures vingt!
STÉPHANE Pas de problème! Merci et à demain!

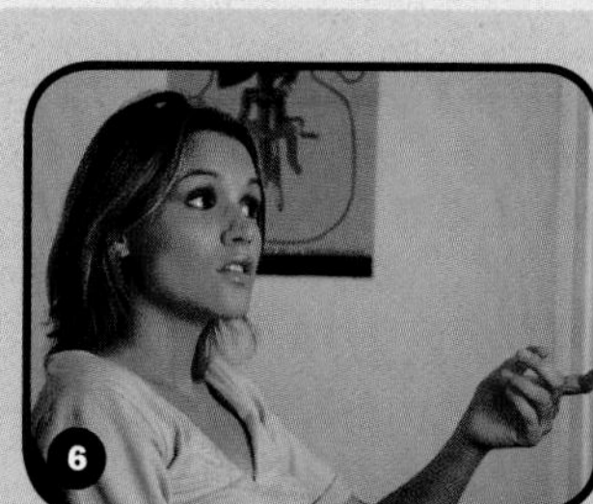

SANDRINE Et puis, en juillet, le Tour de France commence. J'aime bien regarder à la télévision. Et après, c'est mon anniversaire, le 20. Cette année, je fête mes vingt et un ans. Tous les ans, pour célébrer mon anniversaire, j'invite mes amis et je prépare une super soirée. J'adore faire la cuisine, c'est une vraie passion!
DAVID Ah, oui?

SANDRINE En parlant d'anniversaire, Stéphane célèbre ses dix-huit ans samedi prochain. C'est un anniversaire important. ...On organise une surprise. Tu es invité!
DAVID Hmm, c'est très gentil, mais... Tu essaies de ne pas parler deux minutes, s'il te plaît? Parfait!

SANDRINE Pascal! Qu'est-ce que tu fais aujourd'hui? Il fait beau à Paris?
DAVID Encore un peu de patience! Allez, encore dix secondes... Voilà!

ACTIVITÉS

1 Qui? **Identifiez les personnages pour chaque phrase. Écrivez D pour David, R pour Rachid, S pour Sandrine et St pour Stéphane**

1. Cette personne aime faire la cuisine. S
2. Cette personne sort quand il fait froid. D
3. Cette personne aime le Tour de France. S
4. Cette personne n'aime pas la pluie. S
5. Cette personne va boire de l'eau. R
6. Ces personnes ont rendez-vous tous les jeudis. R, St
7. Cette personne fête son anniversaire en janvier. D
8. Ces personnes célèbrent un joli portrait. D, R, S
9. Cette personne fête ses dix-huit ans samedi prochain. St
10. Cette personne prépare des crêpes pour le dîner. S

Practice more at **espaces.vhlcentral.com.**

OPTIONS

Avant de regarder la vidéo Before showing the video, show students individual photos and have them write their own captions. Ask volunteers to write their captions on the board.

Regarder la vidéo Download and print the videoscript found on the Supersite, and white out months, seasons, weather-related expressions, and other new vocabulary items. Distribute the scripts for pairs or groups to complete as cloze paragraphs as they watch the video.

Les anniversaires à travers (*through*) les saisons

À l'appartement de David et de Rachid...

SANDRINE C'est quand, ton anniversaire?

DAVID Qui, moi? Oh, c'est le quinze janvier.

SANDRINE Il neige en janvier, à Washington?

DAVID Parfois... et il pleut souvent à l'automne et en hiver.

SANDRINE Je déteste la pluie. C'est pénible. Qu'est-ce que tu aimes faire quand il pleut, toi?

DAVID Oh, beaucoup de choses! Dessiner, écouter de la musique. J'aime tellement la nature, je sors même quand il fait très froid.

SANDRINE Moi, je préfère l'été. Il fait chaud. On fait des promenades.

RACHID Oh là là, j'ai soif! Mais... qu'est-ce que vous faites, tous les deux?

DAVID Oh, rien! Je fais juste un portrait de Sandrine.

RACHID Bravo, c'est pas mal du tout! Hmm, mais quelque chose ne va pas, David. Sandrine n'a pas de téléphone dans la main!

SANDRINE Oh, Rachid, ça suffit! C'est vrai, tu as vraiment du talent, David. Pourquoi ne pas célébrer mon joli portrait? Vous avez faim, les garçons?

RACHID ET DAVID Oui!

SANDRINE Je prépare le dîner. Vous aimez les crêpes ou vous préférez une omelette?

RACHID ET DAVID Des crêpes... Miam!

Expressions utiles

Talking about birthdays

- **Cette année, je fête mes vingt et un ans.**
  This year, I celebrate my twenty-first birthday.
- **Pour célébrer mon anniversaire, je prépare une super soirée.**
  To celebrate my birthday, I plan a great party.
- **Stéphane célèbre ses dix-huit ans samedi prochain.**
  Stéphane celebrates his eighteenth birthday next Saturday.
- **On organise une surprise.**
  We are planning a surprise.

Talking about hopes and preferences

- **Tu essaies de ne pas parler deux minutes, s'il te plaît?**
  Could you try not to talk for two minutes, please?
- **J'aime tellement la nature, je sors même quand il fait très froid.**
  I like nature so much, I go out even when it's very cold.
- **Moi, je préfère l'été.**
  Me, I prefer summer.
- **Vous aimez les crêpes ou vous préférez une omelette?**
  Do you like crêpes or do you prefer an omelette?

Additional vocabulary

- **encore un peu**
  a little more
- **Quelque chose ne va pas.**
  Something's not right/working.
- **Allez.**
  Come on.
- **main**
  hand
- **Ça suffit!**
  That's enough!
- **Miam!**
  Yum!

ACTIVITÉS

2 Faux! **Toutes ces phrases contiennent une information qui est fausse. Corrigez chaque phrase.** Answers will vary. Suggested answers below.

1. Stéphane a dix-huit ans. Stéphane a dix-sept ans.
2. David et Rachid préfèrent une omelette. Ils préfèrent des crêpes.
3. Il fait froid et il pleut. Il fait beau/bon.
4. On n'organise rien (*anything*) pour l'anniversaire de Stéphane. On organise une surprise pour l'anniversaire de Stéphane.
5. L'anniversaire de Stéphane est au printemps. L'anniversaire de Stéphane est en automne.
6. Rachid et Stéphane ont froid. Ils ont chaud.

3 Conversez Parlez avec vos camarades de classe pour découvrir (*find out*) qui a l'anniversaire le plus proche du vôtre (*closest to yours*). Qui est-ce? Quand est son anniversaire? En quelle saison? Quel mois? En général, quel temps fait-il le jour de son anniversaire?

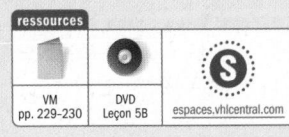

ressources: VM pp. 229–230 | DVD Leçon 5B | espaces.vhlcentral.com

Expressions utiles

- Draw attention to numbers 101 and higher and spelling-change **-er** verbs in the video-still captions, in the **Expressions utiles** box, and as they occur in your conversation with students.
- Have students scan the video-still captions and the **Expressions utiles** box for expressions related to hopes and preferences.
- Ask students about their own preferences. You might ask questions like: **Vous préférez l'été ou l'hiver? l'automne ou le printemps? janvier ou juillet? regarder la télé ou aller au cinéma?** For a more challenging activity, follow up by asking **Pourquoi?**

1 Expansions

- Continue the activity with more statements like these. **11. Cette personne fête son anniversaire samedi prochain. (St) 12. Cette personne parle souvent au téléphone. (S) 13. Cette personne aime écouter de la musique. (D)**
- Assign one of the four main characters in this episode to a small group. Each group should write a brief description of their character's likes, dislikes, and preferences.

2 Suggestion Have students correct false statements on the board.

2 Expansion Give these false items for extra practice. **1. Sandrine n'aime pas parler au téléphone (Faux.) 2. Stéphane et Rachid étudient la psychologie aujourd'hui. (Faux.) 3. Sandrine n'aime pas regarder la télé. (Faux.) 4. Sur son portrait, Sandrine a un téléphone dans la main. (Faux.)**

3 Suggestion Brainstorm questions students might ask to find the person whose birthday is closest to their own. Once they have found that person, have them do this activity in pairs. Ask volunteers to tell the class what they learned about their partner.

OPTIONS

Extra Practice Ask volunteers to ad-lib the episode for the class. Assure them that it is not necessary to memorize the episode or to stick strictly to its content. They should try to get the general meaning across with the vocabulary and expressions they know, and they should feel free to be creative. Give them time to prepare. You may want to assign this as homework and do it the next class period as a review activity.

Game Play a memory game. The first player tells his or her birthday. The next player repeats what the first said, then adds his or her birthday. The third player must state the first two birthdays, then his or her own. Continue until someone makes an error. Replay the game until everyone has had a turn. Or, form teams and alternate sides. If a player makes a mistake, that team gets a strike. After three strikes, the game is over.

Section Goals

In this section, students will:
- learn about French public gardens
- learn terms for natural disasters
- learn names of public gardens and parks in various French-speaking regions
- read about cycling in France

Instructional Resources
espaces.vhlcentral.com: activities; downloads; reference tools

Culture à la loupe

Avant la lecture
- Take a poll of students to find out how many of them come from towns with or without public parks.
- Ask if students know of any French parks or if anyone visited a park in Paris. If so, ask what they remember about them.

Lecture
- Point out the chart comparing **Le bois de Vincennes et le bois de Boulogne**. Ask students what information is shown. Have them compare details about the two parks.
- Look at a detailed map of Paris with the class, so students visualize where **le bois de Vincennes** and **le bois de Boulogne** are located. Introduce **le jardin des Plantes, le parc Monceau, le parc Montsouris**, and **le parc des Buttes Chaumont**.

Après la lecture Have students think of parks in the United States. Have them compare the roles and levels of popularity between French and American parks.

1 Expansion Continue the activity with additional questions like these.
11. Quelles activités y a-t-il pour les adultes au bois de Boulogne? 12. Quels sont les quatre parcs parisiens dans ce texte? 13. Dans quel parc trouve-t-on une cascade?

connections cultures NATIONAL STANDARDS

CULTURE À LA LOUPE

Les jardins publics français

le jardin du Luxembourg

Dans les villes françaises, on trouve des jardins° publics, la plupart du° temps au centre-ville. Ils sont en général entourés° d'une grille° et ouverts° au public pendant° la journée. Certains sont très petits et très simples; d'autres sont très grands avec d'immenses pelouses°, des plantes, des arbres° et de jolis parterres de fleurs°. Il y a aussi des sentiers° pour faire des promenades, des bancs°, des aires de jeux° pour les enfants, des statues, des fontaines ou des bassins°. On y° trouve des parents avec leurs enfants, des personnes qui font un pique-nique, qui jouent à la pétanque° ou au football, etc.

À Paris, le jardin des Tuileries et le jardin du Luxembourg sont deux jardins publics de style classique, très appréciés des Parisiens. Il y a aussi deux grands parcs à côté de Paris: le bois° de Vincennes, à l'est°, qui a un zoo, un jardin tropical et la foire° du Trône, la plus grande fête foraine° de France; et le bois de Boulogne, à l'ouest°, qui a un parc d'attractions° pour les enfants. Tous les deux ont aussi des cafés et des restaurants. Quand il fait beau, on peut faire du canotage° sur leurs lacs° ou pratiquer des activités sportives diverses.

Le bois de Vincennes et le bois de Boulogne

VINCENNES	BOULOGNE
• une superficie° totale de 995 hectares	• une superficie totale de 863 hectares
• un zoo de 15 hectares	• cinq entrées°
• 19 km de sentiers pour les promenades à cheval et à vélo	• 95 km d'allées
• 32 km d'allées pour le jogging	• une cascade° de 10 mètres de large° et 14 mètres de haut°
• la Ferme° de Paris, une ferme de 5 hectares	• deux hippodromes°

jardins *gardens/parks* **la plupart du** *most of* **entourés** *surrounded* **grille** *fence* **ouverts** *open* **pendant** *during* **pelouses** *lawns* **arbres** *trees* **parterres de fleurs** *flower beds* **sentiers** *paths* **bancs** *benches* **aires de jeux** *playgrounds* **bassins** *ponds* **y** *there* **pétanque** *a popular game similar to the Italian game of bocce* **bois** *forest/wooded park* **est** *east* **foire** *fair* **fête foraine** *carnival* **ouest** *west* **parc d'attractions** *amusement park* **canotage** *boating* **lacs** *lakes* **superficie** *area* **Ferme** *Farm* **entrées** *entrances* **cascade** *waterfall* **de large** *wide* **de haut** *high* **hippodromes** *horse racetracks*

Coup de main

In France and in most other countries, units of measurement are different than those used in the United States.

1 hectare = *2.47 acres*

1 kilomètre = *0.62 mile*

1 mètre = *approximately 1 yard (3 feet)*

ACTIVITÉS

1 Répondez Répondez aux questions par des phrases complètes.

1. Où trouve-t-on, en général, les jardins publics des villes françaises? En général, on trouve les jardins publics des villes françaises au centre-ville.
2. Quel type de végétation y a-t-il dans les jardins publics français? Il y a des pelouses, des arbres, des plantes et des parterres de fleurs.
3. Qu'y a-t-il pour les enfants dans les jardins et les parcs français? Il y a des aires de jeux, des parcs d'attractions et des zoos.
4. Où va-t-on, à Paris, si on a envie de voir des animaux? On va au zoo du bois de Vincennes.
5. Quel type de plantes, en particulier, peut-on trouver au bois de Vincennes? On peut trouver des plantes tropicales au bois de Vincennes.
6. Comment s'appelle la plus grande fête foraine de France? Elle s'appelle la foire du Trône.
7. Où les enfants peuvent-ils visiter un parc d'attractions? Les enfants peuvent visiter un parc d'attractions au bois de Boulogne.
8. Que peut-on faire au bois de Vincennes? Answers may vary. Possible answers: On peut faire du jogging, ou des promenades à cheval ou à vélo.
9. Citez deux activités que les Français aiment faire dans les jardins publics. Answers may vary. Possible answers: Ils font des promenades et des pique-niques.
10. Est-il possible de manger dans les jardins et les parcs? Expliquez votre réponse. Answers may vary. Possible answer: Oui. Il y a parfois des restaurants et des cafés, et des personnes font aussi des pique-niques.

OPTIONS

Les jardins publics français Explain the longstanding reputations of **le bois de Vincennes** and **le bois de Boulogne**. **Le bois de Vincennes** was a working-class destination where marginal characters did their business. **Le bois de Boulogne** was a place where the well-heeled hoped to be seen. Eighteenth-century associations say it all: **le Marquis de Sade** was imprisoned at **le bois de Vincennes**, and **Marie-Antoinette** lived in **le château de Bagatelle**, which she commissioned at the western end of **le bois de Boulogne**. There is no longer a socio-economic status attached to each of these green spaces, but many Parisians are familiar with their reputations.

LE FRANÇAIS QUOTIDIEN

Les catastrophes naturelles

tempête (f.) de neige	*blizzard*
canicule (f.)	*heat wave*
inondation (f.)	*flood*
ouragan (m.)	*hurricane*
raz-de-marée (m.)	*tidal wave, tsunami*
sécheresse (f.)	*drought*
tornade (f.)	*tornado*
tremblement (m.) de terre	*earthquake*

LE MONDE FRANCOPHONE

Des parcs publics

Voici quelques parcs publics du monde francophone.

Bruxelles, Belgique
le bois de la Cambre 123 hectares, un lac° avec une île° au centre

Casablanca, Maroc
le parc de la Ligue Arabe des palmiers°, un parc d'attractions pour enfants, des cafés et restaurants

Québec, Canada
le parc des Champs de Batailles («Plaines d'Abraham») 107 hectares, 6.000 arbres°

Tunis, Tunisie
le parc du Belvédère 110 hectares, un zoo de 13 hectares, 230.000 arbres (80 espèces° différentes), situé° sur une colline°

lac *lake* **île** *island* **palmiers** *palm trees* **arbres** *trees* **espèces** *species* **situé** *located* **colline** *hill*

PORTRAIT

Les Français et le vélo

Tous les étés, la course° cycliste du Tour de France attire° un grand nombre de spectateurs, Français et étrangers, surtout lors de° son arrivée sur les Champs-Élysées, à Paris. C'est le grand événement° sportif de l'année pour les amoureux du cyclisme. Les Français adorent aussi faire du vélo pendant° leur temps libre. Beaucoup de clubs organisent des randonnées en vélo de course° le week-end. Pour les personnes qui préfèrent le vélo tout terrain (VTT)°, il y a des sentiers° adaptés dans les parcs régionaux et nationaux. Certaines agences de voyages proposent aussi des vacances «vélo» en France ou à l'étranger°.

course *race* **attire** *attracts* **lors de** *at the time of* **événement** *event* **pendant** *during* **vélo de course** *road bike* **vélo tout terrain (VTT)** *mountain biking* **sentiers** *paths* **à l'étranger** *abroad*

le Tour de France sur les Champs-Élysées

SUR INTERNET

Qu'est-ce que Jacques Anquetil, Eddy Merckx et Bernard Hinault ont en commun?

Go to espaces.vhlcentral.com to find more information related to this **ESPACE CULTURE**.

ACTIVITÉS

2 Vrai ou faux? Indiquez si les phrases sont vraies ou fausses. Corrigez les phrases fausses.

1. Les Français ne font pas de vélo. Faux. Les Français adorent faire du vélo pendant leur temps libre.
2. Les membres de clubs de vélo font des promenades le week-end. Vrai.
3. Les agences de voyages offrent des vacances «vélo». Vrai.
4. On utilise un VTT quand on fait du vélo sur la route. Faux. On utilise un vélo de course.
5. Le Tour de France arrive sur les Champs-Élysées à Paris. Vrai.

3 Les catastrophes naturelles Avec un(e) partenaire, parlez de trois catastrophes naturelles. Quel temps fait-il, en général, pendant (*during*) chaque catastrophe? Choisissez une catastrophe et décrivez-la à vos camarades. Peuvent-ils deviner (*Can they guess*) de quelle catastrophe vous parlez?

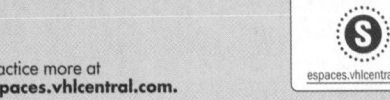

Practice more at **espaces.vhlcentral.com.**

ressources
espaces.vhlcentral.com

Le français quotidien After studying the vocabulary, ask students to close their books and to number from one to five on a piece of paper. Describe five of these **catastrophes naturelles** with new lexical items from **Leçon 5B.** Have the class write down the event you are describing. Go over the answers as a class.

Portrait
- Ask students what they know about the **Tour de France**. They may mention Lance Armstrong, **le maillot jaune** (*yellow jersey*), etc.
- Find out if the class has heard of stereotypes about the French and cycling. Have them list ideas in small groups.
- The importance of the bicycle has increased in France as a response to environmental issues. Cities like Paris, Lyon, Nantes, and Aix-en-Provence have created systems of **vélopartage**, large-scale bike renting whereby people take and leave a "citybike" whenever they want. Also, many municipalities have increased the number of bike paths (**pistes cyclables**).

Le monde francophone
- Look at the francophone world map in **Appendice A** to remind students where these countries are located.
- Practice pronunciation with the descriptions of these parks.

2 Expansion Continue the activity with more true/false statements like these.
6. Le Tour de France est une grande course cycliste. (Vrai.)
7. Le Tour de France est au printemps. (Faux, en été)
8. Les Français et les étrangers sont spectateurs du Tour de France. (Vrai.)

3 Expansion Students can use this as an opportunity to practice contradicting while quizzing each other about weather in the context of these new expressions. Example: **Étudiant(e) 1: Quand il y a un ouragan, fait-il soleil? Étudiant(e) 2: Pas du tout! Il pleut beaucoup.**

OPTIONS

Des parcs publics Assign a francophone country to several students in class. Have everyone do individual research on gardens or a park in the country he or she has been assigned. Students should be prepared to present their findings about the park in at least three clear sentences in French and an image from the Internet, if possible.

Les Français et le vélo Bring in an example of francophone music or film about cycling. For example, play the song ***Mon vélo est blanc*** by Anne Sylvestre. Screen part of the Belgian film ***Le vélo de Ghislain Lambert***. There are also scenes with Charlotte Gainsbourg riding a bicycle in ***La petite voleuse***.

Section Goals

In this section, students will learn:

- numbers 101 and higher
- mathematical terms

Instructional Resources
*espaces.vhlcentral.com: Lab MP3s; WB/VM/LM Answer Key; IRM (**Essayez!** and **Mise en pratique** answers; Lab Audioscript); activities; downloads; reference tools*

Suggestions

- Review numbers 0–100 by asking students questions that call for a number in the answer. Examples: **Combien d'étudiants y a-t-il dans la classe? Quel âge avez-vous? Quel âge a votre grand-mère? Anne a trois crayons. J'ai quatre boîtes de vingt crayons. Combien de crayons avons-nous? (quatre-vingt-trois)**
- Write on the board: **quatre cents étudiants, neuf cents personnes, deux mille livres, onze millions de voyageurs**. Help students deduce the meanings of the numbers.
- Model pronunciation of example numbers. Write other three-to seven-digit numbers on the board and have students read them.
- Go over the example sentences containing **cent**, **mille**, and **million**. Explain that the rules for when to pluralize are different from English.
- Point out that a space may be used instead of a period to indicate thousands and millions.
- Tell students that when writing out the year 1000, the word **mille** is not shortened to **mil: l'an mille**.
- You may also want to teach your students these mathematical terms:
  la différence *difference*
  le produit *product*
  le quotient *quotient*
  la somme *sum*

Successful Language Learning Explain that to count from 101–199, say **cent** followed by 1–99. So, 101: **cent un**, 102: **cent deux**, 103: **cent trois**, and so forth up to 199: **cent quatre-vingt-dix-neuf**. Use the same strategy after **deux cents, trois cents**, etc.

NATIONAL STANDARDS comparisons

5B.1 Numbers 101 and higher

Numbers 101 and higher

101	cent un	**800**	huit cents
125	cent vingt-cinq	**900**	neuf cents
198	cent quatre-vingt-dix-huit	**1.000**	mille
200	deux cents	**1.100**	mille cent
245	deux cent quarante-cinq	**2.000**	deux mille
300	trois cents	**5.000**	cinq mille
400	quatre cents	**100.000**	cent mille
500	cinq cents	**550.000**	cinq cent cinquante mille
600	six cents	**1.000.000**	un million
700	sept cents	**8.000.000**	huit millions

- Note that French uses a period, rather than a comma, to indicate thousands and millions.
- The word **cent** does not take a final **-s** when it is followed by the numbers **1–99**.

Il y a **deux cent cinquante** jours de soleil.
There are 250 sunny days.

but

J'ai **quatre cents** bandes dessinées.
I have 400 comic books.

- The number **un** is not used before the word **mille** to mean *a/one thousand*. It is used, however, before **million** to say *a/one million*.

Mille personnes habitent le village.
One thousand people live in the village.

but

Un million de personnes habitent la région.
One million people live in the region.

- **Mille**, unlike **cent** and **million**, is invariable. It never takes an **-s**.

Aimez-vous *Les **Mille** et Une Nuits*?
Do you like "The Thousand and One Nights"?

Onze mille étudiants sont inscrits.
Eleven thousand students are registered.

- Before a noun, **million** and **millions** are followed by **de/d'**.

Deux millions de personnes sont en vacances.
Two million people are on vacation.

Il y a **onze millions d'habitants** dans la capitale.
There are 11,000,000 inhabitants in the capital.

- When writing out years, the word **mille** is usually shortened to **mil**.

mil huit cent soixante-cinq
eighteen (hundred) sixty-five

MISE EN PRATIQUE

1 Quelle adresse? Vous allez distribuer des journaux (*newspapers*) et vous téléphonez aux clients pour avoir leur adresse. Écrivez les adresses.

MODÈLE
cent deux, rue Lafayette
102, rue Lafayette

1. deux cent cinquante-deux, rue de Bretagne 252, rue de Bretagne
2. quatre cents, avenue Malbon 400, avenue Malbon
3. cent soixante-dix-sept, rue Jeanne d'Arc 177, rue Jeanne d'Arc
4. cinq cent quarante-six, boulevard St. Marc 546, boulevard St. Marc
5. six cent quatre-vingt-huit, avenue des Gaulois 688, avenue des Gaulois
6. trois cent quatre-vingt-douze, boulevard Micheline 392, boulevard Micheline
7. cent vingt-cinq, rue des Pierres 125, rue des Pierres
8. trois cent quatre, avenue St. Germain 304, avenue St. Germain

2 Les maths Faites les opérations et écrivez les réponses. Answers may vary slightly.

MODÈLE
200 + 300 =
Deux cents plus trois cents font cinq cents.

1. 650 + 750 = Six cent cinquante plus sept cent cinquante font mille quatre cents.
2. 2.000.000 + 3.000.000 = Deux millions plus trois millions font cinq millions.
3. 966 – 342 = Neuf cent soixante-six moins trois cent quarante-deux égale six cent vingt-quatre.
4. 155 + 310 = Cent cinquante-cinq plus trois cent dix font quatre cent soixante-cinq.
5. 2.000 – 150 = Deux mille moins cent cinquante font mille huit cent cinquante.
6. 375 × 2 = Trois cent soixante-quinze multiplié par deux égale sept cent cinquante.
7. 1.250 + 2.250 = Mille deux cent cinquante plus deux mille deux cent cinquante font trois mille cinq cents.
8. 4.444 ÷ 4 = Quatre mille quatre cent quarante-quatre divisé par quatre égale mille cent onze.

3 Combien d'habitants? À tour de rôle, demandez à votre partenaire combien d'habitants il y a dans chaque ville d'après (*according to*) les statistiques.

MODÈLE
Dijon: 153.813
Étudiant(e) 1: *Combien d'habitants y a-t-il à Dijon?*
Étudiant(e) 2: *Il y a cent cinquante-trois mille huit cent treize habitants.*

1. Toulouse: 398.423 Il y a trois cent quatre-vingt-dix-huit mille quatre cent vingt-trois habitants.
2. Abidjan: 2.877.948 Il y a deux millions huit cent soixante-dix-sept mille neuf cent quarante-huit habitants.
3. Lyon: 453.187 Il y a quatre cent cinquante-trois mille cent quatre-vingt-sept habitants.
4. Québec: 510.559 Il y a cinq cent dix mille cinq cent cinquante-neuf habitants.
5. Marseille: 807.071 Il y a huit cent sept mille soixante et onze habitants.
6. Papeete: 26.181 Il y a vingt-six mille cent quatre-vingt-un habitants.

Practice more at **espaces.vhlcentral.com.**

OPTIONS

Game Ask students to stand up to create a number chain. The first student states the number 25. The next student says 50. Students continue the chain, using multiples of 25. If a student misses the next number in sequence, he or she must sit down. Continue play until only one student is left standing. If a challenge is required to break a tie, play the game with multiples of 30.

Extra Practice Ask students to make a list of nine items containing the following: a variety of plural and singular nouns, three numerals in the hundreds, three in the thousands, and three in the millions. Once lists are completed, have students exchange them and read the items off their partners' lists aloud. Partners should listen for the correct number and any agreement errors.

COMMUNICATION

4 **Quand?** Avec un(e) partenaire, regardez les dates et dites quand ces événements ont lieu (*take place*).

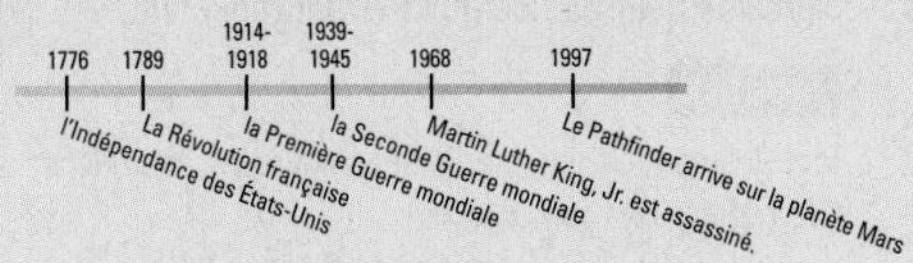

1. Le Pathfinder arrive sur la planète Mars.
   Il arrive en mille neuf cent quatre-vingt-dix-sept.
2. La Première Guerre mondiale commence.
   Elle commence en mille neuf cent quatorze.
3. La Seconde Guerre mondiale prend fin (*ends*).
   Elle prend fin en mille neuf cent quarante-cinq.
4. L'Amérique déclare son indépendance.
   Elle déclare son indépendance en mille sept cent soixante-seize.
5. Martin Luther King, Jr. est assassiné.
   Il est assassiné en mille neuf cent soixante-huit.
6. La Première Guerre Mondiale prend fin.
   Elle prend fin en mille neuf cent dix-huit.

5 **Combien ça coûte?** Vous regardez un catalogue avec un(e) ami(e). À tour de rôle, demandez à votre partenaire le prix des choses. Answers will vary.

MODÈLE

Étudiant(e) 1: *Combien coûte l'ordinateur?*
Étudiant(e) 2: *Il coûte mille huit cents euros.*

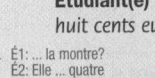

1. É1: ... la montre? É2: Elle ... quatre cent trente-deux ...

3. É1: ... le sac à dos? É2: Il ... cent dix-huit ...

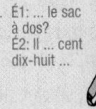

2. É1: ... les dictionnaires? É2: Ils ... cent seize ...

4. É1: ... le vélo? É2: Il ... six cent soixante-quinze ...

6 **Dépensez de l'argent** Vous et votre partenaire avez 100.000€. Décidez quels articles de la liste vous allez prendre. Justifiez vos choix à la classe. Answers will vary.

MODÈLE

Étudiant(e) 1: *On prend un rendez-vous avec Brad Pitt.*
Étudiant(e) 2: *Alors, nous n'avons pas assez d'argent pour la voiture!*

un ordinateur... 2.000€	des vacances à Tahiti... 7.000€
un rendez-vous avec Brad Pitt... 50.000€	un vélo... 1.000€
un rendez-vous avec Madonna... 50.000€	une voiture de luxe... 60.000€

- In French, years before 2000 may be written out in two ways. Notice that in English, the word *hundred* can be omitted, but in French, the word **cent** is required.

mil neuf cent treize *one thousand nine hundred (and) thirteen*	*or*	**dix-neuf cent treize** *nineteen (hundred) thirteen*

- You can talk about mathematical operations both formally and informally.

Mathematical terms

	informal	formal
plus	**et**	**plus**
minus	**moins**	**moins**
multiplied by	**fois**	**multiplié par**
divided by	**sur**	**divisé par**
equals	**font**	**égale**

- The verb **égaler** (*to equal*) is expressed in the singular, but the verb **faire** is plural.

110 et 205 font 315 $110 + 205 = 315$	**110 plus 205 égale 315** $110 + 205 = 315$
60 fois 3 font 180 $60 \times 3 = 180$	**60 multiplié par 3 égale 180** $60 \times 3 = 180$
999 sur 9 font 111 $999 \div 9 = 111$	**999 divisé par 9 égale 111** $999 \div 9 = 111$

- In French, decimal punctuation is inverted. Use **une virgule** (*comma*) instead of **un point** (*period*).

5.419,32	**cinq mille quatre cent dix-neuf virgule trente-deux**
5,419.32	*five thousand four hundred nineteen point thirty-two*

- The expression **pour cent** (*percent*) is two words, not one.

Le magasin offre une réduction de soixante **pour cent**.
The store is offering a sixty percent discount.

Essayez! **Donnez les équivalents en français.**

1. 10.000 dix mille
2. 620 six cent vingt
3. 365 trois cent soixante-cinq
4. 42.000 quarante-deux mille
5. 200.000.000 deux cents millions
6. 480 quatre cent quatre-vingts
7. 1.789 mille sept cent quatre-vingt-neuf
8. 400 quatre cents
9. 150% cent cinquante pour cent
10. 1.250,50 mille deux cent cinquante virgule cinquante

Essayez! Have students think of four more numbers for their partner to write out in French.

1 Suggestion For listening comprehension, have students read numbers from the activity to a partner.

1 Expansion Give students these real addresses in regions **Centre** and **Pays de la Loire**. Model how to pronounce the postal codes. Example: 45000: **quarante-cinq mille. (1) Préfecture de la Région Centre et du Loiret: 181, rue de Bourgogne - 45042 ORLÉANS (2) Espace Région Centre de Tours: 1, rue des Ursulines - 37000 TOURS (3) Auberge de Jeunesse: 23, Avenue Neigre - 28000 CHARTRES (4) Médiathèque Louis Aragon: 54, rue du Port - 72015 LE MANS**

2 Suggestions
- Call on pairs of students to say some of the calculations aloud.
- Give additional math problems if more practice is needed.

2 Expansion Have pairs convert a **calcul** into a word problem. Example: **J'ai deux cents dollars. Ma sœur a trois cents dollars. Combien de dollars avons-nous?**

3 Expansion Write on the board some well-known American cities and your university's city or town. Ask students: **Combien d'habitants...?** Have them guess if they don't know. Then write the accurate number next to each city. Have students come to the board to write out the populations in French.

4 Expansion Ask students to brainstorm other famous years throughout history.

5 & 6 Suggestions
- Before beginning each activity, make sure students know the vocabulary.
- Do the **modèles** with a volunteer to make sure students understand the activities.

OPTIONS

Extra Practice Have small groups of students work together to create a worksheet consisting of five math word problems for their classmates to complete. Have students take turns reading problems to the class or one of the other small groups, who, in turn, will solve the problems. Have groups include an answer key with their worksheets.

Groups Divide the class into groups of ten. Give a flashcard with a number from 0–9 to each person in each group. If one group is smaller, distribute extra numbers to group members, as needed, so some students have more than one card. Call out a three- to nine-digit number in which none of the digits is repeated. Students arrange themselves, showing their flashcard(s) to reflect the number. Repeat with other numbers.

Section Goals

In this section, students will learn **-er** verbs with spelling changes.

Instructional Resources
*espaces.vhlcentral.com: Lab MP3s; WB/VM/LM Answer Key; IRM (**Essayez!** and **Mise en pratique** answers; Lab Audioscript; **Feuilles d'activités**); activities; downloads; reference tools*

Suggestions

- Model pronunciations of forms of **acheter**, **espérer**, and **envoyer**. Go over the example statements as a class.
- Guide students to notice that, like regular **-er** verbs, spelling-change **-er** verbs are "boot verbs."
- Point out that infinitives often follow forms of **espérer**. Example: **Il espère gagner.**
- Ask questions using verbs from this section, encouraging student responses. Examples: **Où est-ce que vous achetez du pain? Quelle saison préférez-vous: l'été ou l'hiver?**
- Explain that when the letter **e** is followed by one pronounced consonant and a silent **e**, you need to add an **accent grave** over the first **e**. If the first **e** already has an **accent aigu**, it becomes an **accent grave**. This causes spelling changes in some verbs, adjectives, and nouns. Remind students to apply this rule whenever this pattern of letters occurs. Exception: **e** with an **accent circonflexe**.
- Go through the meanings of verbs. Note the number of cognates. Make sure students understand that **amener** and **emmener** are only used for people. Ask: What verbs would you use to say *to take* and *to bring* objects? (**prendre**; **apporter**)

5B.2 Spelling-change *-er* verbs

NATIONAL STANDARDS comparisons

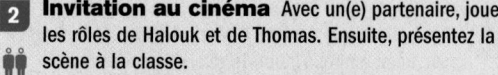

Point de départ Some **-er** verbs, though regular with respect to their verb endings, have spelling changes that occur in the verb stem (what remains after the **-er** is dropped).

- Most infinitives whose next-to-last syllable contains an **e** (no accent) change this letter to **è** in all forms except **nous** and **vous**.

Acheter (to buy)	
j'achète	nous achetons
tu achètes	vous achetez
il/elle achète	ils/elles achètent

Où est-ce que tu **achètes** des skis?
Where do you buy skis?

Ils **achètent** beaucoup sur Internet.
They buy a lot on the Internet.

- Infinitives whose next-to-last syllable contains an **é** change this letter to **è** in all forms except **nous** and **vous**.

Espérer (to hope)	
j'espère	nous espérons
tu espères	vous espérez
il/elle espère	ils/elles espèrent

Elle **espère** arriver tôt aujourd'hui.
She hopes to arrive early today.

Nos profs **espèrent** commencer les cours.
Our professors hope to start classes.

Elle achète quelque chose.

Ils répètent.

- Infinitives ending in **-yer** change **y** to **i** in all forms except **nous** and **vous**.

Envoyer (to send)	
j'envoie	nous envoyons
tu envoies	vous envoyez
il/elle envoie	ils/elles envoient

J'**envoie** une lettre.
I'm sending a letter.

Tes amis **envoient** un e-mail.
Your friends send an e-mail.

MISE EN PRATIQUE

1 Passe-temps Chaque membre de la famille Desrosiers a son passe-temps préféré. Utilisez les éléments pour dire ce qu'ils (*what they*) font.

MODÈLE

Tante Manon fait une randonnée. (acheter / sandwichs)
Elle achète des sandwichs.

1. Nous faisons du vélo. (essayer / vélo) Nous essayons le vélo.
2. Christiane aime chanter. (répéter) Elle répète.
3. Les filles jouent au foot. (espérer / gagner) Elles espèrent gagner.
4. Vous allez à la pêche. (emmener / enfants) Vous emmenez les enfants.
5. Papa fait un tour en voiture. (nettoyer / voiture) Il nettoie la voiture.
6. Mes frères font du camping. (préférer / partir tôt) Ils préfèrent partir tôt.

2 Invitation au cinéma Avec un(e) partenaire, jouez les rôles de Halouk et de Thomas. Ensuite, présentez la scène à la classe.

THOMAS J'ai envie d'aller au cinéma.

HALOUK Bonne idée. Nous (1) ___emmenons___ (emmener, protéger) Véronique avec nous?

THOMAS J' (2) ___espère___ (acheter, espérer) qu'elle a du temps libre.

HALOUK Peut-être, mais je/j' (3) ___envoie___ (envoyer, payer) des e-mails tous les jours et elle ne répond pas.

THOMAS Parce que son ordinateur ne fonctionne pas. Elle (4) ___préfère___ (essayer, préférer) parler au téléphone.

HALOUK D'accord. Alors toi, tu (5) ___achètes___ (acheter, répéter) les tickets au cinéma et moi, je vais chercher Véronique.

3 Que font-ils? Dites ce que (*Say what*) font les personnages. Answers will vary.

MODÈLE

Il achète une baguette.

acheter

1. envoyer

2. payer

3. répéter

4. nettoyer

Practice more at **espaces.vhlcentral.com.**

OPTIONS

Game Divide the class into two teams. Announce one of the infinitives and a subject pronoun. Example: **emmener**; **ils**. At the board, have the first member of Team A say and write the given subject and the conjugated form of the verb. If the team member answers correctly, Team A gets one point. If not, give the first member of Team B the same example. The team with the most points at the end of the game wins.

Video Replay the video episode, having students focus on **-er** verbs with spelling changes. Have them note each one they hear, with subjects if conjugated. Find out how many occurrences students heard before pointing out these examples: **je préfère, célébrer, célèbre, tu essaies,** and **préférer.** Ask for remarks with spelling-change **-er** verbs that describe the characters. Example: **Rachid possède un ordinateur.**

COMMUNICATION

4 Questions À tour de rôle, posez les questions à un(e) partenaire. Answers will vary.

1. Qu'est-ce que tu achètes tous les jours?
2. Qu'est-ce que tu achètes tous les mois?
3. Quand tu sors avec ton/ta petit(e) ami(e), qui paie?
4. Est-ce que ton/ta camarade de chambre et toi partagez les frais (*expenses*)? Qui paie quoi?
5. Est-ce que tu possèdes une voiture?
6. Qui nettoie ta chambre?
7. À qui est-ce que tu envoies des e-mails?
8. Qu'est-ce que tu espères faire cet été?

5 Réponses affirmatives Votre professeur va vous donner une feuille d'activités. Trouvez au moins un(e) camarade de classe qui réponde oui à chaque question. Et si vous aussi, vous répondez oui aux questions, écrivez votre nom. Answers will vary.

MODÈLE

Étudiant(e) 1: *Est-ce que tu achètes exclusivement sur Internet?*
Étudiant(e) 2: *Oui, j'achète exclusivement sur Internet.*

Questions	*Noms*
1. acheter exclusivement sur Internet	*Virginie, Éric*
2. posséder un ordinateur	
3. envoyer des lettres à ses grands-parents	
4. célébrer une occasion spéciale demain	

6 E-mail à l'oncle Marcel Xavier va écrire un e-mail à son oncle pour raconter (*to tell*) ses activités de la semaine prochaine. Il prépare une liste des choses qu'il veut dire (*wants to say*). Avec un(e) partenaire, écrivez son e-mail. Answers will vary.

- lundi: emmener maman chez le médecin
- mercredi: fac envoyer notes
- jeudi: répéter rôle Roméo et Juliette
- vendredi: célébrer anniversaire papa
- vendredi: essayer faire gym
- samedi: parents acheter voiture

- The change of **y** to **i** is optional in verbs whose infinitives end in **-ayer**.

Je **paie** avec une carte de crédit.	Comment est-ce que tu **payes**?
I pay with a credit card.	*How do you pay?*

Other spelling-change -er verbs

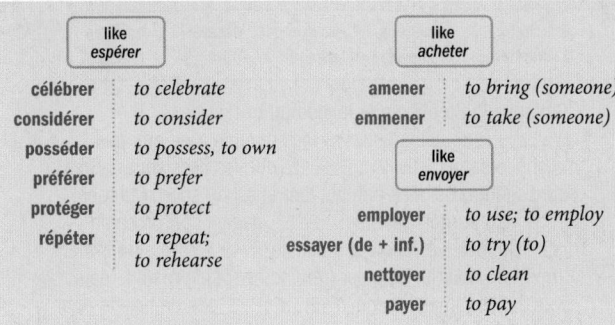

like espérer

célébrer	*to celebrate*
considérer	*to consider*
posséder	*to possess, to own*
préférer	*to prefer*
protéger	*to protect*
répéter	*to repeat; to rehearse*

like acheter

amener	*to bring (someone)*
emmener	*to take (someone)*

like envoyer

employer	*to use; to employ*
essayer (de + inf.)	*to try (to)*
nettoyer	*to clean*
payer	*to pay*

Je préfère l'été.
Il fait chaud.

Tu essaies de
ne pas parler?

- Note that the **nous** and **vous** forms of the verbs presented in this section have no spelling changes.

Vous **achetez** des sandwichs aussi.	Nous **espérons** partir à huit heures.
You're buying sandwiches, too.	*We hope to leave at 8 o'clock.*
Nous **envoyons** les enfants à l'école.	Vous **payez** avec une carte de crédit.
We're sending the children to school.	*You pay with a credit card.*

Essayez! Complétez les phrases avec la forme correcte du verbe.

1. Les bibliothèques ___emploient___ (employer) beaucoup d'étudiants.
2. Vous ___répétez___ (répéter) les phrases en français.
3. Nous ___payons___ (payer) assez pour les livres.
4. Mon camarade de chambre ne ___nettoie___ (nettoyer) pas son bureau.
5. Est-ce que tu ___espères___ (espérer) gagner?
6. Vous ___essayez___ (essayer) parfois d'arriver à l'heure.
7. Tu ___préfères___ (préférer) prendre du thé ou du café?
8. Elle ___emmène___ (emmener) sa mère au cinéma.
9. On ___célèbre___ (célébrer) une occasion spéciale.
10. Les parents ___protègent___ (protéger) leurs enfants.

Essayez! For additional drills with spelling-change **-er** verbs for the whole class or those who need extra practice, do this activity orally and on the board with different subjects.

1 Suggestion Ask for a volunteer to demonstrate the **modèle**.

1 Expansion Have students write four additional statements modeled on the activity about their own family members.

2 Suggestion Explain that students must first choose the logical verb, then write the correct form.

3 Expansion Show additional pictures of people cleaning, using something, trying, sending, etc. Ask a yes/no question about each picture. Example: Showing an image of someone sending a letter, ask: **Est-ce qu'il nettoie?** Students answer: **Mais non, il envoie une lettre.**

4 Expansion Have students write two more questions containing spelling-change **-er** verbs that they would like to ask their partner.

5 Suggestion Call on two volunteers to read the **modèle** aloud. Then distribute the **Feuilles d'activités** found on the Supersite.

6 Expansion Have students think of a family member or friend to whom they would likely write an e-mail. Tell them to first list at least five ideas using as many spelling-change **-er** verbs as possible. Then have them write an e-mail of at least five sentences.

OPTIONS

Extra Practice Arrange students in rows of six. The first person in each row has a piece of paper. Call out an infinitive. Silently, the first student writes the **je** form and passes the paper to the student behind him or her. That student writes the **tu** form and passes the paper on. The last person in the row holds up the paper to show completion. Have students rotate places before calling out another verb.

Small Groups Have small groups write dehydrated sentences with only subjects and infinitives. Examples: **1. tu / amener / ??? 2. Sylvie et Véronique / espérer / ???** Tell groups to switch with another group, who will form a complete sentence by conjugating the verb and inventing an appropriate ending. Ask for volunteers to write one of their group's sentences on the board.

Instructional Resources
espaces.vhlcentral.com:
IRM (Info Gap Activities);
Testing Program, pp. 37–40;
Test Files; Testing Program MP3s; activities; downloads; reference tools
Test Generator

1 Expansion Have students write a story about their preferred sport modeled on the paragraph in this activity.

2 Suggestion Have pairs get together to form groups of four to review each others' sentences. Have students explain any corrections or suggested changes.

3 Suggestion Encourage students to choose places from the French-speaking world that they have learned about in **Espace culture** and **Panorama** sections.

3 Expansion Have students create more questions based on those in the activity to ask their partner. Guide the class to ask about where the partner hopes or prefers to go for various vacations throughout the year. Students may combine reusing weather conditions described in the box and using additional weather descriptions.

4 Expansion For additional numbers practice, have students ask each other: **Combien coûte __________ (type de voyage) avec la commission?**

5 Suggestion Ask for volunteers to do the **modèle** and auction off a few more items to set further examples.

6 Suggestions
- Divide the class into pairs and distribute the Info Gap Handouts found on the Supersite for this activity. Give students ten minutes to complete the activity.
- Act out the **modèle** with a student volunteer playing the role of **Étudiant(e) 2**.

Révision

1 Le basket Avec un(e) partenaire, utilisez les verbes de la liste pour compléter le paragraphe.

acheter	considérer	envoyer	essayer	préférer
amener	employer	espérer	payer	répéter

Je m'appelle Stéphanie et je joue au basket. Je/J' (1) __amène__ toujours (*always*) mes parents avec moi aux matchs le samedi. Ils (2) __considèrent__ que les filles sont de très bonnes joueuses. Mes parents font aussi du sport. Ma mère fait du vélo et mon père (3) __espère__ gagner son prochain match de foot! Le vendredi matin, je/j' (4) __envoie__ un e-mail à ma mère pour lui rappeler (*remind her of*) le match. Mais elle n'oublie jamais! Ils ne/n' (5) __achètent__ pas de tickets pour les matchs, parce que les parents des joueurs ne/n' (6) __paient__ pas. Nous (7) __essayons__ toujours d'arriver une demi-heure avant le match, parce que maman et papa (8) __préfèrent, espèrent__ s'asseoir (*to sit*) tout près du terrain (*court*). Ils sont tellement fiers!

2 Que font-ils? Avec un(e) partenaire, parlez des activités des personnages et écrivez une phrase par illustration. Answers will vary.

1. __________

2. __________

3. __________

4. __________

5. __________

6. __________

3 Où partir? Avec un(e) partenaire, choisissez cinq endroits intéressants à visiter où il fait le temps indiqué sur la liste. Ensuite, répondez aux questions. Answers will vary.

Il fait chaud. Il fait soleil. Il fait du vent. Il neige. Il pleut.

1. Où essayez-vous d'aller cet été? Pourquoi?
2. Où préférez-vous partir cet hiver? Pourquoi?
3. Quelle est la première destination que vous espérez visiter? La dernière? Pourquoi?
4. Qui emmenez-vous avec vous? Pourquoi?

4 J'achète Vous allez payer un voyage aux membres de votre famille et à vos amis. À tour de rôle, choisissez un voyage et donnez à votre partenaire la liste des personnes qui partent. Votre partenaire va vous donner le prix à payer. Answers will vary.

MODÈLE

Étudiant(e) 1: *J'achète un voyage de dix jours dans les Pays de la Loire à ma cousine Pauline et à mon frère Alexandre.*
Étudiant(e) 2: *D'accord. Tu paies deux mille cinq cent soixante-deux euros.*

Voyages	Prix par personne	Commission
Dix jours dans les Pays de la Loire	1.250€	62€
Deux semaines de camping	660€	35€
Sept jours au soleil en hiver	2.100€	78€
Trois jours à Paris en avril	500€	55€
Trois mois en Europe en été	10.400€	47€
Un week-end à Nice en septembre	350€	80€
Une semaine à la montagne en juin	990€	66€
Une semaine à la neige	1.800€	73€

5 La vente aux enchères Par groupes de quatre, organisez une vente aux enchères (*auction*) pour vendre les affaires (*things*) du professeur. À tour de rôle, un(e) étudiant(e) joue le rôle du vendeur/de la vendeuse et les autres étudiants jouent le rôle des enchérisseurs (*bidders*). Vous avez 5.000 euros et toutes les enchères (*bids*) commencent à cent euros. Answers will vary.

MODÈLE

Étudiant(e) 1: *J'ai le cahier du professeur. Qui paie cent euros?*
Étudiant(e) 2: *Moi, je paie cent euros.*
Étudiant(e) 1: *Qui paie cent cinquante euros?*

6 À la bibliothèque Votre professeur va vous donner, à vous et à votre partenaire, deux feuilles d'activités différentes. Attention! Ne regardez pas la feuille de votre partenaire. Answers will vary.

MODÈLE

Étudiant(e) 1: *Est-ce que tu as le livre «Candide»?*
Étudiant(e) 2: *Oui, son numéro de référence est P, Q, deux cent soixante-six, cent quarante-sept, cent dix.*

ressources
WB pp. 65-68 | LM pp. 39-40 | espaces.vhlcentral.com

OPTIONS

Small Groups Have students write a conversation between two friends. One friend tries to convince the other to go out. The other makes excuses to not go. Students should include as many spelling-change **-er** verbs and weather expressions as possible. Example: **Étudiant(e) 1: Faisons une randonnée! Étudiant(e) 2: Mais je nettoie ma chambre. Étudiant(e) 1: Mais il fait beau. Étudiant(e) 2: Il va pleuvoir plus tard.**

Pairs Ask students to imagine they are going on an extended trip. Have them make a list of at least five things they are to do (buy things, take someone somewhere, send mail, etc.) before leaving. Examples: **Je vais acheter un nouveau parapluie. J'espère envoyer une carte d'anniversaire.**

À l'écoute

communication STANDARDS

Audio: Activities

STRATÉGIE

Listening for key words

By listening for key words (**mots-clés**) or phrases, you can identify the subject and main ideas of what you hear, as well as some of the details.

To practice this strategy, you will listen to a short paragraph. Jot down the key words that help you identify the subject of the paragraph and its main ideas.

Préparation

Regardez l'image. Où trouve-t-on ce type d'image? Manque-t-il des éléments (*Is anything missing*) sur cette carte? Faites une liste de mots-clés qui vont vous aider à trouver ces informations quand vous allez écouter la météo (*the weather*).

À vous d'écouter

Écoutez la météo. Puis, écoutez une deuxième fois et complétez le tableau. Notez la température et écrivez un **X** pour indiquer le temps qu'il fait dans chaque ville.

Ville							Température
Paris			X				8°C
Lille				X			6°C
Strasbourg						X	5°C
Brest			X				10°C
Lyon				X			9°C
Bordeaux		X					11°C
Toulouse	X						12°C
Marseille				X			12°C
Nice					X		13°C

Practice more at **espaces.vhlcentral.com.**

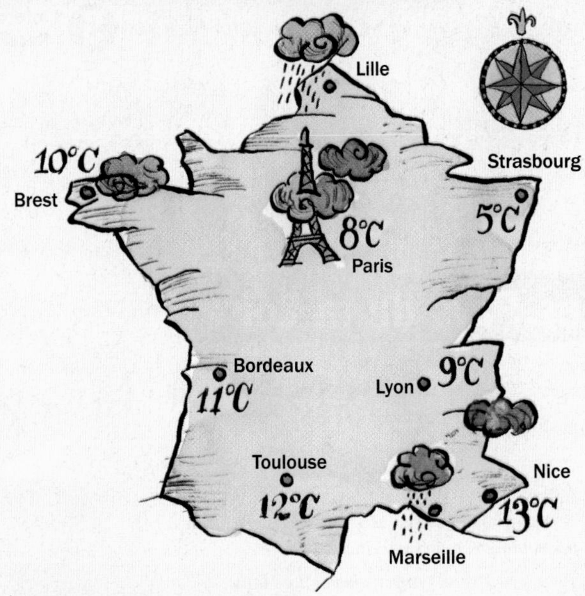

Compréhension

Probable ou improbable? Indiquez si ces (*these*) phrases sont probables ou improbables, d'après la météo d'aujourd'hui.

MODÈLE

	Probable	Improbable
Ève va nager à Strasbourg.	___	✓
1. Lucie fait du vélo à Lille.	___	✓
2. Il fait un temps épouvantable à Toulouse.	___	✓
3. Émilien joue aux cartes à la maison à Lyon.	✓	___
4. Il va neiger à Marseille.	___	✓
5. Jérome et Yves jouent au golf à Bordeaux.	✓	___
6. À Lyon, on a besoin d'un imperméable.	✓	___
7. Il fait froid à Strasbourg.	✓	___
8. Nous allons nager à Nice cet après-midi.	___	✓

Quelle ville choisir? Imaginez qu'aujourd'hui vous êtes en France. Décidez dans quelle ville vous avez envie de passer la journée. Pourquoi? Décrivez le temps qu'il fait et citez des activités que vous allez peut-être faire.

MODÈLE

J'ai envie d'aller à Strasbourg parce que j'aime l'hiver et la neige. Aujourd'hui, il fait froid et il neige. Je vais faire une promenade en ville et après, je vais boire un chocolat chaud au café.

Section Goals

In this section, students will:

- learn to listen for key words
- listen to a short paragraph and note the key words
- answer questions based on the content of a recorded weather forecast

Instructional Resources
espaces.vhlcentral.com: IRM (Textbook Audioscript); Textbook MP3s; downloads; reference tools

Stratégie
Script Qu'est-ce que je fais quand j'ai du temps libre? Eh bien, l'hiver, j'aime faire du ski. Au printemps et en automne, quand il fait bon, je fais du vélo et du cheval. Et l'été, je fais de la planche à voile.

Préparation Have students look at the map and describe what they see. Guide them to think about expressions that are commonly mentioned during a weather forecast. Ask them to brainstorm and write a list of as much weather-related vocabulary as they can in five minutes.

À vous d'écouter
Script Mesdames, Mesdemoiselles, Messieurs, bonjour et bienvenue sur Radio Satellite. Il est 10h00 et voici la météo. Aujourd'hui, sur la capitale, des nuages toute la journée. Eh oui, il fait frais à Paris ce matin, avec une température maximale de huit degrés. À Lille, on va avoir un temps épouvantable. Il fait froid avec six degrés seulement et il va pleuvoir tout l'après-midi et toute la soirée. À Strasbourg, il fait cinq degrés et il neige encore. Il fait assez frais à Brest, avec dix degrés et beaucoup de nuages. À Lyon, il fait neuf degrés aussi avec un temps très orageux, alors ne sortez pas sans votre parapluie! À Bordeaux, il fait bon, onze degrés et quelques nuages. Toulouse va avoir du soleil toute la journée et il va faire douze degrés. À Marseille, la température est de douze degrés maintenant, mais il va pleuvoir dans l'après-midi. Sur la Côte d'Azur, il fait treize degrés à Nice, et il y a beaucoup de vent. Bonne journée!

Section Goals
In this section, students will learn historical and cultural information about **Pays de la Loire** and **Centre**.

Instructional Resources
espaces.vhlcentral.com: Transparency #30; WB/VM/LM Answer Key; activities; downloads; reference tools

Carte des Pays de la Loire et du Centre
- Have students look at the map of the regions **Pays de la Loire** and **Centre** or use **Transparency #30**. Have volunteers read aloud the cities and geographic features. Model French pronunciation of city names, as necessary.
- Ask students to name a geographical feature that was likely an asset to these regions during their development. (the many major rivers)
- Ask students if they recognize any of the town names and to share any prior knowledge they have about the locations.

La région en chiffres
- Ask volunteers to read the sections. After each section, ask other students questions about the content.
- Have students list the many cognates that appear in this section and state the likely English equivalent or what the word might relate to.

Incroyable mais vrai!
Chambord's construction began in 1519 under François Ier, continued under Henri II, and was finally completed in 1685 under Louis XIV.

NATIONAL STANDARDS connections cultures

Interactive Map Reading

Panorama

Les Pays de la Loire

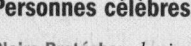

La région en chiffres
- **Superficie:** *32.082 km²°*
- **Population:** *3.344.000*
  SOURCE: INSEE
- **Industries principales:** *aéronautique, agriculture, informatique, tourisme, viticulture°*
- **Villes principales:** *Angers, Laval, Le Mans, Nantes, Saint Nazaire*

Personnes célèbres
- **Claire Bretécher,** *dessinatrice de bandes dessinées (1940–)*
- **Léon Bollée,** *inventeur d'automobiles (1870–1913)*
- **Jules Verne,** *écrivain° (1828–1905)*

Le Centre

La région en chiffres
- **Superficie:** *39.152 km²*
- **Population:** *2.480.000*
- **Industrie principale:** *tourisme*
- **Villes principales:** *Bourges, Chartres, Orléans, Tours, Vierzon*

Personnes célèbres
- **Honoré de Balzac,** *écrivain (1799–1850)*
- **George Sand,** *femme écrivain (1804–1876)*
- **Gérard Depardieu,** *acteur (1948–)*

un pèlerinage° à la cathédrale de Chartres

le Vendée Globe, course° nautique

la Loire

Incroyable mais vrai!
Construit° au XVIe (seizième) siècle°, l'architecture du château de Chambord est influencée par Léonard de Vinci. Le château a 440 pièces°, 84 escaliers° et 365 cheminées (une pour chaque° jour de l'année). Le logis° central a deux escaliers en forme de double hélice°. Les escaliers vont dans la même° direction, mais ne se croisent jamais°.

km² (kilomètres carrés) *square kilometers* **viticulture** *wine-growing* **écrivain** *writer* **Construit** *Constructed* **siècle** *century* **pièces** *rooms* **escaliers** *staircases* **chaque** *each* **logis** *living area* **hélice** *helix* **même** *same* **ne se croisent jamais** *never cross* **pèlerinage** *pilgrimage* **course** *race*

OPTIONS

Tours et Chartres Tours and Chartres are lively cities that have thriving industries and are considered historical, academic, and cultural centers. Tours was at one time the capital of France and the residence of kings. Built on the site of a Roman town, it has remnants of medieval architecture, such as the timber-framed houses present in **place Plumereau**, which is the pedestrian-zoned, medieval heart of the city.

Chartres was named after the Celtic tribe, the Carnutes. The city was attacked and many of its structures destroyed. However, many efforts were put into its restoration. One of the most magnificent architectural masterpieces is **la cathédrale Notre-Dame de Chartres**. The cathedral marks the high point of gothic and medieval art, featuring fine sculptures, over 170 stained-glass windows, and flying buttresses.

Les monuments

La vallée des rois

La vallée de la Loire, avec ses châteaux, est appelée la vallée des rois°. C'est au XVIe (seizième) siècle° que les Valois° quittent Paris pour habiter dans la région, où ils construisent° de nombreux° châteaux de style Renaissance. François Ier inaugure le siècle des «rois voyageurs»: ceux° qui vont d'un château à l'autre avec leur cour° et toutes leurs possessions. Chenonceau, Chambord et Amboise sont aujourd'hui les châteaux les plus° visités.

Les festivals

Le Printemps de Bourges

Le Printemps de Bourges est un festival de musique qui a lieu° chaque année, en avril. Pendant° une semaine, tous les styles de musique sont représentés: variété française, musiques du monde°, rock, musique électronique, reggae, hip-hop, etc... Il y a des dizaines° de spectacles, de nombreux artistes, des milliers de spectateurs et des noms légendaires comme Serge Gainsbourg, Yves Montand, Ray Charles et Johnny Clegg.

Les sports

Les 24 heures du Mans

Les 24 heures du Mans, c'est la course° d'endurance automobile la plus célèbre° du monde. Depuis° 1923, de prestigieuses marques° y° participent. C'est sur ce circuit de 13,6 km que Ferrari gagne neuf victoires et que Porsche détient° le record de 16 victoires avec une vitesse moyenne° de 222 km/h sur 5.335 km. Il existe aussi les 24 heures du Mans moto°.

Les destinations

La route des vins

La vallée de la Loire est réputée pour ses vignobles°, en particulier pour ses vins blancs°. Le Sauvignon et le Chardonnay, par exemple, constituent environ° 75% (pour cent) de la production. La vigne est cultivée dans la vallée depuis l'an 380. Aujourd'hui, les vignerons° de la région produisent 400 millions de bouteilles par an. Pour apprécier le vin, il est nécessaire de l'observer°, de le sentir, de le goûter° et de le déguster°. C'est tout un art!

Qu'est-ce que vous avez appris? Répondez aux questions par des phrases complètes.

1. Quel événement peut-on voir aux Sables d'Olonne? On peut voir le Vendée Globe, une course nautique, aux Sables d'Olonne.
2. Au seizième siècle, qui influence le style de construction de Chambord? Léonard de Vinci influence le style de construction de Chambord.
3. Combien de cheminées y a-t-il à Chambord? Il y a 365 cheminées à Chambord.
4. De quel style sont les châteaux de la Loire? Les châteaux de la Loire sont de style Renaissance.
5. Pourquoi les Valois sont-ils «les rois voyageurs»? Ils sont «les rois voyageurs» parce qu'ils vont d'un château à l'autre avec toutes leurs possessions.
6. Combien de spectateurs vont au Printemps de Bourges chaque année? Des milliers de spectateurs vont au Printemps de Bourges chaque année.
7. Qu'est-ce que les 24 heures du Mans? C'est une course d'endurance automobile.
8. Quel autre type de course existe-t-il au Mans? Il existe aussi une course de moto.
9. Quels vins sont produits dans la vallée de la Loire? Les vins blancs sont principalement produits dans la vallée de la Loire.
10. Combien de bouteilles y sont produites chaque année? 400 millions de bouteilles de vin sont produites chaque année dans la vallée de la Loire.

Practice more at **espaces.vhlcentral.com**.

ressources: WB pp. 69–70 | espaces.vhlcentral.com

SUR INTERNET

Go to **espaces.vhlcentral.com** to find more cultural information related to this **PANORAMA**.

1. Trouvez des informations sur le Vendée Globe. Quel est l'itinéraire de la course? Combien de bateaux (*boats*) y participent chaque année?
2. Qui étaient (*were*) les artistes invités au dernier Printemps de Bourges? En connaissez-vous quelques-uns? (*Do you know some of them?*)

rois *kings* **siècle** *century* **les Valois** *name of a royal dynasty* **construisent** *build* **de nombreux** *numerous* **ceux** *those* **cour** *court* **les plus** *the most* **a lieu** *takes place* **Pendant** *For* **monde** *world* **dizaines** *dozens* **course** *race* **célèbre** *famous* **Depuis** *Since* **marques** *brands* **y** *there* **détient** *holds* **vitesse moyenne** *average speed* **moto** *motorcycle* **vignobles** *vineyards* **vins blancs** *white wines* **environ** *around* **vignerons** *wine-growers* **l'observer** *observe it* **le goûter** *taste it* **le déguster** *savor it*

La vallée des rois François Ier (1515–1547) and his court resided and traveled between his châteaux in Amboise, Blois, and Chambord. The castles were first built as defense structures but later evolved into decorative palaces. With less of a need for defense, elements like moats and towers remained as symbols of rank and ancestry. Other magnificent châteaux of the area are Azay-le-Rideau, Chenonceau, Villandry, Saumur, Ussé, Chaumont, Beauregard, and Cour-Cheverny.

Le Printemps de Bourges This music festival has been taking place every spring since its creation in 1977. Festival goers can listen to the music of the latest up-and-coming talent as well as world-renowned artists. Music shows can be found close to downtown. Musicians also play in restaurants, bars, and at outdoor and indoor stages. Some shows are free to the public.

Les 24 heures du Mans The biggest names in sports car racing come to test their speed, endurance, and reliability on the 13.6 km (8.5 mile) track. The driver of the car to travel the greatest distance within the 24-hour period is the champion. Close to 200,000 fans and 2,000 journalists come to Le Mans in June for one of the best-known automobile races in the world.

La route des vins The Loire River flows through the heart of the Loire Valley, connecting many of the major wine-producing towns. Nantes, home of the Muscadet grape, produces dry white wines. There is a concentration of vineyards closer to the center of the Loire Valley in Saumur, Vouvray, Azay-le-Rideau, Chinon, Bourgueil, among others. Classic white wines are found further east in Pouilly-sur-Loire. The Loire Valley is known for all sorts of white wines, but also produces some red and rosé wines.

OPTIONS

Cultural Activity Considering the historical, architectural, and cultural richness of the regions **Pays de la Loire** and **Centre**, it's no wonder they are part of the World Heritage List of UNESCO (United Nations Education, Scientific, and Cultural Organization). Have students explore UNESCO's website to find out more. Ask students to search the World Heritage List for other places from these regions.

Small Groups During the reign of François Ier, the Renaissance period was at its height. There was an increasing interest in arts and humanism, which was evident in the court life at the châteaux. Have small groups research various aspects of court life, such as the food they ate, activities they participated in, and what kinds of music, literature, and art were preferred. Have each group make a short presentation on their findings.

Section Goals

In this section, students will:

- learn to skim a text
- read a weekly city guide about Montreal

Stratégie Tell students that they can often predict the content of an unfamiliar document in French by skimming it and looking for recognizable format elements.

Examinez le texte Have students skim the text at the top of this calendar of events in and around Montreal. Point out the cognates **arts**, **culture**, **festival**, **musique classique**, and **manifestations culturelles**. Ask them to predict what type of document it is (city guide/calendar of events in a newspaper/weekly). Then ask students to scan the rest of the calendar of events.

Catégories Before students do this activity, ask them to think of three words or expressions that fit each of the three given categories (**les loisirs culturels, les activités sportives, les activités de plein air**) in English.

Trouvez Go over answers with the whole class by pointing out where in the text each piece of information is found. Expand the activity by having students write additional entries for the calendar of events that include information for the unchecked items (**où manger cette semaine, le temps qu'il va faire cette semaine, des prix d'entrée, des adresses**).

Language Note Point out that French-speaking Canadians say **la fin de semaine** instead of **le week-end**.

Lecture

Reading

National Standards: communication, cultures

Avant la lecture

STRATÉGIE

Skimming

Skimming involves quickly reading through a document to absorb its general meaning. This allows you to understand the main ideas without having to read word for word. When you skim a text, look at its title and subtitles and read the first sentence of each paragraph.

Examinez le texte

Regardez rapidement le texte. Quel est le titre (*title*) du texte? En combien de parties le texte est-il divisé? Quels sont les titres des parties? Maintenant, regardez les photos. Quel est le sujet de l'article?

Catégories

Dans le texte, trouvez trois mots ou expressions qui représentent chaque catégorie. Answers will vary. Suggested answers below.

les loisirs culturels
musique classique ______ cinéma africain ______ musée des Beaux-Arts ______

les activités sportives
golf ______ ski ______ tennis ______

les activités de plein air (*outdoor*)
camping ______ randonnées ______ équitation ______

Trouvez

Regardez le document. Indiquez si vous trouvez ces informations.

______ 1. où manger cette semaine
______ 2. le temps qu'il va faire cette semaine
__✓__ 3. où aller à la pêche
______ 4. des prix d'entrée (*entrance*)
__✓__ 5. des numéros de téléphone
__✓__ 6. des sports
__✓__ 7. des spectacles
______ 8. des adresses

CETTE SEMAINE À MONTRÉAL ET DANS LA RÉGION

ARTS ET CULTURE

Festivals et autres manifestations culturelles à explorer:

- Festival de musique classique, samedi de 16h00 à 22h00, à la Salle de concerts Richelieu, à Montréal
- Festival du cinéma africain, dans tous les cinémas de Montréal
- Journée de la bande dessinée, samedi toute la journée, à la Librairie Rochefort, à Montréal
- Festival de reggae, dimanche tout l'après-midi, à l'Espace Lemay, à Montréal

Spectacle à voir°

- *La Cantatrice chauve*, pièce° d'Eugène Ionesco, samedi et dimanche à 20h00, au Théâtre du Chat Bleu, à Montréal

À ne pas oublier°

- Le musée des Beaux-Arts de Montréal, avec sa collection de plus de° 30.000 objets d'art du monde entier°

OPTIONS

TPR Write activities from the calendar of events (**aller à la pêche, jouer au baseball, faire de l'équitation,** etc.) on slips of paper. Divide the class into two teams. Have a member of one team draw a paper. That team member mimes the chosen activity. The other team guesses what it is. Give points for correct answers. The team with the most points wins.

Small Groups Have groups of three students work together to read aloud each section of the calendar of events (**Arts et culture, Sports et jeux, Exploration**). Each student will then write two questions about the section that he or she read. After they have finished, ask groups to exchange their questions with another group. Have groups read the questions to the class and ask volunteers to answer them.

SPORTS ET JEUX

- L'Académie de golf de Montréal organise un grand tournoi° le mois prochain. Pour plus d'informations, contactez le (514) 846-1225.
- Tous les dimanches, le Club d'échecs de Montréal organise des tournois d'échecs en plein air° dans le parc Champellier. Pour plus d'informations, appelez le (514) 846-1085.
- Skiez! Passez la fin de semaine dans les Laurentides° ou dans les Cantons-de-l'Est!
- Et pour la famille sportive: essayez le parc Lafontaine, un centre d'amusement pour tous qui offre: volley-ball, tennis, football et baseball.

PASSIONNÉ° DE PÊCHE?
N'OUBLIEZ PAS LES NOMBREUX
LACS° OÙ LA PÊCHE EST AUTORISÉE.

EXPLORATION

Redécouvrez la nature grâce à° ces activités à ne pas manquer°:

Visite du parc national de la Jacques-Cartier°
- Camping
- Promenades et randonnées
- Observation de la faune et de la flore

Région des Laurentides et Gaspésie°
- Équitation°
- Randonnées à cheval de 2 à 5 jours en camping

voir *see* **pièce (de théâtre)** *play* **À ne pas oublier** *Not to be forgotten* **plus de** *more than* **du monde entier** *from around the world* **tournoi** *tournament* **en plein air** *outdoor* **Laurentides** *region of eastern Quebec* **Passionné** *Enthusiast* **lacs** *lakes* **grâce à** *thanks to* **à ne pas manquer** *not to be missed* **la Jacques-Cartier** *the Jacques-Cartier river in Quebec* **Gaspésie** *peninsula of Quebec* **Équitation** *Horseback riding*

Après la lecture

Répondez Répondez aux questions avec des phrases complètes.

1. Citez deux activités sportives qu'on peut pratiquer à l'extérieur.
   Answers will vary.
2. À quel jeu est-ce qu'on joue dans le parc Champellier?
   On joue aux échecs dans le parc Champellier.
3. Où va peut-être aller un passionné de lecture et de dessin?
   Un passionné de lecture et de dessin va peut-être aller à la Journée de la bande dessinée.
4. Où pratique-t-on des sports d'équipe?
   On pratique des sports d'équipe au parc Lafontaine.
5. Où y a-t-il de la neige au Québec en cette saison?
   Il y a de la neige dans les Laurentides et dans les Cantons-de-l'Est.
6. Si on aime beaucoup la musique, où peut-on aller?
   On peut aller au Festival de musique classique ou au Festival de reggae.

Suggestions **Lucille est étudiante au Québec. Ce week-end, elle invite sa famille à explorer la région. Choisissez une activité à faire ou un lieu à visiter que chaque membre de sa famille va aimer.**

MODÈLE

La sœur cadette de Lucille adore le ski.
Elle va aimer les Laurentides et les Cantons-de-l'Est.

1. La mère de Lucille est artiste.
   Elle va aimer le musée des Beaux-Arts de Montréal.
2. Le frère de Lucille joue au volley-ball à l'université.
   Il va aimer le parc Lafontaine.
3. La sœur aînée de Lucille a envie de voir un film sénégalais.
   Elle va aimer le Festival du cinéma africain.
4. Le grand-père de Lucille joue souvent aux échecs.
   Il va aimer les tournois d'échecs en plein air dans le parc Champellier.
5. La grand-mère de Lucille est fan de théâtre.
   Elle va aimer *La Cantatrice chauve* au Théâtre du Chat Bleu.
6. Le père de Lucille adore la nature et les animaux, mais il n'est pas très sportif.
   Answers will vary. Possible answer: Il va aimer les promenades dans le parc national de la Jacques-Cartier.

Une invitation **Vous allez passer le week-end au Québec. Qu'est-ce que vous allez faire? Par groupes de quatre, discutez des activités qui vous intéressent (*that interest you*) et essayez de trouver trois ou quatre activités que vous avez en commun. Attention! Il va peut-être pleuvoir ce week-end, alors ne choisissez pas (*don't choose*) uniquement des activités de plein air!**

Répondez Present these as items 7–10. **7. Où peut-on voir des films africains? (On peut voir des films africains dans tous les cinémas de Montréal.) 8. Combien d'objets d'art y a-t-il au musée des Beaux-Arts de Montréal? (Il y a plus de 30.000 objets d'art.) 9. Quels sports pratique-t-on au parc Lafontaine? (On propose le volley-ball, le tennis, le football et le baseball.) 10. Si on aime beaucoup les animaux et les fleurs, où peut-on aller? (On peut aller au parc national de la Jacques-Cartier.)**

Suggestions Ask students to write about three more members of Lucille's family. They should model their sentences after the ones in the activity, saying what each person enjoys doing. Then have students read their sentences to a partner. The partner will come up with a suggested activity or place to visit that will suit each person.

Une invitation Give students a couple of minutes to review the **Vocabulaire** on page 146, **Expressions utiles** on page 151, and Expressions with **faire** on page 154. Add activities, such as **faire du surf des neiges, prendre des photos, faire des arts martiaux**, and **faire du skateboard**.

Expansion Have one or two groups act out their conversation from **Une invitation** for the rest of the class. Before the groups begin, have the listeners in the class write a list of ten activities that they think will be mentioned in each of the presentations. As students listen, have them check off on their list the activities they hear.

OPTIONS

Extra Practice Give students true or false statements about the **Lecture.** Example: **On peut faire des randonnées à cheval au parc national de la Jacques-Cartier. (Faux. On peut faire des randonnées à cheval en Région des Laurentides et Gaspésie.)**

Extra Practice Ask students to go through the selection and locate all of the activities that require usage of **faire**. (Encourage them to use their dictionaries, if necessary.) Then have them write sentences saying whether or not they like doing those activities. Example: **Activités avec faire: faire du vélo, faire de l'équitation**, etc. **J'aime faire du vélo. Je n'aime pas faire de l'équitation.**

Section Goals
In this section, students will:
- learn to use a French-English dictionary
- write a brochure including weather-related information and seasonal activities

Stratégie Explain to students that when they look up a translation of an English word in a French-English dictionary, they will frequently find more than one translation. They must decide which one best fits the context. Discuss the meanings of *racket* that might be found in an entry in a French-English dictionary and the usefulness of the explanatory notes and abbreviations found in dictionary entries.

Thème Remind students of some of the common graphic features used in brochures: headings, times and places, brief descriptions of events, and prices.

Écriture

communication cultures NATIONAL STANDARDS

STRATÉGIE

Using a dictionary

A common mistake made by beginning language learners is to embrace the dictionary as the ultimate resource for reading, writing, and speaking. While it is true that the dictionary is a useful tool that can provide valuable information about vocabulary, using the dictionary correctly requires that you understand the elements of each entry.

If you glance at a French-English dictionary, you will notice that the format is similar to that of an English dictionary. The word is listed first, usually followed by its pronunciation. Then come the definitions, organized by parts of speech. Sometimes, the most frequently used meanings are listed first.

To find the best word for your needs, you should refer to the abbreviations and the explanatory notes that appear next to the entries. For example, imagine that you are writing about your pastimes. You want to write *I want to buy a new racket for my match tomorrow*, but you don't know the French word for *racket*.

In the dictionary, you might find an entry like this one:

racket n 1. boucan; 2. raquette (sport)

The abbreviation key at the front of the dictionary says that *n* corresponds to **nom** (*noun*). Then, the first word you see is **boucan**. The definition of **boucan** is *noise or racket,* so **boucan** is probably not the word you want. The second word is **raquette**, followed by the word *sport*, which indicates that it is related to **sports**. This detail indicates that the word **raquette** is the best choice for your needs.

Thème

Écrire une brochure

Avant l'écriture

1. Choisissez le sujet de votre brochure:

   A. Vous travaillez à la Chambre de Commerce de votre région pour l'été. Des hommes et des femmes d'affaires québécois vont visiter votre région cette année, mais ils n'ont pas encore décidé (*have not yet decided*) quand. La Chambre de Commerce vous demande de créer (*asks you to create*) une petite brochure sur le temps qu'il fait dans votre région aux différentes saisons de l'année. Dites quelle saison, à votre avis (*in your opinion*), est idéale pour visiter votre région et expliquez pourquoi.

   B. Vous avez une réunion familiale pour décider où aller en vacances cette année, mais chaque membre de la famille suggère un endroit différent. Choisissez un lieu de vacances où vous avez envie d'aller et créez une brochure pour montrer à votre famille pourquoi vous devriez (*should*) tous y aller (*go there*). Décrivez la météo de l'endroit et indiquez les différentes activités culturelles et sportives qu'on peut y faire.

   C. Vous passez un semestre/trimestre dans le pays francophone de votre choix (*of your choice*). Deux étudiants de votre cours de français ont aussi envie de visiter ce pays. Créez une petite brochure pour partager vos impressions du pays. Présentez le pays, donnez des informations météorologiques et décrivez vos activités préférées.

OPTIONS

Avant l'écriture Reinforce to students that when they look up a word in a French-English dictionary, not all of the translations listed will have the same meaning. Tell them that a good way to check a possible translation of an English word is to look up the French word and see how it is translated back into English.

Discuss the three topics students may wish to write about. Introduce terms such as **comité**, **guide d'orientation**, and **chambre de commerce**. Evaluate the level of formality of each of the brochures described. (The chamber of commerce brochure will be more formal than the family and student brochures.) Remind students to keep this in mind when they create their brochures.

2. Choisissez le sujet de votre brochure et pensez au vocabulaire utile à son écriture. Utilisez le tableau (*chart*) pour noter tous les mots (*words*) en français qui vous viennent à l'esprit (*you can think of*). Ensuite (*Then*), revoyez (*review*) la liste de vocabulaire des unités 1–4 et ajoutez (*add*) le vocabulaire utile pour le sujet. Enfin (*Finally*), regardez votre tableau. Quels sont les mots en anglais que vous pourriez (*could*) ajouter? Créez une nouvelle liste et cherchez les mots dans un dictionnaire.

Mots en français (de moi)	*Mots en français (des listes)*	*Mots en anglais*
		anglais / français:

3. Cherchez les mots dans le dictionnaire. N'oubliez pas d'utiliser la procédure de **Stratégie**.

Écriture

Utilisez le vocabulaire du tableau pour créer votre brochure. N'oubliez pas de penser à un titre (*title*). Ensuite, créez des sections et donnez-leur (*them*) aussi un titre, comme **Printemps, Été, ...; Ville, Campagne (Countryside), ...; France, Tunisie, ...** Vous pouvez (*can*) utiliser des photos pour illustrer.

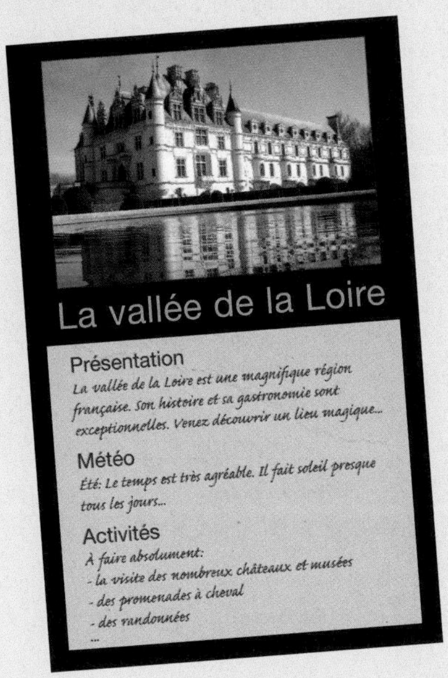

Après l'écriture

1. Échangez votre brochure avec celle (*the one*) d'un(e) partenaire. Répondez à ces questions pour commenter son travail.
   - Votre partenaire a-t-il/elle couvert (*did cover*) le sujet?
   - A-t-il/elle donné (*did give*) un titre à la brochure et aux sections?
   - S'il (*If there*) y a des photos, illustrent-elles le texte?
   - Votre partenaire a-t-il/elle utilisé (*did use*) le vocabulaire approprié?
   - A-t-il/elle correctement conjugué (*did conjugate*) les verbes?

2. Corrigez votre brochure d'après (*according to*) les commentaires de votre partenaire. Relisez votre travail pour éliminer ces problèmes:
   - des fautes (*errors*) d'orthographe
   - des fautes de ponctuation
   - des fautes de conjugaison
   - des fautes d'accord (*agreement*) des adjectifs
   - un mauvais emploi (*use*) de la grammaire

EVALUATION

Criteria

Content Contains all the information included in the subject description the student chose.
Scale: 1 2 3 4 5

Organization Follows a typical brochure organization with a major head, text, and at least one visual.
Scale: 1 2 3 4 5

Accuracy Uses possessive and descriptive adjectives and modifies them accordingly. Spells words and conjugates verbs correctly throughout.
Scale: 1 2 3 4 5

Creativity The student includes additional information that is not included in the task, adds extra features to the brochure such as bulleted lists and boxed text, and/or spends extra time on design and presentation.
Scale: 1 2 3 4 5

Scoring

Excellent	18–20 points
Good	14–17 points
Satisfactory	10–13 points
Unsatisfactory	< 10 points

OPTIONS

Avant l'écriture Group students who have chosen to work on the same brochures and encourage them to share their ideas and personalized vocabulary from step 2 before they begin writing. As a group, have them brainstorm additional vocabulary they may need to look up before they begin writing.

Before students begin writing, have the class discuss some of the features that are typically found in brochures, such as headings, schedules, lists, boxed/highlighted text, photos, graphics, and other visuals. Bring in some brochures for students to analyze before they create their own.

Instructional Resources
espaces.vhlcentral.com: Textbook MP3s; IRM (Textbook Audioscript); downloads; reference tools

Suggestion Tell students that an easy way to study from **Vocabulaire** is to cover up the French half of each section, leaving only the English equivalents exposed. They can then quiz themselves on the French items. To focus on the English equivalents of the French entries, they simply reverse this process.

VOCABULAIRE

Activités sportives et loisirs

aider	*to help*
aller à la pêche	*to go fishing*
bricoler	*to tinker; to do odd jobs*
chanter	*to sing*
désirer	*to want*
gagner	*to win*
indiquer	*to indicate*
jouer (à/de)	*to play*
marcher	*to walk (person); to work (thing)*
pratiquer	*to play regularly, to practice*
skier	*to ski*
une bande dessinée (B.D.)	*comic strip*
le baseball	*baseball*
le basket(-ball)	*basketball*
les cartes (*f.*)	*cards*
le cinéma	*movies*
les échecs (*m.*)	*chess*
une équipe	*team*
le foot(ball)	*soccer*
le football américain	*football*
le golf	*golf*
un jeu	*game*
un joueur/une joueuse	*player*
un loisir	*leisure activity*
un match	*game*
un passe-temps	*pastime, hobby*
un spectacle	*show*
le sport	*sport*
un stade	*stadium*
le temps libre	*free time*
le tennis	*tennis*
le volley(-ball)	*volleyball*

Verbes irréguliers en -ir

courir	*to run*
dormir	*to sleep*
partir	*to leave*
sentir	*to feel; to smell; to sense*
servir	*to serve*
sortir	*to go out, to leave*

Le temps qu'il fait

Il fait 18 degrés.	*It is 18 degrees.*
Il fait beau.	*The weather is nice.*
Il fait bon.	*The weather is good/warm.*
Il fait chaud.	*It is hot (out).*
Il fait (du) soleil.	*It is sunny.*
Il fait du vent.	*It is windy.*
Il fait frais.	*It is cool.*
Il fait froid.	*It is cold.*
Il fait mauvais.	*The weather is bad.*
Il fait un temps épouvantable.	*The weather is dreadful.*
Il neige. (neiger)	*It is snowing. (to snow)*
Il pleut. (pleuvoir)	*It is raining. (to rain)*
Le temps est nuageux.	*It is cloudy.*
Le temps est orageux.	*It is stormy.*
Quel temps fait-il?	*What is the weather like?*
Quelle température fait-il?	*What is the temperature?*
un imperméable	*rain jacket*
un parapluie	*umbrella*

Verbes

acheter	*to buy*
amener	*to bring (someone)*
célébrer	*to celebrate*
considérer	*to consider*
emmener	*to take (someone)*
employer	*to use; to employ*
envoyer	*to send*
espérer	*to hope*
essayer (de + *inf.*)	*to try (to)*
nettoyer	*to clean*
payer	*to pay*
posséder	*to possess, to own*
préférer	*to prefer*
protéger	*to protect*
répéter	*to repeat; to rehearse*

La fréquence

une/deux fois par jour, semaine, mois, an, etc.	*one/two time(s) per day, week, month, year, etc.*
déjà	*already*
encore	*again, still*
jamais	*never*
longtemps	*long time*
maintenant	*now*
parfois	*sometimes*
rarement	*rarely*
souvent	*often*

Les saisons, les mois, les dates

une saison	*season*
l'automne (*m.*)/en automne	*fall/in the fall*
l'été (*m.*)/en été	*summer/in the summer*
l'hiver (*m.*)/en hiver	*winter/in the winter*
le printemps (*m.*)/au printemps	*spring/in the spring*
Quelle est la date?	*What's the date?*
C'est le 1er (premier) octobre.	*It's the first of October.*
C'est quand votre/ton anniversaire?	*When is your birthday?*
C'est le 2 mai.	*It's the second of May.*
C'est quand l'anniversaire de Paul?	*When is Paul's birthday?*
C'est le 15 mars.	*It's March 15th.*
un anniversaire	*birthday*
janvier	*January*
février	*February*
mars	*March*
avril	*April*
mai	*May*
juin	*June*
juillet	*July*
août	*August*
septembre	*September*
octobre	*October*
novembre	*November*
décembre	*December*

Expressions utiles	*See pp. 151 and 165.*
Expressions with *faire*	*See p. 154.*
faire	*See p. 154.*
Il faut...	*See p. 155.*
Numbers 101 and higher	*See p. 168.*

ressources
espaces.vhlcentral.com

Les fêtes

UNITÉ 6

Pour commencer

- Qui est l'invitée sur la photo?
- Qu'est-ce qu'Amina et Valérie vont faire?
- Qu'est-ce qu'elles vont manger? Du pain ou une mousse au chocolat?
- De quelle couleur est le tee-shirt d'Amina? Orange ou violet?

Unit Goals

Leçon 6A

In this lesson, students will learn:
- terms for parties and celebrations
- terms for the stages of life
- more differences between open and closed vowels
- about **carnaval** and France's Bastille Day
- more about festivals and holiday celebrations through specially shot video footage
- demonstrative adjectives
- the **passé composé** with **avoir**
- some irregular past participles
- about the Belgian postal service

Leçon 6B

In this lesson, students will learn:
- terms for clothing, shopping, and colors
- more about open and closed vowels
- about the fashion industry in France
- indirect object pronouns
- more uses of disjunctive pronouns
- regular and irregular **-re** verbs
- to listen for linguistic cues in oral communication

Savoir-faire

In this section, students will learn:
- cultural and historical information about the French regions of **Aquitaine**, **Midi-Pyrénées**, and **Languedoc-Roussillon**
- to recognize word families
- how to report an interview

Pour commencer

- **Amina est l'invitée.**
- **Elles vont faire la fête.**
- **Elles vont manger une mousse au chocolat.**
- **Son tee-shirt est orange.**

RESOURCES

Workbook/Video Manual: WB Activities, pp. 71–84
Laboratory Manual: Lab Activities, pp. 41–48
Workbook/Video Manual: Video Activities, pp. 231–234; pp. 281–282
WB/VM/LM Answer Key
espaces.vhlcentral.com: Textbook MP3s; Lab MP3s; Instructor's Resource Manual [IRM] (Textbook Audioscript; Lab Audioscript; Videoscript; **Roman-photo** Translations; **Vocabulaire supplémentaire**; **Feuilles d'activités**; Info Gap Activities; **Essayez!** and **Mise en pratique** answers); Transparencies #31, #32, #33; Testing Program, pp. 41–48; pp. 129–136; Test Files; Testing Program MP3s
Test Generator
Video on DVD

Section Goals

In this section, students will learn and practice vocabulary related to:
- parties and celebrations
- stages of life and interpersonal relationships

Instructional Resources
*espaces.vhlcentral.com: Transparency #31; IRM (**Vocabulaire supplémentaire; Mise en pratique** answers; Textbook Audioscript; Lab Audioscript; Info Gap Activities); Textbook MP3s; Lab MP3s; WB/VM/LM Answer Key; activities; downloads; reference tools*

Suggestions
- Have students look over the new vocabulary and identify the cognates. Examples: **organiser, fiancé(e), mariage,** and **divorce.**
- Describe what people are doing in the drawing using **Transparency #31.** Examples: **Ils font la fête. Ils boivent du champagne.** Follow up with simple questions based on your narrative.
- Point out the banner and the cake in the illustration. Ask students what **Bon anniversaire** and **Joyeux anniversaire** mean. (*Happy birthday*)
- Point out the similarities and differences between these related words: **aimer, ami(e), l'amitié, un amour, amoureux,** and **amoureuse.**
- Additional vocabulary for this lesson can be found in the **Vocabulaire supplémentaire** on the Supersite.

Leçon 6A

You will learn how to...
- talk about celebrations
- talk about the stages of life

Talking Picture
Audio: Activity

Surprise!

Vocabulaire

faire la fête	*to party*
faire une surprise (à quelqu'un)	*to surprise (someone)*
fêter	*to celebrate*
organiser une fête	*to organize a party*
une fête	*party; celebration*
un jour férié	*holiday*
une bière	*beer*
le vin	*wine*
l'amitié	*friendship*
l'amour	*love*
le bonheur	*happiness*
un(e) fiancé(e)	*fiancé*
des jeunes mariés (m.)	*newlyweds*
un rendez-vous	*date; appointment*
l'adolescence (f.)	*adolescence*
l'âge adulte (m.)	*adulthood*
un divorce	*divorce*
l'enfance (f.)	*childhood*
une étape	*stage*
l'état civil (m.)	*marital status*
la jeunesse	*youth*
un mariage	*marriage; wedding*
la mort	*death*
la naissance	*birth*
la vie	*life*
la vieillesse	*old age*
prendre sa retraite	*to retire*
tomber amoureux/amoureuse	*to fall in love*
ensemble	*together*

ressources
WB pp. 71–72 | LM p. 41 | espaces.vhlcentral.com

OPTIONS

Les fêtes Point out that, in addition to celebrating birthdays, many people in French-speaking cultures celebrate **la fête**, or saint's day, which is based upon their given name. Bring in a French calendar that has the names of **fêtes** and have students find their own saint's day. You may need to help students find the name that most closely resembles their own.

Extra Practice Have students write three fill-in-the-blank sentences based on the drawing above, using the new vocabulary. Then have each student exchange papers with a classmate and complete the sentences. Remind them to verify their answers.

Mise en pratique

1 Chassez l'intrus **Indiquez le mot ou l'expression qui n'appartient pas (*doesn't belong*) à la liste.**

1. l'amour, tomber amoureux, un fiancé, un divorce
2. un mariage, un couple, un jour férié, un fiancé
3. un biscuit, une bière, un dessert, un gâteau
4. une glace, une bière, le champagne, le vin
5. la vieillesse, la naissance, l'enfance, la jeunesse
6. faire la fête, un hôte, des invités, une étape
7. fêter, un cadeau, la vie, une surprise
8. l'état civil, la naissance, la mort, l'adolescence

2 Écoutez **Écoutez la conversation entre Anne et Nathalie. Indiquez si les affirmations sont vraies ou fausses.**

	Vrai	Faux
1. Jean-Marc va prendre sa retraite dans six mois.	☐	☑
2. Nathalie a l'idée d'organiser une fête pour Jean-Marc.	☐	☑
3. Anne va acheter un gâteau.	☑	☐
4. Nathalie va apporter de la glace.	☐	☑
5. La fête est une surprise.	☑	☐
6. Nathalie va envoyer les invitations par e-mail.	☑	☐
7. La fête va avoir lieu (*take place*) dans le bureau d'Anne.	☐	☑
8. La maison d'Anne n'est pas belle.	☐	☑
9. Tout le monde va donner des idées pour le cadeau.	☑	☐
10. Les invités vont acheter le cadeau.	☐	☑

3 Associez **Faites correspondre les mots et expressions de la colonne de gauche avec les définitions de la colonne de droite. Notez que tous les éléments ne sont pas utilisés. Ensuite (*Then*), avec un(e) partenaire, donnez votre propre définition de quatre expressions de la première colonne. Votre partenaire doit deviner (*must guess*) de quoi vous parlez.**

b 1. la naissance
... 2. l'enfance
c 3. l'adolescence
... 4. l'âge adulte
e 5. tomber amoureux
a 6. un jour férié
g 7. le mariage
f 8. le divorce
h 9. prendre sa retraite
d 10. la mort

a. C'est une date importante, comme le 4 juillet aux États-Unis.
b. C'est la fin de l'étape prénatale.
c. C'est l'étape de la vie pendant laquelle (*during which*) on va au lycée.
d. C'est un événement très triste.
e. C'est soudain (*suddenly*) aimer une personne.
f. C'est le futur probable d'un couple qui se dispute (*fights*) tout le temps.
g. C'est un jour de bonheur et de célébration de l'amour.
h. C'est quand une personne décide de ne plus travailler.

Practice more at **espaces.vhlcentral.com.**

1 Expansions
- For additional practice, give students these items. **9. la vieillesse, la jeunesse, la fête, l'âge adulte (la fête) 10. l'amour, le bonheur, l'amitié, la retraite (la retraite)**
- Have students create one or two additional items using at least three of the new vocabulary words in each one. Collect their papers and write some of the items on the board.

2 Tapescript ANNE: Nathalie, je vais organiser une fête pour Jean-Marc. Il va prendre sa retraite dans un mois. Ça va être une surprise. Je vais acheter un gâteau.
NATHALIE: Oh, et moi, qu'est-ce que je fais pour aider, Anne? J'apporte des biscuits?
A: Oui, c'est une bonne idée. Il faut aussi trouver un cadeau original.
N: D'accord, mais je vais avoir besoin d'un peu de temps pour y penser.
A: Qu'est-ce qu'on fait pour les invités?
N: Pour faire une vraie surprise à Jean-Marc, il faut être discrètes. Je propose d'envoyer un e-mail à tout le monde. En plus, comme ça, c'est rapide.
A: Et qu'est-ce qu'on fait pour la décoration?
N: Pourquoi ne pas fêter sa retraite chez toi? Ta maison est belle, et on n'a pas besoin de beaucoup de décoration.
A: Oui, pourquoi pas! Maintenant, il ne reste plus qu'à trouver un cadeau. Pourquoi est-ce qu'on ne demande pas aux autres de donner des idées par e-mail?
N: Oui, et quel beau cadeau pour Jean-Marc si tout le monde participe et donne un peu d'argent!
(On Textbook MP3s)

2 Suggestion Play the conversation again, stopping at the end of each sentence that contains the answer to one of these items. Have students verify true statements and correct the false ones.

3 Suggestion Have volunteers share their definitions with the class.

OPTIONS

Game Write vocabulary words related to celebrations on index cards. On another set of cards, draw or paste pictures to match each term. Tape them face down on the board in random order. Divide the class into two teams. Then play a game of concentration, matching words with pictures. When a player has a match, his/her team collects those cards. When all the cards have been matched, the team with the most cards wins.

Extra Practice Say vocabulary words aloud and have students write or say opposite terms. Examples: **la jeunesse (la vieillesse), le divorce (le mariage), la naissance (la mort), séparé (ensemble),** and **enfant (adulte).**

4 Suggestions
- Go over the answers to the activity with the class before students write their own sentences.
- Ask volunteers to write their sentences on the board and have the class make corrections as needed.

5 Suggestion Have two volunteers read the **modèle** aloud. Then divide the class into pairs and distribute the Info Gap Handouts found on the Supersite for this activity. Give students ten minutes to complete the activity.

6 Suggestion Tell students that they should plan the party first by answering the questions. Then they should use those answers to write the conversation discussing the details of the party.

Communication

4 Le mot juste **Complétez les phrases par le mot illustré. Faites les accords nécessaires. Ensuite (*Then*), avec un(e) partenaire, créez (*create*) une phrase pour laquelle (*for which*) vous illustrez trois mots d'ESPACE CONTEXTES. Échangez votre phrase avec celle d'un autre groupe et résolvez le rébus.**

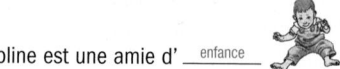

1. Caroline est une amie d' enfance . Je vais lui faire une surprise  samedi. C'est son anniversaire.
2. Marc et Sophie sont inséparables. Ils sont toujours ensemble . C'est le bonheur et le grand amour .
3. Le vin  rouge va bien avec les viandes rouges, alors que le champagne  va mieux (*goes better*) avec les desserts .
4. Les (jeunes) mariés  ont beaucoup de cadeaux .
5. La naissance  de ma sœur est un grand bonheur  pour mes parents.

5 Sept différences **Votre professeur va vous donner, à vous et à votre partenaire, deux feuilles d'activités différentes. À tour de rôle, posez-vous des questions pour trouver les sept différences entre les illustrations de l'anniversaire des jumeaux (*twins*) Boniface. Attention! Ne regardez pas la feuille de votre partenaire.**

MODÈLE

Étudiant(e) 1: *Sur mon image, il y a trois cadeaux. Combien de cadeaux y a-t-il sur ton image?*
Étudiant(e) 2: *Sur mon image, il y a quatre cadeaux.*

6 C'est la fête! **Vous avez terminé (*have finished*) les examens de fin d'année et vous allez organiser une fête! Avec un(e) partenaire, écrivez une conversation au sujet de la préparation de cette fête. N'oubliez pas de répondre aux questions suivantes. Ensuite (*Then*), jouez (*act out*) votre dialogue devant la classe.** Answers will vary.

1. Quand allez-vous organiser la fête?
2. Qui vont être les invités?
3. Où la fête va-t-elle avoir lieu (*take place*)?
4. Qu'allez-vous manger? Qu'allez-vous boire?
5. Qui va apporter quoi?
6. Qui est responsable de la musique? De la décoration?
7. Qu'allez-vous faire pendant (*during*) la fête?
8. Qui va nettoyer après la fête?

OPTIONS

Small Groups In groups of three or four, have students plan and perform a skit in which they depict a particular stage of life (youth, old age, etc.) or marital status (engaged, single, divorced). The rest of the class tries to guess which stage of life or marital status the skit represents.

Pairs Have students write four or five true/false statements based on the illustration on pages 182–183. Then have them get together with a partner and take turns saying their statements and responding **C'est vrai** or **C'est faux.** Call on volunteers to correct the false statements, pointing out the changes on **Transparency #31**.

Les sons et les lettres

S Audio: Concepts, Activities Record & Compare

NATIONAL STANDARDS comparisons

Open vs. closed vowels: Part 2

The letter combinations **au** and **eau** are pronounced like the vowel sound in the English word *coat*, but without the glide heard in English. These are closed **o** sounds.

chaud	**aussi**	**beaucoup**	**tableau**

When the letter **o** is followed by a consonant sound, it is usually pronounced like the vowel in the English word *raw*. This is an open **o** sound.

homme	**téléphone**	**ordinateur**	**orange**

When the letter **o** occurs as the last sound of a word or is followed by a *z* sound, such as a single **s** between two vowels, it is usually pronounced with the closed **o** sound.

trop	**héros**	**rose**	**chose**

When the letter **o** has an **accent circonflexe**, it is usually pronounced with the closed **o** sound.

drôle	**bientôt**	**pôle**	**côté**

Prononcez Répétez les mots suivants à voix haute.

1. rôle
2. porte
3. dos
4. chaud
5. prose
6. gros
7. oiseau
8. encore
9. mauvais
10. nouveau
11. restaurant
12. bibliothèque

Articulez Répétez les phrases suivantes à voix haute.

1. En automne, on n'a pas trop chaud.
2. Aurélie a une bonne note en biologie.
3. Votre colocataire est d'origine japonaise?
4. Sophie aime beaucoup l'informatique et la psychologie.
5. Nos copains mangent au restaurant marocain aujourd'hui.
6. Comme cadeau, Robert et Corinne vont préparer un gâteau.

Dictons Répétez les dictons à voix haute.

La fortune vient en dormant.[2]

Tout nouveau, tout beau.[1]

[1] Shiny and new.
[2] Fortune comes while you sleep.

ressources
LM p. 42
espaces.vhlcentral.com

Section Goals

In this section, students will learn more about open and closed vowels.

Instructional Resources
espaces.vhlcentral.com: Textbook MP3s; Lab MP3s; WB/VM/LM Answer Key; IRM (Textbook Audioscript; Lab Audioscript); activities; downloads; reference tools

Suggestions

- Model the pronunciation of each open and closed vowel sound. Have students watch the shape of your mouth, then repeat the sound after you. Pronounce each of the example words and have students repeat them.
- Remind students that **o** is sometimes nasalized when followed by a single **m** or **n**. Compare the following words: **bon, nom**, and **bonne, homme**.
- Ask students to provide more examples of words from this lesson or previous lessons with these vowel sounds. Examples: **cadeau, gâteau, hôte, octobre,** and **beau**.
- Dictate five familiar words containing the open and closed vowels presented here, repeating each one at least two times. Then write them on the board or on a transparency and have students check their spelling.

Dictons Ask students if they can think of sayings in English that are similar to **«La fortune vient en dormant.»** (*Good things come to those who wait. Patience is a virtue.*)

OPTIONS

Extra Practice Use these sentences with open and closed vowel sounds for additional practice or dictation. **1. Octobre est en automne. 2. Est-ce qu'il fait mauvais aujourd'hui? 3. En août, il fait beau, mais il fait chaud. 4. Aurélie est aussi drôle que Paul.**

Extra Practice Teach students this French tongue-twister that contains a variety of vowel sounds. **Paul se pèle au pôle dans sa pile de pulls et polos pâles. Pas plus d'appel de la poule à l'Opel que d'opale dans la pelle à Paul.**

Section Goals

In this section, students will learn functional phrases for talking about the past and celebrations through comprehensible input.

Instructional Resources
*espaces.vhlcentral.com: Video; WB/VM/LM Answer Key; IRM (Videoscript; **Roman-photo** Translations); activities; downloads; reference tools*
Video on DVD

Video Recap: Leçon 5B Before doing this **Roman-photo**, review the previous one with this true/false activity.

1. Rachid aime boire de l'eau. (Vrai.)
2. L'anniversaire de Stéphane est le 15 janvier. (Faux.)
3. Sandrine déteste la pluie. (Vrai.)
4. Stéphane va avoir 18 ans. (Vrai.)
5. Rachid n'aime pas le portrait de Sandrine. (Faux.)

Video Synopsis Sandrine tells Pascal about her preparations for Stéphane's party. Valérie arrives and offers to help Sandrine carry the desserts to **Le P'tit Bistrot**. Meanwhile, Astrid and Rachid are shopping for birthday gifts. They buy gag gifts and a watch. At the café, Astrid helps Valérie with decorations while Rachid goes to get Stéphane. Amina is in a good mood because her parents are coming to visit.

Suggestions
- Ask students to read the title, glance at the video stills, and predict what they think the episode will be about. Record their predictions.
- Have students scan the video-still captions and find sentences with words or expressions related to party preparations. Have volunteers read their phrases.
- After reading the **Roman-photo**, review their predictions and ask which ones were correct.

Les cadeaux

Video: *Roman-photo*
Record & Compare

PERSONNAGES

Amina

Astrid

Rachid

Sandrine

Valérie

Vendeuse

1

À l'appartement de Sandrine...

SANDRINE Allô, Pascal? Tu m'as téléphoné? Écoute, je suis très occupée, là. Je prépare un gâteau d'anniversaire pour Stéphane... Il a dix-huit ans aujourd'hui... On organise une fête surprise au P'tit Bistrot.

2

SANDRINE J'ai fait une mousse au chocolat, comme pour ton anniversaire. Stéphane adore ça! J'ai aussi préparé des biscuits que David aime bien.

3

SANDRINE Quoi? David!... Mais non, il n'est pas marié. C'est un bon copain, c'est tout!... Désolée, je n'ai pas le temps de discuter. À bientôt.

6

RACHID Écoute, Astrid. Il faut trouver un cadeau... un *vrai* cadeau d'anniversaire.
ASTRID Excusez-moi, Madame. Combien coûte cette montre, s'il vous plaît?
VENDEUSE Quarante euros.
ASTRID Que penses-tu de cette montre, Rachid?
RACHID Bonne idée.

7

VENDEUSE Je fais un paquet cadeau?
ASTRID Oui, merci.
RACHID Eh, Astrid, il faut y aller!
VENDEUSE Et voilà dix euros. Merci, Mademoiselle, bonne fin de journée.

8

Au café...

VALÉRIE Ah, vous voilà! Astrid, aide-nous avec les décorations, s'il te plaît. La fête commence à six heures. Sandrine a tout préparé.
ASTRID Quelle heure est-il? Zut, déjà? En tout cas, on a trouvé des cadeaux.
RACHID Je vais chercher Stéphane.

ACTIVITÉS

1 Vrai ou faux? Indiquez si ces (*these*) affirmations sont vraies ou fausses. Corrigez les phrases fausses.

1. Sandrine prépare un gâteau d'anniversaire pour Stéphane. Vrai.
2. Sandrine est désolée parce qu'elle n'a pas le temps de discuter avec Rachid. Faux. Elle n'a pas le temps de discuter avec Pascal.
3. Rachid ne comprend pas la blague. Vrai.
4. Pour aider Sandrine, Valérie va apporter les desserts. Vrai.
5. Rachid et Astrid trouvent un cadeau pour Valérie. Faux. Ils trouvent un cadeau pour Stéphane.
6. Rachid n'aime pas l'idée de la montre pour Stéphane. Faux. Rachid aime l'idée de la montre pour Stéphane.
7. La fête d'anniversaire pour Stéphane commence à huit heures. Faux. Elle commence à six heures.
8. Sandrine va chercher Stéphane. Faux. Rachid va chercher Stéphane.
9. Amina a apporté de la glace au chocolat. Vrai.
10. Les parents d'Amina vont passer l'été à Aix-en-Provence. Vrai.

Practice more at **espaces.vhlcentral.com.**

OPTIONS

Avant de regarder la vidéo Before viewing the video, have students brainstorm a list of words or expressions that someone might say when preparing for a party and discussing gifts. Write their ideas on the board.

Regarder la vidéo Show the video in three parts, pausing the video before each location change. Have students describe what happens in each place. Write their observations on the board. Then show the entire episode again without pausing and have the class fill in any missing details to summarize the plot.

Tout le monde prépare la surprise pour Stéphane.

4

VALÉRIE Oh là là! Tu as fait tout ça pour Stéphane?!
SANDRINE Oh, ce n'est pas grand-chose.
VALÉRIE Tu es un ange! Stéphane va bientôt arriver. Je t'aide à apporter ces desserts?
SANDRINE Oh, merci, c'est gentil.

5

Dans un magasin...
ASTRID Eh Rachid, j'ai eu une idée géniale... Des cadeaux parfaits pour Stéphane. Regarde! Ce matin, j'ai acheté cette calculatrice et ces livres.
RACHID Mais enfin, Astrid, Stéphane n'aime pas les livres.
ASTRID Oh, Rachid, tu ne comprends rien. C'est une blague.

9

AMINA Bonjour! Désolée, je suis en retard!
VALÉRIE Ce n'est pas grave. Tu es toute belle ce soir!

10

AMINA Vous trouvez? J'ai acheté ce cadeau pour Stéphane. Et j'ai apporté de la glace au chocolat aussi.
VALÉRIE Oh, merci! Il faut aider Astrid avec les décorations.
ASTRID Salut, Amina. Ça va?
AMINA Oui, super. Mes parents ont téléphoné du Sénégal ce matin! Ils vont passer l'été ici. C'est le bonheur!

Expressions utiles

Talking about celebrations

- **J'ai fait une mousse au chocolat, comme pour ton anniversaire.**
  I made a chocolate mousse, (just) like for your birthday.
- **J'ai aussi préparé des biscuits que David aime bien.**
  I have also prepared some cookies that David likes.
- **Je fais un paquet cadeau?**
  Shall I wrap the present?
- **En tout cas, on a trouvé des cadeaux.**
  In any case, we have found some presents.
- **Et j'ai apporté de la glace au chocolat.**
  And I brought some chocolate ice cream.

Talking about the past

- **Tu m'as téléphoné?**
  Did you call me?
- **Tu as fait tout ça pour Stéphane?!**
  You did all that for Stéphane?!
- **J'ai eu une idée géniale.**
  I had a great idea.
- **Sandrine a tout préparé.**
  Sandrine prepared everything.

Pointing out things

- **Je t'aide à apporter ces desserts?**
  Can I help you to carry these desserts?
- **J'ai acheté cette calculatrice et ces livres.**
  I bought this calculator and these books.
- **J'ai acheté ce cadeau pour Stéphane.**
  I bought this present for Stéphane.

Additional vocabulary

- **Ce n'est pas grave.**
  It's okay./No problem.
- **Tu ne comprends rien.**
  You don't understand a thing.
- **désolé(e)**
  sorry
- **discuter**
  to talk
- **zut**
  darn

ACTIVITÉS

2 Le bon mot Choisissez le bon mot entre **ce** (*m.*), **cette** (*f.*) et **ces** (*pl.*) pour compléter les phrases. Attention, les phrases ne sont pas identiques aux dialogues!

1. Je t'aide à apporter __ce__ gâteau?
2. Ce matin, j'ai acheté __ces__ calculatrices et __ce__ livre.
3. Rachid ne comprend pas __cette__ blague.
4. Combien coûtent __ces__ montres?
5. À quelle heure commence __cette__ classe?

3 Imaginez Avec un(e) partenaire, imaginez qu'Amina soit (*is*) dans un grand magasin et qu'elle téléphone à Valérie pour l'aider à choisir le cadeau idéal pour Stéphane. Amina propose plusieurs possibilités de cadeaux et Valérie donne son avis (*opinion*) sur chacune d'entre elles (*each of them*).

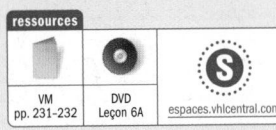

ressources: VM pp. 231-232 | DVD Leçon 6A | espaces.vhlcentral.com

Expressions utiles
- Model the pronunciation of the **Expressions utiles** and have students repeat them.
- As you work through the list, point out forms of the **passé composé** and demonstrative adjectives. Tell students that these grammar structures will be formally presented in the **Structures** section.
- Respond briefly to questions about the **passé composé** and demonstrative adjectives. Reinforce correct forms, but do not expect students to produce them consistently at this time.
- Say some of the **Expressions utiles** and have students react to them. Examples: **1. J'ai eu une idée géniale! (Ah oui? Quelle est ton idée?) 2. Sandrine a tout préparé. (Oh, c'est gentil!)**

1 Expansion For additional practice, give students these items. **11. Sandrine prépare une mousse au chocolat. (Vrai.) 12. David n'aime pas les biscuits. (Faux. David aime les biscuits.) 13. Astrid achète une calculatrice pour Stéphane. (Vrai.)**

2 Suggestion Before beginning the activity, point out the gender of each demonstrative adjective given. Tell students that demonstrative adjectives must agree with the noun they modify just like articles and descriptive adjectives.

2 Expansion For additional practice, give students these items. **6. Je t'aide à apporter ____ desserts? (ces) 7. Tu es très belle ____ soir. (ce) 8. Mes parents ont téléphoné du Sénégal ____ matin. (ce)**

3 Suggestion If time is limited, assign students the roles of Valérie or Amina and tell them to prepare for homework a list of possible questions or responses according to their role. Then allow partners a few minutes to work together before presenting their conversations.

OPTIONS

Les cadeaux Point out the question **Je fais un paquet cadeau?** Explain that many stores gift wrap items free of charge, especially small items. The wrapping is often a simple sack sealed with a small ribbon and a sticker, which usually bears the name of the store.

L'étiquette Point out some basic etiquette regarding gifts in France. For example, if invited to eat at someone's house, one should not bring wine because the host or hostess most certainly will have chosen an appropriate wine to accompany the meal. Instead, choose candy or flowers.

Section Goals

In this section, students will:

- learn about **carnaval**
- learn to express congratulations and best wishes
- learn about some festivals and holidays in various francophone regions
- read about Bastille Day
- view authentic video footage

Instructional Resources
espaces.vhlcentral.com: Video; WB/VM/LM Answer Key; IRM (Videoscript); activities; downloads; reference tools

Culture à la loupe

Avant la lecture Ask if anyone has attended **carnaval** or **Mardi gras** or seen TV news clips of these celebrations. Then ask students to share what they know about these celebrations.

Lecture

- The word **carnaval** is from the Italian *carnevale*, an alteration of the medieval Latin *carnelevare,* meaning *removal of meat.*
- Point out that the plural of **carnaval** is **carnavals.**

Après la lecture Ask students: **Où désirez-vous assister à une célébration: à Nice, à la Nouvelle-Orléans, à Québec ou à la Martinique? Pourquoi?**

1 Expansion For additional practice, give students these items. **11. Quel événement** (*event*) **est-ce qu'on fête au carnaval? (la fin de l'hiver et l'arrivée du printemps)** **12. Où est-ce qu'il fait très froid lors du** (*during*) **carnaval? (à Québec) 13. Combien de défilés y a-t-il pendant le carnaval de la Nouvelle-Orléans? (plus de 70)**

NATIONAL STANDARDS connections cultures

S Video: *Flash culture*

CULTURE À LA LOUPE

Le carnaval

le roi du carnaval de Nice

Tous les ans, beaucoup de pays° et de régions francophones célèbrent le carnaval. Cette tradition est l'occasion de fêter la fin° de l'hiver et l'arrivée° du printemps. En général, la période de fête commence la semaine avant le Carême° et se termine° le jour du Mardi gras. Le carnaval demande très souvent des mois de préparation. La ville organise des défilés° de musique, de masques, de costumes et de chars fleuris°. La fête finit souvent par la crémation du roi° Carnaval, personnage de papier qui représente le carnaval et l'hiver.

Certaines villes et certaines régions sont réputées° pour leur carnaval: Nice, en France, la ville de Québec, au Canada, la Nouvelle-Orléans, aux États-Unis, et la Martinique. Chaque ville a ses traditions particulières. La ville de Nice, lieu du plus grand carnaval français, organise une grande bataille de fleurs° où des jeunes, sur des chars, envoient des milliers° de fleurs aux spectateurs. À Québec, le climat intense transforme le carnaval en une célébration de l'hiver. Le symbole officiel de la fête est le «Bonhomme» (de neige°) et les gens font du ski, de la pêche sous la glace° ou des courses de traîneaux à chiens°. À la Martinique, le carnaval continue jusqu'au° mercredi des Cendres°, à minuit: les gens, tout en noir et blanc°, regardent la crémation de Vaval, le roi Carnaval. Le carnaval de la Nouvelle-Orléans est célébré avec de nombreux bals° et défilés costumés. Ses couleurs officielles sont l'or°, le vert° et le violet.

le carnaval de Québec

Le carnaval en détail

Martinique	Chaque ville choisit une reine°.
Nice	La première bataille de fleurs a eu lieu° en 1876. Chaque année, on envoie entre 80.000 et 100.000 fleurs aux spectateurs.
la Nouvelle-Orléans	Il y a plus de 70 défilés pendant° le carnaval.
la ville de Québec	Le premier carnaval a eu lieu en 1894.

pays *countries* **fin** *end* **arrivée** *arrival* **Carême** *Lent* **se termine** *ends* **défilés** *parades* **chars fleuris** *floats decorated with flowers* **roi** *king* **réputées** *famous* **bataille de fleurs** *flower battle* **milliers** *thousands* **«Bonhomme» (de neige)** *snowman* **pêche sous la glace** *ice-fishing* **courses de traîneaux à chiens** *dogsled races* **jusqu'au** *until* **mercredi des Cendres** *Ash Wednesday* **noir et blanc** *black and white* **bals** *balls (dances)* **or** *gold* **vert** *green* **reine** *queen* **a eu lieu** *took place* **pendant** *during*

ACTIVITÉS

1 Compréhension Répondez par des phrases complètes.

1. En général, quel est le dernier jour du carnaval?
   En général, le dernier jour du carnaval est le jour du Mardi gras.
2. Dans quelle ville des États-Unis est-ce qu'on célèbre le carnaval?
   On célèbre le carnaval à la Nouvelle-Orléans.
3. Où a lieu le plus grand carnaval français?
   Le plus grand carnaval français a lieu à Nice.
4. Qu'est-ce que les jeunes envoient aux spectateurs du carnaval de Nice?
   Les jeunes envoient des fleurs aux spectateurs.
5. Quel est le symbole officiel du carnaval de Québec?
   Le «Bonhomme» est le symbole officiel du carnaval de Québec.
6. Que fait-on pendant (*during*) le carnaval de Québec?
   On pratique des activités d'hiver pendant le carnaval de Québec.
7. Qu'est-ce qui est différent au carnaval de la Martinique?
   Il continue jusqu'au mercredi des Cendres.
8. Qui est Vaval?
   Vaval est le roi du carnaval à la Martinique.
9. Comment est-ce qu'on célèbre le carnaval à la Nouvelle-Orléans?
   On célèbre le carnaval à la Nouvelle-Orléans avec des bals et des défilés.
10. Quelles sont les couleurs officielles du carnaval de la Nouvelle-Orléans?
    Les couleurs officielles du carnaval de la Nouvelle-Orléans sont l'or, le vert et le violet.

OPTIONS

Small Groups Have students work in groups of three. They should choose a country, research its **carnaval**, and create an Internet home page for next year's **carnaval** in that country. Tell them that the home page should include the dates, a list of events with short descriptions, and any other important or interesting information. Have students present their home pages to the class.

Pairs Working in pairs, have students write a conversation between two people who are trying to decide if they should go to the **carnaval** in Nice or in Quebec City. After they have finished, have volunteers act out their conversations for the class.

LE FRANÇAIS QUOTIDIEN

Les vœux

À votre santé!	*To your health!*
Bonne année!	*Happy New Year!*
Bravo! Félicitations!	*Bravo! Congratulations!*
Joyeuses fêtes!	*Have a good holiday!*
Meilleurs vœux!	*Best wishes!*
Santé!	*Cheers!*
Tous mes vœux de bonheur!	*All the best!*

LE MONDE FRANCOPHONE

Fêtes et festivals

Voici d'autres fêtes et festivals francophones.

En Côte d'Ivoire

La fête des Ignames (plusieurs dates) On célèbre la fin° de la récolte° des ignames°, une ressource très importante pour les Ivoiriens.

Au Maroc

La fête du Trône (le 30 juillet) Tout le pays honore le roi° avec des parades et des spectacles.

À la Martinique/À la Guadeloupe

La fête des Cuisinières (en août) Les femmes défilent° en costumes traditionnels et présentent des spécialités locales qu'elles ont préparées pour la fête.

Dans de nombreux pays

L'Aïd el-Fitr C'est la fête musulmane° de la rupture du jeûne° à la fin du Ramadan.

fin *end* **récolte** *harvest* **ignames** *yams* **roi** *king* **défilent** *parade* **musulmane** *Muslim* **jeûne** *fast*

PORTRAIT

Le 14 juillet

Le 14 juillet 1789, sous le règne° de Louis XVI, les Français se sont rebellés contre° la monarchie et ont pris° la Bastille, une forteresse utilisée comme prison. Cette date est très importante dans l'histoire de France parce qu'elle représente le début de la Révolution. Le 14 juillet symbolise la fondation de la République française et a donc° été sélectionné comme date de la Fête nationale. Tous les ans, il y a un grand défilé° militaire sur les Champs-Élysées, la plus grande° avenue parisienne. Partout° en France, les gens assistent à des défilés et à des fêtes dans les rues°. Le soir, il y a de nombreux bals populaires° où les Français dansent et célèbrent cette date historique. Le soir, on assiste aux feux d'artifices° traditionnels.

règne *reign* **se sont rebellés contre** *rebelled against* **ont pris** *stormed* **donc** *therefore* **défilé** *parade* **la plus grande** *the largest* **Partout** *Everywhere* **rues** *streets* **bals populaires** *public dances* **feux d'artifices** *fireworks*

SUR INTERNET

Qu'est-ce que c'est, la fête des Rois?

Go to **espaces.vhlcentral.com** to find more cultural information related to this **ESPACE CULTURE**. Then watch the corresponding **Flash culture**.

ACTIVITÉS

2 Les fêtes Complétez les phrases.

1. Le 14 juillet 1789 est la date ___du début de la Révolution française___.
2. Aujourd'hui, le 14 juillet est la ___Fête nationale de la République française___.
3. En France, le soir du 14 juillet, il y a ___des bals populaires et des feux d'artifices___.
4. À plusieurs dates, les Ivoiriens fêtent ___la fin de la récolte des ignames___.
5. Au Maroc, il y a un festival au mois de ___juillet___.
6. Dans les pays musulmans, l'Aïd el-Fitr célèbre ___la fin du Ramadan___.

Practice more at **espaces.vhlcentral.com.**

3 Faisons la fête ensemble! Vous êtes en vacances dans un pays francophone et vous invitez un(e) ami(e) à aller à une fête ou à un festival francophone avec vous. Expliquez à votre partenaire ce que vous allez faire. Votre partenaire va vous poser des questions.

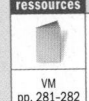

ressources: VM pp. 281–282; espaces.vhlcentral.com

Le français quotidien

- Model the pronunciation of each expression and have students repeat it. Point out that the expression **«Tous mes vœux de bonheur!»** is used primarily at weddings. You might also give them the expression **Bonne chance!** (*Good luck!*)
- Have students identify whether they would use these expressions at **une fête d'anniversaire, une réception de mariage,** or **un anniversaire de mariage.**

Portrait If possible, bring in a photo of the Bastille. Then have students turn to the map of Paris on page 102. Point out that the military parade begins at **Charles de Gaulle-Étoile** and ends at the **Place de la Concorde**. During the French Revolution, the **Place de la Concorde** was known as the **Place de la Révolution** because so many executions took place there, including the execution of Louis XVI on January 21, 1793.

Le monde francophone After students have read the text, have them work in pairs and take turns asking each other questions about the content. Examples: **Où est la fête des Cuisinières? Comment les Marocains fêtent-ils la fête du Trône?**

2 Expansion For additional practice, give students these items. **7. La Bastille était** (*was*) **une forteresse utilisée comme ____ avant la Révolution. (prison) 8. Le défilé militaire pour le 14 juillet a lieu sur ____. (les Champs-Élysées) 9. La fête des Cuisinières a lieu en août ____. (à la Martinique et à la Guadeloupe)**

3 Suggestion Before beginning the activity, have students choose a holiday or festival to discuss.

Flash culture Tell students that they will learn more about French festivals and holiday celebrations by watching a variety of real-life images narrated by Benjamin. Show the video segment, and then have students jot down at least three examples of things they saw. You can also use the activities in the video manual in class to reinforce this **Flash culture** or assign them as homework.

OPTIONS

Cultural Comparison First, ask students: **Quel jour férié aux États-Unis correspond au 14 juillet en France? (la fête de l'indépendance américaine, le 4 juillet)** Then have them work in small groups and compare the two holidays. Tell them to make a list of the similarities (**Similitudes**) and differences (**Différences**) in French. Have groups read their lists to the class.

Le 14 juillet Explain that a Bastille Day celebration would not be complete without a rendering of France's national anthem, ***La Marseillaise***, composed by Claude-Joseph Rouget de Lisle in 1792. Bring the lyrics and a recording of the song for students to listen to. Alternatively, you can have students go to **www.marseillaise.org** to hear the song or read the lyrics.

Section Goals

In this section, students will learn:
- demonstrative adjectives
- to use **-ci** and **-là** to specify demonstratives

Instructional Resources
*espaces.vhlcentral.com: Lab MP3s; WB/VM/LM Answer Key; IRM (**Essayez!** and **Mise en pratique** answers; Lab Audioscript); activities; downloads; reference tools*

Suggestions
- Point to a book on your desk. Say: **Ce livre est sur mon bureau.** Point to a sheet of paper next to the book. Say: **Cette feuille de papier est à côté du livre.** Then point to an object in front of you and say: **Cet objet est devant moi.**
- Write **ce** and **cet** on the board. Point out that the masculine singular demonstrative adjective has two forms. Say the following words and have students give the demonstrative: **garçon**, **homme**, **biscuit**, **ordinateur**, **cadeau**, and **examen**.
- Point out that there is only one plural demonstrative adjective in French, regardless of gender: **ces**.
- Have students identify the demonstrative adjectives in the ad for **La maison Julien**. Ask them what type of store it is.
- Hold up pictures or point to objects, saying either the singular or plural demonstrative to describe each object. Have students give the opposite. Examples: **ces baguettes (cette baguette)**, **ce stylo (ces stylos)**, and **ces invités (cet invité)**.
- Place a short pencil close to you and a long pencil far away. Say: **Ce crayon-ci est court. Ce crayon-là est long.** Continue with other objects until students grasp the concept.

National Standards comparisons

6A.1 Demonstrative adjectives

Point de départ To identify or point out a noun with the French equivalent of *this/these* and *that/those*, use a demonstrative adjective before the noun.

Demonstrative adjectives

	singular: Before consonant	singular: Before vowel sound	plural
masculine	**ce** café	**cet** éclair	**ces** cafés, **ces** éclairs
feminine	**cette** surprise	**cette** amie	**ces** surprises, **ces** amies

Ce copain organise une fête.
This friend is organizing a party.

Cette glace est excellente.
This ice cream is excellent.

Cet hôpital est trop loin du centre-ville.
That hospital is too far from downtown.

Je préfère **ces** cadeaux.
I prefer those gifts.

Combien coûte cette montre?

J'ai ce cadeau pour Stéphane.

- Although the forms of **ce** can refer to a noun that is near (*this/these*) and one that is far (*that/those*), the meaning will usually be clear from context.

Ce dessert est délicieux.
This dessert is delicious.

Ils vont aimer **cette** surprise.
They're going to like this surprise.

Joël préfère **cet** éclair.
Joël prefers that éclair.

Ces glaçons sont pour la limonade.
Those ice cubes are for the lemon soda.

La maison Julien
Pour toutes ces occasions...
pour célébrer tout ce bonheur...
nous pensons à tous les détails.

MISE EN PRATIQUE

1 Remplacez Remplacez les noms au singulier par des noms au pluriel et vice versa.

MODÈLE
J'aime mieux ce dessert.
J'aime mieux ces desserts.

1. Ces glaces au chocolat sont délicieuses. (Cette glace au chocolat est délicieuse.)
2. Ce gâteau est énorme. (Ces gâteaux sont énormes.)
3. Ces biscuits ne sont pas bons. (Ce biscuit n'est pas bon.)
4. Ces invitées sont gentilles. (Cette invitée est gentille.)
5. Ces hôtes parlent japonais. (Cet hôte parle japonais.)
6. Cette bière est allemande. (Ces bières sont allemandes.)

2 Monsieur Parfait Avant la fête, l'hôte donne à sa femme son opinion sur les préparations. Complétez ce texte avec **ce**, **cette** ou **ces**.

Mmm! (1) __Ce__ champagne est parfait. Ah! (2) __Ces__ gâteaux sont magnifiques, (3) __ces__ biscuits sont délicieux et j'adore (4) __cette__ glace. Bah! (5) __Ces__ bonbons sont originaux, mais pas très bons. Ouvre (*Open*) (6) __cette__ bouteille. (7) __Ce__ café sur (8) __cette__ table sent très bon. (9) __Cette__ plante a besoin d'eau. (10) __Ce__ tableau (*painting*) n'est pas droit (*straight*)! Oh là là! Arrange (11) __ces__ chaises autour de (*around*) (12) __ces__ trois tables!

3 Magazine Complétez les phrases.

MODÈLE
Ce cheval est très grand.

1. __Ce gâteau__ au chocolat et __cette glace__ sont délicieux.

3. __Ces jeunes mariés__ sont très heureux.

2. __Cette fille__ aime beaucoup __ces bonbons__.

4. __Cet homme__ est à la retraite.

Practice more at **espaces.vhlcentral.com.**

OPTIONS

Game Divide the class into two teams. Choose one team member at a time to go to the board, alternating between teams. Say a noun. The person at the board must write and say the noun with the correct demonstrative adjective. Example: **fille** (**cette fille**). Give a point for each correct answer. The team with the most points at the end of the game wins.

Extra Practice Hold up or point to various classroom objects. Tell students to write down all forms of demonstrative adjectives that could apply. Example: **chaise (cette chaise, ces chaises, cette chaise-ci, cette chaise-là, ces chaises-ci, ces chaises-là)**.

COMMUNICATION

4 Comparez Avec un(e) partenaire, comparez le contenu (*content*) à tour de rôle. Answers will vary.

MODÈLE

Étudiant(e) 1: *Comment sont ces hommes?*
Étudiant(e) 2: *Cet homme-ci est petit et cet homme-là est grand.*

l'homme

1. la femme

3. le chien

2. l'automobile (*f.*)

4. la fille

5 Préférences Demandez à votre partenaire ses préférences, puis donnez votre opinion. Employez des adjectifs démonstratifs et présentez vos réponses à la classe. Answers will vary.

MODÈLE

Étudiant(e) 1: *Quel film est-ce que tu aimes?*
Étudiant(e) 2: *J'aime bien Casablanca.*
Étudiant(e) 1: *Moi, je n'aime pas du tout ce vieux film.*

acteur/actrice	passe-temps
chanteur/chanteuse	restaurant
dessert	saison
film	sport
magasin	ville
?	?

6 Invitation Vous organisez une fête et vous êtes au supermarché avec un(e) ami(e). Vous n'êtes pas d'accord sur ce que (*what*) vous allez acheter. Avec un(e) partenaire, jouez les rôles. Answers will vary.

MODÈLE

Étudiant(e) 1: *On achète cette glace-ci?*
Étudiant(e) 2: *Je n'aime pas cette glace-ci. Je préfère cette glace-là!*
Étudiant(e) 1: *Mais cette glace-là coûte dix euros!*
Étudiant(e) 2: *D'accord! On prend cette glace-ci.*

- To make it especially clear that you're referring to something near versus something far, add **-ci** or **-là**, respectively, to the noun following the demonstrative adjective.

ce couple-**ci** *this couple (here)*	**ces** biscuits-**ci** *these cookies (here)*
cette invitée-**là** *that guest (there)*	**ces** fêtes-**là** *those parties (there)*

- Use **-ci** and **-là** in the same sentence to contrast similar items.

On prend **cette glace-ci**, pas **cette glace-là**. *We'll have this ice cream, not that ice cream.*	Tu achètes **ce fromage-ci** ou **ce fromage-là**? *Are you buying this cheese or that cheese?*

J'aime bien **cette jupe-ci**.
I like this skirt.

Je n'aime pas **ces chaussures-là**.
I don't like those shoes.

Essayez! **Complétez les phrases avec la forme correcte de l'adjectif démonstratif.**

1. Cette glace au chocolat est très bonne!
2. Qu'est-ce que tu penses de ce cadeau?
3. Cet homme-là est l'hôte de la fête.
4. Tu préfères ces biscuits-ci ou ces biscuits-là?
5. Vous aimez mieux ce dessert-ci ou ce dessert-là?
6. Cette année-ci, on va fêter l'anniversaire de mariage de nos parents en famille.
7. Tu achètes cet éclair-là.
8. Vous achetez cette montre?
9. Cette surprise va être géniale!
10. Cet invité-là est antipathique.

Essayez! Have students create new sentences orally by changing the singular nouns to the plural or vice versa in items 1–5.

1 Expansion For additional practice, give students these items. **7. Ces bonbons sont trop sucrés. 8. Ces vins sont rouges.**

2 Suggestion Tell students to underline the nouns that will correspond to the demonstrative adjectives and identify their number and gender before they write the demonstrative adjective.

3 Suggestion Before beginning the activity, have students identify in French the items pictured.

4 Suggestion Have two volunteers read the **modèle** aloud. Remind students to take turns asking and answering the questions.

5 Suggestion Have two volunteers read the **modèle** aloud. Tell students to add at least two items of their own to the list.

6 Suggestion Before beginning the activity, have students brainstorm items they might buy for the party and write them on the board.

OPTIONS

Video Show the video episode again and have students listen for the demonstrative adjectives. Tell them to write down each demonstrative adjective they hear and the noun it modifies. Then, have students check the Videoscript to see if they were correct.

Pairs Have students turn to **Espace contextes** on pages 182–183. Working in pairs, tell them to make comments about the people and items in the illustration using demonstrative adjectives. Examples: **Ces desserts-là ont l'air délicieux, n'est-ce pas? Oui, mais je préfère ce gâteau-ci.** Use **Transparency #31** when giving examples.

Section Goals

In this section, students will learn:
- the **passé composé** with **avoir**
- some irregular past participles

Instructional Resources
*espaces.vhlcentral.com: Lab MP3s; WB/VM/LM Answer Key; IRM (**Essayez!** and **Mise en pratique** answers; Lab Audioscript); activities; downloads; reference tools*

Suggestions
- Quickly review the present tense of **avoir**.
- Introduce the **passé composé** by describing what you did yesterday. Include adverbs commonly used to indicate past actions, such as **hier** and **hier soir**. Examples: **Hier, j'ai enseigné deux cours de français. Hier soir, j'ai téléphoné à un(e) ami(e) et j'ai écouté de la musique.** Each time you say a **passé composé** form write it on the board.
- Ask students some questions about their activities. Examples: **Avez-vous écouté de la musique hier? Avez-vous regardé la télé?** Ask other students about their classmates' activities. Examples: **Quelle musique est-ce que ____ a écouté hier soir? Qu'est-ce que ____ a regardé?**
- Explain that the **passé composé** has three English equivalents. Example: **Nous avons mangé.** = *We ate. We did eat. We have eaten.*

6A.2 The *passé composé* with *avoir*

NATIONAL STANDARDS comparisons

Point de départ In order to talk about events in the past, French uses two principal tenses: the **passé composé** and the imperfect. In this lesson, you will learn how to form the **passé composé**, which is used to express actions or states of being completed in the past. You will learn about the imperfect in **Leçon 7B**.

- The **passé composé** of most verbs is formed with a present-tense form of **avoir** (the auxiliary verb) followed by the past participle of the verb expressing the action.

AUXILIARY VERB / PAST PARTICIPLE

Nous **avons** **fêté**.
We celebrated / have celebrated.

- The past participle of a regular **-er** verb is formed by replacing the **-er** ending of the infinitive with **-é**.

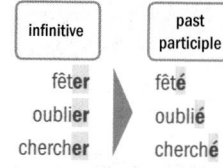

infinitive		past participle
fêt**er**	→	fêt**é**
oubli**er**	→	oubli**é**
cherch**er**	→	cherch**é**

- Most regular **-er** verbs are conjugated in the **passé composé** like the verb **parler** shown below.

The *passé composé*

j'ai parlé	*I spoke/have spoken*	**nous avons parlé**	*we spoke/have spoken*
tu as parlé	*you spoke/have spoken*	**vous avez parlé**	*you spoke/have spoken*
il/elle a parlé	*he/she/it spoke/has spoken*	**ils/elles ont parlé**	*they spoke/have spoken*

- To make a verb negative in the **passé composé**, place **ne/n'** and **pas** around the conjugated form of **avoir**.

On **n'**a **pas** fêté mon anniversaire.
We didn't celebrate my birthday.

Elles **n'**ont **pas** acheté de biscuits hier?
They didn't buy any cookies yesterday?

- To ask questions using inversion in the **passé composé**, invert the subject pronoun and the conjugated form of **avoir**.

Avez-vous fêté votre anniversaire?
Did you celebrate your birthday?

Est-ce qu'elles **ont acheté** des biscuits?
Did they buy any cookies?

MISE EN PRATIQUE

1 Qu'est-ce qu'ils ont fait? Laurent parle de son week-end en ville avec sa famille. Complétez ses phrases avec le **passé composé** du verbe correct.

1. Nous __avons mangé__ (nager, manger) des escargots.
2. Papa __a acheté__ (acheter, apprendre) une nouvelle montre.
3. J'__ai pris__ (prendre, oublier) une glace à la terrasse d'un café.
4. Vous __avez essayé__ (enseigner, essayer) un nouveau restaurant.
5. Mes parents __ont célébré__ (dessiner, célébrer) leur anniversaire de mariage.
6. Ils __ont fait__ (fréquenter, faire) une promenade.
7. Ma sœur __a bu__ (boire, nettoyer) un chocolat chaud.
8. Le soir, nous __avons eu__ (écouter, avoir) sommeil.

2 Pas encore Un copain pose des questions pénibles. Écrivez ses questions, puis donnez des réponses négatives.

MODÈLE
inviter vos amis (vous)
Vous avez invité vos amis?
Non, nous n'avons pas invité nos amis.

1. écouter mon CD (tu) Tu as écouté mon CD? Non, je n'ai pas écouté ton CD.
2. faire ses devoirs (Matthieu) Matthieu a fait ses devoirs? Non, il n'a pas fait ses devoirs.
3. courir dans le parc (elles) Elles ont couru dans le parc? Non, elles n'ont pas couru dans le parc.
4. parler aux profs (tu) Tu as parlé aux profs? Non, je n'ai pas parlé aux profs.
5. apprendre les verbes irréguliers (Yassim) Yassim a appris les verbes irréguliers? Non, il n'a pas appris les verbes irréguliers.
6. être à la piscine (Marie et Lise) Marie et Lise ont été à la piscine? Non, elles n'ont pas été à la piscine.
7. emmener André au cinéma (vous) Vous avez emmené André au cinéma? Non, nous n'avons pas emmené André au cinéma.
8. avoir le temps d'étudier (tu) Tu as eu le temps d'étudier? Non, je n'ai pas eu le temps d'étudier.

3 La semaine À tour de rôle, assemblez les éléments des colonnes pour raconter (*to tell*) à votre partenaire ce que (*what*) tout le monde (*everyone*) a fait cette semaine. Answers will vary.

A	B	C
je	acheter	bonbons
Luc	apprendre	café
mon prof	boire	l'espagnol
Sylvie	faire	famille
mes parents	jouer	foot
mes copains et moi	manger	glace
tu	parler	jogging
vous	prendre	promenade

Practice more at **espaces.vhlcentral.com.**

OPTIONS

Pairs Working in pairs, have students tell each other two things they did last week, two things their best friend did, and two things they did together. Then have each student get together with another classmate and report what the first person told him or her.

Small Groups Divide the class into groups of five. Give each group a list of verbs, including some with irregular past participles. The first student chooses a verb from the list and gives the **je** form. The second student gives the **tu** form, and so on. Students work their way down the list, alternating who chooses the verb.

NATIONAL communication STANDARDS

COMMUNICATION

4 Vendredi soir Vous et votre partenaire avez assisté à une fête vendredi soir. Parlez de la fête à tour de rôle. Qu'est-ce que les invités ont fait? Quelle a été l'occasion? Answers will vary.

5 L'été dernier Vous avez passé l'été dernier avec deux amis, mais vos souvenirs (*memories*) diffèrent. Par groupes de trois, utilisez les expressions de la liste et imaginez le dialogue. Answers will vary.

MODÈLE

Étudiant(e) 1: *Nous avons fait du cheval tous les matins.*
Étudiant(e) 2: *Mais non! Moi, j'ai fait du cheval. Vous deux, vous avez fait du jogging.*
Étudiant(e) 3: *Je n'ai pas fait de jogging. J'ai dormi!*

acheter	essayer	faire une promenade
courir	faire du cheval	jouer aux cartes
dormir	faire du jogging	jouer au foot
emmener	faire la fête	manger

6 Qu'est-ce que tu as fait? Avec un(e) partenaire, posez-vous les questions à tour de rôle. Ensuite, présentez vos réponses à la classe. Answers will vary.

1. As-tu fait la fête samedi dernier? Où? Avec qui?
2. Est-ce que tu as célébré une occasion importante cette année? Quelle occasion?
3. As-tu organisé une fête? Pour qui?
4. Qui est-ce que tu as invité à ta dernière fête?
5. Qu'est-ce que tu as fait pour fêter ton dernier anniversaire?
6. Est-ce que tu as préparé quelque chose à manger pour une fête ou un dîner? Quoi?

- The adverbs **hier** (*yesterday*) and **avant-hier** (*the day before yesterday*) are used often with the **passé composé**.
- Place the adverbs **déjà**, **encore**, **bien**, **mal**, and **beaucoup** between the auxiliary verb or **pas** and the past participle.

Tu as **déjà** mangé ta part de gâteau.
You already ate your piece of cake.

Elle n'a pas **encore** visité notre ville.
She hasn't visited our town yet.

- The past participle of spelling-change **-er** verbs has no spelling changes.

Laurent a-t-il **acheté** le champagne?
Did Laurent buy the champagne?

Vous avez **envoyé** des bonbons.
You sent candy.

- The past participle of most **-ir** verbs is formed by replacing the **-ir** ending with **-i**.

Sylvie a **dormi** jusqu'à dix heures.
Sylvie slept until 10 o'clock.

On a **senti** leurs regards.
We felt their stares.

Some irregular past participles

apprendre	appris	être	été
avoir	eu	faire	fait
boire	bu	pleuvoir	plu
comprendre	compris	prendre	pris
courir	couru	surprendre	surpris

Nous avons **bu** du vin.
We drank wine.

Ils ont **été** très en retard.
They have been very late.

- The **passé composé** of **il faut** is **il a fallu**; that of **il y a** is **il y a eu**.

Il a fallu passer par le supermarché.
It was necessary to stop by the supermarket.

Il y a eu deux fêtes hier soir.
There were two parties last night.

BOÎTE À OUTILS
Some verbs, like **aller**, use **être** instead of **avoir** to form the **passé composé**. You will learn more about these verbs in **Leçon 7A**.

Essayez! **Indiquez les formes du passé composé des verbes.**

1. j' *ai commencé, ai payé, ai bavardé* (commencer, payer, bavarder)
2. tu as servi, as compris, as donné (servir, comprendre, donner)
3. on a parlé, a eu, a dormi (parler, avoir, dormir)
4. nous avons adoré, avons fait, avons amené (adorer, faire, amener)
5. vous avez pris, avez employé, avez couru (prendre, employer, courir)
6. elles ont espéré, ont bu, ont appris (espérer, boire, apprendre)

Essayez! For additional practice, have students create complete sentences orally or in writing using the subjects and verbs given.

1 Expansion Ask follow-up questions about Laurent's weekend. Examples: **1. Qu'est-ce qu'ils ont mangé? 2. Qui a acheté une montre? 3. Qui a pris une glace à la terrasse d'un café? 4. Qu'est-ce que leurs parents ont célébré? 5. Quand est-ce que Laurent et sa famille ont eu sommeil?**

2 Suggestion To check answers, have one student ask the question and call on another student to answer it. This activity can also be done in pairs.

2 Expansion For additional practice, give students these items. **9. parler à ses parents (Stéphane) 10. boire du café (toi et ton copain)**

3 Suggestion Before beginning this activity, call on volunteers to give the past participles of verbs listed.

4 Suggestion Before beginning the activity, have students describe what the people are doing in the present tense.

5 Suggestion Have three volunteers read the **modèle** aloud. Encourage students to be creative.

6 Suggestion Tell students to jot down notes on their partner's responses and to add two of their own questions to the list.

OPTIONS

TPR Working in groups of three, have students write three sentences in the **passé composé**, each with a different verb. After they have finished, have each group mime its sentences for the class. When someone guesses the mimed action, the group writes the sentence on the board.

Extra Practice For homework, have students write a paragraph about what they did yesterday or last weekend. Then, in class, have them exchange papers with a classmate and peer edit each other's work.

Instructional Resources
*espaces.vhlcentral.com: IRM (**Feuilles d'activités**; Info Gap Activities); Testing Program, pp. 41–44; Test Files; Testing Program MP3s; activities; downloads; reference tools Test Generator*

1 Suggestion Before beginning this activity, give students a few minutes to jot down some notes about the previous Thanksgiving.

2 Expansion Have a few volunteers report the common activities they and their partner did.

3 Suggestion Before beginning the activity, have students identify the items on the table.

4 Suggestion Distribute the **Feuilles d'activités** found on the Supersite.

5 Suggestion Tell students that they can talk about a real or imaginary dinner. Encourage students to be creative.

6 Suggestion Divide the class into pairs and distribute the Info Gap Handouts found on the Supersite for this activity. Give students ten minutes to complete the activity.

Révision

1 L'année dernière et cette année Décrivez vos dernières fêtes de Thanksgiving à votre partenaire. Utilisez les verbes de la liste. Parlez aussi de vos projets (*plans*) pour le prochain Thanksgiving. Answers will vary.

MODÈLE

Étudiant(e) 1: *L'année dernière, nous avons fêté Thanksgiving chez mes grands-parents. Cette année, je vais manger au restaurant avec mes parents.*

Étudiant(e) 2: *Moi, j'ai fait la fête avec mes amis l'année dernière. Cette année, je vais visiter New York avec ma sœur.*

aller	donner	fêter	préparer
acheter	dormir	manger	regarder
boire	faire	prendre	téléphoner

2 Ce musée, cette ville Faites par écrit (*Write*) une liste de cinq lieux (villes, musées, restaurants, etc.) que vous avez visités. Avec un(e) partenaire, comparez vos listes. Utilisez des adjectifs démonstratifs dans vos phrases. Answers will vary.

MODÈLE

Étudiant(e) 1: *Ah, tu as visité Bruxelles. Moi aussi, j'ai visité cette ville. Elle est belle.*

Étudiant(e) 2: *Tu as mangé au restaurant La Douce France. Je n'aime pas du tout ce restaurant!*

3 La fête Vous et votre partenaire avez préparé une fête avec vos amis. Vous avez acheté des cadeaux, des boissons et des snacks. À tour de rôle, parlez de ce qu'il y a sur l'illustration. Answers will vary.

MODÈLE

Étudiant(e) 1: *J'aime bien ces biscuits-là.*

Étudiant(e) 2: *Moi, j'ai apporté cette glace-ci.*

4 Enquête Qu'est-ce que vos camarades ont fait de différent dans leur vie? Votre professeur va vous donner une feuille d'activités. Parlez à vos camarades pour trouver une personne différente pour chaque expérience, puis écrivez son nom. Answers will vary.

MODÈLE

Étudiant(e) 1: *As-tu parlé à un acteur?*

Étudiant(e) 2: *Oui! Une fois, j'ai parlé à Bruce Willis!*

Expérience	*Noms*
1. parler à un(e) acteur/actrice	*Julien*
2. passer une nuit entière sans dormir	
3. dépenser plus de $100 pour des CD en une fois	
4. faire la fête un lundi soir	
5. courir cinq kilomètres ou plus	
6. faire une surprise à un(e) ami(e) pour son anniversaire	

5 Conversez Avec un(e) partenaire, préparez une conversation entre deux copains/copines sur les détails d'un dîner romantique du week-end dernier. N'oubliez pas de mentionner dans la conversation: Answers will vary.

- où ils ont mangé
- les thèmes de la conversation
- qui a parlé de quoi
- qui a payé
- la date du prochain rendez-vous

6 Magali fait la fête Votre professeur va vous donner, à vous et à votre partenaire, deux feuilles d'activités différentes. Attention! Ne regardez pas la feuille de votre partenaire. Answers will vary.

MODÈLE

Étudiant(e) 1: *Magali a parlé avec un homme. Cet homme n'a pas l'air intéressant du tout!*

Étudiant(e) 2: *Après, ...*

ressources
WB pp. 73-76 | LM pp. 43-44 | espaces.vhlcentral.com

OPTIONS

Extra Practice Have students create a continuous narration about a person who had a very bad day. Begin the story by saying: **Hier, Robert a passé une très mauvaise journée.** Call on one student to continue the story by telling how Robert began his day. The second person tells what happened next. Students continue adding sentences until only one student remains. He or she must conclude the story.

Extra Practice Have students make a "to do" list (**à faire...**) at the beginning of their day. Then, tell students to review their list at the end of the day and write down which activities they completed and which ones they didn't complete. Example: **acheter de la nourriture: Non, je n'ai pas acheté de nourriture.**

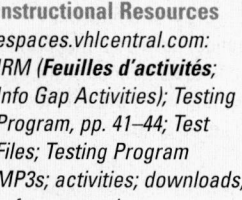

Video: TV Clip

Le Zapping

La Poste

La Poste, le service postal belge, distribue tous les jours les cartes de vœux° (et le reste du courrier°) chez ses clients, comme la poste des États-Unis et celle (*the one*) du Canada. Pourtant°, en Belgique, La Poste offre aussi à ses clients une vaste gamme° de services pour la gestion° de leur argent. Par l'intermédiaire de° la Banque de La Poste, les Belges ont la possibilité d'ouvrir° des comptes° chèques et de posséder des cartes de crédit comme avec une banque traditionnelle. Il existe aussi des prêts° variés pour les grandes dépenses, comme des vacances ou même une maison. Tout ça à La Poste!

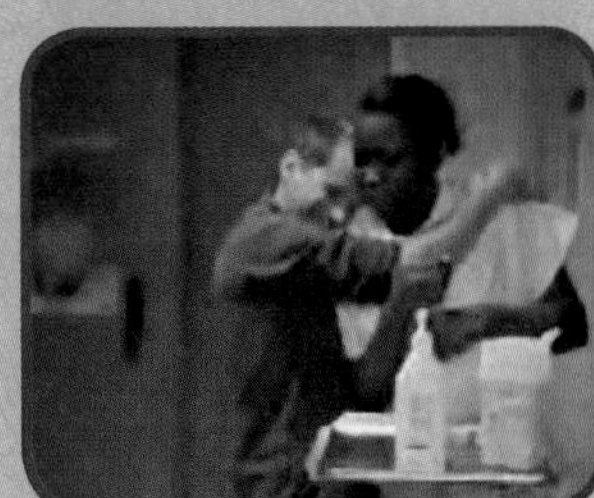

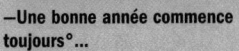

—Une bonne année commence toujours°...

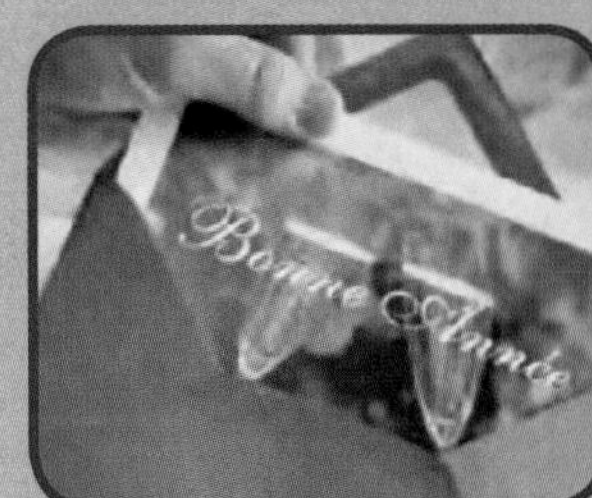

—... par quelqu'un qui vous la souhaite°.

Compréhension **Répondez aux questions.** Some answers will vary.

1. Qui est l'homme dans la publicité (*ad*)? Comment est son année?
   C'est un jeune père. Il a beaucoup de chance cette année.
2. Que fête-t-il cette année?
   Il fête la naissance de son enfant. Il gagne un match de football et un gros contrat au bureau.
3. Pourquoi l'année commence-t-elle par la fin (*end*)?
   C'est pour indiquer que l'homme a eu de la chance toute l'année, parce que quelqu'un a envoyé une carte de vœux.

Discussion **Avec un(e) partenaire, répondez aux questions et discutez.** Answers will vary.

1. Quelles sortes d'événements fêtez-vous? Comment?
2. Envoyez-vous des cartes de vœux? Quel effet ont-elles sur le/la destinataire (*recipient*)?

cartes de vœux *greeting cards* **courrier** *mail* **Pourtant** *However* **gamme** *range* **gestion** *management*
Par l'intermédiaire de *Through* **ouvrir** *to open* **comptes** *accounts* **prêts** *loans*
toujours *always* **par quelqu'un qui vous la souhaite** *with someone who wishes it for you*

Practice more at **espaces.vhlcentral.com.**

Section Goals

In this section, students will:

- read about **La Poste**, the Belgian postal service
- watch a commercial for **La Poste**
- answer questions about the commercial and **La Poste**

Instructional Resources
*espaces.vhlcentral.com: TV commercial; IRM (**Le zapping** TV clip transcription); activities; downloads; reference tools*

Introduction
To check comprehension, ask these questions:
1. Que fait La Poste belge comme les services postaux d'autres pays? (Elle distribue les cartes de voeux.)
2. Qu'offre-t-elle aussi à ses clients? (Elle offre des services pour la gestion de leur argent.)
3. Qu'existe-t-il pour les grandes dépenses? (Il existe des prêts variés.)

Avant de regarder la vidéo

- Have students look at the video stills, read the captions, and predict what is happening in the commercial for each visual. **(1. Cet homme fête la naissance de son enfant. C'est le grand bonheur. 2. Il va avoir une très bonne année, parce qu'un ami a envoyé une carte de voeux.)**
- Before showing the video, explain to students that they do not need to understand every word they hear. Tell them to listen for the text in the captions and for any familiar words. They should also look out for scenes depicting this lesson's vocabulary.

Compréhension Have students work in pairs or groups for this activity. Tell them to write their answers. Then show the video again so that they can check their answers and add any missing information.

Discussion Ask students to share their partner's answers. Keep track of them on the board to determine how many of the same special occasions they celebrate and which one is most common.

OPTIONS

Postal History Belgium has long played a key role in postal history. In the early sixteenth century, François de Tassis, whose ancestors had operated mail delivery services between Italian city states since the late thirteenth century, was appointed by the Holy Roman Emperor Maximilian I to run the first pan-European postal service. François de Tassis consequently moved his family to Brussels, where the operation was to be headquartered. Mail delivery now covered a vast expanse, from Belgium and the Low Countries to modern-day France and Germany, reaching as far south as Spain and Naples. The logo of the Belgian postal service depicts the horn traditionally blown by mail carriers along the extensive routes to announce the arrival or departure of the mail.

Section Goals

In this section, students will learn and practice vocabulary related to:

- clothing and accessories
- shopping
- colors

Instructional Resources
*espaces.vhlcentral.com: Transparency #32; IRM (**Vocabulaire supplémentaire; Mise en pratique** answers; Textbook Audioscript; Lab Audioscript); Textbook MP3s; Lab MP3s; WB/VM/LM Answer Key; activities; downloads; reference tools*

Suggestions

- Use **Transparency #32.** Point out clothing items in the store and describe what the people in the illustration are wearing. Examples: **Cette femme porte une robe. Ce tee-shirt est bon marché.**
- After presenting the new vocabulary, briefly describe what you are wearing.
- Have students name one item of clothing they are wearing today. Then ask: **Que porte ____? De quelle couleur est ____?**
- Point out the difference between **une écharpe** (a heavier scarf or wrap worn in fall or winter) and **un foulard** (a lighter scarf usually worn in spring or summer).
- Tell students that the word **taille** is used to talk about *clothing sizes.* **Pointure** refers to *shoe sizes.*
- Point out the title of this lesson. Tell students that **chic** is an invariable adjective.
- Tell students that the verb **porter** means *to wear* or *to carry.* The verb **mettre** (*to wear; to put on*) is presented on page 207.
- Additional vocabulary for this lesson can be found in the **Vocabulaire supplémentaire** on the Supersite.

Leçon 6B

You will learn how to...

- **describe clothing**
- **offer and accept gifts**

Talking Picture
Audio: Activity

Très chic!

Vocabulaire

aller avec	*to go with*
un anorak	*ski jacket, parka*
une chaussette	*sock*
une chemise (à manches courtes/longues)	*shirt (short-/long-sleeved)*
un chemisier	*blouse*
un gant	*glove*
un jean	*jeans*
une jupe	*skirt*
un manteau	*coat*
un pantalon	*pants*
un pull	*sweater*
un sous-vêtement	*underwear*
une taille	*clothing size*
un tailleur	*(woman's) suit; tailor*
un tee-shirt	*tee shirt*
un vendeur/une vendeuse	*salesman/saleswoman*
des vêtements (*m.*)	*clothing*
De quelle couleur...?	*In what color...?*
des soldes (*m.*)	*sales*
chaque	*each*
large	*loose; big*
serré(e)	*tight*

ressources
WB pp. 77–78 | LM p. 45 | espaces.vhlcentral.com

OPTIONS

Game Have students stand. Toss a beanbag to a student at random and say the name of a sport, place, or activity. The person has four seconds to name a clothing item or accessory that goes with it. That person then tosses the beanbag to another student and says a sport, place, or activity. Students who cannot think of an item in time or repeat an item that has already been mentioned are eliminated. The last person standing wins.

Extra Practice Review the weather and seasons by asking students what they wear in various circumstances. Examples: **Que portez-vous quand il fait chaud/quand il fait frais/quand il neige/au printemps/en hiver?**

Attention!

Note that the adjectives **orange** and **marron** are invariable; they do not vary in gender or number to match the noun they modify.

J'aime l'anorak orange.

Il porte des chaussures marron.

Mise en pratique

1 Les vêtements Choisissez le mot qui ne va pas avec les autres.

1. des baskets, (une cravate), une chaussure
2. un jean, un pantalon, (une jupe)
3. un tailleur, un costume, (un short)
4. (des lunettes), un chemisier, une chemise
5. (un tee-shirt), un pull, un anorak
6. une casquette, (une ceinture), un chapeau
7. un sous-vêtement, une chaussette, (un sac à main)
8. une jupe, une robe, (une écharpe)

2 Écoutez Guillaume prépare ses vacances d'hiver (*winter vacation*). Indiquez quels vêtements il va acheter pour son voyage.

	Oui	Non
1. des baskets	☑	☐
2. un maillot de bain	☐	☑
3. des chemises	☐	☑
4. un pantalon noir	☑	☐
5. un manteau	☑	☐
6. un anorak	☐	☑
7. un jean	☑	☐
8. un short	☐	☑
9. un pull	☐	☑
10. une robe	☐	☑

Guillaume

3 De quelle couleur? Indiquez de quelle(s) couleur(s) sont ces choses.

MODÈLE

l'océan
Il est bleu.
la statue de la Liberté
Elle est verte.

1. le drapeau français Il est bleu, blanc et rouge.
2. les dollars américains Ils sont verts.
3. les pommes (*apples*) Answers will vary. Elles sont rouges, vertes ou jaunes.
4. le soleil Il est jaune.
5. la nuit Elle est noire.
6. le zèbre Il est blanc et noir.
7. la neige Elle est blanche.
8. les oranges Elles sont orange.
9. le café Il est marron ou noir.
10. les bananes Elles sont jaunes.

Practice more at **espaces.vhlcentral.com.**

1 Expansions

- For additional practice, give students these items. **9. un sac à main, une ceinture, une robe (une robe) 10. un pull, un gant, un tee-shirt (un gant) 11. un pantalon, un blouson, un anorak (un pantalon) 12. des chaussettes, des baskets, un chapeau (un chapeau)**
- Have students create one or two additional items using at least three new vocabulary words in each one. Collect their papers and write some of the items on the board.

2 Tapescript Bonjour! Je m'appelle Guillaume. Je vais aller en Suisse pour mes vacances d'hiver. J'ai besoin d'acheter un manteau parce qu'il va faire froid. J'ai déjà acheté un pull gris. J'ai aussi un bel anorak bleu qui est un peu vieux, mais chaud. Pour faire des randonnées, j'ai besoin d'un jean et de nouvelles baskets. Pour aller en boîte, je vais acheter un pantalon noir qui va aller avec toutes mes chemises: j'ai des chemises de toutes les couleurs, des chemises à manches longues, à manches courtes. Bien sûr, je ne vais pas avoir besoin d'un short parce qu'il ne va pas faire chaud.
(On Textbook MP3s)

2 Expansion Play the recording again. Ask students why Guillaume is not going to buy the items marked **Non.** Example: **Pourquoi Guillaume ne va-t-il pas acheter un maillot de bain? (parce qu'il va faire froid en Suisse)**

3 Expansions

- Point out items in the classroom and have students tell what color they are. Examples: **le tableau, ce sac à dos,** and **mon stylo.**
- Have students name items of various colors. Example: **Nommez** (*Name*) **quelque chose de rouge. (le chemisier de ____)**

OPTIONS

TPR Play a game of **Jacques a dit** (*Simon says*). Write **asseyez-vous** and **levez-vous** on the board and model them by sitting and standing as you say them. Start by saying: **Jacques a dit: Si vous portez un jean noir, levez-vous.** Students wearing black jeans stand up and remain standing until further instruction. Work through various items of clothing. Give instructions without saying **Jacques a dit...** once in a while.

Small Groups Divide the class into small groups. Assign each group a season and a vacation destination. Have groups brainstorm a list of items to pack and write a brief explanation for each item. You might want to have groups write two lists, one for a female traveler and one for a male.

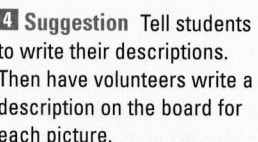

4 Suggestion Tell students to write their descriptions. Then have volunteers write a description on the board for each picture.

4 Expansion Have students describe what they are wearing in detail, including accessories and colors of each item.

5 Suggestion Remind students to include greetings and other polite expressions in their role-plays. Have volunteers perform their role-plays for the rest of the class.

6 Expansion Take a quick class survey to find out students' clothing preferences. Tally the results on the board.

7 Suggestion Have a volunteer read the **modèle** aloud.

NATIONAL communication STANDARDS

Communication

4 Qu'est-ce qu'ils portent? Avec un(e) camarade de classe, regardez les images et à tour de rôle, décrivez ce que les personnages portent. Answers will vary.

MODÈLE

Elle porte un maillot de bain rouge.

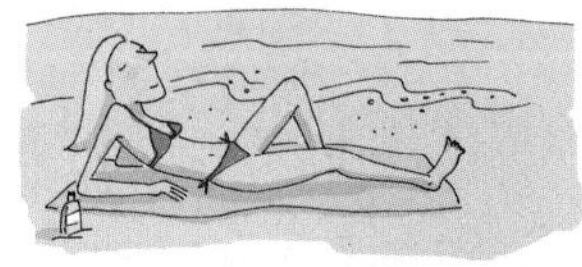

1.

2.

3.

4.

5 On fait du shopping Choisissez deux partenaires et préparez une conversation. Deux client(e)s et un vendeur/une vendeuse sont dans un grand magasin; les client(e)s sont invité(e)s à un événement très chic, mais ils ou elles ne veulent pas (*don't want*) dépenser beaucoup d'argent. Answers will vary.

Client(e)s

- Décrivez l'événement auquel (*to which*) vous êtes invité(e)s.
- Parlez des vêtements que vous cherchez, de vos couleurs préférées, de votre taille. Trouvez-vous le vêtement trop large, trop serré, etc.?
- Demandez les prix et dites si vous trouvez que c'est cher, bon marché, etc.

Vendeur/Vendeuse

- Demandez les tailles, préférences, etc. des client(e)s.
- Répondez à toutes les questions de vos client(e)s.
- Suggérez des vêtements appropriés.

Coup de main

To compare French and American sizes, see the chart on p. 202.

6 Conversez Interviewez un(e) camarade de classe. Answers will vary.

1. Qu'est-ce que tu portes l'hiver? Et l'été?
2. Qu'est-ce que tu portes pour aller à l'université?
3. Qu'est-ce que tu portes pour aller à la plage (*beach*)?
4. Qu'est-ce que tu portes pour faire une randonnée?
5. Qu'est-ce que tu portes pour aller en boîte de nuit?
6. Qu'est-ce que tu portes pour un entretien d'embauche (*job interview*)?
7. Quelle est ta couleur préférée? Pourquoi?
8. Qu'est-ce que tu portes pour aller dans un restaurant très élégant?
9. Où est-ce que tu achètes tes vêtements? Pourquoi?
10. Est-ce que tu prêtes (*lend*) tes vêtements à tes ami(e)s?

7 Défilé de mode Votre classe a organisé un défilé de mode (*fashion show*). Votre partenaire est mannequin (*model*) et vous représentez la marque (*brand*) de vêtements. Pendant que votre partenaire défile, vous décrivez à la classe les vêtements qu'il ou elle porte. Après, échangez les rôles. Answers will vary.

MODÈLE

Et voici la charmante Julie, qui porte les modèles de la dernière collection H&M®: une chemise à manches courtes et un pantalon noir, ensemble idéal pour aller en boîte de nuit. Ses chaussures blanches vont parfaitement avec l'ensemble. Cette collection H&M est très à la mode et très bon marché.

OPTIONS

Extra Practice Have students write a paragraph about a real or imaginary vacation they plan to take and the clothing they will take with them. Tell them to include what kind of weather they expect at their destination and any weather-specific clothing they will need. Ask volunteers to share their paragraphs with the class.

Extra Practice Have students write descriptions of an article of clothing or a complete outfit that best describes them without indicating who they are. Collect the papers and read the descriptions aloud. The rest of the class has to guess who wrote each one.

Les sons et les lettres

Audio: Concepts, Activities
Record & Compare

National Standards: comparisons

Open vs. closed vowels: Part 3

The letter combination **eu** can be pronounced two different ways, open and closed. Compare the pronunciation of the vowel sounds in these words.

cheveux **neveu** **heure** **meilleur**

When **eu** is followed by a pronounced consonant, it has an open sound. The open **eu** sound does not exist in English. To pronounce it, say **è** with your lips only slightly rounded.

peur **jeune** **chanteur** **beurre**

The letter combination **œu** is usually pronounced with an open **eu** sound.

sœur **bœuf** **œuf** **chœur**

When **eu** is the last sound of a syllable, it has a closed vowel sound, similar to the vowel sound in the English word *full*. While this exact sound does not exist in English, you can make the closed **eu** sound by saying **é** with your lips rounded.

deux **bleu** **peu** **mieux**

When **eu** is followed by a *z* sound, such as a single **s** between two vowels, it is usually pronounced with the closed **eu** sound.

chanteuse **généreuse** **sérieuse** **curieuse**

Prononcez Répétez les mots suivants à voix haute.

1. leur
2. veuve
3. neuf
4. vieux
5. curieux
6. acteur
7. monsieur
8. coiffeuse
9. ordinateur
10. tailleur
11. vendeuse
12. couleur

Articulez Répétez les phrases suivantes à voix haute.

1. Le professeur Heudier a soixante-deux ans.
2. Est-ce que Matthieu est jeune ou vieux?
3. Monsieur Eustache est un chanteur fabuleux.
4. Eugène a les yeux bleus et les cheveux bruns.

Dictons Répétez les dictons à voix haute.

Qui vole un œuf, vole un bœuf.[1]

Les conseilleurs ne sont pas les payeurs.[2]

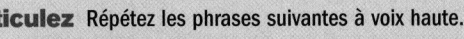

[1] He who steals an egg would steal an ox.
[2] Those who give advice are not the ones who pay the price.

ressources
LM p. 46
espaces.vhlcentral.com

Section Goals

In this section, students will learn about additional open and closed vowel sounds.

Instructional Resources
espaces.vhlcentral.com: Textbook MP3s; Lab MP3s; WB/VM/LM Answer Key; IRM (Textbook Audioscript; Lab Audioscript); activities; downloads; reference tools

Suggestions

- Model the pronunciation of each open and closed vowel sound. Have students watch the shape of your mouth, then repeat each sound after you. Pronounce each of the example words and have students repeat them.
- Point out that the letters **o** and **e** together are usually written as the single character **œ**.
- Ask students to provide more examples of words from this lesson or previous lessons with these vowel sounds. Examples: **tailleur, vendeuse, ordinateur, feuille,** and **chanteuse.**
- Dictate five familiar words containing the open and closed vowels presented in this section to the class, repeating each one at least two times. Then write them on the board or on a transparency and have students check their spelling.

Dictons Ask students to explain the two sayings in their own words.

OPTIONS

Extra Practice Use these sentences with open and closed vowel sounds for additional practice or dictation. **1. Elle a deux ordinateurs neufs. 2. Ma sœur est jeune et sérieuse. 3. J'aime mieux être coiffeur ou ingénieur. 4. Tu veux ce vieux tailleur?**

Extra Practice Teach students these French tongue-twisters that contain the open and closed vowel sounds on this page. **Pépé paie peu, mémé m'émeut. Je veux un feutre bleu.**

Section Goals

In this section, students will learn functional phrases for talking about clothing and gifts through comprehensible input.

Instructional Resources
*espaces.vhlcentral.com: Video; WB/VM/LM Answer Key; IRM (Videoscript; **Roman-photo** Translations); activities; downloads; reference tools*
Video on DVD

Video Recap: Leçon 6A
Before doing this **Roman-photo**, review the previous one with this activity.

1. Qu'est-ce que Sandrine a préparé pour l'anniversaire de Stéphane? (les desserts: une mousse au chocolat, des biscuits et un gâteau)
2. Qu'est-ce que Rachid et Astrid ont acheté comme cadeaux? (une calculatrice, des livres et une montre)
3. Qui a fait la décoration au café? (Astrid, Valérie et Amina)
4. Qu'est-ce qu'Amina a apporté à la fête? (un cadeau et de la glace au chocolat)

Video Synopsis Stéphane arrives at his surprise party. Sandrine explains that David is in Paris with his parents. Sandrine admires Amina's outfit, and Stéphane opens his presents. Valérie gives him a leather jacket and gloves. When he opens the books and calculator from Rachid and Astrid, he tries to act pleased. Then he realizes they were gag gifts when he sees the watch.

Suggestions
- Have students read the title, glance at the video stills, and predict what the episode will be about. Record their predictions.
- Have students read the **Roman-photo** conversation in groups of six.
- Have students scan the captions for vocabulary related to clothing and colors.
- Review students' predictions and ask them which ones were correct.

NATIONAL STANDARDS communication cultures

L'anniversaire

S Video: *Roman-photo* Record & Compare

PERSONNAGES

Amina

Astrid

Rachid

Sandrine

Stéphane

Valérie

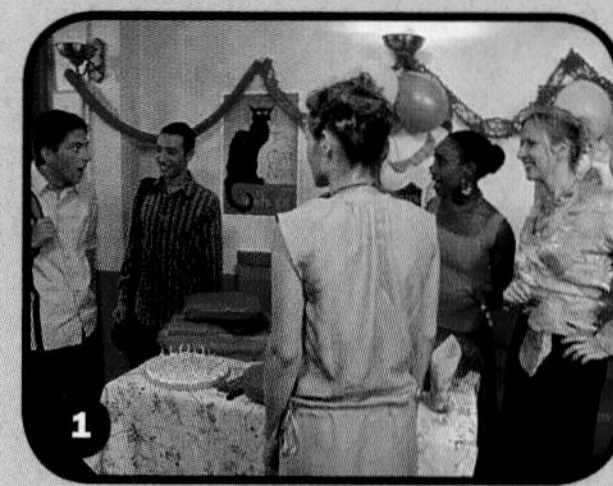
1

Au café...

VALÉRIE, SANDRINE, AMINA, ASTRID ET RACHID Surprise! Joyeux anniversaire, Stéphane!
STÉPHANE Alors là, je suis agréablement surpris!
VALÉRIE Bon anniversaire, mon chéri!
SANDRINE On a organisé cette surprise ensemble...

2

VALÉRIE Pas du tout! C'est Sandrine qui a presque tout préparé.
SANDRINE Oh, je n'ai fait que les desserts et ton gâteau d'anniversaire.
STÉPHANE Tu es un ange.
RACHID Bon anniversaire, Stéphane. Tu sais, à ton âge, il ne faut pas perdre son temps. Alors cette année, tu travailles sérieusement, c'est promis?
STÉPHANE Oui, oui.

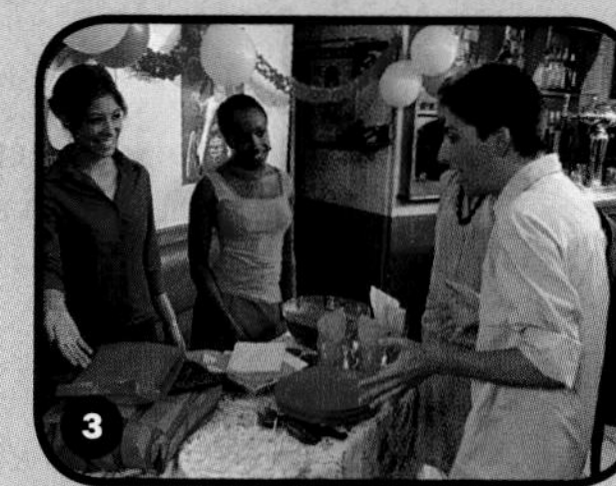
3

AMINA Rachid a raison. Dix-huit ans, c'est une étape importante dans la vie! Il faut fêter ça.
ASTRID Joyeux anniversaire, Stéphane.
STÉPHANE Oh, et en plus, vous m'avez apporté des cadeaux!

6

AMINA Oui. J'ai tout fait moi-même: ce tee-shirt, cette jupe et j'ai acheté ces chaussures.
SANDRINE Tu es une véritable artiste, Amina! Ta jupe est très originale! J'adore!
AMINA J'ai une idée. Tu me prêtes ta robe grise samedi et je te prête ma jupe. D'accord?
SANDRINE Bonne idée!

7

STÉPHANE Eh! C'est super cool, ce blouson en cuir noir. Avec des gants en plus! Merci, maman!
AMINA Ces gants vont très bien avec le blouson! Très à la mode!
STÉPHANE Tu trouves?

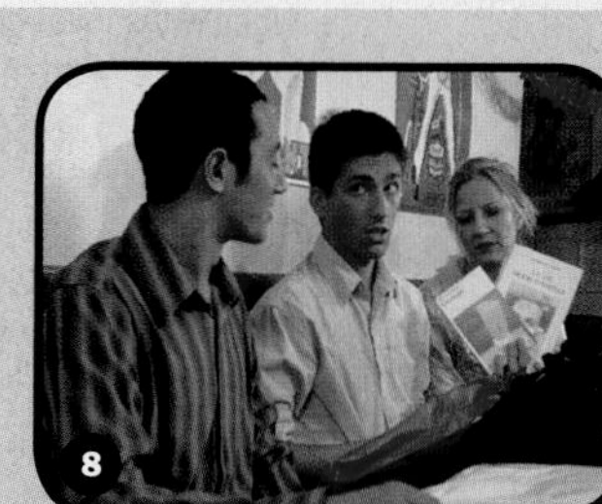
8

RACHID Tiens, Stéphane.
STÉPHANE Mais qu'est-ce que c'est? Des livres?
RACHID Oui, la littérature, c'est important pour la culture générale!
VALÉRIE Tu as raison, Rachid.
STÉPHANE Euh oui... euh... c'est gentil... euh... merci, Rachid.

ACTIVITÉS

1 Vrai ou faux? Indiquez si ces affirmations sont vraies ou fausses. Corrigez les phrases fausses.

1. David ne veut pas (*doesn't want*) aller à la fête.
   Faux. David est désolé de ne pas être là.
2. Sandrine porte une jupe bleue.
   Faux. Sandrine porte une robe grise.
3. Amina a fait sa jupe elle-même (*herself*).
   Vrai.
4. Le tee-shirt d'Amina est en soie.
   Vrai.
5. Valérie donne un blouson en cuir et une ceinture à Stéphane.
   Faux. Valérie donne un blouson en cuir et des gants à Stéphane.
6. Sandrine n'aime pas partager ses vêtements.
   Faux. Sandrine va prêter sa robe à Amina.
7. Pour Amina, 18 ans, c'est une étape importante.
   Vrai.
8. Sandrine n'a rien fait (*didn't do anything*) pour la fête.
   Faux. Sandrine a fait le gâteau et les desserts.
9. Rachid donne des livres de littérature à Stéphane.
   Vrai.
10. Stéphane pense que ses amis sont drôles.
    Faux. Stéphane pense que ses amis ne sont pas drôles.

Practice more at **espaces.vhlcentral.com.**

OPTIONS

Avant de regarder la vidéo Before viewing the video, have students work in pairs and make a list of words and expressions they might hear at a surprise birthday party.

Regarder la vidéo Show the video episode and tell students to check off the words or expressions they hear on their lists. Then show the episode again and have students give you a play-by-play description of the action. Write their descriptions on the board.

Les amis fêtent l'anniversaire de Stéphane.

4

5

SANDRINE Ah au fait, David est désolé de ne pas être là. Ce week-end, il visite Paris avec ses parents. Mais il pense à toi.
STÉPHANE Je comprends tout à fait. Les parents de David sont de Washington, n'est-ce pas?
SANDRINE Oui, c'est ça.

AMINA Merci, Sandrine. Je trouve que tu es très élégante dans cette robe grise! La couleur te va très bien.
SANDRINE Vraiment? Et toi, tu es très chic. C'est du coton?
AMINA Non, de la soie.
SANDRINE Cet ensemble, c'est une de tes créations, n'est-ce pas?

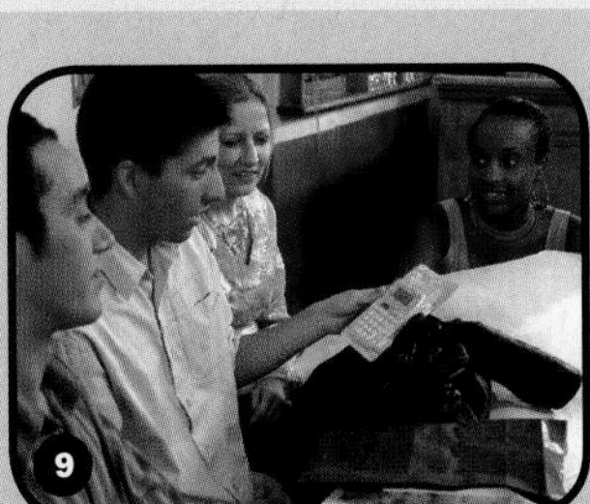
9

10

STÉPHANE Une calculatrice rose... pour moi?
ASTRID Oui, c'est pour t'aider à répondre à toutes les questions en maths, et avec le sourire.
STÉPHANE Euh, merci beaucoup! C'est très... utile.
ASTRID Attends! Il y a encore un cadeau pour toi...

STÉPHANE Ouah, cette montre est géniale, merci!
ASTRID Tu as aimé notre petite blague? Nous, on a bien ri.
RACHID Eh Stéphane! Tu as vraiment aimé tes livres et ta calculatrice?
STÉPHANE Ouais, vous deux, ce que vous êtes drôles.

Expressions utiles

Talking about your clothes

- **Et toi, tu es très chic. C'est du coton/de la soie?**
  And you, you are very chic. Is it cotton/silk?
- **J'ai tout fait moi-même.**
  I did/made everything myself.
- **La couleur te va très bien.**
  The color suits you well.
- **Tu es une véritable artiste! Ta jupe est très originale!**
  You are a true artist! Your skirt is very original!
- **Tu me prêtes ta robe grise samedi et je te prête ma jupe.**
  You lend me your gray dress Saturday and I'll lend you my skirt.
- **C'est super cool, ce blouson en cuir/laine/velours noir(e). Avec des gants en plus!**
  It's really cool, this black leather/wool/velvet jacket. With gloves as well!

Additional vocabulary

- **Vous m'avez apporté des cadeaux!**
  You brought me gifts!
- **Tu sais, à ton âge, il ne faut pas perdre son temps.**
  You know, at your age, one should not waste time.
- **C'est pour t'aider à répondre à toutes les questions en maths, et avec le sourire.**
  It's to help you answer all the questions in math, with a smile.
- **agréablement surpris(e)** *pleasantly surprised*
- **C'est promis?** *Promise?*
- **Il pense à toi.** *He's thinking of you.*
- **tout à fait** *absolutely*
- **Vraiment?** *Really?*
- **véritable** *true, genuine*
- **Pour moi?** *For me?*
- **Attends!** *Wait!*
- **On a bien ri.** *We had a good laugh.*

ACTIVITÉS

2 Identifiez Indiquez qui a dit (*said*) ces phrases: Amina (A), Astrid (As), Rachid (R), Sandrine (S), Stéphane (St) ou Valérie (V).

S 1. Tu es une véritable artiste.
As 2. On a bien ri.
A 3. Très à la mode.
St 4. Je comprends tout à fait.
V 5. C'est Sandrine qui a presque tout préparé.
R 6. C'est promis?

3 À vous! Ce sont les soldes. Sandrine, David et Amina vont dans un magasin pour acheter des vêtements. Ils essaient différentes choses, donnent leur avis (*opinion*) et parlent de leurs préférences, des prix et des matières (*fabrics*). Avec un(e) partenaire, écrivez la conversation et jouez la scène devant la classe.

ressources: VM pp. 233-234 | DVD Leçon 6B | espaces.vhlcentral.com

Expressions utiles
- Model the pronunciation of the **Expressions utiles** and have students repeat them.
- As you work through the list, point out expressions with indirect object pronouns, disjunctive pronouns, and **-re** verbs. Tell students that these grammar structures will be formally presented in **Espace structures**.
- Respond briefly to questions about indirect object pronouns and **-re** verbs. Reinforce correct forms, but do not expect students to produce them consistently at this time.
- Point out that the pronouns **tu**, **te**, and **toi** all mean *you*, but they cannot be used interchangeably because they are different parts of speech.
- To practice different fabrics and other materials, ask students yes/no and either/or questions about their clothing. Examples: ____, **votre chemisier, c'est du coton ou de la soie?** ____, **votre blouson, c'est du cuir ou de la laine? Avez-vous des gants en cuir noir?**

1 Suggestion Have students write their corrections for false statements on the board.

1 Expansion For additional practice, give students these items. **11. Stéphane n'est pas content de la fête. (Faux.) 12. David est à Paris avec ses parents (Vrai.) 13. Sandrine aime bien la jupe d'Amina. (Vrai.) 14. Stéphane n'aime pas la montre. (Faux.)**

2 Expansion In addition to identifying the speaker, have students give the name of the person to whom each one is speaking. **1. Amina 2. Stéphane 3. Stéphane 4. Sandrine 5. Stéphane 6. Stéphane**

3 Suggestion Tell students to use an idea map or outline to plan their conversation before they begin to write it.

OPTIONS

Game Divide the class into two teams. Give one team member a card with the name of an item of clothing or an accessory. This person has 30 seconds to draw the item and one player on his or her team has to guess what it is. Give a point for each correct answer. If a player cannot guess the item within the time limit, the next player on the opposing team may "steal" the point.

Extra Practice Bring in photos from French fashion magazines or catalogues, such as ***3 Suisses*** or ***La Redoute***, and have students give their opinions about the clothing and accessories.

Section Goals

In this section, students will:

- learn about the fashion industry in France and where to buy clothes
- learn terms related to fashion
- read about traditional clothing and fabrics in some francophone regions
- read about Coco Chanel

Instructional Resources
espaces.vhlcentral.com: activities; downloads; reference tools

Culture à la loupe

Avant la lecture Have students read the title, look at the photos, and predict what this reading is about. Then ask them to share any information they know about French fashion or the fashion industry in France.

Lecture

- Point out the **Coup de main** and have students compare the clothing sizes. Example: **Si une femme porte la taille 8 aux États-Unis, quelle taille porte-t-elle en France? (38)**
- Explain that a **hypermarché** is similar to a Wal-Mart in the United States.

Après la lecture Ask students: **Où les Français achètent-ils leurs vêtements? (dans les boutiques indépendantes, dans les chaînes de magasins spécialisés, dans les hypermarchés, dans les centres commerciaux, au marché aux puces, sur catalogue et sur Internet)**

1 Expansion For additional practice, give students these items. **11. Les couturiers ne dessinent pas de modèles pour le prêt-à-porter. (Faux.) 12. On peut (*can*) acheter des vêtements aux marchés aux puces en France. (Vrai.)**

CULTURE À LA LOUPE

La mode en France

Paris est la capitale de la mode et les maisons de haute couture° françaises, comme Chanel, Yves Saint Laurent, Dior ou Christian Lacroix, sont connues° dans le monde entier°. Pendant° une semaine, en été et en hiver, elles présentent leurs collections à la presse et à un public privilégié, au cours de° défilés de mode°. Les modèles° sont uniques et très chers. Certains couturiers° dessinent° aussi des modèles pour le prêt-à-porter°. Ils vendent° ces collections plus abordables° dans leurs boutiques et parfois dans les grands magasins, comme les Galeries Lafayette ou le Printemps à Paris.

Pour la majorité des Français, la mode est un moyen° d'expression. Beaucoup de jeunes, par exemple, personnalisent leurs vêtements «basiques», ce qu'on appelle «customiser». Les magasins préférés des Français sont les boutiques indépendantes et, pour les jeunes, les chaînes de magasins spécialisés, comme Naf Naf ou Kookaï. Les Français achètent également° des vêtements dans les hypermarchés° et les centres commerciaux, comme Auchan ou Carrefour. Des vêtements sont aussi vendus° sur les marchés aux puces°, et par correspondance, dans des catalogues et sur Internet.

maisons de haute couture *high fashion houses* **connues** *known* **monde entier** *entire world* **Pendant** *For* **au cours de** *during* **défilés de mode** *fashion shows* **modèles** *creations (clothing)* **couturiers** *fashion designers* **dessinent** *design* **prêt-à-porter** *ready-to-wear* **vendent** *sell* **plus abordables** *more affordable* **moyen** *means* **également** *also* **hypermarchés** *large supermarkets* **vendus** *sold* **marchés aux puces** *flea markets*

Coup de main

Comparaison des tailles

FEMMES						
France	32	34	36	38	40	42
USA	2	4	6	8	10	12
HOMMES (PANTALONS)						
France	36	38	40	42	44	46
USA	26	28	30	32	34	36

Évolution des dépenses des Français pour la mode (en % du budget)

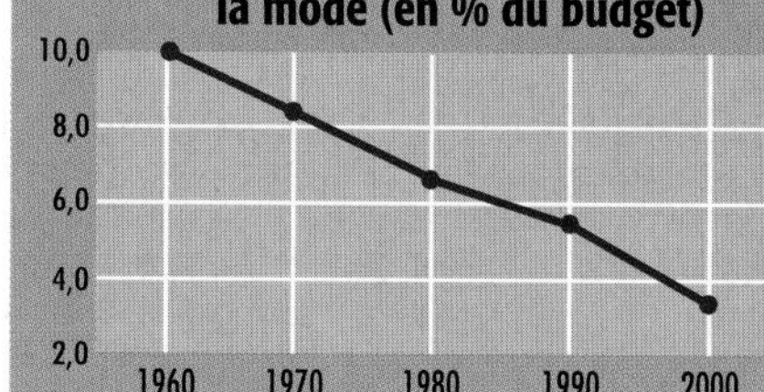

SOURCE: Francoscopie

ACTIVITÉS

1 Vrai ou faux? Indiquez si les phrases sont **vraies** ou **fausses**. Corrigez les phrases fausses.

1. Les grands couturiers français dessinent des modèles de haute couture. Vrai.
2. Les défilés de haute couture ont lieu (*take place*) en mai. Faux. Ils ont lieu en été et en hiver.
3. Le prêt-à-porter est plus cher que (*more expensive than*) la haute couture. Faux. La haute couture est plus chère.
4. Les vêtements de prêt-à-porter sont parfois vendus dans les grands magasins. Vrai.
5. Les jeunes Français aiment personnaliser leurs vêtements. Vrai.
6. En France, on vend des vêtements par correspondance. Vrai.
7. Aujourd'hui, les Français dépensent plus (*more*) d'argent pour leurs vêtements qu'en (*than in*) 1980. Faux. Ils dépensent moins d'argent aujourd'hui.
8. Naf Naf est une maison de haute couture française. Faux. Naf Naf est une chaîne de magasins.
9. On vend des vêtements dans les hypermarchés en France. Vrai.
10. Les Français n'achètent pas de vêtements sur Internet. Faux. Ils achètent des vêtements sur Internet.

Practice more at **espaces.vhlcentral.com.**

202 *deux cent deux*

OPTIONS

Cultural Comparison Have students work in groups of three and compare where French people and Americans shop for clothing. Tell them to list the similarities and differences in a two-column chart under the headings **Similitudes** and **Différences**. After they complet their charts, have two groups get together and compare their lists.

Extra Practice First, ask students what information the graph **Évolution des dépenses des Français pour la mode** shows. (The percentage of total budget that the French spent on fashion from 1960–2000.) Then ask: **Quel pourcentage de leur budget les Français ont-ils dépensé pour la mode en 1960? (10,0%) Et en 1970? (8,2%) En 1980? (6,3%) En 1990? (5,5%) En 2000? (3,7%)** (Accept approximate answers.)

LE FRANÇAIS QUOTIDIEN

Les vêtements et la mode

fringues (*f.*)	*clothes*
look (*m.*)	*style*
vintage (*m.*)	*vintage clothing*
BCBG (bon chic bon genre)	*chic and conservative*
ringard(e)	*out-of-style*
être bien/ mal sapé(e)	*to be well/ badly dressed*
être sur son 31	*to be well dressed*

PORTRAIT

Coco Chanel, styliste parisienne

«La mode se démode°, le style jamais.» —*Coco Chanel*

Coco Chanel (1883-1971) est considérée comme étant° l'icône du parfum et de la mode du vingtième siècle°. Dans les années 1910, elle a l'idée audacieuse° d'intégrer la mode «à la garçonne» dans ses créations: les lignes féminines empruntent aux° éléments de la mode masculine. C'est la naissance du fameux tailleur Chanel. Pour «Mademoiselle Chanel», l'important dans la mode, c'est que les vêtements permettent de bouger°; ils doivent° être simples et confortables. Son invention de «la petite robe noire» illustre l'esprit° classique et élégant de ses collections. De nombreuses célébrités ont immortalisé le nom de Chanel: Jacqueline Kennedy avec le tailleur et Marilyn Monroe avec le parfum No. 5, par exemple.

se démode *goes out of fashion* **étant** *being* **vingtième siècle** *twentieth century* **idée audacieuse** *daring idea* **empruntent aux** *borrow* **bouger** *move* **doivent** *have to* **esprit** *spirit*

LE MONDE FRANCOPHONE

Vêtements et tissus

Voici quelques vêtements et tissus° traditionnels du monde francophone.

En Afrique centrale et de l'Ouest

Le boubou tunique plus ou moins° longue et souvent très colorée

Les batiks tissus traditionnels très colorés

En Afrique du Nord

La djellaba longue tunique à capuche°

Le kaftan sorte de djellaba portée à la maison

À la Martinique

Le madras tissu typique aux couleurs vives

À Tahiti

Le paréo morceau° de tissu attaché au-dessus de la poitrine° ou à la taille°

tissus *fabrics* **plus ou moins** *more or less* **à capuche** *hooded* **morceau** *piece* **poitrine** *chest* **taille** *waist*

SUR INTERNET

Combien de couturiers présentent leurs collections dans les défilés de mode, à Paris, chaque hiver?

Go to **espaces.vhlcentral.com** to find more cultural information related to this **ESPACE CULTURE.**

ACTIVITÉS

2 Coco Chanel Complétez les phrases.

1. Coco Chanel était (*was*) ___stylise de mode___.
2. Le style Chanel est inspiré de ___la mode masculine___.
3. Les vêtements Chanel sont ___simples et confortables___.
4. Jacqueline Kennedy portait souvent des ___tailleurs___ Chanel.
5. D'après «Mademoiselle Chanel», il est très important de pouvoir (*to be able to*) ___bouger___ dans ses vêtements.
6. C'est Coco Chanel qui a inventé ___la petite robe noire___.

3 Le «relookage» Vous êtes conseiller/conseillère en image (*image counselors*), spécialisé(e) dans le «relookage». Votre nouveau (nouvelle) client(e), une célébrité, vous demande de l'aider à sélectionner un nouveau style. Discutez de ce nouveau look avec un(e) partenaire.

ressources

espaces.vhlcentral.com

deux cent trois 203

Le français quotidien
- Model the pronunciation of each term and have students repeat it.
- Ask students to give some examples of vintage clothing.
- Have volunteers create sentences using these words.

Portrait Have students look at the photos of Coco Chanel and describe her appearance and clothing.

Le monde francophone
- Bring in photos from magazines or the Internet of people wearing these types of clothing and fabrics to show the class.
- Ask a few content questions based on the reading. Examples: **1. Comment s'appelle la tunique que les gens portent en Afrique centrale? (le boubou) 2. Qu'est-ce qu'une djellaba? (C'est une longue tunique à capuche.) 3. À la Martinique, on porte des vêtements faits de batik ou de madras? (des vêtements faits de madras) 4. Où porte-t-on le kaftan? (en Afrique du Nord)**

2 Expansion For additional practice, give students these items. **7. Les collections de Chanel sont classiques et ____. (élégantes) 8. Marilyn Monroe a immortalisé ____ de Chanel. (le parfum No. 5)**

3 Suggestions
- Tell students that they can change the person's hairstyle as well as the clothing. Encourage them to include what is wrong with the person's present style in their discussion.
- Have students write their descriptions and read them aloud for the class.

OPTIONS

Vêtements et tissus Have students create five true/false statements based on the content in **Le monde francophone**. Then have students get together with a classmate and take turns reading their statements and responding **vrai** or **faux**.

Les couturiers Have students research one of the **couturiers** from the **Sur Internet** activity and write a short paragraph about the person. Tell them to include information about the person's accomplishments, type(s) of clothing he or she designs, where it is sold, and any other important details.

Section Goals

In this section, students will learn:
- indirect object pronouns
- some additional uses of disjunctive pronouns

Instructional Resources
*espaces.vhlcentral.com: Lab MP3s; WB/VM/LM Answer Key; IRM (**Essayez!** and **Mise en pratique** answers; Lab Audioscript); activities; downloads; reference tools*

Suggestions
- Say and write on the board: **Valérie achète un blouson à Stéphane.** Tell students that an indirect object is a noun or pronoun that answers the question *to whom* or *for whom* an action is done. Ask them what the indirect object of the verb is in the sentence. (Stéphane) Explain that indirect object nouns are introduced by the preposition **à**. Point out that **un blouson** is the direct object of the verb.
- Write the indirect object pronouns on the board. Show students some photos and say: **Je vous montre mes photos.** Give a student an object, such as a book, and say: **Je vous prête mon livre.** Continue the same procedure with the remaining indirect object pronouns.
- Explain that, in French, indirect object pronouns do not follow verbs as they do in English. The word order in French is [*subject*] + (**ne**) [*indirect object pronoun*] + [*verb* or *subject*] + [*conjugated verb*] + [*indirect object pronoun*] + [*infinitive*].
- Ask students to call out the disjunctive pronouns. Explain the use of **-même(s)** and provide a few examples. Then have students create some sentences with the disjunctive pronouns.

6B.1 Indirect object pronouns

National Standards: comparisons

- An indirect object expresses *to whom* or *for whom* an action is done. In the example below, the indirect object answers this question: **À qui parle Claire?** (*To whom does Claire speak?*)

SUBJECT — VERB — INDIRECT OBJECT NOUN

Claire parle à sa mère.
Claire speaks to her mother.

Indirect object pronouns					
singular			plural		
me	te	lui	nous	vous	leur

- Indirect object pronouns replace indirect object nouns.

Claire parle à **sa mère**. *Claire speaks to her mother.*	Claire **lui** parle. *Claire speaks to her.*
J'envoie des cadeaux à **mes nièces**. *I send gifts to my nieces.*	Je **leur** envoie des cadeaux. *I send them gifts.*

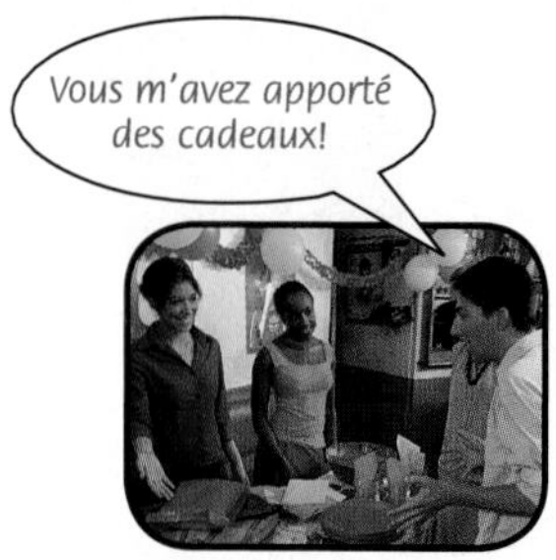

Vous m'avez apporté des cadeaux!

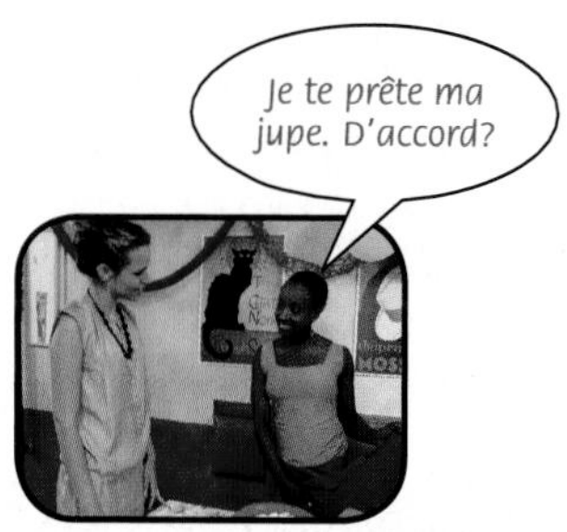

Je te prête ma jupe. D'accord?

- The indirect object pronoun usually precedes the conjugated verb.

Antoine, je **te** parle. *Antoine, I'm speaking to you.*	Notre père **nous** a envoyé un e-mail. *Our father sent us an e-mail.*

- In a negative statement, place the indirect object pronoun between **ne** and the conjugated verb.

Antoine, je **ne te parle** pas de ça. *Antoine, I'm not speaking to you about that.*	Notre père **ne nous a** pas envoyé d'e-mail. *Our father didn't send us an e-mail.*

- When an infinitive follows a conjugated verb, the indirect object pronoun precedes the infinitive.

Nous allons **lui donner** la cravate. *We're going to give him the tie.*	Ils espèrent **vous prêter** le costume. *They hope to lend you the suit.*

MISE EN PRATIQUE

1 Complétez Corinne fait du shopping avec sa copine Célia. Trouvez le bon pronom d'objet indirect pour compléter ses phrases.

1. Je leur achète des baskets. (à mes cousins)
2. Je te prends une ceinture. (à toi, Célia)
3. Nous lui achetons une jupe. (à notre copine Christelle)
4. Célia nous prend des lunettes de soleil. (à ma mère et à moi)
5. Je vous achète des gants. (à ta mère et à toi, Célia)
6. Célia m' achète un pantalon. (à moi)

2 Dialogues Complétez les dialogues.

1. M. SAUNIER Tu m'as posé une question, chérie?
   MME SAUNIER Oui. Je t' ai demandé l'heure.
2. CLIENT Je cherche un beau pull.
   VENDEUSE Je vais vous montrer ce pull noir.
3. PROF 1 Mes étudiants ont passé l'examen.
   PROF 2 Tu leur envoies les résultats?
4. MÈRE Qu'est-ce que vous allez faire?
   ENFANTS On va aller au cinéma. Tu nous donnes de l'argent?
5. PIERRE Tu me téléphones ce soir?
   CHARLOTTE D'accord. Je te téléphone.
6. GÉRARD Christophe a oublié son pull. Il a froid!
   VALENTIN Je lui prête mon blouson.

3 Assemblez Avec un(e) partenaire, assemblez les éléments des colonnes pour comparer vos familles et vos amis. Answers will vary.

MODÈLE
Étudiant(e) 1: *Mon père me prête souvent sa voiture.*
Étudiant(e) 2: *Mon père, lui, il nous prête de l'argent.*

A	B	C
je	acheter	argent
tu	apporter	biscuits
mon père	envoyer	cadeaux
ma mère	expliquer	devoirs
mon frère	faire	e-mails
ma sœur	montrer	problèmes
mon/ma petit(e) ami(e)	parler	vêtements
mes copains	payer	voiture
	prêter	

Practice more at **espaces.vhlcentral.com.**

OPTIONS

Extra Practice Write sentences with indirect objects on the board. Examples: **Anne-Laure ne te donne pas de biscuits. Pierre ne me parle pas. Loïc prête de l'argent à Louise. Marie nous pose une question. Je téléphone à mes amis.** Have students come to the board and circle the indirect objects.

Small Groups Working in groups of three, the first student lends an object to the second and says: **Je te prête mon/ma....** The second student responds: **Tu me prêtes ton/ta....** The third student says: **Marc lui prête son/sa....** Groups repeat the procedure until everyone has begun the chain twice. To practice plural pronouns, have two groups get together. Then two students lend something to two other students.

COMMUNICATION

4 Qu'allez-vous faire? Avec un(e) partenaire, dites ce que vous allez faire pour aider ces personnes. Employez les verbes de la liste et présentez vos réponses à la classe. Answers will vary.

MODÈLE

Un ami a soif.
On va lui donner de l'eau.

apporter	parler
demander	poser des questions
donner	préparer
envoyer	prêter
faire	téléphoner

1. Une personne âgée (*old*) a froid.
2. Des touristes sont perdus (*lost*).
3. Un homme est sans abri (*homeless*).
4. Votre professeur est à l'hôpital.
5. Des amis vous invitent à manger chez eux.
6. Vos nièces ont faim.
7. Votre petit(e) ami(e) fête son anniversaire.
8. Votre meilleur(e) (*best*) ami(e) a des problèmes.

5 Les cadeaux de l'année dernière Par groupes de trois, parlez des cadeaux que vous avez achetés à votre famille et à vos amis l'année dernière. Que vous ont-ils acheté? Présentez vos réponses à la classe. Answers will vary.

MODÈLE

Étudiant(e) 1: *Qu'est-ce que tu as acheté à ta mère?*
Étudiant(e) 2: *Je lui ai acheté un ordinateur.*
Étudiant(e) 3: *Ma copine Dominique m'a acheté une montre.*

6 Au grand magasin Par groupes de trois, jouez les rôles de deux client(e)s et d'un(e) vendeur/vendeuse. Les client(e)s cherchent des vêtements pour faire des cadeaux. Ils parlent de ce qu'ils (*what they*) cherchent et le/la vendeur/vendeuse leur fait des suggestions. Answers will vary.

Verbs used with indirect object pronouns

demander à	*to ask, to request*	**parler à**	*to speak to*
donner à	*to give to*	**poser une question à**	*to pose/ ask a question (to)*
envoyer à	*to send to*	**prêter à**	*to lend to*
montrer à	*to show to*	**téléphoner à**	*to phone, to call*

- The indirect object pronouns **me** and **te** become **m'** and **t'** before a verb beginning with a vowel sound.

Ton petit ami **t'envoie** des fleurs.
Your boyfriend sends you flowers.

Isabelle **m'a** prêté son sac à main.
Isabelle lent me her handbag.

Disjunctive pronouns

BOÎTE À OUTILS

In **Leçon 3B**, you learned to use disjunctive pronouns (**moi**, **toi**, **lui**, **elle**, **nous**, **vous**, **eux**, **elles**) after prepositions: **J'ai une écharpe pour ton frère/pour lui.** (*I have a scarf for your brother/for him.*)

- Disjunctive pronouns can also be used alone or in phrases without a verb.

Qui prend du café? — **Moi**! — **Eux** aussi?
Who's having coffee? — *Me!* — *Them, too?*

- Disjunctive pronouns emphasize the person to whom they refer.

Moi, je porte souvent une casquette.
Me, I often wear a cap.

Mon frère, **lui**, il déteste les casquettes.
My brother, him, he hates caps.

- To say *myself*, *ourselves*, etc., add **-même(s)** after the disjunctive pronoun.

Tu fais ça **toi-même**?
Are you doing that yourself?

Ils organisent la fête **eux-mêmes**.
They're organizing the party themselves.

Essayez! **Complétez les phrases avec le pronom d'objet indirect approprié.**

1. Tu *nous* montres tes photos? (*us*)
2. Luc, je *te* donne ma nouvelle adresse. (*you, fam.*)
3. Vous *me* posez de bonnes questions. (*me*)
4. Nous *leur* avons demandé. (*them*)
5. On *vous* achète une nouvelle robe. (*you, form.*)
6. Ses parents *lui* ont acheté un tailleur. (*her*)
7. Je vais *lui* téléphoner à dix heures. (*him*)
8. Elle va *me* prêter sa jupe. (*me*)

Essayez! Have students restate items 1, 2, 4, 5, and 6 using the **futur proche**. Example: **1. Tu vas nous montrer tes photos?**

1 Expansion Have students write four more sentences with indirect objects (not pronouns). Tell them to exchange papers with a classmate and rewrite the sentences, replacing the indirect object with the corresponding indirect object pronoun.

2 Suggestion To check students' answers, have volunteers read different roles aloud.

3 Expansion Have students convert three of their statements into questions for their partner, using **Qui...?** or **À qui...?** Example: **Qui te prête ses livres?**

4 Suggestion Have pairs write their suggestions. Encourage them to come up with multiple responses for each item.

5 Suggestion Before beginning the activity, give students a few minutes to jot down a list of gifts they bought for their family last year. Then have three volunteers read the **modèle** aloud.

6 Suggestions
- Before beginning the activity, have students describe what is happening in the photo.
- Videotape the scenes in class or have students videotape themselves outside of class. Show the videos so students can critique their role-plays.

OPTIONS

Video Have students read along as you show the video episode again. Tell them to note each time an indirect object pronoun or a disjunctive pronoun is used. After the video, ask them to read the sentences they identified and to say to whom each pronoun refers.

Pairs Have students work in pairs. Tell them to write five questions they would like to ask their partner that require an indirect object pronoun in the answer. They should then take turns asking and answering each other's questions.

Section Goals

In this section, students will learn:

- regular **-re** verbs
- irregular **-re** verbs

Instructional Resources
*espaces.vhlcentral.com: Lab MP3s; WB/VM/LM Answer Key; IRM (**Essayez!** and **Mise en pratique** answers; Lab Audioscript; Info Gap Activities); activities; downloads; reference tools*

Suggestions

- Model the pronunciation of the **-re** verbs and have students repeat them.
- Introduce the verbs by talking about yourself and asking students follow-up questions. Examples: **Je réponds à tous mes e-mails. Et vous, répondez-vous à tous vos e-mails? D'habitude, je mets un pantalon. Aujourd'hui, j'ai mis une jupe/un costume. Et vous, que mettez-vous, en général? Je rends visite à ma famille le week-end. Rendez-vous visite à votre famille le week-end?**
- Ask a volunteer to go to the board and write the conjugation of **donner** as you write the conjugation of **attendre**. Have students compare the endings of the two verb conjugations, noting the similarities and differences.
- Follow the same procedure with the conjugations of **conduire** and **mettre**. Point out that many irregular **-re** verbs have two stems. Examples: **conduire (condui-, conduis-)** and **mettre (met-, mett-)**.
- Explain that the past participles of regular **-re** verbs add **-u** to the stem. Example: **attendre: attendu.** Then say the verbs listed and have students respond with the past participles.
- Point out the irregular past participles.

6B.2 Regular and irregular -re verbs

NATIONAL STANDARDS comparisons

Point de départ You've already seen infinitives that end in **-er** and **-ir**. The infinitive forms of some French verbs end in **-re**.

- Many **-re** verbs, such as **attendre** (*to wait*), follow a regular pattern of conjugation, as shown below.

Attendre

j'attends	**nous attendons**
tu attends	**vous attendez**
il/elle attend	**ils/elles attendent**

Tu **attends** les soldes?
Are you waiting for the sales?

Nous **attendons** dans le magasin.
We're waiting in the store.

Other regular -re verbs

descendre (de)	*to go downstairs; to get off; to take down*	**rendre (à)**	*to give back, to return (to)*
		rendre visite (à)	*to visit someone*
entendre	*to hear*	**répondre (à)**	*to respond, to answer (to)*
perdre (son temps)	*to lose (to waste one's time)*	**vendre**	*to sell*

- The verb **attendre** means *to wait* or *to wait for*. Unlike English, it does not require a preposition.

Marc **attend le bus**.
Marc is waiting for the bus.

Ils **attendent Robert**.
They're waiting for Robert.

- To form the past participle of regular **-re** verbs, drop the **-re** from the infinitive and add **-u**.

Les étudiants ont **vendu** leurs livres.
The students sold their books.

Il a **entendu** arriver la voiture de sa femme.
He heard his wife's car arrive.

J'ai **répondu** à ton e-mail.
I answered your e-mail.

Nous avons **perdu** patience.
We lost patience.

- **Rendre visite à** means *to visit a person*, while **visiter** means *to visit a place*.

Tu **rends visite à ta grand-mère** le lundi.
You visit your grandmother on Mondays.

Cécile va **visiter le musée** aujourd'hui.
Cécile is going to visit the museum today.

MISE EN PRATIQUE

1 Qui fait quoi? Quelles phrases vont avec les illustrations?

1.

3.

2.

4.

__3__ a. Martin attend ses copains.
__4__ b. Nous rendons visite à notre grand-mère.
__1__ c. Tu vends de jolis vêtements.
__2__ d. Je ris en regardant un film.

2 Les clients difficiles Florian et Vincent travaillent dans un grand magasin. Complétez leur conversation.

VINCENT Tu n'as pas encore mangé?
FLORIAN Non, j' (1) __attends__ (attendre) Jérémy.
VINCENT Il ne (2) __descend__ (descendre) pas tout de suite. Il (3) __perd__ (perdre) son temps avec un client difficile. Il (4) __met__ (mettre) des cravates, des costumes, des chaussures...
FLORIAN Nous ne (5) __vendons__ (vendre) pas souvent à des clients comme ça.
VINCENT C'est vrai. Ils (6) __promettent__ (promettre) d'acheter quelque chose, puis ils partent les mains vides (*empty*).

3 La journée de Béatrice Hier, Béatrice a fait une liste des choses à faire. Avec un(e) partenaire, utilisez les verbes de la liste au passé composé pour dire (*to say*) tout ce qu'elle a fait. Answers will vary.

attendre	mettre
conduire	rendre visite
entendre	traduire

1. devoir d'espagnol	4. tante Albertine
2. mon nouveau CD	5. gants dans mon sac
3. e-mail de Sébastien	6. vieille voiture (car)

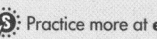

Practice more at **espaces.vhlcentral.com.**

OPTIONS

Extra Practice Do a rapid-response drill. Write an infinitive from the list of **-re** verbs on the board. Call out subject pronouns and/or names, and have students respond with the correct verb form. Then repeat the drill, having students respond with the correct forms of the **passé composé**.

Pairs Have students make a list of five things their parents allow them to do and five things their parents don't allow them to do. Then have them get together in pairs and compare their lists. Have volunteers report to the class the items they have in common. Example: **Mes parents ne me permettent pas de mettre des vêtements trop serrés. Ils me permettent parfois de conduire leur voiture.**

NATIONAL communication STANDARDS

COMMUNICATION

4 Fréquence Employez les verbes de la liste et d'autres verbes pour dire (*to tell*) à un(e) partenaire ce que (*what*) vous faites tous les jours, une fois par mois et une fois par an. Alternez les rôles. Answers will vary.

MODÈLE

Étudiant(e) 1: *J'attends mes copains au resto U tous les jours.*
Étudiant(e) 2: *Moi, je rends visite à mes grands-parents une fois par mois.*

attendre	perdre
conduire	rendre
entendre	répondre
mettre	sourire
?	?

5 La journée des vendeuses Votre professeur va vous donner, à vous et à votre partenaire, une série d'illustrations qui montrent la journée d'Aude et d'Aurélie. Attention! Ne regardez pas la feuille de votre partenaire. Answers will vary.

MODÈLE

Étudiant(e) 1: *Le matin, elles ont conduit pour aller au magasin.*
Étudiant(e) 2: *Après, ...*

6 Les charades Par groupes de quatre, jouez aux charades. Chaque étudiant(e) pense à une phrase différente avec un des verbes en **-re**. La première personne qui devine (*guesses*) propose la prochaine charade. Answers will vary.

- Some verbs whose infinitives end in **-re** are irregular.

Irregular -re verbs

	conduire *(to drive)*	**mettre** *(to put (on))*	**rire** *(to laugh)*
je	conduis	mets	ris
tu	conduis	mets	ris
il/elle	conduit	met	rit
nous	conduisons	mettons	rions
vous	conduisez	mettez	riez
ils/elles	conduisent	mettent	rient

Je **conduis** bien. *I'm driving well.*
Il **met** ses gants. *He puts on his gloves.*
Elles **rient** toujours. *They always laugh.*

Other irregular -re verbs

like *conduire*

construire	*to build, to construct*
détruire	*to destroy*
produire	*to produce*
réduire	*to reduce*
traduire	*to translate*

like *mettre*

permettre	*to allow*
promettre	*to promise*

like *rire*

sourire	*to smile*

- The past participle of the verb **mettre** is **mis**. Verbs derived from **mettre** (**permettre**, **promettre**) follow the same pattern: **permis**, **promis**.
- The past participle of **conduire** is **conduit**. Verbs like it follow the same pattern: **construire → construit**; **détruire → détruit**; **produire → produit**; **réduire → réduit**; **traduire → traduit**.
- The past participle of **rire** is **ri**. The past participle of **sourire** is **souri**.
- Like for the other verb groups, use present tense verb forms to give commands.

Conduis moins vite! *Drive slower!*
Promettez-moi. *Promise me.*
Réponds-lui. *Answer him.*

Essayez! Complétez les phrases avec la forme correcte du présent du verbe.

1. Ils attendent (attendre) l'arrivée du train.
2. Nous répondons (répondre) aux questions du professeur.
3. Je souris (sourire) quand je suis heureuse.
4. Si on construit (construire) trop, on détruit (détruire) la nature.
5. Quand il fait froid, vous mettez (mettre) un pull.
6. Est-ce que les étudiants entendent (entendre) le professeur?

Essayez! For additional practice, change the subjects of the sentences and have students restate them.

1 Expansion Have students create short descriptions of the people, places, and objects in the drawings by putting in additional information.

2 Expansion Ask students comprehension questions about the dialogue. Examples: **1. Pourquoi Henri n'a-t-il pas encore mangé? (Il attend Jean-Michel.) 2. Où est Jean-Michel? (Il est avec un client difficile.) 3. Pourquoi ce client est-il difficile? (parce qu'il met tout, mais il part les mains vides)**

3 Expansion Have students also say what Béatrice did not do.

4 Suggestion Have two volunteers read the **modèle** aloud.

4 Expansion To practice the **passé composé**, have students specify when they did these things. Example: **J'ai rendu visite à mes grands-parents en avril.**

5 Suggestion Divide the class into pairs and distribute the Info Gap Handouts found on the Supersite for this activity.

6 Suggestion This activity can also be used as a game by dividing the class into two teams with players from each team acting out the charades.

OPTIONS

Extra Practice Ask students personalized questions using **-re** verbs. Examples: **1. Comment les étudiants perdent-ils leur temps? 2. Est-ce que l'argent rend les gens heureux? 3. Que vend-on dans une boutique? 4. Vos parents vous permettent-ils d'avoir une carte de crédit à la fac? 5. Conduisez-vous rapidement? 6. Où mettez-vous vos livres en classe?**

Pairs Have students work in pairs. Tell them to write a conversation between a clerk in a clothing store and a customer who has lost some item like sunglasses, a scarf, or gloves. The customer should explain the situation, and the clerk should ask for details, such as when the item was lost and a description. Alternatively, pairs can role-play this situation.

Instructional Resources
espaces.vhlcentral.com: IRM (Info Gap Activities); Testing Program, pp. 45–48; Test Files; Testing Program MP3s; activities; downloads; reference tools
Test Generator

1 Suggestion Have two volunteers read the **modèle** aloud. Remind students that they need to use the preposition **à** before the indirect object in the questions.

2 Expansion Take a quick class survey of students' reactions to each type of e-mail. Tally the results on the board.

3 Suggestion Before beginning the activity, have students jot down a list of objects.

4 Suggestion Before beginning, have the class identify the items in each **ensemble**.

4 Expansion Have students think of two new destinations. Tell them to switch roles and repeat the activity.

5 Suggestion Encourage students to use some of the comments in the **Expressions utiles** on page 201 in their role-plays.

6 Suggestion Divide the class into pairs and distribute the Info Gap Handouts found on the Supersite for this activity.

Révision

1 Je leur téléphone Par groupes de quatre, interviewez vos camarades. Préparez dix questions avec un verbe et une personne de la liste. Écrivez les réponses. Answers will vary.

MODÈLE

Étudiant(e) 1: *Est-ce que tu parles souvent à ton frère?*
Étudiant(e) 2: *Oui, je lui parle le lundi.*

verbes	personnes
donner un cadeau	copain ou copine d'enfance
envoyer une carte/un e-mail	cousin ou cousine
parler	grands-parents
rendre visite	petit(e) ami(e)
téléphoner	sœur ou frère

2 Mes e-mails Ces personnes vous envoient des e-mails. Que faites-vous? Vous ne répondez pas, vous attendez quelques jours, vous leur téléphonez? Par groupes de trois, comparez vos réactions. Answers will vary.

MODÈLE

Étudiant(e) 1: *Ma mère m'envoie un e-mail tous les jours.*
Étudiant(e) 2: *Tu lui réponds tout de suite?*
Étudiant(e) 3: *Tu préfères lui téléphoner?*

1. un e-mail anonyme
2. un e-mail d'un(e) camarade de classe
3. un e-mail d'un professeur
4. un e-mail d'un(e) ami(e) d'enfance
5. un e-mail d'un(e) ex-petit(e) ami(e)
6. un e-mail de vos parents

3 Une liste Des membres de votre famille ou des amis vous ont donné ou acheté des vêtements que vous n'aimez pas du tout. Faites une liste de quatre ou cinq de ces vêtements. Comparez votre liste à la liste d'un(e) camarade. Answers will vary.

MODÈLE

Étudiant(e) 1: *Ma soeur m'a donné une écharpe verte et laide et mon père m'a acheté des chaussettes marron trop petites!*
Étudiant(e) 2: *L'année dernière, mon petit ami m'a donné...*

4 Quoi mettre? Vous et votre partenaire allez faire des choses différentes. Un(e) partenaire va fêter la retraite de ses parents à Tahiti. L'autre va skier dans les Alpes. Qu'allez-vous porter? Demandez des vêtements à votre partenaire si vous n'aimez pas tous les vêtements de votre ensemble. Answers will vary.

MODÈLE

Étudiant(e) 1: *Est-ce que tu me prêtes ton tee-shirt violet?*
Étudiant(e) 2: *Ah non, j'ai besoin de ce tee-shirt. Tu me prêtes ton pantalon?*

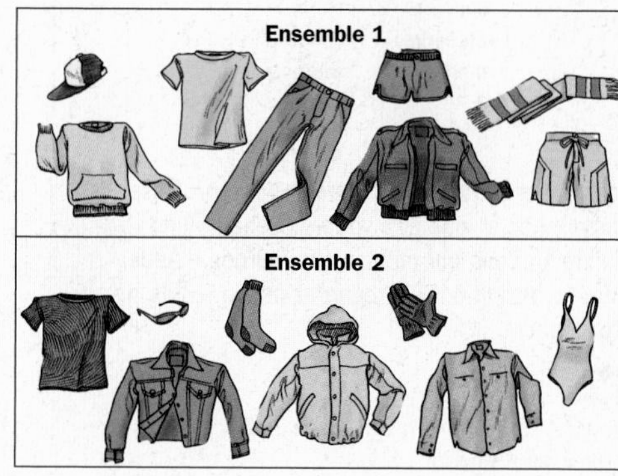

5 S'il te plaît Votre ami(e) a acheté un nouveau vêtement que vous aimez beaucoup. Vous essayez de convaincre (*to convince*) cet(te) ami(e) de vous prêter ce vêtement. Préparez un dialogue avec un(e) partenaire où vous employez tous les verbes. Jouez la scène pour la classe. Answers will vary.

aller avec	montrer
aller bien	prêter
donner	promettre
mettre	rendre

6 Bon anniversaire, Nicolas! Votre professeur va vous donner, à vous et à votre partenaire, deux feuilles d'activités différentes. Attention! Ne regardez pas la feuille de votre partenaire. Answers will vary.

MODÈLE

Étudiant(e) 1: *Les amis de Nicolas lui téléphonent.*
Étudiant(e) 2: *Ensuite, ...*

ressources
WB pp. 79-82 | LM pp. 47-48 | espaces.vhlcentral.com

OPTIONS

Small Groups Have students work in groups of three. Tell them to imagine that it is the holiday season. They have to create a radio commercial for a clothing store. The commercials should include gift ideas for prospective customers, such as what they can buy, for whom, and at what price.

Extra Practice Have students write a conversation between two people sitting at a busy sidewalk café in the city. They are watching the people who walk by, asking each other questions about what the passersby are doing, and making comments about their clothing. Tell students to use as many **-re** verbs and verbs that take indirect object pronouns as possible.

À l'écoute

communication STANDARDS

Audio: Activities

STRATÉGIE

Listening for linguistic cues

You can enhance your listening comprehension by listening for specific linguistic cues. For example, if you listen for the endings of conjugated verbs, or for familiar constructions, such as the **passé composé** with **avoir**, **avoir envie de** + [*infinitive*] or **aller** + [*infinitive*], you can find out whether a person did something in the past, wants to do something, or will do something in the future.

To practice listening for linguistic cues, you will listen to four sentences. As you listen, note whether each sentence refers to a past, present, or future action.

Préparation

Regardez la photo. Où sont Pauline et Sarah? Que font-elles? Décrivez les vêtements qu'elles regardent. À votre avis, pour quelle occasion cherchent-elles des vêtements?

À vous d'écouter

Écoutez la conversation entre Pauline et Sarah. Après une deuxième écoute, indiquez si les actions suivantes sont du **passé (p)**, du **présent (pr)** ou du **futur (f)**.

__p__ 1. aller à la fête de la cousine de Pauline
__p__ 2. beaucoup danser
__p__ 3. rencontrer un musicien
__f__ 4. déjeuner avec un garçon intéressant
__pr__ 5. chercher de nouveaux vêtements
__f__ 6. mettre des chaussures en cuir noir
__pr__ 7. aimer une robe bleue
__f__ 8. acheter la robe bleue

Practice more at **espaces.vhlcentral.com.**

Compréhension

Complétez Complétez les phrases.

1. Pauline cherche des vêtements pour __c__.
   a. un dîner b. une fête c. un rendez-vous
2. Pauline va acheter un pantalon noir et __b__.
   a. un tee-shirt b. une chemise rose c. un maillot de bain
3. Sarah pense que __b__ ne vont pas avec les nouveaux vêtements.
   a. l'écharpe verte b. les baskets roses c. les lunettes de soleil
4. D'après Sarah, les chaussures __a__ sont élégantes.
   a. en cuir noir b. roses c. en soie
5. La couleur préférée de Sarah n'est pas le __c__.
   a. rose b. jaune c. vert
6. Sarah cherche un vêtement pour __b__.
   a. un déjeuner b. la fête de retraite de son père c. un mariage
7. Sarah va acheter une robe en soie __a__.
   a. à manches courtes b. à manches longues c. rouge
8. La robe existe en vert, en bleu et en __c__.
   a. noir b. marron c. blanc

Une occasion spéciale Décrivez la dernière fois que vous avez fêté une occasion spéciale. Qu'est-ce que vous avez fêté? Où? Comment? Avec qui? Qu'est-ce que vous avez mis comme vêtements? Et les autres?

MODÈLE

Samedi, nous avons fêté l'anniversaire de mon petit ami. Nous avons invité nos amis Paul, Marc, Julia et Naomi dans un restaurant élégant. Moi, j'ai mis une belle robe verte en coton. Mon petit ami a mis un costume gris. Paul a mis...

Section Goals

In this section, students will:
- learn to listen for specific linguistic cues
- listen for temporal cues in sentences
- listen to a conversation and complete several activities

Instructional Resources
espaces.vhlcentral.com: IRM (Textbook Audioscript); Textbook MP3s; downloads; reference tools

Stratégie
Script 1. Est-ce que tu vas aller au mariage de tes cousins? (*future*) 2. Elles ont acheté dix nouveaux maillots de bain pour cet été! (*past*) 3. Noémie a envie de parler à Martha de son rendez-vous avec Julien. (*present*) 4. Vous avez vendu tous les tee-shirts? (*past*)

Préparation Have students look at the photo of Pauline and Sarah, describe what they see, and predict what they are talking about.

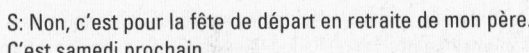

À vous d'écouter
Script PAULINE: Tiens, bonjour, Sarah. Ça va?
SARAH: Ah, bonjour Pauline! Oui, très bien et toi?
P: Bien, merci. Dis, je t'ai cherchée hier soir à la fête de ma cousine...
S: Excuse-moi. J'ai passé une mauvaise journée hier et j'ai complètement oublié. Mais... Et toi? Tu as aimé la fête?
P: Oui, j'ai beaucoup dansé et j'ai rencontré un garçon intéressant. Il s'appelle Boris et il est musicien. Je vais déjeuner avec lui demain midi, alors je cherche de nouveaux vêtements pour notre rendez-vous. Qu'est-ce que tu penses de ce pantalon noir avec cette chemise rose?
S: Oui, c'est bien. Et qu'est-ce que tu vas mettre comme chaussures?
P: Ben, ces baskets roses, non?
S: Ah non. Des chaussures en cuir noir, c'est plus élégant.
P: Oui, tu as raison. Et toi, qu'est-ce que tu cherches?
S: Une jolie robe pas trop chère.
P: Tu as un rendez-vous, toi aussi?
S: Non, c'est pour la fête de départ en retraite de mon père. C'est samedi prochain.
P: Regarde cette robe rouge en coton. Elle est jolie, non?
S: Oui, mais elle a l'air un peu serrée. Je préfère les robes larges.
P: Et cette belle robe en soie à manches courtes?
S: Je déteste le vert. Ils l'ont en bleu?
P: Oui, et en blanc aussi.
S: Super. Je vais prendre la bleue.

Section Goals

In this section, students will read historical and cultural information about **Aquitaine**, **Midi-Pyrénées**, and **Languedoc-Roussillon**.

Instructional Resources
espaces.vhlcentral.com: Transparency #33; WB/VM/LM Answer Key; activities; downloads; reference tools

Carte des régions Aquitaine, Midi-Pyrénées et Languedoc-Roussillon

- Have students look at the map or use **Transparency #33**. Ask volunteers to read aloud the names of cities and geographical features. Model French pronunciation as necessary. Point out the locations of Spain and Andorra.
- Have students identify the locations of the places in the photos.

La région en chiffres

- Point out the three different coats of arms for the regions.
- Have volunteers read the sections aloud. After each section, ask questions about the content.
- Point out that the Bordeaux region is one of the largest producers of fine wines in the world.
- Ask students to share any information they might know about the **Personnes célèbres**.

Incroyable mais vrai! The original cave at Lascaux was closed in 1963 in order to save the paintings from deterioration. A replica of the cave, known as Lascaux II, was built nearby and contains reproductions of the Great Hall of Bulls and the Painted Gallery.

NATIONAL STANDARDS connections cultures

Interactive Map Reading

Panorama

la dune du Pilat

Aquitaine

La région en chiffres

- **Superficie:** *41.308 km²*
- **Population:** *3.049.000*
- **Industrie principale:** *agriculture*
- **Villes principales:** *Bordeaux, Pau, Périgueux*

Midi-Pyrénées

La région en chiffres

- **Superficie:** *45.348 km²*
- **Population:** *2.687.000*
- **Industries principales:** *aéronautique, agriculture*
- **Villes principales:** *Auch, Toulouse, Rodez*

Languedoc-Roussillon

La région en chiffres

- **Superficie:** *27.376 km²*
- **Population:** *2.458.000*
- **Industrie principale:** *agriculture*
- **Villes principales:** *Montpellier, Nîmes, Perpignan*

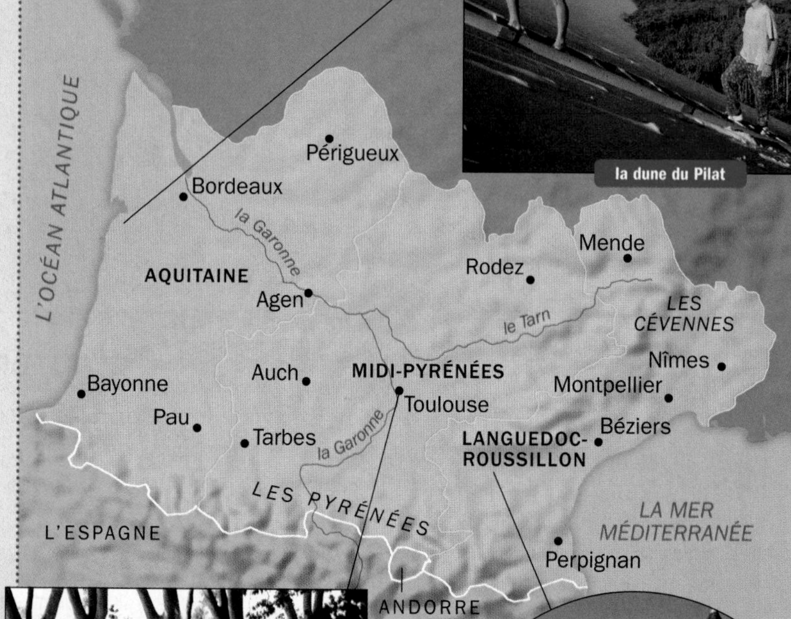

le canal du Midi

la cité de Carcassonne

Personnes célèbres

- **Aliénor d'Aquitaine,** *Aquitaine, reine° de France (1122–1204)*
- **Jean Jaurès,** *Midi-Pyrénées, homme politique (1859–1914)*
- **Henri de Toulouse-Lautrec,** *Midi-Pyrénées, peintre et lithographe (1864–1901)*
- **Georges Brassens,** *Languedoc-Roussillon, chanteur (1921–1981)*
- **Francis Cabrel,** *Aquitaine, chanteur (1953–)*

reine *queen* **grotte** *cave* **gravures** *carvings* **peintures** *paintings* **découvrent** *discover*

Incroyable mais vrai!

Appelée parfois «la chapelle Sixtine préhistorique», la grotte° de Lascaux, en Aquitaine, est décorée de 1.500 gravures° et de 600 peintures°, vieilles de plus de 17.000 ans. En 1940, quatre garçons découvrent° ce sanctuaire. Les fresques, composées de plusieurs animaux, ont jusqu'à ce jour une signification mystérieuse.

OPTIONS

Personnes célèbres **Eleanor of Aquitaine** was one of the most powerful women in Europe during her time. Her first husband was King Louis VII of France. She later became Queen of England when she married Henry II. She was also the mother of Richard the Lionheart. **Francis Cabrel** is a guitarist, composer, and singer of blues-rock, pop, and contemporary folk music.

Jean Jaurès was a leader of the French socialist movement. **Toulouse-Lautrec** established lithography as a major art form with his vivid posters depicting Parisian nightlife in Montmartre. **Georges Brassens** was a poetic songwriter and performer who used his lyrics to address social issues.

La gastronomie

Le foie gras et le cassoulet

Le foie gras° et le cassoulet sont des spécialités du sud-ouest° de la France. Le foie gras est un produit° de luxe, en général réservé aux grandes occasions. On le mange sur du pain grillé ou comme ingrédient d'un plat° élaboré. Le cassoulet est un plat populaire, préparé à l'origine dans une «cassole°». Les ingrédients varient, mais en général, cette spécialité est composée d'haricots° blancs, de viande° de porc et de canard, de saucisses°, de tomates, d'ail° et d'herbes.

Les monuments

Les arènes de Nîmes

Inspirées du Colisée de Rome, les arènes° de Nîmes, en Languedoc-Roussillon, datent de la fin du premier siècle. C'est l'amphithéâtre le plus grand° de France et le mieux° conservé de l'ère° romaine. Les spectacles de gladiateurs d'autrefois°, appréciés par plus de° 20.000 spectateurs, sont aujourd'hui remplacés° par des corridas° et des spectacles musicaux pour le plaisir de 15.000 spectateurs en été et 7.000 spectateurs en hiver.

Le sport

La pelote basque

L'origine de la pelote est ancienne°: on retrouve des versions du jeu chez les Mayas, les Grecs et les Romains. C'est au Pays Basque, à la frontière° entre la France et l'Espagne, en Aquitaine, que le jeu se transforme en véritable sport. La pelote basque existe sous sept formes différentes; le principe de base est de lancer° une balle en cuir°, la «pelote», contre un mur° avec la «paleta», une raquette en bois°, et le «chistera», un grand gant en osier°.

Les traditions

La langue d'Oc

La langue d'Oc (l'occitan) est une langue romane° née° dans le sud de la France. Cette langue a donné son nom à la région: Languedoc-Roussillon. La poésie lyrique occitane et l'idéologie des troubadours° du Moyen Âge° influencent les valeurs° culturelles et intellectuelles européennes. Il existe plusieurs dialectes de l'occitan. «Los cats fan pas de chins» (les chats ne font pas des chiens) et «la bornicarié porta pas pa a casa» (la beauté n'apporte pas de pain à la maison) sont deux proverbes occitans connus°.

Qu'est-ce que vous avez appris? Répondez aux questions par des phrases complètes.

1. Qui était (*was*) peintre, lithographe et d'origine midi-pyrénéenne?
   Henri de Toulouse-Lautrec était peintre, lithographe et d'origine midi-pyrénéenne.
2. Quel est le surnom (*nickname*) de la grotte de Lascaux?
   Le surnom de la grotte de Lascaux est «la chapelle Sixtine préhistorique».
3. Que trouve-t-on dans la grotte de Lascaux?
   On trouve des peintures et des gravures dans la grotte de Lascaux.
4. Quand mange-t-on du foie gras, en général?
   En général, le foie gras est réservé aux grandes occasions.
5. Quels ingrédients utilise-t-on pour le cassoulet?
   On utilise des haricots blancs, de la viande, des saucisses, des tomates, de l'ail et des herbes.
6. Quand les arènes de Nîmes ont-elles été construites?
   Les arènes de Nîmes datent de la fin du premier siècle.
7. Combien de spectateurs y a-t-il dans les arènes de Nîmes en hiver? Il y a 7.000 personnes dans les arènes de Nîmes en hiver.
8. Quelles civilisations ont une version de la pelote?
   Les civilisations des Mayas, des Romains et des Grecs ont une version de la pelote.
9. Combien de formes différentes de pelote basque y a-t-il?
   Il y a sept formes différentes de pelote basque.
10. Qu'est-ce qui influence les valeurs culturelles et intellectuelles européennes? Ce sont la poésie occitane et l'idéologie des troubadours du Moyen Âge.

Practice more at **espaces.vhlcentral.com.**

ressources: WB pp. 83–84 | espaces.vhlcentral.com

SUR INTERNET

Go to espaces.vhlcentral.com to find more cultural information related to this **PANORAMA**.

1. Il existe une forme de la pelote basque aux États-Unis. Comment s'appelle ce sport?
2. Cherchez des peintures de la grotte de Lascaux. Quelles sont vos préférées? Pourquoi?
3. Cherchez plus d'informations sur Henri de Toulouse-Lautrec. Avez-vous déjà vu quelques-unes de ses peintures? Où?

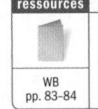

foie gras *fatted liver of an animal served in the form of a pâté* **sud-ouest** *southwest* **produit** *product* **plat** *dish* **cassole** *pottery dish* **haricots** *beans* **viande** *meat* **saucisses** *sausages* **ail** *garlic* **arènes** *amphitheaters* **le plus grand** *the largest* **le mieux** *the most* **ère** *era* **autrefois** *long ago* **plus de** *more than* **remplacés** *replaced* **corridas** *bullfights* **ancienne** *ancient* **frontière** *border* **lancer** *throw* **cuir** *leather* **mur** *wall* **bois** *wood* **osier** *wicker* **langue romane** *romance language* **née** *born* **troubadours** *minstrels* **Moyen Âge** *Middle Ages* **valeurs** *values* **connus** *well-known*

Le foie gras et le cassoulet

- The raising of geese and ducks for **foie gras** dates back to ancient Egypt, Greece, Rome, and Gaul. There is a rivalry amongst the southwestern regions for the best variety of **cassoulet**. The differences occur mostly in the type of meat used.
- Ask students to name some regional dishes in the United States. Also ask if they know of a dish similar to **cassoulet**.

Les arènes de Nîmes

- Throughout the centuries the amphitheater always remained in use. At one time, residences were built within the arena and during another period it was used as a fortress and refuge. In 1909, it was restored to its original design as an arena for entertainment.
- Have students compare today's amphitheaters or arenas to the amphitheaters of the Romans.

La pelote basque

- The courts, gear, and rules used to play **pelote basque** can vary from village to village. But no matter which variety of the game is played, it is always lively and fast. The speed of the **pelote** can get up to 250–300 km/hr or about 155–186 mph.
- Ask students what sports are similar to **pelote basque**.

La langue d'Oc **La langue d'Oc** is spoken by approximately 1.5 million people in the south of France. Although the Occitan dialects have been influenced by modern French, they still strongly resemble dialects of the Middle Ages in which the phonology and grammar are more closely related to Spanish.

OPTIONS

La langue d'Oc The troubadours of southern France were traveling poet-musicians. They wrote and performed courtly love poems or songs for the ladies of the courts in the Occitan dialect Provençal. Eleanor of Aquitaine, a patron of troubadours, used her influence to introduce Provençal poetry at the courts in northern France. This type of poetry thrived in the twelfth and thirteenth centuries, and had a great influence on later lyric poetry.

Cultural Activity Point out that France and Spain share a border. Ask students to give some examples of cross-cultural influences. (**les corridas à Nîmes, la pelote basque,** or jai-alai, and **la poésie lyrique des troubadours**)

Section Goals
In this section, students will:
- learn to recognize word families
- read an invitation to an engagement celebration

Stratégie Write **inviter** on the board and ask students what it means in English. Next to it, write **invitation** and **invité(e)**, then ask them the meaning of these words. Point out that all three words have the same root and belong to a word family. Explain that recognizing the relationship between a known word and unfamiliar words can help them infer the meaning of words they don't know.

Examinez le texte Tell students to scan the text for the new words and try to guess their meaning based on the root and context before they look them up in the dictionary.

Familles de mots Point out the three categories of words. You might want to tell students to look for the words in the **Vocabulaire** on page 216.

Lecture

NATIONAL STANDARDS communication cultures

Reading

Avant la lecture

STRATÉGIE

Recognizing word families

Recognizing related words can help you guess the meaning of words in context, ensuring better comprehension of a reading selection. Using this strategy will enrich your French vocabulary.

Examinez le texte

Voici quelques mots que vous avez déjà appris. Pour chaque mot, trouvez un terme de la même famille dans le texte et utilisez un dictionnaire pour donner son équivalent en anglais.

MODÈLE

ami	*amitié*	*friendship*
1 diplôme	diplômés	*graduates*
2. commencer	le commencement	*beginning*
3. sortir	la sortie	*exit*
4. timide	la timidité	*shyness*
5. difficile	les difficultés	*difficulties*
6. préférer	les préférences	*preferences*

Familles de mots

Avec un(e) partenaire, trouvez le bon mot pour compléter chaque famille de mots. (Note: vous avez appris tous les mots qui manquent (*all the missing words*) dans cette unité et il y a un mot de chaque famille dans le texte.)

MODÈLE

attendre l'attente attendu(e)

VERBE	NOM	ADJECTIF
1. boire	la boisson	bu(e)
2. fêter	la fête	festif/festive
3. vivre	la vie	vif/vive
4. rajeunir	la jeunesse	jeune
5. surprendre	la surprise	surpris(e)
6. répondre	la réponse	répondu(e)

Ça y est; c'est officiel

Bravo, jeunes diplômés°! C'est le commencement d'une nouvelle vie. Il est maintenant temps de fêter ça!

Pour faire retomber la pression°, Mathilde, Christophe, Alexandre et Laurence vous invitent à fêter entre amis votre diplôme bien mérité°!

À laisser chez vous:
La timidité, la fatigue, les soucis° et les difficultés des études et de la vie quotidienne° pour une ambiance festive

Quoi d'autre?
Un groupe de musique (le frère de Mathilde et sa bande) va venir° jouer pour nous!

OPTIONS

Extra Practice Write these words on the board. At least one form will be familiar to students. Have them discuss the relationship between the words and their meanings. **1. idée, idéal(e), idéaliste, idéalement, idéaliser 2. organiser, organisateur/organisatrice, organisation, organisationnel(le), 3. chanter, chanteur/chanteuse, chansonnette, chanson, chantable**

Pairs Working in pairs, have students discuss whether or not they would attend a party like the one in the selection. Tell them to talk about the aspects of the activities that they do and do not like. Afterwards, ask them if they have ever attended a similar event and what types of activities were planned for the guests.

À apporter:
Nourriture° et boissons: Chaque invité apporte quelque chose pour le buffet: salades, plats° froids/chauds, fruits, desserts, boissons
Activités: Jeux de cartes, ballons°, autres jeux selon° vos préférences, chaises pliantes°, maillot de bain (pour la piscine), crème solaire
Surprenez-nous!

Quand:
Le samedi 16 juillet (de 16h00 à minuit)

Où:
Chez les parents de Laurence, 14 route des Mines, Allouagne, Nord-Pas-de-Calais

Comment y aller°:
À la sortie d'Allouagne, prenez la route de Lozinghem. Tournez à gauche sur la route des Mines. Le numéro 14 est la grande maison sur la droite. (Nous allons mettre des ballons° de couleurs sur la route pour indiquer l'endroit.)

Au programme:
Faire la fête, bien sûr! Manger (buffet et barbecue), rire, danser et fêter la fin des cours! Attendez-vous à passer un bon moment!

Autres activités:
Activités en plein air° (football, badmington, volley, piscine... et surtout détente°!)

Pour répondre à cette invitation:
Téléphonez à Laurence (avant le 6 juillet, SVP°) au 06.14.55.85.80 ou par e-mail:
laurence@courriel.fr

Ça y est! *That's it!* **diplômés** *graduates* **faire retomber la pression** *to unwind* **bien mérité** *well deserved* **soucis** *worries* **vie quotidienne** *daily life* **va venir** *is going to come* **Nourriture** *Food* **plats** *dishes* **ballons** *balls* **selon** *depending on* **pliantes** *folding* **y aller** *get there* **ballons** *balloons* **en plein air** *outdoor* **détente** *relaxation* **svp** *please*

Après la lecture

Vrai ou faux? **Indiquez si les phrases sont vraies ou fausses. Corrigez les phrases fausses.** Answers may vary slightly.

1. C'est une invitation à une fête d'anniversaire.
   Faux. C'est une invitation pour fêter le diplôme.
2. Les invités vont passer un mauvais moment.
   Faux. Les invités vont passer un bon moment.
3. On va manger des salades et des desserts.
   Vrai.
4. Les invités vont faire toutes les activités dans la maison.
   Faux. Les invités vont faire des activités en plein air.
5. Un groupe de musique va jouer à la fête.
   Vrai.
6. La fête commence à 16h00.
   Vrai.

Conseillez **Vous êtes Laurence, un des organisateurs de la fête. Les invités veulent (*want*) assister à la fête, mais ils vous contactent pour parler de leurs soucis respectifs. Donnez-leur des conseils (*advice*) pour les mettre à l'aise (*at ease*).** Answers may vary. Suggested answers:

MODÈLE

Isabelle: J'ai beaucoup de soucis cette semaine.
Vous: *Tu vas laisser tes soucis à la maison et venir (come) à la fête.*

1. Thomas: Je ne sais (*know*) pas quoi apporter.
   Vous: Tu vas apporter des boissons gazeuses.
2. Sarah: Je me perds (*get lost*) facilement quand je conduis.
   Vous: Tu vas chercher les ballons de couleurs sur la route.
3. Sylvie: Je ne fais pas de sport.
   Vous: Tu vas jouer aux cartes et discuter.
4. Salim: Je veux (*want*) répondre à l'invitation, mais je n'ai pas d'ordinateur.
   Vous: Tu vas me téléphoner.
5. Sandra: Je n'aime pas le barbecue.
   Vous: Tu vas manger des salades.
6. Véronique: J'aime faire du sport en plein air, mais je n'aime pas le football.
   Vous: Tu vas faire du badmington et du volley.

On va à la fête? **Vous êtes invité(e) à cette fête et vous allez amener un(e) ami(e). Téléphonez à cet(te) ami(e) (votre partenaire) pour l'inviter. Donnez des détails et répondez aux questions de votre ami(e) sur les hôtes, les invités, les activités de l'après-midi et de la soirée, les choses à apporter, etc.**

Vrai ou faux? Go over the answers with the class. For the false items, have students point out where they found the correct answer in the text.

Conseillez
- This activity can be done in pairs. Remind students to switch roles after items 1–3.
- Have pairs write two more situations for the activity. Then have them exchange papers with another pair and complete the situations.

On va à la fête? After students have completed the activity, take a quick class poll. Ask: **Qui va assister à la fête? Qui ne va pas assister à la fête? Pourquoi?**

OPTIONS

Small Groups Have students write an invitation to a birthday party, an anniversary party, or a holiday celebration. Tell them to include the name(s) of the host(s); date, time, and place of the event; what is being celebrated; and any other important details. If possible, provide students with examples of other invitations in French to use as models.

Pairs Working in pairs, have students write three content questions based on the reading. When they have finished, have them get together with another pair and take turns asking and answering each other's questions.

Section Goals
In this section, students will:
- learn to report an interview
- learn to conduct an interview

Stratégie Play the role of an interviewee. Tell students to interview you about your clothing preferences. Allow recording so students can transcribe the interview. Then choose volunteers to report on the interview, transcribing it verbatim, summarizing it, or summarizing and quoting you occasionally.

Proofreading Activity Have the class correct these sentences. **1. Quand est-ce vous avez achete ces vetements? 2. Cette blouson-la est tres cher, mais c'est parfait. 3. Est-ce que vous déjà avez travaille comme styliste? 4. Vous allez parler moi de votre travail?**

Écriture

communication cultures NATIONAL STANDARDS

STRATÉGIE

How to report an interview

There are several ways to prepare a written report about an interview. For example, you can transcribe the interview verbatim, or you can summarize it. In any event, the report should begin with an interesting title and a brief introduction including the five *W*'s (*who, what, when, where, why*) and the *H* (*how*) of the interview. The report should end with an interesting conclusion. Note that when you transcribe a conversation in French, you should pay careful attention to format and punctuation.

Écrire une conversation en français

- Pour indiquer qui parle dans une conversation, on peut mettre le nom de la personne qui parle devant sa phrase.

  MONIQUE Lucie, qu'est-ce que tu vas mettre pour l'anniversaire de Julien?

  LUCIE Je vais mettre ma robe en soie bleue à manches courtes. Et toi, tu vas mettre quoi?

  MONIQUE Eh bien, une jupe en coton et un chemisier, je pense. Ou peut-être mon pantalon en cuir avec... Tiens, tu me prêtes ta chemise jaune et blanche?

  LUCIE Oui, si tu me la rends (*return it to me*) dimanche. Elle va avec le pantalon que je vais porter la semaine prochaine.

- On peut aussi commencer les phrases avec des tirets (*dashes*) pour indiquer quand une nouvelle personne parle.

– Qu'est-ce que tu as acheté comme cadeau pour Julien?

– Une cravate noire et violette. Elle est très jolie. Et toi?

– Je n'ai pas encore acheté son cadeau. Des lunettes de soleil peut-être?

– Oui, c'est une bonne idée! Et il y a des soldes à Saint-Louis Lunettes.

Thème

Écrire une interview

Avant l'écriture

1. Clarisse Deschamps est une styliste suisse. Elle dessine des vêtements pour les jeunes et va présenter sa nouvelle collection sur votre campus. Vous allez interviewer Clarisse pour le journal de votre université.

Préparez une liste de questions à poser à Clarisse Deschamps sur sa nouvelle collection. Vous pouvez (*can*) poser des questions sur:

- les types de vêtements
- les couleurs
- le style
- les prix

Quoi?	1. 2.
Comment?	1. 2.
Pour qui?	1. 2.
Combien?	1. 2.
Pourquoi?	1. 2.
Où?	1. 2.
Quand?	1. 2.

OPTIONS

Avant l'écriture As a preparation, have each student write a short paragraph or list of their ideas about Clarisse Deschamps. What is she like? What does she look like? What kinds of clothes does she like and dislike? Have them write a short profile to use when they write the answers.

Once students have written the answers, discuss various techniques they can use to organize their information. One way is to go back to the chart they used to ask their questions and add the answers to it. Another is to prioritize by level of interest, with the most interesting information first. Ask students if they have other ideas on how to organize their facts.

2. Une fois que vous avez rempli (*filled out*) le tableau (*chart*), choisissez les questions à poser pendant (*during*) l'interview.

3. Une fois (*Once*) vos questions finalisées, notez les réponses. Ensuite (*Then*), organisez les informations en catégories telles que (*such as*) les types de vêtements, les couleurs et les styles, la clientèle, le prix, etc.

Écriture

Écrivez un compte rendu (*report*) de l'interview.

- Commencez par une courte introduction.

  MODÈLE *Voici une interview de Clarisse Deschamps, styliste suisse.*

- Résumez (*Summarize*) les informations obtenues (*obtained*) pour chaque catégorie et présentez ces éléments de manière cohérente. Citez la personne interviewée au moins deux fois (*at least twice*).

  MODÈLE *Je lui ai demandé: —Quel genre de vêtements préférez-vous porter pour sortir? —Elle m'a répondu: —Moi, je préfère porter une robe noire. C'est très élégant.*

- Terminez par une brève (*brief*) conclusion.

  MODÈLE *On vend la collection de Clarisse Deschamps à Vêtements & Co à côté de l'université. Cette semaine, il y a des soldes!*

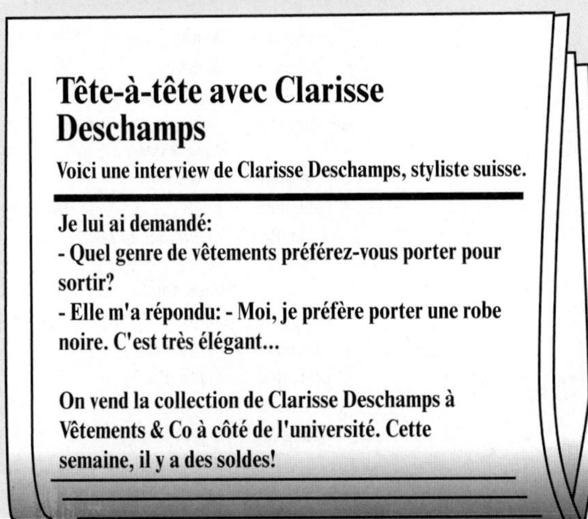

Tête-à-tête avec Clarisse Deschamps

Voici une interview de Clarisse Deschamps, styliste suisse.

Je lui ai demandé:
- Quel genre de vêtements préférez-vous porter pour sortir?
- Elle m'a répondu: - Moi, je préfère porter une robe noire. C'est très élégant...

On vend la collection de Clarisse Deschamps à Vêtements & Co à côté de l'université. Cette semaine, il y a des soldes!

Après l'écriture

1. Échangez votre compte rendu avec celui (*the one*) d'un(e) partenaire. Répondez à ces questions pour commenter son travail.

   - Votre partenaire a-t-il/elle organisé les informations en plusieurs catégories?
   - A-til/elle inclu au moins deux citations (*quotes*) dans son compte rendu?
   - A-t-il/elle utilisé le bon style pour écrire les citations?
   - A-t-il/elle utilisé les bonnes formes verbales?

2. Corrigez votre compte rendu d'après (*according to*) les commentaires de votre partenaire. Relisez votre travail pour éliminer ces problèmes:

   - des fautes (*errors*) d'orthographe
   - des fautes de ponctuation
   - des fautes de conjugaison
   - des fautes d'accord (*agreement*) des adjectifs
   - un mauvais emploi (*use*) de la grammaire

EVALUATION

Criteria

Content Contains all the information included in bulleted list of tasks.
Scale: 1 2 3 4 5

Organization Includes a short introduction, a 10-12 line conversation that represents the interview and a brief conclusion.
Scale: 1 2 3 4 5

Accuracy Uses forms of the **passé composé** (when applicable) and new unit verbs correctly. Spells words, conjugates verbs, and modifies adjectives correctly throughout.
Scale: 1 2 3 4 5

Creativity The student includes additional information that is not included in the task and/or creates a conversation that is longer than 10-12 lines.
Scale: 1 2 3 4 5

Scoring

Excellent	18–20 points
Good	14–17 points
Satisfactory	10–13 points
Unsatisfactory	< 10 points

OPTIONS

Écriture On the board, demonstrate other ways to report direct quotations in writing. One is the name with a colon after it, followed by the quote (dialogue style). Another is the person's name, followed by a comma and a direct quote using quotation marks (**guillemets**).

Bring in some magazines and newspapers showing how interviews are transcribed and presented. Ask students to choose one example and to follow the model.

Flashcards
Audio: Vocabulary

VOCABULAIRE

UNITÉ 6

Instructional Resources
espaces.vhlcentral.com: Textbook MP3s; IRM (Textbook Audioscript); downloads; reference tools

Suggestion Tell students that an easy way to study from **Vocabulaire** is to cover up the French half of each section, leaving only the English equivalents exposed. They can then quiz themselves on the French items. To focus on the English equivalents of the French entries, they simply reverse this process.

Les vêtements

aller avec	*to go with*
porter	*to wear*
un anorak	*ski jacket; parka*
des baskets (*f.*)	*tennis shoes*
un blouson	*jacket*
une casquette	*(baseball) cap*
une ceinture	*belt*
un chapeau	*hat*
une chaussette	*sock*
une chaussure	*shoe*
une chemise (à manches courtes/longues)	*shirt (short-/long-sleeved)*
un chemisier	*blouse*
un costume	*(man's) suit*
une cravate	*tie*
une écharpe	*scarf*
un gant	*glove*
un jean	*jeans*
une jupe	*skirt*
des lunettes (de soleil) (*f.*)	*(sun)glasses*
un maillot de bain	*swimsuit, bathing suit*
un manteau	*coat*
un pantalon	*pants*
un pull	*sweater*
une robe	*dress*
un sac à main	*purse, handbag*
un short	*shorts*
un sous-vêtement	*underwear*
une taille	*clothing size*
un tailleur	*(woman's) suit; tailor*
un tee-shirt	*tee shirt*
des vêtements (*m.*)	*clothing*
des soldes (*m.*)	*sales*
un vendeur/une vendeuse	*salesman/saleswoman*
bon marché	*inexpensive*
chaque	*each*
cher/chère	*expensive*
large	*loose; big*
serré(e)	*tight*

Les fêtes

faire la fête	*to party*
faire une surprise (à quelqu'un)	*to surprise (someone)*
fêter	*to celebrate*
organiser une fête	*to organize a party*
une bière	*beer*
un biscuit	*cookie*
un bonbon	*candy*
le champagne	*champagne*
un dessert	*dessert*
un gâteau	*cake*
la glace	*ice cream*
un glaçon	*ice cube*
le vin	*wine*
un cadeau	*gift*
une fête	*party; celebration*
un hôte/une hôtesse	*host(ess)*
un(e) invité(e)	*guest*
un jour férié	*holiday*
une surprise	*surprise*

Périodes de la vie

l'adolescence (*f.*)	*adolescence*
l'âge adulte (*m.*)	*adulthood*
un divorce	*divorce*
l'enfance (*f.*)	*childhood*
une étape	*stage*
l'état civil (*m.*)	*marital status*
la jeunesse	*youth*
un mariage	*marriage; wedding*
la mort	*death*
la naissance	*birth*
la vie	*life*
la vieillesse	*old age*
prendre sa retraite	*to retire*
tomber amoureux/amoureuse	*to fall in love*
avant-hier	*the day before yesterday*
hier	*yesterday*

Expressions utiles	*See pp. 187 and 201.*
Demonstrative adjectives	*See p. 190.*
Indirect object pronouns	*See p. 204.*
Disjunctive pronouns	*See p. 205.*

Les relations

une amitié	*friendship*
un amour	*love*
le bonheur	*happiness*
un couple	*couple*
un(e) fiancé(e)	*fiancé*
des jeunes mariés (*m.*)	*newlyweds*
un rendez-vous	*date; appointment*
ensemble	*together*

Les couleurs

De quelle couleur...?	*In what color...?*
blanc(he)	*white*
bleu(e)	*blue*
gris(e)	*gray*
jaune	*yellow*
marron	*brown*
noir(e)	*black*
orange	*orange*
rose	*pink*
rouge	*red*
vert(e)	*green*
violet(te)	*purple; violet*

Verbes en -re

attendre	*to wait*
conduire	*to drive*
construire	*to build; to construct*
descendre (de)	*to go down; to get off; to take down*
détruire	*to destroy*
entendre	*to hear*
mettre	*to put (on); to place*
perdre (son temps)	*to lose (to waste one's time)*
permettre	*to allow*
produire	*to produce*
promettre	*to promise*
réduire	*to reduce*
rendre (à)	*to give back; to return (to)*
rendre visite (à)	*to visit someone*
répondre (à)	*to respond; to answer (to)*
rire	*to laugh*
sourire	*to smile*
traduire	*to translate*
vendre	*to sell*

ressources
espaces.vhlcentral.com

En vacances

UNITÉ **7**

Pour commencer
- Indiquez les couleurs qu'on voit (*sees*) sur la photo.
- Quel temps fait-il?
- Quel(s) vêtement(s) Stéphane porte-t-il?
- Quelle(s) activité(s) Stéphane peut-il pratiquer là où il se trouve?

Unit Goals
Leçon 7A
In this lesson, students will learn:
- terms for travel and vacation
- names of countries and nationalities
- the role of diacriticals
- about Tahiti and **le musée d'Orsay**
- more about transportation and lodging through specially shot video footage
- the **passé composé** with **être**
- direct object pronouns
- about **TER** regional train service

Leçon 7B
In this lesson, students will learn:
- terms related to hotels and accommodations
- ordinal numbers
- expressions for sequencing events
- the pronunciation of **ti**, **sti**, and **ssi**
- how and where the French vacation
- the formation and usage of adverbs
- the **imparfait**
- the verbs **dire**, **écrire**, **lire**, and **décrire**
- to recognize the genre of spoken discourse

Savoir-faire
In this section, students will learn:
- cultural and historical information about the French regions of **Provence-Alpes-Côte d'Azur** and **Rhône-Alpes**
- to predict the content of a text from its title
- to make an outline
- to write a brochure

Pour commencer
- **jaune, bleu, vert, noir, blanc**
- **Il fait beau./Il fait (du) soleil./ Il fait chaud.**
- **Il porte un maillot de bain.**
- **Il peut nager.**

RESOURCES

Workbook/Video Manual: WB Activities, pp. 85–98
Laboratory Manual: Lab Activities, pp. 49–56
Workbook/Video Manual: Video Activities, pp. 235–238; pp. 283–284
WB/VM/LM Answer Key
espaces.vhlcentral.com: Textbook MP3s; Lab MP3s; Instructor's Resource Manual [IRM] (Textbook Audioscript; Lab Audioscript; Videoscript; **Roman-photo** Translations; **Vocabulaire supplémentaire**; **Feuilles d'activités**; Info Gap Activities; **Le zapping** TV clip transcription; **Essayez!** and **Mise en pratique** answers); Transparencies #34, #35, #36; Testing Program, pp. 49–56, pp. 161–172; Test Files; Testing Program MP3s
Test Generator
Video on DVD

Section Goals

In this section, students will learn and practice vocabulary related to:
- travel and vacations
- names of countries and nationalities

Instructional Resources
*espaces.vhlcentral.com: Transparency #34; IRM (**Vocabulaire supplémentaire; Mise en pratique** answers; Textbook Audioscript; Lab Audioscript; Info Gap Activities); Textbook MP3s; Lab MP3s; WB/VM/LM Answer Key; activities; downloads; reference tools*

Suggestions
- Use **Transparency #34** and describe what the people are doing. Examples: **Cette femme achète un billet. Cet homme utilise un plan.**
- Ask students questions about travel and transportation using the vocabulary. **Aimez-vous voyager? Comment préférez-vous voyager? Aimez-vous prendre le train? Aimez-vous prendre l'avion? Préférez-vous rouler en voiture ou prendre l'autobus? Quels pays avez-vous visités?** At this time, introduce additional countries, states, provinces, and their prepositions as needed from the **Vocabulaire supplémentaire** on the Supersite.
- Point out that **faire des achats** also means *to go shopping.*
- Point out that **un (auto)bus** is a local bus; a bus that goes from town to town is **un (auto) car**. Then explain the nuance between **une station de train** and **une gare**.
- Point out that **les vacances** is always plural.
- Tell students that **un plan** is a city or town map; **une carte** is a map of a larger area, such as a region or country.
- Explain that the word **un ticket** is used for a bus, subway, or other small ticket. A plane or train ticket or a ticket to an event, such as a concert, is called **un billet**.

Leçon 7A

You will learn how to...
- describe trips you have taken
- tell where you went

Talking Picture
Audio: Activity

Bon voyage!

Vocabulaire

faire du shopping	*to go shopping*
faire les valises	*to pack one's bags*
faire un séjour	*to spend time (somewhere)*
partir en vacances	*to go on vacation*
prendre un train (un taxi, un (auto)bus, un bateau)	*to take a train (taxi, bus, boat)*
rouler en voiture	*to ride in a car*
un aéroport	*airport*
un arrêt d'autobus (de bus)	*bus stop*
un billet aller-retour	*round-trip ticket*
un billet (d'avion, de train)	*(plane, train) ticket*
un (jour de) congé	*day off*
une douane	*customs*
une gare (routière)	*train station (bus terminal)*
une station (de métro)	*(subway) station*
une station de ski	*ski resort*
un ticket (de bus, de métro)	*(bus, subway) ticket*
des vacances (f.)	*vacation*
un vol	*flight*
à l'étranger	*abroad, overseas*
la campagne	*country(side)*
une capitale	*capital*
un pays	*country*
(en/l') Allemagne (f.)	*(to/in) Germany*
(en/l') Angleterre (f.)	*(to/in) England*
(en/la) Belgique (belge)	*(to/in) Belgium (Belgian)*
(au/le) Brésil (brésilien(ne))	*(to/in) Brazil (Brazilian)*
(en/la) Chine (chinois(e))	*(to/in) China (Chinese)*
(en/l') Irlande (irlandais(e)) (f.)	*(to/in) Ireland (Irish)*
(en/l') Italie (f.)	*(to/in) Italy*
(au/le) Japon	*(to/in) Japan*
(en/la) Suisse	*(to/in) Switzerland*

ressources
WB pp. 85-86
LM p. 49
espaces.vhlcentral.com

OPTIONS

Extra Practice Call out names of countries and nationalities at random, including adjectives of nationality from previous lessons. Have students classify them as either **un pays** or **une nationalité**. You might want to list the words on the board in two columns or have students write them on the board.

Game Write vocabulary for means of transportation on index cards. On another set of cards, draw or paste pictures to match each term. Tape them face down on the board in random order. Divide the class into two teams. Play a game of Concentration in which students match words with pictures. When a match is made, that player's team collects those cards. When all pairs have been matched, the team with the most cards wins.

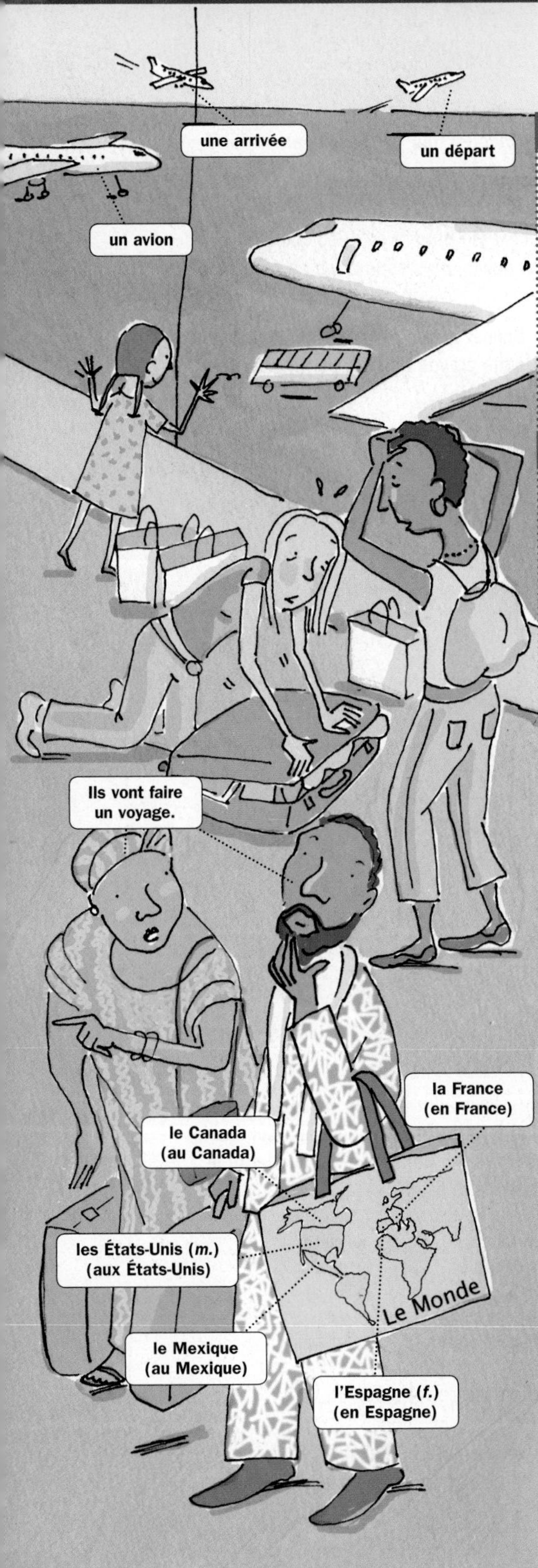

Mise en pratique

1 Chassez l'intrus **Indiquez le mot ou l'expression qui ne convient pas.**

1. faire un séjour, partir en vacances, un jour de congé, une station de ski
2. un aéroport, une station de métro, une arrivée, une gare routière
3. une douane, un départ, une arrivée, une sortie
4. le monde, un pays, le journal, une capitale
5. la campagne, la mer, la plage, des gens
6. prendre un bus, un arrêt de bus, utiliser un plan, une gare routière
7. bronzer, prendre un avion, un vol, un aéroport
8. prendre un taxi, rouler en voiture, un vol, une gare routière

2 Écoutez **Écoutez Cédric et Nathalie parler de leurs vacances. Ensuite (*Then*), complétez les phrases avec un mot ou une expression de la section ESPACE CONTEXTES. Notez que toutes les options ne sont pas utilisées.**

_f_ 1. Nathalie va partir...	a. sont idéales pour bronzer.
_b_ 2. Nathalie a déjà...	b. son billet d'avion.
_j_ 3. Nathalie va peut-être...	c. le plan de Paris de Cédric.
_g_ 4. La famille de Cédric...	d. la capitale du Mexique.
_h_ 5. Paul pense que l'Espagne est...	e. le tour du monde.
	f. à l'étranger.
_a_ 6. Pour Cédric, les plages du Brésil...	g. n'a pas encore décidé entre l'Espagne, le Mexique et le Brésil.
_e_ 7. Un jour, Cédric va faire...	
_c_ 8. Nathalie va utiliser...	h. un pays superbe.
	i. faire un séjour en Italie.

3 Les vacances **Justine va partir en vacances demain. Complétez le paragraphe avec les mots et expressions de la liste. Toutes les options ne sont pas utilisées.**

aller-retour	faire ma valise	sortie
une arrivée	pays	station
faire un séjour	plage	taxi
faire du shopping	prendre un bus	vol

Demain, je pars en vacances. Je vais (1) _faire un séjour_ avec mon frère à l'île Maurice, une petite île (*island*) tropicale dans l'océan Indien. Nous allons (2) _prendre un bus_ pour l'aéroport à 7h00. Mon frère veut (*wants*) prendre un (3) _taxi_, mais moi, je pense qu'il faut économiser parce que j'ai envie de (4) _faire du shopping_ au marché et dans les boutiques de Port-Louis, la capitale. Le (5) _vol_ est à 10h. Nous n'avons pas besoin de visa pour le voyage; pour entrer dans le (6) _pays_, il faut seulement montrer un passeport et un billet (7) _aller-retour_. J'ai acheté un nouveau maillot de bain pour aller à la (8) _plage_. Et maintenant, je vais (9) _faire ma valise_!

Practice more at **espaces.vhlcentral.com.**

1 Suggestion Have students put **l'intrus** with other expressions like it. Example: **une station de ski** goes with item 5. If the word does not fit another set, have students create a set of at least three related words.

2 Tapescript CÉDRIC: Nathalie, où est-ce que tu vas aller en vacances cet été?
NATHALIE: Je vais partir à l'étranger.
C: Moi aussi. Où est-ce que tu vas?
N: Je vais en France pour quinze jours. C'est un pays tellement intéressant. J'ai déjà mon billet d'avion. J'attends le départ avec beaucoup d'impatience. Je vais aller à Paris et aussi à Nice. On va peut-être faire un court séjour en Italie. Ça va être super! Et toi, où est-ce que tu pars en vacances?
C: Moi, je vais faire un voyage mais je ne sais pas où. Ma famille n'a pas encore décidé entre l'Espagne, le Mexique et le Brésil. Qu'en penses-tu?
N: Mon frère Paul fait ses études en Espagne, à Grenade. Il trouve que c'est un pays superbe et que les gens sont très gentils.
C: Moi, je pense que le Brésil, c'est plus exotique et les plages sont idéales pour bronzer.
N: Mexico, la capitale du Mexique, a beaucoup de musées très intéressants.
C: Un jour, je vais faire le tour du monde, mais pour ça, il faut trouver un vol bon marché. Nathalie, tu as besoin de quelqu'un pour t'aider à faire tes valises et te conduire à l'aéroport?
N: Oh oui, merci. C'est vraiment gentil. Est-ce que tu as un plan de Paris à me prêter?
C: Bien sûr, pas de problème.
(On Textbook MP3s)

2 Suggestion Before students listen, have them scan the sentence fragments in this activity and pick out new words. Examples: **bronzer**, **aéroport**, **séjour**, and **pays**.

3 Expansion Have pairs of students add to Justine's paragraph by creating sentences using the three unused words (**arrivée, station, sortie**). Have them rewrite the paragraph, logically adding their sentences. Ask volunteers to read their paragraphs aloud.

OPTIONS

Extra Practice Ask students what means of transportation one might take to go from one place to another. Example: **Quel(s) moyen(s) de transport est-ce qu'on prend pour aller de Paris à Rome? Des États-Unis en Angleterre? De la faculté au supermarché? De la tour Eiffel à l'Arc de Triomphe?**

Game Play a game of **Dix questions**. Ask a volunteer to think of a country. Other students get one chance to ask a yes/no question and guess the country. Encourage students to ask questions about languages spoken there and location. You might want to brainstorm prepositions of location on the board. Examples: **près de**, **loin de**, **à côté de**, etc. Limit attempts to ten questions per place.

4 Suggestion After completing this activity in pairs, combine pairs of students to form groups of four. Have students share what they learned about their partners with the other pair.

4 Expansion Ask each student question 8: **Dans quel pays as-tu envie de voyager?** Accept simple answers like **la France**. Follow up each answer by asking **Pourquoi?**

5 Suggestion Ask volunteers to write their descriptions on the board.

6 Suggestion Before distributing the Info Gap Handouts found on the Supersite, you might want to brainstorm some questions that will elicit the missing information and write them on the board.

7 Suggestion Have students exchange letters for peer editing. Editors should make sure all required elements are included in the letter and underline, rather than correct, grammar and spelling errors.

NATIONAL communication STANDARDS

Communication

4 Répondez Avec un(e) partenaire, posez-vous ces questions et répondez-y (*them*) à tour de rôle. Answers will vary.

1. Où pars-tu en vacances cette année? Quand?
2. Quand fais-tu tes valises? Avec combien de valises voyages-tu?
3. Préfères-tu la mer, la campagne ou les stations de ski?
4. Comment vas-tu à l'aéroport? Prends-tu l'autobus? Le métro?
5. Quelles sont tes vacances préférées?
6. Quand utilises-tu un plan?
7. Quel est ton pays favori? Pourquoi?
8. Dans quel(s) pays as-tu envie de voyager?

5 Décrivez Avec un(e) partenaire, écrivez (*write*) une description des images. Donnez autant de (*as many*) détails que possible. Ensuite (*Then*), rejoignez un autre groupe et lisez vos descriptions. L'autre groupe doit deviner (*must guess*) quelle image vous décrivez (*describe*). Answers will vary.

1.

2.

3.

4.

5.

6.

6 Conversez Votre professeur va vous donner, à vous et à votre partenaire, une feuille d'activités. L'un de vous est un(e) client(e) qui a besoin de faire une réservation pour des vacances, l'autre est l'agent de voyages. Travaillez ensemble pour finaliser la réservation et compléter vos feuilles respectives. Attention! Ne regardez pas la feuille de votre partenaire. Answers will vary.

7 Un voyage Vous allez faire un voyage en Europe et rendre visite à votre cousin, Jean-Marc, qui étudie en Belgique. Écrivez-lui (*Write to him*) une lettre et utilisez les mots de la liste. Answers will vary.

un aéroport	la France
la Belgique	prendre un taxi
un billet	la Suisse
faire un séjour	un vol
faire les valises	un voyage

- Parlez des détails de votre départ.
- Expliquez votre tour d'Europe.
- Organisez votre arrivée en Belgique.
- Parlez de ce que (*what*) vous allez faire ensemble.

OPTIONS

Small Groups Have students work in groups of three to write riddles about people, places, or objects from **Espace contextes**. For each riddle, the group must come up with at least three hints or descriptions. Have students from each group read hints to the rest of the class. Example: **Je suis fait de papier. Je suis souvent en noir et blanc. Je vous donne beaucoup d'informations. (Je suis un journal.)**

Game Write **Dans quel pays parle-t-on…?** on the board. Have students stand. Toss a beanbag to a student and ask where a language is spoken. The player has four seconds to name a country. He or she then tosses the beanbag to a classmate and asks where a language is spoken. Players who cannot think of a country in time are eliminated. Languages may be repeated, but countries may not. The last person standing wins.

Les sons et les lettres

Audio: Concepts, Activities
Record & Compare

comparisons NATIONAL STANDARDS

Diacriticals for meaning

Some French words with different meanings have nearly identical spellings except for a diacritical mark (*accent*). Sometimes a diacritical does not affect pronunciation at all.

ou	**où**	**a**	**à**
or	*where*	*has*	*to, at*

Sometimes, you can clearly hear the difference between the words.

côte	**côté**	**sale**	**salé**
coast	*side*	*dirty*	*salty*

Very often, two similar-looking words are different parts of speech. Many similar-looking word pairs are those with and without an **-é** at the end.

âge	**âgé**	**entre**	**entré (entrer)**
age (n.)	*elderly* (adj.)	*between* (prep.)	*entered* (p.p.)

In such instances, context should make their meaning clear.

Tu as quel âge?
How old are you? / What is your age?

C'est un homme âgé.
He's an elderly man.

Prononcez Répétez les mots suivants à voix haute.

1. la (*the*) là (*there*)
2. êtes (*are*) étés (*summers*)
3. jeune (*young*) jeûne (*fasting*)
4. pêche (*peach*) pêché (*fished*)

Articulez Répétez les phrases suivantes à voix haute.

1. J'habite dans une ferme (*farm*).
   Le magasin est fermé (*closed*).
2. Les animaux mangent du maïs (*corn*).
   Je suis suisse, mais il est belge.
3. Est-ce que tu es prête?
   J'ai prêté ma voiture (*car*) à Marcel.
4. La lampe est à côté de la chaise.
   J'adore la côte ouest de la France.

Dictons Répétez les dictons à voix haute.

À vos marques, prêts, partez! [1]

C'est un prêté pour un rendu. [2]

ressources
LM p. 50
espaces.vhlcentral.com

[1] On your mark, get set, go!
[2] One good turn deserves another. (lit. It is one loaned for one returned.)

Section Goals

In this section, students will learn about the use of diacriticals to distinguish between words with the same or similar spellings.

Instructional Resources
espaces.vhlcentral.com: Textbook MP3s; Lab MP3s; WB/VM/LM Answer Key; IRM (Textbook Audioscript; Lab Audioscript); activities; downloads; reference tools

Suggestions

- Model the pronunciation of the example words and have students repeat after you.
- Write examples of other past participles that are used as adjectives on the board. Examples: **réservé** and **préparé**. Ask students to provide more examples.
- Have students give you the English equivalents for the following words in the **Articulez**: **2. mais 3. prête** and **prêté 4. côté** and **côte**.
- Dictate five simple sentences with words that have diacriticals that distinguish meaning, repeating each one at least two times. Then write the sentences on the board or a transparency and have students check their spelling.

Dictons Have students compare the pronunciation and meaning of **prêts** and **prêté**. Then have them identify their parts of speech.

OPTIONS

Extra Practice Use these sentences that contain words with and without diacriticals for additional practice or as a dictation. **1. Quel âge a-t-il? Mon grand-père est âgé. 2. Le bureau est entre le lit et la porte. Marcel est entré dans la salle. 3. La ligne est occupée. Suzanne s'occupe des enfants. 4. J'ai réservé une table au restaurant. Sylvain est réservé.**

Extra Practice Teach students this French tongue-twister that contains diacriticals that affect meaning. **Un pêcheur péchait sous un pêcher, le pêcher empêchait le pêcheur de pêcher, le pêcheur coupa le pêcher, le pêcher n'empêcha plus le pêcheur de pêcher.**

Section Goals
In this section, students will learn functional phrases for talking about vacations.

Instructional Resources
*espaces.vhlcentral.com: Video; WB/VM/LM Answer Key; IRM (Videoscript; **Roman-photo** Translations); activities; downloads; reference tools*
Video on DVD

Video Recap: Leçon 6B
Before doing this **Roman-photo**, review the previous one with this activity.

1. **____ a fêté ses dix-huit ans. (Stéphane)**
2. **____ a fait un gâteau d'anniversaire. (Sandrine)**
3. **____ a visité Paris avec ses parents. (David)**
4. **____ a fait une jupe originale. (Amina)**
5. **____ ont donné une montre à Stéphane. (Rachid et Astrid)**
6. **____ lui a donné un blouson en cuir noir. (Valérie)**

Video Synopsis At the train station, David tells Rachid about his trip to Paris. At the café, he tells Stéphane about his trip and that he loved the museums. Stéphane wants to go to Tahiti. David gives Stéphane sunglasses for his birthday. When Sandrine hears about David's trip, she remembers she needs to make reservations for her ski trip to Albertville.

Suggestions
- Ask students to read the title, glance at the video stills, and predict what the episode will be about. Record their predictions.
- Have students read the **Roman-photo** aloud in groups of four.
- Point out the expressions **bon voyage** and **bon séjour**. Explain that **un voyage** refers to travel to and from a destination; **un séjour** is extended time spent at the place itself.
- Review predictions and ask which ones were correct.

De retour au P'tit Bistrot

Video: *Roman-photo*
Record & Compare

PERSONNAGES

David

Rachid

Sandrine

Stéphane

À la gare...

RACHID Tu as fait bon voyage?
DAVID Salut! Excellent, merci.
RACHID Tu es parti pour Paris avec une valise et te voici avec ces énormes sacs en plus!
DAVID Mes parents et moi sommes allés aux Galeries Lafayette. On a acheté des vêtements et des trucs pour l'appartement aussi.

RACHID Ah ouais?
DAVID Mes parents sont arrivés des États-Unis jeudi soir. Ils ont pris une chambre dans un bel hôtel, tout près de la tour Eiffel.
RACHID Génial!
DAVID Moi, je suis arrivé à la gare vendredi soir. Et nous sommes allés dîner dans une excellente brasserie. Mmm!

DAVID Samedi, on a pris un bateau-mouche sur la Seine. J'ai visité un musée différent chaque jour: le musée du Louvre, le musée d'Orsay...
RACHID En résumé, tu as passé de bonnes vacances dans la capitale... Bon, on y va?
DAVID Ah, euh, oui, allons-y!

STÉPHANE Pour moi, les vacances idéales, c'est un voyage à Tahiti. Ahhh... la plage, et moi en maillot de bain avec des lunettes de soleil... et les filles en bikini!
DAVID Au fait, je n'ai pas oublié ton anniversaire.
STÉPHANE Ouah! Super, ces lunettes de soleil! Merci, David, c'est gentil.

DAVID Désolé de ne pas avoir été là pour ton anniversaire, Stéphane. Alors, ils t'ont fait la surprise?
STÉPHANE Oui, et quelle belle surprise! J'ai reçu des cadeaux trop cool. Et le gâteau de Sandrine, je l'ai adoré.
DAVID Ah, Sandrine... elle est adorable... Euh, Stéphane, tu m'excuses une minute?

DAVID Coucou! Je suis de retour!
SANDRINE Oh! Salut, David. Alors, tu as aimé Paris?
DAVID Oui! J'ai fait plein de choses... de vraies petites vacances! On a fait...

ACTIVITÉS

1 Les événements Mettez ces événements dans l'ordre chronologique.

__1__ a. Rachid va chercher David.
__6__ b. Stéphane parle de son anniversaire.
__10__ c. Sandrine va faire une réservation.
__5__ d. David donne un cadeau à Stéphane.
__2__ e. Rachid mentionne que David a beaucoup de sacs.
__7__ f. Stéphane met les lunettes de soleil.
__4__ g. Stéphane décrit (*describes*) ses vacances idéales.
__8__ h. David parle avec Sandrine.
__9__ i. Sandrine pense à ses vacances.
__3__ j. Rachid et David repartent en voiture.

Practice more at **espaces.vhlcentral.com.**

OPTIONS

Avant de regarder la vidéo Before viewing the video episode **De retour au P'tit Bistrot**, have pairs of students make a list of things someone might say when describing a trip and talking about means of transportation.

Regarder la vidéo Download and print the videoscript on the Supersite, and white out words related to travel and transportation. Distribute the scripts to pairs or groups to complete as cloze paragraphs as they watch the video.

David parle de ses vacances.

STÉPHANE Alors, ces vacances? Tu as fait un bon séjour?
DAVID Oui, formidable!
STÉPHANE Alors, vous êtes restés combien de temps à Paris?
DAVID Quatre jours. Ce n'est pas très long, mais on a visité pas mal d'endroits.
STÉPHANE Comment est-ce que vous avez visité la ville? En voiture?

DAVID En voiture!? Tu es fou! On a pris le métro, comme tout le monde.
STÉPHANE Tes parents n'aiment pas conduire?
DAVID Si, à la campagne, mais pas en ville, surtout une ville comme Paris. On a visité les monuments, les musées...
STÉPHANE Et Monsieur l'artiste a aimé les musées de Paris?
DAVID Je les ai adorés!

SANDRINE Oh! Des vacances!
DAVID Oui... Des vacances? Qu'est-ce qu'il y a?
SANDRINE Je vais à Albertville pour les vacances d'hiver. On va faire du ski!

SANDRINE Est-ce que tu skies?
DAVID Un peu, oui...
SANDRINE Désolée, je dois partir. J'ai une réservation à faire! Rendez-vous ici demain, David. D'accord? Ciao!

Expressions utiles

Talking about vacations

- **Tu es parti pour Paris avec une valise et te voici avec ces énormes sacs en plus!**
  You left for Paris with one suitcase and here you are with these huge extra bags!
- **Nous sommes allés aux Galeries Lafayette.**
  We went to the Galeries Lafayette.
- **On a acheté des trucs pour l'appartement aussi.**
  We also bought some things for the apartment.
- **Moi, je suis arrivé à la gare vendredi soir et nous sommes allés dîner.**
  I got to/arrived at the station Friday night and we went to dinner.
- **On a pris un bateau-mouche sur la Seine.**
  We took a sightseeing boat on the Seine.
- **Vous êtes restés combien de temps à Paris?**
  How long did you stay in Paris?
- **On a pris le métro, comme tout le monde.**
  We took the subway, like everyone else.
- **J'ai fait plein de choses.**
  I did a lot of things.
- **Les musées de Paris, je les ai adorés!**
  The museums in Paris, I loved them!

Additional vocabulary

- **Alors, ils t'ont fait la surprise?**
  So, they surprised you?
- **J'ai reçu des cadeaux trop cool.**
  I got the coolest gifts.
- **Le gâteau, je l'ai adoré.**
  I loved the cake.
- **Tu m'excuses une minute?**
  Would you excuse me a minute?
- **Oui, formidable!**
  Yes, wonderful!
- **Qu'est-ce qu'il y a?**
  What is the matter?
- **Désolé(e), je dois partir.**
  Sorry, I have to leave.

ACTIVITÉS

2 Questions Répondez aux questions. Answers may vary slightly.

1. David est parti pour Paris avec combien de valises? À son retour (*Upon his return*), est-ce qu'il a le même nombre de valises?
   Il est parti avec une valise. Non, à son retour, il a des sacs en plus.
2. Qu'est-ce que David a fait pour ses vacances?
   Il a visité Paris avec ses parents.
3. Qu'est-ce que David donne à Stéphane comme cadeau d'anniversaire? Stéphane aime-t-il le cadeau?
   Il donne des lunettes de soleil à Stéphane. Oui, Stéphane aime beaucoup le cadeau.
4. Quelles sont les vacances idéales de Stéphane? C'est un voyage à Tahiti. Stéphane est à la plage en maillot de bain avec des lunettes de soleil.
5. Qu'est-ce que Sandrine va faire pour ses vacances d'hiver?
   Elle va faire du ski à Albertville.

3 Écrivez Imaginez: vous êtes David, Stéphane ou Sandrine et vous allez en vacances à Paris, Tahiti ou Albertville. Écrivez un e-mail à Valérie. Quel temps fait-il? Où est-ce que vous restez? Quels vêtements est-ce que vous avez apportés? Qu'est-ce que vous faites chaque jour?

ressources

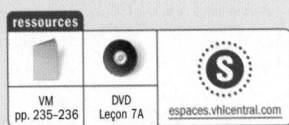

VM pp. 235–236	DVD Leçon 7A	espaces.vhlcentral.com

OPTIONS

Les bateaux-mouches Touring by **bateau-mouche** is an excellent way to see the famous sights along the River Seine. Tourists can listen to narrations in various languages as they pass by **la cathédrale de Notre-Dame, la Conciergerie**, under the ornate **pont Alexandre III**, under the oldest bridge in Paris **le Pont Neuf, la tour Eiffel**, and even a miniature version of the **statue de la Liberté**.

Small Groups Have students work in groups of four to prepare a skit to present to the class. In the skit, the group of friends checks into a hotel and decides what they feel like doing for the rest of the day. Tell them to describe what city they are visiting, describe the hotel and their rooms, and explain what activities they want to do while they are visiting the city.

Expressions utiles

- Model the pronunciation of the **Expressions utiles** and have students repeat them after you.
- Draw attention to expressions with direct object pronouns and the **passé composé** with **être** in the videostill captions, in the **Expressions utiles** box, and as they occur in your conversation with students. Point out that this material will be formally presented in **Espace structures**.
- Respond briefly to questions about direct object pronouns and the **passé composé** with **être**. Reinforce correct forms, but do not expect students to produce them consistently at this time.
- Point out that **cool** is invariable since it is an adopted word.
- Point out to students that the word **formidable** is a **faux ami**, meaning *wonderful*, not *formidable*.
- Remind students that **désolée** in the last sentence is feminine because Sandrine is talking about herself. A man would say, **(je suis) désolé**.

1 Suggestion Form several groups of five students. Write each of these sentences on individual strips of paper and distribute them among the students in each group (two per student). Copy a set of sentences for each group. Have students read their sentences aloud in the proper order.

1 Expansion Have students write sentences to fill in parts of the story not mentioned in this activity.

2 Expansion Give students time to write out their answers to these questions. Then ask volunteers to write them on the board.

3 Suggestion Before starting this activity, review vocabulary for weather, clothing, and activities by asking questions. Examples: **Quel temps fait-il à Paris en été? à Albertville en hiver? Qu'est-ce que vous aimez faire à la plage? à la montagne? Qu'est-ce que vous mettez quand il fait chaud? quand il fait froid?**

Section Goals

In this section, students will:

- learn about Tahiti
- learn terms related to train travel
- find out some unusual facts about transportation in the francophone world
- read about **le musée d'Orsay**
- view authentic video footage

Instructional Resources
espaces.vhlcentral.com: Video; WB/VM/LM Answer Key; IRM (Videoscript); activities; downloads; reference tools

Culture à la loupe

Avant la lecture Ask students: **Où est Tahiti? Quelle(s) langue(s) parle-t-on à Tahiti?** Ask if anyone can explain Tahiti's relationship to France.

Lecture Pointing out the **Coup de main** box, explain the relationship between the verb tenses in the two clauses. Discourage students from experimenting with **si** clauses except those with both verbs in the present or one in the present and the other in **le futur proche**. **Si** clauses with the conditional are presented in **Leçon 13B, Espace structures**.

Après la lecture

- Ask students to say something they learned from the passage that inspires them to visit Tahiti or that dissuades them from visiting. Examples: **J'ai envie de visiter Tahiti parce que j'adore la montagne et la plage. Moi, je n'ai pas envie d'aller à Tahiti parce que je déteste le temps très chaud.**
- You might also ask students to identify any review vocabulary in the passage. Examples: **la pêche, la planche à voile, faire des randonnées**, etc.

1 Expansion Continue the activity with these questions.
11. Comment est le climat de Tahiti? (C'est un climat chaud.)
12. À part les plages, que peut-on visiter? (des montagnes, des lagons, des spas, Papeete)
13. Quelles attractions trouve-t-on à Papeete? (des restaurants, des boîtes de nuit, des boutiques variées et un marché)

Video: *Flash culture*

CULTURE À LA LOUPE

Tahiti

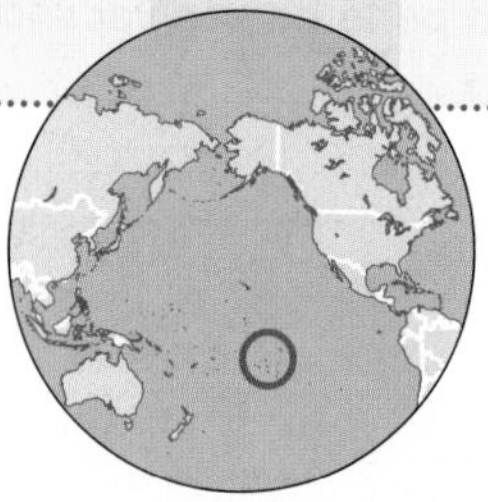

Tahiti, dans le sud° de l'océan Pacifique, est la plus grande île° de la Polynésie française. Elle devient° un protectorat français en 1842, puis° une colonie française en 1880. Depuis 1959, elle fait partie de la collectivité d'outre-mer° de Polynésie française. Les langues officielles de Tahiti sont le français et le tahitien.

Le tourisme est une source d'activité très importante pour l'île. Ses hôtels de luxe et leurs fameux bungalows sur l'eau accueillent° près de 200.000 visiteurs par an. Les touristes apprécient Tahiti pour son climat chaud, ses plages superbes et sa culture riche en traditions. À Tahiti, il y a la possibilité de faire toutes sortes d'activités aquatiques comme du bateau, de la pêche, de la planche à voile ou de la plongée°. On peut aussi faire des randonnées en montagne ou explorer les nombreux lagons bleus de l'île. Si on n'a pas envie de faire de sport, on peut se détendre° dans un spa, bronzer à la plage ou se promener° sur l'île. Papeete, capitale de la Polynésie française et ville principale de Tahiti, offre de bons restaurants, des boîtes de nuit, des boutiques variées et un marché.

sud *south* **la plus grande île** *the largest island* **devient** *becomes* **puis** *then* **collectivité d'outre-mer** *overseas territory* **accueillent** *welcome* **plongée** *scuba diving* **se détendre** *relax* **se promener** *go for a walk*

Coup de main

Si introduces a hypothesis. It may come at the beginning or at the middle of a sentence.

si + subject + verb + subject + verb

Si on n'a pas envie de faire de sport, on peut se détendre dans un spa.

subject + verb + **si** *+ subject + verb*

On peut se détendre dans un spa si on n'a pas envie de faire de sport.

ACTIVITÉS

1 Répondez Répondez aux questions par des phrases complètes.

1. Où est Tahiti?
   Tahiti est dans le sud de l'océan Pacifique.
2. Quand est-ce que Tahiti devient une colonie française?
   Tahiti devient une colonie en 1880.
3. De quoi fait partie Tahiti?
   Tahiti fait partie de la collectivité d'outre-mer de Polynésie française.
4. Quelles langues parle-t-on à Tahiti?
   On parle français et tahitien.
5. Quelle particularité ont les hôtels de luxe à Tahiti?
   Les hôtels de luxe ont des bungalows sur l'eau.
6. Combien de personnes par an visitent Tahiti?
   Près de 200.000 touristes par an visitent Tahiti.
7. Pourquoi est-ce que les touristes aiment visiter Tahiti? Les touristes aiment visiter Tahiti parce qu'il fait chaud et parce que les plages sont superbes.
8. Quelles sont deux activités sportives que les touristes aiment faire à Tahiti?
   Answers may vary. Possible answer: Ils aiment faire du bateau et de la plongée.
9. Comment s'appelle la ville principale de Tahiti?
   La ville principale de Tahiti s'appelle Papeete.
10. Où va-t-on à Papeete pour acheter un cadeau pour un ami?
    On va au marché ou dans les boutiques.

OPTIONS

Pairs Have students imagine arriving in Tahiti to meet a friend who lives there. The "visitor" should ask about possible ways to spend time during the visit and the "resident" should propose activities (basing information on the reading and the vocabulary from **Espace contextes**).

Then combine two pairs for a reflection on each pair's experiences while together in Tahiti. One pair should ask the other pair what they did, using **les pronoms disjoints** for emphasis and contrast. Encourage students to use an array of verbs conjugated in the **passé composé** with **être** and **avoir**.

LE FRANÇAIS QUOTIDIEN

À la gare

contrôleur	*ticket inspector*
couchette	*berth*
guichet	*ticket window*
horaire	*schedule*
quai	*train/metro platform*
voie	*track*
wagon-lit	*sleeper car*
composter	*to punch one's (train) ticket*

LE MONDE FRANCOPHONE

Les transports

Voici quelques faits insolites° dans les transports.

Au Canada Inauguré en 1966, le métro de Montréal est le premier du monde à rouler° sur des pneus° et non sur des roues° en métal. Chaque station a été conçue° par un architecte différent.

En France L'Eurotunnel (le tunnel sous la Manche°) permet aux trains Eurostar de transporter des voyageurs et des marchandises entre la France et l'Angleterre.

En Mauritanie Le train du désert, en Mauritanie, en Afrique, est peut-être le train de marchandises le plus long° du monde. Long de 2 à 3 km en général, le train fait deux ou trois voyages chaque jour du Sahara à la côte ouest°. C'est un voyage de plus de 600 km qui dure jusqu'à° 18 heures. Un des seuls moyens° de transport dans la région, ce train est aussi un train de voyageurs.

faits insolites *unusual facts* **rouler** *ride* **pneus** *tires* **roues** *wheels* **conçue** *designed* **Manche** *English Channel* **le plus long** *the longest* **côte ouest** *west coast* **dure jusqu'à** *lasts up to* **seuls moyens** *only means*

PORTRAIT

Le musée d'Orsay

Le musée d'Orsay est un des musées parisiens les plus° visités. Le lieu n'a pourtant° pas toujours été un musée. À l'origine, ce bâtiment° est une gare, construite par l'architecte Victor Laloux et inaugurée en 1900 à l'occasion de l'Exposition universelle. Les voies° de la gare d'Orsay deviennent° trop courtes et en 1939, on décide de limiter le service aux trains de banlieue. Plus tard, la gare sert de décor à des films, comme *Le Procès* de Kafka adapté par Orson Welles, puis° elle devient théâtre, puis salle de ventes aux enchères°. En 1986, le bâtiment est transformé en musée. Il est principalement dédié° à l'art du dix-neuvième siècle°, avec une magnifique collection d'art impressionniste.

***Danseuses en bleu*, Edgar Degas**

les plus *the most* **pourtant** *however* **bâtiment** *building* **voies** *tracks* **deviennent** *become* **puis** *then* **ventes aux enchères** *auction* **principalement dédié** *mainly dedicated* **siècle** *century*

SUR INTERNET

Qu'est-ce que le funiculaire de Montmartre?

Go to espaces.vhlcentral.com to find more information related to this **ESPACE CULTURE**. Then watch the corresponding **Flash culture**.

ACTIVITÉS

2 Vrai ou faux? Indiquez si les phrases sont **vraies** ou **fausses**. Corrigez les phrases fausses.

1. Le musée d'Orsay a été un théâtre.
   Vrai.
2. Le musée d'Orsay a été une station de métro.
   Faux. Il a été une gare.
3. Le musée d'Orsay est dédié à la sculpture moderne.
   Faux. Le musée d'Orsay est dédié à l'art du dix-neuvième siècle.
4. Il y a un tunnel entre la France et la Guyane française.
   Faux. Il y a un tunnel entre la France et l'Angleterre.
5. Le métro de Montréal roule sur des roues en métal.
   Faux. Le métro de Montréal roule sur des pneus.
6. Le train du désert transporte aussi des voyageurs.
   Vrai.

3 Comment voyager? Vous allez passer deux semaines en France. Vous avez envie de visiter Paris et deux autres régions. Par petits groupes, parlez des moyens (*means*) de transport que vous allez utiliser pendant votre voyage. Expliquez vos choix (*choices*).

Practice more at **espaces.vhlcentral.com.**

ressources: VM pp. 283-284 | espaces.vhlcentral.com

Le français quotidien Explain that French people visit **la SNCF (Société nationale des chemins de fer français)** to get information about rates and to buy train tickets (just as Americans go to an Amtrak station). Bring in a map showing train routes, so students understand the viability of train travel to and from big cities and small towns alike. Remind students of what they learned about **le TGV** in **Unité 2, Panorama**, page 67.

Portrait Show photos of Claude Monet's train paintings ***La Gare Saint-Lazare***, ***Train dans la neige***, and ***Train dans la campagne***, the last of which is in **le musée d'Orsay**.

Le monde francophone Have students work in pairs to ask each other content questions. Examples: **1. Quel est le nom du tunnel entre la France et l'Angleterre? (L'Eurotunnel/ le tunnel sous la Manche) 2. Quelle est une des différences entre le métro de Montréal et le métro de Paris? (Le métro de Montréal roule sur des pneus.)**

2 Expansion Continue the activity with these true/false statements.
7. La gare d'Orsay a servi de décor à des films. (Vrai.)
8. Quand les voies deviennent trop courtes, la gare d'Orsay est limitée au métro. (Faux, aux trains de banlieue)

3 Expansion Once students have agreed on the areas they would like to visit, they should consult road and train maps to see which **moyen de transport** would work best.

Flash culture Tell students that they will learn more about transportation and lodging by watching a variety of real-life images narrated by Csilla. Show the video segment without sound and tell students to call out what they see. Then show the video segment again with sound. You can also use the activities in the video manual in class to reinforce this **Flash culture** or assign them as homework.

OPTIONS

Cultural Comparison Bring in maps of the Paris **métro** and **RER** along with maps of a well-known American public transportation system, such as the New York City subway. Ask students: **Quel moyen de transport préférez-vous à Paris? à New York?** Then have them discuss their answers and plan mock commutes to various destinations in the two cities. Tell them to list similarities (**Similitudes**) and differences (**Différences**) between the American and French subway systems. Have groups compare lists.

Les transports You may want to supplement this section by telling students about travel between **Tanger (Maroc)** and **Algésiras (Espagne)** via hydrofoil; between **la Corse**, **l'Italie**, and **la Tunisie** by ferry; **le funiculaire de Montmartre**; **les canaux** in France; and **le bus amphibie** in **Montréal**.

Section Goals

In this section, students will learn the **passé composé** with **être**.

Instructional Resources
*espaces.vhlcentral.com: Lab MP3s; WB/VM/LM Answer Key; Transparency #34; IRM (**Essayez!** and **Mise en pratique** answers; Lab Audioscript; **Feuilles d'activités**); activities; downloads; reference tools*

Suggestions
- Quickly review the **passé composé** with **avoir**.
- Introduce the **passé composé** with **être** by describing where you went yesterday. Example: **Hier, je suis allé(e) à la bibliothèque de la faculté. Ensuite, je suis allé(e) chez moi.** Then ask students: **Et vous, où êtes-vous allé(e) hier?**
- Write the **passé composé** of **donner** and **aller** on the board. Have students compare the forms of the **passé composé** with **avoir** and **être**.
- Explain the agreement of past participles in the **passé composé** with **être**.
- Point out the verbs that form the **passé composé** with **être** as well as the irregular past participles **mort** and **né**.
- Tell students that the present tense forms of **naître** and **mourir** are rarely used.
- Have students turn to the illustration on pages 218–219 or use **Transparency #34** and have them describe the scene in the past.
- Tell students they will learn about adverbs in **Espace structures 7B**.

NATIONAL STANDARDS comparisons

7A.1 The *passé composé* with *être*

Point de départ In **Leçon 6A**, you learned to form the **passé composé** with **avoir**. Some verbs, however, form the **passé composé** with **être**.

- To form the **passé composé** of these verbs, use a present-tense form of **être** and the past participle of the verb that expresses the action.

	PRESENT TENSE	PAST PARTICIPLE		PRESENT TENSE	PAST PARTICIPLE
Je	**suis**	**allé.**	Il	**est**	**sorti.**

- Many of the verbs that take **être** in the **passé composé** involve motion. You have already learned a few of them: **aller**, **arriver**, **descendre**, **partir**, **passer**, **rentrer**, **sortir**, and **tomber**.

Jean-Luc **est parti** en vacances.
Jean-Luc left on vacation.

Je **suis tombé** de la chaise.
I fell off the chair.

Tu es parti pour Paris.
Mes parents sont arrivés des États-Unis.

- The past participles of verbs conjugated with **être** agree with their subjects in number and gender.

Charles, tu **es allé** à Montréal?
Charles, did you go to Montreal?

Florence **est partie** en vacances.
Florence left on vacation.

Mes frères **sont rentrés**.
My brothers came back.

Elles **sont arrivées** hier soir.
They arrived last night.

- To make a verb negative in the **passé composé**, place **ne/n'** and **pas** around the auxiliary verb, in this case, **être**.

Emma et Élodie **ne sont pas sorties**?
Emma and Élodie didn't go out?

Nous **ne sommes pas allées** à la plage.
We didn't go to the beach.

Je **ne suis pas passé** chez mon amie.
I didn't stop by my friend's house.

Vous **n'êtes pas rentrés** à la maison hier.
You didn't come home yesterday.

MISE EN PRATIQUE

1 Un week-end sympa Carole raconte son week-end à Paris. Complétez l'histoire avec les formes correctes des verbes au passé composé.

Thomas et moi, nous (1) __sommes partis__ (partir) de Lyon samedi et nous (2) __sommes arrivés__ (arriver) à Paris à onze heures. Nous (3) __sommes passés__ (passer) à l'hôtel et puis, je (4) __suis allée__ (aller) au Louvre. En route, je (5) __suis tombée__ (tomber) sur un vieil ami, et nous (6) __sommes allés__ (aller) prendre un café. Ensuite, je (7) __suis entrée__ (entrer) dans le musée. Samedi soir, Thomas et moi (8) __sommes montés__ (monter) au sommet de la tour Eiffel et après, nous (9) __sommes sortis__ (sortir) en boîte. Dimanche, nous (10) __sommes retournés__ (retourner) au Louvre. Ouf... je suis fatiguée!

2 Dimanche dernier Dites ce que (*what*) ces personnes ont fait dimanche dernier. Utilisez les verbes de la liste. Suggested answers

MODÈLE
Laure est allée à la piscine.

Laure

aller	rentrer
arriver	rester
monter	sortir

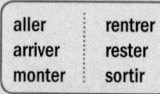

1. je Je suis rentré tard.

3. nous Nous sommes allés à l'église.

2. tu Tu es restée à l'hôtel.

4. Pamela et Caroline Pamela et Caroline sont sorties.

3 L'accident Le mois dernier, Djénaba et Safiatou sont allées au Sénégal. Racontez (*Tell*) leur histoire. Avec un(e) partenaire, complétez les phrases au passé composé. Ensuite, mettez-les dans l'ordre chronologique.

__1__ a. les filles / partir pour Dakar en avion
Les filles sont parties pour Dakar en avion.
__5__ b. Djénaba / tomber de vélo
Djénaba est tombée de vélo.
__4__ c. elles / aller faire du vélo dimanche matin
Elles sont allées faire du vélo dimanche matin.
__2__ d. elles / arriver à Dakar tard le soir
Elles sont arrivées à Dakar tard le soir.
__3__ e. elles / rester à l'hôtel Sofitel
Elles sont restées à l'hôtel Sofitel.
__6__ f. elle / aller à l'hôpital
Elle est allée à l'hôpital.

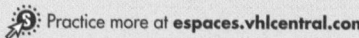

Practice more at **espaces.vhlcentral.com.**

OPTIONS

Extra Practice To practice discriminating between the **passé composé** with **être** and the **passé composé** with **avoir**, call out infinitives and have students respond with **avoir** or **être** and the past participle. Examples: **1. voyager (avoir voyagé) 2. entrer (être entré) 3. aller (être allé) 4. parler (avoir parlé) 5. retourner (être retourné)**

Game Divide the class into two teams. Choose one team member at a time to go to the board, alternating between teams. Say a subject pronoun and an infinitive. The person at the board must write and say the correct **passé composé** form. Example: **je: aller (je suis allé[e])**. Give a point for each correct answer. The team with the most points at the end of the game wins.

National Standards: communication

COMMUNICATION

4 Les vacances de printemps Avec un(e) partenaire, parlez de vos dernières vacances de printemps. Répondez à toutes ses questions. Answers will vary.

MODÈLE

quand / partir
Étudiant(e) 1: *Quand es-tu parti(e)?*
Étudiant(e) 2: *Je suis parti(e) vendredi soir.*

1. où / aller
2. avec qui / partir
3. comment / voyager
4. à quelle heure / arriver
5. où / rester
6. combien de temps / rester
7. que / visiter
8. sortir / souvent le soir
9. que / acheter
10. quand / rentrer

5 Enquête Votre professeur va vous donner une feuille d'activités. Circulez dans la classe et demandez à différents camarades s'ils ont fait ces choses récemment (*recently*). Présentez les résultats de votre enquête à la classe. Answers will vary.

MODÈLE

Étudiant(e) 1: *Es-tu allé(e) au musée récemment?*
Étudiant(e) 2: *Oui, je suis allé(e) au musée jeudi dernier.*

Questions	Noms
1. aller au musée	François
2. passer chez ses amis	
3. sortir en boîte	
4. rester à la maison pour écouter de la musique	
5. partir en week-end avec un copain	
6. monter dans un avion	

6 À l'aéroport Par groupes de quatre, parlez d'une mauvaise expérience dans un aéroport. À tour de rôle, racontez (*tell*) vos aventures et posez le plus (*most*) de questions possible. Utilisez les expressions de la liste et d'autres. Answers will vary.

MODÈLE

Étudiant(e) 1: *Quand je suis rentré(e) de la Martinique, j'ai attendu trois heures à la douane.*
Étudiant(e) 2: *Quelle horreur! Pourquoi?*

arriver	partir
attendre	perdre
avion	prendre un avion
billet (aller-retour)	sortir
douane	vol

- Here are a few more verbs that take **être** instead of **avoir** in the **passé composé.**

Some verbs used with *être*

entrer	*to enter*	**naître**	*to be born*
monter	*to go up; to get in/on*	**rester**	*to stay*
mourir	*to die*	**retourner**	*to return*

Mes parents **sont nés** en 1958 à Paris.
My parents were born in 1958 in Paris.

Ma grand-mère maternelle **est morte** l'année dernière.
My maternal grandmother died last year.

- Note that the verb **passer** takes **être** when it means *to pass by*, but it takes **avoir** when it means *to spend time.*

Maryse **est passée** par la douane.
Maryse passed through customs.

Maryse **a passé** trois jours à la campagne.
Maryse spent three days in the country.

- To form a question using inversion in the **passé composé**, invert the subject pronoun and the conjugated form of **être**.

Est-elle restée à l'hôtel Aquabella?
Did she stay at the Hotel Aquabella?

Vous êtes arrivée ce matin, Madame Roch?
Did you arrive this morning, Mrs. Roch?

- Place short adverbs such as **déjà**, **encore**, **bien**, **mal**, and **beaucoup** between the auxiliary verb **être** or **pas** and the past participle.

Elle **est déjà rentrée** de vacances?
She already came back from vacation?

Nous **ne sommes pas encore arrivés** à Aix-en-Provence.
We haven't arrived in Aix-en-Provence yet.

Essayez! **Choisissez le participe passé approprié.**

1. Vous êtes (nés/né) en 1959, Monsieur?
2. Les élèves sont (partis/parti) le 2 juin.
3. Les filles sont (rentrées/rentrés) de vacances.
4. Simone de Beauvoir est-elle (mort/morte) en 1986?
5. Mes frères sont (sortis/sortie).
6. Paul n'est pas (resté/restée) chez sa grand-mère.
7. Tu es (arrivés/arrivée) avant dix heures, Sophie.
8. Jacqueline a (passée/passé) une semaine en Suisse.

Essayez! For additional practice, change the subjects of the sentences (except items 1 and 7), and have students restate or rewrite them.

1 Suggestion Before beginning the activity, have students identify the past participles of the verbs in parentheses.

2 Expansion Ask students what they did last Sunday.

3 Expansion Have two volunteers play the roles of Djénaba and Safiatou. Tell the rest of the class to ask them questions about their trip. Example: **Quand êtes-vous arrivées à Dakar?**

4 Suggestion Have two volunteers read the **modèle** aloud.

5 Suggestion Distribute the **Feuilles d'activités** found on the Supersite.

6 Suggestion Before beginning the activity, ask the students about their travel experiences. Example: **Êtes-vous déjà allé(e)s dans un autre pays?**

OPTIONS

Video Show the video episode again to give students more input regarding the **passé composé** with **être** and **avoir**. Pause the video where appropriate to discuss how certain verbs were used and to ask comprehension questions.

Extra Practice Using the information in the **Roman-photo**, have students write a summary of David's trip to Paris. Then have students get together with a partner and exchange papers. Tell them to peer edit each other's work. Remind them to check for the correct usage of **avoir** and **être** in the **passé composé,** subject-verb agreement, and the correct forms of past participles.

Section Goals

In this section, students will learn direct object pronouns.

Instructional Resources
*espaces.vhlcentral.com: Lab MP3s; WB/VM/LM Answer Key; IRM (**Essayez!** and **Mise en pratique** answers; Lab Audioscript); activities; downloads; reference tools*

Suggestions

- Write these sentences on the board: **Qui a les tickets? Roger les a.** Underline **les tickets** and explain that it is the direct object. The direct object receives the action of the verb. It answers the questions *what?* or *whom?* Then underline **les** and explain that it is the plural direct object pronoun. Translate both sentences, pointing out the word order. Follow the same procedure with these sentences.
  —Qui prend le bus?
  —Les étudiants le prennent.
  —Qui écrit la lettre?
  —Mon père l'écrit.
- Take various objects from students' desks and ask: **Qui a ____?** Have students respond using the direct object pronoun: **Vous ____ avez.**
- Point out that direct objects are never preceded by a preposition.
- Continue asking questions to elicit other direct object pronouns. Examples: **M'entendez-vous? (Oui, nous vous entendons.) Qui achète vos vêtements? (Je les achète.)**
- Explain the agreement of past participles with direct object pronouns in the **passé composé**.

7A.2 Direct object pronouns

NATIONAL STANDARDS comparisons

Point de départ In **Leçon 6B**, you learned about indirect objects. You are now going to learn about direct objects.

DIRECT OBJECT — INDIRECT OBJECT

J'ai fait **un cadeau** **à ma sœur**.
I gave a gift to my sister.

- Note that a direct object receives the action of a verb directly and an indirect object receives the action of a verb indirectly. While indirect objects are frequently preceded by the preposition **à**, no preposition is needed before the direct object.

J'emmène **mes parents**. *I'm taking my parents.*	*but*	Je parle **à mes parents**. *I'm speaking to my parents.*

- You can use a direct object pronoun in the place of a direct object noun.

Tu fais **les valises**? *Are you packing the suitcases?*	Tu **les** fais? *Are you packing them?*
Ils retrouvent **Luc** à la gare. *They're meeting Luc at the station.*	Ils **le** retrouvent à la gare. *They're meeting him at the station.*

Direct object pronouns

singular		plural	
me/m'	*me*	nous	*us*
te/t'	*you*	vous	*you*
le/la/l'	*him/her/it*	les	*them*

Tes parents sont allés te chercher?

Tu m'excuses une minute?

- Place a direct object pronoun before the conjugated verb.

Les langues? Laurent et Xavier **les** étudient. *Languages? Laurent and Xavier study them.*	Les étudiants **vous** ont entendu. *The students heard you.*

MISE EN PRATIQUE

1 Des activités Dites ce que (*what*) ces gens font le week-end. Employez les pronoms d'objet direct.

MODÈLE

Il l'écoute.

Dominique écoute ce CD.

1. Benoît regarde ses DVD.
Il les regarde.

3. Il mange son gâteau.
Il le mange.

2. Ma mère admire cette robe.
Elle l'admire.

4. Ils achètent ces lunettes.
Ils les achètent.

2 À la plage La famille de Dalila a passé une semaine à la mer. Dalila parle de ce que (*what*) chaque membre de sa famille a fait. Employez des pronoms d'objet direct.

MODÈLE

J'ai conduit Ahmed à la plage. *Je l'ai conduit à la plage.*

1. Mon père a acheté le journal tous les matins. Il l'a acheté tous les matins.
2. Ma sœur a retrouvé son petit ami au café. Elle l'a retrouvé au café.
3. Mes parents ont emmené les enfants au cinéma. Ils les ont emmenés au cinéma.
4. Mon frère a invité sa fiancée au restaurant. Il l'a invitée au restaurant.
5. Anissa a porté ses lunettes de soleil. Elle les a portées.
6. À midi, Chekib a acheté les baguettes pour le repas (*meal*). À midi, il les a achetées.

3 Des doutes Julie et son amie Caroline sont au café. Elle répond à ses questions sur leurs vacances chez ses parents. Formez les questions que pose Caroline. Avec un(e) partenaire, jouez les deux rôles. Ensuite, présentez la scène à la classe. Suggested answers

1. Oui, mes parents t'invitent au bord de la mer. Tes parents m'invitent au bord de la mer?
2. Oui, je vais t'attendre à l'aéroport. Quelqu'un va m'attendre à l'aéroport?
3. Oui, mon frère va nous emmener sur son bateau. Ton frère va-t-il nous emmener sur son bateau?
4. Oui, je pense que ma famille va bien t'aimer. Penses-tu que ta famille va bien m'aimer?
5. J'ai choisi d'emporter (*take*) les chaussures vertes. Quelles chaussures as-tu choisies d'emporter?
6. J'ai pris le maillot de bain bleu. Quel maillot de bain as-tu pris?

Practice more at **espaces.vhlcentral.com.**

OPTIONS

Game Send a student out of the room. Give his or her belongings to other students to hide. Then have the person return. To get the belongings back, the person must ask students yes/no questions. They should respond using direct object pronouns. Example: **Tu as mon livre? (Oui, je l'ai./Non, je ne l'ai pas.)**

Pairs Have students work in pairs. Write the following list on the board. Tell them to take turns asking each other who does these activities: **acheter le billet, prendre le bus, aimer les sports, passer la douane,** and **étudier les mathématiques.** Example: **Qui prend le bus? (Mon ami Patrick le prend.)**

COMMUNICATION

4 **À Tahiti** Vous allez partir à Tahiti. Avec un(e) partenaire, posez-vous ces questions. Il/Elle vous répond en utilisant (*by using*) le pronom d'objet direct approprié. Ensuite, alternez les rôles. Answers will vary.

MODÈLE

Est-ce que tu prends le bus pour aller à la plage?
Non, je ne le prends pas.

1. Est-ce que tu prends l'avion?
2. Qui va t'attendre à l'aéroport?
3. Quand as-tu fait tes valises?
4. Est-ce que tu as acheté ton maillot de bain?
5. Est-ce que tu prends ton appareil photo?
6. Quels vêtements as-tu achetés?
7. Tu vas regarder la télévision tahitienne?
8. Vas-tu essayer les plats typiques de Tahiti?

5 **Le départ** Clémentine va partir au Cameroun chez sa correspondante (*pen pal*) Léa. Sa mère veut (*wants*) être sûre qu'elle n'a pas oublié un objet important, mais sa fille n'a presque rien (*nothing*) fait. Avec un(e) partenaire, jouez leur conversation en utilisant les phrases de la liste. Answers will vary.

MODÈLE

Étudiant(e) 1: *Tu as acheté le cadeau pour ton amie?*
Étudiant(e) 2: *Non, je ne l'ai pas encore acheté.*
Étudiant(e) 1: *Quand vas-tu l'acheter?*
Étudiant(e) 2: *Je vais l'acheter cet après-midi.*

acheter ton billet d'avion	faire tes valises
avoir l'adresse de Léa	prendre tes lunettes
chercher ton maillot de bain	préparer tes vêtements
confirmer l'heure d'arrivée	trouver ton passeport

- In a negative statement, place the direct object pronoun between **ne/n'** and the conjugated verb.

Le chinois? Je **ne le parle pas**.	Elle **ne l'a pas** pris à 14 heures?
Chinese? I don't speak it.	*She didn't take it at 2 o'clock?*

- When an infinitive follows a conjugated verb, the direct object pronoun precedes the infinitive.

Marcel va **nous écouter**.	Tu ne préfères pas **la porter** demain?
Marcel is going to listen to us.	*Don't you prefer to wear it tomorrow?*

- When a direct object pronoun is used with the **passé composé**, the past participle must agree with it in both gender and number.

J'ai mis **la valise** dans la voiture ce matin. *I put the suitcase in the car this morning.*	Je **l'**ai **mise** dans la voiture ce matin. *I put it in the car this morning.*
J'ai attendu **les filles** à la gare. *I waited for the girls at the station.*	Je **les** ai **attendues** à la gare. *I waited for them at the station.*

- In questions using **Quel(s)/Quelle(s)** and the **passé composé**, the past participle must agree with the gender and number of **Quel(s)/Quelle(s)**.

Quel hôtel avez-vous **choisi**? *Which hotel did you choose?*	**Quels** pays as-tu **visités**? *Which countries did you visit?*
Quelle plage as-tu **préférée**? *Which beach did you prefer?*	**Quelles** valises as-tu **apportées**? *Which suitcases did you bring?*

Essayez! **Répondez aux questions en remplaçant (*by replacing*) l'objet direct par un pronom d'objet direct.**

1. Thierry prend le train? Oui, il ___le___ prend.
2. Tu attends ta mère? Oui, je ___l'___ attends.
3. Vous entendez Olivier et Vincent? Oui, on ___les___ entend.
4. Le professeur te cherche? Oui, il ___me___ cherche.
5. Quels copains retrouves-tu au parc? Marc et Cyril? Oui, je ___les___ retrouve au parc.
6. Vous m'invitez? Oui, nous ___t'/vous___ invitons.
7. Tu nous comprends? Oui, je ___vous___ comprends.
8. Quelle valise prends-tu pour aller en vacances? La rouge? Oui, je ___la___ prends.
9. Chloé aime écouter la musique classique? Oui, elle aime ___l'___ écouter.
10. Vous avez regardé le film *Chacun cherche son chat*? Oui, nous ___l'___ avons regardé.

Essayez! For additional practice, have students restate or rewrite the answers in the negative.

1 Suggestion Have students ask questions with a direct object pronoun for each item. Example: **Qui l'écoute?**

2 Suggestion Before beginning the activity, have students identify the direct objects.

3 Suggestion Tell students to add two of their own questions to the list.

4 Suggestions
- Before beginning the activity, have students describe the photo.
- Tell students to add three of their own questions with direct objects to the list.

5 Suggestions
- Before beginning the activity, have students underline the direct objects in the phrases.
- Have two volunteers read the **modèle** aloud.

OPTIONS

Extra Practice Make a list of twenty questions requiring direct object pronouns in the answer. Arrange students in two concentric circles. Students in the inner circle ask questions from the list to those in the outer circle until you say stop (**Arrêtez-vous**). The outer circle then moves one person to the right and the questions begin again. Continue for five minutes, and then have the students in the outer circle ask the questions.

Pairs Have students work in pairs. Tell them to invent a romantic dialogue between Simone and Jean-Claude, two protagonists of a soap opera. They should include direct object pronouns in their dialogues and these verbs: **adorer, aimer, détester,** and **attendre.** Example: **Jean-Claude: Simone, je t'adore.**

Instructional Resources
*espaces.vhlcentral.com: IRM (**Feuilles d'activités**; Info Gap Activities); Testing Program, pp. 49–52; Test Files; Testing Program MP3s; activities; downloads; reference tools*
Test Generator

1 Suggestion Tell students to write their sentences. Remind them that verbs that indicate motion often require the **passé composé** with **être**.

2 Suggestions
- Distribute the **Feuilles d'activités** found on the Supersite.
- Have two volunteers read the **modèle** aloud. Remind students to use direct object pronouns in their responses.

3 Suggestion Tell students to jot down notes during their interviews.

4 Suggestion Before beginning the activity, have the class identify the items.

4 Expansion To practice **vous** forms, bring in a small suitcase with various items and tell the class you just returned from a trip. Students must ask you questions about your vacation based on the items and figure out where you went. Example: a suitcase with gloves, a hat, a parka, and ski goggles.

5 Expansion Have groups decide who had the best or most interesting weekend, then ask them to tell the class about it.

6 Suggestion Divide the class into pairs and distribute the Info Gap Handouts found on the Supersite for this activity. Give students ten minutes to complete the activity.

NATIONAL communication STANDARDS

Révision

1 Il y a dix minutes Avec un(e) partenaire, décrivez (*describe*) dans cette scène les actions qui se sont passées (*happened*) il y a dix minutes. Utilisez les verbes de la liste pour écrire (*write*) des phrases. Ensuite, comparez vos phrases avec les phrases d'un autre groupe. Answers will vary.

MODÈLE

Étudiant(e) 1: *Il y a dix minutes, M. Hamid est parti.*
Étudiant(e) 2: *Il y a dix minutes, ...*

aller	partir
arriver	rentrer
descendre	sortir
monter	tomber

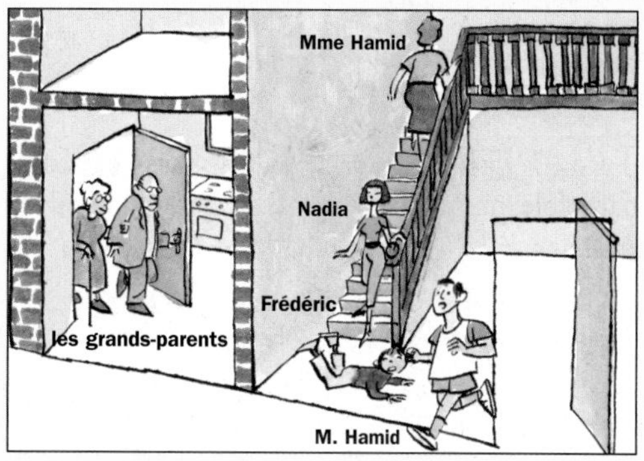

2 Qui aime quoi? Votre professeur va vous donner une feuille d'activités. Circulez dans la classe pour trouver un(e) camarade différent(e) qui aime ou qui n'aime pas chaque lieu de la liste. Answers will vary.

MODÈLE

Étudiant(e) 1: *Est-ce que tu aimes les aéroports?*
Étudiant(e) 2: *Je ne les aime pas du tout; je les déteste.*

3 À l'étranger Par groupes de quatre, interviewez vos camarades. Dans quels pays sont-ils déjà allés? Dans quelles villes? Comparez vos destinations, puis présentez toutes les réponses à la classe. N'oubliez pas de demander: Answers will vary.

- quand vos camarades sont parti(e)s
- où ils/elles sont allé(e)s
- où ils/elles sont resté(e)s
- combien de temps ils/elles ont passé là-bas

4 La valise Sandra et John sont partis en vacances. Voici leur valise. Avec un(e) partenaire, faites une description écrite (*written*) de leurs vacances. Où sont-ils allés? Comment sont-ils partis? Answers will vary.

5 Un long week-end Avec un(e) partenaire, préparez huit questions sur le dernier long week-end. Utilisez les verbes de la liste. Ensuite, par groupes de quatre, répondez à toutes les questions. Answers will vary.

MODÈLE

Étudiant(e) 1: *Où es-tu allé(e) vendredi soir?*
Étudiant(e) 2: *Vendredi soir, je suis resté(e) chez moi. Mais samedi, je suis sorti(e)!*

aller	rentrer
arriver	rester
partir	retourner
passer	sortir

6 Mireille et les Girard Votre professeur va vous donner, à vous et à votre partenaire, une feuille sur le week-end de Mireille et de la famille Girard. Attention! Ne regardez pas la feuille de votre partenaire. Answers will vary.

MODÈLE

Étudiant(e) 1: *Qu'est-ce que Mireille a fait vendredi soir?*
Étudiant(e) 2: *Elle est allée au cinéma.*

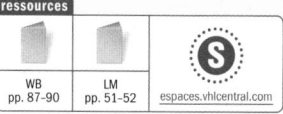

ressources
WB pp. 87-90 | LM pp. 51-52 | espaces.vhlcentral.com

OPTIONS

Extra Practice Write these phrases on the board. Tell students to write complete sentences, using the **passé composé**. **1. Janine et moi / faire du shopping 2. Nous / partir / une heure 3. Nous / prendre / métro / Galeries Lafayette / et / nous / passer / après-midi / là 4. Nous / arriver / chez Janine / fatigué 5. Elle / ne pas / avoir besoin / sortir / pour manger / et / nous / rester / la maison**

Extra Practice Have students write a composition about a memorable vacation they took with friends or family. Remind them to use the **passé composé**. They should also use object pronouns to avoid unnecessary repetition.

Video: TV Clip

Le Zapping

NATIONAL STANDARDS communication cultures

NATIONAL STANDARDS connections communities

Le TER

En 1984, la SNCF (Société nationale des chemins de fer° français) met en place dans 20 régions le TER (Transport Express Régional). Les trains TER relient° les villes d'une même région ou de différentes régions. Il y a, entre autres, le TER Picardie et le TER Alsace. Ces trains sont rapides, confortables et pratiques pour éviter° les embouteillages° du matin et du soir. Les TER concrétisent la décentralisation des chemins de fer français, parce que ce sont les Conseils Régionaux qui financent et décident des trajets°, des dessertes° et des horaires°.

—On devrait° parfois réfléchir avant de° prendre sa voiture.

—Pour être bien, bougeons mieux°.

Compréhension Répondez aux questions. Some answers will vary.

1. Comment le guépard (*cheetah*) chasse-t-il la gazelle? Il roule en voiture.
2. Quelle mauvaise surprise rencontre-t-il? Il rencontre un énorme embouteillage.
3. Pourquoi l'autre guépard va-t-il attraper la gazelle? Il prend le train et évite l'embouteillage.

Discussion Par groupes de trois, répondez aux questions. Answers will vary.

1. Quelle est l'importance du guépard dans cette publicité (*ad*)? Pourquoi pas un autre animal?
2. Quels moyens (*means*) de transport prenez-vous souvent? Pourquoi? Quels sont leurs avantages?

chemins de fer *railroads* **relient** *link* **éviter** *avoid* **embouteillages** *traffic jams* **trajets** *routes* **dessertes** *service* **horaires** *schedules* **devrait** *should* **réfléchir avant de** *think before* **bougeons mieux** *let's move better*

Practice more at **espaces.vhlcentral.com.**

Section Goals

In this section, students will:

- read about the network of regional **TER** trains
- watch a commercial for the regional trains
- answer questions about the commercial and traveling by train

Instructional Resources
*espaces.vhlcentral.com: TV commercial; IRM (**Le zapping** TV clip transcription); activities; downloads; reference tools*

Introduction
To check comprehension, ask these questions:
1. Quelle fonction ont les trains TER? (Ils relient les villes d'une même région ou de différentes régions.)
2. Pourquoi sont-ils pratiques? (On évite les embouteillages du matin et du soir.)

Avant de regarder la vidéo

- Have students look at the video stills, read the captions, and predict what is happening in the commercial for each visual. **(1. Parfois, prendre la voiture n'est pas une bonne idée. 2. Pour être bien et ne pas perdre de temps, le train est une option intelligente.)**
- Before showing the video, explain to students that they do not need to understand every word they hear. Introduce the verb **réfléchir** and ask them to guess the English cognate (*to reflect*). Use the verb **bouger** in a few sample sentences and have students guess its meaning and create sentences of their own with it.

Compréhension Have students work in pairs or groups for this activity. Tell them to write their answers. Then show the video again so that they can check their answers and add any missing information.

Discussion Ask students if they have ever found themselves in a situation where driving turned out unexpectedly to be the slowest option. What type of public transportation would they have picked instead?

OPTIONS

SNCF In 1997, new European Union regulations required the **SNCF** to transfer the management of its network of tracks as well as other components of its infrastructure to a separate, government-subsidized company called the **RFF** (**Réseau ferré de France**). The **SNCF** still operates and maintains the trains themselves. Of course, the **SNCF** for years has collaborated with other rail entities. It has worked with the **RER** (suburban Paris commuter trains) for the purpose of sharing tracks and negotiating rail traffic and schedules. Furthermore, the **SNCF** has long collaborated with the **RATP** (Paris **Métro**) for running its trains on the subway network's lower-voltage tracks.

Section Goals

In this section, students will learn and practice vocabulary related to:
- hotels
- ordinal numbers
- sequencing events

Instructional Resources
*espaces.vhlcentral.com: Transparency #35; IRM (**Vocabulaire supplémentaire**; **Mise en pratique** answers; Textbook Audioscript; Lab Audioscript); Textbook MP3s; Lab MP3s; WB/VM/LM Answer Key; activities; downloads; reference tools*

Suggestions

- Use **Transparency #35.** Point out people and things in the illustration and describe what the people are doing. Example: **Ils sont à la réception d'un hôtel. Ils ont une réservation. Voici la clé de leur chambre.**
- Have students look over the new vocabulary. They should notice that many terms related to hotels and travel are cognates (**réservation, réception, passeport,** and **passager**).
- Point out that **passeport** has an **e** and **passager/passagère** have no **n**.
- Model the difference in pronunciation between **deuxième** and **douzième**, and have students repeat.
- Point out that the word **libre (gratuit(e))** means *free*, as in *available*, not *free of charge*.
- Emphasize that, in this context, **complet/complète** means *full*, not *complete*.
- Tell students that the word **second(e)** is used instead of **deuxième** when there are only two items to list. Example: **La Seconde Guerre mondiale**.
- Additional vocabulary for this lesson can be found in the **Vocabulaire supplémentaire** on the Supersite.

Leçon 7B

Talking Picture
Audio: Activity

You will learn how to...
- **make hotel reservations**
- **give instructions**

À l'hôtel

Vocabulaire

annuler une réservation	*to cancel a reservation*
réserver	*to reserve, to book*
premier/première	*first*
cinquième	*fifth*
neuvième	*ninth*
vingt et unième	*twenty-first*
vingt-deuxième	*twenty-second*
trente et unième	*thirty-first*
centième	*hundredth*
une agence de voyages	*travel agency*
un agent de voyages	*travel agent*
une auberge de jeunesse	*youth hostel*
une chambre individuelle	*single room*
un hôtel	*hotel*
un passager/une passagère	*passenger*
complet/complète	*full (no vacancies)*
libre	*available*
alors	*so, then; at that moment*
après (que)	*after*
avant (de)	*before*
d'abord	*first*
donc	*therefore*
enfin	*finally, at last*
ensuite	*then, next*
finalement	*finally*
pendant (que)	*during, while*
puis	*then*
tout à coup	*suddenly*
tout de suite	*right away*

ressources
WB pp. 91-92
LM p. 53
espaces.vhlcentral.com

OPTIONS

TPR Ask ten volunteers to line up facing the class. Make sure students know what number they are in line. Call out ordinal numbers at random. The student whose cardinal number corresponds to the called ordinal number has three seconds to step forward. If that student is too slow, he or she sits down. The order changes for the rest of the students standing further down the line. The last students standing win.

Les étages Point out to students that a second floor in the U.S. would be called **le premier étage** in the Francophone world. Tell them that an **étage** is a floor above another floor. Elevators usually indicate the ground floor by the letter **R** (or other abbreviation of **rez-de-chaussée**) or the number **0**. Add that, in buildings with only two floors, people say **à l'étage** for *on the second floor.*

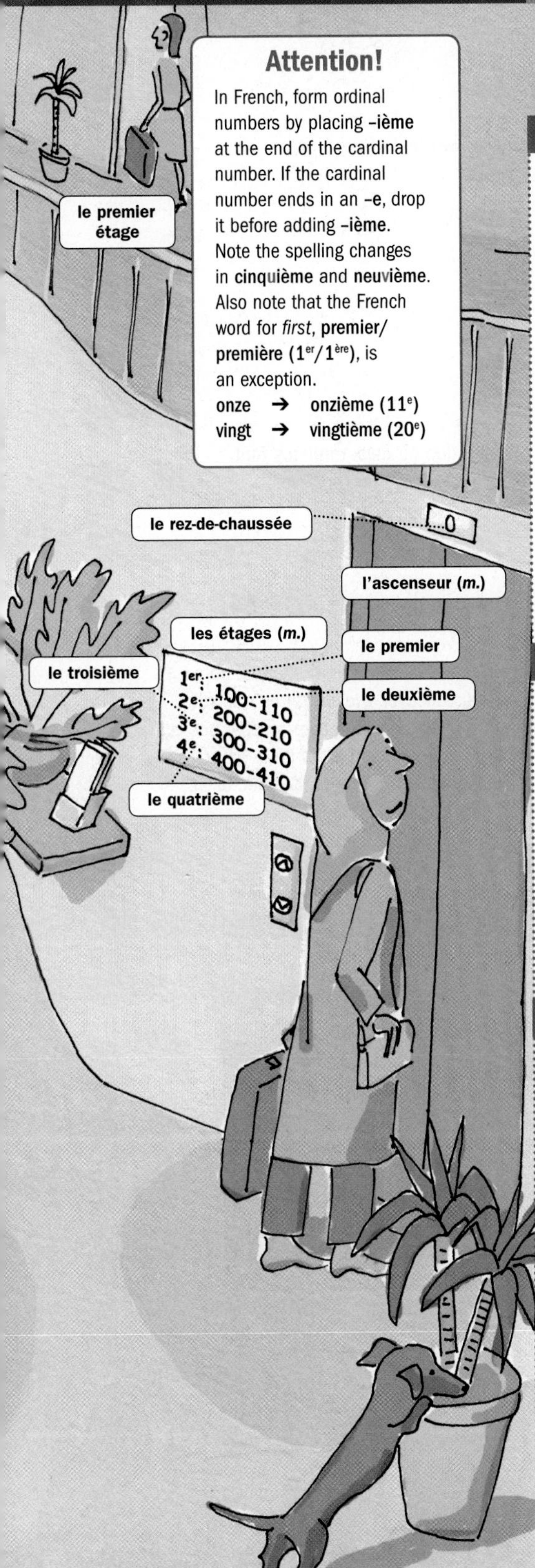

Attention!

In French, form ordinal numbers by placing **-ième** at the end of the cardinal number. If the cardinal number ends in an **-e**, drop it before adding **-ième**. Note the spelling changes in **cinquième** and **neuvième**. Also note that the French word for *first*, **premier/première** (1er/1ère), is an exception.

onze → **onzième** (11e)
vingt → **vingtième** (20e)

Mise en pratique

1 **Remplissez** Complétez les phrases avec le nombre ordinal qui convient (*fits*).

MODÈLE

B est la ____deuxième____ lettre de l'alphabet.

1. Décembre est le ____douzième____ mois de l'année.
2. Mercredi est le ____troisième____ jour de la semaine.
3. Aux États-Unis, le rez-de-chaussée est le ____premier____ étage.
4. Ma classe de français est au ____Answers will vary.____ (étage).
5. Octobre est le ____dixième____ mois de l'année.
6. Z est la ____vingt-sixième____ lettre de l'alphabet.
7. Samedi est le ____sixième____ jour de la semaine.
8. Barack Obama est le ____quarante-quatrième____ président des États-Unis.
9. Mon prénom (*first name*) commence avec la ____Answers will vary.____ lettre de l'alphabet.
10. La fête nationale américaine est le ____quatrième____ jour du mois de juillet.

2 **Écoutez** Écoutez la conversation entre Mme Renoir et un hôtelier et décidez si les phrases sont **vraies** ou **fausses**.

	Vrai	Faux
1. Mme Renoir est à l'agence de voyages.	☐	☑
2. Mme Renoir a fait une réservation.	☑	☐
3. Mme Renoir prend la chambre au cinquième étage.	☐	☑
4. Il y a un ascenseur dans l'hôtel.	☐	☑
5. Mme Renoir a réservé une chambre à deux lits.	☐	☑
6. La cliente s'appelle Margot Renoir.	☑	☐
7. L' hôtel a des chambres libres.	☐	☑
8. L' hôtelier donne à Mme Renoir la clé de la chambre 27.	☑	☐

3 **Hôtel Paradis** Virginie téléphone à l'hôtel Paradis pour faire une réservation. Mettez les phrases dans l'ordre chronologique.

__6__ a. Finalement, il me demande le numéro de ma carte de crédit (*credit card*) pour finaliser la réservation.
__2__ b. Pendant la conversation, je demande une chambre individuelle au troisième étage.
__1__ c. D'abord, j'appelle l'hôtel Paradis pour faire une réservation.
__4__ d. Je ne veux (*want*) pas dormir au rez-de-chaussée, donc je demande une chambre au deuxième étage.
__3__ e. Ensuite, l'hôtel me rappelle (*calls me back*) pour annoncer qu'il n'y a plus de chambre libre au troisième étage, donc ma réservation est annulée.
__5__ f. C'est alors que l'hôtelier me donne une chambre au deuxième étage à côté de l'ascenseur.

Practice more at **espaces.vhlcentral.com.**

1 Expansions
- Point out that the French calendar begins the week with Monday.
- Give students these items. **11. Aujourd'hui est le ____ jour de la semaine. 12. Ce cours est mon ____ cours aujourd'hui. 13. Ma chambre est au ____ étage. 14. Mon anniversaire est pendant le ____ mois de l'année.** (Answers will vary.)
- Have students invent riddles using ordinal numbers. Example: **Je suis le seizième président des États-Unis. Qui suis-je?** (Abraham Lincoln)

2 Tapescript L'HÔTELIER: Bonjour, Madame. Bienvenue à l'hôtel Casablanca! Avez-vous une réservation?
LA CLIENTE: Bonjour, Monsieur. Oui, mon mari et moi avons fait une réservation.
H: Et c'est à quel nom?
C: Je l'ai faite à mon nom, Renoir.
H: Excellent! Vous avez réservé une chambre avec un grand lit. Votre chambre est la numéro 57 au cinquième étage.
C: Ah non, il y a une erreur. J'ai réservé la chambre numéro 27 au deuxième étage. Je refuse de prendre cette chambre, il n'y a pas d'ascenseur dans votre hôtel. Est-ce que vous avez une autre solution?
H: Madame Renoir, je suis désolé, mais l'hôtel est complet.
C: Oh là là. Ce n'est pas possible! Qu'est-ce que je vais faire?
H: Un instant, êtes-vous Marguerite Renoir?
C: Non, je suis Margot Renoir.
H: Madame Renoir, pardonnez-moi. Voici votre clé, chambre 27 au deuxième étage.
(On Textbook MP3s)

3 Suggestion Call students' attention to the sequencing words in these sentences. Examples: **Finalement**, **Pendant**, **D'abord**, etc.

3 Expansion Have pairs of students rewrite the story using the sequencing words, but changing the details. Example: reserve a different kind of room, encounter a different problem, and find a different solution.

OPTIONS

Extra Practice Review seasons, months, and days while practicing ordinal numbers by asking questions like the following: **Quel est le septième mois de l'année? Quelle est la troisième saison de l'année? Quel est le dernier jour de la semaine?**

Extra Practice Ask questions about the **À l'hôtel** illustration. Examples: **Cet hôtel a combien d'étages? Ce monsieur a un passeport de quel pays? Qu'est-ce que l'homme à la réception donne aux clients?** Then ask students personalized questions. Examples: **Préférez-vous aller à une agence de voyages ou faire les réservations sur Internet? Aimez-vous voyager seul(e) ou en groupe? Avez-vous un hôtel préféré?**

4 Expansions
- After students have answered the questions, have them make up a conversation between a customer and a travel agent to arrange the trip.
- Ask volunteers to describe their **vacances idéales** to the class.

5 Suggestion Have students consider other details that might come up while making a hotel reservation and include them in their conversation. Examples: **Est-ce qu'il y a un ascenseur? Il y a une télévision dans la chambre?** Have them refer to the **Vocabulaire supplémentaire** from the Supersite.

6 Expansion Assign each group a different francophone location. Tell students to include any nearby attractions (**la plage, la campagne, le centre-ville**) and hotel amenities (**la piscine, le restaurant**) in their poster. For inspiration, show some French language brochures from actual hotels.

7 Suggestion Before starting this activity, have students brainstorm a list of steps involved in making a hotel reservation. If students have never reserved a room before, have them make up a scenario that includes at least one complication, for instance, their first choice of hotel is full.

Successful Language Learning Remind students to accept some corrections without explanation, especially when they are attempting to use language and structures above their current level. Tell them not to overanalyze and to trust that it will make more sense as their language skills develop.

Communication

NATIONAL communication STANDARDS

4 Conversez Un(e) camarade passe des vacances idéales dans un hôtel. Interviewez-le/la (*him/her*). Answers will vary.

1. Quelles sont les dates de ton séjour?
2. Où vas-tu? Dans quel pays, quelle région ou quelle ville? Vas-tu à la mer, à la campagne, ...?
3. À quel hôtel descends-tu (*do you stay*)?
4. Qui fait la réservation?
5. Comment est l'hôtel? Est-ce que l'hôtel a un ascenseur, une piscine, ...?
6. À quel étage est ta chambre?
7. Combien de lits a ta chambre?
8. Laisses-tu ton passeport à la réception?

5 Notre réservation Par groupes de trois, travaillez pour préparer une présentation où deux touristes font une réservation dans un hôtel ou une auberge de jeunesse francophone. N'oubliez pas d'ajouter (*add*) les informations de la liste. Answers will vary.

- le nom de l'hôtel
- le type de chambre(s)
- l'étage
- le nombre de lits
- les dates
- le prix

6 Mon hôtel Vous allez ouvrir (*open*) votre propre hôtel. Par groupes de quatre, créez une affiche (*poster*) pour le promouvoir (*promote*) avec l'information de la liste et présentez votre hôtel au reste de la classe. Votre professeur va ensuite donner à chaque groupe un budget. Avec ce budget, vous allez faire la réservation à l'hôtel qui convient le mieux (*best suits*) à votre groupe. Answers will vary.

- le nom de votre hôtel
- le nombre d'étoiles (*stars*)
- les services offerts
- le prix pour une nuit

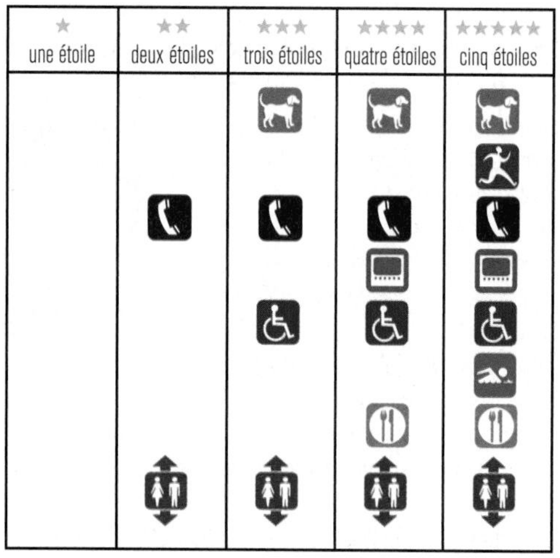

7 Votre dernière réservation Écrivez un paragraphe où vous décrivez (*describe*) ce que vous avez fait la dernière fois que vous avez réservé une chambre. Utilisez au moins cinq mots de la liste. Échangez et comparez votre paragraphe avec celui (*the one*) d'un camarade de classe. Answers will vary.

alors	d'abord	puis
après (que)	donc	tout à coup
avant (de)	enfin	tout de suite

OPTIONS

Extra Practice Give each student a card with either (1) a noun from the **Vocabulaire**, such as **chambre, clé,** or **passeport** or (2) a related verb, such as **réserver, prendre, oublier,** or **perdre**. Tell students to find someone whose word can be combined logically with their own. Then have them write an original sentence in the **passé composé**. Compile the sentences on the board. Then use sequencing expressions to combine them into a story.

Combien d'étoiles préférez-vous? Tell students that the French government regulates hotel ratings and requires that they be posted. Hotels must meet standards to qualify for a certain number of stars. A two-star hotel is a comfortable budget hotel. A five-star hotel is luxurious. While the level of comfort is standardized, prices are not.

Les sons et les lettres

Audio: Concepts, Activities
Record & Compare

National Standards: comparisons

ti, sti, and ssi

The letters **ti** followed by a consonant are pronounced like the English word *tea*, but without the puff released in the English pronunciation.

actif **petit** **tigre** **utiles**

When the letter combination **ti** is followed by a vowel sound, it is often pronounced like the sound linking the English words *miss you*.

dictionnaire **patient** **initial** **addition**

Regardless of whether it is followed by a consonant or a vowel, the letter combination **sti** is pronounced *stee*, as in the English word *steep*.

gestion **question** **Sébastien** **artistique**

The letter combination **ssi** followed by another vowel or a consonant is usually pronounced like the sound linking the English words *miss you*.

passion **expression** **mission** **profession**

Words that end in **-sion** or **-tion** are often cognates with English words, but they are pronounced quite differently. In French, these words are never pronounced with a *sh* sound.

compression **nation** **attention** **addition**

Prononcez Répétez les mots suivants à voix haute.

1. artiste
2. mission
3. réservation
4. impatient
5. position
6. initiative
7. possession
8. nationalité
9. compassion
10. possible

Articulez Répétez les phrases suivantes à voix haute.

1. L'addition, s'il vous plaît.
2. Christine est optimiste et active.
3. Elle a fait une bonne première impression.
4. Laëtitia est impatiente parce qu'elle est fatiguée.
5. Tu cherches des expressions idiomatiques dans le dictionnaire.

Il n'est de règle sans exception.[2]

Dictons Répétez les dictons à voix haute.

De la discussion jaillit la lumière.[1]

[1] Discussion brings light.
[2] The exception proves the rule.

ressources
LM p. 54
espaces.vhlcentral.com

Section Goals

In this section, students will learn about the letter combinations **ti**, **sti**, and **ssi**.

Instructional Resources
espaces.vhlcentral.com: Textbook MP3s; Lab MP3s; WB/VM/LM Answer Key; IRM (Textbook Audioscript; Lab Audioscript); activities; downloads; reference tools

Suggestions

- Pronounce each of the example words and have students repeat them after you.
- To practice **ti**, have students put the palm of their hand in front of their lips and say the English word *tea*. Ask them if they felt the puff of air when they pronounced the letter **t**. Then have them pronounce the French word **petit** holding their hand in front of their mouth. Explain that they should not feel a puff of air when they pronounce the letters **ti** in French.
- Point out that **-sion** as in the word **télévision** has a **[z]** sound. Additionally, **-cia** as in the name **Patricia** has an unvoiced **[s]** sound
- Many words that end in **-sion**, **-ssion**, **-stion**, and **-tion** are cognates. Contrast the French and English pronunciation of words such as **attention** and **mission**.
- Mention words from the **Vocabulaire** that contain **ti**, **sti**, or **ssi**. Then have students repeat after you. Alternatively, ask students to recall such vocabulary. Examples: **réception, réservation, vingtième**. See if a volunteer is able to recall any words from previous lessons. Examples: **pessimiste, dessiner, l'addition**, and **attention**.

Dictons Tell students that the word **lumière** is used figuratively in the proverb **«De la discussion jaillit la lumière.»** Ask students what they think it means in this context (*clarity, ideas*).

OPTIONS

Extra Practice Here are some sentences to use for additional practice with these letter combinations. **1. C'est utile d'étudier la gestion et l'informatique. 2. La profession de Sébastien? Il est dentiste. 3. Patricia utilise un plan de la station de ski. 4. Martine est-elle pessimiste ou optimiste?**

Extra Practice Teach your students the following French tongue-twisters that contain **ti** and **ssi**: **1. Pauvre petit pêcheur, prend patience pour pouvoir prendre plusieurs petits poissons. 2. Un pâtissier qui pâtissait chez un tapissier qui tapissait, dit un jour au tapissier qui tapissait: vaut-il mieux pâtisser chez un tapissier qui tapisse ou tapisser chez un pâtissier qui pâtisse?**

La réservation d'hôtel

Video: *Roman-photo*
Record & Compare

PERSONNAGES

Agent de voyages

Amina

Pascal

Sandrine

À l'agence de voyages...

SANDRINE J'ai besoin d'une réservation d'hôtel, s'il vous plaît. C'est pour les vacances de Noël.

AGENT Où allez-vous? En Italie?

SANDRINE Nous allons à Albertville.

AGENT Et c'est pour combien de personnes?

SANDRINE Nous sommes deux, mais il nous faut deux chambres individuelles.

AGENT Très bien. Quelles sont les dates du séjour, Mademoiselle?

SANDRINE Alors, le 25, c'est Noël, donc je fête en famille. Disons du 26 décembre au 2 janvier.

AGENT Ce n'est pas possible à Albertville, mais à Megève, j'ai deux chambres à l'hôtel Le Vieux Moulin pour 143 euros par personne. Ou alors, à l'hôtel Le Mont Blanc pour 171 euros par personne.

SANDRINE Oh non, mais Megève, ce n'est pas Albertville... et ces prix! C'est vraiment trop cher.

AGENT C'est la saison, Mademoiselle. Les hôtels les moins chers sont déjà complets.

SANDRINE Oh là là. Je ne sais pas quoi faire... J'ai besoin de réfléchir. Merci, Monsieur. Au revoir!

AGENT Au revoir, Mademoiselle.

Chez Sandrine...

SANDRINE Oui, Pascal. Amina nous a trouvé une auberge à Albertville. C'est génial, non? En plus, c'est pas cher!

PASCAL Euh, en fait... Albertville, maintenant, c'est impossible.

SANDRINE Qu'est-ce que tu dis?

PASCAL C'est que... j'ai du travail.

SANDRINE Du travail! Mais c'est Noël! On ne travaille pas à Noël! Et Amina a déjà tout réservé... Oh! C'est pas vrai!

PASCAL (*à lui-même*) Elle n'est pas très heureuse maintenant, mais quelle surprise en perspective!

Un peu plus tard...

AMINA On a réussi, Sandrine! La réservation est faite. Tu as de la chance! Mais, qu'est-ce qu'il y a?

SANDRINE Tu es super gentille, Amina, mais Pascal a annulé pour Noël. Il dit qu'il a du travail... Lui et moi, c'est fini. Tu as fait beaucoup d'efforts pour faire la réservation, je suis désolée.

ACTIVITÉS

1 Vrai ou faux? Indiquez si ces affirmations sont vraies ou fausses. Corrigez les phrases fausses. Answers may vary.

1. Sandrine fait une réservation à l'agence de voyages.
   Faux. Sandrine ne fait pas de réservation à l'agence de voyages.
2. Pascal dit un mensonge (*lie*).
   Vrai.
3. Amina fait une réservation à l'hôtel Le Mont Blanc.
   Faux. Amina fait une réservation à l'auberge de la Costaroche.
4. Il faut annuler la réservation à l'auberge de la Costaroche.
   Vrai.
5. Amina est fâchée (*angry*) contre Sandrine.
   Faux. Amina n'est pas fâchée contre Sandrine.
6. Pascal est fâché contre Sandrine.
   Faux. Pascal n'est pas fâché contre Sandrine.
7. Sandrine est fâchée contre Pascal.
   Vrai.
8. Sandrine a envie de voyager le 25 décembre.
   Faux. Sandrine a envie de voyager le 26 décembre.
9. Cent soixante et onze euros, c'est beaucoup d'argent pour Sandrine.
   Vrai.
10. Il y a beaucoup de touristes à Albertville en décembre.
    Vrai.

Practice more at **espaces.vhlcentral.com.**

Section Goals

In this section, students will learn functional phrases for getting help and making reservations.

Instructional Resources
*espaces.vhlcentral.com: Video; WB/VM/LM Answer Key; IRM (Videoscript; **Roman-photo** Translations); activities; downloads; reference tools*
Video on DVD

Video Recap: Leçon 7A
Before doing this **Roman-photo**, review the previous one with this activity.

1. Où est allé David? (à Paris)
2. Avec qui a-t-il visité Paris? (avec ses parents)
3. Qu'a-t-il fait à Paris? (Il a visité les musées et les monuments. Il a pris un bateau-mouche.)
4. Qu'est-ce qu'il a apporté à Stéphane? (des lunettes de soleil)
5. Où Sandrine va-t-elle passer ses vacances d'hiver? (à Albertville)

Video Synopsis Sandrine goes to a travel agency to find a hotel in Albertville. They are all too expensive, so she leaves without making a reservation. She asks Amina to help find a cheaper hotel. Then Pascal says he can't go to Albertville after all. Disappointed, Sandrine tells Amina to cancel the reservation because she and Pascal are finished. Amina then tells Sandrine about Cyberhomme, her electronic pen pal.

Suggestions
- Ask students to read the title, glance at the video stills, and predict what the episode will be about.
- Have students read the **Roman-photo** aloud in groups of four.
- Have students scan the captions to find at least three sentences that contain words and expressions related to travel and accommodations. Examples: **Ou alors, à l'hôtel Le Mont Blanc, deux chambres individuelles pour 171 euros par personne. Les hôtels les moins chers sont déjà complets.**
- Review students' predictions and ask which ones were correct.

OPTIONS

Avant de regarder la vidéo Before viewing the video episode **La réservation d'hôtel**, have students brainstorm a list of things people might say when arranging a hotel reservation. For example, what questions might a travel agent ask? How might the traveler respond?

Regarder la vidéo Play the video episode once without sound and have the class create a plot summary based on the visual cues. Afterward, show the video with sound and have the class correct any mistaken guesses and fill in any gaps in the plot summary they created.

Sandrine essaie d'organiser son voyage.

4

5

Au P'tit Bistrot...

SANDRINE Amina, je n'ai pas réussi à faire une réservation pour Albertville. Tu peux m'aider?

AMINA C'est que... je suis connectée avec Cyberhomme.

SANDRINE Avec qui?

AMINA J'écris un e-mail à... Bon, je t'explique plus tard. Dis-moi, comment est-ce que je peux t'aider?

Un peu plus tard...

AMINA Bon, alors... Sandrine m'a demandé de trouver un hôtel pas cher à Albertville. Pas facile à Noël... Je vais essayer... Voilà! L'auberge de la Costaroche... 39 euros la nuit pour une chambre individuelle. L'hôtel n'est pas complet et il y a deux chambres libres. Quelle chance, cette Sandrine! Bon, nom... Sandrine Aubry...

9

10

AMINA Bon, la réservation, ce n'est pas un problème. C'était facile de réserver. Mais toi, Sandrine, c'est évident, ça ne va pas.

SANDRINE C'est vrai. Mais, alors, c'est qui, ce «Cyberhomme»?

AMINA Oh, c'est juste un ami virtuel. On correspond sur Internet, c'est tout. Ce soir, c'est son dixième message!

SANDRINE Lis-le-moi!

AMINA Euh non, c'est personnel...

SANDRINE Alors, dis-moi comment il est!

AMINA D'accord... Il est étudiant, sportif mais sérieux. Très intellectuel.

SANDRINE S'il te plaît, écris-lui: «Sandrine cherche aussi un cyberhomme»!

Expressions utiles

Getting help

- **Je ne sais pas quoi faire... J'ai besoin de réfléchir.**
  I don't know what to do... I have to think.
- **Je n'ai pas réussi à faire une réservation pour Albertville.**
  I didn't manage to make a reservation for Albertville.
- **Tu peux m'aider?**
  Can you help me?
- **Dis-moi, comment est-ce que je peux t'aider?**
  Tell me, how can I help you?
- **Qu'est-ce que tu dis?**
  What are you saying/did you say?
- **On a réussi.**
  We succeeded./We got it.
- **S'il te plaît, écris-lui.**
  Please, write to him.

Additional vocabulary

- **C'est trop tard?**
  Is it too late?
- **Disons...**
  Let's say...
- **La réservation est faite.**
  The reservation has been made.
- **C'est fini.**
  It's over.
- **Je suis connectée avec...**
  I am online with...
- **Lis-le-moi.**
  Read it to me.
- **Il dit que...**
  He says that...
- **les moins chers**
  the least expensive
- **en fait**
  in fact

ACTIVITÉS

2 Questions Répondez aux questions.

1. Pourquoi est-il difficile de faire une réservation pour Albertville? C'est difficile parce que c'est Noël.
2. Pourquoi est-ce que Sandrine ne veut pas (*doesn't want*) rester à l'hôtel Le Vieux Moulin? L'hôtel Le Vieux Moulin est très cher.
3. Pourquoi Pascal dit-il qu'il ne peut pas (*can't*) aller à Albertville? Il dit qu'il a du travail.
4. Qui est Cyberhomme? C'est l'ami virtuel d'Amina.
5. À votre avis (*In your opinion*), Sandrine va-t-elle rester (*stay*) avec Pascal? Answers will vary.

3 Devinez Inventez-vous une identité virtuelle. Écrivez un paragraphe dans lequel (*in which*) vous vous décrivez, vous et vos loisirs préférés. Donnez votre nom d'internaute (*cybername*). Votre professeur va afficher (*post*) vos messages. Devinez (*Guess*) à qui correspondent les descriptions.

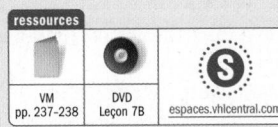

ressources: VM pp. 237–238 | DVD Leçon 7B | espaces.vhlcentral.com

Expressions utiles

- Draw attention to **-ir** verbs and expressions used to ask for help in the captions, in the **Expressions utiles** box, and as they occur in your conversation with students. Point out that this material will be formally presented in **Espace structures**.
- Respond briefly to questions about regular and irregular **-ir** verbs. Reinforce correct forms, but do not expect students to produce them consistently at this time.
- Contrast the pronunciation of the following expressions: **en fait, on fait**.
- Point out the differences between direct and indirect discourse by writing these two sentences on the board: **Il dit qu'il a du travail. Il dit: «J'ai du travail.»**

1 Suggestion Have students correct the items that are false.

1 Expansion Give these statements to the class. **11. Sandrine a besoin de deux chambres individuelles. (Vrai.) 12. Amina ne fait pas de réservation. (Faux.) 13. Cyberhomme est l'ami virtuel de Sandrine. (Faux.)**

2 Suggestion Have students discuss these questions in small groups.

2 Expansion Discuss question #5 as a class. Have students make other predictions about what will happen. Ask what kind of surprise they think Pascal has in mind.

3 Suggestion Without revealing students' identities, match students with common interests and have them write back to one another.

OPTIONS

Extra Practice Ask volunteers to act out the **Roman-photo** episode for the class. Assure them that it is not necessary to memorize the episode or to stick strictly to its content. Give them time to prepare. You may want to assign this as homework and do it the next class period as a review activity.

Pairs Have students write a brief paragraph recapping the major events in this episode and using sequencing expressions, such as **d'abord, donc, ensuite, avant de, alors,** etc. Ask volunteers to read their synopses aloud.

Section Goals

In this section, students will:

- learn about how and where the French vacation
- learn some terms used in youth hostels
- find out about vacation spots in the francophone world
- read about the Alps, a popular destination for skiers

Instructional Resources
espaces.vhlcentral.com: activities; downloads; reference tools

Culture à la loupe

Avant la lecture Ask students how much vacation their parents can take annually, how much is typical in this country, and how much they think working people need to be happy in their work. You might also ask what vacation activities Americans enjoy and what the students imagine is popular in France.

Lecture

- Mention to students that when experts anticipate the **grands départs** on the **autoroutes**, these days are labeled **rouge** throughout France.
- Explain the **Coup de main** box on superlatives to help students understand the text.

Après la lecture Ask students to compare American and French vacation habits. Example: **Les étudiants à l'université ici commencent leurs vacances en mai, mais les étudiants en France terminent leurs études en juin.**

1 Expansion Continue the activity with these fill-in-the-blank statements. **11. Les Français d'aujourd'hui prennent des vacances qui durent ____ en moyenne. (sept jours) 12. Les vacances les moins populaires à l'étranger sont ____. (en Asie) 13. Les étudiants commencent leurs vacances d'été en ____. (juin)**

CULTURE À LA LOUPE

Les vacances des Français

une plage à Biarritz, en France

Les Français, aujourd'hui, ont beaucoup de vacances. En 1936, les Français obtiennent° leurs premiers congés payés: deux semaines par an. En 1956, les congés payés passent à trois semaines, puis à quatre en 1969, et enfin à cinq semaines en 1982. Aujourd'hui, les Français sont parmi ceux qui° ont le plus de vacances en Europe. Pendant longtemps, les Français prenaient° un mois de congés l'été, en août, et beaucoup d'entreprises°, de bureaux et de magasins ferment° tout le mois (la fermeture annuelle). Aujourd'hui, les Français ont tendance à prendre des vacances plus courtes (sept jours en moyenne°), mais plus souvent. Quant aux° destinations de vacances, 90% (pour cent) des Français restent en France. S'ils partent à l'étranger, leurs destinations préférées sont l'Espagne, l'Afrique et l'Italie. Environ° 35% des Français vont à la campagne, 30% vont en ville, 25% vont à la mer et 10% vont à la montagne.

Ce sont les personnes âgées et les agriculteurs° qui partent le moins souvent en vacances et les étudiants qui voyagent le plus, parce qu'ils ont beaucoup de congés. Pour eux, les cours commencent en septembre ou octobre avec la rentrée des classes. Puis, il y a deux semaines de vacances plusieurs fois dans l'année: les vacances de Noël en décembre-janvier, les vacances d'hiver en février-mars et les vacances de printemps en avril-mai. Les élèves (de la maternelle° au lycée) ont une semaine en plus pour les vacances de la Toussaint en octobre-novembre. L'été, les étudiants et les élèves ont les grandes vacances de juin jusqu'à° la rentrée.

obtiennent *obtain* **parmi ceux qui** *among the ones who* **prenaient** *took* **entreprises** *companies* **ferment** *close* **en moyenne** *on average* **Quant aux** *As for* **Environ** *Around* **agriculteurs** *farmers* **maternelle** *pre-school* **jusqu'à** *until*

Coup de main

To form the superlative of nouns, use **le plus (de)** + (*noun*) to say *the most* and **le moins (de)** + (*noun*) to say *the least.*

Les étudiants ont le plus de congés.

Les personnes âgées prennent le moins de congés.

Les destinations de vacances des Français aujourd'hui

PAYS / CONTINENT	SÉJOURS
France	90,1%
Espagne	1,9%
Afrique	1,8%
Italie	1,6%
Amérique	1,3%
Belgique / Luxembourg	0,9%
Grande-Bretagne / Irlande	0,9%
Allemagne	0,8%
Asie / Océanie	0,7%

SOURCE: TNS Sofres

ACTIVITÉS

1 Complétez Complétez les phrases.

1. C'est en 1936 que les Français obtiennent leurs premiers congés payés.
2. Depuis (*Since*) 1982, les Français ont cinq semaines de congés payés.
3. Pendant longtemps, les Français prennent leurs vacances au mois d'août.
4. Pendant la fermeture annuelle, beaucoup de magasins sont fermés.
5. La France est le lieu de vacances préféré de 90% des Français.
6. Les destinations étrangères préférées des Français sont l'Espagne, l'Afrique et l'Italie.
7. Le lieu de séjour favori des Français est la campagne.
8. Les personnes âgées et les agriculteurs ne partent pas souvent en vacances.
9. Ce sont les étudiants qui ont le plus de vacances.
10. Les étudiants ont deux semaines de vacances plusieurs fois par an.

Practice more at **espaces.vhlcentral.com.**

OPTIONS

Extra Practice Ask students what they can learn in the chart **Les destinations de vacances des Français aujourd'hui**. (percentages showing where the French spend their vacations today) Have students quiz each other on the chart, so they can practice geography and percentages.

Pairs Ask students to work with a partner to tell in their own words three main points described in **Les vacances des Français**. You might brainstorm a list on the board: the history of employee vacations, the change in how the French take their vacations, and the time periods of student vacations.

LE FRANÇAIS QUOTIDIEN

À l'auberge de jeunesse

bagagerie (*f.*)	*baggage check room*
cadenas (*m.*)	*padlock*
casier (*m.*)	*locker*
couvre-feu (*m.*)	*curfew*
dortoir (*m.*)	*dormitory*
sac (*m.*) de couchage	*sleeping bag*
mixte	*coed*

LE MONDE FRANCOPHONE

Des vacances francophones

Voici quelques idées de vacances francophones:

Au soleil

- un séjour ou une croisière (un voyage en bateau) aux Antilles, dans la mer des Caraïbes: la Martinique, la Guadeloupe
- un séjour ou une croisière en Polynésie française, dans l'océan Pacifique: l'archipel de la Société (avec Tahiti), les Marquises, les Tuamotu, les îles Gambier et les îles Australes

Pour de l'aventure

- un trekking (une randonnée à pied) ou une randonnée à dos de chameau° dans le désert du Sahara: Maroc, Tunisie, Algérie
- un circuit-aventure dans les forêts de Madagascar, dans l'océan Indien ou dans la forêt équatoriale de la Guyane française, en Amérique du Sud°

à dos de chameau *camelback* **Sud** *South*

PORTRAIT

Les Alpes et le ski

Près de 11% des Français partent à la montagne pendant les vacances d'hiver. Soixante-dix pour cent d'entre eux° choisissent° une station de ski des Alpes françaises. La chaîne° des Alpes est la plus grande chaîne de montagnes d'Europe. Elle fait plus de 1.000 km de long et va de la Méditerranée à l'Autriche°. Plusieurs pays la partagent: entre autres° la France, la Suisse, l'Allemagne et l'Italie. Le Mont-Blanc, le sommet° le plus haut° d'Europe occidentale°, est à 4.811 mètres d'altitude. On trouve d'excellentes pistes° de ski dans les Alpes, comme à Chamonix, Tignes, Val d'Isère et aux Trois Vallées.

d'entre eux *of them* **choisissent** *choose* **chaîne** *range* **l'Autriche** *Austria* **entre autres** *among others* **sommet** *peak* **le plus haut** *the highest* **occidentale** *Western* **pistes** *trails*

SUR INTERNET

Chaque année, depuis (*since*) 1982, plus de 4 millions de Français utilisent des Chèques-Vacances pour payer leurs vacances. Qu'est-ce que c'est, un Chèque-Vacances?

Go to espaces.vhlcentral.com to find more information related to this **ESPACE CULTURE**.

ACTIVITÉS

2 Répondez Répondez aux questions par des phrases complètes.

1. Que peut-on utiliser à la place des draps?
   On peut utiliser un sac de couchage.
2. Quand on passe la nuit dans le dortoir d'une auberge de jeunesse, où met-on ses affaires (*belongings*)?
   On les met dans un casier.
3. Qu'est-ce que c'est, les Alpes?
   C'est une grande chaîne de montagnes partagée entre plusieurs pays d'Europe.
4. Quel est le sommet le plus haut d'Europe occidentale?
   Le Mont-Blanc est le sommet le plus haut d'Europe occidentale.
5. Quel séjour est-ce que vous suggérez à un(e) jeune Américain(e) qui aime l'aventure et qui a envie de pratiquer son français?
   Answers will vary.

3 À l'agence de voyages Vous travaillez dans une agence de voyages en France. Votre partenaire, un(e) client(e), va vous parler des activités et du climat qu'il/elle aime. Faites quelques suggestions de destinations. Votre client(e) va vous poser des questions sur les différents voyages que vous suggérez.

ressources
espaces.vhlcentral.com

Le français quotidien Encourage students to try an **auberge de jeunesse** if they travel overseas. They have no frills, sometimes have curfews, can be noisy, and meals (if offered) are during limited hours. **L'auberge de jeunesse** is the best deal, though; many travelers find lifelong international friends and traveling companions there.

Portrait Explain that the Pyrenees are another important ski destination in France. Show their geographical relationship to the Alps on a map and point out that the Pyrenees create a natural border between France and Spain.

Le monde francophone Call on volunteers to read each bulleted item. Then ask for other volunteers to point out each francophone place mentioned on **Transparencies #2** or **#4**.

2 Expansion Continue the activity with these questions. **6. Quel pourcentage des Français part pour la montagne pendant les vacances d'hiver? (près de 11%) 7. Quels pays partagent les Alpes? (la France, l'Allemagne, la Suisse, l'Autriche et l'Italie) 8. Où trouve-t-on de bonnes pistes de ski? (à Chamonix, Tignes, Val d'Isère et aux Trois Vallées)**

3 Expansion After the trip, the **client(e)** returns to the **agent** to discuss what he or she did on the trip. The **agent** asks: **Qu'est-ce que vous avez fait? Et puis, qu'est-ce que vous avez vu? Ensuite, où êtes-vous allé(e)?** The **client(e)** then volunteers as much information as possible about the trip.

OPTIONS

Pairs Have students imagine that, while studying in France, they are planning a trip for an upcoming vacation. They can speak **au présent** and **au futur proche**. Examples: **Où est-ce qu'on va aller? Qui va réserver l'hôtel/l'auberge de jeunesse? Qu'est-ce qu'on a envie de faire?** Encourage them to consult **Les vacances des Français** to plan a trip when French universities are actually on break. Then have them refer to **Le monde francophone** to discuss which type of vacation they would like best, **au soleil** or **pour de l'aventure**. You might want to come up with some questions as a class before students continue in pairs. Examples: **Que préférez-vous, la plage ou le désert? Entre le Maroc et la Martinique, que préférez-vous? Moi, j'ai envie de faire une croisière, et vous?**

Section Goals

In this section, students will learn:

- the formation of adverbs using [*adjective*] + **-ment**
- irregular adverbs
- adverb placement

Instructional Resources
*espaces.vhlcentral.com: Lab MP3s; WB/VM/LM Answer Key; IRM (**Essayez!** and **Mise en pratique** answers; Lab Audioscript; **Feuilles d'activités**); activities; downloads; reference tools*

Suggestions

- To start the lesson, ask volunteers to give examples of adverbs already learned and use them in a sentence. Examples: **Je vais très bien/mal. Ils ont déjà fait leurs devoirs. Elle travaille souvent le samedi**.
- Use magazine pictures of people doing various things to further review known adverbs and introduce a few new ones. Examples: **Ce chien mange beaucoup. Cette fille-ci nettoie rarement sa chambre. Cet homme-là se sent mal.**
- Brainstorm a list of masculine adjectives with the whole class. Have students write the feminine forms, reminding them that some do not change. Examples: **heureux (heureuse), facile (facile).**
- Point out that many adverbs are formed by adding **-ment** to the end of feminine forms of adjectives. Call attention to the exception for adjectives that already end in a vowel. Then ask questions with adverbs that correspond to the adjectives mentioned. Example: **Faites-vous facilement vos devoirs?**
- Write sentences using regular adverbs with **-ment** on the board. Have volunteers underline the adverb. Example: **Le professeur parle rapidement.**

7B.1 Adverbs

NATIONAL STANDARDS comparisons

Point de départ Adverbs describe how, when, and where actions take place. They modify verbs, adjectives, and even other adverbs. You've already learned some adverbs such as **bien**, **déjà**, **surtout**, and **très**.

- To form an adverb from an adjective that ends in a consonant, take the feminine singular form and add **-ment**. This ending is equivalent to the English *-ly*.

masculine singular adjective	feminine singular adjective	adverb	
actif	active	activement	*actively*
franc	franche	franchement	*frankly, honestly*
heureux	heureuse	heureusement	*fortunately*
malheureux	malheureuse	malheureusement	*unfortunately*

Elle parle **nerveusement**.
She speaks nervously.

Il n'est pas passé **dernièrement**.
He hasn't stopped by lately.

- If the masculine singular form of an adjective ends in a vowel, just add **-ment** to the end.

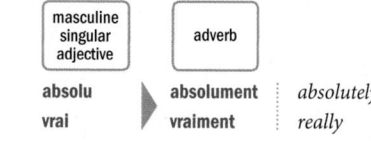

masculine singular adjective	adverb	
absolu	absolument	*absolutely*
vrai	vraiment	*really*

Martin répond **poliment**.
Martin answers politely.

Ils réservent **facilement** la chambre.
They reserve the room easily.

- To form an adverb from an adjective that ends in **-ant** or **-ent** in the masculine singular, replace the ending with **-amment** or **-emment**, respectively. Both endings are pronounced identically, like **femme**.

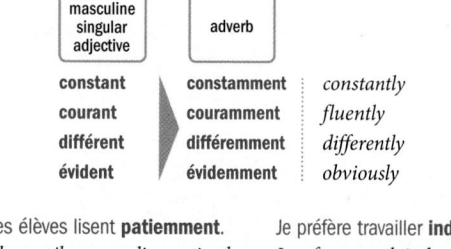

masculine singular adjective	adverb	
constant	constamment	*constantly*
courant	couramment	*fluently*
différent	différemment	*differently*
évident	évidemment	*obviously*

Les élèves lisent **patiemment**.
The pupils are reading patiently.

Je préfère travailler **indépendamment**.
I prefer to work independently.

Elle parle **couramment** français.
She speaks French fluently.

Vous pensez **différemment**.
You think differently.

MISE EN PRATIQUE

1 Assemblez Trouvez l'adverbe opposé.

f	1. gentiment	a. difficilement
e	2. bien	b. rarement
h	3. heureusement	c. faiblement
g	4. lentement	d. impatiemment
a	5. facilement	e. mal
d	6. patiemment	f. méchamment
b	7. fréquemment	g. vite
c	8. fortement	h. malheureusement

2 Invitation aux vacances Béatrice parle de ses vacances chez sa cousine. Complétez les phrases avec les adverbes qui correspondent aux adjectifs entre parenthèses.

Ma cousine Caroline m'a invitée à passer les vacances chez elle, à Nice. (1) ___Évidemment___ (Évident), j'ai été très contente et j'ai (2) ___rapidement___ (rapide) accepté son invitation. J'ai (3) ___attentivement___ (attentif) lu les brochures touristiques et j'ai (4) ___constamment___ (constant) parlé de mon voyage. (5) ___Finalement___ (Final), le jour de mon départ est arrivé. J'ai (6) ___prudemment___ (prudent) fait ma valise. À Paris, j'ai attendu le train très (7) ___impatiemment___ (impatient). (8) ___Franchement___ (Franc), j'avais hâte (*was eager*) d'arriver!

3 Les activités Avec un(e) partenaire, assemblez les éléments des colonnes pour décrire à tour de rôle comment on fait ces activités. Answers will vary.

MODÈLE

Étudiant(e) 1: *Je travaille sérieusement.*
Étudiant(e) 2: *Mon frère joue constamment.*

A	B	C
je	aider	constamment
mon frère	dormir	facilement
ma sœur	faire la cuisine	franchement
mon ami(e)	jouer	gentiment
mes profs	parler	patiemment
ma mère	travailler	rapidement
mon père	voyager	sérieusement
?	?	?

Practice more at **espaces.vhlcentral.com.**

OPTIONS

Video Replay the video episode, having students focus on the use of adverbs. Tell them to jot down a list of all of the adverbs they hear. Make two columns on the board, one for adverbs with **-ment** and another for all other adverbs. Have students write the adverbs under the appropriate column. Then have them create original sentences using each adverb.

Game Divide the class into small groups. Say the name of a famous person or historical figure. Give groups three minutes to write down as many short sentences as possible about that person, using adverbs and adverbial expressions. At the end of each round, have groups read their answers aloud. Award one point after each round to the group with the highest number of correct adverbs. The first group to earn five points wins.

COMMUNICATION

4 **À l'université** Vous désirez mieux connaître (*know better*) vos camarades de classe. Répondez aux questions de votre partenaire avec les adverbes de la liste ou avec d'autres. Answers will vary.

attentivement	mal	rapidement
bien	parfois	rarement
facilement	patiemment	sérieusement
lentement	prudemment	souvent

1. Quand vas-tu à l'université?
2. Comment étudies-tu, en général?
3. Quand tes amis et toi étudiez-vous ensemble?
4. Comment les étudiants écoutent-ils leur prof?
5. Comment ton prof de français parle-t-il?
6. Comment conduis-tu quand tu vas à la fac?
7. Quand ton/ta camarade de chambre fait-il/elle du sport?
8. Quand allez-vous au cinéma, tes amis et toi?

5 **Fréquences** Votre professeur va vous donner une feuille d'activités. Circulez dans la classe et demandez à vos camarades à quelle fréquence ils/elles font ces choses. Trouvez une personne différente pour chaque réponse, puis présentez les réponses à la classe. Answers will vary.

MODÈLE

Étudiant(e) 1: *À quelle fréquence pars-tu en vacances?*
Étudiant(e) 2: *Je pars fréquemment en vacances.*

6 **Notre classe** Par groupes de quatre, choisissez les camarades de votre classe qui correspondent à ces descriptions. Trouvez le plus de (*the most of*) personnes possible. Answers will vary.

Qui dans la classe...

1. ...bavarde constamment avec ses voisins?
2. ...parle bien français?
3. ...chante bien?
4. ...apprend facilement les langues?
5. ...écoute attentivement le prof?
6. ...travaille sérieusement après les cours?
7. ...aime beaucoup les maths?
8. ...travaille trop?
9. ...dessine souvent pendant les cours?
10. ...dort parfois pendant les cours?

- Some adverbs are irregular.

masculine singular adjective	adverb	
bon	**bien**	*well*
gentil	**gentiment**	*nicely*
mauvais	**mal**	*badly*

Son français est bon; il le parle **bien**.
His French is good; he speaks it well.

Leurs devoirs sont mauvais; ils écrivent **mal**.
Their homework is bad; they write badly.

- Although the adverb **rapidement** can be formed from the adjective **rapide**, you can also use the adverb **vite** to say *fast/quickly*. Note that when you use **vite** with a verb in the **passé composé** when meaning *fast*, the adverb needs to be placed after the past participle.

Bérénice a gagné la course? Oui, elle a couru **vite**.
Did Bérénice win the race? Yes, she ran fast.

- You've learned **jamais**, **parfois**, **rarement**, and **souvent**. Here are three more adverbs of frequency: **de temps en temps** (*from time to time*), **en général** (*in general*), **quelquefois** (*sometimes*).

Elle lit **souvent**.
She often reads.

En général, ils prennent le bus.
In general, they take the bus.

- Place an adverb that modifies an adjective or another adverb before the word it modifies.

La chambre est **assez** grande.
The room is pretty big.

Ils font très **vite** les réservations.
They make reservations very quickly.

- Place an adverb that modifies a verb immediately after the verb.

Il parle **bien** le français?
Does he speak French well?

Elles parlent **constamment**.
They talk constantly.

- In the **passé composé**, place short adverbs before the past participle.

Ils sont **vite** partis.
They left quickly.

Ils ont **bien** travaillé.
They worked well.

Essayez! **Donnez les adverbes qui correspondent à ces adjectifs.**

1. complet *complètement*
2. sérieux sérieusement
3. séparé séparément
4. constant constamment
5. mauvais mal
6. actif activement
7. impatient impatiemment
8. bon bien
9. franc franchement
10. difficile difficilement
11. vrai vraiment
12. gentil gentiment

Essayez! Make three columns on the board entitled: **l'adjectif masculin, l'adjectif féminin,** and **l'adverbe avec -ment.** Have students fill in the chart.

1 Expansion Have students use the antonyms in a sentence using **mais**. Example: **Je vais fréquemment à la bibliothèque, mais ma camarade de chambre va rarement à la bibliothèque.**

2 Expansion Tell students to write follow-up yes/no questions about Béatrice's description of her vacation. Then have pairs ask and answer the questions. Example: **Béatrice a accepté l'invitation de sa cousine? (Oui, elle a rapidement accepté l'invitation.)**

3 Suggestion Before beginning the activity, have students identify the adjective from which the adverbs in column C are derived. Review the formation of **-amment** and **-emment** adverbs.

4 Expansion Have students work in pairs to write three more questions like those in the activity. Students then switch questions with another pair and answer them orally.

5 Suggestions
- Have two volunteers read the **modèle** aloud, and then distribute the **Feuilles d'activités** found on the Supersite.
- If some students finish early, have them form pairs or a small group to begin comparing their findings. Teach them to ask questions, such as: **Quels camarades de classe font les choses différemment? Et semblablement** (*similarly*)?

6 Suggestion Remind the class that the adverbs in these sentences modify the verb, so they immediately follow the verb.

OPTIONS

Extra Practice Tell students to research travel to a French-speaking location. For maximum cultural variety, assign a different location to each student or simply have students select their preferred destination. Have them find information online or in the library about what there is to see and do there. After they have completed their research, have them create a brochure with images of the place and write short descriptive captions. After that, tell students to plan an imaginary itinerary, telling what they will and won't do when they go and how often they will do each activity. Remind them to use frequency adverbs like **jamais, parfois, rarement, souvent, de temps en temps,** etc. Finally, have students present their brochures to the class and talk about their plans.

Section Goals

In this section, students will learn:

- the imperfect tense
- **être** in the imperfect tense

Instructional Resources
*espaces.vhlcentral.com: Lab MP3s; WB/VM/LM Answer Key; IRM (**Essayez!** and **Mise en pratique** answers; Lab Audioscript); activities; downloads; reference tools*

Suggestions

- Remind students that they can already express the past using the **passé composé**. Now they will learn another tense needed to express themselves in the past. Mention that the **imparfait** expresses the past in a different way.
- Introduce the **imparfait** by describing something you used to do when you were little. Example: **Quand j'étais petit(e), je passais souvent les vacances chez mes grands-parents. Quand il faisait froid, nous jouions aux cartes à la maison. En été, ma famille louait une maison au bord de la mer.** Then ask students: **Et vous, que faisiez-vous quand vous étiez petits?** Encourage student responses.
- Ask volunteers to answer questions about their childhood. Example: **Quand vous étiez jeune, où alliez-vous en vacances avec votre famille? Aimiez-vous aller au cinéma? Au musée?**
- Review the present-tense **nous** forms of various verbs and explain that the stem without **-ons** is also the **imparfait** stem. Mention the exception with verbs ending in **-ger** and **-cer**.

7B.2 The *imparfait*

NATIONAL STANDARDS comparisons

Point de départ You've learned how the **passé composé** can express past actions. Now you'll learn another past tense, the **imparfait** (*imperfect*).

- The **imparfait** can be translated several ways into English.

Hakim **voyageait** souvent quand il était petit.	Nina **chantait** sous la douche tous les matins.
Hakim traveled often when he was little.	*Nina sang in the shower every morning.*
Hakim used to travel often when he was little.	*Nina used to sing in the shower every morning.*
Hakim was traveling often when he was little.	*Nina was singing in the shower every morning.*

- The **imparfait** is used to talk about actions that took place repeatedly or habitually during an unspecified period of time.

J'**habitais** près de chez toi.	Vous m'**appeliez** tous les jours.
I was living near you.	*You used to call me every day.*

- To form the **imparfait**, drop the **-ons** ending from the **nous** form of the present tense and replace it with these endings.

The *imparfait*

	parler (parl~~ons~~)	finir (finiss~~ons~~)	vendre (vend~~ons~~)	boire (buv~~ons~~)
je	parlais	finissais	vendais	buvais
tu	parlais	finissais	vendais	buvais
il/elle	parlait	finissait	vendait	buvait
nous	parlions	finissions	vendions	buvions
vous	parliez	finissiez	vendiez	buviez
ils/elles	parlaient	finissaient	vendaient	buvaient

- Verbs whose infinitives end in **-ger** add an **e** before all endings of the **imparfait** except in the **nous** and **vous** forms. Verbs whose infinitives end in **-cer** change **c** to **ç** before all endings except in the **nous** and **vous** forms.

tu **voyageais**	*but*	nous **voyagions**
les invités **commençaient**	*but*	vous **commenciez**

- Note that the **nous** and **vous** forms of infinitives ending in **-ier** contain a double **i** in the **imparfait**.

Vous **skiiez** en janvier.	Nous **étudiions** jusqu'à minuit.
You used to ski in January.	*We studied until midnight.*

MISE EN PRATIQUE

1 Nos voyages La famille d'Emmanuel voyageait souvent quand il était petit. Complétez son histoire en mettant (*by putting*) à l'imparfait les verbes entre parenthèses.

Quand j' (1) étais (être) jeune, mon père (2) travaillait (travailler) pour une société canadienne et nous (3) voyagions (voyager) souvent. Quand nous (4) partions (partir), je (5) faisais (faire) ma valise et je (6) préparais (préparer) toutes mes affaires. Ma petite sœur (7) détestait (détester) voyager. Elle (8) disait (dire) qu'elle (9) aimait (aimer) rester chez nous près de ses amis et que ce n' (10) était (être) pas juste!

2 Le samedi Dites ce que (*what*) ces personnes faisaient habituellement le samedi.

MODÈLE

Paul dormait.

Paul / dormir

1. je / faire / jogging
Je faisais du jogging.

2. ils / finir / devoirs
Ils finissaient leurs devoirs.

3. vous / manger / glace
Vous mangiez des glaces/une glace.

4. tu / prendre / café
Tu prenais du café.

3 Maintenant et avant Qu'est-ce qu'Emmanuel et sa famille font différemment aujourd'hui? Avec un(e) partenaire, écrivez des phrases à l'imparfait et trouvez les adverbes opposés. Suggested answers

MODÈLE

beaucoup travailler (je)
Maintenant, je travaille beaucoup, mais avant je travaillais peu.

1. rarement voyager (je)
   ... je voyage rarement, ... je voyageais constamment.
2. facilement prendre le train (nous)
   ... nous prenons facilement le train..., ... nous prenions difficilement le train.
3. souvent aller à la piscine (on)
   ... on va souvent à la piscine, ... on allait rarement à la piscine.
4. parfois acheter des cartes postales (mes parents)
   ... ils achètent parfois des cartes postales, ... ils achetaient souvent...
5. bien bricoler (vous)
   ... vous bricolez bien, ... vous bricoliez mal.
6. patiemment attendre son anniversaire (ma sœur)
   ... elle attend patiemment..., ... elle attendait impatiemment...

Practice more at **espaces.vhlcentral.com.**

OPTIONS

Game Divide the class into two teams. Choose one team member at a time to go to the board, alternating between teams. Say a subject pronoun and an infinitive. The student at the board must write and say the correct **imparfait** form. Example: **je: parler (je parlais)**. Give a point for each correct answer. Play to five or ten points, depending on how much time you have.

Extra Practice Have students write five true/false sentences with the **imparfait** describing things they did while on vacation when they were younger. Have pairs read their descriptions aloud, one sentence at a time, listening for the **imparfait** and guessing what is true or false. Encourage follow-up discussion. Example: **L'hôtel où je suis resté avait 99 étages.** The other students might say: **Ce n'est pas vrai! Combien d'étages avait-il vraiment?**

COMMUNICATION

4 Quand tu avais seize ans À tour de rôle, posez ces questions à votre partenaire pour savoir *(to know)* les détails de sa vie quand il/elle avait seize ans.

Answers will vary.

1. Où habitais-tu?
2. Est-ce que tu conduisais déjà une voiture?
3. Où est-ce que ta famille et toi alliez en vacances?
4. Pendant combien de temps partiez-vous en vacances?
5. Est-ce que tes amis et toi, vous sortiez tard le soir?
6. Que faisaient tes parents le week-end?
7. Quels sports pratiquais-tu?
8. Quel genre de musique écoutais-tu?
9. Comment était ton école?
10. Aimais-tu l'école? Pourquoi?

5 Discutez Regardez l'image. Un(e) partenaire et vous avez passé vos vacances à Saint-Barthélemy. Avec votre partenaire, écrivez un paragraphe d'au moins six phrases. Décrivez le temps qu'il faisait et ce que (*what*) vous faisiez quand vous étiez là-bas. Utilisez l'imparfait dans votre description.

6 Une énigme La nuit dernière, quelqu'un est entré dans le bureau de votre professeur et a emporté (*took away*) l'examen de français. Vous devez (*must*) trouver qui. Qu'est-ce que vos camarades de classe faisaient hier soir? Relisez vos notes et dites qui est le voleur (*thief*). Ensuite, présentez vos conclusions à la classe.

Answers will vary.

- The **imparfait** is used for description, often with the verb **être**, which is irregular in this tense.

The *imparfait* of *être*

j'étais	nous étions
tu étais	vous étiez
il/elle était	ils/elles étaient

J'**étais** dans la chambre.
I was in the bedroom.

Vous **étiez** à l'hôtel.
You were in the hotel.

- Note the imperfect forms of these expressions.

Il **pleuvait** chaque matin.
It rained each morning.

Il **neigeait** parfois au printemps.
It snowed sometimes in the spring.

Il y **avait** deux clés.
There were two keys.

Il **fallait** payer le repas.
It was necessary to pay for the meal

The verbs *dire*, *lire*, and *écrire*

- The verbs **dire** (*to say*), **lire** (*to read*), and **écrire** (*to write*) are conjugated as follows: **je dis, tu dis, il dit, nous disons, vous dites, ils disent; je lis, tu lis, il lit, nous lisons, vous lisez, ils lisent; j'écris, tu écris, il écrit, nous écrivons, vous écrivez, ils écrivent**. The verb **décrire** (*to describe*) is conjugated like **écrire**.

Elle m'**écrit**.
She writes to me.

Ne **dis** pas ton secret.
Don't tell your secret.

Lisez cet e-mail.
Read that e-mail.

- The past participle of **dire**, **écrire**, and **décrire**, respectively, are **dit**, **écrit**, and **décrit**. The past participle of **lire** is **lu**.

Ils l'**ont dit**.
They said it.

Tu l'**as écrit**.
You wrote it.

Nous l'**avons** lu.
We read it.

- In the **imparfait**, these verbs have regular endings.

Je le **disais**.
I used to say it.

Ils **lisaient** souvent.
They read often.

Tu **écrivais** rarement.
You wrote rarely.

Essayez! Choisissez la réponse correcte pour compléter les phrases.

1. Muriel (réservais/réservait) une chambre en ville.
2. Vous (partageait/partagiez) une chambre avec un autre étudiant.
3. Nous (écrivait/écrivions) beaucoup à nos amis.
4. Il y (avait/était) un bon restaurant au premier étage.
5. Il (neigeait/fallait) mettre le chauffage (*heat*) quand il (faisaient/faisait) froid.
6. Qu'est-ce que tu (faisait/faisais) à la plage?
7. Vous (lisiez/lisaient) beaucoup avant?
8. Nous (étaient/étions) trois dans la petite chambre.

Essayez! Have students identify the infinitive of each verb in the activity. Examples: **1. réserver 2. partager**

1 Suggestion Before assigning the activity, review the forms of the imperfect by calling out an infinitive and a series of subject pronouns. Ask volunteers to give the corresponding forms. Example: **détester, nous** (**nous détestions**).

2 Expansion After completing the activity, have students complete the sentences using the **passé composé**. Compare the meanings of each sentence.

3 Suggestion Divide the class into two groups, **l'imparfait** and **le présent**. Have the first group give one phrase about what Emmanuel and his family used to do. The second group should describe what he and his family do differently now, using an opposite verb in the present tense.

4 Expansion Have students share their partner's answers with the class using the third person pronouns **il/elle**.

5 Suggestion Write a few descriptive sentences using the imperfect on the board before having students work in pairs. Examples: **Nous ne partagions pas de chambre. Tous les jours, nous allions à la plage.**

5 Expansion Have pairs of students present their imaginary vacations to another pair or to the whole class. Using the imperfect, compile a list of activities on the board.

6 Suggestion Before doing this activity, remind students that the imperfect form of **être** is irregular.

OPTIONS

Game Label the four corners of the room with different historical periods. Examples: **la Préhistoire, le Moyen Âge, la Renaissance,** and **le Dix-Neuvième siècle**. Tell students to go to the corner that best represents the historical period they would visit if they could. Each group then discusses their reasons for picking that period using the **imparfait**. A spokesperson will summarize his or her group's responses to the class.

Extra Practice Bring in, or choose a few students to bring in, video clips from popular movies. Show clips to the class. Brainstorm important vocabulary. After viewing each clip, have students use the **imparfait** to describe what was happening and what people in the clip were doing.

Instructional Resources
espaces.vhlcentral.com:
*IRM (**Feuilles d'activités**; Info Gap Activities); Testing Program, pp. 53–56; Test Files; Testing Program MP3s; activities; downloads; reference tools*
Test Generator

1 Suggestion Have students write out the questions and answers. Check use of subject pronouns and the **imparfait** forms of **être**.

2 Suggestion Have two volunteers model a question and answer for the class.

2 Expansion After group members finish questioning each other, have a student from each group read the answers from another student. The class will then guess which student's childhood birthday celebration was described.

3 Suggestions
- Ask two students to read the **modèle** aloud. Then distribute the **Feuilles d'activités** found on the Supersite.
- Encourage students to add sports and leisure activities not already found in their survey.

4 Suggestion Before beginning the activity, have students describe what the people in the drawing are doing in the present tense.

5 Expansion Tell students to imagine they are the **ancien(ne) patron(ne)** and have decided to give the employee a second chance. It is time for the three-month review. Have them draft a brief letter to the employee discussing his or her past versus present performance on the job.

6 Suggestion Divide the class into pairs and distribute the Info Gap Handouts for this activity.

Révision

1 Mes affaires Vous cherchez vos affaires (*belongings*). À tour de rôle, demandez de l'aide à votre partenaire. Où étaient-elles la dernière fois? Answers will vary.

MODÈLE

Étudiant(e) 1: *Je cherche mes clés. Où sont-elles?*
Étudiant(e) 2: *Tu n'as pas cherché à la réception? Elles étaient à la réception.*

baskets	passeport
journal	pull
livre	sac à dos
parapluie	valise

à la réception	sur la chaise
au rez-de-chaussée	sous le lit
dans la chambre	dans ton sac
au deuxième étage	à l'auberge de jeunesse

2 Les anniversaires Avec un(e) partenaire, préparez huit questions pour savoir (*know*) comment vos camarades de classe célébraient leur anniversaire quand ils étaient enfants. Employez l'imparfait et des adverbes dans vos questions, puis posez-les à un autre groupe. Answers will vary.

MODÈLE

Étudiant(e) 1: *Que faisais-tu souvent pour ton anniversaire?*
Étudiant(e) 2: *Quand j'étais petit, mes parents organisaient souvent une fête.*

3 Sports et loisirs Votre professeur va vous donner une feuille d'activités. Circulez dans la classe et demandez à vos camarades s'ils pratiquaient ces activités avant d'entrer à la fac. Trouvez une personne différente qui dise (*says*) oui pour chaque activité. Présentez les réponses à la classe. Answers will vary.

MODÈLE

Étudiant(e) 1: *Est-ce que tu faisais souvent du jogging avant d'entrer à la fac?*
Étudiant(e) 2: *Oui, je courais souvent le matin.*

4 Pendant les vacances Par groupes de trois, créez le texte d'un article qui décrit ce que (*what*) faisaient ces gens. Utilisez des verbes à l'imparfait et des adverbes dans vos descriptions. Ensuite, présentez vos articles à la classe. Answers will vary.

5 Mes mauvaises habitudes Vous aviez de mauvaises habitudes, mais vous les avez changées. Maintenant, vous parlez avec votre ancien(ne) patron(ne) (*former boss*) pour essayer de récupérer l'emploi (*job*) que vous avez perdu. Avec un(e) partenaire, préparez la conversation. Answers will vary.

MODÈLE

Étudiant(e) 1: *Impossible de vous employer! Vous dormiez tout le temps.*
Étudiant(e) 2: *Je dormais souvent, mais je travaillais aussi. Cette fois, je vais travailler sérieusement.*

6 Un week-end en vacances Votre professeur va vous donner, à vous et à votre partenaire, une feuille de dessins sur le week-end de M. et Mme Bardot et de leur fille Alexandra. Attention! Ne regardez pas la feuille de votre partenaire. Answers will vary.

MODÈLE

Étudiant(e) 1: *En général, ils restaient dans un hôtel.*
Étudiant(e) 2: *Tous les jours, …*

ressources
WB pp. 93–96 | LM pp. 55–56 | espaces.vhlcentral.com

OPTIONS

Extra Practice Use these sentences containing adverbs and regular and irregular verbs in the **imparfait** as a dictation. Read each sentence twice, pausing after the second time for students to write. **1. Heureusement, il y avait beaucoup d'étudiants dans la classe. 2. Conduisait-il vite ta voiture? 3. J'étais vraiment très heureuse de te voir. 4. Il fallait constamment travailler le samedi.**

Extra Practice Have small groups organize a skit about a birthday or other party that took place recently. Guide them to first make general comments about the party, such as **C'était vraiment amusant!** Then describe a few specific things that were going on, what people were talking about, what they were wearing, and any other appropriate details. After the skits are performed, have students vote for their favorite.

À l'écoute

NATIONAL communication STANDARDS

Audio: Activities

STRATÉGIE

Recognizing the genre of spoken discourse

You will encounter many different types of spoken discourse in French. For example, you may hear a political speech, a radio interview, a commercial, a message on an answering machine, or a news broadcast. Try to identify the context of what you hear so that you can activate your background knowledge about that type of discourse and identify the speaker's motives and intentions.

To practice this strategy, you will listen to two short selections. Identify the genre of each one.

Préparation

Quand vous partez en vacances, qui décide où aller? Qui fait les réservations? Est-ce que vous utilisez les services d'une agence de voyages? Internet?

À vous d'écouter

Écoutez la publicité. Puis écoutez une deuxième fois et notez les informations qui manquent (*that are missing*). Notez aussi un détail supplémentaire pour chaque voyage.

Pays (ville/région)	Nombre de jours/semaines	Prix par personne	Détail supplémentaire
1. Italie (Venise)	3 jours	395 euros	Answers will vary.
2. Brésil	1 semaine	1.500 euros	Answers will vary.
3. Irlande (Dublin)	5 jours	575 euros	Answers will vary.
4. Amérique du Nord (États-Unis, Canada, Mexique)	14 jours	2.000 euros	Answers will vary.
5. France (Avignon)	7 jours	487 euros	Answers will vary.

Practice more at **espaces.vhlcentral.com.**

Compréhension

Où vont-ils? Vous travaillez pour l'agence Vacances Pour Tous cet été. Indiquez où chaque personne va aller.

1. Madame Dupuis n'a pas envie d'aller à l'étranger.
   Madame Dupuis va aller à Avignon.
2. Le fils de Monsieur Girard a besoin de pratiquer son espagnol et son anglais.
   Il va aller en Amérique du Nord.
3. Madame Leroy a envie de visiter une capitale européenne.
   Elle va aller en Irlande.
4. Yves Marignaud a seulement trois jours de congés.
   Il va aller en Italie (Venise).
5. Justine adore la plage et le soleil.
   Elle va aller au Brésil.
6. La famille Abou a envie de passer ses vacances à la campagne.
   Ils vont aller à Avignon.

Votre voyage Vous avez fait un des voyages proposés par l'agence Vacances Pour Tous. C'est le dernier jour et vous écrivez une carte postale (*postcard*) à un(e) ami(e) francophone. Parlez-lui de votre séjour. Quel voyage avez-vous fait? Pourquoi? Comment avez-vous voyagé? Qu'est-ce que vous avez fait pendant votre séjour? Est-ce que vous avez aimé vos vacances? Expliquez pourquoi.

Section Goals

In this section, students will:
- learn to recognize the genre of spoken discourse
- listen to a radio ad for a travel agency

Instructional Resources
espaces.vhlcentral.com: IRM (Textbook Audioscript); Textbook MP3s; activities; downloads; reference tools

Stratégie
Scripts 1. Bonjour et bienvenue à l'hôtel Belle Plage de Monaco. Nous sommes à quelques minutes de la plage, au 14 avenue des Anges, et nous avons des bus directs pour l'aéroport et la gare routière. Ce week-end, notre hôtel a encore six chambres libres. Si vous désirez des informations sur nos chambres, nos prix et notre hôtel en général, faites le 1. Pour faire ou confirmer une réservation, faites le 2. Pour contacter des clients de l'hôtel, faites le 3. Merci de nous avoir appelés et bonne journée. (message enregistré)
2. Mesdames, Messieurs, nous allons bientôt arriver à notre destination. À l'arrivée à l'aéroport de Montréal, sortez vos passeports pour passer la douane. Ensuite, allez au troisième étage pour prendre vos valises. Nous espérons que vous allez passer un agréable séjour au Canada. Merci d'avoir voyagé avec Air Vacances et à bientôt. (annonce d'avion)

Préparation Have students discuss the questions in pairs or groups. Then have them describe the photo.

À vous d'écouter
Script Envie de partir en vacances? Pour un petit week-end en amoureux ou pour des vacances au soleil, l'agence Vacances Pour Tous a la formule idéale!
Nos promotions de la semaine: Week-end à Venise, en Italie. Avion au départ de Paris vendredi matin, retour dimanche soir. Logement à l'hôtel; 395 euros par personne.
Envie de mer et de plage? Séjour d'une semaine au Brésil; 1.500 euros par personne.
Découvrez la capitale irlandaise avec un séjour de 5 jours à Dublin; 575 euros par personne. En train et bateau.
Autre super promotion pour étudiants: un voyage de deux semaines en Amérique. Une semaine aux États-Unis, quatre jours au Canada et trois jours au Mexique; 2.000 euros par personne. En avion et autobus. Logement en auberge de jeunesse.
Vous n'avez pas envie de partir à l'étranger, mais vous avez une semaine de congé? Nous avons une promotion incroyable sur la France. Sept jours à la campagne. Voyage en train. Logement dans un petit hôtel près d'Avignon; 487 euros par personne.
Appelez tout de suite le 01.42.46.46.46 pour faire vos réservations!

Section Goals

In this section, students will learn about the history and culture of **Provence-Alpes-Côte d'Azur** and **Rhône-Alpes**.

Instructional Resources
espaces.vhlcentral.com: Transparency #36; WB/VM/LM Answer Key; activities; downloads; reference tools

Carte des régions Provence-Alpes-Côte d'Azur et Rhône-Alpes

- Have students look at the map of the regions **Provence-Alpes-Côte d'Azur (PACA)** and **Rhône-Alpes** or use **Transparency #36**. Point out that **Provence-Alpes-Côte d'Azur** and **Rhône-Alpes** are popular tourist destinations year-round. Ask students to cite the geographic features that likely make these locations such attractive and diverse vacation spots. (**les Alpes**, **les plages**, etc.)
- Ask students if they are familiar with any of the location names and to share what they know about or associate with these places. Students should recognize Aix-en-Provence for the references in **Roman-photo**.
- Have students find **Mont-Blanc**. It is Europe's highest mountain, reaching 15,780 ft.

La région en chiffres

- Ask volunteers to read the sections. Then ask students questions about the content.
- Point out cognates and clarify any unfamiliar words.
- Tell students that Grenoble was the site of the 1968 Winter Olympics. Ask what other towns of these regions have hosted the Olympic Games. (Chamonix, 1924 and Albertville, 1992)

Incroyable mais vrai! Have students reference the map to see where **la Camargue** is located. **Le parc naturel régional de Camargue** was created to protect the rich flora and fauna found in the region and encompasses 211,740 acres. See if students remember how to convert that into hectares. (211,740 acres ÷ 2.47 = 85,690 hectares)

NATIONAL STANDARDS connections cultures

Interactive Map Reading

Panorama

le ski dans les Alpes

Provence-Alpes-Côte d'Azur

La région en chiffres

- **Superficie:** *31.400 km²*
- **Population:** *4.818.000*
  SOURCE: INSEE
- **Industries principales:** *agriculture, industries agro-alimentaires°, métallurgiques et mécaniques, parfumerie, tourisme*
- **Villes principales:** *Avignon, Gap, Marseille, Nice, Toulon*

Personnes célèbres

- **Nostradamus,** *astrologue et médecin (1503–1566)*
- **Marcel Pagnol,** *cinéaste° et écrivain (1895–1974)*
- **Surya Bonaly,** *athlète olympique (1973–)*

Rhône-Alpes

La région en chiffres

- **Superficie:** *43.698 km²*
- **Population:** *6.058.000*
- **Industries principales:** *agriculture, élevage°, tourisme, industries chimiques, métallurgiques et textiles*
- **Villes principales:** *Annecy, Chambéry, Grenoble, Lyon, Saint-Étienne*

le palais des Papes° à Avignon

la promenade des Anglais à Nice

Personnes célèbres

- **Louise Labé,** *poétesse (1524–1566)*
- **Stendhal,** *écrivain (1783–1842)*

- **Antoine de Saint-Exupéry,** *écrivain, auteur° du* Petit Prince *(1900–1944)*

agro-alimentaires *food-processing* **cinéaste** *filmmaker* **élevage** *livestock raising* **auteur** *author* **confrérie** *brotherhood* **gardians** *herdsmen* **depuis** *since* **sud** *south* **chevaux** *horses* **taureaux** *bulls* **flamants** *flamingos* **Montés** *Riding* **Papes** *Popes*

Incroyable mais vrai!

Tous les cow-boys ne sont pas américains. En Camargue, la confrérie° des gardians° perpétue depuis° 1512 les traditions des cow-boys français. C'est dans le sud° que cohabitent les chevaux° blancs camarguais, des taureaux° noirs et des flamants° roses. Montés° sur des chevaux blancs, les gardians gardent les taureaux noirs.

OPTIONS

Personnes célèbres **Surya Bonaly** has competed in three Olympic Games and has won medals in many national and international figure skating competitions. **Marcel Pagnol** was the first filmmaker to be elected to the **Académie française**. Two of **Stendhal's** best-known novels are ***Le Rouge et le Noir*** and ***La Chartreuse de Parme***. **Louise Labé** wrote passionate poetry in the style of Petrarch. **Antoine de Saint-Exupéry** is the only French author to have three books among the top ten best sellers of the period. He is best known for writing and illustrating ***Le Petit Prince***, which has been translated into numerous languages.

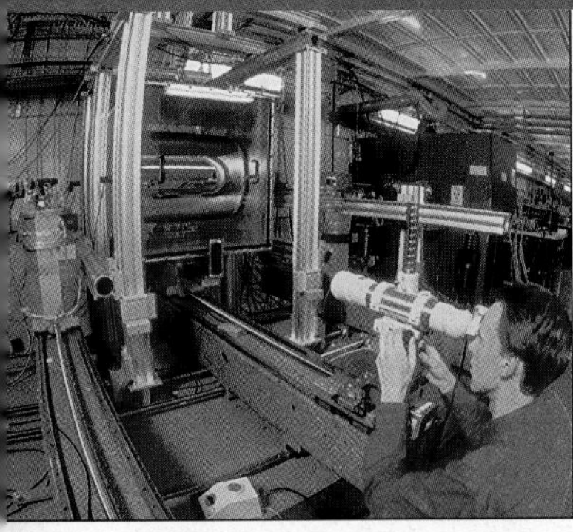

Les destinations

Grenoble

La ville de Grenoble, dans la région Rhône-Alpes, est surnommée «Capitale des Alpes» et «Ville Technologique». Située° à la porte des Alpes, elle donne accès aux grandes stations de ski alpin et est le premier centre de recherche° en France après Paris, avec plus de° 15.000 chercheurs°. Le synchrotron de Grenoble, un des plus grands° accélérateurs de particules du monde, permet à 5.000 chercheurs d'étudier la matière°. Grenoble est également° une ville universitaire avec quatre universités et 60.000 étudiants.

Les arts

Le festival de Cannes

Chaque année depuis° 1946, au mois de mai, de nombreux acteurs, réalisateurs° et journalistes viennent à Cannes, sur la Côte d'Azur, pour le Festival International du Film. Avec près de 4.000 films (courts et longs métrages°), 4.500 journalistes et plus de 90 pays représentés, c'est la manifestation cinématographique annuelle la plus médiatisée°. Après deux semaines de projections, de fêtes, d'expositions et de concerts, le jury international du festival choisit le meilleur° des vingt films présentés en compétition officielle.

La gastronomie

La raclette et la fondue

La Savoie, dans la région Rhône-Alpes, est très riche en fromages et deux de ses spécialités sont à base de fromage. Pour la raclette, on met du fromage à raclette sur un appareil° à raclette pour le faire fondre°. Chaque personne racle° du fromage dans son assiette° et le mange avec des pommes de terre° et de la charcuterie°. La fondue est un mélange° de fromages fondus°. Avec un bâton°, on trempe° un morceau° de pain dans la fondue. Ne le faites pas tomber!

Les traditions

Grasse, France

La ville de Grasse, sur la Côte d'Azur, est le centre de la parfumerie° française. Capitale mondiale du parfum depuis le dix-huitième siècle, Grasse cultive les fleurs depuis le Moyen Âge°: violette, lavande, rose, plantes aromatiques, etc. Au dix-neuvième siècle, ses parfumeurs, comme Molinard, ont conquis° les marchés du monde grâce à° la fabrication industrielle.

Qu'est-ce que vous avez appris? Répondez aux questions par des phrases complètes.

1. Comment s'appelle la région où les gardians perpétuent les traditions des cow-boys français?
   La région s'appelle la Camargue.
2. Qui a écrit *Le Petit Prince*?
   Antoine de Saint-Exupéry a écrit *Le Petit Prince*.
3. Quel est le rôle des gardians?
   Ils gardent les taureaux.
4. Où est située Grenoble?
   Grenoble est située dans la région Rhône-Alpes.
5. À Grenoble, qui vient étudier la matière?
   À Grenoble, les chercheurs viennent étudier la matière.
6. Depuis quand existe le festival de Cannes?
   Le festival de Cannes existe depuis 1946.
7. Qui choisit le meilleur film au festival de Cannes?
   Le jury international choisit le meilleur film.
8. Avec quoi mange-t-on la raclette?
   On mange la raclette avec des pommes de terre et de la charcuterie.
9. Quelle ville est le centre de la parfumerie française?
   La ville de Grasse est le centre de la parfumerie française.
10. Pourquoi Grasse est-elle le centre de la parfumerie française?
    Grasse est le centre de la parfumerie française parce que la ville cultive les fleurs. / grâce à la fabrication industrielle.

ressources

WB pp. 97–98 | espaces.vhlcentral.com

Practice more at **espaces.vhlcentral.com.**

SUR INTERNET

Go to espaces.vhlcentral.com to find more cultural information related to this **PANORAMA**.

1. Quels films étaient (*were*) en compétition au dernier festival de Cannes? Qui composait (*made up*) le jury?
2. Trouvez des informations sur la parfumerie à Grasse. Quelles sont deux autres parfumeries qu'on trouve à Grasse?

Située *Located* **recherche** *research* **plus de** *more than* **chercheurs** *researchers* **des plus grands** *of the largest* **matière** *matter* **également** *also* **depuis** *since* **réalisateurs** *filmmakers* **métrages** *films* **la plus médiatisée** *the most publicized* **meilleur** *best* **appareil** *machine* **fondre** *melt* **racle** *scrapes* **assiette** *plate* **pommes de terre** *potatoes* **charcuterie** *cooked pork meats* **mélange** *mix* **fondus** *melted* **bâton** *stick* **trempe** *dips* **morceau** *piece* **parfumerie** *perfume industry* **Moyen Âge** *Middle Ages* **ont conquis** *conquered* **grâce à** *thanks to*

Grenoble There are a vast number of educational institutions in the city of Grenoble. The city is considered a center for chemical, electronic, and nuclear research. Have students search Grenoble's city web site for information about how many universities are located in Grenoble and in what areas of study they specialize.

Le festival de Cannes Only accredited film industry professionals can attend **le festival de Cannes**. Those not involved in the film industry can obtain invitations to the **Cinéma de la Plage**. Each evening at the **Cinéma de la Plage**, films that are not in the running for the **Palme d'Or** may be viewed on a large open-air screen.

La raclette et la fondue Invented by the Swiss, fondue has become an international dish, and each region has adapted the dish to its own taste. In Savoie, instead of the traditional Gruyère cheese, people use Comté and Beaufort as well as Emmental cheeses. Kirsch and dry white wine, preferably from Savoie, are added to the cheese.

Grasse, France Each summer, people in Grasse celebrate the **Fête du Jasmin**. Over 150,000 flowers are used to decorate the floats and to throw in the battle of flowers. Women throw flowers from the floats and spray the audience with jasmine water. Folk dancers, bands, and artists come from all over Europe to celebrate this festival.

OPTIONS

Cultural Activity Have students look at the web sites for **le festival de Cannes**, **les César du Cinéma**, and a major award show or film festival from their region. Ask students to compare and contrast the award categories, the selection process, the event, and the winners. Have each student share his or her findings with the class.

Pairs Have students imagine that they have gone on vacation in **Provence-Alpes-Côte d'Azur**, **Rhône-Alpes**, or both. Students will work with a partner telling about their experience. Ask students to tell where they went, talk about at least two activities they did there, and what the weather was like. The partner should then ask a question about the trip and tell about his or her vacation.

Section Goals

In this section, students will:
- learn to predict content from the title
- read a travel brochure in French

Stratégie Tell students that they can often predict the content of a newspaper article from its headline. Display or make up several cognate-rich headlines from French newspapers. Examples: **L'ONU critique le changement de règle du vote pour le référendum en Irak; Huit clubs de football français rattrapés par la justice; À la télé américaine, le président est une femme.** Ask students to predict the content of each article.

Examinez le texte Ask volunteers to share their ideas about what type of document it is, and what information they think each section will have. Then go over the correct answers with the entire class.

Des titres Working in pairs to compare their answers, have students discuss how they are able to tell where these titles were found.

Lecture

NATIONAL STANDARDS communication cultures

S Reading

Avant la lecture

STRATÉGIE

Predicting content from the title

Prediction is an invaluable strategy in reading for comprehension. We can usually predict the content of a newspaper article from its headline, for example. More often than not, we decide whether or not to read the article based on its headline. Predicting content from the title will help you increase your reading comprehension in French.

Examinez le texte

Regardez le titre (*title*) et les sous-titres (*subtitles*) du texte. À votre avis, quel type de document est-ce? Avec un(e) camarade, faites une liste des informations que vous allez probablement trouver dans chaque section du document.

Des titres

Regardez ces titres et indiquez en quelques mots le sujet possible du texte qui suit (*follows*) chaque titre. Où pensez-vous qu'on a trouvé ces titres (dans un journal, un magazine, une brochure, un guide, etc.)?

Cette semaine à Paris:
un journal

Encore un nouveau restaurant pour chiens
un journal, un magazine

L'Égypte des pyramides en 8 jours
une brochure, un guide

L'AÉROPORT CHARLES-DE-GAULLE A PERDU LES VALISES D'UN VOL DE TOURISTES ALLEMANDS
un journal

Plan du centre-ville
un guide

Résultats du septième match de football entre la France et l'Angleterre
un journal

Hôtel confortable près de la gare routière
une brochure

TOUR DE CORSE

Voyage organisé de 12 jours

3.000 euros tout compris°
Promotion spéciale de Vacances-Voyages, agence de voyages certifiée

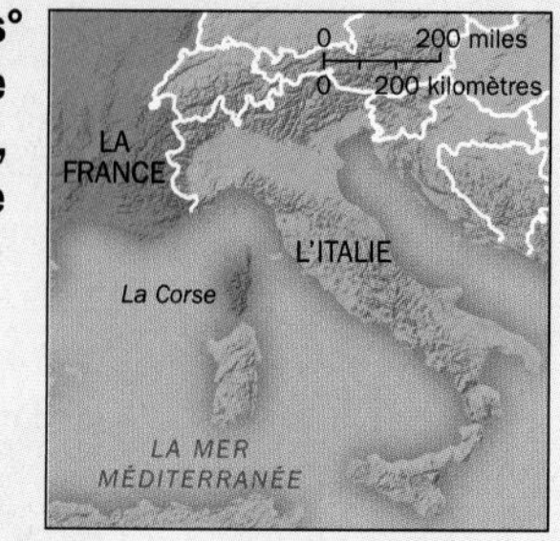

ITINÉRAIRE

JOUR 1 Paris–Ajaccio

Vous partez de Paris en avion pour Ajaccio, en Corse. Vous prenez tout de suite le bus pour aller à votre hôtel. Vous commencez par visiter la ville d'Ajaccio à pied°, puis vous dînez à l'hôtel.

JOUR 2 Ajaccio–Bonifacio

Le matin, vous partez en autobus pour Bonifacio, la belle ville côtière° où vous déjeunez dans un petit restaurant italien avant de visiter la ville. L'après-midi, vous montez à bord° d'un bateau pour une promenade en mer, occasion idéale pour observer les falaises rocailleuses° et les plages blanches de l'île°. Ensuite, vous rentrez à l'hôtel pour dîner et y (*there*) passer la nuit.

JOUR 3 Bonifacio–Corte

La forêt de l'Ospédale est l'endroit idéal pour une randonnée à pied. Vous pique-niquez à Zonza, petite ville montagneuse, avant de continuer vers Corte, l'ancienne° capitale de la Corse. Vous passez la soirée et la nuit à Corte.

JOUR 4 Corte–Bastia

Vous avez la journée pour visiter la ville de Bastia. Vous assistez à un spectacle de danse, puis vous passez la soirée à l'hôtel.

JOUR 5 Bastia–Calvi

Vous visitez d'abord le Cap Corse, la péninsule au nord° de la Corse. Puis, vous continuez vers le désert des Agriates, zone de montagnes désertiques où la chaleur est très forte. Ensuite, c'est l'Île-Rousse et une promenade à vélo dans la ville de Calvi. Vous dînez à votre hôtel.

OPTIONS

Small Groups Have five students work together to brainstorm a list of what would constitute an ideal vacation for them. Each student should contribute at least one idea. Opinions will vary. Ask the group to designate one student to take notes and another to present the information to the class. When each group has its list, ask the presenters to share the group's ideas. How are the group's ideas? Similar or different?

Extra Practice Ask students if they have ever been on an organized tour. If students have not been on a tour similar to the one to Corsica described in **Lecture**, have them interview someone they know who has. Have students answer questions like these: **Où êtes-vous allé(e)? Avec quelle agence? Avez-vous aimé toutes les activités organisées? Expliquez pourquoi.**

JOUR 6 Calvi–Porto

Vous partez en bus le matin pour la vallée du Fango et le golfe de Galéria à l'ouest° de l'île. Puis, vous visitez le parc naturel régional et le golfe de Porto. Ensuite, vous faites une promenade en bateau avant de passer la soirée dans la ville de Porto.

JOUR 7 Porto–Ajaccio

En bateau, vous visitez des calanques°, particularité géographique de la région méditerranéenne, avant de retourner à Ajaccio.

JOURS 8 à 11 Ajaccio

À Ajaccio, vous avez trois jours pour explorer la ville. Vous avez la possibilité de visiter la cathédrale, la maison natale° de Napoléon ou des musées, et aussi de faire du shopping ou d'aller à la plage.

JOUR 12 Ajaccio–Paris

Vous retournez à Paris en avion.

tout compris *all-inclusive* **à pied** *on foot* **côtière** *coastal* **à bord** *aboard* **falaises rocailleuses** *rocky cliffs* **île** *island* **ancienne** *former* **nord** *north* **ouest** *west* **calanques** *rocky coves or creeks* **natale** *birth*

Après la lecture

Les questions du professeur **Vous avez envie de faire ce voyage en Corse et vous parlez du voyage organisé avec votre professeur de français. Répondez à ses questions par des phrases complètes, d'après la brochure.**

1. Comment allez-vous aller en Corse?
   Je vais prendre l'avion à Paris.
2. Où le vol arrive-t-il en Corse?
   Le vol arrive à Ajaccio.
3. Combien de temps est-ce que vous allez passer en Corse?
   Je vais passer douze jours en Corse.
4. Est-ce que vous allez dormir dans des auberges de jeunesse?
   Non. Je vais dormir à l'hôtel./dans des hôtels.
5. Qu'est-ce que vous allez faire à Bastia?
   Je vais visiter la ville, aller à un spectacle de danse, puis passer la soirée à l'hôtel.
6. Est-ce que vous retournez à Ajaccio le neuvième jour?
   Non. Je retourne à Ajaccio le septième jour.
7. Qu'est-ce que vous allez prendre comme transports en Corse?
   Je vais prendre l'autobus et des bateaux.
8. Avez-vous besoin de faire toutes les réservations?
   Non. Le voyage est organisé par une agence de voyages.

C'est sûr, je pars en Corse! **Vous allez passer trois semaines en France et vous avez décidé, avec un(e) ami(e), de faire le voyage organisé en Corse au départ de Paris. Vous et votre ami(e) téléphonez à l'agence de voyages pour avoir plus de détails. Posez des questions sur le voyage et demandez des précisions sur les villes visitées, les visites et les activités au programme, les hôtels, les transports, etc.**

- Vous aimez faire des randonnées, mais votre ami(e) préfère voir (*to see*) des spectacles et faire du shopping.
- L'agent va expliquer pourquoi vous allez aimer ce voyage en Corse.
- Demandez à l'agent de vous trouver un billet d'avion aller-retour pour aller de votre ville à Paris.
- Demandez aussi un hôtel à Paris pour la troisième semaine de votre séjour en France.
- L'agent va aussi suggérer des visites et des activités intéressantes à faire à Paris.
- Vous expliquez à l'agent que vous voulez (*want*) avoir du temps libre pendant le voyage.

Les questions du professeur Have students quickly review the brochure before answering the questions. Suggest that pairs take turns answering them. The student who does not answer a question should find the line of text that contains the answer.

C'est sûr, je pars en Corse! Have groups act out their conversations for the rest of the class.

Expansion Tell students that the travel agency is planning to create additional brochures to help them promote their **Tour de Corse** excursion. Their goal is to have several slightly different brochures about the same trip that may appeal to different types of people. Ask students to come up with 3 or 4 short, interesting titles for these new brochures.

OPTIONS

Pairs Have students work together in pairs. Tell them to divide the twelve-day **Tour de Corse** itinerary between them. Each student will then write at least five questions asking about their chosen parts of the trip. They will then answer each other's questions.

Pairs Bring in additional short, simple French-language magazine or newspaper articles you have read. Have pairs scan the headlines/titles of the articles to determine their content. Have them write down all the clues that help them come to these conclusions. Then ask pairs to present their findings to the class. Confirm the correct predictions.

Section Goals

In this section, students will:
- learn to make an outline
- write a travel brochure

Stratégie Explain that outlines are a great way for a writer to think about what a piece of writing will be like before actually expending much time and effort on writing. An outline is also a great way of keeping a writer on track, and helps him or her keep the whole writing project in mind while focusing on a specific part.

Thème Discuss the travel brochure that students are going to write. Go over the list of information that they might include. You might indicate a specific number of points that should be in the brochure. Tell students that the **Tour de Corse** brochure in **Lecture**, pages 248–249, can serve as a model for their writing. Remind them that they are writing with the purpose of attracting people to take a trip. Suggest that students brainstorm in French as many details as possible about the trip they will describe.

Écriture

NATIONAL STANDARDS communication cultures

STRATÉGIE

Making an outline

When we write to share information, an outline can serve to separate topics and subtopics, providing a framework for presenting the data. Consider the following excerpt from an outline of the tourist brochure on pages 248–249.

I. Itinéraire et description du voyage
   A. Jour 1
      1. ville: Ajaccio
      2. visites: visite de la ville à pied
      3. activités: dîner
   B. Jour 2
      1. ville: Bonifacio
      2. visites: la ville de Bonifacio
      3. activités: promenade en bateau, dîner

II. Description des hôtels et des transports
   A. Hôtels
   B. Transports

Schéma d'idées

Idea maps can be used to create outlines. The major sections of an idea map correspond to the Roman numerals in an outline. The minor sections correspond to the outline's capital letters, and so on. Consider the idea map that led to the outline above.

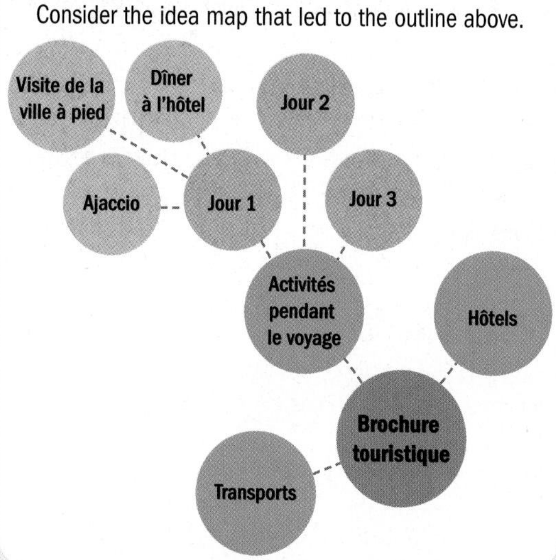

Thème

Écrivez une brochure

Avant l'écriture

1. Vous allez préparer une brochure pour un voyage organisé que vous avez fait ou que vous avez envie de faire dans un pays francophone. Utilisez un schéma d'idées pour vous aider. Voici des exemples d'informations que votre brochure peut (*can*) donner.

- le pays et la ville
- le nombre de jours
- la date et l'heure du départ et du retour
- les transports utilisés (train, avion, ...) et le lieu de départ (aéroport JFK, gare de Lyon, ...)
- le temps qu'il va probablement faire et quelques suggestions de vêtements à porter
- où on va dormir (hôtel, auberge de jeunesse, camping, ...)
- où on va manger (restaurant, café, pique-nique dans un parc, ...)
- les visites culturelles (monuments, musées, ...)
- les autres activités au programme (explorer la ville, aller au marché, faire du sport, ...)
- le prix du voyage par personne

OPTIONS

Avant l'écriture Show how an idea map corresponds to a numerical written outline. Use two large circles for points I and II of the outline. Use four smaller circles for the two sets of A and B points. Finally, add six smaller circles that correspond to the 1, 2, and 3 points. Challenge students to take the existing idea map and convert it to a numerical written outline.

For students who have trouble breaking larger ideas down into smaller ones, recycle the use of question words from Unit 4. Create an idea map that shows a subject in a larger circle. Spinning off from it can be smaller circles each with a different question and answer about that subject.

2. Complétez le schéma d'idées pour vous aider à visualiser ce que (*what*) vous allez présenter dans votre brochure.

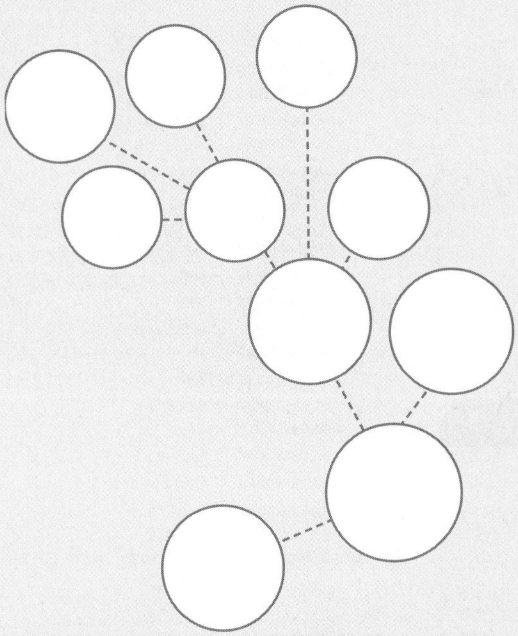

3. Une fois (*Once*) votre schéma d'idées créé, pensez à d'autres informations qui pourraient (*could*) être importantes pour la création de votre brochure.

Écriture

Utilisez votre schéma d'idées pour créer la brochure de votre voyage. Donnez un titre (*title*) à la présentation et aux différentes catégories. Chaque section et sous-section (*minor section*) doit (*must*) avoir son titre et être présentée séparément. Incorporez au moins (*at least*) quatre sous-sections. Vous pouvez inclure (*can include*) des visuels. Faites attention à bien les placer dans les sections correspondantes. Utilisez les constructions grammaticales et le vocabulaire que vous avez appris dans cette unité.

Après l'écriture

1. Échangez votre brochure avec celle (*the one*) d'un(e) partenaire. Répondez à ces questions pour commenter son travail.
   - La brochure de votre partenaire correspond-elle au schéma d'idées qu'il/elle a créé?
   - Votre partenaire a-t-il/elle inclu au moins quatre sections?
   - Toutes les sections et sous-sections ont-elles un titre?
   - Votre partenaire a-t-il/elle décrit en détail chaque catégorie?
   - Chaque sous-section présente-t-elle des informations supplémentaires sur le sujet?
   - Si votre partenaire a ajouté (*added*) des visuels, illustrent-ils vraiment le texte qu'ils accompagnent?
   - Votre partenaire a-t-il/elle correctement utilisé les constructions grammaticales et le vocabulaire de l'unité?

2. Corrigez votre brochure d'après (*according to*) les commentaires de votre partenaire. Relisez votre travail pour éliminer ces problèmes:
   - des fautes (*errors*) d'orthographe
   - des fautes de ponctuation
   - des fautes de conjugaison
   - des fautes d'accord (*agreement*) des adjectifs
   - un mauvais emploi (*use*) de la grammaire

EVALUATION

Criteria

Content Contains both an idea map and an outline that provide all the information requested in bulleted list of tasks.
Scale: 1 2 3 4 5

Organization An outline or idea map that is then converted into a brochure with a title and minor sections that correspond to the outline or idea map.
Scale: 1 2 3 4 5

Accuracy Uses forms of **aller** and direct object pronouns correctly. Spells words, conjugates verbs, and modifies adjectives correctly throughout.
Scale: 1 2 3 4 5

Creativity Includes additional information that is not included in the task and/or designs a brochure with photos, drawings, or extra embellishments.
Scale: 1 2 3 4 5

Scoring

Excellent	18–20 points
Good	14–17 points
Satisfactory	10–13 points
Unsatisfactory	< 10 points

OPTIONS

Écriture Students may need help converting the bulleted information into an outline/idea map. As a class, brainstorm ways to organize the facts. For example: (1st level): **Un voyage à ______**, (2nd level): **Généralités, Que faire et voir** (to see). Then have students associate the following with one of the 2nd level categories: number of days, dates, travel times, transportation, weather, price, hotels, restaurants, cultural visits, other activities.

Review the kind of neutral and formal language typically used in a travel brochure. Have students review command forms from Lessons 2A, 4B, and 6B. You may want to get them started with some useful expressions such as **Nous donnons...** and **Vous allez** [+ *infinitive*], along with a number of adjectives such as **fascinant(e), intéressant(e), beau/belle, historique, ancien(ne), confortable, agréable, délicieux/délicieuse,** and so on.

Instructional Resources
espaces.vhlcentral.com: Textbook MP3s; IRM (Textbook Audioscript); downloads; reference tools

Suggestion Tell students that an easy way to study from **Vocabulaire** is to cover up the French half of each section, leaving only the English equivalents exposed. They can then quiz themselves on the French items. To focus on the English equivalents of the French entries, they simply reverse this process.

Flashcards
Audio: Vocabulary

VOCABULAIRE

Partir en voyage

un aéroport	*airport*
un arrêt d'autobus (de bus)	*bus stop*
une arrivée	*arrival*
un avion	*plane*
un billet aller-retour	*round-trip ticket*
un billet (d'avion, de train)	*(plane, train) ticket*
un départ	*departure*
une douane	*customs*
une gare (routière)	*train station (bus terminal)*
une sortie	*exit*
une station (de métro)	*(subway) station*
une station de ski	*ski resort*
un ticket (de bus, de métro)	*(bus, subway) ticket*
un vol	*flight*
un voyage	*trip*
à l'étranger	*abroad, overseas*
la campagne	*country(side)*
une capitale	*capital*
des gens (*m.*)	*people*
le monde	*world*
un pays	*country*

Les pays

(en/l') Allemagne (*f.*)	*(to/in) Germany*
(en/l') Angleterre (*f.*)	*(to/in) England*
(en/la) Belgique (belge)	*(to/in) Belgium (Belgian)*
(au/le) Brésil (brésilien(ne))	*(to/in) Brazil (Brazilian)*
(au/le) Canada	*(to/in) Canada*
(en/la) Chine (chinois(e))	*(to/in) China (Chinese)*
(en/l') Espagne (*f.*)	*(to/in) Spain*
(aux/les) États-Unis (*m.*)	*(to/in) United States*
(en/la) France	*(to/in) France*
(en/l') Irlande (*f.*) (irlandais(e))	*(to/in) Ireland (Irish)*
(en/l') Italie (*f.*)	*(to/in) Italy*
(au/le) Japon	*(to/in) Japan*
(au/le) Mexique	*(to/in) Mexico*
(en/la) Suisse	*(to/in) Switzerland*

ressources
espaces.vhlcentral.com

Les vacances

bronzer	*to tan*
faire du shopping	*to go shopping*
faire les valises	*to pack one's bags*
faire un séjour	*to spend time (somewhere)*
partir en vacances	*to go on vacation*
prendre un train (un avion, un taxi, un (auto)bus, un bateau)	*to take a train (plane, taxi, bus, boat)*
rouler en voiture	*to ride in a car*
utiliser un plan	*to use/read a map*
un (jour de) congé	*day off*
le journal	*newspaper*
la mer	*sea*
une plage	*beach*
des vacances (*f.*)	*vacation*

Adverbes

absolument	*absolutely*
activement	*actively*
bien	*well*
constamment	*constantly*
couramment	*fluently*
différemment	*differently*
évidemment	*obviously, evidently; of course*
franchement	*frankly, honestly*
gentiment	*nicely*
heureusement	*fortunately*
mal	*badly*
malheureusement	*unfortunately*
vraiment	*really*

Verbes

aller	*to go*
arriver	*to arrive*
descendre	*to go/take down*
entrer	*to enter*
monter	*to go/come up; to get in/on*
mourir	*to die*
naître	*to be born*
partir	*to leave*
passer	*to pass by; to spend time*
rentrer	*to return*
rester	*to stay*
retourner	*to return*
sortir	*to go out*
tomber (sur quelqu'un)	*to fall (to run into somebody)*

Faire une réservation

annuler	*to cancel*
une réservation	*a reservation*
réserver	*to reserve, to book*
une agence de voyages	*travel agency*
un agent de voyages	*travel agent*
un ascenseur	*elevator*
une auberge de jeunesse	*youth hostel*
une chambre individuelle	*single room*
une clé	*key*
un(e) client(e)	*client; guest*
un étage	*floor*
un hôtel	*hotel*
un hôtelier/une hôtelière	*hotel keeper*
un lit	*bed*
un passager/une passagère	*passenger*
un passeport	*passport*
la réception	*reception desk*
le rez-de-chaussée	*ground floor*
complet/complète	*full (no vacancies)*
libre	*available*

Verbes irréguliers

décrire	*to describe*
dire	*to say*
écrire	*to write*
lire	*to read*

Expressions utiles	*See pp. 223 and 237.*
Direct object pronouns	*See pp. 228–229.*
Ordinal numbers	*See pp. 232–233.*

Chez nous

UNITÉ 8

Pour commencer

- Où sont David et Rachid?
  a. dans le salon b. dans la cuisine c. dans la chambre
- Qu'est-ce qu'il n'y a pas sur la photo?
  a. un canapé b. une table c. une télévision
- Que font David et Rachid?
  a. Ils étudient. b. Ils passent un bon moment. c. Ils regardent la télé.

Unit Goals

Leçon 8A

In this lesson, students will learn:
- terms for parts of the house
- terms for furniture
- the pronunciation of **s** and **ss**
- about housing in France and **le château Frontenac**
- more about housing in France through specially shot video footage
- the uses of the **passé composé** and the **imparfait**
- about Century 21 in France

Leçon 8B

In this lesson, students will learn:
- terms for household chores
- terms for appliances
- the pronunciation of semi-vowels
- about the interiors of French homes and the French Quarter in New Orleans
- more about the uses of the **passé composé** and the **imparfait**
- the uses of **savoir** and **connaître**
- to use visual cues to understand spoken French

Savoir-faire

In this section, students will learn:
- cultural and historical information about **Alsace** and **Lorraine**
- to guess the meaning of unknown words from context
- to write a narrative using the **passé composé** and the **imparfait**

Pour commencer

- **a. dans le salon**
- **c. une télévision**
- **b. Ils passent un bon moment.**

RESOURCES

Workbook/Video Manual: WB Activities, pp. 99–112
Laboratory Manual: Lab Activities, pp. 57–64
Workbook/Video Manual: Video Activities, pp. 239–242; pp. 285–286
WB/VM/LM Answer Key

espaces.vhlcentral.com: Textbook MP3s; Lab MP3s; Instructor's Resource Manual [IRM] (Textbook Audioscript; Lab Audioscript; Videoscript; **Roman-photo** Translations; **Vocabulaire supplémentaire**; **Feuilles d'activités**; Info Gap Activities; **Le zapping** TV clip transcription; **Essayez!**and **Mise en pratique** answers); Transparencies #37, #38, #39; Testing Program, pp. 57–64; Test Files; Testing Program MP3s
Test Generator
Video on DVD

Section Goals

In this section, students will learn and practice vocabulary related to:
- housing
- rooms and home furnishings

Instructional Resources
*espaces.vhlcentral.com: Transparency #37; IRM (**Vocabulaire supplémentaire**; **Mise en pratique** answers; Textbook Audioscript; Lab Audioscript; Info Gap Activities); Textbook MP3s; Lab MP3s; WB/VM/LM Answer Key; activities; downloads; reference tools*

Suggestions

- Use **Transparency #37**. Point out rooms and furnishings in the illustration. Examples: **Ça, c'est la salle de bains. Voici un canapé.**
- Ask students questions about their homes using the new vocabulary. Examples: **Habitez-vous dans une maison, dans un appartement ou dans une résidence universitaire? Avez-vous un balcon? Un garage? Combien de salles de bains avez-vous?**
- Point out the difference between **le loyer** (*the rent*) and **louer** (*to rent*).
- Explain that **une chambre** is *a bedroom*, but **une pièce** is the generic term for *a room*.
- Explain that **un salon** is a more formal room used primarily for entertaining guests. Generally, it is not used for watching television or other leisure activities. **Une salle de séjour** is a more functional room, similar to an American family room or den.
- Point out that **un studio** is *a studio apartment*, usually equipped with a couch that converts into a bed and a kitchenette.
- Additional vocabulary for this lesson can be found in the **Vocabulaire supplémentaire** on the Supersite.

Leçon 8A

Talking Picture
Audio: Activity

You will learn how to...
- describe your home
- talk about habitual past actions

La maison

Vocabulaire

déménager	*to move out*
emménager	*to move in*
louer	*to rent*
un appartement	*apartment*
une cave	*cellar; basement*
un couloir	*hallway*
une cuisine	*kitchen*
un escalier	*staircase*
un immeuble	*building*
un jardin	*garden; yard*
un logement	*housing*
un loyer	*rent*
une pièce	*room*
un quartier	*area, neighborhood*
une résidence universitaire	*dorm*
une salle à manger	*dining room*
un salon	*formal living/sitting room*
un studio	*studio (apartment)*
une armoire	*armoire, wardrobe*
une douche	*shower*
un lavabo	*bathroom sink*
un meuble	*piece of furniture*
un placard	*closet, cupboard*
un tiroir	*drawer*
un(e) propriétaire	*owner*

ressources
WB pp. 99-100 | LM p. 57 | espaces.vhlcentral.com

OPTIONS

Extra Practice Ask students what activities they do in various rooms. Examples: **Dans quelle pièce... mangez-vous? étudiez-vous? dormez-vous? faites-vous la cuisine? travaillez-vous sur l'ordinateur? parlez-vous au téléphone?**

TPR Make signs for various rooms in a house and for other parts of a home, such as **le garage** or **le balcon**. Also make several signs for bedrooms and bathrooms. Distribute the signs to students. As other students describe their homes (one floor at a time), those holding signs arrange themselves according to the descriptions. Tell students to use prepositions of location in their descriptions.

Mise en pratique

1 Chassez l'intrus **Indiquez le mot ou l'expression qui ne va pas avec les autres (*that doesn't belong*).**

1. un appartement, un quartier, un logement, un studio
2. une baignoire, une douche, un sous-sol, un lavabo
3. un salon, une salle à manger, une salle de séjour, un jardin
4. un meuble, un canapé, une armoire, une affiche
5. un placard, un balcon, un jardin, un garage
6. une chambre, une cuisine, un rideau, une pièce
7. un meuble, une commode, un couloir, un lit
8. un miroir, un tapis, une fenêtre, une affiche

2 Écoutez **Patrice cherche un appartement. Écoutez sa conversation téléphonique et dites si les affirmations sont vraies ou fausses.**

	Vrai	Faux
1. Madame Dautry est la propriétaire de l'appartement.	☑	☐
2. L'appartement est au 24 rue Pasteur.	☑	☐
3. L'appartement est au cinquième étage.	☐	☑
4. L'appartement est dans un vieil immeuble.	☐	☑
5. L'appartement n'a pas de balcon, mais il a un garage.	☐	☑
6. Il y a une baignoire dans la salle de bains.	☐	☑
7. Les toilettes ne sont pas dans la salle de bains.	☑	☐
8. L'appartement est un studio.	☐	☑
9. Le loyer est de 490€.	☑	☐
10. Patrice va tout de suite emménager.	☐	☑

3 Définitions **Lisez les définitions et trouvez les mots ou expressions d'ESPACE CONTEXTES qui correspondent. Ensuite, avec un(e) partenaire, donnez votre propre définition de cinq mots ou expressions. Rejoignez un autre groupe et lisez vos définitions. L'autre groupe doit deviner (*must guess*) de quoi vous parlez.**

1. C'est ce que (*what*) vous payez chaque mois quand vous n'êtes pas propriétaire de votre appartement. ___un loyer___
2. Vous passez par ici pour aller d'une pièce à une autre. ___un couloir___
3. C'est le fait de (*act of*) partir de votre appartement. ___déménager___
4. C'est là que vous mettez vos livres. ___une étagère___
5. En général, il y en a quatre dans une pièce et ils séparent les pièces de votre appartement. ___les murs___
6. C'est ce que vous utilisez pour lire le soir. ___une lampe___
7. C'est là que vous mettez votre voiture. ___un garage___
8. C'est ce que vous utilisez pour aller du premier au deuxième étage d'un immeuble. ___un escalier/un ascenseur___
9. Quand vous avez des invités, c'est la pièce dans laquelle (*in which*) vous dînez. ___la salle à manger___
10. En général, il est sur le sol (*floor*) d'une pièce. ___un tapis___

Practice more at **espaces.vhlcentral.com.**

1 Expansion Have students create one or two additional sets using at least three of the new vocabulary words in each one. Collect their papers and write some of the items on the board.

2 Tapescript PATRICE: Allô, Madame Dautry, s'il vous plaît.
MADAME: Oui, c'est moi. J'écoute.
P: Mon nom est Patrice Leconte. Je vous appelle au sujet de votre appartement du 24, rue Pasteur. Est-ce qu'il est toujours libre?
M: Oui, jeune homme. Il est toujours libre.
P: Parfait. Comment est-il?
M: Il est au quatrième étage d'un immeuble moderne. Il y a un balcon, mais pas de garage. La chambre est plutôt petite, mais il y a beaucoup de placards.
P: Et la salle de bains?
M: Elle est petite aussi, avec une douche, un lavabo et un grand miroir. Les toilettes sont séparées.
P: Et le salon?
M: C'est la pièce principale. Elle est plutôt grande. La cuisine est juste à côté.
P: C'est combien, le loyer?
M: Le loyer est de 490€.
P: Oh, c'est cher!
M: Mais vous êtes à côté de l'université et l'appartement est libre le premier septembre.
P: Bon, je vais y penser. Merci beaucoup. Au revoir, Madame.
M: Au revoir, Monsieur.
(On Textbook MP3s)

2 Expansion Play the recording again, stopping at the end of each sentence that contains an answer. Have students verify true statements and correct the false ones.

3 Suggestion Before beginning this activity, you might want to teach your students expressions for circumlocution. Examples: **C'est un objet qu'on utilise pour… C'est une pièce où…**

OPTIONS

Game Write vocabulary words related to home furnishings on index cards. On another set of cards, draw or paste pictures to match each term. Tape them face down on the board in random order. Divide the class into two teams. Play a game of Concentration in which students match words with pictures. When a player has a match, his or her team collects those cards. When all cards are matched, the team with the most cards wins.

Extra Practice Write **Logements** and **Meubles** at the top of two columns on the board or on a transparency. Say vocabulary words and have students classify them in the correct category. Examples: **un appartement (logement), une résidence (logement), un studio (logement), un canapé (meuble), un lit (meuble)**, and **une armoire (meuble)**.

4 Suggestion Have students jot down notes during their interviews. Then have them report what they learned to another pair of students.

5 Suggestions
- Before beginning this activity, have students brainstorm vocabulary for furnishings and other items found in a bedroom. Write the words on the board.
- Review the prepositions in **Leçon 3B**.

6 Suggestion Divide the class into pairs and distribute the Info Gap Handouts found on the Supersite for this activity. Have two volunteers read the **modèle** aloud.

7 Suggestion Tell students to include colors in their descriptions.

Successful Language Learning Suggest to students that they study vocabulary words in varying order to avoid relying on the order itself to help them remember. Point out that words at the beginning and the end of lists tend to be easier to recall than those in the middle.

Communication

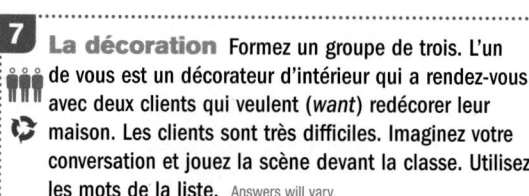

4 **Répondez** À tour de rôle avec un(e) partenaire, posez-vous ces questions et répondez-y (*them*). Answers will vary.

1. Où est-ce que tu habites?
2. Quelle est la taille de ton appartement ou de ta maison? Combien de pièces y a-t-il?
3. Quand as-tu emménagé?
4. Est-ce que tu as un jardin? Un garage?
5. Combien de placards as-tu? Où sont-ils?
6. Quels meubles as-tu? Comment sont-ils?
7. Quels meubles est-ce que tu voudrais (*would like*) avoir dans ton appartement? (Répondez: Je voudrais...)
8. Qu'est-ce que tu n'aimes pas au sujet de ton appartement?

5 **Votre chambre** Écrivez une description de votre chambre. À tour de rôle, lisez votre description à votre partenaire. Il/Elle va vous demander d'autres détails et dessiner un plan. Ensuite, regardez le dessin (*drawing*) de votre partenaire et dites s'il correspond à votre chambre ou non. N'oubliez pas d'inclure (*include*) des prépositions pour indiquer où sont certains meubles et objets. Answers will vary.

6 **Sept différences** Votre professeur va vous donner, à vous et à votre partenaire, deux feuilles d'activités différentes. Il y a sept différences entre les deux images. Comparez vos dessins et faites une liste de ces différences. Quel est le groupe le plus rapide (*the quickest*) de la classe? Attention! Ne regardez pas la feuille de votre partenaire. Answers will vary.

MODÈLE

Étudiant(e) 1: *Dans mon appartement, il y a un lit. Il y a une lampe à côté du lit.*
Étudiant(e) 2: *Dans mon appartement aussi, il y a un lit, mais il n'y a pas de lampe.*

7 **La décoration** Formez un groupe de trois. L'un de vous est un décorateur d'intérieur qui a rendez-vous avec deux clients qui veulent (*want*) redécorer leur maison. Les clients sont très difficiles. Imaginez votre conversation et jouez la scène devant la classe. Utilisez les mots de la liste. Answers will vary.

un canapé	un fauteuil
une chambre	un meuble
une cuisine	un mur
un escalier	un placard
une étagère	un tapis

OPTIONS

Extra Practice Call out words for furnishings and other objects, and have students write or say the room(s) where they might be found. Examples: **la télévision (la salle de séjour), le lit (la chambre),** and **la table (la salle à manger).**

TPR Have the class label various parts of the classroom with the names of rooms one would typically find in a house. Then have groups of three perform a skit in which the owner is showing the house to two exchange students who are going to be spending the semester there.

Les sons et les lettres

Audio: Concepts, Activities
Record & Compare

NATIONAL STANDARDS comparisons

s and ss

You've already learned that an **s** at the end of a word is usually silent.

lavabos **copains** **vas** **placards**

An **s** at the beginning of a word, before a consonant, or after a pronounced consonant is pronounced like the *s* in the English word *set*.

soir **salon** **studio** **absolument**

A double **s** is pronounced like the *ss* in the English word *kiss*.

grosse **assez** **intéressant** **rousse**

An **s** at the end of a word is often pronounced when the following word begins with a vowel sound. An **s** in a liaison sounds like a *z*, like the *s* in the English word *rose*.

très élégant **trois hommes**

The other instance where the French **s** has a *z* sound is when there is a single **s** between two vowels within the same word. The **s** is pronounced like the *s* in the English word *music*.

musée **amusant** **oiseau** **besoin**

These words look alike, but have different meanings. Compare the pronunciations of each word pair.

poison **poisson** **désert** **dessert**

Prononcez Répétez les mots suivants à voix haute.

1. sac
2. triste
3. suisse
4. chose
5. bourse
6. passer
7. surprise
8. assister
9. magasin
10. expressions
11. sénégalaise
12. sérieusement

Articulez Répétez les phrases suivantes à voix haute.

1. Le spectacle est très amusant et la chanteuse est superbe.
2. Est-ce que vous habitez dans une résidence universitaire?
3. De temps en temps, Suzanne assiste à l'inauguration d'expositions au musée.
4. Heureusement, mes professeurs sont sympathiques, sociables et très sincères.

Dictons Répétez les dictons à voix haute.

Si jeunesse savait, si vieillesse pouvait.[1]

Les oiseaux de même plumage s'assemblent sur le même rivage.[2]

[1] Youth is wasted on the young. (lit. If youth but knew, if old age but could.)
[2] Birds of a feather flock together.

ressources
LM p. 58
espaces.vhlcentral.com

Section Goals

In this section, students will learn about the sounds of **s** and **ss**.

Instructional Resources
espaces.vhlcentral.com: Textbook MP3s; Lab MP3s; WB/VM/LM Answer Key; IRM (Textbook Audioscript; Lab Audioscript); activities; downloads; reference tools

Suggestions

- Model the pronunciation of the example words and have students repeat them after you.
- Ask students to provide more examples of words from this lesson or previous lessons with these sounds. Examples: **cuisine, salon, résidence,** and **expression.**
- Dictate five familiar words containing **s** and **ss**, repeating each one at least two times. Then write them on the board or on a transparency and have students check their spelling.

OPTIONS

Extra Practice Use these sentences for additional practice or dictation. **1. Serge est professeur de sociologie. 2. Solange est paresseuse et pessimiste. 3. Ces étudiants sénégalais sont très intelligents. 4. Sylvain essaie les chaussures sans chaussettes.**

Extra Practice Teach students these French tongue-twisters that contain the **s** and **ss** sounds. **1. Ces six saucissons-ci sont si secs qu'on ne sait si c'en sont. 2. Zazie causait avec sa cousine en cousant.**

Section Goals

In this section, students will learn functional phrases for talking about their home.

Instructional Resources
*espaces.vhlcentral.com: Video; WB/VM/LM Answer Key; IRM (Videoscript; **Roman-photo** Translations); activities; downloads; reference tools*
Video on DVD

Video Recap: Leçon 7B Before doing this **Roman-photo**, review the previous one with this activity.

1. Pourquoi Sandrine est-elle allée à l'agence de voyages? (pour faire une réservation d'hôtel à Albertville)
2. Pourquoi n'a-t-elle pas fait la réservation? (Les hôtels moins chers sont complets.)
3. Comment Amina a-t-elle réussi à trouver un hôtel? (Elle a cherché sur Internet.)
4. Pourquoi Sandrine n'est-elle pas contente? (parce que Pascal ne va pas aller à Albertville)

Video Synopsis Pascal arrives in Aix-en-Provence. He runs into Rachid, who helps him pick up his flowers. He has never met Rachid before. Rachid and David then take a tour of Sandrine's apartment, which is very nice and big. Pascal shows up unexpectedly. Sandrine is not pleased by his surprise visit and breaks up with him.

Suggestions
- Have students scan the **Roman-photo** and find words related to the home.
- Have students read the **Roman-photo** conversation in groups of four.
- Review students' predictions and ask them which ones were correct.

NATIONAL STANDARDS communication cultures

La visite surprise

Video: *Roman-photo*
Record & Compare

PERSONNAGES

David

Pascal

Rachid

Sandrine

En ville, Pascal fait tomber (drops) *ses fleurs.*
PASCAL Aïe!
RACHID Tenez. (*Il aide Pascal.*)
PASCAL Oh, merci.
RACHID Aïe!
PASCAL Oh pardon, je suis vraiment désolé!
RACHID Ce n'est rien.
PASCAL Bonne journée!

Chez Sandrine...
RACHID Eh, salut, David! Dis donc, ce n'est pas un logement d'étudiants ici! C'est grand chez toi! Tu ne déménages pas, finalement?
DAVID Heureusement, Sandrine a décidé de rester.
SANDRINE Oui, je suis bien dans cet appartement. Seulement, les loyers sont très chers au centre-ville.

RACHID Oui, malheureusement! Tu as combien de pièces?
SANDRINE Il y a trois pièces: le salon, la salle à manger, ma chambre. Bien sûr, il y a une cuisine et j'ai aussi une grande salle de bains. Je te fais visiter?

SANDRINE Et voici ma chambre.
RACHID Elle est belle!
SANDRINE Oui... j'aime le vert.

RACHID Dis, c'est vrai, Sandrine, ta salle de bains est vraiment grande.
DAVID Oui! Et elle a un beau miroir au-dessus du lavabo et une baignoire!
RACHID Chez nous, on a seulement une douche.
SANDRINE Moi, je préfère les douches, en fait.

Le téléphone sonne (rings).
RACHID Comparé à cet appartement, le nôtre, c'est une cave! Pas de décorations, juste des affiches, un canapé, des étagères et mon bureau.
DAVID C'est vrai. On n'a même pas de rideaux.

ACTIVITÉS

1 Vrai ou faux? **Indiquez si ces affirmations sont vraies ou fausses. Corrigez les phrases fausses.** Answers may vary.

1. C'est la première fois que Rachid visite l'appartement. Vrai.
2. Sandrine ne déménage pas. Vrai.
3. Les loyers au centre-ville ne sont pas chers. Faux. Les loyers au centre-ville sont très chers.
4. Sandrine invite ses amis chez elle. Vrai.
5. Rachid préfère son appartement à l'appartement de Sandrine. Faux. Rachid préfère l'appartement de Sandrine.
6. Chez les garçons, il y a une baignoire et des rideaux. Faux. Les garçons ont une douche et n'ont pas de rideaux.
7. Quand Pascal arrive, Sandrine est contente (*pleased*). Faux. Sandrine n'est pas contente.
8. Pascal doit (*must*) travailler ce week-end. Faux. Pascal ne travaille pas ce week-end.

Practice more at **espaces.vhlcentral.com.**

OPTIONS

Avant de regarder la vidéo Before viewing the video, have students read the title and predict what might happen in this episode. Write their predictions on the board.

Regarder la vidéo Show the video episode without sound and have the class create a plot summary based on the visual cues. Then show the video again with sound and have the class correct any mistakes and fill in any gaps in the plot summary they created.

Pascal arrive à Aix-en-Provence.

SANDRINE Voici la salle à manger.
RACHID Ça, c'est une pièce très importante pour nous, les invités.

SANDRINE Et puis, la cuisine.
RACHID Une pièce très importante pour Sandrine...
DAVID Évidemment!

SANDRINE Mais Pascal... je pensais que tu avais du travail... Quoi? Tu es ici, maintenant? C'est une blague!
PASCAL Mais ma chérie, j'ai pris le train pour te faire une surprise...

SANDRINE Une surprise! Nous deux, c'est fini! D'abord, tu me dis que les vacances avec moi, c'est impossible et ensuite tu arrives à Aix sans me téléphoner!
PASCAL Bon, si c'est comme ça, reste où tu es. Ne descends pas. Moi, je m'en vais. Voilà tes fleurs. Tu parles d'une surprise!

Expressions utiles

Talking about your home

- **Tu ne déménages pas, finalement?**
  You are not moving, after all?
- **Heureusement, Sandrine a décidé de rester.**
  Thankfully/Happily, Sandrine has decided to stay.
- **Seulement, les loyers sont très chers au centre-ville.**
  However, rents are very expensive downtown.
- **Je te fais visiter?**
  Shall I give you a tour?
- **Ta salle de bains est vraiment grande.**
  Your bathroom is really big.
- **Elle a un beau miroir au-dessus du lavabo.**
  It has a nice mirror above the sink.
- **Chez nous, on a seulement une douche.**
  At our place, we only have a shower.

Additional vocabulary

- **Aïe!**
  Ouch!
- **Tenez.**
  Here.
- **Je pensais que tu avais du travail.**
  I thought you had work to do.
- **Mais ma chérie, j'ai pris le train pour te faire une surprise.**
  But sweetie, I took the train to surprise you.
- **sans**
  without
- **Moi, je m'en vais.**
  I am leaving/getting out of here.

ACTIVITÉS

2 **Quel appartement?** Indiquez si ces objets sont dans l'appartement de Sandrine **(S)** ou dans l'appartement de David et Rachid **(D & R)**.

1. baignoire S
2. douche D & R
3. rideaux S
4. canapé D & R, S
5. trois pièces S
6. étagères D & R
7. miroir S
8. affiches D & R

3 **Conversez** Sandrine décide que son loyer est vraiment trop cher. Elle cherche un appartement à partager avec Amina. Avec deux partenaires, écrivez leur conversation avec un agent immobilier (*real estate agent*). Elles décrivent l'endroit idéal, le prix et les meubles qu'elles préfèrent. L'agent décrit plusieurs possibilités.

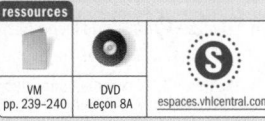

ressources: VM pp. 239-240 | DVD Leçon 8A | espaces.vhlcentral.com

Expressions utiles
- Model the pronunciation of the **Expressions utiles** and have students repeat them.
- As you work through the list, point out adverbs ending in **-ment** and verbs in the **imparfait.** You might want to tell students that the ending **-ment** usually corresponds to the English ending *-ly*. Then tell them that these grammar structures will be formally presented in the **Structures** section.
- Respond briefly to questions about the **imparfait.** Reinforce correct forms, but do not expect students to produce them consistently at this time.
- Point out that **être fâché(e) contre quelqu'un** means *to be angry with someone*, but **être fâché(e) avec quelqu'un,** means *to be no longer on speaking terms with someone.*

1 Suggestion Have students write their corrections for false statements on the board.

1 Expansion For additional practice, give students these items. **9. Rachid et Pascal sont de bons amis. (Faux.) 10. La chambre de Sandrine est rose. (Faux.) 11. L'appartement de Sandrine est une cave. (Faux.)**

2 Expansion For additional practice, give students these items. **9. bureau (D & R) 10. grande salle de bains (S) 11. douche (D & R)**

3 Suggestions
- Before writing the conversation, tell students that the person playing the real estate agent should make a list of questions to ask prospective clients, and the two people playing Sandrine and Amina should decide on the features they are looking for in an apartment.
- You might want to bring in some real estate ads in French from newspapers or the Internet for the agents to use.

OPTIONS

Small Groups Have groups of three interview each other about their dream house, with one student conducting the interview, one answering, and one taking notes. At three-minute intervals, have students switch roles until each has been interviewer, interviewee, and note-taker. Then have two groups get together and take turns describing their dream houses to one another using their notes.

Pairs Have students work in pairs. Tell them to write an alternate ending to this episode, in which Sandrine is pleased to see Pascal and invites him upstairs to meet Rachid and David. Encourage students to use some of the **Expressions utiles**. Then have volunteers perform their role-plays for the class.

connections cultures NATIONAL STANDARDS

Video: *Flash culture*

Section Goals

In this section, students will:
- learn about different types of housing in France
- learn terms related to renting an apartment
- read about traditional houses in various francophone regions
- read about **le château Frontenac**
- view authentic video footage

Instructional Resources
espaces.vhlcentral.com: Video; WB/VM/LM Answer Key; IRM (Videoscript); activities; downloads; reference tools

Culture à la loupe

Avant la lecture Have students look at the photos and describe what they see.

Lecture
- Point out the **Coup de main**.
- Point out the statistics chart. Ask students what information the chart shows. (the change in percentage between 1962 and 1999 of the size of houses as measured by number of rooms) Explain that the kitchen and bathrooms are not included when counting rooms in a French residence.

Après la lecture Ask students: **Dans quel type de logement français désirez-vous habiter? Pourquoi?**

1 Expansion For additional practice, give students these items. **11. Plus de la moitié des Français habitent un appartement. (Faux.) 12. Dans le nord, les maisons sont souvent en bois. (Faux. Elles sont en briques.) 13. Cinquante pour cent des Français sont propriétaires. (Vrai.)**

CULTURE À LA LOUPE

Le logement en France

Les trois quarts des gens habitent en ville et un Français sur cinq habite la région parisienne. Quinze pour cent de la population habitent en banlieue dans des HLM (habitations à loyer modéré°), des appartements réservés aux familles qui n'ont pas beaucoup d'argent. Plus de la moitié des Français habitent une maison individuelle et l'autre partie habite un appartement. Cinquante pour cent des Français sont propriétaires, dont° dix pour cent ont une résidence secondaire.

Le type et la taille° des logements varient. Dans les grandes villes, beaucoup d'anciens hôtels particuliers° ont été transformés en appartements. En banlieue, on trouve de grands ensembles°, des groupes d'immeubles assez° modernes qui bénéficient de certains équipements collectifs°. En général, dans les petites villes et les villages, les gens habitent de petites maisons qui sont souvent assez anciennes.

Le style et l'architecture varient d'une région à l'autre. La région parisienne a de nombreux pavillons (maisons avec de petits jardins). Dans le nord°, on habite souvent des maisons en briques° avec des toits en ardoise°. En Alsace-Lorraine, il y a de vieilles maisons à colombages° avec des parties de mur en bois°. Les maisons traditionnelles de l'ouest° ont des toits de chaume°. Dans le sud°, il y a des villas de style méditerranéen avec des toits en tuiles° rouges et des mas° provençaux (vieilles maisons en pierres°).

habitations à loyer modéré *low-cost government housing* **dont** *of which* **taille** *size* **anciens hôtels particuliers** *former private mansions* **grands ensembles** *high-rise buildings* **assez** *rather* **bénéficient de certains équipements collectifs** *benefit from certain shared facilities* **nord** *north* **briques** *bricks* **toits en ardoise** *slate roofs* **maisons à colombages** *half-timbered houses* **bois** *wood* **ouest** *west* **chaume** *thatch* **sud** *south* **tuiles** *tiles* **mas** *farmhouses* **pierres** *stones*

Coup de main

Here are some terms commonly used in statistics.

un quart = *one quarter*
un tiers = *one third*
la moitié = *half*
la plupart de = *most of*
un sur cinq = *one in five*

Évolution de la taille des logements en France

TAILLE	1999	2005
1 pièce	6,5%	6,0%
2 pièces	12,0%	11,5%
3 pièces	22,0%	20,5%
4 pièces et plus	58,5%	61,0%

SOURCE: INSEE

ACTIVITÉS

1 Vrai ou faux? Indiquez si les phrases sont **vraies** ou **fausses**. Corrigez les phrases fausses. Answers may vary slightly.

1. Il n'y a pas beaucoup de Français qui habitent la région parisienne. Faux. Un Français sur cinq habite la région parisienne.
2. Les familles sans beaucoup d'argent habitent souvent dans des HLM. Vrai.
3. La moitié des Français ont une résidence secondaire. Faux. Peu de Français qui sont propriétaires ont une résidence secondaire.
4. On a transformé beaucoup d'anciens hôtels particuliers en appartements. Vrai.
5. Les grands ensembles sont des maisons en pierres. Faux. Les grands ensembles sont des groupes d'immeubles assez modernes.
6. Les maisons françaises ont des styles d'architecture différents d'une région à l'autre. Vrai.
7. En général, les maisons dans les villages sont assez vieilles. Vrai.
8. Dans le sud de la France, il y a beaucoup de pavillons. Faux. Dans le sud de la France, il y a des villas de style méditerranéen et des mas provençaux.
9. Dans le nord de la France, il y a beaucoup de vieilles maisons à colombages. Faux. C'est dans l'est de la France qu'il y a des maisons à colombages.
10. En France, en 1999, presque (*almost*) un quart des maisons et des appartements avaient (*had*) seulement trois pièces. Vrai.

Practice more at **espaces.vhlcentral.com.**

OPTIONS

Extra Practice Write the following headings on the board and have students identify the different types of housing in each area: **Les grandes villes, La banlieue, Le Nord, L'Alsace-Lorraine, L'Ouest,** and **Le Sud.**

Cultural Comparison Have students work in groups of three to compare the types of housing in France and the United States. Tell them to list the similarities and differences in a two-column chart under the headings **Similitudes** and **Différences**. After completing their charts, have two groups get together and compare their lists.

LE FRANÇAIS QUOTIDIEN

Location d'un logement

agence (*f.*) de location	*rental agency*
bail (*m.*)	*lease*
caution (*f.*)	*security deposit*
charges (*f.*)	*basic utilities*
chauffage (*m.*)	*heating*
électricité (*f.*)	*electricity*
locataire (*m./f.*)	*tenant*
petites annonces (*f.*)	*(rental) ads*

LE MONDE FRANCOPHONE

L'architecture

Voici quelques exemples d'habitations traditionnelles.

En Afrique centrale et de l'Ouest des maisons construites sur pilotis°, avec un grenier à riz°

En Afrique du Nord des maisons en pisé (de la terre° rouge mélangée° à de la paille°) construites autour d'un patio central et avec, souvent, une terrasse sur le toit°

Aux Antilles des maisons en bois de toutes les couleurs avec des toits en métal

En Polynésie française des bungalows, construits sur pilotis ou sur le sol, souvent en bambou avec des toits en paille ou en feuilles de cocotier°

Au Viêt-nam des maisons sur pilotis construites sur des lacs, des rivières ou simplement au-dessus du sol°

pilotis *stilts* **grenier à riz** *rice loft* **terre** *clay* **mélangée** *mixed* **paille** *straw* **toit** *roof* **feuilles de cocotier** *coconut palm leaves* **au-dessus du sol** *off the ground*

PORTRAIT

Le château Frontenac

Le château Frontenac est un hôtel de luxe et un des plus beaux° sites touristiques de la ville de Québec. Construit entre la fin° du XIXe siècle et le début° du XXe siècle sur le Cap Diamant, dans le quartier du Vieux-Québec, le château offre une vue° spectaculaire sur la ville. Aujourd'hui, avec ses 618 chambres sur 18 étages, ses restaurants gastronomiques, sa piscine et son centre sportif, le château Frontenac est classé parmi° les 500 meilleurs° hôtels du monde.

un des plus beaux *one of the most beautiful* **fin** *end* **début** *beginning* **vue** *view* **classé parmi** *ranked among* **meilleurs** *best*

SUR INTERNET

Qu'est-ce qu'une pendaison de crémaillère? D'où vient cette expression?

Go to **espaces.vhlcentral.com** to find more information related to this **ESPACE CULTURE**. Then watch the corresponding **Flash culture**.

ACTIVITÉS

2 **Répondez** Répondez aux questions, d'après les informations données dans les textes.

1. Qu'est-ce que le château Frontenac?
   C'est un hôtel de luxe.
2. De quel siècle date le château Frontenac?
   Le château Frontenac date du XIXe siècle.
3. Dans quel quartier de la ville de Québec le trouve-t-on?
   On le trouve dans le quartier du Vieux-Québec.
4. Où trouve-t-on les maisons sur pilotis?
   On les trouve en Afrique centrale et de l'Ouest, au Viêt-nam et en Polynésie française.
5. Quelles sont les caractéristiques des maisons d'Afrique du Nord?
   Le patio central et la terrasse sur le toit sont des caractéristiques des maisons d'Afrique du Nord.

3 **Une année en France** Vous allez habiter en France. Téléphonez à un agent immobilier (*real estate*) (votre partenaire) et expliquez-lui le type de logement que vous recherchez. Il/Elle va vous donner des renseignements sur les logements disponibles (*available*). Posez des questions pour avoir plus de détails.

ressources: VM pp. 285-286 | espaces.vhlcentral.com

Le français quotidien Model the pronunciation of each term and have students repeat it. Point out that the word **location** is a **faux ami**; it means *rental*. You might also wish to add these terms to the list: **un particulier** (*a private person*), **une chambre de bonne** (*a small room, usually on the top floor, to rent in someone's home; originally it was the maid's room*), **un deux-pièces** (*a two-room apartment*), and **un concierge** (*doorman*).

Portrait

- **Le château Frontenac** is located on a hill overlooking the St. Lawrence River. It is considered the symbol of Quebec City. Have students locate Quebec City on the map of North America in **Appendice A** and point out its strategic location.
- Ask students: **Désirez-vous faire un séjour au château Frontenac? Pourquoi?**

Le monde francophone Bring in photos of the various types of houses from magazines or the Internet. After students have read the text, show them the photos and have them identify the location.

2 Expansion For additional practice, give students these items. **6. Combien de chambres y a-t-il au château? (618) 7. Où trouve-t-on les maisons en bois de toutes les couleurs? (aux Antilles)**

3 Suggestion Have students sit back-to-back and pretend they are holding a phone to their ear to simulate a phone conversation.

Flash culture Tell students that they will learn more about housing by watching a variety of real-life images narrated by Benjamin. Show the video segment, then have students jot down in French at least three types of residences they saw. You can also use the activities in the video manual in class to reinforce this **Flash culture** or assign them as homework.

OPTIONS

Location d'un logement Distribute photocopies of apartment rental ads from a French newspaper or the Internet. Have students guess the meanings of abbreviations, such as **sdb**, **cuis.** and **pisc.**, and explain unfamiliar ones, such as **T3** or **m²**. Then tell students to work in pairs and write five comprehension questions based on the ads. Have volunteers read their questions aloud, and ask other students to answer them.

Cultural Comparison Have students work in groups of three and compare **le château Frontenac** to the hotels in their city or town. Tell them to list the similarities and differences in a two-column chart under the headings **Similitudes** and **Différences**. After completing their charts, have two groups get together and compare their lists.

Section Goals

In this section, students will learn to compare and contrast some of the basic uses and meanings of the **passé composé** and the **imparfait**:

Instructional Resources
*espaces.vhlcentral.com: Lab MP3s; WB/VM/LM Answer Key; IRM (**Essayez!** and **Mise en pratique** answers; Lab Audioscript); activities; downloads; reference tools*

Suggestions

- Draw a timeline on the board and mark events on it and label as follows: **J'ai pris mon petit-déjeuner à 7h30. J'ai quitté la maison à 8h. Je suis allé(e) au cours de biologie à 10h15. J'ai déjeuné à midi. Je suis rentré(e) à cinq heures du soir** etc. Then, write the following sentences randomly around the timeline: **Il faisait un temps épouvantable. Le cours de biologie était intéressant**. Explain to students that these sentences cannot be placed at any specific point since they express feelings, background circumstances, or events that occur over an unspecified period of time.
- Have students make two flashcards. On one they write **passé composé** and on the other they write **imparfait**. Read a short text in which both verb tenses are used. As you read each verb, students show the appropriate card. Then call on a volunteer to write the conjugated verb form on the board.
- Contrast the uses of the **passé composé** and **imparfait** by giving personalized examples of things you and/or your family did yesterday versus things you and your family used to do when you were young. Examples: **Hier soir, je suis allée au centre commercial. Quand j'étais petite, je jouais au foot.** Then make two columns on the board, one labeled **Hier, je/j'...** and the other labeled **Quand j'étais petit(e)...** Have volunteers take turns writing complete sentences about themselves under each column.

8A.1 The *passé composé* vs. the *imparfait* (Part 1)

NATIONAL STANDARDS comparisons

Point de départ Although the **passé composé** and the **imparfait** are both past tenses, they have very distinct uses and are not interchangeable. The choice between these two tenses depends on the context and on the point of view of the speaker.

The *passé composé*

Uses of the *passé composé*

To express specific actions that started and ended in the past and are viewed by the speaker as completed	J'**ai nettoyé** la salle de bains deux fois. *I cleaned the bathroom twice.* Nous **avons acheté** un tapis. *We bought a rug.* L'enfant **est né** à la maison. *The child was born at home.* Il **a plu** hier. *It rained yesterday.*
To tell about events that happened at a specific point in time or within a specific length of time in the past	Je **suis allé** à la pêche avec papa il y a deux ans. *I went fishing with dad two years ago.* Elle **a étudié** à Paris pendant six mois. *She studied in Paris for six months.*
To express the beginning or end of a past action	Le film **a commencé** à huit heures. *The movie began at 8 o'clock.* Ils **ont fini** les devoirs samedi matin. *They finished the homework Saturday morning.*
To narrate a series of past actions or events	Ce matin, j'**ai fait** du jogging, j'**ai nettoyé** la chambre et j'**ai rangé** la cuisine. *This morning, I jogged, I cleaned my bedroom, and I tidied up the kitchen.* Pour la fête d'anniversaire de papa, maman **a envoyé** les invitations, elle **a acheté** un cadeau et elle **a fait** les décorations. *For dad's birthday party, mom sent out the invitations, bought a gift, and did the decorations.*
To signal a change in physical or mental state	Il est mort dans un accident. *He died in an accident.* Tout à coup, elle **a eu** peur. *All of a sudden, she got frightened.*

MISE EN PRATIQUE

1 Une surprise désagréable Récemment, Benoît a fait un séjour à Strasbourg avec un collègue. Complétez son récit (*narration*) avec l'imparfait ou le passé composé.

Ce matin, il (1) __faisait__ (faire) chaud. J' (2) __étais__ (être) content de partir pour Strasbourg. Je (3) __suis parti__ (partir) pour la gare, où j' (4) __ai retrouvé__ (retrouver) Franck. Le train (5) __est arrivé__ (arriver) à Strasbourg à midi. Nous (6) __avons commencé__ (commencer) notre promenade en ville. Nous (7) __avions__ (avoir) besoin d'un plan. J' (8) __ai cherché__ (chercher) mon portefeuille (*wallet*), mais il (9) __était__ (être) toujours dans le train! Franck et moi, nous (10) __avons couru__ (courir) à la gare!

2 Le week-end dernier Qu'est-ce que Lucie a fait samedi dernier? Créez des phrases complètes au passé composé ou à l'imparfait pour décrire sa soirée.

MODÈLE finir / je / mes tâches ménagères / tôt
J'ai fini mes tâches ménagères tôt.

1. froid / faire / et / neiger
   Il faisait froid et il neigeait.
2. cinéma / mes amis / aller / je / avec / alors
   Alors, je suis allée au cinéma avec mes amis.
3. film / sept heures / commencer
   Le film a commencé à sept heures.
4. Audrey Tautou / film / dans / être
   Audrey Tautou était dans le film.
5. après / film / aller / café / mes amis et moi
   Après le film, mes amis moi sommes allés au café.
6. nous / prendre / éclairs / limonades / et
   Nous avons pris des éclairs et des limonades.
7. rentrer / je / chez / minuit / moi
   Je suis rentrée chez moi à minuit
8. fatigué / avoir / sommeil / je / être
   J'étais fatiguée et j'avais sommeil.

3 Vacances à la montagne Hugo raconte ses vacances. Complétez ses phrases avec un des verbes de la liste au passé composé ou à l'imparfait.

aller	neiger	retourner
avoir	passer	skier
faire	rester	venir

1. L'hiver dernier, nous __avons passé__ les vacances à la montagne.
2. Quand nous sommes arrivés sur les pistes de ski, il __neigeait__ beaucoup et il __faisait__ un temps épouvantable.
3. Ce jour-là, nous __sommes restés__ à l'hôtel tout l'après-midi.
4. Le jour suivant, nous __sommes retournés__ sur les pistes.
5. Nous __avons skié__ et papa __est allé__ faire une randonnée.
6. Quand ils __avaient__ mon âge, papa et oncle Hervé __venaient__ tous les hivers à la montagne.

Practice more at **espaces.vhlcentral.com.**

OPTIONS

Pairs Work with a partner to write a critical review about a fashion show you attended last week. Give details about what the models were wearing and how they looked. You might also want to include comparisons between clothing styles you saw last week and how they were different from those in the past.

Small Groups Have students work in groups of four to write a brief account of a surprise party they organized last weekend. Have them tell how they prepared for the party, which rooms they decorated, what the weather was like, and how everyone felt after the party. Then, have them share their summary with the rest of the class.

COMMUNICATION

4 Situations Avec un(e) partenaire, parlez de ces situations en utilisant (*by using*) le passé composé ou l'imparfait. Comparez vos réponses, puis présentez-les à la classe. Answers will vary.

MODÈLE

Le premier jour de cours...
Étudiant(e) 1: *Le premier jour de cours, j'étais tellement nerveux que j'ai oublié mes livres.*
Étudiant(e) 2: *Moi, j'étais nerveux aussi, alors j'ai quitté la résidence universitaire très tôt.*

1. Quand j'étais petit(e), ...
2. L'été dernier, ...
3. Hier soir, mon/ma petit(e) ami(e)...
4. Hier, le professeur...
5. La semaine dernière, mon/ma camarade de chambre...
6. Ce matin, au resto U, ...
7. Quand j'étais au lycée, ...
8. La dernière fois que j'étais en vacances, ...

5 Votre premier/première petit(e) ami(e) Posez ces questions à un(e) partenaire. Ajoutez (*Add*) d'autres questions si vous le voulez (*want*). Answers will vary.

1. Qui a été ton/ta premier/première petit(e) ami(e)?
2. Quel âge avais-tu quand tu as fait sa connaissance?
3. Comment était-il/elle?
4. Est-ce que tu as fait la connaissance de sa famille?
5. Pendant combien de temps êtes-vous sortis ensemble?
6. Où alliez-vous quand vous sortiez?
7. Aviez-vous les mêmes (*same*) centres d'intérêt?
8. Pourquoi avez-vous arrêté (*stopped*) de sortir ensemble?

6 Dialogue Sébastien, qui a seize ans, est sorti avec des amis hier soir. Quand il est rentré à trois heures du matin, sa mère était furieuse parce que ce n'était pas la première fois qu'il rentrait tard. Avec un(e) partenaire, préparez le dialogue entre Sébastien et sa mère. Answers will vary.

MODÈLE

Étudiant(e) 1: *Que faisais-tu à minuit?*
Étudiant(e) 2: *Mes copains et moi, nous sommes allés manger une pizza...*

The *imparfait*

Uses of the *imparfait*

To describe an ongoing past action with no reference to its beginning or end	Vous **dormiez** sur le canapé. *You were sleeping on the couch.* Tu **attendais** dans le café? *You were waiting in the café?* Nous **regardions** la télé chez Fanny. *We were watching TV at Fanny's house.* Les enfants **lisaient** tranquillement. *The children were reading peacefully.*
To express habitual or repeated past actions and events	Nous **faisions** un tour en voiture le dimanche matin. *We used to go for a drive on Sunday mornings.* Elle **mettait** toujours la voiture dans le garage. *She always put the car in the garage.* Maman **travaillait** souvent dans le jardin. *Mom would often work in the garden.* Quand j'**étais** jeune, j'**aimais** faire du camping. *When I was young, I used to like to go camping.*
To describe mental, physical, and emotional states or conditions	Karine **était** très inquiète. *Karine was very worried.* Simon et Marion **étaient** fatigués et ils **avaient** sommeil. *Simon and Marion were tired and sleepy.* Mon ami **avait** faim et il **avait** envie de manger quelque chose. *My friend was hungry and felt like eating something.*

Essayez! Donnez les formes correctes des verbes.

passé composé		imparfait	
1. commencer (il)	*il a commencé*	1. jouer (nous)	*nous jouions*
2. acheter (tu)	tu as acheté	2. être (tu)	tu étais
3. boire (nous)	nous avons bu	3. prendre (elles)	elles prenaient
4. apprendre (ils)	ils ont appris	4. avoir (vous)	vous aviez
5. répondre (je)	j'ai répondu	5. conduire (il)	il conduisait

Essayez! Give items like these as additional practice. For the **passé composé**: **6. descendre (elle) (elle est descendue) 7. lire (je) (j'ai lu)** For the **imparfait**: **6. écrire (je) (j'écrivais) 7. dire (on) (on disait)**

1 Expansion Have volunteers explain why they chose the **passé composé** or **imparfait** in each case. Ask them to point out any words or expressions that triggered one tense or the other.

2 Suggestion Before assigning the activity, remind students that actions viewed as completed by the speaker take the **passé composé**. Have students give personal examples of actions in the past using this verb tense.

3 Expansion Have students use this activity as a model to write a short journal entry about a vacation of their own using the **passé composé** and the **imparfait.**

4 Expansion Have students choose one of these sentences to begin telling a short story in the past. Encourage students to use both the **passé composé** and the **imparfait.**

5 Expansion After completing the pair work, assign this activity as a short written composition.

6 Suggestions Act out the **modèle** with a volunteer before assigning this activity to pairs. Have pairs of students role-play their dialogues in front of the class.

OPTIONS

Extra Practice Make cards that contain a verb or noun and an expression that signals a past tense. Example: **hier / parc** or **Quand j'étais jeune / voyager**. Mix them up in a hat and have each student pick a card at random. Have each student state the cues on his or her card and use them in a sentence with the **passé composé** or **imparfait.** Have the student say which tense he or she will use before formulating the sentence.

Small Groups Have students work in groups to pick a popular holiday and write a few sentences in the past tense to describe it. Students might talk about typical activities they did that day, the weather, or how they felt on that day. Then, have them share their description with the class without revealing the holiday and have their classmates guess what holiday it is.

Section Goals

In this section, students will learn:

- the use of the **passé composé** vs. the **imparfait** in a narration, interrupted actions, and cause and effect
- common expressions indicating the past tense
- the verb **vivre**

Instructional Resources
*espaces.vhlcentral.com: Lab MP3s; WB/VM/LM Answer Key; IRM (**Essayez!** and **Mise en pratique** answers; Lab Audioscript); activities; downloads; reference tools*

Suggestions

- Tell students that the choice of the **passé composé** vs. the **imparfait** is very important since the meaning conveyed can be different based on which tense you use. Example: **J'ai téléphoné quand ma mère est arrivée. Je téléphonais quand ma mère est arrivée.** In the first case, I called after my mother arrived. In the second case, I was in the process of calling when my mother arrived. You might have students come up with other examples of sentences where the message changes based on which past tense is used.
- Point out to students that if both actions in a sentence are ongoing or completed simultaneously, then both verbs can be either in the **passé composé** or the **imparfait**. Example: **Je suis sorti quand tu es entré. Je sortais quand tu entrais.** They will need to pay close attention to the meaning they want to convey.
- Give personalized examples as you contrast the **passé composé** and the **imparfait**. Examples: **La semaine dernière quand je répétais dans le salon, quelqu'un m'a téléphoné. Je n'ai pas entendu le téléphone parce que je jouais du piano.**
- Give students these other expressions that signal the **imparfait: de temps en temps** (*from time to time*), **en général** (*in general, usually*), **quelquefois** (*sometimes*), **autrefois** (*in the past*).

8A.2 The *passé composé* vs. the *imparfait* (Part 2)

NATIONAL STANDARDS comparisons

Point de départ You have already seen some uses of the **passé composé** versus the **imparfait** while talking about things and events in the past. Here are some other contexts in which the choice of the tense you use is important.

- The **passé composé** and the **imparfait** are often used together to narrate a story or an incident. In such cases, the imparfait is usually used to set the scene or the background while the **passé composé** moves the story along.

Uses of the *passé composé* and the *imparfait*

passé composé *It is used to talk about:*	imparfait *It is used to describe:*
• main facts	• the framework of the story: *weather, date, time, background scenery*
• specific, completed events	• descriptions of people: *age, physical and personality traits, clothing, feelings, state of mind*
• actions that advance the plot	• background setting: *what was going on, what others were doing*

Il **était** minuit et le temps **était** orageux. J'**avais** peur parce que j'**étais** seule dans la maison. Soudain, quelqu'un **a frappé** à la porte. J'**ai regardé** par la fenêtre et j'**ai vu** un vieil homme habillé en noir...
It was midnight and it was stormy. I was afraid because I was alone at home. Suddenly, someone knocked on the door. I looked through the window and I saw an old man dressed in black...

Il **était** deux heures de l'après-midi et il **faisait** beau dehors. Les étudiants **attendaient** impatiemment la sortie. C'**était** le dernier jour de l'école! Finalement, le prof **est entré** dans la salle pour nous donner les résultats...
It was 2 o'clock and it was nice outside. The students were waiting impatiently for dismissal. It was the last day of school! Finally, the professor came into the classroom to give us our results...

- When the **passé composé** and the **imparfait** occur in the same sentence, the action in the **passé composé** often interrupts the ongoing action in the **imparfait**.

ACTION IN PROGRESS	INTERRUPTING ACTION
Je **chantais** *I was singing*	quand mon petit ami **est arrivé**. *when my boyfriend arrived.*
Céline et Maxime **dormaient** *Céline and Maxime were sleeping*	quand le téléphone **a sonné**. *when the phone rang.*

MISE EN PRATIQUE

1 Pourquoi? Expliquez pourquoi Sabine a fait ou n'a pas fait ces choses.

MODÈLE ne pas faire de tennis / être fatigué
Sabine n'a pas fait de tennis parce qu'elle était fatiguée.

1. aller au centre commercial / aimer faire les soldes Sabine est allée au centre commercial parce qu'elle aimait faire les soldes.
2. ne pas travailler / avoir sommeil Sabine n'a pas travaillé parce qu'elle avait sommeil.
3. ne pas sortir / pleuvoir Sabine n'est pas sortie parce qu'il pleuvait.
4. mettre un pull / faire froid Sabine a mis un pull parce qu'il faisait froid.
5. manger une pizza / avoir faim Sabine a mangé une pizza parce qu'elle avait faim.
6. acheter une nouvelle robe / sortir avec des amis Sabine a acheté une nouvelle robe parce qu'elle sortait avec des amis.
7. vendre son fauteuil / déménager Sabine a vendu son fauteuil parce qu'elle déménageait.
8. ne pas bien dormir / être inquiet Sabine n'a pas bien dormi parce qu'elle était inquiète.

2 Qu'est-il arrivé quand...? Dites ce qui (*what*) est arrivé quand ces personnes faisaient ces activités. Utilisez les mots donnés et d'autres mots. Suggested answers

MODÈLE
Tu nageais quand ton oncle est arrivé.

tu / oncle / arriver

1. Tristan / entendre / chien Tristan nettoyait sa chambre quand il a entendu le chien.

3. vous / voir / billet Vous partiez pour la France quand vous avez perdu votre billet.

2. nous / petite fille / tomber Nous patinions quand la petite fille est tombée.

4. Paul et Éric / téléphone / sonner Paul et Éric déjeunaient dans la salle à manger quand le téléphone a sonné.

3 Rien d'extraordinaire Matthieu a passé une journée assez banale. Réécrivez ce paragraphe au passé.

Il est 6h30. Il pleut. Je prends mon petit-déjeuner, je mets mon imperméable et je quitte la maison. J'attends une demi-heure à l'arrêt de bus et finalement, je cours au restaurant où je travaille. J'arrive en retard. Le patron (*boss*) n'est pas content. Le soir, après mon travail, je rentre à la maison et je vais directement au lit.
Il était 6h30. Il pleuvait. J'ai pris mon petit-déjeuner, j'ai mis mon imperméable et j'ai quitté la maison. J'ai attendu une demi-heure à l'arrêt de bus et finalement, j'ai couru au restaurant où je travaillais. Je suis arrivé en retard. Le patron n'était pas content. Le soir, après mon travail, je suis rentré à la maison et je suis directement allé au lit.

Practice more at **espaces.vhlcentral.com.**

OPTIONS

Pairs Ask students to narrate an embarrassing moment. Tell them to describe what happened and how they felt, using the **passé composé** and **imparfait.** Then have volunteers retell their partner's embarrassing moment using the third person. You may want to let students make up a fake embarrassing moment.

Small Groups Have students work in groups of four to write a short article about an imaginary road trip they took last summer. Students should use the **imparfait** to set the scene and the **passé composé** to narrate events. Each student should contribute three sentences to the article. When finished, have students read their article to the class.

NATIONAL communication STANDARDS

COMMUNICATION

4 La curiosité Votre tante Louise veut tout savoir. Elle vous pose beaucoup de questions. Avec un(e) partenaire, répondez aux questions d'une manière logique et échangez les rôles. Answers will vary.

MODÈLE retourner au bureau
Étudiant(e) 1: *Pourquoi est-ce que tu es retourné(e) au bureau?*
Étudiant(e) 2: *Je suis retourné(e) au bureau parce que j'avais beaucoup de travail.*

1. aller en boîte de nuit
2. aller au magasin
3. sortir avec des amis
4. téléphoner à ton cousin
5. rentrer tard
6. aller au café
7. inviter des gens
8. être triste

5 Une entrevue Avec un(e) partenaire, posez-vous ces questions à tour de rôle. Answers will vary.

1. Où allais-tu souvent quand tu étais petit(e)?
2. Qu'est-ce que tu aimais lire?
3. Est-ce que tu as vécu dans un autre pays?
4. Comment étais-tu quand tu avais dix ans?
5. Qu'est-ce que ton/ta camarade de chambre faisait quand tu es rentré(e) hier?
6. Qu'est-ce que tu as fait hier soir?
7. Qu'est-ce que tu as pris au petit-déjeuner ce matin?
8. Qu'est-ce que tu as porté aujourd'hui?

6 Scénario Par groupes de trois, créez une histoire au passé. La première personne commence par une phrase. La deuxième personne doit (*must*) continuer l'histoire. La troisième personne reprend la suite d'une manière logique. Continuez l'histoire une personne à la fois jusqu'à ce que vous ayez (*until you have*) un petit scénario. Soyez créatif! Ensuite, présentez votre scénario à la classe. Answers will vary.

- Depending on how you want to express the actions, either the **passé composé** or the **imparfait** can follow **quand**.

  Mes parents **sont arrivés** quand nous **répétions** dans le sous-sol.
  My parents arrived when we were rehearsing in the basement.

- Sometimes the use of the **passé composé** and the **imparfait** in the same sentence expresses a cause and effect.

  J'**avais** faim, alors j'**ai mangé** un sandwich.
  I was hungry so I ate a sandwich.

- Certain adverbs often indicate a particular past tense.

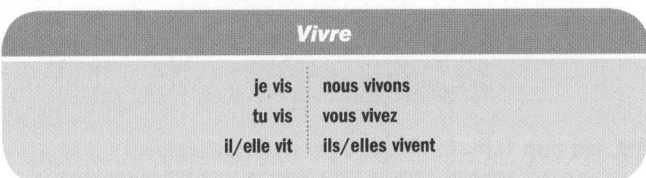

Expressions that signal a past tense

passé composé		imparfait	
soudain	*suddenly*	**d'habitude**	*usually*
tout d'un coup/ tout à coup	*all of a sudden*	**parfois**	*sometimes*
		souvent	*often*
une (deux, etc.) fois	*once (twice, etc.)*	**toujours**	*always*
un jour	*one day*	**tous les jours**	*every day*

- While talking about the past or narrating a tale, you might use the verb **vivre** (*to live*) which is irregular.

Vivre

je vis	**nous vivons**
tu vis	**vous vivez**
il/elle vit	**ils/elles vivent**

Les enfants **vivent** avec leurs grands-parents.
The children live with their grandparents.

- The past participle of **vivre** is **vécu**. The **imparfait** is formed like regular **-re** verbs by taking the **nous** form, dropping the **-ons**, and adding the endings.

  Rémi **a** toujours **vécu** à Nice.
  Rémi always lived in Nice.

  Nous **vivions** avec mon oncle.
  We used to live with my uncle.

Essayez! **Choisissez la forme correcte du verbe au passé.**

1. Lise (a étudié / étudiait) toujours avec ses amis.
2. Maman (a fait / faisait) du yoga hier.
3. Ma grand-mère (passait / a passé) par là tous les jours.
4. D'habitude, ils (arrivaient / sont arrivés) toujours en retard.
5. Tout à coup, le professeur (entrait / est entré) dans la classe.
6. Ce matin, Camille (a lavé / lavait) le chien.

Essayez! Give the following items as additional practice:
9. Autrefois, Nathan (a amené / amenait) sa sœur au cours de danse. (amenait) 10. Je/J' (ai parlé / parlais) deux fois à ma cousine la semaine dernière. (ai parlé) 11. Parfois, nous (faisions / avons fait) une randonnée en montagne. (faisions) 12. Elle (voyait / a vu) mes parents une fois à la mairie. (a vu)

1 Expansion Have students redo this activity, this time coming up with their own explanations for why Sabine did or did not do the activities.

2 Suggestion Have students come up with different sentences using the same illustrations.

3 Suggestion Have students compare their answers with a partner's. For sentences where their answers differ, they should explain why they chose the **passé composé** or the **imparfait** and decide which tense is appropriate.

4 Expansion Have the students do the activity reframing the questions in the negative and asking why their partner did not do those activities. Example: **Pourquoi est-ce que tu n'es pas allé(e) en boîte de nuit?**

5 Suggestion Have students do questions 1, 2, 3, 6, 7, and 8 as a survey by circulating around the classroom and interviewing at least five classmates. Have them tabulate the responses of each classmate in a chart and see how similar or different the responses were.

6 Suggestion This activity can be done either orally or in writing.

OPTIONS

Extra Practice Divide the class into teams. Make a list of all the adverbs or expressions that signal a past tense. As you read out each expression, a member from each team should come to the board and write a sentence in the past using that expression. The team that completes a correct sentence first gets a point.

Small Groups Have students work in small groups to discuss their favorite movie or book. Students should use appropriate past tense forms to describe the main characters and give a brief summary of the plot. Encourage students to ask their classmates questions about the film or text.

Instructional Resources
espaces.vhlcentral.com: Testing Program, pp. 57–60; Test Files; Testing Program MP3s; activities; downloads; reference tools
Test Generator

1 Expansion Have students add an adjective to each object they ask about. Example: **Je cherche mes nouvelles baskets. Où sont-elles? Je cherche mon pull jaune. Où est-il?**

2 Expansion You can expand this activity by having students do this in groups of three or four where one student plays the role of the detective and the others are possible witnesses who all claim to have seen the suspects. When questioned, the witnesses give the detective conflicting information about the suspects.

3 Suggestion As the students take turns being the interviewer and interviewee, have one of them answer the questions as if he or she had a wonderful vacation, the house was lovely, the weather was great, and everything went well while the other person had a negative experience where nothing was satisfactory.

4 Expansion Expand this activity by showing the class an **avant** and **après** picture of a person or place in a magazine. Divide the students into two groups. Have one group describe the person or place in the before picture. Have the other group describe the after picture using the present tense.

5 Suggestion Remind students that the floors are counted differently in France than in the U.S. The first floor in the U.S. would be the **rez-de-chaussée** in France while the second floor would be the **premier étage**. Ask students if they know other countries which refer to floors in the same way as the French do.

Révision

1 Mes affaires Vous cherchez vos affaires (*belongings*). À tour de rôle, demandez de l'aide à votre partenaire. Où étaient-elles pour la dernière fois? Utilisez l'illustration pour les trouver. Answers will vary.

MODÈLE

Étudiant(e) 1: *Je cherche mes baskets. Où sont-elles?*
Étudiant(e) 2: *Tu n'as pas cherché sur l'étagère? Elles étaient sur l'étagère.*

baskets	ordinateur
casquette	parapluie
journal	pull
livre	sac à dos

2 Un bon témoin Il y a eu un cambriolage (*burglary*) chez votre voisin M. Cachetout. Le détective vous interroge parce que vous avez vu deux personnes suspectes sortir de la maison du voisin. Avec un(e) partenaire, créez ce dialogue et jouez cette scène devant la classe. Utilisez ces éléments dans votre scène. Answers will vary.

- une description physique des suspects
- leurs attitudes
- leurs vêtements
- ce que (*what*) vous faisiez quand vous avez vu les suspects

MODÈLE

Étudiant(e) 1: *À quelle heure est-ce que vous avez vu les deux personnes sortir?*
Étudiant(e) 2: *À dix heures. Ils sont sortis du garage.*

3 Quel séjour! Le magazine *Campagne décoration* a eu un concours le mois dernier et vous avez gagné le prix, une semaine de vacances dans une maison à la campagne en France. Vous venez de retourner de (*just came back from*) vos vacances et vous donnez une interview à propos de (*about*) votre séjour. Avec un(e) partenaire, à tour de rôle, posez-vous des questions sur la maison, le temps, les activités dans la région et votre opinion de ces vacances en général. Utilisez l'imparfait et le passé composé. Answers will vary.

MODÈLE

Étudiant(e) 1: *Combien de pièces y avait-il dans cette maison?*
Étudiant(e) 2: *Il y avait six pièces dans la maison.*

4 Avant et après Voici la chambre d'Annette avant et après une visite de sa mère. Comment était sa chambre à l'origine? Avec un(e) partenaire, décrivez la pièce à tour de rôle et cherchez les différences entre les deux illustrations. Answers will vary.

MODÈLE

Avant, la lampe était à côté de l'ordinateur. Maintenant, elle est à côté du canapé.

5 La maison de mon enfance Décrivez l'appartement ou la maison de votre enfance à un(e) partenaire. Où se trouvait-il/elle? Combien de pièces y avait-il? Comment étaient-elles orientées? Y avait-il une piscine, un sous-sol? Qui vivait avec vous dans cet appartement ou cette maison? Racontez (*Tell*) des anecdotes. Donnez beaucoup de détails. Answers will vary.

MODÈLE

Ma maison se trouvait au bord de la mer. C'était une maison à deux étages (floors). Au rez-de-chaussée, il y avait...

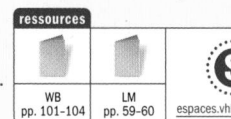

ressources
WB pp. 101-104 | LM pp. 59-60 | espaces.vhlcentral.com

OPTIONS

Pairs Have students work in pairs to draw the floor plan of their dream home on a sheet of paper or cardboard. Have them cut out the floor plan into pieces by individual rooms. Then have them give these pieces to their partner who will reassemble the floor plan based on their description of the house.

Extra Practice Have small groups organize a skit about a birthday or other party that took place recently. Guide them to first make general comments about the party, such as **C'était vraiment amusant!** Then describe a few specific things that were going on, what people were talking about, what they were wearing, and what happened. After the skits are performed, have students vote on their favorite one.

Video: TV Clip

Le Zapping

NATIONAL STANDARDS communication cultures

NATIONAL STANDARDS connections communities

Century 21 France

La société immobilière° Century 21 France commence ses opérations en 1987. Ses agences franchisées ont bientôt un grand succès, et Century 21 devient° une des principales sociétés immobilières de France. Cette société est connue° pour son marketing innovateur, qui diffuse à la télévision et sur Internet des publicités° d'un humour contemporain et parfois hors norme°. Century 21 France crée, par exemple, une campagne publicitaire pour montrer les risques de ne pas utiliser un agent immobilier quand on vend ou quand on achète une maison.

Century 21
L'IMMOBILIER, C'EST PLUS SIMPLE AVEC UN AGENT IMMOBILIER
www.century21france.fr

—Alors, d'abord le salon...

—Des pièces, des pièces, des pièces...

Compréhension Répondez aux questions. Some answers will vary.

1. Quelles pièces le propriétaire de l'appartement montre-t-il au couple? Il leur montre le salon, la chambre et les toilettes.
2. Comment est sa description de l'appartement? Elle est trop courte et superficielle.
3. Que ne mentionne-t-il pas du tout? Sample answer: Il ne parle pas du tout de la cuisine.

Discussion Par groupes de trois, répondez aux questions et discutez. Answers will vary.

1. Un agent immobilier est-il vraiment nécessaire pour vendre ou acheter une maison? Pourquoi?
2. Jouez les rôles d'un agent immobilier très compétent qui montre une maison à deux clients. Quelles pièces montrez-vous? Quels détails donnez-vous? Jouez la scène devant la classe.

société immobilière *real estate company* **devient** *becomes*
connue *known* **publicités** *ads* **hors norme** *unconventional*

Practice more at **espaces.vhlcentral.com.**

Section Goals

In this section, students will:

- read about the real estate franchise Century 21 France
- watch a commercial for the franchise
- answer questions about the commercial and Century 21 France

Instructional Resources
*espaces.vhlcentral.com: TV commercial; IRM (**Le zapping** TV clip transcription); activities; downloads; reference tools*

Introduction
To check comprehension, ask these questions:
1. Où trouve-t-on les agences Century 21 France? (On les trouve en France, en Suisse et à Monaco.)
2. Comment sont les publicités de la société immobilière? (Elles sont d'un humour contemporain.)
3. Que montre une de ses campagnes publicitaires? (Elle montre les risques de ne pas utiliser un agent immobilier.)

Avant de regarder la vidéo

- Have students look at the video stills, read the captions, and predict what is happening in the commercial for each visual. **(1. Les clients sont dans l'appartement avec le propriétaire. Il leur montre le salon. 2. Les clients sont dans le couloir avec le propriétaire. Ils n'entrent pas dans toutes les pièces.)**
- Before showing the video, explain to students that they do not need to understand every word they hear. Tell them to listen for the text in the captions, cognates, and house-related vocabulary.

Compréhension Have students work in pairs or groups for this activity. Tell them to write their answers. Then show the video again so that they can check their answers and add any missing information.

Discussion After students watch each role-play, ask them to say what the competent real estate agent did right.

OPTIONS

Pierre Palmade French actor and comedian Pierre Palmade plays the owner of the apartment in this Century 21 France commercial. Born in Bordeaux in 1968, Palmade moved to Paris at 19 to launch his career as a stand-up comic. Soon he was appearing on television with other well-known comics, among them the now popular Michèle Laroque. However, it was his first co-writing experience with comic Muriel Robin that not only forged a strong professional and personal friendship between them, but also led to their collaboration on multiple other projects and helped secure his celebrity status. Although Palmade has starred in a few films, most of his creative output has involved writing material for other actors. Today he is an enormously popular comedian known for playing unpleasant characters.

Section Goals

In this section, students will learn and practice vocabulary related to:
- household chores
- home appliances

Instructional Resources
*espaces.vhlcentral.com: Transparency #38; IRM (**Vocabulaire supplémentaire**; **Mise en pratique** answers; Textbook Audioscript; Lab Audioscript; **Feuilles d'activités**); Textbook MP3s; Lab MP3s; WB/VM/LM Answer Key; activities; downloads; reference tools*

Suggestions

- Use **Transparency #38.** Point out appliances and talk about what people in the illustration are doing. Examples: **Ça, c'est un four à micro-ondes. Cette femme balaie.**
- Ask students questions about chores using the new vocabulary. Examples: **Préférez-vous balayer ou passer l'aspirateur? Faire la cuisine ou faire la lessive? Mettre la table ou sortir la poubelle?**
- Say vocabulary words and tell students to write or say the opposite terms. Examples: **sale (propre), débarrasser la table (mettre la table),** and **salir les vêtements (faire la lessive).**
- Point out the difference between **un évier** (*kitchen sink*) and **un lavabo** (*bathroom sink*).
- Point out the expressions that use **faire**: **faire la lessive, faire la poussière, faire le ménage, faire le lit,** and **faire la vaisselle**.
- Tell students that the names of several appliances are compounds of verbs and nouns. Examples: **grille-pain, lave-vaisselle,** and **sèche-linge**. Other appliances use the preposition **à**: **un fer à repasser, un four à micro-ondes.**
- Additional vocabulary for this lesson can be found in the **Vocabulaire supplémentaire** on the Supersite.

Leçon 8B

You will learn how to...
- talk about chores
- talk about appliances

S Talking Picture
Audio: Activity

Les tâches ménagères

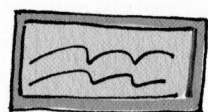

Vocabulaire

débarrasser la table	*to clear the table*
enlever/faire la poussière	*to dust*
essuyer la vaisselle/ la table	*to dry the dishes/ to wipe the table*
faire la lessive	*to do the laundry*
faire le ménage	*to do the housework*
laver	*to wash*
mettre la table	*to set the table*
passer l'aspirateur	*to vacuum*
ranger	*to tidy up; to put away*
salir	*to soil, to make dirty*
propre	*clean*
sale	*dirty*
un appareil électrique/ ménager	*electrical/household appliance*
une cafetière	*coffeemaker*
une cuisinière	*stove; female cook*
un grille-pain	*toaster*
un lave-linge	*washing machine*
un lave-vaisselle	*dishwasher*
un sèche-linge	*clothes dryer*
une tâche ménagère	*household chore*

ressources
WB pp. 105-106
LM p. 61
espaces.vhlcentral.com

OPTIONS

Game Write vocabulary words for appliances on index cards. On another set of cards, draw or paste pictures to match each term. Tape them face down on the board in random order. Divide the class into two teams. Then play a game of Concentration in which students match words with pictures. When a player has a match, that player's team collects those cards. When all the cards have been matched, the team with the most cards wins.

Extra Practice Ask students what chores they do in various rooms. Examples: **Dans quelle pièce... faites-vous la vaisselle? faites-vous le lit? mettez-vous la table? passez-vous l'aspirateur? repassez-vous? balayez-vous?**

Mise en pratique

1 On fait le ménage Complétez les phrases avec le bon mot.

1. On balaie avec un balai.
2. On repasse le linge avec un fer à repasser.
3. On fait la lessive avec un lave-linge.
4. On lave la vaisselle avec un lave-vaisselle.
5. On prépare le café avec une cafetière.
6. On sèche les vêtements avec un sèche-linge.
7. On met la glace dans un congélateur.
8. Pour faire le lit, on doit arranger les draps, la couverture et l'oreiller/les oreillers.

2 Écoutez Écoutez la conversation téléphonique (*phone call*) entre Édouard, un étudiant, et un conseiller (*radio psychologist*) à la radio. Ensuite, indiquez les tâches ménagères que faisaient Édouard et Paul au début du semestre.

	Édouard	Paul
1. Il faisait la cuisine.	☑	☐
2. Il faisait les lits.	☐	☑
3. Il passait l'aspirateur.	☑	☐
4. Il sortait la poubelle.	☐	☑
5. Il balayait.	☐	☑
6. Il faisait la lessive.	☑	☐
7. Il faisait la vaisselle.	☐	☑
8. Il nettoyait le frigo.	☑	☐

3 Les tâches ménagères Avec un(e) partenaire, indiquez quelles tâches ménagères vous faites dans chaque pièce ou partie de votre logement. Il y a plus d'une réponse possible. Answers will vary.

1. La chambre: ____
2. La cuisine: ____
3. La salle de bains: ____
4. La salle à manger: ____
5. La salle de séjour: ____
6. Le garage: ____

Practice more at **espaces.vhlcentral.com.**

1 Expansion Reverse this activity and ask students what each appliance is used for. Example: **Que fait-on avec une cuisinière? (On fait la cuisine.)**

2 Tapescript J'ai un problème avec Paul, mon colocataire, parce qu'il ne m'aide pas à faire le ménage. Quand le semestre a commencé, il faisait la vaisselle, il sortait la poubelle et il balayait. Parfois, il faisait même mon lit. Paul ne faisait jamais la cuisine parce qu'il détestait ça, c'est moi qui la faisais. Je faisais aussi la lessive, je passais l'aspirateur et je nettoyais le frigo. Maintenant, Paul ne fait jamais son lit et il ne m'aide pas. C'est moi qui fais tout. Qu'est-ce que vous me suggérez de faire?
(On Textbook MP3s)

2 Suggestion After listening to the recording, have students identify Paul and Édouard in the photo and describe what they are doing.

2 Expansion Have students describe how they share household chores with their roommate(s) or others in their household.

3 Suggestion Have students get together with another pair and compare their answers.

OPTIONS

Extra Practice Have students complete these analogies.

1. passer l'aspirateur : tapis / lave-vaisselle : ____ (verre/tasse)
2. chaud : froid / cuisinière : ____ (congélateur)
3. ordinateur : bureau / armoire : ____ (chambre)
4. tasse : cuisine / voiture : ____ (garage)
5. café : cafetière / pain : ____ (grille-pain)
6. mauvais : bon / sale : ____ (propre)
7. chaud : four à micro-ondes / froid : ____ (frigo/congélateur)
8. arriver : partir / nettoyer : ____ (salir)
9. table : verre / lit : ____ (draps/couverture/oreiller(s))

4 Suggestion Distribute the **Feuilles d'activités** found on the Supersite. Have two volunteers read the **modèle**.

5 Suggestion Have students jot down notes during their interviews. Then ask them to report what they learned about their partner.

5 Expansion Take a quick survey about household chores using items 4 and 6. Tally the results on the board.

6 Suggestion Before beginning this activity, have students brainstorm desirable and undesirable qualities or habits of roommates. Write a list on the board.

7 Suggestion Have students exchange paragraphs for peer editing. Tell them to underline, rather than correct, grammar and spelling errors.

Communication

4 Qui fait quoi? Votre professeur va vous donner une feuille d'activités. Dites si vous faites les tâches indiquées en écrivant (*by writing*) **Oui** ou **Non** dans la première colonne. Ensuite, posez des questions à vos camarades de classe; écrivez leur nom dans la deuxième colonne quand ils répondent **Oui**. Présentez vos réponses à la classe. Answers will vary.

MODÈLE

mettre la table pour prendre le petit-déjeuner
Étudiant(e) 1: *Est-ce que tu mets la table pour prendre le petit-déjeuner?*
Étudiant(e) 2: *Oui, je mets la table chaque matin./ Non, je prends le petit-déjeuner au resto U, donc je ne mets pas la table.*

Activités	Moi	Mes camarades de classe
1. mettre la table pour prendre le petit-déjeuner		
2. passer l'aspirateur tous les jours		
3. salir ses vêtements quand on mange		
4. nettoyer les toilettes		
5. balayer la cuisine		
6. débarrasser la table après le dîner		
7. souvent enlever la poussière sur son ordinateur		
8. laver les vitres (*windows*)		

5 Conversez Interviewez un(e) camarade de classe. Answers will vary.

1. Qui fait la vaisselle chez toi?
2. Qui fait la lessive chez toi?
3. Fais-tu ton lit tous les jours?
4. Quelles tâches ménagères as-tu faites le week-end dernier?
5. Repasses-tu tous tes vêtements?
6. Quelles tâches ménagères détestes-tu faire?
7. Quels appareils électriques as-tu chez toi?
8. Ranges-tu souvent ta chambre?

6 Camarade de chambre Vous cherchez un(e) camarade de chambre pour votre appartement et deux personnes ont répondu à votre petite annonce (*ad*) dans le journal. Travaillez avec deux camarades de classe et préparez un dialogue dans lequel (*in which*) vous: Answers will vary.

- parlez des tâches ménagères que vous détestez/aimez faire.
- parlez des responsabilités de votre nouveau/nouvelle camarade de chambre.
- parlez de vos passions et de vos habitudes.
- décidez quelle est la personne qui vous convient le mieux (*suits you best*).

7 Écrivez L'appartement de Martine est un désastre: la cuisine est sale et comme vous pouvez (*can*) l'imaginer, le reste de l'appartement est encore pire (*worse*). Préparez un paragraphe où vous décrivez les problèmes que vous voyez (*see*) et que vous imaginez. Ensuite, écrivez la liste des tâches que Martine va faire pour tout nettoyer. Answers will vary.

OPTIONS

Small Groups Have groups of three write riddles about furnishings or appliances. For each riddle, the group comes up with at least three hints. Example: **Je suis très doux. On me met sur le lit. Je vous aide à bien dormir. (Je suis un oreiller.)** Ask them to read their riddles to the class, who will guess the answer.

Extra Practice Have students complete this paragraph. **L'appartement de Roger est un désastre. Il a rarement le temps de faire le ____ (ménage). Il ____ (passe) l'aspirateur une fois par semestre et il ne/n'____ (fait/enlève) pas la poussière. Il y a des tasses et des verres dans l'____ (évier) parce qu'il oublie de les mettre dans le ____ (lave-vaisselle). L'appartement sent mauvais parce qu'il ne sort pas la ____ (poubelle).**

Les sons et les lettres

Audio: Concepts, Activities
Record & Compare

National Standards: comparisons

Semi-vowels

French has three semi-vowels. Semi-vowels are sounds that are produced in much the same way as vowels, but also have many properties in common with consonants. Semi-vowels are also sometimes referred to as *glides* because they glide from or into the vowel they accompany.

Lucien **chien** **soif** **nuit**

The semi-vowel that occurs in the word **bien** is very much like the *y* in the English word *yes*. It is usually spelled with an **i** or a **y** (pronounced *ee*), then glides into the following sound. This semi-vowel sound is also produced when **ll** follows an **i**.

nation **balayer** **bien** **brillant**

The semi-vowel that occurs in the word **soif** is like the *w* in the English words *was* and *we*. It usually begins with **o** or **ou**, then glides into the following vowel.

trois **froid** **oui** **ouistiti**

The third semi-vowel sound occurs in the word **nuit**. It is spelled with the vowel **u**, as in the French word **tu**, then glides into the following sound.

lui **suis** **cruel** **intellectuel**

Prononcez Répétez les mots suivants à voix haute.

1. oui
2. taille
3. suisse
4. fille
5. mois
6. cruel
7. minuit
8. jouer
9. cuisine
10. juillet
11. échouer
12. croissant

Articulez Répétez les phrases suivantes à voix haute.

1. Voici trois poissons noirs.
2. Louis et sa famille sont suisses.
3. Parfois, Grégoire fait de la cuisine chinoise.
4. Aujourd'hui, Matthieu et Damien vont travailler.
5. Françoise a besoin de faire ses devoirs d'histoire.
6. La fille de Monsieur Poirot va conduire pour la première fois.

Dictons Répétez les dictons à voix haute.

Vouloir, c'est pouvoir.[2]

La nuit, tous les chats sont gris.[1]

[1] All cats are *gray* in the dark.
[2] Where there's a will, there's a way.

ressources
LM p. 62
espaces.vhlcentral.com

Section Goals

In this section, students will learn about semi-vowels.

Instructional Resources
espaces.vhlcentral.com: Textbook MP3s; Lab MP3s; WB/VM/LM Answer Key; IRM (Textbook Audioscript; Lab Audioscript); activities; downloads; reference tools

Suggestions

- Model the pronunciation of the example words and have students repeat them after you.
- Ask students to provide more examples of words from this lesson or previous lessons with these sounds. Examples: **balayer, essuyer,** and **évier**.
- Dictate five familiar words containing semi-vowels, repeating each one at least two times. Then write them on the board or on a transparency and have students check their spelling.
- Remind students that many vowels combine to make a single sound with no glide. Examples: **ai** and **ou**.
- Explain that **un ouistiti** is a marmoset.

OPTIONS

Extra Practice Use these sentences with semi-vowels for additional practice or dictation. **1. Nous balayons bien la cuisine. 2. J'ai soif, mais tu as froid. 3. Une fois, ma fille a oublié son parapluie. 4. Parfois, mon chien aime jouer entre minuit et trois heures du matin.**

Extra Practice Teach students these French tongue-twisters that contain semi-vowels. **1. Trois petites truites non cuites, trois petites truites crues. 2. Une bête noire se baigne dans une baignoire noire.**

Section Goals

In this section, students will learn functional phrases for talking about who and what they know.

Instructional Resources
espaces.vhlcentral.com: Video; WB/VM/LM Answer Key; IRM (Videoscript; ***Roman-photo*** *Translations); activities; downloads; reference tools*
Video on DVD

Video Recap: Leçon 8A
Before doing this **Roman-photo**, review the previous one with this activity.
1. Qui a fait une visite surprise à Aix-en-Provence? (Pascal)
2. Combien de pièces y a-t-il chez Sandrine? (trois)
3. Comment est l'appartement de Sandrine? (grand et beau)
4. Comment est l'appartement de Rachid et David? (petit, pas de décorations et pas beaucoup de meubles)
5. Que pense Sandrine de la visite surprise de Pascal? (Elle n'est pas contente.)

Video Synopsis
At the café, Amina talks to Sandrine on the phone. Valérie questions Stéphane about his chores and reminds him to do the dishes before he leaves. Amina arrives at Sandrine's. As Sandrine is baking cookies, she breaks a plate. The two girls talk about how annoying Pascal is. Sandrine asks if Amina plans to meet Cyberhomme in person. Amina is not sure that's a good idea.

Suggestions
- Have students predict what the episode will be about based on the title and video stills.
- Have students scan the **Roman-photo** and find sentences related to chores.
- After reading the captions, review students' predictions.

NATIONAL STANDARDS communication cultures

La vie sans Pascal

S Video: *Roman-photo* Record & Compare

PERSONNAGES

Amina

Michèle

Sandrine

Stéphane

Valérie

Au P'tit Bistrot...
MICHÈLE Tout va bien, Amina?
AMINA Oui, ça va, merci. (*Au téléphone*) Allô?... Qu'est-ce qu'il y a, Sandrine?... Non, je ne le savais pas, mais franchement, ça ne me surprend pas... Écoute, j'arrive chez toi dans quinze minutes, d'accord? ... À tout à l'heure!

MICHÈLE Je débarrasse la table?
AMINA Oui, merci, et apporte-moi l'addition, s'il te plaît.
MICHÈLE Tout de suite.

VALÉRIE Tu as fait ton lit, ce matin?
STÉPHANE Oui, maman.
VALÉRIE Est-ce que tu as rangé ta chambre?
STÉPHANE Euh... oui, ce matin, pendant que tu faisais la lessive.

Chez Sandrine...
SANDRINE Salut, Amina! Merci d'être venue.
AMINA Mmmm. Qu'est-ce qui sent si bon?
SANDRINE Il y a des biscuits au chocolat dans le four.
AMINA Oh, est-ce que tu les préparais quand tu m'as téléphoné?

SANDRINE Tu as soif?
AMINA Un peu, oui.
SANDRINE Sers-toi, j'ai des jus de fruits au frigo.

Sandrine casse () une assiette.
SANDRINE Et zut!
AMINA Ça va, Sandrine?
SANDRINE Oui, oui... passe-moi le balai, s'il te plaît.
AMINA N'oublie pas de balayer sous la cuisinière.
SANDRINE Je sais! Excuse-moi, Amina. Comme je t'ai dit au téléphone, Pascal et moi, c'est fini.

ACTIVITÉS

1 Questions **Répondez aux questions par des phrases complètes.** Answers may vary slightly.

1. Avec qui Amina parle-t-elle au téléphone? Elle parle avec Sandrine.
2. Comment va Sandrine aujourd'hui? Pourquoi? Elle est de mauvaise humeur parce que c'est fini avec Pascal.
3. Est-ce que Stéphane a fait toutes ses tâches ménagères? Non, il n'a pas fait toutes ses tâches ménagères.
4. Qu'est-ce que Sandrine préparait quand elle a téléphoné à Amina? Elle préparait des biscuits au chocolat.
5. Amina a faim et a soif. À votre avis (*opinion*), que va-t-elle prendre? Elle va prendre un jus de fruits et elle va manger des biscuits.
6. Pourquoi Amina n'est-elle pas fâchée (*angry*) contre Sandrine? Elle comprend pourquoi Sandrine est un peu triste/de mauvaise humeur.
7. Pourquoi Amina pense-t-elle que Sandrine aimerait (*would like*) un cyberhomme américain? Amina pense que Sandrine aime David.
8. Sandrine pense qu'Amina devrait (*should*) rencontrer Cyberhomme, mais Amina pense que ce n'est pas une bonne idée. À votre avis, qui a raison? Answers will vary.

OPTIONS

Avant de regarder la vidéo Before playing the video, show students individual photos from the **Roman-photo**, #5 or #8 for example, and have them write their own captions. Ask volunteers to write their captions on the board.

Regarder la vidéo Download and print the videoscript found on the Supersite, then white out words related to household chores and other key vocabulary in order to create a master for a cloze activity. Distribute photocopies and tell students to fill in the missing information as they watch the video episode.

Amina console Sandrine.

VALÉRIE Hmm... et la vaisselle? Tu as fait la vaisselle?
STÉPHANE Non, pas encore, mais...
MICHÈLE Il me faut l'addition pour Amina.
VALÉRIE Stéphane, tu dois faire la vaisselle avant de sortir.
STÉPHANE Bon, ça va, j'y vais!

VALÉRIE Ah, Michèle, il faut sortir les poubelles pour ce soir!
MICHÈLE Oui, comptez sur moi, Madame Forestier.
VALÉRIE Très bien! Moi, je rentre, il est l'heure de préparer le dîner.

SANDRINE Il était tellement pénible. Bref, je suis de mauvaise humeur aujourd'hui.
AMINA Ne t'en fais pas, je comprends.
SANDRINE Toi, tu as de la chance.
AMINA Pourquoi tu dis ça?
SANDRINE Tu as ton Cyberhomme. Tu vas le rencontrer un de ces jours?
AMINA Oh... Je ne sais pas si c'est une bonne idée.

SANDRINE Pourquoi pas?
AMINA Sandrine, il faut être prudent dans la vie, je ne le connais pas vraiment, tu sais.
SANDRINE Comme d'habitude, tu as raison. Mais finalement, un cyberhomme, c'est peut-être mieux qu'un petit ami. Ou alors, un petit ami artistique, charmant et beau garçon.
AMINA Et américain?

Expressions utiles

Talking about what you know

- **Je ne le savais pas, mais franchement, ça ne me surprend pas.**
  I didn't know that, but frankly, I'm not surprised.
- **Je sais!**
  I know!
- **Je ne sais pas si c'est une bonne idée.**
  I don't know if that's a good idea.
- **Je ne le connais pas vraiment, tu sais.**
  I don't really know him, you know.

Additional vocabulary

- **Comptez sur moi.**
  Count on me.
- **Ne t'en fais pas.**
  Don't worry about it.
- **J'y vais!**
  I'm going there!/I'm on my way!
- **pas encore**
  not yet
- **tu dois**
  you must
- **être de bonne/mauvaise humeur**
  to be in a good/bad mood

ACTIVITÉS

2 Le ménage Indiquez qui a fait ou va faire ces tâches ménagères: Amina (A), Michèle (M), Sandrine (S), Stéphane (St), Valérie (V) ou personne (*no one*) (P).

1. sortir la poubelle M
2. balayer S & A
3. passer l'aspirateur P
4. faire la vaisselle St
5. faire le lit St
6. débarrasser la table M
7. faire la lessive V
8. ranger sa chambre St

Practice more at **espaces.vhlcentral.com.**

3 Écrivez Vous avez gagné un pari (*bet*) avec votre colocataire et il/elle doit faire (*must do*) en conséquence toutes les tâches ménagères que vous lui indiquez pendant un mois. Écrivez une liste de dix tâches minimum. Pour chaque tâche, précisez la pièce du logement et combien de fois par semaine il/elle doit l'exécuter.

ressources: VM pp. 241-242 | DVD Leçon 8B | espaces.vhlcentral.com

Expressions utiles

- Model the pronunciation of the **Expressions utiles** and have students repeat them.
- As you work through the list, point out the forms of **savoir** and **connaître**. See if students can discern the difference in meaning between the two verbs from the example sentences. Respond briefly to their questions, but tell them that these verbs will be formally presented in **Espace structures 8B.2**.

1 Suggestion Have volunteers write their answers on the board. Go over them as a class.

2 Expansion Ask students who works the hardest of all these people. Have them support their opinion with details from this episode and previous ones.

3 Suggestion Have students use commands in their lists for review.

OPTIONS

Extra Practice Divide the class into two groups based on their answers to question 8 on page 272 (whether or not Amina should meet Cyberhomme) and have a debate about who is right. Tell groups to brainstorm a list of arguments to support their point of view and anticipate rebuttals for what the other team might say.

Pairs Have students work in pairs. Tell them to reread the last lines of the **Roman-photo** and write a short paragraph predicting what will happen in future episodes. Do they think Amina will meet Cyberhomme in person? What do they think will happen in Sandrine's love life? Have volunteers read their paragraphs to the class aloud.

NATIONAL STANDARDS connections cultures

Section Goals

In this section, students will:

- learn about the interior of French homes
- learn some colloquial terms for describing a home or room
- learn the names of some famous homes in the francophone world
- read about the French Quarter in New Orleans

Instructional Resources
espaces.vhlcentral.com: activities; downloads; reference tools

Culture à la loupe

Avant la lecture

- Have students look at the photos and describe what they see.
- Tell students to read the first sentence of the text. Then ask: **Quel est le sujet du texte?**

Lecture

- Point out the **Coup de main** and have two volunteers read the examples. Demonstrative pronouns will be presented in **Leçon 14A**.
- Point out the statistics chart. Ask students what information the chart shows. (the percentage of French residences that have the appliances listed)

Après la lecture Ask students: **Quelles sont les différences entre l'intérieur des logements français et l'intérieur des logements américains?**

1 Suggestion Go over the answers with the class.

CULTURE À LA LOUPE

L'intérieur des logements français

L'intérieur des maisons et des appartements français est assez° différent de celui des Américains. Quand on entre dans un immeuble ancien en France, on est dans un hall° où il y a des boîtes aux lettres°. Ensuite, il y a souvent une deuxième porte. Celle-ci conduit à° l'escalier. Il n'y a pas souvent d'ascenseur, mais s'il y en a un°, en général, il est très petit et il est au milieu de° l'escalier. Le hall de l'immeuble peut aussi avoir une porte qui donne sur une cour° ou un jardin, souvent derrière le bâtiment°.

À l'intérieur des logements, les pièces sont en général plus petites que° les pièces américaines, surtout les cuisines et les salles de bains. Dans la cuisine, on trouve tous les appareils ménagers nécessaires (cuisinière, four, four à micro-ondes, frigo), mais ils sont plus petits qu'aux États-Unis. Les lave-vaisselle sont assez rares dans les appartements et plus communs dans les maisons. On a souvent une seule° salle de bains et les toilettes sont en général dans une autre petite pièce séparée°. Les lave-linge sont aussi assez petits et on les trouve, en général, dans la cuisine ou dans la salle de bains. Dans les chambres, en France, il n'y a pas de grands placards et les vêtements sont rangés la plupart° du temps dans une armoire ou une commode. Les fenêtres s'ouvrent° sur l'intérieur, un peu comme des portes, et il est très rare d'avoir des moustiquaires°. Par contre°, il y a toujours des volets°.

assez *rather* **hall** *entryway* **boîtes aux lettres** *mailboxes* **conduit à** *leads to* **s'il y en a un** *if there is one* **au milieu de** *in the middle of* **cour** *courtyard* **bâtiment** *building* **plus petites que** *smaller than* **une seule** *only one* **séparée** *separate* **la plupart** *most* **s'ouvrent** *open* **moustiquaires** *screens* **Par contre** *On the other hand* **volets** *shutters*

Combien de logements ont ces appareils ménagers?

Réfrigérateur	96%
Lave-linge	95%
Cuisinière/Four	94%
Four à micro-ondes	72%
Congélateur	55%
Lave-vaisselle	45%
Sèche-linge	27%

SOURCE: GIFAM/Francoscopie

Coup de main

Demonstrative pronouns help to avoid repetition.

	S.	P.
M.	**celui**	**ceux**
F.	**celle**	**celles**

Ce lit est grand, mais le lit de Monique est petit.

Ce lit est grand, mais celui de Monique est petit.

ACTIVITÉS

1 Complétez Complétez chaque phrase logiquement.
Answers will vary. Possible answers provided.

1. Dans le hall d'un immeuble français, on trouve... des boîtes aux lettres et des portes.
2. Au milieu de l'escalier, dans les vieux immeubles français, ... il y a parfois un ascenseur.
3. Derrière les vieux immeubles, on trouve souvent... une cour ou un jardin.
4. Les cuisines et les salles de bains françaises sont... assez petites.
5. Dans les appartements français, il est assez rare d'avoir... un lave-vaisselle.
6. Les logements français ont souvent une seule... salle de bains.
7. En France, les toilettes sont souvent... dans une pièce séparée.
8. Les Français rangent souvent leurs vêtements dans une armoire parce qu'ils... n'ont pas souvent de placards.
9. On trouve souvent le lave-linge... dans la cuisine ou dans la salle de bains.
10. En général, les fenêtres dans les logements français... ont des volets.

OPTIONS

Cultural Comparison Take a quick class survey to find out how many students have the appliances listed in the chart in their homes. Tally the results on the board and have students calculate the percentages. Example: **Combien de personnes ont un réfrigérateur à la maison?** Then have students compare the results of this survey with those in the chart. Examples: **Plus d'Américains ont un sèche-linge dans leur maison./Moins de Français ont un sèche-linge dans leur maison.**

LE FRANÇAIS QUOTIDIEN

Quelles conditions!

boxon (*m.*)	*shambles*
gourbis (*m.*)	*pigsty*
piaule (*f.*)	*pad, room*
souk (*m.*)	*mess*
impeccable	*spic-and-span*
ringard	*cheesy, old-fashioned*
crécher	*to live*
semer la pagaille	*to make a mess*

LE MONDE FRANCOPHONE

Résidences célèbres

Voici quelques résidences célèbres.

En France

l'hôtel Matignon la résidence du Premier ministre°

Au Maroc

le Palais royal de Rabat la résidence du roi° et de sa famille

À la Martinique

la Pagerie la maison natale° de Joséphine de Beauharnais (femme de Napoléon Bonaparte)

À Monaco

le Palais du Prince la résidence de la famille princière° de Monaco (la famille Grimaldi)

Au Sénégal

le Palais présidentiel de Dakar la résidence du président du Sénégal, dans un jardin tropical

Premier ministre *Prime Minister* **roi** *king* **la maison natale** *birthplace* **la famille princière** *the prince and his family*

PORTRAIT

Le Vieux Carré

Le Quartier Français, ou Vieux Carré, est le centre historique de la Nouvelle-Orléans. Il est connu pour sa culture créole, sa vie nocturne°, sa musique et sa fameuse «joie de vivre». Beaucoup de visiteurs viennent° participer à ses fêtes, comme le carnaval de Mardi Gras ou le festival de jazz, en avril. Ils aiment aussi admirer ses nombreux bâtiments° classés monuments historiques, comme le Cabildo ou la cathédrale Saint-Louis, la plus vieille° cathédrale des États-Unis. On ne doit pas quitter le Vieux Carré sans avoir exploré les jardins et les patios cachés° de ses vieilles maisons de planteurs.

vie nocturne *night life* **viennent** *come* **bâtiments** *buildings* **la plus vieille** *the oldest* **cachés** *hidden*

SUR INTERNET

Qu'est-ce qu'on peut voir (see) au musée des Arts décoratifs de Paris?

Go to **espaces.vhlcentral.com** to find more information related to this **ESPACE CULTURE**.

ACTIVITÉS

2 Complétez Complétez les phrases.

1. Le Vieux Carré est le centre historique de la Nouvelle-Orléans.
2. Il est connu pour sa culture créole, sa vie nocturne, sa musique et sa «joie de vivre».
3. Dans le Vieux Carré, il faut explorer les jardins et les patios cachés des vieilles maisons de planteurs.
4. Les Grimaldi habitent dans le Palais du Prince à Monaco.
5. L'hôtel Matignon est la résidence du Premier ministre français.
6. L'impératrice Joséphine est née à la Pagerie, à la Martinique.

Practice more at **espaces.vhlcentral.com.**

3 C'est le souk! Vos parents viennent vous rendre visite ce soir et votre colocataire a semé la pagaille dans tout l'appartement. C'est le souk! Avec un(e) partenaire, inventez une conversation où vous lui donnez des ordres pour nettoyer avant l'arrivée de vos parents. Jouez la scène devant la classe.

ressources

espaces.vhlcentral.com

Le français quotidien
- Model the pronunciation of each term and have students repeat it.
- Have volunteers create sentences using these words.

Portrait Ask students: **Que désirez-vous faire ou visiter dans le Vieux Carré de la Nouvelle-Orléans?**

Le monde francophone
- Bring in photos from magazines, books, or the Internet of these famous homes to show the class.
- Ask a few content questions based on the text. Examples: **1. Où est le Palais du Prince? (à Monaco) 2. Où habite le Premier ministre de la France? (à l'hôtel Matignon) 3. Qui habite le Palais du Prince? (la famille princière de Monaco) 4. Comment s'appelle la maison natale de la femme de Napoléon? (la Pagerie)**

2 Expansion For additional practice, give students these items. **7. ____ sont deux fêtes célèbres à la Nouvelle-Orléans. (Le carnaval de Mardi Gras et le festival de jazz) 8. Le palais du Cabildo est à ____. (la Nouvelle-Orléans) 9. Le roi du Maroc habite ____. (le Palais royal de Rabat)**

3 Suggestion Encourage students to use terms in **Le français quotidien** in their role-plays.

OPTIONS

Le Vieux Carré **Le Cabildo** was completed in 1799. The ceremonies finalizing the Louisiana Purchase were held there in 1803. Since 1903, it has been the Louisiana State Museum. The museum contains a number of objects from Napoleonic history. The present-day **cathédrale Saint-Louis** was completed in 1851. Made of bricks, the cathedral is dedicated to King Louis IX of France (1214–1270), who was canonized in 1297. His life is depicted in ten of the stained glass windows. This building is actually the third cathedral to occupy this site. The first cathedral was completed in 1727, but it burned down in 1788. The second was completed in 1794, but collapsed in 1849.

Section Goals

In this section, students will learn:

- to compare and contrast the uses and meanings of the **passé composé** and the **imparfait**
- common expressions indicating past tenses

Instructional Resources
*espaces.vhlcentral.com: Lab MP3s; WB/VM/LM Answer Key; IRM (**Essayez!** and **Mise en pratique** answers; Lab Audioscript); activities; downloads; reference tools*

Suggestions

- To practice contrasting the **passé composé** vs. the **imparfait**, first do a quick review of each tense and its uses. Then write the following sentences on the board: **1. Je vais au cinéma avec un ami. 2. Nous prenons le bus. 3. Après le film, nous mangeons au restaurant. 4. Ensuite, nous allons danser dans une boîte de nuit. 5. Nous rentrons tard à la maison.** Have students change the sentences above first to the **passé composé** and then to the **imparfait.** Have them add adverbs or expressions they've learned that signal a past tense wherever possible.
- As you are reviewing the **passé composé** vs. the **imparfait**, have students focus on the pronunciation of these tenses since it is very important to be able to distinguish between the respective sounds of the two tenses. You might have them practice the following sentences: **J'ai travaillé. / Je travaillais. Il parlait. / Il a parlé. Tu allais. / Tu es allé(e). Elle chantait. / Elle a chanté.** You could also add the present tense of these sentences and have them practice pronouncing all three tenses.
- Have students interview each other about their childhood activities using the following question: **Quand tu étais petit(e), qu'est-ce que tu faisais… a) après l'école? b) le week-end? c) pendant les grandes vacances** (*summer vacation*)?

NATIONAL STANDARDS comparisons

8B.1 The *passé composé* vs. the *imparfait* (Summary)

Point de départ You have learned the uses of the **passé composé** versus the **imparfait** to talk about things and events in the past. These tenses are distinct and are not used in the same way. Remember always to keep the context and the message you wish to convey in mind while deciding which tense to use.

Uses of the *passé composé*

To talk about events that happened at a specific moment or that took place for a precise duration in the past	Je **suis allé** au concert vendredi. *I went to the concert on Friday.*
To relate a sequence of events or tell about isolated actions that started and ended in the past and are completed from the speaker's viewpoint	Tu **as fait** le lit, tu **as sorti** la poubelle et tu **as mis** la table. *You made the bed, took out the trash, and set the table.*
To indicate a change in the mental, emotional or physical state of a person	Tout à coup, elle **a eu** soif. *Suddenly, she got thirsty.*
To narrate the facts in a story	Nous **avons passé** une journée fantastique à la plage. *We spent a fantastic day at the beach.*
To describe actions that move the plot forward in a narration	Soudain, Thomas **a trouvé** une photo dans l'eau. *Suddenly Thomas found a photograph in the water.*

Uses of the *imparfait*

To talk about actions that lasted for an unspecified duration of time	Elle **dormait** tranquillement. *She was sleeping peacefully.*
To relate events that occurred habitually or repeatedly in the past or tell how things used to be	Nous **faisions** une promenade au parc tous les dimanches matins. *We used to walk in the park every Sunday morning.*
To describe an ongoing mental, emotional or physical state of a person	Elle **avait** toujours soif. *She was always thirsty.*
To describe the background scene and setting of a story	Il **faisait** beau et le ciel **était** bleu. *The weather was nice and the sky was blue.*
To describe people and things	C'**était** une photo d'une jolie fille. *It was a photograph of a pretty girl.*

MISE EN PRATIQUE

1 À l'étranger! Racontez (*Tell*) cette histoire au passé en choisissant (*by choosing*) l'imparfait ou le passé composé.

Lise (1) avait (avoir) vraiment envie de travailler en France après l'université. Alors, un jour, elle (2) a quitté (quitter) son petit village près de Bruxelles et elle (3) a pris (prendre) le train pour Paris. Elle (4) est arrivée (arriver) à Paris. Elle (5) a trouvé (trouver) une chambre dans un petit hôtel. Pendant six mois, elle (6) a balayé (balayer) le couloir et (7) a nettoyé (nettoyer) les chambres. Au bout de (*After*) six mois, elle (8) a pris (prendre) des cours au Cordon Bleu et maintenant, elle est chef dans un petit restaurant!

2 Explique-moi! Dites pourquoi vos amis et vous n'avez pas fait les choses que vous deviez faire. Faites des phrases complètes en disant ce que (*by saying what*) vous n'avez pas fait au passé composé et en donnant (*by giving*) la raison à l'imparfait.

MODÈLE Élise / étudier / avoir sommeil
Élise n'a pas étudié parce qu'elle avait sommeil.

1. Carla / faire une promenade / pleuvoir Carla n'a pas fait de promenade parce qu'il pleuvait.
2. Alexandre et Mia / ranger la chambre / regarder la télé Alexandre et Mia n'ont pas rangé la chambre parce qu'ils regardaient la télé.
3. nous / répondre au prof / ne pas faire attention Nous n'avons pas répondu au prof parce que nous ne faisions pas attention.
4. Jade et Noémie / venir au café / nettoyer la maison Jade et Noémie ne sont pas venues au café parce qu'elles nettoyaient la maison.
5. Léo / mettre un short / aller à un entretien (*interview*) Léo n'a pas mis son short parce qu'il allait à un entretien.

3 Qu'est-ce qu'ils faisaient quand...? Que faisaient ces personnes au moment de l'interruption? Suggested answers

MODÈLE
Papa débarrassait la table quand mon frère est arrivé.

débarrasser / arriver

Ils sortaient la poubelle quand le voisin a dit bonjour.
1. sortir / dire

Sa mère faisait la lessive quand Anne est partie.
3. faire / partir

Michel passait l'aspirateur quand l'enfant est tombé.
2. passer / tomber

Ils lavaient la voiture quand il a commencé à pleuvoir.
4. laver / commencer

Practice more at **espaces.vhlcentral.com.**

OPTIONS

Extra Practice Have students recall a memorable day from their childhood. Ask them to narrate this day, giving as many details as possible: the weather, who was there, what happened, how they felt etc. Alternatively, you could do this as a written activity and have students create a journal entry about their memorable day.

Pairs Distribute illustrations or photos from magazines of everyday activities and vacation activities. Have students arrange the pictures in pairs and create sentences to say that one activity was going on when the other one interrupted it. You might call on pairs of students to hold up their pictures and present their sentences to the rest of the class.

COMMUNICATION

4 Situations Avec un(e) partenaire, complétez ces phrases avec le passé composé ou l'imparfait. Comparez vos réponses, puis présentez-les à la classe. Answers will vary.

1. Autrefois, ma famille...
2. Je faisais une promenade quand...
3. Mon/Ma petit(e) ami(e)... tous les jours.
4. D'habitude, au petit-déjeuner, je...
5. Une fois, mon copain et moi...
6. Hier, je rentrais de l'université quand...
7. Parfois, ma mère...
8. Hier, il faisait mauvais. Soudain, ...

5 À votre tour Demandez à un(e) partenaire de compléter ces phrases avec le passé composé ou l'imparfait. Ensuite, présentez vos phrases à la classe. Answers will vary.

1. Mes profs au collège...
2. Quand je suis rentré(e) chez moi hier, ...
3. Le week-end dernier, ...
4. Quand j'ai fait la connaissance de mon/ma petit(e) ami(e), ...
5. La première fois que mon/ma petit(e) ami(e) et moi sommes sortis, ...
6. Quand j'avais dix ans, ...
7. Le jour où la tragédie du 11 septembre est arrivée, ...
8. Pendant les vacances d'été, ...
9. Quand M. Barack Obama est devenu président des États-Unis, ...
10. Hier soir, je regardais la télé quand...

6 Je me souviens! Racontez à votre partenaire un événement spécial de votre vie qui s'est déjà passé. Votre partenaire vous pose des questions pour avoir plus de détails sur cet événement. Vous pouvez (*can*) parler d'un anniversaire, d'une fête familiale, d'un mariage ou d'un concert. Answers will vary.

MODÈLE

Étudiant(e) 1: *Nous avons fait une grande fête d'anniversaire pour ma grand-mère l'année dernière.*
Étudiant(e) 2: *Quel âge a-t-elle eu?*

- The **imparfait** and the **passé composé** are sometimes used in the same sentence where the former is used to say what was going on when something else happened. To say what happened that interrupted the ongoing activity, use the **passé composé**.

Je **travaillais** dans le jardin quand mon amie **a téléphoné**.
I was working in the garden when my friend called.

Ils **faisaient** de la planche à voile quand j'**ai pris** cette photo.
They were wind-surfing when I took this photo.

- A cause and effect relationship is sometimes expressed by using the **passé composé** and the **imparfait** in the same sentence.

Marie **avait** envie de faire du shopping, alors elle **est allée** au centre commercial.
Marie felt like shopping so she went to the mall.

Mon ami **a balayé** la maison parce qu'elle **était** sale.
My friend swept the house because it was dirty.

- Remember that the verb **avoir** has a different meaning when used in the **imparfait** versus the **passé composé**.

J'**avais** sommeil.
I was sleepy.

J'**ai eu** sommeil.
I got sleepy.

- Certain expressions like **soudain, tout à coup, autrefois, une fois, d'habitude, souvent, toujours,** etc. serve as clues to signal a particular past tense.

Autrefois, mes parents et moi **vivions** en Belgique.
In the past, my parents and I used to live in Belgium.

Un jour, j'**ai rencontré** Nathalie au cinéma.
One day, I met Nathalie at the movies.

D'habitude, j'**allais** au centre-ville avec mes amis.
Usually, I used to go downtown with my friends.

J'**ai fait** du cheval deux fois dans ma vie.
I have gone horseback riding two times in my life.

Essayez! **Écrivez la forme correcte du verbe au passé.**

1. D'habitude, vous _mangiez_ (manger) dans la salle à manger.
2. Quand mes copines étaient petites, elles _jouaient_ (jouer) de la guitare.
3. Tout à coup, ma sœur _est arrivée_ (arriver) à l'école.
4. Ce matin, Matthieu _a repassé_ (repasser) le linge.
5. Ils _ont vécu_ (vivre) en France pendant un mois.
6. Les chats _dormaient_ (dormir) toujours sur le tapis.
7. Je/J' _ai loué_ (louer) un studio en ville pendant trois semaines.
8. Vous _laviez_ (laver) toujours les rideaux?

Essayez! Give the following items as additional practice. **1. La semaine dernière, mon ami et moi ____ (faire) de la planche à voile. (avons fait) 2. Avant, ils ____ (répondre) toujours aux questions du prof. (répondaient) 3. Papa ____ (acheter) un nouveau frigo hier. (a acheté) 4. D'habitude, nous ____ (mettre) nos vêtements dans le placard. (mettions)**

1 & 2 Expansions Have volunteers explain why they chose the **passé composé** or **imparfait** in each case. Ask them to point out any words or expressions that triggered one tense or the other.

3 Expansion Have students come up with a short story for each illustration.

4 Expansion Have students choose one of these sentences to begin telling a short story in the past. Encourage students to use both the **passé composé** and the **imparfait**.

5 Expansion You could also have students do this activity as a survey by making the phrases into questions and adding additional questions in the past if they want. Examples: **Comment étaient tes profs au collège? Que faisait ta mère quand tu es rentré(e) chez toi hier? Qu'est-ce que tu as fait le week-end dernier?**

6 Suggestions
- Act out the **modèle** with a volunteer before assigning this activity to pairs.
- Encourage students to use key adverbs to indicate the appropriate verb tenses in the dialogue. Examples: **soudain, tout à coup, autrefois,** etc.

OPTIONS

Extra Practice Divide the class into groups of five. Have each group imagine that they own a household cleaning service and create a radio or TV commercial for it. Have students create a logo (if it is a TV commercial) and a slogan for their business and maybe a jingle to go with their commercial. As a part of their commercial, they should use testimonials from customers who used their service. The customers should talk in detail about everything the cleaning service did and their opinion of their work.

Pairs Have students work with a partner to write an e-mail to a friend telling about the horrible weekend they had because they had to do a lot of chores and complaining about their siblings who did not do their share of the work.

Section Goals
In this section, students will learn the uses of **savoir** and **connaître**.

Instructional Resources
*espaces.vhlcentral.com: Lab MP3s; WB/VM/LM Answer Key; IRM (**Essayez!** and **Mise en pratique** answers; Lab Audioscript; **Feuilles d'activités**); activities; downloads; reference tools*

Suggestions
- Model **savoir** by asking several questions with it. Examples: ____, **savez-vous faire du ski? Et vous,** ____, **savez-vous où est la bibliothèque?** Next, write **connaître** on the board and ask questions, such as: ____, **connaissez-vous mon frère? Connaissez-vous la Nouvelle-Orléans?** Ask students further questions using both verbs to help them infer the difference in use between the two.
- Point out that the context of the phrase will indicate which verb to use. Using examples in English, have students say which verb would be used for the French translation. Examples: I know how to swim. (**savoir**) He doesn't know the president. (**connaître**)
- Review the changes in meaning when **savoir** and **connaître** are used in the **imparfait** and **passé composé.**
- Prepare dehydrated sentences such as these: **tu / savoir / que tu / ne pas connaître / mon petit ami; nous / connaître / les nouveaux étudiants.** Write them on the board one at a time and have students complete them.

8B.2 The verbs *savoir* and *connaître*

NATIONAL comparisons STANDARDS

Point de départ The verbs **savoir** and **connaître** both mean *to know*. The verb you use will depend on the context.

Savoir

Savoir	
je	sais
tu	sais
il/elle	sait
nous	savons
vous	savez
ils/elles	savent

- Use the verb **savoir** to say you know factual information.

Je **sais** tout sur lui.
I know everything about him.

Vous **savez** qui est venu hier?
Do you know who came yesterday?

- While talking about facts, the verb **savoir** may often be followed by **que**, **qui**, **où**, **quand**, **comment**, or **pourquoi**.

Nous **savons que** tu arrives mardi.
We know that you are arriving on Tuesday.

Ils **savent comment** aller à la gare.
They know how to get to the train station.

Je **sais où** je vais.
I know where I am going.

Tu **sais qui** a fait la lessive?
Do you know who did the laundry?

- Use the verb **savoir** to say how to do something.

Il **sait** jouer du piano.
He knows how to play the piano.

Savez-vous faire la cuisine?
Do you know how to cook?

Je **sais** jouer au tennis.
I know how to play tennis.

Ils **savent** parler espagnol.
They know how to speak Spanish.

- The past participle of **savoir** is **su**. When used in the **passé composé**, **savoir** takes a slightly different meaning.

Je **savais** qu'il allait venir.
I knew he was coming.

J'**ai su** qu'il allait venir.
I found out (discovered) he was coming.

Nous **savions** qu'il y avait une fête.
We knew that there was a party.

Nous **avons su** qu'il y avait une fête.
We found out that there was a party.

MISE EN PRATIQUE

1 Les passe-temps Qu'est-ce que ces personnes savent faire?

MODÈLE
Patrick sait skier.

Patrick

1. Halima
Halima sait faire du roller.

3. tu
Tu sais jouer au tennis.

2. vous
Vous savez nager.

4. nous
Nous savons jouer au foot.

2 Dialogues Complétez les conversations avec le présent du verbe **savoir** ou **connaître.**

1. Marie __sait__ faire la cuisine?
   Oui, mais elle ne __connaît__ pas beaucoup de recettes (*recipes*).
2. Vous __connaissez__ les parents de François?
   Non, je __connais__ seulement sa cousine.
3. Tes enfants __savent__ nager dans la mer.
   Et mon fils aîné __connaît__ toutes les espèces de poissons.
4. Je __sais__ que le train arrive à trois heures.
   Est-ce que tu __sais__ à quelle heure il part?

3 Assemblez Assemblez les éléments des colonnes pour construire des phrases. Answers will vary.

MODÈLE *Je sais parler une langue étrangère.*

A	B	C
Gérard Depardieu	(ne pas) connaître	des célébrités
Oprah	(ne pas) savoir	faire la cuisine
je		jouer au basket
ton/ta camarade de chambre		Julia Roberts
		parler une langue étrangère

Practice more at **espaces.vhlcentral.com.**

OPTIONS

Video Replay the video episode, having students focus on forms of **savoir** and **connaître**, as well as the use of the **imparfait** and the **passé composé.** Tell them to note when each one is used. Afterward, ask the class to describe the conversations that took place and what tenses were used. Have them identify the reason for this verb choice (a series of past actions, ongoing actions in the past, etc.).

Extra Practice Ask individual students questions using **savoir** and **connaître** that are most likely not true for them. When students give a negative answer, they should indicate someone else who would answer in the affirmative. Example: ____, **connaissez-vous le président des États-Unis? (Non, je ne le connais pas, mais le Premier ministre du Canada le connaît.)**

COMMUNICATION

4 **Enquête** Votre professeur va vous donner une feuille d'activités. Circulez dans la classe pour trouver au moins une personne différente qui répond oui à chaque question. Answers will vary.

Sujets	Noms
1. Sais-tu faire une mousse au chocolat?	Jacqueline
2. Connais-tu New York?	
3. Connais-tu le nom des sénateurs de cet État (State)?	
4. Connais-tu quelqu'un qui habite en Californie?	

5 **Questions** À tour de rôle, posez ces questions à un(e) partenaire. Ensuite, présentez vos réponses à la classe. Answers will vary.

1. Quel bon restaurant connais-tu près d'ici? Est-ce que tu y (*there*) manges souvent?
2. Dans ta famille, qui sait chanter le mieux (*best*)?
3. Connais-tu l'Europe? Quelles villes connais-tu?
4. Reconnais-tu toutes les chansons (*songs*) que tu entends à la radio?
5. Tes parents savent-ils utiliser Internet? Le font-ils bien?
6. Connais-tu un(e) acteur/actrice célèbre? Une autre personne célèbre?
7. Ton/Ta meilleur(e) (*best*) ami(e) sait-il/elle écouter quand tu lui racontes (*tell*) tes problèmes?
8. Connais-tu la date d'anniversaire de tous les membres de ta famille et de tous tes amis? Donne des exemples.

6 **Je sais le faire** Votre colocataire et vous invitez un(e) ami(e). Par groupes de trois, un(e) étudiant(e) joue le rôle de l'ami(e) invité(e) et les deux autres jouent le rôle des colocataires. Chacun(e) (*Each one*) essaie de montrer toutes les choses qu'il/elle sait faire. Answers will vary.

MODÈLE

Étudiant(e) 1: *Alors, tu sais faire la vaisselle?*
Étudiant(e) 2: *Je sais faire la vaisselle, et je sais faire la cuisine aussi.*
Étudiant(e) 3: *Moi, je sais faire la cuisine, mais il/elle ne sait pas passer l'aspirateur.*

Connaître

Connaître	
je	connais
tu	connais
il/elle	connaît
nous	connaissons
vous	connaissez
ils/elles	connaissent

- Use the verb **connaître** to say that you *know, have a knowledge of,* or *are familiar with* people.

Mes parents ne **connaissent** pas mon prof de maths.
My parents don't know my math professor.

Tu **connais** la fille qui vend l'appartement?
Do you know the girl who is selling the apartment?

- Use the verb **connaître** to say that you *know, have a knowledge of,* or *are familiar with* places or things.

Sébastien **connaît** ce quartier de Rome.
Sébastien knows (is familiar with) this neighborhood of Rome.

Je ne **connais** pas bien la cuisine marocaine.
I am not familiar with Moroccan cuisine.

- The past participle of **connaître** is **connu**. When used in the **passé composé**, **connaître** has a special connotation. It means *met (for the first time).*

Luca **a connu** Élodie à la fac.
Luca met Élodie at the university.

Luca **connaissait** Élodie à la fac.
Luca knew Élodie at the university.

- **Reconnaître** means *to recognize.* It follows the same conjugation pattern as **connaître**.

Mes profs de lycée me **reconnaissent** encore.
My high school teachers still recognize me.

Nous avons **reconnu** vos enfants à la soirée.
We recognized your children at the party.

Essayez! Complétez les phrases avec les formes correctes des verbes **savoir** et **connaître**.

1. Je _connais_ de bons restaurants.
2. Ils ne _savent_ pas parler allemand.
3. Vous _savez_ faire du cheval?
4. Tu _connais_ une bonne coiffeuse?
5. Nous ne _connaissons_ pas Jacques.
6. Caroline _sait_ jouer aux échecs.
7. Vous ne _connaissez_ pas cet artiste?
8. Nous _savons_ faire le ménage.

Essayez! Have students change the sentences to the past tense. Examples: **1. Je connaissais de bons restaurants. 2. Ils ne savaient pas parler allemand.**

1 Expansion Ask individual students questions about what they know how to do. Example: **Savez-vous parler espagnol? (Non, je ne sais pas parler espagnol.)**

2 Expansion Have students work in pairs to write three more sentences similar to those in the activity. Call on volunteers to present their sentences to the class.

3 Expansion Ask students questions about what certain celebrities know how to do or whom they know. Examples: **Est-ce que Brad Pitt connaît Jennifer Aniston? (Oui, il la connaît.) Est-ce que Jennifer Lopez sait parler espagnol? (Oui, elle sait le parler.)**

4 Suggestions
- Distribute the **Feuilles d'activités** found on the Supersite.
- Have students read through the list of questions using **savoir** and **connaître** for comprehension before completing the activity.

5 Expansion Ask these questions of the whole class. Ask students who answer in the affirmative for additional information. Examples: **Qui sait chanter? Chantez-vous bien? Chantiez-vous avec un groupe quand vous étiez plus jeune?**

6 Suggestion Ask for three volunteers to act out the **modèle** for the class.

OPTIONS

Extra Practice Have students write down three things they know how to do well (using **savoir bien** + [*infinitive*]). Collect the papers, and then read the sentences. Tell students that they must not identify themselves when they hear their sentence. The rest of the class takes turns trying to guess who wrote each sentence. Repeat this activity with **connaître**.

Pairs Ask students to write brief, but creative, paragraphs in which they use **savoir** and **connaître**. Then have them exchange their papers with a partner. Tell students to help each other, through peer editing, to make the paragraphs as error-free as possible. Collect the papers for grading.

Instructional Resources
espaces.vhlcentral.com:
*IRM (**Feuilles d'activités**; Info Gap Activities); Testing Program pp. 61–64; Test Files; Testing Program MP3s; activities; downloads; reference tools*
Test Generator

1 Expansion Tell students to imagine they are hosting their own dinner party. Have them make a list of tasks that must be completed before the guests arrive. Have them use the **passé composé**.

2 Suggestions
- Have two students say the **modèle** before distributing the **Feuilles d'activités** found on the Supersite.
- Before doing the activity, have students practice creating sentences using **connaître** in the **passé composé** and in the **imparfait**. Example: **J'ai connu la petite amie de Jacques en 2005. Je connais son ancienne petite amie.**

3 Suggestion Review the **imparfait** with the verb phrases listed in this activity. Ask volunteers to supply the correct verb forms for the subjects you suggest. Example: **repasser le linge: je (je repassais le linge)**.

4 Suggestion Have students bring photos from magazines or newspapers to supplement this activity. Or, students may prefer to sketch drawings of events.

5 Expansion Ask students to imagine that they are writing an e-mail home to their family expressing what they have learned and whom they have met since arriving at college. Instruct them to use sentence constructions similar to those presented in this activity.

6 Suggestion Divide the class into pairs and distribute the Info Gap Handouts found on the Supersite for this activity. Give students ten minutes to complete the activity.

National Standards: communication

Révision

1 Un grand dîner Émilie et son mari Vincent ont invité des amis à dîner ce soir. Qu'ont-ils fait cet après-midi pour préparer la soirée? Que vont-ils faire ce soir après le départ des invités? Conversez avec un(e) partenaire. Answers will vary.

MODÈLE

Étudiant(e) 1: *Cet après-midi, Émilie et Vincent ont mis la table.*

Étudiant(e) 2: *Ce soir, ils vont faire la vaisselle.*

2 Mes connaissances Votre professeur va vous donner une feuille d'activités. Interviewez vos camarades. Pour chaque activité, trouvez un(e) camarade différent(e) qui réponde affirmativement. Answers will vary.

Étudiant(e) 1: *Connais-tu une personne qui aime faire le ménage?*

Étudiant(e) 2: *Oui, autrefois, mon père aimait bien faire le ménage.*

Activités	*Noms*
1. ne pas souvent faire la vaisselle	
2. aimer faire le ménage	*Farid*
3. dormir avec une couverture en été	
4. faire son lit tous les jours	
5. rarement repasser ses vêtements	

3 Qui faisait le ménage? Par groupes de trois, interviewez vos camarades. Qui faisait le ménage à la maison quand ils habitaient encore chez leurs parents? Préparez des questions avec ces expressions et comparez vos réponses. Answers will vary.

balayer	mettre et débarrasser la table
faire la lessive	passer l'aspirateur
faire le lit	ranger
faire la vaisselle	repasser le linge

4 Soudain! Tout était calme quand soudain... Avec un(e) partenaire, choisissez l'une des deux photos et écrivez un texte de dix phrases. Faites cinq phrases pour décrire la photo, et cinq autres pour raconter (*to tell*) un événement qui s'est passé soudainement (*that suddenly happened*). Employez des adverbes et soyez imaginatifs. Answers will vary.

5 J'ai appris... Qu'avez-vous appris ou qui connaissez-vous depuis que (*since*) vous êtes à la fac? Avec un(e) partenaire, faites une liste de cinq choses et de cinq personnes. À chaque fois, utilisez un imparfait et un passé composé dans vos explications. Answers will vary.

MODÈLE

Étudiant(e) 1: *Avant, je ne savais pas comment dire bonjour en français, et puis j'ai commencé ce cours, et maintenant, je sais le dire.*

Étudiant(e) 2: *Avant, je ne connaissais pas tous les pays francophones, et maintenant, je les connais.*

6 Élise fait sa lessive Votre professeur va vous donner, à vous et à votre partenaire, une feuille avec des dessins représentant (*representing*) Élise et sa journée d'hier. Attention! Ne regardez pas la feuille de votre partenaire. Answers will vary.

MODÈLE

Étudiant(e) 1: *Hier matin, Élise avait besoin de faire sa lessive.*

Étudiant(e) 2: *Mais, elle...*

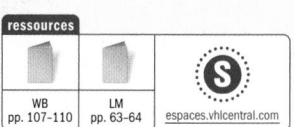

ressources: WB pp. 107–110 | LM pp. 63–64 | espaces.vhlcentral.com

OPTIONS

Extra Practice Divide the class into three groups. One group is **savoir** (present tense with infinitive, **imparfait**), the second group is **connaître** (present tense, **imparfait**), and the third group is **savoir** and **connaître** (**passé composé**). Have each group brainstorm a list of phrases using their assigned verbs and tenses. A volunteer from each group should present their results to the class.

Example: Group 1 – **Je sais chanter.** (**présent**) **Ma mère savait parler français.** (**imparfait**) Group 2 – **Nous connaissons les nouveaux étudiants.** (**présent**) **Il connaissait le président des États-Unis.** (**imparfait**) Group 3 – **J'ai su que l'examen de français était très difficile.** (**passé composé**) **Mon père a connu mon petit ami.** (**passé composé**)

À l'écoute

NATIONAL communication STANDARDS

S Audio: Activities

STRATÉGIE

Using visual cues

Visual cues like illustrations and headings provide useful clues about what you will hear.

To practice this strategy, you will listen to a passage related to the image. Jot down the clues the image gives you as you listen. Answers will vary.

Préparation

Qu'est-ce qu'il y a sur les trois photos à droite? À votre avis, quel va être le sujet de la conversation entre M. Duchemin et Mme Lopez?

À vous d'écouter

Écoutez la conversation. M. Duchemin va proposer trois logements à Mme Lopez. Regardez les annonces et écrivez le numéro de référence de chaque possibilité qu'il propose.

1. Possibilité 1: Réf. 521
2. Possibilité 2: Réf. 522
3. Possibilité 3: Réf. 520

À LOUER

Appartement en ville, moderne, avec balcon
1.200 €
(Réf. 520)

5 pièces, jardin, proche parc Victor Hugo
950 €
(Réf. 521)

Maison meublée en banlieue, grande, tt confort, cuisine équipée
1.200 €
(Réf. 522)

Compréhension

Les détails Après une deuxième écoute, complétez le tableau (*chart*) avec les informations données dans la conversation.

	Où?	Maison ou appartement?	Meublé ou non?	Nombre de chambres?	Garage?	Jardin?
Logement 1	ville	maison	non	trois	non	oui
Logement 2	banlieue	maison	oui	quatre	oui	oui
Logement 3	centre-ville	appartement	non	deux	oui	non

Quel logement pour les Lopez? Lisez cette description de la famille Lopez. Décidez quel logement cette famille va probablement choisir et expliquez votre réponse.

M. Lopez travaille au centre-ville. Le soir, il rentre tard à la maison et il est souvent fatigué parce qu'il travaille beaucoup. Il n'a pas envie de passer son temps à travailler dans le jardin. Mme Lopez adore le cinéma et le théâtre. Elle n'aime pas beaucoup faire le ménage. Les Lopez ont une fille qui a seize ans. Elle adore retrouver ses copines pour faire du shopping en ville. Les Lopez ont beaucoup de beaux meubles modernes. Ils ont aussi une nouvelle voiture: une grosse BMW qui a coûté très cher!

Section Goals
In this section, students will:
- use visual cues to understand an oral description
- listen to a conversation and complete several activities

Instructional Resources
espaces.vhlcentral.com: IRM (Textbook Audioscript); Textbook MP3s; downloads; reference tools

Stratégie
Script Nous avons trouvé un appartement super dans le quartier du Marais. Il est au premier étage, dans un immeuble très calme. Il y a une salle de séjour assez grande, une cuisine avec frigo, cuisinière et lave-linge, une petite salle de bains et deux chambres très jolies. Il y a aussi des placards dans toutes les pièces et un garage en sous-sol pour notre voiture. On peut emménager la semaine prochaine et le loyer n'est pas très cher. Nous sommes vraiment heureux, tu sais!

À vous d'écouter
Script AGENT: Allô, bonjour. Madame Lopez, s'il vous plaît.
CLIENTE: C'est elle-même.
A: Ah, bonjour, Madame. Ici Monsieur Duchemin de l'agence immobilière. Vous cherchez un logement à louer à Avignon ou dans la banlieue, c'est bien ça?
C: Oui, Monsieur, c'est exact. Vous avez une maison à me proposer?
A: Oui, j'ai trois possibilités. La première est une maison en ville, dans un quartier calme près du parc Victor Hugo. Elle n'est pas très grande, mais elle est très jolie et elle a un petit jardin. Il y a un salon, une salle à manger, une grande cuisine avec beaucoup de placards, une salle de bains, les W.-C. et trois chambres.
C: Il y a un garage?
A: Non, Madame, mais il y a toujours des places dans le quartier.
C: Bon. Et qu'est-ce que vous avez d'autre?
A: J'ai aussi une très grande maison meublée avec jardin et garage en banlieue, à une demi-heure de la ville.
C: C'est un peu loin, mais bon... Il y a combien de chambres?
A: Quatre chambres.
C: Et qu'est-ce qu'il y a comme meubles?
A: Un canapé, des fauteuils et des étagères dans le salon, un grand lit et une commode dans la grande chambre... et voyons, quoi d'autre? Ah, oui! La cuisine est équipée avec tout le nécessaire: frigo, congélateur, cuisinière, four à micro-ondes, lave-linge et sèche-linge.
C: Très bien. Et la troisième possibilité?
A: C'est un grand appartement dans le centre-ville, sur la place des Halles. Il n'y a pas de jardin.
C: Et combien de chambres y a-t-il?
A: Deux chambres avec des balcons. Si vous aimez le moderne, cet appartement est parfait pour vous. Et il a un garage.
C: Bon, je vais en parler avec mon mari.
A: Très bien, Madame. Au revoir.
C: Au revoir, Monsieur Duchemin.

Section Goals

In this section, students will read historical and cultural information about Alsace and Lorraine.

Instructional Resources
espaces.vhlcentral.com: Transparency #39; WB/VM/LM Answer Key; activities; downloads; reference tools

Carte de l'Alsace et de la Lorraine

- Have students look at the map or use **Transparency #39**. Ask volunteers to read the names of cities and other geographical features aloud. Model pronunciation as necessary.
- Ask students to name the countries that border these regions. Then have them identify the cities with German names.

La région en chiffres

- Point out the coats of arms for the regions.
- Have volunteers read the sections. After each section, ask questions about the content.

Incroyable mais vrai! The architecture of Alsace and Lorraine exemplifies the regions' changing national identity over the years. Throughout the regions, there are border citadels, feudal and Teutonic castles, fortresses, medieval and Renaissance churches and cathedrals, and timber-framed and stone houses.

NATIONAL STANDARDS connections cultures

Interactive Map Reading

Panorama

le quartier de la Petite France à Strasbourg

L'Alsace

La région en chiffres

- **Superficie:** *8.280 km²*
- **Population:** *1.829.000*
  SOURCE: INSEE
- **Industries principales:** *viticulture, culture du houblon° et brassage° de la bière, exploitation forestière°, industrie automobile, tourisme*
- **Villes principales:** *Colmar, Mulhouse, Strasbourg*

Personnes célèbres

- **Gustave Doré,** *dessinateur° et peintre° (1832–1883)*
- **Auguste Bartholdi,** *sculpteur, statue de la Liberté à New York, (1834–1904)*
-  **Albert Schweitzer,** *médecin, prix Nobel de la paix en 1952 (1875–1965)*

la place Stanislas à Nancy

dans les Vosges

La Lorraine

La région en chiffres

- **Superficie:** *23.547 km²*
- **Population:** *2.343.000*
- **Industries principales:** *industrie automobile, agroalimentaire°, bois° pour le papier, chimie et pétrochimie, métallurgie, verre et cristal*
- **Villes principales:** *Épinal, Forbach, Metz, Nancy*

Personnes célèbres

- **Georges de La Tour,** *peintre (1593–1652)*
- **Bernard-Marie Koltès,** *dramaturge° (1948–1989)*
-  **Patricia Kaas,** *chanteuse (1966–)*

houblon *hops* **brassage** *brewing* **exploitation forestière** *forestry* **dessinateur** *illustrator* **peintre** *painter* **agroalimentaire** *food processing* **bois** *wood* **dramaturge** *playwright* **traité** *treaty* **envahit** *invades* **à nouveau** *once again*

Incroyable mais vrai!

Français depuis 1648, l'Alsace et le département de la Moselle en Lorraine deviennent allemands en 1871. Puis en 1919, le traité° de Versailles les rend à la France. Ensuite, en 1939, l'Allemagne envahit° la région qui redevient allemande entre 1940 et 1944. Depuis, l'Alsace et la Lorraine sont à nouveau° françaises.

OPTIONS

Personnes célèbres **Gustave Doré** was known for his highly imaginative books of illustrations with images from myths and legends. **Auguste Bartholdi** also sculpted ***le Lion de Belfort***. The Statue of Liberty was presented to the United States as a gift from the French people in 1886. **Albert Schweitzer** was awarded the Nobel Prize for his medical missionary work in Africa. He was also a philosopher, musician, and theologian. **Georges de La Tour**'s paintings are mostly of human subjects portrayed in a realistic manner in torch or candlelit scenes. **Bernard-Marie Koltès**'s plays have been translated into over 30 languages. **Patricia Kaas** sings in the style of French **chanson**, mixing traditional elements with pop, jazz, and blues.

La gastronomie

La choucroute

La choucroute est typiquement alsacienne et son nom vient de l'allemand «sauerkraut». Du chou râpé° fermente dans un baril° avec du gros sel° et des baies de genièvre°. Puis, le chou est cuit° dans du vin blanc ou de la bière et mangé avec de la charcuterie° alsacienne et des pommes de terre°. La choucroute, qui se conserve longtemps° grâce à° la fermentation, est une nourriture appréciée° des marins° pendant leurs longs voyages.

L'histoire

Jeanne d'Arc

Jeanne d'Arc est née en 1412, en Lorraine, dans une famille de paysans°. En 1429, quand la France est en guerre avec l'Angleterre, Jeanne d'Arc décide de partir au combat pour libérer son pays. Elle prend la tête° d'une armée et libère la ville d'Orléans des Anglais. Cette victoire permet de sacrer° Charles VII roi de France. Plus tard, Jeanne d'Arc perd ses alliés° pour des raisons politiques. Vendue aux Anglais, elle est condamnée pour hérésie. Elle est exécutée à Rouen, en 1431. En 1920, l'Église catholique la canonise.

Les destinations

Strasbourg

Strasbourg, capitale de l'Alsace, est le siège° du Conseil de l'Europe depuis 1949 et du Parlement européen depuis 1979. Le Conseil de l'Europe est responsable de la promotion des valeurs démocratiques et des droits de l'homme°, de l'identité culturelle européenne et de la recherche de solutions° aux problèmes de société. Les membres du Parlement sont élus° dans chaque pays de l'Union européenne. Le Parlement contribue à l'élaboration de la législation européenne et à la gestion de l'Europe.

La société

Un mélange de cultures

L'Alsace a été enrichie° par de multiples courants° historiques et culturels grâce à sa position entre la France et l'Allemagne. La langue alsacienne vient d'un dialecte germanique et l'allemand est maintenant enseigné dans les écoles primaires. Quand la région est rendue à la France en 1919, les Alsaciens continuent de bénéficier des lois° sociales allemandes. Le mélange° des cultures est visible à Noël avec des traditions allemandes et françaises (le sapin de Noël, Saint Nicolas, les marchés).

Qu'est-ce que vous avez appris? **Répondez aux questions par des phrases complètes.**

1. En 1919, quel document rend l'Alsace et la Moselle à la France?
   Le traité de Versailles les rend à la France.
2. Combien de fois l'Alsace et la Moselle ont-elles changé de nationalité depuis 1871?
   Elles ont changé quatre fois de nationalité depuis 1871.
3. Quel est l'ingrédient principal de la choucroute?
   L'ingrédient principal de la choucroute est le chou.
4. De qui la choucroute est-elle particulièrement appréciée?
   Elle est appréciée des marins.
5. Pourquoi Strasbourg est-elle importante?
   C'est le siège du Conseil de l'Europe et du Parlement européen.
6. Quel est un des rôles du Conseil de l'Europe? Answers will vary. Suggested answer: Il est responsable de la promotion des valeurs démocratiques.
7. Contre qui Jeanne d'Arc a-t-elle défendu la France?
   Elle a défendu la France contre les Anglais.
8. Comment est-elle morte?
   Elle a été exécutée.
9. Quelle langue étrangère enseigne-t-on aux petits Alsaciens?
   On leur enseigne l'allemand.
10. À quel moment de l'année le mélange des cultures est-il particulièrement visible en Alsace?
    Il est particulièrement visible à Noël.

Practice more at **espaces.vhlcentral.com.**

ressources
WB pp. 111-112 | espaces.vhlcentral.com

SUR INTERNET

Go to espaces.vhlcentral.com to find more cultural information related to this **PANORAMA**.

1. Quelle est la différence entre le Conseil européen et le Conseil de l'Europe?
2. Trouvez d'autres informations sur Jeanne d'Arc. Quel est son surnom?
3. Pourquoi l'Alsace et le département de la Moselle sont-ils devenus allemands en 1871?

chou râpé *grated cabbage* **baril** *cask* **gros sel** *coarse sea salt* **baies de genièvre** *juniper berries* **cuit** *cooked* **charcuterie** *cooked pork meats* **pommes de terre** *potatoes* **qui se conserve longtemps** *which keeps for a long time* **grâce à** *thanks to* **appréciée** *valued* **marins** *sailors* **paysans** *peasants* **prend la tête** *takes the lead* **sacrer** *crown* **alliés** *allies* **siège** *headquarters* **droits de l'homme** *human rights* **recherche de solutions** *finding solutions* **élus** *elected* **enrichie** *enriched* **courants** *trends, movements* **lois** *laws* **mélange** *mix*

La choucroute
- In other regions, **la choucroute** may be garnished with smoked beef, goose, and occasionally fish.
- Ask students: **Avez-vous déjà mangé de la choucroute? A-t-on déjà servi de la choucroute chez vous? L'aimez-vous?**

Jeanne d'Arc
- Joan of Arc was accused of witchcraft, wantonness in cutting her hair and wearing men's clothes, and blasphemous pride. She was burned at the stake at the age of 19. In 1456, she was officially declared innocent, and later canonized for her bravery and martyrdom. Her life has been the subject of many famous literary works.
- Ask students if they think it was common for a woman to lead an army into battle in the fifteenth century.

Strasbourg **Le Conseil de l'Europe** is Europe's oldest political organization. It has 47 member countries. Have students research **le Conseil de l'Europe** web site to find out what countries were the original members and what countries are more recent members.

Un mélange de cultures The traditional costumes worn by the Protestant Alsatian women have either a red or black bonnet tied with a bow. The traditional costumes of the Catholic Alsatian women have a white bonnet made of tulle bordered with flowers.

OPTIONS

Cultural Activity Have students work in pairs. Tell them to make a list of examples of Germanic influences in these regions, including those shown in the photos and map. After completing their lists, ask various volunteers to give examples until all are mentioned.

La Petite France This picturesque part of old Strasbourg used to be the fishers', millers', and tanners' district. The half-timbered houses (**les maisons à colombages**) in the alleys, dating from the sixteenth century, have the traditional interior courtyards, sloped roofs, and open attic areas where the pelts used to dry. The covered bridges and the Vauban Barrage played critical roles in uniting Strasbourg to France in 1681.

Section Goals
In this section, students will:
- learn to guess meaning from context
- read an article about **le château de Versailles**

Stratégie Tell students that they can often infer the meaning of an unfamiliar word by looking at the word's context and by using their common sense. Five types of context clues are:
- synonyms
- antonyms
- clarifications
- definitions
- additional details

Have students read this sentence from the letter: **Je cherchais un studio, mais j'ai trouvé un appartement plus grand: un deux-pièces près de la fac!** Point out that the meaning of **un deux-pièces** can be inferred since they already know the words **deux** and **une pièce.** The explanation that follows in the note also helps to clarify the meaning.

Examinez le texte
- Write this sentence on the board: **La pièce la plus célèbre du château de Versailles est la galerie des Glaces**. Point out the phrase **la plus célèbre** and ask a volunteer to explain how the context might give clues to its meaning.
- Go over the answers to the activity with the class.

Expérience personnelle Before beginning the activity, have students brainstorm the names of famous or historic homes they can talk about.

Lecture

Reading

Avant la lecture

STRATÉGIE

Guessing meaning from context

As you read in French, you will often see words you have not learned. You can guess what they mean by looking at surrounding words. Read this note and guess what **un deux-pièces** means.

> Johanne,
>
> Je cherchais un studio, mais j'ai trouvé un appartement plus grand: un deux-pièces près de la fac! Le salon est grand et la chambre a deux placards. La cuisine a un frigo et une cuisinière, et la salle de bains a une baignoire. Et le loyer? Seulement 450 euros par mois!

If you guessed *a two-room apartment*, you are correct. You can conclude that someone is describing an apartment he or she will rent.

Examinez le texte

Regardez le texte et décrivez les photos. Quel va être le sujet de la lecture? Puis, trouvez ces mots et expressions dans le texte. Essayez de deviner leur sens (*to guess their meaning*).

ont été rajoutées (were added)	autour du (around)	de haut (in height)
de nombreux bassins (numerous pools/fountains)	légumes (vegetables)	roi (King)

Expérience personnelle

Avez-vous visité une résidence célèbre ou historique? Où? Quand? Comment était-ce? Un personnage historique a-t-il habité là? Qui? Parlez de cette visite à un(e) camarade.

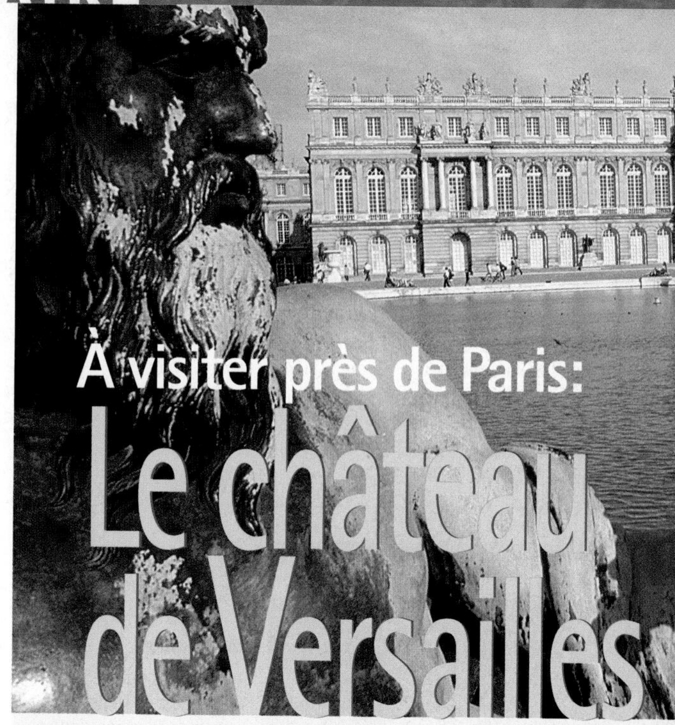

À visiter près de Paris: Le château de Versailles

La construction du célèbre° château de Versailles a commencé en 1623 sous le roi Louis XIII. Au départ, c'était un petit château où le roi logeait° quand il allait à la chasse°. Plus tard, en 1678, Louis XIV, aussi appelé le Roi-Soleil, a décidé de faire de Versailles sa résidence principale. Il a demandé à son architecte, Louis Le Vau, d'agrandir° le château, et à son premier peintre°, Charles Le Brun, de le décorer. Le Vau a fait construire, entre autres°, le Grand Appartement du Roi. La décoration de cet appartement de sept pièces était à la gloire du Roi-Soleil. La pièce la plus célèbre du château de Versailles est la galerie des Glaces°. C'est une immense pièce de 73 mètres de long, 10,50 mètres de large et 12,30 mètres de haut°. D'un côté, 17 fenêtres donnent° sur les jardins, et de l'autre côté, il y a 17 arcades embellies de miroirs immenses. Au nord° de la galerie des Glaces, on trouve le salon de la Guerre°, et, au sud°, le salon de la Paix°. Quand on visite le château de Versailles, on peut également° voir de nombreuses autres pièces, ajoutées à différentes périodes, comme la chambre de la Reine°,

À l'intérieur du palais

OPTIONS

Le château de Versailles Located in the region **Île-de-France, le château de Versailles** is about twelve miles from Paris. **Le château et les jardins de Versailles** are classified as a UNESCO World Heritage Site. Hundreds of masterpieces of seventeenth-century French sculpture can be viewed in the gardens, and it is estimated that seven million people visit the gardens each year.

Extra Practice Ask students to make a list of words from the text whose meanings they guessed. Then have them work with partners and compare their lists. Students should explain to each other what clues they used in the text to help them guess the meanings. Help the class confirm the predictions, or have students confirm the meanings in a dictionary.

Le château de Versailles et une fontaine

plusieurs cuisines et salles à manger d'hiver et d'été, des bibliothèques, divers salons et cabinets, et plus de 18.000 m²° de galeries qui racontent° l'histoire de France en images. L'opéra, une grande salle où plus de° 700 personnes assistaient souvent à divers spectacles et bals, a aussi été ajouté plus tard. C'est dans cette salle que le futur roi Louis XVI et Marie-Antoinette ont été mariés. Partout° dans le château, on peut admirer une collection unique de meubles (lits, tables, fauteuils et chaises, bureaux, etc.) et de magnifiques tissus° (tapis, rideaux et tapisseries°). Le château de Versailles a aussi une chapelle et d'autres bâtiments, comme le Grand et le Petit Trianon. Autour du château, il y a des serres° et de magnifiques jardins avec de nombreux bassins°, fontaines et statues. Dans l'Orangerie, on trouve plus de 1.000 arbres°, et de nombreux fruits et légumes sont toujours cultivés dans le Potager° du Roi. L'Arboretum de Chèvreloup était le terrain de chasse des rois et on y° trouve aujourd'hui des arbres du monde entier°.

célèbre *famous* **logeait** *stayed* **chasse** *hunting* **agrandir** *enlarge* **peintre** *painter* **entre autres** *among other things* **Glaces** *Mirrors* **haut** *high* **donnent** *open* **nord** *north* **Guerre** *War* **sud** *south* **Paix** *Peace* **également** *also* **Reine** *Queen* **m² (mètres carrés)** *square meters* **racontent** *tell* **plus de** *more than* **Partout** *Everywhere* **tissus** *fabrics* **tapisseries** *tapestries* **serres** *greenhouses* **bassins** *ponds* **arbres** *trees* **Potager** *vegetable garden* **y** *there* **entier** *entire*

Après la lecture

Vrai ou faux? Indiquez si les phrases sont **vraies** ou **fausses**. Corrigez les phrases fausses.

1. Louis XIII habitait à Versailles toute l'année.
   Faux. Louis XIII logeait à Versailles quand il allait à la chasse.
2. Louis Le Vau est appelé le Roi-Soleil.
   Faux. Louis XIV est appelé le Roi-Soleil.
3. La galerie des Glaces est une grande pièce avec beaucoup de miroirs et de fenêtres.
   Vrai.
4. Il y a deux salons près de la galerie des Glaces.
   Vrai.
5. Aujourd'hui, au château de Versailles, il n'y a pas de meubles.
   Faux. Il y a une collection unique de meubles (lits, tables, fauteuils et chaises, bureaux, etc.).
6. Le château de Versailles n'a pas de jardins parce qu'il a été construit en ville.
   Faux. Il a des jardins: l'Orangerie, le Potager et l'Arboretum de Chèvreloup.

Répondez Répondez aux questions par des phrases complètes.

1. Comment était Versailles sous Louis XIII? Quand logeait-il là?
   C'était un petit château où le roi logeait quand il allait à la chasse.
2. Qu'est-ce que Louis XIV a fait du château?
   Il a fait de Versailles sa résidence principale. Il l'a agrandi et l'a décoré.
3. Qu'est-ce que Louis Le Vau a fait à Versailles?
   Il a construit, entre autres, le Grand Appartement du Roi.
4. Dans quelle salle Louis XVI et Marie-Antoinette ont-ils été mariés? Comment est cette salle?
   Ils ont été mariés dans l'Opéra. C'est une grande salle où plus de 700 personnes assistaient souvent à divers spectacles et bals.
5. Louis XVI est-il devenu roi avant ou après son mariage?
   Il est devenu roi après son mariage.
6. Le château de Versailles est-il composé d'un seul bâtiment? Expliquez.
   Non, le château a aussi une chapelle et d'autres bâtiments comme le Grand et le Petit Trianon.

Les personnages célèbres de Versailles

Par groupes de trois ou quatre, choisissez une des personnes mentionnées dans la lecture et faites des recherches (*research*) à son sujet. Préparez un rapport écrit (*written report*) à présenter à la classe. Vous pouvez (*may*) utiliser les ressources de votre bibliothèque ou Internet.

Vrai ou faux? Go over the answers with the class. For false items, have students point out where they found the correct information in the text.

Répondez Have students get together with a partner and compare their answers. If they don't agree, tell them to locate the answer in the text.

Les personnages célèbres de Versailles Before assigning this activity, have students identify the people mentioned in the article and write their names on the board. To avoid duplication of efforts, you may want to assign each group a specific person. Encourage students to provide visuals with their presentations.

OPTIONS

Small Groups Working in groups of three or four, have students discuss the features that they find most interesting or appealing about **le château de Versailles** and make a list of them.

Extra Practice Tell students to skim the text and underline all of the verbs in the **passé composé** and **imparfait**. Then go through the text and ask volunteers to explain why each verb is in the **passé composé** or the **imparfait**.

Section Goals
In this section, students will:
- learn to write a narrative using the **passé composé** and the **imparfait**
- write a story about the past

Stratégie Write these sentences on the board. **1. Le film a fini à minuit. 2. J'ai fait mon lit, j'ai rangé ma chambre et j'ai passé l'aspirateur. 3. Le bébé a dormi parce qu'il avait sommeil. 4. Quand nous étions au restaurant, nous avons parlé avec nos copains.** Ask volunteers to explain why the **passé composé** or **imparfait** was used in each case. Then have the class write sentences for their compositions.

Thème Explain that the story they are going to write will be about events that occurred in the past. Encourage them to brainstorm as many details as possible before they begin writing.

Écriture

NATIONAL communication cultures STANDARDS

STRATÉGIE

Mastering the simple past tenses

In French, when you write about events that occurred in the past, you need to know when to use the **passé composé** and when to use the **imparfait**. A good understanding of the uses of each tense will make it much easier to determine which one to use as you write.

Look at the following summary of the uses of the **passé composé** and the **imparfait**. Write your own example sentence for each of the rules described.

Passé composé vs. imparfait

Passé composé

1. Actions viewed as completed

   ____

2. Beginning or end of past actions

   ____

3. Series of past actions

   ____

Imparfait

1. Ongoing past actions

   ____

2. Habitual past actions

   ____

3. Mental, physical, and emotional states and characteristics of the past

   ____

With a partner, compare your example sentences. Use the sentences as a guide to help you decide which tense to use as you are writing a story about something that happened in the past.

Thème

Écrire une histoire

Avant l'écriture

1. Quand vous étiez petit(e), vous habitiez dans la maison ou l'appartement de vos rêves (*of your dreams*).

   - Vous allez décrire cette maison ou cet appartement.
   - Vous allez écrire sur la ville où vous habitiez et sur votre quartier.
   - Vous allez décrire les différentes pièces, les meubles et les objets décoratifs.
   - Vous allez parler de votre pièce préférée et de ce que (*what*) vous aimiez faire dans cette pièce.

   Ensuite, imaginez qu'il y ait eu (*was*) un cambriolage (*burglary*) dans cette maison ou dans cet appartement. Vous allez alors décrire ce qui est arrivé (*what happened*).

Coup de main

Here are some terms that you may find useful in your narration.

le voleur	*thief*
cassé(e)	*broken*
j'ai vu	*I saw*
manquer	*to be missing*

OPTIONS

Avant l'écriture Say or read aloud some French past-tense sentences and have students identify the **passé composé** and **imparfait** forms. For each sentence, have students say why one form or the other was used. Review with them the situations and contexts that trigger the use of each tense.

Preview the use of the arrow diagram. Copy it on the board, making sure it is large enough to write inside. Start out with a description of the setting using the **imparfait** and write those sentences inside the arrow. Then have students volunteer possible completed actions using the **passé composé** and write them on the lines that intersect the arrow.

2. Utilisez le diagramme pour vous aider à analyser les éléments de votre histoire. Écrivez les éléments qui se rapportent à (*that are related to*) l'imparfait dans la partie IMPARFAIT et ceux (*the ones*) qui se rapportent au passé composé dans les parties PASSÉ COMPOSÉ.

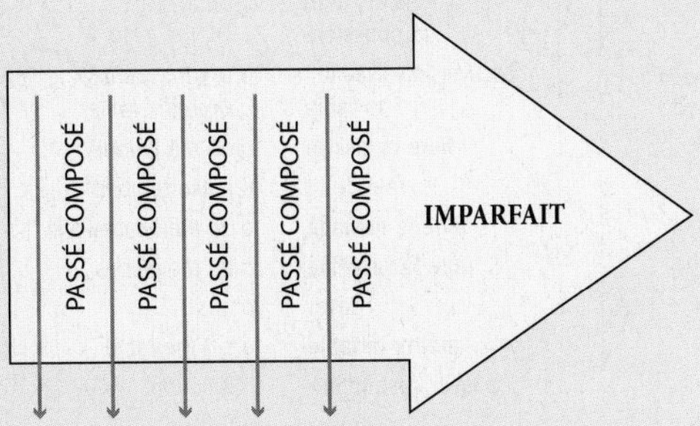

3. Après avoir complété le diagramme, échangez-le avec celui d'un(e) partenaire. Votre partenaire doit-il (*does he/she have to*) changer quelque chose? Expliquez pourquoi.

Écriture

Utilisez le diagramme pour écrire votre histoire. Écrivez trois paragraphes:

- le premier sur la présentation générale de la maison ou de l'appartement et de la ville où vous habitiez,
- le deuxième sur votre pièce préférée et la raison pour laquelle (*the reason why*) vous l'avez choisie,
- le troisième sur le cambriolage, sur ce qui s'est passé (*what happened*) et sur ce que vous avez fait (*what you did*).

Quand j'étais petit(e), j'habitais dans un château, en France. Le château était dans une petite ville près de Paris. Il y avait un grand jardin, avec beaucoup d'animaux. Il y avait douze pièces...

Ma pièce préférée était la cuisine parce que j'aimais faire la cuisine et que j'aidais souvent ma mère...

Un jour, mes parents et moi sommes rentrés de vacances...

Après l'écriture

1. Échangez votre histoire avec celle (*the one*) d'un(e) partenaire. Répondez à ces questions pour commenter son travail.
   - Votre partenaire a-t-il/elle correctement utilisé l'imparfait et le passé composé?
   - A-t-il/elle écrit trois paragraphes qui correspondent aux descriptions de sa maison ou de son appartement et de la ville, de sa pièce préférée et du cambriolage?
   - Quel(s) détail(s) ajouteriez-vous (*would you add*)? Lequel/Lesquels enlèveriez-vous (*Which one(s) would you delete*)? Quel(s) autre(s) commentaire(s) avez-vous pour votre partenaire?

2. Corrigez votre histoire d'après (*according to*) les commentaires de votre partenaire. Relisez votre travail pour éliminer ces problèmes:
   - des fautes (*errors*) d'orthographe
   - des fautes de ponctuation
   - des fautes de conjugaison
   - des fautes d'accord (*agreement*) des adjectifs
   - un mauvais emploi (*use*) de la grammaire

EVALUATION

Criteria

Content Contains a complete description of a house or apartment, its furnishings, and the place where it was located, followed by a complete past-tense narration about a robbery that took place there.
Scale: 1 2 3 4 5

Organization Contains two parts: a complete past-tense description of a place that uses **imparfait** forms followed by a past-tense narration using the **passé composé**.
Scale: 1 2 3 4 5

Accuracy Uses **passé composé** and **imparfait** forms correctly and in the correct context. Spells words, conjugates verbs, and modifies adjectives correctly throughout.
Scale: 1 2 3 4 5

Creativity Includes additional information that is not included in the task and/or uses adjectives and descriptive verbs to make the scene more vivid.
Scale: 1 2 3 4 5

Scoring

Excellent	18–20 points
Good	14–17 points
Satisfactory	10–13 points
Unsatisfactory	< 10 points

OPTIONS

Écriture Supply students with some useful expressions to use for their compositions: 1. Ongoing past-tense description: **toujours, tous les jours, d'habitude, normalement, en général/généralement, chaque fois, de temps en temps** 2. Completed past actions: **tout d'un coup, tous ensemble, dans un moment, à ce moment-là, puis, ensuite, après, plus tard, enfin, finalement**

Après l'écriture When students have completed their stories, have them work in pairs or small groups to create a dramatic reenactment of the story. They can use voiceover narration for the descriptive part, then act out the completed actions that are part of the robbery and its aftermath. Encourage students to be creative and to use props and posters to set the stage and tell the story.

Instructional Resources
espaces.vhlcentral.com: Textbook MP3s; IRM (Textbook Audioscript); downloads; reference tools

Suggestion Tell students that an easy way to study from **Vocabulaire** is to cover up the French half of each section, leaving only the English equivalents exposed. They can then quiz themselves on the French items. To focus on the English equivalents of the French entries, they simply reverse this process.

Flashcards
Audio: Vocabulary

VOCABULAIRE

Les parties d'une maison

un balcon	*balcony*
une cave	*cellar; basement*
une chambre	*bedroom*
un couloir	*hallway*
une cuisine	*kitchen*
un escalier	*staircase*
un garage	*garage*
un jardin	*garden; yard*
un mur	*wall*
une pièce	*room*
une salle à manger	*dining room*
une salle de bains	*bathroom*
une salle de séjour	*living/family room*
un salon	*formal living/ sitting room*
un sous-sol	*basement*
un studio	*studio (apartment)*
les toilettes (*f.*)/ W.-C. (*m.*)	*restrooms/toilet*

Les appareils ménagers

un appareil électrique/ménager	*electrical/household appliance*
une cafetière	*coffeemaker*
un congélateur	*freezer*
une cuisinière	*stove; female cook*
un fer à repasser	*iron*
un four	*oven*
un (four à) micro-ondes	*microwave oven*
un frigo	*refrigerator*
un grille-pain	*toaster*
un lave-linge	*washing machine*
un lave-vaisselle	*dishwasher*
un sèche-linge	*clothes dryer*

Chez soi

un(e) propriétaire	*owner*
un appartement	*apartment*
un immeuble	*building*
un logement	*housing*
un loyer	*rent*
un quartier	*area, neighborhood*
une résidence universitaire	*dorm*
une affiche	*poster*
une armoire	*armoire, wardrobe*
une baignoire	*bathtub*
un balai	*broom*
un canapé	*couch*
une commode	*dresser, chest of drawers*
une couverture	*blanket*
une douche	*shower*
les draps (*m.*)	*sheets*
une étagère	*shelf*
un évier	*kitchen sink*
un fauteuil	*armchair*
une fleur	*flower*
une lampe	*lamp*
un lavabo	*bathroom sink*
un meuble	*piece of furniture*
un miroir	*mirror*
un oreiller	*pillow*
un placard	*closet, cupboard*
un rideau	*drape, curtain*
un tapis	*rug*
un tiroir	*drawer*
déménager	*to move out*
emménager	*to move in*
louer	*to rent*

Les tâches ménagères

une tâche ménagère	*household chore*
balayer	*to sweep*
débarrasser la table	*to clear the table*
enlever/faire la poussière	*to dust*
essuyer la vaisselle/ la table	*to dry the dishes/ to wipe the table*
faire la lessive	*to do the laundry*
faire le lit	*to make the bed*
faire le ménage	*to do the housework*
faire la vaisselle	*to do the dishes*
laver	*to wash*
mettre la table	*to set the table*
passer l'aspirateur	*to vacuum*
ranger	*to tidy up; to put away*
repasser (le linge)	*to iron (the laundry)*
salir	*to soil, to make dirty*
sortir la/les poubelle(s)	*to take out the trash*
propre	*clean*
sale	*dirty*

Verbes

connaître	*to know, to be familiar with*
reconnaître	*to recognize*
savoir	*to know (facts), to know how to do something*
vivre	*to live*

Expressions utiles	See pp. 259 and 273.
Expressions that signal a past tense	See p. 265.

ressources
espaces.vhlcentral.com

La nourriture

UNITÉ 9

Leçon 9A

Leçon 9B

Pour commencer

- Où est Sandrine, dans un supermarché ou une poissonnerie?
- Quand va-t-elle manger ce qu'elle (*what she*) a dans la main? Le matin ou à midi?
- Comment va-t-elle le servir, avec un steak, dans une salade ou dans une tarte?
- Est-ce qu'elle a déjà payé ou pas encore (*not yet*)?

Savoir-faire

Unit Goals

Leçon 9A

In this lesson, students will learn:
- terms for food and meals
- about the **e caduc** and the **e muet**
- about food shopping in France
- more about open-air markets through specially shot video footage
- the verb **venir** and similar verbs
- the **passé récent**
- to use time expressions with **depuis**, **pendant**, and **il y a**
- the verbs **devoir**, **vouloir**, and **pouvoir**
- how to prepare a **far breton**

Leçon 9B

In this lesson, students will learn:
- terms for eating in a restaurant
- terms for specialty food shops
- about stress and rhythm in spoken French
- about French meals and eating habits
- comparatives and superlatives of adjectives and adverbs
- irregular comparative and superlative forms
- double object pronouns
- to take notes as they listen

Savoir-faire

In this section, students will learn:
- cultural and historical information about **Bourgogne** and **Franche-Comté**
- to read for the main idea
- to express and support opinions
- to write a restaurant review

Pour commencer

- **Elle est dans un supermarché.**
- **Elle va le manger à midi.**
- **Elle va le servir dans une salade.**
- **Non, elle n'a pas encore payé.**

RESSOURCES

Workbook/Video Manual: WB Activities, pp. 113–126
Laboratory Manual: Lab Activities, pp. 65–72
Workbook/Video Manual: Video Activities, pp. 243–246; pp. 287–288
WB/VM/LM Answer Key

espaces.vhlcentral.com: Textbook MP3s; Lab MP3s; Instructor's Resource Manual [IRM] (Textbook Audioscript; Lab Audioscript; Videoscript; **Roman-photo** Translations; **Vocabulaire supplémentaire**; **Feuilles d'activités**; Info Gap Activities; **Essayez!** and **Mise en pratique** answers); Transparencies #40, #41, #42; Testing Program, pp. 65–72, pp. 137–144; Test Files; Testing Program MP3s
Test Generator
Video on DVD

Section Goals

In this section, students will learn and practice vocabulary related to:
- foods
- meals

Instructional Resources
*espaces.vhlcentral.com: Transparency #40; IRM (**Vocabulaire supplémentaire**; **Mise en pratique** answers; Textbook Audioscript; Lab Audioscript; **Feuilles d'activités**); Textbook MP3s; Lab MP3s; WB/VM/LM Answer Key; activities; downloads; reference tools*

Suggestions
- Use **Transparency #40.** Point out foods as you describe the illustration. Examples: **Voici des fraises. Elle achète une pêche. Le garçon a acheté des œufs, un poivron vert et une laitue.**
- Ask students questions about their food preferences using the new vocabulary. **Préférez-vous les poires ou les fraises? Les oranges ou les bananes? Les tomates ou les champignons? Les escargots ou le thon? Le porc ou le poulet? La viande ou les fruits de mer?**
- Point out that **une cantine** is a cafeteria in French, while **une cafétéria** is a self-service restaurant.
- Name some dishes and have students explain what ingredients are used to make them. Examples: **une salade de fruits, une salade mixte,** and **un sandwich.**
- Say food items and have students classify them in categories under the headings: **les fruits, les légumes, la viande,** and **le poisson.**
- Additional vocabulary for this lesson can be found in the **Vocabulaire supplémentaire** on the Supersite.

Leçon 9A

Talking Picture
Audio: Activity

You will learn how to...
- talk about food
- express needs, desires, and abilities

Quel appétit!

Vocabulaire

cuisiner	*to cook*
faire les courses (f.)	*to go (grocery) shopping*
une cantine	*(school) cafeteria*
un supermarché	*supermarket*
un aliment	*food item*
un déjeuner	*lunch*
un dîner	*dinner*
un goûter	*afternoon snack*
la nourriture	*food, sustenance*
un petit-déjeuner	*breakfast*
un repas	*meal*
des petits pois (m.)	*peas*
une salade	*salad*
le bœuf	*beef*
un escargot	*escargot, snail*
les fruits de mer (m.)	*seafood*
un pâté (de campagne)	*pâté*
le porc	*pork*
un poulet	*chicken*
une saucisse	*sausage*
un steak	*steak*
le thon	*tuna*
la viande	*meat*
le riz	*rice*
des pâtes (f.)	*pasta*
un yaourt	*yogurt*

ressources
WB pp. 113–114 | LM p. 65 | espaces.vhlcentral.com

OPTIONS

Extra Practice To review colors and practice new vocabulary, ask students to name foods that are different colors. Examples: **jaune (les bananes), rouge (les pommes, les tomates, les fraises), vert (les haricots verts et les petits pois), orange (les oranges et les carottes), blanc (les oignons et le riz).**

Game Divide the class into two teams. Give one player a card with the name of a food item. That player is allowed 30 seconds to draw the item for another player on his or her team to guess. Award a point for a correct answer. If a player doesn't guess the correct answer, the next player on the opposing team may "steal" the point.

Mise en pratique

1 Les invités Vous avez invité quelques amis pour le week-end. Vous vous préparez à les accueillir *(welcome)*. Complétez les phrases suivantes avec les mots ou les expressions qui conviennent le mieux *(fit the best)*.

1. Au petit-déjeuner, Sébastien aime bien prendre un café et manger des croissants et un yaourt. (une salade, des fruits de mer, un yaourt)
2. Pour un petit-déjeuner français, il faut aussi de la confiture. (la confiture, l'ail, l'oignon)
3. J'adore les fruits, alors je vais acheter des pêches. (des petits pois, un repas, des pêches)
4. Mélanie n'aime pas trop la viande, elle va préférer manger des fruits de mer. (des fruits de mer, du pâté de campagne, des saucisses)
5. Je vais aussi préparer une salade pour Mélanie avec des tomates. (de la confiture, des tomates, du bœuf)
6. Jean-François est allergique au lait. Je ne vais donc pas lui servir de yaourt. (carottes, pommes de terre, yaourt)
7. Pour le dessert, je vais préparer une tarte aux fruits avec des fraises. (poivrons, fraises, petits pois)
8. Il faut aller au supermarché pour acheter des oranges pour faire du jus pour le petit-déjeuner. (yaourts, pâtes, oranges)

2 Écoutez Fatima et René se préparent à aller faire des courses. Ils décident de ce qu'ils vont acheter. Écoutez leur conversation. Ensuite, complétez les phrases.

Dans le frigo, il reste six (1) carottes, quelques (2) champignons, une petite (3) laitue et trois (4) tomates. René va utiliser ce qu'il reste dans le frigo pour préparer (5) le déjeuner/une salade. Fatima va acheter des (6) pommes de terre et des (7) oignons. René va acheter des (8) fruits: des (9) fraises, des (10) pêches et quelques (11) poires. René va faire un bon petit repas avec des (12) fruits de mer.

3 Vos habitudes alimentaires Utilisez un élément de chaque colonne pour former des phrases au sujet de vos habitudes alimentaires. N'oubliez pas de faire les accords nécessaires. Answers will vary.

A	B	C
au petit-déjeuner	acheter	des bananes
au déjeuner	adorer	des carottes
au goûter	aimer (bien)	des fruits
au dîner	ne pas tellement aimer	des haricots verts
à la cantine	détester	des légumes
à la maison	manger	des œufs
au restaurant	prendre	du riz
au supermarché		de la viande

Practice more at **espaces.vhlcentral.com.**

1 Expansion Have students explain why the other items are incorrect. Example: **En général, on ne mange pas de fruits de mer au petit-déjeuner.**

2 Tapescript FATIMA: Je n'ai presque plus rien dans le frigo. Il faut aller au supermarché.
RENÉ: D'accord.
F: Regardons d'abord ce qu'il nous reste. Voyons, il nous reste six carottes, quelques champignons, une petite laitue et trois tomates.
R: Parfait. Juste de quoi faire une salade pour le déjeuner. Mais il n'y a plus rien pour le dîner.
F: Dis, nous allons tout le temps au supermarché. Pourquoi ne pas aller au marché plutôt? Il y en a un place Victor Hugo aujourd'hui. Il est là deux fois par semaine: le mercredi et le dimanche. J'ai besoin d'acheter des pommes de terre et des oignons.
R: D'accord. Moi, je vais acheter des fruits: des fraises, des pêches et quelques poires. Et j'ai envie d'acheter des fruits de mer aussi. Je vais te faire un bon petit repas.
F: Alors, allons-y! Au marché!
(On Textbook MP3s)

2 Suggestion Play the complete conversation. Give students a few minutes to complete the paragraph, then play the recording again, stopping at the end of each sentence that contains an answer, so students can check their work or fill in any missing information.

3 Suggestion This activity can be done orally or in writing, in pairs or in groups.

OPTIONS

Extra Practice Have students draw food pyramids based not on what they should eat, but on what they actually do eat. Encourage them to include drawings or magazine photos to enhance their visual presentation. Then have students present their pyramids to the class.

Game Play a memory game in which the first player begins with: **Je vais au supermarché. J'ai besoin d'acheter...** and names one food item. The next player repeats what the first person said and adds another food. The third player must remember what the first two people said before adding an item.

4 Expansion Have students describe what they typically eat at each meal and for snacks.

5 Suggestion Distribute the **Feuilles d'activités** found on the Supersite. Have two volunteers read the **modèle** aloud.

6 Suggestions
- Point out the **Coup de main.**
- Encourage students to include photos or drawings to illustrate their brochures. Have students vote on the best brochure in various categories.

Communication

4 Quel repas? Regardez les dessins et pour chacun d'eux (*each one of them*), indiquez le repas qu'il représente et faites une liste de ce que (*what*) chaque personne mange. Ensuite, avec un(e) partenaire, décrivez une image à tour de rôle. Votre partenaire doit deviner (*must guess*) quel dessin vous décrivez. Answers will vary.

1. ______________

2. ______________

3. ______________

4. ______________

5 Sondage Votre professeur va vous donner une feuille d'activités. Circulez dans la classe et utilisez les éléments du tableau pour former des questions afin de savoir (*in order to find out*) ce que vos camarades de classe mangent. Quels sont les trois aliments les plus (*the most*) souvent mentionnés? Answers will vary.

MODÈLE

Étudiant(e) 1: *À quelle heure est-ce que tu prends ton petit-déjeuner? Que manges-tu?*
Étudiant(e) 2: *Je prends mon petit-déjeuner à sept heures. Je mange du pain avec du beurre et de la confiture, et je bois un café au lait.*

Questions	*Noms*	*Réponses*
1. Petit-déjeuner: Quand? Quoi?	1. ______	1. ______
2. Déjeuner: Où? Quand? Quoi?	2. ______	2. ______
3. Goûter: Quand? Quoi?	3. ______	3. ______
4. Dîner: Quand? Quoi?	4. ______	4. ______
5. Supermarché: Quoi? À quelle fréquence?	5. ______	5. ______
6. Cantine: Quoi? Quand? À quelle fréquence?	6. ______	6. ______

6 La brochure Avec un(e) partenaire, vous allez préparer une brochure pour les nouveaux étudiants français qui viennent (*are coming*) étudier dans votre université. Une partie de la brochure est consacrée (*dedicated*) aux habitudes alimentaires. Faites une comparaison entre la France et les États-Unis. Ensuite, présentez votre brochure à la classe. Answers will vary.

Coup de main

Here are some characteristics of traditional French eating habits.

Le petit-déjeuner is usually light, with bread, butter, and jam, or cereal and coffee or tea. Croissants are normally reserved for the weekend.

Le déjeuner is typically the main meal and may include a starter, a main dish (meat or fish with vegetables), cheese or yogurt, and dessert (often fruit). Lunch breaks may be a half hour to two hours (allowing people to eat at home).

Le goûter is a light afternoon snack such as cookies, French bread with chocolate, pastry, yogurt, or fruit.

Le dîner starts between 7:00 and 8:00 p.m. Foods served at lunch and dinner are similar. However, dinner is typically lighter than lunch and is usually eaten at home.

OPTIONS

Game Play a game of **Dix questions**. Ask a volunteer to think of a food from the new vocabulary. Other students get to ask one yes/no question, and then they can guess what the word is. Limit attempts to ten questions per word. You may want to provide students with some sample questions. Examples: **C'est un fruit? Est-ce qu'il est vert?**

Extra Practice Prepare descriptions of various meals, which include breakfasts, lunches, snacks, and dinners. Have students write down what you say as a dictation. Then have them guess which meal each description represents.

Les sons et les lettres

Audio: Concepts, Activities
Record & Compare

NATIONAL STANDARDS comparisons

e caduc and e muet

In **Leçon 4A**, you learned that the vowel **e** in very short words is pronounced similarly to the *a* in the English word *about*. This sound is called an **e caduc**. An **e caduc** can also occur in longer words and before words beginning with vowel sounds.

rechercher **devoirs** **le haricot** **le onze**

An **e caduc** occurs in order to break up clusters of several consonants.

appartement **quelquefois** **poivre vert** **gouvernement**

An **e caduc** is sometimes called **e muet** (*mute*). It is often dropped in spoken French.

Tu n~~e~~ sais pas. **J~~e~~ veux bien!** **C'est un livr~~e~~ intéressant.**

An unaccented **e** before a single consonant sound is often silent unless its omission makes the word difficult to pronounce.

s~~e~~maine **p~~e~~tit** **final~~e~~ment**

An unaccented e at the end of a word is usually silent and often marks a feminine noun or adjective.

frais~~e~~ **salad~~e~~** **intelligent~~e~~** **jeun~~e~~**

Prononcez Répétez les mots suivants à voix haute.

1. vendredi
2. logement
3. exemple
4. devenir
5. tartelette
6. finalement
7. boucherie
8. petits pois
9. pomme de terre
10. malheureusement

Articulez Répétez les phrases suivantes à voix haute.

1. Tu ne vas pas prendre de casquette?
2. J'étudie le huitième chapitre maintenant.
3. Il va passer ses vacances en Angleterre.
4. Marc me parle souvent au téléphone.
5. Mercredi, je réserve dans une auberge.
6. Finalement, ce petit logement est bien.

Dictons Répétez les dictons à voix haute.

L'habit ne fait pas le moine.¹

Le soleil luit pour tout le monde.²

¹ Clothes don't make the man. (lit. The habit doesn't make the monk.)
² The sun shines for everyone.

ressources
LM p. 66
espaces.vhlcentral.com

Section Goals

In this section, students will learn about **e caduc** and **e muet**.

Instructional Resources
espaces.vhlcentral.com: Textbook MP3s; Lab MP3s; WB/VM/LM Answer Key; IRM (Textbook Audioscript; Lab Audioscript); activities; downloads; reference tools

Suggestions

- Point out that although the pronunciation of the French **e caduc** and that of the *a* in the English word *about* are close, they are not identical. There is a difference in vowel quality and articulation.
- Model the pronunciation of the example words and have students repeat them after you.
- Point out that while the unaccented **e** at the end of a word is itself silent, it can influence the pronunciation of a word, often causing the final consonant to be pronounced. Example: **intelligent / intelligente.**
- Ask students to provide more examples of words from this lesson or previous lessons with **e caduc** and **e muet**. Examples: **repas, petit-déjeuner,** and **petits pois**.
- Dictate five familiar words containing **e caduc** and **e muet**, repeating each one at least two times. Then write them on the board or on a transparency and have students check their spelling.

OPTIONS

Extra Practice Use these sentences with **e caduc** and **e muet** for additional practice or dictation. **1. Je fais mes devoirs le samedi. 2. Malheureusement, elle ne va pas descendre de son appartement. 3. Tu me fais une tartelette aux fraises, s'il te plaît? 4. La semaine dernière, Denise a acheté un immeuble en ville.**

Extra Practice Teach students these French tongue-twisters that contain **e caduc** and **e muet**. **1. Le poivre fait fièvre à la pauvre pieuvre** (*octopus*). (by Pierre Abbat) **2. Je dis que tu l'as dit à Didi ce que j'ai dit jeudi.**

Section Goals

In this section, students will learn functional phrases for discussing meetings, time, and grocery shopping.

Instructional Resources

*espaces.vhlcentral.com: Video; WB/VM/LM Answer Key; IRM (Videoscript; **Roman-photo** Translations); activities; downloads; reference tools*

Video Recap: Leçon 8B

Before doing this **Roman-photo**, review the previous one with this activity.

1. Quelles tâches ménagères a fait Stéphane? (Il a rangé sa chambre, il a fait son lit et il a fait la vaisselle.)

2. Que préparait Sandrine quand Amina est arrivée? (Elle préparait des biscuits au chocolat.)

3. Comment Sandrine décrit-elle Pascal? (Elle dit qu'il est pénible.)

4. Comment était Sandrine? (Elle était de mauvaise humeur.)

5. Pourquoi Sandrine dit-elle qu'Amina a de la chance? (Parce qu'elle a son Cyberhomme.)

Video Synopsis

Amina and David are at the supermarket. Sandrine finally arrives, explaining that her French teacher kept her 20 minutes late, plus she ran into Stéphane who wanted to discuss tonight's dinner. The three friends then discuss what is going to be prepared, and Sandrine picks out the ingredients she needs. At the check-out counter, Amina and David insist on buying the groceries.

Suggestions

- Have students predict what the episode will be about based on the title and video stills.
- Have students scan the captions and find sentences describing foods.
- Review predictions and have students summarize the episode.

Au supermarché

Video: *Roman-photo*
Record & Compare

PERSONNAGES

Amina

Caissière

David

Sandrine

Stéphane

Au supermarché...

AMINA Mais quelle heure est-il? Sandrine devait être là à deux heures et quart. On l'attend depuis quinze minutes!

DAVID Elle va arriver!

AMINA Mais pourquoi est-elle en retard?

DAVID Elle vient peut-être juste de sortir de la fac.

En ville...

STÉPHANE Eh! Sandrine!

SANDRINE Salut, Stéphane, je suis très pressée! David et Amina m'attendent au supermarché depuis vingt minutes.

STÉPHANE À quelle heure est-ce qu'on doit venir ce soir, ma mère et moi?

SANDRINE À sept heures et demie.

STÉPHANE D'accord. Qu'est-ce qu'on peut apporter?

SANDRINE Oh, rien, rien.

STÉPHANE Mais maman insiste.

SANDRINE Bon, une salade, si tu veux.

AMINA Alors, Sandrine. Qu'est-ce que tu vas nous préparer?

SANDRINE Un repas très français. Je pensais à des crêpes.

DAVID Génial, j'adore les crêpes!

SANDRINE Il nous faut des champignons, du jambon et du fromage. Et, bien sûr, des œufs, du lait et du beurre.

SANDRINE Et puis non! Finalement, je vous prépare un bœuf bourguignon.

AMINA Qu'est-ce qu'il nous faut alors?

SANDRINE Du bœuf, des carottes, des oignons...

DAVID Mmm... Ça va être bon!

AMINA Mais le bœuf bourguignon, c'est long à préparer, non?

SANDRINE Tu as raison. Vous ne voulez pas plutôt un poulet à la crème et aux champignons, accompagné d'un gratin de pommes de terre?

AMINA ET DAVID Mmmm!

SANDRINE Alors, c'est décidé.

ACTIVITÉS

1 Les ingrédients Répondez aux questions par des phrases complètes.

1. Quels ingrédients faut-il pour préparer les crêpes de Sandrine? Pour préparer ses crêpes, il faut des champignons, du jambon, du fromage, des œufs, du lait et du beurre.
2. Quels ingrédients faut-il pour préparer le bœuf bourguignon? Pour préparer le bœuf bourguignon, il faut du bœuf, des carottes et des oignons.
3. Quels ingrédients faut-il à Sandrine pour préparer le poulet et le gratin? Pour préparer le poulet et le gratin, il faut du poulet, de la crème, des champignons et des pommes de terre.
4. Quelle va être la salade de Valérie, à votre avis? Quels ingrédients va-t-elle mettre? Answers will vary. Possible answer: Ça va être une salade au thon avec des tomates.
5. À votre avis, quel(s) dessert(s) Sandrine va-t-elle préparer? Answers will vary. Possible answer: Sandrine va préparer une tarte aux fraises.
6. Après avoir lu/regardé cet **ESPACE ROMAN-PHOTO**, quel plat préférez-vous? Pourquoi? Answers will vary.

OPTIONS

Avant de regarder la vidéo Before viewing the video, have students work in pairs and write a list of words and expressions that they might hear in a video episode entitled **Au supermarché**.

Regarder la vidéo Show the video episode and tell students to check off the words and expressions they hear on their lists. Then show the episode again and have students give you a play-by-play description of the action. Write their descriptions on the board.

Amina, Sandrine et David font les courses.

4

5

STÉPHANE Mais quoi, comme salade?
SANDRINE Euh, une salade de tomates ou… peut-être une salade verte… Désolée, Stéphane, je suis vraiment pressée!
STÉPHANE Une salade avec du thon, peut-être? Maman fait une salade au thon délicieuse!
SANDRINE Comme tu veux, Stéphane!

SANDRINE Je suis en retard. Je suis vraiment désolée. Je ne voulais pas vous faire attendre, mais je viens de rencontrer Stéphane et avant ça, mon prof de français m'a retenue pendant vingt minutes!
DAVID Oh, ce n'est pas grave!
AMINA Bon, on fait les courses?

9

10

SANDRINE Voilà exactement ce qu'il me faut pour commencer! Deux beaux poulets!
AMINA Tu sais, Sandrine, le chant, c'est bien, mais tu peux devenir chef de cuisine si tu veux!

CAISSIÈRE Ça vous fait 51 euros et 25 centimes, s'il vous plaît.
AMINA C'est cher!
DAVID Ah non, Sandrine, tu ne paies rien du tout. C'est pour nous!
SANDRINE Mais, c'est mon dîner et vous êtes mes invités.
AMINA Pas question, Sandrine. C'est nous qui payons!

Expressions utiles

Meeting friends

- **Sandrine devait être là à deux heures et quart.**
  Sandrine should have been here at 2:15.
- **On l'attend depuis quinze minutes!**
  We've been waiting for her for fifteen minutes!
- **Elle vient peut-être juste de sortir de la fac.**
  Maybe she just left school.
- **Je suis très pressé(e)!**
  I'm in a big hurry!
- **À quelle heure est-ce qu'on doit venir ce soir?**
  At what time should we come tonight?
- **Je ne voulais pas vous faire attendre, mais je viens de rencontrer Stéphane.**
  I didn't want to make you wait, but I just ran into Stéphane.
- **Mon prof m'a retenue pendant vingt minutes!**
  My professor kept me for twenty minutes!

Additional vocabulary

- **une caissière**
  cashier
- **Vous ne voulez pas plutôt un poulet à la crème accompagné d'un gratin de pommes de terre?**
  Wouldn't you prefer chicken with cream sauce accompanied by potatoes au gratin?
- **Voilà exactement ce qu'il me faut.**
  Here's exactly what I need.
- **Tu peux devenir chef de cuisine si tu veux!**
  You could become a chef if you want!
- **Comme tu veux.**
  As you like./It's up to you./Whatever you want.
- **C'est pour nous.**
  It's on us.

ACTIVITÉS

2 Les événements Mettez les événements dans l'ordre chronologique.

3 a. Sandrine décide de ne pas préparer de bœuf bourguignon.
1 b. Le prof de Sandrine parle avec elle après la classe.
4 c. Amina dit que Sandrine peut devenir chef de cuisine.
6 d. David et Amina paient.
2 e. Stéphane demande à quelle heure il doit arriver.
5 f. Sandrine essaie de payer.

3 À vous! Stéphane arrive chez lui et dit à sa mère qu'il faut préparer une salade pour le dîner de Sandrine. Avec un(e) partenaire, préparez une conversation entre Stéphane et sa mère. Parlez du dîner et décidez des ingrédients pour la salade. Présentez votre conversation à la classe.

Practice more at **espaces.vhlcentral.com.**

ressources: VM pp. 243–244 | DVD Leçon 9A | espaces.vhlcentral.com

Expressions utiles

- Model the pronunciation of the **Expressions utiles.**
- As you work through the list, point out forms of **devoir, pouvoir, vouloir, venir**, and the **passé recent**. Explain that **venir de** can be used to say what just happened or what someone just did. Then tell students that these verbs and structures will be formally presented in **Espace structures**.
- Point out that, although **là** means *there*, in some cases it can be interpreted as *here*. Example: **Sandrine devait être là à deux heures et quart**.
- Explain the difference between **il faut** + *infinitive* (*need to or must do something*) and **il nous faut** (*we need something*).

1 Suggestion Have volunteers write their answers on the board. Then go over them as a class.

2 Suggestion Have students form groups of six. Make a set of individual sentences on strips of paper for each group and distribute them. Tell students to arrange the sentences in the proper order and then read them aloud.

2 Expansion Have students create sentences to fill in parts of the story not mentioned in this activity.

3 Suggestion Tell students to refer to the **Expressions utiles** as they prepare their role-plays.

OPTIONS

Small Groups Have students work in groups of three or four. Tell them to create a menu for a classic French meal, then make a shopping list for the ingredients they need. You might want to suggest some classic dishes, such as **une tarte aux pommes, une soupe à l'oignon,** and **un pot-au-feu** (*beef and vegetable stew*). You can also bring in French cookbooks or simple recipes from magazines or the Internet, for students to use as reference.

Extra Practice Ask volunteers to ad-lib the scenes in video stills 5–10 for the class. Tell them it is not necessary to memorize the episode or to stick strictly to its content. They should try to get the general meaning across with the vocabulary they know, and they should also feel free to be creative. Give them time to prepare.

Section Goals

In this section, students will:
- learn about grocery shopping in France
- learn some colloquial expressions related to foods and meals
- learn about some traditional foods of New Orleans
- read about French cheeses
- view authentic video footage

Instructional Resources
espaces.vhlcentral.com: Video; WB/VM/LM Answer Key; IRM (Videoscript); activities; downloads; reference tools

Culture à la loupe

Avant la lecture Have students look at the photos and describe what they see.

Lecture
- Point out the **Coup de main**.
- Point out the statistics chart. Ask students what information the chart shows. (the amount of each food consumed by a French person in 1970, 1990, and 2006) Then ask how much of each item was consumed. Example: **Combien de kilos de fromage ont consommé les Français en 1970? (14 kg par personne)**

Après la lecture Ask students: **Où les Français font-ils leurs courses? (dans les hypermarchés, les supermarchés, les supérettes, les magasins discount, les petits commerces de quartier, les épiceries de quartier, les épiceries fines, les marchés en plein air ou aux halles) Et les Américains, où font-ils leurs courses?**

1 Expansion Have students create three more fill-in-the-blank sentences. Then tell them to exchange papers with a classmate and complete the activity.

Video: ***Flash culture***

NATIONAL STANDARDS connections cultures

CULTURE À LA LOUPE

Faire des courses

Les Français ont plusieurs possibilités pour faire leurs courses. On peut tout acheter dans les grandes surfaces: les hypermarchés et les supermarchés situés dans les banlieues et à l'extérieur des villes. En plus de l'alimentation, les hypermarchés vendent aussi des vêtements, des chaussures, du matériel audio et vidéo, etc. À l'entrée des hypermarchés, on trouve souvent un ou deux restaurants et quelques magasins. Dans les grandes villes, il y a aussi des supermarchés et des supérettes. Les supérettes sont des petits supermarchés. On trouve aussi des magasins discount qui offrent des produits° moins chers.

Bien souvent, aussi, les habitants d'une ville qui ne peuvent pas° facilement se déplacer° aiment faire leurs courses dans les petits commerces de quartier°. Par exemple, pour le fromage, on va à la crémerie° ou à la fromagerie; pour la viande, on va à la boucherie° ou à la charcuterie°; pour le poisson, à la poissonnerie. Dans les épiceries de quartier, on trouve aussi toutes sortes de produits, par exemple des fruits et des légumes, des produits frais°, des boîtes de conserve°, des produits surgelés°, etc. Les épiceries fines se spécialisent dans les produits de luxe et parfois, dans les plats préparés. La majorité des villes et des villages français ont aussi un marché en plein air° une ou deux fois par semaine. Dans certaines villes, on peut faire ses courses aux halles. Les halles sont comme un marché, mais elles sont dans un bâtiment et, en général, ouvertes tous les jours.

Les Français et l'alimentation
(Consommation par personne par an)

	1970	1990	2006
Bœuf (kg)	16	18	14
Fromage (kg)	14	17	19
Légumes (kg)	71	86	88
Œufs (kg)	12	14	14
Pain (kg)	81	62	54
Poissons, crustacés° (kg)	10	15	12
Volailles° (kg)	15	22	20
Yaourt (kg)	9	16	22

SOURCE: INSEE

produits *products* **ne peuvent pas** *can't* **se déplacer** *move* **commerces de quartier** *neighborhood stores* **crémerie** *cheese shop* **boucherie** *butcher shop* **frais** *fresh* **boîtes de conserve** *canned goods* **surgelés** *frozen* **en plein air** *outdoors* **crustacés** *shellfish* **Volailles** *Poultry*

Coup de main

Weights and measures

un kilogramme
2.2 pounds

une livre (½ kilogramme)
1.1 pound (17.6 ounces)

un litre
1.06 quarts (¼ gallon)

ACTIVITÉS

1 Complétez Complétez les phrases.

1. Dans les hypermarchés, on peut acheter de l'alimentation, des vêtements, des chaussures, du matériel audio et vidéo, etc.
2. En France, les supermarchés sont souvent dans les banlieues.
3. Une supérette est un petit supermarché.
4. Les personnes qui ne peuvent pas se déplacer font leurs courses dans les petits commerces de quartier.
5. Pour acheter du fromage, on peut aller à la crémerie/à la fromagerie.
6. Dans les épiceries de quartier, on peut acheter Answers will vary. Possible answer: des produits frais et des boîtes de conserve.
7. On peut acheter des plats préparés et des produits de luxe dans certaines épiceries fines.
8. Si on aime se promener en plein air, on peut aller faire ses courses au marché.
9. Les halles sont comme un marché, mais en intérieur.
10. La consommation de yaourt a plus que doublé entre 1970 et 2006.

Practice more at **espaces.vhlcentral.com.**

OPTIONS

Les Français et l'alimentation Have students work in pairs. Using the information in the chart, tell them to list the foods with an increase in consumption under the heading **Augmentation de la consommation** and the foods with a decrease in consumption under the heading **Baisse de la consommation**. Then ask: **Qu'apprenez-vous de ces informations?**

Faire des courses Grocery shopping in France is somewhat different from shopping in the United States. Grocery carts are usually locked together in a central place, most often in the parking lot. In order to use a cart, shoppers must insert a token. They get their money back when they return the cart. Also, customers are expected to bag their own groceries.

LE FRANÇAIS QUOTIDIEN

La nourriture

bidoche (*f.*)	*meat*
casse-croûte (*m.*)	*snack*
frometon (*m.*)	*cheese*
poiscaille (*f.*)	*fish*
faire un gueuleton	*to have a large meal*
faire ripaille	*to feast*
se faire une bouffe	*to have a dinner party with friends*

LE MONDE FRANCOPHONE

La cuisine de la Nouvelle-Orléans

À la Nouvelle-Orléans, la cuisine combine les influences créoles des colons° français et les influences cajuns des immigrés acadiens du Canada. Voici quelques spécialités.

le beignet un morceau de pâte frit° et recouvert de sucre, servi à toute heure du jour et de la nuit avec un café à la chicorée° et au lait

le gumbo une soupe à l'okra et aux fruits de mer, souvent accompagnée de riz

le jambalaya un riz très pimenté° préparé avec du jambon, du poulet, des tomates et parfois des saucisses et des fruits de mer

le po-boy de *poor boy* (garçon pauvre), un sandwich au poisson, aux écrevisses°, aux huîtres° ou à la viande dans un morceau de baguette

colons *colonists* **morceau de pâte frit** *fried piece of dough* **chicorée** *chicory* **pimenté** *spicy* **écrevisses** *crawfish* **huîtres** *oysters*

PORTRAIT

Les fromages français

Les Français sont très fiers de leurs fromages, et beaucoup de ces fromages sont connus dans le monde entier. La France produit près de 500 fromages dont° le type varie dans chaque région. Ils sont au lait de vache°, comme le Brie et le Camembert, au lait de chèvre°, comme le crottin de Chavignol, au lait de brebis°, comme le Roquefort, ou faits d'un mélange° de plusieurs laits. Ils sont aussi classés selon° leur fabrication: les fromages à pâte molle°, à pâte cuite° ou non cuite, à pâte persillée° et les fromages frais°. Plus de 95% des Français mangent du fromage et ils dépensent sept milliards° d'euros par an pour le fromage. On célèbre aussi la Journée nationale du fromage avec des débats, des conférences, des démonstrations de recettes° et des dégustations°.

dont *of which* **vache** *cow* **chèvre** *goat* **brebis** *ewe* **mélange** *mix* **selon** *according to* **pâte molle** *soft* **cuite** *cooked* **persillée** *blue cheese* **frais** *fresh* **milliards** *billions* **recettes** *recipes* **dégustations** *tastings*

SUR INTERNET

Peut-on acheter des appareils ménagers dans un hypermarché?

Go to **espaces.vhlcentral.com** to find more information related to this **ESPACE CULTURE**. Then watch the corresponding **Flash culture**.

ACTIVITÉS

2 À table! D'après les textes, répondez aux questions par des phrases complètes.

1. Combien de types de fromage sont produits en France? Près de 500 fromages différents sont produits en France.
2. Quels laits sont utilisés pour faire le fromage en France? Le lait de vache, le lait de chèvre et le lait de brebis sont utilisés pour faire le fromage.
3. Quelles sont trois des catégories de fromages? Answers will vary. Possible answer: Il y a des fromages à pâte cuite, non cuite et persillée.
4. Comment célèbre-t-on la Journée nationale du fromage? On la célèbre avec des débats, des conférences, des démonstrations de recettes et des dégustations.
5. Que met-on dans le jambalaya? On met du riz, du piment, du jambon, du poulet, des tomates et parfois des saucisses et des fruits de mer.
6. Quand peut-on manger des beignets à la Nouvelle-Orléans? On peut manger des beignets à toute heure du jour et de la nuit à la Nouvelle-Orléans.

3 Le pique-nique Vous et un(e) partenaire avez décidé de faire un pique-nique en plein air. Qu'allez-vous manger? Boire? Allez-vous apporter d'autres choses, comme des chaises ou une couverture? Parlez avec un autre groupe et échangez vos idées.

ressources: VM pp. 287-288 | espaces.vhlcentral.com

Le français quotidien
- Model the pronunciation of each term and have students repeat.
- The word **poiscaille** can be masculine or feminine, but it is more commonly used as a feminine noun.

Portrait
- Explain that in a good cheese shop customers can sample the cut cheeses before purchasing them. Also, the shop clerks often give advice on selecting cheese(s).
- Point out that a kind of goat cheese is generally referred to as **un chèvre**; the animal is **une chèvre**.

Le monde francophone Have students read the text. Then ask: **Avez-vous déjà mangé du gumbo? Du jambalaya? Avez-vous envie d'essayer un beignet? Pourquoi? Avez-vous envie d'essayer un po-boy au poisson, aux écrevisses, aux huîtres ou à la viande?**

2 Expansion For additional practice, give students these items. **7. Dans quels pays mange-t-on du fromage français? (dans le monde entier) 8. Combien de Français mangent du fromage? (plus de 95%) 9. Combien les Français dépensent-ils par an pour le fromage? (7 milliards d'euros) 10. Comment s'appelle un sandwich typique de la Nouvelle-Orléans? (un po-boy)**

3 Suggestion Tell students to jot down their ideas so that they will be prepared to discuss them.

Flash culture Tell students they will learn more about open-air markets by watching a variety of real-life images narrated by Csilla. Show the video segment without sound and tell students to call out what they see. Then, show the video segment again with sound. You can also use the activities in the video manual in class to reinforce this **Flash culture** or assign them as homework.

OPTIONS

La cuisine de la Nouvelle-Orléans New Orleans has many excellent chefs, but Paul Prudhomme and Emeril Lagasse are probably the most widely known. Additional specialities of the Crescent City include red beans and rice, crawfish étouffé, dirty rice, barbecued shrimp, blackened redfish, and pralines. Oysters are also popular and are featured in a number of dishes.

Les fromages français Have students go to a grocery store or an online grocery store and make a list of the different varieties or brands of French cheese they can buy there. Also have them note how much each cheese costs per pound and how long it was aged.

Section Goals
In this section, students will learn:
- the verb **venir** and similar verbs
- the **passé récent**
- time expressions with **depuis**, **pendant**, and **il y a**

Instructional Resources
*espaces.vhlcentral.com: Lab MP3s; WB/VM/LM Answer Key; IRM (**Essayez!** and **Mise en pratique** answers; Lab Audioscript); activities; downloads; reference tools*

Suggestions
- Model **venir** with the whole class by asking volunteers questions such as: **Venez-vous souvent au cours? Venez-vous de déjeuner? Venez-vous d'apprendre un nouveau verbe? Venez-vous me parler?** Point out that this verb has different meanings. Explain that when a form of **venir** is followed by **de** + *infinitive*, it means the action has just happened.
- Point out that **venir, devenir,** and **revenir** always take **être** in the **passé composé**.
- Write the conjugation of **venir** in a paradigm. Point out that the **e** changes to **ie** except in the **nous** and **vous** forms.
- Explain that, while other verbs like **tenir, maintenir,** etc. are conjugated like **venir**, they are not verbs of motion and take **avoir** in the **passé composé**.
- Explain that, when used as an interjection, **tiens/tenez** can mean either *here, here you,* or *hey,* depending on the context.
- Tell students that **retenir** means *to remember a piece of information.* Other uses of the verb *to remember* are expressed in French by **se rappeler** or **se souvenir**.
- Ask students questions like these to practice talking about time in the past: **Que faisiez-vous il y a trois ans? (J'étudiais au lycée il y a trois ans.) Depuis quand habitez-vous sur le campus? (J'habite sur le campus depuis le semestre dernier.)**

9A.1 The verb *venir* and the *passé récent*

NATIONAL STANDARDS comparisons

Point de départ In **Leçon 4A**, you learned the verb **aller** and the **futur proche**. Now you will learn how to conjugate and use the irregular verb **venir** (*to come*) and the **passé récent**.

Venir	
je viens	**nous venons**
tu viens	**vous venez**
il/elle vient	**ils/elles viennent**

Vous **venez** souvent ici?
Do you come here often?

Viens vers huit heures.
Come around 8 o'clock.

- **Venir** takes the auxiliary **être** in the **passé composé**. Its past participle is **venu**.

Ils **sont venus** vendredi dernier.
They came last Friday.

Nadine **est venue** déjeuner.
Nadine came to eat lunch.

Nous **sommes venues** à la fac.
We came to campus.

Es-tu **venu** trop tard?
Did you come too late?

- **Venir** can also be used with **de** and an infinitive to say that something has just happened. This is called the **passé récent**.

Je **viens de prendre** mon goûter dans ma chambre.
I just had a snack in my room.

Nous **venons de regarder** cette émission.
We just watched that show.

- **Venir** can be used with an infinitive to say that someone has come to do something.

Papa **est venu** me **chercher**.
Dad came to pick me up.

Elle **venait** nous **rendre** visite.
She used to come visit us.

- The verbs **devenir** (*to become*) and **revenir** (*to come back*) are conjugated like **venir**. They, too, take **être** in the **passé composé**.

Estelle et sa copine **sont devenues** médecins.
Estelle and her friend became doctors.

Il **est revenu** avec une tarte aux fraises.
He came back with a strawberry tart.

- The verbs **tenir** (*to hold*), **maintenir** (*to maintain*), and **retenir** (*to keep, to retain, to remember*) are also conjugated like **venir**. However, they take **avoir** in the **passé composé**.

Corinne **tient** le livre de cuisine.
Corinne is holding the cookbook.

On **a retenu** mon passeport à la douane.
They kept my passport at customs.

MISE EN PRATIQUE

1 Mes tantes Tante Olga téléphone à tante Simone pour lui donner des nouvelles (*news*) de la famille. Complétez ses phrases au passé composé.

1. La semaine dernière, Georges ___est revenu___ (revenir) de vacances.
2. Marc a déménagé, mais je ___n'ai pas retenu___ (ne pas retenir) sa nouvelle adresse.
3. J'ai rencontré Martine ce matin; elle ___est devenue___ (devenir) très jolie.
4. Alfred va avoir 100 ans; c'est parce qu'il ___a maintenu___ (maintenir) une bonne hygiène de vie.
5. Hier midi, Charles et Antoinette ___sont venus___ (venir) déjeuner à la maison.

2 Qu'est-ce qu'ils viennent de faire? Regardez les images et dites ce qu'ils (*what they*) viennent de faire. Answers will vary.

MODÈLE
Julien vient de faire un tour à cheval.

Julien

1. M. et Mme Martin M. et Mme Martin viennent d'assister au concert.

3. nous Nous venons de jouer au tennis.

2. vous Vous venez de dîner.

4. je Je viens de faire des courses.

3 Nos activités Avec un(e) partenaire, dites ce que (*what*) chaque personne vient de faire et ce qu'elle va faire maintenant. Answers will vary.

MODÈLE
Je viens de manger. Maintenant, je vais faire la vaisselle.

A	B	C
je	manger	emménager
tu	faire la lessive	répondre
elle	recevoir une lettre	faire un séjour
nous	acheter une maison	faire la vaisselle
vous	partir en vacances	prendre le train
ils	faire ses valises	repasser le linge

Practice more at **espaces.vhlcentral.com.**

OPTIONS

Extra Practice Do a pattern practice drill. Give an infinitive of a verb like **venir** and ask individual students to provide conjugations for the different subject pronouns and/or names you suggest. Reverse the activity by saying a conjugated form and asking students to give the appropriate subject pronoun. Try this activity with the **passé composé** as well.

Game Divide the class into two teams. Indicate one team member at a time, alternating between teams. Give a verb in its infinitive form and a subject pronoun. The team member goes to the board to write and say the correct **passé récent** form. Give one point per correct answer. Deduct a point for each wrong answer. The team with the most points at the end of play wins.

NATIONAL communication STANDARDS

COMMUNICATION

4 Préparation de la fête Marine a invité ses amis ce soir. Elle a demandé à un(e) ami(e) de l'aider. Ils sont tous/toutes les deux impatient(e)s et ont besoin de savoir si tout est prêt. Avec un(e) partenaire, jouez les rôles de Marine et de son ami(e). Alternez les rôles et utilisez **venir de**, **il y a**, **depuis** et **pendant**. Answers will vary.

MODÈLE

Étudiant(e) 1: *Étienne a téléphoné?*
Étudiant(e) 2: *Oui, il a téléphoné il y a une heure.*

1. Ta mère a apporté les gâteaux?
2. Tu as mis les fleurs dans le vase?
3. Pierre et Stéphanie ont fini de faire les courses?
4. Tu as sorti les boissons depuis quand?
5. Il faut mettre les escargots au four pendant longtemps?
6. Les salades de fruits sont dans le frigo?
7. Tu as préparé les tartes aux poires?
8. Ton petit ami est déjà arrivé?

5 Qui vient? Marc a aussi invité quelques amis ce week-end. Sa mère lui demande qui vient. Avec un(e) partenaire, jouez les rôles de Marc et de sa mère et alternez-les. Utilisez le vocabulaire de la liste. Answers will vary.

MODÈLE

Étudiant(e) 1: *Est-ce que Patricia vient?*
Étudiant(e) 2: *Non, elle ne vient pas.*
Étudiant(e) 1: *Pourquoi?*

absolument	désolé(e)	nous
avec plaisir	impossible	Patricia
bien sûr	je regrette	Paul et Sophie
chez nos grands-parents	mariage de sa sœur	tu

6 Un(e) Américain(e) à Paris Vous êtes à Paris et vous venez de rencontrer un(e) Américain(e) de San Francisco (votre partenaire). Vous lui demandez de vous décrire sa vie à Paris, ses voyages, ce qui (*what*) l'intéresse, etc. Utilisez **depuis**, **il y a** et **pendant**. Ensuite, jouez la scène pour la classe. Answers will vary.

MODÈLE

Étudiant(e) 1: *Tu habites en France depuis longtemps?*
Étudiant(e) 2: *Oui, j'habite à Paris depuis 2004.*

- A command form of **tenir** is often used when handing something to someone.

Tiens, une belle orange pour toi.
Here's a nice orange for you.

Votre sac est tombé! **Tenez**, Madame.
Your bag fell! Here, ma'am.

Depuis, pendant, il y a + [time]

- To say that something happened at a certain time *ago* in the past, use **il y a** + [*time ago*].

Il y a une heure, on était à la cantine.
An hour ago, we were at the cafeteria.

Il a visité Ouagadougou **il y a deux ans**.
He visited Ouagadougou two years ago.

- To say that something happened *for* a particular period of time that has ended, use **pendant** + [*time period*]. Often the verb will be in the **passé composé**.

Salim a fait la vaisselle **pendant deux heures**.
Salim washed dishes for two hours.

Les équipes ont joué au foot **pendant un mois**.
The teams played soccer for one month.

- To say that something has been going on *since* a particular time and continues into the present, use **depuis** + [*time period, date, or starting point*]. Unlike its English equivalent, the verb in the French construction is usually in the present tense.

Elle danse **depuis son arrivée** à la fête.
She has been dancing since she arrived at the party.

Depuis quand **passez**-vous l'été au Québec?
Since when have you been spending summers in Quebec?

Essayez! **Choisissez l'option correcte pour compléter chaque phrase.**

1. Chloé, tu __c__ avec nous à la cantine?
2. Vous __h__ d'où, Monsieur?
3. Les Aubailly __a__ de dîner au café.
4. Julia Child est __g__ célèbre en 1961.
5. Qu'est-ce qu'ils __e__ dans la main?
6. Ils sont __b__ du supermarché à midi.
7. On parlait facilement __d__ dix ans.
8. On mange bien __f__ l'arrivée de maman.

a. viennent
b. revenus
c. viens
d. il y a
e. tiennent
f. depuis
g. devenue
h. venez

Essayez! After completing the activity, have students invent answers to items 1, 2, and 5. Then have them write questions that elicit the responses in items 3, 4, 6, 7, and 8.

1 Expansion Have students work in pairs and create questions that correspond to the sentences in the activity. Example: **1. Depuis quand Georges est-il revenu de vacances?**

2 Expansion Using magazine pictures, show images similar to those in the activity. Students should create sentences using **venir de**. Have volunteers show their pictures to the class and write their sentences on the board.

3 Suggestion Before beginning the activity, review the **futur proche** form **aller** + *infinitive* in **Espace structures 4A.1**.

4 Suggestions
- Ask two students to act out the **modèle**.
- Tell pairs to feel free to create additional questions that fit in the conversation.
- Have volunteers rehearse the conversation, then present it to the class.

5 Expansion After pairs finish the conversation, do this activity with the whole class, alternating who plays the roles of Marc and his mother until all of the vocabulary is used. Encourage the use of additional, creative vocabulary.

6 Suggestion Before beginning the activity, remind students that each expression of time takes a different verb tense when referencing the past. A sentence with **pendant** usually uses the **passé composé** while **depuis** usually uses the **présent**.

OPTIONS

Extra Practice Pass out a copy of a sample French C.V. Explain that the French use this abbreviation for the Latin term *curriculum vitæ* instead of *résumé*. Remind them that **un résumé** is a false cognate meaning *a summary*. Point out differences from an American C.V., such as the incorporation of age and other personal information. Have students invent a job and work in pairs to imagine that they must interview a candidate. They should create a list of questions about the candidate's experience and leisure activities using expressions of time. Example: **Pendant combien de temps avez-vous travaillé à Paris?** Once students have created five questions, have them switch with other pairs and come up with answers. Example: **J'ai travaillé à Paris pendant trois ans.** Finally, have students role-play their interviews in front of the class.

Section Goals

In this section, students will learn the verbs **devoir**, **vouloir**, and **pouvoir**.

Instructional Resources
*espaces.vhlcentral.com: Lab MP3s; WB/VM/LM Answer Key; IRM (**Essayez!** and **Mise en pratique** answers; Lab Audioscript); activities; downloads; reference tools*

Suggestions

- Introduce **devoir**, **vouloir**, and **pouvoir** by taking a survey with questions like these: **Qui doit faire les courses cette semaine? Qui veut devenir chef de cuisine? Qui peut dîner avec moi au restaurant vendredi soir?** Summarize the results on the board.
- Write the paradigm of **devoir** on the board or on a transparency and model its pronunciation. Point out the **-s**, **-s**, **-t** pattern in the singular forms. Then write the paradigms of **vouloir** and **pouvoir**, noting the **-x**, **-x**, **-t** pattern.
- Use magazine pictures to prompt students to make sentences using **devoir**, **vouloir**, and **pouvoir**. Example: picture of someone making a meal (**Elle doit préparer le dîner.**)
- Ask volunteers to translate sentences such as: *We must study for the exam tonight.* (**Nous devons préparer l'examen ce soir.**) *Have you managed to clean your room?* (**As-tu /Avez-vous pu nettoyer ta/votre chambre?**) *My parents refused to eat the meal I prepared.* (**Mes parents n'ont pas voulu manger le repas que j'ai préparé.**)
- Practice by asking the class more questions using the different meanings of **devoir**, **vouloir**, and **pouvoir**. Examples: **Que deviez-vous faire hier soir? Qui vous doit de l'argent? Que veut dire cette phrase? Voulez-vous voyager dans un autre pays? Avez-vous pu faire vos devoirs?**

NATIONAL STANDARDS comparisons

9A.2 The verbs *devoir, vouloir, pouvoir*

Point de départ The verbs **devoir** (*to have to [must]; to owe*), **vouloir** (*to want*), and **pouvoir** (*to be able to [can]*) are all irregular. They all take **avoir** in the **passé composé**.

Devoir, vouloir, pouvoir

	devoir	vouloir	pouvoir
je	dois	veux	peux
tu	dois	veux	peux
il/elle	doit	veut	peut
nous	devons	voulons	pouvons
vous	devez	voulez	pouvez
ils/elles	doivent	veulent	peuvent
past participle	dû	voulu	pu

Je **dois** repasser.
I have to iron.

Veut-elle des pâtes?
Does she want pasta?

Vous **pouvez** entrer.
You can come in.

- **Devoir** can be used with an infinitive to mean *to have to* or *must*. With a direct object, **devoir** means *to owe*.

On **doit** manger des légumes tous les jours.
One must eat vegetables every day.

Tu me **dois** cinq euros pour la salade.
You owe me five euros for the salad.

- **Devoir** is often used in the **passé composé** with an infinitive to speculate on what must have happened.

Ils **ont dû** payer le repas à l'avance.
They had to pay for the meal in advance.

Augustin **a dû** trop manger hier soir.
Augustin must have eaten too much last night.

- In the **imparfait**, **devoir** can be used with an infinitive to express *supposed to*.

Je **devais faire** mes devoirs.
I was supposed to do my homework.

Vous **deviez arriver** à huit heures.
You were supposed to arrive at 8 o'clock.

- When **vouloir** is used with the infinitive **dire**, it is translated as *to mean*.

Nous **voulons dire** exactement le contraire.
We mean exactly the opposite.

Biscuit? Ça **veut dire** *cookie* en français.
Biscuit? *That means* cookie *in French.*

MISE EN PRATIQUE

1 Que doit-on faire? Qu'est-ce que ces personnes doivent faire pour avoir ce qu'elles (*what they*) veulent?

MODÈLE André ___veut___ courir le marathon, alors il ___doit___ faire du jogging.

1. Je ___veux___ grossir, alors je ___dois___ manger des frites.
2. Il ___veut___ être en forme, alors il ___doit___ aller à la gym.
3. Vous ___voulez___ manger des spaghettis, alors vous ___devez___ aller dans un resto italien.
4. Tu ___veux___ manger chez toi, alors tu ___dois___ faire la cuisine.
5. Elles ne ___veulent___ pas arriver en retard (*late*), alors elles ___doivent___ courir.
6. Nous ___voulons___ écouter de la musique, alors nous ___devons___ acheter des CD.

2 Qui peut faire quoi? Ève prépare un grand repas. Dites ce que (*what*) chaque personne peut faire.

MODÈLE
Joseph / faire / courses
Joseph peut faire les courses.

1. Marc / acheter / boissons
Marc peut acheter les/des boissons.
2. Benoît et Anne / préparer / gâteaux
Benoît et Anne peuvent préparer les/des gâteaux.
3. Jean et toi / décorer / salle à manger
Jean et toi pouvez décorer la salle à manger.
4. Patrick et moi / essuyer / verres
Patrick et moi pouvons essuyer les verres.
5. je / prendre / photos
Je peux prendre les/des photos.
6. tu / mettre / table
Tu peux mettre la table.

3 Mes enfants M. Dion est au restaurant avec ses enfants. Le serveur/La serveuse lui demande ce qu'ils (*what they*) veulent prendre. Avec un(e) partenaire, posez les questions et répondez. Alternez les rôles. Answers will vary.

MODÈLE Éric:  ou 

Étudiant(e) 1: *Veut-il un jus d'orange ou un verre de lait?*
Étudiant(e) 2: *Il veut un jus d'orange, s'il vous plaît.*

1. Michèle:  ou 
2. Stéphanie et Éric:  ou 
3. Stéphanie:  ou 
4. Éric:  ou 

Practice more at **espaces.vhlcentral.com.**

OPTIONS

Video Replay the video episode, having students focus on the different uses of **devoir**, **vouloir**, and **pouvoir**. Stop the video where appropriate to discuss how they are used in the conversation and to ask comprehension questions. Example: **À quelle heure doivent-ils arriver chez Sandrine?**

Extra Practice Write a pattern sentence on the board. Example: **Nous ne voulons pas étudier**. Have students copy the model and then dictate a list of different subjects like **Charles, je, les étudiants,** etc. Have students write down the subjects and supply the correct verb form. Ask volunteers to read their answers aloud. Repeat using various forms of **devoir**, **vouloir**, and **pouvoir** expressions.

COMMUNICATION

4 Que faire? À tour de rôle avec un(e) partenaire, dites ce que (*what*) ces personnes peuvent, doivent ou veulent faire ou ne pas faire. Utilisez **pouvoir, devoir** et **vouloir** dans vos réponses. Answers will vary.

MODÈLE

Étudiant(e) 1: *Il veut maigrir.*
Étudiant(e) 2: *Il ne peut pas beaucoup manger.*

1.

4.

2.

5.

3.

6.

5 Ce n'est pas de ma faute. Préparez une liste de cinq choses qui vous sont arrivées (*happened to you*) par accident. Montrez la liste à un(e) partenaire, qui va deviner pourquoi. A-t-il/elle raison? Answers will vary.

MODÈLE

Étudiant(e) 1: *J'ai perdu les clés de ma maison.*
Étudiant(e) 2: *Tu as dû les laisser sur ton lit.*

6 Ce week-end Invitez vos camarades de classe à faire des choses avec vous le week-end prochain. S'ils refusent votre invitation, ils doivent vous donner une excuse. Quelles réponses avez-vous reçues (*received*)? Answers will vary.

MODÈLE

Étudiant(e) 1: *Tu veux jouer au tennis avec moi le week-end prochain?*
Étudiant(e) 2: *Quel jour?*
Étudiant(e) 1: *Samedi matin.*
Étudiant(e) 2: *Je veux bien, mais je dois rendre visite à ma famille.*

Sandrine devait être là. Elle a dû parler à son prof.
J'ai pu vous retrouver au supermarché.

- **Bien vouloir** can be used to express willingness.

Tu veux prendre de la glace?
Do you want to have some ice cream?

Oui, je **veux bien** prendre de la glace.
Yes, I'll gladly have some ice cream.

Voulez-vous dîner avec nous demain soir?
Do you want to have dinner with us tomorrow evening?

Nous **voulons bien** manger avec vous demain soir.
We'd love to eat with you tomorrow evening.

- **Vouloir** is often used in the **passé composé** with an infinitive in negative sentences to express *refused to.*

J'ai essayé, mais il **n'a pas voulu** parler.
I tried, but he refused to talk.

Elles **n'ont pas voulu** débarrasser la table.
They refused to clear the table.

- **Pouvoir** can be used in the **passé composé** with an infinitive to express *managed to do something.*

Nous **avons pu** tout finir.
We managed to finish everything.

Fathia **a pu** nous trouver.
Fathia managed to find us.

Essayez! **Complétez ces phrases avec les formes correctes du présent des verbes.**

devoir

1. Tu ___dois___ revenir à midi?
2. Elles ___doivent___ manger tout de suite.
3. Nous ___devons___ encore vingt euros.
4. Je ne ___dois___ pas assister au pique-nique.
5. Elle ___doit___ nous téléphoner.

vouloir

6. ___Voulez___-vous manger sur la terrasse?
7. Tu ___veux___ quelque chose à boire?
8. Il ___veut___ faire la cuisine.
9. Nous ne ___voulons___ pas prendre de dessert.
10. Ils ___veulent___ préparer un grand repas.

pouvoir

11. Je ___peux___ passer l'aspirateur ce soir.
12. Il ___peut___ acheter de l'ail au marché.
13. Elles ___peuvent___ emménager demain.
14. Vous ___pouvez___ maigrir de quelques kilos.
15. Nous ___pouvons___ mettre la table.

Essayez! Have students rewrite the sentences in the past using the **passé composé** or the **imparfait**. Discuss whether the meaning changes. Example: **1. Tu devais ...** (The meaning changes from *You have to...* to *You were supposed to....*)

1 Expansion Have students create three sentences modeled on those in the activity for their partner to complete. Write some on the board and have the class use the appropriate forms of **devoir**, **vouloir**, and **pouvoir** to complete the sentences.

2 Expansion Have students imagine they are planning a class party and everyone must help out. Ask the class: **Qui peut faire quoi?**

3 Suggestion Have two students act out the **modèle**.

3 Expansion Have pairs repeat this activity in the first and second person, using affirmative and negative sentences with **vouloir**.

4 Suggestion Call on volunteer pairs to say aloud what the people want and what they have to do to attain their goal.

4 Expansion Use photos or magazine pictures to extend the activity. Choose pictures that lend themselves to sentences using **devoir**, **vouloir**, and **pouvoir**.

5 Suggestion Have pairs form groups of four, switch lists, and discuss the reasons why each thing happened. Tell students to suggest alternate or better reasons whenever possible.

6 Suggestions
- Ask two students to act out the **modèle**.
- Before doing the activity, review different ways to refuse an invitation politely using **devoir**, **vouloir**, and **pouvoir**.

OPTIONS

Small Groups In groups of three or four, tell each student to write three sentences using different forms of **devoir, vouloir,** and **pouvoir.** Two of the sentences must be true, and one of them must be false. The other members of the group have to guess which of the sentences is false. This can also be done with the whole class.

Pairs Have students imagine they are going on vacation. Ask them to make a list of tasks **à faire...** (a "to do" list) using **devoir** to prepare for the trip. Example: **1. Avant de partir, je dois faire la lessive.** Then have them create a list of things they can or want to do on the trip using **pouvoir** and **vouloir**. Example: **1. On peut bronzer à la plage. 2. Je veux faire une randonnée.** Call on volunteers to present their lists to the class.

Instructional Resources
espaces.vhlcentral.com: IRM (Info Gap Activities); Testing Program; pp. 65–68; Test Files; Testing Program MP3s; activities; downloads; reference tools Test Generator

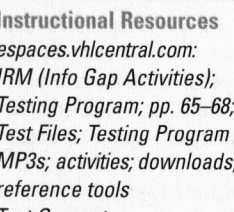

1 Suggestion Before assigning this activity, briefly review the **passé récent** with **venir de** + *infinitive.* Remind students that this tense conveys a different meaning than the **passé composé.**

2 Expansion Have the students state that the mother or father refused to purchase the item for the child using **vouloir** in the **passé composé**. Example: **La mère n'a pas voulu acheter de confiture.**

3 Expansion Have volunteers make comments to the chefs or ask them questions about their recipe. Example: **Je n'aime pas les carottes. Est-ce qu'on peut utiliser des tomates?**

4 Suggestion Before assigning the activity, ask the students questions using the construction **Depuis combien de temps...?** Review the different ways to answer (**il y a** + *time period* and **depuis** + *time period*).

5 Suggestion Have two students act out the **modèle** before assigning this activity.

5 Expansion Have pairs write down their conversation. Call on pairs to perform it for the class.

6 Suggestions
- Act out the **modèle** with a volunteer.
- Divide the class into pairs and distribute the Info Gap Handouts found on the Supersite for this activity. Give students ten minutes to complete the activity.

Révision

1 Au restaurant Avec un(e) partenaire, dites ce que (*what*) ces personnes viennent de faire. Utilisez les verbes de la liste et d'autres verbes. Answers will vary.

apporter	manger
arriver	parler
boire	prendre
demander	téléphoner

2 Au supermarché Un(e) enfant et son père ou sa mère sont au supermarché. L'enfant demande ces choses à manger, mais le père ou la mère ne veut pas les acheter et doit lui donner des raisons. Avec un(e) partenaire, préparez un dialogue, puis jouez-le pour la classe. Employez les verbes **devoir, vouloir** et **pouvoir** et le passé récent. Answers will vary.

MODÈLE

Étudiant(e) 1: *Maman, je veux de la confiture. Achète-moi cette confiture, s'il te plaît.*
Étudiant(e) 2: *Tu ne dois pas manger ça. Tu viens de manger un dessert.*

du chocolat	une glace
des chips	du pâté
un coca	une saucisse
de la confiture	des yaourts aux fruits

3 Le chef de cuisine Vous et votre partenaire êtes deux chefs. Expliquez à votre partenaire comment préparer votre salade préférée. Donnez des conseils (*advice*) avec les verbes **devoir, vouloir** et **pouvoir** et employez le passé récent. Answers will vary.

MODÈLE

Étudiant(e) 1: *Combien de carottes doit-on utiliser?*
Étudiant(e) 2: *On peut utiliser deux ou trois carottes.*

4 Dans le frigo Vous et vos partenaires êtes colocataires et vous nettoyez votre frigo. Qu'allez-vous mettre à la poubelle? Par groupes de trois, regardez l'illustration et décidez. Ensuite, présentez vos décisions à la classe. Answers will vary.

MODÈLE

Étudiant(e) 1: *Depuis combien de temps a-t-on ce fromage dans le frigo?*
Étudiant(e) 2: *Je viens de l'acheter, nous pouvons le garder encore un peu.*

5 Chez moi Vous et votre partenaire voulez manger ensemble après les cours. Vous voulez manger chez vous ou chez votre partenaire, mais pas au resto U. Que pouvez-vous préparer? Que voulez-vous manger ou boire? Answers will vary.

MODÈLE

Étudiant(e) 1: *Chez moi, j'ai du chocolat et du lait, et je peux te faire un chocolat chaud.*
Étudiant(e) 2: *Non merci, je veux plutôt une boisson froide et j'ai des boissons gazeuses à la maison.*

6 Une journée bien occupée Votre professeur va vous donner, à vous et à votre partenaire, une feuille sur les activités d'Alexandra. Attention! Ne regardez pas la feuille de votre partenaire. Answers will vary.

MODÈLE

Étudiant(e) 1: *À quatre heures et demie, Alexandra a pu faire du jogging.*
Étudiant(e) 2: *Après, à cinq heures, elle...*

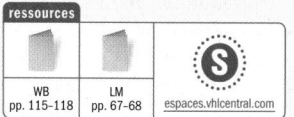

ressources: WB pp. 115–118; LM pp. 67–68; espaces.vhlcentral.com

OPTIONS

Extra Practice Have students write a "how to" paragraph describing a simple task without using commands, but rather the **vous** forms of **devoir, vouloir,** and **pouvoir**. Example: **faire un sandwich—D'abord, vous devez prendre du pain. Vous pouvez mettre du fromage si vous voulez. Ensuite, ...** The paragraph should include five or six basic directions and use vocabulary from this lesson and previous lessons. Then have students exchange their papers with classmates who will ask questions for clarification and provide suggestions for peer editing. Call on volunteers to share their paragraphs with the class. Have one volunteer read an instructional paragraph while another student follows the instructions in front of the class. Encourage the use of props. Have students explain any mistakes they notice.

Video: TV Clip

Le Zapping

National Standards: communication, cultures, connections, communities

Le far breton

En Bretagne, région du nord-ouest de la France, il existe plusieurs variétés de *fars*. Ils ont tous comme ingrédient principal une sorte de farine°, d'où vient leur nom. Les Bretons cuisinaient traditionnellement un far à l'occasion des fêtes religieuses. En Bretagne, il a toujours existé des fars salés° et sucrés°. Pourtant°, c'est une version sucrée avec des pruneaux° qui a traversé les limites régionales pour se populariser dans toute la France sous le nom de "far breton".

—Alors, je vais vous présenter la recette° du far breton.

—Donc, maintenant, je vais casser° les œufs pour les mélanger° ensuite à la farine.

Compréhension **Répondez aux questions.** Some answers will vary.

1. Quels sont les ingrédients du far breton? Il y a du lait, de la farine, du beurre, des œufs, du sucre et des pruneaux.
2. Quel est le verbe de la liste que le chef de cuisine ne dit pas?

ajouter (*to add*), **casser**, **chauffer** (*to heat*), **couper** (*to cut*), **mélanger**, **verser** (*to pour*)

3. À quelle température et pendant combien de temps la pâte (batter) doit-elle rester au four? Elle doit rester au four à 180 degrés pendant une heure.

Discussion **Avec un(e) partenaire, posez-vous ces questions et discutez.** Answers will vary.

Quelle est votre recette préférée? Quels sont les ingrédients? Comment la prépare-t-on?

farine *flour* **salés** *savory* **sucrés** *sweet* **Pourtant** *However* **pruneaux** *prunes*
recette *recipe* **casser** *to crack* **mélanger** *to mix*

Practice more at **espaces.vhlcentral.com.**

Section Goals

In this section, students will:
- read about the history of the **far breton**
- watch a professional chef prepare a **far breton**
- answer questions about the recipe and its preparation

Instructional Resources
*espaces.vhlcentral.com: TV commercial; IRM (**Le zapping** TV clip transcription); activities; downloads; reference tools*

Introduction
To check comprehension, ask these questions:
1. De quelle région de France le far vient-il? (Il vient de Bretagne.)
2. À quelle occasion les Bretons cuisinaient-ils traditionnellement un far? (Ils cuisinaient un far à l'occasion des fêtes religieuses.)
3. Quelle version du far est devenue populaire dans le reste de la France? (Une version sucrée avec des pruneaux est devenue populaire.)

Avant de regarder la vidéo
- Write the word **pâtissier** on the board and explain what it means. Then have students look at the video stills, read the captions, and predict what is happening in the show for each visual. **(1. Le pâtissier est dans une cuisine. Il va préparer un far breton. 2. Il va casser les oeufs pour les mélanger à la farine.)**
- Before showing the video, explain to students that they do not need to understand every word they hear. Tell them to listen for cognates and the text in the captions. They should also listen for food and cooking vocabulary and watch carefully the actions that accompany the pastry chef's description.

Compréhension Have students work in pairs or groups for this activity. Tell them to write their answers. Then show the video again so that they can check their answers and add any missing information.

Discussion Ask students if they know the origin of their favorite recipe. Ask them to bring in photos of the dish or, if possible, a sample to share with the class.

OPTIONS

Une recette française Explain to students that following a French recipe might present a few surprises. When the pastry chef says to put the **far breton** mixture in a 180-degree oven, for instance, he means 180 degrees Celsius, or about 350 degrees Fahrenheit. Here are a few terms specific to cooking that students hear in this lesson's **Le zapping** video and might find unfamiliar:

un appareil *mixture*
une cuisson *cooking, baking (time, process)*
démouler *to turn out of the pan*
dénoyauter *to pit*
une pointe *touch, hint*

Section Goals

In this section, students will learn and practice vocabulary related to:
- setting the table
- eating in a restaurant
- shopping for food

Instructional Resources
*espaces.vhlcentral.com: Transparency #41; IRM (**Vocabulaire supplémentaire**; **Mise en pratique** answers; Textbook Audioscript; Lab Audioscript; Info Gap Activities); Textbook MP3s; Lab MP3s; WB/VM/LM Answer Key; activities; downloads; reference tools*

Suggestions
- Use **Transparency #41.** Describe what people are doing, then point out eating utensils and other items on the tables. Examples: **Le serveur apporte la carte. La femme commande. C'est une fourchette à côté de la serviette.**
- Ask students simple questions based on your narrative. Example: **Que fait le chef?**
- Bring in items for setting the table. Hold up each one and ask: **Qu'est-ce que c'est?**
- Explain that **le menu (fixe)** is a meal with limited choices from the main menu (**la carte**) for a set price, usually **une entrée**, **un plat**, and **un dessert**. Point out the French expression used in English **à la carte**.
- Point out that **une entrée** is *an appetizer*, not *a main course* as in English.
- Point out that **une assiette** is *a plate*, and **un plat** is *a serving dish* or the *food on the serving dish*.
- Explain the **faux ami: commander** means *to order*, not *to command*.
- Bring in photos from magazines or the Internet to introduce the names of the shops listed. Say: **C'est une boulangerie. On vend du pain à la boulangerie.**
- Additional vocabulary for this lesson can be found in the **Vocabulaire supplémentaire** on the Supersite.

Leçon 9B

Talking Picture
Audio: Activity

You will learn how to...
- **describe and discuss food**
- **shop for food**

À table!

Vocabulaire

être au régime	*to be on a diet*
une boîte (de conserve)	*can*
la crème	*cream*
la mayonnaise	*mayonnaise*
la moutarde	*mustard*
une tranche	*slice*
une entrée	*appetizer, starter*
un hors-d'œuvre	*hors-d'oeuvre, appetizer*
un plat (principal)	*(main) dish*
À table!	*Let's eat!/Food is ready!*
compris	*included*
une boucherie	*butcher's shop*
une boulangerie	*bread shop, bakery*
une charcuterie	*delicatessen*
un(e) commerçant(e)	*shopkeeper*
un kilo(gramme)	*kilo(gram)*
une pâtisserie	*pastry shop, bakery; pastry*
une poissonnerie	*fish shop*

ressources
WB pp. 119-120 | LM p. 69 | espaces.vhlcentral.com

304 *trois cent quatre*

OPTIONS

Game On index cards, write vocabulary words related to setting the table. On another set of cards, draw or paste pictures for each term. Tape them face down on the board. Divide the class into two teams. Then play a game of concentration in which students match words with pictures. When a player makes a match, that player's team collects those cards. The team with the most cards at the end of the game wins.

Extra Practice Say the names of foods and have students respond with the type of store that sells each item. Examples: **un steak (une boucherie), des fruits de mer (une poissonnerie), des saucisses (une charcuterie/une boucherie), du pain (une boulangerie), de la moutarde (une épicerie), un gâteau (une pâtisserie), du pâté (une charcuterie),** and **du thon (une poissonnerie).**

Mise en pratique

1 Complétez Complétez ces phrases avec le bon mot.

1. Pour manger de la soupe, on utilise...
   a. un couteau.
   (b.) une cuillère.
   c. une fourchette.
2. On sert la soupe dans...
   a. une assiette.
   b. une carafe.
   (c.) un bol.
3. Au restaurant, le serveur/la serveuse doit... la nourriture.
   a. commander
   (b.) apporter
   c. goûter
4. On vend des baguettes à...
   (a.) la boulangerie.
   b. la charcuterie.
   c. la boucherie.
5. On met... dans le café.
   a. du beurre
   b. du poivre
   (c.) de la crème
6. On vend des gâteaux à...
   a. la boucherie.
   (b.) la pâtisserie.
   c. la poissonnerie.
7. Au restaurant, on commande d'abord...
   (a.) une entrée.
   b. un plat principal.
   c. une serviette.
8. On vend du jambon à...
   (a.) la charcuterie.
   b. la boucherie.
   c. la pâtisserie.

2 Le repas Mettez ces différentes étapes dans l'ordre chronologique.

5 **a.** dire «À table!»
7 **b.** servir le plat principal
4 **c.** mettre les assiettes, les fourchettes, les cuillères et les couteaux sur la table
6 **d.** servir l'entrée
2 **e.** faire les courses
1 **f.** organiser un menu
8 **g.** goûter le dessert avec les invités
3 **h.** faire la cuisine

3 Écoutez Catherine est au régime. Elle parle de ses habitudes alimentaires. Écoutez et indiquez si les affirmations suivantes sont **vraies** ou **fausses**.

	Vrai	Faux
1. Catherine mange beaucoup de desserts.	☐	☑
2. Catherine fait les courses au supermarché.	☐	☑
3. Elle adore la viande.	☐	☑
4. Elle est au régime.	☑	☐
5. Catherine achète des fruits et des légumes au marché.	☑	☐
6. Selon (*According to*) Catherine, le service chez les commerçants est désagréable.	☐	☑
7. Elle va souvent à la boucherie et à la poissonnerie.	☐	☑
8. Elle vient de devenir végétarienne.	☑	☐

Practice more at **espaces.vhlcentral.com.**

1 Expansion For additional practice, give students these items. **9. Pour manger du bœuf, on utilise ____. (une fourchette et un couteau) 10. On sert de la salade dans ____. (un bol/une assiette) 11. Au restaurant, après l'entrée, on mange ____. (le plat principal) 12. On vend du pâté dans les ____. (charcuteries)**

2 Suggestion Have students form groups of eight. Make a set of individual phrases on strips of paper for each group and distribute them. Tell students to arrange the phrases in the proper order and then read them aloud.

3 Tapescript Je suis au régime, alors je ne peux pas manger beaucoup de desserts, ou bien, de pain en général. Parfois, je vais à la boulangerie et j'achète des croissants pour le petit-déjeuner, mais je les prends sans confiture. Quand je mange une salade, je n'utilise jamais d'huile d'olive. Je fais très attention à ce que je mange et je ne mets pas trop de sel dans mes plats. J'utilise très peu de poivre parce que je n'aime pas beaucoup ça. Chaque semaine, quand je fais les courses, je vais à la boulangerie pour acheter du pain. Pour les fruits et les légumes, je vais au marché. Je vais rarement au supermarché; je préfère aller chez les commerçants parce que le service est très agréable. Je ne vais jamais ni à la boucherie ni à la poissonnerie parce que je viens de devenir végétarienne. *(On Textbook MP3s)*

3 Suggestion Have students read the true/false sentences before they listen to the recording.

OPTIONS

Mettre la table A typical French table setting in a restaurant has at least two stemmed glasses per person. If they are not the same size, the larger goblet is for water and the smaller one is for wine. In more formal table settings, there may be several glasses for different types of wine. Champagne is served in tall glasses called **flûtes** or in large shallow glasses called **coupes**; white wine may be served in smaller glasses than red wine. When placing cutlery, knives go on the right with the blade turned toward the plate, and forks go on the left, tines down. Soupspoons are placed next to the forks, on the outside. Teaspoons or dessert forks belong above the plate. A formal French place setting may also include **un porte-couteau**, which serves to protect the tablecloth.

4 Suggestions
- Before beginning the activity, give students a few minutes to think about their responses to these questions.
- Tell students to jot down notes during their interviews. Then have volunteers share their partner's responses with the class.

5 Suggestion Have two volunteers read the **modèle** aloud. Then divide the class into pairs and distribute the Info Gap Handouts found on the Supersite for this activity. Give students ten minutes to complete the activity.

6 Suggestion Give each group a menu from a real French restaurant to use in their role-plays. Many restaurants include sample menus on their websites.

7 Suggestions
- Before beginning the activity, have students describe what they see in the drawing.
- Have students exchange paragraphs for peer editing. Students should make sure all required elements are included and underline grammar and spelling errors.

Communication

4 Conversez **Interviewez un(e) camarade de classe.** Answers will vary.

1. En général, qu'est-ce que tu commandes au restaurant comme entrée? Comme plat principal?
2. Qui fait les courses chez toi? Où? Quand?
3. Est-ce que tu préfères faire les courses au supermarché ou chez les commerçants? Pourquoi?
4. Es-tu au régime? Qu'est-ce que tu manges?
5. Quel est ton plat principal préféré?
6. Aimes-tu la moutarde? Avec quel(s) plat(s) l'utilises-tu?
7. Aimes-tu la mayonnaise? Avec quel(s) plat(s) l'utilises-tu?
8. Dans quel(s) plat(s) mets-tu de l'huile d'olive?

5 Sept différences **Votre professeur va vous donner, à vous et à votre partenaire, deux feuilles d'activités différentes avec le dessin (*drawing*) d'un restaurant. Il y a sept différences entre les deux images. Sans regarder l'image de votre partenaire, comparez vos dessins et faites une liste de ces différences. Quel est le groupe le plus rapide de la classe?**

MODÈLE

Étudiant(e) 1: *Dans mon restaurant, le serveur apporte du beurre à la table.*
Étudiant(e) 2: *Dans mon restaurant aussi, on apporte du beurre à la table, mais c'est une serveuse, pas un serveur.*

6 Au restaurant **Travaillez avec deux camarades de classe pour présenter ce dialogue.** Answers will vary.

- Une personne invite un(e) ami(e) à dîner au restaurant.
- Une personne est le serveur/la serveuse et décrit le menu.
- Vous parlez du menu et de vos préférences.
- Une personne est au régime et ne peut pas manger certains ingrédients.
- Vous commandez les plats.
- Vous parlez des plats que vous mangez.

7 Écriture **Écrivez un paragraphe dans lequel vous:** Answers will vary.

- parlez de la dernière fois que vous avez préparé un dîner, un déjeuner ou un petit-déjeuner pour quelqu'un.
- décrivez les ingrédients que vous avez utilisés pour préparer le(s) plat(s).
- mentionnez les endroits où vous avez acheté les ingrédients et leurs quantités.
- décrivez comment vous avez mis la table.

OPTIONS

Game Toss a beanbag to a student at random and say the name of a store from this lesson or a previous one. The person has four seconds to name a food that is sold there. That person then tosses the beanbag to another student and names a store. Students who cannot think of a food in time or who repeat an item that has already been mentioned are eliminated. The last person standing wins.

Small Groups Have groups of students plan a dinner party for a group of celebrities. Tell them to decide who will attend and what foods will be served. The meal should include several courses and appropriate beverages. You might want to bring in French cookbooks or food magazines for students' reference. Have the class vote on the most delicious-sounding meal and the most interesting guest list.

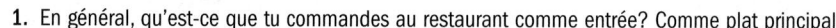

Les sons et les lettres

Audio: Concepts, Activities
Record & Compare

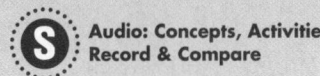

comparisons — NATIONAL STANDARDS

Stress and rhythm

In French, all syllables are pronounced with more or less equal stress, but the final syllable in a phrase is elongated slightly.

Je fais souvent du sport, mais aujourd'hui, j'ai envie de rester à la maison.

French sentences are divided into three basic kinds of rhythmic groups.

Noun phrase	*Verb phrase*	*Prepositional phrase*
Caroline et Dominique	**sont venues**	**chez moi.**

The final syllable of a rhythmic group may be slightly accentuated either by rising intonation (pitch) or elongation.

Caroline et Dominique sont venues chez moi.

In English, you can add emphasis by placing more stress on certain words. In French, you can emphasize the word by adding the corresponding pronoun or you can elongate the first consonant sound.

Je ne sais pas, moi. **Quel idiot!** **C'est fantastique!**

Prononcez Répétez les phrases suivantes à voix haute.

1. Ce n'est pas vrai, ça.
2. Bonjour, Mademoiselle.
3. Moi, je m'appelle Florence.
4. La clé de ma chambre, je l'ai perdue.
5. Je voudrais un grand café noir et un croissant, s'il vous plaît.
6. Nous allons tous au marché, mais Marie, elle va au centre commercial.

Articulez Répétez les phrases en mettant l'emphase (*by emphasizing*) sur les mots indiqués.

1. C'est *impossible*!
2. Le film était *super*!
3. Cette tarte est *délicieuse*!
4. Quelle idée *extraordinaire*!
5. Ma sœur parle *constamment*.

Dictons Répétez les dictons à voix haute.

Le chat parti, les souris dansent.[2]

Les chemins les plus courts ne sont pas toujours les meilleurs.[1]

[1] The shortest paths aren't always the best.
[2] When the cat is away, the mice will play.

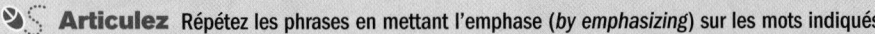

ressources
LM p. 70
espaces.vhlcentral.com

Section Goals

In this section, students will learn about:
- stress and rhythm
- a strategy for emphasizing a word

Instructional Resources
espaces.vhlcentral.com: Textbook MP3s; Lab MP3s; WB/VM/LM Answer Key; IRM (Textbook Audioscript; Lab Audioscript); activities; downloads; reference tools

Suggestions

- Model the pronunciation of the example sentences and have students repeat after you.
- Write these sentences from the **Roman-photo** in **Leçon 9A** on the board or a transparency. **1. Mais quelle heure est-il? 2. Bon, une salade, si tu veux. 3. Mais le bœuf bourguignon, c'est long à préparer, non? 4. Il nous faut des champignons, du jambon et du fromage.** Say the sentences and have students repeat after you. Alternately, have students read the entire video episode aloud in small groups, focusing on correct stress and rhythm.
- Have students read the sentences in the **Articulez** activity more than once, using a variety of methods to place emphasis on the appropriate words, for example, pauses before the word or between syllables.
- Prepare a handout that has several sentences with varied rhythm and stress. Tell students to draw arrows to mark rising and falling intonation as you read the sentences aloud.

OPTIONS

Extra Practice Use these sentences for additional practice with stress and rhythm or as a dictation. **1. Ils préfèrent aller au cinéma. 2. Mon anniversaire, c'est le 14 octobre. 3. Charlotte est professeur d'anglais dans un lycée en France. 4. Pour mes vacances, il me faut un maillot de bain, un short et des lunettes de soleil.**

Extra Practice To practice varying stress and rhythm, teach students these French tongue-twisters. **1. Mur pourrit, trou s'y fit, rat s'y mit; chat l'y vit, rat s'enfuit; chat suivit, rat fut pris. 2. Bonjour, Madame Sans Souci. Combien sont ces six saucissons-ci et combien sont ces six saucissons-là? Six sous, Madame, sont ces six saucissons-ci et six sous aussi sont ces six saucissons-là!**

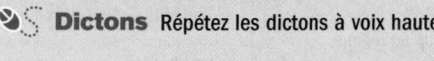

Section Goals

In this section, students will learn functional phrases for making comparisons and discussing a meal.

Instructional Resources
*espaces.vhlcentral.com: Video; WB/VM/LM Answer Key; IRM (Videoscript; **Roman-photo** Translations); activities; downloads; reference tools*
Video on DVD

Video Recap: Leçon 9A
Before doing this **Roman-photo**, review the previous one with this activity.
1. Pourquoi Sandrine a-t-elle retrouvé Amina et David au supermarché? (pour faire les courses pour son dîner)
2. Pourquoi Stéphane a-t-il voulu parler à Sandrine? (Il a voulu savoir à quelle heure il doit arriver chez elle et s'il doit apporter quelque chose.)
3. Qu'est-ce que Sandrine a décidé de préparer? (un poulet à la crème aux champignons avec un gratin de pommes de terre)
4. Qui a payé les courses au supermarché? (Amina et David)

Video Synopsis
David runs into Rachid in town. Rachid has bought a box of chocolates for Sandrine. David decides to buy her a bouquet of flowers. That evening, the guests arrive at Sandrine's. Sandrine is pleased with her gifts. Amina and Stéphane finish setting the table, and they all sit down to eat. The meal is a great success, and everyone compliments Sandrine on her cooking.

Suggestions
- Have students predict what the episode will be about based on the title and video stills.
- Point out that, in **que j'aie jamais reçues,** the subjunctive is used with the superlative.
- After reading the **Roman-photo**, review students' predictions and have them summarize the episode.

NATIONAL STANDARDS communication cultures

Le dîner

Video: *Roman-photo*
Record & Compare

PERSONNAGES

Amina

David

Rachid

Sandrine

Stéphane

Valérie

Au centre-ville...
DAVID Qu'est-ce que tu as fait en ville?
RACHID Des courses à la boulangerie et chez le chocolatier.
DAVID Tu as acheté ces chocolats pour Sandrine?
RACHID Pourquoi? Tu es jaloux? Ne t'en fais pas! Elle nous a invités. Il est normal d'apporter quelque chose.

DAVID Je n'ai pas de cadeau pour elle. Qu'est-ce que je peux lui acheter? Je peux lui apporter des fleurs!
Chez le fleuriste...
DAVID Ces roses sont très jolies, non?
RACHID Tu es tombé amoureux?
DAVID Mais non! Pourquoi tu dis ça?
RACHID Des roses, c'est romantique.
DAVID Ah... Ces fleurs-ci sont jolies. C'est mieux?

RACHID Non, c'est pire! Les chrysanthèmes sont réservés aux funérailles.
DAVID Hmmm. Je ne savais pas que c'était aussi difficile de choisir un bouquet de fleurs!
RACHID Regarde! Celles-là sont parfaites!
DAVID Tu es sûr?
RACHID Sûr et certain, achète-les!

AMINA Sandrine, est-ce qu'on peut faire quelque chose pour t'aider?
SANDRINE Oui, euh, vous pouvez finir de mettre la table, si vous voulez.
VALÉRIE Je vais t'aider dans la cuisine.
AMINA Tiens, Stéphane. Voilà le sel et le poivre. Tu peux les mettre sur la table, s'il te plaît?
SANDRINE À table!

SANDRINE Je vous sers autre chose? Une deuxième tranche de tarte aux pommes peut-être?
VALÉRIE Merci.
AMINA Merci. Je suis au régime.
SANDRINE Et toi, David?
DAVID Oh! J'ai trop mangé. Je n'en peux plus!
STÉPHANE Moi, je veux bien...
SANDRINE Donne-moi ton assiette.

STÉPHANE Tiens, tu peux la lui passer, s'il te plaît?
VALÉRIE Quel repas fantastique, Sandrine. Tu as beaucoup de talent, tu sais.
RACHID Vous avez raison, Madame Forestier. Ton poulet aux champignons était superbe!

ACTIVITÉS

1 **Vrai ou faux?** Indiquez si ces affirmations sont vraies ou fausses. Corrigez les phrases fausses. Answers may vary.

1. Rachid est allé chez le chocolatier. Vrai.
2. Rachid et David sont arrivés en avance. Faux. Rachid et David sont arrivés en retard.
3. David n'a pas apporté de cadeau. Faux. David a apporté des fleurs.
4. Sandrine aime les fleurs de David. Vrai.
5. Personne (*Nobody*) n'aide Sandrine. Faux. Valérie, Amina et Stéphane aident Sandrine.
6. David n'a pas beaucoup mangé. Faux. David a trop mangé.
7. Stéphane n'est pas au régime. Vrai.
8. Sandrine a fait une tarte aux pêches pour le dîner. Faux. Sandrine a fait une tarte aux pommes.
9. Les plats de Sandrine ne sont pas très bons. Faux. Les plats de Sandrine sont bons.
10. Les invités ont passé une soirée très agréable. Vrai.

Practice more at **espaces.vhlcentral.com.**

OPTIONS

Avant de regarder la vidéo Before viewing the video, have students brainstorm a list of things people might say at a dinner party. What expressions might they use before, during, and after a meal? Write the list on the board.

Regarder la vidéo Download and print the videoscript found on the Supersite. Then white out words related to meals, eating, and other key vocabulary in order to create a master for a cloze activity. Distribute the photocopies and tell students to fill in the missing information as they watch the video episode.

Sandrine a préparé un repas fantastique pour ses amis.

4

5

Chez Sandrine...

SANDRINE Bonsoir... Entrez! Oh!
DAVID Tiens. C'est pour toi.
SANDRINE Oh, David! Il ne fallait pas, c'est très gentil!
DAVID Je voulais t'apporter quelque chose.
SANDRINE Ce sont les plus belles fleurs que j'aie jamais reçues! Merci!

RACHID Bonsoir, Sandrine.
SANDRINE Oh, du chocolat! Merci beaucoup.
RACHID J'espère qu'on n'est pas trop en retard.
SANDRINE Pas du tout! Venez! On est dans la salle à manger.

9

10

STÉPHANE Oui, et tes desserts sont les meilleurs! C'est la tarte la plus délicieuse du monde!
SANDRINE Vous êtes adorables, merci. Moi, je trouve que cette tarte aux pommes est meilleure que la tarte aux pêches que j'ai faite il y a quelques semaines.

AMINA Tout ce que tu prépares est bon, Sandrine.
DAVID À Sandrine, le chef de cuisine le plus génial!
TOUS À Sandrine!

Expressions utiles

Making comparisons and judgments

- **Ces fleurs-ci sont jolies. C'est mieux?**
  These flowers are pretty. Is that better?
- **C'est pire! Les chrysanthèmes sont réservés aux funérailles.**
  It's worse! Chrysanthemums are reserved for funerals.
- **Je ne savais pas que c'était aussi difficile de choisir un bouquet de fleurs!**
  I didn't know it was so hard to choose a bouquet of flowers!
- **Ce sont les plus belles fleurs que j'aie jamais reçues!**
  These are the most beautiful flowers I have ever received!
- **C'est la tarte la plus délicieuse du monde!**
  This is the most delicious tart in the world!
- **Cette tarte aux pommes est meilleure que la tarte aux pêches.**
  This apple tart is better than the peach tart.

Additional vocabulary

- **Ah, tu es jaloux? Ne t'en fais pas!**
  Are you jealous? Don't be!/Don't make anything of it!
- **sûr(e) et certain(e)**
  totally sure/completely certain
- **Il ne fallait pas.**
  You shouldn't have./It wasn't necessary.
- **J'ai trop mangé. Je n'en peux plus!**
  I ate too much. I can't fit anymore!
- **Tu peux la lui passer?**
  Can you pass it to her?

2 Questions Répondez aux questions par des phrases complètes.
Answers may vary slightly.

1. Qu'est-ce que Rachid a apporté à Sandrine?
   Il lui a apporté des chocolats.
2. Qu'a fait Amina pour aider?
   Elle a fini de mettre la table.
3. Qui mange une deuxième tranche de tarte aux pommes?
   Stéphane la mange.
4. Quel type de tarte Sandrine a-t-elle préparé il y a quelques semaines?
   Elle a préparé une tarte aux pêches.
5. Pourquoi David n'a-t-il pas acheté les roses?
   Il ne les a pas achetées parce que (Rachid lui a dit que) les roses sont romantiques.

3 Écrivez David veut raconter le dîner de Sandrine à sa famille. Composez un e-mail. Quels ont été les préparatifs (*preparations*)? Qui a apporté quoi? Qui est venu? Qu'est-ce qu'on a mangé? Relisez l'**ESPACE ROMAN-PHOTO** de la Leçon 9A si nécessaire.

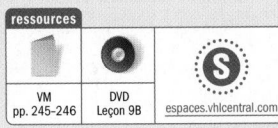

ressources
VM pp. 245-246 | DVD Leçon 9B | espaces.vhlcentral.com

ACTIVITÉS

Expressions utiles

- Model the pronunciation of the **Expressions utiles** and have students repeat them after you.
- As you work through the list, point out the comparative and superlative expressions and double object pronouns. Explain that **mieux** and **meilleur** both mean *better*, but one is an adverb and the other is an adjective. Tell students that these constructions will be formally presented in the **Structures** section.
- Respond briefly to questions about the comparative, the superlative, and double object pronouns. Reinforce correct forms, but do not expect students to produce them consistently at this time.
- Tell students that the expression **je n'en peux plus** is used to say, "*I'm full.*" They should not use the word **plein(e)** in this context.

1 Suggestion Have students write their corrections on the board.

1 Expansion For additional practice, give students these items. **11. David achète les roses. (Faux. Il achète d'autres fleurs.) 12. Valérie aide Sandrine dans la cuisine. (Vrai.) 13. Amina est au régime. (Vrai.) 14. Sandrine n'aime pas sa tarte aux pommes. (Faux. Elle aime sa tarte aux pommes.)**

2 Expansion For additional practice, give students these items. **6. Pourquoi est-ce que David et Rachid ont acheté des cadeaux pour Sandrine? (Ils vont dîner chez elle.) 7. Qu'est-ce que Sandrine a préparé pour le dîner? (Elle a préparé un poulet aux champignons.) 8. Pourquoi est-ce que David n'a pas acheté les chrysanthèmes? (Les chrysanthèmes sont pour les funérailles.)**

3 Suggestion Tell students to jot down the answers to the questions before they begin to compose their e-mail.

OPTIONS

Extra Practice Using the **Roman-photo** as a model, have students write a conversation that takes place at a dinner party. The host or hostess should offer foods, which the guests politely accept or refuse. As each dish is served, guests should comment on the quality of the food. Remind students to use as many of the **Expressions utiles** as they can.

Les fleurs et les sentiments Various flowers are associated with specific sentiments. Much of the symbolism has been forgotten today, but some traditions stemming from the "language" of flowers remain in French culture. For example, red roses are romantic. Chrysanthemums bloom in the fall, so these flowers were placed on graves on Day of the Dead (November 2nd). Now they are a traditional flower for funerals.

Section Goals

In this section, students will:

- learn about meals and eating habits in France
- learn some terms for methods of preparing food
- learn some tips about dining manners in France and North Africa
- read about the popularity of North African food in France

Instructional Resources
espaces.vhlcentral.com: activities; downloads; reference tools

Culture à la loupe

Avant la lecture Have students look at the photos, identify the meals, and describe what they see.

Lecture

- Explain that large family meals consisting of many courses typically take place on Sunday afternoons and on holidays.
- Point out the **Coup de main** and model the pronunciation of the terms. Ask: **Comment préférez-vous votre steak? À point? Bien cuit?**
- Point out the chart **Les Français et les repas**. Ask students what type of information is contained in this chart. (statistics about French meals and eating habits)

Après la lecture Ask students to name the courses in a large French meal in chronological order as you write them on the board.

1 Suggestion Have students read out the sentences in the text where they found the correct answers.

NATIONAL STANDARDS connections cultures

CULTURE À LA LOUPE

Les repas en France

En France, un grand repas traditionnel est composé de beaucoup de plats différents et il peut durer° plusieurs heures. Avant de passer à table, on sert des amuse-gueules° comme des biscuits salés°, des olives ou des cacahuètes°. Ensuite, on commence le repas par un hors-d'œuvre ou directement par une ou deux entrées chaudes ou froides, comme une soupe, de la charcuterie, etc. Puis, on passe au plat principal, qui est en général une viande ou un poisson servi avec des légumes. Après, on apporte la salade (qui peut aussi être servie en entrée), puis le fromage et enfin, on sert le dessert et le café. Le grand repas traditionnel est accompagné de vin, et dans les grandes occasions, de champagne pour le dessert. Bien sûr, les Français ne font pas ce genre de grand repas tous les jours. En général, on mange beaucoup plus simplement.

Au petit-déjeuner, on boit du café au lait, du thé ou du chocolat chaud. On mange des tartines° ou du pain grillé° avec du beurre et de la confiture, et des croissants le week-end.

Le déjeuner est traditionnellement le repas principal, mais aujourd'hui, les Français n'ont pas souvent le temps de rentrer à la maison. Pour cette raison, on mange de plus en plus° au travail ou au café. Après l'école, les enfants prennent parfois un goûter, par exemple du pain avec du chocolat. Et le soir, on dîne à la maison, en famille.

durer *last* **amuse-gueules** *small appetizers* **salés** *salty* **cacahuètes** *peanuts* **tartines** *slices of bread* **pain grillé** *toast* **de plus en plus** *more and more* **moins de** *less than*

Les Français et les repas

- 10% des Français ne prennent pas de petit-déjeuner.
- 60% boivent du café le matin, 20% du thé, 15% du chocolat.
- 99% dînent chez eux en semaine.
- 35% dînent en famille, 30% en couple.
- 75% des dîners consistent en moins de° trois plats successifs.
- Le pain est présent dans plus de 60% des déjeuners et des dîners.

SOURCE: Domoscope Unilever, Francoscopie

Coup de main

You can use these terms to specify how you would like your meat to be cooked.

bleu(e)	*very rare*
saignant(e)	*medium rare*
à point	*medium*
bien cuit(e)	*well-done*

ACTIVITÉS

1 Vrai ou faux? Indiquez si ces phrases sont **vraies** ou **fausses**. Corrigez les phrases fausses.

1. On mange les hors-d'œuvre avant les amuse-gueules. Faux. On mange les amuse-gueules avant les hors-d'œuvre.
2. Le poisson est un plat principal. Vrai.
3. En France, on ne mange jamais la salade en entrée. Faux. On mange la salade en entrée ou après le plat principal.
4. En général, on ne boit pas de vin pendant le repas. Faux. En général, on boit du vin pendant le repas.
5. On sert le fromage entre la salade et le dessert. Vrai.
6. Les Français mangent souvent des œufs au petit-déjeuner. Faux. Ils mangent des tartines ou du pain grillé avec du beurre et de la confiture, ou des croissants le week-end.
7. Tous les Français mangent un grand repas traditionnel chaque soir. Faux. En général, on mange plus simplement.
8. Le déjeuner est traditionnellement le repas principal de la journée en France. Vrai.
9. À midi, les Français mangent toujours à la maison. Faux. Ils mangent de plus en plus souvent au travail ou au café.
10. Les enfants prennent parfois un goûter après l'école. Vrai.

Practice more at **espaces.vhlcentral.com.**

OPTIONS

Cultural Comparison Have students work in groups of three and compare a large, traditional French meal with a typical, large American meal. Tell them to list the similarities and differences in a two-column chart under the headings **Similitudes** and **Différences**. After completing the charts, have volunteers read their lists aloud.

Les Français et les repas Have students write five true/false sentences based on the information in the chart. Then tell them to exchange papers with a classmate and complete the activity. Remind them to verify their answers.

LE FRANÇAIS QUOTIDIEN

Au menu

côtelette (*f.*)	*chop*
escalope (*f.*)	*thin slice of meat or fish*
faux-filet (*m.*)	*sirloin steak*
à la vapeur	*steamed*
farci(e)	*stuffed*
frit(e)	*fried*
garni(e)	*garnished*
rôti(e)	*roasted*

PORTRAIT

La couscousmania des Français

La cuisine du Maghreb est très populaire en France. Les restaurants orientaux sont nombreux et appréciés pour la qualité de leur nourriture et leur ambiance. Les merguez, des petites saucisses rouges pimentées°, sont vendues dans toutes les boucheries. Dans les grandes villes, des pâtisseries au miel° sont dégustées° au goûter. Le plat le plus célèbre reste le couscous, le quatrième plat préféré des Français, devant le steak frites! Aujourd'hui, des restaurants trois étoiles° le proposent en plat du jour et on le sert dans les cantines. Les Français consomment 75.000 tonnes de couscous par an, une vraie couscousmania!

pimentées *spicy* **miel** *honey* **dégustées** *savored* **étoiles** *stars*

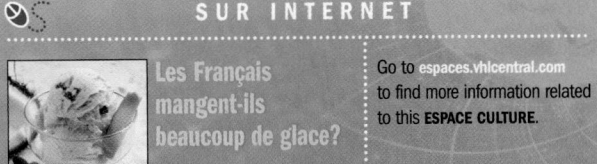

LE MONDE FRANCOPHONE

Si on est invité...

Voici quelques bonnes manières à observer quand on dîne chez des amis.

En Afrique du Nord

- Si quelqu'un vous invite à boire un thé à la menthe, ce n'est pas poli de refuser.
- En général, on enlève ses chaussures avant d'entrer dans une maison.
- On mange souvent avec les doigts°.

En France

- Il est poli d'apporter un petit cadeau pour les hôtes, par exemple des bonbons ou des fleurs.
- On dit parfois «Santé!°» ou «À votre santé°!» avant de boire et «Bon appétit!» avant de manger.
- On mange avec la fourchette dans la main gauche et le couteau dans la main droite et on garde toujours les deux mains sur la table.

doigts *fingers* **Santé!** *Cheers!* **santé** *health*

SUR INTERNET

Les Français mangent-ils beaucoup de glace?

Go to **espaces.vhlcentral.com** to find more information related to this **ESPACE CULTURE**.

ACTIVITÉS

2 Répondez Répondez aux questions d'après les textes.

1. Pourquoi les Français apprécient-ils les restaurants orientaux? *Ils les apprécient pour leur ambiance et la qualité de leur nourriture.*
2. Où sert-on le couscous aujourd'hui? *On le sert dans les restaurants trois étoiles et les cantines.*
3. Qu'est-ce qu'il est impoli de refuser en Afrique du Nord? *Il est impoli de refuser un thé à la menthe.*
4. Quel cadeau peut-on apporter quand on dîne chez des Français? *On peut apporter des bonbons ou des fleurs.*
5. Une fourchette et un couteau sont-ils nécessaires en Afrique du Nord? *Non, on mange souvent avec les doigts.*

3 Que choisir? Avez-vous déjà mangé dans un restaurant nord-africain? Quand? Où? Qu'avez-vous mangé? Du couscous? Si vous n'êtes jamais allé(e) dans un restaurant nord-africain, imaginez que des amis vous invitent à en essayer un. Qu'avez-vous envie de goûter? Pourquoi?

ressources
espaces.vhlcentral.com

Le français quotidien

- Model the pronunciation of each term and have students repeat it.
- Have volunteers describe different dishes using these terms. Examples: **pommes frites, escalope de poulet, légumes à la vapeur**, and **côtelette de porc**.

Portrait

- Have students look at the map of the French-speaking world in **Appendice A**. Point out the proximity of France to North Africa. Explain that **le Maghreb** refers to the three French-speaking nations in North Africa (**le Maroc, l'Algérie,** and **la Tunisie**).
- Explain that couscous is steamed semolina usually served with meat and vegetables.
- Couscous is often considered the national dish of **le Maghreb**.

Le monde francophone Bring in a knife and fork. Demonstrate how Americans typically use these eating utensils, then show students how the French use them.

2 Expansion For additional practice, give students these items. **6. Où peut-on acheter des merguez? (dans toutes les boucheries) 7. Quel type de pâtisserie mange-t-on traditionnellement en Afrique du Nord? (les pâtisseries au miel) 8. Combien de tonnes de couscous les Français mangent-ils par an? (75.000 tonnes) 9. Quand peut-on dire «Santé!»? (avant de boire) 10. Que faut-il enlever avant d'entrer dans une maison en Afrique du Nord? (ses chaussures)**

3 Expansion Take a quick class survey to find out how many students have tried couscous and how many like it. Ask: **Combien d'étudiants ont déjà mangé du couscous? Combien de personnes ont aimé ce plat?** Tally the results on the board.

OPTIONS

La couscousmania des Français Traditionally prepared, couscous is cooked very slowly with meat and vegetables and served on large platters made of colorful **faïence**. When preparing couscous, it is best to use a special couscous cooker called **un couscoussier**. The couscous found in stores is usually instant and requires only hot water.

Si on est invité... It is customary to drink **un thé à la menthe** in small, narrow glasses that are often decorated with faux gold leaf. It is sometimes served with pine nuts floating in the tea. Mint is sold in large bunches at Arab markets in France. For an authentic experience drinking this tea, one should go to the café near **la mosquée** in Paris.

Section Goals

In this section, students will learn:
- comparatives and superlatives of adjectives and adverbs
- irregular comparative and superlative forms

Instructional Resources
*espaces.vhlcentral.com: Lab MP3s; WB/VM/LM Answer Key; IRM (**Essayez!** and **Mise en pratique** answers; Lab Audioscript; **Feuilles d'activités**); activities; downloads; reference tools*

Suggestions
- Write **plus** + *adjective* + **que** and **moins** + *adjective* + **que** on the board, explaining their meaning. Illustrate with examples like this: **Cette classe est plus grande que la classe de l'année dernière.**
- Practice by asking the class questions whose responses require comparisons. Examples: **Qui est aussi jolie que Gwyneth Paltrow? Qui est aussi riche qu'Oprah Winfrey?**
- Practice superlative questions by asking students their opinions. Example: **Quel cours est le plus difficile? Le plus facile?**
- Use magazine pictures to practice the different irregular comparative and superlative forms, for example: uses of **meilleur(e)** (*adjective*) and **mieux** (*adverb*), **pire / plus mauvais(e)** (*adjective*) and **plus mal** (*adverb*).
- Point out that **que** and what follows it are optional if the items being compared are evident. Example: **Le steak est plus cher (que le poulet).**

9B.1 Comparatives and superlatives of adjectives and adverbs

NATIONAL STANDARDS comparisons

- Comparisons in French are formed by placing the words **plus** (*more*), **moins** (*less*), or **aussi** (*as*) before adjectives and adverbs, and the word **que** (*than, as*) after them.

ADJECTIVE	ADVERB
Simone est **plus âgée que** son mari. *Simone is older than her husband.*	Elle parle **plus vite que** son mari. *She speaks more quickly than her husband.*
Guillaume est **moins sportif que** son père. *Guillaume is less athletic than his father.*	Il m'écrit **moins souvent que** son père. *He writes me less often than his father.*
Nina est **aussi indépendante qu'**Anne. *Nina is as independent as Anne.*	Elle joue au golf **aussi bien qu'**Anne. *She plays golf as well as Anne.*

- Superlatives are formed by placing the appropriate definite article after the noun, when it is expressed, and before the comparative form. The preposition **de** often follows the superlative to express *in* or *of*.

NOUN / DEFINITE ARTICLE / COMPARATIVE

Les trains? Le TGV est **(le train) le plus rapide du** monde.
Trains? The TGV is the fastest (train) in the world.

- Some adjectives, like **beau**, **bon**, **grand**, and **nouveau**, precede the nouns they modify. Their superlative forms can also precede the nouns they modify, or they can follow them.

SUPERLATIVE NOUN	NOUN SUPERLATIVE
C'est **la plus grande ville.** *It's the largest city.*	C'est **la ville la plus grande.** *It's the largest city.*

BOÎTE À OUTILS
You learned many of the adjectives that precede the nouns they modify in **Leçon 3A STRUCTURES, page 83.**

MISE EN PRATIQUE

1 Oui, mais... Deux amis comparent deux restaurants. Complétez les phrases avec **bon, bien, meilleur** ou **mieux.**

1. J'ai bien mangé au Café du marché hier.
   Oui, mais nous avons _mieux_ mangé Chez Charles.
2. Les sandwichs au Café du marché sont _bons_.
   Oui, mais les sandwichs de Chez Charles sont meilleurs.
3. Mes amis ont bien aimé le Café du marché.
   Oui, mais mes amis ont _mieux_ mangé Chez Charles.
4. Au Café du marché, le chef prépare _bien_ le poulet.
   Oui, mais le chef de Chez Charles le prépare mieux.
5. Les salades au Café du marché sont bonnes.
   Oui, mais elles sont _meilleures_ Chez Charles.
6. Tout est bon au Café du marché!
   Tout est _meilleur_ Chez Charles!

2 Un nouveau quartier Vous venez d'emménager. Assemblez les éléments des trois colonnes pour poser des questions sur le quartier à un(e) voisin(e). Answers will vary.

MODÈLE
Le jambon est-il moins cher au supermarché ou à la charcuterie?

A	B	C
acheter	aussi	boucherie
aller	meilleur(e)	boulangerie
desserts	mieux	pâtisserie
dîner	moins	quartier
faire les courses	pire	supermarché
pain	plus	voisins

3 Aujourd'hui et autrefois Avec un(e) partenaire, comparez la vie domestique d'aujourd'hui et d'autrefois. Utilisez les adjectifs de la liste à tour de rôle. Ensuite, présentez vos opinions à la classe. Answers will vary.

MODÈLE
Aujourd'hui, les tâches ménagères sont moins difficiles.

compliqué	grand	naturel	rapide
curieux	indépendant	occupé	sophistiqué

1. les congélateurs
2. la nourriture
3. les femmes
4. les voyages
5. les voitures
6. les enfants

Practice more at **espaces.vhlcentral.com.**

OPTIONS

Extra Practice Have students write three original comparative or superlative sentences that describe themselves or compare themselves with a friend, family member, or famous person. Examples: **Je suis la personne la plus intelligente de l'université. Je suis moins égoïste que mon frère.** Then collect the papers and read the sentences aloud. See if the rest of the class can guess who wrote each description.

Game Divide the class into two teams, A and B. Place the names of 20 famous people into a hat. Select a member from each group to draw a name. The student from team A then has ten seconds to compare those two famous people in a complete sentence. If the student has made a logical comparison, team A gets a point. Then it's team B's turn to make a different comparison. The team with the most points at the end wins.

COMMUNICATION

4 Trouvez quelqu'un Votre professeur va vous donner une feuille d'activités. Circulez dans la classe pour trouver des camarades différents qui correspondent aux phrases. Answers will vary.

MODÈLE

Étudiant(e) 1: *Quel âge as-tu?*
Étudiant(e) 2: *J'ai dix-neuf ans.*
Étudiant(e) 1: *Alors, tu es plus jeune que moi.*

Trouvez dans la classe quelqu'un qui...	*Noms*
1. ... est plus jeune que vous.	*Myriam*
2. ... habite plus loin de la fac que vous.	
3. ... prend l'avion aussi souvent que vous.	
4. ... fait moins de gym que vous.	

5 Comparaisons Avec un(e) partenaire, choisissez deux questions et comparez vos réponses. Utilisez des comparatifs et des superlatifs. Answers will vary.

1. Quels jobs d'été as-tu eus?
2. Où as-tu habité?
3. Où es-tu allé(e) en vacances?
4. Qu'as-tu fait le week-end dernier?
5. Quels films as-tu vus (*seen*) récemment?

6 Comparaisons Par groupes de trois, comparez les sujets présentés. Utilisez des comparatifs et des superlatifs. Answers will vary.

MODÈLE

Étudiant(e) 1: *Les vacances à la mer sont plus amusantes que les vacances à la montagne.*
Étudiant(e) 2: *Moi, je pense que les vacances à la montagne sont plus intéressantes.*
Étudiant(e) 3: *D'accord, mais les vacances à l'étranger sont les plus amusantes.*

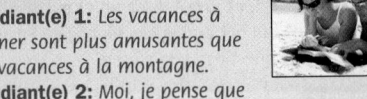

1.

3.

2.

4.

- Since adverbs are invariable, you always use **le** to form the superlative.

M. Duval est le prof qui parle **le plus vite**.
Mr. Duval is the professor who speaks the fastest.

C'est Amandine qui écoute **le moins patiemment**.
Amandine listens the least patiently.

- Some adjectives and adverbs have irregular comparative and superlative forms.

Irregular comparatives and superlatives

Adjective	Comparative	Superlative
bon(ne)(s)	meilleur(e)(s)	le/la/les meilleur(e)(s)
mauvais(e)(s)	pire(s) *or* plus mauvais(e)(s)	le/la/les pire(s) *or* le/la/les plus mauvais(e)(s)
Adverb	**Comparative**	**Superlative**
bien	mieux	le mieux
mal	plus mal	le plus mal

En été, les pêches sont **meilleures** que les pommes.
In summer, the peaches are better than the apples.

Quand on est au régime, les frites sont **pires** que les pâtes.
When you're dieting, fries are worse than pasta.

Johnny Hallyday chante bien, mais Jacques Brel chante **mieux**.
Johnny Hallyday sings well, but Jacques Brel sings better.

Je ne fais pas bien le ménage, mais tu le fais **plus mal** que moi.
I don't do the housework well, but you do it worse than I.

Voilà **la meilleure** boulangerie de la ville.
There's the best bakery in town.

Dans la classe, c'est Clémentine qui écrit **le mieux**.
In the class, Clémentine is the one who writes the best.

Essayez! **Complétez les phrases avec le comparatif ou le superlatif.**

Comparatifs

1. Les étudiants sont *moins âgés que* (- âgés [*old*]) le professeur.
2. Les plages de la Martinique sont-elles mieux que (+ bien) les plages de la Guadeloupe?
3. Évelyne parle aussi poliment que (= poliment) Luc.
4. Les chaussettes sont moins chères que (- chères) les baskets.

Superlatifs

5. Quelle librairie vend les livres *les plus intéressants* (+ intéressants)?
6. Le jean est le moins élégant (- élégant) de tous mes pantalons.
7. Je joue aux cartes avec ma mère. C'est elle qui joue le mieux (+ bien).
8. Les fraises de son jardin sont les moins bonnes (- bonnes).

Essayez! Give additional sentences for extra practice. Examples: **Comparatif: Les roses sentent ____ (+ bon) les chrysanthèmes. (meilleur que) Superlatif: C'est le fromage qui sent (+ mauvais) ____, mais c'est (+ bon) ____. (le plus mauvais/le meilleur)**

1 Expansion In pairs, have students select two local restaurants and describe them using comparatives and superlatives modeled on those in the activity. Ask volunteers to share their sentences with the class.

2 Suggestion You may want to do this as a whole-class activity, giving different students the opportunity to ask and answer questions using the words in the columns.

3 Expansion After completing the activity, ask students to give their opinions about which is better: **la vie d'autrefois ou la vie moderne.** Encourage students to use superlative and comparative forms.

4 Suggestions
- Before beginning the activity, have the class brainstorm additional characteristics to use in this survey. Encourage them to use other vocabulary from past lessons.
- Have two students act out the **modèle**. Then distribute the **Feuilles d'activités** found on the Supersite.

5 Expansion After pairs complete the activity, ask the class questions about their conversations using comparatives and superlatives. Examples: **Qui a eu le pire job de l'été? Le job le plus mal payé?**

6 Suggestion Act out the **modèle** with two volunteers.

6 Expansion Using magazine pictures, show images similar to those in the activity. Have students create additional sentences.

OPTIONS

Extra Practice Give ten comparative and superlative sentences orally to practice listening comprehension. Dictate the sentences, then give students about 30 seconds per sentence to write the direct opposite. Ask volunteers to present their opposite sentences. Example: **La fin de ce livre est meilleure que le début. (La fin de ce livre est pire que le début.)**

TPR Have two or more volunteer students stand up in front of the class with similar objects. Make a comparison between these objects. Example: **John a le cahier le plus grand.** Then call on other volunteers to make different comparisons between other objects. Then ask: **Qui a ____ le/la plus grand(e)?**

Section Goals

In this section, students will learn double object pronouns.

Instructional Resources
*espaces.vhlcentral.com: Lab MP3s; WB/VM/LM Answer Key; IRM (**Essayez!** and **Mise en pratique** answers; Lab Audioscript); activities; downloads; reference tools*

Suggestions

- Briefly review indirect object pronouns (**Leçon 6B**) and direct object pronouns (**Leçon 7A**). Give sentences and have students replace objects with object pronouns. Examples: **Jean nous donne le cours. (Jean nous le donne.) Il écrit la lettre. (Il l'écrit.) Le garçon mange la tarte. (Le garçon la mange.)**
- Explain that object pronouns replace key elements in a conversation or text in order to avoid redundancy.
- To help students visualize which object pronouns are indirect and which are direct, draw a Venn diagram (two intersecting circles) on the board. In the left circle, write direct object pronouns **le**, **la**, **l'**, and **les**. Where there is overlap in the circles, write direct and indirect object pronouns **me**, **te**, **nous**, and **vous**. In the right circle, write the indirect object pronouns **lui** and **leur**. Label the left circle *Direct object pronouns* and the right circle *Indirect object pronouns*.
- Ask students questions to which they respond with third-person double object pronouns. Examples: **Qui rend la monnaie à la cliente? (Le serveur/La serveuse la lui rend.) Qui donne le livre de grammaire aux étudiants? (Le professeur le leur donne.)**

9B.2 Double object pronouns

NATIONAL STANDARDS comparisons

Point de départ In **Leçon 6B** and **Leçon 7A**, respectively, you learned to use indirect and direct object pronouns. Now you will learn to use these pronouns together.

DIRECT OBJECT / INDIRECT OBJECT		DIRECT OBJECT PRONOUN / INDIRECT OBJECT PRONOUN
J'ai rendu **le menu** à **la serveuse**. *I returned the menu to the waitress.*	▶	Je **le lui** ai rendu. *I returned it to her.*

Tu peux la lui passer, s'il te plaît?

Une deuxième tranche? Je te la sers.

- Use this sequence when a sentence contains both a direct and an indirect object pronoun.

me / **te** / **nous** / **vous**	*before*	**le** / **la** / **l'** / **les**	*before*	**lui** / **leur**	+	*[verb]*

Gérard m'envoie les messages de Christiane. Il **me les** envoie tous les jours.
Gérard sends me Christiane's messages.
He sends them to me every day.

Je lui envoie aussi les messages de Laurent. Je **les lui** envoie tous les week-ends.
I send him Laurent's messages, too.
I send them to him every weekend.

Le chef nous prépare son meilleur plat. Les serveurs **nous l'**apportent.
The chef prepares his best dish for us.
The waiters bring it to us.

Nous avons laissé le pourboire des serveurs sur la table. Nous **le leur** avons laissé quand nous sommes partis.
We left a tip for the waiters on the table.
We left it for them when we left.

MISE EN PRATIQUE

1 Les livres Le père de Bertrand lui a acheté des livres. Refaites l'histoire avec deux pronoms pour chaque phrase.

1. Papa a acheté <u>ces livres à Bertrand.</u> Papa les lui a achetés.
2. Il a lu <u>les livres à ses petits frères.</u> Il les leur a lus.
3. Maintenant, ses frères veulent lire <u>les livres à leur père.</u> Maintenant, ses frères veulent les lui lire.
4. Bertrand donne <u>les livres à ses petits frères.</u> Bertrand les leur donne.
5. Les garçons montrent <u>les livres à leur père.</u> Les garçons les lui montrent.
6. Leur père préfère donner <u>sa place à leur mère.</u> Leur père préfère la lui donner.
7. Les enfants lisent <u>les livres à leur mère.</u> Les enfants les lui lisent.
8. «Maintenant, lisez <u>les livres à votre père</u>», dit-elle. «Maintenant, lisez-les-lui», dit-elle.

2 Comment? Un groupe d'amis parle de l'anniversaire de Christelle. Antoine n'entend pas très bien. Il répète tout ce que les gens disent. Utilisez des pronoms pour écrire ses questions.

MODÈLE

Je vais prêter mon pull noir à Christelle.
Tu veux le lui prêter?

1. Son père a acheté la petite voiture bleue à Christelle. Son père la lui a achetée?
2. Nous envoyons les invitations aux amis. Vous les leur envoyez?
3. Le prof a donné la meilleure note à Christelle le jour de son anniversaire. Le prof la lui a donnée?
4. Je vais prêter mon tailleur à Christelle vendredi soir. Tu vas le lui prêter vendredi soir?
5. Est-ce que vous voulez me lire l'invitation? Est-ce que je veux / nous voulons vous la lire?
6. Nous n'avons pas envoyé l'invitation au professeur. Vous ne la lui avez pas envoyée?
7. Gilbert et Arthur vont nous apporter le gâteau. Gilbert et Arthur vont vous l'apporter?
8. Sa mère va payer le repas à sa fille. Sa mère va le lui payer?

3 De quoi parle-t-on? Avec un(e) partenaire, imaginez les questions qui ont donné ces réponses. Ensuite, présentez vos questions à la classe. Answers will vary.

MODÈLE

Il veut le lui vendre.
Il veut vendre son vélo à son camarade?

1. Marc va la lui donner.
2. Nous te l'avons envoyée hier.
3. Elle te les a achetés la semaine dernière.
4. Tu me les prêtes souvent.
5. Micheline ne va pas vous les prendre.
6. Tu ne nous les as pas prises.
7. Rendez-les-moi!
8. Ne le lui disons pas!

Practice more at **espaces.vhlcentral.com.**

OPTIONS

Video Replay the video, having students focus on the use of comparatives, superlatives, and all object pronouns. Stop the video where appropriate to discuss how these forms were used and to ask questions. Ask to whom or to what each object pronoun refers. For example, when David says **Qu'est-ce que je peux lui apporter?**, have students clarify the use of **lui**. **(Il demande ce qu'il peut apporter à Sandrine.)**

Pairs Have students write five sentences that contain both direct and indirect object nouns. When they are finished, have them switch papers with a partner who must restate the sentences using double object pronouns.

COMMUNICATION

4 **Une entrevue** Avec un(e) partenaire, répondez aux questions sur votre enfance. Utilisez deux pronoms dans vos réponses. Answers will vary.

1. Est-ce que tes parents te montraient les films de Disney quand tu étais petit(e)?
2. Est-ce que tu vas montrer les films de Disney à tes enfants un jour?
3. Est-ce que quelqu'un te parlait français quand tu étais petit(e)?
4. Qui t'a acheté ton premier vélo?
5. Qui te faisait à dîner quand tu étais petit(e)?
6. Qui te préparait le petit-déjeuner le matin?

5 **Qui vous aide?** Avec un(e) partenaire, posez des questions avec les pronoms interrogatifs qui et quand. Vous pouvez choisir le présent, le passé composé ou l'imparfait. Répondez aux questions avec deux pronoms. Answers will vary.

MODÈLE prêter sa voiture

Étudiant(e) 1: *Qui te prête sa voiture?*
Étudiant(e) 2: *Ma mère me la prête.*
Étudiant(e) 1: *Quand est-ce qu'elle te la prête?*
Étudiant(e) 2: *Elle me la prête le vendredi.*

faire la cuisine	nettoyer la chambre
faire le lit	payer l'université
laver les vêtements	prêter ses livres

6 **Les courses** Avec un(e) partenaire, préparez deux dialogues basés sur deux des photos. À tour de rôle, jouez le/la client(e) et le/la marchand(e). Utilisez le vocabulaire et deux pronoms, si possible, dans les dialogues. Answers will vary.

commander	être au régime	du poulet
des croissants	les fruits de mer	une saucisse
cuisiner	un plat	un steak
une entrée	du porc	une tarte

- In an infinitive construction, the double object pronouns come after the conjugated verb and precede the infinitive, just like single object pronouns.

Mes notes de français? Je vais **vous les** prêter.
My French notes? I'm going to lend them to you.

Carole veut lire mon poème? Je vais **le lui** montrer.
Carole wants to read my poem? I'm going to show it to her.

- In the **passé composé** the double object pronouns precede the auxiliary verb, just like single object pronouns. The past participle agrees with the preceding direct object.

Rémi a-t-il acheté ces fleurs pour sa mère?
Did Rémi buy those flowers for his mother?

Oui, il **les lui** a **achetées**.
Yes, he bought them for her.

Vous m'avez donné la plus grande chambre?
Did you give me the biggest room?

Non, nous ne **vous** l'avons pas **donnée**.
No, we didn't give it to you.

- In affirmative commands, the verb is followed by the direct object pronoun and then the indirect object pronoun, with hyphens in between. Remember to use **moi** and **toi** instead of **me** and **te**.

Vous avez trois voitures? Montrez-**les-moi**.
You have three cars? Show them to me.

Tu connais la réponse à la question du prof? Dis-**la-nous**.
You know the answer to the professor's question? Tell it to us.

Voici le livre. Donne-**le-leur**.
Here's the book. Give it to them.

Ce poème? Traduisons-**le-lui**.
This poem? Let's translate it for her.

Essayez! Utilisez deux pronoms pour refaire ces phrases.

1. Le prof vous donne les résultats des examens. *Le prof vous les donne.*
2. Tes parents t'achètent le billet. Tes parents te l'achètent.
3. Qui t'a donné cette belle lampe bleue? Qui te l'a donnée?
4. Il nous a réservé les chambres. Il nous les a réservées.
5. Pose-moi tes questions. Pose-les-moi.
6. Explique-leur le problème de maths. Explique-le-leur.
7. Peux-tu me montrer les photos? Peux-tu me les montrer?
8. Tu préfères lui prêter ton dictionnaire? Tu préfères le lui prêter?

Essayez! Have students rewrite the answers from **Essayez!** as negative sentences. Example: **1. Le prof ne vous les donne pas.**

1 Suggestion Have students write the answers on the board and go over them with the class.

2 Suggestion Before assigning this activity, have students underline the direct objects and circle the indirect objects in each sentence on photocopies or a transparency.

3 Expansion Have students write their own sentences using double object pronouns modeled on those in the activity. Pairs exchange papers and invent possible questions that elicit those responses.

4 Expansion Have two pairs get together and ask each other questions in the third person based on what they just learned about their partners.

5 Expansion Have students tell the class their partners' responses using the third person. Example: **Sa mère la lui prête le vendredi.**

6 Suggestions
- Go over the photos with the students so it is clear what stores are pictured.
- Make sure students include at least two affirmative commands including **s'il vous plaît** and double object pronouns in their conversations.
- Call on a few volunteer pairs to act out one of the conversations for the class.

OPTIONS

Extra Practice Here are three questions and answers containing object pronouns to use as a dictation. **1. Qui parle aux étudiants? Le professeur leur parle. 2. Qui m'a invité(e) à la fête? Mon petit ami t'a invité(e) à la fête. 3. Prêtes-tu la voiture à ton frère? Non, je ne la lui prête pas.**

Pairs Have students brainstorm a list of people to whom they relate well. Examples: **le prof de français, les parents, les amis,** etc. Have them describe their relationships with those people to their partner. Encourage them to use object pronouns whenever possible. Example: **le prof de français (Je peux lui poser des questions, lui parler en français et lui demander une bonne note.)**

Instructional Resources
espaces.vhlcentral.com: IRM (Info Gap Activities); Testing Program, pp. 69–72; Test Files; Testing Program MP3s; activities; downloads; reference tools
Test Generator

1 Suggestion Encourage students to use both familiar commands and **pouvoir** + *infinitive* when completing the activity.

2 Expansion You can also do this activity in groups of three. Have the third student imagine he or she is the server. The other students must ask questions about the food in order to make a decision. Example: **La tarte aux pommes est-elle plus fraîche que les pêches à la crème?**

3 Expansion Students should imagine they must create a restaurant ad featuring their favorite dish. Have students make up five sentences using superlatives to convince customers their restaurant is the best and to entice them to order their favorite dish.

4 Suggestion Before assigning this activity, review the different meanings the verbs **devoir, vouloir,** and **pouvoir** can have in the past and negative forms.

5 Suggestions
- Act out the **modèle** with two volunteers.
- Have students brainstorm a list of additional ideas with two options on the board. Example: **étudier dans une grande ou une petite université**

6 Suggestion Divide the class into pairs and distribute the Info Gap Handouts found on the Supersite for this activity. Give students ten minutes to complete the activity.

Révision

1 Fais les courses pour moi Vous n'avez pas le temps d'aller dans tous ces magasins. Choisissez un magasin. Puis, par groupes de quatre, trouvez des camarades qui vont dans d'autres magasins. À tour de rôle, demandez-leur de faire des courses pour vous. Utilisez des pronoms doubles dans vos réponses. Answers will vary.

MODÈLE

Étudiant(e) 1: *J'ai besoin de deux filets de poissons. Tu peux me les prendre à la poissonnerie?*
Étudiant(e) 2: *Pas de problème. Et moi, j'ai besoin de...*

un camembert	six croissants
deux bouteilles de lait	une tarte aux pêches
deux filets de poissons	des tomates
douze œufs	une tranche de jambon
quatre côtes (*chops*) de porc	trois baguettes

2 Je les leur commande Vous êtes au restaurant. Avec un(e) partenaire, choisissez le meilleur plat pour chaque membre de votre famille. Employez des comparatifs, des superlatifs et des pronoms doubles dans vos réponses. Answers will vary.

MODÈLE

Étudiant(e) 1: *Et le poulet?*
Étudiant(e) 2: *Mon père mange du poulet plus souvent que ma mère. Je vais le lui commander.*

Assiette de fruits de mer	Petits pois et carottes
Bœuf avec une sauce au vin	Pizza aux quatre fromages
Hamburger et frites	Sandwich au thon
Pêches à la crème	Tarte aux pommes

3 Mes plats préférés Par groupes de trois, interviewez vos camarades. Quels sont les plats qu'ils aiment le mieux? Quand les ont-ils mangés la dernière fois? Choisissez vos trois plats préférés, puis comparez-les avec les plats de vos camarades. Employez des comparatifs, des superlatifs et le passé récent. Answers will vary.

4 Le week-end dernier Préparez deux listes par écrit, une pour les choses que vous avez pu faire le week-end dernier et une pour les choses que vous n'avez pas pu faire. Ensuite, avec un(e) partenaire, comparez vos listes et expliquez vos réponses. Employez les verbes **devoir, vouloir** et **pouvoir** au passé composé et, si possible, les pronoms doubles. Answers will vary.

MODÈLE

Étudiant(e) 1: *J'ai voulu envoyer un e-mail à ma cousine.*
Étudiant(e) 2: *Est-ce que tu as pu le lui envoyer?*

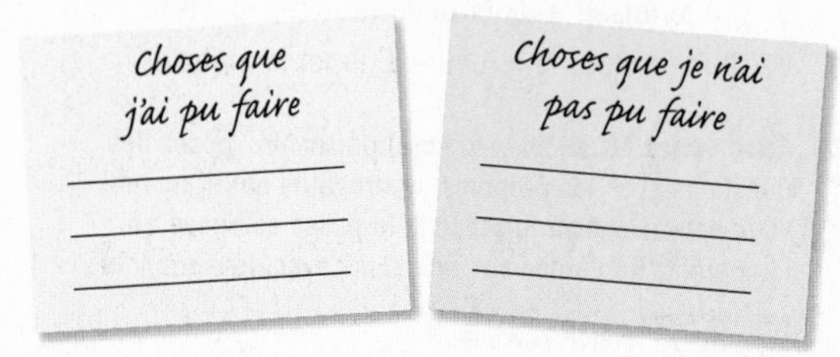

Choses que j'ai pu faire
Choses que je n'ai pas pu faire

5 C'est mieux Par groupes de trois, donnez votre opinion sur ces sujets. Pour chaque sujet, comparez les deux options. Soyez prêts à présenter les résultats de vos discussions à la classe. Answers will vary.

MODÈLE apporter des fleurs ou du vin à un dîner

Étudiant(e) 1: *C'est plus sympa d'apporter des fleurs à un dîner.*
Étudiant(e) 2: *Oui, on peut les mettre sur la table. Elles sont plus jolies qu'une bouteille de vin.*
Étudiant(e) 3: *Peut-être, mais le vin est un cadeau plus généreux.*

- commencer ou finir un régime
- faire les courses ou faire la cuisine
- manger ou faire la cuisine

6 Six différences Votre professeur va vous donner, à vous et à votre partenaire, deux feuilles d'activités différentes. Comparez les deux familles pour trouver les six différences. Attention! Ne regardez pas la feuille de votre partenaire. Answers will vary.

MODÈLE

Étudiant(e) 1: *Fatiha est aussi grande que Samira.*
Étudiant(e) 2: *Non, Fatiha est moins grande que Samira.*

ressources
WB pp. 121-124
LM pp. 71-72
espaces.vhlcentral.com

OPTIONS

Extra Practice Have students imagine that a senior from their old high school wants to attend their university the following year and wrote them an e-mail asking questions about it. Provide a brief sample message. Example: **Je suis en terminale au lycée et je veux être prêt(e) pour l'université. Le campus est plus grand ou plus petit que le lycée? Les cours au lycée sont-ils beaucoup moins difficiles que les cours à la fac? Quel cours est le plus intéressant? Est-ce que les repas sont meilleurs? Quelles sont les autres différences avec le lycée?** Students then write a reply telling about different aspects of the university. Encourage the use of personal experience in their comparisons. Then in groups of three, have each student present his or her e-mail. Students should discuss whether they agree or disagree with their classmates.

À l'écoute

National communication Standards

Audio: Activities

STRATÉGIE

Jotting down notes as you listen

Jotting down notes while you listen to a conversation in French can help you keep track of the important points or details. It will help you to focus actively on comprehension rather than on remembering what you have heard.

To practice this strategy, you will listen to a paragraph. Jot down the main points you hear.

Préparation

Regardez la photo et décrivez la scène. Où sont ces hommes? Que font-ils? Qui sont-ils, à votre avis? Qu'y a-t-il dans la poêle (*frying pan*)? À votre avis, que préparent-ils?

À vous d'écouter

Écoutez les instructions pour préparer une salade niçoise et notez les ingrédients nécessaires.

Pour la salade

des haricots verts	des tomates
des pommes de terre	un poivron
des œufs	du thon
de la salade	des olives noires

Pour la vinaigrette (*dressing*)

de l'huile d'olive	du sel
de la moutarde	du poivre
de l'ail	du vinaigre

Practice more at **espaces.vhlcentral.com.**

Compréhension

Le bon ordre Mettez ces instructions simplifiées dans le bon ordre, d'après la recette de la salade niçoise.

7 a. Mélanger (*Mix*) le vinaigre, l'huile d'olive, la moutarde et l'ail pour faire la vinaigrette.
6 b. Mettre le thon et les olives sur la salade.
4 c. Couper (*Cut*) les œufs et les mettre dans la salade.
1 d. Faire cuire (*Cook*) les pommes de terre, les haricots verts et les œufs.
5 e. Mettre les morceaux de tomates et de poivron sur la salade.
2 f. Laver (*Wash*) la salade et la mettre dans une grande assiette.
3 g. Mettre les haricots verts et les pommes de terre sur la salade.
8 h. Mettre la vinaigrette sur la salade et servir.

Votre recette préférée Quel est votre plat ou dessert favori? Donnez la liste des ingrédients qu'il faut pour le préparer, puis expliquez à un groupe de camarades comment le préparer. Ne leur donnez pas le nom du plat. Ils vont prendre des notes et essayer de le deviner (*to guess*). Ensuite, changez de rôles.

Section Goals

In this section, students will:
- learn to take notes as they listen
- listen to a paragraph and jot down the main points
- listen to a cooking program and complete several activities

Instructional Resources
espaces.vhlcentral.com: IRM (Textbook Audioscript); Textbook MP3s; activities; downloads; reference tools

Stratégie
Script Bon, je vais aller faire les courses. D'abord, je vais passer à la boucherie. J'ai besoin d'un poulet et de quatre steaks. Ensuite, je vais aller à la boulangerie pour acheter du pain et des croissants. Ah oui! Il faut aussi du poisson pour ce soir. Alors, du thon à la poissonnerie. Et au supermarché, des légumes et des fruits.

Préparation Have students look at the photo and describe what they see. Then ask them to guess what dish the chef is preparing.

À vous d'écouter
Script Bonjour à tous et bienvenue à «Cuisiner avec Claude». Aujourd'hui, nous allons préparer une salade bien française: la salade niçoise. C'est une salade très complète qui est parfaite pour l'été. Alors, voici ce que vous devez faire pour préparer cette salade. Tout d'abord, faites cuire les haricots verts et les pommes de terre dans de l'eau très chaude avec un peu de sel. Faites aussi cuire les œufs dans de l'eau. Lavez bien la salade et mettez-la dans une grande assiette. Mettez les pommes de terre et les haricots verts sur la salade. Coupez les œufs, quelques tomates et un poivron et mettez-les dans la salade. Ensuite, mettez du thon et des olives noires. Et maintenant, pour la vinaigrette, mélangez du vinaigre, de l'huile d'olive, de la moutarde et un peu d'ail. Mettez du sel et du poivre dans la vinaigrette et ajoutez-la à la salade. Et voilà! Votre salade est prête!

Vous pouvez la servir avec du pain ou bien des croûtons, si vous le désirez. Cette salade délicieuse est rapide à préparer et vous pouvez la servir en entrée ou bien comme plat principal. Allez! À table! Et bon appétit à tous!

Section Goals

In this section, students will read historical and cultural information about Burgundy and Franche-Comté.

Instructional Resources
espaces.vhlcentral.com: Transparency #42; WB/VM/LM Answer Key; activities; downloads; reference tools

Carte de la Bourgogne et de la Franche-Comté

- Have students look at the map or use **Transparency #42**. Ask volunteers to read the names of cities and rivers aloud. Model the pronunciation as necessary.
- Ask students to name the country that borders Franche-Comté. (**La Suisse**)

La région en chiffres

- Point out the coats of arms for the regions.
- Have volunteers read the sections. After each section, ask students questions about the content.
- Point out that the vineyards of Burgundy produce some of the world's greatest wines.
- Tell students that the town of Dijon is famous for its mustard.
- The town of Nevers is famous for its fine, hand-painted, decorative pottery, known as **faïence**.
- In Franche-Comté, many handcrafted objects are made from wood, such as violins, guitars, pipes, clocks, and toys.

Incroyable mais vrai! Snails have been eaten as food since at least ancient Roman times. They are a rich source of protein and are supposed to help prevent aging.

NATIONAL STANDARDS connections cultures

Interactive Map Reading

Panorama

les vendanges° en Bourgogne

La Bourgogne

La région en chiffres

- **Superficie:** *31.582 km²*
- **Population:** *1.626.000*
  SOURCE: INSEE
- **Industries principales:** *industries automobile et pharmaceutique, tourisme, viticulture°*
- **Villes principales:** *Auxerre, Chalon-sur-Saône, Dijon, Mâcon, Nevers*

Personnes célèbres

- **Gustave Eiffel,** *ingénieur° (la tour Eiffel) (1832–1923)*
- **Colette,** *femme écrivain° (1873–1954)*
- **Claude Jade,** *actrice (1948–2006)*

La Franche-Comté

La région en chiffres

- **Superficie:** *16.202 km²*
- **Population:** *1.151.000*
- **Industries principales:** *agriculture, artisanat, industrie automobile, horlogerie°, tourisme*
- **Villes principales:** *Belfort, Besançon, Dole, Pontarlier, Vesoul*

Personnes célèbres

- **Louis (1864–1948) et Auguste (1862–1954) Lumière,** *inventeurs du cinématographe°*
- **Claire Motte,** *danseuse étoile° à l'Opéra de Paris (1937–1986)*

un marché à Dijon

la ville d'Ornans

Incroyable mais vrai!

Au Moyen Âge, les escargots servaient à° la fabrication de sirops contre la toux°. La recette bourguignonne (beurre, ail, persil°) est popularisée au 19e siècle. La France produit 500 à 800 tonnes d'escargots par an, mais en importe 5.000 tonnes. L'escargot aide à lutter contre° le mauvais cholestérol et les maladies cardio-vasculaires.

viticulture *grape growing* **ingénieur** *engineer* **écrivain** *writer* **horlogerie** *watch and clock making* **cinématographe** *motion picture camera* **danseuse étoile** *principal dancer* **servaient à** *were used for* **toux** *cough* **persil** *parsley* **lutter contre** *fight against* **vendanges** *grape harvest*

OPTIONS

Personnes célèbres **Claude Jade** was an internationally acclaimed actress and won several awards, among them the award for Best Actress for her performance in ***L'École des femmes***. **Gustave Eiffel** was also a noted bridge designer, and he designed the wrought-iron skeleton for the inside of the Statue of Liberty. **Colette** (the pen name of Sidonie-Gabrielle Colette) wrote novels about women and their lovers; some of her novels were autobiographical. One her best-known works, ***Gigi*** (1945), was made into a musical film in 1958. **Louis** and **Auguste Lumière** created the first motion picture, ***La sortie des ouvriers de l'usine Lumière***, in 1895. They also made the first newsreels.

Les sports

Les sports d'hiver dans le Jura

On peut pratiquer de nombreux sports d'hiver dans les montagnes du Jura, en Franche-Comté: ski alpin, surf°, monoski, planche à voile sur neige. Mais le Jura est surtout le paradis du ski de fond°. Avec des centaines de kilomètres de pistes°, on y skie de décembre à avril, y compris° la nuit, sur des pistes éclairées°. La célèbre Transjurassienne est la 2e course° d'endurance du monde avec un parcours° de 76 km et un de 50 km. Il y a aussi la Transjeune, un parcours de 10 km pour les jeunes de moins de 20 ans.

Les destinations

Besançon: ancienne capitale de l'horlogerie

L'artisanat de l'horlogerie commence au 16e siècle avec l'installation de grandes horloges dans les monastères. Au 18e siècle, 400 horlogers suisses viennent s'installer° en Franche-Comté. Au 19e siècle, Montbéliard comptait 5.000 horlogers. En hiver, les paysans°-horlogers s'occupaient°, dans leurs fermes°, de la finition° et de la décoration des horloges. En 1862, une école d'horlogerie est créée° et en 1900, Besançon devient le berceau° de l'horlogerie française avec 8.000 horlogers qui produisent 600.000 montres par an.

L'architecture

Les toits de Bourgogne

Les toits° en tuiles vernissées° multicolores sont typiques de la Bourgogne. Inspirés de l'architecture flamande° et d'Europe centrale, ils forment des dessins géométriques. Le plus célèbre bâtiment° est l'Hôtel-Dieu° de Beaune, construit en 1443 pour accueillir° les pauvres et les victimes de la guerre° de Cent ans. Aujourd'hui, l'Hôtel-Dieu organise la plus célèbre vente aux enchères° de vins du monde.

Les gens

Louis Pasteur (1822–1895)

Louis Pasteur est né à Dole, en Franche-Comté. Il découvre° que les fermentations sont dues à des micro-organismes spécifiques. Dans ses recherches° sur les maladies° contagieuses, il montre la relation entre le microbe et l'apparition d'une maladie. Cette découverte° a des applications dans le monde hospitalier et industriel avec les méthodes de désinfection, de stérilisation et de pasteurisation. Le vaccin contre la rage° est aussi une de ses inventions. L'Institut Pasteur est créé à Paris en 1888. Aujourd'hui, il a des filiales° sur les cinq continents.

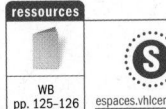

Qu'est-ce que vous avez appris? Répondez aux questions par des phrases complètes.

1. Comment s'appellent les inventeurs du cinématographe?
   Ils s'appellent Louis et Auguste Lumière.
2. À quoi servaient les escargots au Moyen Âge?
   Ils servaient à fabriquer des sirops contre la toux.
3. Avec quoi sont préparés les escargots de Bourgogne?
   Ils sont préparés avec du beurre, de l'ail et du persil.
4. Quel est le sport le plus pratiqué dans le Jura?
   C'est le ski de fond.
5. Qu'est-ce que la Transjurassienne?
   C'est une course d'endurance.
6. D'où viennent les horlogers au 18e siècle?
   Ils viennent de Suisse.
7. Quel style d'architecture a influencé les toits de Bourgogne?
   L'architecture flamande et d'Europe centrale les a influencés.
8. Quel est le bâtiment avec le toit le plus célèbre en Bourgogne?
   C'est l'Hôtel-Dieu de Beaune, un ancien hôpital.
9. Comment les recherches de Pasteur ont-elles été utilisées par les hôpitaux et l'industrie?
   Elles ont été utilisées dans les méthodes de désinfection, de stérilisation et de pasteurisation.
10. Où trouve-t-on des Instituts Pasteur aujourd'hui?
    On trouve des Instituts Pasteur à Paris et sur les cinq continents.

Practice more at **espaces.vhlcentral.com.**

ressources: WB pp. 125–126 | espaces.vhlcentral.com

SUR INTERNET

Go to **espaces.vhlcentral.com** to find more cultural information related to this **PANORAMA**.

1. Quand ont lieu les vendanges en Bourgogne?
2. Cherchez trois recettes à base (*using*) d'escargots.
3. Trouvez des informations sur les vacances d'hiver dans le Jura: logement, prix, activités, etc.
4. Cherchez des informations sur Louis Pasteur. Quel effet ont eu ses découvertes sur des produits alimentaires d'usage courant (*everyday use*)?

surf *snowboarding* **ski de fond** *cross-country skiing* **pistes** *trails* **y compris** *including* **éclairées** *lit* **course** *race* **parcours** *course* **s'installer** *settle* **paysans** *peasants* **s'occupaient** *took care* **fermes** *farms* **finition** *finishing* **créée** *created* **berceau** *cradle* **toits** *roofs* **tuiles vernissées** *glazed tiles* **flamande** *Flemish* **bâtiment** *building* **Hôtel-Dieu** *Hospital* **accueillir** *welcome* **guerre** *war* **vente aux enchères** *auction* **découvre** *discovers* **recherches** *research* **maladies** *illnesses* **découverte** *discovery* **rage** *rabies* **filiales** *branches*

Les sports d'hiver dans le Jura

- The Jura Mountains along the Swiss-French border extend from the Rhône River to the Rhine River.
- Ask students: **Que font les gens sur la photo? (Ils font du ski de fond.) Avez-vous envie de visiter les montagnes du Jura? Pourquoi?**

Besançon: ancienne capitale de l'horlogerie

- The **musée du Temps** in the **palais Granvelle** contains all sorts of time pieces from ancient to modern times. It also chronicles the history of the measurement of time.
- Besançon is no longer the capital of watch/clockmaking. Many businesses have closed, and the region has turned to microtechnics, opticals, and electronics.

Les toits de Bourgogne

- The multicolored tiles appear mostly on buildings dating from the late Middle Ages or the Renaissance, but they were sometimes used on houses built or restored during the nineteenth and twentieth centuries.
- Ask students: **De quelles couleurs sont les tuiles vernissées sur la photo? (blanches, rouges, bleues, vertes, marron)**
- **La guerre de Cent ans** began in 1337 and ended in 1453.

Louis Pasteur Louis Pasteur also discovered ways of preventing silkworm diseases, anthrax, and chicken cholera.

OPTIONS

Bourgogne The duchy of Burgundy enjoyed a golden age from the beginning of Duke Philip the Bold's reign in 1364 to the end of Duke Charles the Bold's reign in 1477. During that time Franche-Comté became part of the Burgundian duchy, as did Flanders and parts of the Netherlands. As a result, Burgundy became a powerful economic and cultural force, and it enjoyed prosperous trade in wine, wool, and grain.

Extra Practice After students have read the **Panorama**, ask them to give examples of industries in Burgundy and Franche-Comté that were influenced by the geography or location of these two regions. Examples: **la viticulture, le tourisme ou les sports d'hiver dans les montagnes du Jura, l'horlogerie (qui a commencé avec l'arrivée des horlogers suisses au 18e siècle)**.

Section Goals

In this section, students will:
- learn to identify the main idea in a text
- read a menu and restaurant review

Stratégie Tell students that recognizing the main idea of a text will help them infer the meanings of unfamiliar words they encounter while reading. Tell them to check the title first because the main idea is often expressed there. Also tell them to read the topic sentence of each paragraph before they read the full text so they will get a sense of the main idea.

Examinez le texte First, have students look at the format of the two texts and ask them if the formats are similar or different. Then, tell them to get together with a partner and discuss the reading strategies they can use to identify the texts' genre.

Comparez les deux textes
- Have students look at the first text (the menu) and ask them if it has a title. Then have them identify the subtitles or subheadings and the type of vocabulary used. Finally, ask them to identify the text's genre.
- Have students look at the second text (the review) and identify the different parts of the reading. Then ask them to compare the formats and vocabulary of the two texts. Write a list of the similarities and differences on the board. Finally, have them identify the genre of the second text.

Lecture

NATIONAL STANDARDS communication cultures

S Reading

Avant la lecture

STRATÉGIE

Reading for the main idea

As you know, you can learn a great deal about a reading selection by looking at its format and by looking for cognates, titles, and subtitles. You can skim to get the gist of the reading selection and scan it for specific information. Reading for the main idea is another useful strategy; it involves locating the topic sentences of each paragraph to determine the author's purpose. Topic sentences can provide clues about the content of each paragraph, as well as the general organization of the reading. Your choice of which reading strategies to use will depend on the style and format of each reading selection.

Examinez le texte

Dans cette lecture, il y a deux textes différents. Regardez ces textes rapidement. Leur format est-il similaire ou différent? Quelles stratégies vont être utiles pour identifier le genre de ces textes, d'après vous? Comparez vos idées avec un(e) camarade.

Comparez les deux textes

Premier texte

Analysez le format du texte. Y a-t-il un titre? Des sous-titres? Plusieurs sections? Comment ce texte est-il organisé? Regardez rapidement le contenu (*content*) du texte. Quel genre de vocabulaire trouvez-vous dans ce texte? D'après vous, qu'est-ce que c'est?

Deuxième texte

Ce texte est-il organisé comme (*like*) le premier texte? Y a-t-il un titre, des sous-titres et plusieurs parties? Y a-t-il des informations similaires aux informations données dans le premier texte? Lesquelles? (*Which ones?*) Le vocabulaire est-il similaire au vocabulaire du premier texte? D'après vous, quel genre de texte est le deuxième texte? Les deux textes parlent-ils du même restaurant?

Chez Michel

12, rue° des Oliviers • 75006 Paris
Tél. 01.42.56.78.90
Ouvert° tous les soirs, de 19h00 à 23h30

Menu à 18 euros • Service compris

Entrée (au choix°)

Assiette de charcuterie
Escargots (1/2 douzaine°)
Salade de tomates au thon
Pâté de campagne
Soupe de légumes

Plat principal (au choix)

Poulet rôti° haricots verts
Steak au poivre pommes de terre
Thon à la moutarde (riz ou légumes au choix)
Bœuf aux carottes et aux champignons
Pâtes aux fruits de mer

Salade verte et plateau de fromages°

Dessert (au choix)

Tarte aux pommes
Tarte aux poires
Fruits de saison
Fraises à la crème Chantilly
Sorbet aux pêches
Gâteau au chocolat
Crème brûlée
Profiteroles au chocolat

OPTIONS

Small Groups Have students work in groups of three. Tell them to create a skit about a waiter or waitress and two customers at **Chez Michel**. The customers should enter the restaurant, ask for a table, order from the menu, and then ask for the check at the end of the meal. The waiter or waitress should respond appropriately and write down the customers' orders on a piece of paper.

Cultural Comparison Have students work in pairs. Tell them to compare the menu from **Chez Michel** with the menu of a restaurant that they frequent. Are they similar or different? Have them consider the format of the menu, the number of dishes and types of food served, and the prices.

À essayer: L'Huile d'Olive

Un nouveau restaurant provençal dans le quartier de Montmartre

L'Huile d'Olive
14, rue Molière
75018 Paris
01.44.53.76.35

Ouvert tous les jours sauf° le lundi
Le midi, de 12h00 à 14h30, Menu à 12 euros et Plat du jour
Le soir, de 19h00 à 23h00, Menus à 15 et 20 euros, Carte

De l'extérieur, L'Huile d'Olive est un restaurant aux murs gris, dans une petite rue triste du quartier de Montmartre. Mais à l'intérieur, tout change. C'est la Provence, avec tout son soleil et toute sa beauté. Les propriétaires, Monsieur et Madame Duchesnes, ont transformé ce vieux restaurant qui est maintenant entièrement décoré dans le style provençal, en bleu et jaune. Dans ce nouveau restaurant très sympathique, les propriétaires vous proposent des plats provençaux traditionnels préparés avec soin°. Comme entrée, je vous recommande la salade de tomates à l'ail ou le carpaccio de thon à l'huile d'olive. Comme plat principal, commandez la daube° provençale, si vous aimez le bœuf, ou le poulet au pastis°. Le plateau de fruits de mer est un excellent choix pour les amoureux du poisson. Comme légumes, essayez les pommes de terre au romarin° ou les petits pois aux oignons. Pour les végétariens, Madame Duchesnes propose des pâtes aux légumes avec une sauce à la crème délicieuse ou bien une ratatouille° de légumes fantastique. À la fin° du repas, commandez le fromage de chèvre° ou si vous préférez les desserts, goûtez la tarte poires-chocolat.

*À L'Huile d'Olive, tout est délicieux et le service est impeccable. Alors, n'hésitez pas! Allez à L'Huile d'Olive pour goûter la Provence! ****

rue *street* **Ouvert** *Open* **choix** *choice* **douzaine** *dozen* **rôti** *roast* **plateau de fromages** *cheeseboard* **sauf** *except* **soin** *care* **daube** *beef stew* **pastis** *anise liquor* **romarin** *rosemary* **ratatouille** *vegetable stew* **fin** *end* **chèvre** *goat*

Après la lecture

Vrai ou faux? Indiquez si les phrases au sujet du premier texte sont **vraies** ou **fausses**. Corrigez les phrases fausses.

1. On peut déjeuner au restaurant Chez Michel.
   Faux. On peut seulement dîner au restaurant Chez Michel.
2. Il n'y a pas de poisson dans les entrées.
   Faux. Il y a du poisson dans la salade de tomates au thon.
3. Comme plat principal, il y a trois viandes.
   Vrai.
4. Le poulet rôti est accompagné de légumes.
   Vrai.
5. Il y a trois plats principaux avec du bœuf.
   Faux. Il y a deux plats principaux avec du bœuf: le steak au poivre pommes de terre et le bœuf aux carottes et aux champignons.
6. On ne peut pas commander de fromage ou de dessert.
   Faux. On peut commander du fromage et des desserts.

Commandez Suggérez une entrée, un plat et un dessert pour ces personnes qui vont dîner au restaurant Chez Michel.
Answers will vary. Possible answers provided.

1. Madame Lonier est au régime et elle n'aime pas la viande.
   Elle peut prendre les escargots, le thon et les fruits de saison.
2. Monsieur Sanchez est végétarien. Il n'aime pas le thon. Il adore les légumes, mais il ne mange jamais de fruits.
   Il peut prendre la soupe de légumes, les pâtes aux fruits de mer et le gâteau au chocolat.
3. Madame Petit a envie de manger de la viande, mais elle n'aime pas beaucoup le bœuf. Elle n'aime ni (*neither*) les gâteaux ni (*nor*) les tartes. Elle peut prendre le pâté de campagne, le poulet rôti haricots verts et les fraises à la crème Chantilly.
4. Et vous, qu'est-ce que vous avez envie de goûter au restaurant Chez Michel? Pourquoi?

Répondez Répondez aux questions par des phrases complètes, d'après le deuxième texte.

1. Comment s'appelle le restaurant?
   Il s'appelle L'Huile d'Olive.
2. Combien coûtent les menus du soir?
   Ils coûtent 15 et 20 euros.
3. Quel est le style de cuisine du restaurant?
   Le style de cuisine est provençal.
4. Quelles viandes le critique (*critic*) recommande-t-il?
   Il recommande la daube provençale et le poulet au pastis.
5. Comment Madame Duchesnes prépare-t-elle les pâtes?
   Elle les prépare avec des légumes et une sauce à la crème délicieuse.
6. Le critique a-t-il aimé ce restaurant? Justifiez votre réponse. Answers may vary. Sample answer: Oui. Le restaurant est très sympathique. Les plats sont préparés avec soin. Tout est délicieux et le service est impeccable.

À Vous Vous et votre partenaire allez sortir manger dans un de ces restaurants. Décidez quel restaurant vous préférez. Est-ce que vous allez déjeuner ou dîner? Combien d'argent allez-vous dépenser? Qu'est-ce que vous allez commander?

Vrai ou faux? Go over the answers with the class.

Commandez
- This activity can be done in pairs.
- For additional practice, give students these situations. **5. David n'aime ni la soupe ni le poisson. Il aime les fruits. 6. Isabelle adore la viande, mais elle n'aime pas les légumes. Elle adore les fruits, surtout les pommes. 7. Claudine adore le thon et les tomates. Elle aime aussi le chocolat.**

Répondez Have students write three more questions about the reading. Then tell them to exchange papers with a partner and answer the questions.

À Vous After completing the activity, take a quick class survey to find out which restaurant was more popular among students. Ask: **Combien de personnes choisissent Chez Michel? Et L'Huile d'Olive?** Tally the results on the board. Then ask pairs to explain why they chose that particular restaurant.

OPTIONS

Montmartre **Le quartier de Montmartre**, located on a hill in Paris (**la butte Montmartre**), is the highest natural point in the city and a popular tourist site. **La Basilique du Sacré-Cœur,** with its large white dome, sits on the top of the hill. Montmartre is famous for its history of bohemian artists and its nightlife, with the **Moulin Rouge** giving it worldwide acclaim.

Extra Practice For additional practice with the restaurant review, give students these true/false items. **1. Le restaurant se trouve en Provence. (Faux.) 2. Le restaurant est fermé le samedi. (Faux.) 3. L'extérieur du restaurant n'est pas très beau. (Vrai.) 4. Il y a des choix de plats si on est végétarien. (Vrai.)**

Section Goals
In this section, students will:
- learn to express and support opinions
- write a restaurant review

Stratégie Explain to students that when they write a restaurant review, it is helpful to have some way of organizing the details required to support the rating. Working in groups of three, have students write a list of questions in French that elicit information readers might want to know and use them to create a rating sheet. Tell them to refer to the list of questions in the **Thème** section as a guide. Encourage students to leave space for comments in each category so they can record details that support their opinions. Suggest that they fill out the rating sheet during the various stages of the meal.

Thème Explain that each student will rate a local restaurant and write a review of a meal there, including a recommendation for future patrons.

Écriture

NATIONAL communication cultures STANDARDS

STRATÉGIE

Expressing and supporting opinions

Written reviews are just one of the many kinds of writing that require you to state your opinions. In order to convince your reader to take your opinions seriously, it is important to support them as thoroughly as possible. Details, facts, examples, and other forms of evidence are necessary. In a restaurant review, for example, it is not enough just to rate the food, service, and atmosphere. Readers will want details about the dishes you ordered, the kind of service you received, and the type of atmosphere you encountered. If you were writing a concert or album review, what kinds of details might your readers expect to find?

It is easier to include details that support your opinions if you plan ahead. Before going to a place or event that you are planning to review, write a list of questions that your readers might ask. Decide which aspects of the experience you are going to rate, and list the details that will help you decide upon a rating. You can then organize these lists into a questionnaire and a rating sheet. Bring these forms with you to remind you of the kinds of information you need to gather in order to support your opinions. Later, these forms will help you organize your review into logical categories. They can also provide the details and other evidence you need to convince your readers of your opinions.

Thème

Écrire une critique

Avant l'écriture

1. Vous allez écrire la critique d'un restaurant de votre ville pour le journal de l'université. Avant de l'écrire, vous allez d'abord créer un questionnaire et une feuille d'évaluation (*rating*) pour vous faire (*to form*) une opinion. Ces éléments vont aussi vous servir pour l'écriture de votre critique.

2. Travaillez avec un(e) partenaire pour créer le questionnaire. Vous pouvez utiliser ces questions ou en inventer *(invent some)* d'autres. Incluez les quatre catégories indiquées.

   - **Cuisine** Quel(s) type(s) de plat(s) y a-t-il au menu? Le restaurant a-t-il une spécialité? Citez quelques plats typiques (entrées et plats principaux) que vous avez goûtés et indiquez les ingrédients utilisés dans ces plats.
   - **Service** Comment est le service? Les serveurs sont-ils gentils et polis? Sont-ils lents ou rapides à apporter la carte, les boissons et les plats?
   - **Ambiance** Comment est le restaurant? Est-il beau? Grand? Bien décoré? Est-ce un restaurant simple ou élégant? Y a-t-il une terrasse? Un bar? Des musiciens?
   - **Informations pratiques** Quel est le prix moyen d'un repas dans ce restaurant (au déjeuner et/ou au dîner)? Où est le restaurant? Quelle est son adresse et comment y (*there*) va-t-on de l'université? Quels sont le numéro de téléphone du restaurant et ses heures d'ouverture (*operating hours*)?

OPTIONS

Avant l'écriture Before students start the assignment, review the difference between fact and opinion and tell them that a good review will contain both. Make various statements and have students say whether they are **fait** (*fact*) or **opinion**: That restaurant has three function rooms. (**fait**) The rooms are beautifully decorated. (**opinion**) Everyone who dines there will have a wonderful time. (**opinion**) The entrees range between 20 and 30 euros each. (**fait**) To warm up and generate vocabulary for the writing assignment, have students work in groups of three to role-play a restaurant scene: two diners (one of whom is a restaurant reviewer) and a waiter/waitress. Have them role-play the diners' conversation with the wait person and then their own conversations while they wait for their food and after it arrives.

3. Après avoir écrit le questionnaire, utilisez les quatre catégories et la liste de questions pour créer une feuille d'évaluation. Un restaurant reçoit (*gets*) trois étoiles (*stars*) s'il est très bon et ne reçoit pas d'étoile s'il est mauvais.

4. Après avoir créé la feuille d'évaluation, utilisez-la pour évaluer un restaurant que vous connaissez. Si (*If*) vous le connaissez bien, peut-être n'est-il pas nécessaire d'aller y (*there*) manger pour compléter la feuille. Si vous ne le connaissez pas bien, vous devez aller l'essayer. Utilisez des comparatifs et des superlatifs quand vous écrivez vos commentaires et vos opinions.

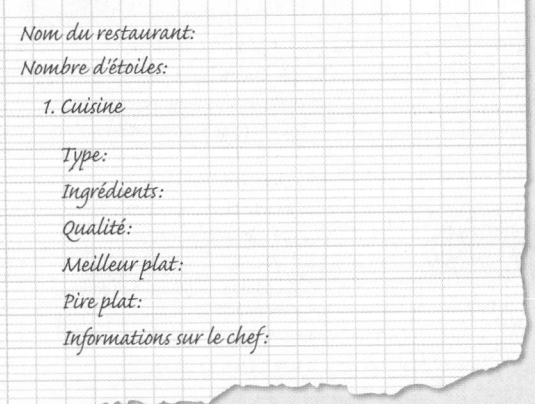

Nom du restaurant:
Nombre d'étoiles:
1. Cuisine
Type:
Ingrédients:
Qualité:
Meilleur plat:
Pire plat:
Informations sur le chef:

Écriture

Utilisez la feuille d'évaluation que vous avez complétée pour écrire votre critique culinaire. Écrivez six brefs paragraphes:

1. une introduction pour indiquer votre opinion générale du restaurant et le nombre d'étoiles qu'il a reçu (*got*)
2. une description de la carte
3. une description du service
4. une description de l'ambiance (*atmosphere*)
5. un paragraphe pour donner les informations pratiques
6. une conclusion pour souligner (*to emphasize*) votre opinion et pour donner des suggestions pour améliorer (*to improve*) le restaurant

Après l'écriture

1. Échangez votre critique avec celle (*the one*) d'un(e) partenaire. Répondez à ces questions pour commenter son travail.
   - Votre partenaire a-t-il/elle écrit une introduction présentant (*presenting*) une opinion générale du restaurant?
   - Votre partenaire a-t-il/elle écrit quatre paragraphes sur la cuisine, le service, l'ambiance et les informations pratiques?
   - Votre partenaire a-t-il/elle écrit une conclusion présentant une nouvelle fois son opinion et proposant (*suggesting*) des suggestions pour le restaurant?
   - Votre partenaire a-t-il/elle utilisé des comparatifs et des superlatifs pour décrire le restaurant?
   - Quel(s) détail(s) ajouteriez-vous (*would you add*)? Quel(s) détail(s) enlèveriez-vous (*would you delete*)? Quel(s) autre(s) commentaire(s) avez-vous pour votre partenaire?

2. Corrigez votre brochure d'après (*according to*) les commentaires de votre partenaire. Relisez votre travail pour éliminer ces problèmes:
   - des fautes (*errors*) d'orthographe et de ponctuation
   - des fautes de conjugaison
   - des fautes d'accord (*agreement*) des adjectifs
   - un mauvais emploi (*use*) de l'imparfait et du passé composé
   - un mauvais emploi des comparatifs et des superlatifs

EVALUATION

Criteria

Content Contains a complete description of a dining experience that includes information about the food, the service, the atmosphere, and factual details about the restaurant.
Scale: 1 2 3 4 5

Organization Organized into six paragraphs: an introduction, four paragraphs corresponding to the four sections of the task, and a conclusion.
Scale: 1 2 3 4 5

Accuracy Uses forms of **devoir, vouloir,** and **pouvoir** correctly. Uses verb tenses correctly and in the correct context. Spells words, conjugates verbs, and modifies adjectives correctly throughout.
Scale: 1 2 3 4 5

Creativity Includes additional information that is not included in the task and/or uses adjectives and descriptive verbs to make the review more interesting and informative.
Scale: 1 2 3 4 5

Scoring

Excellent	18–20 points
Good	14–17 points
Satisfactory	10–13 points
Unsatisfactory	< 10 points

OPTIONS

Écriture Encourage students to use forms of **devoir** in their reviews to make recommendations for improvement. Point out that reviewers frequently express their preferences and opinions in a review while offering advice based on those opinions. They should use **vouloir** to express things they want to see done, **devoir** to say what should be done, and **pouvoir** to say what the restaurant can and can't do well.

Give students some helpful expressions to get them started as they begin each paragraph. Paragraph 1: **J'ai récemment dîné à..., La semaine dernière, j'ai eu l'opportunité d'aller à..., Un nouveau restaurant a ouvert** (*opened*)... Paragraphs 2-5: **Concernant** (*Regarding*)..., **Pour ce qui est de** (*When it comes to*)..., **À noter** (*Note*) **aussi que...** Paragraph 6: **En conclusion..., En résumé.../ Pour résumer..., Je veux finir en disant** (*by saying*) **que...**

Instructional Resources
espaces.vhlcentral.com: Textbook MP3s; IRM (Textbook Audioscript); downloads; reference tools

Suggestion Tell students that an easy way to study from **Vocabulaire** is to cover up the French half of each section, leaving only the English equivalents exposed. They can then quiz themselves on the French items. To focus on the English equivalents of the French entries, they simply reverse this process.

À table!

une assiette	*plate*
un bol	*bowl*
une carafe d'eau	*pitcher of water*
une carte	*menu*
un couteau	*knife*
une cuillère (à soupe/à café)	*spoon (teaspoon/soupspoon)*
une fourchette	*fork*
un menu	*menu*
une nappe	*tablecloth*
une serviette	*napkin*
une boîte (de conserve)	*can*
la crème	*cream*
l'huile (d'olive) (*f.*)	*(olive) oil*
la mayonnaise	*mayonnaise*
la moutarde	*mustard*
le poivre	*pepper*
le sel	*salt*
une tranche	*slice*
une cantine	*(school) cafeteria*
À table!	*Let's eat!/ Food is ready!*
compris	*included*

Les fruits

une banane	*banana*
une fraise	*strawberry*
un fruit	*fruit*
une orange	*orange*
une pêche	*peach*
une poire	*pear*
une pomme	*apple*
une tomate	*tomato*

Autres aliments

un aliment	*food item*
la confiture	*jam*
la nourriture	*food, sustenance*
des pâtes (*f.*)	*pasta*
le riz	*rice*
une tarte	*pie, tart*
un yaourt	*yogurt*

Verbes

devenir	*to become*
devoir	*to have to (must); to owe*
maintenir	*to maintain*
pouvoir	*to be able to (can)*
retenir	*to keep, to retain*
revenir	*to come back*
tenir	*to hold*
venir	*to come*
vouloir	*to want; to mean (with dire)*

Autres mots et locutions

depuis [+ *time*]	*since*
il y a [+ *time*]	*ago*
pendant [+ *time*]	*for*

Les repas

commander	*to order*
cuisiner	*to cook*
être au régime	*to be on a diet*
goûter	*to taste*
un déjeuner	*lunch*
un dîner	*dinner*
un goûter	*afternoon snack*
un petit-déjeuner	*breakfast*
un repas	*meal*
une entrée	*appetizer, starter*
un hors-d'œuvre	*hors-d'œuvre, appetizer*
un plat (principal)	*(main) dish*

Les viandes et les poissons

le bœuf	*beef*
un escargot	*escargot, snail*
les fruits de mer (*m.*)	*seafood*
un œuf	*egg*
un pâté (de campagne)	*pâté, meat spread*
le porc	*pork*
un poulet	*chicken*
une saucisse	*sausage*
un steak	*steak*
le thon	*tuna*
la viande	*meat*

Les légumes

l'ail (*m.*)	*garlic*
une carotte	*carrot*
un champignon	*mushroom*
des haricots verts (*m.*)	*green beans*
une laitue	*lettuce*
un légume	*vegetable*
un oignon	*onion*
des petits pois (*m.*)	*peas*
un poivron (vert, rouge)	*(green, red) pepper*
une pomme de terre	*potato*
une salade	*salad*

Les achats

faire les courses (*f.*)	*to go (grocery) shopping*
une boucherie	*butcher's shop*
une boulangerie	*bread shop, bakery*
une charcuterie	*delicatessen*
une pâtisserie	*pastry shop, bakery; pastry*
une poissonnerie	*fish shop*
un supermarché	*supermarket*
un(e) commerçant(e)	*shopkeeper*
un kilo(gramme)	*kilo(gram)*

Expressions utiles	*See pp. 295 and 309.*
Comparatives and superlatives	*See pp. 312-313.*

ressources
espaces.vhlcentral.com

La santé

UNITÉ **10**

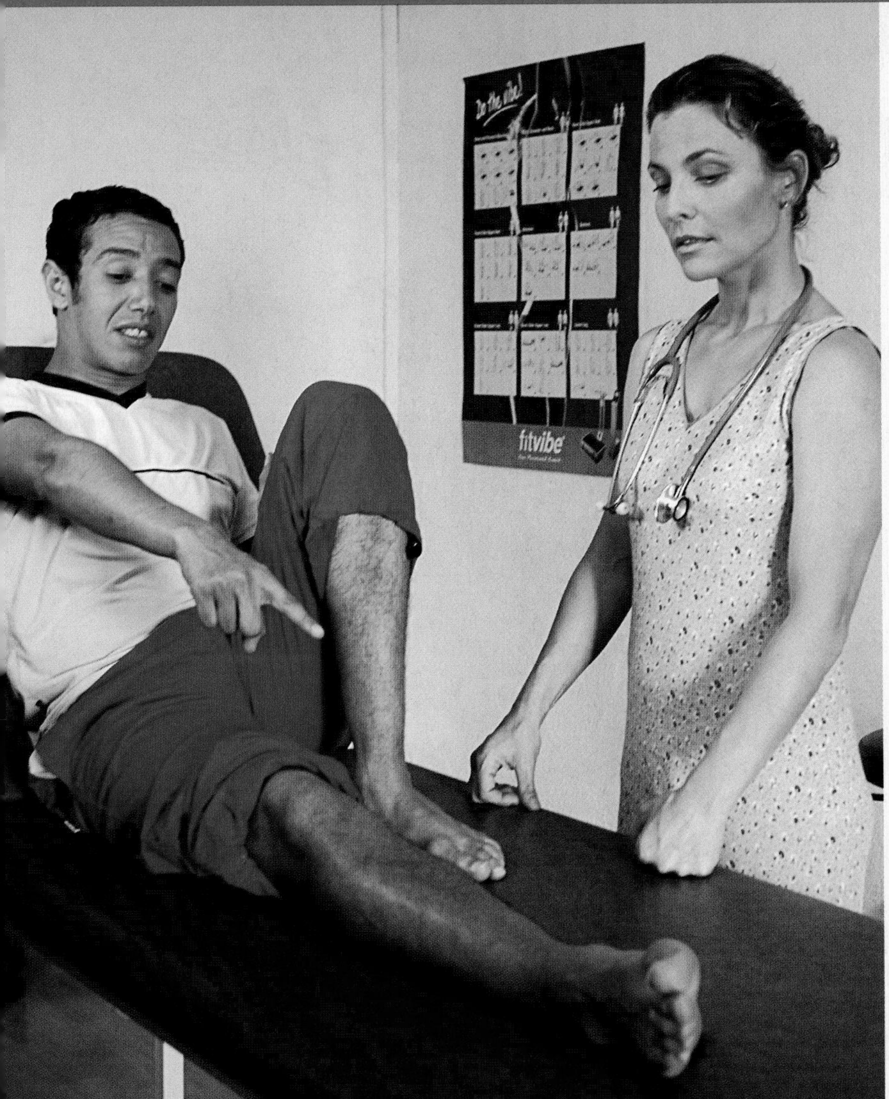

Leçon 10A

ESPACE **CONTEXTES**
pages 326–329
- Parts of the body
- Daily routine
- **Ch**, **qu**, **ph**, **th**, and **gn**

ESPACE **ROMAN-PHOTO**
pages 330–331
- **Drôle de surprise**

ESPACE **CULTURE**
pages 332–333
- Healthcare in France

ESPACE **STRUCTURES**
pages 334–337
- Reflexive verbs
- Reflexives: **Sens idiomatique**

ESPACE **SYNTHÈSE**
pages 338–339
- **Révision**
- **Le zapping**

Leçon 10B

ESPACE **CONTEXTES**
pages 340–343
- Maladies and remedies
- **p**, **t**, and **c**

ESPACE **ROMAN-PHOTO**
pages 344–345
- **L'accident**

ESPACE **CULTURE**
pages 346–347
- **La sécurité sociale**
- **Flash culture**

ESPACE **STRUCTURES**
pages 348–351
- The **passé composé** of reflexive verbs
- The pronouns **y** and **en**

ESPACE **SYNTHÈSE**
pages 352–353
- **Révision**
- **À l'écoute**

Savoir-faire
pages 354–359

Panorama: La Suisse
Lecture: Read an article on healthy living.
Écriture: Write a letter of excuse.

Pour commencer
- Quelle est la profession de la dame? Coiffeuse ou médecin?
- Où sont Rachid et cette dame? À l'hôpital ou à l'épicerie?
- Qu'est-ce qu'il faisait avant de venir, il jouait au foot ou il faisait les courses?

Unit Goals

Leçon 10A
In this lesson, students will learn:
- terms for parts of the body
- terms to discuss one's daily routine
- the pronunciation of **ch**, **qu**, **ph**, **th**, and **gn**
- about healthcare in France
- reflexive verbs
- some common idiomatic reflexive verbs
- about the company Diadermine

Leçon 10B
In this lesson, students will learn:
- terms to describe one's health
- terms for illnesses and remedies
- terms related to medical visits and treatments
- the pronunciation of **p**, **t**, and **c**
- about the national healthcare system in France
- more information on pharmacies and health-related businesses through specially shot video footage
- the **passé composé** of reflexive verbs
- the pronouns **y** and **en**
- to listen for specific information

Savoir-faire
In this section, students will learn:
- cultural and historical information about Switzerland
- to use background knowledge to increase reading comprehension
- to sequence events in a narration

Pour commencer
- **Elle est médecin.**
- **Ils sont à l'hôpital.**
- **Il jouait au foot.**

RESOURCES

Workbook/Video Manual: WB Activities, pp. 127–140
Laboratory Manual: Lab Activities, pp. 73–80
Workbook/Video Manual: Video Activities, pp. 247–250; pp. 289–290
WB/VM/LM Answer Key

espaces.vhlcentral.com: Textbook MP3s; Lab MP3s; Instructor's Resource Manual [IRM] (Textbook Audioscript; Lab Audioscript; Videoscript; **Roman-photo** Translations; **Vocabulaire supplémentaire**; **Feuilles d'activités**; Info Gap Activities; **Le zapping** TV clip transcription; **Essayez!** and **Mise en pratique** answers); Transparencies #43, #44, #45, #46, #47; Testing Program, pp. 73–80, pp. 197–208; Test Files; Testing Program MP3s
Test Generator
Video on DVD

Section Goals

In this section, students will learn and practice vocabulary related to:
- daily routines
- personal hygiene
- some parts of the body

Instructional Resources
*espaces.vhlcentral.com: Transparencies #43, #44; IRM (**Vocabulaire supplémentaire; Mise en pratique** answers; Textbook Audioscript; Lab Audioscript; Info Gap Activities); Textbook MP3s; Lab MP3s; WB/VM/LM Answer Key; activities; downloads; reference tools*

Suggestions
- Using **Transparency #43**, describe what the people in the illustration are doing. Then point out objects and parts of the body. Examples: **Il se rase. Elle se maquille. C'est une serviette de bain.**
- Ask students yes/no questions based on the illustration. Examples: **La fille se lève-t-elle? La femme se regarde-t-elle? Est-ce le bras? Est-ce un peigne?**
- Model the pronunciation of **shampooing**. Mention that they may see the alternate spelling **shampoing**.
- Explain the relationships between these terms: **se raser, un rasoir, une crème à raser; se réveiller, un réveil; se coiffer, un coiffeur, une coiffeuse;** and **se brosser les dents, le dentifrice.**
- Remind students that the plural of **l'œil** is **les yeux**.
- Review the use of partitives with non-count nouns using words from **Espace contextes**. Examples: **du dentifrice** and **du shampooing**.
- Keep in mind that reflexives will only be used in the infinitive and third person singular in the activities until **Espace structures 10A.1**
- Additional vocabulary for this lesson can be found in the **Vocabulaire supplémentaire** on the Supersite.

Leçon 10A

Talking Picture
Audio: Activity

You will learn how to...
- **describe your daily routine**
- **discuss personal hygiene**

La routine quotidienne

Vocabulaire

faire sa toilette	*to wash up*
se brosser les cheveux	*to brush one's hair*
se brosser les dents	*to brush one's teeth*
se coiffer	*to do one's hair*
se coucher	*to go to bed*
se déshabiller	*to undress oneself*
s'endormir	*to go to sleep, to fall asleep*
s'habiller	*to get dressed*
se laver (les mains)	*to wash oneself (one's hands)*
prendre une douche	*to take a shower*
se regarder	*to look at oneself*
se réveiller	*to wake up*
se sécher	*to dry oneself*
le shampooing	*shampoo*
le cœur	*heart*
le corps	*body*
le dos	*back*
la gorge	*throat*
une joue	*cheek*
un orteil	*toe*
la peau	*skin*
la poitrine	*chest*
la taille	*waist*
le visage	*face*

ressources
WB pp. 127-128 | LM p. 73 | espaces.vhlcentral.com

OPTIONS

Game Write vocabulary words for parts of the body on index cards. On another set of cards, draw or paste pictures to match each term. Tape them face down on the board in random order. Divide the class into two teams. Play a game of Concentration in which students match words with pictures. When a player makes a match, that player's team collects those cards. The team with the most cards at the end of the game wins.

Extra Practice Write two columns on the board: **la routine du matin** and **la routine du soir**. Have students classify the verbs in **Espace contextes** according to whether people do the actions when they wake up in the morning or in the evening before they go to bed. Then have students order the actions logically. This activity can also be done in pairs.

Attention!

The verbs following the pronoun **se** are called reflexive verbs. You will learn more about them in **STRUCTURES**. For now, when talking about another person, place the pronoun **se** between the subject and the verb.

Il se regarde. *He looks at himself.*

Elle se réveille. *She wakes up.*

Mise en pratique

1 Association Associez les activités de la colonne de gauche aux parties du corps correspondantes des colonnes de droite. Notez que certains éléments ne sont pas utilisés et que d'autres sont utilisés plus d'une fois.

__e__ 1. écouter	a. la bouche	f. le pied
__a/b__ 2. manger	b. la gorge	g. la taille
__f__ 3. marcher	c. l'orteil	h. la tête
__i__ 4. montrer	d. l'œil	i. le doigt
__a/b__ 5. parler	e. l'oreille	j. le nez
__h__ 6. penser		
__j__ 7. sentir		
__d__ 8. regarder		

2 Quel matin! Complétez les phrases par le mot ou l'expression de la liste qui convient pour trouver ce qui est arrivé à Alexandre aujourd'hui. Notez que tous les mots et expressions ne sont pas utilisés.

le bras	se coucher	se laver	le réveil
se brosser les dents	la gorge	le peigne	le ventre
le cœur	s'habiller	le pied	les yeux

Ce matin, Alexandre n'entend pas son (1) __réveil__. Quand il se lève, il met d'abord le (2) __pied__ gauche par terre. Il entre dans la salle de bains. Là, il ne trouve pas le (3) __peigne__ pour se coiffer ni (*nor*) le dentifrice pour (4) __se brosser les dents__. Il se regarde dans le miroir. Ses (5) __yeux__ sont tout rouges. Comme il a très faim, son (6) __ventre__ commence à faire du bruit (*noise*). Il retourne ensuite dans sa chambre pour (7) __s'habiller__. Il met un pantalon noir et une chemise bleue. Puis, il descend les escaliers et tombe. Après un moment, il retourne dans sa chambre. Après un tel début (*such a beginning*) de journée, Alexandre va (8) __se coucher__.

3 Écoutez Sarah, son grand frère Guillaume et leur père parlent de qui va utiliser la salle de bains en premier ce matin. Écoutez la conversation et indiquez si les affirmations suivantes sont **vraies** ou **fausses**.

	Vrai	Faux
1. Guillaume ne va pas se raser.	☐	☑
2. Guillaume doit encore prendre une douche et se brosser les dents.	☑	☐
3. Sarah n'a pas entendu son réveil.	☑	☐
4. Guillaume demande à Sarah de lui apporter de la crème à raser.	☐	☑
5. Guillaume demande un savon à Sarah.	☐	☑
6. Guillaume demande une grande serviette de bain à Sarah.	☑	☐
7. Sarah doit prendre une douche et s'habiller en moins de vingt minutes.	☑	☐
8. Sarah décide de ne pas se maquiller et de ne pas se sécher les cheveux aujourd'hui.	☑	☐

Practice more at **espaces.vhlcentral.com.**

1 Expansions
- Have students think of other verbs to add to the list and let the class guess the body part(s) associated with them.
- Do this activity in reverse. Name various parts of the body and have students suggest verbs associated with them.

2 Expansion Ask students comprehension questions based on the paragraph. Examples: **1. Pourquoi Alexandre se lève-t-il tard? (Il n'entend pas son réveil.) 2. Que fait-il d'abord? (Il met le pied par terre.) 3. Où va-t-il? (Il va à la salle de bains.) 4. Ça ne va pas bien. Pourquoi? (Il ne peut pas se coiffer./Il ne trouve pas le dentifrice./Ses yeux sont rouges.) 5. Que met-il quand il s'habille? (Il met un pantalon noir et une chemise bleue.) 6. Pourquoi Alexandre veut-il se coucher? (Il veut se coucher parce qu'il est tombé dans les escaliers./La journée commence mal.)**

3 Tapescript SARAH: Allez, Guillaume. J'ai besoin d'utiliser la salle de bains.
GUILLAUME: Une minute! Je viens juste d'y entrer.
S: Mais, je suis en retard pour mes cours. Je n'ai pas entendu mon réveil.
PÈRE: Sarah, laisse ton frère se raser, prendre une douche et se brosser les dents. Il est arrivé le premier.
G: Je fais vite. Tiens! Il n'y a plus de shampooing. Est-ce que tu peux m'apporter une nouvelle bouteille et une grande serviette de bain, s'il te plaît?
S: Et tes pantoufles aussi?
Un peu plus tard…
P: Où est ta sœur?
G: Sarah va prendre sa douche. Elle doit se brosser les dents, s'habiller et se coiffer en moins de vingt minutes. Elle a décidé de ne pas se maquiller et de ne pas se sécher les cheveux pour gagner du temps.
P: Bon, on va te préparer quelque chose à manger dans le bus.
(On Textbook MP3s)

3 Suggestion Have students correct the false statements. If necessary, play the recording again.

OPTIONS

Pairs Have students write down three daily routine activities. Each partner should ask questions using words that indicate time like **pendant**, **avant**, and **après** in order to guess the activities on their partner's list. Example: **Étudiant(e) 1: C'est avant ou après le petit-déjeuner? Étudiant(e) 2: C'est après le petit-déjeuner. Étudiant(e) 1: C'est se brosser les dents? Étudiant(e) 2: Oui, c'est ça.**

Small Groups Have students work in groups of three. Tell them to draw a picture and write a description of a fantastical alien or monster. Example: **C'est un extraterrestre/un monstre. Il a trois nez, quatre yeux et huit bras.** Then have each group read their description while the class draws a picture of the alien or monster. Have students compare their drawings with the group's picture.

4 Expansion Use **Transparency #44**. Assign names to the people in the drawings. Then ask questions about the people's actions. Examples: **Qui se lave les mains? Que fait ____?**

5 Suggestion Have two volunteers read the **modèle** aloud.

5 Expansion For additional practice, give students these items. **13. les doigts de pied 14. la tête 15. le pied**

6 Expansion Have volunteers read their descriptions to the class without saying the person's name. The class has to guess who it is.

7 Suggestions
- Before beginning this activity, you might want to review telling time and adverbs of time.
- Have two volunteers read the **modèle** aloud. Then divide the class into pairs and distribute the Info Gap Handouts found on the Supersite for this activity. Give students ten minutes to complete the activity.

Communication

4 Que font-ils? Écrivez ce que (*what*) font ces personnes et ce qu'elles utilisent pour le faire. Donnez autant de (*as many*) détails que possible. Ensuite, à tour de rôle avec un(e) partenaire, lisez vos descriptions. Votre partenaire doit deviner quelle image vous décrivez. Answers will vary.

1.

2.

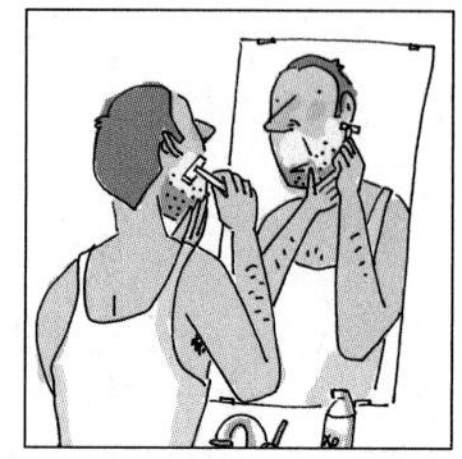
3.

4.

5.

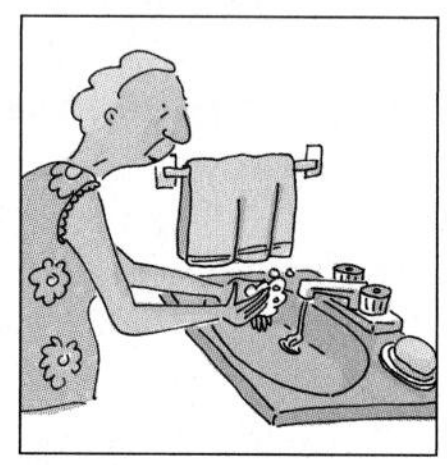
6.

7.

8.

5 Définition Créez votre propre définition des mots de la liste. Ensuite, à tour de rôle, lisez vos définitions à votre partenaire. Il/Elle doit deviner le mot correspondant. Answers will vary.

MODÈLE

cheveux
Étudiant(e) 1: *On utilise une brosse ou un peigne pour les coiffer. Qu'est-ce que c'est?*
Étudiant(e) 2: *Ce sont les cheveux.*

1. le cœur	4. les dents	7. la joue	10. l'orteil
2. le corps	5. le dos	8. le nez	11. la poitrine
3. le cou	6. le genou	9. l'œil	12. le visage

6 Décrivez Avec un(e) partenaire, pensez à votre acteur/actrice préféré(e). Quelle est sa routine du matin? Décrivez-la et utilisez les adjectifs de la liste et les mots et expressions d'**ESPACE CONTEXTES**. Answers will vary.

beau	gros	petit
court	heureux	sincère
égoïste	jeune	de taille moyenne
grand	long	vieux

7 Que fait-elle? Votre professeur va vous donner, à vous et à votre partenaire, deux feuilles d'activités différentes. À tour de rôle, posez-vous des questions pour savoir ce que fait Nadia chaque soir et chaque matin. Attention! Ne regardez pas la feuille de votre partenaire. Answers will vary.

MODÈLE

Étudiant(e) 1: *À vingt-trois heures, Nadia se déshabille et met son pyjama. Que fait-elle ensuite?*
Étudiant(e) 2: *Après, elle...*

OPTIONS

Extra Practice Say the following objects and have students name the body part(s) associated with each one. **1. du shampooing (les cheveux) 2. les lunettes (les yeux) 3. un rasoir (les jambes, le visage) 4. les pantoufles (les pieds) 5. un gant (la main) 6. une écharpe (le cou) 7. un pantalon (les jambes) 8. un peigne (les cheveux) 9. une radio (les oreilles)**

Extra Practice Read these statements to students and have them say whether they are **logique** or **illogique. 1. Alain prend une douche, puis il se sèche. (logique) 2. Gilles s'habille, puis il se couche. (illogique) 3. Solange se coiffe, puis elle s'endort. (illogique) 4. Isabelle se maquille, puis elle se lave. (illogique) 5. Denis se lève, puis il fait sa toilette. (logique)**

Les sons et les lettres

Audio: Concepts, Activities
Record & Compare

comparisons NATIONAL STANDARDS

ch, qu, ph, th, and gn

The letter combination **ch** is usually pronounced like the English *sh*, as in the word *shoe*.

chat **chien** **chose** **enchanté**

In words borrowed from other languages, the pronunciation of **ch** may be irregular. For example, in words of Greek origin, **ch** is pronounced **k**.

psychologie **technologie** **archaïque** **archéologie**

The letter combination **qu** is almost always pronounced like the letter **k**.

quand **pratiquer** **kiosque** **quelle**

The letter combination **ph** is pronounced like an **f**.

téléphone **photo** **prophète** **géographie**

The letter combination **th** is pronounced like the letter **t**. English *th* sounds, as in the words *this* and *with*, never occur in French.

thé **athlète** **bibliothèque** **sympathique**

The letter combination **gn** is pronounced like the sound in the middle of the English word *onion*.

montagne **espagnol** **gagner** **Allemagne**

Prononcez Répétez les mots suivants à voix haute.

1. thé
2. quart
3. chose
4. question
5. cheveux
6. parce que
7. champagne
8. casquette
9. philosophie
10. fréquenter
11. photographie
12. sympathique

Articulez Répétez les phrases suivantes à voix haute.

1. Quentin est martiniquais ou québécois?
2. Quelqu'un explique la question à Joseph.
3. Pourquoi est-ce que Philippe est inquiet?
4. Ignace prend une photo de la montagne.
5. Monique fréquente un café en Belgique.
6. Théo étudie la physique.

Dictons Répétez les dictons à voix haute.

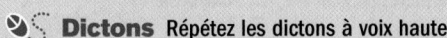

La vache la première au pré lèche la rosée.[1]

N'éveillez pas le chat qui dort.[2]

[1] The early bird gets the worm. (lit. The cow that arrives at the pasture first licks the dew.)
[2] Let sleeping dogs lie. (lit. Don't wake a sleeping cat.)

ressources
LM p. 74
espaces.vhlcentral.com

Section Goals

In this section, students will learn about the sounds **ch**, **qu**, **ph**, **th**, and **gn**.

Instructional Resources
espaces.vhlcentral.com: Textbook MP3s; Lab MP3s; WB/VM/LM Answer Key; IRM (Textbook Audioscript; Lab Audioscript); activities; downloads; reference tools

Suggestions

- Model the pronunciation of each of the example words and have students repeat them.
- Mention words and expressions from the **Vocabulaire** that contain the consonant clusters presented on this page. Then have them repeat after you. Alternatively, ask students to recall such vocabulary. Examples: **campagne, Mexique, Chine,** etc. See if a volunteer is able to recall any words from previous lessons. Examples: **géographie, enseigner, prochain, quatre.**
- Dictate six to eight familiar words containing these letter combinations to the class, repeating each one at least two times. Then write them on the board or on a transparency and have students check and correct their spelling.
- Explain that in the words **pourquoi** and **quoi** there is a **w** sound, which is an effect of **oi** (**moi**, **toi**), not **qu**.
- Tell students that the letter combination **tch** is pronounced as it is in English. Example: **Tchad**. The difference is that **ch** and **tch** are always pronounced differently in French, but often the same in English.

OPTIONS

Extra Practice Here are some sentences to use for additional practice. **1. Charlotte et Michèle ont de la chance. 2. Élisabeth quitte la maison à quatre heures et quart. 3. Chantal a visité l'Allemagne et le Mexique. 4. Thérèse a acheté une photo d'une montagne espagnole.**

Extra Practice Teach students these French tongue-twisters that contain the sounds featured on this page. **1. Une bête noire se baigne dans une baignoire noire. 2. Je suis ce que je suis et si je suis ce que je suis, qu'est-ce que je suis? 3. Cinq chiens chassent six chats.**

Drôle de surprise

Video: *Roman-photo*
Record & Compare

PERSONNAGES

David

Rachid

1

Chez David et Rachid...

DAVID Oh là là, ça ne va pas du tout, toi!

RACHID David, tu te dépêches? Il est sept heures et quart. Je dois me préparer, moi aussi!

2

DAVID Ne t'inquiète pas. Je finis de me brosser les dents!

RACHID On doit partir dans moins de vingt minutes. Tu ne te rends pas compte!

DAVID Excuse-moi, mais on s'est couché tard hier soir.

RACHID Oui et on ne s'est pas réveillé à l'heure, mais mon prof de sciences po, ça ne l'intéresse pas tout ça.

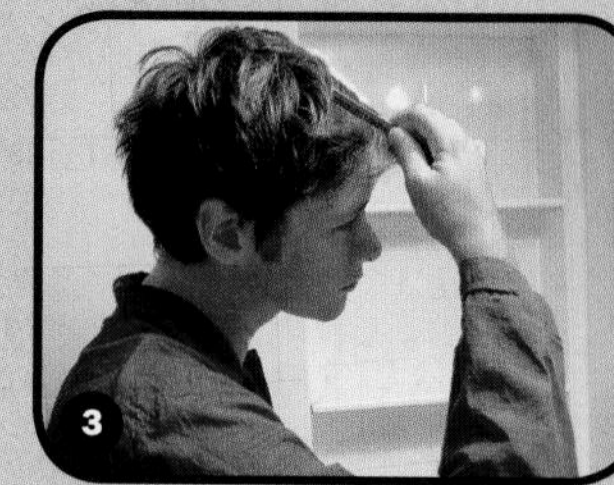
3

DAVID Attends, je ne trouve pas le peigne... Ah, le voilà. Je me coiffe... Deux secondes!

RACHID C'était vraiment sympa hier soir... On s'entend tous super bien et on ne s'ennuie jamais ensemble... Mais enfin, qu'est-ce que tu fais? Je dois me raser, prendre une douche et m'habiller, en exactement dix-sept minutes!

6

RACHID Bon, tu veux bien me passer ma brosse à dents, le dentifrice et un rasoir, s'il te plaît?

DAVID Attends une minute. Je me dépêche.

RACHID Comment est-ce qu'un mec peut prendre aussi longtemps dans la salle de bains?

7

DAVID Euh, j'ai un petit problème...

RACHID Qu'est-ce que tu as sur le visage?

DAVID Aucune idée.

RACHID Est-ce que tu as mal à la gorge? Fais: Ah!

RACHID Et le ventre, ça va?

DAVID Oui, oui, ça va...

8

RACHID Attends, je vais examiner tes yeux... regarde à droite, à gauche... maintenant ferme-les. Bien. Tourne-toi...

DAVID Hé!

ACTIVITÉS

1 Vrai ou faux? Indiquez si ces affirmations sont vraies ou fausses. Corrigez les phrases fausses.
Some answers may vary slightly.

1. David va bien ce matin. Faux. David ne va pas bien ce matin.
2. Rachid est pressé ce matin. Vrai.
3. David se rase. Faux. David se brosse les dents.
4. David se maquille. Faux. David se coiffe.
5. Rachid doit prendre une douche. Vrai.
6. David ne s'est pas réveillé à l'heure. Vrai.
7. David s'est couché tôt hier soir. Faux. David s'est couché tard hier soir.
8. Tout le monde s'est bien amusé (*had a good time*) hier soir. Vrai.
9. Les amis se disputent ce matin. Vrai.
10. Rachid est très inquiet pour David. Faux. Rachid n'est pas inquiet.

Practice more at **espaces.vhlcentral.com.**

Section Goals

In this section, students will learn functional phrases for talking about daily routines and emotional states.

Instructional Resources
espaces.vhlcentral.com: Video; WB/VM/LM Answer Key; IRM (Videoscript; ***Roman-photo*** *Translations); activities; downloads; reference tools*
Video on DVD

Video Recap: Leçon 9B
Before doing this **Roman-photo**, review the previous one with this activity.

1. Quel cadeau Rachid a-t-il apporté à Sandrine? (des chocolats)
2. Et David, qu'a-t-il apporté à Sandrine? (des fleurs)
3. Qui aide à mettre la table? (Amina et Stéphane)
4. Qui est au régime? (Amina)
5. Qu'est-ce que Sandrine a préparé comme dessert? (une tarte aux pommes)

Video Synopsis
In the bathroom, David notices a rash on his face. Rachid needs to use the bathroom, because he woke up late and doesn't want to be late for class. David is taking a long time to get ready. When David finally opens the door, Rachid tricks him into closing his eyes so that he can slip into the bathroom and lock the door. Rachid also advises David to call a doctor about his rash.

Suggestions
- Have students predict what the episode will be about based on the video stills.
- Tell students to scan the **Roman-photo** and find sentences related to daily routines.
- After reading the **Roman-photo** in pairs, have students summarize the episode.

OPTIONS

Avant de regarder la vidéo Tell students to read the title and scene setter. Then have them brainstorm what two roommates might say as they are trying to get ready for class at the same time. Write their ideas on the board.

Regarder la vidéo Show the video episode once without sound and have the class create a plot summary based on the visual cues. Then show the episode with sound and have the class make corrections and fill in any gaps in the plot summary.

David et Rachid se préparent le matin.

4

DAVID Patience, cher ami!
RACHID Tu n'as pas encore pris ta douche?!
DAVID Ne te mets pas en colère. J'arrive, j'arrive! Voilà... un peu de crème sur le visage, sur le cou...
RACHID Tu te maquilles maintenant?

5

DAVID Ce n'est pas facile d'être beau, ça prend du temps, tu sais. Écoute, ça ne sert à rien de se disputer. Lis le journal si tu t'ennuies, j'ai bientôt fini.

9

RACHID Ne t'inquiète pas, c'est probablement une réaction allergique. Téléphone au médecin pour prendre un rendez-vous. Qu'est-ce que tu as mangé hier?
DAVID Eh ben... J'ai mangé un peu de tout! Hé! Je n'ai pas encore fini ma toilette!

10

RACHID Patience, cher ami!

Expressions utiles

Talking about your routine

- **Je dois me préparer.**
  I have to get (myself) ready.
- **Je finis de me brosser les dents!**
  I'm almost done brushing my teeth!
- **On s'est couché tard hier soir.**
  We went to bed late last night.
- **On ne s'est pas réveillé à l'heure.**
  We didn't wake up on time.
- **Je me coiffe.**
  I'm doing my hair.
- **Je dois me raser et m'habiller.**
  I have to shave (myself) and get dressed.
- **Tu te maquilles maintenant?**
  Are you putting makeup on now?

Talking about states of being

- **Ça ne sert à rien de se disputer.**
  It doesn't help to argue.
- **Tu te dépêches?**
  Are you hurrying?/Will you hurry?
- **Ne t'inquiète pas.**
  Don't worry.
- **Tu ne te rends pas compte!**
  You don't realize!
- **On s'entend tous super bien et on ne s'ennuie jamais ensemble.**
  We all get along really well and we never get bored with one another.
- **Ne te mets pas en colère.**
  Don't get angry.
- **Lis le journal si tu t'ennuies.**
  Read the paper if you're bored.

Additional vocabulary

- **Je me dépêche.**
  I'm hurrying.
- **un mec**
  a guy
- **Tourne-toi.**
  Turn around.
- **aucune idée**
  no idea

2 Les opposés Trouvez pour chaque verbe de la colonne de gauche son opposé dans les colonnes de droite. Utilisez un dictionnaire. Attention! Tous les mots ne sont pas utilisés.

_e_ 1. bien s'entendre	a. s'amuser	d. s'appeler
_a/b_ 2. s'ennuyer	b. s'occuper	e. se disputer
_c_ 3. se dépêcher	c. se détendre	f. se coucher
_f_ 4. se lever		
_b_ 5. se reposer		

3 Écrivez Écrivez un paragraphe dans lequel (*in which*) vous décrivez la routine du matin et du soir de David ou de Rachid. Utilisez votre imagination et ce que vous savez d'**ESPACE ROMAN-PHOTO**.

ressources
VM pp. 247-248 | DVD Leçon 10A | espaces.vhlcentral.com

ACTIVITÉS

Expressions utiles
- Model the pronunciation of the **Expressions utiles** and have students repeat them after you.
- As you work through the list, point out reflexive verbs and other expressions used to talk about daily routines. Explain that reflexive pronouns always correspond to their subject pronouns. Examples: **je me, tu te,** and **on se**. Point out that the phrases **On s'est couché** and **On ne s'est pas réveillé** are in the past tense. Tell students that reflexive verbs will be formally presented in **Espace structures**.
- Respond briefly to questions about reflexive verbs. Reinforce correct forms, but do not expect students to produce them consistently at this time.
- Have students combine sentences in **Expressions utiles** with known vocabulary to create mini-conversations.
- If students ask, explain that **j'ai bientôt fini** in video still #5 is an example of a particular use of the **passé composé** to express a future action. Although it is often used with the verb **finir**, they should use the **futur proche** to express an action that occurs in the near future.

1 Suggestion Have students correct the false statements.

1 Expansion For additional practice, give students these items. **11. Rachid est en retard pour son cours de maths. (Faux.) 12. Rachid ne va pas se raser. (Faux.) 13. David dit à Rachid de lire le journal. (Vrai.) 14. Rachid va téléphoner au médecin. (Faux.)**

2 Expansion For additional practice with reflexive verbs, give students these items.
6. s'endormir (se réveiller)
7. s'habiller (se déshabiller)
8. se maquiller (se démaquiller)

3 Suggestion Before beginning this activity, have students brainstorm vocabulary and expressions for describing daily routines and write their suggestions on the board.

OPTIONS

Extra Practice Have students write at least five sentences telling about their roommate's or best friend's actions using the verbs in **Activité 2**. Then tell them to get together with a classmate and take turns reading their descriptions. After students read their descriptions, have them ask their partner to state two facts from the description that has just been read to them.

Extra Practice Ask volunteers to act out the scenes in video stills 6–10 for the class. Tell them it is not necessary to memorize the episode. They should just try to get the general meaning across with the vocabulary they know. Give them time to prepare or have them do their skit as a review activity during the next class period.

Section Goals

In this section, students will:

- learn about medical services and pharmacies in France
- learn some colloquial expressions for parts of the body
- learn some idiomatic expressions associated with body parts
- read about the company L'Occitane

Instructional Resources
espaces.vhlcentral.com: activities; downloads; reference tools

Culture à la loupe

Avant la lecture Ask students: **Que faites-vous quand vous avez une réaction allergique? Et quand vous avez mal? Téléphonez-vous au médecin? Allez-vous à la pharmacie?**

Lecture

- Point out the **Coup de main**. Tell students that **°C** is read **degrés Celsius**. Have students convert the temperatures to degrees Fahrenheit using the formula $\frac{9}{5}$°C + 32 = °F.
- French prescription drug use ranks among the highest in the world, in part due to low cost and generous coverage by **la Sécurité sociale**.

Après la lecture Ask students: **Que peuvent faire les Français quand ils ne se sentent pas bien? (aller chez le médecin, aller à la pharmacie, avoir une visite à domicile, téléphoner à SOS Médecin ou contacter le Samu)**

1 Expansion Have students write two more fill-in-the-blank sentences. Collect their papers and read some of the sentences aloud. Call on volunteers to complete them.

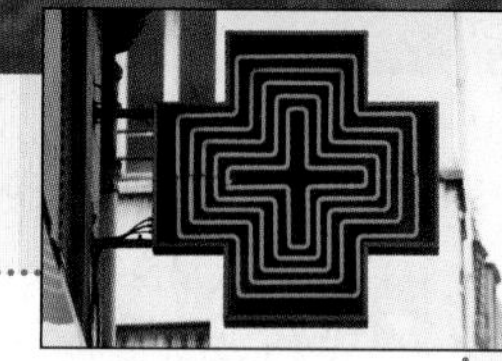

CULTURE À LA LOUPE

Les Français et la santé

Que fait-on en France quand on ne se sent pas bien? On peut, bien sûr, contacter son médecin. Généralement, il vous reçoit° dans son cabinet° pour une consultation et vous donne une ordonnance. Il faut ensuite se rendre à° la pharmacie et présenter son ordonnance pour acheter ses médicaments. Beaucoup de médicaments ne sont pas en vente libre°, donc consulter un médecin est important et nécessaire.

Cependant°, pour leurs petits problèmes de santé, les Français aiment demander conseil° à leur pharmacien. Les pharmaciens en France ont un diplôme spécialisé et font six années d'études supérieures. Ils sont donc très compétents pour donner des conseils de qualité. Les pharmacies sont faciles à trouver: elles ont toutes une grande croix° verte lumineuse° suspendue° à l'extérieur. Elles sont en général ouvertes du lundi au samedi, entre 9h00 et 20h00. Pour les jours fériés et la nuit, il existe des pharmacies de garde°, dont° la liste est affichée sur la porte de chaque pharmacie.

Quand on est très malade, le médecin donne une consultation à domicile°, ce qui° est très pratique pour les enfants et les personnes âgées°! En cas d'urgence, on peut appeler deux autres numéros. SOS Médecin existe dans toutes les grandes villes. Ses médecins répondent aux appels 24 heures sur 24 et font des visites à domicile. Pour les accidents et les gros problèmes, on peut contacter le Samu. C'est un service qui emmène les malades et les blessés° à l'hôpital si nécessaire.

reçoit *sees* **cabinet** *office* **se rendre à** *to go to* **en vente libre** *available over the counter* **Cependant** *However* **conseil** *advice* **croix** *cross* **lumineuse** *illuminated* **suspendue** *hung* **de garde** *emergency* **dont** *of which* **à domicile** *at home* **ce qui** *which* **personnes âgées** *the elderly* **blessés** *injured* **voient** *see* **homéopathie** *homeopathy*

Coup de main

In France, body temperature is measured in Celsius.

37°C is the normal body temperature.

Between **37°** and **38°C** is a slight fever.

For a fever above **38.5°C**, medication should be taken.

Between **39°** and **40°C** is a high fever.

Les habitudes (*habits*) des Français et la santé

- 89% des Français voient° un médecin généraliste dans l'année.
- 54% vont chez le dentiste dans l'année.
- Les médecins donnent une ordonnance dans 80% des consultations.
- 57% des Français utilisent les médecines alternatives.
- 39% utilisent l'homéopathie° au moins une fois dans l'année.

SOURCES: INSEE, CNP/CNAM

ACTIVITÉS

1 Complétez Complétez les phrases, d'après le texte et le tableau.

1. À la fin d'une consultation, le médecin vous donne parfois ___une ordonnance___.
2. ___Beaucoup de médicaments___ en France ne sont pas en vente libre.
3. Les pharmaciens en France font six années ___d'études supérieures___.
4. Les pharmacies sont faciles à trouver grâce à ___la grande croix verte lumineuse suspendue à l'extérieur___.
5. Parfois, le médecin vient à domicile pour donner ___une consultation___.
6. Quand on est très malade, on peut appeler ___Answers will vary. Possible answers: SOS Médecin, le Samu___
7. ___89% des Français___ voient un médecin généraliste dans l'année.
8. 39% des Français utilisent ___l'homéopathie___ au moins une fois dans l'année.
9. La température normale du corps est de ___37°C___.
10. On a une forte fièvre quand on a ___39°C___.

Practice more at **espaces.vhlcentral.com.**

OPTIONS

Cultural Comparison Have students work in pairs and compare medical services and pharmacies in France with those in the United States. Tell them to list the similarities and differences in a two-column chart under the headings **Similitudes** and **Différences.** After completing the charts, have volunteers read their lists to the class.

Les habitudes des Français et la santé Give students these true/false items based on the chart. Examples: **1. La majorité des Français n'utilisent pas de méthodes homéopathiques. (Vrai.) 2. Les Français ne vont pas fréquemment chez le médecin généraliste. (Faux.) 3. Les médecines alternatives ne sont pas populaires en France. (Faux.) 4. Plus de Français doivent aller chez le dentiste tous les ans. (Vrai.)**

LE FRANÇAIS QUOTIDIEN

Les parties du corps

bec (*m.*)	*mouth*
caboche (*f.*)	*head*
carreaux (*m.*)	*eyes*
esgourdes (*f.*)	*ears*
gosier (*m.*)	*throat*
paluche (*f.*)	*hand*
panard (*m.*)	*foot*
pif (*m.*)	*nose*
tifs (*m.*)	*hair*

LE MONDE FRANCOPHONE

Des expressions près du corps

Voici quelques expressions idiomatiques.

En France

avoir le bras long être une personne importante qui peut influencer quelqu'un
avoir un chat dans la gorge avoir du mal à parler
casser les pieds à quelqu'un ennuyer une personne
coûter les yeux de la tête coûter très cher
se mettre le doigt dans l'œil se tromper°

Au Québec

avoir quelqu'un dans le dos détester quelqu'un
coûter un bras coûter très cher
un froid à couper un cheveu un très grand froid
sur le bras gratuit, qu'on n'a pas besoin de payer

En Suisse

avoir des tournements de tête avoir des vertiges°
donner une bonne-main donner un pourboire

se tromper *to be mistaken* **vertiges** *dizziness, vertigo*

PORTRAIT

L'Occitane

En 1976, un jeune étudiant en littérature de 23 ans, Olivier Baussan, a commencé à fabriquer chez lui de l'huile de romarin° et l'a vendue sur les marchés de Provence. Son huile a été très appréciée par le public et Baussan a fondé° L'Occitane, marque° de produits de beauté. La première boutique a ouvert ses portes dans le sud de la France en 1980 et aujourd'hui, la compagnie a plus de 500 boutiques dans 60 pays, y compris aux États-Unis et au Canada. Les produits de L'Occitane, tous faits à base d'ingrédients naturels comme la lavande° ou l'olive, s'inspirent de la Provence et sont fabriqués avec des méthodes traditionnelles. L'Occitane propose° des produits de beauté, des parfums, du maquillage et des produits pour le bain, pour la douche et pour la maison.

huile de romarin *rosemary oil* **fondé** *founded* **marque** *brand* **lavande** *lavender* **propose** *offers*

SUR INTERNET

Les hommes en France dépensent-ils beaucoup d'argent pour les produits de beauté ou de soin?

Go to **espaces.vhlcentral.com** to find more information related to this **ESPACE CULTURE.**

ACTIVITÉS

2 Vrai ou faux? Indiquez si ces phrases sont **vraies** ou **fausses**. Corrigez les phrases fausses.

1. La compagnie L'Occitane a été fondée en Provence. Vrai.
2. Le premier magasin L'Occitane a ouvert ses portes en 1976. Faux. La compagnie a été fondée en 1976, mais le premier magasin a ouvert ses portes en 1980.
3. On trouve l'olive dans certains produits de L'Occitane. Vrai.
4. L'Occitane se spécialise dans les produits pour le corps. Faux. L'Occitane propose aussi des produits pour la maison.
5. Les produits de L'Occitane utilisent des ingrédients naturels et sont fabriqués avec des méthodes traditionnelles. Vrai.

3 Les expressions idiomatiques Regardez bien la liste des expressions dans **Le monde francophone**. En petits groupes, discutez de ces expressions. Lesquelles (*Which*) aimez-vous? Pourquoi? Essayez de deviner l'équivalent de ces expressions en anglais.

ressources
espaces.vhlcentral.com

Le français quotidien
- Model the pronunciation of each term and have students repeat it.
- Say the words and have students point to the corresponding body part.

Portrait
- Have students look at the photo and identify the product. Ask students: **Avez-vous déjà utilisé un produit de l'Occitane? Quel produit?**
- These products contain oils used in homeopathic remedies, a form of alternative medicine. Some product lines are based on honey (**le miel**), verbena (**la verveine**), everlasting flower (**l'immortelle**) from Corsica, or shea (**le karité**) from Africa.

Le monde francophone Model the pronunciation of each expression and have students repeat it. You might also give them these expressions: **prendre ses jambes à son cou (partir très vite)** (France), **perdre la tête (devenir fou)** (France), **être beau/belle comme un cœur (être très beau/belle)** (France/Canada).

2 Expansion For additional practice, give students these items. **6. Les produits de L'Occitane sont vendus seulement en France. (Faux. Il y a plus de 500 boutiques dans 60 pays.) 7. Olivier Baussan étudiait les maths avant de lancer sa compagnie. (Faux. Il étudiait la littérature.) 8. Baussan a d'abord travaillé avec l'huile de lavande. (Faux. Il a d'abord travaillé avec l'huile de romarin.)**

3 Expansion Have students write five sentences using these expressions in a specific context. Example: **Mon billet d'avion m'a coûté les yeux de la tête!**

OPTIONS

Cultural Activity Go to the L'Occitane web site in France at **http://www.loccitane.fr**. Print out a few pages of gift ideas for men and women from their **Boutique cadeaux**, and make photocopies to distribute to pairs. Tell students to take turns asking each other questions about the products and which ones they want to buy.

Les parties du corps Have students write four true/false statements defining the terms from **Le français quotidien**. Examples: **1. Le gosier est le pied. (Faux.) 2. La paluche veut dire la main. (Vrai.)** Then have students get together with a classmate and take turns reading their statements and responding.

Section Goals

In this section, students will learn:

- present-tense reflexive verbs
- the imperative with reflexive verbs

Instructional Resources
*espaces.vhlcentral.com: Lab MP3s; WB/VM/LM Answer Key; IRM (**Essayez!** and **Mise en pratique** answers; Lab Audioscript; **Feuilles d'activités**); activities; downloads; reference tools*

Suggestions

- Model the first person reflexive by talking about yourself. Examples: **Je me réveille très tôt. En général, je me lève à six heures du matin.**
- Model the second person by asking questions using verbs you mentioned in the first person. Examples: **À quelle heure vous réveillez-vous pendant la semaine? Vous levez-vous tôt ou tard en général?** Encourage student responses.
- Introduce the third person by making statements and asking questions about what a student has told you. Examples: ____ **se lève très tard le samedi, n'est-ce pas? (Oui, il/elle se lève entre onze heures et midi.)**
- Write the paradigm of **se laver** on the board and model its pronunciation.
- Use magazine pictures to clarify meanings between third person singular and third person plural forms. Examples: **La femme sur cette photo-ci se maquille. Sur cette photo-là, les enfants se couchent.**
- Compare and contrast reflexive and non-reflexive verbs using examples like these: **Il se réveille à six heures et demie. Il réveille les enfants à sept heures.**
- Point out that to make a question using inversion with a reflexive verb, you simply follow the rule: invert the placement of the subject pronoun with the reflexive verb.

10A.1 Reflexive verbs

NATIONAL STANDARDS comparisons

Point de départ A reflexive verb usually describes what a person does to or for himself or herself. In other words, it "reflects" the action of the verb back to the subject. Reflexive verbs always use reflexive pronouns.

SUBJECT — REFLEXIVE VERB

André **se rase** à huit heures.

Se *laver* (to wash oneself)

je	me lave	*I wash (myself)*
tu	te laves	*you wash (yourself)*
il/elle	se lave	*he/she/it washes (himself/herself/itself)*
nous	nous lavons	*we wash (ourselves)*
vous	vous lavez	*you wash (yourself/yourselves)*
ils/elles	se lavent	*they wash (themselves)*

- The pronoun **se** before an infinitive identifies the verb as reflexive: **se laver**.

Je me coiffe.

Tu te maquilles, maintenant?

- When a reflexive verb is conjugated, the reflexive pronoun agrees with the subject. Except for **se**, reflexive pronouns have the same forms as direct and indirect object pronouns; **se** is used for both singular and plural subjects.

Tu **te couches**.
You're going to bed.

Les enfants **se réveillent**.
The children wake up.

Je **me maquille** aussi.
I put on makeup too.

Nous **nous levons** très tôt.
We get up very early.

- Note that the reflexive pronouns **nous** and **vous** are identical to the corresponding subject pronouns.

Nous **nous regardons** dans le miroir.
We look at ourselves in the mirror.

Vous habillez-vous déjà?
Are you getting dressed already?

MISE EN PRATIQUE

1 Les habitudes Vous allez chez vos amis Frédéric et Pauline. Tout le monde a ses habitudes. Que fait-on tous les jours?

MODÈLE Frédéric / se raser
Frédéric se rase.

1. vous / se réveiller / à six heures
   Vous vous réveillez à six heures.
2. Frédéric et Pauline / se brosser / dents
   Frédéric et Pauline se brossent les dents.
3. tu / se lever / puis / prendre / douche
   Tu te lèves, puis tu prends une douche.
4. nous / sécher / cheveux
   Nous nous séchons les cheveux.
5. on / s'habiller / avant / petit-déjeuner
   On s'habille avant le petit-déjeuner.
6. Frédéric et Pauline / se coiffer / avant / sortir
   Frédéric et Pauline se coiffent avant de sortir.
7. je / se déshabiller / et après / se coucher
   Je me déshabille et après, je me couche.
8. tout le monde / s'endormir / tout de suite
   Tout le monde s'endort tout de suite.

2 La routine Tous les matins, Juliette suit (*follows*) la même routine. Regardez les illustrations et dites ce que (*what*) fait Juliette.

1. Juliette se réveille.

3. Juliette se brosse les dents.

2. Juliette se lève.

4. Juliette se maquille.

3 L'ordre logique À tour de rôle avec un(e) partenaire, indiquez dans quel ordre vous (ou quelqu'un que vous connaissez) faites ces choses. Suggested answers

MODÈLE se lever / se réveiller
D'abord, je me réveille. Ensuite, je me lève.

1. se laver / se sécher
   D'abord, je me lave. Ensuite, je me sèche.
2. se maquiller / prendre une douche
   D'abord, ma sœur prend une douche. Ensuite, elle se maquille.
3. se lever / s'habiller
   D'abord, mon camarade de chambre se lève. Ensuite, il s'habille.
4. se raser / se réveiller
   D'abord, je me réveille. Ensuite, je me rase.
5. se coucher / se brosser les cheveux
   D'abord, nous nous brossons les cheveux. Ensuite, nous nous couchons.
6. s'endormir / se coucher
   D'abord, tu te couches. Ensuite, tu t'endors.
7. se coucher / se déshabiller
   D'abord, je me déshabille. Ensuite, je me couche.
8. se lever / se réveiller
   D'abord, le prof se réveille. Ensuite, il se lève.

Practice more at **espaces.vhlcentral.com.**

OPTIONS

Extra Practice To provide oral practice with reflexive verbs, create sentences that follow the pattern of the sentences in the examples. Say each sentence, have students repeat it, and then say a different subject. Have students then say the new sentence with the new subject, changing pronouns and verb forms as necessary. Example: **Je me brosse les dents deux fois par jour.: on (On se brosse les dents deux fois par jour.)**

TPR Model gestures for a few of the reflexive verbs. Examples: **se coucher** (*lay head on folded hands*), **se coiffer** (*pretend to fix hair*). Have students stand. Begin by practicing as a class using only the **nous** form, saying an expression at random. Example: **Nous nous lavons les mains.** Then vary the verb forms and point to individuals or groups of students who should perform the appropriate gesture. Keep the pace rapid.

COMMUNICATION

4 Tous les jours Que fait votre partenaire tous les jours? Posez-lui les questions et il/elle vous répond. Some answers will vary.

MODÈLE se lever tôt le matin

Étudiant(e) 1: *Te lèves-tu tôt le matin?*
Étudiant(e) 2: *Non, je ne me lève pas tôt le matin.*

1. se réveiller tôt ou tard le week-end
   Te réveilles-tu tôt ou tard le week-end?
2. se lever tout de suite
   Te lèves-tu tout de suite?
3. se maquiller tous les matins
   Te maquilles-tu tous les matins?
4. se laver les cheveux tous les jours
   Te laves-tu les cheveux tous les jours?
5. se raser le soir ou le matin
   Te rases-tu le soir ou le matin?
6. se coucher avant ou après minuit
   Te couches-tu avant ou après minuit?

5 Enquête Votre professeur va vous donner une feuille d'activités. Circulez dans la classe et trouvez un(e) camarade différent(e) pour chaque action. Présentez les réponses à la classe. Answers will vary.

MODÈLE

Étudiant(e) 1: *Est-ce que tu te lèves avant six heures du matin?*
Étudiant(e) 2: *Oui, je me lève parfois à cinq heures!*

Activités	Noms
1. se lever avant six heures du matin	Carole
2. se maquiller pour venir en cours	
3. se brosser les dents trois fois par jour	
4. se laver les cheveux le soir	
5. se coiffer à la dernière mode (fashion)	
6. se reposer le vendredi soir	

6 Jacques a dit Par groupes de quatre, un(e) étudiant(e) donne des ordres au groupe. Attention! Vous devez obéir seulement si l'ordre est précédé de **Jacques a dit...** (*Simon says...*) La personne qui se trompe devient le meneur de jeu (*leader*). Le gagnant (*winner*) est l'étudiant(e) qui n'a pas été le meneur de jeu. Utilisez les expressions de la liste, puis trouvez vos propres expressions. Answers will vary.

se brosser les dents	se laver les mains
se coiffer	se lever
s'endormir	se maquiller
s'habiller	se sécher les cheveux

Common reflexive verbs

se brosser les cheveux	*to brush one's hair*	**se laver (les mains)**	*to wash oneself (one's hands)*
se brosser les dents	*to brush one's teeth*	**se lever**	*to get up, to get out of bed*
se coiffer	*to do one's hair*	**se maquiller**	*to put on makeup*
se coucher	*to go to bed*	**se raser**	*to shave oneself*
se déshabiller	*to undress*	**se regarder**	*to look at oneself*
s'endormir	*to fall asleep*	**se réveiller**	*to wake up*
s'habiller	*to get dressed*	**se sécher**	*to dry oneself*

- **S'endormir** is conjugated like **dormir**. **Se lever** and **se sécher** follow the same spelling-change patterns as **acheter** and **espérer**, respectively.

Il **s'endort** tôt.	Tu **te lèves** à quelle heure?	Elles **se sèchent**.
He falls asleep early.	*What time do you get up?*	*They dry off.*

- Some verbs can be used both reflexively and non-reflexively. If the verb acts upon something other than the subject, the non-reflexive form is used.

La mère **se réveille** à sept heures.	Ensuite, elle **réveille** son fils.
The mother wakes up at 7 o'clock.	*Then, she wakes her son up.*

- When a body part is the direct object of a reflexive verb, it is usually preceded by a definite article.

Vous **vous lavez les** mains.	Je ne **me brosse** pas **les** dents.
You wash your hands.	*I'm not brushing my teeth.*

- You form the imperative of a reflexive verb as you would a non-reflexive verb. Add the reflexive pronoun to the end of an affirmative command. In negative commands, place the reflexive pronoun between **ne** and the verb. (Remember to change **te** to **toi** in affirmative commands.)

Réveille-toi, Bruno!	*but*	**Ne te réveille pas**!
Wake up, Bruno!		*Don't wake up!*

Essayez! **Complétez les phrases avec les formes correctes des verbes.**

1. Ils _se brossent_ (se brosser) les dents.
2. À quelle heure est-ce que vous _vous couchez_ (se coucher)?
3. Tu _t'endors_ (s'endormir) en cours.
4. Nous _nous séchons_ (se sécher) les cheveux.
5. On _s'habille_ (s'habiller) vite! Il faut partir.
6. Les femmes _se maquillent_ (se maquiller) souvent.
7. Tu ne _te déshabilles_ (se déshabiller) pas encore.
8. Je _me lève_ (se lever) vers onze heures.

Essayez! Have students say logical commands for items 2, 3, 4, and 7. (**2. Couchez-vous [de bonne heure]. 3. Ne t'endors pas en cours. 4. Séchons-nous les cheveux. 7. Ne te déshabille pas.**)

1 Suggestion Before assigning this activity, review reflexive verbs by comparing and contrasting weekday versus weekend routines. Example: **Vous couchez-vous plus tôt pendant la semaine?**

2 Expansion Repeat the activity as a pattern drill, supplying different subjects for each drawing. Example: **1. je (Je me réveille.) 2. ils (Ils se lèvent.)**

3 Suggestion Tell students that they may vary the sequencing expressions used, such as **puis** instead of **ensuite**.

3 Expansion Have students say two sentences in which they combine more than two activities. Example: **se lever / se laver / se maquiller (D'abord ma mère se lève, ensuite elle se lave et finalement elle se maquille.)**

4 Expansion Have students come up with four additional items. Pairs then switch papers and form questions.

5 Suggestion Have two students demonstrate the **modèle**. Then distribute the **Feuilles d'activités** found on the Supersite.

6 Suggestion To give winners a chance to lead the game, have **le/la gagnant(e)** from each group come to the front of the room to take turns saying **Jacques a dit...**

OPTIONS

Extra Practice Have students compare their own routines with Juliette's in **Activité 2** on page 334. Have them express each part of the morning routine that they have in common. Example: **Moi aussi, je me réveille, puis je me lève.** Then have them express any differences. Examples: **Je ne me maquille pas (tous les matins). Juliette ne se lave pas le visage. Moi, si, je me lave le visage.**

Small Groups Have groups of three pretend that they share an apartment with only one bathroom. Tell them to have a conversation in which they discuss their morning schedule problems. Example: **Étudiant(e) 1: J'ai cours à huit heures. Je me lève à sept heures et je me lave tout de suite. Étudiant(e) 2: Moi aussi, je dois me laver à sept heures. Étudiant(e) 3: Alors, ____, réveille-toi à sept heures moins le quart.**

Section Goals

In this section, students will learn idiomatic reflexive expressions.

Instructional Resources
*espaces.vhlcentral.com: Lab MP3s; WB/VM/LM Answer Key; IRM (**Essayez!** and **Mise en pratique** answers; Lab Audioscript); activities; downloads; reference tools*

Suggestions

- Remind students what idiomatic expressions are. Ask which types of these expressions students already know. (idiomatic expressions with **avoir** and **faire**)
- Go through the list of common idiomatic reflexives with the class, pronouncing them and having students repeat. Have them point out which verb(s) they have seen before, such as **s'appeler**.
- Ask students to study the list and note related English words. Examples: **s'amuser** *amuse*, **s'occuper** *occupy*.
- Call attention to the spelling change verbs and the irregular **s'asseoir**.
- To show how **s'asseoir** can be polite or abrupt in its imperative form, tell students that **Assieds-toi/Asseyez-vous** can mean *Be seated.*, *Have a seat.*, or *Sit down!*
- Point out that when **que** follows a verb, it means *that*, as in the example: **Je me souviens que tu m'as téléphoné.** = *I remember (that) you phoned me.* Although the word *that* is optional in English, stress that **que** is required in French.

10A.2 Reflexives: *Sens idiomatique*

NATIONAL STANDARDS comparisons

Point de départ You've learned that reflexive verbs "reflect" the action back to the subject. Some reflexive verbs, however, do not literally express a reflexive meaning.

Common idiomatic reflexives

s'amuser	*to play; to have fun*	**s'intéresser (à)**	*to be interested (in)*
s'appeler	*to be called*	**se mettre à**	*to begin to*
s'arrêter	*to stop*	**se mettre en colère**	*to become angry*
s'asseoir	*to sit down*	**s'occuper (de)**	*to take care of, to keep oneself busy*
se dépêcher	*to hurry*	**se préparer**	*to get ready*
se détendre	*to relax*	**se promener**	*to take a walk*
se disputer (avec)	*to argue (with)*	**se rendre compte (de/que)**	*to realize*
s'énerver	*to get worked up, to become upset*		
s'ennuyer	*to get bored*	**se reposer**	*to rest*
bien s'entendre (avec)	*to get along well (with)*	**se souvenir (de)**	*to remember*
		se tromper	*to be mistaken*
s'inquiéter	*to worry*	**se trouver**	*to be located*

- **Se souvenir** is conjugated like **venir**.

Souviens-toi de son anniversaire.
Remember her birthday.

Nous nous souvenons de cette date.
We remember that date.

- **S'ennuyer** has the same spelling changes as **envoyer**. **Se promener** and **s'inquiéter** have the same spelling changes as **acheter** and **espérer**, respectively.

Je **m'ennuie** à mourir aujourd'hui.
I'm bored to death today.

On **se promène** dans le parc.
We take a walk in the park.

Ils **s'inquiètent** pour leur fille.
They worry about their daughter.

MISE EN PRATIQUE

1 Ma sœur et moi Complétez ce texte avec les formes correctes des verbes.

Je (1) m'appelle (s'appeler) Anne, et j'ai une sœur, Stéphanie. Nous (2) nous habillons (s'habiller) souvent de la même manière, mais nous sommes très différentes. Stéphanie (3) s'intéresse (s'intéresser) à la politique et elle étudie le droit, et moi, je (4) m'intéresse (s'intéresser) à l'art et je fais de la peinture (*paint*). Nous habitons ensemble, et nous (5) nous entendons bien (s'entendre bien). On (6) s'arrête (s'arrêter) souvent au parc et on (7) s'assied (s'asseoir) sur un banc (*bench*) pour bavarder. Quelquefois, on (8) se met en colère (se mettre en colère). Heureusement, on (9) se rend compte (se rendre compte) que c'est inutile. En fait, Stéphanie et moi, nous (10) ne nous ennuyons pas (ne pas s'ennuyer) ensemble.

2 Que faire? Que font Diane et ses copains? Utilisez les verbes de la liste pour compléter les phrases. Suggested answers

s'amuser	se disputer	s'occuper
s'appeler	s'énerver	se préparer
s'asseoir	s'ennuyer	se promener
se dépêcher	s'entendre	se reposer
se détendre	s'inquiéter	se tromper

1. Si je suis en retard pour mon cours, je me dépêche.
2. Parfois, Toufik se trompe et ne donne pas la bonne réponse.
3. Quand un cours n'est pas intéressant, nous nous ennuyons.
4. Le week-end, Hubert et Édith sont fatigués, alors ils se reposent.
5. Quand je ne comprends pas mon prof, je m'inquiète.
6. Quand il fait beau, vous allez dans le parc et vous vous promenez.

3 La fête Marc a invité ses amis pour célébrer la fin (*end*) du semestre. Avec un(e) partenaire, décrivez la scène à tour de rôle. Utilisez tous les verbes possibles de la liste de l'**Activité 2**. Answers will vary.

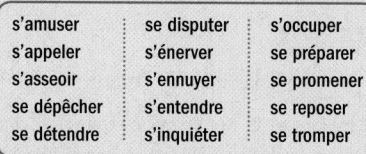

Practice more at **espaces.vhlcentral.com.**

OPTIONS

Pairs Have students write a short account of their own daily routine using both types of reflexives. Pairs then compare and contrast their routines using a Venn Diagram. Have the pair write one of their names in the left circle, the other in the right circle, and **les deux** where the circles overlap. They list their activities in the appropriate locations. Remind them to change the subject pronoun to **nous** in the overlapping section.

Game Have two teams write descriptions of five famous people or places, real or fictional, using idiomatic reflexives. Use **se trouver**. Team members take turns reading their descriptions while the opposing team gets three chances to guess who or what is being described. Each correct guess wins a point, while a team that fools its opponents gets two points. For a tiebreaker, you give clues to both teams. The first to guess correctly wins.

NATIONAL communication STANDARDS

COMMUNICATION

4 Se connaître Vous voulez mieux connaître vos camarades. Par groupes de quatre, posez-vous des questions, puis présentez les réponses à la classe. Answers will vary.

MODÈLE s'intéresser à la politique

Étudiant(e) 1: *Je ne m'intéresse pas à la politique. Et toi, t'intéresses-tu à la politique?*
Étudiant(e) 2: *Je m'intéresse beaucoup à la politique et je lis le journal tous les jours.*

1. s'amuser en cours de français
2. s'inquiéter pour les examens
3. s'asseoir au premier rang (*row*) dans la classe
4. s'énerver facilement
5. se mettre souvent en colère
6. se reposer le week-end

5 Curieux Utilisez ces verbes et expressions pour interviewer un(e) partenaire. Answers will vary.

MODÈLE s'amuser / avec qui

Étudiant(e) 1: *Avec qui est-ce que tu t'amuses?*
Étudiant(e) 2: *Je m'amuse avec mes amis.*

1. s'entendre bien / avec qui
2. s'intéresser / à quoi
3. s'ennuyer / quand, pourquoi
4. se mettre en colère / pourquoi
5. se détendre / quand, comment
6. se promener / avec qui, où, quand
7. se disputer / avec qui, pourquoi
8. se dépêcher / quand, pourquoi

6 Une mère inquiète La mère de Philippe lui a écrit cet e-mail. Avec un(e) partenaire, préparez par écrit la réponse de Philippe. Employez des verbes réfléchis à sens idiomatique. Answers will vary.

> Mon chéri,
>
> Je m'inquiète beaucoup pour toi. Je me rends compte que tu as changé. Tu ne t'amuses pas avec tes amis et tu te mets constamment en colère. Maintenant, tu restes tout le temps dans ta chambre et tu t'intéresses seulement à la télé. Est-ce que tu t'ennuies à l'école? Te souviens-tu que tu as des amis? J'espère que je me trompe.

- Note the spelling changes of **s'appeler** in the present tense.

S'appeler **(to be named, to call oneself)**	
je m'appelle	nous nous appelons
tu t'appelles	vous vous appelez
il/elle s'appelle	ils/elles s'appellent

Tu **t'appelles** comment?
What is your name?

Vous **vous appelez** Laure?
Is your name Laure?

- Note the irregular conjugation of the verb **s'asseoir**.

S'asseoir **(to be seated, to sit down)**	
je m'assieds	nous nous asseyons
tu t'assieds	vous vous asseyez
il/elle s'assied	ils/elles s'asseyent

Asseyez-vous, Monsieur.
Have a seat, sir.

Assieds-toi ici sur le canapé.
Sit here on the sofa.

- Many idiomatical reflexive expressions can be used alone, with a preposition, or with the conjunction **que**.

Tu **te trompes**.
You're wrong.

Il **se trompe** toujours **de** date.
He's always mixing up the date.

Marlène **s'énerve** facilement.
Marlène gets mad easily.

Marlène **s'énerve contre** Thierry.
Marlène gets mad at Thierry.

Ils **se souviennent de** ton anniversaire.
They remember your birthday.

Je **me souviens que** tu m'as téléphoné.
I remember you phoned me.

Essayez! Choisissez les formes correctes des verbes.

1. Mes parents *s'inquiètent* (s'inquiéter) beaucoup.
2. Nous nous entendons (s'entendre) bien, ma sœur et moi.
3. Alexis ne se rend (se rendre) pas compte que sa petite amie ne l'aime pas.
4. On doit se dépêcher (se dépêcher) pour arriver à la fac.
5. Papa s'occupe (s'occuper) toujours de la cuisine.
6. Tu t'amuses (s'amuser) quand tu vas au cinéma?
7. Vous vous intéressez (s'intéresser) au cours d'histoire de l'art?
8. Je ne me dispute (se disputer) pas souvent avec les profs.
9. Tu te reposes (se reposer) un peu sur le lit.
10. Angélique s'assied (s'asseoir) toujours près de la porte.
11. Je m'appelle (s'appeler) Suzanne.
12. Elles s'ennuient (s'ennuyer) chez leurs cousins.

Essayez! Give these sentences for additional practice. Tell students to choose a reflexive verb from the list. **13. La boulangerie ____ à côté de l'épicerie. (se trouve) 14. Cette fête est nulle. On ____. (s'ennuie) 15. Mes copains disent que ce cours est facile, mais je ne suis pas d'accord. Je pense qu'ils ____ (se trompent).**

1 Expansion Give students related sentences like the following. **1. Stéphanie et Anne ____ (se promener) parfois le week-end. (se promènent) 2. Le soir, elles ____ (ne pas s'endormir) tout de suite parce qu'elles parlent beaucoup. (ne s'endorment pas)**

2 Expansion Give additional statements modeled on those in the activity. Examples: **7. Cette étudiante n'est pas très patiente et elle ____ facilement. (s'énerve) 8. Tu t'entends assez bien avec mon frère, mais quelquefois vous ____. (vous disputez)**

3 Suggestion Help pairs get started by asking a question or two to the whole class. Example: **Que fait Fatima? (Elle s'ennuie./ Elle ne parle pas.)**

4 Suggestions
- Have two volunteers act out the **modèle**.
- Give more topics to discuss. Examples: **s'appeler comme son père/sa mère** and **bien s'entendre avec tout le monde**.

5 Expansion Have two pairs form a group of four. Students take turns asking questions in the second person plural. Example: **Vous vous amusez bien avec vos amis? (Oui, nous nous amusons bien avec eux.)** Then have students report back to the class in the third person singular and plural. Examples: ____ **s'entend bien avec sa tante.** ____ **et** ____ **s'intéressent à la médecine.**

6 Suggestion Read the e-mail aloud and ask if students have any questions before assigning this activity.

OPTIONS

Extra Practice Have students think of a friend or family member to whom they are particularly close. Assign a short writing task in which students describe their relationship with this person using at least five different common idiomatic reflexives. Tell them to be creative. They may also refer to **Activité 1** on page 336 for sample sentences.

Video Replay the video episode, having students focus on reflexive verbs. Stop the video strategically to discuss how reflexives are used in various structures. Examples: **Je dois me préparer, moi aussi!** (infinitive) **Ne t'inquiète pas.** (command) **Tu ne te rends pas compte!** (present tense) Have students identify the **passé composé** of reflexive verbs, but tell them it will be formally introduced in **Espace structures 10B.1**.

Instructional Resources
espaces.vhlcentral.com: IRM (Info Gap Activities); Testing Program, pp. 73–76; Test Files; Testing Program MP3s; activities; downloads; reference tools
Test Generator

1 Suggestion First, have students describe the people physically as a brief review activity. Then have them make up names for the people before describing what they are doing.

2 Suggestion Act out the **modèle** with a volunteer. Then point out the use of double object pronouns. Review the correct order if necessary.

3 Suggestion Before assigning groups, go over some of the things that men and women often do differently to get ready to go out. Examples: **Les femmes ne se rasent pas le visage. Les hommes ne se maquillent pas.**

4 Suggestion Ask students what sentence structure they will likely use most in this conversation. (commands)

5 Suggestion Have pairs compare their stories with others. Have students point out any errors or omissions. Vote on the funniest story.

6 Suggestion Divide the class into pairs and distribute the Info Gap Handouts found on the Supersite for this activity. Give students ten minutes to complete the activity.

NATIONAL communication STANDARDS

Révision

1 Les colocataires Avec un(e) partenaire, décrivez cette maison de colocataires. Que font-ils à sept heures du matin? Answers will vary.

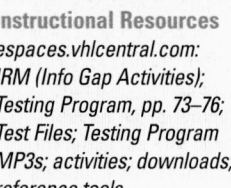

1.

2.

3.

2 Le camping Vous et votre partenaire faites du camping dans un endroit isolé. Malheureusement, vous avez tout oublié. À tour de rôle, parlez de ces problèmes à votre partenaire. Il/Elle va essayer de vous aider. Answers will vary.

MODÈLE

Étudiant(e) 1: *Je veux me laver les cheveux, mais je n'ai pas pris mon shampooing.*
Étudiant(e) 2: *Moi, j'ai apporté mon shampooing. Je te le prête.*

se brosser les cheveux	se laver le visage
se brosser les dents	prendre une douche
se coiffer	se raser
se laver les mains	se sécher les cheveux

3 Débat Par groupes de quatre, débattez cette question: Qui prend plus de temps pour se préparer avant de sortir, les hommes ou les femmes? Préparez une liste de raisons pour défendre votre point de vue. Présentez vos arguments à la classe. Answers will vary.

ressources
WB pp. 129–132 | LM pp. 75–76 | espaces.vhlcentral.com

4 Dépêchez-vous! Avec un(e) partenaire, vous êtes les parents de trois enfants. Ils doivent partir pour l'école dans dix minutes, mais ils viennent juste de se réveiller! Que leur dites-vous? Utilisez des verbes réfléchis. Answers will vary.

MODÈLE

Étudiant(e) 1: *Dépêchez-vous!*
Étudiant(e) 2: *Lève-toi!*

5 Départ en vacances Avec un(e) partenaire, observez les images et décrivez-les. Utilisez tous les verbes de la liste. Ensuite, racontez à la classe l'histoire du départ en vacances de la famille Glassié. Answers will vary.

s'amuser	s'énerver
se dépêcher	se mettre en colère
se détendre	se préparer
se disputer (avec)	se rendre compte

1.

3.

2.

4.

6 La personnalité de Martin Votre professeur va vous donner, à vous et à votre partenaire, une feuille d'information sur Martin. Attention! Ne regardez pas la feuille de votre partenaire. Answers will vary.

MODÈLE

Étudiant(e) 1: *Martin s'habille élégamment.*
Étudiant(e) 2: *Mais il s'ennuie le soir.*

OPTIONS

Extra Practice Ask students to translate these sentences into French using the same verb in each item. They choose reflexive or non-reflexive. 1. My dog is called Buddy. When I call him, he doesn't listen to me. (**Mon chien s'appelle Buddy. Quand je l'appelle, il ne m'écoute pas.**) 2. The children are walking the dog while their parents take a walk. (**Les enfants promènent le chien pendant que leurs parents se promènent.**) 3. We have to get ready. Why are you *(pl.)* preparing for the exam now? (**Nous devons nous préparer. Pourquoi préparez-vous l'examen maintenant?**) 4. Wash your *(sing.)* hands. Then wash your little brother. (**Lave-toi les mains. Puis lave ton petit frère.**) 5. The hairdresser does her hair in the morning. She does her clients' hair all day. (**La coiffeuse se coiffe le matin. Elle coiffe ses clients toute la journée.**)

Video: TV Clip

Le Zapping

1 femme sur 2 ne se démaquille pas...

En 1904, les laboratoires Bonetti, une entreprise (*firm*) française, créent° la crème médicale Diadermine. Cette crème connaît vite un grand succès et est utilisée par toute la famille. Son succès permet à la marque° de lancer° d'autres produits. Le groupe Henkel rachète° les laboratoires Bonetti en 1980. Et en 1998, Diadermine invente les lingettes démaquillantes° qui représentent aujourd'hui presque un quart du marché des démaquillants.

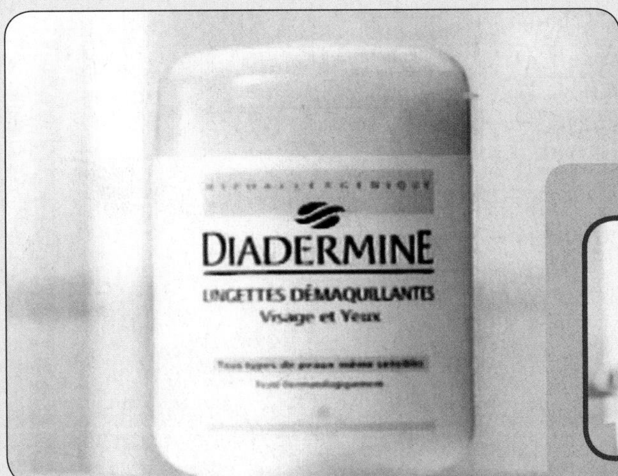

—Trop long, trop compliqué.

—Une seule lingette pour démaquiller et nettoyer le visage et les yeux.

Compréhension Répondez aux questions. Answers will vary.

1. Pourquoi ces lingettes sont-elles une innovation?
2. Quelles femmes vont utiliser ces lingettes?

Discussion Par groupes de quatre, répondez aux questions et discutez. Answers will vary.

1. Que pensez-vous du maquillage?
2. Passez-vous du temps à vous préparer le matin? Expliquez votre réponse.

créent *create* **marque** *brand* **lancer** *launch* **rachète** *buys out*
lingettes démaquillantes *make-up removal tissues*

Practice more at **espaces.vhlcentral.com.**

Section Goals

In this section, students will:

- read about the cosmetic company Diadermine
- watch a commercial for make-up removing towelettes
- answer questions about the commercial and Diadermine

Instructional Resources
*espaces.vhlcentral.com: TV commercial; IRM (**Le zapping** TV clip transcription); activities; downloads; reference tools*

Introduction
To check comprehension, ask these questions.
1. Que créent les laboratoires Bonetti en 1904? (Ils créent la crème médicale Diadermine.)
2. Qu'invente Diadermine en 1998? (Elle invente les lingettes démaquillantes.)
3. Ces lingettes ont-elles du succès? (Oui, elles représentent presque un quart du marché des démaquillants.)

Avant de regarder la vidéo

- Have students look at the video stills, read the captions, and predict what is happening in the commercial for each visual. **(1. La femme n'aime pas enlever son maquillage. Ça prend trop de temps et d'énergie. 2. On présente une solution au problème: les lingettes démaquillantes Diadermine.)**
- Before showing the video, explain to students that they do not need to understand every word they hear. Tell them to listen for cognates, the product name, and its qualities.

Compréhension Have students work in pairs or groups for this activity. Tell them to write their answers. Then show the video again so that they can check their answers and add any missing information.

Discussion Take a quick class survey to find out if makeup is popular among the students.

OPTIONS

Diadermine Here is a list of successful Diadermine products.
1930s: Diadermine talc
1949: sunscreen for outdoor activities
1950: anti-wrinkle cream, which is still one of Diadermine's best sellers
1978: first anti-wrinkle cream with collagen
1994: first complete skincare product with fruit acids called Fruitosome
1995: Réactivance products, for mature skin
1998: makeup removing towelettes
1999: smoothing and anti-wrinkle patches

Section Goals

In this section, students will learn and practice vocabulary related to:

- illnesses and medical conditions
- accidents
- medical visits and treatments

Instructional Resources
*espaces.vhlcentral.com: Transparencies #45, #46; IRM (**Vocabulaire supplémentaire**; **Mise en pratique** answers; Textbook Audioscript; Lab Audioscript); Textbook MP3s; Lab MP3s; WB/VM/LM Answer Key; activities; downloads; reference tools*

Suggestions

- Use **Transparency #45.** Describe the scene at this emergency room. Point out various medical conditions and treatments. Examples: **Ces personnes sont chez le médecin. Ce sont des patients. Elle est enceinte. Il a une blessure. Elle fait une piqûre.**
- Ask questions based on your narrative. Examples: **Est-il en bonne santé? A-t-il un rhume? A-t-il/elle mal?**
- Point out expressions with **avoir (avoir mal au dos, avoir mal au cœur); faire (faire mal, faire une piqûre, faire de l'exercice);** and **être (être en bonne/mauvaise santé, être malade, être en pleine forme).**
- Then point out reflexive verbs (**se fouler, se casser, se sentir**). Tell students to use **se sentir bien** to say they *feel good (feel well)* and **se sentir mal** to say they *feel bad.* **Sentir bon/mauvais** means *to smell good/bad.* Remind them to use the definite article, not a possessive adjective, when describing injuries to body parts. Example: **Il se casse *le* bras** (not ***son* bras**).
- Point out the different spelling of the French word **exercice** and the English *exercise.*
- Additional vocabulary for this lesson can be found in the **Vocabulaire supplémentaire** on the Supersite.

Leçon 10B

Talking Picture
Audio: Activity

You will learn how to...

- **describe your health**
- **talk about remedies and well-being**

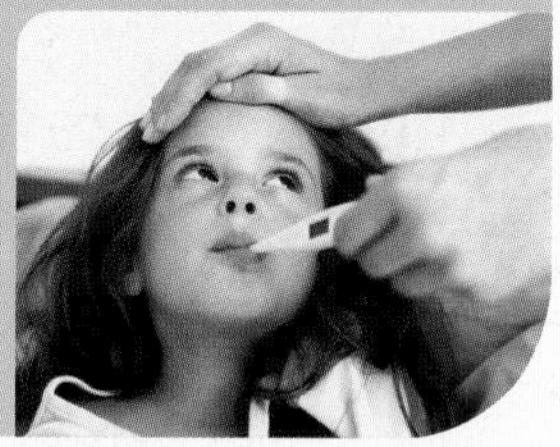

J'ai mal!

Vocabulaire

aller aux urgences/ à la pharmacie	*to go to the emergency room/ to the pharmacy*
avoir mal	*to have an ache*
avoir mal au cœur	*to feel nauseous*
enfler	*to swell*
être en bonne santé	*to be in good health*
être en mauvaise santé	*to be in bad health*
être en pleine forme	*to be in good shape*
éviter de	*to avoid*
faire mal	*to hurt*
garder la ligne	*to stay slim*
guérir	*to get better*
se blesser	*to hurt oneself*
se casser (la jambe/ le bras)	*to break one's (leg/ arm)*
se fouler la cheville	*to twist/sprain one's ankle*
se porter mal/mieux	*to be ill/better*
se sentir	*to feel*
tomber/être malade	*to get/to be sick*
un(e) dentiste	*dentist*
un(e) pharmacien(ne)	*pharmacist*
une allergie	*allergy*
une douleur	*pain*
la grippe	*flu*
un symptôme	*symptom*
une aspirine	*aspirin*
un médicament (contre/pour)	*medication (to prevent/for)*
une ordonnance	*prescription*
les urgences	*emergency room*
déprimé(e)	*depressed*
grave	*serious*
sain(e)	*healthy*

ressources
WB pp. 133-134 | LM p. 77 | espaces.vhlcentral.com

OPTIONS

Extra Practice Write the following headings at the top of three columns on the board: **Les maladies, Les remèdes,** and **Les professions médicales**. Say words and expressions from the **Contextes** and have students classify them. Ask volunteers to write them in the appropriate column.

Game Have students stand. Toss a beanbag to a student at random and say the name of an illness or injury. Tell students they should be creative. (**prendre un thé/de la soupe, se reposer, ne pas marcher...**) The person has five seconds to suggest a remedy or treatment. That person then tosses the beanbag to another student and says an illness or injury. Students who cannot think of a remedy or treatment are eliminated. The last person standing wins.

Mise en pratique

1 Chassez l'intrus **Indiquez le mot qui ne va pas avec les autres.**

1. un médicament, une pilule, une ordonnance, une aspirine
2. un médecin, un dentiste, un patient, une pharmacienne
3. un rhume, une aspirine, la grippe, une allergie
4. tomber malade, guérir, être en bonne santé, se porter mieux
5. éternuer, tousser, fumer, avoir mal à la gorge
6. être en pleine forme, être malade, être en bonne santé, garder la ligne
7. se sentir bien, se porter mieux, être en mauvaise santé, ne pas fumer
8. une blessure, une pharmacie, un symptôme, une douleur

2 Complétez **Complétez ces phrases avec le bon mot choisi dans ESPACE CONTEXTES pour faire des phrases logiques.** Some answers may vary.

1. Vous allez chez le médecin quand vous tombez __malade__.
2. Vous allez chez __le/la dentiste__ quand vous avez mal aux dents.
3. __L'infirmier/ière__ aide les médecins.
4. Une femme qui va avoir un bébé est __enceinte__.
5. Une personne qui a eu un grave accident est emmenée (*taken*) aux __urgences__.
6. On prend une __aspirine__ quand on a mal à la tête.
7. Pour être en forme et garder la ligne, il faut __faire de l'exercice__.
8. Si on n'est pas malade, on est __sain(e)/en bonne santé__.
9. Le médecin peut vous faire __une piqûre__.
10. __Une ordonnance__ est une liste de médicaments à prendre.
11. Être __déprimé__, c'est être tout le temps malheureux.
12. Si les fleurs vous font __éternuer__, vous avez une allergie.

3 Écoutez **Monsieur Sebbar est tombé malade. Vous allez écouter une conversation entre lui et son médecin. Choisissez les éléments de chaque catégorie qui sont vrais.**

Symptômes
1. J'ai mal à la tête. ☑
2. J'ai mal a u ventre. ☐
3. J'ai mal aux yeux. ☑
4. J'ai mal à la gorge. ☐
5. J'ai mal au cœur. ☐
6. J'ai mal à la cheville. ☑
7. J'ai de la fièvre. ☑

Diagnostic
1. la grippe ☑
2. un rhume ☐
3. la cheville cassée ☐

Traitement
1. faire de l'exercice ☐
2. faire une piqûre ☑
3. prendre des médicaments ☑

Practice more at **espaces.vhlcentral.com.**

1 Suggestion Go over the answers with the class. Have volunteers explain why each word doesn't belong.

2 Suggestion Ask volunteers to read the completed sentences aloud.

3 Tapescript MÉDECIN: Monsieur Sebbar, qu'est-ce qui ne va pas?
MONSIEUR SEBBAR: Docteur, j'ai mal partout. J'ai mal aux yeux et j'ai mal à la tête.
M: Laissez-moi voir... je vais prendre votre température. Vous avez de la fièvre, aussi.
S: Ce n'est pas tout! Ce matin, quand je me suis levé pour aller aux toilettes, je suis tombé. J'ai peur de m'être cassé la cheville parce qu'elle me fait très mal.
M: Monsieur Sebbar, ne vous inquiétez pas. Heureusement, vous vous êtes seulement foulé la cheville. Je vais vous donner quelques médicaments contre la douleur. Quant à vos autres symptômes, vous avez la grippe. Restez au lit pendant une semaine. Buvez beaucoup d'eau. L'infirmière va vous faire une piqûre. Comme ça, vous allez guérir plus vite.
(On Textbook MP3s)

3 Suggestion Play the conversation again, stopping at the end of each sentence that contains an answer so students can check their work.

OPTIONS

Pairs Have students work in pairs and take turns asking each other questions based on the illustration on pages 340–341. Tell them to point to the people as they ask their questions. Examples: **1. Qui travaille chez le médecin? 2. Que fait le médecin? 3. Qui prend une pilule? 4. Qu'est-ce que ce patient fait? 5. Qui se sent mal?**

Extra Practice Bring in drawings or magazine photos related to illness, medicine, and medical appointments. Have the class describe what is going on in the images or create stories about the people.

4 Suggestions
- Tell students to jot down notes during their interviews.
- After completing the interviews, have pairs get together with another pair and report what they learned about their partner.

5 Suggestion Tell students to write a description of each illustration. Then ask volunteers to read their descriptions aloud and have the class guess which illustration they are describing.

6 Suggestions
- Provide a model for students by describing an illness or accident you may have had.
- For this activity, you might want to preview the **passé composé** of reflexive verbs by presenting the first person singular form of a few verbs. Example: **Je me suis foulé (cassé/blessé) la cheville (le bras/l'orteil)**.

7 Suggestions
- Before beginning the activity, remind students that the doctor/patient relationship calls for the formal subject pronoun **vous**.
- Have students brainstorm a list of symptoms they might have and write them on the board.

Communication

NATIONAL communication STANDARDS

4 Conversez Interviewez un(e) camarade de classe. Answers will vary.

1. Quand t'a-t-on fait une piqûre pour la dernière fois? Pourquoi? Et une ordonnance?
2. Est-ce que tu as souvent un rhume? Que fais-tu pour te soigner (*to treat yourself*)?
3. Quel médicament prends-tu quand tu as de la fièvre? Et quand tu as mal à la tête?
4. Es-tu allé(e) chez le médecin cette année? À l'hôpital? Pourquoi?
5. Es-tu déjà allé(e) aux urgences? Pourquoi?
6. Un membre de ta famille ou un(e) de tes ami(e)s est-il/elle à l'hôpital en ce moment? Comment se sent cette personne?
7. Est-ce une bonne idée de fumer? Pourquoi?
8. Comment te sens-tu aujourd'hui? Et comment te sentais-tu hier?

5 Qu'est-ce qui ne va pas? Travaillez avec un(e) camarade de classe et à tour de rôle, indiquez ce qui ne va pas chez chaque personne. Proposez un traitement (*treatment*). Answers will vary.

1.

2.

3.

4.

5.

6.

7.

8.

6 Écriture Suivez les instructions et composez un paragraphe. Ensuite, comparez votre paragraphe avec celui d'un(e) camarade de classe. Answers will vary.

- Décrivez la dernière fois que vous étiez malade ou la dernière fois que vous avez eu un accident.
- Dites quels étaient vos symptômes.
- Dites si vous êtes allé(e) chez le médecin ou aux urgences.
- Mentionnez si vous avez eu une ordonnance et quels médicaments vous avez pris.

7 Chez le médecin Travaillez avec un(e) camarade de classe pour présenter un dialogue dans lequel vous: Answers will vary.

- jouez le rôle d'un médecin et d'un(e) patient(e).
- parlez des symptômes du/de la patient(e).
- présentez le diagnostic (*diagnosis*) du médecin.
- proposez une ordonnance au/à la patient(e).

OPTIONS

Pairs Have students work in pairs. Tell them to make a list of suggestions on how to prevent getting a cold (**un rhume**) or the flu (**la grippe**). Examples: **On doit souvent se laver les mains. On doit manger des fruits et des légumes. On doit éviter les personnes malades.** Then have them get together with another pair and compare their lists.

Extra Practice Have the class create a story of a very unfortunate person, **Pauvre Pierre**. The first person starts by saying what happens to him using the present tense. The next person repeats what the first one said, then adds another sentence to the story. Example: **Pauvre Pierre, quand il se réveille, il a mal à la tête.** The last student to speak concludes the story.

Les sons et les lettres

Audio: Concepts, Activities
Record & Compare

p, t, and c

Read the following English words aloud while holding your hand an inch or two in front of your mouth. You should feel a small burst of air when you pronounce each of the consonants.

pan **top** **cope** **pat**

In French, the letters **p**, **t**, and **c** are not accompanied by a short burst of air. This time, try to minimize the amount of air you exhale as you pronounce these consonants. You should feel only a very small burst of air or none at all.

panne **taupe** **capital** **cœur**

To minimize a t sound, touch your tongue to your teeth and gums, rather than just your gums.

taille **tête** **tomber** **tousser**

Similarly, you can minimize the force of a **p** by smiling slightly as you pronounce it.

pied **poitrine** **pilule** **piqûre**

When you pronounce a hard c sound, you can minimize the force by releasing it very quickly.

corps **cou** **casser** **comme**

Prononcez Répétez les mots suivants à voix haute.

1. plat
2. cave
3. tort
4. timide
5. commencer
6. travailler
7. pardon
8. carotte
9. partager
10. problème
11. rencontrer
12. confiture
13. petits pois
14. colocataire
15. canadien

Articulez Répétez les phrases suivantes à voix haute.

1. Paul préfère le tennis ou les cartes?
2. Claude déteste le poisson et le café.
3. Claire et Thomas ont-ils la grippe?
4. Tu préfères les biscuits ou les gâteaux?

Dictons Répétez les dictons à voix haute.

Les absents ont toujours tort.[1]

Il n'y a que le premier pas qui coûte.[2]
Bienvenue les ENFANTS!

ressources
LM p. 78
espaces.vhlcentral.com

[1] Those who are absent are always the ones to blame.
[2] The first step is always the hardest.

Section Goals

In this section, students will learn about the letters **p**, **t**, and **c**.

Instructional Resources
espaces.vhlcentral.com: Textbook MP3s; Lab MP3s; WB/VM/LM Answer Key; IRM (Textbook Audioscript; Lab Audioscript); activities; downloads; reference tools

Suggestions

- Model the pronunciation of the example words and have students repeat them after you.
- Ask students to provide more examples of words from this lesson or previous lessons with these sounds. Examples: **ventre, pleine, patient, santé, thé, café,** and **commander**.
- Dictate five familiar words containing the consonants **p, t** and **c**, repeating each one at least two times. Then write them on the board or a transparency and have students check their spelling.

OPTIONS

Extra Practice Use these sentences with **p**, **t**, and **c** for additional practice or as a dictation. **1. Carole partage son gâteau avec Paul. 2. Ta tante Thérèse nous a apporté du thé. 3. Patricia prend des pilules pour sa grippe. 4. Chloé a très mal au cou parce qu'elle est tombée.**

Extra Practice Teach students this French tongue-twister that contains plosive sounds. **Tu t'entêtes à tout tenter, tu t'uses et tu te tues à tant t'entêter. Tatie, ton thé t'a-t-il ôté ta toux, disait la tortue au tatou. Mais pas du tout, dit le tatou, je tousse tant que l'on m'entend de Tahiti à Tombouctou.**

Section Goals

In this section, students will learn functional phrases for giving instructions or suggestions and for describing ailments or injuries.

Instructional Resources
*espaces.vhlcentral.com: Video; WB/VM/LM Answer Key; IRM (Videoscript; **Roman-photo** Translations); activities; downloads; reference tools*
Video on DVD

Video Recap: Leçon 10A
Before doing this **Roman-photo**, review the previous one with this activity.

1. Qui ne se sent pas bien? (David)
2. Où est David? (dans la salle de bains)
3. Qui est en retard pour son cours de sciences po? (Rachid)
4. Comment est-ce que Rachid entre enfin dans la salle de bains? (Il dit à David de fermer les yeux.)
5. À qui est-ce que David va téléphoner? (au médecin)

Video Synopsis
Rachid and Stéphane are playing soccer at the park. Rachid hurts his ankle so Amina and Stéphane take him to the doctor's. Dr. Beaumarchais says it is only sprained. Then she tells him how to treat his ankle and writes a prescription. At the apartment, David is surprised when Rachid arrives on crutches. Stéphane wants to know what happened to David. He explains that the cream is for his rash, which is an allergic reaction. They also gave him a shot and some medication.

Suggestions
- Have students predict what the episode will be about based on the video stills.
- Have students scan the captions for sentences related to injuries or illnesses.
- After reading the **Roman-photo**, have students summarize the episode.

NATIONAL STANDARDS communication cultures

L'accident

Video: ***Roman-photo***
Record & Compare

PERSONNAGES

Amina

David

Dr Beaumarchais

Rachid

Stéphane

1

Au parc...
RACHID Comment s'appelle le parti politique qui gagne les élections en 1936?
STÉPHANE Le Front Populaire.
RACHID Exact. Qui en était le chef?
STÉPHANE Je ne m'en souviens pas.
RACHID Réfléchis. Qui est devenu président...?

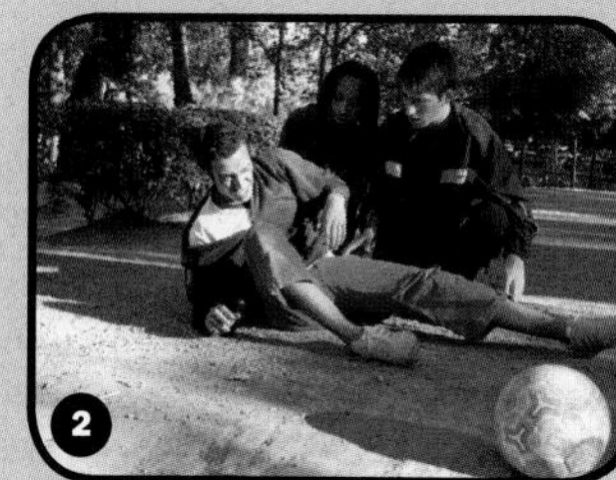
2

AMINA Salut, vous deux!
RACHID Bonjour, Amina! (*Il tombe.*) Aïe!
STÉPHANE Tiens, donne-moi la main. Essaie de te relever.
RACHID Attends... non, je ne peux pas.
AMINA On va t'emmener chez le médecin tout de suite. Stéphane, mets-toi là, de l'autre côté. Hop là! On y va? Allons-y.

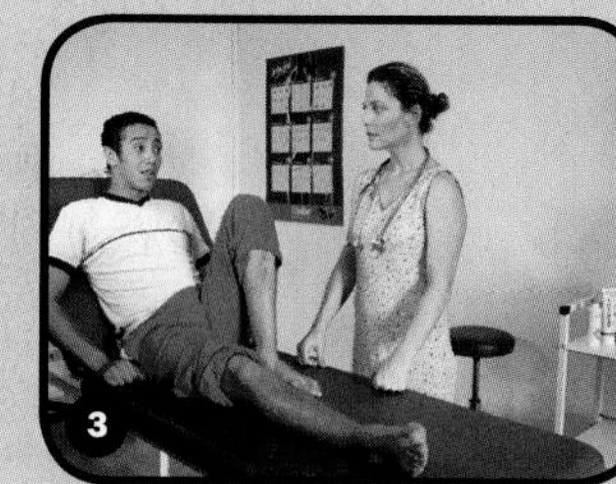
3

Chez le médecin...
DOCTEUR Alors, expliquez-moi ce qui s'est passé.
RACHID Eh bien, je jouais au foot quand tout à coup, je suis tombé.
DOCTEUR Et où est-ce que vous avez mal? Au genou? À la jambe? Ça ne vous fait pas mal ici?
RACHID Non, pas vraiment.

6

AMINA Ah, te voilà, Rachid!
STÉPHANE Alors, tu t'es cassé la jambe? Euh... tu peux toujours jouer au foot?
AMINA Stéphane!
RACHID Pas pour le moment, non; mais ne t'inquiète pas. Après quelques semaines de repos, je vais guérir rapidement et retrouver la forme.

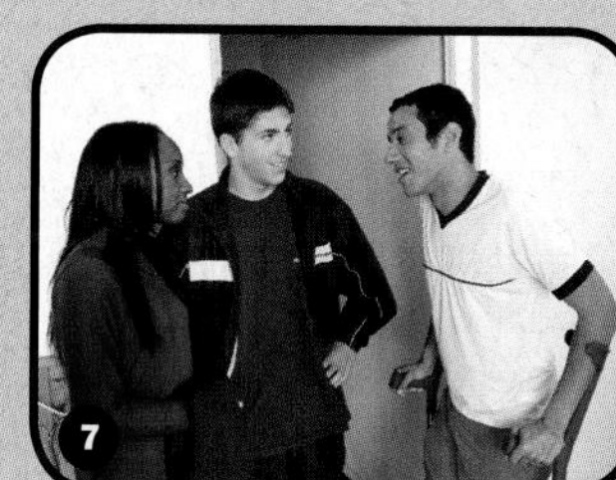
7

AMINA Qu'est-ce que t'a dit le docteur?
RACHID Oh, ce n'est pas grave. Je me suis foulé la cheville. C'est tout.
AMINA Ah, c'est une bonne nouvelle. Bon, on rentre?
RACHID Oui, volontiers. Dis, est-ce qu'on peut passer par la pharmacie?
AMINA Bien sûr!

8

Chez David et Rachid...
DAVID Rachid! Qu'est-ce qui t'est arrivé?
RACHID On jouait au foot et je suis tombé. Je me suis foulé la cheville.
DAVID Oh! C'est idiot!
AMINA Bon, on va mettre de la glace sur ta cheville. Il y en a au congélateur?
DAVID Oui, il y en a.

ACTIVITÉS

1 Les événements Mettez ces événements dans l'ordre chronologique.

__7__ a. Rachid, Stéphane et Amina vont à la pharmacie.
__3__ b. Rachid tombe.
__9__ c. David explique qu'il a eu une réaction allergique.
__1__ d. Rachid et Stéphane jouent au foot.
__5__ e. Le docteur Beaumarchais explique que Rachid n'a pas la cheville cassée.
__2__ f. Stéphane ne se souvient pas de la réponse.
__4__ g. Amina et Stéphane aident Rachid.
__8__ h. Amina et Stéphane sont surpris de voir (*see*) comment est le visage de David.
__10__ i. David dit qu'il est allé aux urgences.
__6__ j. Le docteur Beaumarchais prépare une ordonnance.

Practice more at **espaces.vhlcentral.com.**

OPTIONS

Avant de regarder la vidéo Before viewing the video, have students work in pairs and brainstorm a list of things people might say to a doctor when they get hurt. Also have them write a list of things a doctor might ask a patient who is hurt.

Regarder la vidéo Download and print the videoscript found on the Supersite. Then white out words related to injuries, illnesses, and other key vocabulary in order to create a master for a cloze activity. Distribute the photocopies and tell students to fill in the missing information as they watch the video episode.

Rachid se foule la cheville.

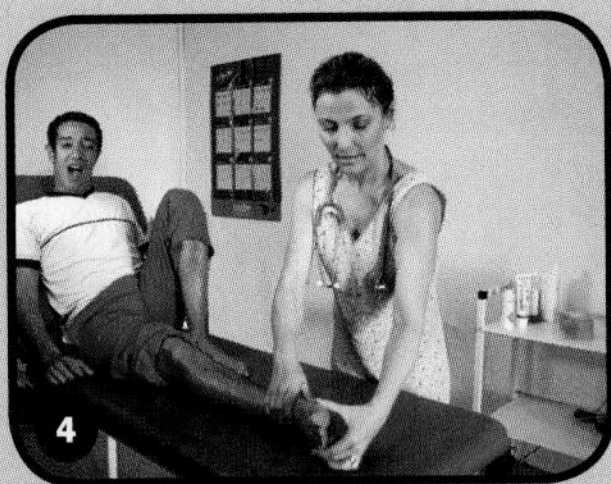
4

DOCTEUR Et là, à la cheville?
RACHID Aïe! Oui, c'est ça!
DOCTEUR Vous pouvez tourner le pied à droite... Et à gauche? Doucement. La bonne nouvelle, c'est que ce n'est pas cassé.
RACHID Ouf, j'ai eu peur.

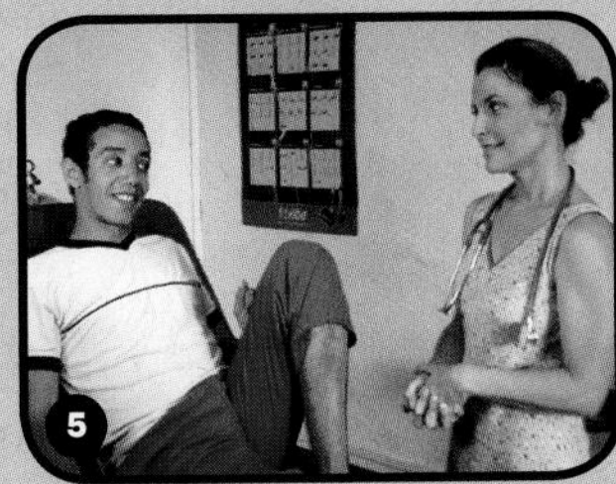
5

DOCTEUR Vous vous êtes simplement foulé la cheville. Alors, voilà ce que vous allez faire: mettre de la glace, vous reposer. Ça veut dire: pas de foot pendant une semaine au moins et prendre des médicaments contre la douleur. Je vous prépare une ordonnance tout de suite.
RACHID Merci, Docteur Beaumarchais.

9

STÉPHANE Et toi, David, qu'est-ce qui t'est arrivé? Tu fais le clown ou quoi?
DAVID Ah! Ah!... Très drôle, Stéphane.
AMINA Ça te fait mal?
DAVID Non. C'est juste une allergie. Ça commence à aller mieux. Je suis allé aux urgences. On m'a fait une piqûre et on m'a donné des médicaments. Ça va passer. En attendant, je dois éviter le soleil.

10

STÉPHANE Vous faites vraiment la paire, tous les deux!
AMINA Allez, Stéphane. Laissons-les tranquilles. Au revoir, vous deux. Reposez-vous bien!
RACHID Merci! Au revoir!
DAVID Au revoir!
DAVID Eh! Rends-moi la télécommande! Je regardais ce film...

Expressions utiles

Giving instructions and suggestions

- **Essaie de te relever.**
  Try to get up.
- **On y va? Allons-y.**
  Ready? Let's go (there).
- **Qu'est-ce qui t'est arrivé?**
  What happened to you?
- **Laissons-les tranquilles.**
  Let's leave them alone.
- **Rends-moi la télécommande.**
  Give me back the remote.

Referring to ideas, quantities, and places

- **Qui en était le chef?**
  Who was the leader of it?
- **Je ne m'en souviens pas.**
  I don't remember it.
- **De la glace. Il y en a au congélateur?**
  Ice. Is there any in the freezer?
- **Oui, il y en a.**
  Yes, there is some (there).

Additional vocabulary

- **la bonne nouvelle**
  the good news
- **ça veut dire**
  that is to say/that means
- **volontiers**
  gladly
- **en attendant**
  in the meantime

ACTIVITÉS

2 À vous! **Sandrine ne sait pas encore ce qui (*what*) est arrivé à David et à Rachid. Avec deux camarades de classe, préparez une conversation dans laquelle Sandrine découvre ce qui s'est passé. Ensuite, jouez les rôles de Sandrine, David et Rachid devant la classe.**

- Imaginez le contexte de la conversation: le lieu, qui fait/a fait quoi.
- Décidez si Sandrine rencontre les garçons ensemble ou séparément.
- Décrivez la surprise initiale de Sandrine. Détaillez ses questions et ses réactions.

3 Écrivez **Rachid et David ont deux problèmes de santé très différents. Qu'est-ce que vous préférez, une cheville foulée pendant une semaine ou une réaction allergique au visage? Écrivez un paragraphe dans lequel vous comparez les deux situations. Quelle situation est la pire? Pourquoi?**

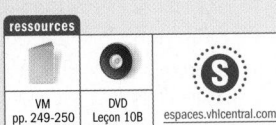

ressources
VM pp. 249-250 | DVD Leçon 10B | espaces.vhlcentral.com

Expressions utiles

- Model the pronunciation of the **Expressions utiles** and have students repeat them.
- As you work through the list, point out the **passé composé** of reflexive verbs and the pronouns **y** and **en**. Tell students that these structures will be formally presented in **Espace structures**.
- Respond briefly to questions about the **passé composé** of reflexive verbs and the pronouns **y** and **en**. Reinforce correct forms, but do not expect students to produce them consistently at this time.
- Point out that the pronoun **en** is not the same as the preposition **en**. To illustrate this point, write the following sentences on the board and compare them. **Il y en a.** (*There is/are **some**.*) **Il est en France.** (*He is **in** France.*)

Successful Language Learning Tell students that before traveling to a French-speaking country, they should make a list of their allergies and medical needs and learn how to say them in French.

1 Suggestion Have students form groups of five. Make a set of individual sentences on strips of paper for each group and distribute them (two sentences per student). Tell students to arrange the sentences in the proper order and read them aloud.

1 Expansion Have students create sentences to fill in parts of the story not mentioned in this activity.

2 Suggestion Assign students a role (Sandrine, David, or Rachid). Encourage them to be creative.

3 Suggestion Before writing their paragraphs, tell students to jot down a list of positive and negative aspects of each situation so that they can make a decision.

OPTIONS

Game Play a game of **Dix questions**. Ask a volunteer to think of an ailment or illness from this lesson. Other students get to ask one yes/no question each. Then they can guess the ailment/illness. Limit attempts to ten questions per item. You may want to provide students with some sample questions. Examples: **As-tu mal à la tête? As-tu mal au cœur? Es-tu blessé(e)?**

Pairs Have students work in pairs and interview each other using these questions. **1. Est-ce que tu tombes souvent malade? 2. Est-ce que tu as souvent mal à la tête? 3. Est-ce que tu manges bien ou mal? 4. Est-ce que tu manges beaucoup de fruits et de légumes? 5. Est-ce que tu fais de l'exercice? 6. Combien de fois par an est-ce que tu vas chez le dentiste?**

National Standards: connections, cultures

Video: *Flash culture*

Section Goals

In this section, students will:

- learn about the national healthcare system in France
- learn some terms for common health problems
- learn about several francophone pioneers in medicine
- read about **L'hôtel des Invalides**
- view authentic video footage

Instructional Resources
espaces.vhlcentral.com: Video; WB/VM/LM Answer Key; IRM (Videoscript); activities; downloads; reference tools

Culture à la loupe

Avant la lecture Have students look at the visuals and describe what they see. Then ask them what they think **la Sécurité sociale** in France is.

Lecture

- Point out the statistics chart. Ask students what information the chart shows. (French medical visits)
- Tell students that the French healthcare system was ranked number one by the World Health Organization in 2000 and in 2002.

Après la lecture Ask students to name the different branches of **la Sécurité sociale** and explain what they do. (**la branche «famille», la branche «vieillesse» et la branche «maladie»**)

1 Expansion Have students write two more true/false statements based on the reading. Then tell them to get into groups of three and take turns reading their sentences and responding.

CULTURE À LA LOUPE

La Sécurité sociale

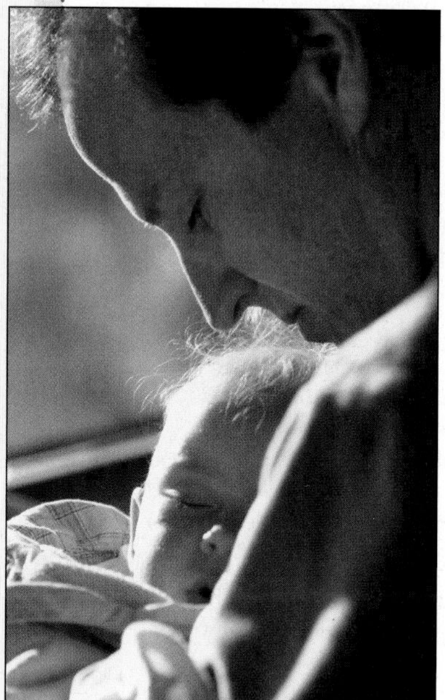

En France, presque tous les habitants sont couverts par le système national de la Sécurité sociale. La Sécurité sociale, ou «la sécu», est un organisme d'État, financé principalement par les cotisations° sociales des travailleurs, qui donne une aide financière à ses bénéficiaires dans différents domaines. La branche «famille», par exemple, s'occupe des allocations° pour la maternité et les enfants. La branche «vieillesse» paie les retraites des personnes âgées°. La branche «maladie» aide les gens en cas de maladies et d'accidents du travail. Chaque personne qui bénéficie des prestations° de la Sécurité sociale a une carte Vitale qui ressemble à une carte de crédit et qui contient° toutes ses informations personnelles.

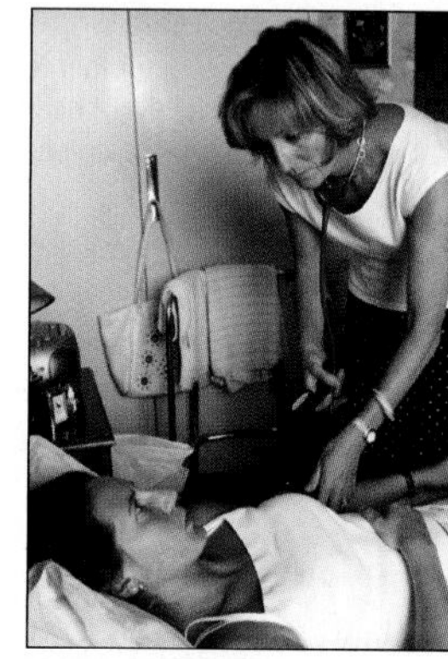

La Sécurité sociale rembourse° en moyenne 75% des frais° médicaux. Les visites chez le médecin sont remboursées à 70%. Le taux° de remboursement varie entre 80 et 100% pour les séjours en clinique ou à l'hôpital et entre 70 et 100% pour les soins dentaires°. Pour les médicaments sur ordonnance, le taux de remboursement varie beaucoup: de 35 à 100% selon° les médicaments achetés. Beaucoup de gens ont aussi une mutuelle, une assurance santé supplémentaire qui rembourse ce que la Sécurité sociale ne rembourse pas. Ceux° qui ne peuvent pas avoir de mutuelle et ceux qui n'ont pas droit à° la Sécurité sociale traditionnelle bénéficient parfois de la Couverture Maladie Universelle (CMU). La CMU garantit le remboursement à 100% des frais médicaux aux gens qui n'ont pas assez de ressources.

cotisations *contributions* **allocations** *allowances* **personnes âgées** *the elderly* **prestations** *benefits* **contient** *holds* **rembourse** *reimburses* **frais** *expenses* **taux** *rate* **soins dentaires** *dental care* **selon** *depending on* **Ceux** *Those* **n'ont pas droit à** *don't qualify for* **En moyenne** *On average* **dont** *of which* **ont lieu** *take place*

Les visites médicales

- En moyenne°, les Français consultent un médecin sept fois par an,
- dont° quatre fois un généraliste
- et trois fois un spécialiste.
- 70% des visites médicales ont lieu° chez le médecin.
- 20% ont lieu à la maison.
- 10% ont lieu à l'hôpital.

SOURCE: Francoscopie

ACTIVITÉS

1 Vrai ou faux? Indiquez si les phrases sont **vraies** ou **fausses**. Corrigez les phrases fausses.

1. Les cotisations des travailleurs financent la Sécurité sociale. Vrai.
2. La Sécurité sociale a plusieurs branches. Vrai.
3. La branche «vieillesse» s'occupe des accidents du travail. Faux. Elle s'occupe des retraites.
4. La carte Vitale est une assurance supplémentaire. Faux. C'est une carte qui contient toutes les informations personnelles d'une personne.
5. La Sécurité sociale rembourse en moyenne 100% des frais médicaux. Faux. Elle rembourse en moyenne 75% des frais médicaux.
6. Entre 70 et 100% des soins dentaires sont remboursés par la sécu. Vrai.
7. La Sécurité sociale ne rembourse pas les médicaments. Faux. Elle rembourse entre 35 et 100% du prix des médicaments sur ordonnance.
8. En plus de la Sécurité sociale, certaines personnes ont des assurances santé supplémentaires. Vrai.
9. Si on n'a pas beaucoup d'argent, on peut bénéficier de la CMU. Vrai.
10. 20% des consultations médicales ont lieu à l'hôpital. Faux. 10% ont lieu à l'hôpital. 20% ont lieu à la maison.

Practice more at **espaces.vhlcentral.com.**

OPTIONS

Cultural Comparison Take a quick class survey to find out how many times students visit a doctor in a year and if they see the doctor at his or her office, at the hospital, or the doctor comes to their home. Tally the results on the board and have students figure out the percentages. Then have students compare the results of this survey with the information in the chart **Les visites médicales**.

La Sécurité sociale France offers a degree of socialized medicine, though the coverage is not as complete as in some other countries. Criticism of the system stems from abuse by those who pay little for services at the expense of those who earn the most, and thus pay the most to the government.

LE FRANÇAIS QUOTIDIEN

Des problèmes de santé

angine (*f.*)	*strep throat*
bronchite (*f.*)	*bronchitis*
carie (*f.*)	*cavity*
frissons (*m.*)	*chills*
migraine (*f.*)	*migraine*
nez bouché	*stuffy nose*
nez qui coule	*runny nose*
sinusite (*f.*)	*sinus infection*
toux (*f.*)	*cough*

LE MONDE FRANCOPHONE

Des pionniers de la médecine

Voici quelques pionniers francophones de la médecine.

En Belgique
Jules Bordet (1870–1961) médecin et microbiologiste qui a découvert° le microbe de la coqueluche°

En France
Bernard Kouchner (1939–) médecin, cofondateur° de Médecins sans frontières° et de Médecins du monde

En Haïti
Yvonne Sylvain (1907–1989) première femme médecin et gynécologue obstétricienne d'Haïti

Au Québec
Jeanne Mance (1606–1673) fondatrice du premier hôpital d'Amérique du Nord

En Suisse
Henri Dunant (1828–1910) fondateur de la Croix-Rouge°

a découvert *discovered* **coqueluche** *whooping cough* **cofondateur** *cofounder* **frontières** *Borders* **Croix-Rouge** *Red Cross*

PORTRAIT

L'hôtel des Invalides

L'hôtel des Invalides est un monument parisien dont le dôme doré° est un chef-d'œuvre° de l'architecture du XVIIe siècle. Le roi° Louis XIV l'a fait construire entre 1670 et 1680 pour accueillir° les vieux soldats° et les soldats invalides°. Pendant la Seconde Guerre mondiale°, le monument a servi de cachette° à des membres de la Résistance. Plusieurs grands hommes de guerre reposent° aux Invalides, notamment Napoléon Bonaparte et Claude Joseph Rouget de Lisle, l'auteur de ***La Marseillaise***, l'hymne national français. Aujourd'hui, l'hôtel des Invalides accueille toujours d'anciens° soldats de l'armée française, mais c'est aussi un site culturel qui a quatre musées.

doré *gold* **chef-d'œuvre** *masterpiece* **roi** *King* **accueillir** *welcome, take in* **soldats** *soldiers* **invalides** *disabled* **Guerre mondiale** *World War* **cachette** *hiding place* **reposent** *are buried* **anciens** *former*

SUR INTERNET

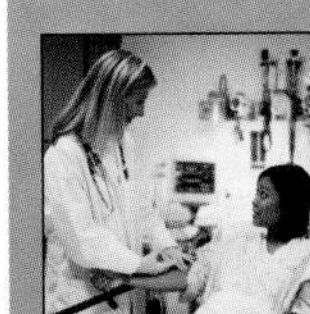

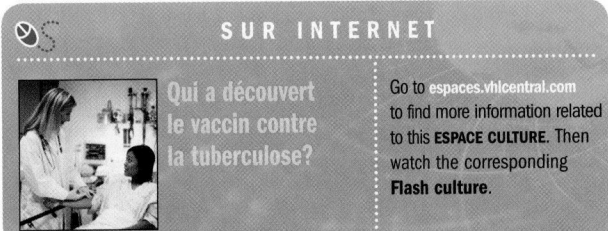

Qui a découvert le vaccin contre la tuberculose?

Go to **espaces.vhlcentral.com** to find more information related to this **ESPACE CULTURE**. Then watch the corresponding **Flash culture**.

ACTIVITÉS

2 Répondez Répondez aux questions par des phrases complètes.

1. Pour qui Louis XIV a-t-il fait construire l'hôtel des Invalides? Il l'a fait construire pour les vieux soldats et les soldats invalides.
2. Quand l'hôtel des Invalides a-t-il été construit? L'hôtel a été construit entre 1670 et 1680.
3. Qui a utilisé l'hôtel des Invalides pendant la Seconde Guerre mondiale? Des membres de la Résistance l'ont utilisé pendant la Seconde Guerre mondiale.
4. Que peut-on faire aujourd'hui à l'hôtel des Invalides? On peut visiter quatre musées.
5. Qui a été la première femme médecin d'Haïti? Yvonne Sylvain a été la première femme médecin d'Haïti.

3 Problèmes de santé Avec un(e) camarade, écrivez cinq phrases dans lesquelles (*in which*) vous utilisez le vocabulaire du **Français quotidien**. Soyez prêts à les présenter devant la classe.

ressources
VM pp. 289-290
espaces.vhlcentral.com

Le français quotidien
- Model the pronunciation of each term and have students repeat it.
- Ask students questions using these terms. Examples: **1. Avez-vous déjà eu une angine (une bronchite/une migraine/une sinusite)? Quand? 2. Les frissons sont-ils un symptôme d'une migraine?**

Portrait **Les Invalides** houses **le musée de l'Armée** (a military museum with a collection of weapons, armor, and uniforms from the Middle Ages to the twentieth century), **le musée des Plans-Reliefs** (a museum with a collection of scale models and maps of fortified French towns during the reigns of Louis XIV and Napoleon III), **le musée de l'Ordre de la Libération** (a memorial museum with galleries dedicated to Free France, the Resistance, and the transportation to concentration camps), and **l'église de St-Louis-des-Invalides**.

Le monde francophone Have students write four true/false statements based on the information given in **Des pionniers de la médecine**. Then have them get together with a classmate and take turns reading their sentences and responding.

2 Expansion For additional practice, give students these items. **6. Où se trouve l'hôtel des Invalides? (à Paris) 7. Qui a fondé** (*founded*) **la Croix-Rouge? (Henri Dunant) 8. Qui a aidé à fonder Médecins sans frontières? (Bernard Kouchner)**

3 Suggestion Have pairs get together with another pair of students and peer edit each other's sentences.

Flash culture Tell students that they will learn more about pharmacies and other health related businesses by watching a variety of real-life images narrated by Benjamin. Show the video segment, then have students jot down in French at least three examples of things they saw. You can also use the activities in the video manual in class or as homework to reinforce this **Flash culture**.

OPTIONS

Small Groups Have students work in groups of three. Tell them to make a list of symptoms and treatments for these illnesses: **l'angine, la bronchite, la migraine**, and **la sinusite**. You might want to give them the words **l'antibiotique** and **la pénicilline**. Then have two groups get together and compare their lists.

Cultural Comparison Have the class discuss and compare how the French and Americans honor their war veterans.

Section Goals

In this section, students will learn:

- the **passé composé** and the **imparfait** of reflexive verbs
- past participle agreement with reflexive verbs

Instructional Resources
*espaces.vhlcentral.com: Lab MP3s; WB/VM/LM Answer Key; IRM (**Essayez!** and **Mise en pratique** answers; Lab Audioscript); activities; downloads; reference tools*

Suggestions

- Briefly review the **passé composé** with **être** and past participle agreement from **Espace structures 7A.1** and **7A.2**.
- To introduce reflexive verbs in the **passé composé**, compare it with the present tense by discussing something out of character that you did one day versus what you usually do. Example: **Hier, je me suis levé(e) à neuf heures, mais d'habitude, je me lève à six heures.** Encourage similar statements from students. Write the sentences on the board, having volunteers underline the auxiliary verbs and circle the past participle agreements.
- Then talk about things that happened to you and to your students in the past. Examples: **Il y a deux ans, je me suis arrêté(e) chez mes amis français pendant mon voyage en Europe.**

NATIONAL STANDARDS comparisons

10B.1 The *passé composé* of reflexive verbs

Point de départ In **Leçon 10A**, you learned to form the present tense and command forms of reflexive verbs. You will now learn how to form the **passé composé** of reflexive verbs.

Vous vous êtes foulé la cheville.

Tu t'es cassé la jambe?

- Use the auxiliary verb **être** with all reflexive verbs in the **passé composé**, and place the reflexive pronoun before it.

Nous **nous sommes fait** mal hier, pendant la randonnée.
We hurt ourselves during the hike yesterday.

Il **s'est lavé** les mains avant de prendre le médicament.
He washed his hands before taking the medicine.

- If the verb is not followed by a direct object, the past participle should agree with the subject in gender and number.

SUBJECT / PAST PARTICIPLE
L'infirmier et le médecin **se sont disputés**.
The nurse and the doctor argued.

SUBJECT / PAST PARTICIPLE
Elle **s'est assise** dans le fauteuil du dentiste.
She sat in the dentist's chair.

- If the verb is followed by a direct object, the past participle should not agree with the subject. Use the masculine singular form.

PAST PARTICIPLE / DIRECT OBJECT
Régine **s'est foulé** les deux chevilles.
Régine twisted both ankles.

PAST PARTICIPLE / DIRECT OBJECT
Ils **se sont cassé** les bras.
They broke their arms.

- To make a reflexive verb negative in the **passé composé**, place **ne** before the reflexive pronoun and **pas** after the auxiliary verb.

Elles **ne se sont pas** mises en colère.
They didn't get angry.

Nous **ne nous sommes pas** sentis mieux.
We didn't feel better.

Je **ne me suis pas** rasé ce matin.
I didn't shave this morning.

Tu **ne t'es pas** coiffée.
You didn't do your hair.

MISE EN PRATIQUE

1 Une lettre Complétez la lettre que Christine a écrite sur sa journée. Mettez les verbes au passé composé.

Hier soir, je (1) me suis couchée (se coucher) trop tard, et quand je (2) me suis réveillée (se réveiller), j'étais fatiguée. Mais je voulais jouer au basket, alors je (3) me suis levée (se lever) et je (4) me suis brossé (se brosser) les dents. Mon amie est venue me chercher et je (5) me suis endormie (s'endormir) dans la voiture! Je pense que mon amie (6) s'est énervée (s'énerver) un peu contre moi. Nous (7) nous sommes préparées (se préparer) pour le match et nous (8) nous sommes mises (se mettre) à jouer.

2 Descriptions Utilisez des verbes réfléchis pour décrire ce que (*what*) les personnages des illustrations ont fait ou n'ont pas fait hier. Mettez les verbes au passé composé. Suggested answers

MODÈLE
Thomas ne s'est pas lavé.

Thomas

1. **mes amis**
Mes amis se sont disputés.

3. **je**
Je me suis ennuyée.

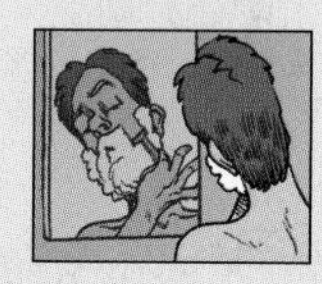
2. **tu**
Tu t'es rasé.

4. **vous**
Vous vous êtes mise en colère.

3 Une mauvaise journée Hier, Djamila a eu toutes sortes de difficultés. Utilisez le vocabulaire de la liste pour raconter sa mauvaise journée. Answers will vary.

MODÈLE
Djamila s'est trompée. Elle s'est brossé les dents avec du savon!

le bras	s'habiller	un rhume
se brosser	la jambe	du savon
se casser	se laver	se sentir
les chaussures	se lever	du shampooing
du dentifrice	le pied	se tromper

Practice more at **espaces.vhlcentral.com.**

OPTIONS

Extra Practice Ask students questions like the following with reflexive verbs. Examples: **Vous êtes-vous souvenu(e)s de vos cours de français pendant l'examen? (Oui, je me suis souvenu[e] de ….) Vous êtes-vous couché(e)s tôt ou tard hier soir? (Je me suis couché[e] tôt/tard.) Vous êtes-vous mis(e) en colère contre un de vos amis? (Oui/Non, je [ne] me suis [pas] mis[e] en colère contre un de mes amis.)**

Game Divide the class into two teams. Choose one student at a time to go to the board, alternating between teams. Say a subject and a reflexive verb in the infinitive. The student at the board writes and says the **passé composé** form. Example: **il: s'asseoir (il s'est assis); nous** (*fem.*)**: s'inquiéter (nous nous sommes inquiétées)** Teams earn a point per correct answer. The team with the most points at the end of the game wins.

NATIONAL communication STANDARDS

COMMUNICATION

4 Et toi? **Avec un(e) partenaire, posez-vous ces questions. Ensuite, présentez vos réponses à la classe.** Answers will vary.

1. À quelle heure t'es-tu réveillé(e) ce matin?
2. Avec quel dentifrice t'es-tu brossé les dents?
3. Avec quel shampooing t'es-tu lavé les cheveux aujourd'hui?
4. T'es-tu énervé(e) cette semaine? Pourquoi?
5. T'es-tu disputé(e) avec quelqu'un cette semaine? Avec qui?
6. T'es-tu endormi(e) facilement hier soir? Pourquoi?
7. T'es-tu promené(e) récemment? Où?
8. Comment t'es-tu détendu(e) le week-end dernier?
9. Comment t'es-tu amusé(e) le week-end dernier?
10. T'es-tu bien entendu(e) avec ton/ta camarade de chambre le premier mois?

5 Enquête criminelle **Il y a eu un crime dans votre quartier et un agent de police vous pose des questions pour son enquête (*investigation*). Avec un(e) partenaire, utilisez le vocabulaire de la liste pour créer le dialogue.** Answers will vary.

appartement	se coucher
blessure	se disputer
corps	s'énerver
déprimé(e)	se lever
grave	se mettre en colère
quartier	se réveiller
revenir	se souvenir
soudain	se trouver

6 Charades **Par groupes de quatre, pensez à une phrase au passé composé avec un verbe réfléchi et jouez-la. La première personne qui devine joue la prochaine phrase.** Answers will vary.

- Ask a question using inversion with a reflexive verb in the **passé composé** as you would with non-reflexive verbs. Place the subject pronoun after the auxiliary verb and keep the reflexive pronoun before the auxiliary.

  Irène **s'est-elle** blessée au genou?
  Did Irène hurt her knee?

  Ne **vous êtes-vous** pas rendu compte de ça?
  Didn't you realize that?

- Place a direct object pronoun between the reflexive pronoun and the auxiliary verb. Make the past participle agree with the direct object pronoun that precedes it.

  Il a la cheville un peu enflée. Il **se l'est cassée** il y a une semaine.
  His ankle is a bit swollen. He broke it a week ago.

  Mes mains? Mais je **me les** suis déjà **lavées**.
  My hands? But I already washed them.

- The irregular past participle of the verb **s'asseoir** is **assis(e)**.

Elle **s'est assise** près de la fenêtre.
She sat near the window.

Les jeunes mariés **se sont assis** dans le salon.
The newlyweds sat in the living room.

- Form the **imparfait** of reflexive verbs just as you would non-reflexive verbs. Just add the corresponding reflexive pronoun.

  Je **me brossais** les dents trois fois par jour.
  I used to brush my teeth three times a day.

  Nous **nous promenions** souvent au parc.
  We used to take walks often in the park.

Essayez! **Complétez ces phrases.**

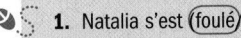

1. Natalia s'est (foulé/foulée) le bras.
2. Sa jambe? Comment Robert se l'est-il (cassé/cassée)?
3. Les deux joueurs de basket se sont (blessé/blessés) au genou.
4. L'infirmière s'est (lavé/lavées) les mains.
5. M. Pinchon s'est (fait/faite) mal à la jambe.
6. S'est-elle (rasé/rasées) les jambes?
7. Elles se sont (maquillé/maquillés) les yeux?
8. Nous nous sommes (cassé/ cassées) la jambe.

Essayez! Review that only direct objects preceding the **passé composé** with **être** require past participle agreement. Clarify that when a direct object comes after the verb in **passé composé** reflexive sentences, the reflexive pronoun acts as an indirect object (no agreement). Where there is no direct object after the verb, the reflexive pronoun acts as a direct object, thereby requiring past participle agreement.

1 Expansion Ask students to think of other details that Christine didn't mention. Examples: **Elle s'est habillée. Elle (ne) s'est (pas) maquillée. Elle (ne) s'est (pas) peigné les cheveux.**

2 Expansion Show photos or magazine pictures, having students describe what happened based on the subject (pronoun) you give. Examples: 5. a couple of young women relaxing (**nous**) (**Nous nous sommes détendues.**) 6. an elderly woman going to bed (**notre grand-mère**) (**Notre grand-mère s'est couchée.**)

3 Suggestions
- Have two students act out the **modèle**.
- Call on pairs to do the activity in front of the class.

4 Expansion Ask volunteers to share some of their answers. The class then adds information by speculating on the reason behind each answer. Have the volunteer confirm or refute the speculation. Allow students to make up answers if the questions are too personal. Example: **Tu t'es énervé(e) cette semaine parce que ton/ta copain/copine et toi vous êtes disputés.**

5 Suggestion Before beginning this activity, ask students warm-up questions. Examples: **Y a-t-il déjà eu un crime dans votre quartier? Vous êtes-vous blessés? Ou quelqu'un que vous connaissez s'est blessé? Y a-t-il eu une investigation?**

6 Suggestion Ask each group to present their best charade to the class.

OPTIONS

TPR Have a volunteer quickly mime two or three activities in front of the class. Examples: stand up, wash hands, and do hair. Then ask: **Qu'a-t-il/elle fait?** Call on students to say what the classmate did in the **passé composé** with reflexive verbs. Example: ____ **s'est levé(e). Ensuite, il/elle s'est lavé les mains. Enfin, il/elle s'est coiffé(e).** Repeat with more than one volunteer miming the activities at the same time.

Small Groups Have groups compile a list of famous people who could be described using one of the reflexive verbs. Then group members must work together to write a sentence with a reflexive verb in the **passé composé** about each person without mentioning the person's name. Other groups guess who it is. Example: **Simone de Beauvoir s'est bien entendue avec cet auteur. (Jean-Paul Sartre)**

Section Goals

In this section, students will learn the pronouns **y** and **en**.

Instructional Resources
*espaces.vhlcentral.com: Lab MP3s; WB/VM/LM Answer Key; IRM (**Essayez!** and **Mise en pratique** answers; Lab Audioscript; **Feuilles d'activités**); activities; downloads; reference tools*

Suggestions
- Ask students to recall expressions containing pronouns **y** and **en** that they have already learned. Examples: **il y a, ne t'en fais pas,** and **je vous en prie**. Make sure they understand when **en** is a preposition instead of a pronoun.
- Have students ask you questions about various locations, first in the present tense and then in the **passé composé**. Examples: **Dînez-vous au restaurant? (Oui, j'y dîne./Non, je n'y dîne pas.) Êtes-vous allé(e) à l'hôtel des Invalides? (Oui, j'y suis allé(e)./Non, je n'y suis pas allé(e).)** Have them make up other questions to ask you that elicit **en** as a pronoun. Then turn the questions back to the students, encouraging their responses with **y** or **en**.
- Clarify that **y** and **en** are not used to refer to people. Examples:
  Je parle des cours. → J'en parle.
  Je parle de mon père. → Je parle de lui.
  Je pense à mes cours. → J'y pense.
  Je pense à ma mère. → Je pense à elle.

NATIONAL STANDARDS comparisons

10B.2 The pronouns *y* and *en*

Point de départ The pronoun **y** replaces a previously mentioned phrase that begins with the prepositions **à**, **chez**, **dans**, **en**, or **sur**. The pronoun **en** replaces a previously mentioned phrase that begins with a partitive or indefinite article, or with the preposition **de**.

PREPOSITIONAL PHRASE		PRONOUN
Nous allons **chez le médecin**.	▶	Nous **y** allons.
Il était le chef **du Front Populaire**.	▶	Il **en** était le chef.

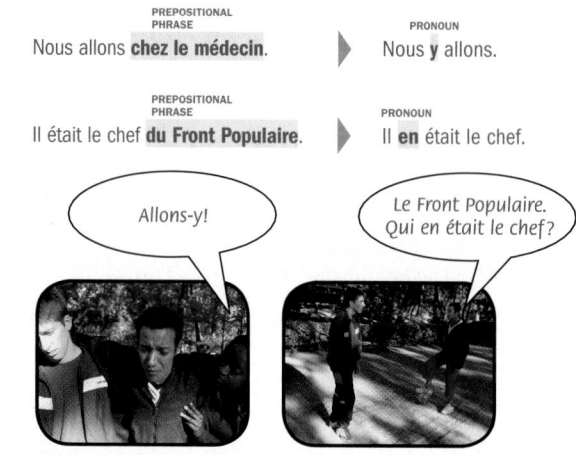

Allons-y!

Le Front Populaire.
Qui en était le chef?

- The pronouns **y** and **en** precede the conjugated verb.

Es-tu allée **à la plage**? *Did you go to the beach?* — Oui, j'**y** suis allée. *Yes, I went there.*

Achètent-elles **de la moutarde**? *Are they buying mustard?* — Oui, elles **en** achètent. *Yes, they're buying some.*

- Never omit **y** or **en** even when the English equivalents can be omitted.

Ah, vous allez **à la boulangerie**. *Oh, you're going to the bakery.* — Tu **y** vas aussi? *Are you going (there), too?*

Est-ce qu'elle prend **du sucre**? *Does she take sugar?* — Non, elle n'**en** prend pas. *No, she doesn't (take any).*

- Always use **en** with a number or expression of quantity when the noun is omitted.

Combien **de frères** a-t-elle? *How many brothers does she have?* — Elle **en** a **un (deux, trois)**. *She has one (two, three).*

Avez-vous acheté **beaucoup de pain**? *Did you buy a lot of bread?* — Oui, j'**en** ai acheté **beaucoup**. *Yes, I bought a lot.*

- Use **en** to replace a prepositional phrase that begins with **de**.

Vous revenez **de vacances**? *Are you coming back from vacation?* — Oui, nous **en** revenons. *Yes, we're coming back (from vacation).*

MISE EN PRATIQUE

1 Sondage M. Renaud répond aux questions d'un journaliste qui fait un sondage (*poll*) pour un magazine français. Utilisez **y** ou **en** pour compléter les notes du journaliste. Answers may vary slightly.

Nombre/Fréquence		Notes
1. Enfant	3	M. Renaud en a trois.
2. Chien	0	M. Renaud n'en a pas.
3. Voiture	2	M. Renaud en a deux.
4. Cinéma	rarement	M. Renaud y va rarement.
5. Argent	peu	M. Renaud en a peu.
6. Thé/café	parfois	M. Renaud en boit parfois.
7. New York	en 2005	M. Renaud y est allé en 2005.
8. Chez le médecin	une fois par an	M. Renaud y va une fois par an.

2 Histoire médicale Avec un(e) partenaire, jouez le rôle de quelqu'un qui va à l'hôpital où on lui pose ces questions. Justifiez toutes vos réponses. Utilisez les pronoms **y** et **en**. Some answers will vary.

1. Avez-vous des allergies? Oui, j'en ai. / Non, je n'en ai pas.
2. Êtes-vous allé(e) aux urgences cette année? Oui, j'y suis allé(e). / Non, je n'y suis pas allé(e).
3. Allez-vous chez le médecin régulièrement? Oui, j'y vais régulièrement. / Non, je n'y vais pas régulièrement.
4. Combien d'aspirines prenez-vous par jour? J'en prends... / Je n'en prends pas.
5. Faites-vous du sport tous les jours? Oui, j'en fais. / Non, je n'en fais pas.
6. Avez-vous des douleurs? Oui, j'en ai. / Non, je n'en ai pas.
7. Avez-vous de la fièvre? Oui, j'en ai. / Non, je n'en ai pas.
8. Vous êtes-vous blessé(e) au travail? Oui, je m'y suis blessé(e). / Non, je ne m'y suis pas blessé(e).

3 Chez le dentiste Mme Hanh emmène ses fils chez un nouveau dentiste. Complétez le dialogue entre le dentiste et les deux garçons. Utilisez les pronoms **y** et **en**. Suggested answers

LE DENTISTE C'est la première fois que vous allez chez le dentiste?
FRÉDÉRIC Oui, (1) c'est la première fois que nous y allons.
LE DENTISTE N'ayez pas peur. Alors, mangez-vous beaucoup de sucre?
HENRI (2) Non, nous n'en mangeons pas beaucoup.
LE DENTISTE Et toi, Frédéric, utilises-tu du dentifrice?
FRÉDÉRIC (3) Oui, j'en utilise.
HENRI Est-ce que vous allez nous faire une piqûre?
LE DENTISTE (4) Oui, je vais vous en faire une.
HENRI Moi, je n'ai pas peur des piqûres... mais j'espère que vous n'allez pas trouver de caries (*cavities*).
LE DENTISTE (5) Je vais peut-être en trouver une ou deux.

Practice more at **espaces.vhlcentral.com**.

OPTIONS

Extra Practice Show pictures of easily identifiable places around town and/or around the world. Ask students if they go, have been, if they want to go, if they used to go, etc., to the various places. Examples: **Y allez-vous souvent? Y alliez-vous quand vous étiez petit(e)s? Voulez-vous y aller?** You could also do a similar activity without pictures. Ask questions with specific places, requiring students to use **y** in their replies.

Game Divide the class into two teams. Choose one student at a time, alternating between teams. Call out a prepositional phrase that could be replaced with **en** or **y**. The student has three seconds to choose. Examples: **chez moi (y); dans la salle de bains (y); des États-Unis (en); en France (y); du pain (en).** Teams earn a point per correct answer. The team with the most points at the end of the game wins.

COMMUNICATION

4 Trouvez quelqu'un qui... Votre professeur va vous donner une feuille d'activités. Circulez dans la classe pour trouver un(e) camarade différent(e) qui donne une réponse affirmative à chaque question. Employez les pronoms **y** et **en**. Answers will vary.

MODÈLE

Étudiant(e) 1: *Je suis né(e) à Los Angeles. Y es-tu né(e) aussi?*
Étudiant(e) 2: *Oui, j'y suis né(e) aussi!*

Qui...	Noms
1. est né(e) dans la même (same) ville que vous?	Mélanie
2. a pris une aspirine aujourd'hui? Pourquoi?	
3. est allé(e) en Suisse? Quand?	
4. a mangé au resto U cette semaine? Combien de fois?	
5. est déjà allé(e) aux urgences? Pourquoi?	
6. est allé(e) chez le dentiste ce mois-ci? Quand?	

5 Interview Posez ces questions à un(e) partenaire. Employez **y** ou **en** dans vos réponses, puis présentez-les à la classe. Answers will vary.

Demandez à un(e) partenaire...

1. s'il/elle va à la bibliothèque (au restaurant, à la plage, chez le dentiste) aujourd'hui. Pourquoi?
2. s'il/elle a besoin d'argent (d'une voiture, de courage, de temps libre). Pourquoi?
3. s'il/elle s'intéresse aux sports (à la littérature, au jazz, à la politique). Que préfère-t-il/elle?
4. combien de personnes il y a dans sa famille (dans la classe de français, dans sa résidence universitaire).
5. s'il/elle a un chien (beaucoup de cousins, un grand-père, un vélo, un ordinateur). Où sont-ils?
6. s'il/elle a des allergies (une blessure, un rhume). Que fait-il/elle contre les symptômes?

6 Chez le docteur Vous avez ces problèmes et vous allez chez le docteur. Votre partenaire va jouer le rôle du docteur. Parlez de vos symptômes. Que faut-il faire? Utilisez les pronoms **y** et **en**. Answers will vary.

- des allergies
- la grippe
- une cheville foulée
- mal à la gorge

- Like other pronouns in an infinitive construction, **y** and **en** precede the infinitive.

Quand préfères-tu manger **chez Fatima**? *When do you prefer to eat at Fatima's?*	Je **préfère y manger** demain soir. *I prefer to eat there tomorrow night.*
Vas-tu prendre **du thé**? *Are you going to have tea?*	Non, je ne **vais** pas **en prendre**. *Yes, we're going to have some.*

- In the **passé composé**, the past participle never agrees with **y** or **en**.

Avez-vous trouvé **des fraises**? *Did you find some strawberries?*	Oui, nous **en** avons trouvé. *Yes, we found some.*

- In an affirmative **tu** command, add an **-s** to any **-er** verb followed by **y** or **en**. Note that **aller** also follows this pattern.

Tu vas chez le médecin? Va**s-y**! *You're going to the doctor's? Go!*	*but*	Va chez le médecin! *Go to the doctor's!*
Il y a des pommes. Mange**s-en**! *There are some apples. Eat a few!*	*but*	Mange des pommes! *Eat apples!*

- When using two pronouns in the same sentence, **y** and **en** always come in second position.

Vous parlez **à Hélène de sa toux**? *Are you talking to Hélène about her cough?*	Oui, nous **lui en** parlons. *Yes, we're talking to her about it.*

- With imperatives, **moi** followed by **y** and **en** becomes **m'y** and **m'en**. **Toi** followed by **y** and **en** becomes **t'y** and **t'en**.

Vous avez **des pêches** aujourd'hui? *You have peaches today?*	Donnez-**m'en** dix. *Give me ten.*

- When used together in the same sentence, **y** is placed before **en**.

Il y a **de bons médecins à l'hôpital**? *Are there good doctors at the hospital?*	Oui, il **y en** a. *Yes, there are.*

Essayez! **Complétez les phrases avec le pronom correct.**

1. Faites-vous du sport? Oui, nous <u>en</u> faisons.
2. Papa est au garage? Oui, il <u>y</u> est.
3. Nous voulons des fraises. Donnez-nous- <u>en</u> un kilo.
4. Mettez-vous du sucre dans votre café? Oui, nous <u>en</u> mettons.
5. Est-ce que tu t'intéresses à la médecine? Oui, je m' <u>y</u> intéresse.
6. Il est allé au cinéma? Oui, il <u>y</u> est allé.
7. Combien de pièces y avait-il? Il y <u>en</u> avait quatre.
8. Avez-vous des lampes? Non, nous n'<u>en</u> avons pas.
9. Elles sont chez leur copine. Elles <u>y</u> sont depuis samedi.
10. Êtes-vous allés en France? Oui, nous <u>y</u> sommes allés.

Essayez! Supplement this activity with items like these: **11. Avez-vous besoin d'une aspirine? (Non, nous n'en avons pas besoin.) 12. Qui joue au foot? (J'y joue. / ____ y joue.) 13. Combien de pièces y avait-il dans la maison? (Il y en avait quatre).**

1 Expansion After completing the activity, have students form the questions that would elicit the responses. Then have them take turns asking each other the questions and answering them. Example: **Combien d'enfants a-t-il? (Il en a trois.)**

2 Suggestion Have students take turns playing the roles of the nurse and the celebrity.

3 Suggestion You may want to assign this activity to groups of three. If so, call on a volunteer group to act out the completed conversation for the class.

4 Suggestions
- Have two volunteers act out the **modèle**.
- Distribute the **Feuilles d'activités** found on the Supersite.

5 Suggestions
- Encourage students to think of a few additional questions modeled on those in the activity.
- Have students report what they learned about their partner in small groups.

6 Suggestions
- Make sure each student plays both the doctor and patient roles.
- Tell students to feel free to talk about other symptoms learned in this lesson.

OPTIONS

Video Replay the video episode, having students focus on the **passé composé** of reflexive verbs and the pronouns **y** and **en**. Pause the video where appropriate to discuss how they were used and to ask comprehension questions. Examples: **Stéphane s'est-il souvenu du nom du chef du Front Populaire? (Non, il ne s'en est pas souvenu.) Qui s'est blessé? (Rachid s'est blessé.) Va-t-il chez le médecin? (Oui, il y va.)**

Pairs Have pairs ask each other if they play sports, musical instruments, or do certain activities. Students respond yes or no in a complete sentence using **y** or **en**. If the answer is no, encourage them to say whether they used to, are going to, want to, if someone else plays, etc. Examples: **Fais-tu de l'exercice? (Oui, j'en fais cinq fois par semaine.) Fais-tu du golf? (Non, je n'en fais pas, mais ma mère en fait.)**

NATIONAL STANDARDS communication cultures

Révision

1 **La salle d'attente** Observez cette salle d'attente (*waiting room*) et, avec un(e) partenaire, décrivez la situation ou la maladie de chaque personne. À tour de rôle, essayez de prescrire un remède. Utilisez les pronoms **y** ou **en** dans vos dialogues. Answers will vary.

MODÈLE

Étudiant(e) 1: *Ce garçon s'est foulé la cheville. Il doit aller aux urgences.*
Étudiant(e) 2: *Oui, et cette fille...*

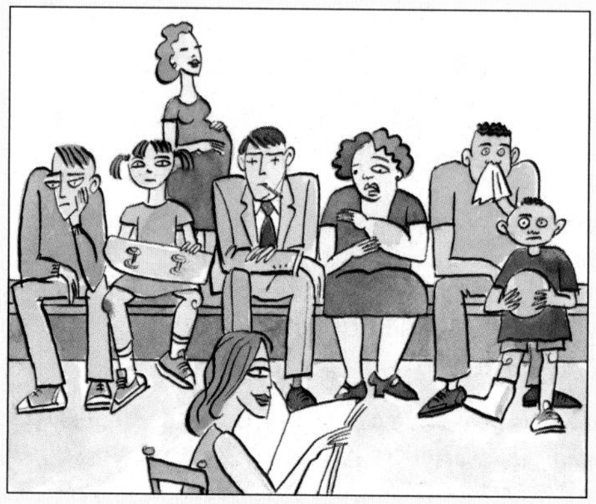

2 **Êtes-vous souvent malade?** Avec un(e) partenaire, préparez huit questions pour savoir si vos camarades de classe sont en bonne ou en mauvaise santé. Ensuite, par groupes de quatre, posez les questions à vos camarades et écrivez leurs réponses. Employez des pronoms. Answers will vary.

3 **Oh! Ça va?!** Vous êtes un(e) piéton(ne) (*pedestrian*) et tout d'un coup, vous voyez (*see*) un(e) cycliste tomber de son vélo. Avec un(e) partenaire, suivez (*follow*) ces instructions et préparez la scène. Utilisez les pronoms **y** et **en**. Answers will vary.

Piéton(ne)	Cycliste
Demandez s'il/elle s'est fait mal.	Dites quel est le problème.
Posez des questions sur les symptômes.	Décrivez les symptômes.
Proposez de l'emmener aux urgences.	Acceptez ou refusez la proposition.

4 **Pour partir loin** Vous et un(e) partenaire allez vivre (*to live*) un mois dans une région totalement isolée. Regardez l'illustration: vous pouvez mettre seulement cinq choses dans votre sac de voyage. Choisissez-les avec votre partenaire. Answers will vary.

MODÈLE

Étudiant(e) 1: *On prend du shampooing pour se laver les cheveux?*
Étudiant(e) 2: *Non, la bouteille est trop grande!*

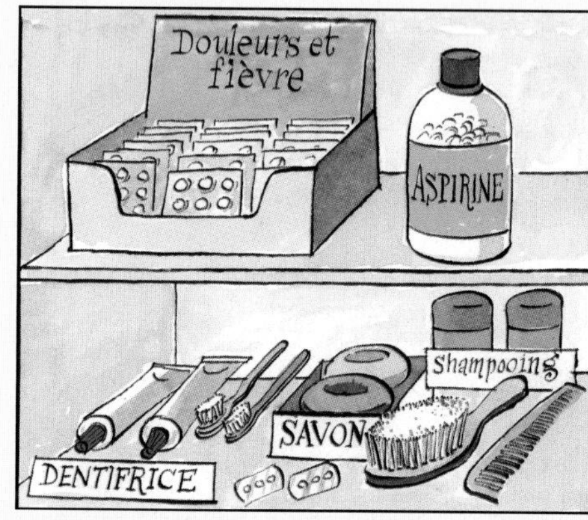

5 **Le malade imaginaire** Vous êtes hypocondriaque et vous pensez être très malade. À tour de rôle, parlez de vos peurs à votre partenaire, qui va essayer de vous rassurer. Utilisez les pronoms **y** et **en** dans votre dialogue. Answers will vary.

MODÈLE

Étudiant(e) 1: *J'ai de la fièvre, n'est-ce pas?*
Étudiant(e) 2: *Mais non, tu n'en as pas!*
Étudiant(e) 1: *J'ai besoin d'un médicament!*
Étudiant(e) 2: *Mais non, tu n'en as pas besoin!*

6 **La famille Valmont** Votre professeur va vous donner, à vous et à votre partenaire, une feuille d'informations sur la famille Valmont. Attention! Ne regardez pas la feuille de votre partenaire. Answers will vary.

MODÈLE

Étudiant(e) 1: *David jouait au baseball.*
Étudiant(e) 2: *Voilà pourquoi il s'est cassé le bras!*

ressources
WB pp. 135–138 | LM pp. 79–80 | espaces.vhlcentral.com

Instructional Resources
espaces.vhlcentral.com:
IRM (Info Gap Activities);
Testing Program, pp. 77–80;
Test Files; Testing Program MP3s; activities; downloads; reference tools
Test Generator

1 Suggestions
- Before assigning this activity, ask for a volunteer pair to complete the **modèle** for the class.
- When the activity is over, have another pair communicate their whole conversation to the class.

2 Suggestions
- To help students get started, have two volunteers act out a **modèle.** Example: **Étudiant(e) 1: Vas-tu souvent chez le médecin? Étudiant(e) 2: Non, heureusement, je n'y vais pas souvent.**
- Provide students with a word bank including expressions like these: **aller chez le docteur/dentiste, avoir des allergies, avoir un rhume, se casser/se fouler le/la/les +** (*body part*)**, faire du sport, faire un régime, fumer, prendre des médicaments**, etc.

3 Expansion To practice more verb forms and review indirect discourse, have pairs tell each other about a minor accident they had. Tell them to say who helped them and what they said to one other.

4 Expansion Have volunteers act out their conversation for the class using props such as empty toiletry bottles and empty medication boxes.

5 Suggestions
- Before assigning this activity, ask some questions. Examples: **Êtes-vous hypocondriaque? Connaissez-vous quelqu'un qui a une maladie «imaginaire»? Que lui dites-vous?**
- Call on two students to act out the **modèle**.

6 Suggestion Divide the class into pairs and distribute the Info Gap Handouts found on the Supersite for this activity. Give students ten minutes to complete the activity.

OPTIONS

Game Divide the class into groups of three. Have each member tell about the strangest, funniest, worst, or most exciting thing that he or she has ever done. Require students to use the **passé composé** with as many reflexive verbs as possible and the pronouns **y** and **en** wherever appropriate to avoid redundancy. Point out that they should also use the **imparfait**. Example: **Quand j'avais seize ans, je suis allé(e) au Mexique. Un jour, quand je me suis réveillé(e), je ne me sentais pas très bien. J'avais mal et j'avais besoin de médicaments, mais je ne savais pas où en trouver...** The group then chooses one account to write down. Read each group's description aloud. Give the class two minutes to question the group to find out whose experience was described. A group that guesses correctly wins a point; a group that fools the class wins two points.

À l'écoute

communication STANDARDS NATIONAL

S Audio: Activities

STRATÉGIE

Listening for specific information

You can listen for specific information effectively once you identify the subject of a conversation. You can also use your background knowledge to predict what kinds of information you might hear.

To practice this strategy, you will listen to a commercial for a flu relief medication. Before you listen, use what you already know about the flu and commercials for medications to predict the content of the commercial. Then, listen and jot down specific information the commercial provides. Compare these details to the predictions you first made.

Préparation

Regardez la photo et décrivez les deux personnes. Comment est l'homme? Est-il sportif, d'après vous? A-t-il l'air en forme? Pensez-vous qu'il a des problèmes de santé? Quels problèmes? Et la femme, comment est-elle? A-t-elle l'air en forme? De quoi parlent-ils?

À vous d'écouter

Écoutez la conversation et indiquez chaque problème que Dimitri mentionne.

1. Il est déprimé. ___X___
2. Il fume trop. ______
3. Il ne fait pas assez d'exercice. ___X___
4. Il a des douleurs à la gorge. ______
5. Il a beaucoup d'allergies. ______
6. Il a mal au dos. ___X___
7. Il ne mange pas sainement. ___X___
8. Il a de la fièvre. ______

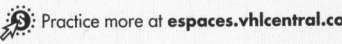

Practice more at **espaces.vhlcentral.com.**

Compréhension

Les conseils de Nadine Écoutez la conversation une deuxième fois. Pour chaque catégorie, donnez un des conseils (*pieces of advice*) de Nadine. Answers will vary. Possible answers provided.

1. Nutrition
   manger plus sainement; manger des fruits, des légumes et du poisson; éviter les régimes
2. Exercice
   faire du sport (de l'exercice); faire de la natation
3. Mode de vie (*Lifestyle*)
   prendre le temps de se reposer; s'amuser un peu tous les jours

Avez-vous deviné? Relisez vos notes de la Préparation. Avez-vous deviné le sujet de la conversation entre Dimitri et Nadine? Comparez avec un(e) camarade.

Un questionnaire Vous travaillez au centre médical de votre université. Il va y avoir beaucoup d'étudiants francophones ce semestre et ils doivent tous passer une visite médicale. Le directeur du centre vous a demandé de créer un questionnaire en français sur la santé et le mode de vie. Par groupes de trois ou quatre, préparez ce questionnaire (10 questions minimum) et soyez prêts à le présenter à la classe. Voici quelques thèmes à considérer:

- les maladies
- les problèmes de santé récents
- la nutrition
- l'exercice
- les régimes
- le stress et les problèmes personnels
- le repos

Section Goals

In this section, students will:
- learn to listen for specific information
- listen to a commercial and jot down information
- listen to a conversation and complete several activities

Instructional Resources
espaces.vhlcentral.com: IRM (Textbook Audioscript); Textbook MP3s; downloads; reference tools

Stratégie
Script Vous ne vous sentez pas bien? Vous avez mal à la tête et au dos? Tout votre corps vous fait mal? Vous éternuez et vous toussez? Vous vous sentez faible et vous n'êtes pas en forme? Vous avez probablement la grippe. Alors, n'attendez pas! Dépêchez-vous d'acheter le médicament homéopathique Grippum. Avec Grippum, la santé est retrouvée en quelques jours! Grippum, en vente chez votre pharmacien.

À vous d'écouter
Script NADINE: Tiens... Dimitri? Dimitri Klein?
DIMITRI: Euh... oui?
N: C'est moi, Nadine Girardot, du cours de littérature de Madame Larose. Tu ne te souviens pas de moi?
D: Ah si, bien sûr! Excuse-moi. Je ne me sens pas très bien, aujourd'hui.
N: Oui, tu as l'air fatigué... Qu'est-ce qui ne va pas?
D: Ben, je ne sais pas trop. Je ne suis pas très en forme depuis deux mois.
N: Ah bon? Et tu es allé chez le médecin?
D: Oui, mais il dit que je ne suis pas malade. Il pense que je suis un peu déprimé parce que je m'ennuie à l'université. Et comme je ne me repose pas beaucoup, il pense aussi que je suis fatigué.
N: C'est très important de se reposer. Tu dois prendre le temps de te reposer et de t'amuser un peu tous les jours.
D: Il dit aussi que je dois manger plus sainement et faire de l'exercice.
N: C'est vrai, tu sais. On est beaucoup plus en forme quand on mange bien et quand on fait du sport.
D: Oui, je sais... Je pense commencer un régime.
N: Ah non! Ce n'est pas une bonne idée. Les régimes sont mauvais pour la santé. Manger sainement, c'est simplement manger plus de fruits, de légumes et de poisson. Tu vas voir, si tu manges sainement, tu vas retrouver la ligne sans problème. Et tu ne fais pas de sport?
D: Non, j'ai souvent des douleurs dans le dos, alors le sport...
N: Fais de la natation! C'est excellent pour le dos.
D: Oui, bonne idée... Mais toi, tu as l'air d'être en forme, dis donc!
N: Oui, j'ai une forme super en ce moment. J'ai arrêté de fumer, je mange bien et je fais de l'exercice trois fois par semaine. Je me sens vraiment très bien!
D: Eh bien, bravo!

Section Goals

In this section, students will read historical and cultural information about Switzerland.

Instructional Resources
espaces.vhlcentral.com: Transparency #47; WB/VM/LM Answer Key; activities; downloads; reference tools

Carte de la Suisse

- Have students look at the map or use **Transparency #47**. Ask volunteers to read aloud the names of cities and geographical features. Model the pronunciation as necessary. Explain that about two-thirds of the country is mountainous.
- Point out the francophone region and have students name the cities that are French-speaking.
- Have students name the countries that border Switzerland.

Le pays en chiffres

- Point out the flag of Switzerland. Then ask students to share any information they know about the country.
- Have volunteers read the sections. After each section, ask students questions about the content.
- Tell students the percentage of the population that speaks each language: Swiss German 64%, French 20%, Italian 6.5%, Romansh 0.5%, and others 9.0%. SOURCE: **Office fédéral de la statistique**.
- Explain that many products in Switzerland have information written in French, German, Italian, and even English.

Incroyable mais vrai! The Swiss play a major role in humanitarian peacekeeping efforts.

NATIONAL STANDARDS connections cultures

Interactive Map Reading

Panorama

La Suisse

Le pays en chiffres

- **Superficie:** *41.285 km²*
- **Population:** *7.594.000*
  SOURCE: Population Division, UN Secretariat
- **Industries principales:** *activités financières° (banques, assurances), agroalimentaire°, élevage bovin°, horlogerie°, métallurgie, tourisme*
- **Villes principales:** *Bâle, Berne, Genève, Lausanne, Zurich*
- **Langues:** *allemand, français, italien, romanche*
  L'allemand, le français et l'italien sont les langues officielles, parlées dans les différentes régions du pays. Le romanche, langue d'origine latine, est parlée dans l'est° du pays. Langue nationale depuis 1938, elle n'est pas utilisée au niveau° fédéral. Aujourd'hui en Suisse, l'italien et le romanche sont moins parlés que d'autres langues étrangères.
- **Monnaie:** *le franc suisse*

Suisses célèbres

- **Johanna Spyri**, *auteur de «Heidi» (1827–1901)*
- **Louis Chevrolet**, *coureur automobile°, fondateur de la société Chevrolet (1878–1941)*

- **Alberto Giacometti**, *sculpteur (1901–1966)*

- **Charles-Édouard Jeanneret Le Corbusier**, *architecte (1887–1965)*
- **Jean-Luc Godard**, *cinéaste (1930–)*
- **Martina Hingis**, *joueuse de tennis (1980–)*

financières *financial* **agroalimentaire** *food processing* **élevage bovin** *livestock farming* **horlogerie** *watch and clock making* **est** *east* **niveau** *level* **coureur automobile** *racecar driver* **barques** *small boats* **guerres** *wars* **Battue** *Defeated* **paix** *peace treaty* **statut** *status* **ne... ni** *neither... nor* **OTAN** *NATO*

le château de Chillon sur le lac Léman

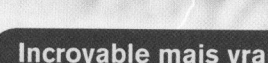

des barques° sur le lac de Saint-Moritz

Incroyable mais vrai!

La Suisse n'a pas connu de guerres° depuis le 16e siècle! Battue° par la France en 1515, elle signe une paix° perpétuelle avec ce pays et inaugure donc sa période de neutralité. Ce statut° est reconnu par les autres pays européens en 1815 et, depuis, la Suisse ne peut participer à aucune guerre ni° être membre d'alliances militaires comme l'OTAN°.

OPTIONS

Suisses célèbres **Johanna Spyri** began her writing career in order to help refugees of the Franco-Prussian War. **Louis Chevrolet** designed the first Chevrolet automobile sold in 1911. General Motors bought the Chevrolet Motor Company in 1918. **Alberto Giacometti**, a painter as well as a sculptor, was best known for his very thin, metal sculptures. Internationally renowned, **Le Corbusier**'s works and ideas had a profound influence on the development of modern architecture and the field of city planning. **Martina Hingis** won five Grand Slam single titles. At age 16, she became the youngest winner of a Grand Slam tournament in the 20th century. **Jean-Luc Godard** was born in Paris, but grew up on the Swiss side of Lake Geneva. He is known for his independent vision and his unconventional, often controversial, films.

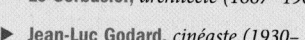

L'économie

Des montres et des banques

L'économie suisse se caractérise par la présence de grandes entreprises° multinationales et par son secteur financier. Les multinationales sont particulièrement actives dans le domaine des banques, des assurances, de l'agroalimentaire (Nestlé), de l'industrie pharmaceutique et de l'horlogerie (Longines, Rolex, Swatch). 50% de la production mondiale° d'articles° d'horlogerie viennent de Suisse. Le franc suisse est une des monnaies les plus stables du monde et les banques suisses ont la réputation de bien gérer° les fortunes de leurs clients.

Les gens

Jean-Jacques Rousseau (1712–1778)

Né à Genève, Jean-Jacques Rousseau a passé sa vie entre la France et la Suisse. Vagabond et autodidacte°, Rousseau est devenu écrivain, philosophe, théoricien politique et musicien. Il a comme principe° que l'homme naît bon et que c'est la société qui le corrompt°. Défenseur de la tolérance religieuse et de la liberté de pensée, les principes de Rousseau, exprimés° principalement dans son œuvre° *Du contrat social*, se retrouvent° dans la Révolution française. À la fin de sa vie, il écrit *Les Confessions*, son autobiographie, un genre nouveau pour l'époque°.

Les traditions

Le couteau suisse

En 1884, Carl Elsener, coutelier° suisse, se rend compte que les soldats° suisses portent des couteaux allemands. Il décide donc de fonder sa propre compagnie en Suisse et invente le «couteau du soldat» à quatre outils°. Depuis 1891, chaque soldat de l'armée suisse en a un. En 1897, Elsener développe le «couteau d'officier°» pour l'armée et aujourd'hui, il est vendu au grand public. Le célèbre couteau, orné de la croix° suisse sur fond° rouge, offre un choix de 90 accessoires.

Les destinations

Genève

La ville de Genève, à la frontière° franco-suisse, est une ville internationale et francophone. C'est une belle ville verte, avec sa rade° sur le lac Léman et son célèbre jet d'eau°. Son horloge fleurie°, ses promenades, ses magasins divers et ses nombreux chocolatiers font de Genève une ville très appréciée des touristes. C'est ici qu'on trouve aussi de nombreuses grandes entreprises internationales et organisations internationales et non gouvernementales, l'ONU°, la Croix- Rouge° et l'OMS° Pour cette raison, 45% de la population de Genève est d'origine étrangère.

Qu'est-ce que vous avez appris? Répondez aux questions par des phrases complètes.

1. Quelles sont les langues officielles de la Suisse?
   L'allemand, le français et l'italien sont les langues officielles de la Suisse.
2. Quand la Suisse a-t-elle commencé sa période de neutralité?
   La Suisse a commencé sa période de neutralité en 1515.
3. Que signifie la neutralité pour la Suisse?
   Elle ne participe pas aux guerres et elle ne peut pas être membre d'alliances militaires.
4. Quels sont deux secteurs importants de l'économie suisse?
   Answers will vary.
5. Quel est le principe fondamental de Rousseau?
   L'homme naît bon, mais c'est la société qui le corrompt.
6. Quel événement les idées de Rousseau ont-elles influencé?
   La Révolution française a été influencée par les idées de Rousseau.
7. À quoi servait le couteau suisse à l'origine?
   C'était un couteau porté par les soldats de l'armée suisse.
8. Pourquoi Carl Elsener a-t-il inventé le couteau suisse?
   Il a inventé le couteau suisse parce que les soldats suisses portaient des couteaux allemands.
9. Où se trouve la ville de Genève en Suisse?
   Genève se trouve à la frontière franco-suisse.
10. Quel pourcentage de la population de Genève est d'origine étrangère?
    45% de sa population est d'origine étrangère.

Practice more at **espaces.vhlcentral.com.**

ressources
WB pp. 139–140 | espaces.vhlcentral.com

SUR INTERNET

Go to **espaces.vhlcentral.com** to find more cultural information related to this **PANORAMA**.

1. Cherchez plus d'informations sur Ella Maillart. Qu'a-t-elle fait de remarquable?
2. Cherchez plus d'informations sur les œuvres de Rousseau. Quelles autres œuvres a-t-il écrites?
3. La Suisse est membre des Nations Unies. Depuis quand en est-elle membre? Quel est son statut (status) dans l'Union européenne?

entreprises *companies* **mondiale** *worldwide* **articles** *products* **gérer** *manage* **autodidacte** *self-taught* **comme principe** *as a principle* **corrompt** *corrupts* **exprimés** *expressed* **œuvre** *work* **se retrouvent** *are found* **époque** *time* **coutelier** *knife maker* **soldats** *soldiers* **outils** *tools* **officier** *officer* **orné de la croix** *adorned with the cross* **fond** *background* **frontière** *border* **rade** *harbor* **jet d'eau** *fountain* **horloge fleurie** *flower clock* **ONU (Organisation des Nations unies)** *U.N.* **Croix-Rouge** *Red Cross* **OMS (Organisation mondiale de la santé)** *W.H.O. (World Health Organization)*

Des montres et des banques

- Located in Zurich, Crédit Suisse and UBS AG are Switzerland's largest international banks. Swiss banks are known for their discretion, confidentiality, and secrecy. Clients are protected through the use of numbered accounts, and only a few top managers actually know who owns a particular account.
- Have students look at the photo and describe what they see. Then ask: **Combien d'étudiants portent une Swatch? Pourquoi ces montres sont-elles populaires? Connaissez-vous quelqu'un qui a une Rolex?**
- Ask students to name some Nestlé products. **Citez quelques produits Nestlé (le chocolat, la nourriture pour bébés, etc.)**

Jean-Jacques Rousseau
People's views of society, family values, and political and ethical thinking were directly affected by Rousseau's writings. Through his involvement with the **Philosophes** and Diderot's ***Encyclopédie***, Rousseau influenced society's taste in music, arguing for freedom of expression rather than strict adherence to rules and traditions.

Le couteau suisse

- Victorinox makes 100 models of Swiss Army knives and sells approximately 7 million of them each year. More than 90% of the knives are exported.
- Have students look at the photo and identify the implements on the Swiss Army knife. Then ask: **Avez-vous un couteau suisse?**

Genève Known as the "City of Peace", Geneva is considered an ideal neutral site for major diplomatic negotiations. Approximately 190 international organizations are located in Geneva.

OPTIONS

Game Create categories for the information on Switzerland. Examples: **Géographie, Suisses célèbres, Langues,** and **Industries/Produits**. For each category, make cards with a question on one side. Tape the cards to the board under the proper category with the question face down. Divide the class into two teams, and have them take turns picking a card and answering the question. Teams win a point per correct reply.

Les montres suisses Watches, clocks, and alarm clocks manufactured in Switzerland must carry the designation "Swiss made" or "Swiss." A lot of technical expertise goes into fitting very complex mechanisms into small casings. A typical luxury watch usually has over 300 parts. The most complex, luxury watch in the world is probably Calibre 89 by Patek Philippe, which contains 1728 parts.

Section Goals

In this section, students will:
- learn to use background knowledge when reading
- read a magazine article on combating fatigue

Stratégie Explain to students that they will find it easier to understand the content of a text by reviewing previous knowledge about the topic before they begin reading.

Examinez le texte Students should mention that the text is a magazine article written by Dr. Émilie Parmentier and published in France.

Questions personnelles
- Point out to students that by answering these **Questions personnelles** they are activating their background knowledge about health habits and fatigue. This will help them to understand the magazine article.
- Have students discuss their answers to the questions in pairs or small groups.

Lecture

Ⓢ Reading

NATIONAL communication cultures STANDARDS

Avant la lecture

STRATÉGIE

Activating background knowledge

Using what you already know about a particular subject will often help you better understand a reading selection. For example, if you read an article about a recent medical discovery, you might think about what you already know about health in order to understand unfamiliar words or concepts.

Examinez le texte

Regardez le document. Analysez le titre de la lecture. Quel est le mot-clé de ce titre? Quel est le sens (*meaning*) du titre? Quel va être le sujet du texte? Faites une liste de vos idées et comparez-les avec les idées d'un(e) camarade. Puis, avec votre partenaire, faites aussi une liste de ce que vous savez déjà sur ce sujet. Essayez de répondre aux questions.

- Quel type de texte est-ce?
- Où pensez-vous que ce texte a été publié?
- Qui a écrit ce texte?
- Quelle est la profession de l'auteur?

Questions personnelles

Répondez aux questions par des phrases complètes.

1. Vous sentez-vous parfois fatigué(e) pendant la journée? Quand? Pourquoi?
2. Êtes-vous souvent fatigué(e) quand vous avez beaucoup de devoirs ou d'examens? Et quand vous faites beaucoup de sport?
3. Dormez-vous bien, en général? Vous couchez-vous tôt ou tard? Et le matin, à quelle heure vous levez-vous, en général?
4. Prenez-vous le temps de vous détendre dans la journée? Que faites-vous pour vous détendre?
5. Mangez-vous sainement? Qu'aimez-vous manger?
6. Faites-vous du sport ou d'autres activités physiques? Lesquel(le)s (*Which ones*)?

Non à la fatigue!

Par le docteur Émilie Parmentier

Selon un sondage° récent, plus de 50% des Français se sentent souvent fatigués. Que faire pour être moins fatigué? Voici les dix conseils° du docteur Émilie Parmentier.

1 Mangez sainement et évitez les régimes

Vous pouvez garder la ligne et la forme si vous évitez les régimes et choisissez les fruits, les légumes et le poisson au lieu de° la viande et des féculents°. Le matin, prenez le temps de vous préparer un bon petit-déjeuner, mais le soir, mangez léger°.

2 Dormez bien

Chaque personne est différente. Certaines ont besoin de 6 heures de sommeil° par nuit, d'autres de 10 heures. Respectez vos besoins et essayez de dormir assez, mais pas trop.

3 Essayez de respecter des horaires réguliers

Avoir des horaires réguliers°, c'est bon pour la forme. Levez-vous à la même heure chaque jour, si possible, puis le soir, essayez aussi de vous coucher toujours à la même heure.

4 Prenez le temps de vous détendre avant de vous coucher

Le soir avant de vous coucher, prenez quelques minutes pour vous détendre et oublier vos préoccupations et vos problèmes. Essayez la méditation ou le yoga.

5 Ne vous dépêchez pas tout le temps

Il est très important d'avoir des moments de calme tous les jours et de ne pas toujours se dépêcher. Promenez-vous dans un parc, asseyez-vous et reposez-vous quelques minutes.

OPTIONS

Small Groups Have students work in groups of three or four. Tell them to create a list of possible reasons why more than 50% of French people often feel tired. Example: **Ils travaillent beaucoup**. Then have them get together with another group and compare their lists. Record the most popular reasons on the board.

Pairs Have students work in pairs. Tell them to go through the article and find all the sentences that contain reflexive verbs. Mention that students should watch for reflexive verbs appearing in the infinitive. Example: **... prenez le temps de *vous préparer*...** Then have them point out which verbs are literally reflexive versus those with an idiomatic sense.

6 **Amusez-vous et détendez-vous avec les personnes que vous aimez**

Passez des moments en famille ou avec des amis et des personnes avec qui vous vous entendez bien. Parlez de sujets agréables, riez et amusez-vous!

7 **Faites du sport ou d'autres activités physiques**

Si on fait trop de sport, on peut être fatigué, mais quand on ne pratique pas assez d'activités physiques, on se sent fatigué aussi. Donc, pour bien vous porter, pratiquez des activités physiques plusieurs fois par semaine. Mais attention! Les activités sportives sont à éviter tard le soir parce qu'elles peuvent causer des troubles du sommeil.

8 **Évitez les discussions importantes le soir**

Il n'est pas bon de s'énerver, de se mettre en colère ou de s'inquiéter avant de se coucher parce que cela rend le sommeil difficile. Le soir, évitez donc les grandes discussions (entre époux, entre colocataires, entre petits amis, sur vos problèmes dans les études).

9 **Attention au tabac°, au café et à l'alcool**

Limitez votre consommation° de café et d'alcool. Et si vous fumez, essayez d'arrêter. Demandez à votre médecin de vous donner une ordonnance pour des médicaments qui peuvent vous aider à arrêter.

10 **Faites des petites siestes**

Parfois, quand vous êtes fatigué, même° une sieste° de vingt minutes peut vous aider à continuer la journée. Alors, quand vous avez juste° quelques minutes de libres, pensez à faire une petite sieste.

Enfin, si vous vous sentez très faible, voire° mal pendant une période de plus de deux semaines, allez voir le médecin. Consultez un médecin si vous tombez malade très souvent ou si vous vous sentez déprimé.

Selon un sondage *According to a survey* **conseils** *pieces of advice* **au lieu de** *instead of* **féculents** *starches* **léger** *light* **sommeil** *sleep* **horaires réguliers** *set schedules* **tabac** *tobacco* **consommation** *consumption* **même** *even* **sieste** *nap* **juste** *just* **voire** *or even*

Après la lecture

Complétez **Complétez les phrases.**

1. Pour être en bonne santé, il est nécessaire de manger sainement.
2. L'alcool et le tabac ne sont pas bons pour la santé. On ne doit donc pas beaucoup boire et on doit arrêter de fumer.
3. Il est bon de faire du yoga ou de la méditation pour se détendre.
4. Il est préférable d'éviter les discussions importantes ou graves le soir.
5. On doit prendre le temps de s'amuser et de se détendre avec ses amis.
6. Si on se sent vraiment très fatigué ou si on est déprimé, c'est toujours une bonne idée d' aller consulter un médecin.
7. Il est bon de toujours se lever et se coucher à la même heure.
8. Pour être en forme, pratiquez des activités physiques plusieurs fois par semaine.

Vrai ou faux? **Indiquez si les phrases sont vraies ou fausses. Corrigez les phrases fausses.**

1. C'est une infirmière qui donne ces conseils.
   Faux. Émilie Parmentier est médecin.
2. Les Français ne sont pas souvent fatigués.
   Faux. Plus de 50% des Français sont souvent fatigués.
3. D'après le docteur Parmentier, il est important de faire un régime pour garder la ligne.
   Faux. Il est important d'éviter les régimes et de manger des fruits, des légumes et du poisson.
4. C'est le soir qu'on doit manger le plus.
   Faux. Le soir, on doit manger léger.
5. Quand on dort trop, on peut se sentir fatigué.
   Vrai.
6. Il est bon de se lever et de se coucher à la même heure tous les jours.
   Vrai.
7. On doit se reposer au calme tous les jours.
   Vrai.
8. Il est recommandé de faire du sport le soir avant de se coucher. Faux. Il est recommandé d'éviter les activités sportives tard le soir parce qu'elles peuvent causer des troubles du sommeil.

Votre opinion compte **Que pensez-vous des conseils du docteur Parmentier? A-t-elle raison ou tort, d'après vous? Avec un(e) camarade, choisissez deux de ses conseils et donnez votre opinion sur chacun (*each one*). Quels conseils allez-vous donner à votre camarade?**

Complétez Go over the answers with the class. Call on volunteers to read the completed sentences aloud.

Vrai ou faux?
- Have students work in pairs. Tell them to take turns reading the statements aloud and deciding whether they are true or false. They should also locate the correct answer to the false items in the text.
- Have students write two more true/false items. Then ask volunteers to read their sentences aloud and have the class respond.

Votre opinion compte After completing the activity, take a quick class survey to find out which pieces of advice students agreed with and which ones they thought were wrong.

OPTIONS

Extra Practice Have students write an additional piece of advice on staying healthy and fighting fatigue. Remind them to use the imperative. Then ask volunteers to read their piece of advice to the class. The class should decide if the advice is valid or not.

Small Groups Have students write the numbers from the reading that correspond to the suggestions that they already follow and the numbers of the suggestions they would like to try. Then have students form groups of four and compare their answers.

Section Goals
In this section, students will:
- learn to sequence events in a narration
- write a letter

Stratégie Discuss the importance of having an introduction (**introduction**), body (**corps**), and a conclusion (**conclusion**). Then read through the list of adverbs with the class. Point out that these words can be used to indicate a sequence of events or activities.

Thème Tell students they should answer the questions before they begin to write their letters.

Proofreading Activity To practice editing skills, have the class correct these sentences. **1. Je finis de se brosser mes dents! 2. Il s'a couchée tard hier soir. 3. On n'est pas fait de l'exercise hier. 4. Je dois me rase et m'habille. 5. Ne te met pas en colére. 6. Lisez le journal si tu t'ennuyes.**

Écriture

NATIONAL STANDARDS communication cultures

STRATÉGIE

Sequencing events

Paying attention to sequencing in a narrative will ensure that your writing flows logically from one part to the next. Of course, every composition should have an introduction, a body, and a conclusion.

The introduction presents the subject, the setting, the situation, and the people involved. The main part, or the body, describes the events and people's reactions to these events. The conclusion brings the narrative to a close.

Adverbs and adverbial phrases are often used as transitions between the introduction, the body, and the conclusion. Here is a list of commonly used adverbs in French.

Adverbes

(tout) d'abord	*first*
premièrement / en premier	*first*
avant (de)	*before*
après	*after*
alors	*then, at that time*
(et) puis	*(and) then*
ensuite	*then*
plus tard	*later*
bientôt	*soon*
enfin	*finally*
finalement	*finally*

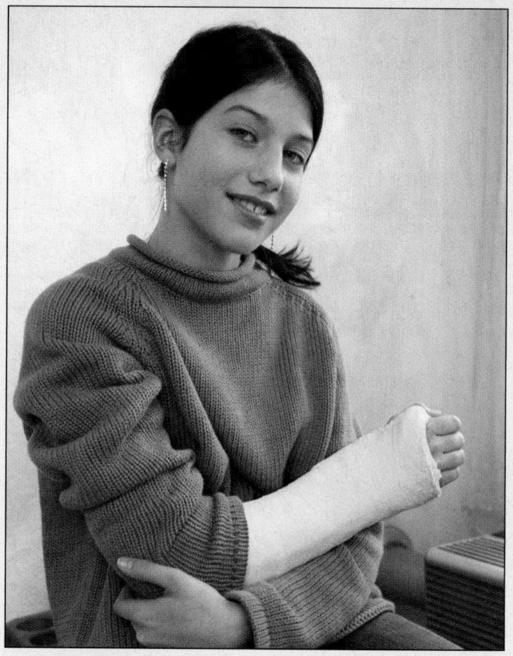

Thème

Écrire une lettre

Avant l'écriture

1. Vous avez été malade le jour du dernier examen de français et vous n'avez pas pu passer l'examen. Vous allez préparer une lettre destinée à votre professeur de français pour lui expliquer ce qui s'est passé. Pour vous y aider, répondez d'abord aux questions:
   - Que s'est-il passé? (maladie, accident, autre problème de santé, etc.)
   - Quels étaient les symptômes ou quelle blessure avez-vous eue? (avoir mal au ventre, avoir de la fièvre, avoir une jambe cassée, etc.)
   - Qu'est-ce qui a peut-être causé ce problème? (accident, pas assez d'exercice physique, ne pas manger sainement, etc.)
   - Qu'avez-vous fait? (prendre des médicaments, aller chez le docteur ou le dentiste, aller aux urgences, etc.)
   - Qu'est-ce qu'on vous a fait là-bas? (une piqûre, une radio [*X-ray*], une ordonnance, etc.)
   - Comment vous sentez-vous maintenant et qu'allez-vous faire pour rester en forme? (ne plus fumer, faire plus attention, faire de l'exercice, etc.)

OPTIONS

Avant l'écriture Working in groups of three, have students practice the adverbs **(tout) d'abord, alors, (et) puis, ensuite, plus tard,** and **enfin** by telling a past-tense story. The first student begins by creating a sentence that starts with **(tout) d'abord**. The second student follows with a sentence that begins with **alors**. The story continues this way until all the adverbs have been used and each student has created two sentences.

Help students turn the list of tasks into an outline for their letter. Then show them how it corresponds to the eight parts of the sequence chart.
Salutation / Paragraph 1: Introduction / Paragraphs 2-7: the six bulleted items / Paragraph 8: Conclusion / Closing and signature

2. Maintenant, vous allez compléter ce schéma d'idées avec vos réponses. Il va vous servir à placer les informations dans l'ordre. Chaque cadre (*box*) représente une information. Ajoutez-y (*Add*) une introduction et une conclusion. Utilisez des verbes réfléchis.

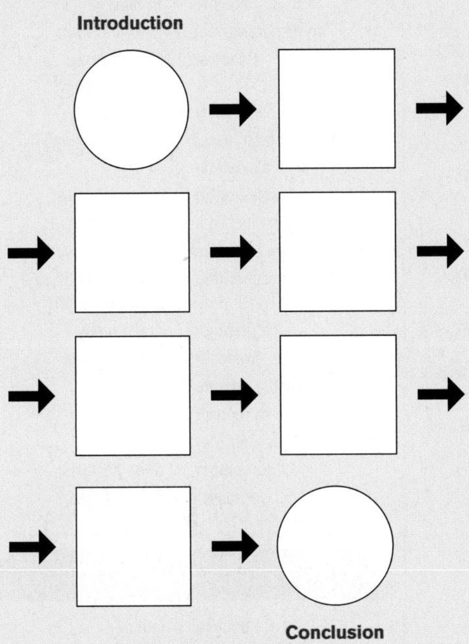

3. Regardez à nouveau (*again*) le schéma d'idées. Quels adverbes pouvez-vous y ajouter pour lier (*link*) les informations? Écrivez-les au-dessus de (*above*) chaque cadre.

Écriture

Utilisez le schéma d'idées pour écrire votre lettre au passé (passé composé et imparfait). Elle doit inclure (*include*) une introduction, une partie centrale (le corps), une conclusion et les adverbes que vous avez écrits au-dessus des cadres. À la fin (*end*) de la lettre, excusez-vous et demandez à votre professeur si (*if*) vous pouvez passer l'examen la semaine prochaine. (Attention! Cette partie de la lettre doit être au présent.)

Après l'écriture

1. Échangez votre lettre avec celle (*the one*) d'un(e) partenaire. Répondez à ces questions pour commenter son travail.

- Votre partenaire a-t-il/elle écrit une introduction et une conclusion?
- Votre partenaire a-t-il/elle écrit une partie centrale présentant (*presenting*) les raisons de son absence?
- Votre partenaire a-t-il/elle inclu les adverbes?
- Votre partenaire s'est-il/elle excusé(e) et a-t-il/elle demandé de repasser (*retake*) l'examen?
- Votre partenaire a-t-il/elle correctement utilisé les verbes réfléchis?
- Quel(s) détail(s) ajouteriez-vous (*would you add*)? Quel(s) détail(s) enlèveriez-vous (*would you delete*)? Quel(s) autre(s) commentaire(s) avez-vous pour votre partenaire?

2. Corrigez votre lettre d'après (*according to*) les commentaires de votre partenaire. Relisez votre travail pour éliminer ces problèmes:

- des fautes (*errors*) d'orthographe
- des fautes de ponctuation
- des fautes de conjugaison
- un mauvais emploi (*use*) du passé
- un mauvais emploi de la grammaire de l'unité
- des fautes d'accord (*agreement*) des adjectifs

EVALUATION

Criteria

Content Contains descriptions of each of the bulleted points of the task, as well as an appropriate introduction and conclusion.
Scale: 1 2 3 4 5

Organization Organized into an eight-paragraph letter with a salutation, an introduction, six descriptive paragraphs, a conclusion, a closing, and a signature.
Scale: 1 2 3 4 5

Accuracy Uses forms of **passé composé**, **imparfait**, and reflexive verbs correctly. Spells words, conjugates verbs, and modifies adjectives correctly throughout.
Scale: 1 2 3 4 5

Creativity Includes additional information that is not included in the task and/or uses adjectives, descriptive verbs, and additional details to make the letter more interesting and persuasive.
Scale: 1 2 3 4 5

Scoring

Excellent	18–20 points
Good	14–17 points
Satisfactory	10–13 points
Unsatisfactory	< 10 points

OPTIONS

Avant l'écriture Before students begin writing, have them jot down a word that relates to each bulleted item in the task inside the sequence diagram. (For example: **problème, symptômes, raison**, etc.) Then, next to each key word, have students indicate the tenses they are likely to use when describing it. (For example: **problème – passé composé** for accidents, **imparfait** for illnesses, and so on.)

Écriture Give students some formal salutations, introductions, and closings they can use in the letter to their instructor.
Salutations: **Monsieur/Madame le Professeur...**
Introductions: **Je vous prie de bien vouloir me faire savoir..., Je vous saurais gré de bien vouloir...**
Closings: **Je vous adresse mes sincères salutations..., Recevez mes cordiales salutations...**

Instructional Resources
espaces.vhlcentral.com: Textbook MP3s; IRM (Textbook Audioscript); downloads; reference tools

Suggestion Tell students that an easy way to study from **Vocabulaire** is to cover up the French half of each section, leaving only the English equivalents exposed. They can then quiz themselves on the French items. To focus on the English equivalents of the French entries, they simply reverse this process.

Flashcards
Audio: Vocabulary

VOCABULAIRE

La routine

faire sa toilette	*to wash up*
se brosser les cheveux	*to brush one's hair*
se brosser les dents	*to brush one's teeth*
se coiffer	*to do one's hair*
se coucher	*to go to bed*
se déshabiller	*to undress*
s'endormir	*to go to sleep, to fall asleep*
s'habiller	*to get dressed*
se laver (les mains)	*to wash oneself (one's hands)*
se lever	*to get up, to get out of bed*
se maquiller	*to put on makeup*
prendre une douche	*to take a shower*
se raser	*to shave oneself*
se regarder	*to look at oneself*
se réveiller	*to wake up*
se sécher	*to dry oneself*

Dans la salle de bains

un réveil	*alarm clock*
une brosse (à cheveux, à dents)	*brush (hairbrush, toothbrush)*
la crème à raser	*shaving cream*
le dentifrice	*toothpaste*
le maquillage	*makeup*
une pantoufle	*slipper*
un peigne	*comb*
un rasoir	*razor*
le savon	*soap*
une serviette (de bain)	*(bath) towel*
le shampooing	*shampoo*

La forme

être en pleine forme	*to be in good shape*
faire de l'exercice	*to exercise*
garder la ligne	*to stay slim*

Expressions utiles	*See pp. 331 and 345.*
The pronouns y and en	*See pp. 350–351.*

La santé

aller aux urgences/ à la pharmacie	*to go to the emergency room/ to the pharmacy*
avoir mal	*to have an ache*
avoir mal au cœur	*to feel nauseous*
enfler	*to swell*
éternuer	*to sneeze*
être en bonne santé	*to be in good health*
être en mauvaise santé	*to be in bad health*
éviter de	*to avoid*
faire mal	*to hurt*
faire une piqûre	*to give a shot*
fumer	*to smoke*
guérir	*to get better*
se blesser	*to hurt oneself*
se casser (la jambe/ le bras)	*to break one's (leg/ arm)*
se faire mal (à la jambe, au bras...)	*to hurt one's (leg, arm...)*
se fouler la cheville	*to twist/sprain one's ankle*
se porter mal/mieux	*to be ill/better*
se sentir	*to feel*
tomber/être malade	*to get/to be sick*
tousser	*to cough*
une allergie	*allergy*
une blessure	*injury, wound*
une douleur	*pain*
une fièvre (avoir de la fièvre)	*(to have) a fever*
la grippe	*flu*
un rhume	*cold*
un symptôme	*symptom*
une aspirine	*aspirin*
un médicament (contre/pour)	*medication (to prevent/for)*
une ordonnance	*prescription*
une pilule	*pill*
les urgences	*emergency room*
déprimé(e)	*depressed*
enceinte	*pregnant*
grave	*serious*
sain(e)	*healthy*
un(e) dentiste	*dentist*
un infirmier/ une infirmière	*nurse*
un(e) patient(e)	*patient*
un(e) pharmacien(ne)	*pharmacist*

Verbes pronominaux

s'amuser	*to play, to have fun*
s'appeler	*to be called*
s'arrêter	*to stop*
s'asseoir	*to sit down*
se dépêcher	*to hurry*
se détendre	*to relax*
se disputer (avec)	*to argue (with)*
s'énerver	*to get worked up, to become upset*
s'ennuyer	*to get bored*
s'entendre bien (avec)	*to get along well (with)*
s'inquiéter	*to worry*
s'intéresser (à)	*to be interested (in)*
se mettre à	*to begin to*
se mettre en colère	*to become angry*
s'occuper (de)	*to take care of, to keep oneself busy*
se préparer	*to get ready*
se promener	*to take a walk*
se rendre compte	*to realize*
se reposer	*to rest*
se souvenir (de)	*to remember*
se tromper	*to be mistaken*
se trouver	*to be located*

Le corps

la bouche	*mouth*
un bras	*arm*
le cœur	*heart*
le corps	*body*
le cou	*neck*
un doigt	*finger*
un doigt de pied	*toe*
le dos	*back*
un genou (genoux *pl.*)	*knee (knees)*
la gorge	*throat*
une jambe	*leg*
une joue	*cheek*
le nez	*nose*
un œil (yeux *pl.*)	*eye (eyes)*
une oreille	*ear*
un orteil	*toe*
la peau	*skin*
un pied	*foot*
la poitrine	*chest*
la taille	*waist*
la tête	*head*
le ventre	*stomach*
le visage	*face*

ressources
espaces.vhlcentral.com

La technologie

UNITÉ 11

Pour commencer

- David et Amina font...
  a. les courses. b. la cuisine.
  c. de l'ordinateur.
- Quel est l'objet présent sur la photo?
  a. un savon b. une télévision c. un ordinateur
- Que font-ils?
  a. Ils surfent sur Internet.
  b. Ils font du sport. c. Ils font la fête.

Unit Goals

Leçon 11A

In this lesson, students will learn:
- terms for electronics products
- Internet terms
- the pronunciation of final consonants
- about technology in France and the Ariane rocket
- the use of prepositions with infinitives
- reciprocal reflexives
- about **NRJ Mobile**

Leçon 11B

In this lesson, students will learn:
- terms for cars and driving
- terms for car maintenance and repair
- the pronunciation of the letter **x**
- about cars and driving in France and the car manufacturer Citroën
- more about city streets and driving in France through specially shot video footage
- the verbs **ouvrir** and **offrir**
- the conditional
- to guess the meaning of words from context in spoken French

Savoir-faire

In this section, students will learn:
- cultural and historical information about Belgium
- to recognize the purpose of a text
- to make a list of key words

Pour commencer

- **c. de l'ordinateur.**
- **c. un ordinateur.**
- **a. Ils surfent sur Internet.**

RESOURCES

Workbook/Video Manual: WB Activities, pp. 141–154
Laboratory Manual: Lab Activities, pp. 81–88
Workbook/Video Manual: Video Activities, pp. 251–254; pp. 291–292
WB/VM/LM Answer Key

espaces.vhlcentral.com: Instructor's Resource Manual [IRM] (Textbook Audioscript; Lab Audioscript; Videoscript; **Roman-photo** Translations; **Vocabulaire supplémentaire**; **Feuilles d'activités**; Info Gap Activities; **Le zapping** TV clip transcription; **Essayez!** and **Mise en pratique** answers);

Transparencies #48, #49, #50; Testing Program, pp. 81–88; Test Files; Testing Program MP3s; Lab MP3s; Textbook MP3s
Test Generator
Video on DVD

Section Goals

In this section, students will learn and practice vocabulary related to:

- electronics products
- the Internet

Instructional Resources
*espaces.vhlcentral.com: Transparency #48; IRM (**Vocabulaire supplémentaire**; **Mise en pratique** answers; Textbook Audioscript; Lab Audioscript; Info Gap Activities); Textbook MP3s; Lab MP3s; WB/VM/LM Answer Key; activities; downloads; reference tools*

Suggestions

- Have students look over the vocabulary. Point out that many words related to electronics and the Internet are cognates. You might also introduce **MP3**, **iPod**, and **blog**.
- Use **Transparency #48.** Point out objects and describe what the people are doing. Examples: **C'est une imprimante. Il a un portable.**
- Ask students questions about electronics and the Internet using the new vocabulary. Examples: **Jouez-vous à des jeux vidéo? Avez-vous un baladeur CD? Un répondeur téléphonique? Un lecteur DVD? Une caméra vidéo? Aimez-vous surfer sur Internet? Quel est votre site web préféré?**
- Tell students that the official French term for *e-mail* is **la messagerie électronique**, but most people say **l'e-mail. Le courriel** is used in Canada.
- Explain that **CD** and **compact-disc** are borrowed from English, so neither changes in the plural (**un CD, des CD**). Since **cédérom** is French, the plural is marked (**des cédéroms**). The British trademark **compact-disc** is often used instead of **disque compact**.
- Point out that **marcher** is used more than **fonctionner** in everyday language.
- Additional vocabulary for this lesson can be found in the **Vocabulaire supplémentaire** on the Supersite.

Leçon 11A

You will learn how to...

- talk about communication
- talk about electronics

Talking Picture
Audio: Activity

Le son et l'image

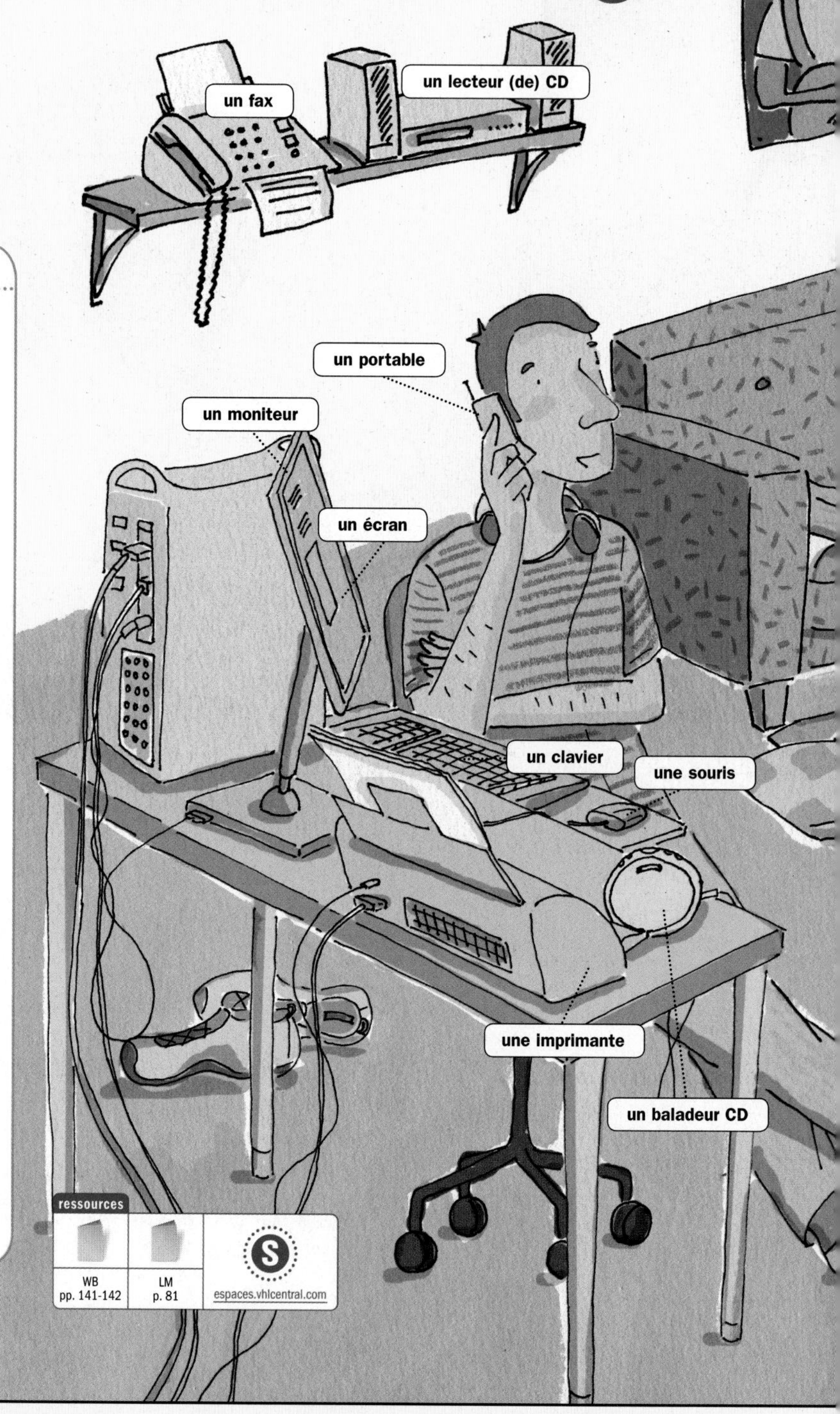

Vocabulaire

allumer	*to turn on*
composer (un numéro)	*to dial (a number)*
démarrer	*to start up*
effacer	*to erase*
enregistrer	*to record*
éteindre	*to turn off; to shut off*
être connecté(e) (avec)	*to be online (with)*
être en ligne (avec)	*to be online/on the phone (with)*
fermer	*to close; to shut off*
fonctionner/marcher	*to function, to work*
graver	*to record, to burn (a CD)*
imprimer	*to print*
sauvegarder	*to save*
surfer sur Internet	*to surf the Internet*
télécharger	*to download*
un CD-ROM/un cédérom (CD-ROM/cédéroms *pl.*)	*CD-ROM(s)*
un e-mail	*e-mail*
un fichier	*file*
un jeu vidéo (jeux vidéo *pl.*)	*video game(s)*
un logiciel	*software, program*
un mot de passe	*password*
une page d'accueil	*homepage*
un site Internet/web	*website*
un appareil photo (numérique)	*(digital) camera*
une caméra vidéo/un caméscope	*camcorder*
une chaîne (de télévision)	*(television) channel*
une chaîne stéréo	*stereo system*
un disque dur	*hard drive*
un lecteur (de) DVD	*DVD player*
un magnétophone	*tape recorder*

ressources
WB pp. 141-142 | LM p. 81 | espaces.vhlcentral.com

OPTIONS

Extra Practice Have students make a list of six electronic devices they have or use frequently. Then tell them to circulate around the room asking others if they have or use the same items. If someone answers affirmatively, the student should ask the person to sign his or her name next to the item. Students should try to get a different signature for each item.

Game Write vocabulary words for electronic equipment on index cards. On another set of cards, draw or paste pictures to match each term. Tape them face down on the board in random order. Divide the class into two teams. Play a game of Concentration in which students match words with pictures. When a player makes a match, that player's team collects those cards. The team with the most cards at the end of the game wins.

Attention!

- The prefix **re-** in French is used much as it is in English. It expresses the idea of doing an action again.

to dial	**composer**
to redial	**recomposer**
to start	**démarrer**
to restart	**redémarrer**

- The conjugation of **éteindre** is irregular:

j'éteins	**nous éteignons**
tu éteins	**vous éteignez**
il/elle éteint	**ils/elles éteignent**

Mise en pratique

1 Chassez l'intrus **Choisissez le mot ou l'expression qui ne va pas avec les autres.**

1. une arobase, une page d'accueil, un site web, (un fax)
2. sonner, (démarrer), un portable, un répondeur
3. une souris, un clavier, un moniteur, (une chaîne stéréo)
4. un baladeur, (un jeu vidéo), une chaîne stéréo, un CD
5. un fichier, sauvegarder, (une télécommande), effacer
6. un site web, être en ligne, télécharger, (composer)

2 Association **Faites correspondre les activités de la colonne de gauche aux objects correspondants de la colonne de droite.**

1. enregistrer une émission e	a. une télécommande
2. faire un film c	b. un appareil photo
3. parler avec un ami à tout moment f	c. une caméra vidéo
4. laisser un message téléphonique d	d. un répondeur
5. écrire un e-mail h	e. un magnétoscope
6. écouter des CD g	f. un portable
7. changer de chaîne a	g. un baladeur
8. prendre des photos b	h. un clavier

3 Écoutez **Écoutez la conversation entre Jérôme et l'employée d'un cybercafé. Ensuite, complétez les phrases suivantes.**

1. Jérôme a pris des photos avec...
   a. une cassette vidéo.
   b. un répondeur téléphonique.
   (c.) un appareil photo.
2. Jérôme voudrait (*would like*)...
   (a.) imprimer et envoyer ses photos.
   b. sauvegarder ses photos sur son disque dur.
   c. effacer ses photos.
3. Jérôme n'a pas... pour regarder ses photos.
   a. de télécommande adaptée
   (b.) de logiciel adapté
   c. de mot de passe adapté
4. Jérôme peut sélectionner les photos...
   (a.) par un clic de la souris.
   b. avec une arobase.
   c. avec le clavier.
5. L'employée propose à Jérôme...
   a. de faire fonctionner le logiciel.
   (b.) de graver un CD.
   c. d'utiliser une imprimante noir et blanc.
6. Pour envoyer les photos, Jérôme doit...
   a. utiliser un fax.
   b. utiliser un écran.
   (c.) les attacher à un e-mail.

Coup de main

Here are some useful terms to help you read e-mail addresses in French.

at sign (@)	**arobase (*f.*)**
dash	**tiret (*m.*)**
dot	**point (*m.*)**
underscore	**tiret bas (*m.*)**

Practice more at **espaces.vhlcentral.com.**

1 Expansion Have students create two more items using words or expressions from the new vocabulary. Collect their papers, write some of the items on the board, and have the class identify **l'intrus**.

2 Expansion Ask students what electronic devices are used to perform these actions. **1. imprimer un document (une imprimante) 2. composer un numéro (un téléphone/ un portable) 3. regarder un film (un magnétoscope/une télévision/ un lecteur de DVD) 4. écouter de la musique (une chaîne stéréo/ une radio/un ordinateur/un baladeur CD/un lecteur de CD)**

3 Tapescript JÉRÔME: Bonjour, Mademoiselle. J'ai besoin de votre aide, s'il vous plaît.
L'EMPLOYÉE: Oui, bien sûr, Monsieur.
J: Voilà. J'ai pris des photos avec mon appareil numérique, mais je n'ai pas de logiciel adapté pour les regarder. Je veux les imprimer et aussi les envoyer par e-mail.
E: Pour imprimer, vous n'avez qu'à utiliser cette imprimante couleur, mais d'abord, il faut télécharger vos photos. Ensuite, vous pouvez les sélectionner par un simple clic de la souris. Vous pouvez aussi les sauvegarder et les graver sur CD.
J: Parfait. Et pour les envoyer par e-mail?
E: Pour envoyer les photos, passer à votre compte d'e-mail. Attachez les photos à l'e-mail, et envoyez-le normalement.
J: C'est finalement simple.
E: Oui, c'est très simple. Avez-vous d'autres questions, Monsieur?
J: Non, c'était le seul problème que j'avais. Je vous remercie beaucoup.
E: De rien. Au revoir, Monsieur.
(On Textbook MP3s)

3 Suggestion Play the conversation again, stopping at the end of each sentence that contains the answer to one of the items so students can check their work.

OPTIONS

Les adresses Internet Most Internet addresses in the United States end in the codes **.com, .org, .gov**, or **.edu**. Write the following codes on the board and have students guess which French-speaking country they refer to. **1. .fr (France) 2. .be (Belgique) 3. .ch (Suisse) 4. .ca (Canada) 5. .ci (Côte d'Ivoire) 6. .ma (Maroc) 7. .sn (Sénégal) 8. .pf (Polynésie française) 9. .mc (Monaco) 10. .lu (Luxembourg) 11. .qc.ca (Québec)**

Game Divide the class into two teams. Give one player a card with the name of an electronic device or technology product. That player is allowed 30 seconds to draw the item for another player on his or her team to guess. Award a point for a correct guess. If a player doesn't guess the correct answer, the next player on the opposing team may "steal" the point.

4 Suggestion Point out that some of the items in column C require verbs to make complete sentences. Tell students to write down their questions.

5 Suggestions
- Tell students that crossword terms can be found **horizontalement** and **verticalement**.
- Have two volunteers read the **modèle** aloud. Then divide the class into pairs and distribute the Info Gap Handouts found on the Supersite for this activity. Give students ten minutes to complete the activity.

6 Suggestion Encourage students to include drawings, clip art, or magazine photos in their brochures. You may wish to assign this activity as homework.

7 Suggestion Before beginning this activity, brainstorm famous people from the past with whom it might be interesting to have such a discussion. Examples: Benjamin Franklin, Thomas Edison, and Alexander Graham Bell.

Communication

4 Qui fait quoi? Avec un(e) partenaire, formez des questions à partir de ces listes d'expressions. Ensuite, à tour de rôle, posez vos questions à votre partenaire afin d'en (*in order to*) savoir plus sur ses habitudes par rapport à la technologie. Answers will vary.

MODÈLE

Étudiant(e) 1: *À qui envoies-tu des e-mails?*
Étudiant(e) 2: *J'envoie des e-mails à mes professeurs pour les devoirs et à mes amis.*

A	B	C
à qui	être en ligne	toi
combien de	télécharger	tes parents
comment	un e-mail	tes grands-parents
où	un disque compact	ton professeur de français
pour qui	un site web	ta sœur
pourquoi	graver	tes amis
quand	un appareil photo numérique	les autres étudiants
quel(le)(s)	un jeu vidéo	les enfants

5 Mots croisés Votre professeur va vous donner, à vous et à votre partenaire, deux grilles de mots croisés (*crossword puzzle*) incomplètes. Votre partenaire a les mots qui vous manquent, et vice versa. Donnez-lui une définition et des exemples pour compléter la grille. Attention! N'utilisez pas le mot recherché.

MODÈLE

Étudiant(e) 1: *Horizontalement (Across), le numéro 1, c'est ce que (what) tu fais pour mettre ton fichier Internet sur ton disque dur.*
Étudiant(e) 2: *Télécharger!*

6 Le cybercafé Le patron d'un cybercafé souhaite (*wishes*) avoir plus de clients et vous demande de créer une brochure. Avec un(e) partenaire, présentez les différents services offerts et tous les avantages de ce cybercafé. Utilisez les mots et expressions d'**ESPACE CONTEXTES**. Incluez ces informations: Answers will vary.

- nom, adresse et horaires du cybercafé
- nombre et type d'appareils (*devices*) électroniques
- description des services
- liste des prix par type de service

7 La technologie d'hier et d'aujourd'hui Avec un(e) partenaire, imaginez une conversation avec une personne célèbre du passé. Vous parlez de l'évolution de la technologie et, bien sûr, cette personne est choquée de voir (*see*) les appareils électroniques du 21e siècle (*century*). Utilisez les mots et expressions d'**ESPACE CONTEXTES**. Answers will vary.

- Choisissez trois ou quatre appareils différents.
- Demandez/Donnez une définition pour chaque objet.
- Demandez/Expliquez comment utiliser chaque appareil.
- Demandez quels sont les points positifs et négatifs de chaque appareil, et expliquez-les.

OPTIONS

Pairs Have students work in pairs. Tell them to role-play a situation between a person who is computer savvy and someone who wants to learn how to use a computer and surf the Internet. If possible, have students use their laptops during the role-play to demonstrate how a computer works.

Extra Practice Stage a debate about the role of technology in today's world. Propose this question: **La technologie est-elle bonne ou mauvaise pour la société?** Divide the class into two groups, assigning each side a position. Allow groups time to plan their arguments before staging the debate. You may also divide the class into four groups and have two debates going on at the same time.

Les sons et les lettres

Audio: Concepts, Activities
Record & Compare

NATIONAL STANDARDS comparisons

Final consonants

You already learned that final consonants are usually silent, except for the letters **c**, **r**, **f**, and **l**.

avec **hiver** **chef** **hôtel**

You've probably noticed other exceptions to this rule. Often, such exceptions are words borrowed from other languages. These final consonants are pronounced.

Latin	*English*	*Inuit*	*Latin*
forum	**snob**	**anorak**	**gaz**

Numbers, geographical directions, and proper names are common exceptions.

cinq **sud** **Agnès** **Maghreb**

Some words with identical spellings are pronounced differently to distinguish between meanings or parts of speech.

fils = *son* — **fils** (silent s) = *threads*
tous (pronoun) = *everyone* — **tous** (silent s) (adjective) = *all*

The word plus can have three different pronunciations.

plus de (silent *s*) **plus que** (*s* sound) **plus ou moins** (*z* sound in liaison)

Prononcez Répétez les mots suivants à voix haute.

1. cap
2. six
3. truc
4. club
5. slip
6. actif
7. strict
8. avril
9. index
10. Alfred
11. bifteck
12. bus

Articulez Répétez les phrases suivantes à voix haute.

1. Leur fils est gentil, mais il est très snob.
2. Au restaurant, nous avons tous pris du bifteck.
3. Le sept août, David assiste au forum sur le Maghreb.
4. Alex et Ludovic jouent au tennis dans un club de sport.
5. Prosper prend le bus pour aller à l'est de la ville.

Dictons Répétez les dictons à voix haute.

[1] The more you drink, the thirstier you are.
[2] All for one and one for all!

ressources
LM p. 82
espaces.vhlcentral.com

Section Goals

In this section, students will learn about final consonants.

Instructional Resources
espaces.vhlcentral.com: Textbook MP3s; Lab MP3s; WB/VM/LM Answer Key; IRM (Textbook Audioscript; Lab Audioscript); activities; downloads; reference tools

Suggestions

- Model the pronunciation of the examples and have students repeat them after you.
- Explain that some words with pronounced final consonants are actually abbreviated forms of longer words. Examples: **gym (*f.*)** = **gymnastique (*f.*)** and **petit-déj** = **petit-déjeuner**.
- Mention that many exceptions must be memorized.
- Dictate five familiar words containing pronounced and silent final consonants, repeating each one at least two times. Then write them on the board or a transparency and have students check their spelling.

Dictons The proverb **«Plus on boit, plus on a soif.»** is a quote from Arthur Schopenhauer. The full quote is **«La richesse est pareille à l'eau de mer: plus on en boit, plus on a soif.»** The proverb **«Un pour tous, tous pour un!»** is the motto of Switzerland.

OPTIONS

Extra Practice For additional practice with silent and pronounced final consonants, have students write sentences on individual index cards using the words below. Then collect the cards and distribute some of them (at least one for each word) for students to read aloud. **1. porc 2. concept 3. œufs 4. bol 5. appareil 6. truc 7. premier 8. four 9. hôtel 10. gentil**

Extra Practice Teach students the following French tongue-twisters that contain silent and pronounced final consonants. **1. Des blancs pains, des bancs peints, des bains pleins. 2. Lily lit le livre dans le lit. 3. Si ton bec aime mon bec comme mon bec aime ton bec, donne-moi le plus gros bec de la Province de Québec!**

Section Goals
In this section, students will learn functional phrases for talking about communication and technology.

Instructional Resources
espaces.vhlcentral.com: WB/VM/LM Answer Key; IRM (Videoscript; ***Roman-photo*** *Translations); activities; downloads; reference tools*
Video on DVD

Video Recap: Leçon 10B
Before doing this **Roman-photo**, review the previous one with this activity.
1. Que faisait Rachid quand il s'est blessé? (Il jouait au foot.) 2. Qu'est-ce qui est arrivé? (Il est tombé et il s'est foulé la cheville.) 3. Que lui a dit le médecin? (Elle lui a dit de mettre de la glace, de se reposer, de prendre des médicaments contre la douleur et de ne pas jouer au football pendant une semaine). 4. Pourquoi David avait-il de la crème sur le visage? (Il a eu une réaction allergique.)

Video Synopsis
Rachid is annoyed because David is playing several electronic devices. Rachid reminds him of a paper that is due in two days. Just as David finishes his paper, he has a computer problem and loses part of his work. He calls Amina for help, and she manages to retrieve his document. When Amina sees Rachid's computer screen, she realizes that he is Cyberhomme.

Suggestions
- Tell students to scan the captions for vocabulary related to electronics and technology.
- After reading the **Roman-photo**, have students summarize the episode.

C'est qui, Cyberhomme?

Video: *Roman-photo*
Record & Compare

PERSONNAGES

Amina

David

Rachid

Sandrine

Valérie

1

Chez David et Rachid...
RACHID Dis donc, David! Un peu de silence. Je n'arrive pas à travailler!
DAVID Qu'est-ce que tu dis?
RACHID Je dis que je ne peux pas me concentrer! La télé est allumée, tu ne la regardes même pas. Et en même temps, la chaîne stéréo fonctionne et tu ne l'écoutes pas!

2

DAVID Oh, désolé, Rachid.
RACHID Ah, on arrive enfin à s'entendre parler et à s'entendre réfléchir! À quoi est-ce que tu joues?
DAVID Un jeu vidéo génial!
RACHID Tu n'étudies pas? Tu n'avais pas une dissertation à faire? Lundi, c'est dans deux jours!
DAVID Okay. Je la commence.

3

Au café...
SANDRINE Tu as un autre e-mail de Cyberhomme? Qu'est-ce qu'il dit?
AMINA Oh, il est super gentil, écoute: «Chère Technofemme, je ne sais pas comment te dire combien j'adore lire tes messages. On s'entend si bien et on a beaucoup de choses en commun. J'ai l'impression que toi et moi, on peut tout se dire.»

6

Chez David et Rachid...
DAVID Et voilà! J'ai fini ma dissert, Rachid.
RACHID Bravo!
DAVID Maintenant, je l'imprime.
RACHID N'oublie pas de la sauvegarder.
DAVID Oh, non!
RACHID Tu n'as pas sauvegardé?

7

DAVID Si, mais... Attends... le logiciel redémarre. Ce n'est pas vrai! Il a effacé les quatre derniers paragraphes! Oh non!
RACHID Téléphone à Amina. C'est une pro de l'informatique. Peut-être qu'elle peut retrouver la dernière version de ton fichier.
DAVID Au secours, Amina! J'ai besoin de tes talents.

8

Un peu plus tard...
AMINA Ça y est, David. Voilà ta dissertation.
DAVID Tu me sauves la vie!
AMINA Ce n'était pas grand-chose, mais tu sais, David, il faut sauvegarder au moins toutes les cinq minutes pour ne pas avoir de problème.
DAVID Oui. C'est idiot de ma part.

ACTIVITÉS

1 Vrai ou faux? **Indiquez si ces affirmations sont vraies ou fausses. Corrigez les phrases fausses.** Answers may vary.

1. Rachid est en train d'écrire (*in the process of writing*) une dissertation pour son cours de sciences po. Faux. Rachid est en train d'écrire à Technofemme.
2. David ne fait pas ses devoirs immédiatement; il a tendance à remettre les choses à plus tard. Vrai.
3. David aime les jeux vidéo. Vrai.
4. David regarde la télévision avec beaucoup d'attention. Faux. David ne regarde pas la télévision.
5. Rachid n'aime pas les distractions. Vrai.
6. Valérie s'inquiète de la sécurité d'Amina. Vrai.
7. David sauvegarde ses documents toutes les cinq minutes. Faux. David ne sauvegarde pas toujours ses documents.
8. David pense qu'il a perdu la totalité de son document. Faux. David pense qu'il a perdu les quatre derniers paragraphes.
9. Amina sait beaucoup de choses sur la technologie. Vrai.
10. Amina et Cyberhomme décident de se rencontrer. Faux. Amina ne veut pas rencontrer Cyberhomme.

Practice more at **espaces.vhlcentral.com.**

OPTIONS

Avant de regarder la vidéo Tell students to read the title and scene setter. Then have them guess who Cyberhomme is. They should support their ideas with details from previous episodes. Write their guesses on the board.

Regarder la vidéo Show the video episode once without sound and have the class create a plot summary based on the visual cues. Then show the episode with sound and have the class make corrections and fill in any gaps in the plot summary.

Amina découvre l'identité de son ami virtuel.

4

5

SANDRINE Il est adorable, ton Cyberhomme! Continue! Est-ce qu'il veut te rencontrer en personne?
VALÉRIE Qui vas-tu rencontrer, Amina? Qui est ce Cyberhomme?
SANDRINE Amina l'a connu sur Internet. Ils s'écrivent depuis longtemps, n'est-ce pas, Amina?

AMINA Oui, mais comme je te l'ai déjà dit, je ne sais pas si c'est une bonne idée de se rencontrer en personne. S'écrire des e-mails, c'est une chose; se donner rendez-vous, ça peut être dangereux.
VALÉRIE Amina a raison, Sandrine. On ne sait jamais.
SANDRINE Mais il est si charmant et tellement romantique...

9

10

RACHID Merci, Amina. Tu me sauves la vie aussi. Peut-être que maintenant, je vais pouvoir me concentrer.
AMINA Ah? Et tu travailles sur quoi? Ce n'est pas possible!... C'est toi, Cyberhomme?!

RACHID Et toi, tu es Technofemme?!
DAVID Évidemment, tu me l'as dit toi-même: Amina est une pro de l'informatique.

Expressions utiles

Expressing how you communicate with others

- **On arrive enfin à s'entendre parler!**
  Finally we can hear each other speak!
- **On s'entend si bien.**
  We get along so well.
- **On peut tout se dire.**
  We can tell each other anything.
- **Ils s'écrivent depuis longtemps.**
  They've been writing to each other for quite a while.
- **S'écrire des e-mails, c'est une chose; se donner rendez-vous, ça peut être dangereux.**
  Writing e-mails to each other, it's one thing; arranging to meet could be dangerous.

Additional vocabulary

- **se rencontrer**
  to meet each other
- **On ne sait jamais.**
  You/One never know(s).
- **Au secours!**
  Help!
- **C'est idiot de ma part.**
  It's stupid of me.
- **une dissertation**
  paper
- **pas grand-chose**
  not much

ACTIVITÉS

2 Questions Répondez aux questions par des phrases complètes.

1. Pourquoi Rachid se met-il en colère?
   Il se met en colère parce qu'il ne peut pas se concentrer.
2. Pourquoi y a-t-il beaucoup de bruit (*noise*) chez Rachid et David?
   Il y a beaucoup de bruit parce que la chaîne stéréo et la télévision sont allumées.
3. Est-ce qu'Amina s'entend bien avec Cyberhomme?
   Oui, elle s'entend bien avec Cyberhomme.
4. Que pense Valérie de la possibilité d'un rendez-vous avec Cyberhomme?
   Elle pense que ça peut être dangereux.
5. Qu'est-ce que Rachid fait pendant que David joue au jeu vidéo et écrit sa dissertation?
   Il écrit des e-mails à Amina/Technofemme.

3 À vous Pour ce qui est des (*With respect to*) études, David et Rachid sont très différents. David aime les distractions et Rachid a besoin de silence pour travailler. Avec un(e) camarade de classe, décrivez vos habitudes en ce qui concerne (*concerning*) les études. Avez-vous les mêmes? Pouvez-vous être de bon(ne)s colocataires? Présentez vos conclusions à la classe.

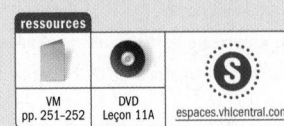

ressources

VM	DVD	
pp. 251-252	Leçon 11A	espaces.vhlcentral.com

Expressions utiles

- Model the pronunciation of the **Expressions utiles** and have students repeat them after you.
- As you work through the list, point out reciprocal verbs and prepositions used with infinitives. Explain the difference between **entendre** and **s'entendre**. Tell students that these grammar points will be formally presented in **Espace structures**.
- Respond briefly to questions about reciprocal verbs and prepositions with infinitives. Reinforce correct forms, but do not expect students to produce them consistently at this time.
- Ask students what **arriver** means. (*to arrive, to happen*) Then point out that **arriver à** + *infinitive* means *to be able to* or *to manage to do something*. Example: **Je n'arrive pas à travailler.**
- Explain that **une dissertation** is a *paper*, such as an essay, not a *dissertation*. The abbreviated form is **dissert**.

1 Suggestion Have students correct the false statements.

2 Suggestion Have students compare their answers in pairs or small groups.

2 Expansion For additional practice, give students these items. **6. David éteint la télé et la chaîne stéréo, puis que se met-il à faire? (Il se met à jouer à un jeu vidéo.) 7. Qu'est-ce que Cyberhomme et Technofemme ont en commun? (Ils aiment la technologie.) 8. Selon Sandrine, comment est Cyberhomme? (Il est adorable, charmant et romantique.)**

3 Suggestion Before beginning this activity, give students a few minutes to think about their study habits and jot down some ideas.

OPTIONS

Small Groups Working in groups of three, have students role-play this situation. One student is an irate customer in a cybercafé who is annoyed by something the customer seated nearby is doing, for example, playing music too loudly or making noises while playing a game. Another student is the customer who defends his or her own actions. The third student is an employee who tries to resolve the situation.

Pairs Have students work in pairs and discuss these questions. **1. Pourquoi Amina n'a-t-elle pas l'intention d'avoir un rendez-vous avec Cyberhomme? 2. Sandrine pense que Cyberhomme est romantique et elle encourage Amina à fixer un rendez-vous avec lui. Qui a raison, Amina ou Sandrine? Pourquoi?**

Section Goals

In this section, students will:

- learn about technology in France
- learn some common Internet terms
- learn about some online francophone radio stations
- read about the Ariane rocket

Instructional Resources
espaces.vhlcentral.com: activities; downloads; reference tools

Culture à la loupe

Avant la lecture Have students look at the photos and describe what the people are doing.

Lecture

- Tell students to make a list of new Internet terms they encounter as they read the article. Examples: **la connexion par câble/ADSL, la connexion haut/bas débit, le graveur**, and **le scanner**.
- In 2008, France was ranked number 8 in the top 20 countries for Internet usage, with over 36 million users. Canada is number 12. (Source: www.marsouin.org)
- Point out the statistics chart. Ask students what information it shows. (the percentage of French households that have the electronics devices listed)

Après la lecture Ask students: **À votre avis, pourquoi est-ce que les cybercafés sont plus populaires en France qu'aux États-Unis?**

1 Suggestion Have students get together with a classmate to check their answers.

communication cultures — NATIONAL STANDARDS

CULTURE À LA LOUPE

La technologie et les Français

le Minitel

Depuis les années 1980, la technologie connaît une grande évolution. En France, cette révolution technologique a commencé par l'invention du Minitel au début des années 1980. Cette invention a été développée par France Télécom, la compagnie nationale française de téléphone, au début des années 1980. Le Minitel peut être considéré comme le prédécesseur d'Internet. C'est un petit terminal qu'on branche° sur sa ligne téléphonique et qui permet d'accéder à toutes sortes d'informations et de jeux, de faire des réservations de train ou d'hôtel, de commander des articles en ligne ou d'acheter des billets de concert, par exemple.

Aujourd'hui, Internet remplace le Minitel et de plus en plus de Français sont équipés chez eux d'un ordinateur et d'une connexion Internet. Les Français ont le choix entre la connexion par câble et la connexion ADSL°. Enfin, pour ceux° qui n'ont pas d'autre moyen de se connecter à Internet, il existe en France, beaucoup plus qu'aux États-Unis, de nombreux cybercafés.

En ce qui concerne les autres appareils électroniques à la mode, on note une augmentation des achats° de consoles de jeux vidéo, de lecteurs de CD/DVD, de caméras vidéo, de téléphones multifonctions, d'appareils photos numériques ou de produits périphériques° pour les ordinateurs, comme les imprimantes, les scanners ou les graveurs. Mais l'appareil qui a connu le plus grand succès en France, c'est sans doute le téléphone portable. En 1996, moins de 2,5 millions de Français avaient un téléphone portable. Aujourd'hui, plus de 86% des Français en possèdent un.

branche *connects* **Environ** *About* **bas débit** *low-speed* **haut débit** *high-speed* **ADSL** *DSL* **ceux** *those* **moyen** *mean* **achats** *purchases* **périphériques** *peripheral*

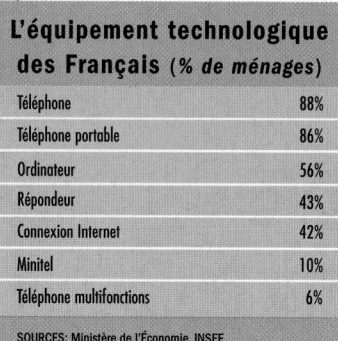

L'équipement technologique des Français (*% de ménages*)

Téléphone	88%
Téléphone portable	86%
Ordinateur	56%
Répondeur	43%
Connexion Internet	42%
Minitel	10%
Téléphone multifonctions	6%

SOURCES: Ministère de l'Économie, INSEE

Coup de main

When saying an e-mail address aloud, follow this example.

claude-monet@yahoo.fr

claude tiret monet arobase yahoo point F R

ACTIVITÉS

1 Répondez Répondez aux questions par des phrases complètes.

1. Quelle invention française est le prédécesseur d'Internet? C'est le Minitel.
2. Qu'est-ce que le Minitel? C'est un petit terminal qu'on branche sur sa ligne téléphonique et qui permet d'accéder à toutes sortes d'informations.
3. Quel est le nom de la compagnie nationale française de téléphone? C'est France Télécom.
4. Quels sont les deux choix de connexion Internet en France? Ce sont les connexions par câble et par ADSL.
5. Où peut-on aller si on n'a pas accès à Internet à la maison? On peut aller dans un cybercafé.
6. Quels sont deux des appareils électroniques qu'on achète souvent en France en ce moment? Answers will vary. Possible answer: Ce sont les lecteurs de CD/DVD et les consoles de jeux vidéo.
7. Quel appareil électronique a eu le plus de succès depuis 1996? C'est le téléphone portable.
8. Quel est le pourcentage de Français qui possèdent un ordinateur? 56% des Français possèdent un ordinateur.
9. Est-il courant (*common*) d'avoir Internet en France? Oui, 42% des Français ont Internet chez eux.
10. La majorité des Français ont-ils encore un Minitel? Non. Seulement 10% des Français ont encore un Minitel.

OPTIONS

Cultural Comparison Take a quick class survey to find out how many students have the electronic devices listed in the chart in their homes. Example: **Combien d'étudiants ont un téléphone à la maison?** Tally the results on the board and have students calculate the percentages. Then have students compare the results of this survey with the percentages in the chart. Example: **Plus d'Américains ont un ordinateur chez eux.**

LE FRANÇAIS QUOTIDIEN

Cyberespace

blog (*m.*)	*blog*
grimace (*f.*)	*frown*
message (*m.*) instantané	*instant message*
moteur (*m.*) de recherche	*search engine*
pseudo(nyme) (*m.*)	*screen name*
smiley (*m.*)	*smiley (face)*
chatter	*to chat*

LE MONDE FRANCOPHONE

Quelques stations de radio francophones

Voici quelques radios francophones en ligne.

En Afrique

Africa 1 radio africaine qui propose des actualités et beaucoup de musique africaine (www.africa1.com)

En Belgique

Classic 21 radio pour les jeunes qui passe° de la musique rock et propose des emplois° pour les étudiants (www.classic21.be)

En France

NRJ radio privée nationale pour les jeunes qui passe tous les grands tubes° (www.nrj.fr)

En Suisse

Fréquence Banane radio universitaire de Lausanne (www.frequencebanane.ch)

passe *plays* **emplois** *jobs* **tubes** *hits*

PORTRAIT

La fusée Ariane

Après la Seconde Guerre mondiale°, la conquête de l'espace° s'est amplifiée. En Europe, le premier programme spatial, le programme Europa, n'a pas eu beaucoup de succès et a été abandonné. En 1970, la France a proposé un nouveau programme spatial, le projet Ariane, qui a eu un succès considérable. La fusée° Ariane est un lanceur° civil de satellites européen. Elle est basée à Kourou, en Guyane française, département et région français d'outre-mer°, en Amérique du Sud. Elle transporte des satellites commerciaux vers° l'espace. La première fusée Ariane a été lancée en 1979 et il y a eu plusieurs générations de fusées Ariane depuis. Aujourd'hui, Ariane V (cinq), un lanceur beaucoup plus puissant° que ses prédécesseurs, est utilisée.

Guerre mondiale *World War* **espace** *space* **fusée** *rocket* **lanceur** *launcher* **outre-mer** *overseas* **vers** *towards* **puissant** *powerful*

SUR INTERNET

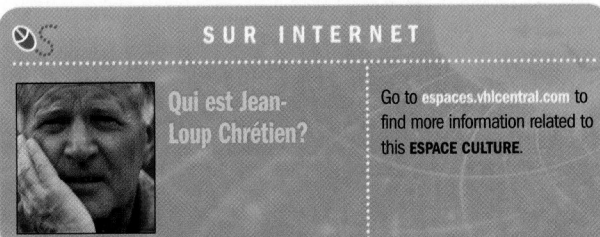

Qui est Jean-Loup Chrétien?

Go to **espaces.vhlcentral.com** to find more information related to this **ESPACE CULTURE**.

ACTIVITÉS

2 Complétez Complétez les phrases d'après les textes.

1. Quand on parle en ligne sur Internet, on chatte.
2. Pour faire une recherche sur Internet, on utilise un moteur de recherche.
3. En Suisse, beaucoup d'étudiants écoutent la radio Fréquence Banane.
4. Le premier programme spatial européen s'appelait Europa.
5. La fusée Ariane est le lanceur civil de satellites européen.

Practice more at **espaces.vhlcentral.com.**

3 À vous... Avec un(e) partenaire, écrivez six phrases où vous utilisez le vocabulaire du Français quotidien. Soyez prêts à les présenter devant la classe.

ressources

espaces.vhlcentral.com

OPTIONS

Quelques stations de radio francophones Have students write a brief critique of one of the radio stations in **Le monde francophone.** Assign each student a station so that all are covered. Tell them to go to the station's website, look at the features, and listen to the music. They should comment on what they like, dislike, or find interesting about the website.

Cultural Comparison Have students research and discuss the similarities and differences between **le projet Ariane** and NASA's Apollo Space Program (**le projet Apollo**), Skylab (**le projet Skylab**), and the space shuttle (**la navette spatiale**).

Le français quotidien

- Model the pronunciation of each term and have students repeat it.
- Ask students questions using these terms. Examples: **1. Écrivez-vous des messages instantanés? Si oui, à qui les écrivez-vous? 2. Quel moteur de recherche préférez-vous? 3. Quels sont les pseudonymes de Rachid et d'Amina dans la vidéo? (Cyberhomme et Technofemme) 4. Aimez-vous chatter en ligne? Avec qui chattez-vous?**

Portrait Point out that the space age began in 1957 with the launch of the satellite *Sputnik*. This touched off a "space race" between the United States and Russia, which culminated in the first man landing on the moon in 1969.

Le monde francophone

- You might want to tell students about **RFI (Radio France Internationale)** at **www.rfi.fr (*news*)**. **RFI** also has a music site at **www.rfimusique.com**.
- After reading the text, ask students what the Internet addresses are for various radio stations. Example: **Quelle est l'adresse Internet de Classic 21? (www.classic21.be)**
- Take a quick class survey to find out which radio station(s) they would be interested in listening to and have them explain why. Example: **Combien d'étudiants aimeraient** (*would like*) **écouter NRJ? Pourquoi?**

2 Expansion For additional practice, give students these items. **6. Pour une réponse immédiate, on peut envoyer ____. (un message instantané) 7. Pour protéger son identité quand on chatte, on peut employer ____. (un pseudonyme) 8. La première fusée Ariane a été lancée en ____. (1979)**

3 Suggestion Have each pair get together with another pair of students to peer edit each other's sentences.

Section Goals
In this section, students will learn verbs that require a preposition before the infinitive.

Instructional Resources
*espaces.vhlcentral.com: Lab MP3s; WB/VM/LM Answer Key; IRM (**Essayez!** and **Mise en pratique** answers; Lab Audioscript); activities; downloads; reference tools*

Suggestions
- Point out that students already know how to use verbs with infinitives by asking questions with **aller**, **pouvoir**, **savoir**, etc. Examples: **Allez-vous faire une promenade après la classe? Pouvons-nous refaire la leçon? Savez-vous danser?**
- Introduce prepositions with the infinitive by using both constructions (*verb + infinitive, verb + preposition + infinitive*) in the same sentence. Ask students what differences they hear. Example: **D'habitude, mon oncle déteste voyager à l'étranger, mais il a décidé d'aller à Paris cet été.**
- After presenting the use of **à** and **de** with the infinitive, write an infinitive on the board and ask volunteers to use it in a sentence with the appropriate preposition. Examples: **hésiter (J'hésite à inviter ton frère à la fête.) rêver (Il rêve d'acheter une nouvelle voiture.)**
- To contrast the use of **à** and **de** with pronouns, review the contractions these prepositions form with definite articles: **au, aux, des**. Point out that prepositions with infinitives and pronouns do not take this form. Example: **Ce film... j'hésite à le voir.**
- Point out that the preposition **pour** + [*infinitive*] can mean *in order to*. Example: **Ils sont allés à la bibliothèque pour étudier.** *(They went to the library [in order] to study.)*

11A.1 Prepositions with the infinitive

NATIONAL STANDARDS comparisons

Point de départ Infinitive constructions, where the first verb is conjugated and the second verb is an infinitive, are common in French.

CONJUGATED VERB	INFINITIVE
Vous **pouvez**	**fermer** le document.
You can	*close the document.*

- Some conjugated verbs are followed directly by an infinitive. Others are followed by the preposition **à** or **de** before the infinitive.

verbs followed directly by infinitive	verbs followed by à before infinitive	verbs followed by de before infinitive
adorer	aider à	arrêter de *to stop*
aimer	s'amuser à *to pass time by*	décider de *to decide to*
aller	apprendre à	éviter de
détester	arriver à *to manage to*	finir de
devoir	commencer à	s'occuper de *to take care of, to see to*
espérer	continuer à	oublier de
pouvoir	hésiter à *to hesitate to*	permettre de
préférer	se préparer à	refuser de *to refuse to*
savoir	réussir à	rêver de *to dream about*
vouloir		venir de *to have just*

Nous **allons manger** à midi.
We are going to eat at noon.

Elle **a appris à conduire** une voiture.
She learned to drive a car.

Il **rêve de visiter** l'Afrique.
He dreams about visiting Africa.

- Place object pronouns before infinitives. Unlike definite articles, they do not contract with the prepositions **à** and **de**.

J'**ai décidé de les télécharger**.
I decided to download them.

Il **est arrivé à le lui donner**.
He managed to give it to him.

- The infinitive is also used after the prepositions **pour** and **sans**.

Nous sommes venus **pour t'aider**.
We came to help you.

Elle part **sans manger**.
She's leaving without eating.

Essayez! Décidez s'il faut ou non une préposition. S'il en faut une, choisissez entre **à** et **de**.

1. Tu sais ___Ø___ cuisiner.
2. Commencez ___à___ travailler.
3. Tu veux ___Ø___ goûter la soupe?
4. Elles vont ___Ø___ revenir.
5. Je finis ___de___ mettre la table.
6. Il hésite ___à___ me poser la question.

MISE EN PRATIQUE

1 Les vacances Paul veut voyager cet été. Il vous raconte ses problèmes. Complétez le paragraphe avec les prépositions à ou de, si nécessaire.

Je n'arrive pas (1) ___à___ décider où passer mes vacances. Je veux (2) ___Ø___ visiter un pays chaud et ensoleillé (*sunny*). J'espère (3) ___Ø___ trouver des billets d'avion pour la Martinique. Cet après-midi, je me suis amusé (4) ___à___ regarder les prix des billets d'avion sur Internet. Je n'ai pas réussi (5) ___à___ trouver un bon tarif (*fare*). Je vais continuer (6) ___à___ chercher. J'hésite (7) ___à___ payer plein tarif, mais je refuse (8) ___de___ voyager en stand-by.

2 Questionnaire Vous cherchez un travail d'été. Complétez les phrases avec les prépositions à ou de, quand c'est nécessaire. Ensuite, indiquez si vous êtes d'accord avec ces affirmations.

oui	non	
___	___	1. Vous savez ___Ø___ parler plusieurs langues.
___	___	2. Vous acceptez ___de___ voyager souvent.
___	___	3. Vous n'hésitez pas ___à___ travailler tard.
___	___	4. Vous oubliez ___de___ répondre au téléphone.
___	___	5. Vous pouvez ___Ø___ travailler le week-end.
___	___	6. Vous commencez ___à___ travailler immédiatement.

3 Le week-end dernier Sophie et ses copains ont fait beaucoup de choses le week-end dernier. Regardez les illustrations et dites ce qu'ils (*what they*) ont fait.

Suggested answers

MODÈLE
J'ai décidé de conduire.

je / décider

1. nous / devoir
Nous avons dû nous réveiller tôt.

3. André / refuser
André a refusé de nager.

2. elles / apprendre
Elles ont appris à jouer au tennis.

4. vous / aider
Vous avez aidé à faire la cuisine.

Practice more at **espaces.vhlcentral.com.**

OPTIONS

Extra Practice Have students write five original sentences using verbs with prepositions and infinitives. Students should use as much active lesson vocabulary as possible. Then have students read their sentences aloud.

Game Divide the class into teams. Call out a verb from the list above. The first member of each team runs to the board and writes a sample sentence, using the verb, its corresponding preposition (if applicable), and an infinitive. If the sentence of the team finishing first is correct, the team gets a point. If not, check the next team, and so on. Practice all verbs from the chart, making sure each team member has had at least two turns. Then tally the points to see which team wins.

COMMUNICATION

4 Assemblez Avez-vous eu de bonnes ou de mauvaises expériences avec la technologie? À tour de rôle, avec un(e) partenaire, assemblez les éléments des colonnes pour créer des phrases logiques. Answers will vary.

MODÈLE

Étudiant(e) 1: *Je déteste télécharger des logiciels.*
Étudiant(e) 2: *Chez moi, ma mère n'arrive pas à envoyer des e-mails.*

A	B	C	D
ma mère		accepter	composer
mon père		aimer	effacer
mon frère		arriver	envoyer
ma sœur		décider	éteindre
mes copains		détester	être en ligne
mon petit ami	(ne pas)	hésiter	fermer
ma petite amie		oublier	graver
notre prof		refuser	ouvrir
nous		réussir	sauvegarder
?		?	télécharger

5 Les voyages Vous et votre partenaire parlez des vacances et de voyages. Utilisez ces éléments pour vous poser des questions. Justifiez vos réponses. Answers will vary.

MODÈLE aimer / faire des voyages

Étudiant(e) 1: *Aimes-tu faire des voyages?*
Étudiant(e) 2: *Oui, j'aime faire des voyages. J'aime faire la connaissance de beaucoup de personnes.*

1. rêver / aller en Asie
2. vouloir / visiter des musées
3. préférer / voyager avec un groupe ou seul(e)
4. commencer / lire des guides touristiques
5. réussir / trouver des vols bon marché
6. aimer / rencontrer des amis à l'étranger

6 Une pub Par groupes de trois, préparez une publicité pour École-dinateur, une école qui enseigne l'informatique aux technophobes. Utilisez le plus de verbes possible de la liste avec un infinitif. Answers will vary.

MODÈLE *Rêvez-vous d'écrire des e-mails? Continuez-vous à travailler comme vos grands-parents? Alors...*

aimer	continuer	refuser
s'amuser	détester	réussir
apprendre	hésiter	rêver
arriver	oublier	savoir

Le français vivant

Internet?
Football?
Musique en ligne?
DVD?
Vous avez toujours rêvé de posséder un ordinateur comme ça. Vous vouliez l'acheter, et vous venez de l'allumer. Maintenant, vous commencez à vous rendre compte de ses possibilités. N'hésitez pas à en profiter. En tout confort.

Identifiez Quels verbes trouvez-vous devant un infinitif dans le texte de cette publicité (*ad*)? Lesquels (*Which ones*) sont suivis (*are followed*) d'une préposition? Quelle préposition?
rêver de, vouloir, venir de, commencer à, hésiter à

Questions À tour de rôle avec un(e) partenaire, posez-vous ces questions. Answers will vary.

1. As-tu toujours rêvé de posséder quelque chose en particulier? De faire quelque chose en particulier? Explique.
2. Que veux-tu acheter en ce moment? Pourquoi?
3. D'habitude, qu'hésites-tu à faire?
4. La technologie peut-elle vraiment apporter le confort?
5. Qu'as-tu commencé à faire grâce à (*thanks to*) la technologie? Qu'as-tu arrêté de faire à cause de la technologie?

Essayez! After completing the activity, have students underline the conjugated verb and preposition (if applicable). Ask volunteers to replace the verbs and prepositions with others from the list on page 370.

1 Suggestion Before starting, ask individuals to identify the infinitives of the conjugated verbs.

2 Expansion Take a survey of students' responses to the statements. Examples: **Qui sait parler plusieurs langues? Qui accepte de voyager souvent? Qui hésite à travailler tard?** Have students expand on their answers. Example: **Pourquoi hésitez-vous à travailler tard?**

3 Expansion Ask volunteers to tell two things they did last weekend.

4 Suggestion Before dividing the class into pairs, introduce the activity using your own situation. Example: **Moi, j'aime envoyer des e-mails à mes amis. J'arrive à sauvegarder tous les messages qu'ils m'envoient.**

5 Expansion Have students continue the activity, using these items **7. arriver / utiliser un plan 8. éviter / bronzer**

6 Expansion After the groups present their ads, have students from other groups imagine they are potential **École-dinateur** clients and ask questions about their services. Examples: **Nous apprenons à graver des CD? Qui nous aide à télécharger des fichiers?**

Le français vivant
- Ask what the ad is for, and then ask a volunteer to read it aloud.
- Have students describe what the person in the photo is doing and identify all of the objects they see.
- Ask students: **Voulez-vous acheter cet ordinateur? Expliquez.**

OPTIONS

Extra Practice Have students write three sentences about themselves using three different types of verbs: verbs followed directly by an infinitive, verbs followed by **à** before the infinitive, and verbs followed by **de** before the infinitive. Collect the papers and read them aloud. The rest of the class tries to guess who wrote the sentences.

Video Show the video again to give the students more input with verbs + [*infinitives*] and verbs + [*prepositions*] + [*infinitives*]. Stop the video where appropriate to discuss how these constructions were used and to ask comprehension questions.

Section Goals

In this section, students will learn reciprocal reflexives.

Instructional Resources
*espaces.vhlcentral.com: Lab MP3s; WB/VM/LM Answer Key; IRM (**Essayez!** and **Mise en pratique** answers; Lab Audioscript); activities; downloads; reference tools*

Suggestions

- Review the reflexive pronouns in the paradigm: **(je) me, (tu) te, (il/elle/on) se, (nous) nous, (vous) vous, (ils/elles) se.**
- Ask volunteers to explain what reflexive verbs are. Ask other students to provide examples. Review reflexive verbs and pronouns by asking students questions about their personal routine. Example: **Je me suis réveillé(e) à sept heures. Et vous, à quelle heure vous êtes-vous réveillé(e)?**
- Use magazine pictures to introduce the concept of reciprocal reflexive verbs.
- After going over the example sentences, ask students questions using reciprocal constructions. Examples: **Les frères s'entendent-ils bien? Vous écrivez-vous des lettres ou des e-mails? Quand vous êtes-vous rencontrés?**

Essayez! Have volunteers create sentences with the verbs in this activity.

NATIONAL comparisons STANDARDS

11A.2 Reciprocal reflexives

Point de départ In **Leçon 10A**, you learned that reflexive verbs indicate that the subject of a sentence does the action to itself. Reciprocal reflexives, on the other hand, express a shared or reciprocal action between two or more people or things. In this context, the pronoun means *(to) each other* or *(to) one another*.

Il **se regarde** dans le miroir. *but* Alain et Diane **se regardent.**
He looks at himself in the mirror. — *Alain and Diane look at each other.*

Common reciprocal verbs

s'adorer	*to adore one another*	s'entendre bien (avec)	*to get along well (with one another)*
s'aider	*to help one another*	se parler	*to speak to one another*
s'aimer (bien)	*to love (to like) one another*	se quitter	*to leave one another*
se connaître	*to know one another*	se regarder	*to look at one another*
se dire	*to tell one another*	se rencontrer	*to meet one another (make an acquaintance)*
se donner	*to give one another*	se retrouver	*to meet one another (planned)*
s'écrire	*to write one another*	se téléphoner	*to phone one another*
s'embrasser	*to kiss one another*		

Annick et Joël **s'écrivent** tous les jours.
Annick and Joël write one another every day.

Vous **vous donnez** souvent rendez-vous le lundi?
Do you arrange to meet often on Mondays?

- The past participle of a reciprocal verb does not agree with the subject when the subject is also the indirect object of the verb.

Marie a aidé son frère.
Marie helped her brother.

Lise a parlé à sa sœur.
Lise spoke to her sister.

Ils se sont **aidés**. *but* Elles se sont **parlé**.
They helped each other. — *They spoke to each other.*

Essayez! Donnez les formes correctes des verbes.

1. (s'embrasser) nous *nous embrassons*
2. (se quitter) vous vous quittez
3. (se rencontrer) ils se rencontrent
4. (se dire) nous nous disons
5. (se parler) elles se parlent
6. (se retrouver) ils se retrouvent

MISE EN PRATIQUE

1 L'amour réciproque Employez des verbes réciproques pour raconter l'histoire d'amour entre Laure et Habib.

MODÈLE Laure retrouve Habib tous les jours. Habib retrouve Laure tous les jours.
Laure et Habib se retrouvent tous les jours.

1. Laure connaît bien Habib. Habib connaît bien Laure. Laure et Habib se connaissent bien.
2. Elle le regarde amoureusement. Il la regarde amoureusement. Ils se regardent amoureusement.
3. Laure écrit des e-mails à Habib. Habib écrit des e-mails à Laure. Laure et Habib s'écrivent des e-mails.
4. Elle lui téléphone tous les soirs. Il lui téléphone tous les soirs. Ils se téléphonent tous les soirs.
5. Elle lui dit tous ses secrets. Il lui dit tous ses secrets. Ils se disent tous leurs secrets.

2 Souvenir Les étudiants de votre classe se retrouvent dix ans après la fin des études. Employez l'imparfait pour parler de vos souvenirs.

MODÈLE Marie et moi / s'aider souvent
Marie et moi, nous nous aidions souvent.

1. Marc et toi / se regarder en cours Marc et toi, vous vous regardiez en cours.
2. Anne et Mouna / se téléphoner Anne et Mouna se téléphonaient.
3. François et moi / s'écrire deux fois par semaine François et moi, nous nous écrivions deux fois par semaine.
4. Paul et toi / s'entendre bien Paul et toi, vous vous entendiez bien.
5. Luc et Sylvie / s'adorer Luc et Sylvie s'adoraient.
6. Patrick et moi / se retrouver après les cours Patrick et moi, nous nous retrouvions après les cours.

3 Une rencontre Regardez les illustrations. Qu'est-ce que ces personnages ont fait? Suggested answers

MODÈLE
Ils se sont rencontrés.

ils

1. Arnaud et moi
Arnaud et moi, nous nous sommes embrassés.

3. elles
Elles se sont téléphoné.

2. vous
Vous vous êtes quittés.

4. nous
Nous nous sommes écrit.

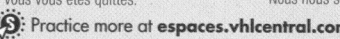

Practice more at **espaces.vhlcentral.com.**

OPTIONS

Video Ask students to write two columns on a piece of paper: Reflexive Verbs and Reciprocal Reflexive Verbs. Replay the video episode. Have students write down any examples they hear. Then form groups of three and have students compare their lists.

Extra Practice To provide oral practice with reciprocal reflexive verbs, create sentences that follow the pattern of the sentences in the examples. Say the sentence, have students repeat it, then give a different subject, varying the number. Have students then say the sentence with the new subject, changing pronouns and verbs as necessary.

COMMUNICATION

4 Curieux Pensez à deux amis qui sont amoureux. Votre partenaire va vous poser beaucoup de questions pour tout savoir sur leur relation. Répondez-lui. Answers will vary.

MODÈLE

Étudiant(e) 1: *Est-ce qu'ils se regardent tout le temps?*
Étudiant(e) 2: *Non, ils ne se regardent pas tout le temps, mais ils n'arrêtent pas de se téléphoner!*

s'adorer	se retrouver	régulièrement
s'aimer	se téléphoner	souvent
s'écrire	bien	tout le temps
s'embrasser	mal	tous les jours
s'entendre	quelquefois	?

5 Un rendez-vous Avec un(e) partenaire, posez-vous des questions sur la dernière fois que vous êtes sorti(e) avec quelqu'un. Answers will vary.

MODÈLE

à quelle heure / se donner rendez-vous
Étudiant(e) 1: *À quelle heure vous êtes-vous donné rendez-vous?*
Étudiant(e) 2: *Nous nous sommes donné rendez-vous à sept heures.*

1. où / se retrouver
2. se parler / longtemps
3. s'entendre / bien
4. à quelle heure / se quitter
5. se téléphoner / plus tard

6 On se quitte Julie a reçu (*received*) cette lettre de son petit ami Sébastien. Elle ne comprend pas du tout, mais elle doit lui répondre. Avec un(e) partenaire, employez des verbes réciproques pour écrire la réponse. Answers will vary.

Chère Julie,

Nous devons nous quitter. Pourquoi sommes-nous encore ensemble? Nous ne nous sommes pas aimés. Nous nous disputons tout le temps et nous ne nous parlons pas souvent. Soyons réalistes. Je te quitte et j'espère que tu comprends.

Sébastien

Le français vivant

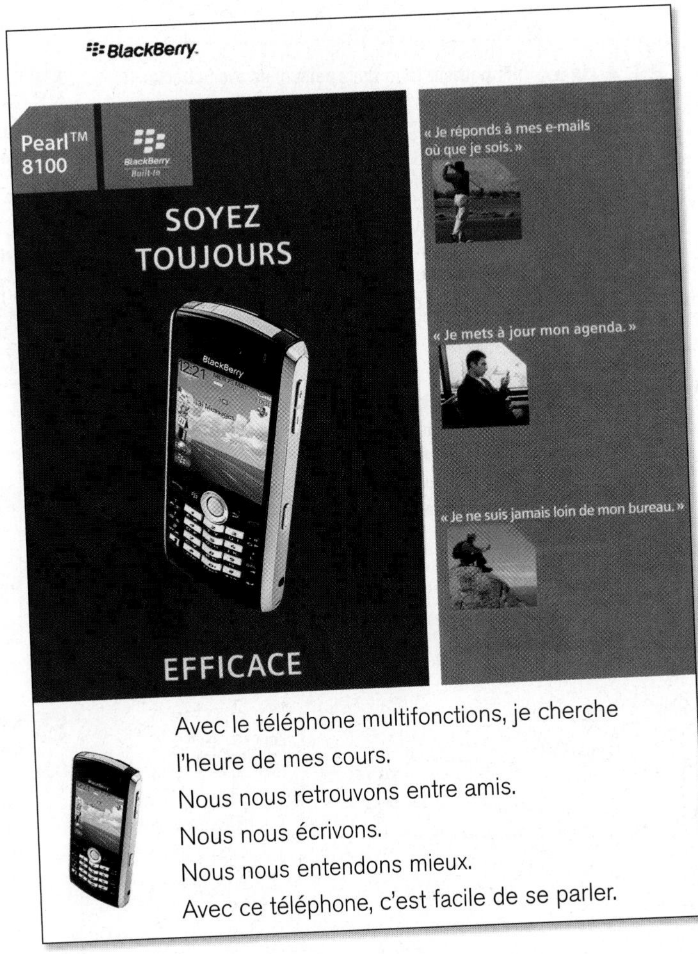

BlackBerry
Pearl™ 8100
BlackBerry Built-In
SOYEZ TOUJOURS
EFFICACE
« Je réponds à mes e-mails où que je sois. »
« Je mets à jour mon agenda. »
« Je ne suis jamais loin de mon bureau. »
Avec le téléphone multifonctions, je cherche l'heure de mes cours.
Nous nous retrouvons entre amis.
Nous nous écrivons.
Nous nous entendons mieux.
Avec ce téléphone, c'est facile de se parler.

Identifiez Quels verbes réciproques avez-vous trouvés dans la publicité (*ad*)? se retrouver, s'écrire, s'entendre mieux, se parler

Questions À tour de rôle avec un(e) partenaire, posez-vous ces questions. Answers will vary.

1. Tes amis et toi, vous envoyez-vous des messages avec un téléphone?
2. Penses-tu que les gens s'entendent mieux grâce à (*thanks to*) la technologie? Pourquoi?
3. Quels gadgets technologiques utilises-tu pour communiquer avec tes amis? Pourquoi les utilises-tu?
4. Quels gadgets technologiques utilisaient tes grands-parents pour communiquer avec leurs amis? Pourquoi les utilisaient-ils?

1 Suggestion Do this as a whole-class activity, giving different students the opportunity to form sentences.

2 Expansion Have students imagine that someone from the class contradicts what is said at the reunion. Ask volunteers to change the sentences in the activity to their negative form.

3 Suggestion Remind students to pay attention to the agreement of the past participle.

3 Expansion After assigning this activity, have pairs find magazine pictures and create three more sentences using reciprocal reflexives and the **passé composé**.

4 Expansion Have pairs use the reciprocal reflexives from the activity to create a short story about two friends falling in love. Encourage them to use the **passé composé,** the **imparfait**, and the present tense.

5 Expansion After completing the activity, have the students imagine they overheard the conversation about the date. Have pairs retell the facts of the conversation using the **passé composé** and the third person.

6 Suggestion Before assigning the activity, have volunteers identify the infinitive forms of each verb.

Le français vivant
- Have students describe what the man in the photos is doing.
- Call on a volunteer to read the ad aloud.
- Ask: **Possédez-vous un téléphone multifonctions?** If any students in the class do own a smartphone, have them note which feature(s) in the ad they use or like most or least. Examples: **Je fais tout avec mon téléphone, mais je l'utilise surtout pour répondre à mes e-mails. / Moi, je ne me sers pas de l'agenda.**

OPTIONS

Pairs Have students write and perform a conversation in which one friend discusses a misunderstanding he or she just had with his or her significant other. One student must explain the misunderstanding while the other must ask questions and offer advice. Encourage students to incorporate verbs with infinitives (and prepositions, where needed) and reciprocal reflexive verbs.

TPR Write reciprocal reflexive verbs on index cards and mix them up in a hat. Have volunteers pick a card at random and act out the reciprocal action. The class will guess the action, using the verb in a sentence.

Révision

Instructional Resources
*espaces.vhlcentral.com: IRM (**Feuilles d'activités**; Info Gap Activities); Testing Program, pp. 81–84; Test Files; Testing Program MP3s; activities; downloads; reference tools Test Generator*

1 Suggestion Before starting the activity, have students brainstorm a list of reciprocal verbs to use.

2 Suggestion Call on two volunteers to act out the **modèle.** Then distribute the **Feuilles d'activités** found on the Supersite.

2 Expansion Have pairs write six original sentences with reciprocal reflexives based on the answers from the survey. Some sentences should be affirmative statements, and some should be negative.

3 Expansion Have pairs invent situations or stories about the people in the drawing.

4 Expansion Ask students questions about how they, their close friends, or their family met their significant others. Example: **____, avez-vous un(e) petit(e) ami(e)? Comment vous êtes-vous rencontrés?**

5 Suggestion Before assigning the activity, have a group act out the **modèle** in front of the class. The third group member ad-libs a piece of advice.

6 Suggestion Divide the class into pairs and distribute the Info Gap Handouts found on the Supersite for this activity. Give students ten minutes to complete the activity.

1 À deux Que peuvent faire deux personnes avec chacun (*each one*) de ces objets? Avec un(e) partenaire, répondez à tour de rôle et employez des verbes réciproques. Answers will vary.

MODÈLE un appareil photo numérique
Avec un appareil photo numérique, deux personnes peuvent s'envoyer des photos tout de suite.

- un portable
- du papier et un stylo
- un ordinateur
- une caméra vidéo
- un fax
- un magnétophone

2 La communication Votre professeur va vous donner une feuille d'activités. Circulez dans la classe pour interviewer vos camarades. Comment communiquent-ils avec leurs familles et leurs amis? Pour chaque question, parlez avec des camarades différents qui doivent justifier leurs réponses. Answers will vary.

MODÈLE
Étudiant(e) 1: *Tes amis et toi, vous écrivez-vous plus de cinq e-mails par jour?*
Étudiant(e) 2: *Oui, parfois nous nous écrivons dix e-mails.*
Étudiant(e) 1: *Pourquoi vous écrivez-vous tellement souvent?*

Activités	Oui	Non
1. s'écrire plus de cinq e-mails par jour	Théo	Corinne
2. s'envoyer des lettres par la poste		
3. se téléphoner le week-end		
4. se parler dans les couloirs		
5. se retrouver au resto U		
6. se donner rendez-vous		
7. se rencontrer sur Internet		
8. bien s'entendre		

3 Dimanche au parc Ces personnes sont allées au parc dimanche dernier. Avec un(e) partenaire, décrivez à tour de rôle leurs activités. Employez des verbes réciproques. Answers will vary.

4 Leur rencontre Comment ces couples se sont-ils rencontrés? Par groupes de trois, inventez une histoire courte pour chaque couple. Utilisez les verbes donnés (*given*) et des verbes réciproques. Answers will vary.

1. venir de

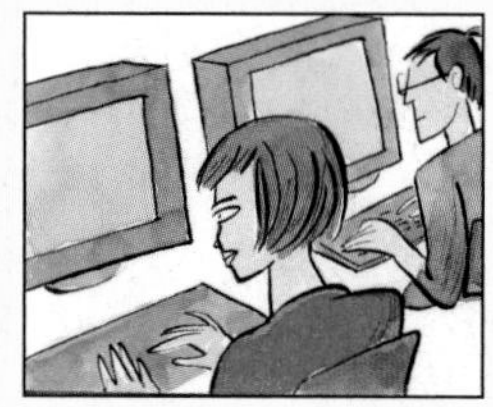
2. commencer à

3. continuer à

4. rêver de

5 Les bonnes relations Parlez avec deux camarades. Que faut-il faire pour maintenir de bonnes relations avec ses amis ou sa famille? À tour de rôle, utilisez les verbes de la liste pour donner des conseils (*advice*). Answers will vary.

MODÈLE
Étudiant(e) 1: *Dans une bonne relation, deux personnes peuvent tout se dire.*
Étudiant(e) 2: *Oui, et elles apprennent à se connaître.*

s'adorer	se connaître	hésiter à
s'aider	se dire	oublier de
apprendre à	s'embrasser	pouvoir
arrêter de	espérer	refuser de
commencer à	éviter de	savoir

6 Rencontre sur Internet Votre professeur va vous donner, à vous et à votre partenaire, une feuille d'illustrations sur la rencontre sur Internet d'Amandine et de Christophe. Attention! Ne regardez pas la feuille de votre partenaire. Answers will vary.

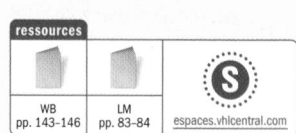

ressources
WB pp. 143-146 | LM pp. 83-84 | espaces.vhlcentral.com

OPTIONS

Extra Practice Have students brainstorm a list of chores that must be done every week at their house using vocabulary from previous lessons. Then ask students: **Qui s'occupe de quoi?** After assigning names to each task, have students create sentences telling who forgets to do their chores (**oublier de**), who refuses to do their chores (**refuser de**), and who receives help with their chores (**aider à**).

Game Divide the class into teams of four. Write a reciprocal verb on the board. Groups have 15 seconds to come up with a sentence in the present, the **imparfait**, or the **passé composé.** All groups with correct sentences earn one point.

Video: TV Clip

Le Zapping

NRJ Mobile

En 1981 est née, à Paris, la Nouvelle Radio Jeune, ou NRJ. La prononciation des trois lettres de son sigle° évoque un ingrédient du caractère de son public: l'énergie. La radio a toujours visé° les jeunes par la programmation de musique contemporaine et internationale. NRJ connaît un énorme succès et on peut aujourd'hui l'écouter partout° en France et dans d'autres pays européens. Débuté en 2005, NRJ Mobile vise aussi les jeunes et leur permet d'entièrement personnaliser leurs portables, y compris° les sonneries°.

—Alors j'ai créé KellyMobile, le premier opérateur qui comprend ce que° c'est d'être un fan.

—L'opérateur avec des sonneries ultra puissantes°, comme nous!

Compréhension Répondez aux questions. Some answers will vary.

1. Pourquoi les filles dans la publicité (*commercial*) sont-elles heureuses? Elles sont heureuses parce qu'elles peuvent personnaliser leurs portables.
2. Quelle réaction ont les personnes qui entendent leurs cris (*screams*)? Elles sont surprises et elles s'énervent.

Discussion Par groupes de trois, répondez aux questions et discutez. Answers will vary.

1. KellyMobile est-il le vrai nom du service mobile? Pourquoi s'appelle-t-il ainsi (*this way*)?
2. Pourquoi la pub montre-t-elle deux filles qui crient? Cette manière de s'exprimer (*expressing oneself*) est-elle normale? Pourquoi?
3. Comment personnalisez-vous votre portable? Pourquoi cette possibilité est-elle importante?

sigle *acronym* **visé** *aimed at* **partout** *everywhere* **y compris** *including*
sonneries *ring tones* **ce que** *what* **puissantes** *powerful*

Practice more at **espaces.vhlcentral.com.**

OPTIONS

NRJ Mobile To show just how customizable their cell phones are, **NRJ Mobile** launched television commercials, such as the one featured in this lesson's **Le zapping**, advertising wireless telephone services named after the ad's fictional main character. In this case, the name is KellyMobile. Although the wireless provider names are not real, the url **toimobile.fr** is and redirects to **nrjmobile.fr.** As with the original **NRJ** radio, **NRJ Mobile** marketing targets 12- to 25-year-olds, establishing a connection between its wireless packages and promotions and the worlds of entertainment, sports, and video games. There is also an **NRJ** television channel with programming that targets the same segment of the market.

Section Goals

In this section, students will:
- read about **NRJ Mobile** wireless provider
- watch a commercial for the company
- answer questions about the commercial and **NRJ Mobile**

Instructional Resources
*espaces.vhlcentral.com: TV commercial; IRM (**Le zapping** TV clip transcription); activities; downloads; reference tools*

Introduction
To check comprehension, ask these questions: **1. Qu'évoque la prononciation du sigle NRJ? (Elle évoque l'énergie de son public.) 2. Quelle sorte de programmation peut-on écouter sur NRJ? (On peut écouter de la musique contemporaine et internationale.) 3. Que permet de faire NRJ Mobile? (Ça permet d'entièrement personnaliser les portables.)**

Avant de regarder la vidéo
- Have students look at the video stills, read the captions, and predict what is happening in the commercial for each visual. **(1. La première fille parle sur son portable. Elle aime bien son opérateur. 2. La deuxième fille parle aussi sur son portable. Il a une sonnerie puissante.)**
- Before showing the video, explain to students that they do not need to understand every word they hear. Tell them to listen for the text in the captions and for any familiar words. Explain that the commercial's visuals are intentionally humorous and the girls' speech is exaggerated to match the humor.

Compréhension Have students work in pairs or groups for this activity. Tell them to write their answers. Then show the video again so that they can check their answers and add any missing information.

Discussion Have volunteers tell the class how the others in their group customize their cell phones. Write on the board any unfamiliar words they might need.

Section Goals

In this section, students will learn and practice vocabulary related to:

- cars and driving
- car maintenance and repair

Instructional Resources
*espaces.vhlcentral.com: Transparency #23; IRM (**Vocabulaire supplémentaire; Mise en pratique** answers; Textbook Audioscript; Lab Audioscript); Textbook MP3s; Lab MP3s; WB/VM/LM Answer Key; activities; downloads; reference tools*

Suggestions

- Use **Transparency #49.** Point out objects and describe what the people are doing. Examples: **Ces personnes sont dans une station-service. C'est une voiture. Il a un pneu crevé. Il fait le plein d'essence.**
- Follow up with simple questions based on your narrative. Examples: **C'est un volant? Qu'est-ce que c'est? Le mécanicien vérifie la pression des pneus?**
- Ask students questions about cars and driving using the new vocabulary. Examples: **Avez-vous une voiture? Attachez-vous votre ceinture de sécurité quand vous conduisez? Quand vous allez à la station-service, faites-vous le plein vous-même? Combien coûte un gallon d'essence?**
- Explain that **dépasser** has two meanings: **dépasser la limitation de vitesse** means *to go over the speed limit* and **dépasser une voiture/un camion** means *to pass a car/truck.*
- Additional vocabulary for this lesson can be found in the **Vocabulaire supplémentaire** on the Supersite.

Leçon 11B

You will learn how to...

- **talk about cars**
- **talk about traffic**
- **say what you would do**

Talking Picture
Audio: Activity

En voiture!

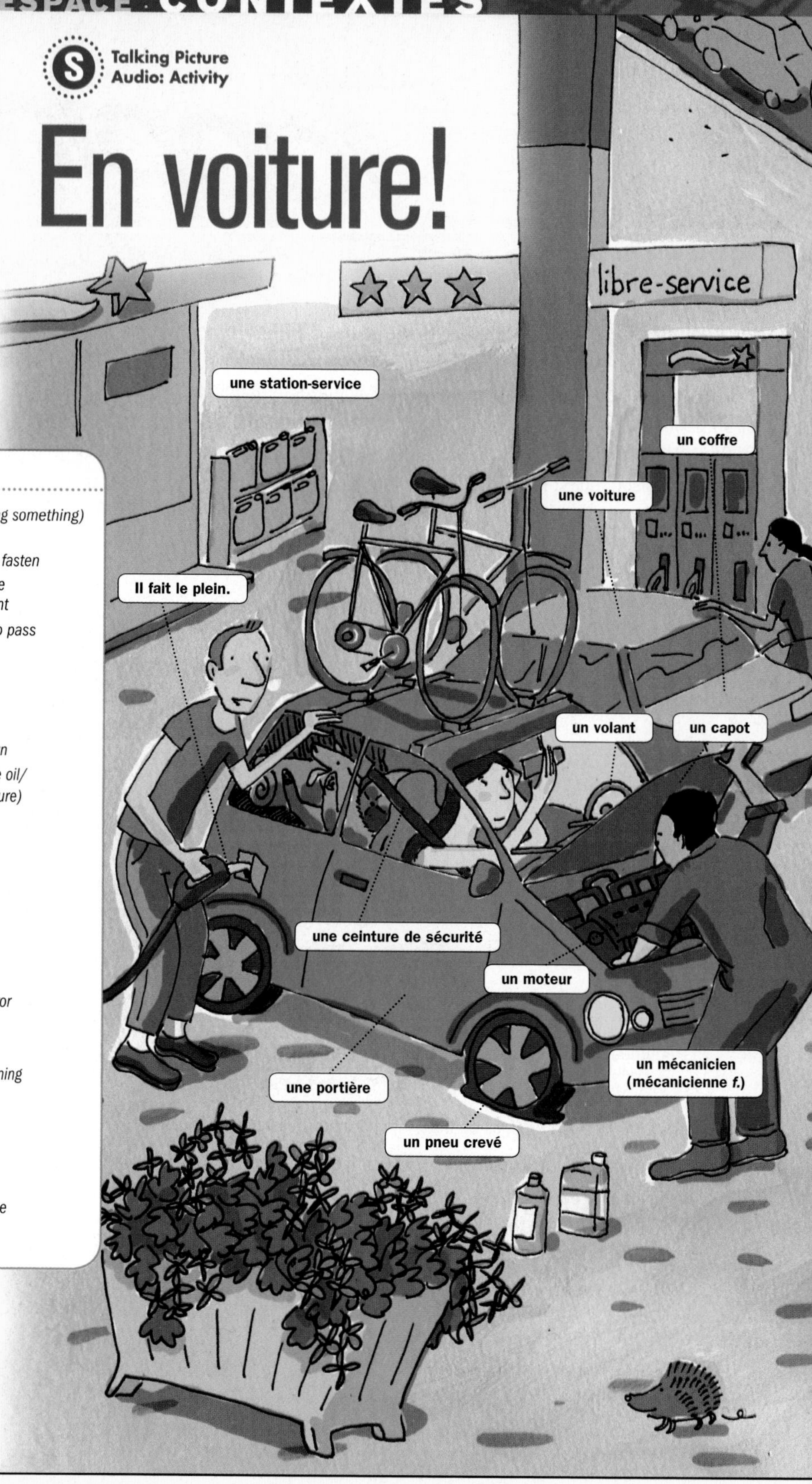

Vocabulaire

arrêter (de faire quelque chose)	*to stop (doing something)*
attacher	*to buckle, to fasten*
avoir un accident	*to have/to be in an accident*
dépasser	*to go over; to pass*
freiner	*to brake*
se garer	*to park*
rentrer dans	*to hit*
réparer	*to repair*
tomber en panne	*to break down*
vérifier (l'huile/ la pression des pneus)	*to check (the oil/ the air pressure)*
l'embrayage (*m.*)	*clutch*
l'essence (*f.*)	*gas*
les freins (*m., pl.*)	*brakes*
l'huile (*f.*)	*oil*
un pare-chocs (pare-chocs *pl.*)	*bumper*
un réservoir d'essence	*gas tank*
un rétroviseur	*rearview mirror*
une roue	*wheel*
une roue de secours	*spare tire*
un voyant (d'essence/ d'huile)	*(gas/oil) warning light*
une amende	*fine*
une autoroute	*highway*
un parking	*parking lot*
un permis de conduire	*driver's license*
une rue	*street*

ressources
WB pp. 147-148 | LM p. 85 | espaces.vhlcentral.com

OPTIONS

Game Play a game of **Dix questions**. Ask a volunteer to think of a car part from the new vocabulary. Other students get to ask one yes/no question, then they can guess what the word is. Limit attempts to ten questions per word. You might want to tell students that they can narrow down the options by asking questions about where the part is on the car and what it does.

Small Groups Distribute pictures of cars to groups of three students. Detailed photos of car interiors and exteriors are available online or from car dealerships. List parts of the car on the board, such as **volant, pneu, coffre,** and **rétroviseur**. Tell students to label the parts on the pictures. Alternatively, ask a student who can draw to sketch a car (inside and out) on the board and have students label its parts.

Mise en pratique

1 **Les correspondances** Reliez (*Link*) les éléments des deux colonnes.

b 1. dépasser	a. les freins
d 2. tomber en panne	b. la limitation de vitesse
a 3. freiner	c. la ceinture de sécurité
e 4. faire le plein	d. une voiture
g 5. réparer une voiture	e. l'essence
f 6. se garer	f. un parking
c 7. attacher	g. un mécanicien
h 8. vérifier la pression	h. les pneus

2 **Complétez** Complétez les phrases avec le bon mot de vocabulaire.

1. La personne qui répare une voiture est un ___mécanicien___.
2. Il faut ouvrir le ___capot___ de la voiture pour vérifier l'huile.
3. On met de l'essence dans le ___réservoir d'essence___.
4. Le ___permis de conduire___ est un document officiel qui vous autorise à conduire.
5. On utilise les ___phares___ pour voir (*see*) quand on conduit la nuit.
6. On utilise les ___essuie-glaces___ pour voir à travers (*through*) le pare-brise quand il pleut.
7. Le ___volant___ sert à diriger (*steer*) la voiture.
8. Vous utilisez le ___rétroviseur___ pour voir la circulation derrière vous.
9. La personne qui peut donner une amende est un ___policier/agent de police___.
10. On peut ranger ses valises dans le ___coffre___ de la voiture.
11. On utilise les ___freins___ quand on veut s'arrêter.
12. Quand il y a beaucoup de voitures sur la route, il y a de la ___circulation___.

3 **Écoutez** Madeleine a eu une mauvaise journée. Écoutez son histoire. Ensuite, indiquez si les phrases suivantes sont **vraies** ou **fausses**.

	Vrai	Faux
Madeleine...		
1. a oublié son permis de conduire.	☐	☑
2. a dépassé la limitation de vitesse.	☑	☐
3. a fait le plein avant d'aller à la fac.	☐	☑
4. a attaché sa ceinture de sécurité.	☑	☐
5. s'est garée à l'université.	☑	☐
6. conduisait quand un policier l'a arrêtée.	☑	☐
Sa voiture...		
7. a redémarré.	☐	☑
8. avait un pneu crevé.	☐	☑
9. n'avait pas d'essence.	☑	☐
10. était en panne.	☑	☐

Practice more at **espaces.vhlcentral.com.**

1 Expansion For additional practice, ask students what parts of a car are associated with these activities. **1. nettoyer le pare-brise (les essuie-glaces) 2. conduire (le volant) 3. arrêter (les freins) 4. changer de vitesse (l'embrayage) 5. regarder ce qui est derrière la voiture (le rétroviseur)**

2 Suggestion Have students work in pairs on this activity. Then go over the answers with the class.

3 Tapescript Hier, j'ai eu une journée terrible! J'avais un examen de maths à 8h00 du matin et je me suis levée en retard. J'étais très pressée, donc je conduisais très vite, quand tout à coup j'ai entendu une sirène. Quand j'ai regardé dans le rétroviseur, c'était un policier. Heureusement, j'avais mon permis de conduire avec moi et j'avais ma ceinture de sécurité attachée, mais comme je roulais plus vite que la vitesse autorisée, j'ai dû payer une amende. Finalement, je suis arrivée à l'université et j'ai trouvé une place pour me garer sans problème. J'ai passé mon examen de maths et je suis partie. Quand je suis retournée à ma voiture pour partir, elle n'a pas démarré. Un mécanicien est venu, il a vérifié la voiture et il m'a dit qu'elle ne démarrait pas parce qu'elle n'avait pas d'essence.
(On Textbook MP3s)

3 Suggestion Play the recording again, stopping at the end of each sentence that contains an answer so students can check their work.

OPTIONS

Les appellations des routes en France The letter preceding the highway number indicates what type of road it is. For example, the **A-8** is **une autoroute** (*freeway*). **Une autoroute à péage** is a *toll road*. The **N-7** is **une route nationale**, a smaller highway. The **D-15** is **une route départementale**, an even smaller road. **Les autoroutes** are much faster than **les routes nationales** or **départementales**, but they are not free and usually less scenic.

Extra Practice Propose various driving situations to your students and then ask: **De quoi avez-vous besoin?** Examples: **1. Vous allez en ville en voiture pour faire vos courses. (un parking) 2. Vous êtes sur l'autoroute et vous avez un pneu crevé. (une roue de secours) 3. Vous avez 18 ans et vous voulez conduire. (un permis de conduire) 4. Vous conduisez et il commence à pleuvoir. (les essuie-glaces)**

4 Suggestions
- Tell students to jot down notes during their interviews.
- After completing the interviews, ask volunteers to share their partner's responses with the class.

5 Suggestion Have two volunteers read the **modèle** aloud. Then divide the class into pairs and distribute the Info Gap Handouts found on the Supersite for this activity. Give students ten minutes to complete the activity.

6 Suggestions
- Before beginning the activity, have students look at the photo and describe what they see.
- Have the class brainstorm a list of potential problems that a car can have and write their suggestions on the board. Example: **Ma voiture consomme beaucoup d'essence.**

7 Suggestion Have students review the use of the **passé composé** and **imparfait** for narrating events in the past before they begin writing. See **Leçon 8B**, pages 276–277.

Communication

4 Conversez Interviewez un(e) camarade de classe. Answers will vary.

1. As-tu une voiture? De quelle sorte?
2. À quel âge as-tu obtenu (*obtained*) ton permis de conduire? Comment s'est passé l'examen?
3. Sais-tu comment changer un pneu crevé? En as-tu déjà changé un?
4. Ta voiture est-elle tombée en panne récemment? Qui l'a réparée?
5. Respectes-tu la limitation de vitesse sur l'autoroute? Et tes amis?
6. As-tu déjà été arrêté(e) par un policier? Pour quelle(s) raison(s)?
7. Combien de fois par mois fais-tu le plein (d'essence)? Combien paies-tu à chaque fois?
8. Quelle(s) autoroute(s) utilises-tu pour aller à l'université?
9. Sais-tu comment conduire une voiture à boîte de vitesses manuelle (*manual*)? Et tes amis?
10. As-tu eu des problèmes de pare-chocs récemment? Et des problèmes d'essuie-glaces?

5 Sept différences Votre professeur va vous donner, à vous et à votre partenaire, deux feuilles d'activités différentes. À tour de rôle, posez-vous des questions pour trouver les sept différences entre vos dessins. Attention! Ne regardez pas la feuille de votre partenaire.

MODÈLE

Étudiant(e) 1: *Ma voiture est blanche. De quelle couleur est ta voiture?*
Étudiant(e) 2: *Oh! Ma voiture est noire.*

6 Chez le mécanicien Travaillez avec un(e) camarade de classe pour présenter un dialogue dans lequel (*in which*) vous jouez les rôles d'un(e) client(e) et d'un(e) mécanicien(ne). Answers will vary.

Le/La client(e)...
- explique le problème qu'il/elle a.
- donne quelques détails sur les problèmes qu'il/elle a eus dans le passé.
- négocie le prix et la date à laquelle (*when*) il/elle peut venir chercher la voiture.

Le/La mécanicien(ne)...
- demande quand le problème a commencé et s'il y en a d'autres.
- explique le problème et donne le prix des réparations.
- accepte les conditions du/de la clien(e).

7 Écriture Écrivez un paragraphe à propos d'un (*about an*) accident de la circulation. Suivez les instructions. Answers will vary.

- Parlez d'un accident (voiture, moto [*f.*], vélo) que vous avez eu récemment. Si vous n'avez jamais eu d'accident, inventez-en un.
- Décrivez ce qui (*what*) s'est passé avant, pendant et après.
- Donnez des détails.
- Comparez votre paragraphe à celui (*that*) d'un(e) camarade de classe.

OPTIONS

Game Write vocabulary words related to cars on index cards. On another set of cards, draw or paste pictures to match each term. Tape them face down on the board in random order. Divide the class into two teams. Play a game of Concentration in which students match words with pictures. When a player makes a match, that player's team collects those cards. The team with the most cards at the end of the game wins.

Pairs Have students work in pairs. Tell them to take turns explaining to a younger brother or sister how to drive a car. Example: **Tout d'abord, tu attaches ta ceinture de sécurité. Puis...**

Les sons et les lettres

Audio: Concepts, Activities
Record & Compare

NATIONAL comparisons STANDARDS

The letter x

The letter **x** in french is sometimes pronounced *-ks*, like the *x* in the English word *axe*.

taxi **expliquer** **mexicain** **texte**

Unlike English, some French words begin with a *gz-* sound.

xylophone **xénon** **xénophile** **Xavière**

The letters **ex-** followed by a vowel are often pronounced like the English word *eggs*.

exemple **examen** **exil** **exact**

Sometimes an x is pronounced s, as in the following numbers.

soixante **six** **dix**

An **x** is pronounced *z* in a liaison. Otherwise, an **x** at the end of a word is usually silent.

deux enfants **six éléphants** **mieux** **curieux**

Prononcez Répétez les mots suivants à voix haute.

1. fax
2. eux
3. dix
4. prix
5. jeux
6. index
7. excuser
8. exercice
9. orageux
10. expression
11. contexte
12. sérieux

Articulez Répétez les phrases suivantes à voix haute.

1. Les amoureux sont devenus époux.
2. Soixante-dix euros! La note (*bill*) du taxi est exorbitante!
3. Alexandre est nerveux parce qu'il a deux examens.
4. Xavier explore le vieux quartier d'Aix-en-Provence.
5. Le professeur explique l'exercice aux étudiants exceptionnels.

Dictons Répétez les dictons à voix haute.

Les belles plumes font les beaux oiseaux.[2]

Les beaux esprits se rencontrent.[1]

[1] Great minds think alike.
[2] Beautiful feathers make beautiful birds.

ressources
LM p. 86
espaces.vhlcentral.com

Section Goals

In this section, students will learn about the letter **x**.

Instructional Resources
espaces.vhlcentral.com: Textbook MP3s; Lab MP3s; WB/VM/LM Answer Key; IRM (Textbook Audioscript; Lab Audioscript); activities; downloads; reference tools

Suggestions

- Model the pronunciation of the example words and have students repeat after you.
- Have students practice saying words that contain the letter **x** in various positions. Examples: Middle: **excellent, expliquer, expérience,** and **extérieur**. End: **yeux, heureux, époux, cheveux, jeux,** and **mieux**.
- Ask students to provide more examples of words with the letter **x**.
- Dictate five simple sentences with words that have the letter **x**, repeating each one at least two times. Then write the sentences on the board or a transparency and have students check their spelling.

Dictons The saying **«Les belles plumes font les beaux oiseaux»** is a quote from the French poet Bonaventure Des Périers (1500–1544).

OPTIONS

Extra Practice For additional practice with the letter **x**, have students write sentences on individual index cards using the words below. Then collect the cards and distribute some of them (at least one for each word) for students to read aloud. **1. excuser 2. deux 3. époux 4. cheveux 5. malheureux 6. roux 7. vieux 8. ennuyeux 9. explorer 10. généreux**

Extra Practice Teach students these French tongue-twisters that contain the letter **x**. **1. Le fisc fixe exprès chaque taxe fixe excessive exclusivement au luxe et à l'acquis. 2. Un taxi attaque six taxis. 3. Je veux et j'exige d'exquises excuses.**

Section Goals
In this section, students will learn functional phrases for talking about dating and cars.

Instructional Resources
*espaces.vhlcentral.com: WB/VM/LM Answer Key; IRM (Videoscript; **Roman-photo** Translations); activities; downloads; reference tools*
Video on DVD

Video Recap: Leçon 11A
Before doing this **Roman-photo**, review the previous one with this true/false activity.
1. Rachid n'arrive pas à travailler à cause de David. (Vrai.) 2. David ne finit pas sa dissertation. (Faux.) 3. Amina n'a pas l'intention de rencontrer Cyberhomme. (Vrai.) 4. Amina retrouve la dissertation de David. (Vrai.) 5. David est Cyberhomme. (Faux.)

Video Synopsis
Rachid goes to the service station to get some gas. Amina is waiting at **Le P'tit Bistrot** for him to pick her up for a date. Rachid brings her flowers and is very attentive. In the car, Rachid notices that an indicator light is on, so he returns to the service station. The car just needs some oil. After fixing the problem, they take off again, but they don't get very far because they have a flat tire.

Suggestions
- Have students predict what the episode will be about based on the video stills.
- Tell students to scan the captions and find vocabulary related to cars and driving.
- After reading the **Roman-photo**, review students' predictions and have them summarize the episode.

La panne

Video: *Roman-photo*
Record & Compare

PERSONNAGES

Amina

Mécanicien

Rachid

Sandrine

Valérie

1

À la station-service...
MÉCANICIEN Elle est belle, votre voiture! Elle est de quelle année?
RACHID Elle est de 2005.
MÉCANICIEN Je vérifie l'huile ou la pression des pneus?
RACHID Non, merci, ça va. Je suis un peu pressé, en fait. Au revoir.

2

Au P'tit Bistrot...
SANDRINE Ton Cyberhomme, c'est Rachid! Quelle coïncidence!
AMINA C'est incroyable, non? Je savais qu'il habitait à Aix, mais...
VALÉRIE Une vraie petite histoire d'amour, comme dans les films!
SANDRINE C'est exactement ce que je me disais!

3

AMINA Rachid arrive dans quelques minutes. Est-ce que cette couleur va avec ma jupe?
SANDRINE Vous l'avez entendue? Ne serait-elle pas amoureuse?
AMINA Arrête de dire des bêtises.

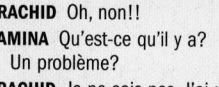

6

RACHID Oh, non!!
AMINA Qu'est-ce qu'il y a? Un problème?
RACHID Je ne sais pas. J'ai un voyant qui s'est allumé.
AMINA Allons à une station-service.
RACHID Oui... c'est une bonne idée.

7

De retour à la station-service...
MÉCANICIEN Ah! Vous êtes de retour. Mais que se passe-t-il? Je peux vous aider?
RACHID J'espère. Il y a quelque chose qui ne va pas, peut-être avec le moteur. Regardez, ce voyant est allumé.
MÉCANICIEN Ah, ça? C'est l'huile. Je m'en occupe tout de suite.

8

MÉCANICIEN Vous pouvez redémarrer? Et voilà.
RACHID Parfait. Au revoir. Bonne journée.
MÉCANICIEN Bonne route!

ACTIVITÉS

1 Vrai ou faux? Indiquez si ces affirmations sont **vraies** ou **fausses**. Corrigez les phrases fausses. Answers may vary.

1. La voiture de Rachid est neuve (*new*). Faux. Elle est de 2005.
2. Quand Rachid va à la station-service la première fois, il a beaucoup de temps. Faux. Il est un peu pressé.
3. Amina savait que Cyberhomme habitait à Aix. Vrai.
4. Sandrine trouve l'histoire de Rachid et Amina très romantique. Vrai.
5. Amina ouvre la portière de la voiture. Faux. Rachid ouvre la portière.
6. Rachid est galant (*a gentleman*). Vrai.
7. Le premier problème que Rachid rencontre est une panne d'essence. Faux. Un voyant s'est allumé.
8. Le mécanicien répare la voiture. Vrai.
9. La voiture a un pneu crevé. Vrai.
10. Rachid n'est pas très content. Vrai.

Practice more at **espaces.vhlcentral.com.**

OPTIONS

Avant de regarder la vidéo Tell students to read the title and scene setter. Then have them predict what might happen in this episode. Write their predictions on the board. After viewing the episode, have them confirm or correct their predictions.

Regarder la vidéo Print out the videoscript found on the Supersite. Then white out words related to cars and other key vocabulary in order to create a master for a cloze activity. Distribute photocopies and tell students to fill in the missing information as they watch the video episode.

Amina sort avec Rachid pour la première fois.

SANDRINE Oh, regarde, il lui offre des fleurs.
RACHID Bonjour, Amina. Tiens, c'est pour toi.
AMINA Bonjour, Rachid. Oh, merci, c'est très gentil.
RACHID Tu es très belle, aujourd'hui.
AMINA Merci.

RACHID Attends, laisse-moi t'ouvrir la portière.
AMINA Merci.
RACHID N'oublie pas d'attacher ta ceinture.
AMINA Oui, bien sûr.

AMINA Heureusement, ce n'était pas bien grave. À quelle heure est notre réservation?
RACHID Oh! C'est pas vrai!

AMINA Qu'est-ce que c'était?
RACHID On a un pneu crevé.
AMINA Oh, non!!

Expressions utiles

Talking about dating

- **Il lui offre des fleurs.**
  He's offering/giving her flowers.
- **Attends, laisse-moi t'ouvrir la portière.**
  Wait, let me open the (car) door for you.

Talking about cars

- **N'oublie pas d'attacher ta ceinture.**
  Don't forget to fasten your seatbelt.
- **J'ai un voyant qui s'est allumé.**
  One of the dashboard lights came on.
- **Il y a quelque chose qui ne va pas.**
  There's something wrong.

Additional vocabulary

- **incroyable**
  incredible

ACTIVITÉS

2 Qui? Indiquez qui dirait (*would say*) ces affirmations: Amina (**A**), le mécanicien (**M**), Rachid (**R**), Sandrine (**S**) ou Valérie (**V**).

1. La prochaine fois, je vais suivre les conseils du mécanicien. R
2. Je suis un peu anxieuse. A
3. C'est comme dans un conte de fées (*fairy tale*)! S/V
4. Taisez-vous (*Be quiet*), s'il vous plaît! A
5. Il aurait dû (*should have*) m'écouter. M

3 Écrivez Que se passe-t-il pour Amina et Rachid après le deuxième incident? Utilisez votre imagination et écrivez un paragraphe qui raconte ce qu'ils ont fait. Est-ce que quelqu'un d'autre les aide? Amina est-elle fâchée? Y aura-t-il (*Will there be*) un deuxième rendez-vous pour Cyberhomme et Technofemme?

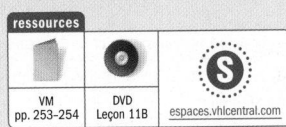

ressources: VM pp. 253–254 | DVD Leçon 11B | espaces.vhlcentral.com

Expressions utiles
- Model the pronunciation of the **Expressions utiles** and have students repeat them after you.
- As you work through the list, point out forms of **offrir** and **ouvrir,** as well as relative pronouns. Tell students that these verbs and structures will be formally presented in **Espace structures**.
- Respond briefly to questions about verbs like **offrir** and **ouvrir** and relative pronouns. Reinforce correct forms, but do not expect students to produce them consistently at this time.
- Tell students that **un mécanicien** is a *car mechanic* and **un garagiste** is a *garage owner.*
- Explain the different words for *light*: **un voyant (lumineux)** is a *warning light* on a vehicle, **les phares** are *headlights*, and the generic term for *light* is **la lumière**.
- Point out that **une portière** is a *car door*; a door in a room or a house is **une porte**. Similarly, a *car window* is **une vitre**, not **une fenêtre**.

1 Suggestion Have students correct the false statements.

2 Expansion Have students create three more items using lines from the **Roman-photo** conversation. Collect their papers, write some of the items on the board, and ask volunteers to identify the speakers.

3 Expansion Have students exchange papers for peer editing. Then ask volunteers to read their paragraphs aloud.

OPTIONS

Extra Practice Assign students a character (**Rachid, Amina,** or **le mécanicien**) and have them prepare a brief summary of the day's events from that character's point of view without saying the person's name. Ask volunteers to read their summaries to the class. Then have the class guess which character would have given each summary.

Le permis de conduire In France, the legal driving age for a regular permit is 18. In order to get a license, students take classes at an **auto-école**. Drivers must know **le code de la route** (*the driving code*) and understand how a car works. Since the lessons are very expensive, it is not unusual for young people to receive them as a gift for their eighteenth birthday.

Section Goals

In this section, students will:

- learn about cars and driving habits in France
- learn some terms for types of vehicles
- learn about the rules of the road in various francophone regions
- read about the car manufacturer Citroën
- view authentic video footage

Instructional Resources
espaces.vhlcentral.com: Video; WB/VM/LM Answer Key; IRM (Videoscript); activities; downloads; reference tools
Video on DVD

Culture à la loupe

Avant la lecture Have students look at the photos and describe what they see.

Lecture

- Explain that in Europe gas is sold in liters, not in gallons (1 gallon = 3.79 liters).
- Point out the statistics chart. Ask students what information it shows. (the percentage of French people in rural and urban areas who own a car)

Après la lecture Have students compare cars, driving habits, and car ownership in France and in the United States.

1 Suggestion Have students work on this activity in pairs.

National Standards: connections, cultures

Video: *Flash culture*

CULTURE À LA LOUPE

Les voitures en France

la Smart

Dans l'ensemble°, les Français utilisent moins leur voiture que les Américains. Il n'est pas rare qu'un couple ou une famille possède une seule voiture. Dans les grandes villes, beaucoup de gens se déplacent° à pied ou utilisent les transports en commun°. Dans les villages ou à la campagne, les gens utilisent un peu plus fréquemment leurs voitures. Pour les grandes distances pourtant°, ils ont tendance, plus que les Américains, à laisser leurs voitures chez eux et à prendre le train ou l'avion. En général, les voitures en France sont beaucoup plus petites que les voitures qu'on trouve aux États-Unis, mais on y trouve des quatre-quatre° (4x4), même dans les grandes villes. La Smart, une voiture minuscule produite par les compagnies Swatch et Mercedes-Benz, a aussi beaucoup de succès en France et en Europe.

Il y a plusieurs raisons qui expliquent ces différences. D'abord, les rues des villes françaises sont beaucoup moins larges. En centre-ville, beaucoup de rues sont piétonnes° et d'autres sont si petites qu'il est parfois difficile de passer, même avec une petite voiture. Il y a aussi de gros problèmes de parking dans la majorité des villes françaises. Il y a peu de places de parking et elles sont en général assez petites. Il est donc nécessaire de faire un créneau° pour se garer et plus la voiture est petite, plus° on a de chance de le réussir. En plus, en France, l'essence est plus chère qu'aux États-Unis. Il vaut donc mieux avoir une petite voiture économique qui ne consomme pas beaucoup d'essence, ou prendre les transports en commun quand c'est possible.

Pourcentage de Français qui possèdent une voiture

Dans les villages et à la campagne	92%
Dans les villes de moins de 20.000 habitants	86%
Dans les villes de 20.000 à 100.000 habitants	84%
Dans les villes de plus de 100.000 habitants	78%
En région parisienne	60%
À Paris	46%

SOURCE: Francoscopie

Dans l'ensemble *By and large* **se déplacent** *get around* **transports en commun** *public transportation* **pourtant** *however* **quatre-quatre** *sport utility vehicles* **piétonnes** *reserved for pedestrians* **faire un créneau** *parallel park* **plus..., plus...** *the more..., the more...*

ACTIVITÉS

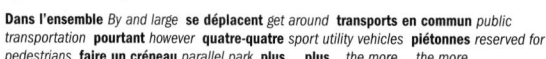

1 Complétez Donnez un début ou une suite logique à chaque phrase, d'après le texte. Answers may vary. Possible answers provided.

1. ... possèdent parfois une seule voiture. Les familles françaises
2. Les Français qui habitent en ville se déplacent souvent... à pied ou utilisent les transports en commun.
3. Beaucoup de Français prennent le train ou l'avion... pour faire de longs voyages.
4. ... sont en général plus petites qu'aux États-Unis. Les voitures en France
5. Comme aux États-Unis, même dans les grandes villes en France, on trouve... des quatre-quatre.
6. ..., on peut facilement faire un créneau pour se garer. Avec la Smart
7. Il n'est pas toujours facile de se garer dans les villes françaises... parce qu'il y a peu de places de parking et parce qu'elles sont en général assez petites.
8. ... parce que l'essence coûte cher en France. Il vaut mieux avoir une petite voiture économique
9. ..., la grande majorité des Français ont une voiture. Dans les villages et à la campagne
10. Le nombre de Français qui ont une voiture est plus important dans les villages et à la campagne qu'... à Paris.

Practice more at **espaces.vhlcentral.com.**

OPTIONS

Pourcentage de Français qui possèdent une voiture Ask students these questions. **1. Où les gens sont-ils 86% à posséder une voiture? (dans les villes de moins de 20.000 habitants) 2. Qui possède le moins de voitures? (les Parisiens) 3. Les habitants de la région parisienne possèdent-ils plus de voitures que les gens dans les villes de plus de 100.000 habitants? (Non)**

Les parcmètres Parking meters in France are not generally located next to the parking spot. The failure to see a parking meter is not a valid excuse for an expired meter. One should look for a meter down the street to avoid getting a parking ticket and having to pay a fine.

LE FRANÇAIS QUOTIDIEN

Pour parler des voitures

bagnole (*f.*)	*car*
berline (*f.*)	*sedan*
break (*m.*)	*station wagon*
caisse (*f.*)	*car*
char (*m.*) (Québec)	*car*
coupé (*m.*)	*coupe*
décapotable (*f.*)	*convertible*
monospace (*m.*)	*minivan*
pick-up (*m.*)	*pickup*

PORTRAIT

Le constructeur automobile Citroën

La marque° Citroën est une marque de voitures française créée° en 1919 par André Citroën, ingénieur et industriel français. La marque est réputée pour son utilisation de technologies d'avant-garde et pour ses innovations dans le domaine de l'automobile. Le premier véhicule construit par Citroën, la voiture type A, a été la première voiture européenne construite en série°. En 1924, Citroën a utilisé la première carrosserie° entièrement faite en acier° d'Europe. Puis, dans les années 1930, Citroën a inventé la traction avant°. Parmi les modèles de voiture les plus vendus de la marque Citroën, on compte la 2CV, ou «deux chevaux», un modèle bon marché et très apprécié des jeunes dans les années 1970 et 1980. En 1976, Citroën a fusionné° avec un autre grand constructeur automobile° français, Peugeot, pour former le groupe PSA Peugeot-Citroën.

marque *make* **créée** *created* **en série** *mass-produced* **carrosserie** *body* **acier** *steel* **traction avant** *front-wheel drive* **a fusionné** *merged* **constructeur automobile** *car manufacturer*

LE MONDE FRANCOPHONE

Conduire une voiture

Voici quelques informations utiles.

En France Il n'existe pas de carrefours° avec quatre panneaux° de stop.

En France, en Belgique et en Suisse Il est interdit d'utiliser un téléphone portable quand on conduit et on n'a pas le droit de tourner à droite quand le feu° est rouge.

À l'île Maurice et aux Seychelles Faites attention! On conduit à gauche.

En Suisse Pour conduire sur l'autoroute, il est nécessaire d'acheter une vignette° et de la mettre sur son pare-brise. On peut l'acheter à la poste ou dans les stations-service, et elle est valable° un an.

Dans l'Union européenne Le permis de conduire d'un pays de l'Union européenne est valable dans tous les autres pays de l'Union.

carrefours *intersections* **panneaux** *signs* **feu** *traffic light* **vignette** *sticker* **valable** *valid*

SUR INTERNET

Qu'est-ce que la Formule 1?

Go to espaces.vhlcentral.com to find more information related to this **ESPACE CULTURE.** Then watch the corresponding **Flash culture.**

ACTIVITÉS

2 Répondez Répondez par des phrases complètes.

1. Quelles sont les caractéristiques de la marque Citroën? Elle est réputée pour son utilisation de technologies d'avant-garde et pour ses innovations.
2. Quelle est une des innovations de la marque Citroën? Answers will vary. Possible answer: La construction en série d'une voiture en Europe a été une innovation.
3. Quel modèle de Citroën a eu beaucoup de succès? La 2CV, ou «deux chevaux», a eu beaucoup de succès.
4. Qu'a fait la compagnie Citroën en 1976? La compagnie a fusionné avec un autre constructeur automobile français, Peugeot.
5. Que faut-il avoir pour conduire sur l'autoroute, en Suisse? Il faut avoir une vignette sur le pare-brise.
6. Les résidents d'autres pays de l'UE ont-ils le droit de conduire en France? Oui, les permis de conduire des autres pays de l'Union européenne sont valables en France.

3 À vous... Quelle est votre voiture préférée? Pourquoi? Avec un(e) partenaire, discutez de ce sujet et soyez prêts à expliquer vos raisons au reste de la classe.

ressources
VM pp. 291–292
espaces.vhlcentral.com

Le français quotidien
- Model the pronunciation of each term and have students repeat it.
- Bring in photos of the different types of vehicles from an automotive magazine and have students identify them. Ask: **Qu'est-ce que c'est? C'est un monospace?**

Portrait
- André Citroën (1878–1935) got the idea of mass producing cars when he visited Henry Ford's new Rouge River plant in Detroit. He was also a master at marketing his cars.
- Have students look at the photo of the car. Ask: **Que pensez-vous de la Citroën sur la photo? Voulez-vous en posséder une? Pourquoi?**

Le monde francophone Have students compare the information given here with driving rules in the United States. Example: **Aux États-Unis, il y a souvent des carrefours avec quatre panneaux de stop. En France, il n'y en a pas.**

2 Expansion For additional practice, give students these items. **7. Qu'est-ce qu'il est interdit de faire au volant dans les pays francophones d'Europe? (utiliser un portable) 8. Dans quels lieux francophones conduit-on à gauche? (à l'île Maurice et aux Seychelles)**

3 Suggestion Have students bring in a photo of their favorite car to use as a visual aid during this activity. Photos can generally be found at a company's or a car dealer's website.

Flash culture Tell students that they will learn more about cars and driving in a city by watching a variety of real-life images narrated by Csilla. Show the video segment. Then ask students to close their eyes and describe from memory what they saw as you write their descriptions on the board. You can also use the activities in the video manual in class to reinforce this **Flash culture** or assign them as homework.

OPTIONS

Les limitations de vitesse Speed limits are generally higher in France than in the United States. For example, speed limits are 130 km/h (about 80 mph) on **les autoroutes**, 110 km/h (about 70 mph) on **les voies (*lanes*) rapides**, 90 km/h (about 55 mph) on **les routes**, and 50 km/h (about 30 mph) in cities and towns.

Cultural Activity Make a color transparency of French road signs (**panneaux de signalisation/signaux routiers**), which can be reproduced from the Internet or other reference sources. Then have the class guess what the signs mean.

NATIONAL STANDARDS comparisons

Section Goals

In this section, students will learn:

- the verbs **ouvrir** and **offrir**
- other verbs with the same conjugation (**couvrir, souffrir,** etc.)

Instructional Resources
*espaces.vhlcentral.com: Lab MP3s; WB/VM/LM Answer Key; IRM (**Essayez!** and **Mise en pratique** answers; Lab Audioscript); activities; downloads; reference tools*

Suggestions

- Review the conjugation of **-er** verbs.
- Write **j'ouvre, tu ouvres, il/elle ouvre** on the board. Point out that the endings are the same as **-er** verbs in the present tense.
- Follow the same procedure with **ouvrir**, but in the imperfect tense. Point out that with this tense, the verb is regular and takes **-ir** verb endings.
- Model verbs like **ouvrir** and **offrir** by asking volunteers questions. Examples: **À quelle heure la bibliothèque ouvre-t-elle? Quels services les grands magasins offrent-ils? Avez-vous souffert quand vous avez eu la varicelle** (*chicken pox*)?

Essayez! Give additional items such as these. **7. Qu'est-ce que je t'____ (offrir) pour ton anniversaire? (offre) 8. Vous ____ (ouvrir) les fichiers. (ouvrez)**

11B.1 The verbs *ouvrir* and *offrir*

Point de départ The verbs **ouvrir** (*to open*) and **offrir** (*to offer*) are irregular. Although they end in **-ir**, they use the endings of regular **-er** verbs in the present tense.

Ouvrir* and *offrir

	ouvrir	offrir
j'	ouvre	offre
tu	ouvres	offres
il/elle	ouvre	offre
nous	ouvrons	offrons
vous	ouvrez	offrez
ils/elles	ouvrent	offrent

La boutique **ouvre** à dix heures.
The shop opens at 10 o'clock.

Nous **offrons** soixante-quinze dollars.
We offer seventy-five dollars.

- The verbs **couvrir** (*to cover*), **découvrir** (*to discover*), and **souffrir** (*to suffer*) use the same endings as **ouvrir** and **offrir**.

Elle **souffre** quand elle est chez le dentiste.
She suffers when she's at the dentist's.

Couvrez la tête d'un enfant quand il fait soleil.
Cover the head of a child when it's sunny.

- The past participles of **ouvrir** and **offrir** are, respectively, **ouvert** and **offert**. Verbs like **ouvrir** and **offrir** follow this pattern.

Nous **avons découvert** un bon logiciel.
We discovered a good software program.

Elles **ont souffert** d'une allergie.
They suffered from an allergy.

- Verbs like **ouvrir** and **offrir** are regular in the **imparfait**.

Nous **souffrions** pendant les moments difficiles.
We suffered during the bad times.

Ils nous **offraient** de beaux cadeaux.
They used to give us nice gifts.

Essayez! **Complétez les phrases avec les formes correctes du présent des verbes.**

1. On *découvre* (découvrir) beaucoup de choses quand on lit.
2. Vous ouvrez (ouvrir) le livre.
3. Tu souffres (souffrir) beaucoup chez le dentiste?
4. Elle offre (offrir) des fleurs à ses amis.
5. Nous offrons (offrir) dix mille dollars pour la voiture.
6. Les profs couvrent (couvrir) les réponses.

MISE EN PRATIQUE

1 Mais non! **Alexandra et sa copine Djamila viennent d'arriver en cours et parlent de leurs camarades. Que se disent-elles?**

MODÈLE Julianne souffre d'un mal de tête. (je)
Je souffre aussi d'un mal de tête.

1. Sylvain ouvre son livre. (Caroline)
   Caroline ouvre aussi son livre.
2. Antoine souffre d'allergies. (le professeur et moi)
   Le professeur et moi souffrons aussi d'allergies.
3. Loïc découvre la réponse. (nous)
   Nous découvrons aussi la réponse.
4. Tu offres ta place à Maéva. (Théo)
   Théo offre aussi sa place à Maéva.
5. Je souffre beaucoup avant les examens. (nous)
   Nous souffrons aussi beaucoup avant les examens.
6. Vous ouvrez votre sac à dos. (Luc et Anne)
   Luc et Anne ouvrent aussi leur sac à dos.
7. Odile et Fatou couvrent leurs devoirs. (Lise)
   Lise couvre aussi ses devoirs.
8. Angèle découvre qu'elle adore les maths. (je)
   Je découvre aussi que j'adore les maths.

2 Je l'ai déjà fait **Maya parle avec sa sœur des choses qu'elle veut faire pour organiser une fête dans leur nouvelle maison. Sophie lui dit qu'elle les a déjà faites.**

MODÈLE Je veux ouvrir les bouteilles.
Je les ai déjà ouvertes.

1. Je veux couvrir les meubles pour les protéger.
   Je les ai déjà couverts.
2. Je veux ouvrir toutes les fenêtres.
   Je les ai déjà ouvertes.
3. Je veux découvrir le centre-ville.
   Je l'ai déjà découvert.
4. Je veux offrir des cadeaux aux voisins.
   Je leur en ai déjà offert.
5. Je veux ouvrir les nouveaux CD.
   Je les ai déjà ouverts.
6. Je veux couvrir les murs d'affiches.
   Je les ai déjà couverts.
7. Je veux découvrir ce que (*what*) nos amis vont nous offrir.
   Je l'ai déjà découvert.
8. Je veux offrir une fleur aux invités.
   Je leur en ai déjà offert une.

3 Que faisaient-ils? **Qu'est-ce que ces personnages faisaient hier? Employez les verbes de la liste.** Answers may vary.

couvrir découvrir offrir ouvrir souffrir

1. Benoît
Benoît ouvrait son livre.

3. vous
Vous découvriez de l'argent.

2. tu
Tu souffrais d'une grippe.

4. ils
Ils offraient un cadeau.

Practice more at **espaces.vhlcentral.com.**

OPTIONS

Video Play the video and have students listen for **-er** and **-ir** verbs. Have them write down those they hear. Afterward, write the verbs on the board. Ask their meanings. Have students write original sentences using each verb.

Extra Practice Here are four sentences containing verbs like **ouvrir** to use as dictation. Read each twice, pausing after the second time for students to write. **1. J'ai découvert que mon frère a eu un accident! 2. Nous couvrons la piscine en hiver. 3. Mon grand-père m'offrait des bonbons après le dîner. 4. Le musée ouvre à dix heures.**

COMMUNICATION

4 Questions Avec un(e) partenaire, posez-vous ces questions à tour de rôle. Ensuite, présentez les réponses à la classe. Answers will vary.

1. Qu'est-ce que tu as offert à ta mère pour la Fête des mères?
2. En quelle saison souffres-tu le plus des allergies? Pourquoi?
3. Est-ce que tu te couvres la tête quand tu bronzes? Avec quoi?
4. Est-ce que tu ouvres la fenêtre de ta chambre quand tu dors? Pourquoi?
5. Qu'est-ce que tes amis t'ont offert pour ton dernier anniversaire?
6. Que fais-tu quand tu souffres d'une grippe?
7. As-tu découvert des sites web intéressants? Quels sites?
8. Quand tu achètes un nouveau CD, est-ce que tu l'ouvres tout de suite? Pourquoi?

5 Une amende Un agent de police vous arrête parce que vous n'avez pas respecté la limitation de vitesse. Vous inventez beaucoup d'excuses. Avec un(e) partenaire, créez le dialogue et utilisez ce vocabulaire. Answers will vary.

amende	dépasser	ouvrir
avoir un accident	freiner	permis de conduire
circulation	freins	pneu crevé
coffre	se garer	rentrer dans
couvrir	limitation de vitesse	rue
découvrir	offrir	souffrir

6 Un cadeau électronique Vous avez de l'argent et vous voulez acheter des cadeaux à des membres de votre famille. Dites à un(e) partenaire les choses que vous voulez acheter et pourquoi. Utilisez les verbes de la liste. Answers will vary.

MODÈLE

Je peux acheter un jeu vidéo pour l'offrir à mon neveu.

couvrir | découvrir | offrir | ouvrir | souffrir

Le français vivant

À Noël, offrez le plus beau des cadeaux
Elle ouvre le paquet, et c'est le bonheur! Quoi de plus beau à offrir? Parlez-vous à cœur ouvert.
Telecom

Identifiez Avez-vous trouvé des formes des verbes **ouvrir** et **offrir** dans cette publicité (*ad*)? Lesquelles (*Which ones*)? offrez, ouvre, offrir, ouvert

Questions Posez ces questions à un(e) partenaire et répondez à tour de rôle. Answers will vary.

1. Qui offre un cadeau dans la pub? Qui reçoit (*receives*) un cadeau?
2. Quel cadeau offre-t-on?
3. Quel est le plus beau cadeau qu'on t'aie (*has*) offert?
4. Quel est le plus beau cadeau que tu aies (*have*) offert à quelqu'un?

1 Suggestion Have students check their answers orally with a partner.

2 Suggestion Before assigning this activity, ask questions using **déjà**. Remind students that **déjà** is placed after the conjugated verb and before the past participle. Example: **Qui a déjà étudié la biologie à l'université?**

3 Expansion Divide the class into groups of four. Have each student pick a photo to present to the group as a verbal portrait. Each one should include an introductory sentence that sets the scene, a body, and a conclusion. The verbal portrait should answer the questions *who, what, where, when,* and *why* based on the photo. After everyone in the group has presented a photo, the group votes on which one to present to the class.

4 Expansion Have pairs create two additional questions using the verbs **couvrir, découvrir, offrir, ouvrir,** and **souffrir**. Then pairs switch their questions with other pairs. Students should answer their classmates' questions in complete sentences.

5 Expansion Ask pairs to perform their conversation for the class or have them videotape it outside of class.

6 Expansion Have pairs use the sentences created in the activity to write a short conversation between two friends shopping for a gift at an electronics store. Then ask for volunteers to present their conversation to the class.

Le français vivant
- Call on a volunteer to read the advertisement aloud.
- Point out the phone number with only four digits. Explain that some toll-free numbers in France are like this. The main format for toll-free numbers is 0800 00 00 00.
- After pairs finish the **Questions** activity, go over the answers as a class.

OPTIONS

Game Divide the class into two teams. Indicate one team member at a time, alternating between teams. Give a certain infinitive from the lesson (**couvrir, découvrir, offrir, ouvrir, souffrir**) and name a subject. The team member uses that subject and verb in a sentence. Give a point per correct sentence. Deduct a point for each erroneous sentence. The team with the most points at the end of play wins.

Small Groups Have small groups prepare a conversation in which two roommates borrow a third roommate's car for the weekend without asking. They returned it in terrible condition. Encourage groups to use vocabulary and verbs from the lesson. Give groups time to prepare and practice their skits before presenting them to the class.

Section Goals

In this section, students will learn:
- the conditional tense
- the use of the conditional for expressing polite requests and future actions in a past tense

Instructional Resources
*espaces.vhlcentral.com: Lab MP3s; WB/VM/LM Answer Key; IRM (**Essayez!** and **Mise en pratique** answers; Lab Audioscript); activities; downloads; reference tools*

Suggestions
- Read the captions of the video stills and ask volunteers to indicate the verbs in the conditional.
- After going through the conjugations, check for understanding by asking volunteers to give different forms of verbs not listed: **finir, rendre, acheter**.
- Explain the concept of the conditional as *the future in the past*. Explain that the conditional is used to express some action that was yet to occur at some past time, and give more examples like this: **Je (ne) savais (pas) que je serais professeur de français.** Encourage students to make statements modeled on yours.
- Tell students to imagine they are shopping at the mall. Ask them what they would like to buy there. Example: **Que voudriez-vous acheter? (Je voudrais acheter ____.)** Tell students that **vouloir** in the conditional is a polite form. Emphasize how the conditional is used to make polite requests.

comparisons NATIONAL STANDARDS

11B.2 *Le conditionnel*

Point de départ The conditional expresses what you *would* do or what *would* happen under certain circumstances.

- The conditional of regular verbs is formed by using the infinitive form of the verb as the stem. To form the conditional of **-er** and **-ir** verbs, add the **imparfait** endings to the infinitive. Drop the **-e** from the infinitive of **-re** verbs before adding the endings to it.

Conditional of regular verbs

	parler	réussir	attendre
je/j'	parlerais	réussirais	attendrais
tu	parlerais	réussirais	attendrais
il/elle	parlerait	réussirait	attendrait
nous	parlerions	réussirions	attendrions
vous	parleriez	réussiriez	attendriez
ils/elles	parleraient	réussiraient	attendraient

Nous ne **conduirions** pas.
We would not drive.

À ta place, je **réparerais** la voiture.
In your place, I would repair the car.

- Note the conditional form of most spelling change **-er** verbs.

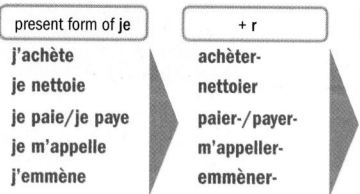

present form of je	+ r	conditional forms
j'achète	achèter-	j'achèterais
je nettoie	nettoier	je nettoierais
je paie/je paye	paier-/payer-	je paierais/payerais
je m'appelle	m'appeller-	je m'appellerais
j'emmène	emmèner-	j'emmènerais

- For **-er** verbs with an **è** before the infinitive ending, form the conditional the same way as regular verbs.

Tu **préférerais** aller à une station-service?
Would you prefer to go to a service station?

Nous **protégerions** les enfants de la chaleur.
We would protect the children from the heat.

- Some verbs use irregular stems in the conditional.

aller	ir-	envoyer	enverr-	recevoir	recevr-
apercevoir	apercevr-	être	ser-	savoir	saur-
avoir	aur-	faire	fer-	venir	viendr-
devoir	devr-	pouvoir	pourr-	vouloir	voudr-

J'**irais** chez toi, mais pas aujourd'hui.
I'd go to your house but not today.

Quand est-ce qu'elle **ferait** le plein?
When would she fill the tank?

MISE EN PRATIQUE

1 Changer de vie Alexandre parle à son ami de ce qu'il (*what he*) aimerait changer dans sa vie. Complétez ses phrases avec les formes correctes du conditionnel.

MODÈLE
Je n' étudierais (étudier) jamais le week-end.

1. Ma petite amie et moi ferions (faire) des études dans la même (*same*) ville.
2. Je vendrais (vendre) ma vieille voiture.
3. Nous achèterions (acheter) une Porsche.
4. J' attacherais (attacher) toujours ma ceinture de sécurité.
5. Nos amis nous rendraient (rendre) souvent visite.
6. Quelqu'un nettoierait (nettoyer) la maison.

2 Les professeurs Que feraient ces personnes si elles étaient profs de français?

MODÈLE tu / donner / examen / difficile
Tu donnerais des examens difficiles.

1. Marc / donner / devoirs
Marc donnerait des devoirs.
2. vous / répondre / à / questions / étudiants
Vous répondriez aux questions des étudiants.
3. nous / permettre / à / étudiants / de / manger / en classe Nous permettrions aux étudiants de manger en classe.
4. tu / parler / français / tout le temps
Tu parlerais français tout le temps.
5. tes parents / boire / café / classe
Tes parents boiraient du café en classe.
6. nous / montrer / films / français
Nous montrerions des films français.

3 Je suis d'accord! Quand on vous dit ce que vos amis font ou ne font pas, dites que vous feriez ou ne feriez pas ces choses. Utilisez le conditionnel dans vos réponses.
Answers will vary.

MODÈLE
Je n'ai pas envie de ranger les valises dans le coffre.
Moi non plus, je n'aurais pas envie de ranger les valises dans le coffre.

Je regarde souvent dans le rétroviseur.
Moi aussi, je regarderais souvent dans le rétroviseur.

1. Élodie ne prend pas le vélo.
Moi non plus, je ne prendrais pas le vélo.
2. Olivier et Solange ne se garent pas devant le café.
Moi non plus, je ne me garerais pas devant le café.
3. Laurent et toi ne vérifiez pas la pression des pneus.
Moi non plus, je ne vérifierais pas la pression des pneus.
4. Tu fais le plein avant de partir.
Moi aussi, je ferais le plein avant de partir.
5. Ma petite amie veut acheter une nouvelle voiture.
Moi aussi, je voudrais acheter une nouvelle voiture.
6. Sylvie ne dépasse pas le policier sur l'autoroute.
Moi non plus, je ne dépasserais pas le policier sur l'autoroute.
7. Nous devons souvent nettoyer le pare-brise.
Moi aussi, je devrais souvent nettoyer le pare-brise.
8. Marie vient chaque semaine à la station-service.
Moi aussi, je viendrais chaque semaine à la station-service.

Practice more at **espaces.vhlcentral.com.**

OPTIONS

Game To prepare for a relay race, line students up in teams of six several feet from the board. Write an infinitive on the board and call out **Commencez!** The first team members go to the board and write the **je** form of the verb in the conditional, then pass the chalk to the next team member, who writes the **tu** form, and so on. The team that finishes first and has all the forms correct wins the round.

Extra Practice Ask students what they would or would not do over the next six months if they could do anything they wanted and money and time were no object. Example: **Je ferais le tour du monde.** Call on volunteers to read their sentences, and then ask the class comprehension questions about what was said. Example: **Qu'est-ce que Paula ferait?**

COMMUNICATION

4 Une grosse fortune Avec un(e) partenaire, parlez de la façon dont (*the way in which*) vous dépenseriez l'argent si quelqu'un vous laissait une grosse fortune. Posez-vous ces questions à tour de rôle. Answers will vary.

1. Partirais-tu en voyage? Où irais-tu?
2. Quelle voiture achèterais-tu?
3. Où habiterais-tu?
4. Qu'est-ce que tu achèterais à tes amis? À ta famille?
5. Donnerais-tu de l'argent à des œuvres de charité (*charities*)? Auxquelles (*To which ones*)?
6. Qu'est-ce qui changerait dans ta vie quotidienne (*daily*)?

5 Sans ça... Par groupes de trois, dites ce qui (*what*) changerait dans le monde sans ces choses. Answers will vary.

MODÈLE sans devoirs?
Les étudiants s'amuseraient plus.

- sans voitures?
- sans télévisions?
- sans téléphones?
- sans ordinateurs?
- sans avions?
- ?

6 Le tour de la France Vous aimeriez faire le tour de la France avec un(e) partenaire. Regardez la carte et discutez de l'itinéraire. Où commenceriez-vous? Que visiteriez-vous? Utilisez ces idées et trouvez-en d'autres. Answers will vary.

MODÈLE
Nous commencerions à Paris.

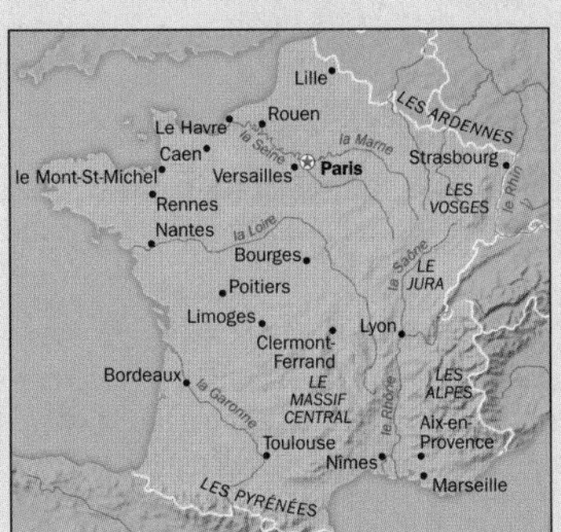

- les plages de la Côte d'Azur
- les randonnées dans le Centre
- le ski dans les Alpes
- les musées à Paris
- les châteaux (*castles*) de la Loire

- The conditional forms of **il y a**, **il faut**, and **il pleut** are, respectively, **il y aurait**, **il faudrait**, and **il pleuvrait**.

Il faudrait ouvrir le capot de la voiture. *We would need to open the hood of the car.*	**Il y aurait** trop de circulation à cette heure-là. *There would be too much traffic at that time.*

- Use the conditional to make a polite request, soften a demand, or express what someone *could* or *should* do.

Je **voudrais** acheter une nouvelle imprimante. *I would like to buy a new printer.*	**Pourriez**-vous nous dire où elles sont? *Could you tell us where they are?*
Tu **devrais** dormir jusqu'à onze heures. *You should sleep until 11 o'clock.*	Nous **aimerions** vérifier la pression des pneus, s'il vous plaît. *We would like to check the tire pressure, please.*

- Use the conditional, along with a past-tense verb, to express what someone said or thought would happen in the future at a past moment in time.

Guillaume a dit qu'il **arriverait** vers midi. *Guillaume said that he would arrive around noon.*	Nous pensions que tu **ferais** tes devoirs. *We thought that you would do your homework.*

- The English *would* can also mean *used to*, in the sense of past habitual action. To express past habitual actions in French, use the **imparfait**.

Je **travaillais** dans un restaurant à Nice. *I would (used to) work at a restaurant in Nice.*	*but*	Je **travaillerais** seulement dans un restaurant à Nice. *I would only work for a restaurant in Nice.*

Essayez! **Indiquez la forme correcte du conditionnel de ces verbes.**

1. je (perdre, devoir, venir) *perdrais, devrais, viendrais*
2. tu (vouloir, aller, essayer) voudrais, irais, essaierais
3. Michel (dire, prendre, savoir) dirait, prendrait, saurait
4. nous (préférer, nettoyer, faire) préférerions, nettoierions, ferions
5. vous (être, pouvoir, avoir) seriez, pourriez, auriez
6. elles (dire, espérer, amener) diraient, espéreraient, amèneraient
7. je (boire, choisir, essuyer) boirais, choisirais, essuierais
8. il (tenir, se lever, envoyer) tiendrait, se lèverait, enverrait

Essayez! Have volunteers make up stories (two or three sentences long) using each of the items.

1 Suggestion Ask six volunteers to write the completed sentences on the board. Have other volunteers correct any errors.

2 Expansion Have students compose questions that would elicit the sentences from the activity as answers. Example: **Marc donnerait-il des devoirs?**

3 Suggestion Have students do this as a written activity.

4 Expansion Have volunteers use the third person to present their partner's responses to the questions.

5 Suggestion Before assigning the activity, have the class brainstorm other items similar to those in the activity. Ask a volunteer to write these items on the board.

6 Expansion Have pairs present their itinerary to the class. Ask volunteers to come up with questions for each pair.

OPTIONS

Pairs Have students take turns asking each other favors, using the conditional for courtesy. Partners respond by saying whether they will do the favor. If partners can't do it, they should make up an excuse. Example: **Pourrais-tu m'aider à faire mes devoirs ce soir? (Je suis désolé, je ne peux pas t'aider. Je dois aller chez mes parents ce soir.)**

Video Show the video again to give students more input on the use of the conditional. Stop the video where appropriate to discuss how and why the conditional was used.

Instructional Resources
*espaces.vhlcentral.com: IRM (**Feuilles d'activités**; Info Gap Activities); Testing Program, pp. 85–88; Test Files; Testing Program MP3s; activities; downloads; reference tools Test Generator*

1 Suggestion Have two volunteers act out the **modèle**. Then distribute the **Feuilles d'activités** found on the Supersite.

1 Expansion Have pairs come up with additional questions related to an automobile that they could ask their classmates.

2 Suggestion Have students compare their sentences with those of other groups and they could vote on the most creative sentence for each image.

3 Expansion Have students reverse roles and imagine that they are going to run a marathon. Have them write a letter to a personal trainer asking five questions about what they should do to get ready for the event. Remind them to use the conditional to phrase their questions in a polite form.

4 Expansion Invite pairs to perform their conversation for the class.

5 Expansion Using magazine and newspaper ads, have pairs invent slogans that advertise an electronic device.

6 Suggestion Divide the class into pairs and distribute the Info Gap Handouts found on the Supersite for this activity. Give students ten minutes to complete the activity.

Révision

1 Dans ma famille... Votre professeur va vous donner une feuille d'activités. Circulez dans la classe pour interviewer un(e) camarade différent(e) pour chaque question. Mentionnez un détail supplémentaire dans vos réponses. Answers will vary.

MODÈLE

Étudiant(e) 1: *Qui, dans ta famille, a peur de conduire?*
Étudiant(e) 2: *Mon oncle Olivier a peur de conduire. Il a eu trop d'accidents.*

Qui, dans ta famille, ...	*Noms*
1. a peur de conduire?	*mon oncle Olivier*
2. aime l'odeur de l'essence?	
3. n'aime pas conduire vite?	
4. n'a jamais eu d'accident?	
5. ne dépasse jamais la limitation de vitesse?	
6. n'a pas son permis de conduire?	
7. ne sait pas faire le plein?	
8. sait vérifier l'huile?	

2 Des explications Avec un(e) partenaire, observez ces personnages et inventez une phrase au conditionnel pour décrire leur situation. Answers will vary.

MODÈLE

Elle ferait du jogging, mais elle s'est foulé la cheville.

1.

3.

2.

4.

3 Le marathon Votre meilleur(e) ami(e) va participer à un marathon dans six mois et il/elle veut savoir ce qu'il/elle (*what he/she*) devrait faire pour s'entraîner (*train himself/herself*). Avec un(e) partenaire, écrivez un e-mail à votre ami(e) pour dire ce que vous feriez à sa place pour vous préparer. Utilisez le conditionnel. Answers will vary.

4 La leçon de conduite Vous êtes moniteur de conduite (*driving instructor*) et c'est la première leçon de conduite que prend votre partenaire. Inventez une scène où il/elle découvre la voiture et où vous lui expliquez la fonction des différentes commandes. Utilisez le conditionnel dans votre dialogue. Answers will vary.

MODÈLE

Étudiant(e) 1: *J'utiliserais ce bouton pour ouvrir le capot?*
Étudiant(e) 2: *Non. Tu utiliserais ce bouton pour ouvrir le coffre.*

5 Les slogans Avec un(e) partenaire, utilisez ces verbes dans des slogans pour vendre cette voiture. Soyez prêts à voter pour les meilleurs slogans de la classe. Answers will vary.

MODÈLE

Étudiant(e) 1: *Qu'est-ce que tu penses de: «Offrez-vous l'évasion»?*
Étudiant(e) 2: *Ce n'est pas mal, mais j'aime bien aussi: «Le monde vous découvre.»*

couvrir découvrir offrir ouvrir souffrir

6 Mots-croisés Votre professeur va vous donner, à vous et à votre partenaire, deux grilles de mots croisés (*crossword*) incomplètes. Attention! Ne regardez pas la feuille de votre partenaire. Utilisez le conditionnel dans vos définitions.

MODÈLE

Étudiant(e) 1: *Horizontalement, le numéro 1, tu les allumerais pour conduire la nuit.*
Étudiant(e) 2: *Les phares!*

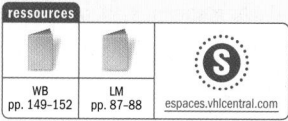

ressources
WB pp. 149–152 | LM pp. 87–88 | espaces.vhlcentral.com

388 *trois cent quatre-vingt-huit*

OPTIONS

Extra Practice Ask students to work in groups of five. One person in each group will play the role of a campus radio talk show host along the lines of "Dear Abby". The other four students will take turns calling in with various problems and the host will give them advice. Students can perform their skits in front of the class or record it and play the "show" for the class.

Game Divide the class into several groups. Tell them to imagine that it is the year 2050. Each team has to write as many phrases as they can using the conditional to describe what the world would be like. Set a time limit for the game. At the end of the allotted time, have each team read their phrases. The team with the most number of grammatically correct phrases at the end of the game wins.

À l'écoute

communication STANDARDS

Audio: Activities

STRATÉGIE

Guessing the meaning of words through context

When you hear an unfamiliar word, you can often guess its meaning by listening to the words and phrases around it.

To practice this strategy, you will listen to a paragraph. Jot down the unfamiliar words that you hear. Then, listen to the paragraph again and jot down the word or words that are the most useful clues to the meaning of each unfamiliar word.

Préparation

Regardez la photo. Que fait la policière? Et l'homme, que fait-il? Où sont-ils? Que se passe-t-il, d'après vous?

À vous d'écouter

Écoutez la conversation entre la policière et l'homme et utilisez le contexte pour vous aider à comprendre les mots et expressions de la colonne A. Trouvez leur équivalent dans la colonne B.

A	B
d 1. la moto	a. un document qui indique une infraction
f 2. la loi	b. un signal pour indiquer dans quelle direction on va aller
a 3. une contravention	c. conduire une voiture
c 4. rouler	d. véhicule à deux roues
b 5. le clignotant	e. faire attention
e 6. être prudent	f. quelque chose qu'il faut respecter

Practice more at **espaces.vhlcentral.com.**

Compréhension

Vrai ou faux? Indiquez si les phrases sont vraies ou fausses. Corrigez les phrases fausses.

1. L'homme a oublié son permis de conduire à l'aéroport.
   Faux. Il va chercher son fils à l'aéroport.
2. L'homme roulait trop vite.
   Vrai.
3. La vitesse est limitée à 150 km/h sur cette route.
   Faux. Elle est limitée à 130.
4. L'homme a dépassé un camion rouge.
   Faux. Il a dépassé une grosse moto.
5. L'agent de police n'accepte pas les excuses de l'homme.
   Vrai.
6. L'agent de police donne une contravention à l'homme.
   Vrai.
7. L'homme préfère payer l'amende tout de suite.
   Faux. Il pense qu'il ne va pas pouvoir payer l'amende.
8. L'agent de police demande à l'homme de faire réparer son rétroviseur avant de repartir.
   Faux. Elle lui demande de bien regarder dans son rétroviseur avant de repartir.

Racontez Choisissez un sujet et écrivez un paragraphe.

1. Avez-vous déjà eu une contravention (*ticket*)? Quand? Où? Que faisiez-vous? Si vous n'avez jamais (*never*) eu de contravention, parlez d'une personne que vous connaissez qui en a déjà eu une.
2. Avez-vous déjà eu de gros problèmes de voiture ou une panne? Quand? Où? Quel était le problème? Êtes-vous allé(e) chez un mécanicien? Qu'a-t-il fait? Est-ce que ça a coûté cher?

Section Goals

In this section, students will:
- learn to guess the meaning of words from context
- listen to a paragraph and jot down unfamiliar words plus clues to their meaning
- listen to a conversation and complete several activities

Instructional Resources
espaces.vhlcentral.com: Textbook MP3s ; IRM (Textbook Audioscript); activities; downloads; reference tools

Stratégie
Script Bonjour, Monsieur. J'ai examiné votre voiture. Suite à l'accident, votre voiture a plusieurs problèmes. En particulier, la portière côté passager ne ferme pas et on ne peut plus remonter la vitre. J'ai regardé sous le capot et le moteur est en bon état. Je vais réparer la voiture et vous pouvez venir la chercher demain.

Préparation Have students look at the photo and describe what they see. Then have them guess what the police officer and the man are talking about.

À vous d'écouter
Script L'AGENT DE POLICE: Bonjour, Monsieur. Votre permis de conduire, s'il vous plaît.
L'HOMME: Oui, Madame. Voilà. Euh... Quel est le problème?
AP: Vous rouliez à 150 kilomètres/heure quand vous avez dépassé la grosse moto et la limitation de vitesse sur cette autoroute est à 130, Monsieur.
H: Vous êtes sûre que j'allais si vite?
AP: Sûre et certaine, Monsieur!
H: Euh... Je suis désolé. C'est que... je suis très, très en retard. Je dois aller chercher mon fils à l'aéroport à vingt heures et...
AP: Ce n'est pas une raison, Monsieur. Vous devez respecter la limitation de vitesse comme tout le monde...
H: Oui, je sais. Je suis vraiment désolé. Vous ne pouvez pas...
AP: Je dois vous donner une contravention.
H: Oh non! Je vous en prie... Je n'ai vraiment pas beaucoup d'argent en ce moment. Je ne sais pas comment je vais pouvoir payer une amende pareille!
AP: Désolée, Monsieur, mais c'est la loi. Tenez. Et roulez moins vite!
H: Oui, Madame.
AP: Et n'oubliez pas d'attacher votre ceinture de sécurité, de mettre votre clignotant et de bien regarder dans votre rétroviseur avant de repartir.
H: Oui, Madame. Au revoir.
AP: Au revoir, Monsieur, et soyez prudent.

Section Goals

In this section, students will read historical and cultural information about Belgium.

Instructional Resources
espaces.vhlcentral.com: Transparency #50; WB/VM/LM Answer Key; activities; downloads; reference tools

Carte de la Belgique
- Have students look at the map or use **Transparency #50**. Ask volunteers to read the names of cities and other geographical features aloud. Model the pronunciation as necessary. Point out the francophone regions.
- Have students identify the countries that border Belgium.

Le pays en chiffres
- Point out the flag of Belgium.
- Have volunteers read the sections aloud. After each section, ask students questions about the content.
- Point out that Belgium is one of the smallest and most densely populated countries of Europe. Have students compare Belgium's size and population to Switzerland's (see page 354).
- Tell students that Belgium is a kingdom.
- About one-tenth of Belgium's population is bilingual, and a majority of the people have some knowledge of both French and Flemish.

Incroyable mais vrai! The beer and cheese made at the monasteries are produced using methods that are centuries old.

NATIONAL STANDARDS connections cultures

SAVOIR-FAIRE

S Interactive Map Reading

Panorama

une barque° sur l'Escaut

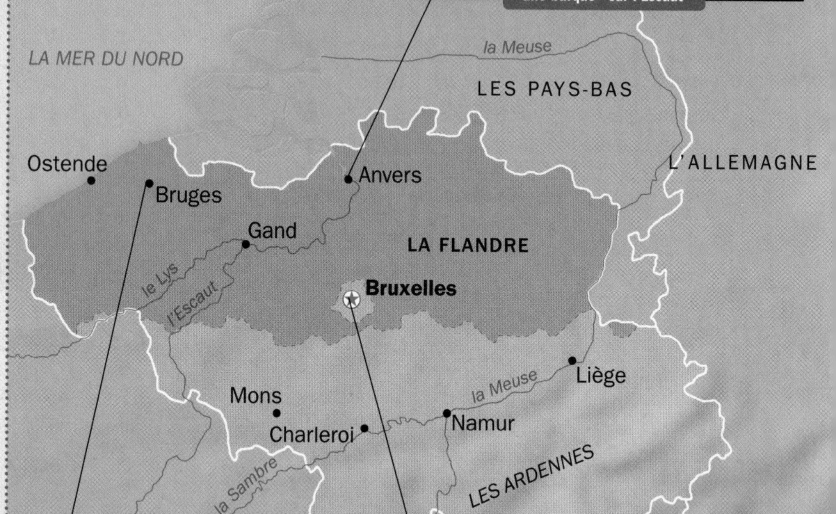

La Belgique

Le pays en chiffres

- **Superficie:** *30.500 km²*
- **Population:** *10.700.000*
  SOURCE: Population Division, UN Secretariat
- **Industries principales:** *agroalimentaire°, chimie, métallurgie, sidérurgie°, textile*
- **Villes principales:** *Anvers, Bruges, Bruxelles, Gand, Liège, Namur*
- **Langues:** *allemand, français, néerlandais°*
  Les Belges néerlandais parlent une variante de la langue néerlandaise qui s'appelle le flamand°. Environ° 60% de la population belge parlent flamand et habitent dans la partie nord° du pays, la Flandre. Le français est surtout parlé dans la partie sud° du pays, la Wallonie, par environ 40% des Belges. L'allemand est parlé par très peu de gens, environ 1%, dans l'est° du pays.
- **Monnaie:** *l'euro*

Belges célèbres

- **Marguerite Yourcenar,** *femme écrivain (1903–1987)*
- **Georges Simenon,** *écrivain (1903–1989)*
- **Jacques Brel,** *chanteur (1929–1978)*
- **Eddy Merckx,** *cycliste, cinq fois vainqueur° du Tour de France (1945–)*
- **Cécile de France,** *actrice (1975–)*
- **Justine Henin,** *joueuse de tennis (1982–)*

Bruges

cortège folklorique° de l'Ommegang

Incroyable mais vrai!

Acheter de la bière ou du fromage au monastère? Pourquoi pas? Les moines° trappistes suivent° des principes monastiques stricts: isolés, ils se consacrent° au travail et à la prière°. Pour subvenir à° leurs besoins, ils font des bières et des fromages de qualité. Seules six bières belges peuvent porter l'appellation «trappiste».

agroalimentaire *food processing* **sidérurgie** *steel industry* **néerlandais** *Dutch* **flamand** *Flemish* **Environ** *About* **nord** *north* **sud** *south* **est** *east* **vainqueur** *winner* **moines** *monks* **suivent** *follow* **se consacrent** *devote themselves* **prière** *prayer* **subvenir à** *provide for* **barque** *small boat* **cortège folklorique** *traditional procession*

OPTIONS

Belges célèbres Known for her historical novels, **Marguerite Yourcenar** (pen name of Marguerite de Crayencour) was the first woman to be elected to the **Académie française**. A prolific writer, **Georges Simenon** wrote mysteries, psychological novels, and pulp fiction. His *Inspector Maigret* series is sold worldwide. Lyricist, composer, singer, and actor, **Jacques Brel** was known for his passionate style and poetic lyrics. **Eddy Merckx** won numerous international competitions. Besides the **Tour de France**, he won the **Tour d'Italie** five times and the **Tour de Flandres** twice. **Cécile de France** has performed on stage and in films. She won **le César du Meilleur Espoir Féminin** for her role in ***L'auberge espagnole***. **Justine Hénin-Hardenne** has won three Grand Slam titles in women's singles and a gold medal at the 2004 Olympics.

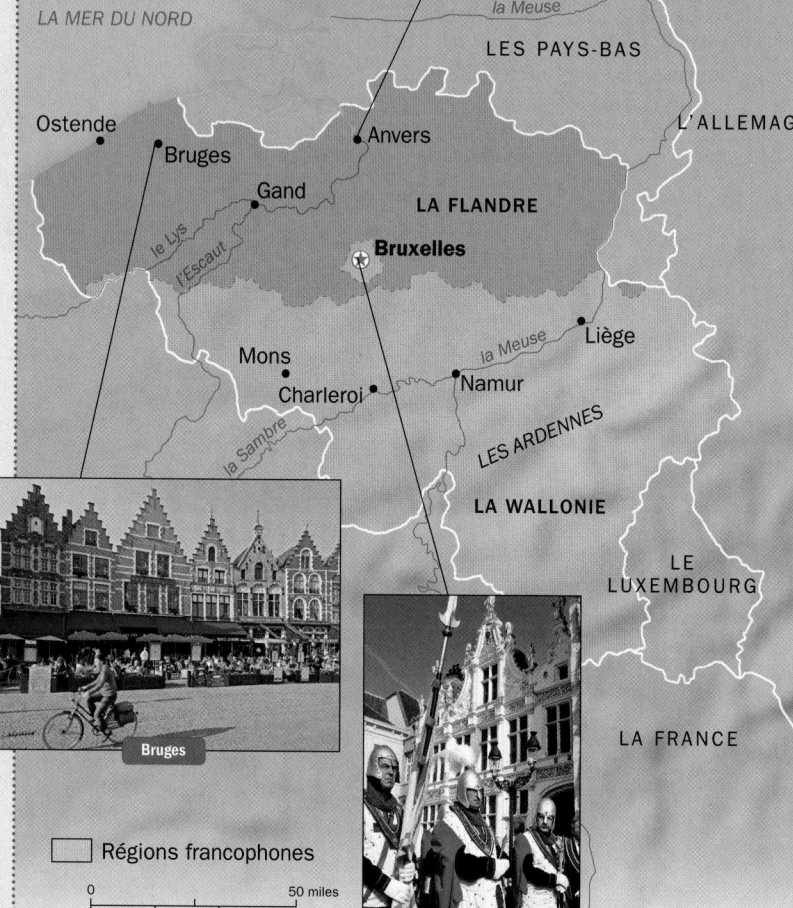

Les destinations

Bruxelles, capitale de l'Europe

Fondée au septième siècle, la ville de Bruxelles a été choisie en 1958 comme siège° de la CEE°. Aujourd'hui, elle reste encore le siège de l'Union européenne (l'UE), lieu central des institutions et des décisions européennes. On y trouve le Parlement européen, organe législatif de l'UE, et depuis 1967, le siège de l'OTAN°. Bruxelles est une ville très cosmopolite, avec un grand nombre d'habitants étrangers. Elle est aussi touristique, renommée pour sa Grand-Place, ses nombreux chocolatiers et la grande qualité de sa cuisine.

Les traditions

La bande dessinée

Les dessinateurs° de bandes dessinées (BD) sont très nombreux en Belgique. À Bruxelles, il y a de nombreuses peintures murales° et statues de personnages de BD. Le dessinateur Peyo est devenu célèbre avec la création des Schtroumpfs° en 1958, mais le père de la BD belge est Hergé, dessinateur qui a créé Tintin et Milou en 1929. Tintin est un reporter qui parcourt° le monde. En 1954, il devient le premier homme, avant Neil Armstrong, à marcher sur la Lune° dans *On a marché sur la Lune*. La BD de Tintin est traduite en 45 langues.

La gastronomie

Les moules frites

Les moules° frites sont une spécialité belge. Les moules, cuites° dans du vin blanc, et les frites sont servies dans des plats séparés, mais on les mange ensemble, et c'est délicieux. Beaucoup de gens ne savent pas que les frites ne sont pas françaises, mais belges! On peut en acheter dans les nombreuses friteries. Elles sont servies dans un cornet° en papier avec une sauce, souvent de la mayonnaise. Il existe même en Belgique une Semaine nationale de la frite et une Union nationale des fituristes.

Les arts

René Magritte (1898–1967)

René Magritte, peintre surréaliste, s'intéressait à la représentation des images mentales. En montrant° la divergence entre un objet et sa représentation, son désir était de «faire hurler° les objets les plus familiers», mais toujours avec humour. Le musée Magritte à Bruxelles se trouve dans la maison où il a habité pendant 24 ans, et qui était aussi le quartier général° des surréalistes belges. Le portrait de Magritte était sur les billets de 500 francs belges. Une de ses œuvres° les plus célèbres, à gauche, est *Le fils de l'homme*.

Qu'est-ce que vous avez appris? Répondez aux questions par des phrases complètes.

1. Quelle est la langue la plus parlée en Belgique?
   Le flamand est la langue la plus parlée.
2. Que produisent les moines trappistes?
   Ils produisent de la bière et du fromage.
3. À quelles activités se consacrent-ils?
   Ils se consacrent au travail et à la prière.
4. Quand Bruxelles a-t-elle été choisie comme capitale de l'Europe? Elle a été choisie en 1958.
5. Qui est le père de la bande dessinée belge?
   Hergé est le père de la bande dessinée belge.
6. Qui est allé sur la Lune avant Armstrong?
   Tintin est allé sur la Lune avant Armstrong.
7. Quelle bande dessinée Peyo a-t-il créée?
   Peyo a créé les Schtroumpfs.
8. Où peut-on acheter des frites?
   On peut acheter des frites dans les friteries.
9. Qu'est-ce que Magritte montre dans ses œuvres?
   Il montre la divergence entre un objet et sa représentation.
10. Quel était le quartier général des surréalistes belges?
    La maison de Magritte était leur quartier général.

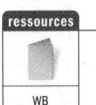

ressources: WB pp. 153–154 | espaces.vhlcentral.com

Practice more at **espaces.vhlcentral.com.**

SUR INTERNET

Go to **espaces.vhlcentral.com** to find more cultural information related to this **PANORAMA.**

1. Quels sont les noms de trois autres personnages de bandes dessinées belges?
2. Dans quelles peintures Magritte a-t-il représenté des parties de la maison (fenêtre, cheminée, escalier)?
3. Cherchez des informations sur la ville de Bruges. Combien de kilomètres de canaux (*canals*) y a-t-il?

siège *headquarters* **CEE** *European Economic Community (predecessor of the European Union)* **OTAN** *NATO* **dessinateurs** *cartoonists* **peintures murales** *murals* **Schtroumpfs** *Smurfs* **parcourt** *travels all over* **Lune** *moon* **moules** *mussels* **cuites** *cooked* **cornet** *cone* **En montrant** *By showing* **faire hurler** *make scream* **quartier général** *headquarters* **œuvres** *works*

Bruxelles, capitale de l'Europe
The city square, **la Grand-Place**, hosts concerts, festivals, and a flower market during the warmer months. Featuring baroque and gothic guild architecture, **la Grand-Place** was used as a merchant's market during the thirteenth century.

La bande dessinée

- In Brussels, one can learn about the creation of comics strips, such as **Tintin** and the **Schtroumpfs**, as well as 670 other cartoonists at the **Centre Belge de la Bande Dessinée**.
- *The Smurfs* was an American TV show from 1981–1990. Ask students: **Combien d'étudiants se souviennent des Schtroumpfs? Qui étaient-ils? Décrivez-les.**

Les moules frites

- Mussels and fries have been served in Belgium since the seventeenth century. The mussels come from the North Sea and are in season from September to February. Although **les moules** are most commonly prepared with white wine, some variations use cream, vegetable stock, or even beer. Today, there are over 4,000 **friteries** in Belgium.
- Ask students: **Voulez-vous goûter des moules frites? Pourquoi?**

René Magritte

- Certain symbols appear repeatedly in Magritte's work, such as a middle-class man wearing a bowler hat, a castle, a window, a rock, and a female torso. Dislocations of space, time, and scale are common elements.
- Have students look at the painting in this section *The Son of Man* (1964) and describe what they see. Then ask: **Que pensez-vous de son style de peinture? Quels objets sont réalistes? Quelle partie est incroyable? Que pensez-vous que la peinture représente?**

OPTIONS

Cultural Comparison Working in small groups, have students compare Brussels to Geneva (page 355), New York City, or Washington, D.C. Tell them to list the similarities and differences in a two-column chart under the headings **Similitudes** and **Différences**. After completing their charts, call on volunteers to read their lists. You might wish to assign a different city to each group.

Le chocolat belge Belgium produces 172,000 tons of chocolate per year and has 2,130 chocolate shops. Godiva, Côte d'Or, Callebaut, and Nirvana are just a few of the many famous Belgian brands. Bring in some Belgian chocolates and conduct a taste test. Ask students how Belgian chocolate compares with well-known American brands of chocolates.

Section Goals
In this section, students will:
- learn to recognize the purpose of a text
- read some cartoons and jokes

Stratégie Tell students that recognizing the writer's purpose will help them understand an unfamiliar text.

Examinez le texte Students should infer that the illustrations are cartoons, the short texts are jokes, the writer's purpose is to make people laugh or to make fun of something or someone, and the language is colloquial.

À propos de l'auteur After reading the text, ask students these comprehension questions.
1. D'où vient Lévy? (Québec)
2. À quel âge a-t-elle commencé à dessiner? (à trois ans)
3. Qui l'a encouragée à être artiste? (son père)
4. Quels sont les sujets de ses dessins humoristiques? (la vie de tous les jours, le travail, les animaux et la politique)

Lecture

National Standards: communication, cultures

Audio: Dramatic Recording

Avant la lecture

STRATÉGIE

Recognizing the purpose of a text

When you are faced with an unfamiliar text, it is important to determine the writer's purpose. If you are reading an editorial in a newspaper, for example, you know that the journalist's objective is to persuade you of his or her point of view. Identifying the purpose of a text will help you better comprehend its meaning.

Examinez le texte

Examinez les illustrations. Quel est le genre de ce texte? Décrivez ce qu'il y a dans chaque illustration. Puis, regardez les trois textes courts. Quel est le genre de ces textes? Quel est leur but (*purpose*)? D'après vous, quel genre de vocabulaire allez-vous trouver dans ces textes?

À propos de l'auteur
Renée Lévy

Renée Lévy est une artiste québécoise. Son père, artiste lui aussi, lui a expliqué les principes du dessin et l'a encouragée à dessiner. Au lycée, Renée Lévy amusait ses camarades de classe avec ses caricatures de professeurs. Ses dessins humoristiques traitent de° nombreux sujets, comme la vie de tous les jours, le travail, les animaux et la politique. On peut voir ses caricatures et ses dessins humoristiques dans plusieurs publications et sur des sites Internet. Renée Lévy est l'auteur des deux dessins que vous allez voir°.

traitent de *deal with* **voir** *see*

Les Technoblagues

Dessin 1

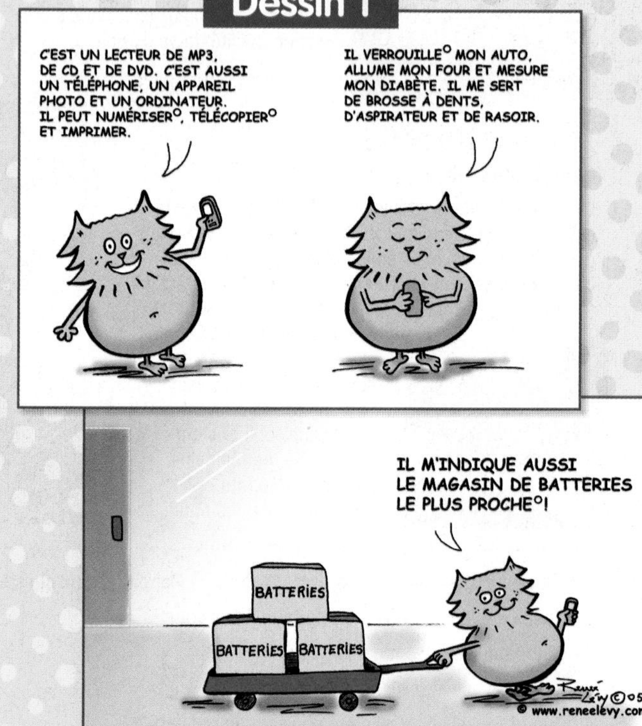

C'EST UN LECTEUR DE MP3, DE CD ET DE DVD. C'EST AUSSI UN TÉLÉPHONE, UN APPAREIL PHOTO ET UN ORDINATEUR. IL PEUT NUMÉRISER°, TÉLÉCOPIER° ET IMPRIMER.
IL VERROUILLE° MON AUTO, ALLUME MON FOUR ET MESURE MON DIABÈTE. IL ME SERT DE BROSSE À DENTS, D'ASPIRATEUR ET DE RASOIR.
IL M'INDIQUE AUSSI LE MAGASIN DE BATTERIES LE PLUS PROCHE°!
BATTERIES
BATTERIES
BATTERIES
Renée Lévy ©05
© www.reneelevy.com

Blague 1

Dans un magasin d'ordinateurs, un père se plaint° du manque d'intérêt° de son fils pour le sport. «Il passe son temps devant son écran, avec ses jeux vidéo», explique le père découragé à l'employé. «Tenez, l'autre jour, je lui ai proposé un match de tennis. Savez-vous ce que mon fils m'a répondu? "Quand tu veux, papa, je vais chercher la disquette."»

OPTIONS

Language Notes Point out that several words in the cartoons are specific to **Québécois** French. In the first cartoon, the word **batterie(s)** is used for *battery*, instead of **pile(s)**. In the second cartoon, **V.U.S.** is used for *SUV*, instead of **4x4 (quatre-quatre)**.

Pairs Have students work in pairs. Tell them to go through the cartoons and jokes, and make a list of all the words they can find in the text related to technology. Then have them get together with another pair and verify their answers.

Blague 2

La maîtresse°, absente de sa classe pendant dix minutes, y retourne et entend un véritable vacarme°. «Quand je suis partie, dit-elle, sévèrement, je vous ai interdit° de bavarder entre vous.» «Mais, dit un élève, on ne s'est pas adressé la parole°. Seulement, pour s'occuper, on a tous sorti nos portables et on a passé un coup de fil° à nos parents.»

Dessin 2

L'ESSENCE COÛTE TRÈS CHER. JE REMPLACE LE MOTEUR DE MON V.U.S°. ...
PAR LE MOTEUR ÉLECTRIQUE DE MA MACHINE À COUDRE°!
SAUF° QU'IL ME FAUDRA° UN PLUS LONG FIL°...
www.reneelevy.com

Blague 3

Un homme vient d'acheter une nouvelle voiture, mais il est obligé de la laisser dans la rue la nuit. Comme il sait que les voleurs° d'autoradios° n'hésitent pas à fracturer° les portières, il met sur son pare-brise la note suivante: IL N'Y A PAS DE RADIO DANS CETTE VOITURE. Le jour d'après, plus de° voiture. À la place où elle se trouvait, il y a seulement la note sur laquelle° on a écrit: *Ce n'est pas grave, on en fera mettre une°.*

numériser *scan* **télécopier** *fax* **verrouille** *locks* **le plus proche** *the closest* **se plaint** *complains* **manque d'intérêt** *lack of interest* **maîtresse** *school teacher* **vacarme** *racket* **interdit** *forbade* **on ne s'est pas adressé la parole** *we didn't speak to each other* **a passé un coup de fil** *made a call* **V.U.S.** *S.U.V.* **machine à coudre** *sewing machine* **sauf** *except* **il me faudra** *I will need* **fil** *cord* **voleurs** *thieves* **autoradios** *car radios* **fracturer** *break* **plus de** *no more* **sur laquelle** *on which* **on en fera mettre une** *we'll have one installed*

Après la lecture

Répondez Répondez aux questions par des phrases complètes.

1. Quelles sont trois des fonctions de l'appareil du **dessin 1**?
   Answers will vary. Possible answer: C'est un lecteur de MP3, un téléphone et un aspirateur.
2. De quoi l'appareil du **dessin 1** a-t-il beaucoup besoin?
   L'appareil a besoin de beaucoup de batteries.
3. Pour jouer au tennis, on a besoin d'une raquette. Dans la **blague 1**, quel mot (*word*) le garçon utilise-t-il au lieu de (*instead of*) «raquette»?
   Il utilise le mot «disquette».
4. Dans la **blague 1**, pourquoi le père est-il découragé?
   Il est découragé parce que son fils ne s'intéresse pas au sport et passe son temps devant son écran d'ordinateur, avec ses jeux vidéo.
5. Dans la **blague 2**, qu'est-ce que la maîtresse a demandé aux élèves?
   Elle a demandé aux élèves de ne pas bavarder entre eux.
6. Qu'ont fait les élèves de la **blague 2** quand la maîtresse est partie?
   Ils ont téléphoné à leurs parents avec leur portable.
7. Pourquoi faut-il remplacer le moteur du V.U.S. dans le **dessin 2**?
   Il faut le remplacer parce que l'essence coûte très cher.
8. De quoi le personnage a-t-il besoin après dans le **dessin 2**?
   Il a besoin d'un fil plus long.
9. Dans la **blague 3**, qu'est-ce que l'homme écrit sur la note qu'il met sur le pare-brise de sa voiture? Pourquoi?
   Il écrit qu'il n'y a pas de radio dans sa voiture. Il pense que les voleurs d'autoradios ne vont pas fracturer les portières s'il n'y a pas de radio dans la voiture.
10. À la fin de la **blague 3**, qu'ont pris les voleurs? Que vont-ils faire?
    Ils ont pris la voiture et vont faire installer un autoradio.

Des inventions **L'appareil du dessin 1 a beaucoup de fonctions. D'après vous, quelle invention de la liste est la plus utile et pourquoi? Soyez prêt à expliquer votre décision à la classe.**

appareil photo	lecteur CD
aspirateur	lecteur DVD
fax	lecteur MP3
imprimante	téléphone

Inventez **Électropuissance, une compagnie d'équipement électronique, vous demande d'inventer l'appareil idéal pour la vie de tous les jours. Dites comment votre invention va vous aider à la maison, à l'école, dans la voiture, en voyage et pour rester en bonne santé.**

Répondez
- Go over the answers with the class.
- Ask various students: **À votre avis, quelle blague est la plus drôle? Quel dessin est le plus drôle? Pourquoi?** Then take a quick poll to find out which cartoon or joke the class considers the funniest or most amusing. Tally the results on the board.

Des inventions
- Give students a few minutes to choose an invention and jot down their reasons before discussing them.
- For each invention listed, ask: **Combien d'étudiants ont choisi ____? Pourquoi?**

Inventez
- If time is limited, you may want to assign this activity as written homework. Then have volunteers present their devices during the next class period. Encourage students to make a drawing of their device so the class can see what it looks like.
- Have the class vote on the most useful invention.

OPTIONS

Pairs Have students work in pairs. Tell them to create a cartoon or write a joke similar to the ones in this reading. They should brainstorm a list of topics first. You might want to suggest that they be related to technology. Then have students present their cartoons or jokes to the class. Have the class vote on the most humorous cartoon and joke.

Cultural Activity Have students go to Renée Lévy's web site to view more of her work. Tell them to find out what other types of artwork she creates, decide which style they prefer, and explain their reasons. Alternatively, you can have them find another cartoon about technology to bring in and share with the class.

Section Goals

In this section, students will:
- learn to make a list of key words before writing
- write a composition about their past and present communication habits

Stratégie Explain that having a list of key words will allow students to maintain their writing flow rather than stopping every few minutes to try and think of a specific word to use.

Thème Tell students to answer the questions first. Then they should make a list of people they communicate with regularly and the means they use to communicate before they begin writing their compositions.

Écriture

NATIONAL communication cultures STANDARDS

STRATÉGIE

Listing key words

Once you have determined the purpose for a piece of writing and identified your audience, it is helpful to make a list of key words you can use while writing. If you were to write a description of your campus, for example, you would probably need a list of prepositions that describe location, such as **devant**, **à côté de**, and **derrière**. Likewise, a list of descriptive adjectives would be useful if you were writing about the people and places of your childhood.

By preparing a list of potential words ahead of time, you will find it easier to avoid using the dictionary while writing your first draft. You will probably also learn a few new words in French while preparing your list of key words.

Listing useful vocabulary is also a valuable organizational strategy since the act of brainstorming key words will help you form ideas about your topic. In addition, a list of key words can help you avoid redundancy when you write.

If you were going to write a composition about your communication habits with your friends, what words would be the most helpful to you? Jot a few of them down and compare your list with a partner's. Did you choose the same words? Would you choose any different or additional words, based on what your partner wrote?

____

____

____

____

____

____

____

____

Thème

Écrire une dissertation

Avant l'écriture

1. Vous allez écrire une dissertation pour décrire vos préférences et vos habitudes en ce qui concerne (*regarding*) les moyens (*means*) de communication d'hier et d'aujourd'hui.

2. D'abord, répondez en quelques mots à ces questions pour vous faire une idée de ce que (*what*) doit inclure votre dissertation.
   - Quel est votre moyen de communication préféré (e-mail, téléphone, lettre, ...)? Pourquoi?
   - En général, comment communiquez-vous avec les gens que vous connaissez? Pourquoi? Avez-vous toujours communiqué avec eux de cette manière (*in this way*)?
   - Communiquez-vous avec tout le monde de la même manière ou cela dépend-il des personnes? Par exemple, restez-vous en contact avec vos grands-parents de la même manière qu'avec votre professeur de français? Expliquez.
   - Comment restez-vous en contact avec les membres de votre famille? Et avec vos amis et vos camarades de classe?
   - Communiquez-vous avec certaines personnes tous les jours? Avec qui? Comment?

OPTIONS

Stratégie Encourage students to rely primarily on known vocabulary when preparing their lists. They should consult a dictionary only if they need a word that is central to their topic and they can't think of it on their own.

Review other strategies for creating a list of useful vocabulary.
- Two or more students can work together to brainstorm a list of words.
- Students can list antonyms for key words related to the topic.
- If necessary, students can look up key words in a bilingual dictionary or a thesaurus and review the entries for related words and synonyms.

3. Ensuite, complétez ce tableau pour faire une liste des personnes avec qui vous communiquez régulièrement, et pour donner le moyen de communication que vous avez utilisé dans le passé et que vous utilisez aujourd'hui. Utilisez aussi votre liste de mots-clés comme point de départ pour votre dissertation.

Personnes	Moyen de communication du passé	Moyen de communication d'aujourd'hui
Personne 1		
Personne 2		
Personne 3		
Personne 4		
Personne 5		

Écriture

1. Servez-vous de la liste de mots-clés que vous avez créée, de vos réponses aux questions et du tableau pour écrire votre dissertation. Utilisez le vocabulaire et la grammaire de l'unité.
2. N'oubliez pas d'inclure ces informations:
   - Toutes les personnes avec qui vous communiquez souvent
   - Les moyens de communications que vous utilisiez avant
   - Les moyens de communications que vous utilisez maintenant
   - La raison pour laquelle vous avez changé de moyen de communication

Après l'écriture

1. Échangez votre dissertation avec celle (*the one*) d'un(e) partenaire. Répondez à ces questions pour commenter son travail.
   - Votre partenaire a-t-il/elle inclu toutes les personnes citées dans le tableau?
   - A-t-il/elle mentionné tous les moyens de communications qu'il/elle utilisait avant?
   - A-t-il/elle mentionné tous les moyens de communications qu'il/elle utilise maintenant?
   - A-t-il/elle mentionné la raison pour laquelle il/elle a changé de moyen de communication?
   - A-t-il/elle utilisé le vocabulaire et la grammaire de l'unité?
   - Quel(s) détail(s) ajouteriez-vous (*would you add*)? Quel(s) détail(s) enlèveriez-vous (*would you delete*)? Quel(s) autre(s) commentaire(s) avez-vous pour votre partenaire?

2. Corrigez votre dissertation d'après (*according to*) les commentaires de votre partenaire. Relisez votre travail pour éliminer ces problèmes:
   - des fautes (*errors*) d'orthographe
   - des fautes de ponctuation
   - des fautes de conjugaison
   - un mauvais emploi (*use*) de la grammaire de l'unité
   - des fautes d'accord (*agreement*) des adjectifs

EVALUATION

Criteria

Content Contains answers to each set of questions called out in the bulleted points of the task, as well as a preliminary list of people and means of communication.
Scale: 1 2 3 4 5

Organization Organized into logical paragraphs that begin with a topic sentence and contain appropriate supporting details.
Scale: 1 2 3 4 5

Accuracy Uses prepositions with the infinitive and relative pronouns correctly. Spells words, conjugates verbs, and modifies adjectives correctly throughout.
Scale: 1 2 3 4 5

Creativity Includes additional information that is not included in the task and/or uses adjectives, descriptive verbs, and additional details to make the composition more interesting.
Scale: 1 2 3 4 5

Scoring

Excellent	18–20 points
Good	14–17 points
Satisfactory	10–13 points
Unsatisfactory	< 10 points

OPTIONS

Avant l'écriture Have students create the list of persons on their own. Then tally the results as a class to see how many people the average student is in touch with, as well as what means of communication he or she used five years ago and what he or she uses today. Create a summary that lists the different means of communication in order of popularity, now and five years ago.

Tell students that they should organize their information around the questions called out by the five bulleted items in the writing task. Here are some transitional phrases they may find useful for moving from one bulleted category to the next: **À mon avis…, Concernant/À propos de/Au sujet de…, Quand il s'agit de…, En général/Généralement, Normalement, D'habitude.**

Instructional Resources
espaces.vhlcentral.com: Textbook MP3s; IRM (Textbook Audioscript); downloads; reference tools

Suggestion Tell students that an easy way to study from **Vocabulaire** is to cover up the French half of each section, leaving only the English equivalents exposed. They can then quiz themselves on the French items. To focus on the English equivalents of the French entries, they simply reverse this process.

Flashcards
Audio: Vocabulary

VOCABULAIRE

L'ordinateur

un CD/compact disc/ disque compact	*CD, compact disc*
(CD/compact disc/ disques compacts *pl.*)	*(CDs, compact discs)*
un CD-ROM/cédérom (CD-ROM/cédéroms *pl.*)	*CD-ROM(s)*
un clavier	*keyboard*
un disque dur	*hard drive*
un écran	*screen*
un e-mail	*e-mail*
un fichier	*file*
une imprimante	*printer*
un jeu vidéo (jeux vidéo *pl.*)	*video game(s)*
un logiciel	*software, program*
un moniteur	*monitor*
un mot de passe	*password*
une page d'accueil	*homepage*
un site Internet/web	*website*
une souris	*mouse*
démarrer	*to start up*
être connecté(e) (avec)	*to be connected (with)*
être en ligne (avec)	*to be online/on the phone (with)*
graver	*to record, to burn (a CD)*
imprimer	*to print*
sauvegarder	*to save*
surfer sur Internet	*to surf the Internet*
télécharger	*to download*

Verbes

couvrir	*to cover*
découvrir	*to discover*
offrir	*to offer*
ouvrir	*to open*
souffrir	*to suffer*

Expressions utiles	*See pp. 367 and 381.*
Prepositions with the infinitive	*See p. 370.*

La voiture

arrêter (de faire quelque chose)	*to stop (doing something)*
attacher sa ceinture de sécurité (*f.*)	*to buckle/to fasten one's seatbelt*
avoir un accident	*to have/to be in an accident*
dépasser	*to go over; to pass*
faire le plein	*to fill the tank*
freiner	*to brake*
se garer	*to park*
rentrer (dans)	*to hit*
réparer	*to repair*
tomber en panne	*to break down*
vérifier (l'huile/la pression des pneus)	*to check (the oil/ the air pressure)*
un capot	*hood*
un coffre	*trunk*
l'embrayage (*m.*)	*clutch*
l'essence (*f.*)	*gas*
un essuie-glace (essuie-glaces *pl.*)	*windshield wiper(s)*
les freins (*m., pl.*)	*brakes*
l'huile (*f.*)	*oil*
un moteur	*engine*
un pare-brise (pare-brise *pl.*)	*windshield*
un pare-chocs (pare-chocs *pl.*)	*bumper*
les phares (*m.*)	*headlights*
un pneu (crevé)	*(flat) tire*
une portière	*car door*
un réservoir d'essence	*gas tank*
un rétroviseur	*rearview mirror*
une roue	*wheel*
une roue de secours	*spare tire*
une voiture	*car*
un volant	*steering wheel*
un voyant (d'essence/ d'huile)	*(gas/oil) warning light*
un agent de police/ un(e) policier/policière	*police officer*
une amende	*fine*
une autoroute	*highway*
la circulation	*traffic*
la limitation de vitesse	*speed limit*
un(e) mécanicien(ne)	*mechanic*
un parking	*parking lot*
un permis de conduire	*driver's license*
une rue	*street*
une station-service	*service station*

Verbes pronominaux réciproques

s'adorer	*to adore one another*
s'aider	*to help one another*
s'aimer (bien)	*to love (like) one another*
se connaître	*to know one another*
se dire	*to tell one another*
se donner	*to give one another*
s'écrire	*to write one another*
s'embrasser	*to kiss one another*
s'entendre bien (avec)	*to get along well (with one another)*
se parler	*to speak to one another*
se quitter	*to leave one another*
se regarder	*to look at one another*
se rencontrer	*to meet one another (make an acquaintance)*
se retrouver	*to meet one another (planned)*
se téléphoner	*to phone one another*

L'électronique

un appareil photo (numérique)	*(digital) camera*
un baladeur CD	*personal CD player*
une caméra vidéo/ un caméscope	*camcorder*
une cassette vidéo	*videotape*
une chaîne (de télévision)	*(television) channel*
une chaîne stéréo	*stereo system*
un fax	*fax (machine)*
un lecteur (de) CD/DVD	*CD/DVD player*
un magnétophone	*tape recorder*
un magnétoscope	*videocassette recorder (VCR)*
un portable	*cell phone*
un poste de télévision	*television set*
un répondeur (téléphonique)	*answering machine*
une télécommande	*remote control*
allumer	*to turn on*
composer (un numéro)	*to dial (a number)*
effacer	*to erase*
enregistrer	*to record*
éteindre	*to turn off; to shut off*
fermer	*to close; to shut off*
fonctionner/marcher	*to work, to function*
sonner	*to ring*

ressources
espaces.vhlcentral.com

En ville

UNITÉ

12

Pour commencer
- Qu'est-ce que David a dans la main?
- Quel temps fait-il?
- Que fait Valérie?
- Est-ce que David va conduire jusqu'à sa destination?

Unit Goals

Leçon 12A
In this lesson, students will learn:
- terms for banking
- terms for business establishments
- terms for the post office
- the pronunciation of the letter **h**
- about methods of payment in France
- more about businesses and small shops through specially shot video footage
- the verbs **voir**, **croire**, **recevoir**, and **apercevoir**
- negative and affirmative expressions
- about the city of Rennes

Leçon 12B
In this lesson, students will learn:
- terms for asking for and giving directions
- rules of French capitalization
- about the centers of French cities and towns
- the formation and usage of **le futur simple**
- irregular future tense forms
- to use background information to understand spoken French

Savoir-faire
In this section, students will learn:
- cultural and historical information about the Canadian province of Quebec
- to identify the narrator's point of view
- to use linking words when writing

Pour commencer
- **Il a un plan dans la main.**
- **Il fait beau./Il fait (du) soleil.**
- **Elle aide David à trouver l'endroit qu'il cherche.**
- **Non, il va y aller à pied.**

RESOURCES

Workbook/Video Manual: WB Activities, pp. 155–168
Laboratory Manual: Lab Activities, pp. 89–96
Workbook/Video Manual: Video Activities, pp. 255–258; pp. 293–294
WB/VM/LM Answer Key

espaces.vhlcentral.com: Instructor's Resource Manual [IRM] (Textbook Audioscript; Lab Audioscript; Videoscript; **Roman-photo** Translations; **Vocabulaire supplémentaire**; **Feuilles d'activités**; Info Gap Activities; **Le zapping** TV clip transcription; **Essayez!** and **Mise en pratique** answers);
Transparencies #51, #52, #53; Testing Program, pp. 89–96; pp. 145–152; Test Files; Testing Program MP3s; Lab MP3s; Textbook MP3s
Test Generator
Video on DVD

Section Goals

In this section, students will learn and practice vocabulary related to:
- banking
- the post office
- business establishments

Instructional Resources
*espaces.vhlcentral.com: Transparency #51; IRM (**Vocabulaire supplémentaire; Mise en pratique** answers; Textbook Audioscript; Lab Audioscript); Textbook MP3s; Lab MP3s; WB/VM/LM Answer Key; activities; downloads; reference tools*

Suggestions
- Use **Transparency #51.** Describe what people are doing. Examples: **Elle poste une lettre. Il retire de l'argent.** Then point out the various stores and other businesses. Have students identify the types of business based on the signs.
- Explain that **un salon de beauté** is a day spa where one gets manicures, pedicures, facials, massages, etc. It is not the same as **un coiffeur/une coiffeuse**.
- Ask students questions using the new vocabulary. Examples: **Que fait le facteur? Que fait l'homme au distributeur automatique? Utilisez-vous les distributeurs automatiques? Que vend-on dans une papeterie? Qu'achète-t-on chez le marchand de journaux? Où est le cybercafé?**
- To introduce banking terms, mime several transactions. Say: **Quand j'ai besoin d'argent, je vais au distributeur.** Follow the same procedure with the post office vocabulary.
- Point out the difference in spelling between the French words **adresse** and **enveloppe** and the English words *address* and *envelope.*
- Additional vocabulary for this lesson can be found in the **Vocabulaire supplémentaire** on the Supersite.

Leçon 12A

Talking Picture
Audio: Activity

You will learn how to...
- make business transactions
- get around town

Les courses

Vocabulaire

accompagner	*to accompany*
avoir un compte bancaire	*to have a bank account*
déposer de l'argent	*to deposit money*
emprunter	*to borrow*
payer par carte (de crédit)	*to pay by credit card*
payer en liquide	*to pay in cash*
payer par chèque	*to pay by check*
remplir un formulaire	*to fill out a form*
retirer de l'argent	*to withdraw money*
signer	*to sign*
une adresse	*address*
une carte postale	*postcard*
une enveloppe	*envelope*
un timbre	*stamp*
une boutique	*boutique, store*
une brasserie	*café, restaurant*
un commissariat de police	*police station*
une laverie	*laundromat*
une mairie	*town/city hall; mayor's office*
un compte-chèques	*checking account*
un compte d'épargne	*savings account*
une dépense	*expenditure, expense*
des pièces de monnaie	*coins*
de la monnaie	*change*
fermé(e)	*closed*
ouvert(e)	*open*

ressources
WB pp. 155-156 | LM p. 89 | espaces.vhlcentral.com

OPTIONS

Extra Practice For additional practice, ask these questions. **1. Avez-vous un compte-chèques? 2. Avez-vous un compte d'épargne? 3. Où y a-t-il un distributeur automatique? 4. Où y a-t-il un bureau de poste? 5. Où y a-t-il une banque? 6. Quelle est votre marchand de journaux préféré? 7. Quelle est votre boutique préférée?**

Game Play a game of **Dix questions**. Ask a volunteer to think of a place listed in the new vocabulary. Other students get to ask one yes/no question, then they can guess what the word is. Limit attempts to ten questions per word. You might want to tell students that they can narrow down their options by asking questions about what can be done at the location.

Mise en pratique

1 Associez Associez chaque activité de la colonne de gauche avec le lieu qui correspond dans la colonne de droite.

d	1. acheter un chemisier	a. un bureau de poste
j	2. acheter du maquillage	b. une banque
i	3. acheter un magazine	c. une bijouterie
c	4. acheter une montre	d. une boutique
e	5. boire un café	e. une brasserie
a	6. envoyer une carte	f. un commissariat de police
g	7. envoyer un e-mail	g. un cybercafé
h	8. faire la lessive	h. une laverie
b	9. ouvrir un compte	i. un marchand de journaux
f	10. payer une amende	j. un salon de beauté

2 Complétez Complétez ces phrases avec le mot ou l'expression qui convient le mieux. N'oubliez pas de faire les accords nécessaires.

1. ___Le facteur___ apporte le courrier tous les jours à la même heure.
2. Quand les magasins sont ___fermés___, on ne peut pas faire de courses.
3. Pour poster une lettre, on peut simplement la mettre dans ___une boîte aux lettres___.
4. Quand on n'a pas beaucoup d'argent, il faut faire attention à ses ___dépenses___.
5. Si la banque n'est pas ouverte, on peut toujours ___retirer de l'argent___ au distributeur automatique.
6. Quand on envoie une lettre, il ne faut pas oublier d'écrire ___l'adresse___ et de mettre ___un timbre___.
7. Pour acheter une voiture, il faut souvent ___emprunter___ de l'argent.
8. Si on n'a pas de lave-linge à la maison, il faut aller à ___la laverie___.

3 Écoutez Écoutez la conversation entre Jean-Pierre et Carole. Ensuite, complétez les phrases avec le bon mot.

1. Carole demande à Jean-Pierre d'acheter des timbres et de ___poster___ un colis. (déposer, poster, retirer)
2. Le ___bureau de poste___ se trouve sur la route de Jean-Pierre. (bureau de poste, papeterie, laverie)
3. Jean-Pierre veut ___déposer___ de l'argent à la banque. (retirer, déposer, emprunter)
4. Jean-Pierre doit ___remplir___ et signer des formulaires. (accompagner, remplir, payer)
5. Jean-Pierre a acheté le journal chez le ___marchand de journaux___. (papeterie, marchand de journaux, bureau de poste)
6. Jean-Pierre n'avait pas assez de ___liquide___ sur lui. (compte-chèques, carte de crédit, liquide)

Practice more at **espaces.vhlcentral.com.**

1 Suggestion Ask students what one does at each place listed. They should respond with the activity. Example: **Que fait-on dans un bureau de poste? (On envoie une lettre/carte.)**

1 Expansion For additional practice, ask students where they might do these activities. **1. poster un colis (au bureau de poste) 2. retirer de l'argent (à la banque/au distributeur automatique) 3. manger quelque chose (dans une brasserie) 4. acheter un cadeau (dans une boutique/dans une bijouterie)**

2 Suggestion Have students check their answers with a classmate.

3 Tapescript JEAN-PIERRE: Carole, je vais aller à la banque. Est-ce que tu as besoin de quelque chose en ville?
CAROLE: Oui. Est-ce que tu peux aller faire des courses pour moi? Tu peux prendre le journal chez le marchand de journaux? J'ai aussi un colis à poster et j'ai besoin de timbres.
J-P: Pas de problème. Le bureau de poste et le marchand de journaux sont sur ma route.
Jean-Pierre est maintenant à la banque.
J-P: Bonjour, Monsieur. J'ai de l'argent à déposer sur mon compte-chèques et sur mon compte d'épargne, s'il vous plaît.
L'EMPLOYÉ: Oui, bien sûr, Monsieur. Voici les formulaires à remplir et à signer. Si vous avez besoin de liquide pendant le week-end, nous avons un nouveau distributeur de billets à l'extérieur.
J-P: Très bien, je vous remercie.
Plus tard, à la maison…
C: Alors, tu as fait mes courses?
J-P: Oui, voici le journal, mais je n'ai pas envoyé le colis. La machine ne fonctionnait pas. Je n'ai pas pu payer avec ma carte de crédit et je n'avais pas assez de liquide sur moi. Je suis désolé.
C: Ce n'est pas grave. Je dois aller à la papeterie plus tard, je peux passer à la poste après.
(On Textbook MP3s)

3 Suggestion Have volunteers read the completed sentences aloud.

OPTIONS

Game Toss a beanbag to a student at random and call out the name of a place. You might also recycle places from **Leçon 4A**. The person has four seconds to name an activity that goes with it. That person then tosses the beanbag to another student and says another place. Students who cannot think of an activity or repeat one that has already been mentioned are eliminated. The last person standing wins.

Small Groups Have students work in groups of four or five. Give each group a different list of errands. Tell them to create a story in which someone goes to various places to complete the errands. Remind them to use sequencing expressions, such as **d'abord, puis**, and **après ça**.

4 Suggestion Encourage students to provide as many details as possible about each photo.

5 Suggestion Tell students to jot down notes during their interviews so that they will remember their partner's responses.

6 Suggestion Encourage students to brainstorm words and expressions they might want to use in their dialogue before they begin writing.

Communication

4 Décrivez **Avec un(e) partenaire, regardez les photos et décrivez où et comment Annick et Charles ont passé la journée samedi dernier. Donnez l'heure exacte pour chaque endroit.** Answers will vary.

1.

2.

3.

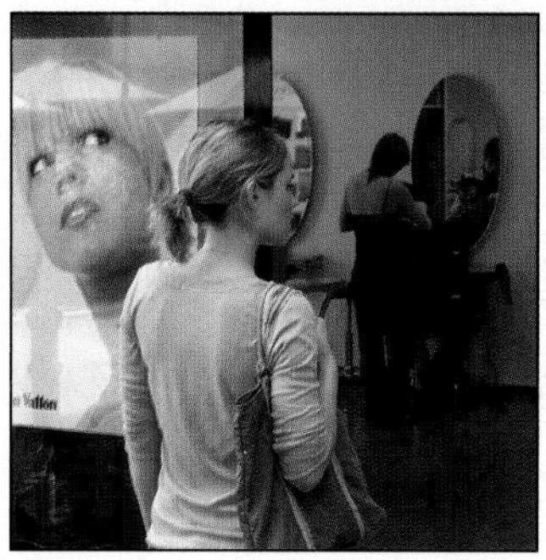

4.

5.

6.

5 Répondez **Avec un(e) partenaire, posez ces questions et répondez-y à tour de rôle. Ensuite, comparez vos réponses avec celles (*the ones*) d'un autre groupe.** Answers will vary.

1. Vas-tu souvent au bureau de poste? Pour quoi faire?
2. Quel genre de courses fais-tu le week-end?
3. Où est-ce que tu fais souvent la queue? Pourquoi?
4. Y a-t-il une laverie près de chez toi? Combien de fois par mois y vas-tu?
5. Comment préfères-tu payer tes achats (*purchases*)? Pourquoi?
6. Combien de fois par semaine utilises-tu un distributeur de billets?

6 À vous de jouer **Par petits groupes, choisissez une de ces situations et écrivez un dialogue. Ensuite, jouez la scène.** Answers will vary.

1. À la banque, un(e) étudiant(e) veut ouvrir un compte bancaire et connaître les services offerts.
2. À la poste, une vieille dame (*lady*) veut envoyer un colis, acheter des timbres et faire un changement d'adresse. Il y a la queue derrière elle.
3. Dans un salon de beauté, deux femmes discutent de leurs courses à la mairie, à la papeterie et chez le marchand de journaux.
4. Dans un cybercafé, des étudiants font des achats en ligne sur différents sites.

OPTIONS

Extra Practice Have students make signs and set up various businesses around the classroom, such as a bank and a post office. Then give students detailed errands to run and have them role-play the situations at the locations. Example: Go to the bank and withdraw 20 euros, then go to the post office and buy six stamps. Tell students to alternate playing employees and customers.

Game Divide the class into two teams. Have a spelling bee using vocabulary words from **Espace contextes**. Pronounce each word, use it in a sentence, and then say the word again. Tell students that they must spell the words in French and include all diacritical marks.

Les sons et les lettres

Audio: Concepts, Activities
Record & Compare

comparisons NATIONAL STANDARDS

The letter h

You already know that the letter **h** is silent in French, and you are familiar with many French words that begin with an **h muet**. In such words, the letter **h** is treated as if it were a vowel. For example, the articles **le** and **la** become **l'** and there is a liaison between the final consonant of a preceding word and the vowel following the **h**.

l'heure **l'homme** **des hôtels** **des hommes**

Some words begin with an **h aspiré**. In such words, the **h** is still silent, but it is not treated like a vowel. Words beginning with **h aspiré**, like these you've already learned, are not preceded by **l'** and there no liaison.

la honte **les haricots verts** **le huit mars** **les hors-d'œuvre**

Words that begin with an **h aspiré** are normally indicated in dictionaries by some kind of symbol, usually an asterisk (*).

Prononcez Répétez les mots suivants à voix haute.

1. le hall	5. le héron	9. l'hilarité	13. les hiéroglyphes
2. la hi-fi	6. l'horloge	10. la Hongrie	14. les hors-d'œuvre
3. l'humeur	7. l'horizon	11. l'hélicoptère	15. les hippopotames
4. la honte	8. le hippie	12. les hamburgers	16. l'hiver

Articulez Répétez les phrases suivantes à voix haute.

1. Hélène joue de la harpe.
2. Hier, Honorine est allée à l'hôpital.
3. Le hamster d'Hervé s'appelle Henri.
4. La Havane est la capitale de Cuba.
5. L'anniversaire d'Héloïse est le huit mars.
6. Le hockey et le handball sont mes sports préférés.

Dictons Répétez les dictons à voix haute.

La honte n'est pas d'être inférieur à l'adversaire, c'est d'être inférieur à soi-même.[1]

L'heure, c'est l'heure; avant l'heure, c'est pas l'heure; après l'heure, c'est plus l'heure.[2]

ressources
LM p. 90
espaces.vhlcentral.com

1 Shame is not being inferior to an adversary; it's being inferior to oneself.
2 On time is on time; before the hour is not on time; after the hour is no longer on time.

Section Goals

In this section, students will learn about the letter **h**.

Instructional Resources
espaces.vhlcentral.com: Textbook MP3s; Lab MP3s; WB/VM/LM Answer Key; IRM (Textbook Audioscript; Lab Audioscript); activities; downloads; reference tools

Suggestions

- Model the pronunciation of the example words and have students repeat them after you.
- Remind students that **h** often combines with other consonants to make different sounds. Examples: **ch** (**chat, chose**) and **ph** (**téléphone**). The **h** is silent when it combines with the letter **t**. Examples: **thé** and **théâtre**.
- Point out that many words beginning with an **h aspiré** are borrowed from other languages. Examples: **le hall, les hamburgers, le handball,** and **la Hollande**.
- Ask students to provide more examples of words that begin with the letter **h**. Examples: **l'huile, l'hôte, l'hôtesse, des habitants,** and **l'hôtel**.
- Dictate five familiar words containing the letter **h**, repeating each one at least two times. Then write them on the board or a transparency and have students check their spelling.

Dictons The saying **«La honte n'est pas d'être inférieur à l'adversaire, c'est d'être inférieur à soi-même»** is a Manchurian proverb. The saying **«L'heure, c'est l'heure; avant l'heure, c'est pas l'heure; après l'heure, c'est plus l'heure»** is a quote from Jules Jouy.

OPTIONS

Extra Practice Use these sentences with the letter **h** for additional practice or dictation. **1. En hiver, Henri va en Hongrie. 2. Horace a honte d'habiter dans cette habitation. 3. Hélène est heureuse de fêter ses huit ans. 4. Notre hôte Hubert sert des huîtres à l'huile d'olive comme hors-d'œuvre.**

Extra Practice Teach students this French tongue-twister that contains the letter **h**. **La pie niche en haut, l'oie niche en bas, le hibou niche ni haut ni bas.**

On fait des courses.

Video: *Roman-photo*
Record & Compare

PERSONNAGES

Amina

David

Employée

Rachid

Sandrine

À la charcuterie...

EMPLOYÉE Bonjour, Mademoiselle, Monsieur. Qu'est-ce que je vous sers?

RACHID Bonjour, Madame. Quatre tranches de pâté et de la salade de carottes pour deux personnes, s'il vous plaît.

EMPLOYÉE Et avec ça?

RACHID Deux tranches de jambon, s'il vous plaît.

RACHID Vous prenez les cartes de crédit?

EMPLOYÉE Ah, désolée, Monsieur. Nous n'acceptons que les paiements en liquide ou par chèque.

RACHID Amina, je viens de m'apercevoir que je n'ai pas de liquide sur moi!

AMINA Ce n'est pas grave, j'en ai assez. Tiens.

Dans la rue...

RACHID Merci, chérie. Passons à la banque avant d'aller au parc.

AMINA Mais, nous sommes samedi midi, la banque est fermée.

RACHID Peut-être, mais il y a toujours le distributeur automatique.

AMINA Bon, d'accord... J'ai quelques courses à faire plus tard cet après-midi. Tu veux m'accompagner?

Dans une autre partie de la ville...

DAVID Tu aimes la cuisine alsacienne?

SANDRINE Oui, j'adore la choucroute!

DAVID Tu veux aller à la brasserie La Petite France? C'est moi qui t'invite.

SANDRINE D'accord, avec plaisir.

DAVID Excellent! Avant d'y aller, il faut trouver un distributeur automatique.

SANDRINE Il y en a un à côté de la banque.

Au distributeur automatique...

SANDRINE Eh, regarde qui fait la queue!

RACHID Tiens, salut, qu'est-ce que vous faites de beau, vous deux?

SANDRINE On va à la brasserie. Vous voulez venir avec nous?

AMINA Non non! Euh... je veux dire... Rachid et moi, on va faire un pique-nique dans le parc.

RACHID Oui, et après ça, Amina a des courses importantes à faire.

SANDRINE Je comprends, pas de problème... David et moi, nous avons aussi des choses à faire cet après-midi.

ACTIVITÉS

1 Vrai ou faux? Indiquez si ces affirmations sont vraies ou fausses. Corrigez les phrases fausses. Answers may vary.

1. Aujourd'hui, la banque est ouverte. Faux. Le samedi midi, la banque est fermée.
2. Amina doit aller à la poste pour envoyer un colis. Faux. Elle doit envoyer des cartes postales.
3. Amina doit aller à la poste pour acheter des timbres. Vrai.
4. Amina va mettre ses cartes postales dans une boîte aux lettres à côté de la banque. Faux. Elle va les mettre dans une boîte aux lettres à côté de la poste.
5. Sandrine n'aime pas la cuisine alsacienne. Faux. Elle adore la cuisine alsacienne.
6. David et Rachid vont retirer de l'argent. Vrai.
7. Il n'y a pas de queue au distributeur automatique. Faux. Il y a la queue au distributeur automatique.
8. David et Sandrine invitent Amina et Rachid à la brasserie. Vrai.
9. Amina et Rachid vont à la brasserie. Faux. Ils vont faire un pique-nique dans le parc.
10. Amina va faire ses courses après le pique-nique. Vrai.

Practice more at **espaces.vhlcentral.com.**

Section Goals

In this section, students will learn functional phrases for talking about errands and money and expressing negation.

Instructional Resources
*espaces.vhlcentral.com: WB/VM/LM Answer Key; IRM (Videoscript; **Roman-photo** Translations); activities; downloads; reference tools*
Video on DVD

Video Recap: Leçon 11B
Before doing this **Roman-photo**, review the previous one with this activity.

1. Où est Rachid quand l'épisode commence? (Il est à une station-service.)
2. Pourquoi y va-t-il? (Il y va pour faire le plein.)
3. Qui attend Rachid au P'tit Bistrot? (Amina l'attend.)
4. Qu'est-ce que Rachid donne à Amina? (Il lui donne des fleurs.)
5. Qu'est-ce qui se passe en route? (Un voyant s'allume. Ils ont un pneu crevé.)

Video Synopsis
Rachid and Amina are buying some food at a **charcuterie** for a picnic. Rachid needs some cash, so they head for an ATM. As they are walking, Amina says she has to go to the post office, the jewelry store, and a boutique that afternoon. David invites Sandrine to eat at a **brasserie**. On the way, they run into Rachid and Amina at the ATM. Sandrine and Amina discuss their new relationships.

Suggestions
- Have students predict what the episode will be about based on the video stills.
- Have students scan the captions for sentences related to places in a city.
- After reading the **Roman-photo**, have students summarize the episode.
- Point out that Amina can buy stamps from a machine even when the post office is closed.

OPTIONS

Avant de regarder la vidéo Tell students to read the title and the scene setter. Then have them predict what might happen in this episode. Write their predictions on the board. After viewing the episode, have them confirm or correct their predictions.

Regarder la vidéo Show the video in four parts, pausing the video before each location change. Have students describe what happens in each place. Write their observations on the board. Then show the entire episode again without pausing and have the class fill in any missing details to summarize the plot.

RACHID Volontiers. Où est-ce que tu vas?
AMINA Je dois aller à la poste pour acheter des timbres et envoyer quelques cartes postales, et puis je voudrais aller à la bijouterie. J'ai reçu un e-mail de la bijouterie qui vend les bijoux que je fais. Regarde.
RACHID Très joli!

AMINA Oui, tu aimes? Et après ça, je dois passer à la boutique Olivia où l'on vend mes vêtements.
RACHID Tu vends aussi des vêtements dans une boutique?
AMINA Oui, mes créations! J'étudie le stylisme de mode, tu ne t'en souviens pas?
RACHID Si, bien sûr, mais... Tu as vraiment du talent.

AMINA Alors! On n'a plus besoin de chercher un cyberhomme?
SANDRINE Pour le moment, je ne cherche personne. David est super.

DAVID De quoi parlez-vous?
SANDRINE Oh, rien d'important.
RACHID Bon, Amina. On y va?
AMINA Oui. Passez un bon après-midi.
SANDRINE Vous aussi.

Expressions utiles

Dealing with money

- **Nous n'acceptons que les paiements en liquide.**
  We only accept payment in cash.
- **Je viens de m'apercevoir que je n'ai pas de liquide.**
  I just noticed/realized I don't have any cash.
- **Il y a toujours le distributeur automatique.**
  There's always the ATM.

Running errands

- **J'ai quelques courses à faire plus tard cet après-midi.**
  I have a few/some errands to run later this afternoon.
- **Je voudrais aller à la bijouterie qui vend les bijoux que je fais.**
  I would like to go to the jewelry shop that sells the jewelry I make.

Expressing negation

- **Pas de problème.**
  No problem.
- **On n'a plus besoin de chercher un cyberhomme?**
  We no longer need to look for a cyberhomme?
- **Pour le moment, je ne cherche personne.**
  For the time being/the moment, I'm not looking for anyone.
- **Rien d'important.**
  Nothing important.

Additional vocabulary

- **J'ai reçu un e-mail.**
  I received an e-mail.
- **Qu'est-ce que vous faites de beau?**
  What are you up to?

2 Complétez Complétez ces phrases.

1. La charcuterie accepte les paiements en liquide et _par chèque_.
2. Amina veut aller à la poste, à la boutique de vêtements et à la _bijouterie_.
3. À côté de la banque, il y a un _distributeur automatique_.
4. Amina paie avec des pièces de monnaie et des _billets_.
5. Amina a des _courses_ à faire cet après-midi.

3 À vous! Que se passe-t-il au pique-nique ou à la brasserie? Avec un(e) camarade de classe, écrivez une conversation entre Amina et Sandrine ou Rachid et David, dans laquelle elles/ils se racontent ce qu'ils ont fait. Qu'ont-ils mangé? Se sont-ils amusés? Était-ce romantique? Jouez la scène devant la classe.

ressources
VM pp. 255-256 | DVD Leçon 12A | espaces.vhlcentral.com

ACTIVITÉS

Expressions utiles
- Model the pronunciation of the **Expressions utiles** and have students repeat them.
- As you work through the list, point out the forms of **recevoir** and **apercevoir**, and negative expressions. Tell students that these verbs and constructions will be formally presented in **Espace structures**.
- Respond briefly to questions about **recevoir**, **apercevoir**, and negative expressions. Reinforce correct forms, but do not expect students to produce them consistently at this time.
- Point out that **les brasseries** usually offer quick, hearty meals. They often specialize in Alsatian dishes, such as **la choucroute**.

1 Suggestion Have students correct the false statements.

1 Expansion For additional practice, give students these items. **11. La charcuterie accepte les cartes de crédit. (Faux. Elle n'accepte que les paiements en liquide ou par chèque.) 12. À la charcuterie, Rachid paie par chèque. (Faux. Amina paie en liquide.) 13. Rachid va accompagner Amina cet après-midi. (Vrai.) 14. Sandrine cherche toujours un cyberhomme. (Faux. Sandrine n'a plus besoin de chercher un cyberhomme.)**

2 Suggestion Have volunteers read the completed sentences aloud.

3 Suggestion Tell students to choose a situation and brainstorm ideas before writing their conversations. Encourage them to be creative.

OPTIONS

Les heures d'ouverture Many small shops close for an hour or two between 12:00 p.m. and 2:00 p.m. It is common to reopen in the afternoon and stay open until around 7:00 p.m. Most stores are not open late in the evening or on Sundays except around the holidays. Stores near popular tourist attractions are exceptions. For example, many businesses along the Champs-Élysées in Paris are open until midnight.

Extra Practice Ask volunteers to ad-lib the scenes in video stills 5–10 for the class. Tell them it is not necessary to memorize the episode. They should just try to get the general meaning across with the vocabulary they know. Give them time to prepare or have them do their skit as a review activity during the next class period.

Section Goals

In this section, students will:

- learn about methods of payment in France
- learn some terms to talk about the **métro**
- learn about some interesting places to shop in the francophone world
- read about Alain Robert, the French "Spiderman"
- view authentic video footage

Instructional Resources
espaces.vhlcentral.com: Video; WB/VM/LM Answer Key; IRM (Videoscript); activities; downloads; reference tools
Video on DVD

Culture à la loupe

Avant la lecture Have students look at the visuals and describe what they see.

Lecture

- Point out that **la Carte Bleue** was widely used in France before the debit card became a common form of payment in the United States.
- Point out the information about opening a bank account in the **Coup de main**.

Après la lecture Ask students: **Comment les Français paient-ils leurs achats et leurs factures? (par prélèvements automatiques sur comptes bancaires, par chèque, par Carte Bleue/carte bancaire/carte de crédit)**

1 Suggestion Have volunteers write the answers on the board. Then go over them with the class.

National Standards: connections, cultures

Video: *Flash culture*

CULTURE À LA LOUPE

Les moyens de paiement en France

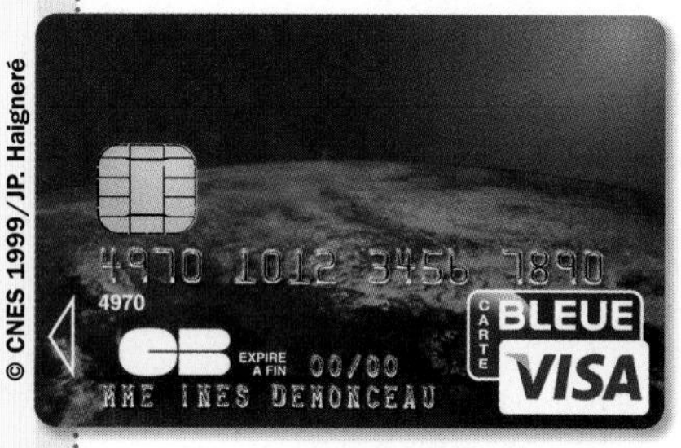

© CNES 1999/JP. Haigneré

À l'exception des petites courses quotidiennes, les Français paient très rarement leurs achats° et leurs factures° en liquide. Pour les paiements réguliers, comme les factures d'électricité ou de téléphone, les virements° et les prélèvements° automatiques sur comptes bancaires sont souvent utilisés. Pour les autres dépenses, le mode de paiement préféré est la carte bancaire. Les Français sont les plus gros utilisateurs de chèques du monde, mais le système de chèques payants° en France les encourage à se servir de leur carte bancaire. Au départ, les cartes bancaires françaises, émises° uniquement par des banques, servaient seulement à retirer de l'argent dans les distributeurs automatiques. Peu de commerces les acceptaient et il fallait° souvent que les achats dépassent° une certaine somme°. Aujourd'hui, l'usage des cartes bancaires est en hausse°, mais on trouve encore des petits commerces qui ne les acceptent pas.

La plupart des Français possèdent actuellement° une carte de la gamme° Carte Bleue. La carte, qui peut être nationale ou internationale, est une carte bancaire liée° à un compte en banque. Certaines cartes peuvent aussi être utilisées comme des cartes de crédit. Dans ce cas, les sommes sont généralement débitées à la fin de chaque mois ou bien on peut faire des paiements mensuels° à la banque. Il existe aussi de plus en plus d'organismes de crédit et de magasins qui offrent leur propre° carte de crédit à leurs clients. Longtemps réticents° devant ce type de crédit, les Français l'utilisent de plus en plus aujourd'hui.

Coup de main

If you are in France for more than three months, you may open a bank account as a **résident** by showing three documents.

- your passport
- your **permis de séjour**
- proof of residence (electric, gas, or phone bill)

achats *purchases* **factures** *bills* **virements** *transfers* **prélèvements** *withdrawals* **payants** *with a fee* **émises** *issued* **il fallait** *it was necessary* **dépassent** *exceed* **somme** *sum* **en hausse** *increasing* **actuellement** *currently* **gamme** *line* **liée** *linked* **mensuels** *monthly* **propre** *own* **réticents** *hesitant*

ACTIVITÉS

1 Répondez Répondez aux questions par des phrases complètes.

1. Comment paie-t-on souvent ses factures en France? On les paie souvent par virement ou par prélèvement automatique.
2. Quel mode de paiement est préféré pour faire des achats? C'est la carte bancaire.
3. Pourquoi de plus en plus de Français utilisent-ils leur carte bancaire? Ils utilisent leur carte bancaire parce qu'il y a, en France, un système de chèques payants.
4. À quoi servait la carte bancaire quand elle est arrivée en France? Elle servait à retirer de l'argent dans les distributeurs automatiques.
5. À l'origine, pourquoi était-il difficile d'utiliser une carte bancaire? Peu de commerces les acceptaient et il fallait souvent que les achats dépassent une certaine somme.
6. Qu'est-ce qu'une carte bancaire? C'est une carte liée à un compte en banque. Certaines peuvent aussi être utilisées comme des cartes de crédit.
7. Quelle carte peut être utilisée à l'étranger? La carte bancaire internationale peut être utilisée à l'étranger.
8. À quel type de carte américaine la carte bancaire française ressemble-t-elle? La carte bancaire française ressemble à la *debit card* américaine.
9. Comment en est-elle différente? Quand on utilise une carte bancaire française, les sommes sont généralement débitées du compte à la fin du mois et non pas immédiatement.
10. Quels organismes offrent leur propre carte de crédit à leurs clients? Les organismes de crédit et les magasins les leur offrent.

OPTIONS

Cultural Comparison Have students work in groups of three. Tell them to compare French and American methods for paying for things. Have them list the similarities and differences in a two-column chart under the headings **Similitudes** and **Différences**. Also tell them to discuss which method of payment they prefer.

Les cartes de crédit Many French people do not approve of the American habit of carrying monthly balances on their credit cards and paying interest for daily expenses. Until recently, many French people did not have any credit cards. Now, most of those who do use them often have only one.

LE FRANÇAIS QUOTIDIEN

Le vocabulaire du métro

bouche (*f.*) de métro	*subway station entrance*
correspondance (*f.*)	*connection*
ligne (*f.*) de métro	*subway line*
rame (*f.*) de métro	*subway train*
strapontin (*m.*)	*foldaway seat*
changer	*to change (subway line)*
monter/descendre	*to get on/to get off*
prendre la direction	*to go in the direction*

PORTRAIT

Le «Spiderman» français

Alain Robert, le «Spiderman» français, découvre l'escalade° quand il est enfant et devient un des meilleurs grimpeurs° de falaises° du monde. Malgré° deux accidents qui l'ont laissé invalide à 60%°, avec des problèmes de vertiges°, il commence sa carrière de grimpeur «urbain» et escalade son premier gratte-ciel° à Chicago, en 1994. Depuis, il a escaladé plus de 70 gratte-ciel et autres structures du monde, dont la tour Eiffel à Paris et la Sears Tower à Chicago. En 1997, il a été arrêté par la police pendant son ascension d'un des plus grands bâtiments du monde, les tours Petronas en Malaisie. Parfois en costume de Spiderman, mais toujours sans corde° et à mains nues°, Robert fait souvent des escalades pour collecter des dons° et il attire° parfois des milliers de spectateurs.

escalade *climbing* **grimpeurs** *climbers* **falaises** *cliffs* **Malgré** *In spite of* **invalide à 60%** *60% disabled* **vertiges** *vertigo* **gratte-ciel** *skyscraper* **corde** *rope* **nues** *bare* **dons** *charitable donations* **attire** *attracts*

LE MONDE FRANCOPHONE

Où faire des courses?

Voici quelques endroits intéressants où faire des courses.

En Afrique du Nord les souks, des marchés couverts ou en plein air° où il y a une grande concentration de magasins et de stands
En Côte d'Ivoire le marché de Cocody à Abidjan où on trouve des tissus° et des objets locaux
À la Martinique le grand marché de Fort-de-France, un marché couvert°, ouvert tous les jours, qui offre toutes sortes de produits
À Montréal la ville souterraine°, un district du centre-ville où il y a de nombreux centres commerciaux reliés° entre eux par des tunnels
À Paris le marché aux puces° de Saint-Ouen où on trouve des antiquités et des objets divers
À Tahiti le marché de Papeete où on propose des produits pour les touristes et pour les Tahitiens

plein air *outdoor* **tissus** *fabrics* **couvert** *covered* **souterraine** *underground* **reliés** *connected* **marché aux puces** *flea market*

SUR INTERNET

Que peut-on acheter chez les bouquinistes, à Paris?

Go to **espaces.vhlcentral.com** to find more information related to this **ESPACE CULTURE**. Then watch the corresponding **Flash culture**.

ACTIVITÉS

2 Vrai ou faux? Indiquez si les phrases sont vraies ou fausses.

1. Alain Robert escalade seulement des falaises. Faux. Il escalade aussi des gratte-ciel et d'autres structures.
2. Alain Robert a escaladé son premier bâtiment (*building*) à Chicago. Vrai.
3. Alain Robert n'a jamais eu de problèmes de santé dans sa carrière de grimpeur. Faux. Il a eu deux accidents graves et il a des problèmes de vertiges.
4. Il y a un quartier souterrain à Montréal. Vrai.
5. Il y a des souks dans les marchés d'Abidjan. Faux. Il y a des souks dans les vieilles villes d'Afrique du Nord.

Practice more at **espaces.vhlcentral.com.**

3 Le marchandage En Afrique du Nord, il est très courant de marchander ou de discuter avec un vendeur pour obtenir un meilleur prix. Avez-vous déjà eu l'occasion de marchander? Où? Quand? Qu'avez-vous acheté? Avez-vous obtenu un bon prix? Discutez de ce sujet avec un(e) partenaire.

ressources: VM pp. 293-294 | espaces.vhlcentral.com

Le français quotidien
- Model the pronunciation of each term and have students repeat it.
- Point out you say **prendre une correspondance.** Remind students that a subway ticket is **un ticket**. In some cities it is possible to purchase **un carnet** or **une carte** for unlimited monthly access.

Portrait
- After two accidents while training in 1982, Robert hasn't suffered any more climbing injuries. He trained mostly on cliffs before starting to climb skyscrapers, which he is now paid to do.
- Ask students: **À votre avis, quel type d'homme est Alain Robert? Avez-vous envie d'escalader un gratte-ciel? Pourquoi?**

Le monde francophone After students have read the text, ask: **Où voulez-vous faire des courses dans le monde francophone? Pourquoi?**

2 Expansion For additional practice, give students these items. **6. Alain Robert escalade les bâtiments en France aussi bien qu'à l'étranger. (Vrai.) 7. Robert réussit à escalader les tours Petronas. (Faux. Il est arrêté par la police.) 8. Le public ne s'intéresse pas à Robert. (Faux. Il attire parfois des milliers de spectateurs.)**

3 Expansion Bring in pictures of objects one might find at a market, such as vegetables, pottery, rugs, and shirts. Have students work in pairs and practice bargaining for the objects pictured. They should take turns playing the customer and the vendor.

Flash culture Tell students that they will learn more about businesses and small shops by watching a variety of real-life images narrated by Benjamin. Show the video segment, then have students jot down in French at least three examples of people or things they saw. You can also use the activities in the video manual in class to reinforce this **Flash culture** or assign them as homework.

OPTIONS

Où faire des courses? Bargaining **(le marchandage)** is a common practice in Arab markets in France and throughout the Arab world. If visiting a souk in North Africa, it is best to go with someone who speaks Arabic. If that isn't possible, it's better to speak French than English, since Americans have a reputation for being wealthy.

Pairs Have students work in pairs. Tell them to write a conversation between two tourists who are taking the **métro** in Paris from the Bastille stop to the Franklin D. Roosevelt stop (line 1) to the Trocadéro stop (line 9), using the vocabulary in **Le français quotidien**. Then have pairs role-play their conversations for the class.

Section Goals

In this section, students will learn:

- the verbs **voir, croire, recevoir,** and **apercevoir**
- the meaning of **revoir** and **s'apercevoir**

Instructional Resources
*espaces.vhlcentral.com: Lab MP3s; WB/VM/LM Answer Key; IRM (**Essayez!** and **Mise en pratique** answers; **Feuilles d'activités**; Lab Audioscript); activities; downloads; reference tools*

Suggestions

- Point out the **-s,-s,-t,-ons,-ez, -ent** endings of both **voir** and **croire** seen before in irregular verbs. Then note that the **nous** and **vous** forms have irregular stems **voy-** and **croy-**.
- Ask students why they think some forms of **recevoir** and **apercevoir** are spelled with a **cédille**. (It helps the reader know to pronounce the sound as [**s**]. Remind them that the letter **c** is pronounced [**s**] in front of the letters **e** and **i,** and [**k**] in front of the letters **a, o,** and **u.**)
- Ask questions to practice **voir**, **croire**, **recevoir**, and **apercevoir** in the present and the **passé composé**. Examples: **Qui a vu un film au cinéma récemment? Qui a reçu le prix Nobel de la paix l'année dernière? Qui croit aux fantômes?**
- Have a volunteer write the paradigm of **revoir** on the board and model its pronunciation.
- Test comprehension of the conditional forms of all four verbs by asking volunteers to supply the correct verb form for the subjects you suggest. Example: **tu / voir (tu verrais)**
- You may want to teach the class the verb **décevoir** and the adjective **déçu** along with **recevoir** and **apercevoir.**
- Point out that **s'apercevoir** is followed by **que/qu'** + [*another verb*] or by **de** + [*noun*].

NATIONAL comparisons STANDARDS

12A.1 *Voir, croire, recevoir, and apercevoir*

Point de départ In this section, you will learn to conjugate four new irregular verbs.

Je m'aperçois que je n'ai pas d'argent.

On vous a vus devant le distributeur!

- Here is the conjugation of the verb **voir** (*to see*).

Voir	
je vois	nous voyons
tu vois	vous voyez
il/elle voit	ils/elles voient

Vous **voyez** la mairie à côté du commissariat de police?
Do you see the city hall next to the police station?

Je ne **vois** pas bien sans mes lunettes.
I don't see well without my glasses.

- The verb **revoir** (*to see again*) is derived from **voir** and is conjugated the same way.

On se **revoit** mercredi ou jeudi?
Will we see each other again Wednesday or Thursday?

Il ne va pas **revoir** ce film avec moi.
He is not going to see this movie again with me.

- Here is the conjugation of the verb **croire** (*to believe*).

Croire	
je crois	nous croyons
tu crois	vous croyez
il/elle croit	ils/elles croient

Tu **crois** que l'homme est innocent.
You believe that the man is innocent.

Nous **croyons** que la boutique est fermée aujourd'hui.
We think that the store is closed today.

MISE EN PRATIQUE

1 Sur le campus Vous parlez avec un(e) ami(e) de votre vie sur le campus. Complétez les phrases avec les verbes appropriés au présent.

1. De sa chambre, mon ami Marc ___voit/aperçoit___ le campus.
2. Mon camarade de chambre et moi, nous ne ___recevons___ pas de visites pendant la semaine.
3. Je ___crois___ que la vie universitaire peut être difficile quelquefois.
4. Ma petite amie et sa sœur ___reçoivent___ souvent des colis de leurs parents.
5. Quand il fait beau, nous ___apercevons/voyons___ les montagnes derrière le stade.
6. Ton meilleur ami et toi, vous ___recevez___ de bonnes notes aux examens?

2 À Québec Mélanie a passé une semaine à Québec avec sa famille. Elle en parle avec son petit ami. Utilisez les verbes donnés au passé composé.

MODÈLE mon frère Paul / voir / la Citadelle
Mon frère Paul a vu la Citadelle.

1. nous / recevoir / journal / à sept heures / du matin
   Nous avons reçu le journal à sept heures du matin.
2. papa et Fabrice / apercevoir / la chute (*waterfalls*) Montmorency / de l'avion
   Papa et Fabrice ont aperçu la chute Montmorency de l'avion.
3. papa et maman / recevoir / des cadeaux / de leurs amis
   Papa et maman ont reçu des cadeaux de leurs amis.
4. je / voir / beaucoup / de spectacles
   J'ai vu beaucoup de spectacles.
5. Simon / croire / à la vieille légende / de Québec
   Simon a cru à la vieille légende de Québec.
6. ta sœur et toi / recevoir / ma carte postale / ?
   Ta sœur et toi avez reçu ma carte postale?

3 Ma vie universitaire Tristan parle de sa vie à la fac. Regardez les illustrations et complétez les phrases avec les verbes **recevoir** et **apercevoir.** Suggested answers

1. Toutes les semaines, je reçois une lettre.

2. De leur fenêtre, les étudiants aperçoivent des arbres.

3. La semaine dernière, mon meilleur ami a reçu son diplôme.

4. Quelquefois, nous apercevons notre prof au resto U.

Practice more at **espaces.vhlcentral.com.**

OPTIONS

Extra Practice Briefly show the class a picture or drawing with numerous objects displayed, for example, a photo of a messy or cluttered room. Ask students to study the objects they see in the photo. Then remove the picture from view and ask students what they remember seeing and what they did not see, using **croire** and/or the **passé composé** of **voir**. Examples: **J'ai vu un lit. Je crois avoir vu…**

Game Tell pairs of students to write an obviously illogical sentence with **recevoir** or **apercevoir**. Example: **J'ai reçu une mauvaise note pour mon anniversaire**. Have students read their sentences aloud while their classmates correct the sentences so that they are logical. Then award prizes for the funniest, most ridiculous, and most creative sentences.

COMMUNICATION

4 Enquête Votre professeur va vous donner une feuille d'activités. Circulez dans la classe et demandez à vos camarades s'ils connaissent quelqu'un qui pratique chaque activité de la liste. S'ils répondent oui, demandez-leur qui est la personne et écrivez la réponse. Ensuite, présentez vos réponses à la classe. Answers will vary.

MODÈLE

Étudiant(e) 1: *Connais-tu quelqu'un qui reçoit rarement des e-mails?*
Étudiant(e) 2: *Oui, mon frère aîné reçoit très peu d'e-mails.*

Activités	Noms	Réponses
1. recevoir / rarement / e-mails	Quang	son frère aîné
2. s'inquiéter / quand / ne pas / recevoir / e-mails		
3. apercevoir / e-mail bizarre / le / ouvrir		

5 Assemblez Achetez-vous sur Internet? Avec un(e) partenaire, assemblez les éléments des colonnes pour raconter vos expériences. Utilisez les verbes **voir, recevoir, apercevoir, croire** et **s'apercevoir** dans votre conversation. Answers will vary.

MODÈLE

Étudiant(e) 1: *Je commande parfois des livres sur Internet. Une fois, je n'ai pas reçu mes livres!*
Étudiant(e) 2: *Mon père adore acheter sur Internet. Il aperçoit souvent des objets qui l'intéressent.*

A	B	C
je	apercevoir	adresse
tu	s'apercevoir	bureau de poste
un(e) ami(e)	commander	carte de crédit
nous	croire	colis
vous	payer	compte-chèques
tes parents	recevoir	formulaire
tes profs	voir	liquide
?	?	?

6 Curieux! Avec un(e) partenaire, posez-vous ces questions à tour de rôle. Answers will vary.

1. Reçois-tu souvent des e-mails? De qui?
2. Tes parents recevaient-ils souvent des amis quand tu étais petit(e)?
3. Crois-tu aux extraterrestres? Pourquoi?
4. Qu'aperçois-tu de ta chambre? Des arbres?
5. Qui as-tu vu le week-end dernier?

- In **Leçon 9A**, you learned to conjugate **devoir**. You will now learn two verbs that are conjugated similarly.

Recevoir and *apercevoir*

	recevoir (*to receive*)	**apercevoir** (*to catch sight of, to see*)
je/j'	reçois	aperçois
tu	reçois	aperçois
il/elle	reçoit	aperçoit
nous	recevons	apercevons
vous	recevez	apercevez
ils/elles	reçoivent	aperçoivent

Je **reçois** de l'argent de mon père.
I receive money from my father.

D'ici, on **aperçoit** le bureau de poste.
From here, you see the post office.

- The verb **s'apercevoir** means *to notice, to be aware of,* or *to realize.*

Cela ne **s'aperçoit** pas.
It is not noticeable.

Il **s'aperçoit** de son erreur.
He realizes his mistake.

- **Voir, croire, recevoir,** and **apercevoir** all take **avoir** as the auxiliary verb in the **passé composé**. Their past participles are respectively, **vu, cru, reçu,** and **aperçu.**

Tu **as vu** son ami au parc?
Did you see his friend at the park?

Nous **avons reçu** un colis.
We received a package.

BOÎTE À OUTILS
Recall that in **Leçon 2A**, you learned the expression **être reçu(e) à un examen** (*to pass an exam*).

- The **conditionnel** of **voir, croire, recevoir,** and **apercevoir** are formed respectively with the stems **verr-, croir-, recevr-,** and **apercevr-.**

On **croirait** que c'est facile à faire.
One would think it's easy to do.

Nous **verrions** le film ce soir.
We would watch the movie tonight.

Essayez! **Complétez les phrases avec les formes correctes des verbes au présent.**

1. Je ne ___vois___ (voir) pas la banque d'ici.
2. Vous ___croyez___ (croire) à son histoire (*story*)?
3. Nous ___recevons___ (recevoir) toujours une lettre de Marie à Noël.
4. Mes amis ___croient___ (croire) que je dors.
5. Ils ___aperçoivent___ (apercevoir) le facteur au coin (*corner*) de la rue.
6. Nous ___voyons___ (voir) encore nos amis d'enfance.
7. Le prof ___reçoit___ (recevoir) un cadeau des étudiants.
8. Tu ___aperçois___ (apercevoir) le marchand de journaux?

Essayez! Have students create sentences in the **passé composé** and the **conditionnel**.

1 Suggestion If students find this first activity difficult, provide a list of the conjugated verbs in random order and ask them to pick the correct verb for each sentence.

2 Expansion Change the subjects of the dehydrated sentences in the activity and have students write or say the new sentences.

3 Expansion Have students create sentences with **recevoir** and **apercevoir** that describe their own life at the university. Tell them that they can illustrate the sentences if they wish.

4 Suggestion Call on volunteers to do the **modèle**. Then distribute the **Feuilles d'activités** found on the Supersite.

4 Expansion Ask students questions about themselves based on the sentence fragments given for the activity. Examples: **Qui reçoit rarement des e-mails? Vous inquiétez-vous quand vous ne recevez pas d'e-mails?** You may want to let students invent answers.

5 Suggestion Tell students to use each expression in the columns at least once.

6 Expansion Have students retell their partner's answers using third person subjects. Example: **Nathalie a récemment reçu une lettre de son copain du Canada.**

OPTIONS

Small Groups Ask small groups of students to compose sentences with **s'apercevoir**. Give them a point for each sentence in which the verb is used and conjugated correctly, and a prize to the group with the most points.

Game Divide the class into teams of three. Each team has a piece of paper. Call out a subject, an infinitive, and a verb tense. Example: **je / voir (conditionnel)**. Each team composes a sentence with the given elements. As soon as a team finishes their sentence, one team member should run to the board and write it out. The first team to write a correct sentence on the board wins. Team members should take turns going to the board.

Section Goals

In this section, students will learn negative and affirmative expressions.

Instructional Resources
*espaces.vhlcentral.com: Lab MP3s; WB/VM/LM Answer Key; IRM (**Essayez!** and **Mise en pratique** answers; Lab Audioscript); activities; downloads; reference tools*

Suggestions

- To help students distinguish between the negative expressions on this page, make a transparency with a set of six fill-in-the-blank sentences with only the second negative particle (**personne, rien,** etc.) missing from each one. Examples: **Je n'ai ____ d'argent! (pas) Il n'y a ____ dans le couloir. (personne)**
- Point out to students that when **personne** and **rien** are used as subjects, the verbs that accompany them are singular. You could also point out that when **de** + [*adjective*] is used to modify **personne, rien, quelque chose,** and **quelqu'un,** the adjective is a masculine singular form.
- You might give students some more sentences with several negative particles so that they get a feel for those kinds of emphatic constructions. Examples: **Je n'ai jamais rien dit à personne! Il n'y a plus rien sur mon compte en banque.**
- To practice adverb placement in the **passé composé**, write sentences on sets of index cards, so that a word is on each card. Give out the cards for a sentence to a group of students and have them put the cards in order.

12A.2 Negative/Affirmative expressions

NATIONAL STANDARDS comparisons

Point de départ In **Leçon 2A**, you learned how to negate verbs with **ne... pas**, which is used to make a general negation. In French, as in English, you can also use a variety of expressions that add a more specific meaning to the negation.

- The other negative expressions are also made up of two parts: **ne** and a second negative word.

Negative expressions

ne... aucun(e)	*none (not any)*	**ne... plus**	*no more (not anymore)*
ne... jamais	*never (not ever)*	**ne... que**	*only*
ne... ni... ni	*neither... nor*	**ne... rien**	*nothing (not anything)*
ne... personne	*nobody, no one*		

Je **n'**ai **aucune** envie de manger.
I have no desire to eat.

Il **n'**a **plus** faim.
He's not hungry anymore.

Le bureau de poste **n'**est **jamais** ouvert.
The post office is never open.

Ils **n'**ont **que** des timbres pour l'Europe.
They only have stamps for Europe.

Elle **ne** parle à **personne**.
She doesn't talk to anyone.

Le facteur **n'**avait **rien** pour nous.
The mailman had nothing for us.

- To negate the expression **il y a**, place **n'** before **y** and the second negative word after the form of **avoir**.

Il **n'**y a **aucune** banque près d'ici?
Aren't there any banks nearby?

Il **n'**y avait **rien** sur mon compte.
There wasn't anything in my account.

- The negative words **personne** and **rien** can be the subject of a verb, in which case they are placed before the verb.

Personne n'était là.
No one was there.

Rien n'est arrivé dans le courrier.
Nothing arrived in the mail.

- Note that **aucun(e)** can be either an adjective or a pronoun. Therefore, it must agree with the noun it modifies. It is always used in the singular.

Tu ne trouves **aucune banque**?
Can't you find any banks?

Je n'en trouve **aucune** par ici.
I can't find any around here.

- **Jamais**, **personne**, **plus**, and **rien** can be doubled up with **ne**.

Elle **ne** parle **jamais** à **personne**.
She never talks to anyone.

Il **n'**y a **plus personne** ici.
There isn't anyone here anymore.

Elle **ne** dit **jamais rien**.
She never says anything.

Il **n'**y a **plus rien** ici.
There isn't anything here anymore.

MISE EN PRATIQUE

1 À la banque Vous voulez ouvrir un nouveau compte et vous posez des questions au banquier. Écrivez ses réponses à la forme négative.

MODÈLE La banque ferme-t-elle à midi? (jamais)
Non, la banque ne ferme jamais à midi.

1. La banque est-elle ouverte le samedi? (jamais) Non, la banque n'est jamais ouverte le samedi.
2. Peut-on ouvrir un compte sans papier d'identité? (personne) Non, personne ne peut ouvrir de compte sans papier d'identité.
3. Avez-vous des distributeurs automatiques dans les supermarchés? (aucun) Non, nous n'avons aucun distributeur automatique dans les supermarchés./Non, nous n'avons de distributeur automatique dans aucun supermarché.
4. Pour retirer de l'argent, ai-je encore besoin de remplir ce document? (plus) Non, vous n'avez plus besoin de remplir ce document.
5. Avez-vous des billets et des pièces dans vos distributeurs automatiques? (que) Non, nous n'avons que des billets dans nos distributeurs automatiques.
6. Est-ce que tout le monde peut retirer de l'argent de mon compte bancaire? (personne) Non, personne ne peut retirer d'argent de votre compte bancaire.

2 Les jumelles Olivia et Anaïs sont des jumelles (*twin sisters*) bien différentes. Expliquez pourquoi.

MODÈLE Olivia est toujours heureuse.
Anaïs n'est jamais heureuse.

1. Olivia rit tout le temps. Anaïs ne rit jamais.
2. Olivia remarque (*notes*) tout. Anaïs ne remarque rien.
3. Olivia voit (*sees*) encore ses amies d'enfance. Anaïs ne voit plus/aucune de ses amies d'enfance.
4. Olivia aime le chocolat et la glace. Anaïs n'aime ni le chocolat ni la glace.
5. Olivia connaît beaucoup de monde. Anaïs ne connaît personne.
6. Olivia reçoit beaucoup de colis. Anaïs ne reçoit aucun colis.

3 Pas exactement Tristan exagère souvent. Il a écrit cet e-mail et vous lui répondez pour dire que les choses ne sont pas arrivées exactement comme ça. Mettez toutes ses phrases à la forme négative dans votre réponse.

MODÈLE
Tu n'es pas arrivé tard à la banque...

Je suis arrivé tard à la banque. Quelqu'un m'a ouvert la porte. J'ai regardé les affiches et les catalogues. J'ai demandé quelque chose. Il y avait encore de l'argent sur mon compte. Je vais souvent revenir dans cette banque.

Tu n'es pas arrivé tard à la banque. Personne ne t'a ouvert la porte. Tu n'as regardé ni les affiches ni les catalogues. Tu n'as rien demandé. Il n'y avait plus d'argent sur ton compte. Tu ne vas jamais revenir dans cette banque.

Practice more at **espaces.vhlcentral.com.**

OPTIONS

Video Replay the video episode while students listen for negative expressions in the last scene. Tell them to raise their hands when they hear one. Then replay the video, pausing each time a negative expression is used for students to say it aloud or write it down.

Pairs Give pairs of students a set of negative sentences and have them give you an affirmative version of each sentence. Example: **Il n'y a personne à la porte. (Il y a quelqu'un à la porte.)** Go over the sentences with the class, asking students to give all the different positive sentences possible.

COMMUNICATION

4 De mauvaise humeur Aujourd'hui, Anne-Marie est très négative. Elle répond négativement à toutes les questions. Avec un(e) partenaire, jouez les rôles d'Anne-Marie et de son amie. Rajoutez (*Add*) deux lignes de dialogue supplémentaires à la fin. Answers will vary.

MODÈLE

tu / sortir avec quelqu'un en ce moment
Étudiant(e) 1: *Est-ce que tu sors avec quelqu'un en ce moment?*
Étudiant(e) 2: *Non, je ne sors avec personne.*

1. tu / faire quelque chose ce soir
2. tes parents / venir chez toi ce week-end
3. ton frère / avoir encore sa vieille voiture
4. tes amis et toi / déjà aller en vacances au Canada
5. quelqu'un / habiter dans ta maison cet été
6. tu / avoir encore faim
7. ?
8. ?

5 Activités dangereuses Avec un(e) partenaire, faites une liste de dix activités dangereuses. Ensuite, travaillez avec un autre groupe et demandez à vos camarades s'ils pratiquent ces activités. Répondent-ils toujours par des phrases négatives? Answers will vary.

MODÈLE

Étudiant(e) 1: *Fais-tu du jogging la nuit?*
Étudiant(e) 2: *Non! Je ne fais jamais de jogging la nuit.*

6 À la banque En vacances, vous vous apercevez que votre valise a disparu (*disappeared*) avec votre argent liquide, vos papiers et vos cartes de crédit. Vous avez besoin de retirer de l'argent à la banque. Par groupes de trois, préparez un dialogue entre vous et deux employés de banque. Utilisez les expressions de la liste. Answers will vary.

jamais	ne... que	quelqu'un
ne... aucun(e)	ne... rien	rien
ne... ni... ni	quelque chose	toujours
ne... plus		

- To say *neither... nor*, use three negative words: **ne... ni... ni**. Note that partitive and indefinite articles are usually omitted.

Le facteur **n'**est **ni** sympa **ni** sociable.
The mailman is neither nice nor sociable.

Je **n'**ai **ni** frères **ni** sœurs.
I have neither brothers nor sisters.

- Note that in the **passé composé**, the words **jamais**, **plus**, and **rien** are placed between the auxiliary verb and the past participle. **Aucun(e)**, **personne**, and **que** follow the past participle.

Elle **n'**est **jamais** revenue.
She's never returned.

Nous **n'**avons **plus** emprunté d'argent.
We haven't borrowed money anymore.

Je **n'**ai **rien** dit aujourd'hui.
I didn't say anything today.

Vous **n'**avez signé **aucun** papier.
You didn't sign any paper.

Il **n'**a parlé à **personne**.
He didn't speak to anyone.

Ils **n'**en ont posté **que** deux.
They only mailed two.

- These expressions can be used in affirmative phrases. Note that when **jamais** is not accompanied by **ne**, it can mean *ever*.

jamais	*ever*	**quelqu'un**	*someone*
quelque chose	*something*	**toujours**	*always; still*

As-tu **jamais** été à cette brasserie?
Have you ever been to that brasserie?

Il y a **quelqu'un**?
Is someone there?

Vous cherchez **quelque chose**?
Are you looking for something?

Il est **toujours** aussi réservé?
Is he still so reserved?

- Note that **personne**, **quelque chose**, **quelqu'un**, and **rien** can be modified with an adjective after **de**.

Nous cherchons **quelque chose de joli**.
We're looking for something pretty.

Je ne sais **rien de nouveau**.
I don't know anything new.

BOÎTE À OUTILS
Remember to use **de** instead of the indefinite article in a negative construction:
Il n'y a plus de billets dans le distributeur. Personne ne poste de lettre le dimanche.

Essayez! **Choisissez l'expression correcte.**

1. (Jamais / Personne) ne trouve cet homme agréable.
2. Je ne veux (rien / jamais) faire aujourd'hui.
3. Y a-t-il (quelqu'un / personne) à la banque?
4. Je n'ai reçu (pas de / aucun) colis.
5. Il n'y avait (ne / ni) lettres ni colis dans la boîte aux lettres.
6. Il n'y a (plus / aucun) d'argent à la banque?
7. Jérôme ne va (toujours / jamais) à la poste.
8. Le facteur n'arrive (toujours / qu') à trois heures.

Essayez! Go over the answers to the activity with the class and have students with the correct responses explain them to the class.

1 Suggestion After students have completed item 6, you may wish to teach them the expression **personne d'autre** (*no one else*): **Non, personne d'autre ne peut retirer d'argent de votre compte bancaire.**

2 Expansion Ask students to give additional negative sentences for the activity. Example: **3. Anaïs ne voit jamais ses amies d'enfance.**

3 Suggestion Have pairs of students complete this activity and act it out in front of the class. One student plays Tristan and one plays his friend.

4 Expansion Once students have written two additional lines of dialogue, alternately call on pairs of students to share the questions they composed and call on other pairs to answer those questions in the negative.

5 Suggestion To get students warmed up for this activity, ask them if they do some unsafe things. Examples: **Vous retirez de l'argent du distributeur automatique à deux heures du matin? Vous ne fermez pas la porte quand vous quittez la maison?**

6 Suggestion Tell students that each member should write the lines for one of the characters (the traveler and the two bank employees). Help them as they collaborate on the dialogue, and encourage them to be as creative as possible.

OPTIONS

Extra Practice Have the class collaborate on a description of a ghost town or a haunted house using expressions from pages 408–409. Write the sentences on the board or on a transparency as they are said and make sure that all seven negative expressions (including **ne... ni... ni...**) are used.

Game Give students index cards with one negative expression from pages 408–409 and another expression that could be used with it on each card. Then tell the students to produce sentences. Example: *(on the card)* **ne... personne + l'école (Personne ne va à l'école le dimanche.)**

Instructional Resources
*espaces.vhlcentral.com: IRM (**Feuilles d'activités**; Info Gap Activities); Testing Program, pp. 89–92; Test Files; Testing Program MP3s; activities; downloads; reference tools Test Generator*

1 Suggestion Have two volunteers read the **modèle** aloud. Then distribute the **Feuilles d'activités** found on the Supersite.

2 Expansion Once students have completed this activity, ask them the following questions about other students. **Qu'est-ce que ____ reçoit dans son courrier? Est-ce que ____ envoie des lettres par la poste de temps en temps? Des colis?**

3 Suggestion To get the class started, have students read the instructions and then make up different kinds of questions. Examples: **Y a-t-il un(e) ____ près d'ici? Où se trouve le/la ____ ?**

4 Suggestion Have students formulate **vrai** or **faux** statements about any subject using the negative expressions listed for the activity.

5 Expansion Remind students of the difference in meaning between **apercevoir** and **s'apercevoir**. Then ask them to make up a couple of sentences with the phrases **s'est aperçu(e) de/que** and **sans m'en apercevoir**.

6 Suggestion Divide the class into pairs and distribute the Info Gap Handouts found on the Supersite for this activity. Give students ten minutes to complete the activity.

Révision

1 Je ne vais jamais... Votre professeur va vous donner une feuille d'activités. Circulez dans la classe pour trouver un(e) camarade différent(e) qui fait ses courses à ces endroits. Où ne vont-ils jamais? Où ne vont-ils plus? Justifiez toutes vos réponses. Answers will vary.

MODÈLE

Étudiant(e) 1: *Vas-tu à la laverie?*
Étudiant(e) 2: *Non, je n'y vais plus parce que j'ai acheté un lave-linge. Mais, je vais toujours à la banque le lundi.*

Endroits	*Noms*
1. banque	*Sabrina*
2. bijouterie	
3. boutique de vêtements	
4. cybercafé	
5. laverie	

2 Le courrier Avec un(e) partenaire, préparez six questions pour interviewer vos camarades. Que reçoivent-ils dans leur courrier? Qu'envoient-ils? Utilisez les expressions négatives et les verbes **recevoir** et **envoyer**. Ensuite, par groupes de quatre, posez vos questions et écrivez les réponses. Answers will vary.

MODÈLE

Étudiant(e) 1: *Est-ce que tu ne reçois que des lettres dans ton courrier?*
Étudiant(e) 2: *Non, je reçois des cadeaux parfois, mais je n'en envoie jamais.*

3 Au village Vous visitez un petit village pour la première fois. Malheureusement, tout y est fermé. Vous posez des questions à un(e) habitant(e) sur les endroits de la liste et il/elle vous répond par des expressions négatives. Préparez le dialogue avec un(e) partenaire. Answers will vary.

MODÈLE

Étudiant(e) 1: *À quelle heure le bureau de poste ouvre-t-il aujourd'hui?*
Étudiant(e) 2: *Malheureusement, le bureau de poste n'existe plus, Monsieur!*

banque	laverie
bureau de poste	mairie
commissariat de police	salon de beauté

4 Vrai ou faux? Par groupes de quatre, travaillez avec un(e) partenaire pour préparer huit phrases au sujet des deux autres partenaires de votre groupe. Essayez de deviner ce qu'ils/elles (*what they*) ont fait et n'ont pas fait. Utilisez dans vos phrases le passé composé et les expressions négatives indiquées. Ensuite, lisez les phrases à vos deux camarades, qui vont vous dire si elles sont vraies ou fausses. Answers will vary.

MODÈLE

Étudiant(e) 1: *Tu n'es jamais allé(e) dans le bureau du prof.*
Étudiant(e) 2: *C'est faux. J'ai dû y aller hier pour lui poser une question.*

- ne... aucun(e)
- ne... jamais
- ne... personne
- ne... plus
- ne... que
- ne... rien

5 Au secours! Avec un(e) partenaire, préparez un dialogue pour représenter la scène de cette illustration. Utilisez les verbes **s'apercevoir**, **voir** et **croire** et des expressions négatives et affirmatives. Answers will vary.

6 Dix ans plus tard Votre professeur va vous donner, à vous et à votre partenaire, deux plans d'une ville. Attention! Ne regardez pas la feuille de votre partenaire. Answers will vary.

MODÈLE

Étudiant(e) 1: *Il y a dix ans, la laverie avait beaucoup de clients.*
Étudiant(e) 2: *Aujourd'hui, il n'y a personne dans la laverie.*

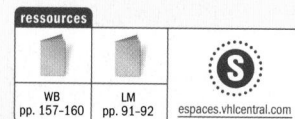

ressources
WB pp. 157–160 | LM pp. 91–92 | espaces.vhlcentral.com

OPTIONS

Extra Practice State that someone is wearing a certain article of clothing and then ask students who it is. Example: **Est-ce que vous voyez quelqu'un dans la classe qui porte un tee-shirt rouge? Qui?** In some cases, name an article not present in the classroom so that students will answer negatively: **Personne ne porte de jupe.**

Extra Practice Read a series of logical and illogical statements that use the verbs **voir**, **recevoir**, **croire**, **apercevoir**, and **s'apercevoir**. Tell students to raise their right hand and say **logique** for logical ones, and to raise their left hand and say **illogique** for illogical ones. Example: **Je reçois toujours de mauvaises notes quand je fais tous mes devoirs. (illogique)**

Video: TV Clip

Le Zapping

Rennes: capitale bretonne

La ville de Rennes devient capitale de la Bretagne en 1532, année où cette région est annexée à la France. Elle commence sa longue histoire de plus de 2.000 ans à l'époque des Gaulois°. Rennes se trouve sur le confluent de deux fleuves°, l'Ille et la Vilaine, emplacement stratégique qui attire° ses premiers habitants. Au centre-ville, on peut admirer son architecture de différentes périodes historiques, comme les maisons médiévales à colombages° et le Parlement de Bretagne du XVIIe siècle.

—Au centre-ville, on trouve des cafés, la mairie, des boutiques, des distributeurs automatiques...

—Une promenade à travers° les rues anciennes du centre historique vous fait découvrir la magnifique architecture bretonne...

Compréhension Répondez aux questions. Some answers will vary.

1. Quelles courses peut-on faire dans un centre-ville français? On peut aller à la poste ou à la banque.
2. Quels lieux d'intérêt culturel peut-on visiter à Rennes? On peut visiter le musée des Beaux-Arts ou la bibliothèque municipale.
3. Comment peut-on s'y détendre? On peut faire une promenade en bateau ou visiter le parc du Thabor.

Discussion Avec un(e) partenaire, discutez de ces questions. Answers will vary.

1. Y a-t-il des villes dans votre pays avec des centres-villes de style français? Lesquelles (*Which ones*)?
2. Que pensez-vous des centres-villes français? Aimeriez-vous habiter à Rennes? Pourquoi?

Gaulois *Gauls (ancient Celtic people)* **fleuves** *rivers* **attire** *attracts* **à colombages** *half-timbered* **à travers** *through*

Practice more at **espaces.vhlcentral.com.**

Section Goals

In this section, students will:
- read about the city of Rennes
- watch a promotional video for the city
- answer questions about the video and Rennes

Instructional Resources
*espaces.vhlcentral.com: TV commercial; IRM (**Le zapping** TV clip transcription); activities; downloads; reference tools*

Introduction
To check comprehension, ask these questions:
1. Quel événement a lieu en 1532? (La Bretagne est annexée à la France et Rennes devient capitale de la région.)
2. Qu'est-ce qui attire les premiers habitants de Rennes? (L'emplacement stratégique sur le confluent de l'Ille et de la Vilaine attire les premiers habitants.)
3. Que peut-on admirer au centre-ville de Rennes? (On peut admirer l'architecture de différentes périodes historiques.)

Avant de regarder la vidéo
- Have students look at the video stills, read the captions, and predict what is happening for each visual. (**1. Ces gens sont au centre-ville de Rennes. 2. Dans le centre historique, on découvre la magnifique architecture bretonne.**)
- Before showing the video, explain to students that they do not need to understand every word they hear. Tell them to listen for the text in the captions and for vocabulary from this lesson. They should also watch every scene carefully and jot down further examples of this lesson's vocabulary.

Compréhension Have students work in pairs or groups for this activity. Tell them to write their answers. Then show the video again so that they can check their answers and add any missing information.

Discussion Ask students who might have traveled outside the United States or Canada to describe the cities they visited. How do their city centers compare to that of Rennes? How do they compare to a typical downtown area in the U.S.?

OPTIONS

Here is a full list of the places and activities shown in the center of Rennes:
- Le marché des Lices
- Des promenades en bateau sur la Vilaine
- Le palais Saint-Georges
- Des maisons à colombages
- Le Parlement de Bretagne
- L'Opéra de Rennes
- Le palais du commerce
- La place de la République
- Le musée des Beaux-Arts
- La cathédrale Saint-Pierre
- Les Champs Libres: la bibliothèque municipale, l'Espace des sciences, le musée de Bretagne
- L'Alignement du XXIe siècle
- Le parc du Thabor
- L'Hôtel de Ville

Section Goals

In this section, students will learn and practice vocabulary related to:
- asking for and giving directions
- landmarks

Instructional Resources
*espaces.vhlcentral.com: Transparency #52; IRM (**Vocabulaire supplémentaire**; **Mise en pratique** answers; Textbook Audioscript; Lab Audioscript); Textbook MP3s; Lab MP3s; WB/VM/LM Answer Key; activities; downloads; reference tools*

Suggestions
- Tell students to look over the new vocabulary and identify the cognates.
- Use **Transparency #52.** Point out objects and describe what the people are doing. Examples: **Il est perdu. C'est une statue. Il y a deux feux de signalisation au carrefour.**
- Define and contrast the words for types of roads: **une rue, une autoroute, un boulevard, une avenue,** and **un chemin**. Also give examples using local roads students know.
- Point out that **coin** and **angle** both mean *corner.*
- Point out the difference between **tout droit** (*straight ahead*) and **à droite** (*to the right*).
- You might want to teach students the expression **point de repère** (*landmark; point of reference*).
- Additional vocabulary for this lesson can be found in the **Vocabulaire supplémentaire** on the Supersite.

Leçon 12B

Talking Picture
Audio: Activity

You will learn how to...
- ask for directions
- tell what you will do

Où se trouve...?

Vocabulaire

continuer	*to continue*
se déplacer	*to move (change location)*
suivre	*to follow*
tourner	*to turn*
traverser	*to cross*
un angle	*corner*
une avenue	*avenue*
un bâtiment	*building*
un boulevard	*boulevard*
un chemin	*way; path*
un coin	*corner*
des indications (f.)	*directions*
un office du tourisme	*tourist office*
au bout (de)	*at the end (of)*
au coin (de)	*at the corner (of)*
autour (de)	*around*
jusqu'à	*until*
(tout) près (de)	*(very) close (to)*
tout droit	*straight ahead*

ressources
WB pp. 161-162 | LM p. 93 | espaces.vhlcentral.com

OPTIONS

Extra Practice Ask students which vocabulary words they associate with these verbs. **1. descendre (rue/escalier) 2. suivre (rue/boulevard/chemin) 3. tourner (gauche/droite) 4. demander (indications) 5. monter (escaliers) 6. traverser (un pont/une rue) 7. regarder (une statue) 8. boire (une fontaine) 9. téléphoner (une cabine téléphonique) 10. s'arrêter (un feu de signalisation)**

TPR Label four points in your classroom with the cardinal directions. Play a game of **Jacques a dit** (*Simon says*) in which students respond to commands using the four directions. Example: **Regardez vers le nord.** Tell students to respond only if they hear the words **Jacques a dit**. If a student responds to a command not preceded by **Jacques a dit**, he or she is eliminated. The last person standing wins.

Attention!

The verb **suivre** (*to follow*) is an important verb for giving and getting directions. Its first person singular form (**je**) is the same as the **je** form of the present tense of **être**. Context will determine the meaning.

je suis	**nous suivons**
tu suis	**vous suivez**
il/elle suit	**ils/elles suivent**

Mise en pratique

1 Écoutez Écoutez cette conversation entre un touriste et une dame (*lady*) à qui il demande son chemin. Ensuite, dites si les affirmations suivantes sont vraies ou fausses.

	Vrai	Faux
1. Le touriste est perdu.	☑	☐
2. Il cherche la rue Saint-Antoine.	☐	☑
3. Il cherche l'hôtel Étoile.	☑	☐
4. L'hôtel est loin d'où il se trouve.	☐	☑
5. Le touriste doit traverser le pont de Sully.	☑	☐
6. Il doit tourner une fois à gauche.	☑	☐
7. La rue de Rivoli se trouve au bout de la rue Saint-Antoine.	☑	☐
8. Le touriste a peur de ne pas se souvenir des indications.	☑	☐
9. Le touriste a oublié le numéro de téléphone de l'hôtel.	☑	☐
10. La dame suggère au touriste de prendre un taxi.	☐	☑

2 Les antonymes Quel est le contraire de ces expressions et de ces mots?

1. continuer tout droit tourner
2. descendre monter
3. sud nord
4. est ouest
5. à droite à gauche
6. devant derrière
7. très loin de tout près de
8. s'orienter être perdu(e)
9. rester se déplacer
10. au début de au bout de

3 Complétez Complétez les phrases avec le bon mot de vocabulaire pour faire des phrases cohérentes. Notez que tous les mots ne sont pas utilisés.

angles	cabine téléphonique	continuer	pont
avenue	chemin	se déplacer	statue
banc	coin	feu de signalisation	traverser

1. On peut s'asseoir sur un banc au parc.
2. L' avenue des Champs-Élysées est très populaire à Paris.
3. La statue de la Liberté se trouve à New York.
4. Le pont du Golden Gate se trouve à San Francisco.
5. Il y a quatre angles à un carrefour.
6. On peut téléphoner dans une cabine téléphonique.
7. Il faut toujours s'arrêter quand le feu de signalisation est au rouge.
8. Il faut toujours regarder à gauche et à droite avant de traverser la rue.
9. En ville, on peut se déplacer rapidement en métro.
10. Quand on est perdu, on demande son chemin.

Practice more at **espaces.vhlcentral.com.**

1 Tapescript TOURISTE: Pardon, Madame, je suis perdu. Où se trouve l'hôtel Étoile, s'il vous plaît?
FEMME: L'hôtel Étoile? Désolée, Monsieur, je ne sais pas. Avez-vous l'adresse?
T: Oui, c'est 37 rue de Rivoli.
F: Ah, ce n'est pas loin d'ici. Suivez cette avenue tout droit jusqu'au pont de Sully. Traversez le pont et continuez sur le boulevard Henri IV. Tournez à gauche sur la rue Saint-Antoine et tout au bout, c'est la rue de Rivoli.
T: Merci, Madame. J'espère pouvoir me souvenir de vos indications.
F: Voulez-vous appeler l'hôtel? Il y a une cabine téléphonique devant nous. Peut-être que quelqu'un peut venir vous chercher?
T: Non, je n'ai pas leur numéro de téléphone. Je l'ai oublié à l'hôtel, mais, merci.
(On Textbook MP3s)

1 Suggestion Have students correct the false statements.

2 Expansions
- Have volunteers create sentences with the words in the activity.
- For additional practice, have students give synonyms for these words. **1. angle (coin) 2. chemin (rue) 3. un grand boulevard (une avenue) 4. un immeuble (un bâtiment)**

3 Suggestion Have volunteers read the completed sentences aloud.

OPTIONS

Pairs Write the following expressions for circumlocution on the board: **C'est un endroit où..., Ça sert à..., C'est où on va pour..., C'est le contraire de..., C'est un synonyme de..., C'est une sorte de....** Tell students to work in pairs and write definitions for these vocabulary words. **1. un boulevard 2. un pont 3. une fontaine 4. des escaliers 5. un bâtiment 6. un office du tourisme 7. une cabine téléphonique**

Then have pairs get together with another pair of students and take turns reading their definitions and guessing the word. Ask each group to choose their best definition and write it on the board for the whole class to guess.

4 Suggestions
- Model the pronunciation of the roads on the map and have students repeat after you.
- Have two volunteers read the **modèle** aloud. Make sure students understand that they are supposed to give directions to the first place from the second place.

5 Expansion Have volunteers report what they learned about their partner to the class.

6 Suggestion Distribute real maps of French towns for students to use in their conversations. Such maps are available through tourist offices and online.

Communication

NATIONAL communication STANDARDS

4 Le plan de la ville **À tour de rôle avec un(e) partenaire, demandez des indications pour pouvoir vous rendre (*to get*) aux endroits de la liste. Indiquez votre point de départ.** Answers will vary.

- Café de la Gare
- Boulangerie Le Pain Chaud
- Hôpital St-Jean
- Office du tourisme
- Épicerie Bresson
- Bureau de poste
- Pharmacie Molière
- Banque
- Université Joseph Fourier
- Cabine téléphonique

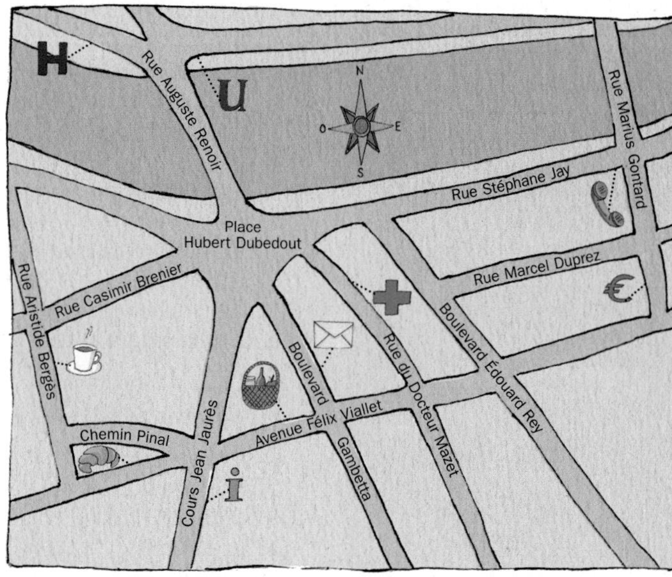

MODÈLE

la boulangerie Le Pain Chaud, le bureau de poste

Étudiant(e) 1: *Excusez-moi, où se trouve la boulangerie Le Pain Chaud, s'il vous plaît?*

Étudiant(e) 2: *Du bureau de poste, suivez le boulevard jusqu'à l'avenue Félix Viallet, ensuite prenez à droite, continuez tout droit, la boulangerie est à droite, juste après le cours Jean Jaurès.*

1. l'hôpital, la pharmacie
2. le café, l'office du tourisme
3. la banque, le bureau de poste
4. l'université, l'épicerie
5. la cabine téléphonique, la boulangerie
6. l'office du tourisme, la pharmacie
7. la banque, l'université
8. la boulangerie, la pharmacie

5 Conversez **Interviewez un(e) camarade de classe.** Answers will vary.

1. Quelles statues célèbres connais-tu? Connais-tu aussi des ponts, des bâtiments célèbres?
2. Quand t'es-tu perdu(e) pour la dernière fois? Où? Qui t'a aidé(e)?
3. Quand as-tu utilisé une cabine téléphonique pour la dernière fois? Où étais-tu?
4. Es-tu déjà allé(e) dans un office du tourisme? Pour quoi faire?
5. Qu'est-ce qui se trouve au coin de la rue où tu habites? Et au bout de la rue?
6. Qui, de ta famille ou de tes ami(e)s, habite près de chez toi?

6 En vacances **Avec un(e) partenaire, préparez cette conversation. Soyez prêt(e)s à jouer la scène devant la classe.** Answers will vary.

- Vous êtes un(e) touriste perdu(e) en ville.
- Vous demandez où se trouvent deux endroits différents.
- Quelqu'un vous indique le chemin.

OPTIONS

Game Arrange furniture to form meandering pathways around the classroom. Blindfold a student and point out to the class a destination somewhere in the room. Have the class give the blindfolded student directions to arrive at the destination. Example: **Tourne(z) à gauche/à droite.** To make this a competitive game, divide the class into two teams. Blindfold two students and have them race to different destinations.

Extra Practice Have students ask for and give directions to and from specific places on campus. Example: **Comment va-t-on du resto U à la bibliothèque?** Other campus landmarks can include: **la librairie, la statue de _____, la fontaine, l'amphithéâtre, le stade,** and **la piscine**.

Les sons et les lettres

Audio: Concepts, Activities
Record & Compare

NATIONAL comparisons STANDARDS

Les majuscules et les minuscules

Some of the rules governing capitalization are the same in French as they are in English. However, many words that are capitalized in English are not capitalized in French. For example, the French pronoun **je** is never capitalized except when it is the first word in a sentence.

Aujourd'hui, je vais au marché. *Today, I am going to the market.*

Days of the week, months, and geographical terms are not capitalized in French.

Qu'est-ce que tu fais lundi après-midi? **Mon anniversaire, c'est le 14 octobre.**
Cette ville est au bord de la mer Méditerranée.

Languages are not capitalized in French, nor are adjectives of nationality. However, if the word is a noun that refers to a person or people of a particular nationality, it is capitalized.

Tu apprends le français.
You are learning French.

C'est une voiture allemande.
It's a German car.

Elle s'est mariée avec un Italien.
She married an Italian.

Les Français adorent le foot.
The French love soccer.

As a general rule, you should write capital letters with their accents. Diacritical marks can change the meaning of words, so not including them can create ambiguities.

LES AVOCATS SERONT JUGÉS.
Lawyers will be judged.

LES AVOCATS SERONT JUGES.
Lawyers will be the judges.

Corrigez Corrigez la capitalisation des mots suivants.

1. MAI mai
2. QUÉBEC Québec
3. VENDREDI vendredi
4. ALLEMAND allemand
5. L'OCÉAN PACIFIQUE l'océan Pacifique
6. LE BOULEVARD ST-MICHEL le boulevard St-Michel

Écrivez Écrivez correctement les phrases en utilisant (*by writing*) les minuscules et les majuscules.

1. LE LUNDI ET LE MERCREDI, J'AI MON COURS D'ITALIEN. Le lundi et le mercredi, j'ai mon cours d'italien.
2. CHARLES BAUDELAIRE ÉTAIT UN POÈTE FRANÇAIS. Charles Baudelaire était un poète français.
3. LES AMÉRICAINS AIMENT BEAUCOUP LE LAC MICHIGAN. Les Américains aiment beaucoup le lac Michigan.
4. UN MONUMENT SE TROUVE SUR L'AVENUE DES CHAMPS-ÉLYSÉES. Un monument se trouve sur l'avenue des Champs-Élysées.

Dictons Répétez les dictons à voix haute.

Si le Français est "tout yeux", l'Anglais est "tout oreilles."[2]

La France, c'est le français quand il est bien écrit.[1]

1 France is French (when it is) well written.
2 If the Frenchman is all eyes, the Englishman is all ears.

ressources
LM p. 94
espaces.vhlcentral.com

Section Goals

In this section, students will learn about French capitalization.

Instructional Resources
espaces.vhlcentral.com: Lab MP3s; WB/VM/LM Answer Key ; IRM (Lab Audioscript); activities; downloads; reference tools

Suggestions
- Model the pronunciation of the example sentences and have students repeat them after you.
- Have students translate the sentences in the second set of examples into English and compare capitalization rules in the two languages.
- You might want to tell students that diacritical marks are sometimes omitted on capital letters in French, especially on signs or headlines. In such cases, they should use the context to ascertain meaning.
- You might want to tell students that the names of religions are not capitalized in French. Example: **Paul est catholique.**
- Dictate three sentences that contain days of the week, months, countries, nationalities or languages, repeating each one at least two times. Then write them on the board or a transparency and have students check their spelling.

Dictons The saying **«La France, c'est le français quand il est bien écrit.»** is a quote from Napoléon Bonaparte. The saying **«Si le Français est "tout yeux", l'Anglais est "tout oreilles".»** is a quote from Jules Verne.

OPTIONS

Extra Practice Use these sentences for additional practice with capitalization. **1. EN FÉVRIER, LISE VA EN ITALIE. 2. LOUIS A UNE VOITURE JAPONAISE. 3. MA COUSINE LAURE S'EST MARIÉE AVEC UN ESPAGNOL. 4. EUGÈNE HABITE AU 28 AVENUE GEORGE V. 5. LES TOURISTES BELGES ONT VISITÉ LA CATHÉDRALE DE NOTRE-DAME DE PARIS.**

Extra Practice Teach students these French tongue-twisters that model French capitalization conventions. **1. Je suis ce que je suis et si je suis ce que je suis, qu'est-ce que je suis? 2. Je dis que tu l'as dit à Didi ce que j'ai dit jeudi.**

Section Goals

In this section, students will learn functional phrases for giving directions and talking about weekend plans.

Instructional Resources
espaces.vhlcentral.com: WB/VM/LM Answer Key; IRM (Videoscript; ***Roman-photo*** *Translations); activities; downloads; reference tools Video on DVD*

Video Recap: Leçon 12A
Before doing this **Roman-photo**, review the previous one with this activity.

1. Pourquoi Rachid et Amina sont-ils à la charcuterie? (Ils achètent de la nourriture pour un pique-nique.)
2. Pourquoi Amina paie-t-elle? (Rachid n'a pas de liquide et la charcuterie n'accepte pas les cartes de crédit.)
3. Où Amina invite-t-elle Rachid à l'accompagner pendant l'après-midi? (dans une boutique et dans une bijouterie)
4. Où David invite-t-il Sandrine à aller avec lui? (dans une brasserie)

Video Synopsis
A tourist asks Monsieur Hulot for directions to the post office. He doesn't know, so he sends him to **Le P'tit Bistrot**. At the café, the four friends are discussing their weekend plans. When the tourist asks for directions, Rachid and David give him conflicting information. Stéphane asks the tourist, more confused than ever, if he can help and then proceeds to give him clear directions.

Suggestions
- Have students predict what the episode will be about based on the video stills.
- Have students scan the captions, and identify places and landmarks in a city.
- After reading the **Roman-photo**, have students summarize the episode.

NATIONAL communication cultures STANDARDS

Chercher son chemin

Video: *Roman-photo*
Record & Compare

PERSONNAGES

Amina

David

M. Hulot

Rachid

Sandrine

Stéphane

Touriste

Au kiosque de M. Hulot...
M. HULOT Bonjour, Monsieur.
TOURISTE Bonjour.
M. HULOT Trois euros, s'il vous plaît.
TOURISTE Je n'ai pas de monnaie.
M. HULOT Voici cinq, six, sept euros qui font dix. Merci.
TOURISTE Excusez-moi, où est le bureau de poste, s'il vous plaît?

M. HULOT Euh... c'est par là... Ah... non... euh... voyons... vous prenez cette rue, là et... euh, non non... je ne sais pas vraiment comment vous expliquer... Attendez, vous voyez le café qui est juste là? Il y aura certainement quelqu'un qui saura vous dire comment y aller.
TOURISTE Ah, merci, Monsieur. Au revoir!

Au P'tit Bistrot...
SANDRINE Qu'est-ce que vous allez faire le week-end prochain?
RACHID Je pense que nous irons faire une randonnée à la Sainte-Victoire.
AMINA Oui, j'espère qu'il fera beau!
DAVID S'il ne pleut pas, nous irons au concert en plein air de Pauline Ester. C'est la chanteuse préférée de Sandrine, n'est-ce pas, chérie?

DAVID Non! À droite!
RACHID Non, à gauche! Puis, vous continuez tout droit, vous traversez le cours Mirabeau et c'est juste là, en face de la fontaine de La Rotonde, à côté de la gare.
DAVID Non, c'est à côté de l'office du tourisme.

TOURISTE Euh merci, je... je vais le trouver tout seul. Au revoir.
TOUS Bonne journée, Monsieur.

À la terrasse...
STÉPHANE Bonjour, je peux vous aider?
TOURISTE J'espère que oui.
STÉPHANE Vous êtes perdu?
TOURISTE Exactement. Je cherche le bureau de poste.

ACTIVITÉS

1 Questions Répondez par des phrases complètes.

1. Qu'est-ce que Rachid et Amina vont faire ce week-end? Ils vont faire une randonnée à la Sainte-Victoire.
2. Qu'est-ce que Sandrine et David vont faire ce week-end? Ils vont aller à un concert en plein air.
3. Quels points de repères (*landmarks*) Stéphane donne-t-il au touriste? Il mentionne le cours Mirabeau, La Rotonde et la fontaine.
4. Est-ce que vous pensez que la musique de Pauline Ester est très appréciée aujourd'hui? Pourquoi? Answers will vary.
5. Est-ce que vous pensez que les choses vont bien entre Amina et Rachid? Pourquoi? Answers will vary.
6. Est-ce que vous pensez que les choses vont bien entre Sandrine et David? Pourquoi? Answers will vary.
7. Comment pensez-vous que le touriste se sent quand il sort du P'tit Bistrot? Answers will vary.
8. Qui avait raison, à votre avis (*in your opinion*), David ou Rachid? Answers will vary.

OPTIONS

Avant de regarder la vidéo Before viewing the video, have students work in pairs and brainstorm a list of words and expressions they might hear in an episode involving people asking for directions.

Regarder la vidéo Show the video episode and tell students to check off the words or expressions they hear on their lists. Then show the episode again and have students give you a play-by-play description of the action. Write their descriptions on the board.

Un touriste se perd à Aix... heureusement, il y a Stéphane!

4

5

SANDRINE Absolument! «Oui, je l'adore, c'est mon amour, mon trésor...»
AMINA Pauline Ester! Tu aimes la musique des années quatre-vingt-dix?
SANDRINE Pas tous les styles de musique, mais Pauline Ester, oui.
AMINA Comme on dit, les goûts et les couleurs, ça ne se discute pas!
RACHID Tu n'aimes pas Pauline Ester, mon cœur?

TOURISTE Excusez-moi, est-ce que vous savez où se trouve le bureau de poste, s'il vous plaît?
RACHID Oui, ce n'est pas loin d'ici. Vous descendez la rue, juste là, ensuite vous continuez jusqu'au feu rouge et vous tournez à gauche.

9

10

STÉPHANE Le bureau de poste? C'est très simple.
TOURISTE Ah bon! C'est loin d'ici?
STÉPHANE Non, pas du tout. C'est tout près. Vous prenez cette rue, là, à gauche. Vous continuez jusqu'au cours Mirabeau. Vous le connaissez?
TOURISTE Non, je ne suis pas d'ici.
STÉPHANE Bon... Le cours Mirabeau, c'est le boulevard principal de la ville.

STÉPHANE Alors, une fois que vous serez sur le cours Mirabeau, vous tournerez à gauche et suivrez le cours jusqu'à La Rotonde. Vous la verrez... Il y a une grande fontaine. Derrière la fontaine, vous trouverez le bureau de poste, et voilà!
TOURISTE Merci beaucoup.
STÉPHANE De rien. Au revoir!

Expressions utiles

Giving directions

- **Attendez, vous voyez le café qui est juste là?**
  Wait, do you see the café right over there?
- **Il y aura certainement quelqu'un qui saura vous dire comment y aller.**
  There will surely be someone there who will know how to tell you how to get there.
- **Vous tournerez à gauche et suivrez le cours jusqu'à La Rotonde.**
  You will turn left and follow the street until the Rotunda.
- **Vous la verrez.**
  You will see it.
- **Derrière la fontaine, vous trouverez le bureau de poste.**
  Behind the fountain, you will find the post office.

Talking about the weekend

- **Je pense que nous irons faire une randonnée.**
  I think we will go for a hike.
- **J'espère qu'il fera beau!**
  I hope it will be nice/the weather will be good!
- **Nous irons au concert en plein air.**
  We will go to the outdoor concert.

Additional vocabulary

- **voyons**
  let's see
- **le boulevard principal**
  the main drag/principal thoroughfare

2 Comment y aller? Remettez les indications pour aller du P'tit Bistrot au bureau de poste dans l'ordre. Écrivez un **X** à côté de l'indication qu'on ne doit pas suivre.

_3_ a. Suivez le cours Mirabeau jusqu'à la fontaine.
_4_ b. Le bureau de poste se trouve derrière la fontaine.
_2_ c. Tournez à gauche.
_X_ d. Tournez à droite au feu rouge.
_1_ e. Prenez cette rue à gauche jusqu'au boulevard principal.

3 Écrivez Le touriste est soulagé (*relieved*) d'enfin arriver au bureau de poste. Il était très découragé; presque personne ne savait lui expliquer comment y aller. Il écrit une carte postale à sa petite amie pour lui raconter son aventure. Composez son message.

Practice more at **espaces.vhlcentral.com.**

ressources: VM pp. 257–258 | DVD Leçon 12B | espaces.vhlcentral.com

ACTIVITÉS

Expressions utiles
- Model the pronunciation of the **Expressions utiles** and have students repeat them after you.
- As you work through the list, point out forms of **le futur simple**. Tell students that this tense will be formally presented in **Espace structures.**
- Respond briefly to questions about **le futur**. Reinforce correct forms, but do not expect students to produce them consistently at this time.
- Point out in caption 4 where Amina says: **Les goûts et les couleurs, ça ne se discute pas**. Ask students to interpret it. Then point out that English expresses the same idea with the saying *"To each his own."*

1 Suggestions
- Go over the answers with the class.
- For item 4, point out that Pauline Ester recorded the song ***Oui, je l'adore*** in 1989, and it remained popular in the 1990s. In this episode, Amina is surprised that Sandrine likes such an old song.

1 Expansion For additional practice, give students these questions. **9. Où va le touriste pour demander son chemin? (Il va chez le marchand de journaux et au café.) 10. Que cherche le touriste? (Il cherche le bureau de poste.) 11. Est-ce que le bureau de poste est loin du P'tit Bistrot? (Non, il est tout près.)**

2 Suggestion Have students form groups of five. Make a set of individual sentences on strips of paper for each group and distribute them. Tell students to arrange the sentences in the proper order and then read them aloud. The person who receives the sentence that does not fit should read that sentence last.

3 Suggestions
- Remind students to use appropriate salutations and closings. (See page 106.)
- If time is limited, this activity may be assigned as homework.

OPTIONS

La Rotonde The large fountain located at one end of **le cours Mirabeau** is called **La Rotonde**. Built in 1860, it features bronze lions and stone cherubs riding swans. The source of the water is the city's underground springs. Every evening, this beautiful fountain is illuminated. If possible, bring in photos of **La Rotonde** to show the class.

Extra Practice Have students find the verbs used to give directions in this episode and list them on the board. Examples: **prendre, tourner, descendre, traverser**, and **continuer**. Then have students write directions from campus to various places in town using as many of these verbs as possible. You may wish to assign students different locations.

connections cultures

NATIONAL STANDARDS

Section Goals

In this section, students will:

- learn about main squares in French cities and towns
- learn more terms for small shops or businesses
- learn the names of famous areas in the hearts of several francophone cities
- read about the Baron Georges Eugène Haussmann

Instructional Resources
espaces.vhlcentral.com: activities; downloads; reference tools

Culture à la loupe

Avant la lecture Have students read the first sentence of the text. Then ask: **Votre ville natale a-t-elle une place principale ou un centre-ville? Quels bâtiments trouvez-vous souvent dans ces endroits?**

Lecture

- Point out the **Coup de main**. Explain that people in Paris customarily refer to a locale as **le 1er** or **le 13ème**, without using the word **arrondissement**. Paris has 20 **arrondissements**.
- Explain that the term **la mairie** is related to the title of the person who works there, **le maire**.

Après la lecture Have students describe what they see in the photos. Then ask: **Pensez-vous que c'est une photo d'un village, d'une petite ville ou d'une grande ville? Pourquoi?**

1 Suggestion Have students work in pairs on this activity.

CULTURE À LA LOUPE

Villes et villages français

Quand on regarde le plan d'un village, d'une petite ville ou celui d'un quartier d'une grande ville, on remarque qu'il y a souvent une place au centre, autour de laquelle° la ville ou le quartier s'organise. Elle est un peu comme «le cœur» de la ville ou du quartier.

Sur la place principale des villes et villages français, on trouve souvent une église. Il peut s'y trouver aussi l'hôtel de ville (la mairie), ainsi que° d'autres bâtiments administratifs comme la poste, le commissariat de police ou l'office du tourisme, s'il y en a un. La grande place est aussi le quartier commercial d'une petite ville et beaucoup de gens y vont pour faire leurs courses dans les magasins ou pour se détendre dans un café, un restaurant ou au cinéma. On y trouve aussi parfois un musée ou un théâtre. La place peut être piétonne° ou ouverte à la circulation, mais dans les deux cas, elle est souvent très animée°.

En général, la grande place est bien entretenue° et décorée d'une fontaine, d'un parterre de fleurs° ou d'une statue. La majorité des rues principales de la ville ou du quartier partent ensuite de la place. Le nom de la place reflète souvent ce qu'on y trouve, par exemple la place de l'Église, la place de la Mairie ou la place de la Comédie. Beaucoup de rues portent le nom d'un écrivain ou d'un personnage célèbre de l'histoire de France, comme rue Victor Hugo ou avenue du général de Gaulle. Au centre-ville, les rues sont souvent très étroites et beaucoup sont à sens unique°.

laquelle *which* **ainsi que** *as well as* **piétonne** *pedestrian* **animée** *busy* **entretenue** *cared for* **parterre de fleurs** *flower bed* **sens unique** *one-way*

Coup de main

Paris, Lyon, and Marseille, the three major French cities, are divided into **arrondissements**, or districts. You can determine in which **arrondissement** something is located by the final numbers of its zip code. For example, 75011 indicates the 11th **arrondissement** in Paris and 13001 is the 1st **arrondissement** in Marseille.

ACTIVITÉS

1 Complétez Donnez un début logique à chaque phrase, d'après le texte. Answers will vary. Possible answers provided.

1. ... au centre de la majorité des petites villes françaises.
   Il y a une place
2. ... autour de sa grande place.
   Une petite ville française s'organise
3. ... se situe souvent sur la place principale d'une ville française.
   Une église
4. ... pour faire leurs courses ou pour se détendre.
   Beaucoup de gens vont sur la grande place de leur ville
5. ... décorent souvent les places.
   Une fontaine, une statue ou un parterre de fleurs
6. ... sont réservées exclusivement aux piétons.
   Les places piétonnes
7. ... détermine souvent le nom d'une place.
   Un bâtiment
8. ... donnent souvent leur nom aux rues françaises.
   Des écrivains ou d'autres personnages célèbres
9. ... sont souvent à sens unique.
   Les rues du centre-ville
10. ... sont divisées en arrondissements.
    Paris, Lyon et Marseille

OPTIONS

Cultural Comparison Have students work in groups of three. Tell them to compare the center of French towns and cities with the center of the town or city in which their campus is located. Have them list the similarities and differences in a two-column chart under the headings **Similitudes** and **Différences**. Alternatively, you can let students choose another location to compare.

Villes et villages français Having a book of maps (**un plan détaillé**) is essential when visiting a French city because roads are often short, narrow, and organized on uneven grids or no grids at all. Even many lifelong residents of Paris and Lyon keep their maps with them.

LE FRANÇAIS QUOTIDIEN

Des magasins

cordonnerie (*f.*)	*cobbler's*
disquaire (*m.*)	*music store*
fleuriste (*m.*)	*florist*
parfumerie (*f.*)	*perfume/beauty shop*
photographe (*m.*)	*photo shop*
quincaillerie (*f.*)	*hardware store*
tailleur (*m.*)	*tailor's*
teinturerie (*f.*)	*dry cleaner's*
vidéoclub (*m.*)	*video store*

PORTRAIT

Le baron Haussmann

En 1853, Napoléon III demande au baron Georges Eugène Haussmann (1809-1891) de moderniser Paris. Le baron imagine alors un programme de transformation de la ville entière°. Il en est le premier vrai urbaniste. Il multiplie sa surface par deux. Pour améliorer° la circulation, il ouvre de larges avenues et des boulevards, comme le boulevard Haussmann, qu'il borde° d'immeubles bourgeois. Il crée de grands carrefours, comme l'Étoile ou la place de la Concorde, et de nombreux parcs et jardins. Plus de 600 km d'égouts° sont construits. Parce qu'il a aussi détruit beaucoup de bâtiments historiques, les Français ont longtemps détesté le baron Haussmann. Pourtant°, son influence a été remarquable.

entière *entire* **améliorer** *improve* **borde** *lines with* **égouts** *sewers* **Pourtant** *However*

LE MONDE FRANCOPHONE

Le centre des villes

Voici le «cœur» de quelques villes francophones.

En Belgique

la Grand-Place à Bruxelles cœur de la vieille ville avec l'hôtel de ville, la maison du roi et de nombreux restaurants et cafés

Au Maroc

la médina de Fès centre historique avec ses monuments, ses boutiques et surtout ses artisans

En Nouvelle-Calédonie

le marché municipal de Nouméa ouvert tous les jours, on y vend du poisson, des fleurs, des légumes et des fruits

Au Québec

la Place-Royale à Québec rues étroites° et maisons en pierres° restaurées des premiers colons° français

étroites *narrow* **pierres** *stones* **colons** *colonists*

SUR INTERNET

Quelle est la particularité de la ville de Rocamadour, en France?

Go to **espaces.vhlcentral.com** to find more information related to this **ESPACE CULTURE.**

ACTIVITÉS

2 Complétez Donnez une suite logique à chaque phrase.

1. En 1853, Napoléon III demande à Haussmann... de moderniser Paris.
2. Pour améliorer la circulation dans Paris, le baron Haussmann a créé... de larges avenues et des boulevards.
3. Les Français ont longtemps détesté le baron Haussmann... parce qu'il a détruit beaucoup de bâtiments historiques.
4. La médina représente... le centre historique de Fès.
5. Au marché de Nouméa, on peut acheter... du poisson, des fleurs, des légumes et des fruits.

Practice more at **espaces.vhlcentral.com.**

3 Une école de langues Vous et un(e) partenaire dirigez une école de langues située en plein centre-ville. Préparez une petite présentation de votre école où vous expliquez où elle se situe, les choses à faire au centre-ville, etc. Vos camarades ont-ils envie de s'y inscrire (*enroll*)?

ressources
espaces.vhlcentral.com

Le français quotidien

- Model the pronunciation of each term and have students repeat it.
- Have volunteers explain what service(s) each store offers or what product(s) each one sells. Example: **Chez le fleuriste, on vend des fleurs.** Alternatively, you can have them write definitions in French. Then tell them to get together with a partner, and take turns reading their definitions and guessing the kind of shop.

Portrait

- Haussmann was born in Paris and began his **carrière préfectorale** in 1831, working in several regions of France before being asked to modernize Paris. The transformation of Paris took place in three stages between 1858 and 1870. The city's sewer system was rebuilt to help prevent disease after a cholera epidemic.
- Have students describe the photos of **le boulevard Haussmann** and **la place de la Concorde.**

Le monde francophone

- After reading the text, ask students in what countries or cities these places are located. Examples: **1. Où est la Place-Royale? (Elle est à Québec.) 2. Dans quel pays est la Grand-Place? (en Belgique)**
- Then ask questions about the individual places. Examples: **1. Dans quels endroits pouvez-vous manger? (sur la Grand-Place) 2. Où pouvez-vous trouver des objets artisanaux? (dans la médina de Fès) 3. Où pouvez-vous voir des monuments et des bâtiments historiques? (sur la Grand-Place, à la médina et sur la Place-Royale)**

2 Expansion For additional practice, give students these items. **6. Haussmann est le premier vrai... (urbaniste de Paris.) 7. Pour rendre Paris plus belle, Haussmann a créé... (de nombreux parcs et jardins.) 8. Le marché municipal de Nouméa est ouvert... (tous les jours.)**

3 Expansion After the presentations have been completed, have students vote on the school they most wish to attend.

OPTIONS

Le baron Haussmann Have students turn to the map of Paris on page 102. Tell them to find **le boulevard Haussmann, la place de la Concorde,** and **l'Étoile (l'Arc de Triomphe)** and describe each location. Then have them find other boulevards and describe the locations of various parks and gardens.

Small Groups Have students work in groups of three or four. Tell them to discuss these topics: **Les Français ont-ils eu raison de détester Haussmann? Faut-il détruire des bâtiments historiques au nom du progrès?** Then ask volunteers to report the results of their discussion to the class.

Section Goals

In this section, students will learn:

- the **futur simple** of regular verbs
- the **futur simple** with spelling-change **-er** verbs

Instructional Resources
*espaces.vhlcentral.com: Lab MP3s; WB/VM/LM Answer Key; IRM (**Essayez!** and **Mise en pratique** answers; Lab Audioscript); activities; downloads; reference tools*

Suggestions

- Before introducing the **futur simple**, review **futur proche** constructions by asking students questions about theirplans for the upcoming weekend. Examples: **Qui va sortir ce week-end? Vous allez faire quoi ce week-end, _______ ?**
- Go over the pronunciation of spelling-change **-er** verbs in the table. Then ask students for other verbs they've learned that end in **-yer** (**employer, essayer, balayer, essuyer,** and **s'ennuyer**).
- You might want to teach the expressions **à l'avenir** and **dans l'avenir** (*in the future*) to the class. In addition, you might give students a list of other adverbial expressions to use with the **futur simple: l'année/la semaine/le mois prochain(e), ...** (*day of the week*) **prochain, dans ... ans/mois/semaines, en ...** (*name of month or year*), etc.

Essayez! Have students create sentences using these phrases.

12B.1 Le futur simple

NATIONAL STANDARDS comparisons

Point de départ In **Leçon 4A**, you learned to use **aller** + [*infinitive*] to express actions that are going to happen in the immediate future (**le futur proche**). You will now learn the future tense to say what *will happen*.

Future tense of regular verbs

	parler	réussir	attendre
je/j'	parlerai	réussirai	attendrai
tu	parleras	réussiras	attendras
il/elle	parlera	réussira	attendra
nous	parlerons	réussirons	attendrons
vous	parlerez	réussirez	attendrez
ils/elles	parleront	réussiront	attendront

- Note that you form the future tense of **-er** and **-ir** verbs by adding the future endings to the infinitive. The **-e** of the infinitive is dropped before adding the endings to **-re** verbs.

Nous **voyagerons** cet été. *We will travel this summer.*
Tu ne **sortiras** pas. *You won't go out.*
Ils **attendront** Sophie. *They will wait for Sophie.*

- Note the future tense forms of most spelling-change **-er** verbs:

present form of je	+r	future forms
j'achète	achèter-	j'achèterai
je nettoie	nettoier-	je nettoierai
je paie/paye	paier-/payer-	je paierai/payerai
je m'appelle	m'appeller-	je m'appellerai

- For **-er** verbs with an **é** before the infinitive ending, form the future tense as you would with regular **-er** verbs.

Elle **répétera** ses questions. *She will repeat her questions.*
Elles **considéreront** le pour et le contre. *They'll consider the pros and cons.*

- The words **le futur** and **l'avenir** (*m.*) both mean *future*. Use the first word when referring to the grammatical future; use the second word when referring to events that haven't occurred yet.

On étudie **le futur** en cours. *We're studying the future (tense) in class.*
Je parlerai de **mon avenir** au prof. *I'll speak to the professor about my future.*

Essayez! **Complétez les phrases avec la forme correcte du futur des verbes.**

1. je *mangerai* (manger)
2. il _prendra_ (prendre)
3. on _boira_ (boire)
4. ils _achèteront_ (acheter)
5. vous _choisirez_ (choisir)
6. tu _connaîtras_ (connaître)

MISE EN PRATIQUE

1 Projets Cécile et ses amis parlent de leurs projets (*plans*) d'avenir. Employez le futur pour refaire ses phrases.

MODÈLE Je vais chercher une belle maison.
Je chercherai une belle maison.

1. Je vais finir mes études. Je finirai mes études.
2. Philippe va me dire où trouver un travail. Philippe me dira où trouver un travail.
3. Tu vas gagner beaucoup d'argent. Tu gagneras beaucoup d'argent.
4. Mes amis vont habiter près de chez moi. Mes amis habiteront près de chez moi.
5. Mon petit ami et moi, nous allons acheter un chien. Mon petit ami et moi, nous achèterons un chien.
6. Vous allez nous rendre visite de temps en temps. Vous nous rendrez visite de temps en temps.

2 Dans l'avenir Qu'est-ce qu'Habib et sa famille vont faire cet été?

MODÈLE mon cousin / lire / dix livres
Mon cousin lira dix livres.

1. mon neveu / apprendre / nager Mon neveu apprendra à nager.
2. mes grands-parents / voyager / en voiture Mes grands-parents voyageront en voiture.
3. en août / je / conduire / ma nouvelle voiture En août, je conduirai ma nouvelle voiture.
4. mon père / écrire / cartes postales Mon père écrira des cartes postales.
5. tante Yamina / maigrir Tante Yamina maigrira.
6. nous / vendre / notre vieille voiture Nous vendrons notre vieille voiture.

3 Je cherche du travail Regardez ces deux annonces (*ads*). Ensuite, avec un(e) partenaire, posez-vous ces questions et parlez du travail que vous préférez. Answers will vary.

NOUVEAU RESTAURANT CHERCHE SERVEUR/SERVEUSE
Cinq ans d'expérience minimum.
Cuisine française.
Du mardi au samedi de 16h30 à 23h30;
le dimanche de 11h30 à 22h30
Salaire 1.200 euros par mois, avec une augmentation après six mois
Métro: Goncourt
Téléphonez au: 01.40.96.31.15

TRAVAILLEZ COMME COIFFEUR/COIFFEUSE
Excellent salaire: 1.000 euros par mois
Deux ans d'expérience
Pour commencer immédiatement
Horaires: mardi, mercredi, jeudi, de 9h00 à 15h00
Téléphonez pour rendez-vous au: 01.38.18.42.90

1. Quel emploi préfères-tu? Pourquoi?
2. À quelle heure arriveras-tu au travail? À quelle heure sortiras-tu?
3. T'amuseras-tu au travail? Pourquoi?
4. Combien gagneras-tu?
5. Prendras-tu le métro? Conduiras-tu? Pourquoi?
6. Chercheras-tu un autre emploi l'année prochaine? Pourquoi?

Practice more at **espaces.vhlcentral.com.**

OPTIONS

Extra Practice Write the following on the board: **L'année prochaine, je/j'....** Then ask students to complete the sentence using a verb in the **futur simple**. If they wish to use a verb with an irregular stem (such as **aller**), give them the form and tell them that they'll learn it in **Espace structures 12B.2**.

Extra Practice Read predictions about the future while students react by saying **Oui, c'est probable** or **Non, c'est peu probable.** Write the two phrases on the board before you get started and be sure to use only verbs with regular stems in the future. Example: **En l'an 3000, personne ne parlera ni français ni anglais.**

COMMUNICATION

4 Chez la voyante Vous voulez savoir ce qui (*what*) vous attend dans l'avenir. Vous allez chez une voyante (*fortune-teller*) et vous lui posez ces questions. Jouez les deux rôles avec un partenaire, puis échangez les rôles. Answers will vary.

1. Où est-ce que je travaillerai après l'université?
2. Où est-ce que j'habiterai dans 20 ans?
3. Avec qui est-ce que je partagerai ma vie?
4. Quelle voiture est-ce que je conduirai?
5. Est-ce que je m'occuperai de ma santé?
6. Qu'est-ce que j'aimerai faire pour m'amuser?
7. Où est-ce que je passerai mes vacances?
8. Où est-ce que je dépenserai mon argent?

5 L'horoscope Avec un(e) partenaire, préparez par écrit l'horoscope d'une célébrité. Ensuite, par groupes de quatre, lisez cet horoscope à vos camarades qui essaieront de découvrir l'identité de la personne. Answers will vary.

MODÈLE

Vous travaillerez comme acteur de cinéma. Vous jouerez dans beaucoup de films français et américains. Vous jouerez des rôles divers dans des films comiques comme Last Holiday et dans des films classiques comme Jean de Florette. (réponse: Gérard Depardieu)

6 Partir très loin Vous et votre partenaire avez décidé de prendre des vacances très loin de chez vous. Regardez les photos et choisissez deux endroits où vous voulez aller, puis comparez-les. Utilisez ces questions pour vous guider. Ensuite, présentez vos réponses à la classe. Answers will vary.

- Qu'apporterez-vous?
- Quand partirez-vous?
- Que visiterez-vous?
- Comment vous détendrez-vous?
- Quand rentrerez-vous?

Le français vivant

Le Nouveau-Brunswick vous enchantera!
Le Nouveau-Brunswick vous habitera pour toujours.
Vous aimerez ses villes cosmopolites et historiques,
au style jeune et moderne. Venez faire un tour.

Identifiez Quelles formes de verbes au futur trouvez-vous dans cette publicité (*ad*)? enchantera, habitera, aimerez

Questions À tour de rôle, avec un(e) partenaire, posez-vous ces questions et répondez. Some answers will vary.

1. Que veut dire «Le Nouveau-Brunswick vous habitera pour toujours»?
   a. Vous habiterez toujours au Nouveau-Brunswick.
   (b.) Vous penserez toujours au Nouveau-Brunswick.
   c. Le Nouveau-Brunswick existera toujours.
2. Pourquoi le touriste aimera-t-il le Nouveau-Brunswick?
3. Dans quel pays se trouve le Nouveau-Brunswick? au Canada
4. Dans quelle région du monde veux-tu voyager? Cette région t'enchantera-t-elle?
5. Voyageras-tu un jour au Nouveau-Brunswick? Pourquoi?

1 Suggestion Have students do this activity in pairs. One student should read items 1–3, and the other one should restate the sentence with **futur simple**. Then they should switch roles.

2 Suggestion Students could complete this activity in phases, first writing out the sentences in the present tense and then changing the verbs from the present to the future tense.

3 Expansion When students have finished, have them write an ad for their ideal job and write sentences about it based on the activity's questions. Allow them to create humorous job descriptions, such as for TV watchers.

4 Expansion Have fortune-tellers record predictions. Then ask volunteers to read the most interesting predictions to the class.

5 Suggestion Discreetly assign a picture of a celebrity from magazines or the Internet to each pair.

6 Suggestion You might suggest that students use **on** rather than **nous** in their sentences so that they are typical of informal, everyday speech.

Le français vivant Ask students to find New Brunswick on the map on page 426. Point out that it is an officially bilingual province whose languages are French and English, and that it borders Quebec and Maine.

OPTIONS

Extra Practice Read a set of statements about what will happen in the future with some good events and some bad ones. Students should react to the statements by giving a thumbs-up (for good events) or a thumbs-down (for bad events). Example: **On gagnera des millions à la loterie.** (thumbs-up)

Small Groups Have students write a half-page description of a place in the future. It can be a utopia or a dystopia. You might suggest that they use ideas from science fiction. You may need to give them forms for some verbs with irregular stems in the future.

Section Goals

In this section, students will learn irregular forms of the **futur simple**.

Instructional Resources
*espaces.vhlcentral.com: Lab MP3s; WB/VM/LM Answer Key; IRM (**Essayez!** and **Mise en pratique** answers; Lab Audioscript); activities; downloads; reference tools*

Suggestions
- Ask students if they'll be doing certain things this coming year. Example: **Irez-vous à l'étranger?** As they give you their answers, write the subject pronoun and verb for each statement on the board and have the class repeat the combination after you.
- Ask students: **Que ferez-vous cet été?** As they tell you what they'll be doing, ask the other students if they'll be doing the same thing. Example: **Qui d'autre habitera à New York?**
- Make index cards with future forms of some of the verbs on this page (**j'irai, ils voudront**) and divide them equally between small groups of students. Have the groups formulate a sentence for each verb form with a statement about what will happen in the future. Example: **Rico deviendra médecin.**
- Have the class make a set of resolutions for the new year using the future tense. Write the resolutions on the board. Example: **Je ferai mes devoirs tous les jours.**

Essayez! If students are struggling to remember endings, write a paradigm for a verb in the future tense on the board and underline the endings. Then ask the class what the endings remind them of. (They resemble the present tense of **avoir**.)

12B.2 Irregular future forms

NATIONAL STANDARDS comparisons

Point de départ In the previous grammar point, you learned how to form the future tense. Although the future endings are the same for all verbs, some verbs use irregular stems in the future tense.

Irregular verbs in the future

infinitive	stem	future forms
aller	ir-	j'irai
apercevoir	apercevr-	j'apercevrai
avoir	aur-	j'aurai
devoir	devr-	je devrai
envoyer	enverr-	j'enverrai
être	ser-	je serai
faire	fer-	je ferai
pouvoir	pourr-	je pourrai
recevoir	recevr-	je recevrai
savoir	saur-	je saurai
venir	viendr-	je viendrai
vouloir	voudr-	je voudrai

Vous **aurez** des vacances?
Will you have vacation?

Nous **irons** en Tunisie.
We will go to Tunisia.

Il **enverra** des cartes postales.
He will send postcards.

Tu les **recevras** dans une semaine.
You will receive them in a week.

- The verbs **devenir**, **maintenir**, **retenir**, **revenir**, and **tenir** are patterned after **venir** in the future tense, just as they are in the present tense.

Nous **reviendrons** bientôt.
We will come back soon.

Tu **deviendras** architecte un jour?
Will you become an architect one day?

- The future forms of **il y a**, **il faut**, and **il pleut** are, respectively, **il y aura**, **il faudra**, and **il pleuvra**.

Il **faudra** apporter le parapluie.
We'll need to bring the umbrella.

Tu penses qu'il **pleuvra** ce week-end?
Do you think it will rain this weekend?

Essayez! Conjuguez ces verbes au futur.

1. je/j' (aller, vouloir, savoir) *irai, voudrai, saurai*
2. tu (faire, pouvoir, envoyer) feras, pourras, enverras
3. Marc (venir, être, apercevoir) viendra, sera, apercevra
4. nous (avoir, devoir, faire) aurons, devrons, ferons
5. vous (recevoir, tenir, aller) recevrez, tiendrez, irez
6. elles (vouloir, faire, être) voudront, feront, seront
7. je/j' (devenir, pouvoir, envoyer) deviendrai, pourrai, enverrai
8. elle (aller, avoir, vouloir) ira, aura, voudra

MISE EN PRATIQUE

1 Que ferai-je? Que feront ces personnes la semaine prochaine?

MODÈLE
J'étudierai.

je / étudier

1. nous / faire
Nous ferons du shopping.

3. vous / aller
Vous irez au cinéma.

2. tu / être
Tu seras à la plage.

4. Yves / devoir
Yves devra travailler.

2 Le rêve de Stéphanie Complétez les phrases pour décrire le rêve (*dream*) de Stéphanie. Employez le futur des verbes.

Quand j' (1) [aurai] (avoir) 26 ans, j' (2) [irai] (aller) habiter au bord de la mer. Mon beau mari (3) [sera] (être) avec moi et nous (4) [aurons] (avoir) une grande maison. Je ne (5) [ferai] (faire) rien à la maison. Nos amis (6) [viendront] (venir) nous rendre visite tous les week-ends.

3 Si... Avec un(e) partenaire, finissez ces phrases à tour de rôle. Employez le futur des verbes de la liste dans toutes vos réponses. Answers will vary.

MODÈLE Si mon ami(e) ne me téléphone pas ce soir, ...
Si mon amie ne me téléphone pas ce soir, je ne ferai pas de gym demain.

aller	devoir	faire	venir
avoir	être	pouvoir	vouloir

1. Si on m'invite à une fête samedi soir, ...
2. Si mes parents me donnent $1.000, ...
3. Si mon ami(e) me prête sa voiture, ...
4. Si le temps est mauvais, ...
5. Si je suis fatigué(e) vendredi, ...
6. Si ma famille me rend visite, ...

Practice more at **espaces.vhlcentral.com.**

OPTIONS

Video Replay the video episode, having students focus on the conversation at the café. Afterwards, ask them questions about it. Examples: **Pourquoi Amina dit-elle qu'elle espère qu'il fera beau ce week-end? Que feront David et Sandrine ce week-end?**

Game Play a game of Bingo. Distribute Bingo cards with infinitives of verbs written in the squares. Then read aloud sentences, each with a future form of one of the verbs in it. Students should block out the verbs they recognize with tokens or scraps of paper and call Bingo! when they've blocked out a whole row.

communication NATIONAL STANDARDS

COMMUNICATION

4 Faites des projets Travaillez avec un(e) camarade de classe pour faire des projets (*plans*) pour ces événements qui auront lieu dans l'avenir. Answers will vary.

MODÈLE

Étudiant(e) 1: *Après l'université, je chercherai un travail à San Diego. J'enseignerai dans un lycée où je pourrai travailler avec les adolescents.*
Étudiant(e) 2: *Moi, après l'université, j'irai en Europe. Je travaillerai comme serveuse dans un café.*

1. Samedi soir: Décidez où vous irez et comment vous y arriverez.
2. Les prochaines vacances: Parlez de ce que (*what*) vous ferez. Que visiterez-vous?
3. Votre prochain anniversaire: Quel âge aurez-vous? Que ferez-vous? Avec qui ferez-vous la fête?
4. Votre vie professionnelle: Que ferez-vous après l'université? Où irez-vous?
5. À 65 ans: Où serez-vous? Que ferez-vous? Avec qui partagerez-vous votre vie?

5 Prédictions Par groupes de trois, parlez de comment sera le monde en 2020, 2050 et 2100. Utilisez votre imagination. Answers will vary.

6 Demain Avec un(e) partenaire, parlez de ce que (*what*) vous, votre famille et vos amis ferez demain. Answers will vary.

MODÈLE

Étudiant(e) 1: *Que feras-tu demain à midi?*
Étudiant(e) 2: *Demain à midi, j'irai poster une lettre. Mon camarade de chambre fera ses devoirs.*

8h00 ______	8h00 ______
______	10h00 ______
10h00 ______	12h00 ______
______	14h00 ______
12h00 ______	16h00 ______
______	18h00 ______
14h00 ______	20h00 ______
______	22h00 ______
16h00 ______	**dimanche**
______	8h00 ______
18h00 ______	10h00 ______
______	12h00 ______
20h00 ______	14h00 ______
______	16h00 ______
22h00 ______	18h00 ______
______	20h00 ______
	22h00 ______

Le français vivant

Un emplacement unique, près du parc Vendôme

Le Voltaire à Nice

À 500 mètres du magnifique parc Vendôme, il y aura bientôt la Villa Adriana: une belle architecture, de grands appartements, avec terrasses et balcons. Vous viendrez visiter et vous ne voudrez plus repartir. Vous serez charmé.

AGENCE IMMO

Identifiez Quelles formes de verbes au futur trouvez-vous dans cette publicité (*ad*)? aura, viendrez, voudrez, serez

Questions À tour de rôle, avec un(e) partenaire, posez-vous ces questions et répondez. Some answers will vary.

1. Où se trouvera bientôt le Voltaire? Il se trouvera à 500 mètres du magnifique parc Vendôme.
2. Quelle sera l'architecture des appartements? L'architecture sera belle avec de grands appartements, avec terrasses et balcons.
3. D'après (*According to*) la pub, quel effet une visite au Voltaire peut-elle avoir? Vous ne voudrez plus repartir. Vous serez charmé.
4. As-tu été dans un appartement que tu n'as pas voulu quitter? Habiteras-tu un jour dans un appartement comme ça?
5. Quelles boutiques et quels bureaux y aura-t-il autour du Voltaire?

1 Expansion Have students create a series of illustrations accompanied by text telling what they'll be doing next week.

2 Suggestion To make sure that students understand the passage they just completed, read each sentence back to them and ask the class if their dream life would be similar. Example: **Et vous? Est-ce que vous rêvez d'avoir une grande maison?**

3 Suggestion Write this paradigm on the board to help students with the activity: **si** + *present tense verb* → *future tense verb*. Make certain that the class remembers and understands the concept of **si** clauses before they complete the activity.

4 Suggestion If students aren't comfortable sharing personal information, tell them that they can answer the questions in the activity for a well-known person (Sarah Michelle Geller, one of the Wayans brothers, etc.) or a fictional character (Rambo, Barbie, etc.).

5 Expansion For the presentation part of this activity, you might write a few reactions on the board for students to repeat. Examples: **Ah, oui, c'est sûr! Mais non! C'est une blague ou quoi?**

6 Suggestion To simplify the presentations, have students present only their partner's plans for tomorrow.

Le français vivant After students have read the ad aloud, point out the phrase **vous ne voudrez plus repartir.** Ask the class what they think it means. Then ask individual students what they think of the building: **Comment trouvez-vous le Voltaire?**

OPTIONS

Extra Practice Make up a transparency with a set of **si** clauses, each beginning a sentence. Allow students to complete the sentences by supplying clauses with the verb in the future tense. Example: **S'il pleut cet après-midi, … (je resterai à la maison avec mon chat.)**

Pairs Teach the expression **Quand les poules auront des dents** and then add ellipses (…) after it and tell the class to complete the thought by describing an improbable scenario with a partner. Example: **…moi, j'irai à la bibliothèque le samedi soir.** When students have completed their work in pairs, have them share it with the class.

Instructional Resources
espaces.vhlcentral.com: IRM (Info Gap Activities); Testing Program, pp. 93–96; Test Files; Testing Program MP3s; activities; downloads; reference tools
Test Generator

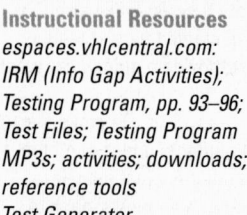

1 Suggestion You might wish to hand out campus maps as a visual aid to help students complete this activity. Students with difficulty visualizing space could trace the routes their partner describes to them on their maps. You could mark the classroom with an X and the words **Vous êtes ici.**

2 Suggestion Tell students to include a time reference (**le matin, jeudi soir,** etc.) in each sentence.

3 Suggestion Before students begin this activity, you may wish to review the vocabulary for houses in **Leçon 8A.**

4 Suggestion So that students have a point of reference to verify the original instructions, have the student that first gives directions write them. Then he or she can read the directions aloud to the first person and verify them while the second person recalls what he or she heard.

5 Suggestion To get the class warmed up for this activity, read a set of logical and illogical statements about what you will do given certain weather conditions. Tell students to qualify each statement as **logique** or **illogique**. Examples: **Il pleuvra samedi, donc j'irai à la plage. (illogique) S'il fait beau dimanche, on ira au parc. (logique)**

6 Suggestion Divide the class into pairs and distribute the Info Gap Handouts found on the Supersite for this activity. Give students ten minutes to complete the activity.

Révision

1 Le campus À tour de rôle, donnez des indications à un(e) partenaire pour aller d'où vous vous trouvez en ce moment jusqu'à d'autres endroits sur le campus. Employez le futur. Answers will vary.

MODÈLE

Étudiant(e) 1: *Tu sortiras du bâtiment et tu tourneras à gauche. Ensuite, tu traverseras la rue. Où seras-tu?*
Étudiant(e) 2: *Je serai à la bibliothèque.*

2 La visite de Québec Avec un(e) partenaire, vous visitez la ville de Québec. Préparez un itinéraire de votre visite où vous vous arrêterez souvent pour visiter ou acheter quelque chose, manger, boire, etc. Soyez prêts à présenter votre itinéraire à la classe. Answers will vary.

MODÈLE

Étudiant(e) 1: *Le matin, nous prendrons le petit-déjeuner dans l'hôtel.*
Étudiant(e) 2: *Ensuite, nous irons visiter le musée de la Civilisation.*

Québec vous attend!
Visitez:
le château Frontenac
la terrasse Dufferin
le musée de la Civilisation
la basilique Notre Dame-de-Québec
le musée de l'Amérique française
et beaucoup plus!

3 Ma future maison Avec un(e) partenaire, parlez de votre future maison et de ses pièces, de son jardin, du quartier et de vos voisins. Utilisez le futur et ces prépositions pour les décrire. Ensuite, présentez les projets (*plans*) de votre partenaire à la classe. Answers will vary.

MODÈLE

Étudiant(e) 1: *Il y aura un énorme jardin devant ma future maison.*
Étudiant(e) 2: *Je n'aurai aucun voisin en face de ma future maison.*

à droite (de)	autour (de)	en face (de)
à gauche (de)	derrière	loin (de)
au bout (de)	devant	(tout) près (de)
au milieu de		

4 Ma ville Vous invitez votre partenaire à venir vous rendre visite dans votre ville d'origine. Expliquez-lui le chemin de l'aéroport jusqu'à votre maison. Ensuite, votre partenaire donnera ces indications à un(e) autre camarade, qui vous les répétera. Les indications sont-elles toujours correctes? Utilisez le futur et alternez les rôles. Answers will vary.

MODÈLE

Étudiant(e) 1: *Tu sortiras de l'aéroport, tu iras jusqu'au centre-ville et tu passeras la mairie où tu tourneras à droite.*
Étudiant(e) 2: *D'accord, à droite à la mairie. Et après, j'irai où?*

5 Des prévisions météo Avec un(e) partenaire, parlez des prévisions météo pour le week-end prochain. Chacun (*Each one*) doit faire cinq prévisions et dire ce qu'on (*what one*) peut faire par ce temps. Soyez prêts à parler de vos prévisions et des possibilités pour le week-end devant la classe. Answers will vary.

MODÈLE

Étudiant(e) 1: *Samedi, il fera beau dans le nord. On pourra faire une promenade.*
Étudiant(e) 2: *Dimanche, il pleuvra dans l'ouest. On devra passer la journée dans l'appartement.*

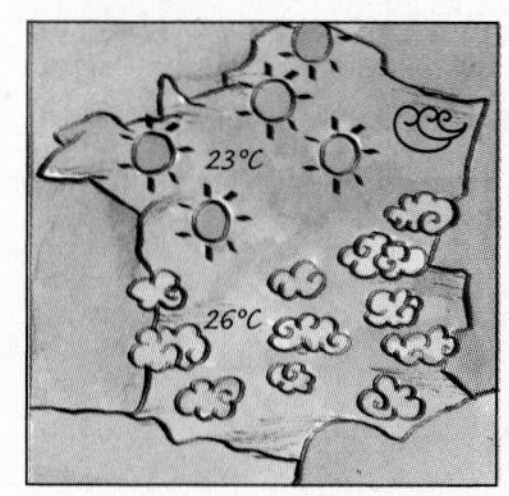

samedi

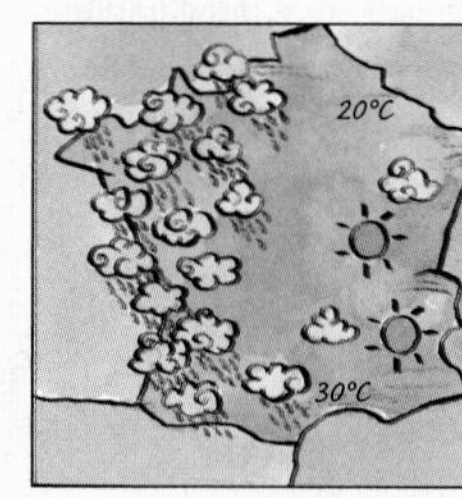

dimanche

6 La vie de Gaëlle et de Marc Votre professeur va vous donner, à vous et à votre partenaire, deux feuilles d'activités différentes sur l'avenir de Gaëlle et de Marc. Attention! Ne regardez pas la feuille de votre partenaire. Answers will vary.

MODÈLE

Étudiant(e) 1: *Marc et Gaëlle finiront leurs études au lycée.*
Étudiant(e) 2: *Ensuite, ...*

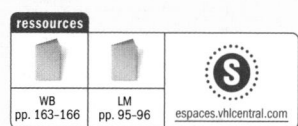

ressources
WB pp. 163-166 | LM pp. 95-96 | espaces.vhlcentral.com

OPTIONS

Extra Practice Read answers and have students produce questions that could have prompted the responses. The answers should contain verbs in the future tense. Challenge the class to come up with as many different questions as possible. Example: **J'habiterai une maison au bord de la mer. (Qu'est-ce que vous ferez après la retraite?)**

Game Make two oversized dice out of paper. Stick labels with subject pronouns on all the facets of one die. Then label the facets of the other die with infinitives of verbs with irregular future stems. Have students take turns rolling the dice so that they know which future-tense verb form to produce for their classmates. Example: **nous + avoir (nous aurons)**

À l'écoute

NATIONAL communication STANDARDS

Audio: Activities

STRATÉGIE

Using background information

Once you discern the topic of a conversation, take a minute to think about what you already know about the subject. Using this background information will help you guess the meaning of unknown words or linguistic structures.

To help you practice this strategy, you will listen to a short paragraph. Jot down the subject of the paragraph, and then use your knowledge of the subject to listen for and write down the paragraph's main points.

Préparation

Regardez la photo. Combien de personnes y a-t-il? Où sont-elles? Que font-elles? D'après vous, de quoi parlent-elles?

À vous d'écouter

Écoutez la conversation entre Amélie et Christophe. Puis, écoutez une deuxième fois et notez les quatre choses qu'ils vont faire ce matin. Comparez vos notes avec celles d'un(e) camarade.

ouvrir un compte en banque

acheter des livres à la librairie

aller à la mairie

aller à la laverie

Practice more at **espaces.vhlcentral.com.**

Compréhension

Vrai ou faux? Indiquez si les phrases sont **vraies** ou **fausses**. Corrigez les phrases fausses.

1. Amélie habite cette ville depuis toujours. Faux. Elle habite cette ville depuis un mois.
2. Amélie ne connaît pas bien la ville. Vrai.
3. Christophe recommande la Banque de l'Ouest parce qu'il aime beaucoup son architecture. Faux. Il la recommande parce qu'elle est tout près et parce qu'il y a un distributeur automatique ouvert 24 heures sur 24.
4. La Banque de l'Ouest est en face d'une bijouterie. Faux. Elle est en face d'une pharmacie.
5. Amélie a besoin d'emprunter de l'argent à la banque. Faux. Elle veut ouvrir un compte en banque.
6. Amélie veut aller à la bibliothèque pour chercher des livres. Faux. Elle veut aller à une librairie pour acheter des livres.
7. La librairie Molière est près d'un jardin public. Vrai.
8. Christophe demande à Amélie si elle peut aller chercher un colis à la poste. Faux. Il lui demande de déposer un formulaire à la mairie.
9. Pour aller à la mairie, on doit traverser un pont. Vrai.
10. Ce matin, Christophe doit aller à la papeterie. Faux. Il doit aller à la laverie.

Dans votre ville Amélie passe un semestre à votre université. Elle vous pose les mêmes questions qu'elle a posées à Christophe. Écrivez-lui un petit mot pour lui expliquer comment aller, d'abord, de l'université à une banque qui se trouve dans le quartier universitaire. Puis, expliquez-lui comment aller de cette banque à un supermarché où les étudiants de votre université font souvent leurs courses. Demandez aussi à Amélie si elle peut faire une petite course pour vous et expliquez-lui où se trouve l'endroit où elle devra aller.

Section Goals

In this section, students will:

- learn to use background information
- listen for the subject and main points in a paragraph
- listen to a conversation and complete several activities

Instructional Resources
espaces.vhlcentral.com: Textbook MP3s; IRM (Textbook Audioscript); downloads; reference tools

Stratégie
Script La nuit dernière, il y a eu un cambriolage à la Banque Monet. Le directeur, Monsieur Dumais, a appelé le commissariat de police aussitôt qu'il est arrivé à la banque, vers huit heures trente ce matin. Pour l'instant, on ne sait pas encore combien d'argent a été volé.

Préparation Tell students to describe the photo. Then have them guess what the people are talking about.

À vous d'écouter
Script AMÉLIE: Dis, Christophe, j'habite ici depuis un mois et je n'ai pas encore ouvert de compte en banque. Quelle banque est-ce que tu me recommandes?
CHRISTOPHE: La Banque de l'Ouest. Elle est tout près d'ici et il y a un distributeur automatique ouvert 24 heures sur 24. Tu sais où elle se trouve?
A: Non. Elle est où?
C: Dans la rue Flaubert. Pour y aller, tu prends le boulevard Jean Jaurès et au carrefour, tu tournes à droite. La banque est à l'angle de la rue Victor Hugo, en face de la pharmacie.
A: D'accord. Et je dois aussi acheter des livres pour la fac. Tu connais une bonne librairie?
C: Oui, la meilleure, c'est la librairie Molière, dans l'avenue de la République. Alors, pour y aller de la banque, tu prends la rue du Ménil et au bout de la rue, tu traverses la place d'Armes. Ensuite, tu descends l'avenue Girard et tu tournes à droite dans l'avenue de la République. Là-bas, tu trouveras la librairie, près du jardin public. Dis, est-ce que tu voudras bien faire une petite course pour moi?
A: Oui, bien sûr.
C: C'est dans le quartier. J'ai besoin de déposer ce formulaire à la mairie.
A: OK. Elle est où, la mairie?
C: Alors, la mairie est sur la place Bellevue. De la librairie, tu continues tout droit dans l'avenue de la République. Ensuite, tu prends à gauche sur le boulevard Henri IV. Tu prends le pont Alexandre Dumas et la mairie sera juste là, de l'autre côté du pont, sur la place Bellevue.
A: Bon, d'accord, pas de problème. Et toi, qu'est-ce que tu vas faire ce matin?
C: Je vais aller à la laverie. J'ai plein de lessive à faire.
A: Eh bien bon courage, alors! À tout à l'heure.
C: Salut!

Section Goals

In this section, students will read historical and cultural information about Quebec.

Instructional Resources
espaces.vhlcentral.com: Transparency #53; WB/VM/LM Answer Key; activities; downloads; reference tools

Carte du Québec

- Have students look at the map or use **Transparency #53**. Ask volunteers to read the names of cities and other geographical features aloud. Model pronunciation as necessary.
- Point out the St. Lawrence River and have students locate the three major cities on its banks.

La province en chiffres

- Point out the flag of Québec province.
- Have volunteers read the sections aloud. After each section, ask students questions about the content.
- Explain that the people of France began using Bourgeois French instead of the King's French after the French Revolution. From then on, the language evolved differently in France and in Québec.

Incroyable mais vrai! Ice bricks are used to build the snow palace. The palace has electrical installations for lighting displays and special effects for the festival.

NATIONAL STANDARDS connections cultures

Interactive Map Reading

Panorama

un traîneau à chiens°

Le Québec

La province en chiffres

- **Superficie:** *1.667.441 km²*
- **Population:** *7.550.000*
  SOURCE: Statistique Canada
- **Industries principales:** *agriculture, exploitation forestière°, hydroélectricité, industrie du bois (papier), minerai° (fer°, cuivre°, or°)*
- **Villes principales:** *Montréal, Québec, Trois-Rivières*
- **Langues:** *anglais, français*

Le français parlé par les Québécois a une histoire très intéressante. La population française qui s'installe° au Québec en 1608 est composée en majorité de Français du nord-ouest de la France. Ils parlent tous leur langue régionale, comme le normand ou le breton. Beaucoup d'entre eux parlent aussi le français de la cour du roi°, langue qui devient la langue commune de tous les Québécois. Assez isolés du reste du monde francophone et ardents défenseurs de leur langue, les Québécois continuent à parler un français considéré plus pur même° que celui° des Français.

- **Monnaie:** *le dollar canadien*

la ville de Trois-Rivières

le Stade olympique, Montréal

Québécois célèbres

- **Antonine Maillet,** *écrivain (1929–)*
- **Jean Chrétien,** *ancien premier ministre du Canada (1934–)*
- **Robert Charlebois,** *chanteur (1944–)*

- **Carole Laure,** *actrice (1948–)*
- **Julie Payette,** *astronaute (1963–)*
- **Mario Lemieux,** *joueur de hockey sur glace (1965–)*

exploitation forestière *forestry* **minerai** *ore* **fer** *iron* **cuivre** *copper* **or** *gold* **s'installe** *settles* **cour du roi** *king's court* **même** *even* **celui** *that* **traîneau à chiens** *dogsled* **loger** *house* **Bonhomme** *Snowman (mascot of the carnival)* **haut** *high* **large** *wide*

Incroyable mais vrai!

Chaque année, pour le carnaval d'hiver de la ville de Québec, 15 personnes travaillent pendant deux mois à la construction d'un immense palais de glace pour loger° le Bonhomme° Carnaval. L'architecture et la taille du palais changent chaque année, mais il mesure parfois jusqu'à 50 mètres de long, 20 m de haut° et 20 m de large°.

OPTIONS

Québécois célèbres **Antonine Maillet** writes plays and novels based on Acadian life. She was awarded France's **Prix Goncourt**. **Jean Chrétien** served as prime minister of Canada from 1993–2003. **Robert Charlebois** is a singer, songwriter, actor, and musician. Internationally acclaimed for his music, Charlebois was one of three men to found the modern **chanson** in Québec. **Carole Laure** is a singer and actress. She performs concerts with her husband and has starred in over 40 films. **Julie Payette** is the chief astronaut for the Canadian Space Agency. She was the first **Québécoise** woman in space and the first Canadian to participate in an International Space Station assembly mission. **Mario Lemieux** has been awarded Most Valuable Player three times and led the Canadian hockey team to its gold medal victory in 2002.

La société

Un Québec indépendant

Pour des raisons politiques, économiques et culturelles, un grand nombre de Québécois, surtout les francophones, luttent°, depuis les années soixante, pour un Québec indépendant du Canada. Ils forment le mouvement souverainiste° et font des efforts pour conserver l'identité culturelle québécoise. Ces Canadiens francophones ont pris le nom de Québécois pour montrer leur «nationalisme». Les séparatistes ont perdu deux référendums en 1980 et en 1995, mais aujourd'hui, l'indépendance est une idée toujours d'actualité°.

Les destinations

Montréal

Montréal, deuxième ville francophone du monde après Paris, est située sur une île du fleuve° Saint-Laurent et présente une ambiance américano-européenne. Elle a été fondée° en 1642 et a, à la fois, l'énergie d'un centre urbain moderne et le charme d'une vieille ville de style européen. Ville cosmopolite et largement bilingue de 1,8 millions d'habitants, elle attire° beaucoup de touristes et accueille° de nombreux étudiants dans ses quatre universités. La majorité des Montréalais, 68%, est de langue maternelle française; 12% parlent l'anglais et 19% une autre langue. Pourtant°, 57% de la population montréalaise peuvent communiquer en français et en anglais.

La musique

Le festival de jazz de Montréal

Le festival international de jazz de Montréal est parmi° les plus prestigieux du monde. Avec 500 concerts, dont 350 donnés gratuitement en plein air°, le festival attire 3.000 artistes de plus de 30 pays, et près de 2,5 millions de spectateurs. Le centre-ville, fermé à la circulation, se transforme en un village musical. De grands noms internationaux comme Miles Davis, Ella Fitzgerald, Dizzy Gillespie ou Pat Metheny sont venus au festival, ainsi que° des jazzmen locaux.

L'histoire

La ville de Québec

Capitale de la province de Québec, la ville de Québec est la seule ville d'Amérique au nord du Mexique qui a conservé ses fortifications. Fondée par l'explorateur français Samuel de Champlain en 1608, Québec est située sur un rocher°, au bord du fleuve Saint-Laurent. Elle est connue en particulier pour sa vieille ville, son carnaval d'hiver et le château Frontenac. Les plaines d'Abraham, où les Britanniques ont vaincu° les Français en 1759 pour prendre le contrôle du Canada, servent aujourd'hui de vaste parc public. De nombreux étudiants de l'Université Laval profitent° du charme de cette ville francophone.

Qu'est-ce que vous avez appris? Répondez aux questions par des phrases complètes.

1. Quelle était la deuxième langue de beaucoup de Français quand ils sont arrivés au Québec?
   La deuxième langue de beaucoup de Français était le français de la cour du roi.
2. Quel est le nom d'un chanteur québécois célèbre?
   Robert Charlebois est un chanteur québécois célèbre.
3. Combien de temps et combien de personnes sont nécessaires à la construction du palais de glace?
   Quinze personnes construisent le palais pendant deux mois.
4. Le palais est-il identique pour chaque carnaval?
   Non, son architecture change chaque année.
5. Que désire le mouvement souverainiste pour le Québec?
   Il désire un Québec indépendant.
6. Quelles sont les deux langues principales parlées à Montréal?
   Ce sont le français et l'anglais.
7. Pourquoi le centre-ville de Montréal est-il fermé pour le festival de jazz?
   Il est transformé en village musical où il y a de nombreux concerts de jazz en plein air.
8. Y a-t-il seulement de grandes stars du jazz au festival?
   Non, il y a aussi des musiciens locaux.
9. Où se situe la ville de Québec?
   Elle se situe sur un rocher, au bord du fleuve Saint-Laurent.
10. Qui a fondé la ville de Québec?
    Samuel de Champlain a fondé la ville de Québec.

Practice more at **espaces.vhlcentral.com.**

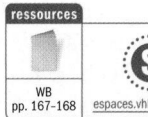

ressources: WB pp. 167–168 | espaces.vhlcentral.com

SUR INTERNET

Go to **espaces.vhlcentral.com** to find more cultural information related to this **PANORAMA**.

1. Quelles sont quelques-unes des expressions qui sont particulières au français des Québécois?
2. Quels sont les autres grands festivals du Québec? Quand ont-ils lieu?
3. Cherchez plus d'informations sur le carnaval d'hiver de Québec. Le palais de glace a-t-il toujours été fait de glace?

luttent *fight* **souverainiste** *in support of sovereignty for Quebec* **d'actualité** *current, relevant* **fleuve** *river* **fondée** *founded* **attire** *attracts* **accueille** *welcomes* **Pourtant** *However* **parmi** *among* **en plein air** *outside* **ainsi que** *as well as* **rocher** *rock* **ont vaincu** *defeated* **profitent** *take advantage of, benefit from*

Un Québec indépendant

- The Quebec flag and its saying **«Je me souviens»,** which appears on Quebec license plates, are symbols of Quebec's nationalism and reflect its French heritage.
- Ask students: **Quels sont les avantages et les inconvénients d'un Québec indépendant?**

Montréal Montreal's name is derived from the name of the mountain on which it is built, Mont-Royal. Due to the fur trade, Montreal grew rapidly in the eighteenth century. The majority of the population was French until around 1830. Between 1830 and 1865, the British became the majority as a result of immigration. Today, Montreal is one of Canada's chief ports.

Le festival de jazz de Montréal The festival has taken place for over 25 years. It is a non-profit event; any surplus funds are used to promote local and international jazz year round.

La ville de Québec

- The historic district of Old Quebec has been designated a World Heritage City by UNESCO. **Vieux Québec** is surrounded by 4.6 kilometers (3 miles) of ramparts. Inside the walls are museums, shops, restaurants, buildings, churches, monuments, museums, and **la Citadelle**.
- Ask students what they remember about **le château Frontenac** from **Leçon 8A**, page 261.

OPTIONS

Game Create categories for the information on Quebec, for example, **Québécois célèbres, La ville de Québec, Montréal,** and **Culture**. For each category, make index cards with a question on one side. Tape the cards to the board under the appropriate category. Divide the class into two teams, and have them take turns selecting a card and answering the question. Teams receive a point for each correct answer. The team with the most points at the end of the game wins.

Pairs Have students work in pairs. Tell them to make a list of reasons why a tourist should visit Quebec and Montreal. After students have completed their lists, call on volunteers to read one item from their list until all options are exhausted.

Section Goals

In this section, students will:
- learn to identify the narrator's point of view
- read a poem in French

Stratégie Tell students that recognizing the point of view from which something is written will help them comprehend it. Write the following two excerpts on the board and ask students to identify the points of view.

En sortant de l'école
Nous avons rencontré
Un grand chemin de fer
(first person)

Trois enfants marchant le long d'une grève (*seashore*). **[...] Ils ont sensiblement la même taille, et sans doute aussi le même âge: une douzaine d'années.** (omniscient narrator)

Examinez le texte Students should infer that the poem is about a city as seen from above and the feelings it conveys.

À propos de l'auteur Charles Baudelaire was interested in politics, taking part in the Revolutions of 1848 and later despising Napoleon III. But he didn't reveal it in his work, as in «Paysage» (**L'Émeute, tempêtant vainement à ma vitre, Ne fera pas lever mon front de mon pupitre**).

Lecture

NATIONAL STANDARDS communication cultures

S Audio: Dramatic Recording

Avant la lecture

STRATÉGIE

Identifying point of view

You can understand a text more completely if you identify the point of view of the narrator. You can do this by simply asking yourself from whose perspective the story is being told. Some stories are narrated in the first person. That is, the narrator is a character in the story, and everything you read is filtered through that person's thoughts, emotions, and opinions. Other texts have an omniscient narrator who is not a character in the story but who reports the thoughts and actions of the story's characters.

Examinez le texte

Regardez le titre du texte et l'image. De quoi va parler ce texte, à votre avis? Décrivez l'image.

À propos de l'auteur
Charles Baudelaire (1821–1867)

Charles Baudelaire est aujourd'hui considéré comme un des plus grands poètes français du dix-neuvième siècle. Né à Paris, où il passera la plus grande partie de sa vie, il connaît une enfance et une adolescence difficiles avec un beau-père, général dans l'armée, qu'il n'aime pas. Baudelaire devient poète, mais est peu apprécié de ses contemporains. En 1857, son recueil° de poèmes Les Fleurs du mal, dont Paysage est tiré, paraît. Cette œuvre°, qui reflète ses pensées° sur la société, est qualifiée de scandaleuse et il est condamné à payer une amende. Il part alors s'installer° pour quelques temps à Bruxelles, en Belgique, où il devient critique d'art et où il réussit enfin à publier° une partie de son recueil hors de° la juridiction française. Il meurt à Paris sans avoir exaucé° son rêve° de publier Les Fleurs du mal dans son intégralité°.

recueil *collection* **œuvre** *work* **pensées** *thoughts* **s'installer** *to settle* **publier** *publish* **hors de** *outside* **exaucé** *satisfied* **rêve** *dream* **intégralité** *entirety*

Paysage

Je veux, pour composer chastement mes églogues°,
Coucher auprès du ciel°, comme les astrologues,
Et, voisin des clochers°, écouter en rêvant°
Leurs hymnes solennels emportés° par le vent.
Les deux mains au menton°, du haut de ma mansarde°,
Je verrai l'atelier° qui chante et qui bavarde°;
Les tuyaux°, les clochers, ces mâts° de la cité,
Et les grands ciels qui font rêver d'éternité.

Il est doux, à travers les brumes°, de voir naître
L'étoile° dans l'azur°, la lampe à la fenêtre,
Les fleuves de charbon° monter au firmament
Et la lune° verser° son pâle° enchantement.

«Paysage» dans *Les Fleurs du mal*
de Charles Baudelaire

OPTIONS

Extra Practice Ask students these questions based on the author's biography. **1. Où est né Charles Baudelaire? (à Paris) 2. Où a-t-il vécu pendant quelques temps? (à Bruxelles, en Belgique) 3. En plus d'être poète, quelle autre profession avait-il? (Il était critique d'art.) 4. Quel est le nom de son recueil de poèmes? (*Les Fleurs du mal*)**

Pairs Remind students that they can appreciate the lyrical nature of poetry by reading a poem aloud. Have partners read **«Paysage»** to each other. Tell them to pay close attention to how the lines are punctuated and how the stanzas are arranged.

Charles Baudelaire

Je verrai les printemps, les étés, les automnes;
Et quand viendra l'hiver aux neiges monotones,
Je fermerai partout° portières et volets°
Pour bâtir° dans la nuit mes féeriques° palais.
Alors je rêverai des horizons bleuâtres,
Et tout ce que° l'Idylle° a de plus enfantin.
L'Émeute°, tempêtant vainement à ma vitre°,
Ne fera pas lever mon front de mon pupitre;
Car je serai plongé° dans cette volupté°
D'évoquer le Printemps avec ma volonté°,
De tirer un soleil de mon cœur, et de faire
De mes pensers brûlants une tiède° atmosphère.

églogues *eclogues (poem about shepherds)* **ciel** *sky* **clochers** *bell towers* **en rêvant** *while dreaming* **emportés** *carried away* **menton** *chin* **mansarde** *attic* **atelier** *workshop* **bavarde** *chats* **tuyaux** *pipes* **mâts** *masts* **brumes** *mists* **étoile** *star* **azur** *blue sky* **fleuves de charbon** *rivers of coal* **lune** *moon* **verser** *to pour* **partout** *everywhere* **volets** *shutters* **bâtir** *to build* **féeriques** *enchanted* **albâtres** *alabaster fountains* **baisers** *kisses* **ce que** *that* **Idylle** *Romance* **Émeute** *Riot* **vitre** *windowpane* **plongé** *immersed* **volupté** *voluptuousness* **volonté** *will* **tiède** *warm*

Après la lecture

Vrai ou faux? Indiquez si les phrases sont **vraies** ou **fausses**. Citez le texte pour justifier vos réponses.
Answers may vary slightly.

	Vrai	Faux
1. Le narrateur est un berger et vit à la campagne. «ces mâts de la cité»	☐	☑
2. Le narrateur aime être à sa fenêtre et regarder l'horizon en rêvant. «écouter en rêvant» «du haut de ma mansarde, Je verrai l'atelier» «Les tuyaux, les clochers, ces mâts de la cité, Et les grands ciels qui font rêver d'éternité.»	☑	☐
3. Il regarde les gens passer. «Je verrai l'atelier/Les tuyaux, les clochers»	☐	☑
4. Il aime être à sa fenêtre au milieu (*middle*) de la journée. «de voir naître/L'étoile dans l'azur, la lampe à la fenêtre»	☐	☑
5. Il est à sa fenêtre à toutes les saisons de l'année. «Et quand viendra l'hiver aux neiges monotones/ Je fermerai partout portières et volets»	☐	☑
6. En hiver, il s'arrête de rêver. «Alors je rêverai des horizons bleuâtres»	☐	☑
7. Il aime la nature. «des jardins, des jets d'eau..., des oiseaux»	☑	☐
8. Il aime les choses simples. «Et tout ce que l'Idylle a de plus enfantin.»	☑	☐
9. Rien ne peut le perturber (*disturb*) pendant qu'il écrit ses poèmes. «Ne fera pas lever mon front de mon pupitre»	☑	☐
10. Il est heureux quand il pense au printemps. «D'évoquer le Printemps» «De tirer un soleil de mon cœur, et de faire/De mes pensers brûlants une tiède atmosphère.»	☑	☐

Le narrateur Regardez rapidement tout le texte et notez les pronoms sujets utilisés dans ce poème. D'après vous, qui est le narrateur? Qui voudrait-il être? Expliquez votre réponse.

Réflexions Et vous, si (*if*) vous deviez écrire un poème sur la vie à la campagne tout en habitant (*living*) en ville, ou vice versa, comment feriez-vous pour trouver l'inspiration? Comme l'auteur du haut de sa fenêtre? Expliqez votre réponse.

Vrai ou faux? Have volunteers write the answers and text quotes on the board. Then go over them with the class.

Le narrateur Take a class survey to find out how many students think it is the poet himself. Have students justify their answers.

Réflexions Have students discuss this question in small groups.

OPTIONS

Small Groups Have groups of three or four students discuss the following questions regarding images in the poem. **1. À quoi «les fleurs de charbon» font-elles allusion (ligne 11)? 2. Que sont «mes féeriques palais» (ligne 16)?**

Extra Practice Have students try to find inspiration the way the author did. Have them choose a place, a city, or a country they never went to, and ask them to brainstorm ideas about it. Then ask them if they find it to be the best way to get inspiration about something they don't know.

Section Goals

In this section, students will:
- learn to use linking words
- write a description of a new business idea

Stratégie Review the list of linking words with the class and have volunteers create sentences with the words.

Thème Tell students to answer the questions first. Remind them to use linking words so that their descriptions won't sound like the first paragraph in the **Stratégie**.

Proofreading Activity Have the class correct these sentences.
1. Je vens de m'apercevoir que je n'ai pas liquide. 2. Il y est toujours le distributeur automatic. 3. Vous tournerez à gauche et suivez le cours jusque à la rotonde. 4. Derriere la fontaine, vous trouverez la bureau poste.

Écriture

NATIONAL STANDARDS communication cultures

STRATÉGIE

Using linking words

You can make your writing more sophisticated by using linking words to connect simple sentences or ideas in order to create more complex sentences. Consider these passages that illustrate this effect:

Without linking words

Aujourd'hui, j'ai fait beaucoup de courses. Je suis allé à la poste. J'ai fait la queue pendant une demi-heure. J'ai acheté des timbres. J'ai aussi posté un colis. Je suis allé à la banque. La banque est rue Girardeau. J'ai perdu ma carte de crédit hier. Je devais aussi retirer de l'argent. Je suis allé à la brasserie pour déjeuner avec un ami. Cet ami s'appelle Marc. Je suis rentré à la maison. Ma mère rentrait du travail.

With linking words

Aujourd'hui, j'ai fait beaucoup de courses. D'abord, je suis allé à la poste où j'ai fait la queue pendant une demi-heure. J'ai acheté des timbres et j'ai aussi posté un colis. Après, je suis allé à la banque qui est rue Girardeau, parce que j'ai perdu ma carte de crédit hier et parce que je devais aussi retirer de l'argent. Ensuite, je suis allé à la brasserie pour déjeuner avec un ami qui s'appelle Marc. Finalement, je suis rentré à la maison alors que ma mère rentrait du travail.

Linking words

alors	*then*	**mais**	*but*
alors que	*as*	**ou**	*or*
après	*then, after that*	**où**	*where*
d'abord	*first*	**parce que**	*because*
donc	*so*	**pendant (que)**	*while*
dont	*of which*	**(et) puis**	*(and) then*
enfin	*finally*	**puisque**	*since*
ensuite	*then, after that*	**quand**	*when*
et	*and*	**que**	*that, which*
finalement	*finally*	**qui**	*who, that*

Thème

Faire la description d'un nouveau commerce

Avant l'écriture

1. Avec des amis, vous allez ouvrir un commerce (*business*) dans le quartier de votre université. Vous voulez créer quelque chose d'original qui n'existe pas encore et qui sera très utile aux étudiants: un endroit où ils pourront faire plusieurs choses en même temps (par exemple, une laverie/salon de coiffure).
2. Lisez ces questions et utilisez votre imagination comme point de départ de votre description.
   - Quel sera le nom du commerce?
   - Quel type de commerce voulez-vous ouvrir?
   - Quels seront les produits (*products*) que vous vendrez? Quels seront les prix? Donnez quelques détails sur l'activité commerciale.
   - Où se trouvera le commerce?
   - Comment sera l'intérieur du commerce (style, décoration, etc.)?
   - Quels seront ses jours et heures d'ouverture (*business hours*)?
   - En quoi consistera l'originalité de votre commerce? Expliquez pourquoi votre commerce sera unique et donnez les raisons pour lesquelles (*which*) des étudiants fréquenteront votre commerce.

OPTIONS

Stratégie Review the linking words with students. Point out that they have seen some of these words in the **Écriture** section of previous units, in particular Unit 8, which involved narration in the past, and Unit 10, which focused on sequencing events. If needed, refer them back to the explanation and practice in these units.

Have students analyze the two sample paragraphs and comment on the writing style used in each. Which sounds less sophisticated? Which sounds more sophisticated? How does the use of linking words affect style? Tell students that as they begin to master accuracy in their writing, they need to develop their writing style, which is an important part of the writing process because of the subtle messages it conveys.

3. Avant d'écrire votre description détaillée, complétez ce tableau par des phrases complètes, à l'aide (*with the help*) des questions que vous venez de lire. Vous devez inventer les détails (le nom du commerce, les produits, les prix...).

Le commerce	**1. le nom:** **2. le type:**
Les produits	**1. le type:** **2. le prix:** **3. détails:**
L'endroit	**1. l'adresse:** **2. près de (monument, grand magasin, ...):**
L'intérieur	**1. le style:** **2. la décoration:** **3. autre information:**
Les jours et heures d'ouverture	**1. les horaires:** **2. les jours d'ouverture:**
L'originalité	**1. le style:** **2. détails:**
...?	

4. Après avoir complété le tableau, regardez les phrases que vous avez écrites. Est-il possible de les combiner avec des mots de liaison (*linking words*) de la liste de **Stratégie**? Regardez cet exemple:

   Le commerce est une laverie, mais aussi un salon de coiffure, parce que nous savons que les étudiants aiment pouvoir faire plusieurs choses en même temps.

5. Réécrivez les phrases que vous pouvez combiner.

Écriture

1. Utilisez les phrases du tableau et celles (*the ones*) que vous venez de combiner pour écrire la description de votre commerce.
2. Pendant que vous écrivez, trouvez d'autres phrases à combiner avec des mots de liaison.
3. Utilisez le vocabulaire de l'unité.
4. Utilisez les verbes voir, recevoir, apercevoir et croire, des expressions négatives et le futur simple.

Après l'écriture

1. Échangez votre description avec celle (*the one*) d'un(e) partenaire. Répondez à ces questions pour commenter son travail.
   - Votre partenaire a-t-il/elle inclu toutes les informations du tableau?
   - A-t-il/elle utilisé des mots de liaison pour combiner les phrases?
   - A-t-il/elle utilisé le vocabulaire de l'unité?
   - A-t-il/elle utilisé les verbes voir, recevoir, apercevoir et croire, des expressions négatives et le futur simple?
   - A-t-il/elle utilisé le conditionnel?
   - Quel(s) détail(s) ajouteriez-vous (*would you add*)? Quel(s) détail(s) enlèveriez-vous (*would you delete*)? Quel(s) autre(s) commentaire(s) avez-vous pour votre partenaire?

2. Corrigez votre description d'après (*according to*) les commentaires de votre partenaire. Relisez votre travail pour éliminer ces problèmes:
   - des fautes (*errors*) d'orthographe
   - des fautes de ponctuation
   - des fautes de conjugaison
   - des fautes d'accord (*agreement*) des adjectifs
   - un mauvais emploi (*use*) de la grammaire

EVALUATION

Criteria

Content Contains answers to each question called out in the bulleted points of the task.
Scale: 1 2 3 4 5

Organization Organized into logical paragraphs that begin with a topic sentence and contain appropriate supporting details.
Scale: 1 2 3 4 5

Accuracy Uses the simple future tense and linking words correctly. Spells words, conjugates verbs, and modifies adjectives correctly throughout.
Scale: 1 2 3 4 5

Creativity Includes additional information that is not included in the task and/or uses adjectives, descriptive verbs, and additional details to make the composition more interesting.
Scale: 1 2 3 4 5

Scoring

Excellent	18–20 points
Good	14–17 points
Satisfactory	10–13 points
Unsatisfactory	< 10 points

OPTIONS

Stratégie Have students practice the linking words by writing a sentence on the board. Ask students to think of a linking word and a second sentence that could be joined to the first. Once you have tried this several times as a class, put students in pairs and have each write single sentences individually and then try to combine them using different linking words.

Point out to students that although the strategy they are practicing is the use of linking words, the writing task itself calls for use of the simple future tense. Have them look carefully at the words used in the questions and review the future tense forms of those verbs in particular before they begin writing.

Flashcards
Audio: Vocabulary

VOCABULAIRE

Instructional Resources
espaces.vhlcentral.com: Textbook MP3s; IRM (Textbook Audioscript); downloads; reference tools

Suggestion Tell students that an easy way to study from **Vocabulaire** is to cover up the French half of each section, leaving only the English equivalents exposed. They can then quiz themselves on the French items. To focus on the English equivalents of the French entries, they simply reverse this process.

Retrouver son chemin

continuer	*to continue*
se déplacer	*to move (change location)*
descendre	*to go/come down*
être perdu(e)	*to be lost*
monter	*to go up/come up*
s'orienter	*to get one's bearings*
suivre	*to follow*
tourner	*to turn*
traverser	*to cross*
un angle	*corner*
une avenue	*avenue*
un banc	*bench*
un bâtiment	*building*
un boulevard	*boulevard*
une cabine téléphonique	*phone booth*
un carrefour	*intersection*
un chemin	*way; path*
un coin	*corner*
des indications (*f.*)	*directions*
un feu de signalisation (feux *pl.*)	*traffic light(s)*
une fontaine	*fountain*
un office du tourisme	*tourist office*
un pont	*bridge*
une rue	*street*
une statue	*statue*
est	*east*
nord	*north*
ouest	*west*
sud	*south*

Pour donner des indications

au bout (de)	*at the end (of)*
au coin (de)	*at the corner (of)*
autour (de)	*around*
jusqu'à	*until*
(tout) près (de)	*(very) close (to)*
tout droit	*straight ahead*

À la poste

poster une lettre	*to mail a letter*
une adresse	*address*
une boîte aux lettres	*mailbox*
une carte postale	*postcard*
un colis	*package*
le courrier	*mail*
une enveloppe	*envelope*
un facteur	*mailman*
un timbre	*stamp*

À la banque

avoir un compte bancaire	*to have a bank account*
déposer de l'argent	*to deposit money*
emprunter	*to borrow*
payer par carte (de crédit)	*to pay by credit card*
payer en liquide	*to pay in cash*
payer par chèque	*to pay by check*
retirer de l'argent	*to withdraw money*
les billets (*m.*)	*bills, notes*
un compte-chèques	*checking account*
un compte d'épargne	*savings account*
une dépense	*expenditure, expense*
un distributeur (automatique/ de billets)	*ATM*
les pièces de monnaie (*f.*)	*coins*
de la monnaie	*change*

En ville

accompagner	*to accompany*
faire la queue	*to wait in line*
remplir un formulaire	*to fill out a form*
signer	*to sign*
une banque	*bank*
une bijouterie	*jewelry store*
une boutique	*boutique, store*
une brasserie	*café, restaurant*
un bureau de poste	*post office*
un cybercafé	*cybercafé*
une laverie	*laundromat*
un marchand de journaux	*newsstand*
une papeterie	*stationery store*
un salon de beauté	*beauty salon*
un commissariat de police	*police station*
une mairie	*town/city hall; mayor's office*
fermé(e)	*closed*
ouvert(e)	*open*

La négation

jamais	*never; ever*
ne... aucun(e)	*none (not any)*
ne... jamais	*never (not ever)*
ne... ni... ni	*neither... nor*
ne... personne	*nobody, no one*
ne... plus	*no more (not anymore)*
ne... que	*only*
ne... rien	*nothing (not anything)*
pas (de)	*no, none*
personne	*no one*
quelque chose	*something*
quelqu'un	*someone*
rien	*nothing*
toujours	*always; still*

Verbes

apercevoir	*to catch sight of, to see*
s'apercevoir	*to notice; to realize*
croire	*to believe*
recevoir	*to receive*
voir	*to see*

Expressions utiles	*See pp. 403 and 417.*
Le futur simple	*See p. 420.*

ressources
espaces.vhlcentral.com

L'avenir et les métiers

UNITÉ 13

Leçon 13A

ESPACE **CONTEXTES**
pages 434–437
- At the office
- Making phone calls
- **La ponctuation française**

ESPACE **ROMAN-PHOTO**
pages 438–439
- **Le bac**

ESPACE **CULTURE**
pages 440–441
- Telephones in France

ESPACE **STRUCTURES**
pages 442–445
- **Le futur simple** with **quand** and **dès que**
- The interrogative pronoun **lequel**

ESPACE **SYNTHÈSE**
pages 446–449
- **Révision**
- **Le zapping**

Leçon 13B

ESPACE **CONTEXTES**
pages 450–453
- Professions
- **Les néologismes et le franglais**

ESPACE **ROMAN-PHOTO**
pages 454–455
- **Je démissionne!**

ESPACE **CULTURE**
pages 456–457
- Unions and strikes
- **Flash culture**

ESPACE **STRUCTURES**
pages 458–461
- **Si** clauses
- Relative pronouns **qui**, **que**, **dont**, **où**

ESPACE **SYNTHÈSE**
pages 462–463
- **Révision**
- **À l'écoute**

Pour commencer
- Quel genre de travail Amina fera-t-elle?
- Est-ce qu'elle travaillera dans un bureau?
- Est-ce qu'elle aimera son travail?
- Que porte-t-elle aujourd'hui?

Savoir-faire
pages 464–469

Panorama: L'Afrique du Nord
Lecture: Read a fable.
Écriture: Write a plan for your professional goals.

Unit Goals

Leçon 13A
In this lesson, students will learn:
- terms for the workplace
- terms for job interviews
- terms for making and receiving phone calls
- rules of punctuation in French
- about telephones, text messages, and **les artisans**
- the future tense with **quand** and **dès que**
- interrogative pronouns **lequel**, **laquelle**, **lesquels**, and **lesquelles**
- about the short film ***Mi-Temps***

Leçon 13B
In this lesson, students will learn:
- terms for professions
- more terms for discussing one's work
- about neologisms and **franglais**
- about labor unions, strikes, and civil servants
- more about professions and work through specially shot video footage
- **si** clauses
- the relative pronouns **qui**, **que**, **dont**, and **où**
- to use background knowledge and listen for specific information

Savoir-faire
In this section, students will learn:
- cultural, geographical, and historical information about Algeria, Morocco, and Tunisia
- to summarize a text in their own words
- to use note cards to organize their writing

Pour commencer
- **Elle fera du stylisme de mode.**
- Answers will vary.
- **Oui, elle l'aimera beaucoup.**
- **Elle porte une robe rose.**

RESOURCES

Workbook/Video Manual: WB Activities, pp. 169–182
Laboratory Manual: Lab Activities, pp. 97–104
Workbook/Video Manual: Video Activities, pp. 259–262; pp. 295–296
WB/VM/LM Answer Key

espaces.vhlcentral.com: Textbook MP3s; Lab MP3s; Instructor's Resource Manual [IRM] (Textbook Audioscript; Lab Audioscript; Videoscript; **Roman-photo** Translations; **Vocabulaire supplémentaire**; **Feuilles d'activités**; Info Gap Activities; **Le zapping** Short Film transcription; **Essayez!** and **Mise en pratique** answers);

Transparencies #54, #55, #56; Testing Program, pp. 97–104; Test Files; Testing Program MP3s; Test Generator
Video on DVD

Section Goals

In this section, students will learn and practice vocabulary related to:
- the workplace
- job interviews
- phone calls

Instructional Resources
*espaces.vhlcentral.com: Transparency #54; IRM (**Vocabulaire supplémentaire**; **Mise en pratique** answers; Textbook Audioscript; Lab Audioscript); Textbook MP3s; Lab MP3s; WB/VM/LM Answer Key; activities; downloads; reference tools*

Suggestions
- Tell students to look over the new vocabulary and identify the cognates.
- Use **Transparency #54**. Point out objects and describe what the people are doing. Examples: **Il patiente. C'est une employée. Il passe un entretien.**
- Point out that **un salaire modeste** is a figurative rather than literal equivalent of *low salary*. One might also say **un bas salaire**.
- Point out the difference between **un poste** (*a job*) and **la poste** (*the post office*).
- Explain that **une lettre de motivation** is a letter a job candidate writes in response to a want ad or when introducing him or herself to a prospective employer.
- Point out the **Attention!** Explain that **chercher** is a general term, while **rechercher** refers to more thorough, methodical research.
- Tell students that **les petites annonces** are short, telegraphic-style ads, usually for low-level or temporary jobs rather than career positions.
- Additional vocabulary for this lesson can be found in the **Vocabulaire supplémentaire** on the Supersite.

Leçon 13A

Talking Picture
Audio: Activity

You will learn how to...
- make and receive phone calls
- talk about your goals

Au bureau

Vocabulaire

chercher un/du travail	*to look for work*
embaucher	*to hire*
faire des projets	*to make plans*
obtenir	*to get, to obtain*
postuler	*to apply*
prendre (un) rendez-vous	*to make an appointment*
trouver un/du travail	*to find a job*
un(e) candidat(e)	*candidate, applicant*
un conseil	*advice*
un domaine	*field*
une entreprise	*firm, business*
une expérience professionnelle	*professional experience*
une formation	*education; training*
une lettre de recommandation	*letter of reference/ recommendation*
une lettre de motivation	*letter of application*
une mention	*distinction*
un métier	*profession*
un poste	*position*
une référence	*reference*
un salaire (élevé, modeste)	*(high, low) salary*
un(e) spécialiste	*specialist*
un stage	*internship; professional training*
appeler	*to call*
laisser un message	*to leave a message*
l'appareil (*m.*)	*telephone*
une télécarte	*phone card*
Qui est à l'appareil?	*Who's calling please?*
C'est de la part de qui?	*On behalf of whom?*
C'est M./Mme/Mlle... (à l'appareil.)	*It's Mr./Mrs./Miss... (on the phone.)*
Ne quittez pas.	*Please hold.*

ressources
WB pp. 169–170
LM p. 97
espaces.vhlcentral.com

OPTIONS

Extra Practice For additional practice, ask students these questions. **1. Quel est votre numéro de téléphone? 2. Quels projets avez-vous faits pour votre carrière? 3. Préférez-vous travailler dans une grande entreprise ou dans une petite compagnie? Pourquoi? 4. Est-il plus important d'avoir un salaire élevé ou un métier qu'on aime bien? 5. Avez-vous déjà écrit une lettre de motivation?**

Game Divide the class into two teams. Have a spelling bee using vocabulary words from **Espace contextes**. Pronounce each word, use it in a sentence, and then say the word again. Tell students that they must spell the words in French and include all diacritical marks.

Attention!

Note the difference in the usage and meaning of **chercher** and **rechercher**.

Il cherche du travail.
He is looking for work.

Cette compagnie recherche un chef du personnel.
This company is looking for a human resources director.

Mise en pratique

1 Complétez

Complétez ces phrases avec le verbe de la liste qui convient le mieux. N'oubliez pas de faire les accords nécessaires.

appeler	lire les annonces	postuler
décrocher	métier	prendre (un) rendez-vous
conseil	obtenir	raccrocher
embaucher	passer un entretien	salaire
laisser des messages	patienter	trouver un/du travail

1. Quand on cherche du travail, il faut ___lire les annonces___ tous les jours.
2. Il est toujours plus facile de trouver un ___métier___ intéressant quand on a une bonne formation.
3. Le téléphone sonne. Est-ce que tu peux ___décrocher___, s'il te plaît?
4. Il y a peu d'entreprises qui ___embauchent___ en ce moment. L'économie ne va pas très bien.
5. —Bonjour, Madame. Je vous ___appelle___ pour ___prendre (un) rendez-vous___.
   —Vous pouvez venir lundi 15, à 16h00?
6. J'ai envoyé mon CV. J'espère qu'ils vont m'appeler pour ___passer un entretien___.
7. ___Patientez___ quelques minutes, s'il vous plaît. Madame Benoît va bientôt arriver.
8. Il ___a raccroché___ parce que la ligne n'était pas bonne.
9. Sophie vient juste de ___trouver un travail___. Elle va organiser une petite fête vendredi pour célébrer son nouveau poste.
10. Une messagerie permet de ___laisser des messages___.

2 Corrigez

Lisez ces phrases et dites si elles sont vraies ou fausses. Corrigez les phrases qui ne sont pas cohérentes.

1. Il faut décrocher le combiné avant de composer un numéro de téléphone.
   Vrai.
2. Quand on appelle d'une cabine téléphonique, on utilise des billets.
   Faux. Quand on appelle d'une cabine téléphonique, on utilise une télécarte.
3. Quand on est embauché, on perd son travail.
   Faux. Quand on est embauché, on trouve un travail.
4. Quand on travaille, on reçoit un salaire à la fin de chaque mois.
   Vrai.
5. À la fin d'un CV américain, il ne faut pas oublier de mentionner ses références.
   Vrai.
6. Pour savoir qui vous appelle au téléphone, vous demandez: «Ne quittez pas.»
   Faux. Vous demandez:«Qui est à l'appareil?»
7. Un(e) patron(ne) dirige (*manages*) une entreprise ou des employés.
   Vrai.
8. Avant d'obtenir un poste, il faut souvent passer une entreprise.
   Faux. Il faut souvent passer un entretien.
9. Quand on travaille dans une entreprise, on est un(e) employé(e).
   Vrai.

3 Écoutez

Armand et Michel cherchent du travail. Écoutez leur conversation et répondez ensuite aux questions.

1. Quel genre de travail Armand recherche-t-il?
   Armand recherche un travail d'assistant.
2. Où est-ce qu'Armand a lu l'annonce?
   Armand a lu l'annonce dans le journal ce matin.
3. Quel(s) document(s) faut-il envoyer pour le stage?
   Il faut envoyer un CV accompagné d'une lettre de motivation.
4. Qui est M. Dupont?
   M. Dupont est le chef du personnel.
5. Que doit faire Armand pour obtenir un entretien?
   Armand doit appeler M. Dupont pour prendre (un) rendez-vous.
6. Quel est le domaine professionnel de Michel?
   Son domaine professionnel est l'informatique.
7. Pourquoi Michel a-t-il des difficultés à trouver du travail?
   Michel a des difficultés à trouver du travail parce qu'il ne sait pas où postuler ni comment obtenir un entretien.
8. Comment est-ce qu'Armand aide Michel?
   Armand trouve deux entreprises qui recherchent des spécialistes dans le domaine de Michel.

Practice more at **espaces.vhlcentral.com.**

1 Expansion Have students write sentences with the unused words from the list: **conseil, obtenir, postuler,** and **salaire.**

2 Suggestion Have students check their answers with a classmate.

3 Tapescript MICHEL: Alors Armand, est-ce que tu as trouvé un travail pour l'été?
ARMAND: Chut, je suis au téléphone!
M: Oh, je suis désolé.
A: Allô. Oui, bonjour, Madame. C'est Armand Lemaire à l'appareil. Je vous appelle au sujet de l'annonce que j'ai lue dans le journal ce matin.
LA SECRÉTAIRE: Oui, très bien. Pour le stage, il faut envoyer votre CV accompagné d'une lettre de motivation.
A: En fait, je n'appelle pas pour le stage, mais pour le poste d'assistant.
S: Oh, excusez-moi. Dans ce cas, il vous faut appeler Monsieur Dupont, notre chef du personnel, pour prendre un rendez-vous et obtenir un entretien. Ne quittez pas. Je vous le passe. (*Musique*) Je suis désolée, mais ça ne répond pas. Je vous passe sa messagerie. Vous pouvez laisser un message avec votre numéro de téléphone.
A: Je vous remercie, Madame.
Plus tard…
M: Voilà, tu n'as plus besoin de chercher du travail! Je suis sûr qu'ils vont t'embaucher!
A: Je préfère attendre. Et toi, comment ça va, ta recherche de travail?
M: Je ne sais pas vraiment où postuler et je ne sais pas comment obtenir un entretien.
A: Avec ta formation et ton expérience professionnelle, je pense que tu trouveras facilement un travail dans l'informatique. Tiens, regarde le journal, cette compagnie et cette autre entreprise-là recherchent des spécialistes dans ton domaine. En plus, je suis certain qu'elles offrent un bon salaire. Tiens, prends le combiné et appelle-les.
(On Textbook MP3s)

3 Suggestion Go over the answers with the class. If students have difficulty, play the conversation again.

OPTIONS

Pairs Write these expressions for circumlocution on the board: **C'est quand on…, C'est ce qu'on fait quand…, C'est un objet/une machine qu'on utilise pour…, C'est quelqu'un qui…** Then have pairs of students write definitions for the following vocabulary words. **1. chercher du travail 2. postuler 3. un appareil 4. un patron 5. raccrocher 6. un entretien 7. une télécarte 8. un spécialiste**

Have pairs get together with another pair of students and take turns reading their definitions and guessing the words. Ask each group to choose its best definition and write it on the board for the whole class to guess.

4 Suggestions
- Tell students to jot down notes during the interviews.
- After completing the interviews, have pairs get together with another pair and report what they learned about their partner.

5 Suggestion If time is limited, have students role-play the conversations in groups of six. Each pair will act out one of the conversations instead of all three.

6 Suggestions
- Before beginning the activity, ask volunteers to read each ad aloud.
- Have the class brainstorm questions a manager might ask. Write the questions on the board.
- Model the activity by role-playing one of the situations with a student. Remind students to use appropriate greetings.

7 Suggestions
- Before beginning this activity, write a list of professional fields on the board. Examples: **les sciences, les affaires, l'éducation,** and **le commerce**.
- Have the class brainstorm questions an advisor might ask in this situation. Write the questions on the board.

Communication

4 Répondez Avec un(e) partenaire, posez-vous ces questions à tour de rôle. Answers will vary.

1. Est-ce que tu as fait des projets d'avenir? Quels sont-ils?
2. Après tes études, dans quel domaine est-ce que tu vas chercher du travail?
3. As-tu déjà fait un stage en entreprise? Comment était-ce?
4. As-tu une expérience professionnelle? Dans quel(s) domaine(s)?
5. As-tu déjà répondu à des annonces pour trouver du travail? Est-ce qu'on t'a embauché(e)?
6. À ton avis, qu'est-ce qui est le plus important pour réussir un entretien d'embauche?
7. Pour qui imagines-tu pouvoir écrire une bonne lettre de recommandation un jour?
8. As-tu déjà préparé ton curriculum vitæ? Quels types d'informations as-tu inclus?

5 Les conversations Avec un(e) partenaire, complétez et remettez dans l'ordre ces conversations. Ensuite, jouez les scènes devant la classe.

Conversation 1

3 —C'est Mlle Grandjean à l'appareil. Est-ce que vous pouvez me passer le chef du personnel, s'il vous plaît?
1 —Allô. Bonjour, Monsieur.
2 —Bonjour. Qui est à l'appareil?
4 Ne quittez pas. Je vous le passe.

Conversation 2

3 —Tu n'as donc pas vu le poste que la compagnie Petit et Fils offre.
1 —Est-ce que tu as lu les annonces ce matin?
4 —Non, mais je connais cette entreprise et elle n'est pas dans mon domaine.
2 —Non, je n'ai pas encore acheté le journal.

Conversation 3

2 —Non, appelle plutôt son portable.
4 —C'est le 06-22-28-80-83.
5 —Oh, encore sa messagerie! Elle ne décroche jamais.
3 —Tu as raison. Quel est son numéro de téléphone?
1 —Stéphanie ne décroche pas. Je vais lui laisser un message.

6 Les petites annonces Lisez ces annonces et choisissez-en une. Avec un(e) partenaire, imaginez votre conversation avec le directeur de l'entreprise que vous avez sélectionnée. Vous devez parler de votre expérience professionnelle, de votre formation et de vos projets. Ensuite, choisissez une autre annonce et changez de rôle. Answers will vary.

Nous recherchons des professionnels de la gestion. Première expérience ou expert(e) dans votre domaine, notre groupe vous offre d'intéressantes opportunités d'évolution. Retrouvez nos postes sur www.comptaparis.fr/métiers.

France Conseil recherche un analyste financier bilingue anglais. Vous travaillez avec nos bureaux à l'étranger pour développer les projets du département. De formation supérieure, vous avez une expérience de chef de projet de 2 à 4 ans. Nous contacter à: France Conseil, 80, rue du Faubourg Saint-Antoine, 75012 Paris

SARLA recherche un(e) assistant(e) commercial(e) trilingue anglais et espagnol avec expérience en informatique (logiciels et Internet). **Envoyer CV et lettre de motivation à SARLA, 155, avenue de Gerland, BP 72, 69007 Lyon**

7 Le poste idéal Vous souhaitez travailler à l'étranger pendant les vacances d'été, mais vous ne savez pas par où commencer. Vous allez donc dans un Centre d'Information Jeunesse pour rencontrer un conseiller/une conseillère (*advisor*) qui va déterminer le pays et le domaine professionnel les mieux adaptés. Travaillez à deux et échangez les rôles avec votre partenaire. Answers will vary.

OPTIONS

Extra Practice Brainstorm a list of professions learned in earlier lessons. Have each student pick a profession or randomly assign one to each student. Tell students to write an advertisement in search of someone in that profession, using the ads in **Activité 6** as models.

Pairs Have students role-play a phone call. Tell pairs to sit back-to-back to simulate the phone conversation. Then give them the following situation: The person they want to speak to is not there, so the caller should leave a message. Tell students to use as much phone-related vocabulary as possible in their conversations.

Les sons et les lettres

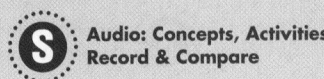

Audio: Concepts, Activities
Record & Compare

NATIONAL comparisons STANDARDS

La ponctuation française

Although French uses most of the same punctuation marks as English, their usage often varies. Unlike English, no period (**point**) is used in abbreviations of measurements in French.

200 m *(meters)* **30 min** *(minutes)* **25 cl** *(centiliters)* **500 g** *(grams)*

In other abbreviations, a period is used only if the last letter of the abbreviation is different from the last letter of the word it represents.

Mme Bonaire = Madame Bonaire **M. Bonaire = Monsieur Bonaire**

French dates are written with the day before the month, so if the month is spelled out, no punctuation is needed. When using digits only, use slashes to separate them.

le 25 février 1954 **25/2/1954** **le 15 août 2006** **15/8/2006**

Notice that a comma (**une virgule**) is not used before the last item in a series or list.

Lucie parle français, anglais et allemand. *Lucie speaks French, English, and German.*

Generally, in French, a direct quotation is enclosed in **guillemets**. Notice that a colon (**deux points**), not a comma, is used before the quotation.

Charlotte a dit: «Appelle-moi!» **Marc a demandé: «Qui est à l'appareil?»**

Réécrivez Ajoutez la ponctuation et remplacez les mots en italique par leurs abréviations.

1. Depuis le *21 mars 1964 Madame Pagny* habite à 500 *mètres* de chez moi
   Depuis le 21.03.1964, Mme Pagny habite à 500 m de chez moi.
2. Ce matin j'ai acheté 2 *kilos* de poires *Monsieur* Florent m'a dit Lucien tu as très bien fait
   Ce matin, j'ai acheté 2 kg de poires. M. Florent m'a dit: «Lucien, tu as très bien fait!»

Corrigez Lisez le paragraphe et ajoutez la bonne ponctuation et les majuscules.

hier michel le frère de ma meilleure amie sylvie m'a téléphoné il a dit carole on va fêter l'anniversaire de sylvie le samedi 13 novembre est-ce que tu peux venir téléphone-moi

Answers may vary. Possible answer: Hier, Michel, le frère de ma meilleure amie, Sylvie, m'a téléphoné. Il a dit: «Carole, on va fêter l'anniversaire de Sylvie, le samedi 13 novembre. Est-ce que tu peux venir? Téléphone-moi!»

Dictons Répétez les dictons à voix haute.

Ne parle jamais des princes: si tu en dis du bien, tu mens; si tu en dis du mal, tu t'exposes.[2]

1 Time is money.
2 Never talk about princes. If you talk nicely about them, you lie. If you say bad things about them, you reveal yourself.

ressources
LM p. 98
espaces.vhlcentral.com

Section Goals

In this section, students will learn about French punctuation.

Instructional Resources
espaces.vhlcentral.com: Textbook MP3s; Lab MP3s; WB/VM/LM Answer Key; IRM (Textbook Audioscript; Lab Audioscript); activities; downloads; reference tools

Suggestions

- Tell students that the semi-colon (**le point-virgule**) is used much more often in French than in English. They will also see a space before a colon (**deux-points**), a question mark (**un point d'interrogation**), an exclamation mark (**un point d'exclamation**), a semi-colon (**un point-virgule**), or between a word and quotation marks (**guillemets**).
- Remind students that phone numbers are written in sets of two digits separated by periods or spaces in French. Examples: **01.23.45.67.99** or **01 23 45 67 99**.
- Review the use of a comma (**une virgule**) for decimals and of the use of a period or a space instead of a comma to separate groups of three digits. Examples: **10,5** = 10.5, **1.000.000** or **1 000 000** = 1,000,000.
- Explain that the lines of different speakers in a dialogue may be preceded by an em dash (**un tiret**):
  —Tu viens avec moi?
  —Non, je reste chez moi.
  —Avez-vous déjà parlé à la patronne?
  —Oui, j'ai un rendez-vous avec elle demain.

Dictons The saying **«Le temps, c'est de l'argent»** is based on an English proverb (*Time is money*).

OPTIONS

Extra Practice Use these sentences for additional practice with French punctuation and have students replace the italicized words with abbreviations. **1. Mon anniversaire c'est le *17 avril 1988* 2. Est-ce que vous avez bu 75 *centilitres* de lait 3. Caroline a visité le musée du Louvre l'Arc de Triomphe et la tour Eiffel 4. L'homme a crié** (*shouted*) **Au secours**

Extra Practice Teach students this French tongue-twister that models some French punctuation conventions.
—Ta tante t'attend.
—J'ai tant de tantes. Quelle tante m'attend?
—Ta tante Antoinette t'attend.

Section Goals
In this section, students will learn functional phrases for talking about tests, future plans, and successes.

Instructional Resources
espaces.vhlcentral.com: WB/VM/LM Answer Key; IRM (Videoscript; ***Roman-photo*** *Translations); activities; downloads; reference tools Video on DVD*

Video Recap: Leçon 12B
Before doing this **Roman-photo**, review the previous one with this activity.

1. Que cherche le touriste? (le bureau de poste)
2. À qui demande-t-il des indications? (d'abord à M. Hulot, puis à David et à Rachid et finalement à Stéphane)
3. Qui lui donne de bonnes indications? (Stéphane)
4. Où est le bureau de poste? (derrière la fontaine, la Rotonde)

Video Synopsis
Stéphane and Astrid just took their **bac**. Stéphane tells Astrid he wants to study architecture at the **Université de Marseille**. She plans to study medicine at the **Université de Bordeaux**. Stéphane calls his mother to tell her the exam is over. At **Le P'tit Bistrot**, a young woman inquires about a job. Unbeknownst to Valérie, Michèle has an interview for a receptionist's job at Dupont.

Suggestions
- Have students predict what the episode will be about based on the video stills.
- Have students scan the captions to find sentences related to jobs and future plans.
- After reading the **Roman-photo**, have students summarize the episode.

Le bac

Video: *Roman-photo*
Record & Compare

PERSONNAGES

Astrid

Jeune femme

Michèle

Stéphane

Valérie

Après le bac...
STÉPHANE Alors, Astrid, tu penses avoir réussi le bac?
ASTRID Franchement, je crois que oui. Et toi?
STÉPHANE Je ne sais pas, c'était plutôt difficile. Mais au moins, c'est fini, et ça, c'est le plus important pour moi!

ASTRID Qu'est-ce que tu vas faire une fois que tu auras le bac?
STÉPHANE Aucune idée, Astrid. J'ai fait une demande à l'université pour étudier l'architecture.
ASTRID Vraiment? Laquelle?
STÉPHANE L'université de Marseille, mais je n'ai pas encore de réponse. Alors, Mademoiselle Je-pense-à-tout, tu sais déjà ce que tu feras?

ASTRID Bien sûr! J'irai à l'université de Bordeaux et dès que je réussirai l'examen de première année, je continuerai en médecine.
STÉPHANE Ah oui? Pour moi, les études, c'est fini pour l'instant. On vient juste de passer le bac, il faut fêter ça! C'est loin, la rentrée.

VALÉRIE Mais bien sûr que je m'inquiète! C'est normal.
STÉPHANE Tu sais, finalement, ce n'était pas si difficile.
VALÉRIE Ah bon? Tu sais quand tu auras les résultats?
STÉPHANE Ils seront affichés dans deux semaines.
VALÉRIE En attendant, il faut prendre des décisions pour préparer l'avenir.

STÉPHANE L'avenir! L'avenir! Vous n'avez que ce mot à la bouche, Astrid et toi. Oh maman, je suis tellement content aujourd'hui. Pour le moment, je voudrais juste faire des projets pour le week-end.
VALÉRIE D'accord, Stéphane. Je comprends. Tu rentres maintenant?
STÉPHANE Oui, maman. J'arrive dans quinze minutes.

Au P'tit Bistrot...
JEUNE FEMME Bonjour, Madame. Je cherche un travail pour cet été. Est-ce que vous embauchez en ce moment?
VALÉRIE Eh bien, c'est possible. L'été en général nous avons beaucoup de clients étrangers. Est-ce que vous parlez anglais?
JEUNE FEMME Oui, c'est ce que j'étudie à l'université.

ACTIVITÉS

1 Complétez Complétez les phrases suivantes.

1. Stéphane et Astrid viennent de passer __le bac__.
2. Stéphane doit téléphoner à __sa mère/Valérie__.
3. Astrid prête une __télécarte__ à Stéphane.
4. Aujourd'hui, Stéphane est très __content/heureux__.
5. Il aura les résultats du bac dans __deux semaines__.
6. Stéphane ne veut pas parler de l' __avenir__.
7. La jeune femme étudie __l'anglais__ à l'université.
8. Valérie dit que de nombreux clients du P'tit Bistrot sont __étrangers__.
9. __Michèle__ est en train (*in the process*) de chercher un nouveau travail.
10. Elle ne veut pas demander __une lettre de recommandation__ à Valérie.

Practice more at **espaces.vhlcentral.com.**

OPTIONS

Avant de regarder la vidéo Before viewing the video, have students work in pairs and brainstorm a list of things a student might say after taking a difficult exam and what a parent might say to a son or daughter after the exam.

Regarder la vidéo Download and print the videoscript from the Supersite. Then white out words related to tests, jobs, and other key vocabulary in order to create a master for a cloze activity. Distribute the photocopies and tell students to fill in the missing information as they watch the video.

Stéphane et Astrid ont passé l'examen.

4

5

STÉPHANE Écoute, je dois téléphoner à ma mère. Je peux emprunter ta télécarte, s'il te plaît?
ASTRID Oui, bien sûr. Tiens.
STÉPHANE Merci.
ASTRID Bon... Je dois rentrer chez moi. Ma famille m'attend. Au revoir.
STÉPHANE Salut.

Stéphane appelle sa mère...
VALÉRIE Le P'tit Bistrot. Bonjour.
STÉPHANE Allô.
VALÉRIE Allô. Qui est à l'appareil?
STÉPHANE Maman, c'est moi!
VALÉRIE Stéphane! Alors, comment ça a été? Tu penses avoir réussi?
STÉPHANE Oui, bien sûr, maman. Ne t'inquiète pas!

9

10

VALÉRIE Et vous avez déjà travaillé dans un café?
JEUNE FEMME Eh bien, l'été dernier j'ai travaillé à la brasserie les Deux Escargots. Vous pouvez les appeler pour obtenir une référence si vous le désirez. Voici leur numéro de téléphone.
VALÉRIE Au revoir, et peut-être à bientôt!

Près de la terrasse...
MICHÈLE J'ai un rendez-vous pour passer un entretien avec l'entreprise Dupont... C'est la compagnie qui offre ce poste de réceptionniste... Tu es fou, je ne peux pas demander une lettre de recommandation à Madame Forestier... Bien sûr, nous irons dîner pour fêter ça dès que j'aurai un nouveau travail.

Expressions utiles

Talking about tests

- **Tu penses avoir réussi le bac?**
  Do you think you passed the ***bac****?*
- **Je crois que oui.**
  I think so.
- **Qu'est-ce que tu vas faire une fois que tu auras le bac?**
  What are you going to do once you have the ***bac****?*
- **Tu sais quand tu auras les résultats?**
  Do you know when you will have the results?
- **Ils seront affichés dans deux semaines.**
  They will be posted in two weeks.

Enjoying successes

- **L'avenir! Vous n'avez que ce mot à la bouche.**
  The future! That's all you talk about.
- **Je suis tellement content(e) aujourd'hui.**
  I am so happy today.
- **Pour le moment, je voudrais juste faire des projets pour le week-end.**
  For the time being, I would only like to make plans for the weekend.
- **Nous irons dîner pour fêter ça dès que j'aurai un nouveau travail.**
  We will go to dinner to celebrate as soon as I have a new job.

Additional vocabulary

- **laquelle**
  which one (f.)

2 Répondez Répondez aux questions suivantes par des phrases complètes.

1. Quels sont les projets d'avenir d'Astrid?
   Elle ira à l'université de Bordeaux et étudiera la médecine.
2. Qu'est-ce que Stéphane veut faire l'année prochaine?
   Il veut étudier l'architecture à l'université de Marseille.
3. Est-ce que les projets d'Astrid et de Stéphane sont certains? (Supposez que les deux auront le bac.) Les projets d'Astrid sont certains, mais Stéphane n'a pas encore de réponse de l'université de Marseille.
4. Quel est le projet de Michèle pour l'avenir?
   Michèle veut travailler comme réceptionniste pour une compagnie.
5. Son projet est-il certain? Non, son projet n'est pas certain: elle doit passer l'entretien d'embauche d'abord. Elle ne sait pas encore s'ils vont lui donner le poste.

3 À vous! La jeune femme qui veut travailler au P'tit Bistrot rencontre Michèle. Elle veut savoir comment est le travail et comment est Valérie comme patronne. Michèle, qui n'est pas vraiment heureuse au P'tit Bistrot en ce moment, lui raconte tout. Avec un(e) camarade de classe, composez le dialogue et jouez la scène devant la classe.

ressources

VM pp. 259–260	DVD Leçon 13A	espaces.vhlcentral.com

ACTIVITÉS

Expressions utiles
- Model the pronunciation of the **Expressions utiles** and have students repeat them.
- As you work through the list, point out **le futur** with **dès que** and **quand**. Also point out the use of the interrogative pronoun **laquelle** in caption 2. Tell students that these grammar points will be formally presented in **Espace structures**.
- Respond briefly to students' questions about these points.
- Remind students that **le futur** is a grammatical term referring to the future tense. To talk about the future as in time, they should use **l'avenir**.

1 Suggestion Have volunteers read the completed sentences aloud.

1 Expansion Have students write additional sentences to fill in the gaps in the storyline.

2 Suggestion Have volunteers write the answers to the questions on the board. Then go over them with the class.

2 Expansion Ask students personalized questions. Allow students to invent answers if they prefer. Examples: **1. Quels sont vos projets d'avenir? 2. Que voulez-vous faire l'année prochaine? 3. Est-ce que vos projets sont sûrs?**

3 Suggestion If time is limited, this activity may be assigned as homework. Assign each student a role (Michèle or the young woman). Have partners prepare their parts at home, then allow them a few minutes to rehearse before presenting their conversation to the class.

OPTIONS

Extra Practice Ask students yes/no questions based on the **Roman-photo**. Tell them to answer **Je crois que oui** or **Je crois que non**. Examples: **1. Stéphane a-t-il réussi au bac? 2. Stéphane va-t-il étudier l'architecture à l'université? 3. Astrid va-t-elle étudier la médecine? 4. La jeune femme va-t-elle être embauchée au P'tit Bistrot? 5. Michèle va-t-elle trouver un autre travail?**

Small Groups Have students work in groups of three. Tell them to write a résumé for a famous person. Write this format on the board for students to follow: **Objectif(s) professionnel(s), Formation, Expérience professionnelle,** and **Références**. Then have volunteers read the résumé to the class without saying the person's name. The class should try to guess whose résumé it is.

Section Goals

In this section, students will:
- learn about phone usage in France
- learn some common terms used in text messages
- read about well-paying jobs in the francophone world
- read about **les artisans** in France

Instructional Resources
espaces.vhlcentral.com; activities; downloads; reference tools

Culture à la loupe
Avant la lecture
- Have students look at the photos and describe what they see.
- Take a quick class survey to find out how many students use public phones, phone cards, cell phones, and text messaging. Tally the results on the board.

Lecture
- Point out the **Coup de main**. Tell students that the commonly used term **SMS** stands for *short message service*.
- Point out the statistics chart. Ask students what information it shows. (the percentage of French people who had cell phones from 1998–2008)

Après la lecture Have students compare the French usage of telephones and phone cards with their own usage based on the results in the survey in **Avant la lecture**.

1 Suggestion Have students read the completed sentences aloud.

CULTURE À LA LOUPE

Le téléphone en France

Pour téléphoner en France, on peut utiliser une cabine publique avec une télécarte. Les télécartes sont vendues dans les bureaux de tabac°, à la poste et dans tous les endroits qui affichent° «Télécartes en vente ici». Si vous devez téléphoner avec de la monnaie, il vaut mieux° essayer un café ou un hôtel. Les cabines publiques à pièces sont très rares.

Les Français sont surtout accros° à leur téléphone portable. Aujourd'hui, plus de 58 millions de personnes sont abonnées°. Soixante-six pour cent d'entre elles choisissent le forfait° et payent un tarif mensuel°. Ce type d'abonnement° exige° d'avoir un compte bancaire en France. Sinon, on a la possibilité de choisir des cartes prépayées ou de louer un portable pour une courte période.

Comme les appels sont chers, les gens communiquent beaucoup par SMS°. En moyenne, chaque abonné envoie 30 SMS par mois. Ces messages sont écrits dans un langage particulier, qui permet de taper° plus vite. Le langage SMS est très phonétique et joue avec le son des lettres et des chiffres°. Tous les jeunes l'utilisent. Les jeunes aiment aussi beaucoup télécharger les logos et sonneries° du moment. En France, le marché de la téléphonie mobile a beaucoup d'avenir.

bureaux de tabac *tobacco shops* **affichent** *post* **il vaut mieux** *it is better* **accros** *addicted* **sont abonnées** *have a subscription* **forfait** *package* **tarif mensuel** *monthly fee* **abonnement** *subscription* **exige** *requires* **SMS** *text message* **taper** *type* **chiffres** *numbers* **sonneries** *ringtones*

Coup de main

A cell phone has many names in French: **téléphone, portable, GSM, mobile.**

A text message may be called an **SMS** or a **texto.**

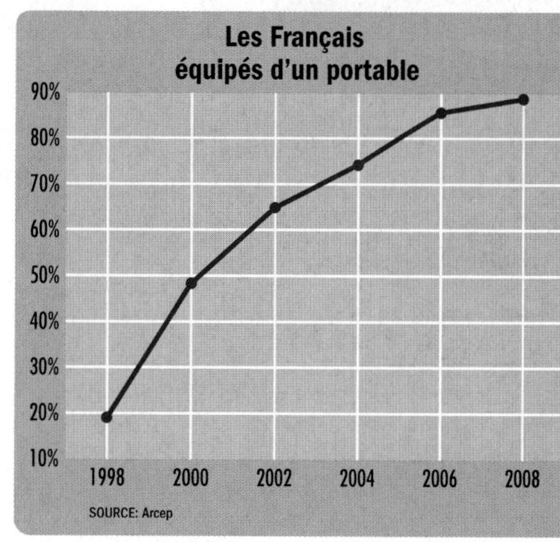

ACTIVITÉS

1 Complétez **Donnez le début ou la suite de chaque phrase, d'après le texte et le tableau.** Answers may vary. Possible answers provided.

1. Pour téléphoner en France, on peut utiliser... une cabine publique avec une télécarte.
2. ... dans les bureaux de tabac, à la poste et dans tous les endroits qui affichent «Télécartes en vente ici». Les télécartes sont vendues
3. Si vous devez téléphoner avec de la monnaie, il vaut mieux... essayer un café ou un hôtel.
4. ... des abonnés choisissent le forfait. 66%
5. En moyenne, chaque abonné envoie... 30 SMS par mois.
6. ... joue avec le son des lettres et des chiffres. Le langage SMS
7. Les jeunes aiment aussi... télécharger des logos et des sonneries.
8. En 1998, 19% seulement des Français... possédaient un portable.
9. ... sont d'autres noms pour désigner le portable. Téléphone, GSM et mobile
10. Un SMS s'appelle aussi... un texto.

Practice more at **espaces.vhlcentral.com.**

OPTIONS

La télécarte When purchasing **une télécarte,** it is less expensive per unit (**unité**) to buy **une grande** for 120 units than **une petite** for 50 units. The disposable **télécarte** works without a code. The French phone booth has two advantages: the quick, efficient insertion system for **la télécarte** and the caller's ability to view the remaining units on the phone card while talking on the phone.

Pairs Have students work in pairs. Tell them to take turns quizzing each other about the information on cell phones in the chart. Write a sample question on the board for students to use as a model. Example: **En quelle année est-ce que 50 pour cent des Français étaient équipés d'un portable? (2000)**

LE FRANÇAIS QUOTIDIEN

Le SMS, C pratik!

A+	*À plus (tard).*
Bap	*Bon après-midi.*
C pa 5pa	*C'est pas sympa!*
Dak	*D'accord.*
GT o 6né	*J'étais au ciné.*
Je t'M	*Je t'aime.*
Jenémar	*J'en ai marre!*
Kestufé	*Qu'est-ce que tu fais?*
Komencava	*Comment ça va?*
MDR	*Mort de rire!*

LE MONDE FRANCOPHONE

Comment gagner sa vie

Voici des métiers et des secteurs où on peut gagner sa vie dans le monde francophone.

Quelques exemples de métiers bien payés

En France avocat(e)
En Haïti prêtre°
Au Sénégal joueur de football professionnel
En Suisse banquier d'affaires

Quelques exemples de secteurs lucratifs

En Belgique l'industrie chimique, du pétrole
Au Québec l'industrie du papier
En Suisse les banques et les assurances
En Tunisie le tourisme

prêtre *priest*

PORTRAIT

Les artisans

L'artisanat en France emploie 2,5 millions de personnes. On le décrit souvent comme «la plus grande entreprise de France». Bouchers, plombiers, fleuristes, bijoutiers... les artisans travaillent dans plus de 300 secteurs d'activité différents. Leurs entreprises sont de petite taille, avec moins de dix employés. Les artisans sont plus nombreux dans les villes, mais ils jouent un grand rôle en milieu rural. En plus d°'y apporter les services nécessaires, ils aident à créer le «lien social°». Artisans et artisans d'art sont considérés comme les gardiens° de la tradition française et de son savoir-faire°, qu'ils se transmettent depuis des générations, grâce au° système de l'apprentissage°.

En plus de *In addition to* **lien social** *social cohesion* **gardiens** *guardians* **savoir-faire** *expertise* **grâce au** *thanks to* **apprentissage** *apprenticeship*

SUR INTERNET

Combien d'hommes a-t-il fallu pour installer les ampoules (*lights*) sur la tour Eiffel?

Go to **espaces.vhlcentral.com** to find more information related to this **ESPACE CULTURE**.

ACTIVITÉS

2 Complétez Complétez les phrases.

1. L'artisanat en France emploie 2,3 millions de personnes.
2. Answer will vary. Possible answer: Bouchers, plombiers, fleuristes, bijoutiers sont des exemples d'artisans.
3. Artisans et artisans d'art sont les gardiens de la tradition française et de son savoir-faire.
4. Le savoir-faire des artisans est transmis grâce au système de l'apprentissage
5. Au Sénégal, joueur de football professionnel est un métier bien payé.
6. En Tunisie, le tourisme est un secteur lucratif.

3 Échange de textos Vous et un(e) partenaire allez faire connaissance par SMS. Préparez un dialogue en français facile, puis transformez-le en messages SMS. Comparez ensuite votre conversation SMS à la conversation d'un autre groupe. Présentez-la devant la classe.

ressources
espaces.vhlcentral.com

Le français quotidien
- Model the pronunciation of both columns so students can hear the sound-symbol correspondence between the abbreviations and the actual expressions.
- Point out that **après-midi** is one of the few words in French that can be either masculine or feminine. This book refers to it as masculine.

Portrait
- It is a point of pride in France to work as an **artisan** and to sell something one can label **artisanal**.
- Ask students: **Considérez-vous qu'un plombier est un artisan? Pourquoi? Et un fleuriste? Un boucher? Un bijoutier?**

Le monde francophone Ask students: **Quels métiers ou secteurs de la liste sont bien/mal payés aux États-Unis? Pourquoi?**

2 Expansion For additional practice, give students these items. **7. Au Québec ____ est un secteur lucratif. (l'industrie du papier) 8. Si on veut bien gagner sa vie en tant que prêtre, on peut vivre ____. (en Haïti)**

3 Expansion Collect the text messages, choose a few, and write them on the board or a transparency. Tell the class to write the messages in standard French.

OPTIONS

Les artisans The French government supports small family businesses. Also, the general public is accustomed to walking from shop to shop to do errands for services and products that may cost more than in chain stores, but are consistently of higher quality.

Extra Practice Have students write five true/false statements based on the information on this page. Then have them get together with a classmate, and take turns reading their statements aloud and responding.

comparisons
NATIONAL STANDARDS

Section Goals

In this section, students will learn the future tense with **quand** and **dès que**.

Instructional Resources
*espaces.vhlcentral.com: Lab MP3s; WB/VM/LM Answer Key; IRM (**Essayez!** and **Mise en pratique** answers; **Feuilles d'activités**; Lab Audioscript); activities; downloads; reference tools*

Suggestions

- Quickly review the **futur simple**.
- Explain that the future tense with **quand** and **dès que** is for expressing an act that has not yet taken place. Point out that in English one usually uses the present tense after *when* or *as soon as*. Check for understanding by asking individuals to supply the future tense of phrases using **quand** and **dès que**. Example: **Quand je ____ (voyager) en Europe, je ____ (louer) une voiture. (voyagerai; louerai)** Contrast with the English equivalent *When I travel to Europe, I will rent a car.*
- Explain that expressions with **quand** and **dès que** that express generalities do not use the future tense. Example: **Quand on veut trouver un travail, on doit écrire une lettre de motivation.**
- Write two columns on the board: **quand** and **dès que**. Have students give example sentences using each clause in the present and future tenses.
- Model the use of **quand** and **dès que** by asking questions about what others will do when they begin looking for a job. Examples: **Où habiterez-vous quand vous chercherez un travail? Dès que vous obtiendrez un travail, que ferez-vous?**

Essayez! Before assigning this activity, have students underline the verbs in the sentences and identify their tense. Example: **1. on l'<u>embauchera</u>** (*future*)

13A.1 *Le futur simple* with *quand* and *dès que*

Point de départ In **Leçon 12B**, you learned how to form **le futur simple**, which is generally equivalent to the English future with *will*. You will now learn how to use **le futur simple** where English uses the present tense.

Je me **mettrai** (FUTURE) à chercher du travail, quand je n'**aurai** (FUTURE) plus d'argent.
*I **will start** looking for work when I **don't have** any more money.*

Dès que je réussirai l'examen de première année, je continuerai en médecine.

Nous irons dîner pour célébrer dès que j'aurai un nouveau travail.

- In a clause that begins with **quand** or **dès que** (*as soon as*), use the future tense if the clause describes an event that will happen in the future.

Il enverra son CV **quand il aura** le temps.	Je posterai mon CV **dès que je pourrai**.
He will send his résumé when he has time.	*I will post my résumé as soon as I can.*

- If a clause with **quand** or **dès que** does not describe a future action, another tense may be used for the verb.

Quand avez-vous fait le stage?	La patronne nous parle **dès qu'elle arrive**.
When did you do the internship?	*The boss talks to us as soon as she arrives.*

Essayez! **Écrivez la forme correcte des verbes indiqués.**

1. On l'embauchera dès qu'on __aura__ (avoir) de l'argent.
2. Nous commencerons le stage quand nous __connaîtrons__ (connaître) les résultats.
3. Il a téléphoné dès qu'il __a reçu__ (recevoir) la lettre.
4. On a envie de sortir quand il __fait__ (faire) beau.
5. Dès que vous __prendrez__ (prendre) rendez-vous, on vous indiquera le salaire.
6. Ils enverront leurs CV dès qu'ils __achèteront__ (acheter) l'ordinateur.
7. Nous passerons un entretien quand il __reviendra__ (revenir) de vacances.
8. Je décroche quand le téléphone __sonne__ (sonner).

MISE EN PRATIQUE

1 Projets Nathalie et Brigitte discutent des problèmes de travail. Nathalie explique ce qu'elle fait quand elle est sans travail. Brigitte approuve.

MODÈLE Je lis les annonces quand je cherche un travail.
Moi aussi, je lirai les annonces quand je chercherai un travail.

1. J'envoie mon CV quand je cherche du travail. Moi aussi, j'enverrai mon CV quand je chercherai du travail.
2. Mon mari lit mon CV dès qu'il a le temps. Mon mari aussi lira mon CV dès qu'il aura le temps.
3. Je suis contente quand tu passes un entretien. Moi aussi, je serai contente quand tu passeras un entretien.
4. Je prends rendez-vous dès que je reçois une lettre d'une compagnie. Moi aussi, je prendrai rendez-vous dès que je recevrai une lettre d'une compagnie.
5. Ta famille et toi, vous êtes heureux quand des chefs du personnel me téléphonent. Ta famille et toi aussi, vous serez heureux quand des chefs du personnel me téléphoneront.
6. Je fais des projets quand j'ai un travail. Moi aussi, je ferai des projets quand j'aurai un travail.

2 Plus tard Aurélien parle de ses projets et des projets de sa famille et de ses amis. Mettez les verbes au futur.

MODÈLE dès que / je / avoir / le bac / je / aller / à l'université
Dès que j'aurai le bac, j'irai à l'université.

1. quand / je / être / à l'université / ma sœur et moi / habiter ensemble Quand je serai à l'université, ma sœur et moi habiterons ensemble.
2. quand / ma sœur / étudier plus / elle / réussir Quand ma sœur étudiera plus, elle réussira.
3. quand / mes parents / être / à la retraite / je / emprunter pour payer mes études Quand mes parents seront à la retraite, j'emprunterai pour payer mes études.
4. dès que / vous / finir vos études / vous / envoyer vos CV / tout / entreprises de la ville Dès que vous finirez vos études, vous enverrez vos CV à toutes les entreprises de la ville.
5. quand / tu / travailler / tu / acheter une voiture Quand tu travailleras, tu achèteras une voiture.
6. quand / nous / trouver / nouveau travail / nous / ne plus lire / les annonces Quand nous trouverons un nouveau travail, nous ne lirons plus les annonces.

3 Conseils Quels conseils pouvez-vous donner à un(e) ami(e) qui cherche du travail? Avec un(e) partenaire, assemblez les éléments des colonnes pour formuler vos conseils. Utilisez **quand** ou **dès que**. Answers will vary.

MODÈLE
Quand tu auras ton diplôme, tu chercheras un travail.

A	B
avoir son diplôme	s'amuser
avoir un métier	chercher un travail
passer un entretien	être riche
réussir ses examens	gagner beaucoup d'argent
trouver un emploi	lire les annonces
	se marier
	parler de son expérience professionnelle

Practice more at **espaces.vhlcentral.com.**

OPTIONS

Extra Practice Write these statements on the board, then ask students to finish them using the appropriate verb tense. **1. Quand on a envie de passer un entretien… 2. Dès qu'il a trouvé un travail… 3. Quand je voyagerai à Paris… 4. Quand je recevrai un salaire élevé… 5. Dès que je parlerai avec mon patron…**

Game Have students write three important things they will or will not do when they graduate on a slip of paper and put it in a box. Example: **Quand j'obtiendrai le diplôme, je n'habiterai plus chez mes parents.** Have students draw a paper from the box, then walk around the room, asking others if they will do what is listed, until they find the person who wrote the slip of paper. The first person to find a match wins.

COMMUNICATION

4 L'avenir Qu'est-ce que l'avenir nous réserve? Avec un(e) partenaire, complétez ces phrases. Ensuite, présentez vos réponses à la classe. Answers will vary.

1. Dès que je réussirai mes examens, je...
2. Ton ami(e) et toi, vous lirez les annonces quand...
3. Mon/Ma meilleur(e) ami(e) travaillera dès que...
4. Tu enverras ton CV quand...
5. Mes amis se marieront dès que...
6. Quand nous aurons beaucoup d'argent, nous...

5 Content(e) Votre professeur va vous donner une feuille d'activités. Circulez dans la classe pour trouver une personne qui réponde oui et une qui réponde non à chaque question. Justifiez toutes vos réponses. Answers will vary.

MODÈLE

Étudiant(e) 1: *Est-ce que tu seras plus content(e) quand tu auras du temps libre?*
Étudiant(e) 2: *Oui, je serai plus content(e) dès que j'aurai du temps libre, parce que je ferai plus souvent de la gym.*

6 Les métiers Vous allez bientôt exercer ces métiers (*have these jobs*). Dites à un(e) partenaire ce qui (*what*) sera possible et ce qui ne sera pas possible quand vous commencerez votre nouveau poste. Alternez les rôles. Answers will vary.

MODÈLE

Étudiant(e) 1: *Dès que je commencerai ce travail, je chercherai un nouvel appartement.*
Étudiant(e) 2: *Je n'aurai plus le temps de sortir quand j'aurai ce poste.*

1.

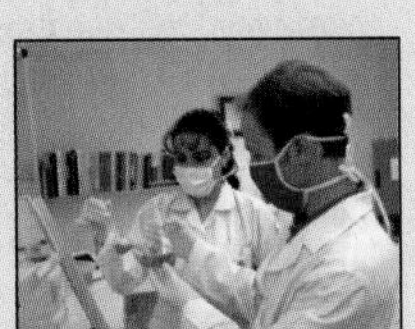
3.

2.

4.

Le français vivant

PRENEZ EN MAIN VOTRE AVENIR
FORUM
RENCONTRE
Vous prendrez en main votre avenir quand vous irez à ce forum. Dès que vous entrerez, vous rencontrerez des gens qui vous aideront à rencontrer d'autres gens, à trouver un emploi.
FORUM Rencontre
IAE
IG2I
ENSIAME
iteem

Identifiez Quelles formes de verbes au futur trouvez-vous après **quand** et **dès que** dans cette publicité (*ad*)? Quels autres verbes au futur trouvez-vous? irez, entrerez, rencontrerez, aideront

Questions À tour de rôle, avec un(e) partenaire, posez-vous ces questions. Answers will vary.

1. Qui assistera au Forum rencontre? Pourquoi?
2. Que trouvera-t-on au Forum rencontre? Que fera-t-on?
3. Que feras-tu dès que tu finiras tes études universitaires?
4. Que penses-tu faire pour trouver un emploi quand tu seras prêt(e) à travailler?

1 Expansion Have pairs model the activity and write three more sentences expressing generalities. Then have students switch their sentences with other pairs.

2 Suggestion Have volunteers write each sentence with the future tense on the board. Ask other volunteers to change the sentences into the present or the past tense and discuss how the meanings change.

3 Suggestion Before beginning the activity, have students talk about the last job they had. Encourage them to use **quand** and **dès que** with the past tense.

4 Expansion Have students write three original sentences modeled after the activity. Then ask volunteers to share their sentences with the class.

5 Suggestion Have two volunteers act out the **modèle**. Then hand out the **Feuilles d'activités** from the Supersite.

6 Expansion Ask volunteers to tell you the job of their dreams. Modeling the activity, have them talk about what will and will not be possible once they have begun their job.

Le français vivant Call on a volunteer to read the ad aloud. Ask students: **Quelles sont les questions qu'on doit poser à un forum pour l'emploi?** Encourage students to use the future tense with **quand** and **dès que**.

OPTIONS

Extra Practice Have students imagine they are taking a vacation to Europe. Ask them to write six things they will do when they arrive. Then in pairs have students imagine they are calling home after their first few days of vacation. Have one student ask questions about what they did upon arrival. The second student should answer the questions using **quand** and **dès que.**

Video Show the video episode again to give students more input on the use of the future tense. Ask the students to write down all the examples of the future tense they hear in the conversation. When the video has finished, review the lists as a class. Discuss the use of **quand**, **dès que**, and **une fois que**.

Section Goals

In this section, students will learn:

- interrogative pronouns **lequel, laquelle**, **lesquels**, and **lesquelles**
- contractions with prepositions and forms of **lequel**

Instructional Resources
*espaces.vhlcentral.com: Lab MP3s; WB/VM/LM Answer Key; IRM (**Essayez!** and **Mise en pratique** answers; **Feuilles d'activités**; Lab Audioscript); activities; downloads; reference tools*

Suggestions

- Review the use and forms of **quel: quel(s), quelle(s).** Remind students that **quel** agrees with the noun it modifies.
- Point out that students already use other interrogative pronouns (**qui, que**). **Lequel** differs in that it has a specific antecedent (a person or thing already mentioned).
- Brainstorm a list of movies and write them on the board. Demonstrate the use of **lequel** by pointing to the list and asking students: **Lequel préférez-vous?**
- Practice **de + lequel** and **à + lequel** by asking students questions that elicit its use. Examples: **Je parle des films étrangers avec mes amis. Desquels parlez-vous? Je m'intéresse à l'histoire américaine. À laquelle vous intéressez-vous?**

Essayez! Before assigning this activity, have students underline the noun (and preposition, if applicable) that the appropriate form of **lequel** should replace.

13A.2 The interrogative pronoun *lequel*

NATIONAL STANDARDS comparisons

Point de départ In **Leçon 4A**, you learned how to use the interrogative adjective **quel**, as in **Quelle heure est-il?** You will now learn how to use the interrogative pronoun **lequel**.

- If a person or thing has already been mentioned, use a form of **lequel**, translated as *which one(s)*, in place of **quel(le)(s)** + [*noun*].

Quel métier choisirez-vous? *Which profession will you choose?*	**Lequel** choisirez-vous? *Which one will you choose?*

- **Lequel** agrees with the noun to which it refers.

	singular	plural
masculine	lequel	lesquels
feminine	laquelle	lesquelles

Quelle entreprise l'a embauché? *Which company hired him?*	**Laquelle** l'a embauché? *Which one hired him?*

- Place the form of **lequel** wherever you would place **quel(le)(s)** + [*noun*] in a question.

Dans **quel domaine** travaille-t-il? *Which field does he work in?*	Dans **lequel** travaille-t-il? *Which one does he work in?*

- Remember that past participles agree with preceding direct objects.

Laquelle avez-vous **choisie**? *Which one did you choose?*	**Lesquels** as-tu **faits**? *Which ones did you do?*

- Forms of **lequel** contract with the prepositions **à** and **de**.

à + form of *lequel*

	singular	plural
masculine	auquel	auxquels
feminine	à laquelle	auxquelles

de + form of *lequel*

	singular	plural
masculine	duquel	desquels
feminine	de laquelle	desquelles

Auxquels vous intéressez-vous? *Which ones interest you?*	Vous parlez **duquel**? *Which one are you talking about?*

Essayez! **Réécrivez les phrases avec des formes de lequel.**

1. Pour quelle compagnie travaillez-vous? *Pour laquelle travaillez-vous?*
2. Quel métier préférez-vous? Lequel préférez-vous?
3. À quel métier t'intéresses-tu? Auquel t'intéresses-tu?
4. De quels stages est-ce que vous parlez? Desquels est-ce que vous parlez?

MISE EN PRATIQUE

1 Au bureau Hubert parle à ses collègues. Complétez ses phrases avec une forme du pronom interrogatif **lequel**.

1. J'ai deux stylos. __Lequel__ veux-tu emprunter?
2. Voici la liste des entreprises. À __laquelle__ devons-nous téléphoner?
3. Avez-vous contacté les employés avec __lesquels__ il faut travailler?
4. Sais-tu le nom des stages __auxquels__ tu as assisté?
5. __Lesquelles__ de ces lettres avez-vous lues?
6. Je suis allé dans plusieurs bureaux. __Desquels/Duquel__ parlez-vous?

2 Répétez Vous rencontrez M. Dupont pendant un dîner où il y a beaucoup de bruit (*noise*). Il vous pose des questions, mais il n'entend pas vos réponses. Avec un(e) partenaire, alternez les rôles. Some answers will vary.

MODÈLE examen / avoir réussi

Étudiant(e) 1: *Quel examen avez-vous réussi?*
Étudiant(e) 2: *L'examen de chimie.*
Étudiant(e) 1: *Lequel avez-vous réussi?*

1. métier / s'intéresser à
   À quel métier vous intéressez-vous? Auquel vous intéressez-vous?
2. CV / avoir envoyé
   Quel CV avez-vous envoyé? Lequel avez-vous envoyé?
3. entreprise / avoir embauché
   Quelle entreprise vous a embauché(e)? Laquelle vous a embauché(e)?
4. candidats / ne pas avoir obtenu de poste
   Quels candidats n'ont pas obtenu de poste? Lesquels n'ont pas obtenu de poste?
5. formations / devoir suivre
   Quelles formations devez-vous suivre? Lesquelles devez-vous suivre?
6. domaine / se spécialiser dans
   Dans quel domaine vous spécialisez-vous? Dans lequel vous spécialisez-vous?

3 La culture francophone Vous voulez savoir si votre partenaire connaît la culture francophone. À tour de rôle, posez-vous ces questions et répondez-y. Ensuite, posez-vous une question avec une forme de **lequel**. Some answers will vary.

MODÈLE Qui chante en français?

a. Madonna (b.) Céline Dion c. Mariah Carey
Laquelle/Lesquelles de ces chanteuses aimes-tu?

1. Qui est un acteur français?
   (a.) Gérard Depardieu b. Tom Hanks c. Johnny Depp
   Lequel/Lesquels de ces acteurs préfères-tu?
2. Où parle-t-on français?
   a. Philadelphie (b.) Montréal c. Athènes
   Laquelle/Lesquelles de ces villes voudras-tu visiter un jour?
3. Quelle voiture est française?
   a. Lotus b. Ferrari (c.) Peugeot
   Laquelle/Lesquelles de ces voitures as-tu déjà conduite(s)?
4. Quelle marque (*brand*) est française?
   a. Mabelle b. Versace (c.) L'Oréal
   Laquelle/Lesquelles de ces marques vas-tu essayer?
5. Qui est un metteur en scène (*director*) français?
   a. Visconti (b.) Besson c. Spielberg
   Lequel/Lesquels de ces metteurs en scène connais-tu?

Practice more at **espaces.vhlcentral.com.**

OPTIONS

Video Replay the video episode, having students focus on the use of **laquelle**. Point out that forms of **lequel** are often used in conversation to clarify a point. Stop the video where appropriate and ask students to which noun each **laquelle** refers.

Game Use a ball to play a game that practices the use of the interrogative pronoun **lequel**. Say a sentence that can be restated using a form of **lequel**. Example: **De quelle université parlez-vous?** Toss the ball to a student who must repeat the sentence using the appropriate form of **lequel**. (**De laquelle parlez-vous?**) When the student has given the appropriate form, he or she tosses the ball back to you. Include both feminine and masculine, singular and plural nouns, and the prepositions **à** and **de** with **lequel**. Keep the pace rapid.

COMMUNICATION

4 **Des choix** Cet été, vous irez en vacances avec des amis et vous visiterez plusieurs endroits. Avec un(e) partenaire, parlez de vos projets et posez des questions pour demander des détails. Answers will vary.

MODÈLE visiter des châteaux (*castles*)

Étudiant(e) 1: *Quand je serai en Suisse, je visiterai des châteaux.*
Étudiant(e) 2: *Lesquels visiteras-tu?*

aller dans des musées	marcher dans les rues
bronzer sur la plage	se promener au parc
dîner au restaurant	sortir en boîte
faire du sport	visiter des sites touristiques
?	?

5 **Enquête** Votre professeur va vous donner une feuille d'activités. Circulez dans la classe et parlez à différent(e)s camarades pour trouver, pour chaque question, une personne qui réponde oui. Demandez des détails. Answers will vary.

MODÈLE

Étudiant(e) 1: *Écoutes-tu de la musique?*
Étudiant(e) 2: *Oui.*
Étudiant(e) 1: *Laquelle aimes-tu?*
Étudiant(e) 2: *J'écoute toujours de la musique classique.*

Activités	*Noms*	*Réponses*
1. écouter de la musique	*Sam*	*musique classique*
2. avoir des passe-temps		
3. bien s'entendre avec des membres de sa famille		
4. s'intéresser aux livres		
5. travailler avec d'autres étudiant(e)s		
6. habiter dans un appartement		

6 **Ce semestre** Avec un(e) partenaire, parlez des bons et des mauvais aspects de votre vie à la fac ce semestre. Employez des formes du pronom interrogatif **lequel**. Ensuite, présentez vos réponses à la classe. Answers will vary.

MODÈLE

Étudiant(e) 1: *J'ai des cours très difficiles ce semestre.*
Étudiant(e) 2: *Lesquels?*
Étudiant(e) 1: *Le cours de biologie et le cours de chimie.*

- les cours
- la résidence
- les livres
- les camarades
- les profs
- ?

Le français vivant

Recherchons candidats avec talents particuliers.
Lequel ou laquelle choisir?
La question traditionnelle:
Lesquels ont un diplôme? Quel diplôme?
La question d'aujourd'hui:
Lequel ou laquelle a une personnalité inhabituelle?
BNP PARIBAS | La banque d'un monde qui change

Identifiez Quelles formes du pronom interrogatif **lequel** trouvez-vous dans cette publicité (*ad*)? Lequel, laquelle, Lesquels

Questions À tour de rôle, avec un(e) partenaire, posez-vous ces questions. Answers will vary.

1. Quel est le but (*goal*) de cette pub?
2. Quelle question posait-on traditionnellement?
3. Quelle question pose-t-on aujourd'hui?
4. Les formations traditionnelles fonctionnent-elles toujours pour trouver un travail? Pourquoi?
5. Pourquoi faut-il aujourd'hui avoir une personnalité inhabituelle?

1 Suggestion Ask six volunteers to write the completed sentences on the board. Have other volunteers correct any spelling or grammar errors.

2 Expansion Have students work in pairs to brainstorm other nouns and verbs similar to those in the activity. Ask volunteers to write their examples on the board. Have other volunteers formulate questions aloud using **lequel**.

3 Suggestion Before assigning the activity, use magazine pictures of popular movies, TV programs, etc., to ask some general questions about students' likes and preferences.

4 Expansions
- Have students bring in photos from a past vacation. Working in pairs, students should ask questions similar to those in the activity, but using the past tense.
- Ask volunteers to present their photos to the class. Have classmates ask questions using the appropriate form of **lequel**.

5 Suggestion Have two volunteers act out the **modèle**. Then hand out the **Feuilles d'activités** from the Supersite

6 Suggestion Brainstorm vocabulary about university life before assigning the activity. Examples: **un emploi sur le campus, les examens**, etc.

OPTIONS

Pairs Have your students interview each other in pairs about where they want to be and what they want to be doing in five years, in ten years, in thirty years, and so forth. Encourage students to use the future tense and ask clarifying questions using the appropriate forms of **lequel**. Have each student take notes on his or her partner's plans. Then ask for a few volunteers to report on their partner's plans for the future.

Small Groups Divide the class into groups of three. Ask each group to work together to write a prediction of a classmate's future, using the future tense with **quand** and **dès que**. The group should not include the name of their subject. Then circulate the description and ask other groups to identify the name of the classmate whose future is being predicted.

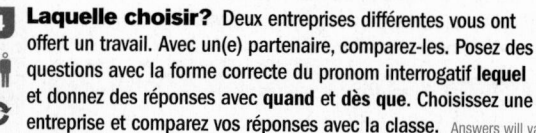

Instructional Resources
espaces.vhlcentral.com: IRM (Info Gap Activities); Testing Program, pp. 97–100; Test Files; Testing Program MP3s; activities; downloads; reference tools Test Generator

1 Expansion Have pairs repeat the activity referring to their budgets. Example: **Quelles choses achèterez-vous dès que vous aurez le budget nécessaire?** Give students magazine pictures to represent what items they will buy.

2 Suggestion Review the use of the relative pronoun **qui** when giving details about a person.

3 Expansion Have students write a letter to a friend giving career advice. Ask students to include the strategies they developed in the activity as part of their letter.

4 Suggestion Before assigning this activity, do the **modèle** with a volunteer. Ask students to describe any companies for which they have worked. Write two of the company names and characteristics on the board.

5 Suggestion Brainstorm typical interview questions with the class before assigning groups for this activity.

6 Suggestion Divide the class into pairs and distribute the Info Gap Handouts found on the Supersite for this activity. Give students ten minutes to complete the activity.

Révision

1 Mon premier emploi Avec un(e) partenaire, dites ce que (*what*) vous ferez et utilisez **quand** ou **dès que**. Answers will vary.

MODÈLE
mon premier emploi
Dès que je serai embauché(e), je téléphonerai à ma mère.

1. mon premier entretien
2. mon premier jour dans l'entreprise
3. rencontrer les autres employés
4. mon premier salaire
5. travailler sur mon premier projet
6. changer de poste
7. me disputer avec le patron
8. quitter l'entreprise

2 Lequel? Avec un(e) partenaire, imaginez un dialogue entre un(e) patron(ne) et son assistant(e). L'assistant(e) demande des précisions. Alternez les rôles. Answers will vary.

MODÈLE
Étudiant(e) 1: *Vous appellerez notre client, s'il vous plaît?*
Étudiant(e) 2: *Oui, mais lequel?*
Étudiant(e) 1: *Le client qui est venu hier après-midi.*

accompagner un visiteur	envoyer un colis
appeler un client	laisser un message à un(e) employé(e)
chercher un numéro de téléphone	prendre un rendez-vous
faire une lettre de recommandation	préparer une réunion (*meeting*)

3 Mes stratégies Avec un(e) partenaire, faites une liste de dix stratégies pour bien mener (*to lead*) votre carrière. Pour chaque stratégie, utilisez **quand** ou **dès que**. Answers will vary.

MODÈLE
Étudiant(e) 1: *Dès que je m'ennuierai, je chercherai un nouveau poste.*
Étudiant(e) 2: *Quand je serai trop fatigué(e), je prendrai des vacances.*

4 Laquelle choisir? Deux entreprises différentes vous ont offert un travail. Avec un(e) partenaire, comparez-les. Posez des questions avec la forme correcte du pronom interrogatif **lequel** et donnez des réponses avec **quand** et **dès que**. Choisissez une entreprise et comparez vos réponses avec la classe. Answers will vary.

MODÈLE
Étudiant(e) 1: *Laquelle te propose un meilleur salaire?*
Étudiant(e) 2: *Verrin me propose un meilleur salaire, mais dès que je commencerai, je devrai travailler jusqu'à neuf heures du soir.*

5 Un entretien Par groupes de trois, jouez cette scène: un chef du personnel visite votre université et vous et un(e) ami(e) passez un entretien informel. Utilisez le pronom interrogatif **lequel** et le futur avec **quand** et **dès que**. Answer will vary.

Le chef du personnel...
- décrit le poste.
- pose des questions.
- répond aux questions des candidat(e)s.
- dit aux candidat(e)s quand il/elle va les contacter.

Les candidat(e)s...
- L'un doit donner toutes les bonnes réponses.
- L'autre ne donne que de mauvaises réponses.
- Les deux posent des questions pour en savoir plus sur l'entreprise et sur les postes.

6 Quand nous chercherons du travail... Votre professeur va vous donner, à vous et à votre partenaire, deux feuilles d'activités différentes. Attention! Ne regardez pas la feuille de votre partenaire. Answers will vary.

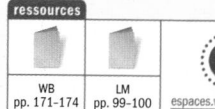

ressources
WB pp. 171–174 | LM pp. 99–100 | espaces.vhlcentral.com

OPTIONS

Extra Practice Tell students to imagine they were fired from a job. Now they must write a letter convincing their **patron(ne)** that they deserve a second chance. Give students fifteen minutes to complete this activity. Encourage the use of the lesson vocabulary and the future tense with **quand** and **dès que**. Then have students switch letters with a classmate for peer editing.

Small Groups Divide the class into groups of three. Have students take turns telling the group three things they hope will be true when they are ten years older. Example: **Quand j'aurai 30 ans, je gagnerai beaucoup d'argent.**

Le Zapping

S Video: Short Film

NATIONAL STANDARDS connections communities

Une jeune étudiante, qui a besoin d'argent pour payer ses études, travaille à mi-temps° dans un supermarché. Elle déteste ce travail, méprise° ses collègues et n'en fait qu'à sa tête°, se croyant supérieure° à tous les autres. Jusqu'au jour où, à cause de ses propres° actions, elle se retrouve dans une situation qui pourrait avoir des conséquences très fâcheuses°.

mi-temps *part time* **méprise** *looks down on* **n'en fait qu'à sa tête** *does whatever she feels like doing* **se croyant supérieure** *thinking she's better* **ses propres** *her own* **fâcheuses** *regrettable*

Expressions utiles

C'est foutu. (*fam.*) *It's ruined.*

J'ai tout foiré. (*fam.*) *I messed up everything.*

C'est plein pot. *It's full price.*

Laisse tomber! *Forget it!*

Dégagez! (*fam.*) *Get lost!*

On s'en fout. (*fam.*) *Who cares.*

Je ne vous empêche pas de... *I'm not keeping you from...*

prendre en compte *to take into consideration*

se donner à fond *to give it one's all*

Vocabulaire du court métrage

un achat *purchase*

bosser (*fam.*) *to work*

le boulot (*fam.*) *work, job*

une bourse *scholarship*

une caisse *cash register*

faire le compte de la caisse *to count the money*

un(e) caissier/caissière *cashier*

la clientèle *customers*

une grève *strike*

un horaire *shift*

un(e) raté(e) *loser*

surveiller *to watch, to keep an eye on*

Préparation

1 Synonymes Remplacez les termes soulignés par des synonymes appropriés du vocabulaire.

1. J'aime énormément mon travail. mon boulot
2. Mon ami déteste ses heures de travail cette année. son horaire
3. Désolé! Il n'y a pas de promotion en ce moment. C'est plein pot.
4. Le patron vient d'annoncer qu'il faut travailler plus vite pour arriver à tout finir. bosser
5. N'y pense plus! C'est trop tard, de toute façon! Laisse tomber!
6. Allez, partez! Il n'y a rien à voir, ici! dégagez

2 Réactions Avec un(e) partenaire, complétez les réactions à ces commentaires avec des mots et expressions du vocabulaire.

1. —Il pleut, nous avons raté le train. Ils sont partis sans nous.
   —Et notre week-end à la plage! __C'est foutu__, c'est sûr!
2. —Mais, bien sûr! Vous pouvez toujours faire tout ce que vous voulez!
   —Oui, c'est vrai, tu __ne nous empêches pas de__ sortir, en général.
3. —Les études ne sont pas très chères en France.
   —Oui, c'est vrai, mais il faut aussi __prendre en compte__ le logement, la nourriture, les transports, les loisirs...
4. —Ta cousine fait tout ce qu'elle peut pour réussir en médecine.
   —Oui, elle __se donne à fond__ dans ses études.
5. —Alors, comment s'est passé ton examen de chimie?
   —Oh là là, une vraie catastrophe. Je crois que __j'ai tout foiré__!
6. —Carole a reçu 5.000 euros du gouvernement pour ses études.
   —C'est vrai? Elle a eu __une bourse__? C'est génial!

Introduction To check comprehension, ask these questions:
1. D'après l'introduction, quel est le sujet du court métrage que vous allez regarder?
2. Pourquoi la jeune fille travaille-t-elle au supermarché?
3. À votre avis, qu'est-ce qu'on veut dire par «elle se retrouve dans une situation qui pourrait avoir des conséquences très fâcheuses»?

Préparation Have students look at the poster and predict what the short film will be about.

1 Expansion Write all the vocabulary words and expressions on strips of paper and have students pick one. Ask them to create logical sentences in which they use the words or expressions they picked.

2 Expansion Ask students if they currently have or if they have ever had a part time job. Have volunteers share their experiences with their classmates. Then ask students to brainstorm the types of jobs students often have while attending university and ask them why they think these jobs are typical student jobs. As a class, briefly discuss the impact having a part time job can have on one's studies. Ask for advantages and disadvantages, and have students give reasons and examples to support their opinions.

OPTIONS

Note culturelle When looking for work, French people can turn to the **ANPE**, which stands for **Agence Nationale pour l'Emploi**. Created in 1967 by the French Government, its goal is to help jobseekers find jobs, help companies recruit new employees, and fight against discrimination in the labor market. The ANPE has a partnership with over 500.000 companies.

Note culturelle The **SMIC (salaire minimum interprofessionnel de croissance)** is the French equivalent of the US minimum wage. It is currently € 8,82 per hour. The **SMIC** is reevaluated every year on January 1st.

Mi-temps

National Standards: communication, cultures

ROSA Bonjour, Alice. Tu travailles, aujourd'hui? Ce n'était pas Viviane, ce matin? Ça fait trois semaines que tu lui laisses le vendredi après-midi.

ALICE Je n'y peux rien. J'ai mes examens à la fac.

ROSA Et elle, ça lui bouffe° tous ses week-ends.

UNE CLIENTE C'est à partir de combien, le parking gratuit°?

ALICE C'est à partir de 500 francs d'achat, Madame. Pour 50 francs, ça ira. Rosa, tu peux me passer le tampon° pour le parking?

ROSA C'est à partir de 500 francs d'achat.

ALICE Rosa, tu peux prendre mes clients? Il faut que je téléphone pour les résultats de mon examen.

ROSA Ça ne peut pas attendre la pause°?

ALICE Allô? C'est moi. GL304. C'est la littérature générale. LM311. Langues vivantes. LP204. Linguistique. C'est pas possible. Il faut que je raccroche, je suis au boulot.

ALICE Elle n'est pas terrible, la musique, aujourd'hui. Tu ne pourrais pas changer?

ABDEL C'est la radio.

ALICE Ben, change de station.

UNE FEMME Alice! Alors, c'était aujourd'hui?

ALICE Ouais, et j'ai tout foiré! C'est foutu.

UNE FEMME Bon, écoute, si t'es occupée, je vais te laisser, d'accord?

ALICE Le poulet de Bresse est en promotion°. Vous pouvez passer à la caisse d'à côté? Je n'en peux plus de ce boulot! Je travaille à mi-temps. Sans ma bourse, laisse tomber! Je me suis donnée à fond et j'ai tout foiré. Je suis une ratée. Le poulet, il est en promotion.

UN HOMME C'est plein pot, le poulet.

ALICE Il est en promo. Cadeau, le poulet!

ALICE 114,80, s'il vous plaît. Bonjour. Au revoir.

UN CLIENT Bonjour.

ALICE Bonjour. Merci. Voilà, au revoir.

UN CLIENT Bonjour.

ALICE Bonjour. Vous n'auriez pas plus petit?

UN CLIENT Non, c'est tout ce que j'ai.

ALICE Rosa, tu n'aurais pas de la monnaie sur 500 francs? Merci. Vous avez le ticket? Au revoir. Vous payez par chèque ou par carte bleue?

UNE CLIENTE Carte bleue.

LE DIRECTEUR Vous ne partez pas sans faire le compte de la caisse.

ALICE C'est Viviane qui le fait en fin de journée.

LE DIRECTEUR Les caisses sont vérifiées à la fin de chaque horaire.

ALICE Non, mais d'habitude, ce n'est pas comme ça. Pourquoi vous ne faites ça qu'à moi? Vous me lâchez°? Vous n'avez pas le droit°. C'est Rosa qui vous a dit de m'emmerder°?

ROSA Le temps de vérification des caisses n'est pas pris en compte dans l'horaire. Vous n'avez pas le droit de demander à Alice de vérifier sa caisse. Ce n'est pas syndical.

ROSA Nous informons notre aimable clientèle que suite à des mesures anti-syndicales° prises par la direction, l'ensemble des caissiers entame° une grève surprise. La sortie des articles est libre°.

UNE CAISSIÈRE Je vais devoir quitter ma caisse et vous laisser, si vous voulez, partir avec vos articles.

UNE CAISSIÈRE Le magasin ferme. Oui, oui, vous pouvez prendre... vous pouvez passer.

UN CLIENT Celui-là...

UNE CAISSIÈRE Au revoir.

bouffe *eats up* **gratuit** *free* **tampon** *stamp* **pause** *break* **en promotion** *on sale* **lâchez** *let go* **droit** *right* **m'emmerder** *bother me* **mesures anti-syndicales** *decisions in violation of workers' rights* **entame** *begins* **libre** *free*

Avant de regarder le film Write the following two heads on the board: **Égoïste** and **Généreux**. As a class, brainstorm ideas for things that a selfish coworker might do and for things that a generous coworker might do. Keep these lists on the board for reference.

Suggestion Stop after each segment and ask students to summarize what happened using their own words. Ask them to point out examples of Alice's selfish behavior in each segment and explain why they feel each behavior is selfish. Example: **Il est interdit de fumer dans le bureau, mais Alice allume quand même une cigarette. Elle ne respecte ni le règlement ni la santé de ses collègues.** After each segment, ask students to try and guess what might happen in the next segment.

Compréhension Have students look at the stills and read the dialogues. Then ask these questions: **1. Qui sont Alice et Rosa? Sont-elles amies, à votre avis? 2. Qu'est-ce que le magasin offre aux clients qui dépensent plus de 500 francs? 3. Pourquoi Alice veut-elle téléphoner? 4. Comment Alice réagit-elle quand Rosa lui demande si elle avait besoin de sortir? 5. De quoi Alice et la jeune femme à la casquette discutent-elles? 6. Pourquoi Alice est-elle obligée de demander de la monnaie à Rosa? 7. Qui suit Alice quand elle quitte sa caisse? Que veut-il? 8. Que fait Rosa à la fin?**

OPTIONS

L'euro Tell students that the Euro started to be used in France, as well as in 10 other European countries, on January 1st, 1999. National currencies were still accepted, though. Then, on January 1st, 2002, it became the official European currency in 12 countries. And since February 28th, 2002, the Euro has been the only currency in use.

Extra Practice Once students have viewed the various segments, ask them to describe and contrast the two main characters, Rosa and Alice, in detail. How would they define their interactions? What is their reaction to Rosa's actions at the end? Why do they think she acted the way she did? Does Alice deserve Rosa's help? What is ironic about the situation?

NATIONAL communication STANDARDS

Analyse

3 Associez D'abord, faites correspondre les images aux phrases. Ensuite, mettez les images dans l'ordre chronologique.

__e__ 1. Rosa donne de la monnaie à Alice.
__a__ 2. Alice attend sa pause pour passer un coup de téléphone (*to phone*) important.
__d__ 3. Le directeur veut qu'Alice vérifie sa caisse maintenant.
__f__ 4. Alice vole (*steals*) dans la caisse.
__b__ 5. Alice sait qu'elle a raté ses examens.
__c__ 6. Les caissiers font la grève. Les clients peuvent partir sans payer.

a. __1__

b. __2__

c. __6__

d. __5__

e. __4__

f. __3__

4 Les relations au supermarché Avec un(e) partenaire, répondez à ces questions sur le film.
Answers will vary.

1. Quelles actions d'Alice créent ou pourraient créer des problèmes pour Viviane? Expliquez.
2. Dans la salle de pause, pourquoi Rosa dit-elle à Alice que les autres employés ont aussi besoin de pauses? Quelle est la réaction d'Alice? Qu'est-ce qui explique peut-être cette réaction?
3. Que fait Alice à plusieurs reprises (*several times*) quand elle ne veut pas s'occuper de ses clients? Qu'en pensez-vous?
4. Pourquoi Alice dit-elle au client qu'il y a une promotion sur le poulet? Que pensez-vous de son comportement (*behavior*)?
5. À votre avis, Rosa a-t-elle dit au directeur qu'Alice avait pris de l'argent? Expliquez votre réponse.
6. D'après vous, Rosa savait-elle qu'Alice avait volé dans la caisse? Expliquez votre réponse.

Practice more at **espaces.vhlcentral.com.**

5 Après la grève Par groupes de trois ou quatre, préparez un dialogue qui a lieu (*that takes place*) après la grève des caissiers.Servez-vous de ces questions comme base. Answers will vary.

- Qu'arrive-t-il à Rosa?
- Alice change-t-elle de comportement et aide-t-elle Rosa?
- Que font les autres employés?
- Que fait le directeur?

3 Expansion Have students justify their answers by quoting relevant sentences from the film.

4 Expansion Have students consider the selfish and generous behaviors they came up with in the **Avant de regarder** activity. Ask them to consider each item in Activity 4 and add to the two columns in **Avant de regarder**. Ask them to hypothesize on why Alice might act in such a selfish manner.

5 Suggestion Before pairs begin work on this activity, brainstorm ideas to incorporate in the dialogues, using the following questions: **Est-ce que la relation de Rosa et d'Alice va être affectée par ce qui s'est passé au magasin? En quoi? Alice va-t-elle se rendre compte de son égoïsme? Va-t-elle changer? Va-t-elle s'excuser ou bien va-t-elle faire comme si de rien n'était** (*as if nothing had happened*)**?**

OPTIONS

Small Groups Have students write a description of what they consider to be a typical selfish person. Encourage them to use elements from the film and to make inferences and draw conclusions.

Extra Practice Have students imagine they are employees at a supermarket where they catch a coworker, whom they do not like very much, steal from the cash register. Ask them to write a paragraph explaining what they would do and why.

Section Goals

In this section, students will learn and practice vocabulary related to:

- professions and occupations
- the workplace

Instructional Resources

*espaces.vhlcentral.com: Transparency #55; IRM (**Vocabulaire supplémentaire**; **Mise en pratique** answers; Textbook Audioscript; Lab Audioscript; Info Gap Activities); Textbook MP3s; Lab MP3s; WB/VM/LM Answer Key; activities; downloads; reference tools*

Suggestions

- Tell students to look over the new vocabulary and identify the cognates.
- Use **Transparency #55.** Identify the professions of people in the illustration. Examples: **C'est un agriculteur. C'est un banquier.**
- Explain that whenever there is no feminine form (**un agriculteur/une agricultrice**) nor article change (**un/une psychologue**) nor a term in apposition (**un homme/une femme politique**), the French say **elle est** followed by the masculine form of the profession. Examples: **Elle est plombier. Elle est chef d'entreprise.**
- Ask students questions using the new vocabulary. Examples: **1. Avez-vous un emploi à mi-temps? 2. Êtes-vous au chômage? 3. Avez-vous une assurance maladie? 4. Pourquoi est-il important d'avoir une assurance maladie? 5. Quelles professions sont exigeantes, à votre avis? 6. Connaissez-vous une femme politique célèbre?**
- Additional vocabulary for this lesson can be found in the **Vocabulaire supplémentaire** on the Supersite.

Leçon 13B

You will learn how to...

- **discuss your work**
- **say what you would do**

Talking Picture
Audio: Activity

Les professions

Vocabulaire

démissionner	*to resign*
diriger	*to manage*
être au chômage	*to be unemployed*
être bien/mal payé(e)	*to be well/badly paid*
gagner	*to earn; to win*
prendre un congé	*to take time off*
renvoyer	*to dismiss, to let go*
une carrière	*career*
un chômeur/une chômeuse	*unemployed person*
un emploi à mi-temps/à temps partiel	*part-time job*
un emploi à plein temps	*full-time job*
un niveau	*level*
une profession (exigeante)	*(demanding) profession*
un(e) retraité(e)	*retired person*
une réunion	*meeting*
une réussite	*success*
un syndicat	*union*
une assurance-maladie	*health insurance*
une assurance-vie	*life insurance*
une augmentation (de salaire)	*raise (in salary)*
une promotion	*promotion*
un cadre/une femme cadre	*executive*
un chef d'entreprise	*head of a company*
un conseiller/une conseillère	*consultant; advisor*
une femme au foyer	*housewife*
un(e) gérant(e)	*manager*
un homme/une femme politique	*politician*
un ouvrier/une ouvrière	*worker, laborer*
un plombier	*plumber*

ressources

WB pp. 175-176 | LM p. 101 | espaces.vhlcentral.com

OPTIONS

TPR Have students mime the work of different professionals. Write the names of professions on slips of paper or whisper them to each person. Examples: **comptable, pompier,** and **chauffeur**. The rest of the class should guess what profession the person is miming. The student who guesses correctly gets to mime the next profession.

Extra Practice Give French words that are related to a profession. Then ask students to guess the profession. Example: **la nourriture, un restaurant, cuisiner, une fourchette, un menu, le dîner (un chef de cuisine)**

Mise en pratique

1 Les professions Pour chaque profession de la colonne de gauche, trouvez la définition qui correspond dans la colonne de droite.

g 1. un chef d'entreprise	a. travaille avec des budgets
j 2. une femme au foyer	b. est employé dans une usine (*factory*)
k 3. un chauffeur	c. répare les fuites (*leaks*) d'eau
i 4. une banquière	d. loue et vend des appartements
h 5. un cuisinier	e. travaille dans un laboratoire
a 6. une comptable	f. s'occupe de la santé des animaux
b 7. un ouvrier	g. dirige des employés
f 8. une vétérinaire	h. prépare des plats dans un restaurant
d 9. un agent immobilier	i. travaille avec de l'argent
c 10. un plombier	j. s'occupe de la maison et des enfants
	k. conduit un taxi ou un camion
	l. donne des conseils

2 Le monde du travail Complétez le paragraphe en utilisant les mots de vocabulaire de la liste pour faire des phrases cohérentes.

à mi-temps	un conseil
à plein temps	mal payés
l'assurance maladie	un niveau
une augmentation	d'une promotion
leur carrière	un salaire élevé

Quand les étudiants ont un travail, en général c'est un emploi (1) à mi-temps parce qu'ils doivent aussi étudier pour préparer (2) leur carrière. Souvent, ils sont (3) mal payés. Mais avec leur diplôme, ils auront la possibilité de trouver un poste (4) à plein temps, avec (5) un salaire élevé et bien souvent (6) l'assurance maladie. Plus tard, ils pourront demander (7) une augmentation de salaire ou bien attendre l'opportunité (8) d'une promotion pour gagner plus d'argent.

3 Écoutez Écoutez la conversation entre Henri et Margot, deux jeunes élèves, et indiquez si les phrases suivantes sont **vraies** ou **fausses**.

Henri

Margot

1. Henri veut être comptable. Faux.
2. Il aidera ses employés. Vrai.
3. Ses employés seront bien payés. Vrai.
4. Il offrira à tous une assurance vie. Faux.
5. Margot veut être chef d'entreprise. Faux.
6. Elle aidera les femmes au foyer. Faux.
7. Margot ne parlera pas aux syndicats. Faux.
8. Une de ses priorités sera le chômage. Vrai.

Practice more at **espaces.vhlcentral.com.**

1 Expansions
- Ask students what professions item e. (**travaille dans un laboratoire**) and item l. (**donne des conseils**) describe. (item e.: **chercheur/chercheuse** and item l.: **conseiller/conseillère**)
- Have students write definitions for other professions not listed. Examples: **un agriculteur, un électricien,** and **un psychologue.**

2 Expansion Have students write three comprehension questions based on the paragraph. Then tell them to get together in groups of three and take turns asking and answering each other's questions.

3 Tapescript HENRI: Quand je serai grand, je serai chef d'entreprise. J'aiderai mes employés. Ils auront un salaire élevé et bien sûr l'assurance maladie et les congés payés.
MARGOT: Moi aussi, quand je serai grande, j'aiderai les gens, spécialement les ouvriers. Je serai femme politique. J'assisterai aux réunions des différents syndicats, j'écouterai les besoins des chômeurs et je travaillerai pour développer les emplois.
(On Textbook MP3s)

3 Suggestions
- Before playing the recording, have students describe the people in the photos.
- After playing the recording, tell students to correct the false statements.

OPTIONS

Game Brainstorm a list of professions from previous lessons and write them on the board. Distribute or have students make a Bingo card (a 5 X 5 grid of 25 squares) and write the name of a profession from this lesson or a previous one in each square. Write the name of each profession on a separate card and put the cards in a box. Draw cards one by one from the box and read the profession aloud. If students have that profession on their cards, they put a check mark in the corner of the box. To win, a student must have five professions in a row. The first person to have five in a row should say Bingo! To verify a win, have the student read the names of the professions in the winning row.

4 Expansion Have pairs get together with another pair and report what information they collected from their partners.

5 Suggestion Before beginning the activity, give students a few minutes to jot down some ideas about their job, boss, and/or employees.

6 Suggestion Have two volunteers read the **modèle** aloud. Then divide the class into pairs and distribute the Info Gap Handouts found on the Supersite for this activity. Give students ten minutes to complete the activity.

7 Suggestion Tell students to use the ads on page 436 as models. Encourage them to invent information for the company, such as a telephone number, a street address, or an e-mail address.

NATIONAL communication STANDARDS

Communication

4 Conversez **Interviewez un(e) camarade de classe. Les réponses peuvent être réelles ou imaginaires.** Answers will vary.

1. Où travailles-tu en ce moment? Es-tu bien payé(e)?
2. Préfères-tu travailler à mi-temps ou à plein temps? Pourquoi?
3. Est-ce le métier que tu feras plus tard? Pourquoi?
4. Est-ce que tu as des congés payés? Une assurance maladie? Qu'en penses-tu?
5. As-tu déjà demandé une augmentation de salaire? As-tu réussi à en obtenir une? Comment?
6. As-tu déjà obtenu une promotion? Quand? Pourquoi?
7. As-tu déjà été au chômage? Pendant combien de temps? Qu'est-ce que tu as fait pendant ce temps-là?
8. Quel genre de carrière veux-tu faire? Ta profession sera-t-elle exigeante? Pourquoi?

5 Votre carrière **Voilà cinq ans que vous n'avez pas vu votre ami(e) de la fac. Depuis, vous avez obtenu tous/toutes les deux votre diplôme et trouvé un travail. Travaillez avec un(e) camarade de classe pour présenter un dialogue avec ces éléments:** Answers will vary.

- Vous vous retrouvez et vous parlez de votre métier.
- Vous décrivez votre poste.
- Vous parlez de votre patron/patronne et/ou de vos employés.
- Vous parlez des avantages et des inconvénients (*drawbacks*) de votre travail.

6 Décrivez **Votre professeur va vous donner, à vous et à votre partenaire, deux feuilles d'activités différentes. À tour de rôle, posez-vous des questions pour trouver ce que font les personnages de chaque profession pendant la journée.** Answers will vary.

MODÈLE

Étudiant(e) 1: *Sur mon dessin, j'ai un plombier qui répare une fuite (leak) d'eau sous un évier.*
Étudiant(e) 2: *Moi, j'ai un homme...*

7 L'offre d'emploi **Vous êtes le chef d'entreprise de Cartalis, une agence immobilière. Vous développez votre entreprise et avez besoin de rapidement embaucher un(e) nouvel(le) employé(e). Avec deux partenaires, écrivez une annonce que vous enverrez à votre journal local. Utilisez les mots de la liste.** Answers will vary.

agent immobilier	poste exigeant
carrière	promotion
congés payés	réussite
diriger	salaire élevé
entretien	temps partiel

OPTIONS

Extra Practice Have students categorize professions according to various paradigms. Examples: **les emplois de bureau/les emplois en plein air; les métiers physiques/les métiers intellectuels;** and **les métiers qui exigent une longue formation/les métiers qui n'exigent pas ou peu de formation.**

Pairs Have students work in pairs. Tell them to make a list of reasons people resign from a job (**Raisons pour démissionner d'un poste**) and a list of reasons people are let go from a job (**Raisons pour être renvoyé[e]**). Then call on volunteers to read one item from their list.

Les sons et les lettres

Audio: Concepts, Activities
Record & Compare

Les néologismes et le franglais

The use of words or neologisms of English origin in the French language is called **franglais**. These words often look identical to the English words, but they are pronounced like French words. Most of these words are masculine, and many end in **-ing**. Some of these words have long been accepted and used in French.

le sweat-shirt **le week-end** **le shopping** **le parking**

Some words for foods and sports are very common, as are expressions in popular culture, business, and advertising.

un milk-shake **le base-ball** **le top-modèle** **le marketing**

Many **franglais** words are recently coined terms (**néologismes**). These are common in contemporary fields, such as entertainment and technology. Some of these words do have French equivalents, but the **franglais** terms are used more often.

un e-mail = un courriel **le chat = la causette** **une star = une vedette**

Some **franglais** words do not exist in English at all, or they are used differently.

un brushing = *a blow-dry* **un relooking =** *a makeover* **le zapping =** *channel surfing*

Prononcez Répétez les mots suivants à voix haute.

1. flirter
2. un fax
3. cliquer
4. le look
5. un clown
6. le planning
7. un scanneur
8. un CD-ROM
9. le volley-ball
10. le shampooing
11. une speakerine
12. le chewing-gum

Articulez Répétez les phrases suivantes à voix haute.

1. Le cowboy porte un jean et un tee-shirt.
2. Julien joue au base-ball et il fait du footing.
3. J'ai envie d'un nouveau look, je vais faire du shopping.
4. Au snack-bar, je commande un hamburger, des chips et un milk-shake.
5. Tout ce qu'il veut faire, c'est rester devant la télé dans le living et zapper!

Dictons Répétez les dictons à voix haute.

Ce n'est pas la star qui fait l'audience, mais l'audience qui fait la star.[1]

Un gentleman est un monsieur qui se sert d'une pince à sucre, même lorsqu'il est seul.[2]

ressources
LM p. 102
espaces.vhlcentral.com

1 It's not the star that makes the fans, it's the fans that make the star.
2 A gentleman is a man who uses sugar tongs, even when he is alone.

Section Goals

In this section, students will learn about neologisms and **franglais**.

Instructional Resources
espaces.vhlcentral.com: Textbook MP3s; Lab MP3s; WB/VM/LM Answer Key; IRM (Textbook Audioscript; Lab Audioscript); activities; downloads; reference tools

Suggestions

- Model the pronunciation of the example words and have students repeat after you.
- Ask students to provide more examples of words that are neologisms or **franglais**. Examples: **cool, le basket-ball, un site web, un toaster** and **surfer.**
- Dictate five familiar words that are neologisms or **franglais**, repeating each one at least two times. Then write them on the board or a transparency and have students check their spelling. Examples: **un GPS, un cowboy, un penalty, un pressing, un blog.**

Dictons The saying **«Ce n'est pas la star qui fait l'audience, mais l'audience qui fait la star»** is a quote from Noël Mamère, a journalist and politician. The saying **«Un gentleman est un monsieur qui se sert d'une pince à sucre, même lorsqu'il est seul»** is a quote from Alphonse Allais, a writer and humorist.

OPTIONS

Extra Practice Write these Internet words on the board or a transparency. Have the class guess the English equivalents. **1. arrosage** (*spamming*) **2. accès** (*hit*) **3. bombardement** (*bombing*) **4. balise** (*tag*) **5. moteur de recherche** (*search engine*) **6. téléchargement** (*downloading*)

Small Groups Have the class work in groups of three or four. Tell them to write a humorous paragraph using as many neologisms or **franglais** terms as possible. Ask a few volunteers to read their paragraphs to the class.

Section Goals

In this section, students will learn functional phrases for talking about hypothetical situations and making polite requests or suggestions.

Instructional Resources
espaces.vhlcentral.com: WB/VM/LM Answer Key; IRM (Videoscript; ***Roman-photo*** *Translations); activities; downloads; reference tools*
Video on DVD

Video Recap: Leçon 13A
Before doing this **Roman-photo**, review the previous one with this activity.
1. Qu'est-ce que Stéphane et Astrid viennent de faire? (passer le bac)
2. Qu'est-ce que Stéphane veut étudier à l'université? (l'architecture)
3. Qu'est-ce qu'Astrid veut étudier à l'université? (la médecine)
4. Qu'est-ce que cherche la jeune femme au P'tit Bistrot? (un emploi)
5. Qu'est-ce que cherche Michèle? (un nouveau travail)

Video Synopsis
Sandrine is anxious about her first public performance as a singer. Amina offers to make her a dress to give her confidence. Stéphane and Astrid get their **bac** results. Astrid passed with honors, but Stéphane has to retake one part of the exam. At **Le P'tit Bistrot**, Michèle asks Valérie for a raise. When Valérie refuses, Michèle quits. Then Stéphane arrives and tells his mother his bad news.

Suggestions
- Tell students to scan the captions to find job-related vocabulary.
- After reading the **Roman-photo**, review students' predictions and have them summarize the episode.

NATIONAL communication cultures STANDARDS

Je démissionne!

Video: *Roman-photo*
Record & Compare

PERSONNAGES

Amina

Astrid

Michèle

Sandrine

Stéphane

Valérie

En ville...
AMINA Alors, Sandrine, ton concert, ce sera la première fois que tu chantes en public?
SANDRINE Oui, et je suis un peu anxieuse!
AMINA Ah! Tu as le trac!
SANDRINE Un peu, oui. Toi, tu es toujours tellement chic, tu as confiance en toi, tu n'as peur de rien...

AMINA Mais Sandrine, la confiance en soi, c'est ici dans le cœur et ici dans la tête. J'ai une idée! Ce qui te donnerait du courage, c'est de porter une superbe robe.
SANDRINE Tu crois? Mais, je n'en ai pas...
AMINA Je m'en occupe. Quel style de robe est-ce que tu aimerais? Suis-moi!

Au marché...
AMINA Que penses-tu de ce tissu noir?
SANDRINE Oh! C'est ravissant!
AMINA Oui et ce serait parfait pour une robe du soir.
SANDRINE Bon, si tu le dis. Moi, si je faisais cette robe moi-même, elle finirait sans doute avec une manche courte et avec une manche longue!

STÉPHANE Attends. Forestier, Stéphane... Oh! Ce n'est pas possible!
ASTRID Quoi, qu'est-ce qu'il y a?
STÉPHANE Je dois repasser une partie de l'examen la semaine prochaine.
ASTRID Oh, ce n'est pas vrai! Il y a peut-être une erreur. Stéphane, attends!

Au P'tit Bistrot...
MICHÈLE Excusez-moi, Madame. Auriez-vous une petite minute?
VALÉRIE Oui, bien sûr!
MICHÈLE Voilà, ça fait deux ans que je travaille ici au P'tit Bistrot... Est-ce qu'il serait possible d'avoir une augmentation?

VALÉRIE Michèle, être serveuse, c'est un métier exigeant, mais les salaires sont modestes!
MICHÈLE Oui, je sais, Madame. Je ne vous demande pas un salaire très élevé, mais... c'est pour ma famille.
VALÉRIE Désolée, Michèle, j'aimerais bien le faire, mais, en ce moment, ce n'est pas possible. Peut-être dans quelques mois...

ACTIVITÉS

1 **Vrai ou faux?** Indiquez si ces affirmations sont **vraies** ou **fausses**. Corrigez les phrases fausses. Answers may vary.

1. Sandrine a un peu peur avant son concert.
   Vrai.
2. Amina ne sait pas comment aider Sandrine.
   Faux. Amina va faire une robe pour Sandrine.
3. Amina va faire une robe de velours noir.
   Faux. Amina va faire une robe en soie noire.
4. Sandrine ne sait pas faire une robe.
   Vrai.
5. Pour la remercier (*To thank her*), Sandrine va préparer un dîner pour Amina.
   Faux. Sandrine va préparer un gâteau pour Amina.
6. Stéphane doit repasser tout le bac.
   Faux. Stéphane doit repasser une partie du bac.
7. Astrid a reçu une très bonne note.
   Vrai.
8. Michèle travaille au P'tit Bistrot depuis deux ans.
   Vrai.
9. Valérie offre à Michèle une toute petite augmentation de salaire.
   Faux. Valérie n'offre pas d'augmentation de salaire à Michèle.
10. Michèle va retourner au P'tit Bistrot après ses vacances.
    Faux. Michèle ne va pas retourner au P'tit Bistrot.

Practice more at **espaces.vhlcentral.com.**

OPTIONS

Avant de regarder la vidéo Tell students to look at the video stills and to read the title and the scene setter. Then have them predict what might happen in this episode. Write their predictions on the board. After viewing the episode, have them confirm or correct their predictions.

Regarder la vidéo Show the video in four parts, pausing it before each location change. Have students describe what happens in each place. Write their observations on the board. Then show the entire episode again without pausing and have the class fill in any missing details to summarize the plot.

Valérie et Stéphane rencontrent de nouveaux problèmes.

4

AMINA Je pourrais en faire une comme ça, si tu veux.
SANDRINE Je préférerais une de tes créations. Si tu as besoin de quoi que ce soit un jour, dis-le-moi.
AMINA Oh, Sandrine, je vais te faire une robe qui te fera plaisir.
SANDRINE Je pourrais te préparer un gâteau au chocolat?
AMINA Mmmm... Je ne dirais pas non.

5

Au lycée...
ASTRID Oh, Stéphane, c'est le grand jour! On va enfin connaître les résultats du bac! Je suis tellement nerveuse. Pas toi?
STÉPHANE Non, pas vraiment. Seulement si j'échoue, ma mère va m'étrangler. Eh! Félicitations, Astrid! Tu as réussi! Avec mention bien en plus!
ASTRID Et toi?

9

MICHÈLE Non, Madame! Dans quelques mois, je serai déjà partie. Je démissionne! Je prends le reste de mes vacances à partir d'aujourd'hui.
VALÉRIE Michèle, attendez! Mais Michèle! Ah, Stéphane, te voilà. Hé! Où vas-tu? Tu as eu les résultats du bac, non? Qu'est-ce qu'il y a?

10

STÉPHANE Maman, je suis désolé, mais je vais devoir repasser une partie de l'examen.
VALÉRIE Oh là là! Stéphane!
STÉPHANE Bon, écoute maman, voici ce que je vais faire: je vais étudier nuit et jour jusqu'à la semaine prochaine: pas de sports, pas de jeux vidéo, pas de télévision. J'irai à l'université, maman. Je te le promets.

Expressions utiles

Talking about hypothetical situations

- **Ce qui te donnerait du courage, c'est de porter une superbe robe.**
  Wearing a great dress would give you courage.
- **Ce serait parfait pour une robe du soir.**
  This would be perfect for an evening gown.
- **Si je faisais cette robe, elle finirait avec une manche courte et avec une manche longue!**
  If I made this dress, it would end up with one short sleeve and one long sleeve!
- **Je préférerais une de tes créations.**
  I would prefer one of your creations.
- **Je ne dirais pas non.**
  I wouldn't say no.
- **Si tu as besoin de quoi que ce soit un jour, dis-le-moi.**
  If you ever need anything someday, tell me.
- **Si j'échoue, ma mère va m'étrangler.**
  If I fail, my mother is going to strangle me.

Making polite requests and suggestions

- **Quel style de robe est-ce que tu aimerais? J'aimerais...**
  What kind of dress would you like? I would like...
- **Je pourrais en faire une comme ça, si tu veux.**
  I could make you one like this, if you would like.
- **Auriez-vous une petite minute?**
  Would you have a minute?
- **Est-ce qu'il serait possible d'avoir une augmentation?**
  Would it be possible to get a raise?

Additional vocabulary

- **le trac**
  stage fright
- **ravissant(e)**
  beautiful; delightful
- **faire plaisir à quelqu'un**
  to make someone happy

ACTIVITÉS

2 **Les mauvaises nouvelles** Stéphane, Valérie et Michèle ont été très déçus (*disappointed*) aujourd'hui pour des raisons différentes. Avec deux partenaires, décidez qui a passé la pire journée et pourquoi. Ensuite, discutez-en avec le reste de la classe.

3 **Écrivez** Pensez à un examen très important de votre vie et écrivez un paragraphe, en répondant à (*by answering*) ces questions. Quel était l'examen? Qu'est-ce que vous avez fait pour le préparer? Comment était-ce? Comme l'histoire de Stéphane ou d'Astrid? Comment cet examen a-t-il affecté vos projets d'avenir?

ressources
VM pp. 261–262 | DVD Leçon 13B | espaces.vhlcentral.com

Expressions utiles
- Model the pronunciation of the **Expressions utiles** and have students repeat them after you.
- As you work through the list, point out **le conditionnel** forms and **si** clauses. Tell students that these grammar points will be formally presented in **Espace structures**.
- Respond briefly to questions about **le conditionnel** and **si** clauses. Reinforce correct forms, but do not expect students to produce them consistently at this time.

1 Suggestion Have students correct the false statements.

1 Expansion For additional practice, give students these items. **11. Amina refuse le gâteau au chocolat parce qu'elle est au régime. (Faux.) 12. Astrid dit que la note de Stéphane est peut-être une erreur. (Vrai.) 13. Michèle veut une augmentation pour acheter une nouvelle voiture. (Faux.) 14. Stéphane promet d'étudier nuit et jour pour réussir son bac. (Vrai.)**

2 Suggestion If time is limited, this activity may be assigned as homework. Group students according to the person they believe had the worst day—Stéphane, Michèle, or Valérie. Have them prepare their arguments at home, then allow the groups a few minutes to rehearse before presenting their case to the class.

3 Expansion Have students exchange compositions for peer editing.

OPTIONS

Pairs Working in pairs, have students write a conversation between a boss and an employee, based on the conversation between Michèle and Valérie. In the conversation, the employee should negotiate something with the boss, such as extra vacation time, permission to come in late one day, or a day off. At first, the boss refuses, but eventually the two compromise and come to an agreement.

Extra Practice Write **j'aimerais** and **vous aimeriez** on the board. Ask students variations of the question: **Quel style de robe est-ce que vous aimeriez porter?** Tell them to respond with **J'aimerais...**. Examples: **1. Quelle profession est-ce que vous aimeriez avoir? 2. Quel salaire est-ce que vous aimeriez recevoir? 3. Quel film est-ce que vous aimeriez voir ce week-end?**

Video: *Flash culture*

Des passagers attendent un train pendant une grève de la SNCF.

CULTURE À LA LOUPE

Syndicats et grèves en France

Les gens se plaignent° souvent des grèves° en France, mais faire la grève est un droit. Ce sont les grandes grèves historiques qui ont apporté aux Français la majorité des avantages sociaux°: retraite, sécurité sociale, congés payés, instruction publique, etc. Les grèves en France sont accompagnées de manifestations ou de pétitions, et beaucoup d'entre elles ont lieu° en automne, après les vacances d'été. Des grèves peuvent avoir lieu dans tous les secteurs de l'économie, en particulier le secteur des transports et celui° de l'enseignement°. Une grève de la SNCF, par exemple, peut immobiliser tout le pays et causer des ennuis à des millions de voyageurs.

une manifestation de la CGT, un syndicat

Les syndicats organisent les trois quarts° de ces mouvements sociaux. La France est pourtant° le pays industrialisé le moins syndiqué° du monde. En 2009, seulement six à huit pour cent des salariés français étaient syndiqués contre environ° 13% aux États-Unis ou 91% en Suède.

De plus en plus, des non-salariés, comme les médecins et les commerçants, font aussi la grève. Dans ce cas, ils cherchent surtout à faire changer les lois°.

En général, le public soutient° les grévistes, mais il demande aussi la création d'un service minimum obligatoire dans les transports publics et l'enseignement pour éviter la paralysie totale du pays. Ce service minimum obligerait° un petit nombre d'employés à travailler pendant chaque grève. La fréquence des grèves a diminué pendant les années 1970, 1980 et 1990, mais a vu° une certaine augmentation depuis l'année 2000.

Les Français favorables à un service minimum

Dans le ramassage des ordures°	84%
Dans l'enseignement public	79%
Dans les transports aériens	77%
Dans les transports publics	74%

SOURCE: Francoscopie

se plaignent *complain* **grèves** *strikes* **avantages sociaux** *benefits* **ont lieu** *take place* **celui** *the one* **enseignement** *education* **trois quarts** *three quarters* **pourtant** *however* **syndiqué** *unionized* **environ** *around* **faire changer les lois** *have the laws changed* **soutient** *supports* **obligerait** *would force* **a vu** *has seen* **ramassage des ordures** *trash collection*

ACTIVITÉS

1 Répondez Répondez aux questions d'après les textes.

1. Quel est un des droits des Français? Faire la grève est un des droits des Français.
2. Qu'est-ce que la grève a apporté aux Français? Elle leur a apporté des avantages sociaux.
3. Quand ont souvent lieu les grèves? Elles ont souvent lieu en automne.
4. Par qui la majorité des grèves sont-elles organisées? Elles sont organisées par les syndicats.
5. Les travailleurs français sont-ils très syndiqués? Non, la France est le pays industrialisé le moins syndiqué du monde.
6. Combien de travailleurs français étaient syndiqués en 2000? Entre six et huit pour cent des travailleurs étaient syndiqués en 2009.
7. Pourquoi les médecins et les commerçants font-ils la grève? Ils font la grève pour changer les lois.
8. Y a-t-il toujours eu un grand nombre de grèves en France? Non, la fréquence des grèves a diminué pendant les années 1970, 1980 et 1990.
9. Combien de Français sont favorables au service minimum dans l'enseignement public? 79% y sont favorables.
10. À quoi sont favorables 77% des Français? 77% des Français sont favorables à un service minimum dans les transports aériens.

Section Goals

In this section, students will:

- learn about unions and strikes in France
- learn some colloquial terms for talking about money
- learn about paid vacations and holidays in various francophone regions
- read about civil servants in France
- view authentic video footage

NATIONAL STANDARDS connections cultures

Instructional Resources
espaces.vhlcentral.com: Video; WB/VM/LM Answer Key; IRM (Videoscript); activities; downloads; reference tools
Video on DVD

Culture à la loupe

Avant la lecture Have students look at the photo of the people protesting and describe what they see. Ask what they are protesting.

Lecture

- Point out the statistics chart. Ask students what information it shows. (the percentage of French people in favor of minimum service for the sectors listed) Then ask: **Pourquoi pensez-vous que tant de gens veulent un service minimum pour ces secteurs? Pourquoi ces services sont-ils très importants?**
- See **Unité 2 Panorama** on page 67 for more information on the SNCF.

Après la lecture Ask students: **Pourquoi fait-on la grève? Qu'espère-t-on obtenir quand on fait la grève?**

1 Suggestion Have volunteers write the answers to the questions on the board. Then go over the answers with the class.

OPTIONS

Les grèves During a strike, people in France march in large or small numbers, as is true in the United States. The media coverage of participants in a strike is also similar: unions consistently report a higher rate of participation than the police. In France, however, one might see police carrying body shields and using tear gas when large groups assemble to strike.

Small Groups Have students work in groups of three or four. Have them discuss the various options unions have for making their demands known: **la pétition, la grève, la manifestation,** and **le boycott**. Tell them to decide which means they think are the most and least effective and explain why.

LE FRANÇAIS QUOTIDIEN

L'argent

Voici d'autres noms familiers souvent utilisés pour parler de l'argent.

avoine (*f.*)	**oseille (*f.*)**
biffeton (*m.*)	**pépètes (*f., pl.*)**
blé (*m.*)	**pèze (*m.*)**
cash (*m.*)	**pognon (*m.*)**
flouze (*m.*)	**radis (*m.*)**
fric (*m.*)	**rond (*m.*)**
grisbi (*m.*)	**thune (*f.*)**

LE MONDE FRANCOPHONE

La durée des vacances et les jours fériés

Voici la durée des congés payés dans quelques pays francophones.

En Belgique 20 jours après une année de travail, plus 10 jours fériés par an
En France 25 jours et 10 jours fériés par an
Au Luxembourg 25 jours et 12 jours fériés par an
Au Maroc 18 jours par an
Au Québec 10 jours et 8 jours fériés par an
Au Sénégal un minimum de 24 jours par an, plus pour les travailleurs avec ancienneté° et pour les mères de famille
En Suisse 20 jours pour les plus de 20 ans, 25 jours pour les moins de 20 ans
En Tunisie 12 jours par an pour les plus de 20 ans, 18 jours pour les 18-20 ans et 24 jours pour les moins de 18 ans

ancienneté *seniority*

PORTRAIT

Les fonctionnaires

Avec environ six millions de fonctionnaires° dans le pays, ou 21% de la population active°, la France bat des records°. Ces fonctionnaires travaillent pour l'État (dans le gouvernement, les universités, les lycées, les compagnies nationales), pour la fonction publique territoriale (le département, la région) ou pour la fonction publique hospitalière. Ils ont de nombreux avantages: des salaires compétitifs, une bonne retraite et une grande protection de l'emploi. Pour devenir fonctionnaire, il faut passer un concours°. Chaque année, près de 40.000 emplois sont ainsi° ouverts au public.

fonctionnaires *civil servants* **population active** *working population* **bat des records** *breaks records* **concours** *competitive examination* **ainsi** *thus*

SUR INTERNET

Quelle est la durée des congés de maternité et de paternité en France?

Go to **espaces.vhlcentral.com** to find more information related to this **ESPACE CULTURE**. Then watch the corresponding **Flash culture**.

ACTIVITÉS

2 Complétez Donnez une suite logique à chaque phrase.

1. La France bat des records avec... environ six millions de fonctionnaires dans le pays.
2. Les fonctionnaires sont employés par... l'État.
3. Ils bénéficient de nombreux... avantages.
4. On peut devenir fonctionnaire après avoir passé... un concours.
5. Au Sénégal, on a des journées de vacances supplémentaires si on est... travailleur avec ancienneté ou mère de famille.
6. La durée des vacances dépend de l'âge en... Tunisie et en Suisse.

3 La grève Vous êtes journaliste et votre partenaire est un fonctionnaire en grève. Vous allez l'interviewer pour le journal télévisé de 20 heures. Préparez un dialogue où vous cherchez à comprendre pourquoi il ou elle est en grève et depuis combien de temps. Soyez prêts à jouer le dialogue devant la classe.

Practice more at **espaces.vhlcentral.com.**

ressources: VM pp. 295-296 | espaces.vhlcentral.com

Le français quotidien
- Model the pronunciation of each term and have students repeat it.
- Point out that **l'avoine** literally means *oats* and **le blé** means *wheat*.

Portrait
- Point out that the **concours** mentioned here is similar to a civil service exam in the United States.
- Ask students: **Quels sont les avantages des fonctionnaires en France? (des salaires compétitifs, une bonne retraite et une grande protection de l'emploi)**

Le monde francophone
- Explain that the number of days off refers to weekdays.
- Ask students: **Dans quel pays la durée des congés payés est-elle la plus longue? (au Luxembourg)**

2 Expansion Have students create three more items for this activity. Then tell them to exchange papers with a classmate and complete the sentences. Remind them to verify their answers.

3 Suggestion If time is limited, assign this activity as homework, so students can prepare their interview questions or responses. Then allow partners a few minutes to rehearse during the next class before presenting their interviews.

Flash culture Tell students that they will learn more about professions by watching a variety of real-life images narrated by Csilla. Show the video segment without sound and tell students to call out what they see. Then show the video segment again with sound. You can also use the activities in the video manual in class to reinforce this **Flash culture** or assign them as homework.

OPTIONS

Extra Practice Tell students that federal civil service employees in the United States get ten paid holidays per year. Then ask these questions. **1. Quels pays ont le plus de jours fériés? (la Belgique et le Luxembourg) 2. Quelle région a le moins de jours fériés? (le Québec)**

Pairs Have students work in pairs to make a list of the sectors in which civil servants in France work. Also tell them to list some of the occupations these sectors include. Then have them get together with another pair and compare their lists.

NATIONAL STANDARDS comparisons

Section Goals

In this section, students will learn:

- the use of **si** clauses with the conditional
- **si** clauses with the present and **imparfait**

Instructional Resources
*espaces.vhlcentral.com: Lab MP3s; WB/VM/LM Answer Key; IRM (**Essayez!** and **Mise en pratique** answers; Lab Audioscript); activities; downloads; reference tools*

Suggestions

- To help students sort out the possibilities with **si** clauses, make a chart with these headings: Condition, **Si** clause, Main clause. Under the first column, list the three types of **si** clauses introduced in this lesson: *contrary-to-fact, possible or likely*, and *suggestion or wish*. Under the second column, write these three items in order: **si** + [*imperfect*], **si** + [*present*], **si** + [*imperfect*]. Under the third column, write *imperfect, future or near future*, and *N/A*.
- Compare and contrast contrary-to-fact situations (which use the imperfect and the conditional) with events that are possible or likely to occur (which use the present and future) using the example sentences. Check understanding by providing main clauses and having volunteers finish the sentence with a **si** clause. Examples: **Je n'irais pas à Paris… (si je n'avais pas d'argent.) Elle travaillera comme professeur… (si elle obtient son doctorat.)**
- Explain that a **si** clause in the past can also express something that is habitual in the past. Example: **Si mon amie m'invitait à une fête, j'y allais toujours.**
- Point out that **si** and **il/ils** contract to become **s'il** and **s'ils**, respectively.

Essayez! Have students change the sentences from a contrary-to-fact situation to a possible or likely situation, and vice versa. Example: **1. Si on visite la Tunisie, on ira admirer les ruines.**

13B.1 *Si* clauses

Point de départ **Si** (*If*) clauses describe a condition or event upon which another condition or event depends. Sentences with **si** clauses consist of a **si** clause and a main (or result) clause.

Si je faisais cette robe, elle serait laide.

- **Si** clauses can speculate or hypothesize about a current event or condition. They express what *would happen* if an event or condition *were to occur*. This is called a contrary-to-fact situation. In such instances, the verb in the **si** clause is in the **imparfait** while the verb in the main clause is in the conditional.

Si j'**étais** au chômage, je lui **enverrais** mon CV.
If I were unemployed, I'd send her my résumé.

Vous **partiriez** souvent en vacances si vous **aviez** de l'argent.
You would go on vacation often if you had money.

- **Si** clauses can also express conditions or events that are possible or likely to occur. In such instances, the **si** clause is in the present while the main clause uses the **futur** or **futur proche**.

Si le patron me **renvoie**, je **trouverai** un emploi à mi-temps.
If the boss fires me, I'll find a part-time job.

Si vous ne **signez** pas le contrat, vous **allez perdre** votre poste.
If you don't sign the contract, you're going to lose your job.

- Use a **si** clause alone with the **imparfait** to make a suggestion or to express a wish.

Si nous **faisions** des projets pour le week-end?
What about making plans for the weekend?

Ah! S'il **obtenait** un meilleur emploi!
Oh! If only he got a better job!

Essayez! **Complétez les phrases avec la forme correcte des verbes.**

1. Si on __visitait__ (visiter) la Tunisie, on irait admirer les ruines.
2. Vous __serez__ (être) plus heureux si vous faites vos devoirs.
3. Si tu __as__ (avoir) la grippe, tu devras aller chez le médecin.
4. S'ils __avaient__ (avoir) un million d'euros, que feraient-ils?
5. Mes parents me __rendront__ (rendre) visite ce week-end s'ils ont le temps.
6. J'__écrirais__ (écrire) au conseiller si j'avais son adresse.

MISE EN PRATIQUE

1 Questions **Vous cherchez un emploi. Indiquez vos réponses aux questions du chef du personnel.**

MODÈLE Quand est-ce que vous pourriez commencer? (vous / avoir besoin de moi / je / pouvoir commencer demain)
Si vous aviez besoin de moi, je pourrais commencer demain.

1. Est-ce que vous aimeriez travailler à plein temps? (vous / offrir un travail à plein temps / je / l'accepter)
   Si vous m'offriez un travail à plein temps, je l'accepterais.
2. Auriez-vous besoin d'une assurance-vie? (je / en avoir besoin / je / vous le dire)
   Si j'en avais besoin d'une, je vous le dirais.
3. Quand prendriez-vous un congé? (mon/ma petite ami(e) / prendre un congé / nous / partir en mai)
   Si mon/ma petit(e) ami(e) prenait un congé, nous partirions en mai.
4. Voudriez-vous devenir cadre un jour? (vous / le permettre / je / devenir cadre dans deux ans)
   Si vous le permettiez, je deviendrais cadre dans deux ans.
5. Quand rentreriez-vous le soir? (nous / devoir travailler très tard / je / rentrer vers minuit)
   Si nous devions travailler très tard, je rentrerais vers minuit.

2 Et si... **D'abord, complétez les questions. Ensuite, employez le conditionnel pour y répondre. Comparez vos réponses aux réponses d'un(e) partenaire.** Answers will vary.

MODÈLE Que ferais-tu si... tu / être malade?
Que ferais-tu si tu étais malade? Si j'étais malade, je dormirais toute la journée.

Situation 1: Que ferais-tu si...

1. tu / être fatigué(e)? ... si tu étais fatigué(e)?
2. il / pleuvoir? ... s'il pleuvait?
3. il / faire beau? ... s'il faisait beau?

Situation 2: Que feraient tes parents si...

1. tu / quitter l'université? ... si tu quittais l'université?
2. tu / choisir de devenir avocat(e)? ... si tu choisissais de devenir avocat(e)?
3. tu / partir habiter en France? ... si tu partais habiter en France?

3 Des réactions **À tour de rôle avec un(e) partenaire, dites ce que (*what*) vous ferez dans ces circonstances.** Answers will vary.

MODÈLE Vous trouvez votre petit(e) ami(e) avec un(e) autre garçon/fille.
Si je trouve mon petit ami..., je ne lui parlerai plus.

1. Vous n'avez pas de devoirs ce week-end.
2. Votre ami(e) organise une fête sans rien vous dire.
3. Vos parents ne vous téléphonent pas pendant un mois.
4. Le prof de français vous donne une mauvaise note.
5. Vous tombez malade.

Practice more at **espaces.vhlcentral.com.**

OPTIONS

Video Replay the video episode, having students focus on **si** clauses. Ask students to write each one down as they hear it. Afterward, have them compare their notes in groups of four.

Extra Practice Ask each student to write a question that contains a **si** clause. Then have students walk around the room until you signal them to stop. On your cue, each student should turn to the nearest classmate. Give students three minutes to ask and answer one another's question before having them begin walking around the room again. Each time you say "stop," students should ask a new partner their question.

COMMUNICATION

4 L'imagination Par groupes de trois, choisissez un de ces sujets et préparez un paragraphe par écrit. Ensuite, lisez votre paragraphe à la classe. Vos camarades décideront quel groupe est le gagnant (*winner*). Answers will vary.

- Si je pouvais devenir invisible, ...
- Si j'étais un extraterrestre à New York, ...
- Si j'inventais une machine, ...
- Si j'étais une célébrité, ...
- Si nous pouvions prendre des vacances sur Mars, ...

5 Le portefeuille Vos camarades de classe trouvent un portefeuille (*wallet*) plein d'argent. Par groupes de quatre, parlez avec un(e) de vos camarades pour deviner ce que (*what*) feraient les deux autres. Ensuite, rejoignez-les pour comparer vos prédictions. Answers will vary.

MODÈLE

Étudiant(e) 1: *Si vous trouviez le portefeuille, vous le rendriez à la police.*
Étudiant(e) 2: *Oui, mais nous garderions l'argent pour aller dans un bon restaurant.*

6 Interview Par groupes de trois, préparez cinq questions pour un(e) candidat(e) à la présidence des États-Unis. Ensuite, jouez les rôles de l'interviewer et du/de la candidat(e). Alternez les rôles. Answers will vary.

MODÈLE

Étudiant(e) 1: *Que feriez-vous au sujet du sexisme dans l'armée?*
Étudiant(e) 2: *Alors, si j'étais président(e), nous...*

Le français vivant

Viendriez-vous nous consulter si vous cherchiez une hôtesse?
Que trouveriez-vous si vous parliez à une autre entreprise?
Une hôtesse d'accueil ou une hôtesse de l'air? Vous voudriez une hôtesse compétente, non?
VediorBis
Si vous parlez à quelqu'un d'autre, vous risquerez beaucoup.

Identifiez Combien de phrases avec **si** trouvez-vous dans cette publicité (*ad*)? Lesquelles? Three: 1. Viendriez-vous nous consulter si vous cherchiez une hôtesse? 2. Que trouveriez-vous si vous parliez à une autre entreprise? 3. Si vous parlez à quelqu'un d'autre, vous risquerez beaucoup.

Questions À tour de rôle, avec un(e) partenaire, posez-vous ces questions. Answers will vary.

1. Pourquoi irait-on chez VediorBis?
2. Quelle erreur pourrait-on éviter?
3. Comment font les conseillers de VediorBis pour trouver l'emploi et l'employé(e) idéal(e) pour tous leurs clients?
4. Irais-tu consulter VediorBis si tu étais au chômage? Pourquoi?

1 Expansion Have students come up with three more questions for their **chef du personnel**. Then have students swap their questions with their classmates and answer their questions using **si** clauses.

2 Expansion Write more situations like those in the activity. Example: **Situation 3: Que feriez-vous si... 1. vous / gagner à la loterie? 2. le club de français / propose un voyage en France? 3. le professeur de français / être malade?**

3 Suggestion Organize the class into two groups: **si + le présent** and **si + l'imparfait**. Have each group complete the activity using the tenses according to their groups. Then discuss the different meanings of the sentences produced by each group.

4 Suggestion Before assigning this activity, write **Si nous pouvions prédire** (*predict*) **l'avenir...** on the board. Brainstorm possible main clauses with the whole class.

5 Expansion Have groups of four brainstorm other moral dilemmas using **Que feraient vos camarades de classe si...** Example: **...s'ils trouvaient les réponses de l'examen de français.**

6 Suggestions
- You may wish to have students pick a different prominent politician that interests them.
- Videotape the interviews and show parts during the next class or check out the tape to students for viewing out of class.

Le français vivant Call on a volunteer to read the ad aloud. Have students point out all the instances of the conditional.

OPTIONS

Pairs Ask students to reflect on their French study habits. Then assign them partners to write a list of eight complex sentences to express what they could do better. Example: **Si je lisais un journal français tous les jours, je pourrais mieux comprendre la langue.**

Small Groups Ask students to bring in the most outlandish news report they can find. In groups of four, have students write a list of statements that use **si** clauses about each report. Example: **Si les extraterrestres venaient à Washington, D.C. pour avoir un rendez-vous avec le président des États-Unis...**

Section Goals

In this section, students will learn the relative pronouns **qui**, **que**, **dont**, and **où**.

Instructional Resources
*espaces.vhlcentral.com: Lab MP3s; WB/VM/LM Answer Key; IRM (**Essayez!** and **Mise en pratique** answers; Lab Audioscript); activities; downloads; reference tools*

Suggestions

- Give an example of an optional relative pronoun in English. *The movie (that) we just watched was very sad.* Emphasize to students that relative pronouns are required in French. Example: **Le film que nous venons de regarder était très triste.**
- Explain that **que** can refer to both people and things. Example: **Le chanteur que tu écoutes est très populaire.**
- Point out that the relative pronoun **qui** is always followed by a conjugated verb. **Qui** acts as the subject. **Qui** can also refer to people or things. Example: **Le stylo (qui est) sur la table est vert.**
- Emphasize that, although the interrogative word **où?** means *where?*, the relative pronoun **où** can also be translated as *when* or *in which*.
- Point out that any expression with **de** can use **dont: avoir besoin de, avoir peur de, parler de, rêver de,** etc. Example: **C'est le voyage dont je rêvais.**

13B.2 Relative pronouns *qui, que, dont, où*

NATIONAL comparisons STANDARDS

Point de départ Relative pronouns link two phrases together into a longer, more complex sentence. The second phrase gives additional information about the first phrase. In English, relative pronouns can sometimes be omitted, but the relative pronoun in French cannot be.

Je suis allé voir **le docteur**.
I went to see the doctor.

Tu m'as parlé de **ce docteur**.
You talked to me about this doctor.

Je suis allé voir le docteur **dont** tu m'as parlé.
I went to see the doctor that you talked to me about.

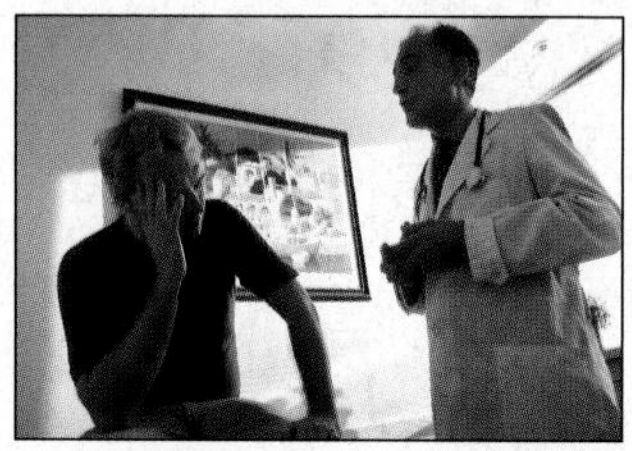

Relative pronouns

qui	*who, that, which*	dont	*of which, of whom*
que	*that, which*	où	*where*

- Use **qui** if an element of the first phrase is the subject of the second phrase.

ELEMENT — Il a renvoyé **la comptable**.
He dismissed the accountant.

SUBJECT — **La comptable** travaillait à mi-temps.
The accountant worked part-time.

Il a renvoyé la comptable **qui** travaillait à mi-temps.
He dismissed the accountant who was working part-time.

ELEMENT — **Le café** est bon.
The café is good.

SUBJECT — **Le café** se trouve près de la fac.
The café is near the university.

Le café **qui** se trouve près de la fac est bon.
The café that is near the university is good.

MISE EN PRATIQUE

1 Notre entreprise Sophie et Thierry discutent de leur bureau et de leurs collègues. Complétez leurs phrases en utilisant (*by using*) les pronoms relatifs **qui, que, dont** ou **où**.

MODÈLE Ils ont une cafétéria *qui* n'est pas trop chère.

1. C'est une entreprise __où__ les employés peuvent suivre des formations supplémentaires.
2. Nous avons une profession __qui__ est exigeante.
3. Notre chef d'entreprise a commandé les nouveaux ordinateurs __dont__ nous avions besoin.
4. La personne __qui__ a un entretien aujourd'hui est l'ami du gérant.
5. La réunion __que__ tu as ratée (*missed*) hier était vraiment intéressante.
6. La femme __dont__ tu as peur est notre chef du personnel, n'est-ce pas?
7. L'homme __qu'__ on a embauché est le mari de Sandra.
8. Tu te souviens du jour __où__ on a fait la connaissance du patron?

2 Les villageois Isabelle vient de déménager dans un petit village et son agent immobilier lui parle des gens qui y habitent. Assemblez les deux phrases avec **qui, que, dont** ou **où** pour en faire une seule.

1. Voici le bureau de M. Dantès. Vous pouvez vous adresser à ce bureau pour obtenir une assurance-vie. Voici le bureau de M. Dantès où vous pouvez vous adresser pour obtenir une assurance-vie.
2. Je vous ai parlé d'une banquière. La banquière s'appelle Murielle Marteau. La banquière dont je vous ai parlé s'appelle Murielle Marteau.
3. Vous avez vu la grande boutique. M. Descartes est le patron de cette boutique. M. Descartes est le patron de la grande boutique que vous avez vue.
4. Je ne connais pas le pompier. Le pompier habite en face de chez vous. Je ne connais pas le pompier qui habite en face de chez vous.
5. Madame Thibaut sert beaucoup de plats régionaux. Vous allez adorer ces plats. Madame Thibaut sert beaucoup de plats régionaux que vous allez adorer.
6. Les cuisinières travaillent à temps partiel. Vous avez rencontré les cuisinières chez moi. Les cuisinières que vous avez rencontrées chez moi travaillent à temps partiel.

3 Les choses que je préfère Marianne parle des choses qu'elle préfère. À tour de rôle avec un(e) partenaire, utilisez les pronoms relatifs pour écrire ses phrases. Présentez vos phrases à la classe. Answers will vary.

1. Marc est l'ami... (qui, dont)
2. «Chez Henri», c'est le restaurant... (où, que)
3. Ce CD est le cadeau... (que, qui)
4. Ma sœur est la personne... (dont, que)

Practice more at **espaces.vhlcentral.com.**

OPTIONS

Video Replay the video episode, having students focus on relative pronouns. Have students divide their paper into two columns: **qui** and **que**. Ask them to write down each example they hear under its appropriate column. Then form groups of three and have students compare their papers.

Extra Practice Have students make complete sentences with phrases like the following. **1. Le tennis est un sport que... 2. Le tennis est un sport qui... 3. Gwyneth Paltrow est une actrice que... 4. Gwyneth Paltrow est une actrice qui... 5. *Le fabuleux destin d'Amélie Poulain*** (*Amélie*) **est un film que... 6. *Amélie* est un film qui...**

COMMUNICATION

4 Des opinions Avec un(e) partenaire, donnez votre opinion sur ces thèmes. Utilisez les pronoms relatifs **qui, que, dont** et **où.** Answers will vary.

MODÈLE

le printemps / saison
Étudiant(e) 1: *Le printemps est la saison que je préfère parce que j'aime les fleurs.*
Étudiant(e) 2: *L'hiver est la saison que je préfère, parce que j'aime la neige.*

1. le petit-déjeuner / repas
2. surfer sur Internet / passe-temps
3. mon/ma camarade de chambre / personne
4. le samedi / jour
5. la chimie / cours
6. la France / pays
7. Tom Cruise / acteur
8. le prof de français / prof

5 Des endroits intéressants Par groupes de trois, organisez un voyage. Parlez des endroits qui vous intéressent et expliquez pourquoi vous voulez y aller. Utilisez des pronoms relatifs dans vos réponses et décidez où vous allez. Answers will vary.

MODÈLE

Allons à Bruxelles où nous pouvons acheter des chocolats délicieux.

6 Chère Madame Avec un(e) partenaire, écrivez un e-mail à votre gérante dans lequel (*in which*) vous expliquez pourquoi vous n'avez pas fini le document qu'elle voulait pour la réunion. Utilisez des pronoms relatifs dans votre e-mail. Answers will vary.

De: clement@entreprise.fr
À: madame.giraud@entreprise.fr
Objet: Document

Chère Madame Giraud,

Je suis désolé, mais je n'ai pas fini le document que vous vouliez aujourd'hui. Ce matin, je suis allé à l'entreprise François et Fils où...

- Use **que** if an element of the first phrase is the direct object of the second. The past participle following **que** agrees in number and gender with the direct object.

ELEMENT	DIRECT OBJECT
Le banquier a deux **voitures** bleues. *The banker has two blue cars.*	Il a acheté **les voitures** hier. *He bought the cars yesterday.*

Le banquier a deux voitures bleues **qu'**il a achetées hier.
The banker has two blue cars that he bought yesterday.

ELEMENT	DIRECT OBJECT
Samir est à côté de **la porte**. *Samir is by the door.*	Nicole lui a ouvert **la porte**. *Nicole opened the door for him.*

Samir est à côté de la porte **que** Nicole lui a ouverte.
Samir is by the door (that) Nicole opened for him.

- Use **dont**, meaning *that* or *of which*, to replace an element in the first phrase that is the object of the preposition **de** in the second phrase.

ELEMENT	OBJECT OF PREPOSITION DE
Stéphane est **pompier**. *Stéphane is a firefighter.*	Tu m'as parlé de **ce pompier**. *You talked to me about this firefighter.*

Stéphane est le pompier **dont** tu m'as parlé?
Is Stéphane the firefighter (that) you talked to me about?

- Use **où**, meaning *where*, *when*, or *in which*, if an element of the first phrase is a place or a period of time.

ELEMENT	PERIOD OF TIME
Venez me parler à **ce moment-là**. *Come speak with me at that moment.*	Vous arrivez à **ce moment-là**. *You arrive at that moment.*

Venez me parler au moment **où** vous arrivez.
Come speak with me at the moment (that) you arrive.

Essayez! **Complétez les phrases avec qui, que, dont, où.**

1. La France est le pays __que__ j'aime le plus.
2. Tu te souviens du jour __où__ tu as fait ma connaissance?
3. M. Valois est le gérant __dont__ mon employé m'a parlé.
4. C'est la voiture __que__ vous avez louée?
5. Voici l'enveloppe __dont__ tu as besoin.
6. Vous connaissez le plombier __qui__ a réparé le lavabo chez Lucas?
7. On passe devant la fac __où__ j'ai fait mes études.
8. Je reconnais le chauffeur de taxi __qui__ a conduit Lucie à l'hôtel.

Essayez! Ask volunteers to create questions or answers that correspond to the sentences in the activity. Example: **1. Quel est le pays que tu aimes le plus?**

1 Suggestion Ask a volunteer to read the **modèle** aloud. Ask another volunteer to explain the use of the relative pronoun in that example. (The answer is **qui** because it is a subject followed by the verb **est.**)

2 Expansion Have pairs write two or more sentences that contain relative pronouns and refer to other people in the village where Isabelle has moved.

3 Expansion Expand the activity by asking students to talk about what they prefer. Have them model their sentences on Marianne's.

4 Expansion In addition to **surfer sur Internet** from #2, brainstorm a list of pastimes with the class. Conduct a conversation with the whole class about which pastimes they prefer and why.

5 Expansion Using magazine or real pictures, have students create a brief travel ad for the destination they chose. The ad should contain at least three uses of relative pronouns. Have students present their ads to the class.

6 Suggestion Do this activity orally, having pairs role-play the manager and the employee talking on the phone.

OPTIONS

Game Ask students to bring in some interesting pictures from magazines or the Internet, but tell them not to show these photos to one another. Divide the class into groups of three. Each group should pick a picture. One student will write an accurate description of it, and the others will write imaginary descriptions. Tell them to use relative pronouns in the descriptions. Each group will read its three descriptions aloud without showing the picture. Give the rest of the class two minutes to ask questions about the descriptions before guessing which is the accurate description. Award one point for a correct guess and two points to a team that fools the class.

Instructional Resources
espaces.vhlcentral.com: Testing Program, pp. 101–104; Test Files; Testing Program MP3s; activities; downloads; reference tools
Test Generator

1 Suggestion Have volunteers share their list with the class.

2 Expansion Ask groups to choose a **métier** not listed in the activity. Then have them write a short paragraph describing what they would and would not do in that position. Have one volunteer from each group read the group's paragraph aloud.

3 Suggestion Point out that this activity elicits sentences that are contrary to fact. Remind students that their sentences should include the conditional tense in the main clause and the imperfect tense in the **si** clause.

4 Suggestion Before assigning the activity, identify the genre of each film. ***Le dernier métro***: drama / ***Les visiteurs***: comedy, sci-fi / ***Toto le héros***: comedy, drama / ***La chèvre***: comedy / ***L'argent de poche***: documentary-style portrait / ***Le professionnel***: action, thriller

5 Suggestion Before assigning the activity, ask the class polite questions using **pouvoir** in the conditional tense. Examples: **Pourriez-vous me prêter votre livre? Pourrais-je vous poser une question? Pourriez-vous m'expliquer...?**

6 Expansion Before assigning the activity, encourage students to brainstorm ideas for different people and places in the office that they are going to ask questions about.

NATIONAL communication STANDARDS

Révision

1 Du changement Avec un(e) partenaire, observez ces bureaux. Faites une liste d'au minimum huit changements que les employés feraient s'ils en avaient les moyens (*means*). Answers will vary.

MODÈLE

Étudiant(e) 1: *Si ces gens pouvaient changer quelque chose, ils achèteraient de nouveaux ordinateurs.*
Étudiant(e) 2: *Si les affaires allaient mieux, ils déménageraient.*

2 Si j'étais... Par groupes de quatre, discutez et faites votre propre (*own*) portrait à travers (*through*) ces métiers. Utilisez la phrase **Si j'étais...** Comparez vos réponses et présentez le portrait d'un(e) camarade à la classe. Answers will vary.

MODÈLE

Étudiant(e) 1: *Si j'étais cuisinier/cuisinière, je ne préparerais que des desserts.*
Étudiant(e) 2: *Si je travaillais comme chauffeur, je ne conduirais que sur autoroute.*

artiste	conseiller/ conseillère	médecin
chauffeur	cuisinier/cuisinière	patron(ne)
chef d'entreprise	femme au foyer	professeur
chercheur/chercheuse		

3 Je démissionnerais... Pour quelles raisons seriez-vous prêt(e)s à démissionner de votre travail? Par groupes de trois, donnez chacun(e) (*each one*) au minimum deux raisons positives et deux raisons négatives. Answers will vary.

MODÈLE

Étudiant(e) 1: *Je démissionnerais si je devais suivre ma famille et déménager loin.*
Étudiant(e) 2: *Moi, je démissionnerais tout de suite si je m'ennuyais dans mon travail.*

4 C'est l'histoire de... Avec un(e) partenaire, commentez ces titres de films français et imaginez les histoires. Utilisez des pronoms relatifs. Ensuite, comparez vos histoires avec les histoires d'un autre groupe. Qui a l'histoire la plus proche (*closest*) du vrai film? Answers will vary.

MODÈLE

Étudiant(e) 1: *C'est l'histoire d'un homme qui...*
Étudiant(e) 2: *... et que la police recherche...*

- *Le dernier métro*
- *Les visiteurs*
- *Toto le héros*
- *La chèvre* (goat)
- *L'argent de poche* (pocket)
- *Le professionnel*

5 Un(e) patron(ne) poli(e) Avec un(e) partenaire, inventez un dialogue entre un(e) patron(ne) et son/sa secrétaire. Le/La patron(ne) demande plusieurs services au/à la secrétaire, qui refuse. Le/La patron(ne) recommence alors ses demandes, mais plus poliment, et le/la secrétaire accepte. Answers will vary.

MODÈLE

Étudiant(e) 1: *Apportez-moi le téléphone!*
Étudiant(e) 2: *Si vous me parlez comme ça, je ne vous apporterai rien.*
Étudiant(e) 1: *Pourriez-vous m'apporter le téléphone, s'il vous plaît?*
Étudiant(e) 2: *Avec plaisir!*

6 Il y a longtemps! Au bout de (*After*) cinq ans, vous retournez dans la ville où vous avez travaillé(e) et vous déjeunez avec un(e) ancien(ne) collègue. Jouez cette scène avec un(e) partenaire. Vous posez des questions à propos d'autres (*about other*) collègues du bureau. Utilisez autant de (*as many*) pronoms relatifs que possible dans votre dialogue. Answers will vary.

MODÈLE

Étudiant(e) 1: *Est-ce que la fille qui faisait un stage travaille toujours avec Paul?*
Étudiant(e) 2: *Ah non! La fille dont tu parles a quitté l'entreprise.*

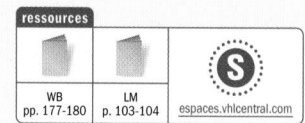

ressources
WB pp. 177-180 | LM p. 103-104 | espaces.vhlcentral.com

OPTIONS

Extra Practice Ask students to finish the following sentences logically: **1. S'il ne pleut pas demain... 2. Si j'avais assez d'argent... 3. Si mon/ma petit(e) ami(e) gagnait à la loterie... 4. Si j'étais psychologue... 5. S'il faisait beau...** Encourage them to be creative.

Pairs Have pairs write ten sentences about what they would do to improve their campus. First, ask them to list the problems they would change and how they would do so. Then have them form their sentences as contrary-to-fact statements. Example: **S'il y avait plus d'aides financières, les étudiants n'auraient pas de prêts étudiants** (*student loans*).

À l'écoute

NATIONAL communication STANDARDS

Audio: Activities

STRATÉGIE

Using background knowledge/ Listening for specific information

If you know the subject of something you are going to listen to, your background knowledge will help you anticipate words and phrases you are going to hear. It will also help you determine important information that you should listen for.

To practice these strategies, you will listen to a radio advertisement for a culinary school. Before you listen, make a list of the things you expect the advertisement to contain. Make another list of information you would listen for if you were considering this school. After listening, look at your lists. Did they help you anticipate the content of the advertisement and focus on key information?

Préparation

Dans la conversation que vous allez entendre, un homme passe un entretien pour obtenir un nouvel emploi. De quoi cet homme et le chef du personnel discuteront-ils pendant l'entretien? Faites une liste des choses dont ils parleront probablement.

À vous d'écouter

Écoutez la conversation. Après une deuxième écoute, complétez les notes du chef du personnel.

Nom: Patrick Martin
Emploi demandé: chercheur en biologie
Diplôme en: biologie
Expérience professionnelle:
- stage (chercheur) au Laboratoire Roche
- Chercheur dans une entreprise de médicaments
- Emploi à mi-temps à l'Hôpital Saint-Jean
- Cherche un emploi à: plein temps

Practice more at **espaces.vhlcentral.com.**

Compréhension

Répondez Répondez aux questions d'après la conversation par des phrases complètes. Answers may vary slightly.

1. Le chef du personnel est-il un homme ou une femme?
   C'est une femme.
2. Patrick a-t-il envoyé son CV avant d'aller à l'entretien?
   Oui, il l'a envoyé.
3. Pourquoi ne travaille-t-il plus pour l'entreprise de médicaments?
   Il a perdu son emploi.
4. Où devra-t-il voyager s'il est choisi pour l'emploi de chercheur?
   Il devra voyager à l'étranger.
5. Est-il d'accord pour voyager? Pourquoi?
   Oui. Il est d'accord parce qu'il aime beaucoup voyager.
6. D'après le chef du personnel, l'emploi de chercheur est-il facile?
   Non, c'est un travail exigeant.
7. Quels sont deux des avantages (*benefits*) qu'on proposera à Patrick s'il est choisi pour l'emploi?
   Possible answer: On lui proposera un bon salaire et la possibilité de souvent avoir des promotions.
8. Quand Patrick commencera-t-il à travailler si on l'embauche pour cet emploi?
   Il commencera à travailler le mois prochain.

Une lettre de candidature Vous allez chercher un stage d'été dans une entreprise en France ou dans un autre pays francophone. Préparez une lettre dans laquelle vous expliquez au chef du personnel quel genre de stage vous intéresse et pourquoi vous voulez faire un stage dans cette entreprise. Parlez aussi de votre formation et de votre expérience professionnelle et expliquez comment ce stage sera utile à votre future carrière.

Section Goals

In this section, students will:
- learn to use background knowledge and listen for specific information
- listen to a radio advertisement for a culinary school
- listen to a job interview and complete several activities

Instructional Resources
espaces.vhlcentral.com: Textbook MP3s; IRM (Textbook Audioscript); downloads; reference tools

Stratégie
Script Envie d'une nouvelle carrière? Notre école propose une formation exceptionnelle de cuisinier. Pendant deux ans, nos étudiants suivent des cours trois jours par semaine et les deux autres jours, ils font des stages dans de nombreux restaurants parisiens. Avec leur diplôme, tous nos étudiants trouvent un emploi bien payé, très facilement. N'hésitez pas, appelez l'École de Cuisine Rochefort au 01.42.34.67.90 pour plus d'informations.

À vous d'écouter
Script CHEF DU PERSONNEL: Bonjour, Monsieur Martin. Entrez.
M. MARTIN: Bonjour, Madame.
C: Alors, voyons... C'est l'emploi de chercheur en biologie qui vous intéresse, c'est bien cela?
M: Oui, Madame, c'est exact.
C: Et vous avez une maîtrise en biologie. Avez-vous déjà de l'expérience professionnelle dans ce domaine?
M: Oui, après mon diplôme, j'ai fait un stage de six mois au Laboratoire Roche pendant lequel j'ai travaillé comme chercheur. Ensuite, j'ai encore travaillé comme chercheur pour une entreprise de médicaments, mais malheureusement, j'ai perdu mon emploi.
C: Et depuis, vous travaillez à l'Hôpital Saint-Jean?
M: Oui, j'ai été embauché en mars, mais ce travail est un emploi à mi-temps et je désire travailler à plein temps. C'est pour cette raison que je vous ai envoyé mon CV.
C: Ah, d'accord... Si vous êtes choisi, vous devrez voyager à l'étranger deux fois par mois, parce que nous avons des bureaux dans plusieurs pays d'Europe. Est-ce que cela vous posera des problèmes?

M: Non, pas du tout. Je suis prêt à aller à l'étranger quand cela sera nécessaire et j'aime beaucoup voyager.
C: Très bien. Vous savez, ce poste est très exigeant, mais si vous êtes travailleur, vous aurez la possibilité d'obtenir des promotions et vous serez très bien payé. Bien sûr, vous aurez cinq semaines de congés payés et la mutuelle de l'entreprise. Notre compagnie offre en plus la possibilité d'avoir une augmentation de salaire tous les six mois.
Avez-vous des questions?
M: Oui. Si je suis choisi, quand est-ce que je commencerai?
C: Le mois prochain. Je vous contacterai dans la semaine si vous êtes choisi.
M: Bon. Merci, Madame. Au revoir.
C: Au revoir.

Section Goals

In this section, students will learn historical, geographical, and cultural information about Algeria, Morocco, and Tunisia.

Instructional Resources
espaces.vhlcentral.com: Transparency #56; WB/VM/LM Answer Key; activities; downloads; reference tools

Carte du Maroc, de la Tunisie et de l'Algérie

- Have students look at the map or use **Transparency #56**. Ask volunteers to read the names of the cities and geographical features aloud.
- Ask students to name the countries that border Algeria, Morroco, and Tunisia.
- Point out that Douz (see photo) is an oasis on the edge of the Sahara Desert.

Le pays en chiffres

- Point out the flags. Ask students what elements these flags have in common. Then explain that the crescent, star, and color green are traditional symbols of Islam.
- Point out that Morocco is a kingdom.
- Have volunteers read the sections aloud. After each section, ask students questions about the content.
- Have students compare the size and population of the countries. Then ask them to guess why Algeria's population is smaller in relation to its size than the other countries. (The southern region is sparsely populated due to the harsh conditions of the Sahara Desert.)
- Ask students: **Où est la mosquée Hassan II? (à Casablanca)** Then point out that approximately 98% of the population in these countries is Muslim.

Incroyable mais vrai! The word *Sahara* comes from *Sahra'*, which means *desert* in Arabic. In reality, the Sahara is not one desert but many deserts. It encompasses 3.5 million square miles and extends over portions of 11 countries.

connections cultures NATIONAL STANDARDS

Interactive Map Reading

Panorama

le marché de Douz, en Tunisie

L'Algérie

Le pays en chiffres

- **Superficie:** *2.381.741 km²*
- **Population:** *38.100.000*
  SOURCE: Population Division, UN Secretariat
- **Industries principales:** *agriculture, gaz naturel, pétrole°*
- **Ville capitale:** *Alger* ▶ **Monnaie:** *dinar algérien*
- **Langues:** *arabe, français, tamazight*

Le Maroc

Le pays en chiffres

- **Superficie:** *446.550 km²*
- **Population:** *36.150.000*
- **Industries principales:** *agriculture, tourisme*
- **Ville capitale:** *Rabat* ▶ **Monnaie:** *dirham*
- **Langues:** *arabe, français*

La Tunisie

Le pays en chiffres

- **Superficie:** *163.610 km²*
- **Population:** *11.140.000*
- **Industries principales:** *agriculture, tourisme*
- **Ville capitale:** *Tunis* ▶ **Monnaie:** *dinar tunisien*
- **Langues:** *arabe, français*

Personnes célèbres

- **Juliette Smája-Zerah,** *Tunisie, première avocate de Tunisie (1890–1973)*
- **Saïd Aouita,** *Maroc, coureur de fond° (1959–)*

- **Khaled,** *Algérie, chanteur (1960–)*

pétrole *oil* **coureur de fond** *long-distance runner* **Grâce aux** *Thanks to* **sources** *springs* **sable** *sand* **faire pousser** *grow* **En plein milieu** *Right in the middle*

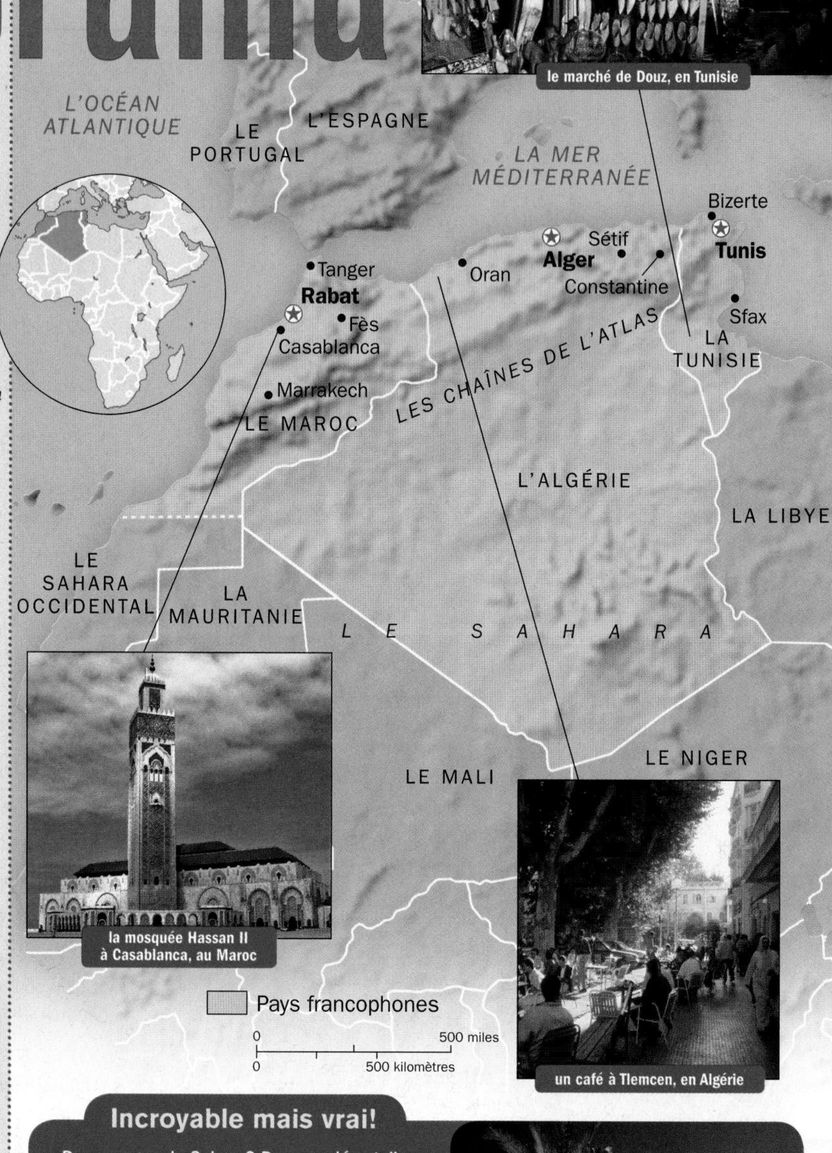

la mosquée Hassan II à Casablanca, au Maroc

un café à Tlemcen, en Algérie

Incroyable mais vrai!

Des oranges du Sahara? Dans ce désert, il ne tombe que 12 cm de pluie par an. Grâce aux° sources° et aux rivières sous le sable°, les Sahariens ont développé un système d'irrigation pour faire pousser° des fruits et des légumes dans les oasis. En plein milieu° du désert, on peut trouver des tomates, des abricots ou des oranges!

OPTIONS

Personnes célèbres **Khaled** has become one of the most popular singers of rai music. His fame spread from North Africa to France to other countries in Europe. **Idir**, another famous singer from Algeria, uses his talent to promote Tamazight, the Berber people's language and culture. **Saïd Aouita** won an Olympic gold medal in the 5000 meter in 1984, a bronze medal in the 800 meter in 1988, as well as world championships.

Les Berbères The Berbers are an indigenous nomadic people of the Maghreb region who live mainly in the mountains. At **le festival du Sahara de Douz** one can observe the arts and traditions of the Berbers. There are shows, dances, music, traditional marriage ceremonies, a horse race, and an endurance race on camelback in the desert.

Les régions

Le Maghreb

La région du Maghreb, en Afrique du Nord, se compose° du Maroc, de l'Algérie et de la Tunisie. Envahis° aux 7e et 8e siècles par les Arabes, les trois pays deviennent plus tard des colonies françaises avant de retrouver leur indépendance dans les années 1950–1960. La population du Maghreb est composée d'Arabes, d'Européens et de Berbères, les premiers résidents de l'Afrique du Nord. Le Grand Maghreb inclut ces trois pays, plus la Libye et la Mauritanie. En 1989, les cinq pays ont formé l'Union du Maghreb Arabe dans l'espoir° de créer une union politique et économique.

Les arts

Assia Djebar (1936–)

Lauréate de nombreux prix littéraires et cinématographiques, Assia Djebar fait partie des écrivains et cinéastes algériens les plus talentueux. Dans ses œuvres°, Djebar présente le point de vue° féminin avec l'intention de donner une voix° aux femmes algériennes. *La Soif*, son premier roman°, sort en 1957. C'est plus tard, pendant qu'elle enseigne l'histoire à l'Université d'Alger, qu'elle devient cinéaste et sort son premier film, *La Nouba des femmes du Mont Chenoua*, en 1979. Le film reçoit le prix de la critique internationale au festival du film de Venise. En 2005, Assia Djebar est élue° à l'Académie française.

Les destinations

Marrakech

La ville de Marrakech, fondée en 1062, est un grand symbole du Maroc médiéval. Sa médina, ou vieille ville, est entourée° de fortifications et fermée aux automobiles. On y trouve la mosquée de Kutubiyya et la place Djema'a el-Fna. La mosquée est le joyau° architectural de la ville, et la place Djema'a el-Fna est la plus active de toute l'Afrique à tout moment de la journée, avec ses nombreux artistes et vendeurs. La médina a aussi le plus grand souk (grand marché couvert°) du Maroc, où toutes sortes d'objets sont proposés, au milieu de délicieuses odeurs de thé à la menthe°, d'épices et de pâtisseries au miel°.

Les traditions

Les hammams

Inventés par les Romains et adoptés par les Arabes, les hammams, ou «bains turcs», sont très nombreux et populaires en Afrique du Nord. Ce sont des bains de vapeur° composés de plusieurs pièces—souvent trois—où la chaleur est plus ou moins forte. L'architecture des hammams varie d'un endroit à un autre, mais ces bains de vapeur servent tous de lieux où se laver et de centres sociaux très importants dans la culture régionale. Les gens s'y réunissent aux grandes occasions de la vie, comme les mariages et les naissances, et y vont aussi de manière habituelle pour se détendre et bavarder entre amis.

Qu'est-ce que vous avez appris? Répondez aux questions par des phrases complètes.

1. Qui est un chanteur algérien célèbre?
   Khaled est un chanteur algérien célèbre.
2. Où fait-on pousser des fruits et des légumes dans le Sahara?
   On en fait pousser dans les oasis.
3. Pourquoi le français est-il parlé au Maghreb?
   Parce que ces trois pays ont été des colonies françaises.
4. Combien de pays composent le Grand Maghreb? Lesquels?
   Cinq pays le composent: l'Algérie, la Libye, le Maroc, la Mauritanie et la Tunisie.
5. Qui est Assia Djebar?
   C'est une femme écrivain et une cinéaste algérienne.
6. Qu'essaie-t-elle de faire dans ses œuvres?
   Elle essaie de présenter le point de vue féminin et de donner une voix aux femmes algériennes.
7. Qu'est-ce qu'un souk?
   C'est un grand marché couvert.
8. Quel est l'autre nom pour la vieille ville de Marrakech?
   Elle s'appelle aussi la médina.
9. Où peut-on aller au Maghreb pour se détendre et bavarder entre amis?
   On peut aller au hammam.
10. Qui a inventé les hammams?
    Les Romains les ont inventés.

ressources: WB pp. 181–182 | espaces.vhlcentral.com

Practice more at **espaces.vhlcentral.com.**

SUR INTERNET

Go to **espaces.vhlcentral.com** to find more cultural information related to this **PANORAMA**.

1. Cherchez plus d'information sur les Berbères. Où se trouvent les grandes populations de Berbères? Ont-ils encore une identité commune?
2. Le henné est une tradition dans le monde maghrébin. Comment et pourquoi est-il employé?
3. Cherchez des informations sur les oasis du Sahara. Comment est la vie là-bas? Que peut-on y faire?

se compose *is made up* **Envahis** *Invaded* **espoir** *hope* **œuvres** *works* **point de vue** *point of view* **voix** *voice* **roman** *novel* **élue** *elected* **entourée** *surrounded* **joyau** *jewel* **couvert** *covered* **menthe** *mint* **miel** *honey* **vapeur** *steam*

Le Maghreb In Arabic, *Maghreb* means *west*. Prior to the Arab conquest, the Maghreb region was part of the Roman Empire.

Assia Djebar (1936–) Assia Djebar (whose given name is Fatima-Zohra Imalayen) is the best-known and most prolific Algerian woman writer. She has chronicled the complexities and evolution of life for North-African women in the Muslim world. Her works have been translated into over 20 languages.

Marrakech
- The **mosquée de Kutubiyya**, or **mosquée des Libraires**, was built in the twelfth century. It is a symbol of the Berber city and a principal landmark. The mosque got its name from the Arabic word for book, *koutoub*, because there used to be a bookseller's market nearby. Ask students: **Avez-vous déjà visité une mosquée? Où? Comment décririez-vous l'intérieur?**
- The souk district is an intricate maze of covered streets where vendors sell their wares, such as carpets, iron work, leather products, clothes, and basketwork. Have students describe what they see in the photo.

Les hammams
- The **hammams** usually offer separate quarters or special days for men and women. The experience begins with a warm steam room where people relax and socialize, then a massage and an exfoliating scrub and soak, ending with a period of relaxation.
- Ask students: **Avez-vous déjà pris un bain turc? Où? Comment vous êtes-vous senti(e)(s) après le bain?**

OPTIONS

Cultural Comparison Have students work in groups of three. Tell them to compare a **hammam** to a spa in the United States. Have them list the similarities and differences in a two-column chart under the headings **Similitudes** and **Différences**. Then have groups get together with another group and compare their lists.

Cultural Activity Have students discuss the various elements these three countries have in common. Tell them to give specific examples. Ask: **Quels sont les éléments que ces trois pays ont en commun?** Examples: **les langues, la religion, l'histoire et la culture.**

Section Goals

In this section, students will:

- learn to summarize a text in their own words
- read a fable in French

Stratégie Tell students that summarizing a text in their own words will help them understand it. Explain that a summary is a restatement of the main idea and major points of a text without the details. As they read a text, they should list the important points and then use linking words to join the ideas.

Examinez le texte Students should mention that the text is a poem, and the main characters are an ant and a cicada. In the first illustration, the ant is working hard, and the cicada is having fun. In the second illustration, it's winter. The cicada is cold and hungry, while the ant has food and shelter.

À propos de l'auteur

- The house in which La Fontaine was born in Château-Thierry is now the **Musée Jean de La Fontaine**.
- Ask students these comprehension questions. **1. Où est né Jean de La Fontaine? (à Château-Thierry) 2. Avant de devenir écrivain, que faisait-il? (Il était avocat.) 3. A-t-il écrit seulement des fables? (Non, il a écrit des poèmes, des nouvelles en vers et des contes.) 4. Quelles fables ont influencé La Fontaine? (les fables d'Ésope) 5. Pourquoi La Fontaine a-t-il écrit des fables? Comment les a-t-il employées? (Les fables de La Fontaine ont critiqué la société contemporaine et la nature humaine.)**

Lecture

NATIONAL STANDARDS: communication, cultures

Audio: Dramatic Recording

Avant la lecture

STRATÉGIE

Summarizing a text in your own words

Summarizing a text in your own words can help you comprehend it better. Before summarizing a text, you may find it helpful to skim it and jot down a few notes about its general meaning. You can then read the text again, writing down the important details. Your notes will help you summarize what you have read. If the text is particularly long, you may want to subdivide it into smaller segments so that you can summarize it more easily.

Examinez le texte

D'abord, regardez la forme du texte. Quel genre de texte est-ce? Puis, regardez les illustrations. Qu'y a-t-il sur ces illustrations? Qui sont les personnages de l'histoire (*story*)? Que font les insectes dans la première illustration? Et dans la deuxième?

À propos de l'auteur
Jean de La Fontaine (1621–1695)

Jean de La Fontaine est un auteur et un poète français très connu du dix-septième siècle. Né à Château-Thierry, à l'est de Paris, il a passé toute son enfance à la campagne avant de devenir avocat et de s'installer à Paris. C'est à la capitale qu'il a rencontré des écrivains célèbres et qu'il a décidé d'écrire. Il est l'auteur de poèmes, de nouvelles en vers° et de contes°, mais il est connu surtout pour ses fables, considérées comme des chefs-d'œuvre° de la littérature française. Au total, La Fontaine a publié 12 livres de fables dans lesquels il a créé des histoires autour de concepts fondamentaux de la morale qu'il a empruntés principalement aux fables d'Ésope. Les fables de La Fontaine, avec leurs animaux et leurs histoires assez simples, étaient, pour lui, une manière° subtile de critiquer la société contemporaine et la nature humaine. Deux de ses fables les plus connues sont *La Cigale et la Fourmi* et *Le Corbeau et le Renard*.

nouvelles en vers *short stories in verse* **contes** *tales* **chefs-d'œuvre** *masterpieces* **manière** *way*

La Cigale et

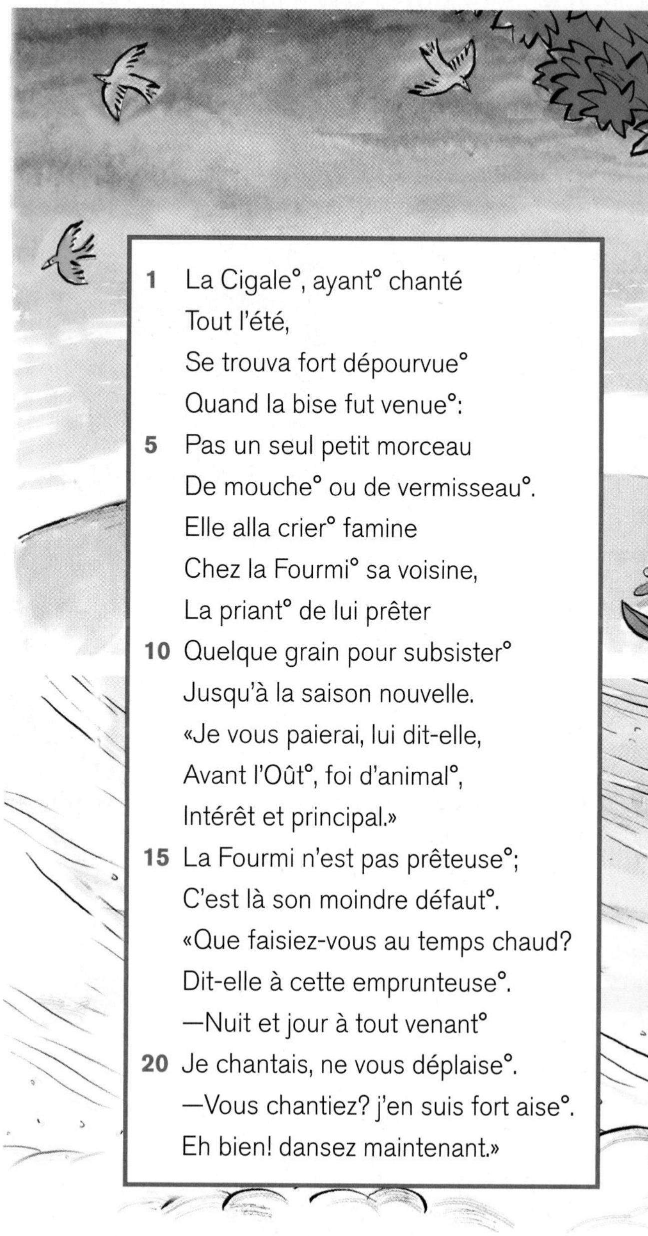

La Cigale°, ayant° chanté
Tout l'été,
Se trouva fort dépourvue°
Quand la bise fut venue°:
Pas un seul petit morceau
De mouche° ou de vermisseau°.
Elle alla crier° famine
Chez la Fourmi° sa voisine,
La priant° de lui prêter
Quelque grain pour subsister°
Jusqu'à la saison nouvelle.
«Je vous paierai, lui dit-elle,
Avant l'Oût°, foi d'animal°,
Intérêt et principal.»
La Fourmi n'est pas prêteuse°;
C'est là son moindre défaut°.
«Que faisiez-vous au temps chaud?
Dit-elle à cette emprunteuse°.
—Nuit et jour à tout venant°
Je chantais, ne vous déplaise°.
—Vous chantiez? j'en suis fort aise°.
Eh bien! dansez maintenant.»

OPTIONS

Extra Practice Have students write speech or thought balloons in French for **la cigale** and **la fourmi** in each illustration. Encourage them to use their own words. You might want to photocopy the illustrations and distribute them to the class so students can draw speech balloons and write the text in them.

Pairs Have students discuss these questions. Why did La Fontaine choose **une cigale** and **une fourmi** as the two insects in this fable? Do his choices make sense? What two insects or animals could replace **la cigale** and **la fourmi**? Tell students to justify their answers.

la Fourmi

de Jean de La Fontaine

Cigale *Cicada* **ayant** *having* **Se trouva fort dépourvue** *Found itself left without a thing* **la bise fut venue** *the cold winds of winter arrived* **mouche** *fly* **vermisseau** *small worm* **alla crier** *went crying* **Fourmi** *Ant* **La priant** *Begging her* **subsister** *survive* **Oût** *August* **foi d'animal** *on my word as an animal* **n'est pas prêteuse** *doesn't like lending things* **moindre défaut** *the least of her shortcomings* **emprunteuse** *borrower* **à tout venant** *all the time* **ne vous déplaise** *whether you like it or not* **fort aise** *overjoyed*

Après la lecture

Répondez Répondez aux questions par des phrases complètes. Answers may vary slightly.

1. Qu'est-ce que la Cigale a fait tout l'été?
   La Cigale a chanté tout l'été.
2. Quel personnage de la fable a beaucoup travaillé pendant l'été?
   C'est la Fourmi.
3. Pourquoi la Cigale n'a-t-elle rien à manger quand l'hiver arrive?
   Elle n'a rien à manger parce qu'elle n'a pas travaillé.
4. Que fait la Cigale quand elle a faim?
   Elle va chez la Fourmi pour lui demander quelque chose à manger.
5. Que fera la Cigale si la Fourmi lui donne à manger?
   Elle lui dit qu'elle la payera.
6. Qu'est-ce que la Fourmi demande à la Cigale?
   Elle lui demande ce qu'elle a fait pendant tout l'été.
7. Quel est le moindre défaut de la Fourmi?
   Elle n'est pas prêteuse.
8. La Fourmi va-t-elle donner quelque chose à manger à la Cigale? Expliquez.
   Non, elle dit à la Cigale d'aller danser.

Un résumé Écrivez un résumé (*summary*) de la fable de La Fontaine. Regardez le texte et prenez des notes sur ce qui se passe aux différents moments de l'histoire. Faites aussi une liste des mots importants que vous ne connaissez pas et trouvez-leur des synonymes que vous pourrez utiliser dans votre résumé. Par exemple, vous connaissez déjà le mot «vent», synonyme de «bise».

La morale de la fable Comme les fables en général, *La Cigale et la Fourmi* a une morale, mais La Fontaine ne la donne pas explicitement. À votre avis, quelle est la morale de cette fable? Êtes-vous d'accord avec cette morale? Discutez ces questions en petits groupes.

Les fables Connaissiez-vous déjà l'histoire de cette fable? Connaissez-vous d'autres fables, comme celles du Grec Ésope, de l'Américain James Thurber, de l'Allemand Gotthold Lessing ou de l'Espagnol Félix Maria Samaniego? Que pensez-vous des fables en général? Aimez-vous les lire? À quoi servent-elles? Quels thèmes trouve-t-on souvent dans les fables? Quels animaux sont souvent utilisés? Discutez ces questions en petits groupes.

Répondez Go over the answers with the class.

Un résumé After completing the activity, have students compare their summaries with a classmate or ask a few volunteers to read their summaries aloud.

La morale de la fable Ask groups to state the moral of the fable. Then ask students why animals are used as characters in fables.

Les fables Before beginning the activity, take a quick class survey to find out how many students have read fables by Thurber, Aesop, Lessing, or Samaniego.

OPTIONS

Pairs Have students work in pairs. Tell them to think of some real-life situations that would mirror the moral taught in this fable. Then have volunteers give examples and ask the class if they think the situation is appropriate or not.

Small Groups Have students work in groups of three or four. Tell them to create a fable of their own. They should decide what the purpose or moral of their fable is, what situation would illustrate it, and which animals should be the main characters. Encourage them to include an illustration. Have volunteer groups act out their fable for the class.

Section Goals

In this section, students will:
- learn to use note cards
- write a composition about their professional goals

Stratégie Explain that using note cards in preparation for writing a composition will help organize and sequence information or ideas.

Thème Tell students to answer the questions first, using note cards for each category (**Types de professions, Recherche d'un emploi,** and **Évolution de carrière**). Remind them to number the cards by category.

Proofreading Activity Have students correct these sentences. **1. Tu penses avoir reussir au bac? 2. Qu'est ce que tu allez faire une fois que tu as le bac? 3. Nous allons diner pour célébrer des que j'ai un nouveau travail. 4. Si je ferais cette robe, elle finirais avec une manche courte et avec une manche longue! 5. Si tu avoir besoin de quoi que c'est un jour, dites-le-moi.**

Écriture

communication cultures NATIONAL STANDARDS

STRATÉGIE

Using note cards

Note cards serve as valuable study aids in many different contexts. When you write, note cards can help you organize and sequence the information you wish to present.

If you were going to write a personal narrative about a trip you took, you would jot down notes about each part of the trip on a different note card. Then you could easily arrange them in chronological order or use a different organization, such as the best parts and the worst parts, traveling and staying, before and after, etc.

Here are some helpful techniques:

- Label the top of each card with a general subject, such as **l'avion** or **l'hôtel**.
- Number the cards in each subject category in the upper right corner to help you organize them.
- Use only the front side of each note card so that you can easily flip through them to find information.

Study this example of a note card used to prepare a composition.

l'avion
- *arrivée à l'aéroport de Chicago à 14h30*
- *départ pour Paris à 16h45, Vol 47 d'Air France*
- *arrivée à Paris (aéroport Charles-de-Gaulle) à 7h15 le lendemain matin*
- *douane*
- *voyage long mais agréable*

Thème

Écrire une rédaction

Avant l'écriture

1. Vous allez écrire une rédaction (*composition*) dans laquelle vous expliquez vos projets d'avenir en ce qui concerne (*concerning*) votre carrière professionnelle.
2. D'abord, préparez des petites fiches (*cards*) avec des notes pour chacune (*each*) des catégories suivantes. Vous avez trois catégories de fiches:
   - types de professions
   - recherche d'un emploi
   - évolution de carrière
3. Pour chaque catégorie, écrivez vos idées sur la fiche correspondante. Utilisez une fiche pour chaque idée. Basez-vous sur ces questions pour trouver des idées.

TYPES DE PROFESSIONS

- Quels domaines professionnels ou quelles professions vous intéressent? Pourquoi? Correspondent-ils à vos études?
- Connaissez-vous déjà des compagnies pour lesquelles vous avez envie de travailler? Lesquelles? Pourquoi?

OPTIONS

Stratégie Have students analyze the topic, notes, and organization of the sample note card shown in the strategy box. Then, as a class, brainstorm other kinds of information you could add to it. Tell students that once they have completed each note card, they should look at it and decide which pieces of information are pertinent to their topic and which are extraneous.

Talk about different ways to organize the note cards. For example, you could organize each card chronologically. Or you could divide it in half, with one side tracking the pros of the subject and the other half indicating the cons. Another way is to record facts in one column and opinions in a second column. Reinforce that students should customize the cards to suit their particular purpose.

RECHERCHE D'UN EMPLOI

- Resterez-vous dans la région où vous habitez maintenant?
- Comment chercherez-vous du travail? Chercherez-vous dans le journal ou sur Internet?
- Chercherez-vous un emploi à temps partiel ou à plein temps? Quel salaire vous proposera-t-on, à votre avis?

ÉVOLUTION DE CARRIÈRE

- Travaillerez-vous pour la même entreprise toute votre carrière ou changerez-vous d'emploi?
- Votre emploi évoluera-t-il beaucoup (promotions, salaire et autres avantages,...), à votre avis?
- Finirez-vous par créer votre propre entreprise?
- À quel âge prendrez-vous votre retraite?

4. Regardez cet exemple pour la catégorie numéro 1.

Types de professions

Je travaillerai dans le domaine de la science. Je deviendrai astronome et j'étudierai l'univers. J'ai toujours voulu savoir s'il y avait de la vie sur d'autres planètes.

5. Avant de noter vos idées sur les fiches, organisez-les selon (*according to*) les trois catégories. Vous aurez ainsi toutes vos idées prêtes pour l'écriture de votre rédaction.

Écriture

1. Servez-vous des fiches pour écrire votre rédaction. Écrivez trois paragraphes en utilisant (*by using*) les catégories comme thèmes de chaque paragraphe.
2. Employez les points de grammaire de cette unité dans votre rédaction.

Après l'écriture

1. Échangez votre rédaction avec celle (*the one*) d'un(e) partenaire. Répondez à ces questions pour commenter son travail.
    - Votre partenaire a-t-il/elle écrit trois paragraphes qui correspondent aux trois catégories d'information?
    - A-t-il/elle répondu à toutes les questions de la liste qui apparaît dans **Avant l'écriture**?
    - A-t-il/elle bien utilisé les points de grammaire de l'unité?
    - Quel(s) détail(s) ajouteriez-vous (*would you add*)? Quel(s) détail(s) enlèveriez-vous (*would you delete*)? Quel(s) autre(s) commentaire(s) avez-vous pour votre partenaire?

2. Corrigez votre rédaction d'après (*according to*) les commentaires de votre partenaire. Relisez votre travail pour éliminer ces problèmes:
    - des fautes (*errors*) d'orthographe
    - des fautes de ponctuation
    - des fautes de conjugaison
    - un mauvais emploi (*use*) des temps
    - un mauvais emploi de la grammaire de l'unité
    - des fautes d'accord (*agreement*) des adjectifs

EVALUATION

Criteria

Content Contains answers to each set of questions called out in the bulleted points of the task.
Scale: 1 2 3 4 5

Organization Organized into a set of note cards with preliminary answers to the questions, followed by a composition that is organized into logical paragraphs, each of which begins with a topic sentence and contains appropriate supporting detail.
Scale: 1 2 3 4 5

Accuracy Uses the simple future tense and forms of **lequel** correctly. Spells words, conjugates verbs, and modifies adjectives correctly throughout.
Scale: 1 2 3 4 5

Creativity Includes additional information that is not specified in the task and/or uses adjectives, descriptive verbs, and additional details to make the composition more interesting.
Scale: 1 2 3 4 5

Scoring

Excellent	18–20 points
Good	14–17 points
Satisfactory	10–13 points
Unsatisfactory	< 10 points

OPTIONS

Avant l'écriture To activate vocabulary for the topic, have students work in pairs and role-play an interview. Students should take turns asking and answering questions from the list and taking notes on their answers and the words they use in their responses. Then, as needed, they can use a dictionary to add any specific words that will personalize these responses.

Point out that most of the questions in the writing task require answers using the simple future tense. Review its formation and the irregular forms from **Unité 12**, and its use with **quand** and **dès que** from this unit. Review also the use of **lequel** and its various combined forms. Practice by asking simple questions using these forms and calling upon individual students to respond.

Instructional Resources
espaces.vhlcentral.com: Textbook MP3s; IRM (Textbook Audioscript); downloads; reference tools

Suggestion Tell students that an easy way to study from **Vocabulaire** is to cover up the French half of each section, leaving only the English equivalents exposed. They can then quiz themselves on the French items. To focus on the English equivalents of the French entries, they simply reverse this process.

Flashcards
Audio: Vocabulary

VOCABULAIRE

Au travail

démissionner	*to resign*
diriger	*to manage*
être au chômage	*to be unemployed*
être bien/mal payé(e)	*to be well/badly paid*
gagner	*to earn; to win*
prendre un congé	*to take time off*
renvoyer	*to dismiss, to let go*
une carrière	*career*
un emploi à mi-temps/à temps partiel	*part-time job*
un emploi à plein temps	*full-time job*
un(e) employé(e)	*employee*
un niveau	*level*
un(e) patron(ne)	*manager; boss*
une profession (exigeante)	*(demanding) profession*
un(e) retraité(e)	*retired person*
une réunion	*meeting*
une réussite	*success*
un syndicat	*union*
une assurance (maladie, vie)	*(health, life) insurance*
une augmentation (de salaire)	*raise (in salary)*
une promotion	*promotion*

Vocabulaire supplémentaire

dès que	*as soon as*
quand	*when*
lequel	*which one (m. sing.)*
lesquels	*which ones (m. pl.)*
laquelle	*which one (f. sing.)*
lesquelles	*which ones (f. pl.)*

Pronoms relatifs

dont	*of which, of whom*
où	*where*
que	*that, which*
qui	*who, that, which*

Qualifications

un domaine	*field*
une expérience professionnelle	*professional experience*
une formation	*education; training*
une lettre de recommandation	*letter of reference/recommendation*
une mention	*distinction*
une référence	*reference*
un(e) spécialiste	*specialist*
un stage	*internship; professional training*

Les métiers

un agent immobilier	*real estate agent*
un agriculteur/une agricultrice	*farmer*
un banquier/une banquière	*banker*
un cadre/une femme cadre	*executive*
un chauffeur de taxi/de camion	*taxi/truck driver*
un chef d'entreprise	*head of a company*
un chercheur/une chercheuse	*researcher*
un(e) comptable	*accountant*
un conseiller/une conseillère	*consultant; advisor*
un cuisinier/une cuisinière	*cook, chef*
un(e) électricien(ne)	*electrician*
une femme au foyer	*housewife*
un(e) gérant(e)	*manager*
un homme/une femme politique	*politician*
un ouvrier/une ouvrière	*worker, laborer*
un plombier	*plumber*
un pompier/une femme pompier	*firefighter*
un(e) psychologue	*psychologist*
un(e) vétérinaire	*veterinarian*

La recherche d'emploi

chercher un/du travail	*to look for work*
embaucher	*to hire*
faire des projets	*to make plans*
lire les annonces (f.)	*to read the want ads*
obtenir	*to get, to obtain*
passer un entretien	*to have an interview*
postuler	*to apply*
prendre (un) rendez-vous	*to make an appointment*
trouver un/du travail	*to find a job*
un(e) candidat(e)	*candidate, applicant*
un chef du personnel	*human resources director*
un chômeur/une chômeuse	*unemployed person*
une compagnie	*company*
un conseil	*advice*
un curriculum vitæ (un CV)	*résumé*
une entreprise	*firm, business*
une lettre de motivation	*letter of application*
un métier	*profession*
un poste	*position*
un salaire (élevé, modeste)	*(high, low) salary*

Au téléphone

appeler	*to call*
décrocher	*to pick up*
laisser un message	*to leave a message*
patienter	*to wait (on the phone), to be on hold*
raccrocher	*to hang up*
l'appareil (m.)	*telephone*
le combiné	*receiver*
la messagerie	*voicemail*
un numéro de téléphone	*phone number*
une télécarte	*phone card*
Allô!	*Hello! (on the phone)*
Qui est à l'appareil?	*Who's calling please?*
C'est de la part de qui?	*On behalf of whom?*
C'est M./Mme/Mlle... (à l'appareil.)	*It's Mr./Mrs./Miss... (on the phone.)*
Ne quittez pas.	*Please hold.*

Expressions utiles	*See pp. 439 and 455*

ressources
espaces.vhlcentral.com

L'espace vert

UNITÉ 14

Leçon 14A

ESPACE CONTEXTES
pages 472–475
- Environmental concerns
- French and English spelling

ESPACE ROMAN-PHOTO
pages 476–477
- **Une idée de génie**

ESPACE CULTURE
pages 478–479
- The ecological movement in France

ESPACE STRUCTURES
pages 480–483
- Demonstrative pronouns
- The subjunctive (Part 1)

ESPACE SYNTHÈSE
pages 484–485
- **Révision**
- **Le zapping**

Leçon 14B

ESPACE CONTEXTES
pages 486–489
- Nature
- Homophones

ESPACE ROMAN-PHOTO
pages 490–491
- **La randonnée**

ESPACE CULTURE
pages 492–493
- National parks
- **Flash culture**

ESPACE STRUCTURES
pages 494–497
- The subjunctive (Part 2)
- Comparatives and superlatives of nouns

ESPACE SYNTHÈSE
pages 498–499
- **Révision**
- **À l'écoute**

Pour commencer
- Où est le groupe d'amis?
  a. à la mer b. à la campagne c. en ville
- Qu'est-ce qu'ils vont faire?
  a. un pique-nique b. les courses c. du vélo
- Qu'est-ce qu'il y a derrière eux?
  a. une jungle b. une montagne c. un pont

Savoir-faire

pages 500–505
Panorama: L'Afrique de l'Ouest et l'Afrique centrale
Lecture: Read an excerpt from a book.
Écriture: Write a letter or an article about an ecological concern.

Unit Goals

Leçon 14A

In this lesson, students will learn:
- terms related to ecology and the environment
- common differences in French and English spelling
- about the ecological movement and nuclear energy in France
- the demonstrative pronouns **celui**, **celle**, **ceux**, and **celles**
- to form **le subjonctif**
- common impersonal expressions that take the subjunctive
- about the **Banque Marocaine du Commerce Extérieur**

Leçon 14B

In this lesson, students will learn:
- terms to discuss nature and conservation
- about homophones
- about France's national park system and Madagascar
- more about the diverse geography of the francophone world through specially shot video footage
- about the subjunctive with verbs and expressions of will and emotion
- verbs with irregular subjunctive forms
- the comparative and superlative of nouns
- to listen for the gist and cognates

Savoir-faire

In this section, students will learn:
- cultural and historical information about the francophone countries of West and Central Africa
- to recognize chronological order in a text
- to consider audience and purpose when writing

Pour commencer

- **b. à la campagne**
- **a. un pique-nique**
- **b. une montagne**

RESOURCES

Workbook/Video Manual: WB Activities, pp. 183–196
Laboratory Manual: Lab Activities, pp. 105–112
Workbook/Video Manual: Video Activities, pp. 263–266; pp. 297–298
WB/VM/LM Answer Key

espaces.vhlcentral.com: Textbook MP3s; Lab MP3s; Instructor's Resource Manual [IRM] (Textbook Audioscript; Lab Audioscript; Videoscript; **Roman-photo** Translations; **Vocabulaire supplémentaire**; **Feuilles d'activités**; Info Gap Activities; **Le zapping** TV clip transcription; **Essayez!** and **Mise en pratique** answers) Transparencies #57, #58, #59;

Testing Program, pp. 105–112; Test Files; Testing Program MP3s
Test Generator
Video on DVD

Section Goals

In this section, students will learn and practice vocabulary related to:
- ecology
- the environment

Instructional Resources
*espaces.vhlcentral.com: Transparency #57; IRM (**Vocabulaire supplémentaire**; **Mise en pratique** answers; Textbook Audioscript; Lab Audioscript); Textbook MP3s; Lab MP3s; WB/VM/LM Answer Key; activities; downloads; reference tools*

Suggestions
- Tell students to look over the new vocabulary and identify the cognates.
- Use **Transparency #57.** Point out people and things as you describe the illustration. Examples: **Elle recycle. Ils ont pollué. C'est une centrale nucléaire.**
- Point out the double consonants in the words **développer** and **environnement**.
- Point out the verb **interdire** and the sign next to it. Write on the board: **Il est interdit de...** Then have students finish the sentence with various things people might be forbidden to do, such as **gaspiller de l'énergie**.
- Ask students questions using the new vocabulary. Examples: **L'université a-t-elle un programme de recyclage? Quels objets recyclez-vous? Que faites-vous pour réduire la pollution? Quel est le plus gros problème écologique de votre région? L'énergie solaire est-elle mieux que l'énergie nucléaire? Pourquoi? Où y a-t-il souvent des glissements de terrain?**
- Additional vocabulary for this lesson can be found in the **Vocabulaire supplémentaire** on the Supersite.

Leçon 14A

Talking Picture
Audio: Activity

You will learn how to...
- talk about pollution
- talk about what needs to be done

Sauvons la planète!

Vocabulaire

abolir	*to abolish*
améliorer	*to improve*
développer	*to develop*
gaspiller	*to waste*
préserver	*to preserve*
prévenir l'incendie	*to prevent a fire*
proposer une solution	*to propose a solution*
sauver la planète	*to save the planet*
une catastrophe	*catastrophe*
un danger	*danger, threat*
des déchets toxiques (*m.*)	*toxic waste*
l'effet de serre (*m.*)	*greenhouse effect*
le gaspillage	*waste*
un glissement de terrain	*landslide*
une population croissante	*growing population*
le réchauffement climatique	*global warming*
la surpopulation	*overpopulation*
le trou dans la couche d'ozone	*hole in the ozone layer*
une usine	*factory*
l'écologie (*f.*)	*ecology*
un emballage en plastique	*plastic wrapping/packaging*
l'environnement (*m.*)	*environment*
un espace	*space, area*
un produit	*product*
la protection	*protection*
écologique	*ecological*
en plein air	*outdoor, open-air*
pur(e)	*pure*
un gouvernement	*government*
une loi	*law*

ressources
WB pp. 183–184 | LM p. 105 | espaces.vhlcentral.com

OPTIONS

Extra Practice Whisper a vocabulary word in a student's ear. That student should draw a picture or a series of pictures that represent the word on the board. The class must guess the word, then spell it in French as a volunteer writes the word on the board.

Game Divide the class into two teams. Have a spelling bee using vocabulary words from **Espace contextes**. Pronounce each word, use it in a sentence, and then say the word again. Tell students that they must spell the words in French and include all diacritical marks.

Mise en pratique

1 Écoutez Écoutez l'annonce radio suivante. Ensuite, complétez les phrases avec le mot ou l'expression qui convient le mieux.

1. C'est l'annonce radio ______
   a. d'un groupe d'étudiants.
   b. d'une entreprise commerciale.
   (c.) d'une agence écologiste.
2. La protection de l'environnement, c'est l'affaire ______
   (a.) de tous.
   b. du gouvernement.
   c. des centres de recyclage.
3. L'annonce dit qu'on peut recycler ______
   (a.) les emballages en plastique et en papier.
   b. les boîtes de conserve.
   c. les bouteilles en plastique.
4. Pour les déchets toxiques, il y a ______
   a. le ramassage des ordures.
   (b.) le centre de recyclage.
   c. l'effet de serre.
5. Pour ne pas gaspiller l'eau, on peut ______
   a. acheter des produits écologiques.
   b. développer les incendies.
   (c.) prendre des douches plus courtes.

2 Complétez Complétez ces phrases avec le mot ou l'expression qui convient le mieux pour parler de l'environnement. N'oubliez pas les accords.

1. Nous avons trois poubelles différentes pour pouvoir ___recycler___.
2. ___L'effet de serre___ contribue au réchauffement de la Terre.
3. ___Les centrales nucléaires___ produisent près de 80% de l'énergie en France.
4. Les pluies ont provoqué ___un glissement de terrain___. À présent, la route est fermée.
5. Chez moi, ___le ramassage___ des ordures se fait tous les lundis.
6. L'accident à l'usine chimique a provoqué un ___nuage de pollution___.

3 Composez Utilisez les éléments de chaque colonne pour former six phrases logiques au sujet de l'environnement. Vous pouvez composer des phrases affirmatives ou négatives. Answers will vary.

Les gens	Les actions	Les éléments
vous	développer	l'eau
on	gaspiller	le covoiturage
les gens	polluer	l'énergie solaire
les politiciens	préserver	l'environnement
les entreprises	proposer	la planète
les centrales nucléaires	sauver	la Terre

Practice more at **espaces.vhlcentral.com.**

1 Tapescript L'écologie, c'est l'affaire de tous! Aidez-nous à préserver et à améliorer l'environnement. Tout commence avec le ramassage des ordures: recyclez vos emballages en plastique et en papier! Ne polluez pas: votre centre de recyclage local est là pour s'occuper de vos déchets toxiques. Ne gaspillez pas l'eau, surtout en cette période de réchauffement de la Terre: comment? Prenez des douches plus courtes! Nous vous rappelons également qu'une loi interdit de laver sa voiture dans certaines régions de France quand il fait extrêmement chaud l'été. Ne gaspillez pas non plus l'énergie: faites attention à la consommation inutile d'énergie de vos appareils électriques. Enfin, évitez d'acheter des produits qui peuvent mettre l'environnement en danger: choisissez des produits écologiques. Ensemble, nous sommes plus forts! Nous développons et proposons des solutions simples. Alors, la prochaine fois que vous entendrez parler de pluies acides, de trou dans la couche d'ozone, de l'effet de serre, de pollution et de catastrophe écologique, vous pourrez être fier de dire que vous faites partie de la solution.

Ceci était un message de l'agence nationale pour la protection de l'environnement. *(On Textbook MP3s)*

1 Suggestion Go over the answers with the class. Ask volunteers to read the complete sentences.

2 Expansion For additional practice, give students these items. **7. Une nouvelle étude des Nations Unies confirme qu'il y a un risque de ____. (surpopulation) En 2050, il y aura neuf milliards (*billions*) de personnes sur Terre. 8. Le parti écologiste veut améliorer ____ de l'environnement. (la protection) 9. Le gouvernement vient de passer ____ sur le transport des déchets toxiques. (une loi) 10. Nous évitons de laisser ____ derrière nous quand nous mangeons dans le parc. (des ordures)**

3 Suggestion This activity can be done orally or in writing in pairs or groups.

OPTIONS

Game Play a game of **Dix questions**. Ask a volunteer to think of a word or expression from the new vocabulary. Other students get to ask one yes/no question, then they can guess what the word is. Limit attempts to ten questions per word. You may want to write some phrases on the board to cue students' questions.

Pairs Have students work in pairs. Write the following list of dangers facing our planet on the board. Tell students to rank them from the most serious to least serious and explain why. Dangers: **la surpopulation, le réchauffement de la Terre, les déchets toxiques, la pollution de l'environnement, la pluie acide, l'effet de serre, le risque d'accident dans une centrale nucléaire**, and **la crise de l'énergie**

4 Suggestion Tell students that their descriptions should include the weather, the time of day, and a possible location.

4 Expansion Bring in additional photos from magazines or the Internet that illustrate ecological problems and have students describe what they see.

5 Suggestion You may wish to assign groups specific situations so that all of them are covered.

6 Suggestion Ask a volunteer to read the **modèle** aloud. Then have students brainstorm a list of words and expressions that are used to inform, persuade, or register a complaint.

Communication

4 Décrivez Avec un(e) partenaire, décrivez ces photos et donnez autant de détails et d'informations que possible. Soyez prêt(e)s à présenter vos descriptions à la classe Answers will vary.

1.

3.

2.

4.

5 À vous de jouer Par petits groupes, préparez une conversation au sujet d'une de ces situations. Ensuite jouez la scène devant la classe. Answers will vary.

- Un(e) employé(e) du centre de recyclage local vient dans votre université pour expliquer aux étudiants un nouveau système de recyclage. De nombreux étudiants posent des questions.
- Un groupe d'écologistes rencontre le patron d'une entreprise accusée de polluer la rivière (*river*) locale.
- Le ministre de l'environnement donne une conférence de presse au sujet d'une nouvelle loi sur la protection de l'environnement.
- Votre colocataire oublie systématiquement de recycler les emballages. Vous avez une conversation animée avec lui/elle.

6 L'article Vous êtes journaliste et vous devez écrire un article pour le journal local au sujet de la pollution. Vous en expliquez les causes et les conséquences sur l'environnement. Vous suggérez aussi des solutions pour améliorer la situation. Answers will vary.

MODÈLE

Les dangers de la pollution chimique

Les usines chimiques de notre région polluent! C'est une catastrophe pour notre environnement. Il faut leur interdire de fonctionner jusqu'à ce qu'elles améliorent leurs systèmes de recyclage…

OPTIONS

Pairs Write these expressions for circumlocution on the board: **C'est un endroit où…, Ça sert à…, C'est le contraire de…, C'est un synonyme de…, C'est quand on….** Then have pairs of students write definitions for these vocabulary words. **1. améliorer 2. un incendie 3. le recyclage 4. le covoiturage 5. la pollution 6. une catastrophe 7. une loi 8. une usine 9. le réchauffement de la Terre**

Have pairs get together with another pair of students and take turns reading their definitions and guessing the word. Ask each group to choose their best definition and write it on the board for the whole class to guess.

Les sons et les lettres

Audio: Concepts, Activities
Record & Compare

NATIONAL comparisons STANDARDS

French and English spelling

You have seen that many French words only differ slightly from their English counterparts. Many differ in predictable ways. English words that end in *-y* often end in **-ie** in French.

biologie **psychologie** **énergie** **écologie**

English words that end in *-ity* often end in **-ité** in French.

qualité **université** **cité** **nationalité**

French equivalents of English words that end in *-ist* often end in **-iste**.

artiste **optimiste** **pessimiste** **dentiste**

French equivalents of English words that end in *-or* and *-er* often end in **-eur**. This tendency is especially common for words that refer to people.

docteur **acteur** **employeur** **agriculteur**

Other English words that end in *-er* end in **-re** in French.

centre **membre** **litre** **théâtre**

Other French words vary in ways that are less predictable, but they are still easy to recognize.

problème **orchestre** **carotte** **calculatrice**

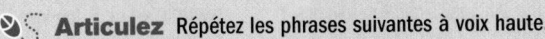

Prononcez Répétez les mots suivants à voix haute.

1. tigre
2. bleu
3. lettre
4. salade
5. poème
6. banane
7. tourisme
8. moniteur
9. pharmacie
10. écologiste
11. conducteur
12. anthropologie

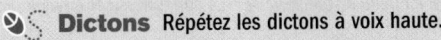

Articulez Répétez les phrases suivantes à voix haute.

1. Ma cousine est vétérinaire.
2. Le moteur ne fonctionne pas.
3. À la banque, Carole paie par chèque.
4. Mon oncle écrit l'adresse sur l'enveloppe.
5. À la station-service, le mécanicien a réparé le moteur.

Dictons Répétez les dictons à voix haute.

On ne fait pas d'omelette sans casser des œufs.[2]

On reconnaît l'arbre à son fruit.[1]

ressources
LM p. 106 | espaces.vhlcentral.com

[1] You can recognize a tree by its fruit.
[2] You can't make an omelet without breaking some eggs.

Section Goals

In this section, students will learn about:
- differences between French and English spelling
- various strategies for recognizing cognates

Instructional Resources
espaces.vhlcentral.com: Textbook MP3s; Lab MP3s; WB/VM/LM Answer Key; IRM (Textbook Audioscript; Lab Audioscript); activities; downloads; reference tools

Suggestions
- Point out that all the words in the explanation section are cognates.
- Model the pronunciation of the example words and have students repeat them after you.
- Ask students to provide more examples of French words that are spelled only slightly differently from their English counterparts. Examples: **allergie, journaliste, spécialiste, géographie, économie, appartement, couleur, développer,** and **espace.**
- Point out that English adjectives ending in *-ous* often end in **-eux** in the masculine form and **-euse** in the feminine form in French. Examples: **nerveux/nerveuse, curieux/curieuse,** and **sérieux/sérieuse.**
- Explain that words that end in *-al* in English often end in **-el** in French. Examples: **naturel, personnel, culturel,** and **fraternel.**
- Explain that English words that end in *-ory* may end in **-oire** in French. Examples: **histoire, laboratoire,** and **victoire.**
- Ask students to think of additional French words that follow these patterns.

OPTIONS

Extra Practice Use these words for additional practice or dictation. **1. anxieux 2. essentiel 3. délicieuse 4. environnement 5. intellectuel 6. serveuse 7. journaliste 8. développer 9. exercice 10. distributeur**

Extra Practice Teach students these French tongue-twisters that contain French words that are similar to English words. **1. Papier, panier, piano 2. Un généreux déjeuner régénérerait des généraux dégénérés.**

Section Goals

In this section, students will learn functional phrases for talking about necessities, asking for opinions, and expressing denial.

Instructional Resources
espaces.vhlcentral.com: WB/VM/LM Answer Key; IRM (Videoscript; ***Roman-photo*** *Translations); activities; downloads; reference tools*
Video on DVD

Video Recap: Leçon 13B
Before doing this **Roman-photo**, review the previous one with this activity.

1. Pourquoi Sandrine est-elle anxieuse? (à cause de son concert)
2. Que propose Amina? (de lui faire une jolie robe)
3. Pourquoi Stéphane n'est-il pas content? (Il doit repasser une partie du bac.)
4. Qu'a demandé Michèle à Valérie? (une augmentation de salaire)
5. Qu'est-ce que Michèle a décidé de faire finalement? (Elle a démissionné.)

Video Synopsis
Valérie asks Stéphane to recycle some bottles and plastic packaging. Amina wants to know where Michèle is. Valérie explains that she quit. David announces that he has to return home to the States in three weeks. To cheer everyone up, Rachid suggests a weekend trip to **la montagne Sainte-Victoire**. They all agree that it's a great idea.

Suggestions
- Have students scan the captions to find sentences related to ecology and the environment.
- After reading the **Roman-photo**, have students summarize the episode.

Une idée de génie

Video: *Roman-photo*
Record & Compare

PERSONNAGES

Amina

David

Rachid

Sandrine

Stéphane

Valérie

1

Au P'tit Bistrot...
VALÉRIE Stéphane, mon chéri, tu peux porter ces bouteilles en verre à recycler, s'il te plaît?
STÉPHANE Oui, bien sûr, maman.
VALÉRIE Oh, et puis, ces emballages en plastique aussi.
STÉPHANE Oui, je m'en occupe tout de suite.

2

RACHID ET AMINA Bonjour, Madame Forestier!
VALÉRIE Bonjour à vous deux.
AMINA Où est Michèle?
VALÉRIE Je n'en sais rien.
RACHID Mais elle ne travaille pas aujourd'hui?
VALÉRIE Non, elle ne vient ni aujourd'hui, ni demain, ni la semaine prochaine.

3

AMINA Elle est en vacances?
VALÉRIE Elle a démissionné.
RACHID Mais pourquoi?
AMINA Ça ne nous regarde pas!
VALÉRIE Oh, ça va, je peux vous le dire. Michèle voulait un autre travail.
RACHID Quelle sorte de travail?
VALÉRIE Plus celui-ci... Elle voulait une augmentation, ce n'était pas possible.

6

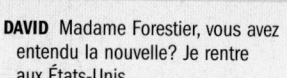

DAVID Madame Forestier, vous avez entendu la nouvelle? Je rentre aux États-Unis.
VALÉRIE Tu repars aux États-Unis?
DAVID Dans trois semaines.
VALÉRIE Il te reste très peu de temps à Aix, alors!
SANDRINE Oui. On sait.
DAVID Il faut que nous passions le reste de mon séjour de bonne humeur, hein?

7

RACHID Ah, mais vraiment, tout le monde a l'air triste aujourd'hui!
AMINA Oui. Pensons à quelque chose pour améliorer la situation. Tu as une idée?
RACHID Oui, peut-être.
AMINA Dis-moi! (*Il lui parle à l'oreille.*) Excellente idée!
RACHID Tu crois? Tu es sûre? Bon... Écoutez, j'ai une idée.

8

DAVID C'est quoi, ton idée?
RACHID Tout le monde a l'air triste aujourd'hui. Si on allait au mont Sainte-Victoire ce week-end. Ça vous dit?
DAVID Oui! J'aimerais bien y aller. J'adore dessiner en plein air.

ACTIVITÉS

1 Les événements Remettez ces événements dans l'ordre chronologique.

6 a. David dit qu'il part dans trois semaines.
3 b. Valérie explique que Michèle ne travaille plus au P'tit Bistrot.
9 c. Amina dit qu'elle veut aller à la montagne Sainte-Victoire ce week-end.
1 d. Stéphane va porter les bouteilles et les emballages à recycler.
2 e. Amina veut savoir où est Michèle.
4 f. David dit au groupe ce qu'il a lu dans le journal.
5 g. Sandrine semble (*seems*) avoir le trac.
10 h. Ils décident de passer le week-end tous ensemble.
8 i. Rachid essaie de remonter le moral à ses amis.
7 j. David console Sandrine.

Practice more at **espaces.vhlcentral.com.**

OPTIONS

Avant de regarder la vidéo Based on the title **Une idée de génie** and video still 7, have students guess what idea Rachid might be suggesting to Amina and why he is suggesting it.

Regarder la vidéo Show the first half of the video episode and have students describe what happened. Write their observations on the board. Then ask them to guess what will happen in the second half of the episode. Write their ideas on the board. Show the entire episode and have students confirm or correct their predictions.

Rachid propose une excursion en montagne.

DAVID Bonjour, tout le monde. Vous avez lu le journal ce matin? Il faut que je vous parle de cet article sur la pollution. J'ai appris beaucoup de choses au sujet des pluies acides, du trou dans la couche d'ozone, de l'effet de serre...
AMINA Oh, David, la barbe.
RACHID Allez, assieds-toi et déjeune avec nous.

Un peu plus tard...
RACHID Ton concert est dans une semaine, n'est-ce pas Sandrine?
SANDRINE Oui.
RACHID Qu'est-ce que tu vas chanter?
SANDRINE Écoute, Rachid, je n'ai pas vraiment envie de parler de ça.

SANDRINE Oui, peut-être...
AMINA Allez! Ça nous fera du bien! Adieu pollution de la ville. À nous, l'air pur de la campagne! Qu'en penses-tu, Sandrine?
SANDRINE Bon, d'accord.

AMINA Super! Et vous, Madame Forestier? Vous et Stéphane avez besoin de vous reposer aussi, vous devez absolument venir avec nous!
VALÉRIE En effet, je crois que c'est une excellente idée!

Expressions utiles

Talking about necessities

- **Il faut que je vous parle de cet article sur la pollution.**
  I have to tell you about this article on pollution.
- **Il faut que nous passions le reste de mon séjour de bonne humeur.**
  We have to spend the rest of my stay in a good mood.

Getting someone's opinion

- **Qu'en penses-tu?**
  What do you think (about that)?
- **Je pense que...**
  I think that...

Expressing denial

- **Je n'en sais rien.**
  I have no idea.
- **Ça ne nous regarde pas.**
  That is none of our business.
- **Quelle sorte de travail? Plus celui-ci.**
  What kind of job? Not this one anymore.

Additional vocabulary

- **au sujet de**
  about
- **Adieu!**
  Farewell!
- **Il te reste très peu de temps.**
  You don't have much time left.
- **en effet**
  indeed/in fact
- **je crois**
  I think/believe
- **Ça te/vous dit?**
  Does that appeal to you?

2 Répondez Répondez à ces questions par des phrases complètes.

1. Que se passe-t-il avec Sandrine? Elle est nerveuse avant son concert et elle est triste parce que David part dans trois semaines.
2. Qu'est-ce qu'Amina croit (*believe*) qu'il se passe avec Michèle? Elle croit que Michèle est peut-être en vacances.
3. Pourquoi Rachid veut-il aller à la montagne Sainte-Victoire? Il trouve que ses amis ont l'air triste et il veut les aider à changer d'humeur.
4. À votre avis, qu'est-ce que David a appris après avoir lu le journal? Answers will vary.

3 Écrivez Imaginez comment se passera le week-end du groupe d'amis à la montagne Sainte-Victoire. Composez un paragraphe qui explique comment ils vont y aller, ce qu'ils y feront, s'ils s'amuseront...

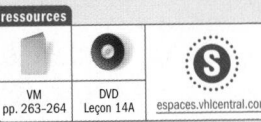

ressources: VM pp. 263–264 | DVD Leçon 14A | espaces.vhlcentral.com

ACTIVITÉS

Expressions utiles
- Model the pronunciation of the **Expressions utiles** and have students repeat them after you.
- As you work through the list, point out forms of the present subjunctive with impersonal expressions and demonstrative pronouns. Tell students that these grammar points will be formally presented in **Espace structures**.
- Respond briefly to questions about the present subjunctive and demonstrative pronouns. Reinforce correct forms, but do not expect students to produce them consistently at this time.
- Point out the different meanings of the word **reste**. Write these sentences and phrases on the board and have students translate them. **1. Il reste des pommes.** (*There are some apples left.*) **2. Il reste là.** (*He stays there.*) **3. Il me reste cinq euros.** (*I have five euros left.*) **4. le reste de la famille** (*the rest of the family*)

1 Suggestion Have students work in groups of five. Make a set of individual sentences on strips of paper for each group and distribute them (two sentences per student). Tell students to arrange the sentences in the proper order and read them aloud.

2 Suggestion Have volunteers write the answers on the board. Go over them with the class.

2 Expansion For additional practice, ask students: **Qu'est-ce que le groupe d'amis veut faire à la montagne Sainte-Victoire? (David veut dessiner en plein air, Amina veut respirer l'air pur et Valérie veut se reposer.)**

3 Suggestion Before beginning the activity, have students brainstorm a list of activities the group might do at **la montagne Sainte-Victoire**. Write them on the board.

OPTIONS

Extra Practice Ask volunteers to ad-lib the **Roman-photo** episode for the class. Tell them it is not necessary to memorize the episode. They should just try to get the general meaning across with the vocabulary they know. Give them time to prepare or have them do their skit as a review activity during the next class period.

Extra Practice Have students write two sentences that a character in this **Roman-photo** episode would say. Tell them they can look at the text for ideas, but they shouldn't copy sentences word for word. Then have volunteers read their sentences aloud. The class has to guess who would say them.

NATIONAL STANDARDS connections cultures

Section Goals

In this section, students will:
- learn about the ecological movement and environmental concerns in France
- learn some ecological terms
- learn about ecotourism in the francophone world
- read about nuclear power in France

Instructional Resources
espaces.vhlcentral.com: activities; downloads; reference tools

Culture à la loupe
Avant la lecture Have students look at the photo of the Green Party protest and describe what they see. Point out the words on the flag «**les verts**». Ask students to guess what it means.

Lecture
- France was a pioneer in **l'agriculture biologique** during the 1980s. Organic production in France then slowed, while it increased elsewhere in Europe. French organic production has been back on the rise since the late 1990s.
- Some of the steps the French government has taken in regard to environmental concerns are: **le Grenelle de l'environnement** (series of meetings begun in 2007 that have led to the passage of new laws), **les crédits d'impôts** (tax deduction for people who have energy-saving work done on their house), **les bonus (ou malus) écologiques** (depending on what car a person buys).
- Point out the statistics chart. Ask students what information it shows. (the percentages of French people who are concerned about the environmental problems listed)

Après la lecture Ask students: **Quelles similitudes et quelles différences pouvez-vous trouver entre l'attitude française et l'attitude américaine concernant l'environnement?**

1 Suggestion Have students read the completed sentences aloud.

CULTURE À LA LOUPE

L'écologie

l'agriculture française

une manifestation° des Verts

Le mouvement écologique a commencé en France dans les années 1970, mais ne s'est réellement développé que dans les années 1980. Ce sont surtout les crises majeures comme le nuage de Tchernobyl en 1986, la destruction de la couche d'ozone, l'effet de serre et les marées noires° qui ont réveillé la conscience écologique des Français. Le désir de préserver la qualité de la vie et les espaces naturels s'est développé en même temps.

Aujourd'hui, l'environnement n'est pas le seul sujet d'inquiétude° des Français. L'emploi, la baisse des revenus° et l'avenir des retraites les préoccupent° plus. Pourtant, le score aux élections du parti écologique des Verts est en hausse° depuis 1999 et on considère que le parti des Verts est le deuxième parti de gauche.

De manière générale, les problèmes liés à° l'environnement qui retiennent° le plus l'attention des Français sont la pollution atmosphérique des villes, la pollution de l'eau, le réchauffement climatique et la prolifération des déchets nucléaires. Pour l'opinion publique, le plus urgent à régler° est la qualité de l'eau. En effet, à cause de° l'agriculture française, les taux° de nitrates et de phosphates dans l'eau sont presque partout largement supérieurs à la normale. Depuis la crise de la vache folle°, les Français sont aussi sensibles aux menaces alimentaires°. Les cultures OGM° ont porté le débat écologique dans les assiettes.

Les inquiétudes sur l'environnement

• les Français qui sont préoccupés par la pollution de l'air et de l'eau	92%
• les Français qui s'opposent à la culture de plantes génétiquement modifiées	86%
• les Français qui sont inquiets pour l'avenir de la planète	83%
• les Français qui s'inquiètent de plus en plus des changements climatiques	76%

SOURCE: www.ifen.fr, www.actu-environnement.com

marées noires *oil spills* **inquiétude** *concern* **baisse des revenus** *lowering of incomes* **préoccupent** *worry* **en hausse** *on the rise* **liés à** *linked to* **retiennent** *hold* **régler** *solve* **à cause de** *because of* **taux** *levels* **vache folle** *mad cow* **alimentaires** *food-related* **OGM (organismes génétiquement modifiés)** *GMO* **manifestation** *demonstration*

ACTIVITÉS

1 Complétez Complétez les phrases.

1. Le mouvement écologique s'est développé dans les années 1980.
2. Les crises majeures comme le nuage de Tchernobyl, la destruction de la couche d'ozone, l'effet de serre et les marées noires ont réveillé la conscience écologique des Français.
3. L'environnement n'est pas la seule préoccupation des Français.
4. Les problèmes d'emploi, la baisse des revenus et l'avenir des retraites préoccupent aussi les Français.
5. Le score du parti écologique des Verts est en hausse depuis 1999.
6. Le problème écologique le plus urgent à régler est la qualité de l'eau.
7. À cause de l'agriculture, les taux de nitrates et de phosphates dans l'eau sont presque partout largement supérieurs à la normale.
8. 92% des Français sont préoccupés par la pollution de l'air et de l'eau.
9. 86% des Français s'opposent à la culture de plantes génétiquement modifiées.
10. 76% des Français s'inquiètent de plus en plus des changements climatiques.

Practice more at **espaces.vhlcentral.com.**

OPTIONS

Pairs Write the following list of problems on the board: **la pollution de l'eau, la pollution de l'air, les changements climatiques, l'emploi, l'urbanisation, les cultures OGM, l'avenir des retraites,** and **les marées noires**. Tell students to take turns making comparisons based on the information in the reading. Example: **La catastrophe des marées noires est moins importante pour les Français que l'emploi**.

Extra Practice Have a class debate. Divide the class into two groups. Assign each group one of these positions: **Il est important de protéger l'environnement. / Il est important de développer l'économie et l'emploi**. Allow groups time to prepare their arguments before staging the debate. You may also divide the class into four groups and have two debates going on at the same time.

LE FRANÇAIS QUOTIDIEN

L'écologie

agriculture (*f.*) bio	*organic farming*
bac (*m.*) de recyclage	*recycling bin*
écologiste (*m., f.*)	*ecologist*
énergie (*f.*) éolienne	*wind power*
énergie (*f.*) renouvelable	*renewable energy*
panneau (*m.*) solaire	*solar panel*
produit (*m.*) bio	*organic product*
seuil (*m.*) de tolérance	*threshold*

LE MONDE FRANCOPHONE

L'écotourisme

Voici quelques destinations francophones de l'écotourisme.

En Afrique du Nord avec le désert du Sahara, en Algérie, au Maroc et en Tunisie
À la Guadeloupe avec le volcan de la Soufrière, ses nombreuses cascades° et ses forêts tropicales
En Guyane française avec sa forêt tropicale humide qui couvre 90% du pays
Au Québec avec sa géographie variée, ses communautés indigènes° et ses trois réserves de biosphère
Aux Seychelles les 115 îles de l'archipel, avec leurs nombreuses réserves naturelles et leurs récifs de corail°
Au Viêt-nam le delta du Mékong, avec son paysage de canaux° et ses cultures de riz

cascades *waterfalls* **indigènes** *native* **récifs de corail** *coral reefs* **canaux** *canals*

PORTRAIT

L'énergie nucléaire

En France, le nucléaire produit 75 à 80% de l'électricité. C'est EDF (Électricité de France) qui a construit les premières centrales° du pays. Aujourd'hui, le pays possède 58 réacteurs et une usine de traitement°, Areva NC. Les déchets radioactifs de France, d'Europe et d'Asie y sont traités°. La France est un exemple de réussite de l'énergie nucléaire, mais sa population est inquiète. L'explosion de Tchernobyl en 1986 a démontré les risques d'accidents des centrales. Dix pour cent des déchets, dits «à vie longue», ne sont pas traitables° et deviennent un problème de santé publique. Le rôle des énergies renouvelables ne peut donc qu'augmenter° à l'avenir.

centrales *power plants* **usine de traitement** *reprocessing plant* **traités** *reprocessed* **ne sont pas traitables** *cannot be reprocessed* **augmenter** *become larger*

SUR INTERNET

Quand la dernière marée noire a-t-elle eu lieu en France?

Go to **espaces.vhlcentral.com** to find more information related to this **ESPACE CULTURE**.

ACTIVITÉS

2 Répondez Répondez aux questions d'après les textes.

1. En France, quelle quantité d'électricité le nucléaire produit-il?
   Le nucléaire produit 75% à 80% de l'électricité en France.
2. Qui a construit les premières centrales françaises?
   EDF (Électricité de France) a construit les premières centrales françaises.
3. Quel type de déchets l'entreprise Areva NC traite-t-elle?
   Areva NC traite les déchets radioactifs de France, d'Europe et d'Asie.
4. Les Français sont-ils contents du nucléaire?
   Non, en majorité, ils sont inquiets.
5. Où peut-on faire de l'écotourisme au Québec?
   On peut faire de l'écotourisme dans les trois réserves de biosphère.

3 Nucléaire et environnement Vous travaillez pour Areva NC et votre partenaire est un militant écologiste. Imaginez ensemble un dialogue où vous parlez de vos opinions pour et contre l'usage (*use*) de l'énergie nucléaire en France. Soyez prêts à jouer votre dialogue devant la classe.

ressources
espaces.vhlcentral.com

Le français quotidien
- Model the pronunciation of each term and have students repeat it. Point out that **bio** is short for **biologique**.
- Have volunteers create sentences using this vocabulary.

Portrait Ask students: **Y a-t-il une centrale nucléaire près de chez vous? Voudriez-vous habiter près d'une centrale nucléaire? Y a-t-il un problème avec les déchets nucléaires aux États-Unis?**

Le monde francophone After reading the text, take a quick class survey to find out which are the most popular ecotourism destinations. Example: **Combien d'étudiants aimeraient faire de l'écotourisme en Afrique du Nord?** Tally the results on the board.

2 Expansion For additional practice, give students these items. **6. Quand a eu lieu la catastrophe nucléaire à Tchernobyl? (en 1986) 7. Quel pourcentage des déchets nucléaires ne sont pas traitables en France? (10 pour cent) 8. Où peut-on faire de l'écotourisme en Afrique du Nord? (dans le désert du Sahara, en Algérie, au Maroc et en Tunisie) 9. Où peut-on faire de l'écotourisme dans une forêt tropicale? (à la Guadeloupe et en Guyane française)**

3 Suggestion Give students time to review the material on both pages and jot down some ideas before they begin their discussion.

OPTIONS

Areva NC Based in La Hague (Normandy), **Areva NC** reprocesses spent power reactor fuel in order to recycle uranium and plutonium and to condition the waste. **Areva NC** has been criticized for its disposal of radioactive waste in the English Channel and in the air. The site in La Hague houses the world's largest stockpile of separated plutonium.

Les énergies renouvelables The windmill (**le moulin à vent**) has existed in Europe since the twelfth century. Today it has evolved into the powerful wind turbine (**l'éolienne moderne**), which owes its technology to the aviation industry. Other renewable energy sources include solar energy (**l'énergie solaire**), hydroelectric power (**l'énergie hydroélectrique**), and geothermal energy (**l'énergie géothermique**).

NATIONAL STANDARDS comparisons

Section Goals

In this section, students will learn:

- the demonstrative pronouns **celui**, **celle**, **ceux**, and **celles**
- to use **-ci** and **-là** with forms of **celui**

Instructional Resources
*espaces.vhlcentral.com: Lab MP3s; WB/VM/LM Answer Key; IRM (**Essayez!** and **Mise en pratique** answers; Lab Audioscript); activities; downloads; reference tools*

Suggestions

- Tell the class that adjectives modifying forms of **celui** agree in gender and number. Use the **Point de départ** example. Past participles also agree in gender and number with any preceding direct object form of **celui**. Example: **La centrale nucléaire de Belleville est celle qu'on a vue à la télé cet après-midi.**
- Make sure students understand that forms of **celui** in relative clauses can be used with the relative pronoun **dont**. Example: **La voiture hybride est celle dont on parle le plus.**
- When using forms of **celui** in prepositional phrases, make sure students understand how possession can be expressed with the construction **celui de** + *a person's name*: **Quel sac cherches-tu? Celui d'Isabelle.**
- Have the class play a guessing game about articles in the classroom (such as clothing and school supplies). Say phrases with the construction **celui de** + [*a person's name*]. Students should respond with an antecedent for your statement. Examples: **Celui de Shayne est bleu. (le tee-shirt) Celles de Roger sont noires. (les lunettes)**

Essayez! Here are some additional items. **7. La population de l'Inde est croissante. (Celle / Celui) de la Russie est en déclin. (Celle) 8. Les bouteilles en verre sont-elles plus écologiques que (ceux / celles) en plastique? (celles) 9. Le gaspillage de l'eau n'est pas plus excusable que (celui / celle) de l'électricité. (celui)**

14A.1 Demonstrative pronouns

Point de départ In **Leçon 6A**, you learned how to use demonstrative adjectives. Demonstrative *pronouns* refer to a person or thing that has already been mentioned. Examples of English demonstrative pronouns include *this one* and *those*.

L'énergie qui coûte moins cher est plus dangereuse. *The energy that costs less is more dangerous.*	▶	**Celle** qui coûte moins cher est plus dangereuse. *The one that costs less is more dangerous.*

- Demonstrative pronouns agree in number and gender with the noun to which they refer.

Demonstrative pronouns

	singular		plural	
masculine	**celui**	*this one; that one; the one*	**ceux**	*these; those; the ones*
feminine	**celle**	*this one; that one; the one*	**celles**	*these; those; the ones*

- Demonstrative pronouns must be followed by one of three constructions: **-ci** or **-là**, a relative clause, or a prepositional phrase.

-ci; -là	**Quels emballages? Ceux-ci?** *Which packages? These here?*	**Quelle bouteille? Celle-là en verre?** *Which bottle? The glass one there?*
relative clause	**Quelle femme? Celle qui parle?** *Which woman? The one who is talking?*	**C'est celui qu'on a entendu à la radio.** *He is the one we heard on the radio.*
prepositional phrase	**Quel problème? Celui de l'effet de serre?** *What problem? The one about the greenhouse effect?*	**Ces sacs coûtent plus cher que ceux en papier.** *Those bags cost more than the paper ones.*

Essayez! Choisissez le pronom démonstratif correct.

1. Le recyclage du plastique coûte plus cher que (celle / celui) du verre.
2. La protection des arbres est aussi importante que (celle / celui) des animaux.
3. Les espaces verts sont (ceux / celles) dont on a le plus besoin en ville.
4. Les ordures les plus sales sont (ceux / celles) des industries.
5. De tous les problèmes écologiques, l'effet de serre est (celui / ceux) dont on parle le plus.
6. Quels sacs préfères-tu: (ceux / celui)-ci?

MISE EN PRATIQUE

1 Le marché aux puces Vous êtes au marché aux puces (*flea market*) pour trouver des cadeaux. Complétez les phrases avec des pronoms démonstratifs.

1. Ce magnifique vase bleu, je pense que c'est __celui__ que maman voulait.
2. Ces deux jolis sacs: __celui-ci__ est pour Sylvie et __celui-là__ est pour Soraya.
3. Cette casquette rouge est pour moi. Elle ressemble à __celle__ de Françoise.
4. Il y avait des boîtes pleines de livres anciens. __Ceux__ que j'ai achetés étaient les plus beaux.
5. J'adore ces deux affiches. __Celle-ci__ est pour Julien et __celle-là__ est pour André.
6. Ce cadeau? __Celui-ci__... C'est une surprise!

2 Entretien Camille doit passer un entretien et elle parle à sa copine Alice. Ajoutez des pronoms démonstratifs avec **-ci** et **-là**. Suggested answers

CAMILLE Qu'est-ce que je peux mettre pour cet entretien? J'ai plusieurs tailleurs sympas.

ALICE Ces deux tailleurs gris font sérieux. Tu devrais plutôt mettre (1) __celui-là__. Il est élégant et classique.

CAMILLE Et comme chemisier, qu'est-ce que je mets?

ALICE (2) __Celui-ci__ est joli, mais (3) __celui-là__ ira mieux avec le style de ton tailleur.

CAMILLE Tu penses que je devrais mettre ces chaussures-ci ou (4) __celles-là__?

ALICE (5) __Celles-ci__ sont très à la mode mais (6) __celles-là__ sont plus classiques.

3 Cadeau d'anniversaire C'est bientôt l'anniversaire d'Houda et vous discutez avec un(e) partenaire des cadeaux que vous pourriez lui offrir. Refaites leur conversation. Answers will vary.

MODÈLE des tee-shirts / plus joli

Étudiant(e) 1: *Tu aimes ce tee-shirt?*
Étudiant(e) 2: *Non, pas trop.*
Étudiant(e) 1: *Alors, lequel préfères-tu?*
Étudiant(e) 2: *Je préfère celui-ci. Il est plus joli.*

- des robes / élégant
- des lunettes de soleil / trop cher
- des CD / plus classique
- des livres / très intéressant

Practice more at **espaces.vhlcentral.com.**

OPTIONS

Extra Practice Have the class identify all the nouns in **Espace contextes**, pages 472–473. Then tell students to work in pairs to write a couple of sentences in which nouns from the list are replaced with forms of **celui.** Example: **des déchets toxiques (Ceux des usines de Sugar Land sont-ils dangereux?)**

Game Make up a set of enigmatic sentences using forms of **celui**. The sentences should contain enough clues to suggest an antecedent. Tell students to guess at possible antecedents for each sentence and encourage them to be creative. Example: **Ceux de Cameron Diaz sont blonds. (les cheveux)**

COMMUNICATION

4 La pollution Que pensent vos camarades de la pollution? Posez ces questions à un(e) partenaire. Ensuite, présentez les réponses à la classe. Utilisez **celui, celle, ceux** ou **celles.** Answers will vary.

1. Quelles voitures polluent le moins: les voitures hybrides ou les voitures de sport? Lesquelles préfères-tu?
2. Si tu devais choisir entre ces deux voitures, laquelle prendrais-tu: celle qui est la plus rapide ou celle qui pollue le moins? Pourquoi?
3. Connais-tu quelqu'un qui fait régulièrement du covoiturage? Qui? Pourquoi le fait-il/elle?
4. Les emballages en plastique polluent-ils plus que ceux en papier? Pourquoi?
5. Est-ce que ceux qui recyclent leurs déchets aident à préserver la nature? Pourquoi?
6. Parmi (*Among*) les pays industrialisés, lesquels polluent le plus? Lesquels polluent le moins?

5 Définitions Votre petit frère vous demande de lui expliquer ces expressions. Avec un(e) partenaire, alternez les rôles pour donner leurs définitions. Utilisez **celui qui, celle qui, ceux qui** ou **celles qui.** Answers will vary.

MODÈLE

un pollueur
Étudiant(e) 1: *Qu'est-ce que c'est, un pollueur?*
Étudiant(e) 2: *C'est celui qui laisse des papiers sales dans la rue.*

- les déchets toxiques
- un(e) écologiste
- un écoproduit
- l'énergie solaire
- la pluie acide
- les voitures hybrides

6 D'accord, pas d'accord Par groupes de quatre, faites ce sondage (*survey*). Qui est d'accord ou qui n'est pas d'accord avec ces phrases? Justifiez vos réponses. Ensuite, comparez-les avec celles d'un autre groupe. Answers will vary.

	D'accord	Pas d'accord
1. Les déchets toxiques d'une centrale nucléaire sont plus dangereux que ceux d'une centrale électrique.	____	____
2. Les sacs en plastique sont aussi facilement recyclables que ceux en papier.	____	____
3. En ce qui concerne la voiture du futur, la voiture hybride est celle dont on parle le plus.	____	____
4. Les déchets qui polluent le plus sont ceux des centrales nucléaires.	____	____

Le français vivant

L'île de Corse
Celle qui a les plus belles plages de la Méditerranée. Tous ceux qui habitent ce paradis sont fiers de le partager avec tous ceux qui leur rendent visite. Celui qui vient en Corse une fois y reviendra toujours.
beautécorse

Identifiez Quels pronoms démonstratifs trouvez-vous dans la publicité (*ad*)? Celle, ceux, Celui

Questions À tour de rôle, avec un(e) partenaire, posez-vous ces questions. Employez des pronoms démonstratifs dans vos réponses, si possible. Answers will vary.

1. D'après (*According to*) la pub, quelles sont les plus belles plages de la Méditerranée? celles de la Corse
2. Qui est fier de partager la Corse? tous ceux qui y habitent
3. Que veut celui qui vient une fois en Corse? Celui qui vient en Corse veut y revenir.
4. Y a-t-il un endroit dans le monde qui a eu cet effet sur toi? Lequel?
5. Voudrais-tu visiter la Corse un jour? Pourquoi?

1 Suggestion You might want to have students complete items 1, 3, and 4 first. Then remind them of the suffixes **-ci** and **-là** before proceeding to items 2, 5, and 6.

2 Suggestion Remind students that French speakers usually refer to a near object with **-ci** before referring to a far object with **-là** in the same sentence.

3 Suggestion Have two volunteers read the **modèle** aloud to the class. Then review forms of the relative pronoun **lequel**. Make sure students understand the different ways **lequel** and **celui** are used.

4 Expansion Introduce students to a concept of personal responsibility from existentialism: **la mauvaise foi**. A person that acts in **mauvaise foi** behaves in a way that is inconsistent with his or her true beliefs. Ask the class to categorize certain behaviors as a **politique de bonne foi** or a **politique de mauvaise foi** for an environmentalist. Examples: **le covoiturage (bonne foi)** and **promouvoir le covoiturage, mais aller seul(e) au travail avec une grosse voiture (mauvaise foi).**

5 Suggestion Have students draw pictures like those in children's books to accompany their definitions.

6 Expansion Have groups select a topic from the list and prepare a small debate. Regardless of their personal beliefs, one student should advocate **d'accord** and the other **pas d'accord**.

Le français vivant Hand out or have students copy the text in the advertisement. Tell them to underline the demonstrative pronouns. Then ask them what they think the antecedents are.

OPTIONS

Extra Practice Have small groups of students prepare a fashion outlook for the season. They should make collages with pictures from magazines or the Internet of the latest styles and tell the class what they think of them, using forms of the demonstrative pronoun **celui** whenever possible. Example: **Ce jean-ci est laid! J'aime mieux celui-là.**

Extra Practice Make a set of index cards, organized in pairs with two similar objects, one on each card. Then prompt students to evaluate the objects with questions using forms of **lequel** and **celui.** Example: (*two pictures of automobiles*) **Laquelle pollue moins, à votre avis? Celle-ci ou celle-là? (La voiture rouge!)**

Section Goals

In this section, students will learn:

- the present subjunctive of regular verbs
- to use the subjunctive after some impersonal expressions

NATIONAL STANDARDS comparisons

Instructional Resources
*espaces.vhlcentral.com: Lab MP3s; WB/VM/LM Answer Key; IRM (**Essayez!** and **Mise en pratique** answers; Lab Audioscript); activities; downloads; reference tools*

Suggestions

- Remind students that verbs ending in **-ier** have a double **i** in the **nous** and **vous** forms of the present subjunctive: **étudiiez, skiions**, etc. (They learned this in **Leçon 8A** with the **imparfait**.)
- Tell the class that to negate impersonal expressions they should place the negative particles around the conjugated verb in the indicative, not around the subjunctive verb that follows in the next clause. Example: **Il ne faut pas qu'elle mette ces ordures dans le bac à recyclage.**
- Point out to students that the expressions **il faut** and **il vaut mieux** can be followed by an infinitive. Example: **Il vaut mieux partager sa voiture de temps en temps.** You could also point out that the other expressions in the list can be followed by **de/d'** + *infinitive*. Example: **Il est nécessaire de partager sa voiture de temps en temps.**
- Read aloud a set of logical and illogical statements about environmentalism that make use of impersonal expressions and the subjunctive. Students should respond by saying **logique** or **illogique.** Example: **Pour éviter de gaspiller l'essence, il vaut mieux qu'on recycle le verre. (illogique)**

14A.2 The subjunctive (Part 1)

Introduction, regular verbs, and impersonal expressions

Point de départ With the exception of commands and the conditional, the verb forms you have learned have been in the indicative mood. The indicative is used to state facts and to express actions or states that the speaker considers real and definite. In contrast, the subjunctive mood expresses the speaker's subjective attitudes toward events and actions or states the speaker's views as uncertain or hypothetical.

Present subjunctive of one-stem verbs

	parler	finir	attendre
que je/j'	parle	finisse	attende
que tu	parles	finisses	attendes
qu'il/elle	parle	finisse	attende
que nous	parlions	finissions	attendions
que vous	parliez	finissiez	attendiez
qu'ils/elles	parlent	finissent	attendent

- The **je**, **tu**, **il/elle**, and **ils/elles** forms of the three verb types form the subjunctive the same way. They add the subjunctive endings to the stem of the **ils/elles** form of the present indicative.

INFINITIVE	PRESENT INDICATIVE OF ILS/ELLES	PRESENT SUBJUNCTIVE
parler	parlent	que je parle
finir	finissent	que je finisse
attendre	attendent	que j'attende

Il est nécessaire qu'on **évite** le gaspillage.
It is necessary that we avoid waste.

Il est important que tu **réfléchisses** aux dangers.
It is important that you think about the dangers.

- The **nous** and **vous** forms of the present subjunctive are the same as those of the **imparfait**.

Il vaut mieux que nous **préservions** l'environnement.
It is better that we preserve the environment.

Il est essentiel que vous **trouviez** un meilleur travail.
It is essential that you find a better job.

Il faut que nous **commencions**.
It is necessary that we start.

Il est bon que vous **réfléchissiez.**
It is good that you're thinking.

BOÎTE À OUTILS
English also uses the subjunctive. It used to be very common, but now survives mostly in expressions such as *if I were you* and *be that as it may*.

MISE EN PRATIQUE

1 Prévenir et améliorer Complétez ces phrases avec la forme correcte des verbes au présent du subjonctif.

1. Il est essentiel que je __recycle__ (recycler).
2. Il est important que nous __réduisions__ (réduire) la pollution.
3. Il faut que le gouvernement __interdise__ (interdire) les voitures polluantes (*polluting*).
4. Il vaut mieux que vous __amélioriez__ (améliorer) les transports en commun (*public transportation*).
5. Il est possible que les pays __prennent__ (prendre) des mesures pour réduire les déchets toxiques.
6. Il est indispensable que tu __boives__ (boire) de l'eau pure.

2 Sur le campus Quelles règles les étudiants qui habitent sur le campus doivent-ils suivre? Transformez ces phrases avec **il faut** et le présent du subjonctif.

MODÈLE Vous devez vous coucher avant minuit.
Il faut que vous vous couchiez avant minuit.

1. Le matin, vous devez vous lever à sept heures.
   Le matin, il faut que vous vous leviez à sept heures.
2. Ils doivent fermer leur porte avant de partir.
   Il faut qu'ils ferment leur porte avant de partir.
3. Tu dois prendre le bus au coin de la rue.
   Il faut que tu prennes le bus au coin de la rue.
4. Je dois déjeuner au resto U à midi.
   Il faut que je déjeune au resto U à midi.
5. Nous devons rentrer tôt pendant la semaine.
   Il faut que nous rentrions tôt pendant la semaine.
6. Elle doit travailler pour payer ses études.
   Il faut qu'elle travaille pour payer ses études.

3 Éviter une catastrophe Que devons-nous faire pour préserver notre planète? Avec un(e) partenaire, faites des phrases avec des expressions impersonnelles.
Answers will vary.

MODÈLE
Il est essentiel que tu évites le gaspillage.

A	B	C
je/j'	améliorer	les écoproduits
tu	développer	les emballages
on	éviter	le gaspillage
nous	préserver	les glissements de terrain
vous	prévenir	les industries propres
le président	recycler	la nature
les pays	sauver	la pollution
?	trouver	le ramassage des ordures

Practice more at **espaces.vhlcentral.com.**

OPTIONS

Video Distribute copies of the script for the last scene of the video for **Leçon 14A** and have students underline all the verbs. Ask them to identify the mood (indicative, imperative, or subjunctive) of each verb. When they realize that the subjunctive is used rarely, point out that native speakers often avoid the subjunctive because it can be tricky for them, too.

Extra Practice Have the class make up a list of ten environmental resolutions using some of the impersonal expressions listed on page 483. Help them when they need expressions such as *a recycling bin* (**un bac à recyclage**). Example: **Il est essentiel qu'on préserve la nature.**

COMMUNICATION

4 Oui ou non? Vous discutez avec un(e) partenaire des problèmes d'environnement. À tour de rôle, parfois, vous confirmez ce qu'il/elle dit, mais parfois, vous n'êtes pas d'accord. Answers will vary.

MODÈLE

Étudiant(e) 1: *Il faut que les pays industrialisés réduisent les émissions à effet de serre.*
Étudiant(e) 2: *C'est vrai, il faut qu'ils réduisent les émissions à effet de serre.*

1. Il est nécessaire que tu recycles les bouteilles.
2. Il est dommage que les étudiants prennent le bus pour aller à la fac.
3. Il est bon qu'on développe des énergies propres.
4. Il est essentiel qu'on signe le protocole de Kyoto.
5. Il est indispensable que nous évitions le gaspillage.
6. Il faut que les pays développent de nouvelles technologies pour réduire les émissions toxiques.

5 Les opinions Vous discutez avec un(e) partenaire des problèmes de pollution. À tour de rôle, répondez à ces questions. Justifiez vos réponses. Answers will vary.

MODÈLE

Étudiant(e) 1: *Faut-il que nous préservions l'environnement?*
Étudiant(e) 2: *Oui, il faut que nous préservions l'environnement pour éviter le réchauffement de la Terre.*

1. Est-il important qu'on s'intéresse à l'écologie?
2. Faut-il qu'on évite de gaspiller?
3. Est-il essentiel que nous construisions des centrales nucléaires?
4. Vaut-il mieux que j'utilise des bacs (*bins*) à recyclage pour le ramassage des ordures?
5. Est-il indispensable qu'on prévienne les incendies?
6. Est-il possible qu'on développe l'énergie solaire?

6 L'écologie Par groupes de quatre, regardez les deux photos et parlez des problèmes écologiques qu'elles évoquent. Ensuite, préparez par écrit une liste des solutions. Comparez votre liste avec celles de la classe. Answers will vary.

MODÈLE

Étudiant(e) 1: *Aujourd'hui, il y a trop d'ordures.*
Étudiant(e) 2: *Il faut qu'on développe le recyclage.*

- The verbs on the preceding page are called one-stem verbs because the same stem is used for all the endings. Two-stem verbs have a different stem for **nous** and **vous**, but the rule still applies: the forms are identical to those of the **imparfait**.

Present subjunctive of two-stem verbs

	acheter	venir	prendre	boire
que je/j'	achète	vienne	prenne	boive
que tu	achètes	viennes	prennes	boives
qu'il/elle	achète	vienne	prenne	boive
que nous	achetions	venions	prenions	buvions
que vous	achetiez	veniez	preniez	buviez
qu'ils/elles	achètent	viennent	prennent	boivent

- The subjunctive is usually used in complex sentences that consist of a main clause and a subordinate clause. The main clause contains a verb or expression that triggers the subjunctive. The word **que** connects the two clauses.

- These impersonal expressions of opinion are often followed by clauses in the subjunctive. They are followed by the infinitive, without **que**, if no person or thing is specified. Add **de** before the infinitive after expressions with **être**.

Il est bon que...	*It is good that...*	**Il est indispensable que...**	*It is essential that...*
Il est dommage que...	*It is a shame that...*	**Il est nécessaire que...**	*It is necessary that...*
Il est essentiel que...	*It is essential that...*	**Il est possible que...**	*It is possible that...*
Il est important que...	*It is important that...*	**Il faut que...**	*One must... / It is necessary that...*
		Il vaut mieux que...	*It is better that...*

Il est essentiel qu'on **réduise** le gaspillage. *but* **Il est essentiel de réduire** le gaspillage.
It is essential that we reduce waste. — *It is essential to reduce waste.*

Il faut qu'on **ferme** l'usine. *but* **Il faut fermer** l'usine.
We must close the factory. — *We must close the factory.*

Essayez! **Indiquez la forme correcte du présent du subjonctif de ces verbes.**

1. (améliorer, choisir, vendre) que je/j' améliore, choisisse, vende
2. (mettre, renvoyer, maigrir) que tu mettes, renvoies, maigrisses
3. (dire, partir, devenir) qu'elle dise, parte, devienne
4. (appeler, enlever, revenir) que nous appelions, enlevions, revenions
5. (démissionner, obtenir, apprendre) que vous démissionniez, obteniez, appreniez
6. (payer, répéter, lire) qu'ils paient, répètent, lisent

Essayez! Toss a tennis ball or a crumpled piece of paper to a student while saying a subject pronoun and the infinitive of a regular verb. He or she gives the present subjunctive form and tosses the object to another student while you call another pronoun and infinitive.

1 Expansion To ensure students' comprehension, ask them to categorize each statement as **une responsabilité gouvernementale, une responsabilité personnelle,** or **les deux**.

2 Expansion Have students reformulate each answer so that the subject is **je/j'**. Then ask them **C'est vrai?** to see if the statement is true for them personally. Example: **Le matin, il faut que je me lève à sept heures. (Ce n'est pas vrai! D'habitude, je me lève à neuf heures.)**

3 Suggestion Remind students to use each of the expressions in the columns at least once.

4 Expansion When students have completed this activity, suggest that they prepare a conversation between a passionate environmentalist and an environmentalism skeptic. Encourage them to use humor and to perform their conversation for the class.

5 Suggestion Have students develop two responses for each question, one that begins with **oui** and one that begins with **non**. They should summarize their arguments in writing when they've completed the activity and place a check next to the argument for each topic that they find most persuasive.

6 Expansion After completing the activity, write this statement on the board: **L'avenir de l'écologie, c'est les technologies.** Then ask students to find arguments that support or contradict it. You might suggest that they do Internet or library research to support their arguments.

OPTIONS

Extra Practice Have students complete the following sentences to practice the subjunctive with impersonal expressions. **1. Il ne faut pas qu'on ____ l'eau. (gaspille) 2. Pour prévenir les incendies, il vaut mieux que les visiteurs du camping ne ____ pas. (fument) 3. L'écologiste nous a dit qu'il fallait qu'on ____ la planète. (sauve)**

Extra Practice Make a set of statements about the environment that use impersonal expressions and the subjunctive. Ask students to pretend that they are ecologists and to give a thumbs-up if they like what they hear or a thumbs-down if they don't. Example for thumbs-up: **Il faut qu'on réduise les déchets toxiques des usines.**

Instructional Resources
espaces.vhlcentral.com: IRM (Info Gap Activities); Testing Program, pp. 105–108; Test Files; Testing Program MP3s; activities; downloads; reference tools
Test Generator

1 Suggestion Tell students to complete this activity in phases. In the first phase, they describe the problem. In the second, they formulate a solution, using a sentence with the present subjunctive. In the third, they rewrite their solution using a form of **celui**.

2 Suggestion Explain to students that French speakers tend to write formal, respectful letters in these sorts of situations. Then supply them with a few of the formulas commonly used by native speakers in formal letters of complaint. Example: **Je vous prie d'agréer, Monsieur/Madame, l'expression de mes salutations respectueuses.**

3 Expansion For an extra challenge, suggest that students also give advice telling what *not* to do. Example for **votre camarade de chambre**: **Il ne faut pas que tu t'énerves quand tu lui expliques le problème.**

4 Suggestion This activity could also be completed by groups of three, so that each student comes up with a suggestion about how to address the situation. Tell students to rotate the order in which they give their suggestions.

5 Suggestion To make sure that students understand others' suggestions, ask the class to rate each suggestion on a scale of 1 (**C'est facile à faire!**) to 5 (**C'est très difficile à faire!**).

6 Suggestion Divide the class into pairs and distribute the Info Gap Handouts found on the Supersite for this activity. Give students ten minutes to complete the activity.

Révision

1 Des solutions Avec un(e) partenaire, décrivez ces problèmes et donnez des solutions. Utilisez le présent du subjonctif et un pronom démonstratif pour chaque photo. Présentez vos solutions à la classe. Answers will vary.

MODÈLE

Étudiant(e) 1: *Cette eau est sale.*
Étudiant(e) 2: *Il faut que celui qui a pollué cette eau paie une grosse amende.*

1.

2.

3.

4.

2 Une lettre Vous habitez dans un village où les autorités veulent construire un grand aéroport. Avec un(e) partenaire, écrivez une lettre aux responsables dans laquelle vous expliquez vos inquiétudes (*worries*). Utilisez des expressions impersonnelles, puis lisez la lettre à la classe. Answers will vary.

3 Les plaintes Par groupes de trois, interviewez vos camarades à tour de rôle. Que vous conseillent-ils de faire quand vous vous plaignez (*complain*) d'une de ces personnes? Écrivez leurs réponses, puis comparez-les à celles d'un autre groupe. Answers will vary.

MODÈLE

Il est important que tu écrives une lettre au gérant.

- vos parents
- votre professeur
- votre camarade de chambre
- un(e) serveur/serveuse
- un(e) patron(ne)
- un médecin

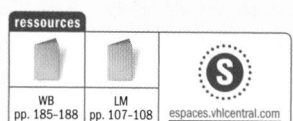

ressources
WB pp. 185–188 | LM pp. 107–108 | espaces.vhlcentral.com

4 Si... Avec un(e) partenaire, observez ces scènes et lisez les phrases. Pour chaque scène, faites trois phrases au présent du subjonctif, puis présentez-les à la classe. Answers will vary.

MODÈLE

Étudiant(e) 1: *Si l'eau est sale, il ne faut pas que les gens mangent les poissons.*
Étudiant(e) 2: *Oui, il faut qu'ils les achètent à la poissonnerie.*

1. Si l'eau est sale, ...

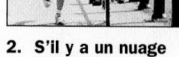

2. S'il y a un nuage de pollution, ...

3. S'il tombe une pluie acide, ...

4. S'il y a un glissement de terrain, ...

5 Des propositions Que peut-on faire pour préserver l'environnement? Avec un(e) partenaire, utilisez le présent du subjonctif et, si nécessaire, des pronoms pour faire des propositions. Ensuite, comparez-les à celles d'un autre groupe. Answers will vary.

MODÈLE

Étudiant(e) 1: *Celui qui change l'huile de sa voiture? Il est essentiel qu'il recycle l'huile et qu'il l'apporte à un garagiste.*
Étudiant(e) 2: *Il ne faut pas qu'il change l'huile trop souvent ou qu'il utilise de l'huile de mauvaise qualité.*

6 Non, Solange! Votre professeur va vous donner, à vous et à votre partenaire, deux feuilles d'activités différentes sur les mauvaises habitudes de Solange. Attention! Ne regardez pas la feuille de votre partenaire. Answers will vary.

MODÈLE

Étudiant(e) 1: *Il est dommage que Solange conduise une voiture qui pollue.*
Étudiant(e) 2: *Il faut qu'elle conduise une voiture plus écologique.*

OPTIONS

TPR Read a list of admonishments that make use of the impersonal expressions on page 483 and the present subjunctive. Ask students to pantomime what you are asking them to do. Example: **Il faut que tu passes l'aspirateur dans ta chambre cet après-midi, Mike!**

Game Make two sets of cards, one labeled with **que/qu'** + [*subject pronouns*], the other labeled with the infinitives of regular verbs. Students in small groups can "play" their hands by providing subjunctive verb forms suggested by pairs of cards. They should put down cards they've used and then draw more to collect as many as possible.

Video: TV Clip

Le Zapping

La BMCE

La Banque Marocaine du Commerce Extérieur est la deuxième plus grande banque du Maroc. Elle a non seulement des agences en Europe et en Asie, mais elle vise° aussi constamment à étendre° les liens° entre le Maroc et le reste du monde. À travers la Fondation BMCE Éducation et Environnement, la banque se soucie° également° de la protection de l'environnement et du développement de la société marocaine. En 2000, elle a lancé le projet Medersat.com, dont un des objectifs les plus importants est la scolarisation des enfants dans les villages marocains.

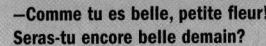

—Comme tu es belle, petite fleur! Seras-tu encore belle demain?

—Attends-moi! Moi aussi, j'ai envie d'apprendre.

Compréhension Répondez aux questions.

1. Sur quoi le garçon est-il debout (*standing*) dans la première scène? Il est debout sur la Terre/la planète.
2. Que demande-t-il à la colombe (*dove*)? Il lui demande si elle peut lui montrer le chemin de la Liberté.
3. Où vont le garçon et sa sœur à la fin? Ils vont à l'école.

Discussion Par groupes de trois, répondez aux questions et discutez. Answers will vary.

1. Pourquoi le garçon pose-t-il des questions? Pourquoi à une fleur, aux étoiles (*stars*), à une colombe et à un arbre (*tree*)? Quels sont leurs attributs?
2. Quels messages concernant les missions de la BMCE la publicité (*commercial*) nous transmet-elle?

vise *aims* **étendre** *to extend* **liens** *links* **se soucie** *cares* **également** *also*

Practice more at **espaces.vhlcentral.com.**

Section Goals

In this section, students will:
- read about the **Banque Marocaine du Commerce Extérieur**
- watch a commercial for the bank
- answer questions about the commercial and the BMCE

Instructional Resources
*espaces.vhlcentral.com: TV commercial; IRM (**Le zapping** TV clip Transcription); activities; downloads; reference tools*

Introduction
To check comprehension, ask these questions:
1. Que vise constamment à faire la BMCE? (Elle vise à étendre les liens entre le Maroc et le reste du monde.)
2. De quoi la banque se soucie-t-elle aussi? (Elle se soucie de la protection de l'environnement et du développement de la société marocaine.)
3. Quel est un des objectifs importants du projet Medersat.com? (Un de ses objectifs les plus importants est la scolarisation des enfants dans les villages marocains.)

Avant de regarder la vidéo
- Have students look at the video stills, read the captions, and predict what is happening in the commercial for each visual. **(1. Le garçon est sur la planète et il parle à une fleur. 2. Un groupe d'enfants court. Ils vont à l'école.)**
- Before showing the video, explain to students that they do not need to understand every word they hear. Tell them to listen for the text in the captions and jot down any familiar words.

Compréhension Have students work in pairs or groups for this activity. Tell them to write their answers. Then show the video again so that they can check their answers and add any missing information.

Discussion Ask groups to explain the connection between all the boy's questions and Medersat.com's educational objective referenced in the introductory paragraph.

OPTIONS

La langue tamazight One of the BMCE's social missions is the promotion of the Tamazight language of Moroccan Berbers. Most Tamazight speakers today live in central Morocco, but people of Berber descent live across most of North Africa. Tamazight is only one of many Berber dialects, though the term is often used generically to denote all of its dialects, some of which are spoken as far south as Burkina Faso and as far east as Egypt. After gaining independence from France in the 1960s, several North African countries, including Morocco, instituted policies to promote the use of Arabic in schools. However, in the process they also suppressed or outright banned the teaching of Tamazight. In the case of Morocco, new policies are today reversing the trend and introducing Tamazight-language instruction in schools.

Section Goals

In this section, students will learn and practice vocabulary related to:
- nature and conservation
- animals

Instructional Resources
*espaces.vhlcentral.com: Transparency #58; IRM (**Vocabulaire supplémentaire**; **Mise en pratique** answers; Textbook Audioscript; Lab Audioscript); Textbook MP3s; Lab MP3s; WB/VM/LM Answer Key; activities; downloads; reference tools*

Suggestions

- Tell students to look over the new vocabulary and identify the cognates.
- Use **Transparency #58.** Point out people and things as you describe the illustration. Examples: **Ils voient une étoile. C'est une vache.**
- To practice the vocabulary, show drawings or magazine photos and ask students questions. Examples: **Qu'est-ce que c'est? C'est un lapin ou un écureuil? Y a-t-il un fleuve sur le dessin?**
- Explain that **jeter**, like **appeler**, doubles the stem's final consonant in all singular forms as well as the third person plural form of the present tense: **je jette, tu jettes, il/elle jette, nous jetons, vous jetez, ils/elles jettent**.
- Additional vocabulary for this lesson can be found in the **Vocabulaire supplémentaire** on the Supersite.

Leçon 14B

Talking Picture
Audio: Activity

You will learn how to...
- **discuss nature and the environment**
- **make comparisons**

En pleine nature

Vocabulaire

chasser	*to hunt*
jeter	*to throw away*
un animal	*animal*
un bois	*woods*
un champ	*field*
une côte	*coast*
un désert	*desert*
un fleuve	*river*
une forêt (tropicale)	*(tropical) forest*
la jungle	*jungle*
la nature	*nature*
une région	*region*
une rivière	*river*
un sentier	*path*
un volcan	*volcano*
la chasse	*hunt*
le déboisement	*deforestation*
l'écotourisme (*m.*)	*ecotourism*
une espèce (menacée)	*(endangered) species*
l'extinction (*f.*)	*extinction*
la préservation	*protection*
une ressource naturelle	*natural resource*
le sauvetage des habitats naturels	*natural habitat preservation*

ressources
WB pp. 189-190
LM p. 109
espaces.vhlcentral.com

OPTIONS

TPR Make a series of true/false statements related to the lesson theme using the new vocabulary. Tell students to remain seated if a statement is true and to stand if it is false. Examples: **Les lapins habitent dans les arbres.** (Students stand.) **On voit des étoiles dans le ciel.** (Students remain seated or sit down.)

Extra Practice Write these categories on the board: **Animaux** and **Éléments naturels** (*Natural features*). Dictate words from the vocabulary. Tell students to write the words under the correct heading on their papers. Examples: **serpent, île, désert, écureuil, volcan, falaise, vallée,** and **vache.**

Mise en pratique

1 Par catégorie Faites correspondre les éléments de la colonne de gauche avec l'élément des colonnes de droite qui convient.

- d 1. la Seine
- j 2. la Martinique
- h 3. une vache
- a 4. l'Etna
- i 5. le pétrole
- g 6. le Sahara
- e 7. un arbre
- c 8. Érié

a. un volcan	f. une forêt
b. une jungle	g. un désert
c. un lac	h. un animal
d. un fleuve	i. une ressource naturelle
e. une plante	j. une île

2 La nature Choisissez le terme qui correspond à chaque définition. Ensuite choisissez trois autres termes d'**ESPACE CONTEXTES** et écrivez leur définition. Avec un partenaire, lisez vos définitions et devinez quels sont les termes que vous avez choisis.

le déboisement	une falaise	la préservation
l'écotourisme	une jungle	le sauvetage des habitats naturels
l'environnement	une pierre	un sentier
l'extinction	un pique-nique	une vache

1. Là où l'homme vit: l'environnement
2. Sauver et protéger: la préservation
3. Lieu très chaud, très humide: une jungle
4. Chemin très étroit (*narrow*): un sentier
5. Quand une espèce n'existe plus: l'extinction
6. Conséquence de la destruction des arbres: le déboisement
7. Action de sauver le lieu où vivent des animaux: le sauvetage des habitats naturels
8. Vacances qui favorisent la protection de l'environnement: l'écotourisme
9. Un animal de taille importante qui mange de l'herbe: une vache
10. Quand on mange dans la nature: un pique-nique
11. Élément minéral solide, parfois gris: une pierre
12. Sur le dessin de gauche, c'est la masse rocheuse (*rocky*) à droite: une falaise

3 Écoutez Écoutez Armand parler de quelques-unes de ses expériences avec la nature. Après une deuxième écoute, écrivez les termes qui se réfèrent au ciel, à la terre et aux plantes. Some answers may vary.

Terre	Ciel	Plantes
nature	étoiles	forêt(s) tropicale(s)
forêt(s) tropicale(s)	Lune	arbres
sentiers		fleurs
campagne		nature

Practice more at **espaces.vhlcentral.com.**

1 Expansion Ask students questions about the location of each item in this activity. Examples: **Dans quelle grande ville se trouve la Seine? (à Paris) Où trouve-t-on des vaches? (dans les vallées/ à la campagne)**

2 Suggestions
- Tell students to compare their answers with their partner's.
- Have students describe what they see in the photo.

3 Tapescript ARMAND: Moi, j'adore la nature. Quand j'ai le temps, je quitte la vie en ville et je fais de l'écotourisme. C'est l'idéal pour profiter de la nature et protéger l'environnement en même temps. Je n'aime pas aller à la pêche parce qu'il y a déjà beaucoup de poissons qui sont en danger d'extinction. J'aime beaucoup les forêts tropicales. L'année dernière, je suis allé visiter la forêt tropicale du Cameroun. C'était magnifique! Il y avait des espèces d'arbres et de fleurs variées et j'ai marché des heures dans des sentiers très différents. Aussi, quand je peux, je vais rendre visite à mon grand-père pour me reposer. Il habite à la campagne. Le soir, on peut se coucher dans l'herbe et regarder les étoiles et la Lune. *(On Textbook MP3s)*

3 Suggestion Go over the answers with the class.

OPTIONS

Game Have students fold a sheet of paper into 16 squares (four folds in half) and write a new vocabulary word in each square. Say definitions for words. If students have the defined word, they mark their paper. The first student to mark four words in a row (across, down or diagonally) calls out **«gagné!»** To verify a win, the student should read the words in the row aloud.

Extra Practice To practice the new vocabulary, ask students these questions. **1. Préférez-vous la montagne ou la mer? 2. Êtes-vous déjà allé(e) dans le désert? dans une forêt tropicale? à la montagne? dans la jungle? 3. Quel est votre animal préféré? 4. Où préféreriez-vous faire un pique-nique? 5. Est-ce que vous chassez? Pourquoi ou pourquoi pas?**

4 Expansion Have pairs get together with another pair of students and share what they learned about their partners.

5 Suggestion If time is limited, this activity may be assigned as homework. Then allow partners time to work together for peer editing in class.

6 Suggestion Encourage students to illustrate their brochures with drawings, magazine photos, or clip art.

7 Suggestion Have a volunteer read the **modèle**. You might suggest that students incorporate information from **Le monde francophone**, page 479, in their radio ads.

Communication

4 Conversez Interviewez un(e) camarade de classe. Answers will vary.

1. As-tu déjà fait de l'écotourisme? Où? Si non, où as-tu envie d'en faire?
2. Aimes-tu les pique-niques? Quand en as-tu fait un pour la dernière fois? Avec qui?
3. Quelles activités aimes-tu pratiquer dans la nature?
4. As-tu déjà visité une forêt? Laquelle?
5. Connais-tu un lac? Quand y es-tu allé(e)? Quelles activités y as-tu pratiquées?
6. Es-tu déjà allé(e) dans un désert? Lequel?
7. Es-tu déjà allé(e) sur une île? Laquelle? Comment as-tu passé le temps?
8. Quelles sont les régions du monde que tu veux visiter? Pour quelle(s) raison(s)?
9. Si tu étais un animal, lequel serais-tu? Pourquoi?
10. Quand tu regardes le ciel, que trouves-tu de beau? Pourquoi?

5 La nature et moi Écrivez un paragraphe dans lequel vous racontez votre expérience avec la nature. Ensuite, à tour de rôle, lisez votre description à votre partenaire et comparez vos paragraphes. Answers will vary.

- Choisissez au minimum deux lieux naturels différents.
- Utilisez un minimum de huit mots de vocabulaire d'**ESPACE CONTEXTES.**
- Faites votre description avec le plus de détails possible.
- Expliquez ce que vous aimez ou ce que vous n'aimez pas à propos de chaque lieu.

6 Les écologistes Vous faites partie d'un club d'écologistes à l'université. Avec deux camarades de classe et les informations suivantes, préparez une brochure pour informer les étudiants du campus d'un grave problème écologique. Présentez ensuite votre brochure au reste de la classe. Quel groupe a présenté le problème le plus sérieux? Quel groupe a proposé les solutions les plus originales? Answers will vary.

- le nom de votre club
- la situation géographique du problème écologique
- la description du problème
- les causes du problème
- les conséquences du problème
- les solutions possibles au problème

7 À la radio Vous travaillez pour le ministère du Tourisme d'un pays francophone et vous devez préparer un texte qui sera lu à la radio. L'objectif de ce message est de faire la promotion de ce pays pour son écotourisme. Décrivez la nature et les activités offertes. Utilisez les mots que vous avez appris dans **ESPACE CONTEXTES.** Answers will vary.

MODÈLE

Venez découvrir la beauté de l'île de Madagascar. Chaque région vous offre des sentiers qui permettent d'admirer des plantes rares et des arbres magnifiques et de rencontrer des animaux extraordinaires…
À Madagascar, la nature est unique, préservée. Le charme et l'exotisme sont ici!

OPTIONS

Game Play a game of **Dix questions**. Ask a volunteer to think of a word from the new vocabulary. Other students get one chance to ask one yes/no question, then they can guess what the word is. Limit attempts to ten questions per word. You may want to write some phrases on the board to cue students' questions.

Game Write vocabulary words related to animals and nature on index cards. On another set of cards, draw or paste pictures to match each term. Tape them face down on the board in random order. Divide the class into two teams. Play a game of Concentration in which students match words with pictures. When a player makes a match, that player's team collects those cards. The team with the most cards at the end of the game wins.

Les sons et les lettres

Audio: Concepts, Activities
Record & Compare

NATIONAL STANDARDS comparisons

Homophones

Many French words sound alike, but are spelled differently. As you have already learned, sometimes the only difference between two words is a diacritical mark. Other words that sound alike have more obvious differences in spelling.

a / à **ou / où** **sont / son** **en / an**

Several forms of a single verb may sound alike. To tell which form is being used, listen for the subject or words that indicate tense.

je parle **tu** parles **ils** parlent
vous parlez **j'ai** parlé **je vais** parler

Many words that sound alike are different parts of speech. Use context to tell them apart.

VERB	POSSESSIVE ADJECTIVE	PREPOSITION	NOUN
Ils sont belges.	**C'est son mari.**	**Tu vas en France?**	**Il a un an.**

You may encounter multiple spellings of words that sound alike. Again, context is the key to understanding which word is being used.

je peux *I can*	**elle peut** *she can*	**peu** *a little, few*
le foie *liver*	**la foi** *faith*	**une fois** *one time*
haut *high*	**l'eau** *water*	**au** *at, to, in the*

Prononcez Répétez les paires de mots suivants à voix haute.

1. ce se	4. foi fois	7. au eau	10. lis lit
2. leur leurs	5. ces ses	8. peut peu	11. quelle qu'elle
3. né nez	6. vert verre	9. où ou	12. c'est s'est

Choisissez Choisissez le mot qui convient à chaque phrase.

1. Je (lis / lit) le journal tous les jours.
2. Son chien est sous le (lis / lit).
3. Corinne est (née / nez) à Paris.
4. Elle a mal au (née / nez).

Jeux de mots Répétez les jeux de mots à voix haute.

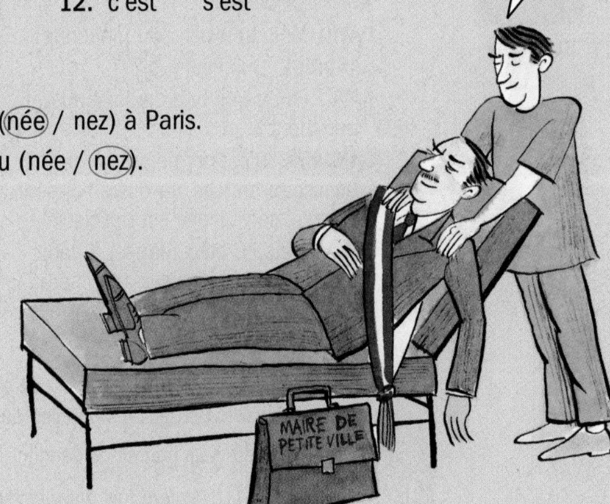

Le ver vert va vers le verre.[1]

Mon père est maire, mon frère est masseur.[2]
MAIRE DE PETITE VILLE

[1] The green worm is going toward the glass.
[2] My father is a mayor, my brother is a masseur.

ressources
LM p. 110
espaces.vhlcentral.com

Section Goals

In this section, students will learn about homophones.

Instructional Resources
espaces.vhlcentral.com: Textbook MP3s; Lab MP3s; WB/VM/LM Answer Key; IRM (Textbook Audioscript; Lab Audioscript); activities; downloads; reference tools

Suggestions
- Model the pronunciation of the example words and have students repeat them after you.
- Point out these additional homophones: **là** (*there*) **/ la** (*the*); **ont** (*have*) **/ on** (*one*); **je vois** (*I see*) **/ il voit** (*he sees*) **/ une voie** (*a way*) **/ une voix** (*a voice*).
- Read each sentence in the **Choisissez** activity aloud. Then have students select the correct word to complete each one.
- Have students look in the end vocabulary or verb charts in **Appendice D** and identify other homophones.
- Dictate five sentences that contain familiar homophones, repeating each one at least two times. Then write them on the board or a transparency and have students check their spelling.

Jeux de mots Make sure students understand the humor in the saying **«Mon père est maire, mon frère est masseur.»** Point out that it sounds like **«Mon père est mère, mon frère est ma sœur.»**

OPTIONS

Extra Practice Tell students to write six pairs of sentences using words in the **Prononcez** activity. Then have volunteers write their sentences on the board and go over them with the class.

Extra Practice Teach students this French tongue-twister that contains homophones. **Si six scies scient six cyprès, six cent six scies scient six cent six cyprès.**

Section Goals
In this section, students will learn functional phrases for expressing regrets, preferences, comparisons, and suggestions.

Instructional Resources
*espaces.vhlcentral.com: WB/VM/LM Answer Key; IRM (Videoscript; **Roman-photo** Translations); activities; downloads; reference tools*
Video on DVD

Video Recap: Leçon 14A
Before doing this **Roman-photo**, review the previous one with this activity.
1. Pourquoi Valérie est-elle de mauvaise humeur? (Michèle a démissionné. Stéphane n'a pas réussi son bac.)
2. Pourquoi Sandrine est-elle de mauvaise humeur? (Elle est/était anxieuse à cause de son concert/du départ de David.)
3. Quelle idée Rachid a-t-il eue? (d'aller à la montagne Sainte-Victoire)
4. Qui va aller à la montagne Sainte-Victoire? (Rachid, Amina, David, Sandrine, Valérie et Stéphane)

Video Synopsis
At **la montagne Sainte-Victoire**, the group visits the **Maison Sainte-Victoire**, an eco-museum. The guide explains that the mountain is a nature preserve. After a picnic, Sandrine wants David to draw her portrait. Rachid and Amina share a romantic moment, until Stéphane interrupts them.

Suggestions
- Have students predict what the episode will be about based on the video stills.
- Tell students to scan the captions for vocabulary related to nature and conservation.
- After reading the **Roman-photo**, have students summarize the episode.

La randonnée

Video: *Roman-photo*
Record & Compare

PERSONNAGES

Amina

David

Guide

Rachid

Sandrine

Stéphane

Valérie

1

À la montagne...
DAVID Que c'est beau!
VALÉRIE C'est la première fois que tu viens à la montagne Sainte-Victoire?
DAVID Non, en fait, je viens assez souvent pour dessiner, mais malheureusement c'est peut-être la dernière fois. C'est dommage que j'aie si peu de temps.

2

SANDRINE Je préférerais qu'on parle d'autre chose.
AMINA Elle a raison, nous sommes venus ici pour passer un bon moment.
STÉPHANE Tiens, et si on essayait de trouver des serpents?
AMINA Des serpents ici?
RACHID Ne t'inquiète pas, ma chérie. Par précaution, je suggère que tu restes près de moi.

3

RACHID Mais il ne faut pas que tu sois aussi anxieuse.
SANDRINE C'est romantique ici, n'est-ce pas?
DAVID Comment? Euh, oui, enfin...
VALÉRIE Avant de commencer notre randonnée, je propose qu'on visite la Maison Sainte-Victoire.
AMINA Bonne idée. Allons-y!

6

Après le pique-nique...
DAVID Mais tu avais faim, Sandrine!
SANDRINE Oui. Pourquoi?
DAVID Parce que tu as mangé autant que Stéphane!
SANDRINE C'est normal, on a beaucoup marché, ça ouvre l'appétit. En plus, ce fromage est délicieux!
DAVID Mais, tu peux manger autant de fromage que tu veux, ma chérie.

7

Stéphane laisse tomber une serviette...
VALÉRIE Stéphane! Mais qu'est-ce que tu jettes par terre? Il est essentiel qu'on laisse cet endroit propre!
STÉPHANE Oh, ne t'inquiète pas, maman. J'allais mettre ça à la poubelle plus tard.

8

SANDRINE David, j'aimerais que tu fasses un portrait de moi, ici, à la montagne. Ça te dit?
DAVID Peut-être un peu plus tard... Cette montagne est tellement belle!
VALÉRIE David, tu es comme Cézanne. Il venait ici tous les jours pour dessiner. La montagne Sainte-Victoire était un de ses sujets favoris.

ACTIVITÉS

1 Vrai ou faux? Indiquez si ces affirmations sont vraies ou fausses. Corrigez les phrases fausses. Answers may vary.

1. David fait un portrait de Sandrine sur-le-champ (*on the spot*). Faux. David ne veut pas faire un portrait de Sandrine tout de suite.
2. C'est la première fois que Stéphane visite la Maison Sainte-Victoire. Vrai.
3. Valérie traite la nature avec respect. Vrai.
4. Sandrine mange beaucoup au pique-nique. Vrai.
5. David et Sandrine passent un après-midi très romantique. Faux. L'après-midi de David et Sandrine n'est pas romantique.
6. Le guide confirme qu'il y a des serpents sur la montagne Sainte-Victoire. Faux. Le guide ne parle pas des serpents.
7. David est un peu triste de devoir bientôt retourner aux États-Unis. Vrai.
8. Valérie pense que David ressemble à Cézanne. Vrai.
9. Rachid est très romantique. Answers will vary.
10. Stéphane laisse Rachid et Amina tranquilles. Faux. Stéphane ne les laisse pas tranquilles.

Practice more at **espaces.vhlcentral.com.**

OPTIONS

Avant de regarder la vidéo Before viewing the video, have students work in pairs and brainstorm a list of words and expressions they expect to hear in an episode about a hike in the mountains.

Regarder la vidéo Show the video episode and tell students to check off the words or expressions on their lists when they hear them. Then show the episode again and have students give you a play-by-play description of the action. Write their descriptions on the board.

Les amis se promènent à la montagne Sainte-Victoire.

À la Maison Sainte-Victoire

GUIDE Mesdames, Messieurs, bonjour et bienvenue. C'est votre première visite de la Maison Sainte-Victoire?

STÉPHANE Pour moi, oui.

GUIDE La Maison Sainte-Victoire a été construite après l'incendie de 1989.

DAVID Un incendie?

GUIDE Oui, celui qui a détruit une très grande partie de la forêt.

GUIDE Maintenant, la montagne est un espace protégé.

DAVID Protégé? Comment?

GUIDE Eh bien, nous nous occupons de la gestion de la montagne et de la forêt. Notre mission est la préservation de la nature, le sauvetage des habitats naturels et la prévention des incendies. Je vous fais visiter le musée?

VALÉRIE Oui, volontiers!

RACHID Tiens, chérie.

AMINA Merci, elle est très belle cette fleur.

RACHID Oui, mais toi, tu es encore plus belle. Tu es plus belle que toutes les fleurs de la nature réunies!

AMINA Rachid...

RACHID Chut! Ne dis rien... Stéphane! Laisse-nous tranquilles.

Expressions utiles

Expressing regrets and preferences

- **C'est dommage que j'aie si peu de temps.**
  It's a shame that I have so little time.
- **Je préférerais qu'on parle d'autre chose.**
  I would prefer to talk about something else.
- **J'aimerais que tu fasses un portrait de moi.**
  I would like you to do a portrait of me.

Making suggestions

- **Par précaution, je suggère que tu restes près de moi.**
  As a precaution, I suggest that you stay close to me.
- **Il ne faut pas que tu sois si anxieuse.**
  There's no need to be so anxious.
- **Je propose qu'on visite...**
  I propose we visit...

Making comparisons

- **Tu as mangé autant que Stéphane!**
  You ate as much as Stéphane!
- **Tu peux manger autant de fromage que tu veux.**
  You can eat as much cheese as you want.

ACTIVITÉS

2 À vous! Imaginez que vous êtes allé(e) à la montagne Sainte-Victoire avec des amis. À l'entrée du parc, il y a une liste de règles (*rules*) à suivre pour protéger la nature. Avec un(e) camarade de classe, imaginez quelles sont ces règles et écrivez une liste. Qu'est-ce qu'il faut faire si vous faites un pique-nique? Une randonnée? Quelles sont les activités interdites? Présentez votre liste à la classe.

3 Écrivez Il y a deux couples dans notre histoire, Sandrine et David, Amina et Rachid. Composez un paragraphe dans lequel vous expliquez quel couple va rester ensemble et quel couple va se séparer. Pourquoi? Attention! Le départ de David n'entre pas en jeu (*doesn't come into play*).

ressources

VM pp. 265–266	DVD Leçon 14B	espaces.vhlcentral.com

Expressions utiles

- Model the pronunciation of the **Expressions utiles** and have students repeat them after you.
- As you work through the list, point out the use of the subjunctive with verbs of will and emotion as well as comparatives and superlatives of nouns. Tell students that these constructions will be formally presented in the **Structures** section.
- Respond briefly to questions about the use of the subjunctive with verbs of will and emotion, comparatives, and superlatives. Reinforce correct forms, but do not expect students to produce them consistently at this time.
- Have students scan the **Roman-photo** and find other expressions used to make comparisons. Examples: **David, tu es comme Cézanne. Tu es plus belle que toutes les fleurs....**

1 Suggestion Have students correct the false statements.

1 Expansion For additional practice, give students these items. **11. David va assez souvent à la montagne Sainte-Victoire. (Vrai.) 12. Sandrine ne veut pas parler du départ de David. (Vrai.) 13. Stéphane prend une photo de David et de Sandrine. (Faux.)**

2 Suggestions

- If time is limited, this activity may be assigned as homework. As an alternative, you can have students create posters instead of lists.
- Encourage students to create symbols for the forbidden activities similar to the "No littering" sign on page 473.

3 Suggestion As students write, circulate around the room to help with unfamiliar vocabulary and expressions.

OPTIONS

Paul Cézanne Born in Aix-en-Provence, Paul Cézanne (1839–1906) lived much of his life as a recluse in Provence. A master of Postimpressionism, he is considered one of the greatest modern French painters. Bring in some photos of Cézanne's sketches and paintings of **la montagne Sainte-Victoire** and have students describe them.

Le mistral The south of France is at high risk for wildfires. Because of the extremely strong wind, **le mistral**, fires can get out of control and spread rapidly. **Le mistral** is caused by air that cools over the mountains and then flows into the valleys, creating a funnel effect and generating extremely strong wind currents. **Le mistral** occurs most often in the spring or winter.

connections cultures NATIONAL STANDARDS

Section Goals

In this section, students will:
- learn about France's national parks
- learn some conservation-related terms
- learn about some famous natural sites in the francophone world
- read about Madagascar
- view authentic video footage

Instructional Resources
espaces.vhlcentral.com: Video; WB/VM/LM Answer Key; IRM (Videoscript); activities; downloads; reference tools
Video on DVD

Culture à la loupe
Avant la lecture
- Have students look at the photos and describe what they see.
- Ask students: **Quels parcs nationaux avez-vous déjà visités?**

Lecture
- Point out the list of French natural sites that hold records.
- Explain that Guadeloupe has been an overseas department of France since 1946. Tourism is one of the main industries.

Après la lecture Ask students: **Quel(s) parc(s) français voudriez-vous visiter? Pourquoi?**

1 Expansion For additional practice, give students these items. **11. Que trouve-t-on dans tous les parcs nationaux? (On trouve des sentiers de randonnée et des activités d'écotourisme guidées.) 12. Combien de parcs nationaux sont montagneux? (sept sur neuf) 13. Quand est-ce que le premier parc national a été créé en France? (en 1963) 14. Où peut-on trouver des bouquetins? (dans la Vanoise)**

S Video: *Flash culture*

CULTURE À LA LOUPE

Les parcs nationaux

des perroquets°, Guadeloupe

le parc de la Vanoise

Les neuf parcs nationaux français sont protégés par le gouvernement, qui s'occupe de leur gestion. Tous offrent des sentiers de randonnée et la possibilité de découvrir la nature pendant des activités d'écotourisme guidées. Ce sont aussi des endroits où les visiteurs peuvent pratiquer différentes activités sportives. Par exemple, ils peuvent pratiquer des sports d'hiver dans cinq des sept parcs montagneux, qui ont de nombreux sommets° et glaciers.

Les Cévennes, en Languedoc-Roussillon, est le plus grand parc national forestier français avec 3.200 km² de forêts, mais on y trouve aussi des montagnes et des plateaux. La Vanoise, un parc de haute montagne dans les Alpes, a été le premier parc créé° en France, en 1963. Avec ses 107 lacs et sa vingtaine° de glaciers, c'est une réserve naturelle où le bouquetin° est protégé. Deux autres parcs, les Écrins et le Mercantour, sont aussi situés dans la région des Alpes. Autre parc montagneux, le parc national des Pyrénées est composé de six vallées principales, riches en forêts, cascades° et autres formations naturelles. C'est aussi un refuge pour de nombreuses espèces menacées, comme l'ours° et l'aigle royal°. Quand il fait beau l'été, le parc marin de Port-Cros, composé d'îles méditerranéennes, est idéal pour des activités aquatiques. Aux Antilles°, il fait chaud et humide toute l'année dans le parc national de la Guadeloupe. Situé dans la forêt tropicale, les paysages° du parc sont très variés: forestiers, volcaniques, côtiers° et maritimes. Ouverts depuis 2007, les deux parcs nationaux les plus récents sont le Parc Amazonien de Guyane, en Amérique du Sud, et le Parc national de La Réunion, dans l'océan Indien.

Les records naturels de la France en Europe de l'Ouest

- Le Mont-Blanc, dans les Alpes, est la plus haute montagne d'Europe de l'Ouest. Il mesure 4.811 mètres.
- La forêt de pins des Landes, en Aquitaine, est le plus grand massif forestier d'Europe. Il fait plus d'un million d'hectares.
- La dune du Pilat, en Aquitaine, est la plus haute dune de sable° d'Europe. Elle mesure 117 mètres.
- Le cirque° de Gavarnie, dans les Pyrénées, a la plus grande cascade d'Europe. Elle mesure 422 mètres.

sommets *summits* **créé** *created* **vingtaine** *about twenty* **bouquetin** *ibex, a type of wild goat* **cascades** *waterfalls* **ours** *bear* **aigle royal** *golden eagle* **Antilles** *the French West Indies* **paysages** *landscapes* **côtiers** *coastal* **perroquets** *parrots* **sable** *sand* **cirque** *steep-walled, mountainous basin*

ACTIVITÉS

1 Répondez Répondez aux questions par des phrases complètes.

1. Combien de parcs nationaux français y a-t-il? Il y a neuf parcs nationaux français.
2. Quel type de parc est le parc des Cévennes? Le parc des Cévennes est un parc forestier.
3. Quel parc est situé sur des îles méditerranéennes? Le parc marin de Port-Cros est situé sur des îles méditerranéennes.
4. Quels sont deux animaux qu'on peut trouver dans les Pyrénées? On peut trouver des ours et des aigles royaux dans les Pyrénées.
5. Quels sont deux types de paysages du parc de la Guadeloupe? Answers will vary. Possible answer: Les paysages forestiers et volcaniques sont deux types de paysages du parc de la Guadeloupe.
6. Comment s'appellent deux des parcs nationaux français et où se trouvent-ils (à la montagne, etc.)? Answers will vary. Possible answer: La Vanoise se trouve dans les montagnes et Port-Cros se trouve sur des îles.
7. Quelle est la plus haute montagne d'Europe? C'est le Mont-Blanc.
8. Où se trouve le plus grand massif forestier d'Europe? Il se trouve dans les Landes, en France.
9. Combien mesure la dune du Pilat? Elle mesure 117 mètres.
10. Combien mesure la plus grande cascade d'Europe? Elle mesure 422 mètres.

OPTIONS

Cultural Comparison Have the class brainstorm a list of famous national parks in the Unites States and write them on the board. Examples: Yellowstone, Yosemite, Death Valley, the Everglades, the Grand Canyon, Hawaii Volcanoes, Hot Springs, and Rocky Mountain.
Then tell students to work in groups of three and compare these national parks to those in France. They should consider geographical features and recreational activities. Have them list the similarities and differences in a two-column chart under the headings **Similitudes** and **Différences**. After completing their charts, have volunteers read their lists and ask the class if they agree or disagree with the observations.

LE FRANÇAIS QUOTIDIEN

La protection de la nature

essence (*f.*) sans plomb	*unleaded gas*
protection du littoral	*shoreline restoration*
mesures (*f.*) antipollution	*pollution control*
reboisement (*m.*)	*reforestation*
valorisation (*f.*) des terres	*land improvement*

LE MONDE FRANCOPHONE

Grands sites naturels

Voici quelques exemples d'espaces naturels remarquables du monde francophone.

En Algérie Plus de 80% de la superficie de l'Algérie, deuxième plus grand pays d'Afrique, sont occupés par le Sahara.

Au Cambodge Le lac Tonle Sap est le plus grand lac d'Asie du sud-est.

Au Cameroun La réserve Dja Faunal est l'une des plus grandes forêts tropicales d'Afrique.

À l'île Maurice L'île est presque entièrement entourée° de plus de 150 km de récifs de corail.

Au Sénégal Le parc national du Niokolo Koba, site du Patrimoine° mondial (UNESCO) et Réserve de la biosphère internationale, est l'une des réserves naturelles les plus importantes d'Afrique de l'Ouest.

Aux Seychelles L'atoll Aldabra abrite la plus grande population de tortues géantes du monde.

entièrement entourée *entirely surrounded* **Patrimoine** *Heritage*

PORTRAIT

Madagascar

Madagascar, ancienne colonie française, est la quatrième plus grande île du monde, et, avec plus de 20 parcs nationaux et réserves naturelles, elle est un paradis pour l'écotourisme. Madagascar (plus de 20 millions d'habitants) est située à 400 km à l'est du Mozambique, dans l'océan Indien. Sa faune et sa flore sont exceptionnelles avec 250.000 espèces différentes, dont 1.000 orchidées. 90% de ces espèces sont uniques au monde. Ses mangroves, rivières, lacs et récifs coralliens° offrent des milieux écologiques variés et ses forêts abritent° 90% des lémuriens° du monde. Caméléons, tortues terrestres°, tortues de mer° et baleines à bosse° sont aussi typiques de l'île.

récifs coralliens *coral reefs* **abritent** *provide a habitat for* **lémuriens** *lemurs* **tortues terrestres** *tortoises* **tortues de mer** *sea turtles* **baleines à bosse** *humpback whales*

SUR INTERNET

Quel est le sujet de l'émission *Thalassa*?

Go to **espaces.vhlcentral.com** to find more information related to this **ESPACE CULTURE**. Then watch the corresponding **Flash culture**.

ACTIVITÉS

2 Complétez Complétez les phrases.

1. Madagascar est une grande ___île___ près du Mozambique.
2. Madagascar est une bonne destination pour ___l'écotourisme___.
3. À Madagascar, la majorité des espèces sont ___uniques au monde___.
4. ___Caméléons, tortues terrestres, tortues de mer et baleines à bosse___ sont des espèces typiques de l'île.
5. L'une des plus grandes forêts tropicales d'Afrique se trouve ___au Cameroun___.

Practice more at **espaces.vhlcentral.com.**

3 À la découverte Vous et deux partenaires voulez visiter ensemble plusieurs pays francophones et découvrir la nature. Quelles destinations choisissez-vous? Comparez les activités qui vous intéressent et les endroits que vous voulez visiter. Soyez prêts à présenter votre itinéraire à la classe.

ressources: VM pp. 297-298 | espaces.vhlcentral.com

Le français quotidien

- Model the pronunciation of each term.
- Ask students questions using these terms. Examples: **1. Votre voiture consomme-t-elle de l'essence sans plomb? 2. Combien cela coûte-t-il par gallon? 3. Pourquoi a-t-on besoin de mesures antipollution? 4. Quand faut-il reboiser? 5. Pourquoi faut-il protéger le littoral?**

Portrait

- Have students locate the island of Madagascar on the map in **Appendice A**.
- Tell students to look at the photo and ask: **Quelle espèce d'animal est-ce? (un lémurien) Avez-vous déjà vu un lémurien? Si oui, où?**

Le monde francophone

- Have students locate the countries or islands on the map of the francophone world in **Appendice A**.
- Point out that an atoll is a ribbon of coral reef around a lagoon. Along the top there are often flat islands or strips of flat land.

2 Expansion For additional practice, give students these items. **6. Madagascar a plus de ____ parcs nationaux et réserves naturelles. (vingt) 7. Madagascar se trouve à l'est du ____. (Mozambique) 8. Dix pour cent des ____ au monde n'habitent pas à Madagascar. (lémuriens)**

3 Suggestion Before beginning the activity, have the class brainstorm a list of possible destinations for ecotourism and write them on the board.

Flash culture Tell students that they will learn more about the diverse geography of France and the French-speaking world by watching a variety of real-life images narrated by Benjamin. Show the video segment. Then ask students to close their eyes and describe from memory what they saw as you write their descriptions on the board. You can also use the activities in the video manual in class to reinforce this **Flash culture** or assign them as homework.

OPTIONS

Madagascar Madagascar was settled by Indonesian migrants around A.D. 700. It became **un protectorat français** in 1885, **une colonie** in 1896, and an independent state in 1960. The official languages are Malagasy (**malgache**), French, and English. More than 90 percent of the people earn their living from the forest, where most of the biodiversity can be found, but 85 percent of the country has already suffered deforestation. The island's population is also growing.

Pairs Have students write five true/false statements using the information on these pages. Then have them get together in pairs and take turns reading their statements and responding.

Section Goals

In this section, students will learn:
- to use the subjunctive to express will or emotion
- the present subjunctive forms of **avoir**, **être**, and **faire**

Instructional Resources
*espaces.vhlcentral.com: Lab MP3s; WB/VM/LM Answer Key; IRM (**Essayez!** and **Mise en pratique** answers; Lab Audioscript); activities; downloads; reference tools*

Suggestions
- Read these sentences to the class: **Je veux manger au resto U ce midi. Je veux que tu manges avec moi au resto U ce midi.** Ask why an infinitive is used in the first sentence and a conjugated verb in the subjunctive mood in the second. (In the first one, the subject is the same for both verbs. In the second one, there are two different subjects.)
- Point out that the subjunctive is sometimes used in English to express will. Example: *The professor demands that we pay attention in class.* **Le prof exige que nous soyons attentifs en classe.** English speakers often use an infinitive instead after a verb that expresses will, even if the subjects of the two verbs are different. Example: *I want you to get out now!* **Je veux que tu sortes d'ici tout de suite!**
- Read statements that begin with **Je propose que vous...**, **Je recommande que vous...**, and **Je suggère que vous...**. Have students qualify each piece of advice you give them as **un bon conseil** or **un mauvais conseil**. Example: **Je recommande que vous ne mangiez que des gâteaux au déjeuner. (C'est un mauvais conseil.)**
- Ask students if the present subjunctive forms of the verbs **avoir** and **être** seem familiar to them. (They resemble the imperative forms for those verbs.)

14B.1 The subjunctive (Part 2)

Will and emotion

- Use the subjunctive with verbs and expressions of will and emotion. Verbs and expressions of will are often used when someone wants to influence the actions of other people. Verbs and expressions of emotion express someone's feelings or attitude.

Je suggère que tu restes près de moi.

Je propose qu'on visite la Maison Sainte-Victoire.

BOÎTE À OUTILS
See **Leçon 14A** for an introduction to the subjunctive and the structure of clauses containing verbs in the subjunctive.

- When the main clause contains an expression of will or emotion and the subordinate clause has a different subject, the subjunctive is required.

MAIN CLAUSE VERB OF WILL	CONNECTOR	SUBORDINATE CLAUSE SUBJUNCTIVE
Mes parents exigent	que	**je dorme** huit heures.
My parents demand	*that*	*I sleep eight hours.*

MAIN CLAUSE EXPRESSION OF EMOTION	CONNECTOR	SUBORDINATE CLAUSE SUBJUNCTIVE
Tu es triste	que	**Sophie ne vienne pas** avec nous.
You are sad	*that*	*Sophie isn't coming with us.*

MAIN CLAUSE VERB OF WILL	CONNECTOR	SUBORDINATE CLAUSE SUBJUNCTIVE
Je préfère	que	**tu travailles** ce soir.
I prefer	*that*	*you work tonight.*

- Here are some verbs and expressions of will commonly followed by the subjunctive.

Verbs of will

demander que...	*to ask that...*	recommander que...	*to recommend that...*
désirer que...	*to want/ desire that...*	souhaiter que...	*to wish that...*
exiger que...	*to demand that...*	suggérer que...	*to suggest that...*
préférer que...	*to prefer that...*	vouloir que...	*to want that...*
proposer que...	*to propose that...*		

MISE EN PRATIQUE

1 Des opinions Que devraient faire les personnages sur les illustrations? Employez ces expressions pour donner vos opinions. Suggested answers

MODÈLE
Je propose que vous mangiez quelque chose.

vous (proposer que)

acheter une décapotable (*convertible*)	garder le secret
boire de l'eau	manger quelque chose
faire la fête	me donner de l'argent
	trouver des amis

1. tu (suggérer que)
Je suggère que tu boives de l'eau.

2. mes voisins (vouloir que)
Je veux que mes voisins me donnent de l'argent.

3. vous (exiger que)
J'exige que vous gardiez le secret.

4. Yves (souhaiter que)
Je souhaite qu'Yves trouve des amis.

5. elle (recommander que)
Je recommande qu'elle achète une décapotable.

6. tu (désirer que)
Je désire que tu fasses la fête.

2 Des opinions Complétez ces phrases avec le présent du subjonctif. Ensuite, comparez vos réponses avec celles d'un(e) partenaire. Answers will vary.

1. Nous sommes furieux que les examens...
2. Notre prof exige que...
3. Nous aimons que le prof...
4. Je propose que... le vendredi.
5. Les étudiants veulent que les cours...
6. Je recommande que... tous les jours.
7. C'est triste que cette université...
8. Nous préférons que le resto U...

Practice more at **espaces.vhlcentral.com.**

OPTIONS

Game Play a variation of **Jacques a dit** (*Simon Says*) with direct and indirect commands. Students should obey indirect commands that use the subjunctive and ignore all direct commands (those that use the imperative). Examples: **Jacques demande que vous vous leviez.** (*Students stand up.*) **Levez-vous!** (*Students remain seated.*)

Extra Practice Tell students to pretend that they've just seen a documentary on an environmental subject and that they should react to what they've seen with an expression of emotion from page 495. Example: **Je suis contente que l'on fasse quelque chose pour protéger les espèces d'oiseaux menacées.**

COMMUNICATION

3 Enquête Comparez vos idées sur la nature et l'environnement avec celles d'un(e) partenaire. Posez-vous ces questions. Answers will vary.

1. Que suggères-tu qu'on fasse pour protéger les forêts tropicales?
2. Vaut-il mieux qu'on ne chasse plus? Pourquoi?
3. Que recommandes-tu qu'on fasse pour arrêter la pollution?
4. Comment souhaites-tu que nous préservions nos ressources naturelles?
5. Quels produits recommandes-tu qu'on développe?
6. Quel problème écologique veux-tu qu'on traite tout de suite?

4 Mme Quefège... Mme Quefège donne des conseils à la radio. Pensez à une difficulté que vous avez et préparez par écrit un paragraphe que vous lui lirez. Elle va vous faire des recommandations. Avec un(e) partenaire, alternez les rôles pour jouer les scènes. Answers will vary.

MODÈLE

Étudiant(e) 1: *Ma petite amie fait constamment ses devoirs et elle ne quitte plus son appartement.*
Étudiant(e) 2: *Je suis désolée qu'elle n'arrête pas de travailler. Si elle ne quitte toujours pas l'appartement ce week-end, je suggère que vous écriviez à ses parents.*

5 Les habitats naturels Par groupes de trois, préparez le texte pour cette affiche où vous expliquez ce qu'on doit faire pour sauver les habitats naturels. Utilisez des verbes au présent du subjonctif. Answers will vary.

- These are some verbs and expressions of emotion followed by the subjunctive.

Verbs and expressions of emotion

aimer que...	*to like that...*	**être heureux / heureuse que...**	*to be happy that...*
avoir peur que...	*to be afraid that...*	**être surpris(e) que...**	*to be surprised that...*
être content(e) que...	*to be glad that...*	**être triste que...**	*to be sad that...*
être désolé(e) que...	*to be sorry that...*	**regretter que...**	*to regret that...*
être furieux / furieuse que...	*to be furious that...*		

- In English, the word *that* introducing the subordinate clause may be omitted. In French, never omit **que** between the two clauses.

Ils sont heureux **que** j'arrive.
They're happy (that) I'm arriving.

Elle préfère **que** tu partes.
She prefers (that) you leave.

- If the subject doesn't change, use the infinitive with expressions of will and emotion. In the case of **avoir peur**, **regretter**, and expressions with **être**, add **de** before the infinitive.

Tu souhaites faire un pique-nique?
Do you wish to have a picnic?

Nous sommes tristes d'entendre la mauvaise nouvelle.
We're sad to hear the bad news.

- Some verbs have irregular subjunctive forms.

Present subjunctive of *avoir*, *être*, *faire*

	avoir	être	faire
que je/j'	aie	sois	fasse
que tu	aies	sois	fasses
qu'il/elle	ait	soit	fasse
que nous	ayons	soyons	fassions
que vous	ayez	soyez	fassiez
qu'ils/elles	aient	soient	fassent

Elle veut que je **fasse** le lit.
She wants me to make the bed.

Tu es désolé qu'elle **soit** loin.
You are sorry that she is far away.

Essayez! Indiquez les formes correctes du présent du subjonctif des verbes.

1. que je *finisse* (finir)
2. qu'il *fasse* (faire)
3. que vous *soyez* (être)
4. que leur enfant *ait* (avoir)
5. que nous *prenions* (prendre)
6. que nous *fassions* (faire)
7. qu'ils *aient* (avoir)
8. que tu *attendes* (attendre)

Essayez! Assign an infinitive to each row of students. They should take turns giving present subjunctive forms for their appointed verb. The first student should give the **que je/j'...** form, the second student the **que tu...** form, and so on. Example for one row of students: (*first student*) **que je fasse,** (*second student*) **que tu fasses,** etc.

1 Suggestion Encourage students to come up with creative suggestions for the people pictured and to share the most interesting suggestions with the class.

2 Suggestion Have one pair of students share their sentences with the class. Ask their classmates to say **d'accord** if they agree or **pas d'accord** if they don't agree with the statements.

3 Expansion Students could also answer these questions. **Avez-vous peur que des espèces soient menacées dans votre région? Que proposez-vous que l'on fasse pour éviter la destruction des habitats naturels autour des villes?**

4 Suggestion Ask students why they think the radio personality is named **Quefège.** (It sounds like the phrase **Que fais-je?**)

5 Expansion Have the class vote on the best text for the poster. Then have small groups create a television ad campaign in the same vein. They should produce a script modeled on the poster text and a storyboard that shows the visuals to appear on the screen. Remind the class that successful TV ads often use striking images and catchy slogans.

OPTIONS

Extra Practice Read aloud some sentence starters that refer to current events or celebrities. Each one should use an expression of emotion from page 493. Students should complete the sentences appropriately. Example: **Emeril Lagasse est furieux que... (qu'il n'y ait plus d'ail au supermarché.)**

Video As students watch the last scene of the video for **Leçon 14B** again, pause periodically and ask them these questions. **Qu'est-ce que Valérie veut que Stéphane fasse? Qu'est-ce que Sandrine veut que David fasse? Qu'est-ce que Rachid veut qu'Amina fasse? Qu'est-ce que Rachid veut que Stéphane fasse?**

Section Goals

In this section, students will learn:

- comparatives with noun
- superlatives with nouns

Instructional Resources
*espaces.vhlcentral.com: Lab MP3s; WB/VM/LM Answer Key; IRM (**Essayez!** and **Mise en pratique** answers; Lab Audioscript); activities; downloads; reference tools*

Suggestions

- Ask students what words are used in comparatives and superlatives for adjectives and adverbs. You might need to remind them by asking a few questions. Example: **Qui est le plus drôle de la classe?** Once students have identified **plus/moins/aussi** + [*adjective/adverb*] + **que**, tell them that the words used to compare quantities for nouns are similar.
- Point out that **de** is used in all the examples of comparative noun constructions just as **que** is used with comparative adjectives and adverbs. You might copy the paradigms that appear under the photos on the board, adding **+ que**.
- Make statements about things in the classroom using comparatives and superlatives of nouns while students qualify them as **vrai** or **faux**. Example: **Sean a plus de livres que Jennifer.**
- Point out that native speakers distinguish **plus de** meaning *more of* from **plus de** meaning *anymore of* by pronouncing the **s** in the former. Example: **Je n'ai plus d'argent!** (**s** not pronounced) **J'ai plus d'argent que toi!** (**s** pronounced)

Essayez! Show a transparency with false statements and have students correct them. Examples: **Il y a plus d'habitants en France qu'aux États-Unis. Il y a autant d'ail dans un gâteau que dans une pizza. Le Grand Canyon est moins grand qu'un timbre postal.**

14B.2 Comparatives and superlatives of nouns

Point de départ In **Leçon 9B**, you learned how to compare nouns and verbs by using comparative and superlative forms of adjectives and adverbs. You will now learn how to compare nouns when talking about quantities.

Tu peux manger autant de fromage que tu veux.

Nous nous occupons de la forêt pour avoir moins d'incendies.
Sainte Victoire

- To compare the amount of something, use these expressions:

plus de	+	[noun]	*more*
moins de	+	[noun]	*less; fewer*
autant de	+	[noun]	*as much; as many*

Elle fait **plus d'heures** que sa sœur.
She works more hours than her sister (does).

Il y a **moins d'arbres** dans le jardin que dans la forêt.
There are fewer trees in the garden than in the forest.

Vous recevez **autant de courrier** que vos amis.
You receive as much mail as your friends (do).

Il n'y a pas **autant d'animaux** dans la ville que dans la jungle.
There aren't as many animals in the city as (there are) in the jungle.

- To express the superlative quantity of a noun (*the most, the least/fewest*), add the definite article **le**: **le plus de**, **le moins de**.

Ce sont les forêts tropicales qui ont **le plus de plantes**.
Tropical rainforests have the most plants.

Ce sont les pays pauvres qui ont **le moins d'argent**.
Poor countries have the least money.

Essayez! **Complétez les phrases avec les comparatifs ou les superlatifs corrects.**

1. Mon ami n'a pas autant de (*as much*) travail que moi.
2. Qui a le moins de (*the fewest*) cousins?
3. La Corse a-t-elle autant de (*as many*) falaises que la Sicile?
4. Il y a moins de (*fewer*) déserts en Amérique du Nord qu'en Afrique.
5. Quel pays a le plus de (*the most*) rivières polluées?
6. Malheureusement, on a plus de (*more*) problèmes que de solutions.

MISE EN PRATIQUE

1 Avec qui sortir? **Amaia compare deux garçons pour voir avec qui elle va accepter de sortir le week-end prochain. Assemblez ses phrases.**

MODÈLE Kadir / avoir / plus / énergie / Jacques
Kadir a plus d'énergie que Jacques.

1. Kadir / avoir / moins / problèmes / Jacques
   Kadir a moins de problèmes que Jacques.
2. Jacques / avoir / plus / humour / Kadir
   Jacques a plus d'humour que Kadir.
3. Kadir / donner / plus / cadeaux / Jacques
   Kadir donne plus de cadeaux que Jacques.
4. Jacques / avoir / autant / amis / Kadir
   Jacques a autant d'amis que Kadir.
5. Kadir / avoir / moins / patience / Jacques
   Kadir a moins de patience que Jacques.
6. Jacques / avoir / plus / ambition / Kadir
   Jacques a plus d'ambition que Kadir.

2 À la campagne **Lise parle de son séjour à la campagne et compare le nombre de choses qu'elle a observées dans la nature. Que dit-elle?**

MODÈLE
J'ai observé autant de nuages blancs que de nuages gris.

1. J'ai observé moins d'arbres que de fleurs./J'ai observé plus de fleurs que d'arbres.

3. J'ai observé moins de chiens que de chats./J'ai observé plus de chats que de chiens.

2. J'ai observé moins d'écureuils que de lapins./J'ai observé plus de lapins que d'écureuils.

4. J'ai observé moins de vaches que de serpents./J'ai observé plus de serpents que de vaches.

3 Combien de calories? **Vous et votre partenaire êtes au régime. Faites au moins quatre comparaisons entre ces aliments. Dites à la classe quel aliment contient le plus de calories et lequel en contient le moins.**
Answers will vary.

MODÈLE
Il y a autant de calories dans un café que dans un thé.

banane	carotte	glace	poulet
biscuits	frites	pain	saucisses
bonbons	gâteau	porc	thon

Practice more at **espaces.vhlcentral.com.**

OPTIONS

Extra Practice Ask students questions about themselves using comparative and superlative noun constructions. They should be able to answer each question by saying **Moi!** or remaining silent. Examples: **Qui a le plus de fichiers audio** (*audio files*) **de la classe? Qui a autant de stylos que Luan? Qui a moins de paires de chaussures que Nisha?**

Extra Practice Challenge students to formulate sentences that use comparatives and superlatives of nouns with the pronoun **en.** Ask them how they would substitute **en** for the nouns in the examples on this page. Example: **Elle fait plus d'heures que sa sœur. (Elle en fait plus que sa sœur.)**

NATIONAL communication STANDARDS

COMMUNICATION

4 **Eh bien, moi...** Posez ces questions à un(e) partenaire, puis faites une comparaison. Answers will vary.

MODÈLE

Étudiant(e) 1: *Pendant combien d'heures par jour regardes-tu la télévision?*
Étudiant(e) 2: *Je regarde la télévision deux heures par jour.*
Étudiant(e) 1: *Je regarde plus d'heures de télévision que toi: Je la regarde trois heures par jour.*

1. Combien de frères (sœurs, cousins) as-tu?
2. Combien d'heures par jour étudies-tu?
3. Combien d'e-mails reçois-tu par jour?
4. Combien d'heures dors-tu chaque nuit?
5. Combien de cours as-tu ce semestre?
6. Combien de cafés prends-tu par jour?

5 **Où habiter?** Avec un(e) partenaire, comparez la vie dans une résidence universitaire à la vie dans un appartement. Décidez où vous préféreriez habiter si vous aviez le choix. Utilisez le vocabulaire de la liste. Answers will vary.

MODÈLE

Étudiant(e) 1: *Dans un appartement, nous pouvons mettre plus d'affiches sur les murs.*
Étudiant(e) 2: *Oui, et dans une résidence, il y a moins d'espace.*

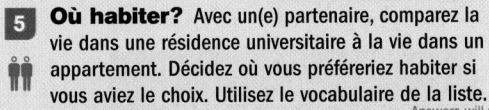

affiches	armoire	meuble	supervision
amis	espace	protection	télé
argent	fêtes	repas	?

6 **Un dialogue** Par groupes de trois, vous voulez voyager dans un pays francophone. Vous consultez une agence de voyages et vous posez des questions. Préparez un dialogue où vous utilisez **autant de, moins de** et **plus de** et alternez les rôles. Answers will vary.

MODÈLE

Étudiant(e) 1: *Où y a-t-il moins de pollution, au Cameroun ou à Paris?*
Étudiant(e) 2: *Il y a de la pollution aux deux endroits. Mais il y a plus de forêts tropicales au Cameroun.*
Étudiant(e) 3: *Où y a-t-il plus de sentiers? On voudrait faire des randonnées.*

Le français vivant

Le Québec
Là où il y a le plus de calme,
le plus de sérénité. Moins de stress que
chez vous, mais autant de confort et
autant de bonheur.
Venez découvrir le Québec...
pour plus d'émotions.

Identifiez Quels comparatifs et superlatifs trouvez-vous dans cette publicité (*ad*)? le plus de calme; le plus de sérénité; Moins de stress; autant de confort; autant de bonheur; plus d'émotions

Questions Posez ces questions à un(e) partenaire et répondez à tour de rôle. Employez des comparatifs et des superlatifs dans vos réponses, si possible. Answers will vary.

1. D'après (*According to*) cette pub, que cherche le touriste qui voudrait passer des vacances au Québec?
2. Quelle comparaison la pub fait-elle entre le Québec et l'endroit où habite le lecteur/la lectrice (*reader*)?
3. As-tu déjà passé des vacances au Québec? Voudrais-tu y aller un jour?
4. Si tu vas ou retournes au Québec un jour, voudras-tu y faire un séjour comme celui que la pub décrit? Pourquoi?

1 Expansion Tell students to write down six statements in which they compare themselves to a good friend or to a sibling.

2 Expansion Ask students to make similar observations about the campus by looking out the window or walking around outside.

3 Suggestion You can focus students' attention by grouping items from the list. Example: **gâteau / carotte (Il y a plus de calories dans un gâteau que dans une carotte.)**

4 Expansion When students have completed the activity, find out which student has the most of each item in the questions. Example: **1. Qui a le plus de frères de toute la classe?**

5 Suggestion Tally on the board how many students prefer apartments and dormitories. Then ask: **Y a-t-il plus d'étudiants qui préfèrent les appartements ou plus d'étudiants qui préfèrent les résidences universitaires?**

6 Expansion Ask students to take notes on their conversation for reference and then verify the travel agent's answers by doing some research on French-language Internet sites.

Le français vivant When students are working on question 3, ask them why the last statement might strike someone as contradicting the first two. Then ask them what you call a contradictory statement that may be true nonetheless (*a paradox*/ **un paradoxe**).

OPTIONS

Extra Practice Ask the class questions about objects around the classroom using comparative and superlative noun constructions. Example: **Qui a plus de crayons, Max ou Lina?** Students should answer in complete sentences.

Game Tell students to write three statements about themselves using comparatives or superlatives of nouns. Suggest that they mention characteristics that would allow their classmates to identify them. Example: **J'ai moins de cheveux que Jason.** Then collect the papers and read them aloud while students guess the identity of each writer. The student with the most correct guesses wins.

Révision

1 Des changements Avec un(e) partenaire, observez ces endroits et dites, à tour de rôle, si vous aimeriez qu'il y ait **plus de** ou **moins de** certaines choses. Ensuite, comparez vos phrases à celles d'un autre groupe. Answers will vary.

MODÈLE

Étudiant(e) 1: *Je préférerais qu'il y ait plus d'eau dans cette rivière.*
Étudiant(e) 2: *J'aimerais mieux qu'il y ait plus d'herbe.*

1.

3.

2.

4.

2 Visite de votre région Interviewez vos camarades. Que recommandent-ils à des visiteurs qui ne connaissent pas votre région? Écrivez leurs réponses, puis comparez vos résultats à ceux d'un autre groupe. Utilisez ces expressions. Answers will vary.

MODÈLE

Étudiant(e) 1: *Que devraient faire les visiteurs de cette région?*
Étudiant(e) 2: *Je recommande qu'ils visitent les musées du centre-ville. Il serait bon qu'ils assistent aussi à un match de baseball.*

il est bon que	proposer que
il est indispensable que	recommander que
il faut que	suggérer que
?	?

3 Plus d'arbres Avec un(e) partenaire, pensez à votre environnement et dites si vous voulez qu'il y ait **plus de**, **moins de** ou **autant de** choses ou d'animaux. Quand vous n'êtes pas d'accord, justifiez vos réponses. Answers will vary.

MODÈLE

Étudiant(e) 1: *Je souhaite qu'il y ait plus d'arbres.*
Étudiant(e) 2: *Oui, il faut plus d'arbres sur le campus et en ville.*

4 Voyage en Afrique centrale Avec un(e) partenaire, vous voulez visiter ces endroits en Afrique centrale. Préparez un dialogue avec des verbes au présent du subjonctif et des comparatifs ou des superlatifs. Ensuite, alternez les rôles. Answers will vary.

MODÈLE

Étudiant(e) 1: *J'aimerais qu'on visite Kribi, au Cameroun. Il y a plus de plages.*
Étudiant(e) 2: *Il vaut mieux que nous visitions le marché, au Gabon.*

- la forêt de Dzanga-Sangha (République centrafricaine)
- le lac Kivu (Rwanda)
- les marchés (Gabon)
- le parc national de Lobéké (Cameroun)
- le parc national de l'Ivindo (Congo)
- les plages de Kribi (Cameroun)

5 Échange d'opinions Avec un(e) partenaire, imaginez une conversation entre un chasseur (*hunter*) et un défenseur de la nature. Préparez un dialogue où les deux se font des suggestions. Ensuite, jouez votre dialogue pour la classe. Answers will vary.

MODÈLE

Étudiant(e) 1: *Il est dommage que vous disiez que les chasseurs n'aiment pas la nature.*
Étudiant(e) 2: *Je souhaite que vous respectiez plus les animaux.*

6 La maman de Carine Votre professeur va vous donner, à vous et à votre partenaire, deux feuilles d'activités différentes sur Carine et sa mère. Attention! Ne regardez pas la feuille de votre partenaire. Answers will vary.

MODÈLE

Étudiant(e) 1: *Si Carine prend l'avion,...*
Étudiant(e) 2: *... sa mère veut qu'elle l'appelle de l'aéroport.*

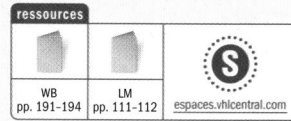

ressources: WB pp. 191-194 | LM pp. 111-112 | espaces.vhlcentral.com

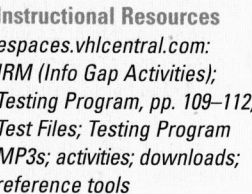

Instructional Resources
espaces.vhlcentral.com: IRM (Info Gap Activities); Testing Program, pp. 109–112; Test Files; Testing Program MP3s; activities; downloads; reference tools
Test Generator

1 Expansion Write items like these on the board and ask students to say whether they would like more or fewer of them in town: **voitures, arrêts de bus, bars, musées, restaurants français, boutiques, prisons, commissariats de police, parcs, criminels, poubelles.** Example: **J'aimerais qu'il y ait moins de voitures dans notre ville.**

2 Suggestion Give students categories to help them think of tourist attractions to mention. Examples: restaurants, shopping, sports, museums, architecture, festivals, etc.

3 Suggestion Ask students to summarize what they said. Example: **C'est dommage qu'il n'y ait pas assez de poubelles sur le campus. Je souhaite qu'il y en ait plus à l'avenir.**

4 Suggestion Have the class identify the expressions listed on pages 483, 494, and 495 that would be useful in this activity. Examples: **Il faut que..., Je propose que... , Je regrette que...**, etc.

5 Expansion When students have finished, tell them to write a new conversation that includes a third speaker—an environmentalist hunter. Have them imagine what this person thinks about hunting while preserving animal species. (Environmental hunters tend to advocate strict controls that assure only overpopulated animal species are hunted, but not overhunted.)

6 Suggestion Divide the class into pairs and distribute the Info Gap Handouts found on the Supersite for this activity. Give students ten minutes to complete the activity.

OPTIONS

Game Ask small groups to write down three statements using comparative or superlative noun constructions. Two of the statements should be true; the third one should be false. Read the statements aloud. Groups identify the false statement in each set. The group with the most correct answers wins.

Extra Practice Put slips of paper, each with the names of two celebrities on it, in a bin. Have students draw slips, and then ask a question using a comparative or superlative that prompts them to identify one of the celebrities. Example: (1. Bill Cosby 2. Bill Gates) **C'est celui des deux qui a le plus d'argent.** (Bill Gates)

À l'écoute

National communication Standards

Audio: Activities

STRATÉGIE

Listening for the gist/ Listening for cognates

Combining these two strategies is an easy way to get a good sense of what you hear. When you listen for the gist, you get the general idea of what you're hearing, which allows you to interpret cognates and other words in a meaningful context. Similarly, the cognates give you information about the details of the story that you might not have understood when listening for the gist.

To practice these strategies, you will listen to a short paragraph. Write down the gist of what you hear and jot down a few cognates. What conclusions can you draw about what you heard?

Préparation

Regardez la photo. Que se passe-t-il à votre avis? Combien de personnes y a-t-il? Pour quelle cause ces personnes manifestent-elles (*demonstrate*)? De quoi vont-elles parler?

À vous d'écouter

Écoutez la personne qui a organisé la manifestation (*demonstration*) et encerclez les sujets mentionnés.

la chasse	les lois sur la protection de l'environnement
les déchets toxiques	
l'effet de serre	la pluie acide
l'énergie nucléaire	la pollution
l'extinction de certaines espèces	la pollution des rivières
	le ramassage des ordures
le gaspillage	la surpopulation

Practice more at **espaces.vhlcentral.com.**

Compréhension

Complétez Choisissez la bonne réponse pour terminer chaque phrase, d'après ce que vous venez d'entendre.

1. On peut recycler ___a___.
   a. le verre b. les déchets toxiques c. tous les déchets
2. Les emballages recyclables aident à ___c___.
   a. éviter le ramassage des ordures
   b. trier (*to sort*) les déchets c. combattre la pollution de la Terre
3. Il faut ___b___ le gaspillage.
   a. développer b. éviter c. polluer
4. Le gouvernement doit ___a___.
   a. passer des lois plus strictes en ce qui concerne l'écologie
   b. éviter l'effet de serre c. réduire le trou dans la couche d'ozone
5. Il y a beaucoup de ___a___ dans les rivières.
   a. déchets toxiques b. ressources naturelles c. verre
6. Trop ___b___ sont en train de disparaître.
   a. d'écoproduits b. d'espèces c. d'océans

Les lois Un(e) représentant(e) du Congrès vient à votre université pour discuter de l'environnement. Par petits groupes, choisissez un problème écologique qui est très important pour vous. Préparez des arguments à lui présenter. Vous voulez lui faire comprendre que le gouvernement doit faire plus dans le domaine que vous avez choisi. Soyez prêts à bien expliquer la situation actuelle (*today*) et les changements nécessaires pour l'améliorer. Pensez aussi à quelques nouvelles lois sur la protection de l'environnement que vous pourrez suggérer à votre représentant(e) du Congrès.

Section Goals

In this section, students will:

- learn to listen for the gist and for cognates
- listen to a paragraph and jot down the gist and some cognates
- listen to a speech at an environmental demonstration and complete several activities

Instructional Resources
espaces.vhlcentral.com: Textbook MP3s; IRM (Textbook Audioscript); downloads; reference tools

Stratégie
Script Les Français choisissent de plus en plus de passer des vacances «vertes», c'est-à-dire des vacances qui proposent des activités d'écotourisme. Ces voyages, qui sont souvent des voyages organisés, permettent à leurs participants de passer du temps dans la nature et de découvrir ce qu'ils peuvent faire pour contribuer plus activement à la protection de notre planète.

Préparation Have students look at the photo and describe what is happening. Then have them guess what the people might be saying.

À vous d'écouter
Script Bonjour à tous et merci beaucoup d'être venus participer à notre manifestation aujourd'hui. Si nous travaillons tous ensemble, nous pourrons trouver des solutions concrètes pour moins polluer notre environnement. Tout d'abord, il est essentiel que nous prenions tous l'habitude de trier nos déchets. Le verre et beaucoup d'autres emballages ménagers peuvent être recyclés. Il est aussi indispensable que vous achetiez des produits emballés dans des emballages recyclables. Ils aident à combattre la pollution de notre planète. Il est aussi nécessaire d'éviter le gaspillage. Ces suggestions sont un bon début, mais malheureusement, nous ne pouvons pas réussir seuls. Il faut absolument que notre gouvernement fasse plus d'efforts en ce qui concerne le recyclage et le ramassage des ordures. Il est également nécessaire que tous les gouvernements d'Europe ainsi que ceux des autres pays et continents fassent passer des lois beaucoup plus strictes en ce qui concerne les déchets toxiques. Nous ne voulons plus de déchets toxiques dans nos rivières ni dans nos océans! La pollution de l'eau, comme celle du reste de la Terre, est un véritable danger qu'il faut prendre très au sérieux. Trop d'espèces aussi sont en train de disparaître et je souhaite qu'aujourd'hui, nous promettions tous d'essayer de faire plus d'efforts pour favoriser l'écologie. Je propose en plus que nous écrivions tous au ministre de l'environnement pour demander des changements dès aujourd'hui!

Section Goals

In this section, students will learn historical and cultural information about West Africa and Central Africa.

Instructional Resources
espaces.vhlcentral.com: Transparency #59; WB/VM/LM Answer Key; activities; downloads; reference tools

Carte de l'Afrique de l'Ouest et de l'Afrique centrale

- Have students look at the map or use **Transparency #59**. Ask volunteers to read the names of countries and major cities aloud. Model pronunciation as necessary.
- Point out the photos of Abidjan, the administrative and commercial center of **la Côte d'Ivoire**, and Kinshasa. Abidjan is a major port city, whereas Kinshasa is an inland city connected by rail to an Atlantic port city.

La région en chiffres

- For the countries of French-speaking West and Central Africa, French is the language of administration, education, and international communication. French is the official language and may share official status with English, Arabic, and other languages native to the country.
- Rwanda has three official languages, and Cameroon recognizes two official and 24 unofficial languages. The minimum number of recognized languages for any country in West or Central Africa is three.

Incroyable mais vrai! Today there is an estimated total of 250 mountain gorillas in Kahuzi-Biega National Park that the World Conservation Society is trying to protect.

SAVOIR-FAIRE

connections cultures NATIONAL STANDARDS

Interactive Map Reading

Panorama

un marché en Afrique

L'Afrique de l'Ouest

La région en chiffres

- **Bénin:** *(11.217.000 habitants), Porto Novo*
- **Burkina-Faso:** *(17.678.000), Ouagadougou*
- **Côte d'Ivoire:** *(21.553.000), Yamoussoukro*
- **Guinée:** *(11.890.000), Conakry*
- **Mali:** *(18.093.000), Bamako*
- **Mauritanie:** *(3.988.000), Nouakchott*
- **Niger:** *(19.283.000), Niamey*
- **Sénégal:** *(14.538.000), Dakar*
- **Togo:** *(7.847.000), Lomé*

SOURCE: Population Division, UN Secretariat

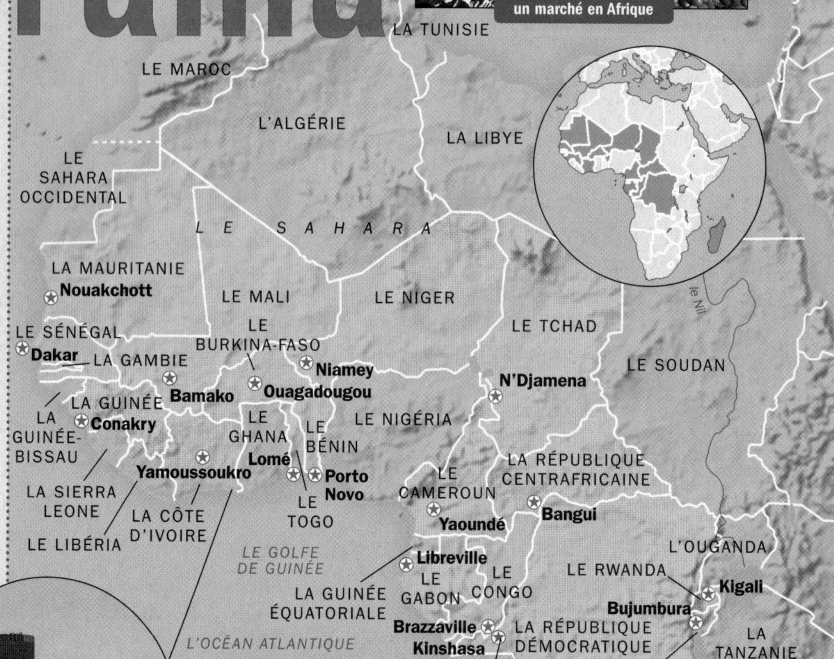

L'Afrique centrale

la ville d'Abidjan

La région en chiffres

- **Burundi:** *(10.617.000), Bujumbura*
- **Cameroun:** *(19.040.000), Yaoundé*
- **Congo:** *(5.441.000), Brazzaville*
- **Gabon:** *(1.605.000), Libreville*
- **République centrafricaine:** *(4.647.000), Bangui*
- **République démocratique du Congo (R.D.C.):** *(78.016.000), Kinshasa*
- **Rwanda:** *(11.262.000), Kigali*
- **Tchad:** *(12.832.000), N'Djamena*

une femme à Kinshasa

Personnes célèbres

- **Mory Kanté**, *Guinée et Mali, chanteur et musicien (1950–)*

- **Djimon Hounsou**, *Bénin, acteur (1964–)*
- **Françoise Mbango-Etone**, *Cameroun, athlète olympique (1976–)*

Incroyable mais vrai!

Progrès ou destruction? Dans le parc Kahuzi-Biega, en R.D.C., habite une espèce menacée d'extinction: le gorille de montagne. Il est encore plus menacé, depuis peu, par l'exploitation d'un minerai qu'on trouve dans ce parc, le coltan, utilisé, entre autres, dans la fabrication de téléphones portables. Aujourd'hui, le parc est sur la liste du patrimoine mondial en péril°.

liste du patrimoine mondial en péril *World Heritage in Danger List*

OPTIONS

Personnes célèbres **Mory Kanté** uses traditional African instruments and rhythms in his music. He plays the kora, which is a large harp-lute. Kanté is the first African musician to sell a million singles, and his music has topped European charts. **Djimon Hounsou** immigrated to France at the age of 13, where he was discovered and made a fashion model by Thierry Mugler. He has starred in major American and French films. He is also the first African male to be nominated for an Academy Award for his role in the movie *In America*. **Françoise Mbango-Etone** competes in the triple jump. She has won world championships, and she won an Olympic gold medal in 2004 and in 2008. She is the first Cameroonian athlete to win an Olympic medal.

Les gens

Léopold Sédar Senghor, le président poète (1906–2001)

Senghor, homme politique et poète sénégalais, était professeur de lettres en France avant de mener° le Sénégal à l'indépendance et de devenir le premier président du pays en 1960. Humaniste et homme de culture, il est un des pères fondateurs° de la Négritude, un mouvement littéraire d'Africains et d'Antillais noirs qui examinent et mettent en valeur leur identité culturelle. Il a aussi organisé le premier Festival mondial des arts nègres, à Dakar, en 1966. Senghor a produit une importante œuvre° littéraire dans laquelle il explore le métissage° des cultures africaines, européennes et américaines. Docteur honoris causa de nombreuses universités, dont Harvard et la Sorbonne, il a été élu° à l'Académie française en 1983.

La musique

Le reggae ivoirien

Alpha Blondy

La Côte d'Ivoire est un des pays d'Afrique où le reggae africain est le plus développé. Ce type de reggae se distingue du reggae jamaïcain par les instruments de musique utilisés et les thèmes abordés°. En fait, les artistes ivoiriens incorporent souvent des instruments traditionnels d'Afrique de l'Ouest et les thèmes sont souvent très politiques. Alpha Blondy, par exemple, est le plus célèbre des chanteurs ivoiriens de reggae et fait souvent des commentaires sociopolitiques. Le chanteur Tiken Jah Fakoly critique la politique occidentale et les gouvernants africains, et Ismaël Isaac dénonce les ventes d'armes° dans le monde. Le reggae ivoirien est chanté en français, en anglais et dans les langues africaines.

Les lieux

Les parcs nationaux du Cameroun

Avec la forêt, la savane et la montagne dans ses réserves et parcs nationaux, le Cameroun présente une des faunes et flores les plus riches et variées d'Afrique. Deux cent quarante empreintes° de dinosaures sont fossilisées au site de dinosaures de Manangia, dans la province du Nord. Les différentes réserves du pays abritent°, entre autres, éléphants, gorilles, chimpanzés, antilopes et plusieurs centaines d'espèces de reptiles, d'oiseaux et de poissons. Le parc national Korup est une des plus anciennes forêts tropicales du monde. Il est connu surtout récemment pour une liane°, découverte là-bas, qui pourrait avoir un effet sur la guérison° de certains cancers et du VIH°.

Les arts

Le FESPACO

Le FESPACO (Festival Panafricain du Cinéma et de la télévision à Ouagadougou), créé en 1969 pour favoriser la promotion du cinéma africain, est le plus grand festival du cinéma africain du monde et le plus grand événement culturel d'Afrique qui revient régulièrement. Vingt films et vingt courts métrages° africains sont présentés en compétition officielle, tous les deux ans, à ce festival du Burkina-Faso. Le FESPACO est aussi une fête populaire avec une cérémonie d'ouverture à laquelle assistent 40.000 spectateurs et des stars de la musique africaine.

Qu'est-ce que vous avez appris? Répondez aux questions par des phrases complètes.

1. Qu'est-ce qui menace la vie des gorilles de montagne?
   L'exploitation du coltan menace la vie des gorilles.
2. Quelle est une des utilisations du coltan?
   Il est utilisé dans la fabrication de portables.
3. Pourquoi Senghor est-il important dans l'histoire du Sénégal?
   Il a mené le Sénégal à l'indépendance et a été le premier président du pays.
4. De quel mouvement Senghor était-il un des fondateurs?
   Il était un des fondateurs du mouvement de la Négritude.
5. Qu'est-ce qui fait la spécificité du son (*sound*) du reggae ivoirien?
   Les artistes utilisent des instruments traditionnels d'Afrique de l'Ouest.
6. De quoi parlent souvent les chanteurs de reggae en Côte d'Ivoire?
   Ils parlent souvent de politique.
7. Qu'a-t-on trouvé sur le site de Manangia?
   On a trouvé des empreintes de dinosaures.
8. Pourquoi le parc national Korup est-il bien connu récemment?
   Il est connu pour la liane qu'on y a trouvée qui pourrait avoir des effets avantageux dans la guérison de cancers et du VIH.
9. Pourquoi le FESPACO a-t-il été créé?
   Le festival a été créé pour favoriser la promotion du cinéma africain.
10. Le FESPACO est-il un festival réservé exclusivement aux professionnels du cinéma?
    Non, c'est aussi une fête populaire.

Practice more at **espaces.vhlcentral.com.**

ressources
WB pp. 195-196
espaces.vhlcentral.com

SUR INTERNET

Go to espaces.vhlcentral.com to find more cultural information related to this **PANORAMA**.

1. Trouvez des informations sur le mouvement de la Négritude. Qui en étaient les autres principaux fondateurs?
2. Écoutez des chansons (*songs*) de reggae ivoirien. De quoi parlent-elles?
3. Cherchez plus d'informations sur le gorille de montagne et le coltan. Quel est le statut (*status*) du gorille aujourd'hui?

mener *lead* **pères fondateurs** *founding fathers* **œuvre** *body of work* **métissage** *mixing* **élu** *elected* **abordés** *dealt with* **ventes d'armes** *weapons sales* **empreintes** *footprints* **abritent** *provide a habitat for, shelter* **liane** *vine* **guérison** *cure* **VIH** *HIV* **métrages** *films*

Léopold Sédar Senghor Senghor was president from 1960–1980. The concept of **la Négritude** is best exemplified in his ***Anthologie de la nouvelle poésie nègre et malgache*** (1948).

Le reggae ivoirien Some of the traditional African musical instruments are talking drums, djembe, balafone, kora, bolon, daro, and the gourd rattle. Many are made from natural materials such as seeds, grass, or wood.

Les parcs nationaux du Cameroun Cameroon's national parks are Waza, Boubandjidah, Bénoué, Kalamaloué, Faro, Mozogo-Gokoro, Korup, Dja, Boumba Bek, and Nki. Ask students: **Quelles espèces d'animaux peut-on voir dans les réserves du Cameroun? (éléphants, gorilles, chimpanzés, antilopes, reptiles, oiseaux et poissons)**

Le FESPACO
- One of the objectives of **FESPACO** is to contribute to the expansion and development of African films. The festival arranges free screenings of African films in rural areas and also offers monetary prizes to its winners.
- Have students locate Ouagadougou on the map on page 500.

OPTIONS

La Négritude **La Négritude** was a literary movement in the 1930s, 1940s, and 1950s. It began among French-speaking African and Caribbean writers living in Paris as a way to protest French colonial rule and forced assimilation into Western culture. A basic tenant of **Négritude** is to look to one's own cultural heritage, traditions, history, and beliefs with pride and to use them in the modern world. In literary works, the value and dignity of African traditions and peoples is manifested through the use of African subject matter and poetic traditions. For example, in poetry some of the traditional values are closeness to nature and constant contact with ancestors.

Section Goals

In this section, students will:
- learn to recognize chronological order
- read an excerpt from a French novel

Stratégie Tell students that understanding the order of events allows a reader to follow what is happening in the narrative.

Successful Language Learning Tell students to look for connecting words and transitions, because they are helpful in following a chain of events.

Examinez le texte
- Point out that geographers study the Earth's surface, its features, the distribution of life on the planet's surface, and the effect of climate and geography on human activity.
- Have volunteers describe the characters in the illustrations.

À propos de l'auteur
- Point out that ***Le Petit Prince*** is considered to be Saint-Exupéry's masterpiece.
- The wreckage from Saint-Exupéry's downed airplane was found in the Mediterranean seabed between Marseille and Cassis in 2000, and was officially attributed as his in 2004.
- The international airport in Lyon (**Aéroport Lyon-Saint-Exupéry**) is named after the famous writer and pilot.
- Ask these comprehension questions. **1. Où est-ce qu'Antoine de Saint-Exupéry est né? (à Lyon) 2. Était-il seulement écrivain? (Non, il était aussi aviateur/pilote.) 3. Quel genre de littérature a-t-il écrit? (des romans) 4. Où est-ce que le Petit Prince a voyagé? (vers d'autres planètes)**

Lecture

NATIONAL STANDARDS communication cultures

Audio: Dramatic Recording

Avant la lecture

STRATÉGIE

Recognizing chronological order

Recognizing the chronological order of events in a narrative is key to understanding the cause and effect relationship between them. When you are able to establish the chronological chain of events, you will easily be able to follow the plot. In order to be more aware of the order of events in a narrative, you may find it helpful to prepare a numbered list of the events as you read.

Examinez le texte

Dans l'extrait (*excerpt*) du *Petit Prince* que vous allez lire, le petit prince rencontre un géographe. Que fait un géographe? En quoi consiste son travail exactement? Est-ce un travail facile ou difficile, à votre avis? Regardez les illustrations et décrivez le géographe et le petit prince.

À propos de l'auteur

Antoine de Saint-Exupéry

Antoine de Saint-Exupéry est né à Lyon, en France, en 1900. C'est un écrivain français très apprécié dans le monde entier qui a aussi eu une carrière d'aviateur. En 1921, il entre dans l'armée, où il est formé comme pilote. Plus tard, en 1926, il devient pilote pour la compagnie Aéropostale et voyage entre la France, l'Afrique du Nord et l'Amérique du Sud. À cette époque, il écrit ses deux premiers romans°, *Courrier Sud* et *Vol de nuit*. De nouveau dans l'armée française, Saint-Exupéry écrit, en 1943, alors qu'il est en Afrique du Nord, son œuvre la plus célèbre, *Le Petit Prince*. Elle sera traduite en plus de 150 langues. Saint-Exupéry disparaît° en 1944 lors d'°une mission en avion.

Le Petit Prince raconte l'histoire d'un jeune garçon qui a quitté sa planète pour visiter d'autres planètes. Pendant son voyage, il rencontre des personnages et des animaux différents. Dans cet extrait, le petit prince arrive sur la sixième planète, où habite un vieux monsieur qui est géographe.

romans *novels* **disparaît** *disappears* **lors d'** *during*

Le Petit Prince

[...]

La sixième planète était une planète dix fois plus vaste. Elle était habitée par un vieux Monsieur qui écrivait d'énormes livres.

—Tiens! voilà un explorateur! s'écria-t-il°, quand il aperçut° le petit prince.

Le petit prince s'assit° sur la table et souffla° un peu. Il avait déjà tant° voyagé!

—D'où viens-tu? lui dit le vieux Monsieur.

—Quel est ce gros livre? dit le petit prince. Que faites-vous ici?

—Je suis géographe, dit le vieux Monsieur.

—Qu'est-ce qu'un géographe?

—C'est un savant° qui connaît où se trouvent les mers, les fleuves, les villes, les montagnes et les déserts.

—Ça, c'est intéressant, dit le petit prince. Ça, c'est enfin un véritable métier! Et il jeta un coup d'œil autour° de lui sur la planète du géographe. Il n'avait jamais vu encore une planète aussi majestueuse.

—Elle est bien belle, votre planète. Est-ce qu'il y a des océans?

—Je ne puis° pas le savoir, dit le géographe.

—Ah! (Le petit prince était déçu°.) Et des montagnes?

—Je ne puis pas le savoir, dit le géographe.

—Et des villes et des fleuves et des déserts?

—Je ne puis pas le savoir non plus, dit le géographe.

—Mais vous êtes géographe!

—C'est exact, dit le géographe, mais je ne suis pas explorateur. Je manque° absolument d'explorateurs. Ce n'est pas le géographe qui va faire le compte° des villes, des fleuves, des montagnes, des mers et des océans. Le géographe est trop important pour flâner°. Il ne quitte pas son bureau. Mais il reçoit les explorateurs. Il les interroge, et il prend note de leurs souvenirs°. Et si les souvenirs de l'un d'entre eux lui paraissent° intéressants, le géographe fait une enquête° sur la moralité de l'explorateur.

—Pourquoi ça?

—Parce qu'un explorateur qui mentirait° entraînerait° des catastrophes dans les livres de géographie. Et aussi un explorateur qui boirait° trop.

—Pourquoi ça? fit° le petit prince.

—Parce que les ivrognes° voient double. Alors le géographe noterait deux montagnes, là où il n'y en a qu'une seule.

—Je connais quelqu'un, dit le petit prince, qui serait mauvais explorateur.

OPTIONS

Extra Practice Have students research and write a summary about Saint-Exupéry's plane crash. They should find out what sort of a mission he was on, who found the plane's wreckage, and any other important or interesting details. Remind them to jot down notes of the events or details in chronological order.

Language Note Tell students that some verbs in this text are in the **passé simple**, which is the literary way of expressing the past tense in French. Have students give the **passé composé** form that corresponds to the **passé simple** form. Examples: **il fit (il a fait)**, **il dit (il a dit)**, **il s'assit (il s'est assis)**, and **il aperçut (il s'est aperçu)**.

—C'est possible. Donc, quand la moralité de l'explorateur paraît° bonne, on fait une enquête sur sa découverte°.

—On va voir?

—Non. C'est trop compliqué. Mais on exige qu'il en rapporte° de grosses pierres.

Le géographe soudain s'émut°.

—Mais toi, tu viens de loin! Tu es explorateur! Tu vas me décrire ta planète!

Et le géographe, ayant ouvert son registre°, tailla° son crayon. On note d'abord au crayon les récits des explorateurs. On attend, pour noter à l'encre°, que l'explorateur ait fourni des preuves°.

—Alors? interrogea le géographe.

—Oh! chez moi, dit le petit prince, ce n'est pas très intéressant, c'est tout petit. J'ai trois volcans. Deux volcans en activité, et un volcan éteint. [...]

s'écria-t-il *he exclaimed* **aperçut** *noticed* **s'assit** *sat down* **souffla** *breathed* **tant** *so much* **savant** *scholar* **jeta un coup d'œil autour** *glanced around* **puis** *can* **déçu** *disappointed* **manque** *lack* **faire le compte** *count* **flâner** *stroll* **souvenirs** *memories* **paraissent** *seem* **enquête** *investigation* **mentirait** *would lie* **entraînerait** *would cause* **boirait** *would drink* **fit** *said* **ivrognes** *drunks* **paraît** *seems* **découverte** *discovery* **rapporte** *brings back* **s'émut** *became emotional* **ayant ouvert son registre** *having opened his book* **tailla** *sharpened* **encre** *ink* **ait fourni des preuves** *has provided proof*

Après la lecture

Le travail d'un géographe Cherchez, dans le texte, les différentes étapes du travail du géographe et mettez-les dans l'ordre chronologique.

8 1. Le géographe écrit la version du récit des explorateurs à l'encre.
2 2. Le géographe demande aux explorateurs de raconter leurs récits.
3 3. Le géographe note les découvertes des explorateurs au crayon.
1 4. Le géographe reçoit des explorateurs.
7 5. Les explorateurs donnent des preuves au géographe.
5 6. Le géographe fait une enquête sur les découvertes des explorateurs.
4 7. Le géographe fait une enquête sur la moralité des explorateurs.
6 8. Le géographe demande aux explorateurs de lui rapporter (*bring back*) des pierres.

Répondez Répondez aux questions par des phrases complètes.

1. Où habite le géographe? Il habite sur la sixième planète.
2. Que faisait le géographe quand le petit prince est arrivé sur sa planète? Il écrivait d'énormes livres.
3. Pourquoi est-ce que le petit prince est fatigué quand il arrive chez le géographe? Il est fatigué parce qu'il a beaucoup voyagé.
4. D'après le géographe, quel est le métier du petit prince? Il pense que le petit prince est explorateur.
5. Pourquoi est-ce qu'un géographe n'explore jamais les endroits qu'il veut connaître? Il est trop important pour flâner.
6. Si un explorateur ment, quelles peuvent être les conséquences, d'après le géographe? Il peut y avoir des catastrophes dans les livres de géographie.
7. Qu'est-ce que le géographe demande au petit prince à la fin de l'extrait? Il lui demande de lui parler de sa planète.
8. Comment est la planète du petit prince? Elle est toute petite, avec deux volcans en activité et un volcan éteint.

Dans le futur Nous sommes en 2650 et on peut voyager dans l'espace. Avez-vous envie de visiter les autres planètes, comme le petit prince? Expliquez. Comment sont les autres planètes, à votre avis? Sont-elles comme la Terre ou pas?

Une lettre au géographe Vous êtes un(e) des explorateurs/exploratrices qui travaillent pour le géographe. Aidez-le à mieux connaître la Terre. Écrivez-lui une lettre dans laquelle vous lui expliquez comment est votre région, votre pays ou un autre endroit dans le monde, si vous préférez.

Le travail d'un géographe If students have difficulty putting the events in order, have them refer to the text and mark the item number next to the corresponding line(s).

Répondez Go over the answers with the class.

Dans le futur This activity can be done in pairs or groups.

Une lettre au géographe Have students exchange their letters for peer editing. Then tell them to ask questions about the letter's content as if they were **le géographe** in the story.

OPTIONS

Extra Practice Have the class discuss these topics. **1. *Le Petit Prince* est-il écrit pour les adultes ou pour les enfants?** Students should justify their opinions with examples from the reading. **2. Comment caractériseriez-vous (*would you characterize*) le géographe et le petit prince? 3. À votre avis, qu'est-ce que le géographe et le petit prince symbolisent (*symbolize*)?**

Extra Practice Have students research and compile a list of titles of Saint-Exupéry's literary works. Tell them to read a brief description of each title, choose a book that they would like to read, and explain why.

Section Goals

In this section, students will:

- learn about a writer's audience and purpose
- write a letter or an article about an environmental issue

Stratégie Review with the class the importance of considering the purpose and audience when writing. Then go through questions 1–5. If possible, provide students with samples of persuasive letters in French, such as letters to the editor. Tell them to identify the audience and the author's purpose for each letter.

Thème Tell students to follow the steps outlined here when writing their letter or article.

Proofreading Activity Have students correct these sentences. **1. Il faut que je vous parler de cette article sur le pollution. 2. C'est dommage que j'ai si peu de temp. 3. J'aimerais que tu fasse une portraite de moi. 4. Il ne faut pas que tu être si anxieuse.**

Écriture

STRATÉGIE

Considering audience and purpose

Writing always has a purpose. During the planning stages, you must determine to whom you are addressing the piece, and what you want to express to your reader. Once you have defined both your audience and your purpose, you will be able to decide which genre, vocabulary, and grammatical structures will best serve your literary composition.

Let's say you want to share your thoughts on local traffic problems. Your audience can be either the local government or the community. You could choose to write a newspaper article, a letter to the editor, or a letter to the city's governing board. You should first ask yourself these questions:

1. Are you going to comment on traffic problems in general, or are you going to point out several specific problems?
2. Are you intending to register a complaint?
3. Are you simply intending to inform others and increase public awareness of the problems?
4. Are you hoping to persuade others to adopt your point of view?
5. Are you hoping to inspire others to take concrete actions?

The answers to these questions will help you establish the purpose of your writing and determine your audience. Of course, your writing can have more than one purpose. For example, you may intend for your writing to both inform others of a problem and inspire them to take action.

Thème

Écrire une lettre ou un article

Avant l'écriture

1. Vous allez écrire au sujet d'un (*about a*) problème de l'environnement qui est important pour vous. Choisissez d'abord le problème dont vous voulez parler. Lisez les trois sujets et choisissez à propos duquel (*about which one*) vous voulez écrire.
    - Écrivez au sujet des programmes qui existent pour protéger l'environnement dans votre communauté. Sont-ils efficaces (*effective*)? Tout le monde (*Everybody*) participe-t-il? Avez-vous des doutes sur le futur de l'environnement dans votre communauté?
    - Décrivez un des attraits (*attractions*) naturels de votre région. Êtes-vous optimiste sur le futur environnemental de votre région? Que font le gouvernement et les habitants de votre région pour protéger l'environnement? Faut-il faire plus?
    - Écrivez au sujet d'un programme pour la protection de l'environnement au niveau national ou international. Est-ce un programme du/des gouvernement(s) ou d'une entreprise privée? Est-il efficace? Qui y participe? Avez-vous des doutes au sujet de ce programme? Pensez-vous qu'on devrait le changer ou l'améliorer? Comment?
2. Décidez qui sera votre public: Voulez-vous écrire une lettre à un membre du gouvernement, à une association universitaire, etc.? Préférez-vous écrire un article pour un journal, un magazine? Complétez ce tableau (*chart*).

OPTIONS

Stratégie Review the strategy with students. Then list some possible audiences for a writing task: the general public, someone you don't know well, someone you know very well. Ask how your language would change for each audience. Then do the same thing with various purposes: to entertain, to inform, to persuade. How would your language change to reflect your purpose in writing?

If possible, provide students with samples of persuasive letters in French, such as letters to the editor from actual or digital newspapers. Ask them: Who is the intended audience for a letter to the editor? Do different newspapers have different kinds of audiences? Then have students work in pairs to analyze each letter and to identify the writer's purpose in writing.

Audience: Cochez (select) les options qui décrivent votre audience.

- ______ *un(e) ami(e) (lequel/laquelle?)*
- ______ *une association universitaire (laquelle?)*
- ______ *un membre du/d'un gouvernement (lequel?)*
- ______ *les lecteurs (readers) d'un journal/magazine (lequel?)*
- ______ *les lecteurs d'un magazine (lequel?)*

Décrivez votre audience ici.

Mots (Words) et expressions pour atteindre (reach) ces lecteurs:

3. Identifiez le but de votre lettre ou article: Voulez-vous simplement informer le public ou allez-vous aussi donner votre opinion personnelle? Complétez ce tableau.

But: Cochez toutes les options qui décrivent votre but.

______ *informer les lecteurs*	______ *se plaindre (to complain)*
______ *exprimer vos sentiments (feelings)*	______ *examiner différents problèmes et situations*
______ *persuader les lecteurs*	______ *examiner un seul problème ou une seule situation*
______ *inspirer les lecteurs*	

Décrivez votre but ici.

Détails qui soutiennent (support) votre but:

4. Après avoir complété les deux tableaux, décidez quel type de rédaction vous allez écrire.

Écriture

1. Préparez une courte introduction, puis présentez le problème que vous avez choisi.
2. N'oubliez pas de répondre à toutes les questions posées dans la présentation du sujet en page précédente.
3. Utilisez le subjonctif pour exprimer la volonté et l'émotion, des comparatifs et des superlatifs, et des pronoms démonstratifs dans votre rédaction.
4. Si vous avez choisi d'exprimer votre opinion personnelle, justifiez-la pour essayer de persuader votre/vos lecteur(s).
5. Préparez la conclusion de votre lettre ou article.

Après l'écriture

1. Échangez votre lettre/article avec celle/celui d'un(e) partenaire. Répondez à ces questions pour commenter son travail.
   - Votre partenaire a-t-il/elle identifié un but et une audience spécifiques?
   - Sa lettre/Son article montre-t-elle/il clairement le but?
   - Sa lettre/Son article est-elle/il réellement destiné(e) (*aimed*) à un type de lecteurs spécifiques?
   - Votre partenaire a-t-il/elle répondu à toutes les questions posées dans la présentation du sujet?
   - A-t-il/elle utilisé les points de grammaire de l'unité?
   - Quel(s) détail(s) ajouteriez-vous (*would you add*)? Quel(s) détail(s) enlèveriez-vous (*would you delete*)? Quel(s) autre(s) commentaire(s) avez-vous pour votre partenaire?

2. Corrigez votre lettre/article d'après (*according to*) les commentaires de votre partenaire. Relisez votre travail pour éliminer ces problèmes:
   - des fautes (*errors*) d'orthographe, de ponctuation et de conjugaison
   - un mauvais emploi (*use*) des temps et de la grammaire de l'unité
   - des fautes d'accord (*agreement*) des adjectifs

EVALUATION

Criteria

Content Includes evidence of and information related to each of the numbered items in the writing task.
Scale: 1 2 3 4 5

Organization Organized into a letter or an article that contains logical paragraphs that begin with a topic sentence and contain appropriate supporting detail.
Scale: 1 2 3 4 5

Accuracy Uses the subjunctive verb forms correctly. Spells words, conjugates verbs, and modifies adjectives correctly throughout.
Scale: 1 2 3 4 5

Creativity Includes additional information that is not requested in the task and/or uses adjectives, descriptive verbs, and additional details to make the composition more interesting.
Scale: 1 2 3 4 5

Scoring

Excellent	18–20 points
Good	14–17 points
Satisfactory	10–13 points
Unsatisfactory	< 10 points

OPTIONS

Avant l'écriture Talk about persuasive language and the kinds of words that inspire people to take action. As a class, brainstorm a list of useful words and expressions that could be used in a typical letter to the editor. Possible items for inclusion: **À mon avis, Je pense que/Je crois que..., Il est urgent/nécessaire/important que..., Nous ne pouvons pas/Nous ne devrions pas..., Je vous exhorte de (*urge*)/Je vous demande de/Je vous prie de (*beg*)...**

Tell students that many of these persuasive expressions and verbs will trigger the use of the subjunctive, such as impersonal expressions with **être (Il est bon que...**, etc.), verbs and expressions of will (**Je demande que...**, etc.), and verbs and expressions of emotion (**J'aimerais que...**, etc.). These can be found on pages 483, 494, and 495 of this unit.

Instructional Resources
espaces.vhlcentral.com: Textbook MP3s; IRM (Textbook Audioscript); downloads; reference tools

Suggestion Tell students that an easy way to study from **Vocabulaire** is to cover up the French half of each section, leaving only the English equivalents exposed. They can then quiz themselves on the French items. To focus on the English equivalents of the French entries, they simply reverse this process.

La nature

un espace	*space, area*
une espèce (menacée)	*(endangered) species*
la nature	*nature*
un pique-nique	*picnic*
une région	*region*
une ressource naturelle	*natural resource*
un arbre	*tree*
un bois	*wood*
un champ	*field*
le ciel	*sky*
une côte	*coast*
un désert	*desert*
une étoile	*star*
une falaise	*cliff*
un fleuve	*river*
une forêt (tropicale)	*(tropical) forest*
l'herbe (f.)	*grass*
une île	*island*
la jungle	*jungle*
un lac	*lake*
la Lune	*moon*
une pierre	*stone*
une plante	*plant*
une rivière	*river*
un sentier	*path*
une vallée	*valley*
un volcan	*volcano*
en plein air	*outdoor, open-air*
pur(e)	*pure*

Verbes de volonté

demander que...	*to ask that...*
désirer que...	*to want/desire that...*
exiger que...	*to demand that...*
préférer que...	*to prefer that...*
proposer que...	*to propose that...*
recommander que...	*to recommend that...*
souhaiter que...	*to wish that...*
suggérer que...	*to suggest that...*
vouloir que...	*to want that...*

L'écologie

améliorer	*to improve*
chasser	*to hunt*
développer	*to develop*
gaspiller	*to waste*
jeter	*to throw away*
polluer	*to pollute*
préserver	*to preserve*
prévenir l'incendie	*to prevent a fire*
proposer une solution	*to propose a solution*
recycler	*to recycle*
sauver la planète	*to save the planet*
une catastrophe	*catastrophe*
une centrale nucléaire	*nuclear plant*
la chasse	*hunt*
le covoiturage	*carpooling*
un danger	*danger, threat*
le déboisement	*deforestation*
des déchets toxiques (m.)	*toxic waste*
l'écologie (f.)	*ecology*
l'écotourisme (m.)	*ecotourism*
l'effet de serre (m.)	*greenhouse effect*
un emballage en plastique	*plastic wrapping/ packaging*
l'énergie nucléaire (f.)	*nuclear energy*
l'énergie solaire (f.)	*solar energy*
l'environnement (m.)	*environment*
l'extinction (f.)	*extinction*
le gaspillage	*waste*
un glissement de terrain	*landslide*
un nuage de pollution	*pollution cloud*
la pluie acide	*acid rain*
la pollution	*pollution*
une population croissante	*growing population*
la préservation	*protection*
un produit	*product*
la protection	*protection*
le ramassage des ordures	*garbage collection*
le réchauffement climatique	*global warming*
le recyclage	*recycling*
le sauvetage des habitats naturels	*natural habitat preservation*
la surpopulation	*overpopulation*
le trou dans la couche d'ozone	*hole in the ozone layer*
une usine	*factory*
écologique	*ecological*

Les animaux

un animal	*animal*
un écureuil	*squirrel*
un lapin	*rabbit*
un serpent	*snake*
une vache	*cow*

Les lois et les règlements

abolir	*to abolish*
interdire	*to forbid, to prohibit*
un gouvernement	*government*
une loi	*law*

Pronoms démonstratifs

celui	*this one; that one; the one (m., sing.)*
ceux	*these; those; the ones (m., pl.)*
celle	*this one; that one; the one (f., sing.)*
celles	*these; those; the ones (f., pl.)*

Expressions impersonnelles

Il est bon que...	*It is good that...*
Il est dommage que...	*It is a shame that...*
Il est essentiel que...	*It is essential that...*
Il est important que...	*It is important that...*
Il est indispensable que...	*It is essential that...*
Il est nécessaire que...	*It is necessary that...*
Il est possible que...	*It is possible that...*
Il faut que...	*One must..., It is necessary that...*
Il vaut mieux que...	*It is better that...*

Expressions utiles	*See pp. 477 and 491.*
Verbs and expressions of emotion	*See p. 495.*
Comparatives and superlatives of nouns	*See p. 496.*

ressources
espaces.vhlcentral.com

Les arts

UNITÉ 15

Leçon 15A

ESPACE CONTEXTES
pages 508–511
- Performance arts
- **Les liaisons obligatoires et les liaisons interdites**

ESPACE ROMAN-PHOTO
pages 512–513
- **Après le concert**

ESPACE CULTURE
pages 514–515
- Theater in France
- **Flash culture**

ESPACE STRUCTURES
pages 516–519
- The subjunctive (Part 3)
- Possessive pronouns

ESPACE SYNTHÈSE
pages 520–523
- **Révision**
- **Le zapping**

Leçon 15B

ESPACE CONTEXTES
pages 524–527
- Literary arts
- TV and movies
- **Les abréviations et les sigles**

ESPACE ROMAN-PHOTO
pages 528–529
- **Au revoir, David!**

ESPACE CULTURE
pages 530–531
- Haitian painting

ESPACE STRUCTURES
pages 532–535
- The subjunctive (Part 4)
- Review of the subjunctive

ESPACE SYNTHÈSE
pages 536–537
- **Révision**
- **À l'écoute**

Savoir-faire

pages 538–543

Panorama: Les Antilles and **la Polynésie française**
Lecture: Read a poem.
Écriture: Write a critique.

Pour commencer

- Où est David? Sur une falaise? Dans une classe? Dans un champ?
- Que dessine-t-il?
- Est-il nécessaire qu'il ait un modèle pour dessiner?
- Est-il possible qu'il soit déjà un artiste connu?

Unit Goals

Leçon 15A

In this lesson, students will learn:
- terms related to the theater and performance arts
- rules for making liaisons and some exceptions
- about the theater in France and Molière
- more about movie theaters and kiosks through specially shot video footage
- about the subjunctive with expressions of doubt, disbelief, and uncertainty
- some irregular forms of the subjunctive
- the possessive pronouns
- about the short film ***La tartine***

Leçon 15B

In this lesson, students will learn:
- terms for television and film
- terms for literature and fine arts
- about abbreviations and acronyms
- about Haitian painting and **le Cirque du Soleil**
- the subjunctive with conjunctions
- to listen for key words and use context

Savoir-faire

In this section, students will learn:
- cultural, economic, and historical information about the Antilles and French Polynesia
- to make inferences and recognize metaphors
- to write strong introductions and conclusions

Pour commencer

- **David est dans une classe.**
- **Il dessine des fruits.**
- Answers may vary.
- Answers may vary.

RESOURCES

Workbook/Video Manual: WB Activities, pp. 197–210
Laboratory Manual: Lab Activities, pp. 113–120
Workbook/Video Manual: Video Activities, pp. 267–270; pp. 299–300
WB/VM/LM Answer Key

espaces.vhlcentral.com: Textbook MP3s; Lab MP3s; Instructor's Resource Manual [IRM] (Textbook Audioscript; Lab Audioscript; Videoscript; **Roman-photo** Translations; **Vocabulaire supplémentaire**; **Feuilles d'activités**; Info Gap Activities; **Le zapping** short film transcription; **Essayez!** and **Mise en pratique** answers); Transparencies #60, #61, #62; Testing Program, pp. 113–120, pp. 153–160, pp. 173–184; pp. 209–220; Test Files; Testing Program MP3s
Test Generator
Video on DVD

Section Goals

In this section, students will learn and practice vocabulary related to:

- theater
- performance arts

Instructional Resources

*espaces.vhlcentral.com: Transparency #60; IRM (**Vocabulaire supplémentaire**; **Mise en pratique** answers; Textbook Audioscript; Lab Audioscript; Info Gap Activities); Textbook MP3s; Lab MP3s; WB/VM/LM Answer Key; activities; downloads; reference tools*

Suggestions

- Tell students to look over the new vocabulary and identify the cognates.
- Use **Transparency #60**. Point out people and things as you describe the illustration. Examples: **Il joue du piano. C'est un opéra. La spectatrice applaudit.**
- Point out the differences in spelling between the French words **danse** and **membre** and the English words *dance* and *member.*
- Model the pronunciation of the word **début**, contrasting it with its English pronunciation.
- Point out the difference between **un personnage** and **une personne**.
- Tell students that **profiter de** does not necessarily have the negative connotation that *to take advantage of* does in English.
- Remind students to use **jouer à** with sports, but **jouer de** with musical instruments. Examples: **Il joue *au* tennis. Il joue *de* la guitare.**
- Ask students questions using the new vocabulary. Examples: **Quels réalisateurs célèbres connaissez-vous? Quelle est votre chanson préférée? Jouez-vous d'un instrument de musique? Si oui, lequel? Aimez-vous aller au théâtre? À l'opéra?**
- Additional vocabulary for this lesson can be found in the **Vocabulaire supplémentaire** on the Supersite.

Leçon 15A

Talking Picture
Audio: Activity

You will learn how to...

- talk about performance arts
- express your feelings and opinions

Que le spectacle commence!

Vocabulaire

jouer un rôle	*to play a role*
présenter	*to present*
profiter de quelque chose	*to take advantage of/ to enjoy something*
un applaudissement	*applause*
une chanson	*song*
un chœur	*choir, chorus*
une comédie (musicale)	*comedy (musical)*
un compositeur	*composer*
un concert	*concert*
une danse	*dance*
un dramaturge	*playwright*
un entracte	*intermission*
un membre	*member*
un metteur en scène	*director (of a play, a show)*
un personnage (principal)	*(main) character*
une pièce de théâtre	*play*
un réalisateur/ une réalisatrice	*director (of a movie)*
une séance	*show; screening*
une troupe	*company, troop*
le début	*beginning; debut*
la fin	*end*
un genre	*genre*
une sorte	*sort, kind*
célèbre	*famous*

ressources

WB pp. 197–198	LM p. 113	espaces.vhlcentral.com

OPTIONS

Extra Practice Have students identify familiar artists, songs, films, plays, etc., by completing your statements with vocabulary from **Espace contextes**. Examples: **1. *Carmen* est ____ de Bizet. (un opéra) 2. *La vie en rose* est ____. (une chanson) 3. *Giselle* est ____. (un ballet) 4. Steven Spielberg est ____. (un réalisateur)**

Extra Practice Write or have students write the names of well-known artists on sticky notes and put them on the backs of other students. Then tell them to walk around the room asking their classmates yes/no questions to determine their identity. Examples: **Est-ce que je suis dramaturge? Est-ce que j'écris des tragédies? Est-ce que je suis William Shakespeare?**

Mise en pratique

1 Choisissez **Choisissez la phrase de la colonne B qui complète le mieux les phrases de la colonne A. Notez que tous les éléments de la colonne B ne sont pas utilisés.**

A

a **1.** Pour entrer dans une salle de spectacle,
g **2.** Georges Bizet a écrit **Carmen** en 1875;
e **3.** Au milieu d'une pièce de théâtre
d **4.** Un metteur en scène est chargé de
h **5.** La tragédie **Hamlet** est une
b **6.** Une comédie musicale est

B

a. il faut un billet.
b. un spectacle de musique et de danse.
c. un membre de la troupe.
d. guider les comédiens dans leur travail.
e. il y a souvent un entracte.
f. il faut danser à l'entracte.
g. c'est un des opéras français les plus célèbres.
h. des pièces de théâtre les plus connues de Shakespeare.

2 Associez **Complétez les analogies suivantes par le mot ou l'expression d'ESPACE CONTEXTES qui convient le mieux.**

1. chanter ⟷ chanson / applaudir ⟷ applaudissement
2. heureux ⟷ comédie / triste ⟷ tragédie
3. théâtre ⟷ pièce / cinéma ⟷ séance
4. concert ⟷ orchestre / chanson ⟷ chœur
5. film ⟷ acteur / ballet ⟷ danseur
6. opéra ⟷ chanter / concert ⟷ faire de la musique
7. livre ⟷ écrivain / musique ⟷ compositeur
8. classe ⟷ étudiant / troupe ⟷ membre
9. film ⟷ réalisateur / pièce de théâtre ⟷ metteur en scène
10. danse ⟷ danseur / chanson ⟷ chanteur

3 Écoutez **Écoutez la conversation entre Hakim et Nadja pendant le spectacle de *Notre-Dame de Paris*, ensuite indiquez la bonne réponse.**

1. Hakim et Nadja donnent leurs...
a. places.
(b.) billets.
c. détails.

2. Leurs places sont situées...
a. très loin de l'orchestre.
b. au balcon.
(c.) près de l'orchestre.

3. Le spectacle est...
(a.) une comédie musicale.
b. un concert.
c. une tragédie.

4. Gilles Maheu est...
a. un dramaturge.
(b.) un metteur en scène.
c. un personnage.

5. Hakim...
a. n'a pas applaudi.
b. a très peu applaudi.
(c.) a beaucoup applaudi.

6. Nadja pense qu'Hakim...
a. va devenir célèbre.
(b.) n'est pas un bon danseur.
c. est un bon compositeur.

Practice more at **espaces.vhlcentral.com.**

1 Suggestion Write each of the phrases in column B on separate pieces of paper and distribute them. Have students read the items in column A aloud. Those with the correct ending finish the sentences.

2 Suggestion Have students explain the relationship between the first set of words, then give the answer.

3 Tapescript L'EMPLOYÉ: Soyez les bienvenus à *Notre-Dame de Paris*. Vos billets, s'il vous plaît.
NADJA: Oui, tenez.
E: Si vous voulez bien me suivre. Voici vos places.
HAKIM: C'est parfait. On n'est pas loin de l'orchestre. On pourra profiter de tous les détails du spectacle.
N: Ce soir, c'est la première de cette comédie musicale. C'est aussi les débuts de Julie Zenatti dans un des rôles principaux.
H: Tu sais qui est le metteur en scène?
N: Oui. C'est Gilles Maheu. Pourquoi?
H: Juste pour savoir. Oh, regarde! Le spectacle va commencer. On continuera de parler à l'entracte.
Un peu plus tard...
H: Tu ne m'avais pas dit qu'en plus de chansons, il y aurait de la danse.
N: Tu n'aimes pas ce genre de spectacle?
H: Si, j'adore. J'ai même mal aux mains tellement j'ai applaudi. Ça me donne envie de faire partie de la troupe. Je pourrais peut-être jouer un petit rôle, non?
N: Je ne suis pas sûre. Tu sais, il faut être très bon danseur. Et puis, en plus, tu ne fais pas de musique...
H: Ce n'est pas vrai. Je te rappelle que je joue de la guitare.
N: Ah, oui... Tu peux toujours te présenter à une audition, mais ne t'attends pas à beaucoup d'applaudissements.
H: Eh bien, si c'est comme ça, tu n'auras pas de place pour mon premier concert!
(On Textbook MP3s)

3 Suggestion Go over the answers with the class.

OPTIONS

Game Write words for various types of artists on index cards. On another set of cards, write words for their works. Tape them face down on the board in random order. Divide the class into two teams. Play a game of Concentration in which students match artists with their works. Example: **dramaturge/pièce de théâtre.** When a player makes a match, that player's team collects those cards. The team with the most cards wins.

Notre-Dame de Paris Gilles Maheu (from Québec) is the actual director of the musical ***Notre-Dame de Paris***, which was adapted from Victor Hugo's novel (titled *The Hunchback of Notre Dame* in English). In addition, Julie Zenatti is the actress and singer who played Fleur-de-Lys in the 1999 movie version of the musical.

4 Expansion Have pairs create two more illustrated sentences using the words from **Espace contextes**. Then tell them to exchange papers with another pair and complete the sentences.

5 Suggestions
- Tell students to jot down notes during their interviews.
- Have students add two of their own questions to the interview.

6 Suggestion Divide the class into pairs and distribute the Info Gap Handouts found on the Supersite for this activity. Give students ten minutes to complete the activity.

7 Suggestions
- If time is limited, have students write their critiques as homework.
- Give students a set amount of time to write their comments before passing the papers on to the next student.

Communication

NATIONAL communication STANDARDS

4 Le mot juste **Avec un(e) partenaire, remplissez les espaces par le mot qui est illustré. Faites les accords nécessaires.**

1. Ma petite sœur apprend à <u>jouer de la batterie</u>  . Ça fait beaucoup de bruit (*noise*) dans la maison. Elle prépare son premier <u>concert</u>  qui sera en décembre.
2. Je dois me dépêcher de trouver une <u>place</u>  parce que la <u>séance</u>  va bientôt commencer.

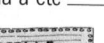

3. Marie-Claude Pietragalla a été <u>danseuse</u>  étoile de l'Opéra de Paris. Je l'ai beaucoup aimée dans le <u>rôle</u>  de Giselle.

4. Je sais <u>jouer du piano</u>  et je voudrais apprendre à <u>jouer du violon</u>  , mais je n'ai pas beaucoup de temps.

5 Répondez **Avec un(e) partenaire, posez-vous les questions suivantes et répondez-y à tour de rôle. Ensuite, comparez vos réponses avec celles d'un autre groupe.** Answers will vary.

1. Quelle sorte de chanson préfères-tu? Pour quelle(s) raison(s)?
2. Quel est le dernier concert auquel tu as assisté? Comment était-ce?
3. Quel est ton genre de spectacle favori? Pourquoi?
4. Quel réalisateur admires-tu le plus? Décris un de ses films.
5. Est-ce que tu fais de la musique? De quel genre?
6. Es-tu un(e) bon(ne) danseur/danseuse? Pour quelle(s) raison(s)?
7. Si tu pouvais jouer un rôle, lequel choisirais-tu? Pourquoi?
8. Est-ce que les arts sont importants pour toi? Lesquels? Pourquoi?

6 Les sorties **Votre professeur va vous donner, à vous et à votre partenaire, une feuille d'activités. Attention! Ne regardez pas la feuille de votre partenaire.** Answers will vary.

MODÈLE

Étudiant(e) 1: *Bonjour.*
Étudiant(e) 2: *Bonjour. J'aimerais voir quelques spectacles ce week-end. Pourriez-vous me dire quels sont les spectacles proposés?*
Étudiant(e) 1: *Bien sûr! Eh bien, vendredi soir...*

7 Le blog virtuel **Formez un petit groupe. Chaque membre du groupe choisit un film ou un spectacle différent.** Answers will vary.

- Écrivez une critique de ce film/spectacle.
- Passez-la à votre partenaire de gauche.
- Il/Elle écrit ensuite ses réactions.
- Continuez le processus pour faire un tour complet.
- Ensuite, discutez de tous vos commentaires.

OPTIONS

Game Have students stand. Toss a beanbag to a student at random and say the name of a famous artist or work. The player has four seconds to classify the work or artist. He or she then tosses the beanbag to another student and says a person or work. Example: *Macbeth* (**C'est une tragédie.**) Students who cannot classify the item in time or repeat one that has already been named are eliminated. The last person standing wins.

Pairs Have pairs of students create posters advertising performances or other types of artistic events on campus or in the community. To ensure variety, you might want to assign specific events. Tell students to use at least six vocabulary words in their posters. Then have students present them to the rest of the class.

Les sons et les lettres

Audio: Concepts, Activities
Record & Compare

NATIONAL STANDARDS comparisons

Les liaisons obligatoires et les liaisons interdites

Rules for making liaisons are complex and have many exceptions. Generally, a liaison is made between pronouns, and between a pronoun and a verb that begins with a vowel or vowel sound.

vous en avez **nous habitons** **ils aiment** **elles arrivent**

Make liaisons between articles, numbers, or the verb **est** and a noun or adjective that begins with a vowel or a vowel sound.

un éléphant **les amis** **dix hommes** (z) **Roger est enchanté.**

There is a liaison after many single-syllable adverbs, conjunctions, and prepositions.

très intéressant **chez eux** **quand elle** (t) **quand on décidera** (t)

Many expressions have obligatory liaisons that may or may not follow these rules.

C'est-à-dire... **Comment allez-vous?** **plus ou moins** **avant-hier**

Never make a liaison before or after the conjunction **et** or between a noun and a verb that follows it. Likewise, do not make a liaison between a singular noun and an adjective that follows it.

un garçon et une fille **Gilbert adore le football.** **un cours intéressant**

There is no liaison before **h aspiré** or before the word **oui** and before numbers.

un hamburger **les héros** **un oui et un non** **mes onze animaux**

Prononcez Répétez les mots suivants à voix haute.

1. les héros 2. mon petit ami 3. un pays africain 4. les onze étages

Articulez Répétez les phrases suivantes à voix haute.

1. Ils en veulent onze.
2. Vous vous êtes bien amusés hier soir?
3. Christelle et Albert habitent en Angleterre.
4. Quand est-ce que Charles a acheté ces objets?

Dictons Répétez les dictons à voix haute.

Les murs ont des oreilles.[2]

Deux avis valent mieux qu'un.[1]

[1] Two heads are better than one. (lit. Two opinions are better than one.)
[2] The walls have ears.

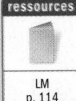

ressources
LM p. 114
espaces.vhlcentral.com

Section Goals

In this section, students will learn about:
- obligatory liaisons
- exceptions to liaison rules

Instructional Resources

espaces.vhlcentral.com: Textbook MP3s; Lab MP3s; WB/VM/LM Answer Key; IRM (Textbook Audioscript; Lab Audioscript); activities; downloads; reference tools

Suggestions

- Model the pronunciation of the example phrases and have students repeat them after you.
- Tell students to avoid making liaisons with proper names.
- Point out that liaisons are optional in certain circumstances, such as after plural nouns or within compound verb phrases. Examples: **des enfants espagnols, tu es allé**.
- Ask students to provide additional examples of each type of liaison.
- Write the phrases in the **Prononcez** activity on the board or a transparency. Have students listen to the recording and tell you where they hear liaisons. Alternately, have students rewrite the phrases on their own paper and draw lines linking letters that form liaisons and crossing out silent final consonants.

OPTIONS

Extra Practice Write the following sentences on the board and have students copy them. Then read the sentences aloud. Tell students to mark the liaisons they hear and cross out silent letters. **1. Nous en prenons une. 2. Ils aiment bien aller aux concerts. 3. Magali et Simon ont un animal de compagnie. 4. Elles iront chercher six oranges et un gâteau pour ce soir.**

Extra Practice Teach students this French tongue-twister that contains liaisons. **Un ange qui songeait à changer de visage se trouva soudain si changé que jamais plus ange ne songea à se changer.**

Section Goals

In this section, students will learn functional phrases for talking about a performance and for expressing certainty, doubt, necessities and desires.

Instructional Resources
espaces.vhlcentral.com: WB/VM/LM Answer Key; IRM (Videoscript; ***Roman-photo*** *Translations); activities; downloads; reference tools Video on DVD*

Video Recap: Leçon 14B
Before doing this **Roman-photo**, review the previous one with this activity.

1. Le groupe a fait un pique-nique à ____. (la montagne Sainte-Victoire)
2. D'abord, ils ont visité ____. (la Maison Sainte-Victoire)
3. Sandrine voulait que David fasse ____, mais il préférait dessiner ____. (un portrait d'elle/la montagne)
4. Stéphane a essayé de prendre une photo de ____. (Rachid et Amina)

Video Synopsis
Rachid, Amina, and David discuss the musical comedy they just saw and Sandrine's performance in it. At **Le P'tit Bistrot**, Valérie wants to know about the show and Sandrine's performance. David says she's not a bad actress, but she can't sing very well. Sandrine overhears his comments and confronts him. They argue and Sandrine breaks up with him.

Suggestions
- Tell students to scan the captions for vocabulary related to shows and performances.
- After reading the **Roman-photo**, have students summarize the episode.

Après le concert

Video: *Roman-photo* Record & Compare

PERSONNAGES

Amina

David

Rachid

Sandrine

Valérie

Après le concert...
RACHID Bon... que pensez-vous du spectacle?
AMINA Euh... c'est ma comédie musicale préférée... Les danseurs étaient excellents.
DAVID Oui, et l'orchestre aussi!

RACHID Et les costumes, comment tu les as trouvés, Amina?
AMINA Très beaux!
RACHID Moi, je trouve que la robe que tu as faite pour Sandrine était le plus beau des costumes.
AMINA Vraiment?
DAVID Eh, voilà Sandrine.

SANDRINE Vous avez entendu ces applaudissements? Je n'arrive pas à croire que c'était pour moi... et toute la troupe, bien sûr!
DAVID Oui c'est vraiment incroyable!
SANDRINE Alors, vous avez aimé notre spectacle?
RACHID Oui! Amina vient de nous dire que c'était sa comédie musicale préférée.

VALÉRIE Et Sandrine?
DAVID Euh, comme ci, comme ça... À vrai dire, ce n'était pas terrible... C'est le moins que l'on puisse dire.
VALÉRIE Ah bon?
DAVID Comme actrice elle n'est pas mal. Elle a bien joué son rôle, mais il est évident qu'elle ne sait pas chanter.
VALÉRIE Tu ne lui as pas dit ça, j'espère!

DAVID Ben, non, mais... Je doute qu'elle devienne une chanteuse célèbre! C'est ça, son rêve. Croyez-vous que ce soit mieux qu'elle le sache?
SANDRINE Tu en as suffisamment dit...
DAVID Sandrine! Je ne savais pas que tu étais là.
SANDRINE De toute évidence! Il vaut mieux que je m'en aille.

À la terrasse...
DAVID Sandrine! Attends!
SANDRINE Pour quoi faire?
DAVID Je voudrais m'expliquer... Il est clair que...
SANDRINE Écoute, ce qui est clair, c'est que tu n'y connais rien en musique et que tu ne sais rien de moi!

ACTIVITÉS

1 Vrai ou faux? **Indiquez si ces affirmations sont vraies ou fausses. Corrigez les phrases fausses.** Answers may vary.

1. Le spectacle est la comédie musicale préférée de Rachid. Faux. Rachid n'a pas aimé le spectacle.
2. Amina a beaucoup aimé les costumes. Vrai.
3. David a apporté des fleurs à Sandrine. Vrai.
4. David n'aime pas vraiment la robe de Sandrine. Faux. David aime bien la robe de Sandrine.
5. Finalement, Sandrine a dû acheter sa robe elle-même. Faux. Amina a fait la robe de Sandrine.
6. Valérie est surprise d'apprendre que Sandrine n'est pas une très bonne chanteuse. Vrai.
7. Sandrine est furieuse quand elle découvre la véritable opinion de David. Vrai.
8. David voulait être méchant avec Sandrine. Faux. Il ne voulait pas être méchant avec elle.
9. Sandrine rompt (*breaks up*) avec David. Vrai.
10. David veut rompre avec Sandrine. Faux. Sandrine veut rompre avec David.

Practice more at **espaces.vhlcentral.com.**

OPTIONS

Avant de regarder la vidéo Before viewing the video, have students work in pairs and brainstorm a list of things people might say after a concert or musical. What aspects of the show might they mention? What expressions might they use to praise or criticize a performance?

Regarder la vidéo Photocopy the videoscript from the IRM. Then white out words related to performance arts and other important vocabulary in order to create a master for a cloze activity. Distribute photocopies and tell students to fill in the missing information as they watch the video episode.

Les amis échangent leurs opinions.

4

5

SANDRINE C'est vrai? C'est la mienne aussi. (*Elle chante.*) J'adore cette chanson!
DAVID Euh... Sandrine, que tu es ravissante dans cette robe!
SANDRINE Merci, David. Elle me va super bien, non? Et toi, Amina, merci mille fois!

Au P'tit Bistrot...
VALÉRIE Alors c'était comment, la pièce de théâtre?
DAVID C'était une comédie musicale.
VALÉRIE Oh! Alors, c'était comment?
DAVID Pas mal. Les danseurs et l'orchestre étaient formidables.
VALÉRIE Et les chanteurs?
DAVID Mmmm... pas mal.

9

10

DAVID Sandrine, je suis désolé de t'avoir blessée, mais il faut bien que quelqu'un soit honnête avec toi.
SANDRINE À quel sujet?
DAVID Eh bien..., la chanson... je doute que ce soit ta vocation.
SANDRINE Tu doutes? Eh bien, moi, je suis certaine... certaine de ne plus jamais vouloir te revoir. C'est fini, David.

DAVID Mais, Sandrine, écoute-moi! C'est pour ton bien que je dis...
SANDRINE Oh ça suffit. Toi, tu m'écoutes... Je suis vraiment heureuse que tu repartes bientôt aux États-Unis. Dommage que ce ne soit pas demain!

Expressions utiles

Talking about a performance

- **Je n'arrive pas à croire que ces applaudissements étaient pour moi!**
  I can't believe all that applause was for me!
- **À vrai dire, ce n'était pas terrible... C'est le moins que l'on puisse dire.**
  To tell the truth, it wasn't great... That's the least that you can say.

Expressing doubts

- **Je doute qu'elle devienne une chanteuse célèbre!**
  I doubt that she will become a famous singer!
- **Croyez-vous que ce soit mieux qu'elle le sache?**
  Do you think it would be better if she knew it?
- **Je doute que ce soit ta vocation.**
  I doubt that it's your vocation/ professional calling.

Expressing certainties

- **Il est évident qu'elle ne sait pas chanter.**
  It's obvious that she does not know how to sing.
- **Ce qui est clair, c'est que tu n'y connais rien en musique.**
  What's clear is that you don't know anything about music.
- **Il est clair que tu ne sais rien de moi.**
  It's clear that you know nothing about me.
- **Je suis certaine de ne plus jamais vouloir te revoir.**
  I'm certain that I never want to see you again.

Talking about necessities and desires

- **Il vaut mieux que je m'en aille.**
  It's better that I go.
- **Il faut bien que quelqu'un soit honnête avec toi.**
  It's really necessary that someone be honest with you.

ACTIVITÉS

2 À vous! David rentre chez lui et explique à Rachid qu'il s'est disputé avec Sandrine. Avec un(e) camarade de classe, préparez une conversation dans laquelle David dit ce qu'il a fait et explique la réaction de Sandrine. Rachid doit lui donner des conseils.

3 Écrivez Pauvre Sandrine! C'est vrai qu'elle ne chante pas bien, mais que son petit ami le dise, c'est blessant (*hurtful*). À votre avis, David a-t-il bien fait d'en parler? Pourquoi? Pour Sandrine, est-ce mieux de savoir ce que pense réellement David? Composez un paragraphe dans lequel vous expliquez votre point de vue.

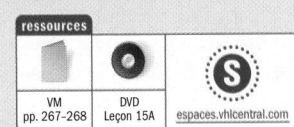

ressources
VM pp. 267–268 | DVD Leçon 15A | espaces.vhlcentral.com

Expressions utiles

- Model the pronunciation of the **Expressions utiles** and have students repeat them after you.
- As you work through the list, point out the use of the subjunctive with verbs of doubt, irregular forms of the subjunctive, and forms of **croire** and **revoir**. Tell students that these grammar points will be formally presented in the **Structures** section.
- Respond briefly to questions about the subjunctive, **croire**, and **revoir**. Reinforce correct forms, but do not expect students to produce them consistently at this time.
- Remind students that **terrible** often means *great* or *terrific*, not *terrible*. The phrase **pas terrible** (*not so great*) is an example of French understatement (**la litote**).
- Explain that **«Il vaut mieux que je m'en aille»** is a subjunctive version of **«Je m'en vais.»**

1 Suggestion Have students correct the false statements.

1 Expansion For additional practice, give students these items. **11. David pense que Sandrine est une bonne actrice. (Vrai.) 12. Amina n'aime pas les comédies musicales. (Faux.) 13. Selon Rachid, la robe de Sandrine est le plus beau des costumes. (Vrai.) 14. David repart aux États-Unis demain. (Faux.)**

2 Suggestion Remind students to use discourse connectors, such as **d'abord**, **puis**, and **après** in their conversations. Rachid should use a variety of structures when giving advice. Examples: **Dis-lui que...** and **À ta place je** [+ *conditional*]....

3 Expansion Have the class divide into two groups and debate whether or not David did the right thing by telling Sandrine what he thought of her singing.

OPTIONS

Pairs Have students work in pairs. Tell them to write predictions about what will happen in the final episode of the **Roman-photo**. Then have volunteers read their predictions aloud and ask the class if they agree or disagree.

Extra Practice Write a few expressions of doubt, certainty, and necessity from the **Roman-photo** on the board. Examples: **Je doute que...**, **Il est évident que...**, and **Il faut bien que...** Then have students create statements about the characters or their actions using these expressions. You might ask other students to react to their statements.

Section Goals

In this section, students will:

- learn about the theater in France
- learn some terms related to the theater
- learn about some famous francophone musicians
- read about Molière
- view authentic video footage

Instructional Resources
espaces.vhlcentral.com: Video; WB/VM/LM Answer Key; IRM (Videoscript); activities; downloads; reference tools Video on DVD

Culture à la loupe

Avant la lecture Have students describe the photo of the actors. Then ask: **Avez-vous déjà vu la représentation d'une pièce par une troupe professionnelle? Où? Quelle pièce de théâtre a-t-elle présentée?**

Lecture

- Point out the **Coup de main**. Ask: **Comment indique-t-on le début d'un spectacle aux États-Unis?**
- Explain that the word **amateur** is a cognate when it refers to a non-professional, such as an amateur actor, but it can also mean *lover of* (something), for example, **un amateur d'art** (*art lover*).
- Point out the statistics chart. Ask students what information it shows. (key statistics about theater performances in France during three seasons)

Après la lecture Ask students: **Comment savez-vous que le théâtre est populaire en France? Quelles parties du texte soutiennent cette idée?**

1 Suggestion Go over the answers with the class.

NATIONAL STANDARDS connections cultures

Video: *Flash culture*

CULTURE À LA LOUPE

Le théâtre, un art vivant et populaire

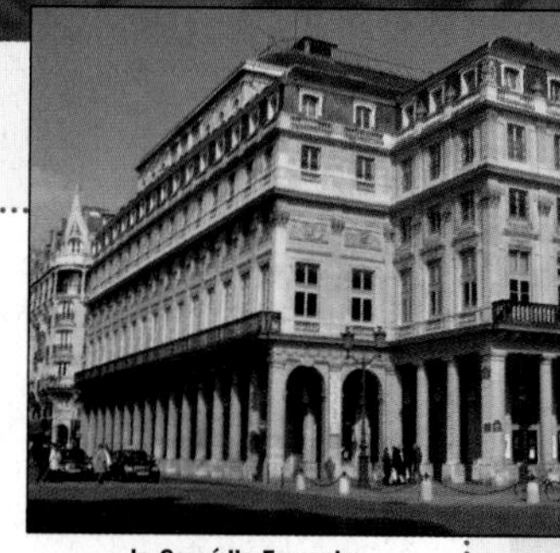

la Comédie-Française

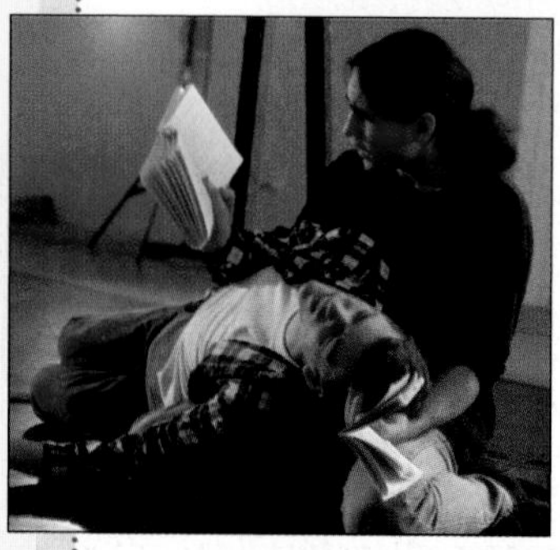

Les Français sont de plus en plus nombreux à fréquenter les théâtres: un Français sur trois voit° au moins une pièce par an. Ce public fréquente les théâtres privés, les théâtres municipaux et les cinq théâtres nationaux, dont le plus ancien est la Comédie-Française. Les spectacles d'amateurs sont aussi très appréciés. Les comédiens° de théâtre ont beaucoup de prestige et reçoivent des récompenses° professionnelles spéciales, les Molières. Le théâtre joue aussi un rôle social important, en particulier pour les jeunes.

Le théâtre français est né au XVIIe siècle. Le roi Louis XIV était un grand amateur° de spectacles et la cour° de Versailles offrait les divertissements° les plus extravagants°. Les œuvres° d'auteurs célèbres, comme Molière ou les tragédiens Pierre Corneille et Jean Racine, datent de cette époque. En 1680, Louis XIV crée l'institution théâtrale la plus prestigieuse de France, la Comédie-Française.

Aujourd'hui, elle s'appelle aussi «Maison de Molière» ou «Théâtre-Français» et elle est toujours le symbole de la tradition théâtrale française. Elle compte parfois jusqu'à 70 comédiens et elle est subventionnée par l'État. Elle a plus de 3.000 pièces à son répertoire et ses comédiens jouent dans près de 900 représentations° par an. Ils partent aussi en tournée° en province et à l'étranger et participent à des enregistrements° pour la radio et pour la télévision.

Pour assister à un de ces spectacles, il faut prendre une réservation et retirer des billets avant le début de la représentation. Au théâtre Richelieu, on peut admirer le fauteuil dans lequel Molière a joué° il y a plus de 300 ans!

voit *sees* **comédiens** *actors* **récompenses** *awards* **amateur** *lover* **cour** *royal court* **divertissements** *entertainment* **les plus extravagants** *wildest* **œuvres** *works* **représentations** *performances* **en tournée** *on tour* **enregistrements** *recordings* **a joué** *acted* **lever de rideau** *rise of the curtain* **mises en scène** *productions*

Coup de main

Les trois coups du lever de rideau°

A French tradition is to signal the beginning of a theater performance with three knocks. At the **Comédie-Française**, a six-knock signal is used instead.

Les chiffres clés du théâtre français sur trois saisons

- 2.638 textes différents ont été joués
- 7.044 mises en scène° ont été programmées
- 31.884 représentations ont été données
- il y a eu entre 1 et 323 représentations par pièce

ACTIVITÉS

1 Complétez Complétez les phrases.

1. Un Français sur trois voit au moins une pièce par an.
2. Les comédiens de théâtre reçoivent des récompenses professionnelles spéciales, les Molières.
3. Le théâtre français est né au XVIIe siècle.
4. Trois auteurs qui datent de cette époque sont Molière, Pierre Corneille et Jean Racine.
5. La Comédie-Française a été créée par Louis XIV en 1680.
6. Maison de Molière et Théâtre-Français sont deux autres noms pour la Comédie-Française.
7. La Comédie-Française a un répertoire de plus de 3.000 pièces.
8. Ses comédiens partent aussi en tournée en province et à l'étranger.
9. Au théâtre Richelieu se trouve le fauteuil dans lequel Molière a joué il y a plus de 300 ans.
10. 2.638 textes ont été joués en France sur trois saisons.

Practice more at **espaces.vhlcentral.com.**

514 *cinq cent quatorze*

OPTIONS

Les dramaturges français Pierre Corneille (1606–1684) helped shape the French classic theatre and was a master at creating tragic protagonists of heroic dimension. ***Le Cid*** (1637) is one of his masterpieces.

Jean Racine (1639–1699) also exemplifies French classicism and replaced Corneille as France's leading tragic dramatist. His most memorable characters are the fierce and tender women of his tragedies. Early in his career Racine became friends with Molière, who produced his first two tragedies. ***Andromaque*** (1667), ***Bajazet*** (1672), ***Mithradate*** (1673), ***Iphigénie en Aulide*** (1674), and ***Phèdre*** (1677) are considered his greatest plays.

LE FRANÇAIS QUOTIDIEN

Les spectacles

billetterie (*f.*)	*box office*
jour (*m.*) de relâche	*day with no performances*
orchestre (*m.*)	*orchestra seats*
poulailler (*m.*)	*gallery*
rentrée (*f.*) théâtrale	*start of theatrical season*
reprise (*f.*)	*revival; rerun*
à l'affiche	*now playing*
incontournable	*must-see*

LE MONDE FRANCOPHONE

Des musiciens

Voici quelques musiciens francophones célèbres.

En Algérie Khaled, chanteur de raï, un mélange° de chanson arabe et d'influences occidentales

Aux Antilles le groupe Kassav, inventeur de la musique zouk

Au Cameroun Manu Dibango, célèbre joueur de saxophone

Au Mali Amadou et Mariam, couple de chanteurs aveugles°

À la Réunion Danyèl Waro, la voix° du maloya, musique typique de l'île

À Saint-Pierre-et-Miquelon Henri Lafitte, auteur, compositeur et interprète° de plus de 500 chansons

Au Sénégal Youssou N'Dour, compositeur et interprète de musique mbalax, un mélange de musique traditionnelle d'Afrique de l'Ouest et de musique occidentale

mélange *mix* **aveugles** *blind* **voix** *voice* **interprète** *performer*

PORTRAIT

Molière (1622–1673)

LE THÉATRE A TRAVERS LES AGES
Molière et sa troupe.

Molière, dont le vrai nom est Jean-Baptiste Poquelin, est le génie de la Comédie-Française. D'origine bourgeoise, il choisit la vie difficile du théâtre. En 1665, il obtient le soutien° de Louis XIV et devient le premier acteur comique, auteur et metteur en scène de France. Molière est un innovateur: il écrit des satires et des farces quand la mode est aux tragédies néoclassiques. Avec le compositeur Lully, il invente la comédie-ballet. Après une vie riche en aventures, il meurt après une représentation° du *Malade imaginaire*, dans laquelle il tenait° le rôle principal. Aujourd'hui, ses pièces sont toujours d'actualité° et Molière reste l'auteur le plus joué en France.

soutien *support* **représentation** *performance* **tenait** *played* **d'actualité** *current*

SUR INTERNET

Qu'est-ce que le festival d'Avignon?

Go to **espaces.vhlcentral.com** to find more information related to this **ESPACE CULTURE**. Then watch the corresponding **Flash culture**.

2 Répondez Répondez aux questions par des phrases complètes.

1. Molière était-il d'origine populaire?
   Non, il était d'origine bourgeoise.
2. Que s'est-il passé dans la vie de Molière en 1659? Il obtient le soutien de Louis XIV et devient le premier acteur comique, auteur et metteur en scène de France.
3. Pourquoi Molière est-il un innovateur?
   Il écrit des satires et des farces quand la mode est aux tragédies néoclassiques.
4. Comment Molière est-il mort?
   Il est mort sur scène, dans le rôle du *Malade imaginaire*.
5. Qu'est-ce que le raï?
   C'est un mélange de chanson traditionnelle arabe et d'influences occidentales.
6. De quel instrument joue Manu Dibango?
   Il joue du saxophone.

3 Un festival Vous et un(e) partenaire allez organiser un festival de culture francophone. Faites des recherches sur des artistes francophones et choisissez qui vous allez inviter. Où vont-ils jouer? Indiquez les genres d'œuvres. Comparez ensuite votre programme avec celui d'un autre groupe.

ressources
VM pp. 299–300
espaces.vhlcentral.com

ACTIVITÉS

Le français quotidien

- Model the pronunciation of each term and have students repeat it.
- Point out that **reprise** is a **faux ami** for the English word *reprise.*

Portrait Have students describe the theater poster. Then ask students: **Avez-vous déjà lu ou vu une comédie de Molière? Laquelle?**

Le monde francophone Have students write four true/false statements based on the information in this section. Then have them get together with a classmate and take turns reading their statements and responding.

2 Expansion For additional practice, give students these items. **7. Quel est le vrai nom de Molière? (Jean-Baptiste Poquelin) 8. Qu'a-t-il inventé avec le compositeur Lully? (la comédie-ballet) 9. Où a-t-on inventé la musique zouk? (aux Antilles)**

3 Suggestion Many festivals post their programs on the Internet. Provide students with a model of an actual program for a cultural festival to follow. Encourage them to be creative and use information they already know.

Flash culture Tell students that they will learn more about movie theaters and types of publications available at kiosks by watching a variety of real-life images narrated by Csilla. Show the video segment without sound and tell students to call out what they see. Then show the video segment again with sound. You can also use the activities in the video manual to reinforce this **Flash culture**.

OPTIONS

Molière Sometimes referred to as the father of modern French comedy, Molière's plays often ridicule human vices and excesses, which are embodied in his characters. These characters encompass a broad spectrum and offer a wide view of seventeenth-century French society. ***L'École des femmes*** (1662), ***Le Tartuffe*** (1664), ***Don Juan*** (1665), ***Le Misanthrope*** (1666), ***Le Bourgeois gentilhomme*** (1670), and ***Les Femmes savantes*** (1672) are among his masterpieces.

Pairs Distribute a French theater schedule, including titles of plays, times of performances, and prices of seats. Then have students work in pairs, with one person playing the role of the theatergoer who wants to buy a ticket and the other person acting as the ticket seller.

NATIONAL STANDARDS comparisons

Section Goals

In this section, students will learn:

- the subjunctive with expressions of doubt, disbelief, or uncertainty
- the subjunctive of irregular verbs **aller**, **pouvoir**, **savoir**, and **vouloir**

Instructional Resources
*espaces.vhlcentral.com: Lab MP3s; WB/VM/LM Answer Key; IRM (**Essayez!** and **Mise en pratique** answers; Lab Audioscript); activities; downloads; reference tools*

Suggestions

- Review the subjunctive verb forms from **Espace structures 14A**, pages 482–483 and **14B**, pages 494–495.
- Explain that, although *that* is often optional in English, **que** is required in French. Example: *I doubt (that) the concert is good.* **Je doute que le concert soit bon.**
- Check for understanding by writing on the board main clauses ending in **que** that require a subjunctive in the subordinate clause. Invite volunteers to suggest several endings for each, using verbs they have just reviewed. Example: **Il est douteux que/qu'...(qu'il y ait un examen la semaine prochaine/que j'achète une nouvelle voiture/qu'on aille à Paris).**
- Point out that the subjunctive is used when there is a change of subject as well as an expression of doubt, disbelief, or uncertainty. If the subject does not change, the infinitive is used. Example: **Jacques n'est pas sûr de pouvoir aller à Paris cet été.**

15A.1 The subjunctive (Part 3)

Verbs of doubt, disbelief, and uncertainty

- The subjunctive is used in a subordinate clause when there is a change of subject and the main clause implies doubt, disbelief, or uncertainty.

MAIN CLAUSE	CONNECTOR	SUBORDINATE CLAUSE
Je doute	**que**	le concert **soit** bon.
I doubt	*that*	*the concert is good.*

Je doute qu'elle devienne une chanteuse célèbre!

Je suis certaine que je ne veux plus jamais te revoir!

Expressions of doubt, disbelief, and uncertainty

douter que...	*to doubt that...*	**Il est impossible que...**	*It is impossible that...*
ne pas croire que...	*not to believe that...*	**Il n'est pas certain que...**	*It is uncertain that...*
ne pas penser que...	*not to think that...*	**Il n'est pas sûr que...**	*It is not sure that...*
Il est douteux que...	*It is doubtful that...*	**Il n'est pas vrai que...**	*It is untrue that...*

Il n'est pas sûr qu'il y **ait** un entracte.
It's not sure that there is an intermission.

Je ne crois pas qu'on **vende** les billets ici.
I don't believe that they sell the tickets here.

- The indicative is used in a subordinate clause when the main clause expresses certainty.

Expressions of certainty

croire que...	*to believe that...*	**Il est clair que...**	*It is clear that...*
penser que...	*to think that...*	**Il est évident que...**	*It is obvious that...*
savoir que...	*to know that...*	**Il est sûr que...**	*It is sure that...*
Il est certain que...	*It is certain that...*	**Il est vrai que...**	*It is true that...*

On **sait que** l'histoire **finit** mal.
We know the story ends badly.

Il est certain qu'elle **comprend**.
It is certain that she understands.

MISE EN PRATIQUE

1 Fort-de-France Vous discutez de vos projets avec votre ami(e) martiniquais(e). Complétez les phrases avec les formes correctes du présent de l'indicatif ou du subjonctif.

1. Je crois que Fort-de-France ___est___ (être) plus loin de Paris que de New York.
2. Il n'est pas certain que je ___vienne___ (venir) à Fort-de-France cet été.
3. Il n'est pas sûr que nous ___partions___ (partir) en croisière (*cruise*) ensemble.
4. Il est clair que nous ___ne partons pas___ (ne pas partir) sans toi.
5. Nous savons que ce voyage ___va___ (aller) te plaire.
6. Il est douteux que le ski alpin ___soit___ (être) un sport populaire ici.

2 Un camarade pénible Vous faites une présentation sur la Martinique devant la classe. Un(e) camarade pénible critique toutes vos idées. Avec un(e) partenaire, jouez la scène. Answers will vary.

MODÈLE
Étudiant(e) 1: *Le carnaval martiniquais est populaire.*
Étudiant(e) 2: *Je doute qu'il soit populaire.*

1. Les ressources naturelles sont protégées.
2. Tout le monde va se promener dans la forêt.
3. Les Martiniquais font des pique-niques tous les jours.
4. L'île a de belles plages.
5. Les enfants y font des randonnées.
6. On y boit des jus de fruits délicieux.

3 Le Tour de France Maxime veut participer un jour au Tour de France. Employez des expressions de doute et de certitude pour lui dire ce que vous pensez de ses habitudes. Answers will vary.

MODÈLE
Je ne crois pas que tu puisses dormir jusqu'à midi!

1.

2.

Practice more at **espaces.vhlcentral.com.**

OPTIONS

TPR Call out a series of sentences, using either an expression of certainty or an expression of doubt, disbelief, or uncertainty. Have students stand if they hear an expression of certainty or remain seated if they hear an expression of doubt. Example: **Il est impossible que j'apprenne une autre langue.** (Students remain seated.)

Pairs Have students write five absurd or strange sentences. Then have them switch sentences with a classmate. Students should write their reactions using a different expression of doubt, disbelief, or uncertainty. Example: **Toutes les femmes aiment bien faire le ménage. (Je ne crois pas que toutes les femmes aiment bien faire le ménage!)**

COMMUNICATION

4 Assemblez Vous avez l'occasion de faire un séjour aux Antilles françaises. À tour de rôle avec un(e) partenaire, assemblez les éléments de chaque colonne pour parler de ces vacances. Answers will vary.

MODÈLE

Il n'est pas certain que nous allions visiter une plantation.

A	B	C
Il est certain que Il n'est pas certain que Il est évident que Il est impossible que Il est vrai que Il n'est pas sûr que Je doute que Je pense que Je sais que ?	je/j' tu mon copain ma sœur mon frère nous les touristes mes parents ?	être content(e)(s) faire des excursions faire beau temps faire du bateau jouer sur la plage pouvoir parler créole visiter une plantation ?

5 Comédie musicale Votre classe prépare une comédie musicale et vous organisez le spectacle. Votre partenaire voudrait y participer et il/elle postule pour un rôle. Alternez les rôles, puis présentez vos dialogues à la classe. Answers will vary.

MODÈLE

Étudiant(e) 1: *Est-il possible que je chante dans la chorale?*
Étudiant(e) 2: *Je doute qu'il soit possible que vous y chantiez. Il n'y a plus de place, mais je crois que...*

- acteur/actrice
- compositeur
- metteur en scène
- animateur/animatrice (*emcee*)
- chorale
- danseurs
- musiciens
- ouvreur/ouvreuse (*usher*)

6 Je doute Votre partenaire veut mieux vous connaître. Écrivez cinq phrases qui vous décrivent: quatre fausses et une vraie. Votre partenaire doit deviner laquelle est vraie et justifier sa réponse. Ensuite, alternez les rôles. Answers will vary.

MODÈLE

Étudiant(e) 1: *Je finis toujours mes devoirs avant de me coucher.*
Étudiant(e) 2: *Je doute que tu finisses tes devoirs avant de te coucher, parce que tu as toujours beaucoup de devoirs.*

- Sometimes a speaker may opt to use the subjunctive in a question to indicate that he or she feels doubtful or uncertain of an affirmative response.

Crois-tu que cet acteur **fasse** un bon Charles de Gaulle?
Do you believe that actor makes a good Charles de Gaulle?

Est-il vrai que vous **partiez** déjà en vacances?
Is it true that you're already leaving on vacation?

Croyez-vous que ce soit mieux qu'elle le sache?
Il vaut mieux que je m'en aille.

Present subjunctive of *aller, pouvoir, savoir, vouloir*

	aller	pouvoir	savoir	vouloir
que je/j'	aille	puisse	sache	veuille
que tu	ailles	puisses	saches	veuilles
qu'il/elle	aille	puisse	sache	veuille
que nous	allions	puissions	sachions	voulions
que vous	alliez	puissiez	sachiez	vouliez
qu'ils/elles	aillent	puissent	sachent	veuillent

Il faut qu'on **aille** au théâtre ce soir.
We have to go to the theater tonight.

Il vaut mieux que tu **saches** la nouvelle.
It's better that you know the news.

Je doute que la pièce **puisse** causer un effet comme celui-là.
I doubt that the play could cause an effect like that.

Est-il possible qu'il **veuille** apprendre à jouer du violon?
Is it possible that he wants to learn to play the violin?

Essayez! **Choisissez la forme correcte du verbe.**

1. Il est douteux que le metteur en scène (sait / **sache**) où est l'acteur.
2. Je sais que Carole Bouquet et Gérard Depardieu (**sont** / soient) mariés.
3. Il est impossible qu'il (est / **soit**) amoureux d'elle.
4. Ne crois-tu pas que l'histoire du Titanic (finit / **finisse**) bien?
5. Est-il vrai que les Français (font / **fassent**) uniquement des films intellectuels?
6. Je ne crois pas qu'il (peut / **puisse**) jouer le rôle du jeune prisonnier.
7. Tout le monde sait que le ballet (**est** / soit) d'origine française.
8. Il n'est pas certain qu'ils (peuvent / **puissent**) terminer le spectacle.

Essayez! Have students underline the main clauses in these sentences. Then have them create original sentences, using the indicative or subjunctive where appropriate.

1 Expansion Have pairs discuss why each subordinate clause is in the indicative or subjunctive. If the sentence is in the indicative, have pairs make the necessary changes in the main clause to elicit the subjunctive. Example: **1. Je ne crois pas que Fort-de-France soit plus loin de Paris que de New York.**

2 Expansion For emphasis, have **Étudiant(e) 1** counter the statement of doubt made by **Étudiant(e) 2** with another statement of certainty. Example: **Mais si! Il est sûr que le carnaval martiniquais est très populaire!**

3 Suggestion Before starting, have the class brainstorm what would be necessary for someone to do or be in order to participate successfully in the **Tour de France**. Examples: **Je sais qu'il faut être en pleine forme. Il est clair qu'on doit faire de l'exercice tous les jours avant d'y participer.**

4 Suggestion Have volunteers give sentences using elements from each of the three columns. Have other volunteers act as secretaries, writing examples on the board. Ask the class to help you correct the grammar and spelling.

5 Suggestion Ask two volunteers to read the **modèle** aloud. Correct any pronunciation errors.

6 Expansion Call on a student to read two statements about his or her partner, without revealing which one is true and which one is false. Have the class guess which statement is which, using expressions of doubt and certainty.

OPTIONS

Video Replay the video episode, having students focus on expressions of certainty, uncertainty, doubt, and disbelief. Stop the video where appropriate and ask students to repeat any construction that includes [*main clause*] + **que** + [*subordinate clause*] and explain why the indicative or subjunctive was used in each instance.

Extra Practice Have students write sentences about three things of which they are certain and three things they doubt or cannot believe. Students should use a different expression for each of their sentences. Have students share some of their sentences with the class.

National Standards: comparisons

Section Goals

In this section, you will learn:
- the possessive pronouns
- the use of the expression **être à quelqu'un**

Instructional Resources
*espaces.vhlcentral.com: Lab MP3s; WB/VM/LM Answer Key; IRM (**Essayez!** and **Mise en pratique** answers; Lab Audioscript); activities; downloads; reference tools*

Suggestions
- You might want to quickly review the possessive adjectives and their usage from **Leçon 3A** with your students before presenting the possessive pronouns. Call out different phrases in English, for example *my hats, their dogs, his boat* etc. and have students give the equivalent in French.
- Practice the difference in pronunciation between **notre** vs. **nôtre** and **votre** vs. **vôtre**. Be sure to stress that the possessive pronouns are pronounced with the closed **o** sound. After students practice this a few times, have them write down the four words on separate index cards. Say one of these words at a time and have them hold up the correct card to check if they are able to hear the difference.
- Once students are comfortable with the concept of the possessive pronouns, you might want to contrast the different ways one can indicate possession using the possessive adjective, the expression **être à quelqu'un**, the possessive pronouns, and the demonstrative pronouns. Example: **C'est le piano de Didier.** *(This is Didier's piano.)* **C'est son piano.** *(It's his piano.)* **C'est le sien./Il est à lui.** *(It's his.)* **Il est meilleur que celui d'Armand.** *(It is better than Armand's.)*

15A.2 Possessive pronouns

Point de départ In **Leçon 3A**, you learned how possessive adjectives function in French. You will now learn about possessive pronouns and how they are different in French and English.

- Possessive pronouns are the words which replace nouns modified by possessive adjectives. In French, the possessive pronouns have different forms depending on whether the noun is masculine or feminine, singular or plural. These are the forms of the French possessive pronouns.

Singular possessive pronouns

masculine	feminine	
le mien	la mienne	*mine*
le tien	la tienne	*yours* (fam./sing.)
le sien	la sienne	*his/hers/its*
le nôtre	la nôtre	*ours*
le vôtre	la vôtre	*yours* (form./pl.)
le leur	la leur	*theirs*

Plural possessive pronouns

masculine	feminine	
les miens	les miennes	*mine*
les tiens	les tiennes	*yours* (fam./sing.)
les siens	les siennes	*his/hers/its*
les nôtres		*ours*
les vôtres		*yours* (form./pl.)
les leurs		*theirs*

Je connais **ton frère**, mais je ne connais pas **le sien**.
I know your brother, but I don't know his/hers.

- French and English possessive pronouns are very similar in usage. They can refer to an object or a person. However, the French possessive pronouns consist of two parts: the definite article and the possessive word. Both parts must agree in number and gender with the noun to which they refer.

Ils aiment mes pièces, mais ils préfèrent **les tiennes**. (**tes pièces**)
They like my plays, but they prefer yours.

- Possessive pronouns, like possessive adjectives, reflect the object or person possessed, *not* the possessor.

sa voiture → *his car* — **la sienne** *(referring to the car)* → *his*
sa voiture → *her car* — **la sienne** *(referring to the car)* → *hers*

MISE EN PRATIQUE

1 Pas de répétitions! Remplacez les mots indiqués par les bons pronoms possessifs.

MODÈLE
Je vois mon frère, mais je ne vois pas ton frère.
Je vois le mien, mais je ne vois pas le tien.

1. Tu préfères mes chansons ou leurs chansons? Tu préfères les miennes ou les leurs?
2. Mes danseurs sont arrivés, mais vos danseurs pas encore. Les miens sont arrivés, mais les vôtres pas encore.
3. Ta comédie est amusante, mais sa comédie est ennuyeuse. La tienne est amusante, mais la sienne est ennuyeuse.
4. Mon petit ami et ton petit ami sont allés au match ensemble. Le mien et le tien sont allés au match ensemble.
5. Ma grand-mère habite à Bruxelles. Et leur grand-mère? La mienne habite à Bruxelles. Et la leur?
6. Nos chansons sont meilleures que vos chansons. Les nôtres sont meilleures que les vôtres.
7. Sa maison est près de la banque. Où est votre maison? La sienne est près de la banque. Où est la vôtre?
8. Leurs séances sont moins longues que tes séances. Les leurs sont moins longues que les tiennes.

2 Quel chaos! Madame Mercier emmène ses enfants et leurs copains à la plage, mais tout le monde a oublié d'apporter quelque chose. Faites des phrases complètes pour dire qui a oublié quoi.

MODÈLE
je / serviette / David
J'ai ma serviette, mais David a oublié la sienne.

1. tu / lunettes de soleil / Marie et Claire Tu as tes lunettes de soleil, mais Marie et Claire ont oublié les leurs.
2. nous / chaussures / Christophe Nous avons nos chaussures, mais Christophe a oublié les siennes.
3. Tristan et Benjamin / casquettes / Élisa et toi Tristan et Benjamin ont leurs casquettes, mais Élisa et toi avez oublié les vôtres.
4. vous / maillot de bain / nous Vous avez votre maillot de bain, mais nous avons oublié les nôtres.
5. Thomas / crème solaire (*sunscreen*) / vous Thomas a sa crème solaire, mais vous avez oublié la vôtre.
6. je / lecteur MP3 / tu J'ai mon lecteur MP3, mais tu as oublié le tien.

3 Les mêmes choses Votre cousin va faire exactement les mêmes choses que vous, aujourd'hui. Écrivez ses réponses avec des pronoms possessifs.

MODÈLE
Tu vas écrire une carte postale à tes grands-parents?
Alors, je vais aussi écrire une carte postale aux miens.

1. Tu vas jouer avec ton petit frère? Alors, je vais aussi jouer avec le mien.
2. Tu vas téléphoner à tes amies? Alors, je vais aussi téléphoner aux miennes.
3. Tu vas donner à manger à tes chats? Alors, je vais aussi donner à manger aux miens.
4. Tu vas dire bonjour à ton prof? Alors, je vais aussi dire bonjour au mien.
5. Tu vas prendre une photo de ta maison? Alors, je vais aussi prendre une photo de la mienne.
6. Tu vas t'occuper de tes affaires? Alors, je vais aussi m'occuper des miennes.

Practice more at **espaces.vhlcentral.com.**

OPTIONS

Extra Practice Have students come up with additional sentences using the indefinite pronoun **on** with **le sien/les siens**. Here are some examples that you can give them. **On s'occupe du sien. On ne se fâche pas contre les siens. On s'intéresse aux siens. On se souvient des siens.**

Extra Practice Have students work in pairs to write at least eight questions on a variety of topics to ask the other. The goal is to use possessive pronouns in the questions or the answers. Ex: **1. Mes grands-parents habitent à Houston. Et les tiens? 2. Ma famille est très grande. Et la tienne? 3. Mon/Ma petit(e) ami(e) est très intelligent(e). Et le tien/la tienne? 4. J'adore mes cours. Et toi? Les miens sont trop difficiles.**

COMMUNICATION

4 **C'est à qui?** Vous êtes responsable du bureau des objets trouvés dans votre université. Avec un(e) partenaire, créez un dialogue et jouez la scène devant la classe. Answers will vary.

MODÈLE

Étudiant(e) 1: *Ces cahiers sont à toi?*
Étudiant(e) 2: *Non, ce ne sont pas les miens.*
Étudiant(e) 1: *Tu es sûr(e)?*
Étudiant(e) 2: *Oui, les miens sont plus grands.*

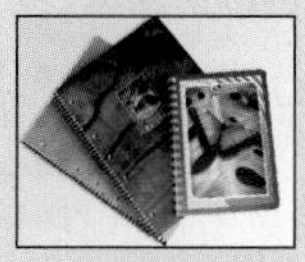

1.

2.

3.

4.

5 **Au spectacle** Catherine est au théâtre avec son ami Rémi. Elle est metteur en scène et compare la pièce qu'elle voit avec la sienne. Avec un(e) partenaire, jouez la conversation. Utilisez autant de pronoms possessifs possibles. Answers will vary.

MODÈLE

Étudiant(e) 1: *Le début de ma pièce est plus intéressant que le sien.*
Étudiant(e) 2: *Je ne suis pas d'accord. Le sien est aussi intéressant que le tien.*

6 **Questions personnelles** Vous voulez mieux connaître votre partenaire. Posez-vous ces questions à tour de rôle. Utilisez des pronoms possessifs dans vos réponses. Answers will vary.

1. Est-ce que tes idées (*ideas*) sont vraiment différentes de celles de tes parents?
2. Est-ce que ton style de vêtements est le même que celui de ton frère ou ta sœur?
3. D'habitude, est-ce que tu t'occupes de tes affaires ou de celles de tes amis?
4. Tu t'entends mieux avec tes parents ou avec ceux de ton/ta petit(e) ami(e)?
5. Tu aimes ton quartier ou celui de tes amis?
6. Tu préfères ta voiture ou celle d'un de tes amis?

- The articles **le** and **les** of the possessive pronouns contract with **à**.

à + le mien	**au mien**
à + la mienne	**à la mienne**
à + les miens	**aux miens**
à + les miennes	**aux miennes**

Tu vas téléphoner **à mes amis** ou **aux tiens**?
Are you going to call my friends or yours?

Avez-vous récemment parlé **à leurs parents** ou **aux vôtres**?
Did you speak recently to their parents or yours?

- The articles **le** and **les** of the possessive pronouns contract also with **de**.

de + le mien	**du mien**
de + la mienne	**de la mienne**
de + les miens	**des miens**
de + les miennes	**des miennes**

Pourquoi t'occupes-tu **de ses problèmes** au lieu **des tiens**?
Why are you concerned with his/her problems instead of yours?

Les critiques parlent **de votre tragédie**, pas **de la nôtre**.
The critics are talking about your tragedy, not ours.

- With the indefinite pronoun **on**, always use the masculine possessive pronoun **le sien/les siens**.

On est fier **des siens**.
One is proud of one's own (people).

- The possessive pronoun is never used after the verb **être** in the construction [*noun/pronoun (subject)*] + **être**. In such a case, use the expression **être à** + [*noun/disjunctive pronoun*].

Ce pull **est à** Nathan.
This sweater belongs to Nathan.

Ce pull **est à** lui.
This sweater is his.

- You can however use the possessive pronouns after the expressions **C'est** and **Ce sont**.

C'est **la nôtre**.
It's ours.

Ce sont **les miennes**.
These are mine.

Essayez! **Écrivez le pronom possessif qui correspond.**

1. Où est ma feuille d'examen? *Où est la mienne?*
2. Ce sont tes sœurs qui reviennent de Grèce? Ce sont les tiennes qui reviennent de Grèce?
3. J'ai revu mon amie d'enfance hier soir! J'ai revu la mienne hier soir!
4. C'est votre lampe qui ne marche plus! C'est la vôtre qui ne marche plus!
5. Ils viennent d'acheter leur piano. Ils viennent d'acheter le leur.
6. Ce sont nos chansons qui passent à la radio! Ce sont les nôtres qui passent à la radio!
7. Ses fauteuils sont toujours en bon état (*condition*). Les siens sont toujours en bon état.
8. Quand ton concert a-t-il lieu (*takes place*)? Quand le tien a-t-il lieu?

Essayez! Here are some additional items that you could give the students. **9. Sa tragédie est longue. (La sienne est longue.) 10. Avez-vous écouté leur chœur? (Avez-vous écouté le leur?) 11. Notre opéra est moderne. (Le nôtre est moderne.) 12. Leurs spectateurs sont contents d'être venus. Les leurs sont contents d'être venus.**

1 Suggestion Have students do this as a written activity. Then, have them exchange their papers and correct each other's work.

2 Expansion Change the subjects of the dehydrated sentences in the activity and have students say or write the new sentences.

3 Expansion Have students redo this activity, this time saying that they have already done what their partner did. Example: **Moi, j'ai déjà écrit une carte postale aux miens.**

4 Suggestion Before they start this activity, have students brainstorm a variety of adjectives they could use to describe their belongings.

4 Expansions
- They could extend the activity by using their personal belongings and asking their partner if the item belongs to him/her.
- Have students use the third person to share their partner's response with the class. Example: **Ces cahiers ne sont pas à lui/elle. Les siens sont plus grands.**

5 Expansion Have pairs volunteer to perform this as a skit in front of the class.

6 Expansion You might have students circulate around the class and ask at least five other students these questions. Then, have them write five sentences to summarize the information obtained through the interviews.

OPTIONS

Game Split the class into four teams. Using the **Essayez!** activity as a model, have each team come up with a list of additional words from the vocabulary they have learned so far and use them with different possessive adjectives. Then, have each team take turns calling out one of their words. The next team should give the corresponding possessive pronoun. The team that answers then gets a chance to call out its word. If a team gives a wrong answer, the following team gets a chance to answer and score a point. The game should proceed at a fairly fast pace. Set a time limit for the game. You could make the game more challenging by having each responding team not only give the corresponding possessive pronoun, but also use it in a logical sentence.

Révision

Instructional Resources
espaces.vhlcentral.com: IRM (Info Gap Activities); Testing Program, pp. 113–116; Test Files; Testing Program MP3s; activities; downloads; reference tools
Test Generator

1 Expansion Brainstorm other hobbies and occupations with the whole class. Then have pairs continue this activity using magazine pictures.

2 Expansion Give these additional items to the class.

- **Il n'y a pas de place pour les femmes dans les films d'action.**
- **La plupart des films américains sont violents.**
- **Les gens plus âgés n'aiment pas la musique rock.**

3 Suggestion Divide the class into pairs and distribute the Info Gap Handouts found on the Supersite for this activity. Give students ten minutes to complete the activity.

4 Expansion Have pairs create a new **annonce** for a **rôle principal**. Encourage students to be creative. Then have students exchange their **annonce** with another pair and repeat the activity.

5 Suggestion Ask a volunteer from each group to take notes on their conversations. After the groups have compared lists, have each volunteer write their group's selections on the board. Each group should take turns summarizing their selections and relating the expressions of doubt and certainty used in the activity.

6 Suggestion Before students begin this activity, have pairs make a list of university supplies they are going to ask to borrow and possible excuses. After they finish the activity, have them share their most creative excuses with the rest of the class. Students should vote for the best excuse they hear.

1 Il est clair que... Observez ces personnes et imaginez leurs activités artistiques préférées. Avec un(e) partenaire, utilisez des expressions de doute et de certitude pour répondre aux questions et pour décrire chaque personnage. Answers will vary.

chanteur de chorale ou de comédie musicale?

danseur ou acteur?

chef d'orchestre ou metteur en scène?

compositeur d'opéra ou dramaturge?

2 Je ne pense pas Que pensent vos camarades de ces affirmations? Par groupes de quatre, trouvez au moins une personne qui soit d'accord avec chaque phrase et une qui ne soit pas d'accord. Utilisez des expressions de doute et de certitude. Ensuite, présentez vos arguments à la classe. Answers will vary.

MODÈLE La télévision fait du mal au cinéma.

Étudiant(e) 1: *Penses-tu que la télévision fasse du mal au cinéma?*
Étudiant(e) 2: *Non, je ne crois pas que ce soit vrai. Il est clair que les acteurs de cinéma sont plus célèbres que ceux de la télé.*

- Jimi Hendrix est le meilleur joueur de guitare.
- Mozart est le meilleur compositeur de musique classique.
- Personne n'aime les comédies musicales aujourd'hui.
- Un danseur est autant un sportif qu'un artiste.
- L'opéra est un genre trop ésotérique et ennuyeux.

3 Les arts Votre professeur va vous donner, à vous et à votre partenaire, deux feuilles d'activités différentes sur les arts. Attention! Ne regardez pas la feuille de votre partenaire. Answers will vary.

4 C'est tout moi! Avec un(e) partenaire, vous voyez ces annonces dans le journal. Vous pensez qu'un de ces rôles est pour vous. Un(e) ami(e) n'est pas du tout d'accord, mais vous insistez. Utilisez des expressions de doute et de certitude dans votre dialogue. Answers will vary.

Cherchons jeune homme
de 27-30 ans, sportif et musclé, avec permis moto et avion, pour rôle principal. Doit être un acteur expérimenté qui sache jouer du piano comme un professionnel et qui puisse monter à cheval. Doit avoir les yeux noirs, beaucoup de charme, de la présence et un look aventurier.

Cherchons jeune femme
de 18-20 ans avec beaucoup de personnalité et qui ait une formation de chanteuse classique, pour rôle dans une comédie musicale en espagnol. Doit pouvoir danser le tango, la salsa et la rumba.
Venez rencontrer le compositeur et le metteur en scène, jeudi à 20 heures, au Théâtre du Boulevard.

5 Le meilleur Avec un(e) partenaire, trouvez un exemple pour chaque catégorie de la liste. Ensuite, comparez votre liste avec celle d'un autre groupe et parlez de vos opinions. Utilisez des expressions de doute et de certitude. Answers will vary.

le/la meilleur(e) ... en ce moment

- film
- chanson à la radio
- danseur/danseuse
- chanteur/chanteuse
- acteur/actrice

6 Mal organisé Vous étiez très pressé(e) ce matin et vous avez oublié de mettre beaucoup de choses dans votre sac à dos. Demandez à votre partenaire si vous pouvez lui emprunter cinq choses dont vous avez besoin pour l'université. Votre partenaire va vous donner des excuses pour ne pas vous les prêter. Utilisez des pronoms possessifs. Jouez votre dialogue devant la classe. Answers will vary.

MODÈLE

Étudiant(e) 1: *Je peux emprunter ta calculatrice?*
Étudiant(e) 2: *Désolé(e). J'ai besoin de la mienne pour faire ce devoir.*

ressources

WB	LM	
pp. 199-202	pp. 115-116	espaces.vhlcentral.com

OPTIONS

Extra Practice Have students imagine they are writing to a friend who is just about to start his or her freshman year of college. In their letter, students should give advice about the uncertainties of university life. Encourage students to use the expressions listed on page 516. You may want to collect students' papers and grade them.

Game Divide the class into two teams. One team writes sentences with expressions of certainty, while the other writes sentences with expressions of doubt, disbelief, or uncertainty. Put all the sentences in a hat. Students take turns drawing sentences for their team and stating the opposite of what the sentence says. The team with the most correct sentences wins.

Le Zapping

S **Video: Short Film**

National Standards: connections, communities

Dans ce film d'animation musical de Guillaume Colomb et Olivier Derivière, les objets et les aliments qu'on associe à un petit-déjeuner français typique prennent vie° pour transformer ce moment simple de la journée en une compétition pleine d'humour entre un pot de miel et un pot de confiture qui convoitent° tous les deux une belle tartine. Lequel d'entre eux sera le vainqueur°? Découvrez-le!

prennent vie *come to life* **convoitent** *covet* **vainqueur** *winner*

Préparation

1 Le bon choix Trouvez le mot ou l'expression la plus proche du terme souligné dans chaque phrase.

1. Arrête de faire l'andouille! c	a. n'est pas content
2. Quel bruit! Mets la musique en sourdine! f	b. se dépêcher
3. Déjà dix heures? Il faut se bouger! b	c. l'idiot
4. J'en soupe avec ce cours! e	d. fort
5. Cet homme râle depuis ce matin. a	e. suis fatigué de
6. Ce café est vraiment corsé. d	f. moins fort

2 À compléter Avec un(e) camarade, complétez ce dialogue avec des mots et expressions des listes.

—Je n'arrête pas de (1) ___bâiller___. J'ai mal dormi.
—Qu'est-ce que tu veux ce matin pour le petit-déjeuner?
—Du pain bien (2) ___croustillant___ avec du beurre et de la confiture.
—Tu veux du café?
—Oui, mais fais-le bien (3) ___corsé___, pas comme hier matin, alors, parce qu'il n'était vraiment pas bon!
—Oh, écoute, arrête de (4) ___râler___! Tu n'es jamais content! Tiens, voilà le jus d'orange...
—(5) ___Bon sang___, fais attention! Tu en as renversé (*spilled*) partout!
—Dis donc, il est déjà huit heures. On doit (6) ___se grouiller___ si on veut arriver à la gare à l'heure!

Expressions utiles

Arrête de faire l'andouille! (*fam.*)
Stop goofing around!

Bon sang! (*fam.*)
Darn it!

Grouille-toi! (*fam.*)
Hurry up!

vouloir du bol (*fam.*)
to want good luck

J'en ai soupé. (*fam.*)
I've had enough.

espèce de feignasse (*fam.*)
you, lazy bum

Si vous n'y mettez pas du vôtre...
If you don't make an effort . . .

Vocabulaire du court métrage

bâiller *to yawn*	**marioles (*m.*)** *jokers*
conte (*m.*) de fée *fairy tale*	**(mettre) en sourdine** *(to play) quietly, softly*
coquin(e)s *rascals*	**pétale (*m.*)** *flake*
corsé *strong*	**râler** *to groan, to complain*
croustillant *crusty*	**se bouger (*fam.*)** *to get moving*
fatidique *fateful*	**tartiner** *to spread*

Introduction
- To check comprehension, ask these questions:
  1. Quel type de film est le court métrage de Guillaume Colomb et Olivier Derivière?
  2. À quel moment de la journée l'action se passe-t-elle?
  3. Qui sont les personnages principaux du court métrage?
  4. Quel est le problème?
- Have students look at the poster of the film and predict what the film will be about.

Expressions utiles Point out that most of the expressions in **Expressions utiles** are familiar language and that students should be careful when using them.

1 Expansion Have students come up with additional multiple choice options using some of the remaining words and expressions from the lists.

2 Expansion Have pairs of students create their own "breakfast" dialogue using as many of the words and expressions as they can. Ask for volunteers to act out their dialogue for the class.

OPTIONS

Expressions Utiles Point out the humor in the use of some of the familiar expressions that are heard in the film: **vouloir du bol** (meaning *luck* in this case, but also meaning *bowl*) and **j'en ai soupé** (meaning *I've had enough*, but also alluding to **le souper** *[dinner]*).

Note Culturelle **La tartine** is a slice of **pain de mie**, which is typically used for toasts in France. **Baguettes** and other types of French breads are also commonly eaten for breakfast, but are not usually toasted. **Croissants** and **pains au chocolat** are also common breakfast choices, especially when having breakfast at a café. Coffee is typically served black or with hot milk, in which case it is often served in a bowl.

Avant de regarder le film Before showing the film, have students brainstorm the names of all the items that would typically be found on a typical "French" breakfast table. Then tell them that the film they are going to watch is an animated film where all these items come to life. Have them imagine the "personality" of each of these items and the kinds of interactions they may have with one another.

Suggestions

- Stop the film right before the end (before the tragic end of the honey and the slice of bread) and ask students to guess how the film is going to end. Then play the rest of the film and have students react to the actual ending. Did anyone guess correctly?
- Replay the film, asking students to make a list of all the characters along with their respective roles. Have them write down adjectives that describe each character. Then ask them to say which character they like best and explain why.

La tartine

National Standards: communication, cultures

1

L'OUVRE-BOÎTE° Le réveil a sonné. Le petit-déjeuner va bientôt commencer. Tous nos amis sont-ils prêts? Où sont ces petits coquins? Ah tiens! En voilà un!

LE BOL Si vous voulez du bol, me voilà, les petits marioles!

LE CAFÉ Et moi, je suis corsé, tout aromatisé°. Et nous formons une équipe idyllique.

LA CONFITURE Et moi, la confiture, je suis prête pour l'aventure.

LE MIEL Et moi?! Il n'y a pas que toi!

L'OUVRE-BOÎTE Ah, décidément, ce miel... toujours en train de râler!

2

L'OUVRE-BOÎTE Elle en a de la chance, cette petite tranche! Car c'est aujourd'hui le jour de sa vie.

LA TARTINE Alors, c'est aujourd'hui? C'est vraiment le jour de ma vie?

3

LA TARTINE Quelle belle journée pour déjeuner! J'en ai rêvé.

LA CONFITURE Tu es si belle!

LE MIEL Elle sera mienne.

LA CONFITURE Viens avec moi!

LA TARTINE Un conte de fée est arrivé.

LE MIEL Ne l'écoute pas!

LA TARTINE Mon aimé! Mon amant°!

LA CONFITURE Mon adorée! Mon amour!

4

LE MIEL Moi, j'en ai marre! J'en ai soupé! Toujours pareil! Il y en a que pour lui, ce pot de confiture!

L'HOMME Nous allons vous départager°. Devant vous, deux bols, un chacun. Derrière, des sucres. Vous allez lancer° un maximum de sucres dans votre bol. Quand la tartine sera prête, celui qui aura le plus de sucres dans son bol aura le droit° de se faire tartiner.

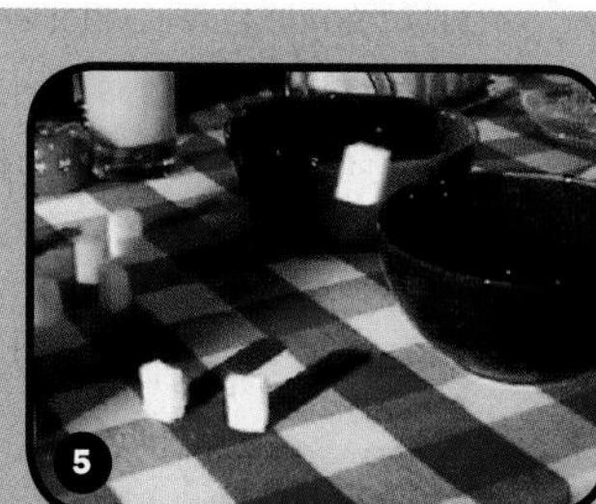

5

L'HOMME Un, deux, trois, quatre, cinq... Un, deux, trois, quatre, cinq, six, sept, huit. Ce sera donc une tartine de confiture.

L'OUVRE-BOÎTE Formidable!

LE MIEL À chaque fois, ce n'est jamais moi. Je vous le dis... Ce n'est pas fini!

6

L'OUVRE-BOÎTE Elle en a eu de la chance, cette petite tranche. Ce fut° aujourd'hui le jour de sa vie.

ouvre-boîte *can opener* **aromatisé** *flavored* **amant** *lover* **départager** *to decide between* **lancer** *to throw* **le droit** *the right* **fut** *was*

OPTIONS

Extra Practice Have students look at the video stills and read the dialogues. Then ask these questions: **1. D'après le narrateur, qui n'est jamais content? 2. Pourquoi la tartine a-t-elle l'air contente? 3. Qui entre dans la pièce? Que va-t-il faire? 4. Qui est amoureux de la tartine? 5. En quoi consiste le défi** (*challenge*)**? 6. Combien de sucres a la confiture à la fin?**

Small Groups Once students have viewed the film, divide the class into small groups and have each group work on a synopsis for an animated story featuring a typical American breakfast. Have students use the film for inspiration and ask these questions to help them get started: **Qui sont les personnages d'un petit-déjeuner américain typique? Comment sont-ils? Y a-t-il aussi un conflit? Si oui, lequel? Sinon, que pourrait-il se passer d'autre à table?**

Analyse

3 Associez Faites correspondre les images aux phrases.

__e__ 1. La tartine est prête à être tartinée.

__c__ 2. L'homme décide de départager le miel et la confiture.

__a__ 3. L'ouvre-boîte réveille tout le monde pour le petit-déjeuner.

__b__ 4. Le miel tombe de la table.

__d__ 5. C'est la compétition entre la confiture et le miel.

__f__ 6. L'homme mange finalement autre chose.

a.

b.

c.

d.

e.

f.

4 Une fin tragique Avec un(e) partenaire, discutez de la fin du film en répondant à (*by answering*) ces questions.

1. Êtes-vous surpris(es) par la fin du film?
2. Comment décririez-vous cette fin? Inattendue (*Unexpected*)? Inévitable? Comique? Tragique?...
3. Que pensez-vous du comportement du miel?
4. Pensez-vous que la fin du film va avec le ton humoristique (*humorous tone*) du reste du film? Expliquez.
5. Que pensez-vous de la réaction de l'homme après la fin tragique du miel et de la tartine?

Practice more at **espaces.vhlcentral.com.**

5 Une autre fin Par groupes de trois ou quatre, imaginez une fin différente en vous aidant (*by getting help*) de ces questions. Dessinez les images qui pourraient apparaître dans votre court métrage. Ensuite, jouez la scène devant la classe, qui choisira la meilleure.

- Est-ce une autre fin tragique ou une fin heureuse?
- Y a-t-il l'intervention d'autres personnages?
- Que fait finalement l'homme?

Compréhension To check comprehension, ask these additional questions: **1. Que fait l'ouvre-boîte au début? 2. Comment est la tartine? Décrivez sa personnalité. 3. Pourquoi est-ce qu'aujourd'hui est un jour spécial pour elle? 4. Qu'est-ce que l'ouvre-boîte dit à l'homme? 5. Avec quoi l'homme veut-il d'abord tartiner la tartine? 6. Quand la compétition prend-elle fin?**

3 Expansion Have pairs or small groups write the draft of a short summary of the film's plot.

4 Expansion Ask students to imagine how tomorrow's breakfast might be different, now that the honey is "dead".

5 Expansion Have students compare the story in the film to famous love stories, such as the ones in *Romeo and Juliet* or *Gone with the Wind*.

OPTIONS

Small Groups Have groups of students use the synopses they prepared in **Small Groups** in the Options box on page 522 to write a short skit of their typical American breakfast. Have students take on the various characters' roles, have a volunteer act as director, and have the groups act out their skits for the class.

Extra Practice In the film, **la tartine** compares its experience to a fairy tale. Have students answer these questions: **Quels sont les éléments typiques d'un conte de fée? Ces éléments sont-ils aussi présents dans le film? En quoi le film peut-il être comparé à un conte de fée?** Ask them to give examples to explain their answers.

Section Goals

In this section, students will learn and practice vocabulary related to:
- fine arts
- films and television
- books

Instructional Resources
*espaces.vhlcentral.com: Transparency #61; IRM (**Vocabulaire supplémentaire; Mise en pratique** answers; Textbook Audioscript; Lab Audioscript; **Feuilles d'activités**); Textbook MP3s; Lab MP3s; WB/VM/LM Answer Key; activities; downloads; reference tools*

Suggestions
- Tell students to look over the new vocabulary and identify the cognates.
- Use **Transparency #61**. Point out people and things as you describe the illustration. Examples: **Elle fait de la peinture. C'est un film d'horreur.**
- Point out that the **f** in **chef-d'œuvre** and the **p** in **sculpture** are silent.
- Point out the difference in spelling between the French word **aventure** and the English word *adventure*.
- Explain that in France you say **une femme écrivain/auteur/peintre/sculpteur** or **elle est écrivain/auteur/peintre/sculpteur**. The terms **écrivaine** and **auteure** are used in Québec. Mention that the term **auteur** is more general than **écrivain**. **Auteur** can also mean *creator*.
- Explain that **les beaux-arts** (*fine arts*) is a term that refers collectively to a variety of artistic fields, particularly those concerned with the creation of beautiful things, such as painting and sculpture.
- Additional vocabulary for this lesson can be found in the **Vocabulaire supplémentaire** on the Supersite.

Leçon 15B

You will learn how to...
- **discuss films and television**
- **discuss books**

Talking Picture
Audio: Activity

Au festival d'art

Vocabulaire

faire les musées	*to go to museums*
publier	*to publish*
les beaux-arts (*m.*)	*fine arts*
un chef-d'œuvre	*masterpiece*
un conte	*tale*
une critique	*review; criticism*
un dessin animé	*cartoon*
un documentaire	*documentary*
un drame psychologique	*psychological drama*
une émission (de télévision)	*(television) program*
un festival (festivals *pl.*)	*festival*
un feuilleton	*soap opera*
un film (d'aventures, policier)	*(adventure, crime) film*
une histoire	*story*
les informations (infos) (*f.*)	*news*
un jeu télévisé	*game show*
la météo	*weather*
les nouvelles (*f.*)	*news*
une œuvre	*artwork, piece of art*
un programme	*program*
une publicité (pub)	*advertisement*
les variétés (*f.*)	*popular music*
ancien(ne)	*ancient; old; former*
doué(e)	*talented, gifted*
gratuit(e)	*free*
littéraire	*literary*
récent(e)	*recent*
à la radio	*on the radio*
à la télé(vision)	*on television*

ressources
WB pp. 203–204 | LM p. 117 | espaces.vhlcentral.com

OPTIONS

Game Write types of television shows or movies on index cards and place them in a box. Divide the class into two teams. Have students draw a card and describe the genre without saying the word, but they may use French titles as clues. Award points as follows: after one clue = 3 points, after two clues = 2 points, and after three clues = 1 point. If a team does not guess the answer after three tries, the other team has one chance to "steal" the point by guessing correctly.

Extra Practice Tell students that they have just returned from an arts festival. Ask them to describe what they did, saw, and heard. Example: **J'ai vu beaucoup de beaux tableaux et j'ai parlé à deux peintres.**

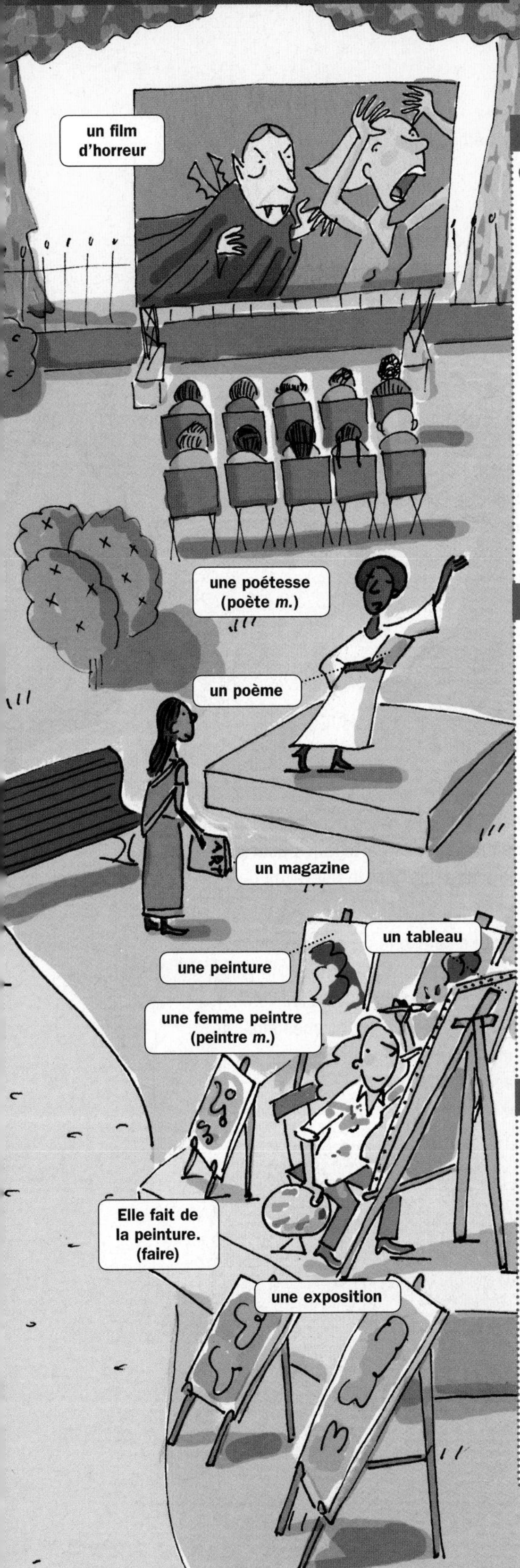

Mise en pratique

1 **Vous les connaissez?** **Faites correspondre les œuvres, personnages et programmes télévisés de la colonne de gauche avec le mot de la colonne de droite qui convient.**

__e__ 1. *La Belle et la Bête*	a. une sculpture
__d__ 2. *Whistler's Mother*	b. un auteur
__a__ 3. Le *David*	c. un film de science-fiction
__h__ 4. *Jeopardy*	d. une peinture
__l__ 5. Claude Monet	e. un conte
__g__ 6. *Les Trois Mousquetaires*	f. un feuilleton
__b__ 7. Victor Hugo	g. un roman
__f__ 8. *All My Children*	h. un jeu télévisé
__i__ 9. *Vogue*	i. un magazine
__c__ 10. *2001, l'Odyssée de l'espace*	j. une exposition
	k. un film d'horreur
	l. un peintre

2 **Complétez** **Complétez ces phrases avec le mot de vocabulaire d'ESPACE CONTEXTES qui convient.**

1. La peinture et la sculpture font partie des __beaux-arts__.
2. Une __poétesse__ est une personne qui écrit des poèmes.
3. Un __auteur__ est quelqu'un qui est à l'origine d'une œuvre.
4. Art de juger (*to judge*) les créations littéraires ou artistiques: __une critique__.
5. Un __documentaire__ est basé sur la réalité.
6. Une __publicité__ est une activité commerciale pour vendre un produit.
7. *Bugs Bunny* et *Mickey Mouse* sont des exemples de __dessin animé__.
8. *Indiana Jones* est un exemple de film __d'aventures__.
9. Si on n'a pas besoin de payer pour entrer dans un musée, c'est __gratuit__.
10. On peut écouter les informations __à la radio__.

3 **Écoutez** **Écoutez la conversation entre Nora et Jeanne et indiquez si Nora (N), Armand (A), Jeanne (J) ou Charles (C) ont fait les choses suivantes.**

__N__ 1. s'est bien amusée au Festival des beaux-arts.
__N et A__ 2. ont vu une exposition d'art contemporain.
__J et C__ 3. ont vu un film d'aventures.
__N et A__ 4. ont assisté à une critique littéraire sur Assia Djebar.
__J et C__ 5. sont restés chez eux.
__N et A__ 6. sont allés à la librairie pour acheter un roman.
__C__ 7. a promis de faire les musées le week-end prochain.
__J__ 8. a fait de la peinture.

Practice more at **espaces.vhlcentral.com.**

cinq cent vingt-cinq 525

1 Expansion Ask students to provide additional examples for each term in the right-hand column.

2 Expansion Have students write three more fill-in-the-blank sentences. Then have them exchange papers with a classmate and fill in the missing words.

3 Tapescript JEANNE: Salut Nora, es-tu allée au Festival des beaux-arts et de la littérature de l'université?
NORA: Oui, j'y suis allée avec Armand. Nous nous sommes bien amusés. D'abord, nous avons vu une exposition d'art contemporain d'artistes locaux. Après, nous avons assisté à une critique des œuvres littéraires d'Assia Djebar, tu sais, la femme écrivain algérienne. À la fin de la présentation, Armand était tellement intéressé par ses œuvres que nous sommes allés à la librairie pour acheter un de ses romans. Et toi, y es-tu allée? Je ne t'ai pas vue.
J: Malheureusement, non. Tu sais que Charles n'aime pas vraiment l'art. Pour lui, c'est ennuyeux, sauf le cinéma. Nous sommes restés à la maison et nous avons vu deux films. J'ai choisi un drame psychologique et lui, un film d'aventures. C'était bien. Après ça, j'ai fait de la peinture et Charles s'est endormi. Il m'a promis que le week-end prochain, il ferait les musées avec moi quand nous serons en Italie.
(On Textbook MP3s)

3 Expansion For review, ask students: **Qui est Assia Djebar?** Students should remember that she is an Algerian feminist author and filmmaker, and the first writer from the Maghreb to be admitted into the **Académie française** (2005). See page 465.

OPTIONS

Game Distribute an authentic French-language television guide. Discuss the genres of the programs listed. Then write titles of various programs from the guide on cards and place them in a hat or box. Write categories for the programs on the board or a transparency. Examples: **un dessin animé, un jeu télévisé, un drame psychologique, un feuilleton, les informations, un film policier**, and **un film d'aventures**. Divide the class into two teams. Have teams take turns drawing titles and classifying them according to their genres. If a player guesses incorrectly, the other team may "steal" the point. Remind students that answers called out of turn do not count. The team with the most points wins.

4 Suggestions
- Tell students to jot down notes during their interviews.
- Have pairs get together with another pair of students and share what they learned about their partners.

5 Suggestions
- Distribute the **Feuilles d'activités** found on the Supersite.
- Give students three to four minutes to complete the first column before having them work in pairs. Then have two volunteers read the **modèle**.

6 Suggestion If time is limited, have students write their paragraphs as homework, then discuss their thoughts with a partner in class.

7 Expansion Have groups write a script for their program and perform it for the class.

Communication

NATIONAL communication STANDARDS

4 Conversez **Interviewez un(e) camarade de classe au sujet de l'art et des médias.** Answers will vary.

1. Quel(s) genre(s) de film préfères-tu? Pourquoi?
2. Quel film récent as-tu vu? Quelle en est l'histoire?
3. As-tu un auteur favori? Lequel?
4. Quel(s) genre(s) d'œuvres littéraires aimes-tu?
5. Qu'est-ce que tu écoutes à la radio? Quand?
6. As-tu fait les musées récemment? Quelle(s) exposition(s) as-tu vue(s)?
7. Quel(s) chef(s)-d'œuvre admires-tu?
8. Qui considères-tu être un peintre doué? Pour quelle(s) raison(s)?
9. Es-tu un(e) artiste? Dans quel domaine?
10. Lis-tu des magazines? Lesquels?

5 À la télévision et à la radio **Votre professeur va vous donner, à vous et à votre partenaire, une feuille d'activités. Remplissez d'abord la première colonne avec vos préférences pour chaque catégorie. Ensuite, comparez vos réponses avec celles d'un(e) camarade de classe.** Answers will vary.

MODÈLE

un dessin animé
Étudiant(e) 1: *Quel est ton dessin animé préféré?*
Étudiant(e) 2: *J'adore regarder les Simpson.*

Programmes	*Moi*	*Noms*
1. un dessin animé		
2. une émission		
3. un feuilleton		

6 L'art et vous **Écrivez un paragraphe d'après (*according to*) ces instructions. Ensuite, à tour de rôle, discutez-en avec un(e) camarade de classe.** Answers will vary.

- Décrivez l'importance que vous donnez à l'art dans votre vie.
- Parlez de l'influence positive et/ou négative de l'art sur le monde.
- Parlez de comment vous aimeriez contribuer à cette influence.

7 Regardons la télé **Avec les éléments donnés, travaillez avec trois autres partenaires pour présenter une émission pour la chaîne de télévision de votre université.** Answers will vary.

- Choisissez une catégorie de programme télévisé. Chaque groupe doit choisir un genre différent, par exemple un jeu, un feuilleton, les informations, la météo, un documentaire, etc.
- Donnez un nom à votre programme et aux personnages de l'émission.
- Annoncez le contenu de votre programme.

OPTIONS

Small Groups Have students work in groups of three. Tell them to role-play a situation in which three roommates share a single television and no one can agree on which shows to watch. Students should discuss what shows are on that night, which are better and why, and so forth. Tell students to resolve the argument in their conversation.

Pairs Have students work in pairs. Give them a list of movie titles and/or TV shows to discuss. Brainstorm expressions for giving favorable and unfavorable opinions and write them in two columns on the board. Examples: **C'est très amusant. C'est trop violent. On ne s'ennuie jamais. Il n'y a pas d'histoire. Le metteur en scène est doué.**

Les sons et les lettres

Audio: Concepts, Activities
Record & Compare

NATIONAL comparisons STANDARDS

Les abréviations

French speakers use many acronyms. This is especially true in newspapers, televised news programs, and in political discussions. Many stand for official organizations or large companies.

EDF = Électricité de France **ONU = Organisation des Nations Unies**

People often use acronyms when referring to geographical place names and transportation.

É-U = États-Unis **RF = République Française**
RN = Route Nationale **TGV = Train à Grande Vitesse**

Many are simply shortened versions of common expressions or compound words.

SVP = S'il Vous Plaît **RV = Rendez-Vous** **RDC = Rez-De-Chaussée**

When speaking, some acronyms are spelled out, while others are pronounced like any other word.

Cedex = Courrier d'Entreprise à Distribution Exceptionnelle *(an overnight delivery service)*

Prononcez Répétez les abréviations suivantes à voix haute.

1. W-C = *Water-Closet*
2. HS = Hors Service (*out of order*)
3. VF = Version Française
4. CV = Curriculum Vitæ
5. TVA = Taxe à la Valeur Ajoutée (*added*)
6. DELF = Diplôme d'Études en Langue Française
7. RATP = Régie Autonome (*independent administration*) des Transports Parisiens
8. SMIC = Salaire Minimum Interprofessionnel de Croissance (*growth*)

Assortissez-les Répétez les abréviations à voix haute. Que représentent-elles?

d	1. ECP	a. objet volant non identifié
e	2. GDF	b. toutes taxes comprises
f	3. DEUG	c. président-directeur général
b	4. TTC	d. École centrale de Paris
c	5. PDG	e. Gaz de France
a	6. OVNI	f. diplôme d'études universitaires générales

Expressions Répétez les expressions à voix haute.

Elle est BCBG (Bon Chic, Bon Genre).²

RSVP (Répondez, S'il Vous Plaît).¹
RSVP AVANT LE 14 MAI 2011
24 rue des roses
06000 NICE

1 Please reply.
2 She is preppy (in a conservatively classic fashion)

ressources
LM p. 118
espaces.vhlcentral.com

Section Goals

In this section, students will learn about:
- abbreviations
- acronyms

Instructional Resources
espaces.vhlcentral.com: Textbook MP3s; Lab MP3s; WB/VM/LM Answer Key; IRM (Textbook Audioscript; Lab Audioscript); activities; downloads; reference tools

Suggestions
- Model the pronunciation of the abbreviations and acronyms and have students repeat them after you.
- Explain that an **acronyme** refers to an abbreviation that can be pronounced as a word and is written without periods, such as **ONU**. A **sigle** is a set of letters forming an abbreviation that is pronounced as separate letters, for example, **RATP** The general tendency is to omit the periods in everyday French.
- Ask students to provide additional examples of French abbreviations or acronyms they have seen or heard.
- Distribute French newspapers or magazines and tell students to find acronyms and abbreviations. Ask them to guess what words they stand for.

OPTIONS

Language Note Tell students that French speakers use many abbreviated forms of words. Some of them are considered slang, so they should be careful about using them in formal situations. Then write the shortened forms of the words below on the board or a transparency and ask students what the original word is. **1. métro (métropolitain) 2. ciné (cinéma) 3. ado (adolescent) 4. micro (microphone) 5. moto (motocyclette) 6. appart (appartement) 7. frigo (réfrigérateur) 8. pub (publicité) 9. petit-déj (petit-déjeuner)**

Extra Practice Write the following abbreviations in a column on the board and their meanings in another column. Have students match the abbreviations and words. **1. K7 (cassette) 2. PJ (police judiciaire) 3. Cie (compagnie) 4. VO (version originale) 5. RP (relations publiques) 6. DOM (département d'outre-mer)**

Section Goals

In this section, students will learn functional phrases for expressing conditions and possible actions.

Instructional Resources
*espaces.vhlcentral.com: WB/ VM/LM Answer Key; IRM (Videoscript; **Roman-photo** Translations); activities; downloads; reference tools Video on DVD*

Video Recap: Leçon 15A
Before doing this **Roman-photo**, review the previous one with this true/false activity.

1. Le spectacle de Sandrine, c'est la comédie musicale préférée d'Amina. (Vrai.)
2. Rachid admire la robe qu'Amina a faite. (Vrai.)
3. Sandrine chante mal, mais elle est une assez bonne actrice. (Vrai.)
4. David dit directement à Sandrine ce qu'il pense de son concert. (Faux.)
5. Sandrine accepte gracieusement ce que David lui dit. (Faux.)

Video Synopsis
Sandrine is making a cake for David's farewell party. She tells Amina that David helped her find her true passion, cooking, and she has decided to become a professional chef. At the party, Amina explains that some of her clothes are going to be in a fashion show for young designers in Paris. Rachid announces that he got his diploma with honors. David says he plans to return next year and have an exhibit of his paintings at **Le P'tit Bistrot**.

Suggestions
- Have students predict what the episode will be about based on the video stills.
- After reading the **Roman-photo**, have students summarize the episode.

Au revoir, David!

Video: *Roman-photo*
Record & Compare

PERSONNAGES

Amina

Astrid

David

Rachid

Sandrine

Stéphane

Valérie

1

2

3

Chez Sandrine...
AMINA Qu'est-ce qui sent si bon?
SANDRINE C'est un gâteau pour David. Il repart demain aux États-Unis tu sais.
AMINA David et toi, vous avez décidé de ne plus vous disputer?
SANDRINE C'est de l'histoire ancienne.
AMINA C'est comme dans un feuilleton. Vous vous disputez, vous vous détestez. Vous vous réconciliez.

SANDRINE J'étais tellement en colère contre lui ce jour-là, mais depuis, j'ai beaucoup réfléchi à ce qu'il m'a dit.
AMINA Et alors...?
SANDRINE En fait, David m'a aidée.
AMINA Comment ça?
SANDRINE Ma vraie passion, ce n'est pas la musique.
AMINA Non? Mais alors, c'est quoi, ta vraie passion?

SANDRINE J'ai décidé de devenir chef de cuisine!
AMINA Ça, c'est une excellente idée.
SANDRINE N'est-ce pas? Et j'ai aussi décidé de préparer ce gâteau pour la fête de ce soir.
AMINA Et moi qui pensais que tu ne voudrais pas y aller...
SANDRINE Mais... David ne peut pas partir sans que je lui dise au revoir!

6

7

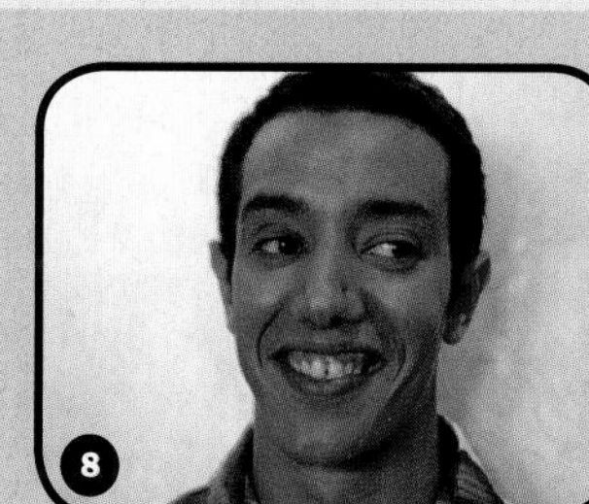
8

À la fête de David...
ASTRID Elle est jolie, ta jupe. C'est une de tes créations, n'est-ce pas?
SANDRINE Cet été, Amina participe à un défilé de mode à Paris.
AMINA N'exagérons rien... C'est une petite présentation des collections de plusieurs jeunes stylistes.
SANDRINE Tu vas montrer ce chef-d'œuvre?

AMINA Oui, cette jupe-ci, la robe que j'ai faite pour toi et d'autres modèles.
RACHID Elle n'est pas géniale, ma chérie? Belle, intelligente, douée...
AMINA Toi aussi, tu as de bonnes nouvelles, n'est-ce pas?
SANDRINE Ah bon?
RACHID Oh, ce n'est pas grand-chose.

AMINA Au contraire, c'est très important!
SANDRINE Vas-y, dis-nous tout, avant que je ne perde patience!
RACHID Eh bien, ça y est, j'ai mon diplôme!
AMINA Ah, mais ce n'est pas tout! Il a eu mention très bien!
SANDRINE Bravo, Rachid!
ASTRID Oui, félicitations!

ACTIVITÉS

1 Les événements Remettez les événements suivants dans l'ordre chronologique.

6 a. Rachid annonce une bonne nouvelle.
4 b. Stéphane veut absolument réussir son bac.
9 c. David promet qu'il va revenir à Aix.
2 d. Sandrine dit qu'elle n'est plus fâchée avec David.
5 e. Amina explique qu'elle va à Paris cet été.
1 f. Amina arrive chez Sandrine.
10 g. Valérie prend une photo du groupe.
7 h. Valérie attire (*gets*) l'attention du groupe.
8 i. David fait un petit discours (*speech*).
3 j. Sandrine annonce qu'elle souhaite devenir chef de cuisine.

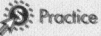

Practice more at **espaces.vhlcentral.com.**

OPTIONS

Avant de regarder la vidéo Before viewing the video, have students work in pairs and brainstorm a list of things people might say at a farewell party. What questions might they ask? What might they talk about?

Regarder la vidéo Download and print the videoscript found on the Supersite. Then white out key vocabulary in order to create a master for a cloze activity. Distribute photocopies and tell students to fill in the missing information as they watch the video episode.

Les amis organisent une fête pour David.

4

5

Au P'tit Bistrot...

SANDRINE Stéphane, tu ne veux pas nous aider à préparer la fête?

STÉPHANE Une minute s'il te plaît.

SANDRINE Mais, qu'est-ce que tu lis de si intéressant? Oh là là, *L'Histoire des Républiques françaises*. Ah, oui je vois... j'ai entendu dire que tu devais repasser une partie du bac.

STÉPHANE Oui, je dois absolument réussir cette fois-ci, mais une fois l'examen passé, je retourne à mes passions—le foot, les jeux vidéo...

SANDRINE Chut... ta mère va t'entendre.

STÉPHANE (*parlant plus fort et de manière sérieuse*) Oui, je t'assure, les documentaires et les infos sont mes nouvelles passions.

9

10

VALÉRIE S'il vous plaît. Nous sommes ici ce soir pour dire au revoir et bon voyage à David, qui repart demain aux États-Unis. Alors, David, comment s'est passée ton année à Aix?

DAVID Oh ça a été fantastique! Je ne connaissais personne à mon arrivée, mais j'ai rapidement trouvé un coloc super! J'ai fait la connaissance de quelques femmes formidables.

DAVID Mais surtout, je me suis fait des amis pour la vie...

ASTRID Quand est-ce que tu vas revenir nous voir, David?

DAVID Eh bien, j'ai l'intention de revenir l'année prochaine pour organiser une exposition de tous mes tableaux au P'tit Bistrot, à condition, bien sûr, que Madame Forestier accepte!

VALÉRIE Allez, une photo. Souriez!

Expressions utiles

Relating conditions and possible actions

- **David ne peut pas partir sans que je lui dise au revoir!**
  David can't leave without my saying good-bye to him!
- **Dis-nous tout, avant que je (ne) perde patience!**
  Tell us everything, before I lose patience!
- **J'ai l'intention de revenir à condition que Madame Forestier accepte.**
  I intend to return on the condition that Madame Forestier accepts.

Additional vocabulary

- **repartir**
  to go back
- **repasser**
  to take again
- **chut**
  shh/hush
- **au contraire**
  on the contrary
- **félicitations**
  congratulations
- **se réconcilier**
  to make up

ACTIVITÉS

2 **À vous!** Sandrine est bien plus calme maintenant. Elle a même dit qu'elle voulait dire au revoir à David à la fête. Avec un(e) camarade de classe, préparez une conversation entre David et Sandrine à cette occasion. Comment finit leur histoire?

3 **Écrivez** Pendant la fête de David, certains ont parlé de leurs projets d'avenir. À votre avis, qu'est-ce qui va arriver l'année prochaine? Écrivez vos prédictions pour chacun d'entre eux, au niveau professionnel et au niveau personnel.

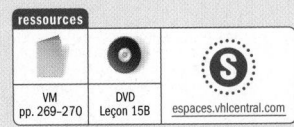

ressources

VM	DVD	
pp. 269–270	Leçon 15B	espaces.vhlcentral.com

Expressions utiles

- Model the pronunciation of the **Expressions utiles** and have students repeat them after you.
- As you work through the list, point out the use of the subjunctive with conjunctions. Tell students that this construction will be formally presented in **Espace structures.**
- Have students scan the **Roman-photo** captions and find expressions used to express intentions. Example: **... une fois l'examen passé, je retourne à mes passions...**

1 Suggestion Have students form groups of five. Make a set of individual sentences on strips of paper for each group and distribute them (two per student). Tell students to arrange the sentences in the proper order and then read them aloud.

1 Expansion Have students write sentences to fill in parts of the story not mentioned in this activity.

2 Suggestion If time is limited, assign each student the role of either Sandrine or David and tell them to prepare their parts at home. Then allow partners a few minutes to rehearse before presenting their conversation to the class.

2 Expansion Have students write a conversation between Rachid and Amina in which they discuss recent events and future plans. How might their story end?

3 Suggestion Tell students to write a paragraph of at least three sentences for each character in the **Roman-photo**.

OPTIONS

Game Have students fold small strips of paper in half. On the outside of the folded paper, they should write an original sentence that one of the characters might say. On the inside, they should write the name of the character. Divide the class into two teams. Put the sentences in a box and have students draw one, read it aloud, and then guess who might say it. Award a point for each correct guess.

Extra Practice Assign each student one of the characters from this **Roman-photo** and have them prepare a brief summary of the party from that character's point of view. Ask volunteers to read their summaries to the class. Then have the class guess which character would give each summary.

Section Goals

communication cultures NATIONAL STANDARDS

In this section, students will:
- learn about Haitian painting
- learn some terms for talking about books
- learn about traditional arts in the francophone world
- read about **le Cirque du Soleil**

Instructional Resources
espaces.vhlcentral.com: activities; downloads; reference tools

Culture à la loupe
Avant la lecture Have students locate Haiti on the map on page 538. Point out that Haiti shares the island with the Dominican Republic.

Lecture
- Point out the **tréma** on the **i** of **Haïti**, a version of *Ayiti* in Creole, is the name given to the land by the original inhabitants, the Taino-Arawak peoples. It means *mountainous country.*
- The country was named Haiti after it gained its independence from France in 1804.

Après la lecture Ask students: **Quels éléments de la peinture haïtienne pouvez-vous identifier sur les tableaux? Que représentent-ils?**

1 Suggestion Go over the answers with the class.

CULTURE À LA LOUPE

La peinture haïtienne

L'art haïtien est surtout connu grâce à° sa peinture. Cette tradition artistique est très ancienne sur l'île, mais ses débuts officiels datent de 1804, quand le roi Christophe crée la première Académie de peinture. Les thèmes les plus fréquents à cette époque sont les thèmes historiques de l'émancipation° et les thèmes religieux du vaudou°.

La peinture haïtienne ne devient célèbre dans le monde qu'à partir de 1943. Cette année-là, Dewitt Peters, un professeur américain du lycée de Port-au-Prince, capitale d'Haïti, rencontre plusieurs jeunes peintres haïtiens. Il aime leurs toiles° et fonde avec eux un centre d'art et de peinture. Ce centre va donner à la majorité des peintres haïtiens les ressources nécessaires pour accéder au° succès. Aujourd'hui, on en est à la quatrième génération d'artistes. Ces peintres appartiennent à° diverses écoles d'art et leurs styles sont très variés, du plus naïf au plus sophistiqué. Ils peuvent être surréalistes, impressionnistes ou même primitifs modernes.

La peinture haïtienne est souvent très colorée et d'une grande vitalité. Quand elle n'est pas abstraite, elle illustre des scènes de la vie quotidienne°, des cérémonies religieuses et des paysages°. En Haïti, la peinture est partout. Elle décore les rues, les murs et les bus. On la trouve aussi bien sur les marchés que dans les galeries d'art. Grâce à des expositions dans le monde entier, les peintres haïtiens séduisent un public de plus en plus large.

un peintre haïtien devant son œuvre

grâce à *thanks to* **émancipation** *liberation* **vaudou** *voodoo* **toiles** *paintings* **accéder au** *achieve* **appartiennent à** *belong to* **quotidienne** *everyday* **paysages** *landscapes*

ACTIVITÉS

1 Répondez Répondez aux questions par des phrases complètes.

1. Quel est l'art le plus connu à Haïti? C'est la peinture.
2. Pourquoi ses débuts officiels datent-ils de 1804? Le roi Christophe crée la première Académie de peinture en 1804.
3. Quels sont les thèmes les plus fréquents à cette époque? Ce sont les thèmes historiques de l'émancipation et les thèmes religieux du vaudou.
4. À partir de quand la peinture haïtienne est-elle devenue célèbre dans le monde? Elle est devenue célèbre à partir de 1943.
5. Quel était le métier de Dewitt Peters? Il était professeur au lycée de Port-au-Prince.
6. Qu'a-t-il créé? Il a créé un centre d'art et de peinture avec des jeunes peintres haïtiens.
7. À quelles écoles d'art les peintres haïtiens appartiennent-ils et comment est leur style? Ils appartiennent à diverses écoles et leurs styles sont très variés.
8. Comment est la peinture haïtienne? Elle est souvent très colorée et d'une grande vitalité.
9. Quels sont les sujets les plus souvent peints? Les scènes de la vie quotidienne, les cérémonies religieuses et les paysages sont les sujets les plus souvent peints.
10. Où peut-on voir de la peinture à Haïti? On peut en voir dans les rues, sur les murs, sur les bus, sur les marchés et dans les galeries d'art.

OPTIONS

Haïti Haiti's official languages are French and Creole. Columbus landed on the island in 1492 and called it Española; it was later renamed Hispaniola. The island was under Spanish rule until 1697, when Haiti became a French colony and was renamed Saint-Domingue. The colony relied on African slaves to work the sugar plantations there. Today over 90% of Haiti's inhabitants are descendants of those slaves.

Small Groups Have students work in groups of three. Tell them that they are owners of a gallery specializing in Haitian art. Each student should research one Haitian painting on the Internet and print an image of the work for his or her gallery. In class, the owners of each gallery should describe the style of their paintings and what they represent to the potential buyers (the class).

LE FRANÇAIS QUOTIDIEN

Les livres

bouquin (*m.*)	*book*
dico (*m.*)	*dictionary*
lecture (*f.*)	*reading*
manuel (*m.*)	*textbook*
nouvelle (*f.*)	*short story*
recueil (*m.*)	*collection*
bouquiner	*to read*
feuilleter	*to leaf through*
parcourir	*to skim*

PORTRAIT

Le Cirque du Soleil

En 1982, des saltimbanques° et des cracheurs de feu° sur échasses° se rencontrent et montent un spectacle à Baie-Saint-Paul, au Québec. En 1984, le gouvernement les embauche pour célébrer le 450e anniversaire de l'arrivée de l'explorateur Jacques Cartier. Ainsi° est né le Cirque du Soleil. Depuis, il a connu un succès international sous la direction de son fondateur principal, Guy Laliberté. Ses spectacles pleins de féerie° et de poésie ravissent° tous les publics et, à la différence de ceux du cirque traditionnel, ils n'ont aucun animal. Ils intègrent plutôt les numéros° acrobatiques de contorsionnistes, trapézistes, équilibristes° et jongleurs à ceux de danseurs et de clowns. Leur univers magique a apporté à la troupe une popularité incroyable et a transformé le monde du cirque.

saltimbanques *acrobats, performers* **cracheurs de feu** *fire-eaters* **échasses** *stilts* **Ainsi** *In this way* **féerie** *enchantment* **ravissent** *delight* **numéros** *acts* **équilibristes** *tightrope walkers*

LE MONDE FRANCOPHONE

Des arts traditionnels

Voici quelques exemples d'art traditionnel du monde francophone.

Aux Antilles la fabrication de poupées° en costumes de madras° traditionnels
Au Burkina Faso les poteries en terre cuite° décorées à la teinture° végétale et la fabrication de masques traditionnels
Au Cambodge le théâtre d'ombres°, avec ses marionnettes en cuir°
Au Maroc l'art de la tapisserie° et du métal
En Polynésie française la sculpture et l'art du tatouage corporel
En Tunisie les arts céramiques et l'art de la calligraphie
Au Viêt-nam la peinture à la laque° et la peinture sur soie°

poupées *dolls* **madras** *brightly-colored cotton or silk fabric* **terre cuite** *terra-cotta* **teinture** *dye* **ombres** *shadows* **marionnettes en cuir** *leather puppets* **tapisserie** *tapestry* **laque** *lacquer* **soie** *silk*

SUR INTERNET

Qu'est-ce que Jean-Pierre Jeunet et Gaston Kaboré ont en commun?

Go to **espaces.vhlcentral.com** to find more information related to this **ESPACE CULTURE**.

ACTIVITÉS

2 Complétez Complétez les phrases.

1. En 1982, des saltimbanques et des cracheurs de feu sur échasses montent un spectacle au Québec.
2. Le Cirque du Soleil est né en 1984.
3. Ses spectacles pleins de féerie et de poésie ravissent tous les publics.
4. Ils intègrent les numéros acrobatiques de contorsionnistes, de trapézistes, d'équilibristes, de jongleurs, de danseurs et de clowns.
5. La fabrication de poupées en costumes de madras traditionnels est un art traditionnel aux Antilles.
6. En Polynésie française, le tatouage corporel est un art.

3 Au cirque Interviewez votre partenaire. Est-il/elle déjà allé(e) au cirque? Au Cirque du Soleil? Combien de fois? Quels numéros a-t-il/elle préférés? En a-t-il/elle un souvenir particulier? A-t-il/elle envie d'y retourner? Soyez prêts à présenter vos résultats à la classe.

ressources
espaces.vhlcentral.com

Practice more at **espaces.vhlcentral.com.**

Le français quotidien
- Model the pronunciation of each term and have students repeat it.
- You may wish to show photos of **les bouquinistes** and present these terms: **poche** or **broché** (*paperback*), **cartonné** (*hardback*), and **relié** (*bound*).
- Have volunteers create sentences with these terms.

Portrait
- In 2004, Guy Laliberté earned **l'Ordre du Canada** the highest distinction of its type in Canada.
- Ask students: **Les gens sur les photos sont des danseurs, des clowns, des jongleurs, des contorsionnistes, des équilibristes ou des trapézistes? (des contorsionnistes et des trapézistes) Voudriez-vous trouver un travail comme celui-là? Pourquoi?**

Le monde francophone Bring in some books or magazines with examples of these art forms to show students. Then have students identify the country that creates each type of art.

2 Expansion For additional practice, give students these items. **7. L'explorateur ____ arrive au Canada au seizième siècle. (Jacques Cartier) 8. Dans les spectacles du Cirque du Soleil il n'y a aucun ____. (animal) 9. Le théâtre ____ est bien connu au Cambodge. (d'ombres) 10. La calligraphie est un exemple d'art traditionnel ____. (en Tunisie)**

3 Suggestion Have students jot down notes during their interviews.

OPTIONS

Le Cirque du Soleil Unlike the American three-ring circus, **le Cirque du Soleil** is rooted in the European tradition of a one-ring circus. It does not show animals or freaks, but focuses instead on human skills highlighted by state-of-the-art sets, artistic costumes, and contemporary music.

Pairs Have students write five true/false statements based on the information on this page. Then have them get together with a classmate and take turns reading their sentences and responding.

Section Goals

In this section, students will learn:

- conjunctions that require the subjunctive
- when to use the infinitive instead of the subjunctive

Instructional Resources
*espaces.vhlcentral.com: Lab MP3s; WB/VM/LM Answer Key; IRM (**Essayez!** and **Mise en pratique** answers; Lab Audioscript); activities; downloads; reference tools*

Suggestions

- To introduce conjunctions that require the subjunctive, make a few statements about yourself. Examples: **Je n'arrive pas en retard au cours, à moins que ma voiture ne démarre pas. Je range mes livres avant que la classe finisse. Je vais à pied au cours, à condition qu'il ne pleuve pas.** Write each conjunction on the board as you say it.
- Have a volunteer read the example sentences from the lesson. Point out that these conjunctions must be followed by a change in subject in order to elicit the subjunctive mood.
- Write sentences that use **avant de** and **pour**, and ask volunteers to rewrite them so that each ends with a subordinate clause with the subjunctive instead of a preposition and infinitive. Example: **Je vais parler avec Chantal avant d'aller au cours. (… avant qu'elle aille au cours/… avant qu'il lui parle)**
- You might want to explain the use of the **ne explétif** at this point. Example: **Je vais parler avec Chantal avant qu'elle n'achète cette voiture.**
- Write the six conjunctions on the board. Ask students to call out some main clauses and subordinate clauses in order to make six logical sentences.

Essayez! Have students form sentences with these phrases. Example: **Avant que nous partions, il faut que j'aille chercher un pull.**

15B.1 The subjunctive (Part 4)

The subjunctive with conjunctions

Point de départ Conjunctions are words or phrases that connect other words and clauses in sentences. Certain conjunctions commonly introduce adverbial clauses, which describe *how*, *why*, *when*, and *where* an action takes place.

- Conjunctions that express a condition upon which an action is dependent are followed by the subjunctive form of the verb.

Conjunctions that require the subjunctive

à condition que...	*on the condition that..., provided that...*	**jusqu'à ce que...**	*until...*
à moins que...	*unless...*	**pour que...**	*so that...*
avant que...	*before...*	**sans que...**	*without...*

main clause	conjunction	subordinate clause
Je vous laisse la clé *I'll leave you the key*	**à condition que** *provided that*	vous me la rendiez. *you return it to me.*
Nous n'irons pas au cinéma *We won't go to the cinema*	**à moins que** *unless*	tu viennes avec nous. *you come with us.*
Elle me montre les photos *She shows me the pictures*	**pour que** *so that*	je connaisse sa famille. *I get to know her family.*

- When the subject of the main clause is the same as the subject of the subordinate clause, use the infinitive after these frequently used conjunctions. Note the change in their forms.

avant que → **avant de**   **sans que** → **sans**   **pour que** → **pour**

Je lis **avant de m'endormir**.
I read before falling asleep.

Elle travaille **pour gagner** de l'argent.
She works in order to earn some money.

Essayez! Indiquez les formes correctes du présent du subjonctif des verbes.

1. avant que nous <u>partions</u> (partir)
2. pour que je ne <u>me mette</u> (se mettre) pas en colère
3. à condition que nous <u>soyons</u> (être) prudents
4. à moins que tu <u>dises</u> (dire) oui
5. sans que les spectateurs les <u>applaudissent</u> (applaudir)
6. à moins qu'il <u>fasse</u> (faire) beau
7. avant que tu <u>saches</u> (savoir) conduire
8. pour que vous <u>appreniez</u> (apprendre) des choses

MISE EN PRATIQUE

1 Je veux bien y aller si... Richard veut que Louise aille avec lui au cinéma ce week-end, mais elle y met plusieurs conditions. Complétez les phrases avec la forme correcte du verbe.

1. Je veux bien aller avec toi au cinéma à moins qu'il <u>fasse</u> (faire) beau.
2. S'il fait beau, je préfère aller à la plage pour <u>bronzer</u> (bronzer).
3. Regarde la météo pour que nous <u>sachions</u> (savoir) le temps qu'il fera.
4. S'il ne fait pas beau, j'irai avec toi à condition que ce <u>ne soit pas</u> (ne pas être) un film d'horreur.
5. J'aime bien les films policiers à moins qu'il y <u>ait</u> (avoir) trop de violence.
6. Nous pouvons voir un documentaire à condition qu'il ne <u>soit</u> (être) pas sur les animaux.
7. Souviens-toi que je ne vois pas de film sans <u>manger</u> (manger) de pop-corn.
8. Si j'ai sommeil, je veux rentrer chez moi avant que le film <u>finisse</u> (finir).

2 Au musée des Beaux-Arts Myriam et Delphine passent la journée au musée. Faites les changements nécessaires pour créer leur conversation. Suggested answers

MYRIAM (1) je / pouvoir / regarder / ce / chef-d'œuvre/ jusqu'à ce que / le musée / fermer
Je pourrais regarder ce chef-d'œuvre jusqu'à ce que le musée ferme.
DELPHINE (2) le peintre / avoir / faire / ce / tableau / avant / avoir / douze ans
Le peintre a fait ce tableau avant d'avoir douze ans.
MYRIAM (3) certain / enfants / être / vraiment doué / sans que / les parents / le / savoir
Certains enfants sont vraiment doués sans que les parents le sachent.
DELPHINE (4) je / vouloir bien / voir / sculptures / Rodin / avant que / nous / partir
Je voudrais bien voir les sculptures de Rodin avant que nous partions.
MYRIAM (5) pouvoir / nous / voir / documentaire sur Rodin / avant / partir
Pouvons-nous voir le documentaire sur Rodin avant de partir?
DELPHINE (6) d'accord / je / aller / le voir / à condition que / il / ne pas être / ennuyeux
D'accord, j'irai le voir à condition qu'il ne soit pas ennuyeux.

3 Opinions Complétez ces phrases de manière originale. Ensuite, comparez vos réponses avec celles d'un(e) partenaire. Answers will vary.

1. J'aime les films d'horreur à moins que...
2. Les gens regardent les feuilletons pour...
3. Je ferai les musées de Paris jusqu'à ce que...
4. On fait des publicités pour que les gens...
5. Je lis des romans à condition que...
6. Je regarde la météo avant de...

Practice more at **espaces.vhlcentral.com.**

OPTIONS

Extra Practice Write the following partial sentences on the board. Have students complete them with true or fictional information about their own lives. **1. Je vais finir mes études à condition que… 2. Je voudrais avoir 500 $ pour que… 3. Je peux sortir ce soir à moins que… 4. Le monde change sans que… 5. Je dois… avant que… 6. Je continuerai à travailler jusqu'à ce que…**

Video Show the video again to give students more input on the use of conjunctions with the subjunctive. Stop the video where appropriate to discuss how and why the subjunctive was used.

COMMUNICATION

4 **Questions** Avec un(e) partenaire, répondez à ces questions. Ensuite, présentez vos réponses à la classe. Answers will vary.

1. Que fais-tu tous les soirs avant de te coucher?
2. Que font tes parents pour que tu puisses étudier à la fac?
3. Que peux-tu faire pour améliorer (*to improve*) ton français?
4. Que veux-tu faire demain à moins qu'il fasse mauvais?
5. Que fais-tu pendant les cours sans que les profs le sachent?
6. Que fais-tu seulement à condition qu'un(e) ami(e) t'accompagne?
7. Quelles stratégies utilises-tu pour avoir de bonnes notes?
8. Quelle activité pratiques-tu sans t'arrêter jusqu'à ce que tu la finisses?

5 **Le week-end** Avec un(e) partenaire, parlez de vos projets pour ce week-end. Utilisez ce vocabulaire. Answers will vary.

MODÈLE

Samedi, je vais aller à la piscine à moins que mes amis veuillent aller à la plage.

à condition que	jusqu'à ce que
à moins que	pour (que)
avant de/que	sans (que)

6 **Tic-Tac-Toe** Formez deux équipes. Une personne commence une phrase et une autre de son équipe la finit avec les mots de la grille. La première équipe à créer trois phrases d'affilée (*in a row*) gagne. Answers will vary.

MODÈLE

Étudiant(e) 1: *J'aime bien admirer un chef-d'œuvre...*
Étudiant(e) 2: *...à moins que ce soit une sculpture.*

pour que	sans que	avant que
à condition que	jusqu'à ce que	pour
à moins que	sans	avant de

Le français vivant

MAURICE QUENTIN DE LA TOUR
Magnifique exposition sur ce grand peintre. Venez au château de Versailles du 2 au 29 septembre avant que ces peintures retournent dans leurs musées d'origine. Nous avons beaucoup travaillé pour que vous ayez l'occasion de voir ces superbes portraits. Venez contempler ces magnifiques tableaux qui vous feront voyager dans une autre époque... à moins que vous restiez indifférent à la beauté éternelle.

Identifiez Quelles conjonctions trouvez-vous avec le présent du subjonctif dans la publicité? avant que, pour que, jusqu'à ce que, à moins que

Questions Posez ces questions à un(e) partenaire et répondez à tour de rôle.

1. Qui était Maurice Quentin de La Tour? un grand peinture
2. Pourquoi faut-il voir l'exposition avant le 29 septembre? Après cette date, les peintures retournent dans leurs musées d'origine.
3. Pourquoi a-t-on beaucoup travaillé au château de Versailles? pour que vous ayez l'occasion de voir ces portraits
4. Quel effet ont les magnifiques tableaux sur les visiteurs? Ils vous font voyager dans une autre époque.
5. D'après (*According to*) la pub, quelle sorte de personne ne voudrait pas visiter l'exposition? Answers will vary.
6. Aimes-tu visiter les musées? Pourquoi? Quels musées as-tu visités? Answers will vary.

1 Suggestion Before assigning the activity, have students circle the conjunctions that always require the subjunctive.

2 Expansion Have students create three similar dehydrated sentences for a partner to complete.

3 Suggestion As you go through the items, ask students which conjunctions require the subjunctive and which could be followed by either the subjunctive or the indicative. For those that could take either, discuss why.

4 Expansion Have students react to individual responses. Example: ____ **fait de l'exercice tous les jours avant de se coucher. Qui fait plus d'exercice? Qui regarde la télévision? Qui lit avant de s'endormir?**

5 Expansion Have partners guess what their friends and family will do for the weekend. Have them do the same with celebrities, taking guesses about their weekend plans.

6 Suggestions
- Have groups prepare tic-tac-toe cards like the one shown in the activity.
- Have the students form new groups and do a second round of tic-tac-toe.

Le français vivant Before reading the ad aloud, ask students to describe the image. Then ask what they think is being advertised. Say: **Regardez bien cette publicité. Que voyez-vous?**

OPTIONS

Pairs Ask partners to interview each other about what they must do today in order to reach their future goals. Students should state what their goals are, the necessary conditions to achieve them, and talk about obstacles they may encounter. They should use as many conjunctions as possible in their interviews. Have pairs present their interviews to the class.

Extra Practice Prepare several statements, some with clauses followed by the infinitive and some with the subjunctive. After each statement, hold up two flashcards, one with **I** for infinitive and one with **S** for subjunctive. Students point to the card that represents what they heard. Examples: **Le professeur parle lentement pour que les étudiants le comprennent. (S) Je n'ai pas besoin de voiture pour aller à l'université. (I)**

Section Goals

In this section, students will review the subjunctive.

Instructional Resources
*espaces.vhlcentral.com: Lab MP3s; WB/VM/LM Answer Key; IRM (**Essayez!** and **Mise en pratique** answers; Lab Audioscript); activities; downloads; reference tools*

Suggestions

- Review the subjunctive by summing up the year in statements that use the subjunctive. Example: **Je veux que vous continuiez à étudier le français. Je doute que vous oubliiez ce qu'on a appris pendant l'année scolaire. Il faut que vous parliez souvent avec vos amis francophones. Avant que nous finissions le cours, vous allez réviser les usages particuliers du subjonctif.** Ask volunteers to identify the subjunctive form in each sentence.
- Have students look over the one-stem and two-stem forms of the subjunctive of regular verbs. Ask them on which form the present subjunctive is based. (One-stem is based on present tense, third person plural **ils/elles**; two-stem is based on present tense, first person plural **nous.**) Then have them close their books. Have them give the present subjunctive of irregular verbs such as **avoir, être, faire, pouvoir, savoir,** and **vouloir.**
- Before working through the summary of subjunctive usage, review the concepts of indicative and subjunctive. Explain that in most discourse verbs are in the indicative. Then ask volunteers to tell you when the subjunctive is used. Write their statements on the board and discuss them.
- Compare the uses of the subjunctive and indicative. When comparing the subjunctive and infinitive in expressions of emotion, doubt, and certainty, discuss cases where the infinitive is used instead of the subjunctive. Compare and contrast the use of subjunctive and indicative with conjunctions.

15B.2 Review of the subjunctive

Point de départ Since **Leçon 14A**, you have been learning about subjunctive verb forms. Because there is no exact English equivalent of the subjunctive in French, do not rely on translation. Learn to recognize the contexts and cues that trigger the subjunctive. The charts on this and the following page will help you review and synthesize what you have learned about the subjunctive.

D'accord, je vous dis tout avant que vous perdiez patience.
Je pense qu'il a raison. Ma vraie passion, ce n'est pas la musique.

Summary of subjunctive forms

one-stem

	parler	finir	attendre	partir
que je/j'	parle	finisse	attende	parte
que tu	parles	finisses	attendes	partes
qu'il/elle	parle	finisse	attende	parte
que nous	parlions	finissions	attendions	partions
que vous	parliez	finissiez	attendiez	partiez
qu'ils/elles	parlent	finissent	attendent	partent

two-stem / irregular forms

	prendre	aller	avoir	être
que je/j'	prenne	aille	aie	sois
que tu	prennes	ailles	aies	sois
qu'il/elle	prenne	aille	ait	soit
que nous	prenions	allions	ayons	soyons
que vous	preniez	alliez	ayez	soyez
qu'ils/elles	prennent	aillent	aient	soient

irregular forms

	faire	pouvoir	savoir	vouloir
que je	fasse	puisse	sache	veuille
que tu	fasses	puisses	saches	veuilles
qu'il/elle	fasse	puisse	sache	veuille
que nous	fassions	puissions	sachions	voulions
que vous	fassiez	puissiez	sachiez	vouliez
qu'ils/elles	fassent	puissent	sachent	veuillent

MISE EN PRATIQUE

1 Oui, maman... La mère de Tarik et d'Aïcha veut que ses enfants soient très instruits (*educated*) sur l'art et la musique. Mettez les verbes à l'infinitif, à l'indicatif ou au subjonctif pour compléter ses phrases.

1. Il est nécessaire de __lire__ (lire) tous les jours.
2. Il ne faut pas que nous __regardions__ (regarder) trop la télévision.
3. Je pense que Tarik __ne va pas__ (ne pas aller) assez souvent au musée.
4. Je ne pense pas que vous __fassiez__ (faire) assez de peinture.
5. Il faut que vous __étudiiez__ (étudier) la peinture et la musique.
6. Il est impossible que vous __puissiez__ (pouvoir) tout comprendre, bien sûr.
7. Je veux que votre père vous __apprenne__ (apprendre) à reconnaître les chefs-d'œuvre de Van Gogh.
8. Il croit que Van Gogh __est__ (être) le plus grand peintre du dix-neuvième siècle (*century*).

2 Parle-moi de ta famille... Marc, le petit ami de Marion, veut tout savoir sur sa famille. Que lui dit-elle? Complétez les phrases. Answers will vary.

1. Il est clair que mes parents...
2. Je ne pense pas que mon frère...
3. Je crois que ma grand-mère...
4. Il est possible que je...
5. Je sais que mon frère et moi, nous...
6. Il est évident que ma famille...
7. Je ne suis pas sûre que...
8. Nous avons peur que...

3 Et nous? Marc veut épouser Chantal, mais elle n'est pas sûre. Comment répond-elle à ses questions? Avec un(e) partenaire, jouez les rôles. Answers will vary.

1. De quoi as-tu peur, Chantal?
2. N'est-il pas clair que je t'aime?
3. Est-il possible que tu sois malheureuse avec moi?
4. Que faut-il que je fasse pour te persuader?
5. De quoi n'es-tu pas sûre?
6. De quoi doutes-tu?
7. Que pensent tes amis?
8. Et tes parents, que veulent-ils que tu fasses?

Practice more at **espaces.vhlcentral.com.**

OPTIONS

Video Have students divide a sheet of paper into four sections, labeling them *Impersonal expressions, Will and emotion, Doubt,* and *Conjunctions.* Replay the video. Have them listen for each use of the subjunctive, writing the examples they hear in the appropriate section. Play the video again, then have students write a short summary that includes each use of the subjunctive.

Extra Practice Here are five sentences to use as a dictation. Read each twice, pausing after the second time for students to write. **1. Il est important que nous regardions cette émission de télévision ce soir. 2. Je vais au mariage à condition qu'il ne pleuve pas. 3. Le patron demande que les employés travaillent plus d'heures. 4. Nathalie est en France jusqu'à ce qu'elle finisse ses études.**

COMMUNICATION

4 Mon émission préférée Avec un(e) partenaire, parlez de vos émissions de télévision préférées. Utilisez ces phrases dans votre conversation. Answers will vary.

1. Je la regarde à condition que...
2. Je suis furieux/furieuse que...
3. Tu devrais la regarder pour que...
4. Je ne suis pas sûr(e) que...
5. Il est important que...
6. Je ne pense pas que...

5 Une pub Par groupes de trois, inventez un produit et faites sa publicité. Utilisez autant de ces expressions que possible. Ensuite, présentez vos produits et vos pubs à la classe, qui votera pour les meilleurs. Answers will vary.

MODÈLE

Voulez-vous que votre maison soit propre? Il faut que vous achetiez «Nettoitou»! Il est formidable! Utilisez-le pour que toute votre maison soit belle!

avant que	il est évident	ne pas penser que
croire que	il est impossible que	pour que
il est douteux que	il faut que	sans que
il est essentiel que	jusqu'à ce que	vouloir que

6 Vos opinions Avec un(e) partenaire, écrivez un paragraphe pour donner votre opinion sur un de ces thèmes. Ensuite, échangez vos feuilles avec un groupe qui a choisi un thème différent et discutez de toutes les opinions. Answers will vary.

MODÈLE

Il est important que les profs écoutent les problèmes de leurs étudiants.

- Le coût (*cost*) élevé des études universitaires
- Les relations entre la France et les États-Unis
- Le rôle du gouvernement dans la vie privée
- La nécessité des armes et de la guerre
- La séparation de l'Église et de l'État (*State*)

- Certain expressions trigger the subjunctive in the subordinate clause when the subject of the main clause is different.

Summary of subjunctive uses

Subjunctive trigger in main clause	Subjunctive in subordinate clause
Verb or expression of opinion	**Il est bon que Djamel conduise.** *It is good (that) Djamel drives.*
Verb or expression of necessity or obligation	**Il est essentiel que les étudiants fassent** leurs devoirs. *It's essential that students do their homework.*
Verb or expression of will or emotion	Nous **avons peur que vous ayez** trop de travail. *We're afraid (that) you have too much work.*
Verb or expression of doubt, disbelief, or uncertainty	Tu **ne crois pas que nous soyons** américaines. *You don't believe (that) we're American.*
Conjunction	Il chantera **à condition que tu saches** jouer du piano. *He'll sing provided that you know how to play the piano.*

- Use the indicative in the subordinate clause when there is an expression of belief, certainty, or truth in the main clause.

Je crois que nous sommes à l'heure. *but* **Je doute que nous soyons** en retard.
I believe (that) we're on time. *I doubt (that) we're late.*

- Use the infinitive when the subject of the main clause is the same as that of the subordinate clause.

Préfères-tu jouer de la guitare? *Do you prefer to play the guitar?*
Nous sommes ici **pour voir** l'auteur. *We're here to see the author.*

Essayez! **Choisissez les formes correctes des verbes.**

1. Veut-il qu'elle (vient / vienne) avec nous?
2. Montre-moi tes photos pour que je (vois / voie) les belles plages.
3. Il faut que tu (as / aies) de la patience.
4. Elle ne doute pas que cette pièce (finit / finisse) tard.
5. Il est vrai que Dahlia (est / soit) malade.
6. Nous sommes contents que vous (allez / alliez) au musée du Louvre.
7. Il est dommage que nous ne (voyons / voyions) pas de peintures.
8. J'espère rentrer avant que mes parents (font / fassent) la cuisine.

Essayez! Have students change the main clause from affirmative to negative, and vice versa. Discuss the impact this change has on the subordinate clause, if any.

1 Expansion Ask volunteers to read the completed sentences and state their reason for choosing the infinitive, subjunctive, or indicative form.

2 Suggestion Model the activity by giving a personal example. Write, for example, **Je doute que mon frère...** on the board, then complete the sentence. **(Je doute que mon frère se souvienne de la date de mon anniversaire.)**

3 Suggestion Call on several pairs to role-play their conversation for the class.

4 Expansion Write on the board all of the **émissions de télévision préférées** that the pairs discussed. Have students who chose the same program sit together. Then ask questions to elicit class discussion about the different programs. Example: **Il y a trois étudiants qui disent qu' *Entourage* est leur émission de télévision préférée. Pourquoi? Il est important que vous la regardiez toutes les semaines?**

5 Expansion Give each group member a task when presenting the ad to the class. The first member should explain the target audience of the ad. The second member should read the text to the class. The third member should pretend to be a client, giving a testimonial about the product's benefits.

6 Suggestion Before dividing the class into groups, give individuals two minutes to choose a topic. Then have them write down three ideas about the topic. Divide the class according to the subject they chose.

OPTIONS

Game Write verbs and expressions of will or emotion on slips of paper and put them in a box or bag. On separate strips, write an equal number of infinitives and subject pronouns. Place these in a separate box or bag. Divide the class into two teams. One member of each team draws a slip of paper from each box and writes a sentence on the board using the elements on both slips. If the sentence makes sense and the grammar is correct, that team gets a point. Play until every team member has had a chance to go to the board. The team with the most points at the end of play wins.

Pairs Have students tell a partner three things he or she doubts and three things of which he or she is certain.

Révision

Instructional Resources
espaces.vhlcentral.com: IRM (Info Gap Activities); Testing Program, pp. 117–120; Test Files; Testing Program MP3s; activities; downloads; reference tools
Test Generator

1 Suggestion Assign students to groups of three. Tell them to appoint a mediator to lead the discussion, a secretary to write out the eight phrases, and a proofreader to check what was written.

2 Expansion Ask each group to choose one art museum and exhibit that they have visited. Have students create an ad to promote the exhibit. Refer them to the ad in **Le français vivant** on page 533 or Internet sites as a resource. Students must use at least three subjunctive phrases in their ad.

3 Suggestion Before assigning this activity, remind students that **vouloir** takes the subjunctive only when there is a subject change. Ask a volunteer to give an example of a sentence with **vouloir** + **que** + [*subjunctive*]. Then have another volunteer give an example of **vouloir** + [*infinitive*].

4 Expansion Have pairs imagine that their friend needs advice about becoming a writer and draft an e-mail to their friend using the sentences created in the activity. Then have pairs exchange their letters with other groups for peer editing.

5 Suggestion Divide the class into pairs and distribute the Info Gap Handouts found on the Supersite for this activity. Give students ten minutes to complete the activity.

1 Un film d'horreur Que doit-on faire pour qu'un film d'horreur soit une réussite? Avec un(e) partenaire, faites par écrit une liste de huit phrases pour expliquer les critères. Utilisez tout ce vocabulaire. Answers will vary.

MODÈLE

Le film peut être une réussite à condition que les acteurs soient des célébrités.

à condition que	jusqu'à ce que
à moins que	pour que
avant que	sans que

2 Quels artistes? Par groupes de trois, interviewez vos camarades pour leur demander quels artistes et quelles œuvres ils vous recommandent de découvrir la prochaine fois que vous visiterez un musée. Écrivez leurs réponses, puis présentez leurs recommandations à la classe. Utilisez ces expressions avec le présent du subjonctif. Answers will vary.

MODÈLE La télévision fait du mal au cinéma.

Je suggère que tu ailles voir les tableaux de Monet. Tu aimeras les couleurs et la représentation des personnages.

il est important que	proposer que
il est indispensable que	recommander que
(ne pas) penser que	suggérer que
?	?

3 Mes enfants Avec un(e) partenaire, préparez un dialogue où ces parents se disent ce qu'ils veulent que leurs enfants fassent plus tard. Utilisez au moins huit verbes au présent du subjonctif. Ensuite, jouez votre scène devant la classe. Answers will vary.

4 Un bon écrivain Que faut-il pour devenir un bon écrivain? Trouvez huit qualités qu'il faut avoir et utilisez l'infinitif pour faire une liste de conseils. À tour de rôle, utilisez votre liste pour donner des conseils à votre partenaire au présent du subjonctif. Answers will vary.

MODÈLE

Étudiant(e) 1: *Conseil numéro 1: Pour être un bon écrivain, il faut avoir beaucoup d'imagination.*
Étudiant(e) 2: *Si tu veux être un bon écrivain, il est essentiel que tu développes ton imagination.*

5 Au Louvre Votre professeur va vous donner, à vous et à votre partenaire, deux feuilles d'activités différentes. Attention! Ne regardez pas la feuille de votre partenaire. Answers will vary.

ressources
WB pp. 205–208 | LM pp. 119–120 | espaces.vhlcentral.com

OPTIONS

Extra Practice Write a cloze paragraph, making remarks about the course. Give students a word bank or let them pick a logical word from the context. Example: **Il est difficile de croire que nous ____ (soyons/arrivions) déjà à la fin du semestre. Je ____ (vous) conseille de bien réviser vos cours pour le dernier examen qui ____ (sera/aura lieu) le vendredi 15 mai à 8 heures. J'espère que vous ____ (avez/aurez) beaucoup appris, non seulement en français, mais aussi à propos du monde francophone. Je souhaite que vous ____ (continuiez) à apprendre cette belle langue, à moins, bien sûr, que vous ne ____ (décidiez) d'arrêter vos études universitaires, mais ce ____ (serait) dommage! N'hésitez pas à me ____ (rendre) visite au bureau à l'avenir. ____ (Tenez)-moi au courant de vos projets!**

À l'écoute

communication NATIONAL STANDARDS

Audio: Activities

STRATÉGIE

Listening for key words/ Using the context

The comprehension of key words is vital to understanding spoken French. You can use your background knowledge of the subject to help you anticipate some key words. When you hear unfamiliar words, remember that you can use context to figure out their meaning.

To practice these strategies, you will listen to a paragraph from a letter sent to a job applicant. Jot down key words, as well as any other words you figured out from the context.

Préparation

Regardez et décrivez la photo. Où sont ces personnes? Que font-elles? Que vont-elles aller voir, à votre avis?

À vous d'écouter

Vous êtes en France et vous voulez inviter un(e) ami(e) à sortir ce week-end. Vous écoutez la radio et vous entendez une annonce pour un spectacle qui plaira peut-être à votre ami(e). Notez les informations principales pour pouvoir ensuite décrire ce spectacle à votre ami(e) et pour lui dire quand vous pourrez aller le voir. Answers will vary.

____
____
____
____
____
____
____
____

Practice more at **espaces.vhlcentral.com.**

Compréhension

Complétez Complétez les phrases.

1. Molière est __a__ de *L'Avare*.
   a. l'auteur **b.** le metteur en scène **c.** le personnage principal
2. *L'Avare* est __c__.
   a. une exposition **b.** un jeune comédien très dynamique
   c. une pièce de théâtre
3. *L'Avare* est drôle. C'est __b__.
   a. une tragédie **b.** une comédie **c.** un drame psychologique
4. Yves Lemoîne est __c__ de *L'Avare*.
   a. l'auteur **b.** le journaliste qui a écrit la critique
   c. le metteur en scène
5. Harpagon est le nom du __a__.
   a. personnage principal **b.** spectacle **c.** poète
6. Dans le journal, il y avait __b__ positive de *L'Avare*.
   a. une pub **b.** une critique **c.** un applaudissement

Invitez votre ami(e)! Vous avez maintenant toutes les informations importantes nécessaires pour inviter votre ami(e) (un[e] camarade) à aller voir *L'Avare* ce week-end.

- Invitez-le/la au spectacle et dites-lui quand vous pourrez y aller.
- Il/Elle va vous poser quelques questions pour obtenir plus de détails sur le spectacle (histoire, personnages, acteurs, etc.).
- Ensuite, comme il/elle n'a pas très envie d'aller voir le spectacle, il/elle va faire plusieurs suggestions d'autres activités artistiques (films, concerts, expositions, etc.).
- Discutez de ces possibilités et choisissez-en une ensemble.

Section Goals

In this section, students will:

- learn to listen for key words and use context
- listen to a letter sent to a job applicant and jot down key words
- listen to a radio advertisement for a play and complete several activities

Instructional Resources
espaces.vhlcentral.com: Textbook MP3s; IRM (Textbook Audioscript); downloads; reference tools

Stratégie
Script Monsieur, Nous vous remercions de votre lettre de candidature pour le poste d'ingénieur informatique et pour l'intérêt que vous portez à notre compagnie. Malheureusement, nous regrettons de vous informer que nous avons déjà retenu un candidat pour cet emploi. Nous vous prions d'agréer, Monsieur, l'expression de nos sentiments distingués.

Préparation Have students look at the photo and describe what they see. They should mention that the people are waiting in line at a box office of a theater.

À vous d'écouter
Script Les amateurs de Molière ne doivent surtout pas manquer *L'Avare* au Théâtre Monfort. Le metteur en scène, Yves Lemoîne, réinvente ce grand classique avec beaucoup de créativité. Avec dans le rôle d'Harpagon, le personnage principal qui a toujours peur qu'on lui prenne son argent, Julien Roche; un jeune comédien très talentueux qui a fait ses débuts il y a trois ans avec la troupe Comédia. *L'Avare* est une comédie très amusante et je suis certain que cette adaptation aura un grand succès. La première représentation a eu lieu hier soir et déjà les applaudissements étaient nombreux et enthousiastes. La pièce a aussi reçu une critique très positive dans le journal *Le Monde*. Si vous souhaitez voir *L'Avare* par Yves Lemoîne, les billets sont en vente au guichet du théâtre tous les jours de 10h00 à 18h00. Il y a deux représentations le vendredi et le samedi, à 19h00 et à 21h30 et une à 14h00 le dimanche.

Successful Language Learning Ask students if they approach listening to French or English differently after using the strategies presented in **ESPACES**.

Section Goals
In this section, students will learn historical and cultural information about the Antilles and French Polynesia.

Instructional Resources
espaces.vhlcentral.com: Transparency #62; WB/VM/LM Answer Key; activities; downloads; reference tools

Carte des Antilles et de la Polynésie française
- Have students look at the map or use **Transparency #62**. Ask volunteers to read the names of countries and islands aloud.
- Point out the location of **la mer des Antilles** or **la mer des Caraïbes**.
- Give students a geographical description of a few locations and have them guess which francophone place you are describing.
- Mention that the tropical islands, which are mostly mountainous, have fertile soils that make for rich, abundant vegetation.

L'archipel en chiffres
- Have volunteers read the sections aloud. After each section, ask students questions about the content.
- Explain that an archipelago is a large group of islands. Point out that the **îles Gambier** and **îles de la Société** are composed of atolls.

Incroyable mais vrai! After the eruption, the accumulated ash and rock raised the summit of Mount Pelée from 5,000 feet to 6,000 feet. After a few more minor eruptions, the volcano now stands at 4,584 feet.

NATIONAL STANDARDS connections cultures

Interactive Map Reading

Panorama

la ville de Gustavia, à Saint-Barthélemy

Les Antilles

L'archipel en chiffres
- **Guadeloupe:** *(472.000 habitants), Pointe-à-Pitre, Basse-Terre*
- **Haïti:** *(9.751.000), Port-au-Prince*
- **Martinique:** *(404.000), Fort-de-France*
- **Saint-Barthélemy:** *(8.400), Gustavia*
- **Saint-Martin:** *(en partie) (35.700), Marigot*

SOURCE: Population Division, UN Secretariat

Antillais célèbres

- **Aimé Césaire,** *Martinique, poète (1913–2008)*
- **Raphaël Confiant,** *Martinique, écrivain° (1951–)*

- **Garcelle Beauvais,** *Haïti, actrice (1966–)*
- **Wyclef Jean,** *Haïti, chanteur de rap (1972–)*

La Polynésie française

L'archipel en chiffres
- **Îles Australes:** *(6.386), Tubuai*
- **Îles de la Société:** *(214.445), Papeete*
- **Îles Gambier:** *(1.097), Mangareva*
- **Îles Marquises:** *(8.712), Nuku-Hiva*
- **Îles Tuamotu:** *(16.959), Fakarava, Rankiroa*

Polynésiens célèbres
- **Henri Hiro,** *Tahiti, îles de la Société, poète (1944–1991)*
- **Rodolphe Vinh Tung,** *Raiatea, îles de la Société, professionnel du wakeboard (1974–)*

les courses de pirogues° en Polynésie française

Incroyable mais vrai!
Jusqu'au vingtième siècle, Saint-Pierre était le port le plus actif des Antilles et la capitale de la Martinique. Mais en 1902, un volcan, la montagne Pelée, entre en éruption. Il n'y a eu que deux survivants°, dont un qui a été protégé par les murs de la prison où il était enfermé°. Certains historiens doutent de l'authenticité de l'histoire de cet homme.

écrivain *writer* **survivants** *survivors* **enfermé** *detained* **pirogues** *dugout canoes*

OPTIONS

Antillais et Polynésiens célèbres **Aimé Césaire** coined the term **«Négritude»**, which came from his poem **«Cahier d'un retour au pays natal»**. **Raphaël Confiant** has won many literary prizes for his works, which have been published in French, Creole, and English. He has championed Creole as a literary language and has been involved in social and political activities in Martinique. **Garcelle Beauvais** is a model and actress. She has appeared in American films and TV shows. **Wyclef Jean**'s music draws from his memories of his youth in Haiti and his multicultural experiences in a Creole environment after immigrating to the United States. **Henri Hiro** was responsible for a cultural resurgence of the traditional Polynesian customs in Tahitian theater, dance, music, and film.

Les arts

Les peintures de Gauguin

En 1891, le peintre° Paul Gauguin (1848–1903) vend ses œuvres° à Paris et déménage à Tahiti, dans les îles de la Société, pour échapper à° la vie moderne. Il y reste deux ans avant de rentrer en France et, en 1895, il retourne en Polynésie française pour y habiter jusqu'à sa mort en 1903. Inspirée par le nouvel environnement du peintre et la nature qui l'entoure°, l'œuvre «tahitienne» de Gauguin est célèbre° pour sa représentation du peuple indigène et l'emploi° de couleurs vives°. Ses peintures° de femmes font partie de ses meilleurs tableaux°.

Les destinations

Haïti, première République noire

En 1791, un ancien esclave°, Toussaint Louverture, mène° une rébellion pour l'abolition de l'esclavage en Haïti, ancienne colonie française. Après avoir gagné le combat, Louverture se proclame gouverneur de l'île d'Hispaniola (Haïti et Saint-Domingue) et abolit l'esclavage. Il est plus tard capturé par l'armée française et renvoyé en France. Son successeur, Jean-Jacques Dessalines, lui-même ancien esclave, vainc° l'armée en 1803 et proclame l'indépendance d'Haïti en 1804. C'est la première République noire du monde et le premier pays du monde occidental à abolir l'esclavage.

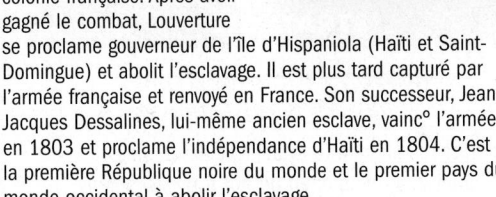

L'économie

La perle noire

La Polynésie française est le principal producteur de perles° noires. Dans la nature, les perles sont très rares; on en trouve dans une huître° sur 15.000. Par contre°, aujourd'hui, la Polynésie française produit plusieurs tonnes de perles noires chaque année. Des milliers de Tahitiens vivent de° l'industrie perlière. Parce qu'elle s'est développée dans les lagons, la perliculture° a même aidé à repeupler° certaines îles et certains endroits ruraux, abandonnés par les gens partis en ville. Les perles sont très variées et présentent différentes formes et nuances de noir.

Les gens

Maryse Condé

Née en Guadeloupe, puis étudiante à la Sorbonne, à Paris, Maryse Condé a vécu° huit ans en Afrique (Ghana, Sénégal, Guinée, etc.). En 1973, elle enseigne dans les universités françaises et commence sa carrière° d'écrivain°. Elle sera ensuite professeur en Californie et à l'Université de Columbia. Ses nombreux romans°, y compris° *Moi, Tituba Sorcière*, ont reçu de multiples récompenses°. Ses romans mêlent° souvent fiction et événements historiques pour montrer la complexité de la culture antillaise, culture liée° à celle de l'Europe et à celle de l'Afrique.

Qu'est-ce que vous avez appris? Répondez aux questions par des phrases complètes.

1. Que s'est-il passé en Martinique au début du vingtième siècle?
   La montagne Pelée est entrée en éruption.
2. L'éruption a-t-elle tué tous les habitants de Saint-Pierre?
   Non, deux habitants n'ont pas été tués.
3. Pour quelle raison Gauguin a-t-il déménagé à Tahiti?
   Il voulait échapper à la vie moderne.
4. Pour quelles raisons l'œuvre «tahitienne» de Gauguin est-elle célèbre?
   Elle est célèbre pour sa représentation du peuple indigène et pour l'emploi de couleurs vives.
5. Quelle est la principale particularité d'Haïti?
   C'est la première République noire du monde.
6. Qui a réussi à abolir l'esclavage en Haïti?
   Toussaint Louverture a réussi à abolir l'esclavage en Haïti.
7. D'où viennent la majorité des perles noires?
   Elles viennent de Polynésie française.
8. Comment la perliculture a-t-elle changé la population de la Polynésie?
   Elle a aidé à repeupler certaines îles et certains endroits ruraux.
9. Où Maryse Condé a-t-elle étudié? Où est-elle née?
   Elle a fait ses études à Paris. Elle est née en Guadeloupe.
10. Ses romans sont-ils entièrement des œuvres de fiction?
    Non, ils mêlent la fiction et l'histoire.

ressources: WB pp. 209–210 | espaces.vhlcentral.com

Practice more at **espaces.vhlcentral.com.**

SUR INTERNET

Go to **espaces.vhlcentral.com** to find more cultural information related to this **PANORAMA**.

1. Cherchez des informations sur Aimé Césaire. Qu'a-t-il en commun avec Léopold Sédar Senghor, poète et homme politique mentionné dans le panorama précédent?
2. Trouvez des informations sur la ville de Saint-Pierre. Comment est-elle aujourd'hui?
3. Cherchez des informations sur les courses de pirogues en Polynésie française. Quelle est leur signification?

peintre *painter* **œuvres** *artworks* **échapper à** *escape* **entoure** *surrounds* **célèbre** *famous* **emploi** *use* **vives** *bright* **peintures** *paintings* **tableaux** *paintings* **esclave** *slave* **mène** *leads* **vainc** *defeats* **perles** *pearls* **huître** *oyster* **Par contre** *On the other hand* **vivent de** *make a living from* **perliculture** *pearl farming* **repeupler** *repopulate* **a vécu** *lived* **carrière** *career* **écrivain** *writer* **romans** *novels* **y compris** *including* **récompenses** *awards* **mêlent** *mix* **liée** *tied*

Les peintures de Gauguin
- Gauguin tried to capture authentic aspects of traditional Tahitian culture, emulated Oceanic traditions in his woodcuts, and often used the Tahitian language for titles of his works.
- Have students describe the painting. Ask: **Qui reconnaît ce tableau. Devinez comment il s'appelle. (*Femmes de Tahiti [sur la plage]*) Savez-vous où le tableau original se trouve aujourd'hui? (Il est au musée d'Orsay à Paris.)**

Haïti, première République noire Haitian Creole and French are the two official languages of Haiti. The grammar of Haitian Creole is similar to languages of West Africa and other Caribbean creoles. Distribute examples of Haitian Creole and have students compare the language with French.

La perle noire Baby oysters are collected from the ocean and raised in pearl farms for three years. A small round piece of mother-of-pearl is inserted into the oyster, and the oyster begins the natural process of secreting nacre in layers onto the foreign substance which becomes a pearl after several years.

Maryse Condé In her historical novels, Maryse Condé has chronicled the migration and experience of the African people from West Africa to the United States and the Caribbean. Her books explore the clash of races and cultures using personal experiences of historical characters.

OPTIONS

Une tradition tahitienne The **Hawaiki Nui Va'a** is one of the world's premier outrigger canoe competitions, and it is an important celebration of Tahiti's traditional sports. Each year in late October or early November, canoeists compete on an 80-mile, four-island course over the span of three days.

Régions d'outre-mer Martinique and Guadeloupe are **départements** or **régions d'outre-mer (DOM/ROM)** of France. They have the same status and responsibilities as any other department of metropolitan France. French Polynesia is referred to as a **collectivité d'outre-mer** (previously **territoire d'outre-mer**) which is more independent, but still has some administrative ties to France.

Section Goals
In this section, students will:
- learn to make inferences and recognize metaphors
- read an African poem

Stratégie
- Tell students that poets do not generally spell out everything for their readers. They will need to look for clues in the poem to infer what is unstated and then draw conclusions in order to comprehend the poet's message.
- Review metaphors. Then write these sentences on the board. **Ses cheveux sont comme de la soie. Ses mots sont de la poésie.** Ask students which sentence is a metaphor. Then have students make up a metaphor in French and share it with the class.

Examinez le texte Students should mention that the text is a poem, the title is **«Note à mes lecteurs»**, and it is written in the first person. The illustrations indicate that the writer is a mother, she is writing outdoors under the starry night, and the people climbing the mountain are her readers.

À propos de l'auteur
- Mariama Mbengue Ndoye's hometown in Senegal is Rufisque. An old port city, Rufisque is now a distant suburb of Dakar.
- Ask students these comprehension questions.
1. Où est née Mariama Mbengue Ndoye? (au Sénégal)
2. Où a-t-elle reçu son doctorat? (à l'Université de Dakar)
3. Qu'a-t-elle étudié à l'École du Louvre? (la muséologie)
4. Qu'avait-elle comme travail entre 1977–1986? (Elle était Conservateur du musée d'Art africain de l'Institut fondamental d'Afrique noire.)
5. Où habite-t-elle actuellement? (en Tunisie)
6. Quels thèmes trouve-t-on dans ses livres? (l'Afrique, la femme africaine et la vie dans les villages)

Lecture

NATIONAL communication cultures STANDARDS

S Audio: Dramatic Recording

Avant la lecture

STRATÉGIE

Making inferences and recognizing metaphors

For dramatic effect and to achieve a smoother writing style, authors often do not explicitly supply the reader with all the details of a story or a poem. Clues (**indices**) in the text can help you infer (**déduire**) those things the writer chooses not to state in a direct manner. You simply "read between the lines" to fill in the missing information.

Metaphors (**Métaphores**) are figures of speech used in literature to make descriptions more vivid. They identify one thing with the attributes and qualities of another, as in *all the world's a stage.*

Examinez le texte

Regardez le texte. Est-ce un extrait de roman? Une nouvelle (*short story*)? Un poème? Quel en est le titre? Qu'indiquent le format et le titre à propos du genre du texte? Regardez aussi les illustrations. Qu'indiquent-elles sur le thème de la lecture?

À propos de l'auteur
Mariama Mbengue Ndoye

Mariama Mbengue Ndoye est née au Sénégal en 1953. Elle fait des études de lettres à l'Université de Dakar, où elle reçoit son doctorat en 1982. Elle obtient un certificat de muséologie de l'École du Louvre à Paris en 1977 et devient ensuite Conservateur du musée d'Art africain de l'Institut fondamental d'Afrique noire à Dakar. Après 15 ans passés en Côte d'Ivoire, elle habite maintenant en Tunisie, où elle écrit. Son œuvre comprend° plusieurs romans, dont *Soukey* et *De vous à moi*, des recueils° de nouvelles et des livres pour enfants. Dans ses livres, elle parle de l'Afrique, de la femme africaine et de la vie dans les villages.

comprend *includes* **recueils** *collections*

Note à mes

En forme de poème (1996)

Je m'appelle Mariama, Marie, Myriem, Marème,
Mouskeba, Maamou à votre aise°

Le O de mon nom Ndoye ouvre son gros œil sur
le monde

Je suis femme, je suis mère, je suis fille
porteuse de nichées d'espoirs°
lourde de hottes° de secrets
pourvoyeuse° de caresses et de claques°

OPTIONS

Pairs Remind students that they can appreciate the lyrical nature of poetry by reading a poem aloud. Have partners read **«Note à mes lecteurs»** to each other. Tell them to pay close attention to how the lines are punctuated and how the stanzas are arranged.

Extra Practice At the end of the poem the author says, **«Je "nous" écris, lisez-moi.»** Have students discuss why she makes that statement. What were her reasons? Then ask them if this poem makes them want to read more of her works. Have them justify their answers.

lecteurs°

7 Je suis une nuit noire étoilée°
8 noire de la souffrance° des femmes en gésine°
9 noire du carbone d'où jaillit° le diamant
10 étoilée du sourire de mes sœurs d'Afrique

11 Je vais déambulant° dans les méandres de mon être et du temps
12 confiant° au papier blanc-ami les songes° fragiles de mon âme° d'enfant

13 Je gravis° ma colline° parfois je m'égratigne°

14 Je regarde mes compagnons de cordée°: Vous.

15 Je «nous» écris, lisez-moi.

16 Mariama Ndoye

lecteurs *readers* **à votre aise** *as you please* **porteuse de nichées d'espoirs** *carrier of broods of hopes* **lourde de hottes** *heavy with baskets* **pourvoyeuse** *provider* **claques** *slaps* **étoilée** *starry* **souffrance** *suffering* **en gésine** *giving birth* **jaillit** *springs up* **déambulant** *wandering* **confiant** *confiding* **songes** *dreams* **âme** *soul* **gravis** *climb up* **colline** *hill* **m'égratigne** *scratch myself* **compagnons de cordée** *fellow climbers*

Après la lecture

Vrai ou faux? Indiquez si les phrases sont **vraies** ou **fausses**. Attention! Beaucoup de choses ne sont que suggérées dans le poème. Citez (*Quote*) le poème pour justifier votre réponse.

1. La femme du poème représente toutes les femmes.
   Vrai. «Je m'appelle Mariama, Marie, Myriem, Marème, Mouskeba, Maamou à votre aise»
2. Elle ne s'intéresse pas au monde.
   Faux. «Le O de mon nom Ndoye ouvre son gros œil sur le monde»
3. Elle n'a pas d'enfants.
   Faux. «je suis mère»
4. C'est une femme qui ne sait pas réprimander.
   Faux. «Je suis [...] pourvoyeuse de caresses et de claques»
5. Elle ressent (*feels*) le bonheur et la douleur des femmes.
   Vrai. «Je suis [...] noire de la souffrance des femmes en gésine [...] étoilée du sourire de mes sœurs d'Afrique»
6. Quand elle écrit, elle parle de ses rêves (*dreams*).
   Vrai. «confiant au papier blanc-ami les songes fragiles de mon âme d'enfant»
7. Elle trouve que c'est facile d'écrire.
   Faux. «Je gravis ma colline parfois je m'égratigne»
8. Quand elle parle de ses compagnons de cordée, elle fait référence à ses enfants.
   Faux. «Note à mes lecteurs [...] je regarde mes compagnons de cordée: Vous.»
9. Elle écrit seulement à propos d'elle-même et pour elle.
   Faux. «Je "nous" écris, lisez-moi.»
10. Ce poème a un ton plutôt pessimiste.
    Faux. «Je suis [...] porteuse de nichées d'espoir»

Métaphores Avez-vous trouvé des métaphores dans ce poème? Trouvez celles qui indiquent que l'auteur vient d'Afrique. Que signifient ces métaphores? L'auteur est-elle fière d'être Africaine?

Answers will vary. Suggested answers: «Je suis une nuit noire étoilée», «noire de la souffrance des femmes en gésine», etc. Les métaphores du poème illustrent la complexité de la vie des femmes africaines.

Escalader ensemble L'auteur compare ses lecteurs à des compagnons de cordée. Pourquoi, à votre avis? Que doit-on faire quand on escalade (*climb*) une montagne? Avez-vous déjà escaladé une montagne ou une colline? Discutez en petit groupe.

Vrai ou faux? Go over the answers with the class.

Métaphores
- Have students work on this activity in pairs or have them compare their answers with a classmate.
- Ask students to think about conversations that they have had recently in which they used a metaphor. As a starting point, you might mention that the quote "All the world's a stage" from Shakespeare's *As You Like It* is an example of a metaphor.

Escalader ensemble Ask groups to share their opinions and ideas with the class.

Successful Language Learning Ask students if they approach reading in French or English differently after using the strategies presented in **ESPACES**.

OPTIONS

Extra Practice Have students write a short poem about themselves using this poem as a model. Encourage them to use metaphors. Ask volunteers to read their poems to the class.

Extra Practice Assign individual students one of the works by Mariama Mbengue Ndoye listed in the author biography or another work such as ***Sur des chemins pavoisés, Parfums d'enfance, La légende de Rufisque***, and ***Le sceptre de Justice***. Tell them to research and write a paragraph about the book that includes the themes, the main characters, and a brief plot summary.

Section Goals

In this section, students will:
- learn to write introductions and conclusions
- write a critique of a film, show, or theatrical work

Stratégie Explain that a strong introduction presents the topic and outlines the important points that will be addressed.

Thème Tell students to follow the steps outlined here when writing their critique.

Proofreading Activity Have students correct these sentences. **1. Croyez-vous que ce soit meilleur qu'elle le sache? 2. Il est évidente qu'elle ne connaît pas chanter. 3. Il est clair que tu ne saches rien de moi.**

Écriture

STRATÉGIE

Writing strong introductions and conclusions

Introductions and conclusions serve a similar purpose: both are intended to focus the reader's attention on the topic being covered. The introduction presents a brief preview of the topic. In addition, it informs your reader of the important points that will be covered in the body of your writing. The conclusion reaffirms those points and concisely sums up the information that has been provided. A compelling fact or statistic, a humorous anecdote, or a question directed to the reader are all interesting ways to begin or end your writing.

For example, if you were writing a biographical report on Antoine de Saint-Exupéry, whom you learned about in **Unité 14 LECTURE**, you might start by noting that Saint-Exupéry's Le Petit Prince is considered to be one of the most widely read books ever. The rest of your introductory paragraph would outline the areas you would cover in the body of your paper, such as the author's life, his works, and the impact that Le Petit Prince has had on adult and children's literature. In your conclusion, you might sum up the most important information in the report and tie this information together in a way that would make your reader want to learn even more about the topic. You could write, for example, "Antoine de Saint-Exupéry, with his imagination and unique view on the world, has created one of the most well-known and enduring characters in world literature."

Thème

Écrire la critique d'une œuvre artistique

Avant l'écriture

1. Vous allez écrire la critique d'un film, d'une pièce de théâtre ou d'un spectacle de votre choix. Votre critique doit avoir trois parties: l'introduction, le développement et la conclusion. Dans l'introduction, vous allez rapidement présenter l'œuvre. Ensuite, dans le développement, vous allez la décrire en détail. Enfin, dans la conclusion, vous allez donner votre opinion et expliquer pourquoi vous recommandez ce spectacle ou non. Utilisez ce plan pour la recherche des idées et pour leur organisation.

Introduction

- Le titre de l'œuvre et le nom de son créateur
- Description du sujet et/ou du genre de l'œuvre
- Quand et où vous l'avez vu

Développement

- Un petit résumé de l'histoire
- Les noms des personnages ou des artistes
- Description des personnages, du/des décor(s) et des costumes

OPTIONS

Avant l'écriture Ask students why an introduction to a biography of Antoine de Saint-Exupéry that does not mention *Le Petit Prince* is not a strong introduction. Explain that a strong conclusion summarizes the information given. Ask students how this conclusion could be stronger: **Saint-Exupéry était un grand écrivain.**

Tell students that the sample introduction uses a summarizing statement as a starting point. Other ways to begin an introduction are with statistics or other factual information related to your topic, with a quotation that summarizes the point of view you plan to develop, or with an anecdote that sets the stage for the rest of your evaluation.

Conclusion

- Votre opinion de l'œuvre
- Explication des raisons pour lesquelles vous la recommandez ou non

Écriture

1. Pour vous assurer (*ensure*) que vous allez écrire une introduction et une conclusion bien développées, remplissez (*fill in*) ce diagramme. Ces deux sections doivent contenir la même information sur les idées principales de votre critique, mais doivent aussi avoir au moins (*at least*) une idée différente. Référez-vous à la stratégie, si nécessaire.

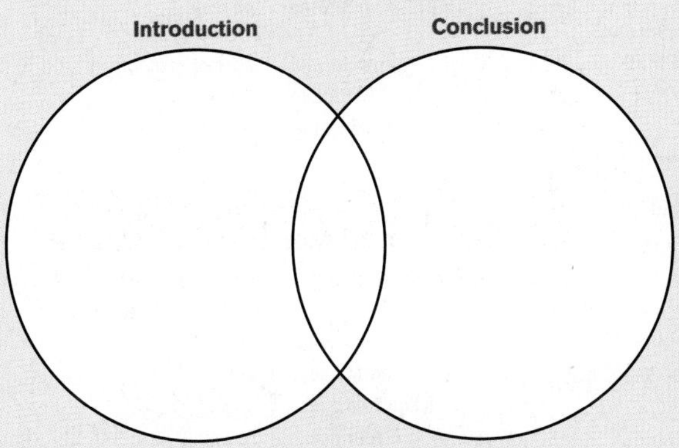

2. Ensuite, utilisez vos idées de la section précédente et du diagramme pour écrire votre critique.

3. Utilisez aussi des formes du subjonctif et, si possible, des pronoms possessifs dans votre critique.

Critique d'une pièce de théâtre

Le malade imaginaire de Molière est une comédie théâtrale que j'ai eu la chance de voir hier soir au Théâtre des Capucins.

L'histoire, qui se passe au XVIIe siècle, est celle d'un vieux bourgeois, Argan, qui se croit constamment malade, alors qu'il ne l'est pas. Béline, sa femme, ...

Cette pièce, qui est d'ailleurs un des nombreux chefs-d'œuvre de Molière, m'a donné l'occasion de passer un très bon moment...

Après l'écriture

1. Échangez votre critique avec celle d'un(e) partenaire. Répondez à ces questions pour commenter son travail.

- Votre partenaire a-t-il/elle inclu une introduction développée?
- A-t-il/elle écrit une partie centrale détaillée?
- A-t-il/elle écrit une conclusion bien développée et en relation avec l'introduction, mais contenant (*containing*) aussi au moins une nouvelle idée?
- A-t-il/elle présenté toutes les informations de la section **Avant l'écriture**?
- A-t-il/elle utilisé des formes du subjonctif?
- Quel(s) détail(s) ajouteriez-vous (*would you add*)? Quel(s) détail(s) enlèveriez-vous (*would you delete*)? Quel(s) autre(s) commentaire(s) avez-vous pour votre partenaire?

2. Corrigez votre lettre d'après (*according to*) les commentaires de votre partenaire. Relisez votre travail pour éliminer ces problèmes:

- des fautes (*errors*) d'orthographe
- des fautes de ponctuation
- des fautes de conjugaison
- un mauvais emploi (*use*) de la grammaire de l'unité
- des fautes d'accord (*agreement*) des adjectifs

EVALUATION

Criteria

Content Contains a complete evaluation of a film, drama, or show that addresses all the information called out in the bulleted list.
Scale: 1 2 3 4 5

Organization Organized into a clear introduction, body, and conclusion, each of which is made up of logical paragraphs that begin with topic sentences and contain appropriate supporting detail.
Scale: 1 2 3 4 5

Accuracy Uses present and past tense forms correctly. Spells words, conjugates verbs, and modifies adjectives correctly throughout.
Scale: 1 2 3 4 5

Creativity Includes additional information that is not requested in the task and/or uses adjectives, descriptive verbs, and additional details to make the composition more interesting.
Scale: 1 2 3 4 5

Scoring

Excellent	18–20 points
Good	14–17 points
Satisfactory	10–13 points
Unsatisfactory	< 10 points

OPTIONS

Avant l'écriture Allow students who may have difficulty with the task to watch a French movie or dramatization of a one-act play together. Give them extra support by supplying some facts about the presentation and then discussing it afterwards with the group. More advanced students who don't need this level of help may either join this group or elect to do the assignment on a piece of their own choosing.

Écriture Supply students with some useful expressions for critiquing a play or film: **À mon avis..., Beaucoup de personnes considèrent (que)/pensent que...., Comme tout le monde le sait..., D'un point de vue artistique/historique..., Selon les critiques...** etc. You may also want to supply a list of adjectives such as **brillant(e), éblouissant(e), réussi(e), avant-gardiste, innovant(e), innovateur/innovatrice, génial(e), surestimé(e), lamentable, médiocre**, and so on.

VOCABULAIRE

Instructional Resources
espaces.vhlcentral.com: Textbook MP3s; IRM (Textbook Audioscript); downloads; reference tools

Suggestion Tell students that an easy way to study from **Vocabulaire** is to cover up the French half of each section, leaving only the English equivalents exposed. They can then quiz themselves on the French items. To focus on the English equivalents of the French entries, they simply reverse this process.

Aller au spectacle

applaudir	*to applaud*
présenter	*to present*
profiter de quelque chose	*to take advantage of/ to enjoy something*
un applaudissement	*applause*
une chanson	*song*
un chœur	*choir, chorus*
une comédie (musicale)	*comedy (musical)*
un concert	*concert*
une danse	*dance*
le début	*beginning; debut*
un entracte	*intermission*
un festival (festivals *pl.*)	*festival*
la fin	*end*
un genre	*genre*
un opéra	*opera*
une pièce de théâtre	*play*
une place	*seat*
une séance	*show; screening*
une sorte	*sort, kind*
un spectateur/ une spectatrice	*spectator*
une tragédie	*tragedy*
gratuit(e)	*free*

Le cinéma et la télévision

un dessin animé	*cartoon*
un documentaire	*documentary*
un drame psychologique	*psychological drama*
une émission (de télévision)	*(television) program*
un feuilleton	*soap opera*
un film (d'aventures, d'horreur, policier, de science-fiction)	*(adventure, horror, crime, science fiction) film*
une histoire	*story*
les informations (infos) (*f.*)	*news*
un jeu télévisé	*game show*
la météo	*weather*
les nouvelles (*f.*)	*news*
un programme	*program*
une publicité (pub)	*advertisement*
les variétés (*f.*)	*popular music*
à la radio	*on the radio*
à la télé(vision)	*on television*

ressources

espaces.vhlcentral.com

Expressions de doute et de certitude

douter que...	*to doubt that...*
ne pas croire que...	*not to believe that...*
ne pas penser que...	*not to think that...*
Il est douteux que...	*It is doubtful that...*
Il est impossible que...	*It is impossible that...*
Il n'est pas certain que...	*It is uncertain that...*
Il n'est pas sûr que...	*It is not sure that...*
Il n'est pas vrai que...	*It is untrue that...*
croire que...	*to believe that...*
penser que...	*to think that...*
savoir que...	*to know that...*
Il est certain que...	*It is certain that...*
Il est clair que...	*It is clear that...*
Il est évident que...	*It is obvious that...*
Il est sûr que...	*It is sure that...*
Il est vrai que...	*It is true that...*

Les artistes

faire de la musique	*to play music*
faire de la peinture	*to paint*
jouer un rôle	*to play a role*
jouer de la batterie/ de la guitare/ du piano/du violon	*to play the drums/ the guitar/the piano/ the violin*
un auteur/ une femme auteur	*author*
un compositeur	*composer*
un danseur/ une danseuse	*dancer*
un dramaturge	*playwright*
un écrivain/ une femme écrivain	*writer*
un membre	*member*
un metteur en scène	*director (of a play, a show)*
un orchestre	*orchestra*
un peintre/ une femme peintre	*painter*
un personnage (principal)	*(main) character*
un poète/ une poétesse	*poet*
un réalisateur/ une réalisatrice	*director (of a movie)*
un sculpteur/ une femme sculpteur	*sculptor*
une troupe	*company, troop*
célèbre	*famous*
doué(e)	*talented; gifted*

Les arts

faire les musées	*to go to museums*
publier	*to publish*
les beaux-arts (*m.*)	*fine arts*
un chef-d'œuvre (chefs-d'œuvre *pl.*)	*masterpiece*
un conte	*tale*
une critique	*review; criticism*
une exposition	*exhibit*
un magazine	*magazine*
une œuvre	*artwork, piece of art*
une peinture	*painting*
un poème	*poem*
un roman	*novel*
une sculpture	*sculpture*
un tableau	*painting*
ancien(ne)	*ancient; old; former*
littéraire	*literary*
récent(e)	*recent*

Conjonctions suivies du subjonctif

à condition que...	*on the condition that..., provided that...*
à moins que...	*unless...*
avant que...	*before...*
jusqu'à ce que...	*until...*
pour que...	*so that...*
sans que...	*without...*

Expressions utiles	*See pp. 513 and 529.*
Possessive pronouns	*See pp. 518–519.*

Le monde francophone

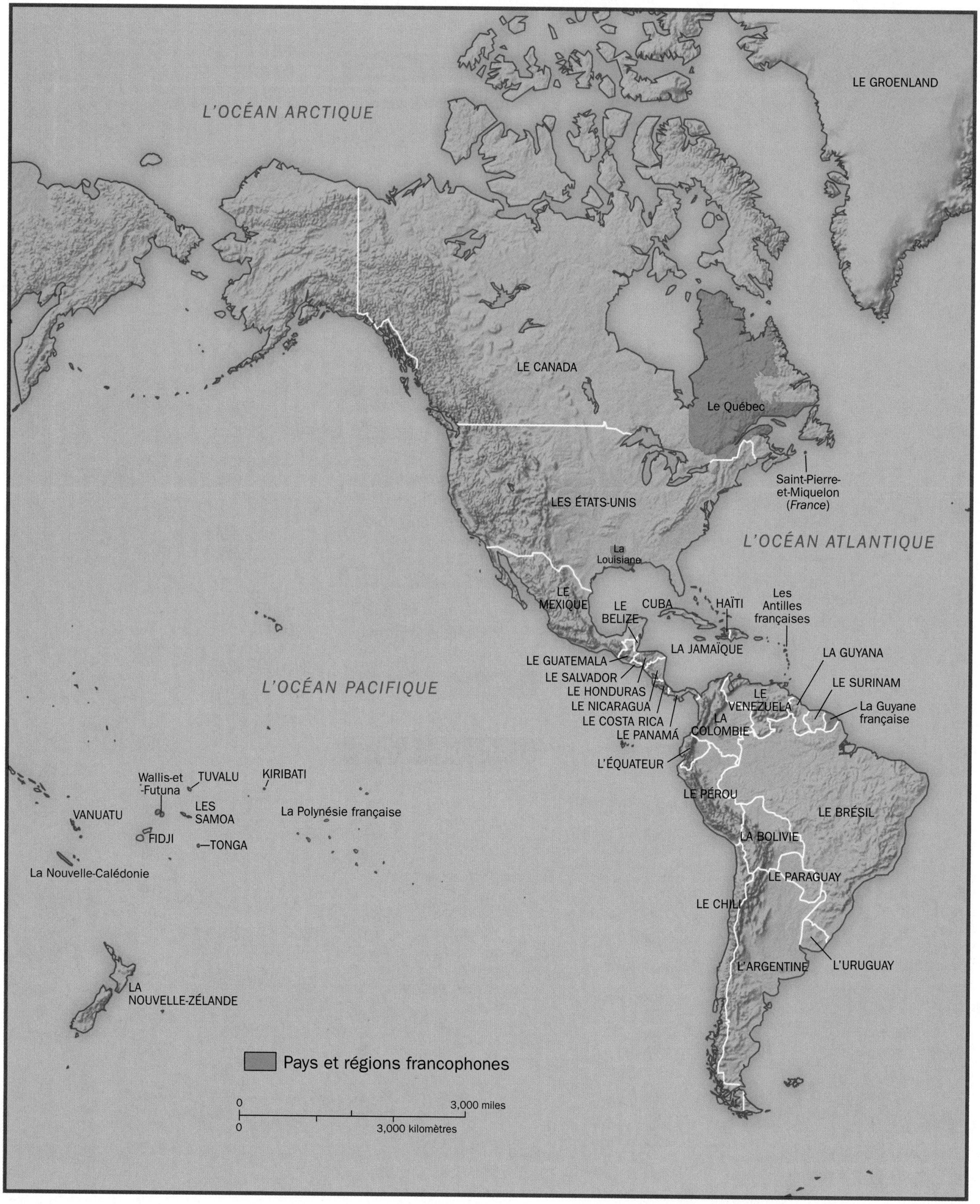
L'OCÉAN ARCTIQUE
LE GROENLAND
LE CANADA
Le Québec
Saint-Pierre-et-Miquelon (France)
LES ÉTATS-UNIS
L'OCÉAN ATLANTIQUE
La Louisiane
LE MEXIQUE
LE BELIZE
CUBA
HAÏTI
Les Antilles françaises
LA JAMAÏQUE
LE GUATEMALA
LE SALVADOR
LE HONDURAS
LE NICARAGUA
LE COSTA RICA
LE PANAMÁ
LA GUYANA
LE SURINAM
La Guyane française
LE VENEZUELA
LA COLOMBIE
L'ÉQUATEUR
LE PÉROU
LE BRÉSIL
LA BOLIVIE
LE PARAGUAY
LE CHILI
L'ARGENTINE
L'URUGUAY
L'OCÉAN PACIFIQUE
Wallis-et-Futuna
TUVALU
KIRIBATI
LES SAMOA
VANUATU
FIDJI
TONGA
La Polynésie française
La Nouvelle-Calédonie
LA NOUVELLE-ZÉLANDE
Pays et régions francophones
0
3,000 miles
0
3,000 kilomètres

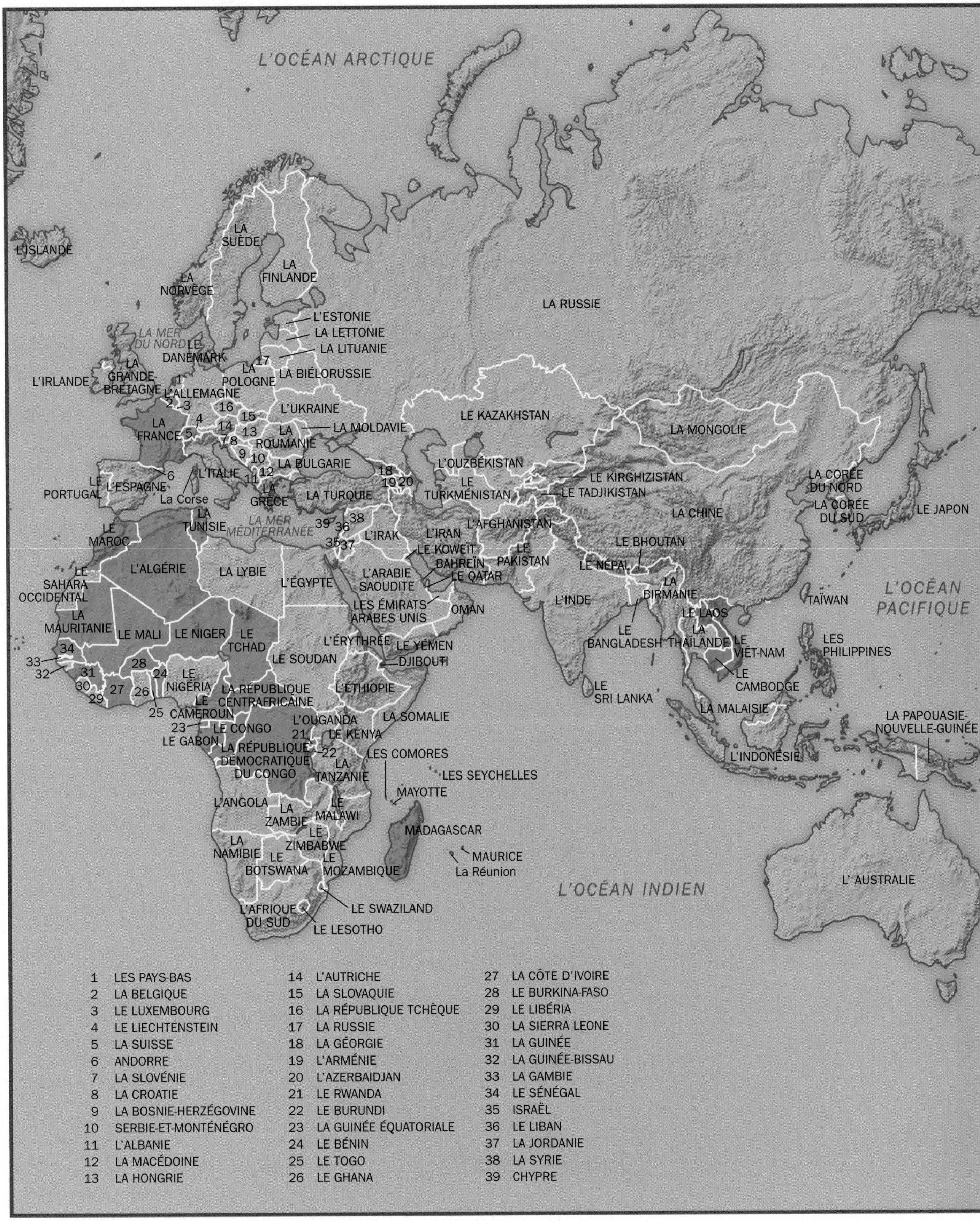

1	LES PAYS-BAS	14	L'AUTRICHE	27	LA CÔTE D'IVOIRE
2	LA BELGIQUE	15	LA SLOVAQUIE	28	LE BURKINA-FASO
3	LE LUXEMBOURG	16	LA RÉPUBLIQUE TCHÈQUE	29	LE LIBÉRIA
4	LE LIECHTENSTEIN	17	LA RUSSIE	30	LA SIERRA LEONE
5	LA SUISSE	18	LA GÉORGIE	31	LA GUINÉE
6	ANDORRE	19	L'ARMÉNIE	32	LA GUINÉE-BISSAU
7	LA SLOVÉNIE	20	L'AZERBAIDJAN	33	LA GAMBIE
8	LA CROATIE	21	LE RWANDA	34	LE SÉNÉGAL
9	LA BOSNIE-HERZÉGOVINE	22	LE BURUNDI	35	ISRAËL
10	SERBIE-ET-MONTÉNÉGRO	23	LA GUINÉE ÉQUATORIALE	36	LE LIBAN
11	L'ALBANIE	24	LE BÉNIN	37	LA JORDANIE
12	LA MACÉDOINE	25	LE TOGO	38	LA SYRIE
13	LA HONGRIE	26	LE GHANA	39	CHYPRE

La France

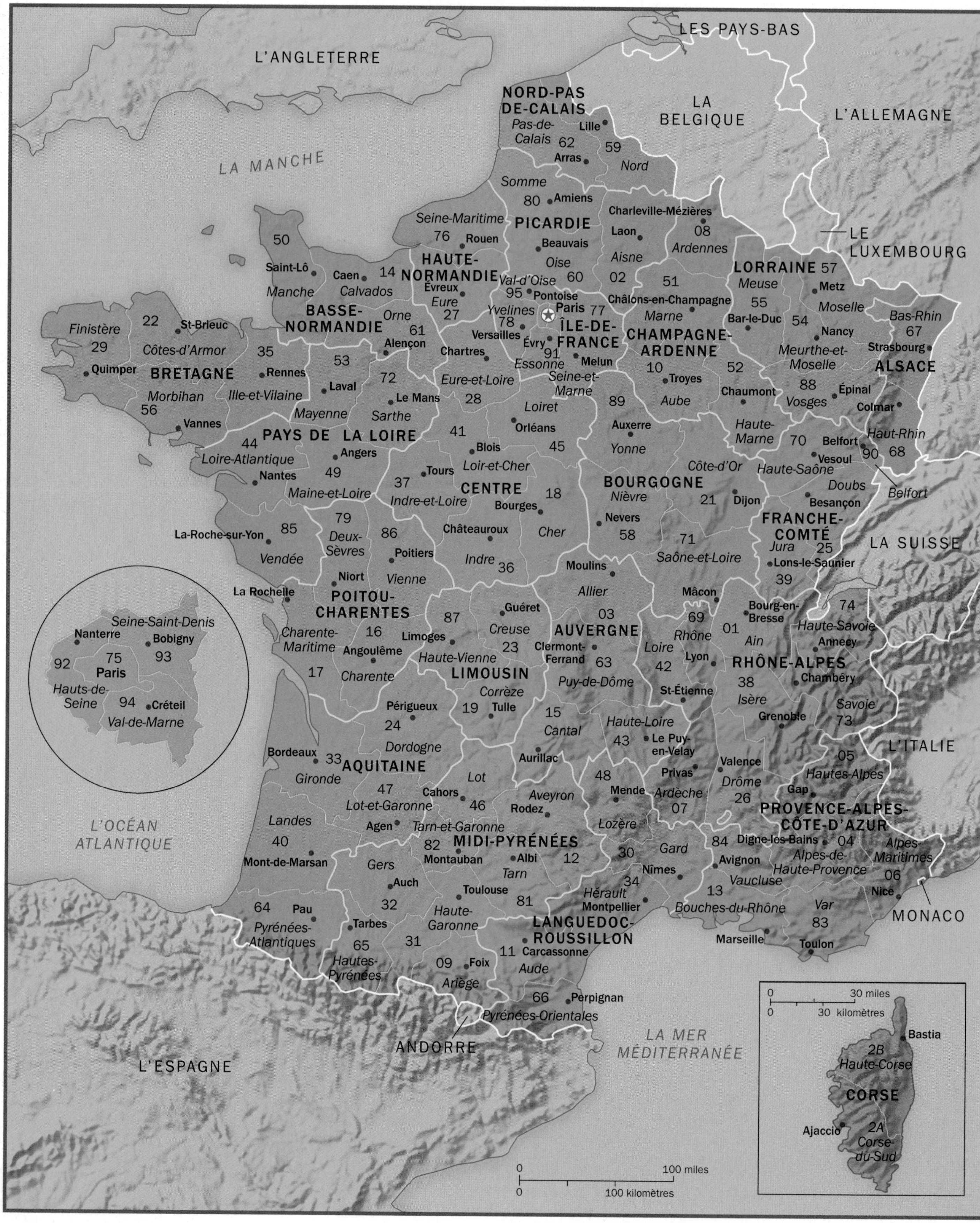

L'ANGLETERRE
LES PAYS-BAS
LA BELGIQUE
L'ALLEMAGNE
LE LUXEMBOURG
LA SUISSE
L'ITALIE
MONACO
ANDORRE
L'ESPAGNE
LA MANCHE
L'OCÉAN ATLANTIQUE
LA MER MÉDITERRANÉE
NORD-PAS DE-CALAIS
Pas-de-Calais 62
Lille
Arras
59 Nord
PICARDIE
Somme 80
Amiens
Oise 60
Beauvais
Aisne 02
Laon
HAUTE-NORMANDIE
Seine-Maritime 76
Rouen
Eure 27
Évreux
BASSE-NORMANDIE
Manche 50
Saint-Lô
Calvados 14
Caen
Orne 61
Alençon
BRETAGNE
Finistère 29
Quimper
Côtes-d'Armor 22
St-Brieuc
Ille-et-Vilaine 35
Rennes
Morbihan 56
Vannes
PAYS DE LA LOIRE
Loire-Atlantique 44
Nantes
Maine-et-Loire 49
Angers
Mayenne 53
Laval
Sarthe 72
Le Mans
Vendée 85
La-Roche-sur-Yon
ÎLE-DE-FRANCE
Val-d'Oise 95
Pontoise
Yvelines 78
Versailles
Paris
77 Seine-et-Marne
Melun
Essonne 91
Évry
CHAMPAGNE-ARDENNE
Ardennes 08
Charleville-Mézières
Marne 51
Châlons-en-Champagne
Aube 10
Troyes
Haute-Marne 52
Chaumont
LORRAINE
Meuse 55
Bar-le-Duc
Moselle 57
Metz
Meurthe-et-Moselle 54
Nancy
Vosges 88
Épinal
ALSACE
Bas-Rhin 67
Strasbourg
Haut-Rhin 68
Colmar
CENTRE
Eure-et-Loire 28
Chartres
Loiret 45
Orléans
Loir-et-Cher 41
Blois
Indre-et-Loire 37
Tours
Cher 18
Bourges
Indre 36
Châteauroux
BOURGOGNE
Yonne 89
Auxerre
Côte-d'Or 21
Dijon
Nièvre 58
Nevers
Saône-et-Loire 71
Mâcon
FRANCHE-COMTÉ
Haute-Saône 70
Vesoul
Doubs 25
Besançon
Jura 39
Lons-le-Saunier
Belfort 90
POITOU-CHARENTES
Deux-Sèvres 79
Niort
Vienne 86
Poitiers
Charente-Maritime 17
La Rochelle
Charente 16
Angoulême
LIMOUSIN
Haute-Vienne 87
Limoges
Creuse 23
Guéret
Corrèze 19
Tulle
AUVERGNE
Allier 03
Moulins
Puy-de-Dôme 63
Clermont-Ferrand
Cantal 15
Aurillac
Haute-Loire 43
Le Puy-en-Velay
RHÔNE-ALPES
Ain 01
Bourg-en-Bresse
Rhône 69
Lyon
Loire 42
St-Étienne
Haute-Savoie 74
Annecy
Savoie 73
Chambéry
Isère 38
Grenoble
Drôme 26
Valence
Ardèche 07
Privas
AQUITAINE
Dordogne 24
Périgueux
Gironde 33
Bordeaux
Lot-et-Garonne 47
Agen
Landes 40
Mont-de-Marsan
Pyrénées-Atlantiques 64
Pau
MIDI-PYRÉNÉES
Lot 46
Cahors
Aveyron 12
Rodez
Tarn-et-Garonne 82
Montauban
Tarn 81
Albi
Gers 32
Auch
Haute-Garonne 31
Toulouse
Hautes-Pyrénées 65
Tarbes
Ariège 09
Foix
LANGUEDOC-ROUSSILLON
Lozère 48
Mende
Gard 30
Nîmes
Hérault 34
Montpellier
Aude 11
Carcassonne
Pyrénées-Orientales 66
Perpignan
PROVENCE-ALPES-CÔTE-D'AZUR
Hautes-Alpes 05
Gap
Alpes-de-Haute-Provence 04
Digne-les-Bains
Alpes-Maritimes 06
Nice
Vaucluse 84
Avignon
Bouches-du-Rhône 13
Marseille
Var 83
Toulon
Seine-Saint-Denis 93
Bobigny
Nanterre
92 Hauts-de-Seine
75 Paris
94 Val-de-Marne
Créteil
CORSE
2B Haute-Corse
Bastia
2A Corse-du-Sud
Ajaccio
0 30 miles
0 30 kilomètres
0 100 miles
0 100 kilomètres

L'Europe

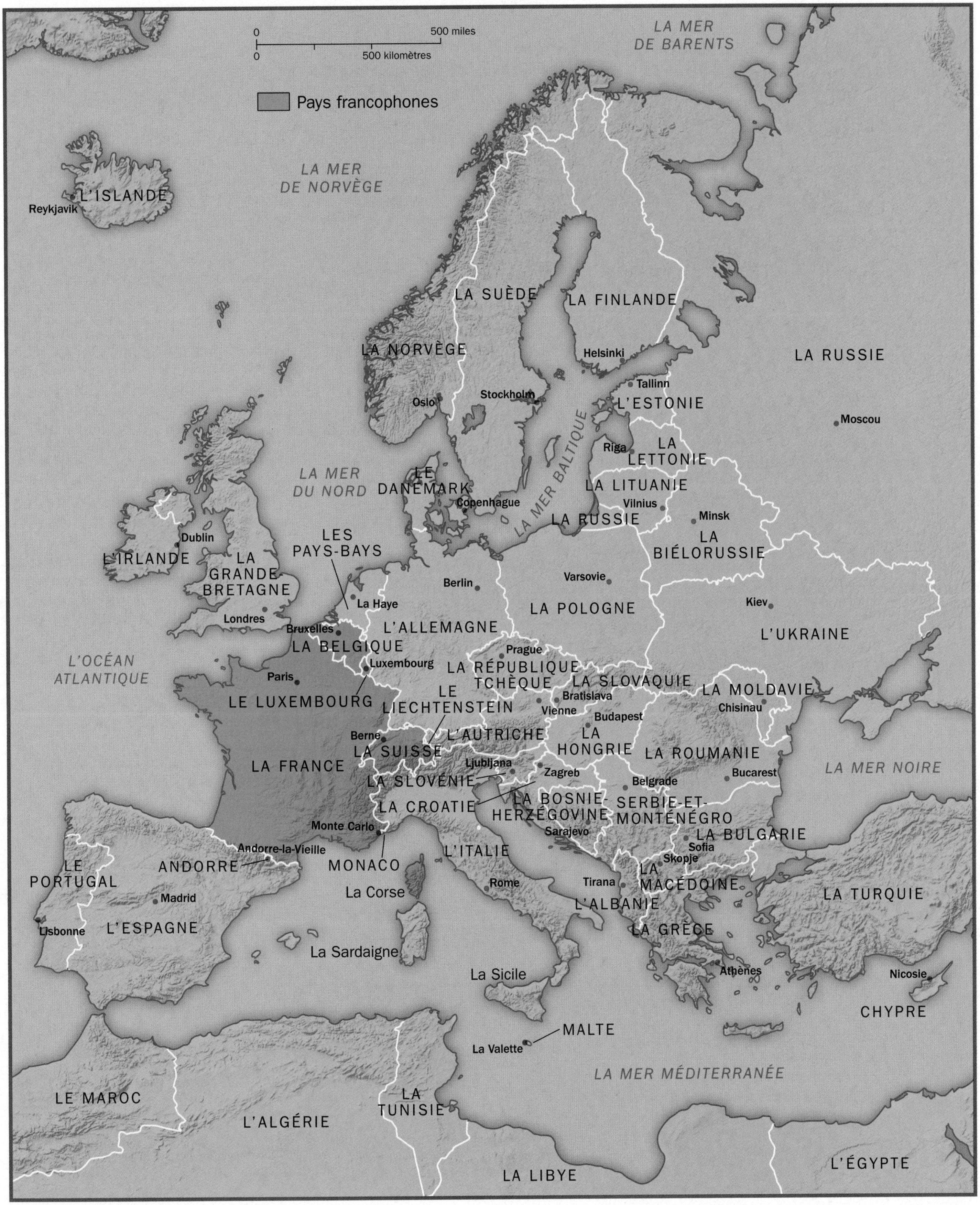

0
500 miles
0
500 kilomètres
Pays francophones
LA MER DE BARENTS
LA MER DE NORVÈGE
L'ISLANDE
Reykjavik
LA SUÈDE
LA FINLANDE
LA NORVÈGE
Helsinki
LA RUSSIE
Tallinn
Stockholm
Oslo
L'ESTONIE
Moscou
LA MER BALTIQUE
Riga
LA LETTONIE
LA MER DU NORD
LE DANEMARK
LA LITUANIE
Copenhague
Vilnius
Minsk
LA RUSSIE
Dublin
LES PAYS-BAYS
LA BIÉLORUSSIE
L'IRLANDE
LA GRANDE-BRETAGNE
Berlin
Varsovie
La Haye
Kiev
LA POLOGNE
Londres
Bruxelles
L'ALLEMAGNE
L'UKRAINE
LA BELGIQUE
Prague
L'OCÉAN ATLANTIQUE
Luxembourg
LA RÉPUBLIQUE TCHÈQUE
Paris
LA SLOVAQUIE
LA MOLDAVIE
LE LIECHTENSTEIN
Bratislava
LE LUXEMBOURG
Vienne
Chisinau
Budapest
Berne
L'AUTRICHE
LA HONGRIE
LA SUISSE
LA ROUMANIE
LA FRANCE
Ljubljana
Zagreb
LA MER NOIRE
Bucarest
LA SLOVÉNIE
Belgrade
LA CROATIE
LA BOSNIE-HERZÉGOVINE
SERBIE-ET-MONTÉNÉGRO
Monte Carlo
Sarajevo
LA BULGARIE
Andorre-la-Vieille
Sofia
L'ITALIE
LE PORTUGAL
ANDORRE
MONACO
Skopje
LA MACÉDOINE
Rome
Tirana
Madrid
La Corse
LA TURQUIE
L'ALBANIE
Lisbonne
L'ESPAGNE
LA GRÈCE
La Sardaigne
Athènes
La Sicile
Nicosie
CHYPRE
MALTE
La Valette
LA MER MÉDITERRANÉE
LE MAROC
LA TUNISIE
L'ALGÉRIE
L'ÉGYPTE
LA LIBYE

L'Afrique

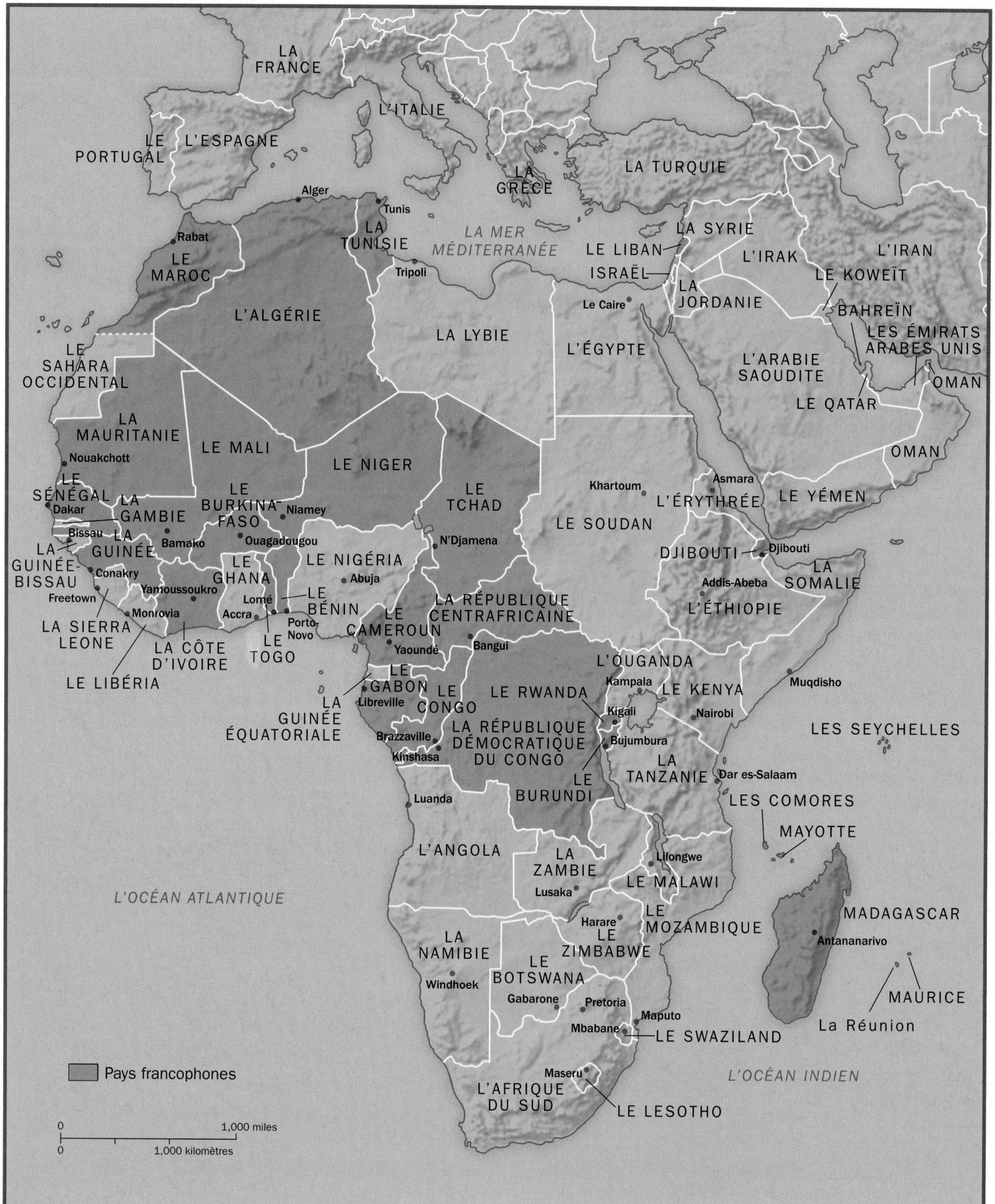
LA FRANCE
L'ITALIE
LE PORTUGAL
L'ESPAGNE
LA GRÈCE
LA TURQUIE
Alger
Tunis
LA TUNISIE
LA MER MÉDITERRANÉE
LA SYRIE
LE LIBAN
ISRAËL
L'IRAK
L'IRAN
Rabat
LE MAROC
Tripoli
LA JORDANIE
LE KOWEÏT
L'ALGÉRIE
Le Caire
BAHREÏN
LA LYBIE
LES ÉMIRATS ARABES UNIS
LE SAHARA OCCIDENTAL
L'ÉGYPTE
L'ARABIE SAOUDITE
OMAN
LE QATAR
LA MAURITANIE
LE MALI
OMAN
Nouakchott
LE NIGER
LE SÉNÉGAL
Dakar
LA GAMBIE
LE BURKINA-FASO
Niamey
LE TCHAD
Khartoum
Asmara
L'ÉRYTHRÉE
LE YÉMEN
LE SOUDAN
Bissau
LA GUINÉE-BISSAU
LA GUINÉE
Bamako
Ouagadougou
N'Djamena
DJIBOUTI
Djibouti
Conakry
LE GHANA
LE NIGÉRIA
LA SOMALIE
Abuja
Addis-Abeba
Freetown
Yamoussoukro
Lomé
LE BÉNIN
LA RÉPUBLIQUE CENTRAFRICAINE
L'ÉTHIOPIE
LA SIERRA LEONE
Monrovia
Accra
Porto-Novo
LE CAMEROUN
LE TOGO
LA CÔTE D'IVOIRE
Yaoundé
Bangui
LE LIBÉRIA
L'OUGANDA
LE GABON
Kampala
Muqdisho
LA GUINÉE ÉQUATORIALE
Libreville
LE CONGO
LE RWANDA
LE KENYA
Kigali
Nairobi
Brazzaville
LA RÉPUBLIQUE DÉMOCRATIQUE DU CONGO
LES SEYCHELLES
Bujumbura
Kinshasa
LA TANZANIE
Dar es-Salaam
LE BURUNDI
Luanda
LES COMORES
MAYOTTE
L'ANGOLA
LA ZAMBIE
Lilongwe
L'OCÉAN ATLANTIQUE
LE MALAWI
Lusaka
MADAGASCAR
Harare
LE MOZAMBIQUE
LE ZIMBABWE
LA NAMIBIE
Antananarivo
LE BOTSWANA
Windhoek
MAURICE
Gabarone
Pretoria
Maputo
La Réunion
Mbabane
LE SWAZILAND
Pays francophones
Maseru
L'OCÉAN INDIEN
L'AFRIQUE DU SUD
LE LESOTHO
0
1,000 miles
0
1,000 kilomètres

L'Amérique du Nord et du Sud

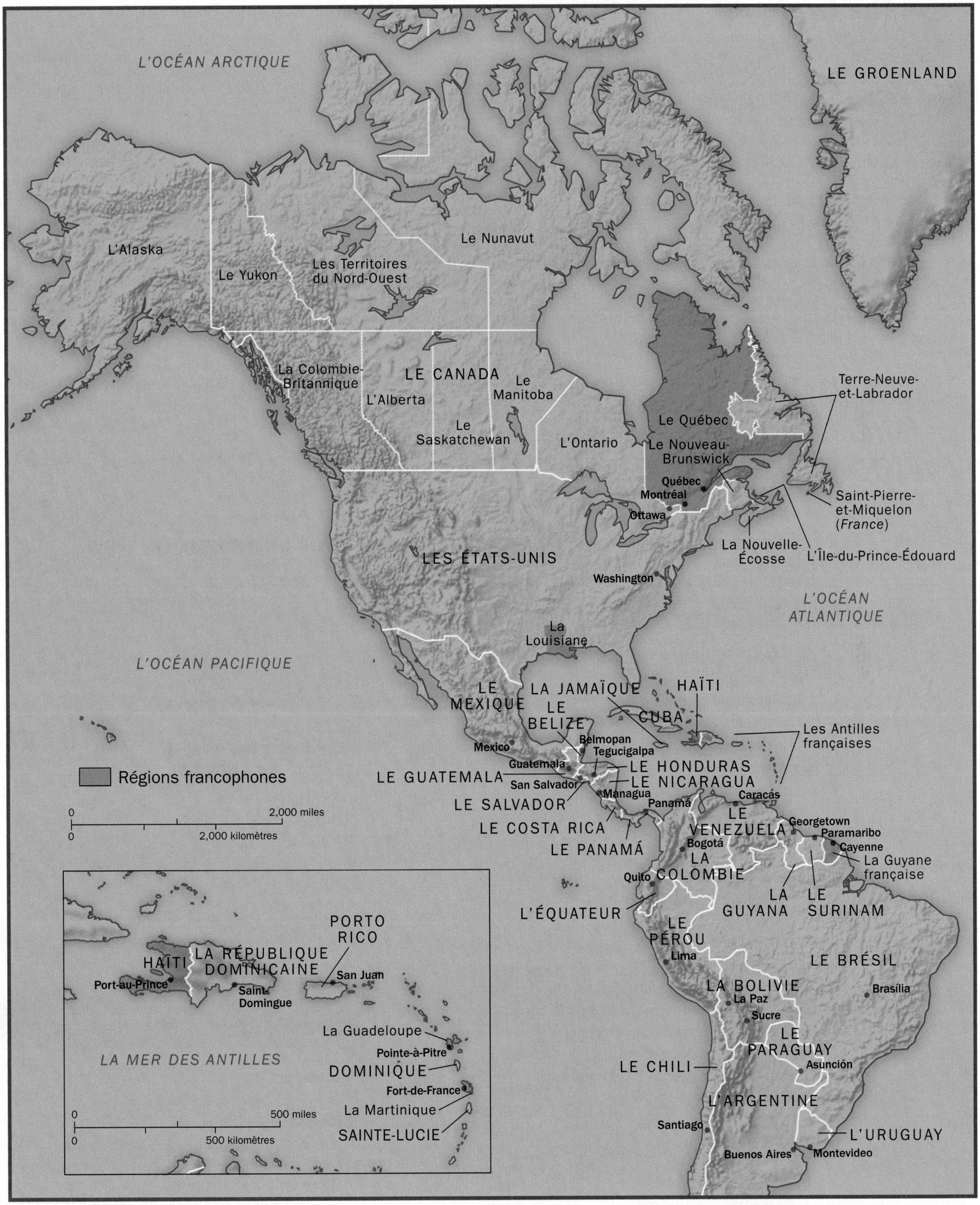
L'OCÉAN ARCTIQUE
LE GROENLAND
L'Alaska
Le Yukon
Les Territoires du Nord-Ouest
Le Nunavut
La Colombie-Britannique
LE CANADA
L'Alberta
Le Saskatchewan
Le Manitoba
L'Ontario
Le Québec
Le Nouveau-Brunswick
Terre-Neuve-et-Labrador
Québec
Montréal
Ottawa
Saint-Pierre-et-Miquelon (France)
La Nouvelle-Écosse
L'Île-du-Prince-Édouard
LES ÉTATS-UNIS
Washington
L'OCÉAN ATLANTIQUE
La Louisiane
L'OCÉAN PACIFIQUE
LE MEXIQUE
LA JAMAÏQUE
HAÏTI
LE BELIZE
CUBA
Les Antilles françaises
Mexico
Belmopan
Tegucigalpa
Guatemala
LE HONDURAS
LE GUATEMALA
San Salvador
LE NICARAGUA
Managua
LE SALVADOR
Panamá
Caracas
LE COSTA RICA
LE PANAMÁ
LE VENEZUELA
Georgetown
Paramaribo
Cayenne
La Guyane française
Bogotá
LA COLOMBIE
Quito
L'ÉQUATEUR
LA GUYANA
LE SURINAM
LE PÉROU
Lima
LE BRÉSIL
Brasília
LA BOLIVIE
La Paz
Sucre
LE PARAGUAY
Asunción
LE CHILI
L'ARGENTINE
Santiago
Buenos Aires
Montevideo
L'URUGUAY
Régions francophones
0 2,000 miles
0 2,000 kilomètres
PORTO RICO
HAÏTI
LA RÉPUBLIQUE DOMINICAINE
San Juan
Port-au-Prince
Saint-Domingue
La Guadeloupe
Pointe-à-Pitre
LA MER DES ANTILLES
DOMINIQUE
Fort-de-France
La Martinique
SAINTE-LUCIE
0 500 miles
0 500 kilomètres

The *impératif*

The **impératif** is the form of a verb that is used to give commands or to offer directions, hints, and suggestions. With command forms, you do not use subject pronouns.

- Form the **tu** command of **-er** verbs by dropping the **-s** from the present tense form. Note that **aller** also follows this pattern.

Réserve deux chambres.	**Ne travaille pas.**	**Va** au marché.
Reserve two rooms.	*Don't work.*	*Go to the market.*

- The **nous** and **vous** command forms of **-er** verbs are the same as the present tense forms.

Nettoyez votre chambre.	**Mangeons** au restaurant ce soir.
Clean your room.	*Let's eat at the restaurant tonight.*

- For **-ir** verbs, **-re** verbs, and most irregular verbs, the command forms are identical to the present tense forms.

Finis la salade.	**Attendez** dix minutes.	**Faisons** du yoga.
Finish the salad.	*Wait ten minutes.*	*Let's do some yoga.*

- The forms of **avoir** and **être** in the **impératif** are irregular.

avoir	**(tu) aie**	**(nous) ayons**	**(vous) ayez**
être	**(tu) sois**	**(nous) soyons**	**(vous) soyez**

Aie confiance.	Ne **soyons** pas en retard.
Have confidence.	*Let's not be late.*

- An object pronoun can be added to the end of an affirmative command. Use a hyphen to separate them. Use **moi** and **toi** for the first- and second-person object pronouns.

Permettez-moi de vous aider.	Achète le dictionnaire et **utilise-le**.
Allow me to help you.	*Buy the dictionary and use it.*

- In negative commands, place object pronouns between **ne** and the verb. Use **me** and **te** for the first- and second-person object pronouns.

Ne **me montre** pas les réponses.	Ne **la touchez** pas.
Please don't show me the answers.	*Don't touch it.*

French Terms for Direction Lines and Classroom Use

Mots utiles *Useful words*

une affirmation	*statement, sentence*
une brochure	*brochure*
un brouillon	*draft*
un but	*purpose, goal*
le contenu	*content*
une conversation	*conversation*
le début	*beginning*
le(s) devoir(s)	*homework*
une enquête	*survey*
une étape	*step*
un indice, une piste	*clue*
la lecture	*reading*
un nom	*name*
l'orthographe	*spelling*
un(e) partenaire	*partner*
un personnage	*a character*
la/les personne(s) décrite(s)	*person (people) described*
une phrase complète	*complete sentence*
un point de départ	*starting point*
le prochain examen	*next test*
une pub/publicité	*ad/advertisement; commercial*
une question	*question*
le rapport	*report*
les ressources	*resources*
un sondage	*opinion poll*
la suite	*ending*
le tableau	*blackboard*
un thème, un sujet	*topic*
dans lequel/laquelle/lesquel(le)s	*in which*
par exemple	*for example*
avant	*before*
chaque	*each*
d'abord	*first*
dernier	*last*
efficace	*efficient*
ensemble	*together*
maintenant	*now*

Pour parler à vos camarades de classe *To talk with your classmates*

C'est ton tour./C'est mon tour.	*It's your/my turn.*
Épelez./Épelle.	*Spell.*
Je commence./Tu commences.	*I start./You start.*
Je suis d'accord/pas d'accord avec toi.	*I agree/disagree with you.*
Ne me dis pas la réponse.	*Don't tell me the answer.*
Veux-tu travailler avec moi?	*Do you want to work with me?*

Verbes utiles *Useful verbs*

ajouter	*to add*
combiner	*to combine*
converser	*to talk; to chat*
créer	*to create*
demander	*to ask*
deviner	*to guess*
dire	*to say*
discuter	*to talk; to discuss*
échanger	*to exchange*
écrire	*to write*
essayer	*to try*
inclure	*to include*
justifier	*to justify*
noter	*to jot down*
raconter	*to tell, to relate (a story)*
relier	*to link*
remplacer	*to replace*
souligner	*to underline*
suivre	*to follow*
traduire	*to translate*
utiliser	*to use*
vérifier	*to check*

Expressions utiles *Useful expressions*

Allez à la page 2.	*Go to page 2.*
Alternez les rôles.	*Switch roles.*
À tour de rôle...	*Take turns...*
À voix haute	*Aloud*
À votre/ton avis	*In your opinion*
Après une deuxième écoute...	*After a second listening...*
Articulez.	*Enunciate.; Pronounce carefully.*
Au sujet de, À propos de	*Regarding, about*
Avec un(e) partenaire/ un(e) camarade de classe	*With a partner/a classmate*
Avez-vous/As-tu des questions?	*Do you have any questions?*
Avez-vous/As-tu fini/terminé?	*Are you done?; Have you finished?*
Chassez l'intrus.	*Choose the item that doesn't belong.*
Choisissez le bon mot.	*Choose the right word.*
Circulez dans la classe.	*Walk around the classroom.*
Comment dit-on ____ en français?	*How do you say ____ in French?*
Comment écrit-on ____ en français?	*How do you spell ____ in French?*
Corrigez les phrases fausses.	*Correct the false statements.*
Créez/Formez des phrases...	*Create/Form sentences...*
D'après vous/Selon vous...	*According to you...*
Décrivez les images/dessins...	*Describe the images/ drawings...*
Désolé(e), j'ai oublié.	*I'm sorry, I forgot.*
Déterminez si...	*Decide whether...*
Dites si vous êtes/Dis si tu es d'accord ou non.	*Say if you agree or not.*
Écrivez une lettre/une phrase.	*Write a letter/a sentence.*
Employez les verbes de la liste.	*Use the verbs from the list.*
En utilisant...	*Using...*
Est-ce que vous pouvez/ tu peux choisir un(e) autre partenaire/ quelqu'un d'autre?	*Can you please choose another partner/ someone else?*
Êtes vous prêt(e)?/ Es-tu prêt(e)?	*Are you ready?*
Excusez-moi, je suis en retard.	*Excuse me for being late.*
Faites correspondre...	*Match...*
Faites les accords nécessaires.	*Make the necessary agreements.*
Félicitations!	*Congratulations!*
Indiquez le mot qui n'appartient pas.	*Indicate the word that doesn't belong.*
Indiquez qui a dit...	*Indicate who said...*
J'ai gagné!/Nous avons gagné!	*I won!/We won!*
Je n'ai pas/Nous n'avons pas encore fini.	*I/We have not finished yet.*
Je ne comprends pas.	*I don't understand.*
Je ne sais pas.	*I don't know.*
Je ne serai pas là demain.	*I won't be here tomorrow.*
Je peux continuer?	*May I continue?*
Jouez le rôle de.../la scène...	*Play the role of.../the scene...*
Lentement, s'il vous plaît.	*Slowly, please.*
Lisez...	*Read...*
Mettez dans l'ordre...	*Put in order...*
Ouvrez/Fermez votre livre.	*Open/Close your books.*
Par groupes de trois/quatre...	*In groups of three/four...*
Partagez vos résultats...	*Share your results...*
Posez-vous les questions suivantes.	*Ask each other the following questions.*
Pour demain, faites...	*For tomorrow, do...*
Pour demain, vous allez/ tu vas faire...	*Tomorrow you are going to do...*
Prononcez.	*Pronounce.*
Qu'est-ce que ____ veut dire?	*What does ____ mean?*
Que pensez-vous/penses-tu de...	*What do you think about...*
Qui a gagné?	*Who won?*
...qui convient le mieux.	*...that best completes/is the most appropriate.*
Rejoignez un autre groupe.	*Get together with another group.*
Remplissez les espaces.	*Fill in the blanks.*
Répondez aux questions suivantes.	*Answer the following questions.*
Soyez prêt(e)s à...	*Be ready to...*
Venez/Viens au tableau.	*Come to the board.*
Vous comprenez?/ Tu comprends?	*Do you understand?*
Vous pouvez expliquer encore une fois, s'il vous plaît?	*Could you explain again, please?*
Vous pouvez répéter, s'il vous plaît?	*Could you repeat that, please?*
Vrai ou faux?	*True or false?*

Glossary of Grammatical Terms

ADJECTIVE A word that modifies, or describes, a noun or pronoun.

des livres **amusants** *some **funny** books*	un homme **grand** *a **tall** man*
de **jolies** fleurs *some **pretty** flowers*	

Demonstrative adjective An adjective that specifies which noun a speaker is referring to.

cette chemise ***this** shirt*	**ce** placard ***this** closet*
cet hôtel ***this** hotel*	**ces** boîtes ***these** boxes*

Possessive adjective An adjective that indicates ownership or possession.

ma belle montre ***my** beautiful watch*	C'est **son** cousin. *This is **his/her** cousin.*
tes crayons ***your** pencils*	Ce sont **leurs** tantes. *Those are **their** aunts.*

ADVERB A word that modifies, or describes, a verb, adjective, or other adverb.

Michael parle **couramment** français.
*Michael speaks French **fluently**.*

Ces enfants sont **vraiment** intelligents.
*These children are **really** smart.*

Elle lui parle **très** franchement.
*She speaks to him **very** candidly.*

ARTICLE A word that points out a noun in either a specific or a non-specific way.

Definite article An article that points out a noun in a specific way.

le marché ***the** market*	**la** valise ***the** suitcase*
les dictionnaires ***the** dictionaries*	**les** mots ***the** words*

Indefinite article An article that points out a noun in a general, non-specific way.

un vélo ***a** bike*	**une** fille ***a** girl*
des oiseaux ***some** birds*	**des** affiches ***some** posters*

CLAUSE A group of words that contains both a conjugated verb and a subject, either expressed or implied.

Main (or Independent) clause A clause that can stand alone as a complete sentence.

J'ai un manteau vert.
I have a green coat.

Subordinate (or Dependent) clause A clause that does not express a complete thought and therefore cannot stand alone as a sentence.

Je travaille dans un restaurant **parce que j'ai besoin d'argent**.
*I work in a restaurant **because I need money.***

COMPARATIVE A construction used with an adjective or adverb to express a comparison between two people, places, or things.

Thomas est **plus petit** qu'Adrien.
*Thomas is **shorter than** Adrien.*

En Corse, il pleut **moins souvent qu'**en Alsace.
*In Corsica, it rains **less often than** in Alsace.*

Cette maison n'a pas **autant de fenêtres** que l'autre.
*This house does not have **as many windows as** the other one.*

CONJUGATION A set of the forms of a verb for a specific tense or mood, or the process by which these verb forms are presented.

Imparfait conjugation of **chanter**:

je chant**ais**	nous chant**ions**
tu chant**ais**	vous chant**iez**
il/elle chant**ait**	ils/elles chant**aient**

CONJUNCTION A word used to connect words, clauses, or phrases.

Suzanne **et** Pierre habitent en Suisse.
*Suzanne **and** Pierre live in Switzerland.*

Je ne dessine pas très bien, **mais** j'aime les cours de dessin.
*I don't draw very well, **but** I like art classes.*

CONTRACTION The joining of two words into one. In French, the contractions are **au**, **aux**, **du**, and **des**.

Ma sœur est allée **au** concert hier soir.
*My sister went **to a** concert last night.*

Il a parlé **aux** voisins cet après-midi.
*He talked **to the** neighbors this afternoon.*

Je retire de l'argent **du** distributeur automatique.
*I withdraw money **from the** ATM machine.*

Nous avons campé près **du** village.
*We camped **near the** village.*

DIRECT OBJECT A noun or pronoun that directly receives the action of the verb.

Thomas lit **un livre**.	Je **l'**ai vu hier.
*Thomas reads **a book**.*	*I saw **him** yesterday.*

GENDER The grammatical categorizing of certain kinds of words, such as nouns and pronouns, as masculine, feminine, or neuter.

Masculine
articles **le, un**
pronouns **il, lui, le, celui-ci, celui-là, lequel**
adjective **élégant**

Feminine
articles **la, une**
pronouns **elle, la, celle-ci, celle-là, laquelle**
adjective **élégante**

IMPERSONAL EXPRESSION A third-person expression with no expressed or specific subject.

Il pleut.	**C'est** très important.
***It's raining**.*	***It's** very important.*

INDIRECT OBJECT A noun or pronoun that receives the action of the verb indirectly; the object, often a living being, to or for whom an action is performed.

Éric donne un livre **à Linda**.
*Éric gave a book **to Linda**.*

Le professeur **m'**a donné une bonne note.
*The teacher gave **me** a good mark.*

INFINITIVE The basic form of a verb. Infinitives in French end in **-er**, **-ir**, **-oir**, or **-re**.

parler	**finir**	**savoir**	**prendre**
to speak	*to finish*	*to know*	*to take*

INTERROGATIVE An adjective or pronoun used to ask a question.

Qui parle?
***Who** is speaking?*

Combien de biscuits as-tu achetés?
***How many** cookies did you buy?*

Que penses-tu faire aujourd'hui?
***What** do you plan to do today?*

INVERSION Changing the word order of a sentence, often to form a question.

Statement: Elle a vendu sa voiture.

Inversion: A-t-elle vendu sa voiture?

MOOD A grammatical distinction of verbs that indicates whether the verb is intended to make a statement or command or to express a doubt, emotion, or condition contrary to fact.

Conditional mood Verb forms used to express what would be done or what would happen under certain circumstances, or to make a polite request, soften a demand, express what someone could or should do, or to state a contrary-to-fact situation.

Il irait se promener s'il avait le temps.
***He would go** for a walk if he had the time.*

Pourrais-tu éteindre la lumière, s'il te plaît?
***Would you** turn off the light, please?*

Je devrais lui parler gentiment.
***I should** talk to her nicely.*

Imperative mood Verb forms used to make commands or suggestions.

Parle lentement.	**Venez** avec moi.
***Speak** slowly.*	***Come** with me.*

Indicative mood Verb forms used to state facts, actions, and states considered to be real.

Je sais qu'**il a** un chat.
***I know** that **he has** a cat.*

Subjunctive mood Verb forms used principally in subordinate (dependent) clauses to express wishes, desires, emotions, doubts, and certain conditions, such as contrary-to-fact situations.

Il est important que **tu finisses** tes devoirs.
*It's important that **you finish** your homework.*

Je doute que **Louis ait** assez d'argent.
*I doubt that **Louis has** enough money.*

NOUN A word that identifies people, animals, places, things, and ideas.

homme *man*	**chat** *cat*
Belgique *Belgium*	**maison** *house*
amitié *friendship*	**livre** *book*

NUMBER A grammatical term that refers to singular or plural. Nouns in French and English have number. Other parts of a sentence, such as adjectives, articles, and verbs, can also have number.

Singular	Plural
une chose ***a** thing*	**des** choses ***some** things*
le professeur ***the** professor*	**les** professeurs ***the** professors*

NUMBERS Words that represent amounts.

Cardinal numbers Words that show specific amounts.

cinq minutes
***five** minutes*

l'année **deux mille six**
*the year **2006***

Ordinal numbers Words that indicate the order of a noun in a series.

le **quatrième** joueur *the **fourth** player*	la **dixième** fois *the **tenth** time*

PAST PARTICIPLE A past form of the verb used in compound tenses. The past participle may also be used as an adjective, but it must then agree in number and gender with the word it modifies.

Ils ont beaucoup **marché**.
*They have **walked** a lot.*

Je n'ai pas **préparé** mon examen.
*I haven't **prepared** for my exam.*

Il y a une fenêtre **ouverte** dans le salon.
*There is an **open** window in the living room.*

PERSON The form of the verb or pronoun that indicates the speaker, the one spoken to, or the one spoken about. In French, as in English, there are three persons: first, second, and third.

Person	Singular	Plural
1st	**je** *I*	**nous** *we*
2nd	**tu** *you*	**vous** *you*
3rd	**il/elle** *he/she/it* **on** *one*	**ils/elles** *they*

PREPOSITION A word or words that describe(s) the relationship, most often in time or space, between two other words.

Annie habite **loin de** Paris.
*Annie lives **far from** Paris.*

Le blouson est **dans** la voiture.
*The jacket is **in** the car.*

Martine s'est coiffée **avant de** sortir.
*Martine combed her hair **before** going out.*

PRONOUN A word that takes the place of a noun or nouns.

Demonstrative pronoun A pronoun that takes the place of a specific noun.

Je veux **celui-ci**.
*I want **this one**.*

Vas-tu acheter **celle-là**?
*Are you going to buy **that one**?*

Marc préférait **ceux-là**.
*Marc preferred **those**.*

Object pronoun A pronoun that functions as a direct or indirect object of the verb.

Elle **lui** donne un cadeau.
*She gives **him** a present.*

Frédéric **me l'**a apporté.
*Frédéric brought **it** to **me**.*

Reflexive pronoun A pronoun that indicates that the action of a verb is performed by the subject on itself. These pronouns are often expressed in English with *-self*: *myself*, *yourself*, etc.

Je **me lave** avant de sortir.
*I **wash (myself)** before going out.*

Marie **s'est couchée** à onze heures et demie.
*Marie **went to bed** at eleven-thirty.*

Relative pronoun A pronoun that connects a subordinate clause to a main clause.

Le garçon **qui** nous a écrit vient nous voir demain.
*The boy **who** wrote us is coming to visit tomorrow.*

Je sais **que** nous avons beaucoup de choses à faire.
*I know **that** we have a lot of things to do.*

Subject pronoun A pronoun that replaces the name or title of a person or thing, and acts as the subject of a verb.

Tu vas partir bientôt.
***You** are going to leave soon.*

Il arrive demain.
***He** arrives tomorrow.*

SUBJECT A noun or pronoun that performs the action of a verb and is often implied by the verb.

Marine va au supermarché.
***Marine** goes to the supermarket.*

Ils travaillent beaucoup.
***They** work a lot.*

Ces livres sont très chers.
***Those books** are very expensive.*

SUPERLATIVE A word or construction used with an adjective, adverb or a noun to express the highest or lowest degree of a specific quality among three or more people, places, or things.

Le cours de français est **le plus intéressant**.
*The French class is **the most interesting**.*

Romain est le garçon qui court **le moins rapidement**.
*Romain is the boy who runs **the least fast**.*

C'est son jardin qui a **le plus d'arbres**.
*It is her garden that has **the most trees**.*

TENSE A set of verb forms that indicates the time of an action or state: past, present, or future.

Compound tense A two-word tense made up of an auxiliary verb and a present or past participle. In French, there are two auxiliary verbs: **être** and **avoir**.

Le colis n'**est** pas encore **arrivé**.
*The package **has** not **arrived** yet.*

Elle **a réussi** son examen.
*She **has passed** her exam.*

Simple tense A tense expressed by a single verb form.

Timothée **jouait** au volley-ball pendant les vacances.
*Timothée **played** volleyball during his vacation.*

Joëlle **parlera** à sa mère demain.
*Joëlle **will speak** with her mom tomorrow.*

VERB A word that expresses actions or states-of-being.

Auxiliary verb A verb used with a present or past participle to form a compound tense. **Avoir** is the most commonly used auxiliary verb in French.

Les enfants **ont** vu les éléphants.
*The children **have** seen the elephants.*

J'espère que tu **as** mangé.
*I hope you **have** eaten.*

Reflexive verb A verb that describes an action performed by the subject on itself and is always used with a reflexive pronoun.

Je **me suis acheté** une voiture neuve.
*I **bought myself** a new car.*

Pierre et Adeline **se lèvent** très tôt.
*Pierre and Adeline **get (themselves) up** very early.*

Spelling-change verb A verb that undergoes a predictable change in spelling in the various conjugations.

acheter	e → è	nous achetons	j'ach**è**te
espérer	é → è	nous espérons	j'esp**è**re
appeler	l → ll	nous appelons	j'appe**ll**e
envoyer	y → i	nous envoyons	j'envo**i**e
essayer	y → i	nous essayons	j'essa**i**e/ j'essa**y**e

Verb Conjugation Tables

The list of verbs below and the model verb tables that start on page 561 show you how to conjugate the verbs that appear in **ESPACES**. Each verb in the list is followed by a model verb conjugated according to the same pattern. The number in parentheses indicates where in the verb tables you can find the conjugated forms of the model verb. For example, if you want to find out how to conjugate the verb **offrir**, look up number 31 to refer to its model verb, **ouvrir**. The phrase **p.c.** with **être** after a verb means that it is conjugated with **être** in the **passé composé**. Reminder: All reflexive (pronominal) verbs use **être** as their auxiliary verb in the **passé composé**. The infinitives of reflexive verbs begin with **se** (**s'**).

In the tables you will find the infinitive, past participles, and all the forms of each model verb you have learned.

abolir like finir (2)
aborder like parler (1)
abriter like parler (1)
accepter like parler (1)
accompagner like parler (1)
accueillir like ouvrir (31)
acheter (7)
adorer like parler (1)
afficher like parler (1)
aider like parler (1)
aimer like parler (1)
aller (13); **p.c.** with **être**
allumer like parler (1)
améliorer like parler (1)
amener like acheter (7)
animer like parler (1)
apercevoir like recevoir (36)
appeler (8)
applaudir like finir (2)
apporter like parler (1)
apprendre like prendre (35)
arrêter like parler (1)
arriver like parler (1) *except* **p.c.** with **être**
assister like parler (1)
attacher like parler (1)
attendre like vendre (3)
attirer like parler (1)
avoir (4)
balayer like essayer (10)
bavarder like parler (1)
boire (15)
bricoler like parler (1)
bronzer like parler (1)
célébrer like préférer (12)
chanter like parler (1)
chasser like parler (1)
chercher like parler (1)
choisir like finir (2)
classer like parler (1)
commander like parler (1)
commencer (9)
composer like parler (1)
comprendre like prendre (35)
compter like parler (1)
conduire (16)
connaître (17)
consacrer like parler (1)
considérer like préférer (12)
construire like conduire (16)
continuer like parler (1)
courir (18)
coûter like parler (1)
couvrir like ouvrir (31)
croire (19)
cuisiner like parler (1)
danser like parler (1)
débarrasser like parler (1)
décider like parler (1)
découvrir like ouvrir (31)
décrire like écrire (22)
décrocher like parler (1)
déjeuner like parler (1)
demander like parler (1)
démarrer like parler (1)
déménager like manger (11)
démissionner like parler (1)
dépasser like parler (1)
dépendre like vendre (3)
dépenser like parler (1)
déposer like parler (1)
descendre like vendre (3) *except* **p.c.** with **être; p.c.** w/**avoir** if takes a direct object
désirer like parler (1)
dessiner like parler (1)
détester like parler (1)
détruire like conduire (16)
développer like parler (1)
devenir like venir (41); **p.c.** with **être**
devoir (20)
dîner like parler (1)
dire (21)
diriger like parler (1)
discuter like parler (1)
divorcer like commencer (9)
donner like parler (1)
dormir like partir (32) *except* **p.c.** with **avoir**
douter like parler (1)
durer like parler (1)
échapper like parler (1)
échouer like parler (1)
écouter like parler (1)
écrire (22)
effacer like commencer (9)
embaucher like parler (1)
emménager like manger (11)
emmener like acheter (7)
employer like essayer (10)

emprunter like parler (1)
enfermer like parler (1)
enfler like parler (1)
enlever like acheter (7)
enregistrer like parler (1)
enseigner like parler (1)
entendre like vendre (3)
entourer like parler (1)
entrer like parler (1) *except* **p.c.** with **être**
entretenir like tenir (40)
envahir like finir (2)
envoyer like essayer (10)
épouser like parler (1)
espérer like préférer (12)
essayer (10)
essuyer like essayer (10)
éteindre (24)
éternuer like parler (1)
étrangler like parler (1)
être (5)
étudier like parler (1)
éviter like parler (1)
exiger like manger (11)
expliquer like parler (1)
explorer like parler (1)
faire (25)
falloir (26)
fermer like parler (1)
fêter like parler (1)
finir (2)
fonctionner like parler (1)
fonder like parler (1)
freiner like parler (1)
fréquenter like parler (1)
fumer like parler (1)
gagner like parler (1)
garder like parler (1)
garer like parler (1)
gaspiller like parler (1)
goûter like parler (1)
graver like parler (1)
grossir like finir (2)
guérir like finir (2)
habiter like parler (1)
imprimer like parler (1)
indiquer like parler (1)
interdire like dire (21)
inviter like parler (1)
jeter like appeler (8)
jouer like parler (1)
laisser like parler (1)
laver like parler (1)
lire (27)
loger like manger (11)
louer like parler (1)
lutter like parler (1)
maigrir like finir (2)
maintenir like tenir (40)
manger (11)
marcher like parler (1)
mêler like préférer (12)
mener like parler (1)
mettre (28)
monter like parler (1) *except* **p.c.** with **être**; **p.c.** w/**avoir** if takes a direct object
montrer like parler (1)
mourir (29); **p.c.** with **être**
nager like manger (11)
naître (30); **p.c.** with **être**
nettoyer like essayer (10)
noter like parler (1)
obtenir like tenir (40)
offrir like ouvrir (31)
organiser like parler (1)
oublier like parler (1)
ouvrir (31)
parler (1)
partager like manger (11)
partir (32); **p.c.** with **être**
passer like parler (1)
patienter like parler (1)
patiner like parler (1)
payer like essayer (10)
penser like parler (1)
perdre like vendre (3)
permettre like mettre (28)
pleuvoir (33)
plonger like manger (11)
polluer like parler (1)
porter like parler (1)
poser like parler (1)
posséder like préférer (12)
poster like parler (1)
pouvoir (34)
pratiquer like parler (1)
préférer (12)
prélever like parler (1)
prendre (35)
préparer like parler (1)
présenter like parler (1)
préserver like parler (1)
prêter like parler (1)
prévenir like tenir (40)
produire like conduire (16)
profiter like parler (1)
promettre like mettre (28)
proposer like parler (1)
protéger like préférer (12)
provenir like venir (41)
publier like parler (1)
quitter like parler (1)
raccrocher like parler (1)
ranger like manger (11)
réaliser like parler (1)
recevoir (36)
recommander like parler (1)
reconnaître like connaître (17)
recycler like parler (1)
réduire like conduire (16)
réfléchir like finir (2)
regarder like parler (1)
régner like préférer (12)
remplacer like parler (1)
remplir like finir (2)
rencontrer like parler (1)
rendre like vendre (3)
rentrer like parler (1) *except* **p.c.** with **être**
renvoyer like essayer (10)
réparer like parler (1)
repasser like parler (1)
répéter like préférer (12)
repeupler like parler (1)
répondre like vendre (3)
réserver like parler (1)
rester like parler (1) *except* **p.c.** with **être**
retenir like tenir (40)
retirer like parler (1)
retourner like parler (1) *except* **p.c.** with **être**
retrouver like parler (1)
réussir like finir (2)
revenir like venir (41); **p.c.** with **être**
revoir like voir (42)
rire (37)
rouler like parler (1)
salir like finir (2)
s'amuser like se laver (6)
s'asseoir (14)
sauvegarder like parler (1)
sauver like parler (1)
savoir (38)
se brosser like se laver (6)
se coiffer like se laver (6)
se composer like se laver (6)
se connecter like se laver (6)
se coucher like se laver (6)
se croiser like se laver (6)
se dépêcher like se laver (6)
se déplacer like se laver (6)
se déshabiller like se laver (6)
se détendre like vendre (3) *except* **p.c.** with **être**
se disputer like se laver (6)
s'embrasser like se laver (6)
s'endormir like partir (32) *except* **p.c.** with **être**
s'énerver like se laver (6)
s'ennuyer like essayer (10) *except* **p.c.** with **être**
s'excuser like se laver (6)
se fouler like se laver (6)

s'installer like se laver (6)
se laver (6)
se lever like se laver (6)
se maquiller like se laver (6)
se marier like se laver (6)
se promener like acheter (7) *except* **p.c.** with **être**
se rappeler like se laver (6)
se raser like se laver (6)
se rebeller like se laver (6)
se réconcilier like se laver (6)
se relever like se laver (6)
se reposer like se laver (6)
se réveiller like se laver (6)
servir like partir (32) *except* **p.c.** with **avoir**
se sécher like préférer (12) *except* **p.c.** with **être**
se souvenir like venir (41)
se tromper like se laver (6)
s'habiller like se laver (6)
sentir like partir (32) *except* **p.c.** with **avoir**
signer like parler (1)
s'inquiéter like préférer (12) *except* **p.c.** with **être**
s'intéresser like se laver (6)
skier like parler (1)
s'occuper like se laver (6)
sonner like parler (1)
s'orienter like se laver (6)
sortir like partir (32)
sourire like rire (37)
souffrir like ouvrir (31)
souhaiter like parler (1)
subvenir like venir (41) *except* **p.c.** with **avoir**
suffire like lire (27)
suggérer like préférer (12)
suivre (39)
surfer like parler (1)
surprendre like prendre (35)
télécharger like parler (1)
téléphoner like parler (1)
tenir (40)
tomber like parler (1) *except* **p.c.** with **être**
tourner like parler (1)
tousser like parler (1)
traduire like conduire (16)
travailler like parler (1)
traverser like parler (1)
trouver like parler (1)
tuer like parler (1)
utiliser like parler (1)
valoir like falloir (26)
vendre (3)
venir (41); **p.c.** with **être**
vérifier like parler (1)
visiter like parler (1)
vivre like suivre (39)
voir (42)
vouloir (43)
voyager like manger (11)

Regular verbs

Infinitive / Past participle	INDICATIVE					CONDITIONAL	SUBJUNCTIVE	IMPERATIVE
	Subject Pronouns	Present	Passé composé	Imperfect	Future	Present	Present	
1 parler	je (j')	parle	ai parlé	parlais	parlerai	parlerais	parle	
(to speak)	tu	parles	as parlé	parlais	parleras	parlerais	parles	parle
	il/elle/on	parle	a parlé	parlait	parlera	parlerait	parle	
parlé	nous	parlons	avons parlé	parlions	parlerons	parlerions	parlions	parlons
	vous	parlez	avez parlé	parliez	parlerez	parleriez	parliez	parlez
	ils/elles	parlent	ont parlé	parlaient	parleront	parleraient	parlent	
2 finir	je (j')	finis	ai fini	finissais	finirai	finirais	finisse	
(to finish)	tu	finis	as fini	finissais	finiras	finirais	finisses	finis
	il/elle/on	finit	a fini	finissait	finira	finirait	finisse	
fini	nous	finissons	avons fini	finissions	finirons	finirions	finissions	finissons
	vous	finissez	avez fini	finissiez	finirez	finiriez	finissiez	finissez
	ils/elles	finissent	ont fini	finissaient	finiront	finiraient	finissent	
3 vendre	je (j')	vends	ai vendu	vendais	vendrai	vendrais	vende	
(to sell)	tu	vends	as vendu	vendais	vendras	vendrais	vendes	vends
	il/elle/on	vend	a vendu	vendait	vendra	vendrait	vende	
vendu	nous	vendons	avons vendu	vendions	vendrons	vendrions	vendions	vendons
	vous	vendez	avez vendu	vendiez	vendrez	vendriez	vendiez	vendez
	ils/elles	vendent	ont vendu	vendaient	vendront	vendraient	vendent	

Auxiliary verbs: *avoir* and *être*

		Infinitive / Past participle	INDICATIVE					CONDITIONAL	SUBJUNCTIVE	IMPERATIVE
			Subject Pronouns	Present	Passé composé	Imperfect	Future	Present	Present	
4	avoir	j'	ai	ai eu	avais	aurai	aurais	aie	
	(to have)	tu	as	as eu	avais	auras	aurais	aies	aie
		il/elle/on	a	a eu	avait	aura	aurait	ait	
	eu	nous	avons	avons eu	avions	aurons	aurions	ayons	ayons
		vous	avez	avez eu	aviez	aurez	auriez	ayez	ayez
		ils/elles	ont	ont eu	avaient	auront	auraient	aient	
5	être	je (j')	suis	ai été	étais	serai	serais	sois	
	(to be)	tu	es	as été	étais	seras	serais	sois	sois
		il/elle/on	est	a été	était	sera	serait	soit	
	été	nous	sommes	avons été	étions	serons	serions	soyons	soyons
		vous	êtes	avez été	étiez	serez	seriez	soyez	soyez
		ils/elles	sont	ont été	étaient	seront	seraient	soient	

Reflexive (Pronominal)

	Infinitive / Past participle	INDICATIVE					CONDITIONAL	SUBJUNCTIVE	IMPERATIVE
		Subject Pronouns	Present	Passé composé	Imperfect	Future	Present	Present	
6	se laver	je	me lave	me suis lavé(e)	me lavais	me laverai	me laverais	me lave	
	(to wash oneself)	tu	te laves	t'es lavé(e)	te lavais	te laveras	te laverais	te laves	lave-toi
		il/elle/on	se lave	s'est lavé(e)	se lavait	se lavera	se laverait	se lave	
	lavé	nous	nous lavons	nous sommes lavé(e)s	nous lavions	nous laverons	nous laverions	nous lavions	lavons-nous
		vous	vous lavez	vous êtes lavé(e)s	vous laviez	vous laverez	vous laveriez	vous laviez	lavez-vous
		ils/elles	se lavent	se sont lavé(e)s	se lavaient	se laveront	se laveraient	se lavent	

Verbs with spelling changes

	Infinitive / Past participle	INDICATIVE					CONDITIONAL	SUBJUNCTIVE	IMPERATIVE
		Subject Pronouns	Present	Passé composé	Imperfect	Future	Present	Present	
7	acheter	j'	achète	ai acheté	achetais	achèterai	achèterais	achète	
	(to buy)	tu	achètes	as acheté	achetais	achèteras	achèterais	achètes	achète
		il/elle/on	achète	a acheté	achetait	achètera	achèterait	achète	
	acheté	nous	achetons	avons acheté	achetions	achèterons	achèterions	achetions	achetons
		vous	achetez	avez acheté	achetiez	achèterez	achèteriez	achetiez	achetez
		ils/elles	achètent	ont acheté	achetaient	achèteront	achèteraient	achètent	
8	appeler	j'	appelle	ai appelé	appelais	appellerai	appellerais	appelle	
	(to call)	tu	appelles	as appelé	appelais	appelleras	appellerais	appelles	appelle
		il/elle/on	appelle	a appelé	appelait	appellera	appellerait	appelle	
	appelé	nous	appelons	avons appelé	appelions	appellerons	appellerions	appelions	appelons
		vous	appelez	avez appelé	appeliez	appellerez	appelleriez	appeliez	appelez
		ils/elles	appellent	ont appelé	appelaient	appelleront	appelleraient	appellent	
9	commencer	je (j')	commence	ai commencé	commençais	commencerai	commencerais	commence	
	(to begin)	tu	commences	as commencé	commençais	commenceras	commencerais	commences	commence
		il/elle/on	commence	a commencé	commençait	commencera	commencerait	commence	
	commencé	nous	commençons	avons commencé	commencions	commencerons	commencerions	commencions	commençons
		vous	commencez	avez commencé	commenciez	commencerez	commenceriez	commenciez	commencez
		ils/elles	commencent	ont commencé	commençaient	commenceront	commenceraient	commencent	
10	essayer	j'	essaie	ai essayé	essayais	essaierai	essaierais	essaie	
	(to try)	tu	essaies	as essayé	essayais	essaieras	essaierais	essaies	essaie
		il/elle/on	essaie	a essayé	essayait	essaiera	essaierait	essaie	
	essayé	nous	essayons	avons essayé	essayions	essaierons	essaierions	essayions	essayons
		vous	essayez	avez essayé	essayiez	essaierez	essaieriez	essayiez	essayez
		ils/elles	essayent	ont essayé	essayaient	essaieront	essaieraient	essaient	
11	manger	je (j')	mange	ai mangé	mangeais	mangerai	mangerais	mange	
	(to eat)	tu	manges	as mangé	mangeais	mangeras	mangerais	manges	mange
		il/elle/on	mange	a mangé	mangeait	mangera	mangerait	mange	
	mangé	nous	mangeons	avons mangé	mangions	mangerons	mangerions	mangions	mangeons
		vous	mangez	avez mangé	mangiez	mangerez	mangeriez	mangiez	mangez
		ils/elles	mangent	ont mangé	mangeaient	mangeront	mangeraient	mangent	

	Infinitive / Past participle	INDICATIVE: Subject Pronouns	INDICATIVE: Present	INDICATIVE: Passé composé	INDICATIVE: Imperfect	INDICATIVE: Future	CONDITIONAL: Present	SUBJUNCTIVE: Present	IMPERATIVE
12	préférer	je (j')	préfère	ai préféré	préférais	préférerai	préférerais	préfère	
	(to prefer)	tu	préfères	as préféré	préférais	préféreras	préférerais	préfères	préfère
		il/elle/on	préfère	a préféré	préférait	préférera	préférerait	préfère	
	préféré	nous	préférons	avons préféré	préférions	préférerons	préférerions	préférions	préférons
		vous	préférez	avez préféré	préfériez	préférerez	préféreriez	préfériez	préférez
		ils/elles	préfèrent	ont préféré	préféraient	préféreront	préféreraient	préfèrent	

Irregular verbs

	Infinitive / Past participle	INDICATIVE: Subject Pronouns	INDICATIVE: Present	INDICATIVE: Passé composé	INDICATIVE: Imperfect	INDICATIVE: Future	CONDITIONAL: Present	SUBJUNCTIVE: Present	IMPERATIVE
13	aller	je (j')	vais	suis allé(e)	allais	irai	irais	aille	
	(to go)	tu	vas	es allé(e)	allais	iras	irais	ailles	va
		il/elle/on	va	est allé(e)	allait	ira	irait	aille	
	allé	nous	allons	sommes allé(e)s	allions	irons	irions	allions	allons
		vous	allez	êtes allé(e)s	alliez	irez	iriez	alliez	allez
		ils/elles	vont	sont allé(e)s	allaient	iront	iraient	aillent	
14	s'asseoir	je	m'assieds	me suis assis(e)	m'asseyais	m'assiérai	m'assiérais	m'asseye	
	(to sit down,	tu	t'assieds	t'es assis(e)	t'asseyais	t'assiéras	t'assiérais	t'asseyes	assieds-toi
	to be seated)	il/elle/on	s'assied	s'est assis(e)	s'asseyait	s'assiéra	s'assiérait	s'asseye	
		nous	nous asseyons	nous sommes assis(e)s	nous asseyions	nous assiérons	nous assiérions	nous asseyions	asseyons-nous
	assis	vous	vous asseyez	vous êtes assis(e)s	vous asseyiez	vous assiérez	vous assiériez	vous asseyiez	asseyez-vous
		ils/elles	s'asseyent	se sont assis(e)s	s'asseyaient	s'assiéront	s'assiéraient	s'asseyent	
15	boire	je (j')	bois	ai bu	buvais	boirai	boirais	boive	
	(to drink)	tu	bois	as bu	buvais	boiras	boirais	boives	bois
		il/elle/on	boit	a bu	buvait	boira	boirait	boive	
	bu	nous	buvons	avons bu	buvions	boirons	boirions	buvions	buvons
		vous	buvez	avez bu	buviez	boirez	boiriez	buviez	buvez
		ils/elles	boivent	ont bu	buvaient	boiront	boiraient	boivent	

	Infinitive / Past participle	INDICATIVE: Subject Pronouns	INDICATIVE: Present	INDICATIVE: Passé composé	INDICATIVE: Imperfect	INDICATIVE: Future	CONDITIONAL: Present	SUBJUNCTIVE: Present	IMPERATIVE
16	conduire	je (j')	conduis	ai conduit	conduisais	conduirai	conduirais	conduise	
	(to drive; to lead)	tu	conduis	as conduit	conduisais	conduiras	conduirais	conduises	conduis
		il/elle/on	conduit	a conduit	conduisait	conduira	conduirait	conduise	
	conduit	nous	conduisons	avons conduit	conduisions	conduirons	conduirions	conduisions	conduisons
		vous	conduisez	avez conduit	conduisiez	conduirez	conduiriez	conduisiez	conduisez
		ils/elles	conduisent	ont conduit	conduisaient	conduiront	conduiraient	conduisent	
17	connaître	je (j')	connais	ai connu	connaissais	connaîtrai	connaîtrais	connaisse	
	(to know, to be	tu	connais	as connu	connaissais	connaîtras	connaîtrais	connaisses	connais
	acquainted with)	il/elle/on	connaît	a connu	connaissait	connaîtra	connaîtrait	connaisse	
		nous	connaissons	avons connu	connaissions	connaîtrons	connaîtrions	connaissions	connaissons
	connu	vous	connaissez	avez connu	connaissiez	connaîtrez	connaîtriez	connaissiez	connaissez
		ils/elles	connaissent	ont connu	connaissaient	connaîtront	connaîtraient	connaissent	
18	courir	je (j')	cours	ai couru	courais	courrai	courrais	coure	
	(to run)	tu	cours	as couru	courais	courras	courrais	coures	cours
		il/elle/on	court	a couru	courait	courra	courrait	coure	
	couru	nous	courons	avons couru	courions	courrons	courrions	courions	courons
		vous	courez	avez couru	couriez	courrez	courriez	couriez	courez
		ils/elles	courent	ont couru	couraient	courront	courraient	courent	
19	croire	je (j')	crois	ai cru	croyais	croirai	croirais	croie	
	(to believe)	tu	crois	as cru	croyais	croiras	croirais	croies	crois
		il/elle/on	croit	a cru	croyait	croira	croirait	croie	
	cru	nous	croyons	avons cru	croyions	croirons	croirions	croyions	croyons
		vous	croyez	avez cru	croyiez	croirez	croiriez	croyiez	croyez
		ils/elles	croient	ont cru	croyaient	croiront	croiraient	croient	
20	devoir	je (j')	dois	ai dû	devais	devrai	devrais	doive	
	(to have to; to owe)	tu	dois	as dû	devais	devras	devrais	doives	dois
		il/elle/on	doit	a dû	devait	devra	devrait	doive	
	dû	nous	devons	avons dû	devions	devrons	devrions	devions	devons
		vous	devez	avez dû	deviez	devrez	devriez	deviez	devez
		ils/elles	doivent	ont dû	devaient	devront	devraient	doivent	

	Infinitive / Past participle	INDICATIVE: Subject Pronouns	Present	Passé composé	Imperfect	Future	CONDITIONAL: Present	SUBJUNCTIVE: Present	IMPERATIVE
21	dire	je (j')	dis	ai dit	disais	dirai	dirais	dise	
	(to say, to tell)	tu	dis	as dit	disais	diras	dirais	dises	dis
		il/elle/on	dit	a dit	disait	dira	dirait	dise	
	dit	nous	disons	avons dit	disions	dirons	dirions	disions	disons
		vous	dites	avez dit	disiez	direz	diriez	disiez	dites
		ils/elles	disent	ont dit	disaient	diront	diraient	disent	
22	écrire	j'	écris	ai écrit	écrivais	écrirai	écrirais	écrive	
	(to write)	tu	écris	as écrit	écrivais	écriras	écrirais	écrives	écris
		il/elle/on	écrit	a écrit	écrivait	écrira	écrirait	écrive	
	écrit	nous	écrivons	avons écrit	écrivions	écrirons	écririons	écrivions	écrivons
		vous	écrivez	avez écrit	écriviez	écrirez	écririez	écriviez	écrivez
		ils/elles	écrivent	ont écrit	écrivaient	écriront	écriraient	écrivent	
23	envoyer	j'	envoie	ai envoyé	envoyais	enverrai	enverrais	envoie	
	(to send)	tu	envoies	as envoyé	envoyais	enverras	enverrais	envoies	envoie
		il/elle/on	envoie	a envoyé	envoyait	enverra	enverrait	envoie	
	envoyé	nous	envoyons	avons envoyé	envoyions	enverrons	enverrions	envoyions	envoyons
		vous	envoyez	avez envoyé	envoyiez	enverrez	enverriez	envoyiez	envoyez
		ils/elles	envoient	ont envoyé	envoyaient	enverront	enverraient	envoient	
24	éteindre	j'	éteins	ai éteint	éteignais	éteindrai	éteindrais	éteigne	
	(to turn off)	tu	éteins	as éteint	éteignais	éteindras	éteindrais	éteignes	éteins
		il/elle/on	éteint	a éteint	éteignait	éteindra	éteindrait	éteigne	
	éteint	nous	éteignons	avons éteint	éteignions	éteindrons	éteindrions	éteignions	éteignons
		vous	éteignez	avez éteint	éteigniez	éteindrez	éteindriez	éteigniez	éteignez
		ils/elles	éteignent	ont éteint	éteignaient	éteindront	éteindraient	éteignent	
25	faire	je (j')	fais	ai fait	faisais	ferai	ferais	fasse	
	(to do; to make)	tu	fais	as fait	faisais	feras	ferais	fasses	fais
		il/elle/on	fait	a fait	faisait	fera	ferait	fasse	
	fait	nous	faisons	avons fait	faisions	ferons	ferions	fassions	faisons
		vous	faites	avez fait	faisiez	ferez	feriez	fassiez	faites
		ils/elles	font	ont fait	faisaient	feront	feraient	fassent	
26	falloir	il	faut	a fallu	fallait	faudra	faudrait	faille	
	(to be necessary)								
	fallu								

	Infinitive / Past participle	INDICATIVE					CONDITIONAL	SUBJUNCTIVE	IMPERATIVE
		Subject Pronouns	Present	Passé composé	Imperfect	Future	Present	Present	
27	lire	je (j')	lis	ai lu	lisais	lirai	lirais	lise	
	(to read)	tu	lis	as lu	lisais	liras	lirais	lises	lis
		il/elle/on	lit	a lu	lisait	lira	lirait	lise	
	lu	nous	lisons	avons lu	lisions	lirons	lirions	lisions	lisons
		vous	lisez	avez lu	lisiez	lirez	liriez	lisiez	lisez
		ils/elles	lisent	ont lu	lisaient	liront	liraient	lisent	
28	mettre	je (j')	mets	ai mis	mettais	mettrai	mettrais	mette	
	(to put)	tu	mets	as mis	mettais	mettras	mettrais	mettes	mets
		il/elle/on	met	a mis	mettait	mettra	mettrait	mette	
	mis	nous	mettons	avons mis	mettions	mettrons	mettrions	mettions	mettons
		vous	mettez	avez mis	mettiez	mettrez	mettriez	mettiez	mettez
		ils/elles	mettent	ont mis	mettaient	mettront	mettraient	mettent	
29	mourir	je	meurs	suis mort(e)	mourais	mourrai	mourrais	meure	
	(to die)	tu	meurs	es mort(e)	mourais	mourras	mourrais	meures	meurs
		il/elle/on	meurt	est mort(e)	mourait	mourra	mourrait	meure	
	mort	nous	mourons	sommes mort(e)s	mourions	mourrons	mourrions	mourions	mourons
		vous	mourez	êtes mort(e)s	mouriez	mourrez	mourriez	mouriez	mourez
		ils/elles	meurent	sont mort(e)s	mouraient	mourront	mourraient	meurent	
30	naître	je	nais	suis né(e)	naissais	naîtrai	naîtrais	naisse	
	(to be born)	tu	nais	es né(e)	naissais	naîtras	naîtrais	naisses	nais
		il/elle/on	naît	est né(e)	naissait	naîtra	naîtrait	naisse	
	né	nous	naissons	sommes né(e)s	naissions	naîtrons	naîtrions	naissions	naissons
		vous	naissez	êtes né(e)s	naissiez	naîtrez	naîtriez	naissiez	naissez
		ils/elles	naissent	sont né(e)s	naissaient	naîtront	naîtraient	naissent	
31	ouvrir	j'	ouvre	ai ouvert	ouvrais	ouvrirai	ouvrirais	ouvre	
	(to open)	tu	ouvres	as ouvert	ouvrais	ouvriras	ouvrirais	ouvres	ouvre
		il/elle/on	ouvre	a ouvert	ouvrait	ouvrira	ouvrirait	ouvre	
	ouvert	nous	ouvrons	avons ouvert	ouvrions	ouvrirons	ouvririons	ouvrions	ouvrons
		vous	ouvrez	avez ouvert	ouvriez	ouvrirez	ouvririez	ouvriez	ouvrez
		ils/elles	ouvrent	ont ouvert	ouvraient	ouvriront	ouvriraient	ouvrent	

	Infinitive Past participle	INDICATIVE Subject Pronouns	Present	Passé composé	Imperfect	Future	CONDITIONAL Present	SUBJUNCTIVE Present	IMPERATIVE
32	partir	je	pars	suis parti(e)	partais	partirai	partirais	parte	
	(to leave)	tu	pars	es parti(e)	partais	partiras	partirais	partes	pars
		il/elle/on	part	est parti(e)	partait	partira	partirait	parte	
	parti	nous	partons	sommes parti(e)s	partions	partirons	partirions	partions	partons
		vous	partez	êtes parti(e)(s)	partiez	partirez	partiriez	partiez	partez
		ils/elles	partent	sont parti(e)s	partaient	partiront	partiraient	partent	
33	pleuvoir	il	pleut	a plu	pleuvait	pleuvra	pleuvrait	pleuve	
	(to rain)								
	plu								
34	pouvoir	je (j')	peux	ai pu	pouvais	pourrai	pourrais	puisse	
	(to be able)	tu	peux	as pu	pouvais	pourras	pourrais	puisses	
		il/elle/on	peut	a pu	pouvait	pourra	pourrait	puisse	
	pu	nous	pouvons	avons pu	pouvions	pourrons	pourrions	puissions	
		vous	pouvez	avez pu	pouviez	pourrez	pourriez	puissiez	
		ils/elles	peuvent	ont pu	pouvaient	pourront	pourraient	puissent	
35	prendre	je (j')	prends	ai pris	prenais	prendrai	prendrais	prenne	
	(to take)	tu	prends	as pris	prenais	prendras	prendrais	prennes	prends
		il/elle/on	prend	a pris	prenait	prendra	prendrait	prenne	
	pris	nous	prenons	avons pris	prenions	prendrons	prendrions	prenions	prenons
		vous	prenez	avez pris	preniez	prendrez	prendriez	preniez	prenez
		ils/elles	prennent	ont pris	prenaient	prendront	prendraient	prennent	
36	recevoir	je (j')	reçois	ai reçu	recevais	recevrai	recevrais	reçoive	
	(to receive)	tu	reçois	as reçu	recevais	recevras	recevrais	reçoives	reçois
		il/elle/on	reçoit	a reçu	recevait	recevra	recevrait	reçoive	
	reçu	nous	recevons	avons reçu	recevions	recevrons	recevrions	recevions	recevons
		vous	recevez	avez reçu	receviez	recevrez	recevriez	receviez	recevez
		ils/elles	reçoivent	ont reçu	recevaient	recevront	recevraient	reçoivent	
37	rire	je (j')	ris	ai ri	riais	rirai	rirais	rie	
	(to laugh)	tu	ris	as ri	riais	riras	rirais	ries	ris
		il/elle/on	rit	a ri	riait	rira	rirait	rie	
	ri	nous	rions	avons ri	riions	rirons	ririons	riions	rions
		vous	riez	avez ri	riiez	rirez	ririez	riiez	riez
		ils/elles	rient	ont ri	riaient	riront	riraient	rient	

	Infinitive / Past participle	INDICATIVE Subject Pronouns	Present	Passé composé	Imperfect	Future	CONDITIONAL Present	SUBJUNCTIVE Present	IMPERATIVE
38	savoir	je (j')	sais	ai su	savais	saurai	saurais	sache	
	(to know)	tu	sais	as su	savais	sauras	saurais	saches	sache
		il/elle/on	sait	a su	savait	saura	saurait	sache	
	su	nous	savons	avons su	savions	saurons	saurions	sachions	sachons
		vous	savez	avez su	saviez	saurez	sauriez	sachiez	sachez
		ils/elles	savent	ont su	savaient	sauront	sauraient	sachent	
39	suivre	je (j')	suis	ai suivi	suivais	suivrai	suivrais	suive	
	(to follow)	tu	suis	as suivi	suivais	suivras	suivrais	suives	suis
		il/elle/on	suit	a suivi	suivait	suivra	suivrait	suive	
	suivi	nous	suivons	avons suivi	suivions	suivrons	suivrions	suivions	suivons
		vous	suivez	avez suivi	suiviez	suivrez	suivriez	suiviez	suivez
		ils/elles	suivent	ont suivi	suivaient	suivront	suivraient	suivent	
40	tenir	je (j')	tiens	ai tenu	tenais	tiendrai	tiendrais	tienne	
	(to hold)	tu	tiens	as tenu	tenais	tiendras	tiendrais	tiennes	tiens
		il/elle/on	tient	a tenu	tenait	tiendra	tiendrait	tienne	
	tenu	nous	tenons	avons tenu	tenions	tiendrons	tiendrions	tenions	tenons
		vous	tenez	avez tenu	teniez	tiendrez	tiendriez	teniez	tenez
		ils/elles	tiennent	ont tenu	tenaient	tiendront	tiendraient	tiennent	
41	venir	je	viens	suis venu(e)	venais	viendrai	viendrais	vienne	
	(to come)	tu	viens	es venu(e)	venais	viendras	viendrais	viennes	viens
		il/elle/on	vient	est venu(e)	venait	viendra	viendrait	vienne	
	venu	nous	venons	sommes venu(e)s	venions	viendrons	viendrions	venions	venons
		vous	venez	êtes venu(e)(s)	veniez	viendrez	viendriez	veniez	venez
		ils/elles	viennent	sont venu(e)s	venaient	viendront	viendraient	viennent	
42	voir	je (j')	vois	ai vu	voyais	verrai	verrais	voie	
	(to see)	tu	vois	as vu	voyais	verras	verrais	voies	vois
		il/elle/on	voit	a vu	voyait	verra	verrait	voie	
	vu	nous	voyons	avons vu	voyions	verrons	verrions	voyions	voyons
		vous	voyez	avez vu	voyiez	verrez	verriez	voyiez	voyez
		ils/elles	voient	ont vu	voyaient	verront	verraient	voient	
43	vouloir	je (j')	veux	ai voulu	voulais	voudrai	voudrais	veuille	
	(to want, to wish)	tu	veux	as voulu	voulais	voudras	voudrais	veuilles	veuille
		il/elle/on	veut	a voulu	voulait	voudra	voudrait	veuille	
	voulu	nous	voulons	avons voulu	voulions	voudrons	voudrions	voulions	veuillons
		vous	voulez	avez voulu	vouliez	voudrez	voudriez	vouliez	veuillez
		ils/elles	veulent	ont voulu	voulaient	voudront	voudraient	veuillent	

Guide to Vocabulary

Abbreviations used in this glossary

adj.	adjective	*form.*	formal	*p.p.*	past participle
adv.	adverb	*imp.*	imperative	*pl.*	plural
art.	article	*indef.*	indefinite	*poss.*	possessive
comp.	comparative	*interj.*	interjection	*prep.*	preposition
conj.	conjunction	*interr.*	interrogative	*pron.*	pronoun
def.	definite	*inv.*	invariable	*refl.*	reflexive
dem.	demonstrative	*i.o.*	indirect object	*rel.*	relative
disj.	disjunctive	*m.*	masculine	*sing.*	singular
d.o.	direct object	*n.*	noun	*sub.*	subject
f.	feminine	*obj.*	object	*super.*	superlative
fam.	familiar	*part.*	partitive	*v.*	verb

French-English

A

à *prep.* at; in; to 4
À bientôt. See you soon. 1
à condition que on the condition that, provided that 15
à côté de *prep.* next to 3
À demain. See you tomorrow. 1
à droite (de) *prep.* to the right (of) 3
à gauche (de) *prep.* to the left (of) 3
à … heure(s) at … (o'clock) 4
à la radio on the radio 15
à la télé(vision) on television 15
à l'étranger abroad, overseas 7
à mi-temps half-time (*job*) 13
à moins que unless 15
à plein temps full-time (*job*) 13
À plus tard. See you later. 1
À quelle heure? What time?; When? 2
À qui? To whom? 4
À table! Let's eat! Food is on! 9
à temps partiel part-time (*job*) 13
À tout à l'heure. See you later. 1
au bout (de) *prep.* at the end (of) 12
au contraire on the contrary 15
au fait *by the way* 3
au printemps in the spring 5
Au revoir. Good-bye. 1
au secours help 11
au sujet de on the subject of, about 14
abolir *v.* to abolish 14
absolument *adv.* absolutely 7
accident *m.* accident 11
avoir un accident to have/to be in an accident 11
accompagner *v.* to accompany 12
acheter *v.* to buy 5
acteur *m.* actor 1
actif/active *adj.* active 3
activement *adv.* actively 7
actrice *f.* actress 1
addition *f.* check, bill 4
adieu farewell 14
adolescence *f.* adolescence 6
adorer *v.* to love 2
J'adore… I love… 2
adresse *f.* address 12
aérobic *m.* aerobics 5
faire de l'aérobic *v.* to do aerobics 5
aéroport *m.* airport 7
affaires *f., pl.* business 3
affiche *f.* poster 8
afficher *v.* to post 13
âge *m.* age 6
âge adulte *m.* adulthood 6
agence de voyages *f.* travel agency 7
agent *m.* officer; agent 11
agent de police *m.* police officer 11
agent de voyages *m.* travel agent 7
agent immobilier *m.* real estate agent 13
agréable *adj.* pleasant 1
agriculteur/agricultrice *m., f.* farmer 13
aider (à) *v.* to help (*to do something*) 5
aie (avoir) *imp. v.* have 7
ail *m.* garlic 9
aimer *v.* to like 2
aimer mieux to prefer 2
aimer que… to like that… 14
J'aime bien… I really like… 2
Je n'aime pas tellement… I don't like … very much. 2
aîné(e) *adj.* elder 3
algérien(ne) *adj.* Algerian 1
aliment *m.* food item; a food 9
Allemagne *f.* Germany 7
allemand(e) *adj.* German 1
aller *v.* to go 4
aller à la pêche to go fishing 5
aller aux urgences to go to the emergency room 10
aller avec to go with 6
aller-retour *adj.* round-trip 7
billet aller-retour *m.* round-trip ticket 7
Allons-y! Let's go! 2
Ça va? What's up?; How are things? 1
Comment allez-vous? *form.* How are you? 1
Comment vas-tu? *fam.* How are you? 1
Je m'en vais. I'm leaving. 8
Je vais bien/mal. I am doing well/badly. 1
J'y vais. I'm going/coming. 8
Nous y allons. We're going/coming. 9
allergie *f.* allergy 10
Allez. Come on. 5
allô *(on the phone)* hello 1
allumer *v.* to turn on 11
alors *adv.* so, then; at that moment 2
améliorer *v.* to improve 13
amende *f.* fine 11
amener *v.* to bring (*someone*) 5
américain(e) *adj.* American 1
football américain *m.* football 5

ami(e) *m., f.* friend 1
petit(e) ami(e) *m., f.* boyfriend/girlfriend 1
amitié *f.* friendship 6
amour *m.* love 6
amoureux/amoureuse *adj.* in love 6
tomber amoureux/amoureuse *v.* to fall in love 6
amusant(e) *adj.* fun 1
an *m.* year 2
ancien(ne) *adj.* ancient, old; former 15
ange *m.* angel 1
anglais(e) *adj.* English 1
angle *m.* corner 12
Angleterre *f.* England 7
animal *m.* animal 14
année *f.* year 2
cette année this year 2
anniversaire *m.* birthday 5
C'est quand l'anniversaire de ... ? When is ...'s birthday? 5
C'est quand ton/votre anniversaire? When is your birthday? 5
annuler (une réservation) *v.* to cancel (a reservation) 7
anorak *m.* ski jacket, parka 6
antipathique *adj.* unpleasant 3
août *m.* August 5
apercevoir *v.* to see, to catch sight of 12
aperçu (apercevoir) *p.p.* seen, caught sight of 12
appareil *m.* (on the phone) telephone 13
appareil (électrique/ménager) *m.* (electrical/household) appliance 8
appareil photo (numérique) *m.* (digital) camera 11
C'est M./Mme/Mlle ... à l'appareil. It's Mr./Mrs./Miss ... on the phone. 13
Qui est à l'appareil? Who's calling, please? 13
appartement *m.* apartment 7
appeler *v.* to call 13
applaudir *v.* to applaud 15
applaudissement *m.* applause 15
apporter *v.* to bring, to carry (*something*) 4
apprendre (à) *v.* to teach; to learn (*to do something*) 4
appris (apprendre) *p.p., adj.* learned 6
après (que) *adv.* after 2
après-demain *adv.* day after tomorrow 2
après-midi *m.* afternoon 2
cet après-midi this afternoon 2
de l'après-midi in the afternoon 2
demain après-midi *adv.* tomorrow afternoon 2
hier après-midi *adv.* yesterday afternoon 7
arbre *m.* tree 14
architecte *m., f.* architect 3
architecture *f.* architecture 2
argent *m.* money 12
dépenser de l'argent *v.* to spend money 4
déposer de l'argent *v.* to deposit money 12
retirer de l'argent *v.* to withdraw money 12
armoire *f.* armoire, wardrobe 8
arrêt d'autobus (de bus) *m.* bus stop 7
arrêter (de faire quelque chose) *v.* to stop (doing something) 11
arrivée *f.* arrival 7
arriver (à) *v.* to arrive; to manage (*to do something*) 2
art *m.* art 2
beaux-arts *m., pl.* fine arts 15
artiste *m., f.* artist 3
ascenseur *m.* elevator 7
aspirateur *m.* vacuum cleaner 8
passer l'aspirateur to vacuum 8
aspirine *f.* aspirin 10
Asseyez-vous! (s'asseoir) *imp. v.* Have a seat! 10
assez *adv.* *(before adjective or adverb)* pretty; quite 7
assez (de) *(before noun)* enough (of) 4
pas assez (de) not enough (of) 4
assiette *f.* plate 9
assis (s'asseoir) *p.p., adj.* *(used as past participle)* sat down; (*used as adjective*) sitting, seated 10
assister *v.* to attend 2
assurance (maladie/vie) *f.* (health/life) insurance 13
athlète *m., f.* athlete 3
attacher *v.* to attach 11
attacher sa ceinture de sécurité to buckle one's seatbelt 11
attendre *v.* to wait 6
attention *f.* attention 5
faire attention (à) *v.* to pay attention (to) 5
au (à + le) *prep.* to/at the 4
auberge de jeunesse *f.* youth hostel 7
aucun(e) *adj.* no; *pron.* none 10
ne... aucun(e) none, not any 12
augmentation (de salaire) *f.* raise (in salary) 13
aujourd'hui *adv.* today 2
auquel (à + lequel) *pron., m., sing.* which one 13
aussi *adv.* too, as well; as 1
Moi aussi. Me too. 1
aussi ... que *(used with an adjective)* as ... as 9
autant de ... que *adv.* *(used with noun to express quantity)* as much/as many ... as 14
auteur/femme auteur *m., f.* author 15
autobus *m.* bus 7
arrêt d'autobus (de bus) *m.* bus stop 7
prendre un autobus to take a bus 7
automne *m.* fall 5
à l'automne in the fall 5
autoroute *f.* highway 11
autour (de) *prep.* around 12
autrefois *adv.* in the past 7
aux (à + les) to/at the 4
auxquelles (à + lesquelles) *pron., f., pl.* which ones 13
auxquels (à + lesquels) *pron., m., pl.* which ones 13
avance *f.* advance 2
en avance *adv.* early 2
avant (de/que) *adv.* before 7
avant-hier *adv.* day before yesterday 7
avec *prep.* with 1
Avec qui? With whom? 4
aventure *f.* adventure 15
film d'aventures *m.* adventure film 15
avenue *f.* avenue 12
avion *m.* airplane 7
prendre un avion *v.* to take a plane 7
avocat(e) *m., f.* lawyer 3
avoir *v.* to have 2
aie *imp. v.* have 2
avoir besoin (de) to need (*something*) 2
avoir chaud to be hot 2
avoir de la chance to be lucky 2
avoir envie (de) to feel like (*doing something*) 2
avoir faim to be hungry 4
avoir froid to be cold 2
avoir honte (de) to be ashamed (of) 2
avoir mal to have an ache 10
avoir mal au cœur to feel nauseated 10

avoir peur (de/que) to be afraid (of/that) 2
avoir raison to be right 2
avoir soif to be thirsty 4
avoir sommeil to be sleepy 2
avoir tort to be wrong 2
avoir un accident to have/to be in an accident 11
avoir un compte bancaire to have a bank account 12
en avoir marre to be fed up 3
avril *m.* April 5
ayez (avoir) *imp. v.* have 7
ayons (avoir) *imp. v.* let's have 7

B

bac(calauréat) *m.* an important exam taken by high-school students in France 2
baguette *f.* baguette 4
baignoire *f.* bathtub 8
bain *m.* bath 6
salle de bains *f.* bathroom 8
baladeur CD *m.* personal CD player 11
balai *m.* broom 8
balayer *v.* to sweep 8
balcon *m.* balcony 8
banane *f.* banana 9
banc *m.* bench 12
bancaire *adj.* banking 12
avoir un compte bancaire *v.* to have a bank account 12
bande dessinée (B.D.) *f.* comic strip 5
banlieue *f.* suburbs 4
banque *f.* bank 12
banquier/banquière *m., f.* banker 13
barbant *adj.*, **barbe** *f.* drag 3
baseball *m.* baseball 5
basket(-ball) *m.* basketball 5
baskets *f., pl.* tennis shoes 6
bateau *m.* boat 7
prendre un bateau *v.* to take a boat 7
bateau-mouche *m.* riverboat 7
bâtiment *m.* building 12
batterie *f.* drums 15
bavarder *v.* to chat 4
beau (belle) *adj.* handsome; beautiful 3
faire quelque chose de beau *v.* to be up to something interesting 12
Il fait beau. The weather is nice. 5
beaucoup (de) *adv.* a lot (of) 4
Merci (beaucoup). Thank you (very much). 1
beau-frère *m.* brother-in-law 3
beau-père *m.* father-in-law; stepfather 3
beaux-arts *m., pl.* fine arts 15
belge *adj.* Belgian 7
Belgique *f.* Belgium 7
belle *adj., f. (feminine form of* **beau***)* beautiful 3
belle-mère *f.* mother-in-law; stepmother 3
belle-sœur *f.* sister-in-law 3
besoin *m.* need 2
avoir besoin (de) to need (*something*) 2
beurre *m.* butter 4
bibliothèque *f.* library 1
bien *adv.* well 7
bien sûr *adv.* of course 2
Je vais bien. I am doing well. 1
Très bien. Very well. 1
bientôt *adv.* soon 1
À bientôt. See you soon. 1
bienvenu(e) *adj.* welcome 1
bière *f.* beer 6
bijouterie *f.* jewelry store 12
billet *m. (travel)* ticket 7; (*money*) bills, notes 12
billet aller-retour *m.* round-trip ticket 7
biologie *f.* biology 2
biscuit *m.* cookie 6
blague *f.* joke 2
blanc(he) *adj.* white 6
blessure *f.* injury, wound 10
bleu(e) *adj.* blue 3
blond(e) *adj.* blonde 3
blouson *m.* jacket 6
bœuf *m.* beef 9
boire *v.* to drink 4
bois *m.* wood 14
boisson (gazeuse) *f.* (carbonated) drink/beverage 4
boîte *f.* box; can 9
boîte aux lettres *f.* mailbox 12
boîte de conserve *f.* can (of food) 9
boîte de nuit *f.* nightclub 4
bol *m.* bowl 9
bon(ne) *adj.* kind; good 3
bon marché *adj.* inexpensive 6
Il fait bon. The weather is good/warm. 5
bonbon *m.* candy 6
bonheur *m.* happiness 6
Bonjour. Good morning.; Hello. 1
Bonsoir. Good evening.; Hello. 1
bouche *f.* mouth 10
boucherie *f.* butcher's shop 9
boulangerie *f.* bread shop, bakery 9
boulevard *m.* boulevard 12
suivre un boulevard *v.* to follow a boulevard 12
bourse *f.* scholarship, grant 2
bout *m.* end 12
au bout (de) *prep.* at the end (of) 12
bouteille (de) *f.* bottle (of) 4
boutique *f.* boutique, store 12
bras *m.* arm 10
brasserie *f.* café; restaurant 12
Brésil *m.* Brazil 7
brésilien(ne) *adj.* Brazilian 7
bricoler *v.* to tinker; to do odd jobs 5
brillant(e) *adj.* bright 1
bronzer *v.* to tan 6
brosse (à cheveux/à dents) *f.* (hair/tooth)brush 10
brun(e) *adj.* (*hair*) dark 3
bu (boire) *p.p.* drunk 6
bureau *m.* desk; office 1
bureau de poste *m.* post office 12
bus *m.* bus 7
arrêt d'autobus (de bus) *m.* bus stop 7
prendre un bus *v.* to take a bus 7

C

ça *pron.* that; this; it 1
Ça dépend. It depends. 4
Ça ne nous regarde pas. That has nothing to do with us.; That is none of our business. 14
Ça suffit. That's enough. 5
Ça te dit? Does that appeal to you? 14
Ça va? What's up?; How are things? 1
ça veut dire that is to say 10
Comme ci, comme ça. So-so. 1
cabine téléphonique *f.* phone booth 12
cadeau *m.* gift 6
paquet cadeau wrapped gift 6
cadet(te) *adj.* younger 3
cadre/femme cadre *m., f.* executive 13
café *m.* café; coffee 1
terrasse de café *f.* café terrace 4
cuillére à café *f.* teaspoon 9
cafetière *f.* coffeemaker 8
cahier *m.* notebook 1
calculatrice *f.* calculator 1
calme *adj.* calm 1; *m.* calm 1
camarade *m., f.* friend 1
camarade de chambre *m., f.* roommate 1
camarade de classe *m., f.* classmate 1

caméra vidéo *f.* camcorder **11**
caméscope *m.* camcorder **11**
campagne *f.* country(side) **7**
pain de campagne *m.* country-style bread **4**
pâté (de campagne) *m.* pâté, meat spread **9**
camping *m.* camping **5**
faire du camping *v.* to go camping **5**
Canada *m.* Canada **7**
canadien(ne) *adj.* Canadian **1**
canapé *m.* couch **8**
candidat(e) *m., f.* candidate; applicant **13**
cantine *f.* (school) cafeteria **9**
capitale *f.* capital **7**
capot *m.* hood **11**
carafe (d'eau) *f.* pitcher (of water) **9**
carotte *f.* carrot **9**
carrefour *m.* intersection **12**
carrière *f.* career **13**
carte *f.* map **1**; menu **9**; card **12**
payer avec une carte de crédit to pay with a credit card **12**
carte postale *f.* postcard **12**
cartes *f. pl.* (*playing*) cards **5**
casquette *f.* (baseball) cap **6**
cassette vidéo *f.* videotape **11**
catastrophe *f.* catastrophe **14**
cave *f.* basement, cellar **8**
CD *m.* CD(s) **11**
CD-ROM *m.* CD-ROM(s) **11**
ce *dem. adj., m., sing.* this; that **6**
ce matin this morning **2**
ce mois-ci this month **2**
Ce n'est pas grave. It's no big deal. **6**
ce soir this evening **2**
ce sont... those are... **1**
ce week-end this weekend **2**
cédérom(s) *m.* CD-ROM(s) **11**
ceinture *f.* belt **6**
attacher sa ceinture de sécurité *v.* to buckle one's seatbelt **11**
célèbre *adj.* famous **15**
célébrer *v.* to celebrate **5**
célibataire *adj.* single **3**
celle *pron., f., sing.* this one; that one; the one **14**
celles *pron., f., pl.* these; those; the ones **14**
celui *pron., m., sing.* this one; that one; the one **14**
cent *m.* one hundred **3**
cent mille *m.* one hundred thousand **5**
cent un *m.* one hundred one **5**
cinq cents *m.* five hundred **5**
centième *adj.* hundredth **7**
centrale nucléaire *f.* nuclear plant **14**
centre commercial *m.* shopping center, mall **4**
centre-ville *m.* city/town center, downtown **4**
certain(e) *adj.* certain **9**
Il est certain que... It is certain that... **15**
Il n'est pas certain que... It is uncertain that... **15**
ces *dem. adj., m., f., pl.* these; those **6**
c'est... it/that is... **1**
C'est de la part de qui? On behalf of whom? **13**
C'est le 1er (premier) octobre. It is October first. **5**
C'est M./Mme/Mlle ... (à l'appareil). It's Mr./Mrs./Miss ... (on the phone). **13**
C'est quand l'anniversaire de... ? When is ...'s birthday? **5**
C'est quand ton/votre anniversaire? When is your birthday? **5**
Qu'est-ce que c'est? What is it? **1**
cet *dem. adj., m., sing.* this; that **6**
cet après-midi this afternoon **2**
cette *dem. adj., f., sing.* this; that **6**
cette année this year **2**
cette semaine this week **2**
ceux *pron., m., pl.* these; those; the ones **14**
chaîne (de télévision) *f.* (television) channel **11**
chaîne stéréo *f.* stereo system **11**
chaise *f.* chair **1**
chambre *f.* bedroom **8**
chambre (individuelle) *f.* (single) room **7**
camarade de chambre *m., f.* roommate **1**
champ *m.* field **14**
champagne *m.* champagne **6**
champignon *m.* mushroom **9**
chance *f.* luck **2**
avoir de la chance *v.* to be lucky **2**
chanson *f.* song **15**
chanter *v.* to sing **5**
chanteur/chanteuse *m., f.* singer **1**
chapeau *m.* hat **6**
chaque *adj.* each **6**
charcuterie *f.* delicatessen **9**
charmant(e) *adj.* charming **1**
chasse *f.* hunt **14**
chasser *v.* to hunt **14**
chat *m.* cat **3**
châtain *adj.* (*hair*) brown **3**
chaud *m.* heat **2**
avoir chaud *v.* to be hot **2**
Il fait chaud. (*weather*) It is hot. **5**
chauffeur de taxi/de camion *m.* taxi/truck driver **13**
chaussette *f.* sock **6**
chaussure *f.* shoe **6**
chef d'entreprise *m.* head of a company **13**
chef-d'œuvre *m.* masterpiece **15**
chemin *m.* path; way **12**
suivre un chemin *v.* to follow a path **12**
chemise (à manches courtes/longues) *f.* (short-/long-sleeved) shirt **6**
chemisier *m.* blouse **6**
chèque *m.* check **12**
compte-chèques *m.* checking account **12**
payer par chèque *v.* to pay by check **12**
cher/chère *adj.* expensive **6**
chercher *v.* to look for **2**
chercher un/du travail to look for work **12**
chercheur/chercheuse *m., f.* researcher **13**
chéri(e) *adj.* dear, beloved, darling **2**
cheval *m.* horse **5**
faire du cheval *v.* to go horseback riding **5**
cheveux *m., pl.* hair **9**
brosse à cheveux *f.* hairbrush **10**
cheveux blonds blond hair **3**
cheveux châtains brown hair **3**
se brosser les cheveux *v.* to brush one's hair **9**
cheville *f.* ankle **10**
se fouler la cheville *v.* to twist/sprain one's ankle **10**
chez *prep.* at (*someone's*) house **3**, at (*a place*) **3**
passer chez quelqu'un *v.* to stop by someone's house **4**
chic *adj.* chic **4**
chien *m.* dog **3**
chimie *f.* chemistry **2**
Chine *f.* China **7**
chinois(e) *adj.* Chinese **7**
chocolat (chaud) *m.* (hot) chocolate **4**
chœur *m.* choir, chorus **15**
choisir *v.* to choose **4**
chômage *m.* unemployment **13**

être au chômage *v.* to be unemployed 13
chômeur/chômeuse *m., f.* unemployed person 13
chose *f.* thing 1
quelque chose *m.* something; anything 4
chrysanthèmes *m., pl.* chrysanthemums 9
chut shh 15
-ci *(used with demonstrative adjective* **ce** *and noun or with demonstrative pronoun* **celui***)* here 6
ce mois-ci this month 2
ciel *m.* sky 14
cinéma (ciné) *m.* movie theater, movies 4
cinq *m.* five 1
cinquante *m.* fifty 1
cinquième *adj.* fifth 7
circulation *f.* traffic 11
clair(e) *adj.* clear 15
Il est clair que… It is clear that… 15
classe *f.* *(group of students)* class 1
camarade de classe *m., f.* classmate 1
salle de classe *f.* classroom 1
clavier *m.* keyboard 11
clé *f.* key 7
client(e) *m., f.* client; guest 7
cœur *m.* heart 10
avoir mal au cœur to feel nauseated 10
coffre *m.* trunk 11
coiffeur/coiffeuse *m., f.* hairdresser 3
coin *m.* corner 12
colis *m.* package 12
colocataire *m., f.* roommate *(in an apartment)* 1
Combien (de)… ? *adv.* How much/many… ? 1
Combien coûte… ? How much is... ? 4
combiné *m.* receiver 13
comédie (musicale) *f.* comedy (musical) 15
commander *v.* to order 9
comme *adv.* how; like, as 2
Comme ci, comme ça. So-so. 1
commencer (à) *v.* to begin *(to do something)* 2
comment *adv.* how 4
Comment? *adv.* What? 4
Comment allez-vous?, *form.* How are you? 1
Comment t'appelles-tu? *fam.* What is your name? 1
Comment vas-tu? *fam.* How are you? 1
Comment vous appelez-vous? *form.* What is your name? 1
commerçant(e) *m., f.* shop-keeper 9
commissariat de police *m.* police station 12
commode *f.* dresser, chest of drawers 8
compact disque *m.* compact disc 11
complet (complète) *adj.* full (no vacancies) 7
composer (un numéro) *v.* to dial (a number) 11
compositeur *m.* composer 15
comprendre *v.* to understand 4
compris (comprendre) *p.p., adj.* understood; included 6
comptable *m., f.* accountant 13
compte *m.* account *(at a bank)* 12
avoir un compte bancaire *v.* to have a bank account 12
compte de chèques *m.* checking account 12
compte d'épargne *m.* savings account 12
se rendre compte *v.* to realize 10
compter sur quelqu'un *v.* to count on someone 8
concert *m.* concert 15
condition *f.* condition 15
à condition que on the condition that…, provided that… 15
conduire *v.* to drive 6
conduit (conduire) *p.p., adj.* driven 6
confiture *f.* jam 9
congé *m.* day off 7
jour de congé *m.* day off 7
prendre un congé *v.* to take time off 13
congélateur *m.* freezer 8
connaissance *f.* acquaintance 5
faire la connaissance de *v.* to meet *(someone)* 5
connaître *v.* to know, to be familiar with 8
connecté(e) *adj.* connected 11
être connecté(e) avec quelqu'un *v.* to be online with someone 7, 11
connu (connaître) *p.p., adj.* known; famous 8
conseil *m.* advice 13
conseiller/conseillère *m., f.* consultant; advisor 13
considérer *v.* to consider 5
constamment *adv.* constantly 7
construire *v.* to build, to construct 6
conte *m.* tale 15
content(e) *adj.* happy 13
être content(e) que… *v.* to be happy that… 14
continuer (à) *v.* to continue *(doing something)* 12
contraire *adj.* contrary 15
au contraire on the contrary 15
copain/copine *m., f.* friend 1
corbeille (à papier) *f.* wastebasket 1
corps *m.* body 10
costume *m.* *(man's)* suit 6
côte *f.* coast 14
coton *m.* cotton 12
cou *m.* neck 10
couche d'ozone *f.* ozone layer 14
trou dans la couche d'ozone *m.* hole in the ozone layer 14
couleur *f.* color 6
De quelle couleur... ? What color... ? 6
couloir *m.* hallway 8
couple *m.* couple 6
courage *m.* courage 13
courageux/courageuse *adj.* courageous, brave 3
couramment *adv.* fluently 7
courir *v.* to run 5
courrier *m.* mail 12
cours *m.* class, course 2
course *f.* errand 9
faire les courses *v.* to go (grocery) shopping 9
court(e) *adj.* short 3
chemise à manches courtes *f.* short-sleeved shirt 6
couru (courir) *p.p.* run 6
cousin(e) *m., f.* cousin 3
couteau *m.* knife 9
coûter *v.* to cost 4
Combien coûte... ? How much is... ? 4
couvert (couvrir) *p.p.* covered 11
couverture *f.* blanket 8
couvrir *v.* to cover 11
covoiturage *m.* carpooling 14
cravate *f.* tie 6
crayon *m.* pencil 1
crème *f.* cream 9
crème à raser *f.* shaving cream 10
crêpe *f.* crêpe 5
crevé(e) *adj.* deflated; blown up 11
pneu crevé *m.* flat tire 11
critique *f.* review; criticism 15
croire (que) *v.* to believe (that) 12
ne pas croire que... to not believe that… 15
croissant *m.* croissant 4
croissant(e) *adj.* growing 14
population croissante *f.* growing population 14

cru (croire) *p.p.* believed 15
cruel/cruelle *adj.* cruel 3
cuillère (à soupe/à café) *f.* (soup/tea)spoon 9
cuir *m.* leather 12
cuisine *f.* cooking; kitchen 5
faire la cuisine *v.* to cook 5
cuisiner *v.* to cook 9
cuisinier/cuisinière *m., f.* cook 13
cuisinière *f.* stove 8
curieux/curieuse *adj.* curious 3
curriculum vitæ (C.V.) *m.* résumé 13
cybercafé *m.* cybercafé 12

D

d'abord *adv.* first 7
d'accord *(tag question)* all right? 2; (*in statement*) okay 2
être d'accord to be in agreement 2
d'autres *m., f.* others 4
d'habitude *adv.* usually 7
danger *m.* danger, threat 14
dangereux/dangereuse *adj.* dangerous 11
dans *prep.* in 3
danse *f.* dance 15
danser *v.* to dance 4
danseur/danseuse *m., f.* dancer 15
date *f.* date 5
Quelle est la date? What is the date? 5
de/d' *prep.* of 3; from 1
de l'après-midi in the afternoon 2
de laquelle *pron., f., sing.* which one 13
De quelle couleur... ? What color... ? 6
De rien. You're welcome. 1
de taille moyenne of medium height 3
de temps en temps *adv.* from time to time 7
débarrasser la table *v.* to clear the table 8
déboisement *m.* deforestation 14
début *m.* beginning; debut 15
décembre *m.* December 5
déchets toxiques *m., pl.* toxic waste 14
décider (de) *v.* to decide (*to do something*) 11
découvert (découvrir) *p.p.* discovered 11
découvrir *v.* to discover 11
décrire *v.* to describe 7
décrocher *v.* to pick up 13
décrit (décrire) *p.p., adj.* described 7
degrés *m., pl.* (*temperature*) degrees 5
Il fait ... degrés. *(to describe weather)* It is ... degrees. 5
déjà *adv.* already 5
déjeuner *m.* lunch 9; *v.* to eat lunch 4
de l' *part. art., m., f., sing.* some 4
de la *part. art., f., sing.* some 4
délicieux/délicieuse delicious 8
demain *adv.* tomorrow 2
À demain. See you tomorrow. 1
après-demain *adv.* day after tomorrow 2
demain matin/après-midi/soir *adv.* tomorrow morning/afternoon/evening 2
demander (à) *v.* to ask (*someone*), to make a request (*of someone*) 6
demander que... *v.* to ask that... 14
démarrer *v.* to start up 11
déménager *v.* to move out 8
demie half 2
et demie half past ... (o'clock) 2
demi-frère *m.* half-brother, stepbrother 3
demi-sœur *f.* half-sister, stepsister 3
démissionner *v.* to resign 13
dent *f.* tooth 9
brosse à dents *f.* toothbrush 10
se brosser les dents *v.* to brush one's teeth 9
dentifrice *m.* toothpaste 10
dentiste *m., f.* dentist 3
départ *m.* departure 7
dépasser *v.* to go over; to pass 11
dépense *f.* expenditure, expense 12
dépenser *v.* to spend 4
dépenser de l'argent *v.* to spend money 4
déposer de l'argent *v.* to deposit money 12
déprimé(e) *adj.* depressed 10
depuis *adv.* since; for 9
dernier/dernière *adj.* last 2
dernièrement *adv.* lastly, finally 7
derrière *prep.* behind 3
des *part. art., m., f., pl.* some 4
des (de + les) *m., f., pl.* of the 3
dès que *adv.* as soon as 13
désagréable *adj.* unpleasant 1
descendre (de) *v.* to go downstairs; to get off; to take down 6
désert *m.* desert 14
désirer (que) *v.* to want (that) 5
désolé(e) *adj.* sorry 6
être désolé(e) que... to be sorry that... 14
desquelles (de + lesquelles) *pron., f., pl.* which ones 13
desquels (de + lesquels) *pron., m., pl.* which ones 13
dessert *m.* dessert 6
dessin animé *m.* cartoon 15
dessiner *v.* to draw 2
détester *v.* to hate 2
Je déteste... I hate... 2
détruire *v.* to destroy 6
détruit (détruire) *p.p., adj.* destroyed 6
deux *m.* two 1
deuxième *adj.* second 7
devant *prep.* in front of 3
développer *v.* to develop 14
devenir *v.* to become 9
devoir *m.* homework 2; *v.* to have to, must 9
dictionnaire *m.* dictionary 1
différemment *adv.* differently 7
différence *f.* difference 1
différent(e) *adj.* different 1
difficile *adj.* difficult 1
dimanche *m.* Sunday 2
dîner *m.* dinner 9; *v.* to have dinner 2
diplôme *m.* diploma, degree 2
dire *v.* to say 7
Ça te dit? Does that appeal to you? 14
ça veut dire that is to say 10
veut dire *v.* means, signifies 9
diriger *v.* to manage 13
discret/discrète *adj.* discreet; unassuming 3
discuter *v.* discuss 6
disque *m.* disk 11
compact disque *m.* compact disc 11
disque dur *m.* hard drive 11
dissertation *f.* essay 11
distributeur automatique/de billets *m.* ATM 12
dit (dire) *p.p., adj.* said 7
divorce *m.* divorce 6
divorcé(e) *adj.* divorced 3
divorcer *v.* to divorce 3
dix *m.* ten 1
dix-huit *m.* eighteen 1
dixième *adj.* tenth 7
dix-neuf *m.* nineteen 1
dix-sept *m.* seventeen 1
documentaire *m.* documentary 15
doigt *m.* finger 10
doigt de pied *m.* toe 10
domaine *m.* field 13

dommage *m.* harm 14
Il est dommage que... It's a shame that... 14
donc *conj.* therefore 7
donner (à) *v.* to give (*to someone*) 2
dont *rel. pron.* of which; of whom; that 13
dormir *v.* to sleep 5
dos *m.* back 10
sac à dos *m.* backpack 1
douane *f.* customs 7
douche *f.* shower 8
prendre une douche *v.* to take a shower 10
doué(e) *adj.* talented, gifted 15
douleur *f.* pain 10
douter (que) *v.* to doubt (that) 15
douteux/douteuse *adj.* doubtful 15
Il est douteux que... It is doubtful that... 15
doux/douce *adj.* sweet; soft 3
douze *m.* twelve 1
dramaturge *m.* playwright 15
drame (psychologique) *m.* (psychological) drama 15
draps *m., pl.* sheets 8
droit *m.* law 2
droite *f.* the right (side) 3
à droite de *prep.* to the right of 3
drôle *adj.* funny 3
du *part. art., m., sing.* some 4
du (de + le) *m., sing.* of the 3
dû (devoir) *p.p., adj. (used with infinitive)* had to; *(used with noun)* due, owed 9
duquel (de + lequel) *pron., m., sing.* which one 13

E

eau (minérale) *f.* (mineral) water 4
carafe d'eau *f.* pitcher of water 9
écharpe *f.* scarf 6
échecs *m., pl.* chess 5
échouer *v.* to fail 2
éclair *m.* éclair 4
école *f.* school 2
écologie *f.* ecology 14
écologique *adj.* ecological 14
économie *f.* economics 2
écotourisme *m.* ecotourism 14
écouter *v.* to listen (to) 2
écran *m.* screen 11
écrire *v.* to write 7
écrivain/femme écrivain *m., f.* writer 15
écrit (écrire) *p.p., adj.* written 7
écureuil *m.* squirrel 14
éducation physique *f.* physical education 2
effacer *v.* to erase 11
effet de serre *m.* greenhouse effect 14
égaler *v.* to equal 3
église *f.* church 4
égoïste *adj.* selfish 1
Eh! *interj.* Hey! 2
électrique *adj.* electric 8
appareil électrique/ménager *m.* electrical/household appliance 8
électricien/électricienne *m., f.* electrician 13
élégant(e) *adj.* elegant 1
élevé *adj.* high 13
élève *m., f.* pupil, student 1
elle *pron., f.* she; it 1; her 3
elle est... she/it is... 1
elles *pron., f.* they 1; them 3
elles sont... they are... 1
e-mail *m.* e-mail 11
emballage (en plastique) *m.* (plastic) wrapping/packaging 14
embaucher *v.* to hire 13
embrayage *m.* (*automobile*) clutch 11
émission (de télévision) *f.* (television) program 15
emménager *v.* to move in 8
emmener *v.* to take (*someone*) 5
emploi *m.* job 13
emploi à mi-temps/à temps partiel *m.* part-time job 13
emploi à plein temps *m.* full-time job 13
employé(e) *m., f.* employee 25
employer *v.* to use, to employ 5
emprunter *v.* to borrow 12
en *prep.* in 3
en automne in the fall 5
en avance early 2
en avoir marre to be fed up 6
en effet indeed; in fact 14
en été in the summer 5
en face (de) *prep.* facing, across (from) 3
en fait in fact 7
en général *adv.* in general 7
en hiver in the winter 5
en plein air in fresh air 14
en retard late 2
en tout cas in any case 6
en vacances on vacation 7
être en ligne to be online 11
en *pron.* some of it/them; about it/them; of it/them; from it/them 10
Je vous en prie. *form.* Please.; You're welcome. 1
Qu'en penses-tu? What do you think about that? 14
enceinte *adj.* pregnant 10
Enchanté(e). Delighted. 1
encore *adv.* again; still 3
endroit *m.* place 4
énergie (nucléaire/solaire) *f.* (nuclear/solar) energy 14
enfance *f.* childhood 6
enfant *m., f.* child 3
enfin *adv.* finally, at last 7
enfler *v.* to swell 10
enlever la poussière *v.* to dust 8
ennuyeux/ennuyeuse *adj.* boring 3
énorme *adj.* enormous, huge 2
enregistrer *v.* to record 11
enseigner *v.* to teach 2
ensemble *adv.* together 6
ensuite *adv.* then, next 7
entendre *v.* to hear 6
entracte *m.* intermission 15
entre *prep.* between 3
entrée *f.* appetizer, starter 9
entreprise *f.* firm, business 13
entrer *v.* to enter 7
entretien: passer un entretien *to have an interview* 13
enveloppe *f.* envelope 12
envie *f.* desire, envy 2
avoir envie (de) to feel like (*doing something*) 2
environnement *m.* environment 14
envoyer (à) *v.* to send (*to someone*) 5
épargne *f.* savings 12
compte d'épargne *m.* savings account 12
épicerie *f.* grocery store 4
épouser *v.* to marry 3
épouvantable *adj.* dreadful 5
Il fait un temps épouvantable. The weather is dreadful. 5
époux/épouse *m., f.* husband/wife 3
équipe *f.* team 5
escalier *m.* staircase 8
escargot *m.* escargot, snail 9
espace *m.* space 14
Espagne *f.* Spain 7
espagnol(e) *adj.* Spanish 1
espèce (menacée) *f.* (endangered) species 14
espérer *v.* to hope 5
essayer *v.* to try 5
essence *f.* gas 11
réservoir d'essence *m.* gas tank 11

voyant d'essence *m.* gas warning light 11
essentiel(le) *adj.* essential 14
Il est essentiel que... It is essential that... 14
essuie-glace *m.* **(essuie-glaces** *pl.***)** windshield wiper(s) 11
essuyer (la vaisselle/la table) *v.* to wipe (the dishes/ the table) 8
est *m.* east 12
Est-ce que... ? *(used in forming questions)* 2
et *conj.* and 1
Et toi? *fam.* And you? 1
Et vous? *form.* And you? 1
étage *m.* floor 7
étagère *f.* shelf 8
étape *f.* stage 6
état civil *m.* marital status 6
États-Unis *m., pl.* United States 7
été *m.* summer 5
en été in the summer 5
été (être) *p.p.* been 6
éteindre *v.* to turn off 11
éternuer *v.* to sneeze 10
étoile *f.* star 14
étranger/étrangère *adj.* foreign 2
langues étrangères *f., pl.* foreign languages 2
étranger *m.* *(places that are)* abroad, overseas 7
à l'étranger abroad, overseas 7
étrangler *v.* to strangle 13
être *v.* to be 1
être bien/mal payé(e) to be well/badly paid 13
être connecté(e) avec quelqu'un to be online with someone 7, 11
être en ligne avec to be online with 11
être en pleine forme to be in good shape 10
études (supérieures) *f., pl.* studies; (higher) education 2
étudiant(e) *m., f.* student 1
étudier *v.* to study 2
eu (avoir) *p.p.* had 6
eux *disj. pron., m., pl.* they, them 3
évidemment *adv.* obviously, evidently; of course 7
évident(e) *adj.* evident, obvious 15
Il est évident que... It is evident that... 15
évier *m.* sink 8
éviter (de) *v.* to avoid *(doing something)* 10
exactement *adv.* exactly 9
examen *m.* exam; test 1
être reçu(e) à un examen *v.* to pass an exam 2
passer un examen *v.* to take an exam 2
Excuse-moi. *fam.* Excuse me. 1
Excusez-moi. *form.* Excuse me. 1
exercice *m.* exercise 10
faire de l'exercice *v.* to exercise 10
exigeant(e) *adj.* demanding 13
profession (exigeante) *f.* a (demanding) profession 13
exiger (que) *v.* to demand (that) 14
expérience (professionnelle) *f.* (professional) experience 13
expliquer *v.* to explain 2
explorer *v.* to explore 4
exposition *f.* exhibit 15
extinction *f.* extinction 14

F

facile *adj.* easy 2
facilement *adv.* easily 7
facteur *m.* mailman 12
faculté *f.* university; faculty 1
faible *adj.* weak 3
faim *f.* hunger 4
avoir faim *v.* to be hungry 4
faire *v.* to do; to make 5
faire attention (à) *v.* to pay attention (to) 5
faire quelque chose de beau *v.* to be up to something interesting 12
faire de l'aérobic *v.* to do aerobics 5
faire de la gym *v.* to work out 5
faire de la musique *v.* to play music 13
faire de la peinture *v.* to paint 15
faire de la planche à voile *v.* to go windsurfing 5
faire de l'exercice *v.* to exercise 10
faire des projets *v.* to make plans 13
faire du camping *v.* to go camping 5
faire du cheval *v.* to go horseback riding 5
faire du jogging *v.* to go jogging 5
faire du shopping *v.* to go shopping 7
faire du ski *v.* to go skiing 5
faire du sport *v.* to do sports 5
faire du vélo *v.* to go bike riding 5
faire la connaissance de *v.* to meet *(someone)* 5
faire la cuisine *v.* to cook 5
faire la fête *v.* to party 6
faire la lessive *v.* to do the laundry 8
faire la poussière *v.* to dust 8
faire la queue *v.* to wait in line 12
faire la vaisselle *v.* to do the dishes 8
faire le lit *v.* to make the bed 8
faire le ménage *v.* to do the housework 8
faire le plein *v.* to fill the tank 11
faire les courses *v.* to run errands 9
faire les musées *v.* to go to museums 15
faire les valises *v.* to pack one's bags 7
faire mal *v.* to hurt 10
faire plaisir à quelqu'un *v.* to please someone 13
faire sa toilette *v.* to wash up 10
faire une piqûre *v.* to give a shot 10
faire une promenade *v.* to go for a walk 5
faire une randonnée *v.* to go for a hike 5
faire un séjour *v.* to spend time *(somewhere)* 7
faire un tour (en voiture) *v.* to go for a walk (drive) 5
faire visiter *v.* to give a tour 8
fait (faire) *p.p., adj.* done; made 6
falaise *f.* cliff 14
faut (falloir) *v. (used with infinitive)* is necessary to... 5
Il a fallu... It was necessary to... 6
Il fallait... One had to... 8
Il faut que... One must.../It is necessary that... 14
fallu (falloir) *p.p. (used with infinitive)* had to... 6
Il a fallu... It was necessary to... 6
famille *f.* family 3
fatigué(e) *adj.* tired 3
fauteuil *m.* armchair 8
favori/favorite *adj.* favorite 3
fax *m.* fax (machine) 11
félicitations congratulations 15
femme *f.* woman; wife 1
femme d'affaires business-woman 3
femme au foyer housewife 13
femme auteur author 15

femme cadre executive 13
femme écrivain writer 15
femme peintre painter 15
femme politique politician 13
femme pompier firefighter 13
femme sculpteur sculptor 15
fenêtre *f.* window 1
fer à repasser *m.* iron 8
férié(e) *adj.* holiday 6
jour férié *m.* holiday 6
fermé(e) *adj.* closed 12
fermer *v.* to close; to shut off 11
festival (festivals *pl.***)** *m.* festival 15
fête *f.* party 6; celebration 6
faire la fête *v.* to party 6
fêter *v.* to celebrate 6
feu de signalisation *m.* traffic light 12
feuille de papier *f.* sheet of paper 1
feuilleton *m.* soap opera 15
février *m.* February 5
fiancé(e) *adj.* engaged 3
fiancé(e) *m., f.* fiancé 6
fichier *m.* file 11
fier/fière *adj.* proud 3
fièvre *f.* fever 10
avoir de la fièvre *v.* to have a fever 10
fille *f.* girl; daughter 1
film (d'aventures, d'horreur, de science-fiction, policier) *m.* (adventure, horror, science-fiction, crime) film 15
fils *m.* son 3
fin *f.* end 15
finalement *adv.* finally 7
fini (finir) *p.p., adj.* finished, done, over 4
finir (de) *v.* to finish (*doing something*) 4
fleur *f.* flower 8
fleuve *m.* river 14
fois *f.* time 8
une fois *adv.* once 7
deux fois *adv.* twice 7
fonctionner *v.* to work, to function 11
fontaine *f.* fountain 12
foot(ball) *m.* soccer 5
football américain *m.* football 5
forêt (tropicale) *f.* (tropical) forest 14
formation *f.* education; training 13
forme *f.* shape; form 10
être en pleine forme *v.* to be in good shape 10
formidable *adj.* great 7
formulaire *m.* form 12
remplir un formulaire to fill out a form 12
fort(e) *adj.* strong 3
fou/folle *adj.* crazy 3
four (à micro-ondes) *m.* (microwave) oven 8
fourchette *f.* fork 9
frais/fraîche *adj.* fresh; cool 5
Il fait frais. (*weather*) It is cool. 5
fraise *f.* strawberry 9
français(e) *adj.* French 1
France *f.* France 7
franchement *adv.* frankly, honestly 7
freiner *v.* to brake 11
freins *m., pl.* brakes 11
fréquenter *v.* to frequent; to visit 4
frère *m.* brother 3
beau-frère *m.* brother-in-law 3
demi-frère *m.* half-brother, stepbrother 3
frigo *m.* refrigerator 8
frisé(e) *adj.* curly 3
frites *f., pl.* French fries 4
froid *m.* cold 2
avoir froid to be cold 2
Il fait froid. *(weather)* It is cold. 5
fromage *m.* cheese 4
fruit *m.* fruit 9
fruits de mer *m., pl.* seafood 9
fumer *v.* to smoke 10
funérailles *f., pl.* funeral 9
furieux/furieuse *adj.* furious 14
être furieux/furieuse que... *v.* to be furious that... 14

G

gagner *v.* to win 5; to earn 13
gant *m.* glove 6
garage *m.* garage 8
garanti(e) *adj.* guaranteed 5
garçon *m.* boy 1
garder la ligne *v.* to stay slim 10
gare (routière) *f.* train station (bus station) 7
gaspillage *m.* waste 14
gaspiller *v.* to waste 14
gâteau *m.* cake 6
gauche *f.* the left (side) 3
à gauche (de) *prep.* to the left (of) 3
gazeux/gazeuse *adj.* carbonated, fizzy 4
boisson gazeuse *f.* carbonated drink/beverage 4
généreux/généreuse *adj.* generous 3
génial(e) *adj.* great 3
genou *m.* knee 10
genre *m.* genre 15
gens *m., pl.* people 7
gentil/gentille *adj.* nice 3
gentiment *adv.* nicely 7
géographie *f.* geography 2
gérant(e) *m., f.* manager 13
gestion *f.* business administration 2
glace *f.* ice cream 6
glaçon *m.* ice cube 6
glissement de terrain *m.* landslide 14
golf *m.* golf 5
gorge *f.* throat 10
goûter *m.* afternoon snack 9; *v.* to taste 9
gouvernement *m.* government 14
grand(e) *adj.* big 3
grand magasin *m.* department store 4
grandir *v.* to grow 4
grand-mère *f.* grandmother 3
grand-père *m.* grandfather 3
grands-parents *m., pl.* grandparents 3
gratin *m.* gratin 9
gratuit(e) *adj.* free 15
grave *adj.* serious 10
Ce n'est pas grave. It's okay.; No problem. 6
graver *v.* to record, to burn (CD, DVD) 11
grille-pain *m.* toaster 8
grippe *f.* flu 10
gris(e) *adj.* gray 6
gros(se) *adj.* fat 3
grossir *v.* to gain weight 4
guérir *v.* to get better 10
guitare *f.* guitar 15
gym *f.* exercise 5
faire de la gym *v.* to work out 5
gymnase *m.* gym 4

H

habitat *m.* habitat 14
sauvetage des habitats *m.* habitat preservation 14
habiter (à) *v.* to live (in/at) 2
haricots verts *m., pl.* green beans 9
Hein? *interj.* Huh?; Right? 3
herbe *f.* grass 14
hésiter (à) *v.* to hesitate (*to do something*) 11
heure(s) *f.* hour, o'clock; time 2
à ... heure(s) at ... (o'clock) 4
À quelle heure? What time?; When? 2
À tout à l'heure. See you later. 1

Quelle heure avez-vous? *form.* What time do you have? 2
Quelle heure est-il? What time is it? 2
heureusement *adv.* fortunately 7
heureux/heureuse *adj.* happy 3
être heureux/heureuse que... to be happy that... 14
hier (matin/après-midi/soir) *adv.* yesterday (morning/afternoon/evening) 7
avant-hier *adv.* day before yesterday 7
histoire *f.* history; story 2
hiver *m.* winter 5
en hiver in the winter 5
homme *m.* man 1
homme d'affaires *m.* businessman 3
homme politique *m.* politician 13
honnête *adj.* honest 15
honte *f.* shame 2
avoir honte (de) *v.* to be ashamed (of) 2
hôpital *m.* hospital 4
horloge *f.* clock 1
hors-d'œuvre *m.* hors d'œuvre, appetizer 9
hôte/hôtesse *m., f.* host 6
hôtel *m.* hotel 7
hôtelier/hôtelière *m., f.* hotel keeper 7
huile *f.* oil 9
huile *f.* (automobile) oil 11
huile d'olive *f.* olive oil 9
vérifier l'huile to check the oil 11
voyant d'huile *m.* oil warning light 11
huit *m.* eight 1
huitième *adj.* eighth 7
humeur *f.* mood 8
être de bonne/mauvaise humeur *v.* to be in a good/bad mood 8

I

ici *adv.* here 1
idée *f.* idea 3
il *sub. pron.* he; it 1
il est... he/it is... 1
Il n'y a pas de quoi. It's nothing.; You're welcome. 1
Il vaut mieux que... It is better that... 14
Il faut (falloir) *v. (used with infinitive)* It is necessary to... 6
Il a fallu... It was necessary to... 6
Il fallait... One had to... 8
Il faut (que)... One must.../ It is necessary that... 14
il y a there is/are 1
il y a eu there was/were 6
il y avait there was/were 8
Qu'est-ce qu'il y a? What is it?; What's wrong? 1
Y a-t-il... ? Is/Are there... ? 2
il y a... *(used with an expression of time)* ... ago 9
île *f.* island 14
ils *sub. pron., m., pl.* they 1
ils sont... they are... 1
immeuble *m.* building 8
impatient(e) *adj.* impatient 1
imperméable *m.* rain jacket 5
important(e) *adj.* important 1
Il est important que... It is important that... 14
impossible *adj.* impossible 15
Il est impossible que... It is impossible that... 15
imprimante *f.* printer 11
imprimer *v.* to print 11
incendie *m.* fire 14
prévenir l'incendie to prevent a fire 14
incroyable *adj.* incredible 11
indépendamment *adv.* independently 7
indépendant(e) *adj.* independent 1
indications *f.* directions 12
indiquer *v.* to indicate 5
indispensable *adj.* essential, indispensable 14
Il est indispensable que... It is essential that... 14
individuel(le) *adj.* single, individual 7
chambre individuelle *f.* single (hotel) room 7
infirmier/infirmière *m., f.* nurse 10
informations (infos) *f., pl.* news 15
informatique *f.* computer science 2
ingénieur *m.* engineer 3
inquiet/inquiète *adj.* worried 3
instrument *m.* instrument 1
intellectuel(le) *adj.* intellectual 3
intelligent(e) *adj.* intelligent 1
interdire *v.* to forbid, to prohibit 14
intéressant(e) *adj.* interesting 1
inutile *adj.* useless 2
invité(e) *m., f.* guest 6
inviter *v.* to invite 4
irlandais(e) *adj.* Irish 7
Irlande *f.* Ireland 7
Italie *f.* Italy 7
italien(ne) *adj.* Italian 1

J

jaloux/jalouse *adj.* jealous 3
jamais *adv.* never 5
ne... jamais never, not ever 12
jambe *f.* leg 10
jambon *m.* ham 4
janvier *m.* January 5
Japon *m.* Japan 7
japonais(e) *adj.* Japanese 1
jardin *m.* garden; yard 8
jaune *adj.* yellow 6
je/j' *sub. pron.* I 1
Je vous en prie. *form.* Please.; You're welcome. 1
jean *m., sing.* jeans 6
jeter *v.* to throw away 14
jeu *m.* game 5
jeu télévisé *m.* game show 15
jeu vidéo (des jeux vidéo) *m.* video game(s) 11
jeudi *m.* Thursday 2
jeune *adj.* young 3
jeunes mariés *m., pl.* newlyweds 6
jeunesse *f.* youth 6
auberge de jeunesse *f.* youth hostel 7
jogging *m.* jogging 5
faire du jogging *v.* to go jogging 5
joli(e) *adj.* handsome; beautiful 3
joue *f.* cheek 10
jouer (à/de) *v.* to play *(a sport/a musical instrument)* 5
jouer un rôle *v.* to play a role 15
joueur/joueuse *m., f.* player 5
jour *m.* day 2
jour de congé *m.* day off 7
jour férié *m.* holiday 6
Quel jour sommes-nous? *What day is it?* 2
journal *m.* newspaper; journal 7
journaliste *m., f.* journalist 3
journée *f.* day 2
juillet *m.* July 5
juin *m.* June 5
jungle *f.* jungle 14
jupe *f.* skirt 6
jus (d'orange/de pomme) *m.* (orange/apple) juice 4
jusqu'à (ce que) *prep.* until 12
juste *adv.* just; right 3
juste à côté right next door 3

K

kilo(gramme) *m.* kilo(gram) **9**
kiosque *m.* kiosk **4**

L

l' *def. art., m., f. sing.* the **1**; *d.o. pron., m., f. him; her; it* **7**
la *def. art., f. sing.* the **1**; *d.o. pron., f. her; it* **7**
là(-bas) (over) there **1**
-là *(used with demonstrative adjective* **ce** *and noun or with demonstrative pronoun* **celui***)* there **6**
lac *m.* lake **14**
laid(e) *adj.* ugly **3**
laine *f.* wool **12**
laisser *v.* to let, to allow **11**
  laisser tranquille *v.* to leave alone **10**
  laisser un message *v.* to leave a message **13**
  laisser un pourboire *v.* to leave a tip **4**
lait *m.* milk **4**
laitue *f.* lettuce **9**
lampe *f.* lamp **8**
langues (étrangères) *f., pl.* (foreign) languages **2**
lapin *m.* rabbit **14**
laquelle *pron., f., sing.* which one **13**
  à laquelle *pron., f., sing.* which one **13**
  de laquelle *pron., f., sing.* which one **13**
large *adj.* loose; big **6**
lavabo *m.* bathroom sink **8**
lave-linge *m.* washing machine **8**
laver *v.* to wash **8**
laverie *f.* laundromat **12**
lave-vaisselle *m.* dishwasher **8**
le *def. art., m. sing.* the **1**; *d.o. pron.* him; it **7**
lecteur de CD/DVD *m.* CD/DVD player **11**
légume *m.* vegetable **9**
lent(e) *adj.* slow **3**
lequel *pron., m., sing.* which one **13**
  auquel (à + lequel) *pron., m., sing.* which one **13**
  duquel (de + lequel) *pron., m., sing.* which one **13**
les *def. art., m., f., pl.* the **1**; *d.o. pron., m., f., pl.* them **7**
lesquelles *pron., f., pl.* which ones **13**
  auxquelles (à + lesquelles) *pron., f., pl.* which ones **13**
  desquelles (de + lesquelles) *pron., f., pl.* which ones **13**
lesquels *pron., m., pl.* which ones **13**
  auxquels (à + lesquels) *pron., m., pl.* which ones **13**
  desquels (de + lesquels) *pron., m., pl.* which ones **13**
lessive *f.* laundry **8**
  faire la lessive *v.* to do the laundry **8**
lettre *f.* letter **12**
  boîte aux lettres *f.* mailbox **12**
  lettre de motivation *f.* letter of application **13**
  lettre de recommandation *f.* letter of recommendation, reference letter **13**
lettres *f., pl.* humanities **2**
leur *i.o. pron., m., f., pl.* them **6**
leur(s) *poss. adj., m., f.* their **3**
  le leur *poss. pron.* their **15**
  la leur *poss. pron.* their **15**
  les leurs *poss. pron.* theirs **15**
librairie *f.* bookstore **1**
libre *adj.* available **7**
lieu *m.* place **4**
ligne *f.* figure, shape **10**
  garder la ligne *v.* to stay slim **10**
limitation de vitesse *f.* speed limit **11**
limonade *f.* lemon soda **4**
linge *m.* laundry **8**
  lave-linge *m.* washing machine **8**
  sèche-linge *m.* clothes dryer **8**
liquide *m.* cash *(money)* **12**
  payer en liquide *v.* to pay in cash **12**
lire *v.* to read **7**
lit *m.* bed **7**
  faire le lit *v.* to make the bed **8**
littéraire *adj.* literary **15**
littérature *f.* literature **1**
livre *m.* book **1**
logement *m.* housing **8**
logiciel *m.* software, program **11**
loi *f.* law **14**
loin de *prep.* far from **3**
loisir *m.* leisure activity **5**
long(ue) *adj.* long **3**
  chemise à manches longues *f.* long-sleeved shirt **6**
longtemps *adv.* a long time **5**
louer *v.* to rent **8**
loyer *m.* rent **8**
lu (lire) *p.p.* read **7**
lui *pron., sing.* he **1**; him **3**; *i.o. pron. (attached to imperative)* to him/her **9**
l'un(e) à l'autre to one another **11**
l'un(e) l'autre one another **11**
lundi *m.* Monday **2**
Lune *f.* moon **14**
lunettes (de soleil) *f., pl.* (sun)glasses **6**
lycée *m.* high school **1**
lycéen(ne) *m., f.* high school student **2**

M

ma *poss. adj., f., sing.* my **3**
Madame *f.* Ma'am; Mrs. **1**
Mademoiselle *f.* Miss **1**
magasin *m.* store **4**
  grand magasin *m.* department store **4**
magazine *m.* magazine **15**
magnétophone *m.* tape recorder **11**
magnétoscope *m.* videocassette recorder (VCR) **11**
mai *m.* May **5**
maigrir *v.* to lose weight **4**
maillot de bain *m.* swimsuit, bathing suit **6**
main *f.* hand **5**
  sac à main *m.* purse, handbag **6**
maintenant *adv.* now **5**
maintenir *v.* to maintain **9**
mairie *f.* town/city hall; mayor's office **12**
mais *conj.* but **1**
  mais non (but) of course not; no **2**
maison *f.* house **4**
  rentrer à la maison *v.* to return home **2**
mal *adv.* badly **7**
  Je vais mal. I am doing badly. **1**
  le plus mal *super. adv.* the worst **9**
  se porter mal *v.* to be doing badly **10**
mal *m.* illness; ache, pain **10**
  avoir mal *v.* to have an ache **10**
  avoir mal au cœur *v.* to feel nauseated **10**
  faire mal *v.* to hurt **10**
malade *adj.* sick, ill **10**
  tomber malade *v.* to get sick **10**
maladie *f.* illness **13**
  assurance maladie *f.* health insurance **13**
malheureusement *adv.* unfortunately **2**
malheureux/malheureuse *adj.* unhappy **3**
manche *f.* sleeve **6**
  chemise à manches courtes/longues *f.* short-/long-sleeved shirt **6**
manger *v.* to eat **2**
  salle à manger *f.* dining room **8**
manteau *m.* coat **6**
maquillage *m.* makeup **10**

marchand de journaux *m.* newsstand 12
marché *m.* market 4
bon marché *adj.* inexpensive 6
marcher *v.* to walk *(person)* 5; to work *(thing)* 11
mardi *m.* Tuesday 2
mari *m.* husband 3
mariage *m.* marriage; wedding *(ceremony)* 6
marié(e) *adj.* married 3
mariés *m., pl.* married couple 6
jeunes mariés *m., pl.* newlyweds 6
marocain(e) *adj.* Moroccan 1
marron *adj., inv.* (not for hair) brown 3
mars *m.* March 5
martiniquais(e) *adj.* from Martinique 1
match *m.* game 5
mathématiques (maths) *f., pl.* mathematics 2
matin *m.* morning 2
ce matin *adv.* this morning 2
demain matin *adv.* tomorrow morning 2
hier matin *adv.* yesterday morning 7
matinée *f.* morning 2
mauvais(e) *adj.* bad 3
Il fait mauvais. The weather is bad. 5
le/la plus mauvais(e) *super. adj.* the worst 9
mayonnaise *f.* mayonnaise 9
me/m' *pron., sing.* me; myself 6
mec *m.* guy 10
mécanicien *m.* mechanic 11
mécanicienne *f.* mechanic 11
méchant(e) *adj.* mean 3
médecin *m.* doctor 3
médicament (contre/pour) *m.* medication (against/for) 10
meilleur(e) *comp. adj.* better 9
le/la meilleur(e) *super. adj.* the best 9
membre *m.* member 15
même *adj.* even 5; same
-même(s) *pron.* -self/-selves 6
menacé(e) *adj.* endangered 14
espèce menacée *f.* endangered species 14
ménage *m.* housework 8
faire le ménage *v.* to do housework 8
ménager/ménagère *adj.* household 8
appareil ménager *m.* household appliance 8
tâche ménagère *f.* household chore 8
mention *f.* distinction 13
menu *m.* menu 9
mer *f.* sea 7
Merci (beaucoup). Thank you (very much). 1
mercredi *m.* Wednesday 2
mère *f.* mother 3
belle-mère *f.* mother-in-law; stepmother 3
mes *poss. adj., m., f., pl.* my 3
message *m.* message 13
laisser un message *v.* to leave a message 13
messagerie *f.* voicemail 13
météo *f.* weather 15
métier *m.* profession 13
métro *m.* subway 7
station de métro *f.* subway station 7
metteur en scène *m.* director *(of a play)* 15
mettre *v.* to put, to place 6
mettre la table to set the table 8
meuble *m.* piece of furniture 8
mexicain(e) *adj.* Mexican 1
Mexique *m.* Mexico 7
Miam! *interj.* Yum! 5
micro-onde *m.* microwave oven 8
four à micro-ondes *m.* microwave oven 8
midi *m.* noon 2
après-midi *m.* afternoon 2
le mien *poss. pron.* mine 15
la mienne *poss. pron.* mine 15
les miens *poss. pron.* mine 15
les miennes *poss. pron.* mine 15
mieux *comp. adv.* better 9
aimer mieux *v.* to prefer 2
le mieux *super. adv.* the best 9
se porter mieux *v.* to be doing better 10
mille *m.* one thousand 5
cent mille *m.* one hundred thousand 5
million, un *m.* one million 5
deux millions *m.* two million 5
minuit *m.* midnight 2
miroir *m.* mirror 8
mis (mettre) *p.p.* put, placed 6
mode *f.* fashion 2
modeste *adj.* modest 13
moi *disj. pron., sing.* I, me 3; *pron. (attached to an imperative)* to me, to myself 9
Moi aussi. Me too. 1
Moi non plus. Me neither. 2
moins *adv.* before ... (o'clock) 2
moins (de) *adv.* less (of); fewer 4
le/la moins *super. adv. (used with verb or adverb)* the least 9
le moins de... *(used with noun to express quantity)* the least... 14
moins de... que... *(used with noun to express quantity)* less... than... 14
mois *m.* month 2
ce mois-ci this month 2
moment *m.* moment 1
mon *poss. adj., m., sing.* my 3
monde *m.* world 7
moniteur *m.* monitor 11
monnaie *f.* change, coins; money 12
Monsieur *m.* Sir; Mr. 1
montagne *f.* mountain 4
monter *v.* to go up, to come up; to get in/on 7
montre *f.* watch 1
montrer (à) *v.* to show *(to someone)* 6
morceau (de) *m.* piece, bit (of) 4
mort *f.* death 6
mort (mourir) *p.p., adj. (as past participle)* died; *(as adjective)* dead 7
mot de passe *m.* password 11
moteur *m.* engine 11
mourir *v.* to die 7
moutarde *f.* mustard 9
moyen(ne) *adj.* medium 3
de taille moyenne of medium height 3
mur *m.* wall 8
musée *m.* museum 4
faire les musées *v.* to go to museums 15
musical(e) *adj.* musical 15
comédie musicale *f.* musical 15
musicien(ne) *m., f.* musician 3
musique: faire de la musique *v.* to play music 15

N

nager *v.* to swim 4
naïf/naïve *adj.* naïve 3
naissance *f.* birth 6
naître *v.* to be born 7
nappe *f.* tablecloth 9
nationalité *f.* nationality 1
Je suis de nationalité... I am of ... nationality. 1
Quelle est ta nationalité? *fam.* What is your nationality? 1
Quelle est votre nationalité? *fam., pl., form.* What is your nationality? 1
nature *f.* nature 14
naturel(le) *adj.* natural 14
ressource naturelle *f.* natural resource 14

né (naître) *p.p., adj.* born 7
ne/n' no, not 1
ne... aucun(e) none, not any 12
ne... jamais never, not ever 12
ne... ni... ni... neither... nor... 12
ne... pas no, not 2
ne... personne nobody, no one 12
ne... plus no more, not anymore 12
ne... que only 12
ne... rien nothing, not anything 12
N'est-ce pas? *(tag question)* Isn't it? 2
nécessaire *adj.* necessary 14
Il est nécessaire que... It is necessary that... 14
neiger *v.* to snow 5
Il neige. It is snowing. 5
nerveusement *adv.* nervously 7
nerveux/nerveuse *adj.* nervous 3
nettoyer *v.* to clean 5
neuf *m.* nine 1
neuvième *adj.* ninth 7
neveu *m.* nephew 3
nez *m.* nose 10
ni nor 12
ne... ni... ni... neither... nor 12
nièce *f.* niece 3
niveau *m.* level 13
noir(e) *adj.* black 3
non no 2
mais non (but) of course not; no 2
nord *m.* north 12
nos *poss. adj., m., f., pl.* our 3
note *f. (academics)* grade 2
notre *poss. adj., m., f., sing.* our 3
le nôtre *poss. pron.* ours 15
la nôtre *poss. pron.* ours 15
les nôtres *poss. pron.* ours 15
nourriture *f.* food, sustenance 9
nous *pron.* we 1; us 3; ourselves 10
nouveau/nouvelle *adj.* new 3
nouvelles *f., pl.* news 15
novembre *m.* November 5
nuage de pollution *m.* pollution cloud 14
nuageux/nuageuse *adj.* cloudy 5
Le temps est nuageux. It is cloudy. 5
nucléaire *adj.* nuclear 14
centrale nucléaire *f.* nuclear plant 14
énergie nucléaire *f.* nuclear energy 14
nuit *f.* night 2
boîte de nuit *f.* nightclub 4
nul(le) *adj.* useless 2
numéro *m.* (telephone) number 11
composer un numéro *v.* to dial a number 11
recomposer un numéro *v.* to redial a number 11

O

obéir (à) *v.* to obey 4
objet *m.* object 1
obtenir *v.* to get, to obtain 13
occupé(e) *adj.* busy 1
octobre *m.* October 5
œil (les yeux) *m.* eye (eyes) 10
œuf *m.* egg 9
œuvre *f.* artwork, piece of art 15
chef-d'œuvre *m.* masterpiece 15
hors-d'œuvre *m.* hors d'œuvre, starter 9
offert (offrir) *p.p.* offered 11
office du tourisme *m.* tourist office 12
offrir *v.* to offer 11
oignon *m.* onion 9
oiseau *m.* bird 3
olive *f.* olive 9
huile d'olive *f.* olive oil 9
omelette *f.* omelette 5
on *sub. pron., sing.* one (we) 1
on y va let's go 10
oncle *m.* uncle 3
onze *m.* eleven 1
onzième *adj.* eleventh 7
opéra *m.* opera 15
optimiste *adj.* optimistic 1
orageux/orageuse *adj.* stormy 5
Le temps est orageux. It is stormy. 5
orange *adj. inv.* orange 6; *f.* orange 9
orchestre *m.* orchestra 15
ordinateur *m.* computer 1
ordonnance *f.* prescription 10
ordures *f., pl.* trash 14
ramassage des ordures *m.* garbage collection 14
oreille *f.* ear 10
oreiller *m.* pillow 8
organiser (une fête) *v.* to organize/to plan (a party) 6
origine *f.* heritage 1
Je suis d'origine... I am of... heritage. 1
orteil *m.* toe 10
ou *or* 3
où *adv., rel. pron.* where 4, 13
ouais *adv.* yeah 2
oublier (de) *v.* to forget *(to do something)* 2
ouest *m.* west 12
oui *adv.* yes 2
ouvert (ouvrir) *p.p., adj. (as past participle)* opened; *(as adjective)* open 11
ouvrier/ouvrière *m., f.* worker, laborer 13
ouvrir *v.* to open 11
ozone *m.* ozone 14
trou dans la couche d'ozone *m.* hole in the ozone layer 14

P

page d'accueil *f.* home page 11
pain (de campagne) *m.* (country-style) bread 4
panne *f.* breakdown, malfunction 11
tomber en panne *v.* to break down 11
pantalon *m., sing.* pants 6
pantoufle *f.* slipper 10
papeterie *f.* stationery store 12
papier *m.* paper 1
corbeille à papier *f.* wastebasket 1
feuille de papier *f.* sheet of paper 1
paquet cadeau *m.* wrapped gift 6
par *prep.* by 3
par jour/semaine/mois/an per day/week/month/year 5
parapluie *m.* umbrella 5
parc *m.* park 4
parce que *conj.* because 2
Pardon. Pardon (me). 1
Pardon? What? 4
pare-brise *m.* windshield 11
pare-chocs *m.* bumper 11
parents *m., pl.* parents 3
paresseux/paresseuse *adj.* lazy 3
parfait(e) *adj.* perfect 4
parfois *adv.* sometimes 5
parking *m.* parking lot 11
parler (à) *v.* to speak (to) 6
parler (au téléphone) *v.* to speak (on the phone) 2
partager *v.* to share 2
partir *v.* to leave 5
partir en vacances *v.* to go on vacation 7
pas (de) *adv.* no, none 12
ne... pas no, not 2
pas de problème no problem 12
pas du tout not at all 2
pas encore not yet 8
Pas mal. Not badly. 1
passager/passagère *m., f.* passenger 7

passeport *m.* passport 7
passer *v.* to pass by; to spend time 7
passer chez quelqu'un *v.* to stop by someone's house 4
passer l'aspirateur *v.* to vacuum 8
passer un examen *v.* to take an exam 2
passe-temps *m.* pastime, hobby 5
pâté (de campagne) *m.* pâté, meat spread 9
pâtes *f., pl.* pasta 9
patiemment *adv.* patiently 7
patient(e) *m., f.* patient 10; *adj.* patient 1
patienter *v.* to wait (on the phone), to be on hold 13
patiner v. to skate 4
pâtisserie *f.* pastry shop, bakery, pastry 9
patron(ne) *m., f.* boss 25
pauvre *adj.* poor 3
payé (payer) *p.p., adj.* paid 13
être bien/mal payé(e) *v.* to be well/badly paid 13
payer *v.* to pay 5
payer avec une carte de crédit *v.* to pay with a credit card 12
payer en liquide *v.* to pay in cash 12
payer par chèque *v.* to pay by check 12
pays *m.* country 7
peau *f.* skin 10
pêche *f.* fishing 5; peach 9
aller à la pêche *v.* to go fishing 5
peigne *m.* comb 10
peintre/femme peintre *m., f.* painter 15
peinture *f.* painting 15
pendant (que) *prep.* during, while 7
pendant *(with time expression) prep.* for 9
pénible *adj.* tiresome 3
penser (que) *v.* to think (that) 2
ne pas penser que... to not think that... 15
Qu'en penses-tu? What do you think about that? 14
perdre *v.* to lose 6
perdre son temps *v.* to lose/ to waste time 6
perdu *p.p., adj.* lost 12
être perdu(e) to be lost 12
père *m.* father 3
beau-père *m.* father-in-law; stepfather 3
permettre (de) *v.* to allow *(to do something)* 6
permis *m.* permit; license 11
permis de conduire *m.* driver's license 11
permis (permettre) *p.p., adj.* permitted, allowed 6
personnage (principal) *m.* (main) character 15
personne *f.* person 1; *pron.* no one 12
ne... personne nobody, no one 12
pessimiste *adj.* pessimistic 1
petit(e) *adj.* small 3; short *(stature)* 3
petit(e) ami(e) *m., f.* boy-friend/girlfriend 1
petit-déjeuner *m.* breakfast 9
petite-fille *f.* granddaughter 3
petit-fils *m.* grandson 3
petits-enfants *m., pl.* grand-children 3
petits pois *m., pl.* peas 9
peu (de) *adv.* little; not much (of) 2
peur *f.* fear 2
avoir peur (de/que) *v.* to be afraid (of/that) 2
peut-être *adv.* maybe, perhaps 2
phares *m., pl.* headlights 11
pharmacie *f.* pharmacy 10
pharmacien(ne) *m., f.* pharmacist 10
philosophie *f.* philosophy 2
photo(graphie) *f.* photo(graph) 3
physique *f.* physics 2
piano *m.* piano 15
pièce *f.* room 8
pièce de théâtre *f.* play 15
pièces de monnaie *f., pl.* change 12
pied *m.* foot 10
pierre *f.* stone 14
pilule *f.* pill 10
pique-nique *m.* picnic 14
piqûre *f.* shot, injection 10
faire une piqûre *v.* to give a shot 10
pire *comp. adj.* worse 9
le/la pire *super. adj.* the worst 9
piscine *f.* pool 4
placard *m.* closet; cupboard 8
place *f.* square; place 4; *f.* seat 15
plage *f.* beach 7
plaisir *m.* pleasure, enjoyment 13
faire plaisir à quelqu'un *v.* to please someone 13
plan *m.* map 7
utiliser un plan *v.* to use a map 7
planche à voile *f.* windsurfing 5
faire de la planche à voile *v.* to go windsurfing 5
planète *f.* planet 14
sauver la planète *v.* to save the planet 14
plante *f.* plant 14
plastique *m.* plastic 14
emballage en plastique *m.* plastic wrapping/packaging 14
plat (principal) *m.* (main) dish 9
plein air *m.* outdoor, open-air 14
pleine forme *f.* good shape, good state of health 10
être en pleine forme *v.* to be in good shape 10
pleurer *v.* to cry
pleuvoir *v.* to rain 5
Il pleut. It is raining. 5
plombier *m.* plumber 13
plu (pleuvoir) *p.p.* rained 6
pluie acide *f.* acid rain 14
plus *adv. (used in comparatives, superlatives, and expressions of quantity)* more 4
le/la plus ... *super. adv. (used with adjective)* the most 9
le/la plus mauvais(e) *super. adj.* the worst 9
le plus *super. adv. (used with verb or adverb)* the most 9
le plus de... *(used with noun to express quantity)* the most... 14
le plus mal *super. adv.* the worst 9
plus... que *(used with adjective)* more... than 9
plus de more of 4
plus de... que *(used with noun to express quantity)* more... than 14
plus mal *comp. adv.* worse 9
plus mauvais(e) *comp. adj.* worse 9
plus *adv.* no more, not anymore 12
ne... plus no more, not any-more 12
plusieurs *adj.* several 4
plutôt *adv.* rather 2
pneu (crevé) *m.* (flat) tire 11
vérifier la pression des pneus *v.* to check the tire pressure 11
poème *m.* poem 15
poète/poétesse *m., f.* poet 15
point *m. (punctuation mark)* period 11
poire *f.* pear 9
poisson *m.* fish 3
poissonnerie *f.* fish shop 9
poitrine *f.* chest 10
poivre *m. (spice)* pepper 9
poivron *m. (vegetable)* pepper 9
poli(e) *adj.* polite 1
police *f.* police 11
agent de police *m.* police officer 11

commissariat de police *m.* police station 12
policier *m.* police officer 11
film policier *m.* detective film 15
policière *f.* police officer 11
poliment *adv.* politely 7
politique *adj.* political 2
femme politique *f.* politician 13
homme politique *m.* politician 13
sciences politiques (sciences po) *f., pl.* political science 2
polluer *v.* to pollute 14
pollution *f.* pollution 14
nuage de pollution *m.* pollution cloud 14
pomme *f.* apple 9
pomme de terre *f.* potato 9
pompier/femme pompier *m., f.* firefighter 13
pont *m.* bridge 12
population croissante *f.* growing population 14
porc *m.* pork 9
portable *m.* cell phone 11
porte *f.* door 1
porter *v.* to wear 6
portière *f.* car door 11
portrait *m.* portrait 5
poser une question (à) *v.* to ask (*someone*) a question 6
posséder *v.* to possess, to own 5
possible *adj.* possible 15
Il est possible que... *It is possible that...* 14
poste *f.* postal service; post office 12
bureau de poste *m.* post office 12
poste *m.* position 13
poste de télévision *m.* television set 11
poster une lettre *v.* to mail a letter 12
postuler *v.* to apply 13
poulet *m.* chicken 9
pour *prep.* for 5
pour qui? for whom? 4
pour rien for no reason 4
pour que so that 15
pourboire *m.* tip 4
laisser un pourboire *v.* to leave a tip 4
pourquoi? *adv.* why? 2
poussière *f.* dust 8
enlever/faire la poussière *v.* to dust 8
pouvoir *v.* to be able to; can 9
pratiquer *v.* to play regularly, to practice 5
préféré(e) *adj.* favorite, preferred 2
préférer (que) *v.* to prefer (that) 5
premier *m.* the first (*day of the month*) 5
C'est le 1er (premier) octobre. It is October first. 5
premier/première *adj.* first 2
prendre *v.* to take 4; to have 4
prendre sa retraite *v.* to retire 6
prendre un train/avion/taxi/autobus/bateau *v.* to take a train/plane/taxi/bus/boat 7
prendre un congé *v.* to take time off 13
prendre une douche *v.* to take a shower 10
prendre (un) rendez-vous *v.* to make an appointment 13
préparer *v.* to prepare (for) 2
près (de) *prep.* close (to), near 3
tout près (de) very close (to) 12
présenter *v.* to present, to introduce 15
Je te présente... *fam.* I would like to introduce... to you. 1
Je vous présente... *fam., form.* I would like to introduce... to you. 1
préservation *f.* protection 14
préserver *v.* to preserve 14
presque *adv.* almost 2
pressé(e) *adj.* hurried 9
pression *f.* pressure 11
vérifier la pression des pneus to check the tire pressure 11
prêt(e) *adj.* ready 3
prêter (à) *v.* to lend (*to someone*) 6
prévenir l'incendie *v.* to prevent a fire 14
principal(e) *adj.* main, principal 9
personnage principal *m.* main character 15
plat principal *m.* main dish 9
printemps *m.* spring 5
au printemps in the spring 5
pris (prendre) *p.p., adj.* taken 6
prix *m.* price 4
problème *m.* problem 1
prochain(e) *adj.* next 2
produire *v.* to produce 6
produit *m.* product 14
produit (produire) *p.p., adj.* produced 6
professeur *m.* teacher, professor 1
profession (exigeante) *f.* (demanding) profession 13
professionnel(le) *adj.* professional 13
expérience professionnelle *f.* professional experience 13
profiter (de) *v.* to take advantage (of); to enjoy 15
programme *m.* program 15
projet *m.* project 13
faire des projets *v.* to make plans 13
promenade *f.* walk, stroll 5
faire une promenade *v.* to go for a walk 5
promettre *v.* to promise 6
promis (promettre) *p.p., adj.* promised 6
promotion *f.* promotion 13
proposer (que) *v.* to propose (that) 14
proposer une solution *v.* to propose a solution 14
propre *adj.* clean 8
propriétaire *m., f.* owner 8; landlord/landlady 8
protection *f.* protection 14
protéger *v.* to protect 5
psychologie *f.* psychology 2
psychologique *adj.* psychological 15
psychologue *m., f.* psychologist 13
pu (pouvoir) *p.p. (used with infinitive)* was able to 9
publicité (pub) *f.* advertisement 15
publier *v.* to publish 15
puis *adv.* then 7
pull *m.* sweater 6
pur(e) *adj.* pure 14

Q

quand *adv.* when 4
C'est quand l'anniversaire de ... ? When is ...'s birthday? 5
C'est quand ton/votre anniversaire? When is your birthday? 5
quarante *m.* forty 1
quart *m.* quarter 2
et quart a quarter after... (o'clock) 2
quartier *m.* area, neighborhood 8
quatorze *m.* fourteen 1
quatre *m.* four 1
quatre-vingts *m.* eighty 3
quatre-vingt-dix *m.* ninety 3
quatrième *adj.* fourth 7
que/qu' *rel. pron.* that; which 13; *conj.* than 9, 14
plus/moins ... que *(used with adjective)* more/less ... than 9
plus/moins de ... que *(used with noun to express quantity)* more/less ... than 14
que/qu'...? *interr. pron.* what? 4
Qu'en penses-tu? What do you think about that? 14

Qu'est-ce que c'est? What is it? 1
Qu'est-ce qu'il y a? What is it?; What's wrong? 1
que *adv.* only 12
ne... que only 12
québécois(e) *adj.* from Quebec 1
quel(le)(s)? *interr. adj.* which? 4; what? 4
À quelle heure? What time?; When? 2
Quel jour sommes-nous? What day is it? 2
Quelle est la date? What is the date? 5
Quelle est ta nationalité? *fam.* What is your nationality? 1
Quelle est votre nationalité? *form.* What is your nationality? 1
Quelle heure avez-vous? *form.* What time do you have? 2
Quelle heure est-il? What time is it? 2
Quelle température fait-il? *(weather)* What is the temperature? 5
Quel temps fait-il? What is the weather like? 5
quelqu'un *pron.* someone 12
quelque chose *m.* something; anything 4
Quelque chose ne va pas. Something's not right. 5
quelquefois *adv.* sometimes 7
quelques *adj.* some 4
question *f.* question 6
poser une question (à) to ask (*someone*) a question 6
queue *f.* line 12
faire la queue *v.* to wait in line 12
qui? *interr. pron.* who? 4; whom? 4; *rel. pron.* who, that 13
à qui? to whom? 4
avec qui? with whom? 4
C'est de la part de qui? On behalf of whom? 13
Qui est à l'appareil? Who's calling, please? 13
Qui est-ce? Who is it? 1
quinze *m.* fifteen 1
quitter (la maison) *v.* to leave (the house) 4
Ne quittez pas. Please hold. 13
quoi? *interr. pron.* what? 1
Il n'y a pas de quoi. It's nothing.; You're welcome. 1
quoi que ce soit whatever it may be 13

R

raccrocher *v.* to hang up 13
radio *f.* radio 15
à la radio on the radio 15
raide *adj.* straight 3
raison *f.* reason; right 2
avoir raison *v.* to be right 2
ramassage des ordures *m.* garbage collection 14
randonnée *f.* hike 5
faire une randonnée *v.* to go for a hike 5
ranger *v.* to tidy up, to put away 8
rapide *adj.* fast 3
rapidement *adv.* rapidly 7
rarement *adv.* rarely 5
rasoir *m.* razor 10
ravissant(e) *adj.* beautiful; delightful 13
réagir *v.* to react 4
réalisateur/réalisatrice *m., f.* director (*of a movie*) 15
récent(e) *adj.* recent 15
réception *f.* reception desk 7
recevoir *v.* to receive 12
réchauffement de la Terre *m.* global warming 14
rechercher *v.* to search for, to look for 13
recommandation *f.* recommendation 13
recommander (que) *v.* to recommend (that) 14
recomposer (un numéro) *v.* to redial (a number) 11
reconnaître *v.* to recognize 8
reconnu (reconnaître) *p.p., adj.* recognized 8
reçu *m.* receipt 12
reçu (recevoir) *p.p., adj.* received 7
être reçu(e) à un examen to pass an exam 2
recyclage *m.* recycling 14
recycler *v.* to recycle 14
redémarrer *v.* to restart, to start again 11
réduire *v.* to reduce 6
réduit (réduire) *p.p., adj.* reduced 6
référence *f.* reference 13
réfléchir (à) *v.* to think (about), to reflect (on) 4
refuser (de) *v.* to refuse (*to do something*) 11
regarder *v.* to watch 2
Ça ne nous regarde pas. That has nothing to do with us.; That is none of our business. 14
régime *m.* diet 10
être au régime *v.* to be on a diet 9
région *f.* region 14
regretter (que) *v.* to regret (that) 14
remplir (un formulaire) *v.* to fill out (a form) 12
rencontrer *v.* to meet 2
rendez-vous *m.* date; appointment 6
prendre (un) rendez-vous *v.* to make an appointment 13
rendre (à) *v.* to give back, to return (to) 6
rendre visite (à) *v.* to visit 6
rentrer (à la maison) *v.* to return (home) 2
rentrer (dans) *v.* to hit 11
renvoyer *v.* to dismiss, to let go 13
réparer *v.* to repair 11
repartir *v.* to go back 15
repas *m.* meal 9
repasser *v.* to take again 15
repasser (le linge) *v.* to iron (the laundry) 8
fer à repasser *m.* iron 8
répéter *v.* to repeat; to rehearse 5
répondeur (téléphonique) *m.* answering machine 11
répondre (à) *v.* to respond, to answer (to) 6
réservation *f.* reservation 7
annuler une réservation *v.* to cancel a reservation 7
réservé(e) *adj.* reserved 1
réserver *v.* to reserve 7
réservoir d'essence *m.* gas tank 11
résidence universitaire *f.* dorm 8
ressource naturelle *f.* natural resource 14
restaurant *m.* restaurant 4
restaurant universitaire (resto U) *m.* university cafeteria 2
rester *v.* to stay 7
résultat *m.* result 2
retenir *v.* to keep, to retain 9
retirer (de l'argent) *v.* to withdraw (money) 12
retourner *v.* to return 7
retraite *f.* retirement 6
prendre sa retraite *v.* to retire 6
retraité(e) *m., f.* retired person 13
retrouver *v.* to find (again); to meet up with 2
rétroviseur *m.* rear-view mirror 11
réunion *f.* meeting 13
réussir (à) *v.* to succeed (*in doing something*) 4
réussite *f.* success 13
réveil *m.* alarm clock 10
revenir *v.* to come back 9
rêver (de) *v.* to dream about 11

revoir *v.* to see again 12
Au revoir. Good-bye. 1
revu (revoir) *p.p.* seen again 12
rez-de-chaussée *m.* ground floor 7
rhume *m.* cold 10
ri (rire) *p.p.* laughed 6
rideau *m.* curtain 8
rien *m.* nothing 12
De rien. You're welcome. 1
ne... rien nothing, not anything 12
ne servir à rien *v.* to be good for nothing 9
rire *v.* to laugh 6
rivière *f.* river 14
riz *m.* rice 9
robe *f.* dress 6
rôle *m.* role 14
jouer un rôle *v.* to play a role 15
roman *m.* novel 15
rose *adj.* pink 6
roue (de secours) *f.* (emergency) tire 11
rouge *adj.* red 6
rougir *v.* to blush 4
rouler en voiture *v.* to ride in a car 7
rue *f.* street 11
suivre une rue *v.* to follow a street 12

S

s'adorer *v.* to adore one another 11
s'aider *v.* to help one another 11
s'aimer (bien) *v.* to love (like) one another 11
s'allumer *v.* to light up 11
s'amuser *v.* to play; to have fun 10
s'amuser à *v.* to pass time by 11
s'apercevoir *v.* to notice; to realize 12
s'appeler *v.* to be named, to be called 10
Comment t'appelles-tu? *fam.* What is your name? 1
Comment vous appelez-vous? *form.* What is your name? 1
Je m'appelle... My name is... 1
s'arrêter *v.* to stop 10
s'asseoir *v.* to sit down 10
sa *poss. adj., f., sing.* his; her; its 3
sac *m.* bag 1
sac à dos *m.* backpack 1
sac à main *m.* purse, handbag 6
sain(e) *adj.* healthy 10
saison *f.* season 5
salade *f.* salad 9
salaire (élevé/modeste) *m.* (high/low) salary 13
augmentation de salaire *f.* raise in salary 13
sale *adj.* dirty 8
salir *v.* to soil, to make dirty 8
salle *f.* room 8
salle à manger *f.* dining room 8
salle de bains *f.* bathroom 8
salle de classe *f.* classroom 1
salle de séjour *f.* living/family room 8
salon *m.* formal living room, sitting room 8
salon de beauté *m.* beauty salon 12
Salut! Hi!; Bye! 1
samedi *m.* Saturday 2
sandwich *m.* sandwich 4
sans *prep.* without 8
sans que *conj.* without 15
santé *f.* health 10
être en bonne/mauvaise santé *v.* to be in good/bad health 10
saucisse *f.* sausage 9
sauvegarder *v.* to save 11
sauver (la planète) *v.* to save (the planet) 14
sauvetage des habitats *m.* habitat preservation 14
savoir *v.* to know (*facts*), to know how to do something 8
savoir (que) *v.* to know (that) 15
Je n'en sais rien. I don't know anything about it. 14
savon *m.* soap 10
sciences *f., pl.* science 2
sciences politiques (sciences po) *f., pl.* political science 2
sculpture *f.* sculpture 15
sculpteur/femme sculpteur *m., f.* sculptor 15
se/s' *pron., sing., pl. (used with reflexive verb)* himself; herself; itself; 10 (*used with reciprocal verb*) each other 11
séance *f.* show; screening 15
se blesser *v.* to hurt oneself 10
se brosser (les cheveux/les dents) *v.* to brush one's (hair/teeth) 9
se casser *v.* to break 10
sèche-linge *m.* clothes dryer 8
se coiffer *v.* to do one's hair 10
se connaître *v.* to know one another 11
se coucher *v.* to go to bed 10
secours *m.* help 11
Au secours! Help! 11
s'écrire *v.* to write one another 11
sécurité *f.* security; safety
attacher sa ceinture de sécurité *v.* to buckle one's seatbelt 11
se dépêcher *v.* to hurry 10
se déplacer *v.* to move, to change location 12
se déshabiller *v.* to undress 10
se détendre *v.* to relax 10
se dire *v.* to tell one another 11
se disputer (avec) *v.* to argue (with) 10
se donner *v.* to give one another 11
se fouler (la cheville) *v.* to twist/to sprain one's (ankle) 10
se garer *v.* to park 11
seize *m.* sixteen 1
séjour *m.* stay 7
faire un séjour *v.* to spend time (*somewhere*) 7
salle de séjour *f.* living room 8
sel *m.* salt 9
se laver (les mains) *v.* to wash oneself (one's hands) 10
se lever *v.* to get up, to get out of bed 10
semaine *f.* week 2
cette semaine this week 2
s'embrasser *v.* to kiss one another 11
se maquiller *v.* to put on makeup 10
se mettre *v.* to put (*something*) on (yourself) 10
se mettre à *v.* to begin to 10
se mettre en colère *v.* to become angry 10
s'endormir *v.* to fall asleep, to go to sleep 10
s'énerver *v.* to get worked up, to become upset 10
sénégalais(e) *adj.* Senegalese 1
s'ennuyer *v.* to get bored 10
s'entendre bien (avec) *v.* to get along well (with one another) 10
sentier *m.* path 14
sentir *v.* to feel; to smell; to sense 5
séparé(e) *adj.* separated 3
se parler *v.* to speak to one another 11
se porter mal/mieux *v.* to be ill/better 10
se préparer (à) *v.* to get ready; to prepare (*to do something*) 10
se promener *v.* to take a walk 10
sept *m.* seven 1
septembre *m.* September 5

septième *adj.* seventh 7
se quitter *v.* to leave one another 11
se raser *v.* to shave oneself 10
se réconcilier *v.* to make up 15
se regarder *v.* to look at oneself; to look at each other 10
se relever *v.* to get up again 10
se rencontrer *v.* to meet one another, to make each other's acquaintance 11
se rendre compte *v.* to realize 10
se reposer *v.* to rest 10
se retrouver *v.* to meet one another (*as planned*) 11
se réveiller *v.* to wake up 10
se sécher *v.* to dry oneself 10
se sentir *v.* to feel 10
sérieux/sérieuse *adj.* serious 3
serpent *m.* snake 14
serre *f.* greenhouse 14
  effet de serre *m.* greenhouse effect 14
serré(e) *adj.* tight 6
serveur/serveuse *m., f.* server 4
serviette *f.* napkin 9
  serviette (de bain) *f.* (bath) towel 10
servir *v.* to serve 5
ses *poss. adj., m., f., pl.* his; her; its 3
se souvenir (de) *v.* to remember 10
se téléphoner *v.* to phone one another 11
se tourner *v.* to turn (oneself) around 10
se tromper (de) *v.* to be mistaken (about) 10
se trouver *v.* to be located 10
seulement *adv.* only 7
s'habiller *v.* to dress 10
shampooing *m.* shampoo 10
shopping *m.* shopping 7
  faire du shopping *v.* to go shopping 7
short *m., sing.* shorts 6
si *conj.* if 13
si *adv.* (*when contradicting a negative statement or question*) yes 2
le sien *poss. pron.* his/hers 15
la sienne *poss. pron.* his/hers 15
les siens *poss. pron.* his/hers 15
les siennes *poss. pron.* his/hers 15
signer *v.* to sign 12
S'il te plaît. *fam.* Please. 1
S'il vous plaît. *form.* Please. 1
sincère *adj.* sincere 1
s'inquiéter *v.* to worry 10
s'intéresser (à) *v.* to be interested (in) 10
site Internet/web *m.* web site 11
six *m.* six 1
sixième *adj.* sixth 7
ski *m.* skiing 5
  faire du ski *v.* to go skiing 5
  station de ski *f.* ski resort 7
skier *v.* to ski 5
s'occuper (de) *v.* to take care (*of something*), to see to 10
sociable *adj.* sociable 1
sociologie *f.* sociology 1
sœur *f.* sister 3
  belle-sœur *f.* sister-in-law 3
  demi-sœur *f.* half-sister, stepsister 3
soie *f.* silk 12
soif *f.* thirst 4
  avoir soif *v.* to be thirsty 4
soir *m.* evening 2
  ce soir *adv.* this evening 2
  demain soir *adv.* tomorrow evening 2
  du soir *adv.* in the evening 2
  hier soir *adv.* yesterday evening 7
soirée *f.* evening 2
sois (être) *imp. v.* be 2
soixante *m.* sixty 1
soixante-dix *m.* seventy 3
solaire *adj.* solar 14
  énergie solaire *f.* solar energy 14
soldes *f., pl.* sales 6
soleil *m.* sun 5
  Il fait (du) soleil. It is sunny. 5
solution *f.* solution 14
  proposer une solution *v.* to propose a solution 14
sommeil *m.* sleep 2
  avoir sommeil *v.* to be sleepy 2
son *poss. adj., m., sing.* his; her; its 3
sonner *v.* to ring 11
s'orienter *v.* to get one's bearings 12
sorte *f.* sort, kind 15
sortie *f.* exit 7
sortir *v.* to go out, to leave 5; to take out 8
  sortir la/les poubelle(s) *v.* to take out the trash 8
soudain *adv.* suddenly 7
souffrir *v.* to suffer 11
souffert (souffrir) *p.p.* suffered 11
souhaiter (que) *v.* to wish (that) 14
soupe *f.* soup 4
  cuillère à soupe *f.* soupspoon 9
sourire *v.* to smile 6; *m.* smile 12
souris *f.* mouse 11
sous *prep.* under 3
sous-sol *m.* basement 8
sous-vêtement *m.* underwear 6
souvent *adv.* often 5
soyez (être) *imp. v.* be 7
soyons (être) *imp. v.* let's be 7
spécialiste *m., f.* specialist 13
spectacle *m.* show 5
spectateur/spectatrice *m., f.* spectator 15
sport *m.* sport(s) 5
  faire du sport *v.* to do sports 5
sportif/sportive *adj.* athletic 3
stade *m.* stadium 5
stage *m.* internship; professional training 13
station (de métro) *f.* (subway) station 7
station de ski *f.* ski resort 7
station-service *f.* service station 11
statue *f.* statue 12
steak *m.* steak 9
studio *m.* studio (*apartment*) 8
stylisme *m.* **de mode** *f.* fashion design 2
stylo *m.* pen 1
su (savoir) *p.p.* known 8
sucre *m.* sugar 4
sud *m.* south 12
suggérer (que) *v.* to suggest (that) 14
sujet *m.* subject 14
  au sujet de on the subject of; about 14
suisse *adj.* Swiss 1
Suisse *f.* Switzerland 7
suivre (un chemin/une rue/un boulevard) *v.* to follow (a path/a street/a boulevard) 12
supermarché *m.* supermarket 9
sur *prep.* on 3
sûr(e) *adj.* sure, certain 9
  bien sûr of course 2
  Il est sûr que... It is sure that... 15
  Il n'est pas sûr que... It is not sure that... 15
surfer sur Internet *v.* to surf the Internet 11
surpopulation *f.* overpopulation 14
surpris (surprendre) *p.p., adj.* surprised 6
  être surpris(e) que... *v.* to be surprised that... 14
  faire une surprise à quelqu'un *v.* to surprise someone 6
surtout *adv.* especially; above all 2
sympa(thique) *adj.* nice 1
symptôme *m.* symptom 10
syndicat *m.* (*trade*) union 13

T

ta *poss. adj., f., sing.* your **3**
table *f.* table **1**
À table! Let's eat! Food is ready! **9**
débarrasser la table *v.* to clear the table **8**
mettre la table *v.* to set the table **8**
tableau *m.* blackboard; picture **1**; *m.* painting **15**
tâche ménagère *f.* household chore **8**
taille *f.* size; waist **6**
de taille moyenne of medium height **3**
tailleur *m.* (*woman's*) suit; tailor **6**
tante *f.* aunt **3**
tapis *m.* rug **8**
tard *adv.* late **2**
À plus tard. See you later. **1**
tarte *f.* pie; tart **9**
tasse (de) *f.* cup (of) **4**
taxi *m.* taxi **7**
prendre un taxi *v.* to take a taxi **7**
te/t' *pron., sing., fam.* you **7**; yourself **10**
tee-shirt *m.* tee shirt **6**
télécarte *f.* phone card **13**
télécharger *v.* to download **11**
télécommande *f.* remote control **11**
téléphone *m.* telephone **2**
parler au téléphone *v.* to speak on the phone **2**
téléphoner (à) *v.* to telephone (*someone*) **2**
téléphonique *adj.* (*related to the*) telephone **12**
cabine téléphonique *f.* phone booth **12**
télévision *f.* television **1**
à la télé(vision) on television **15**
chaîne de télévision *f.* television channel **11**
tellement *adv.* so much **2**
Je n'aime pas tellement... I don't like… very much. **2**
température *f.* temperature **5**
Quelle température fait-il? What is the temperature? **5**
temps *m., sing.* weather **5**
Il fait un temps épouvantable. The weather is dreadful. **5**
Le temps est nuageux. It is cloudy. **5**
Le temps est orageux. It is stormy. **5**
Quel temps fait-il? What is the weather like? **5**
temps *m., sing.* time **5**
de temps en temps *adv.* from time to time **7**
emploi à mi-temps/à temps partiel *m.* part-time job **13**
emploi à plein temps *m.* full-time job **13**
temps libre *m.* free time **5**
Tenez! (tenir) *imp. v.* Here! **9**
tenir *v.* to hold **9**
tennis *m.* tennis **5**
terrasse (de café) *f.* (café) terrace **4**
Terre *f.* Earth **14**
réchauffement de la Terre *m.* global warming **14**
tes *poss. adj., m., f., pl.* your **3**
tête *f.* head **10**
thé *m.* tea **4**
théâtre *m.* theater **15**
thon *m.* tuna **9**
ticket de bus/métro *m.* bus/subway ticket **7**
le tien *poss. pron.* yours **15**
la tienne *poss. pron.* yours **15**
les tiens *poss. pron.* yours **15**
les tiennes *poss. pron.* yours **15**
Tiens! (tenir) *imp. v.* Here! **9**
timbre *m.* stamp **12**
timide *adj.* shy **1**
tiret *m. (punctuation mark)* dash; hyphen **11**
tiroir *m.* drawer **8**
toi *disj. pron., sing., fam.* you **3**; *refl. pron., sing., fam. (attached to imperative)* yourself **10**
toi non plus you neither **2**
toilette *f.* washing up, grooming **10**
faire sa toilette to wash up **10**
toilettes *f., pl.* restroom(s) **8**
tomate *f.* tomato **9**
tomber *v.* to fall **7**
tomber amoureux/amoureuse *v.* to fall in love **6**
tomber en panne *v.* to break down **11**
tomber/être malade *v.* to get/be sick **10**
tomber sur quelqu'un *v.* to run into someone **7**
ton *poss. adj., m., sing.* your **3**
tort *m.* wrong; harm **2**
avoir tort *v.* to be wrong **2**
tôt *adv.* early **2**
toujours *adv.* always **7**
tour *m.* tour **5**
faire un tour (en voiture) *v.* to go for a walk (drive) **5**
tourisme *m.* tourism **12**
office du tourisme *m.* tourist office **12**
tourner *v.* to turn **12**
tousser *v.* to cough **10**
tout *m., sing.* all **4**
tous les *(used before noun)* all the... **4**
tous les jours *adv.* every day **7**
toute la *f., sing. (used before noun)* all the... **4**
toutes les *f., pl. (used before noun)* all the... **4**
tout le *m., sing. (used before noun)* all the... **4**
tout le monde everyone **9**
tout(e) *adv. (before adjective or adverb)* very, really **3**
À tout à l'heure. See you later. **1**
tout à coup suddenly **7**
tout à fait absolutely; completely **12**
tout de suite right away **7**
tout droit straight ahead **12**
tout d'un coup *adv.* all of a sudden **7**
tout près (de) really close by, really close (to) **3**
toxique *adj.* toxic **14**
déchets toxiques *m., pl.* toxic waste **14**
trac *m.* stage fright **13**
traduire *v.* to translate **6**
traduit (traduire) *p.p., adj.* translated **6**
tragédie *f.* tragedy **15**
train *m.* train **7**
tranche *f.* slice **9**
tranquille *adj.* calm, serene **10**
laisser tranquille *v.* to leave alone **10**
travail *m.* work **12**
chercher un/du travail *v.* to look for work **12**
trouver un/du travail *v.* to find a job **13**
travailler *v.* to work **2**
travailleur/travailleuse *adj.* hard-working **3**
traverser *v.* to cross **12**
treize *m.* thirteen **1**
trente *m.* thirty **1**
très *adv. (before adjective or adverb)* very, really **8**
Très bien. Very well. **1**
triste *adj.* sad **3**
être triste que... *v.* to be sad that… **14**
trois *m.* three **1**
troisième *adj.* third **7**
trop (de) *adv.* too many/much (of) **4**

tropical(e) *adj.* tropical **14**
forêt tropicale *f.* tropical forest **14**
trou (dans la couche d'ozone) *m.* hole (in the ozone layer) **14**
troupe *f.* company, troupe **15**
trouver *v.* to find; to think **2**
trouver un/du travail *v.* to find a job **13**
truc *m.* thing **7**
tu *sub. pron., sing., fam.* you **1**

U

un *m. (number)* one **1**
un(e) *indef. art.* a; an **1**
universitaire *adj. (related to the)* university **1**
restaurant universitaire (resto U) *m.* university cafeteria **2**
université *f.* university **1**
urgences *f., pl.* emergency room **10**
aller aux urgences *v.* to go to the emergency room **10**
usine *f.* factory **14**
utile *adj.* useful **2**
utiliser (un plan) *v.* use (a map) **7**

V

vacances *f., pl.* vacation **7**
partir en vacances *v.* to go on vacation **7**
vache *f.* cow **14**
vaisselle *f.* dishes **8**
faire la vaisselle *v.* to do the dishes **8**
lave-vaisselle *m.* dishwasher **8**
valise *f.* suitcase **7**
faire les valises *v.* to pack one's bags **7**
vallée *f.* valley **14**
variétés *f., pl.* popular music **15**
vaut (valloir) *v.*
Il vaut mieux que It is better that **14**
vélo *m.* bicycle **5**
faire du vélo *v.* to go bike riding **5**
velours *m.* velvet **12**
vendeur/vendeuse *m., f.* seller **6**
vendre *v.* to sell **6**
vendredi *m.* Friday **2**
venir *v.* to come **9**
venir de *v. (used with an infinitive)* to have just **9**
vent *m.* wind **5**
Il fait du vent. It is windy. **5**
ventre *m.* stomach **10**
vérifier (l'huile/la pression des pneus) *v.* to check (the oil/the tire pressure) **11**
véritable *adj.* true, real **12**
verre (de) *m.* glass (of) **4**
vers *adv.* about **2**
vert(e) *adj.* green **3**
haricots verts *m., pl.* green beans **9**
vêtements *m., pl.* clothing **6**
sous-vêtement *m.* underwear **6**
vétérinaire *m., f.* veterinarian **13**
veuf/veuve *adj.* widowed **3**
veut dire (vouloir dire) *v.* means, signifies **9**
viande *f.* meat **9**
vie *f.* life **6**
assurance vie *f.* life insurance **13**
vieille *adj., f. (feminine form of* **vieux***)* old **3**
vieillesse *f.* old age **6**
vieillir *v.* to grow old **4**
vietnamien(ne) *adj.* Vietnamese **1**
vieux/vieille *adj.* old **3**
ville *f.* city; town **4**
vin *m.* wine **6**
vingt *m.* twenty **1**
vingtième *adj.* twentieth **7**
violet(te) *adj.* purple; violet **6**
violon *m.* violin **15**
visage *m.* face **10**
visite *f.* visit **6**
rendre visite (à) *v.* to visit *(a person or people)* **6**
visiter *v.* to visit *(a place)* **2**
faire visiter *v.* to give a tour **8**
vite *adv.* quickly **1**; quick, hurry **4**
vitesse *f.* speed **11**
voici here is/are **1**
voilà there is/are **1**
voir *v.* to see **12**
voisin(e) *m., f.* neighbor **3**
voiture *f.* car **11**
faire un tour en voiture *v.* to go for a drive **5**
rouler en voiture *v.* to ride in a car **7**
vol *m.* flight **7**
volant *m.* steering wheel **11**
volcan *m.* volcano **14**
volley(-ball) *m.* volleyball **5**
volontiers *adv.* willingly **10**
vos *poss. adj., m., f., pl.* your **3**
votre *poss. adj., m., f., sing.* your **3**
le vôtre *poss. pron.* yours **15**
la vôtre *poss. pron.* yours **15**
les vôtres *poss. pron.* yours **15**
vouloir *v.* to want; to mean *(with* **dire***)* **9**
ça veut dire that is to say **10**
veut dire *v.* means, signifies **9**
vouloir (que) *v.* to want (that) **14**
voulu (vouloir) *p.p., adj. (used with infinitive)* wanted to... ; *(used with noun)* planned to/ for **9**
vous *pron., sing., pl., fam., form.* you **1**; *d.o. pron.* you **7**; yourself, yourselves **10**
voyage *m.* trip **7**
agence de voyages *f.* travel agency **7**
agent de voyages *m.* travel agent **7**
voyager *v.* to travel **2**
voyant (d'essence/d'huile) *m.* (gas/oil) warning light **11**
vrai(e) *adj.* true; real **3**
Il est vrai que... It is true that... **15**
Il n'est pas vrai que... It is untrue that... **15**
vraiment *adv.* really, truly **5**
vu (voir) *p.p.* seen **15**

W

W.-C. *m., pl.* restroom(s) **8**
week-end *m.* weekend **2**
ce week-end this weekend **2**

Y

y *pron.* there; at *(a place)* **10**
j'y vais I'm going/coming **8**
nous y allons we're going/ coming **9**
on y va let's go **10**
Y a-t-il... ? Is/Are there... ? **2**
yaourt *m.* yogurt **9**
yeux (œil) *m., pl.* eyes **3**

Z

zéro *m.* zero **1**
zut *interj.* darn **6**

English-French

A

a **un(e)** *indef. art.* 1
able: to be able to **pouvoir** *v.* 9
abolish **abolir** *v.* 14
about **vers** *adv.* 2
abroad **à l'étranger** 7
absolutely **absolument** *adv.* 7; **tout à fait** *adv.* 6
accident **accident** *m.* 10
 to have/to be in an accident **avoir un accident** *v.* 11
accompany **accompagner** *v.* 12
account *(at a bank)* **compte** *m.* 12
 checking account **compte** *m.* **de chèques** 12
 to have a bank account **avoir un compte bancaire** *v.* 12
accountant **comptable** *m., f.* 13
acid rain **pluie acide** *f.* 14
across from **en face de** *prep.* 3
acquaintance **connaissance** *f.* 5
active **actif/active** *adj.* 3
actively **activement** *adv.* 7
actor **acteur/actrice** *m., f.* 1
address **adresse** *f.* 12
administration: business administration **gestion** *f.* 2
adolescence **adolescence** *f.* 6
adore **adorer** 2
 I love... **J'adore...** 2
 to adore one another **s'adorer** *v.* 11
adulthood **âge adulte** *m.* 6
adventure **aventure** *f.* 15
 adventure film **film** *m.* **d'aventures** 15
advertisement **publicité (pub)** *f.* 15
advice **conseil** *m.* 13
advisor **conseiller/conseillère** *m., f.* 13
aerobics **aérobic** *m.* 5
 to do aerobics **faire de l'aérobic** *v.* 5
afraid: to be afraid of/that **avoir peur de/que** *v.* 14
after **après (que)** *adv.* 7
afternoon **après-midi** *m.* 2
 ... (o'clock) in the afternoon **... heure(s) de l'après-midi** 2
afternoon snack **goûter** *m.* 9
again **encore** *adv.* 3
age **âge** *m.* 6
agent: travel agent **agent de voyages** *m.* 7
 real estate agent **agent immobilier** *m.* 13
ago *(with an expression of time)* **il y a...** 9
agree: to agree (with) **être d'accord (avec)** *v.* 2
airport **aéroport** *m.* 7
alarm clock **réveil** *m.* 10
Algerian **algérien(ne)** *adj.* 1
all **tout** *m., sing.* 4
 all of a sudden **soudain** *adv.* 7; **tout à coup** *adv.*; **tout d'un coup** *adv.* 7
all right? *(tag question)* **d'accord?** 2
allergy **allergie** *f.* 10
allow *(to do something)* **laisser** *v.* 11; **permettre (de)** *v.* 6
allowed **permis (permettre)** *p.p., adj.* 6
all the... *(agrees with noun that follows)* **tout le...** *m., sing;* **toute la...** *f., sing;* **tous les...** *m., pl.*; **toutes les...** *f., pl.* 4
almost **presque** *adv.* 5
a lot (of) **beaucoup (de)** *adv.* 4
alone: to leave alone **laisser tranquille** *v.* 10
already **déjà** *adv.* 3
always **toujours** *adv.* 7
American **américain(e)** *adj.* 1
an **un(e)** *indef. art.* 1
ancient *(placed after noun)* **ancien(ne)** *adj.* 15
and **et** *conj.* 1
 And you? **Et toi?**, *fam.*; **Et vous?** *form.* 1
angel **ange** *m.* 1
angry: to become angry **s'énerver** *v.* 10; **se mettre en colère** *v.* 10
animal **animal** *m.* 14
ankle **cheville** *f.* 10
answering machine **répondeur téléphonique** *m.* 11
apartment **appartement** *m.* 7
appetizer **entrée** *f.* 9; **hors-d'œuvre** *m.* 9
applaud **applaudir** *v.* 15
applause **applaudissement** *m.* 15
apple **pomme** *f.* 9
appliance **appareil** *m.* 8
 electrical/household appliance **appareil** *m.* **électrique/ménager** 8
applicant **candidat(e)** *m., f.* 13
apply **postuler** *v.* 13
appointment **rendez-vous** *m.* 13
 to make an appointment **prendre (un) rendez-vous** *v.* 13
April **avril** *m.* 5
architect **architecte** *m., f.* 3
architecture **architecture** *f.* 2
Are there... ? **Y a-t-il... ?** 2
area **quartier** *m.* 8
argue (with) **se disputer (avec)** *v.* 10
arm **bras** *m.* 10
armchair **fauteuil** *m.* 8
armoire **armoire** *f.* 8
around **autour (de)** *prep.* 12
arrival **arrivée** *f.* 7
arrive **arriver (à)** *v.* 2
art **art** *m.* 2
 artwork, piece of art **œuvre** *f.* 15
 fine arts **beaux-arts** *m., pl.* 15
artist **artiste** *m., f.* 3
as *(like)* **comme** *adv.* 6
 as ... as *(used with adjective to compare)* **aussi ... que** 9
 as much ... as *(used with noun to express comparative quantity)* **autant de ... que** 14
 as soon as **dès que** *adv.* 13
ashamed: to be ashamed of **avoir honte de** *v.* 2
ask **demander** *v.* 2
 to ask *(someone)* **demander (à)** *v.* 6
 to ask *(someone)* a question **poser une question (à)** *v.* 6
 to ask that... **demander que...** 14
aspirin **aspirine** *f.* 10
at **à** *prep.* 4
 at ... (o'clock) **à ... heure(s)** 4
 at the doctor's office **chez le médecin** *prep.* 2
 at (someone's) house **chez...** *prep.* 2
 at the end (of) **au bout (de)** *prep.* 12
 at last **enfin** *adv.* 11
athlete **athlète** *m., f.* 3
ATM **distributeur** *m.* **automatique/de billets** *m.* 12
attend **assister** *v.* 2
August **août** *m.* 5
aunt **tante** *f.* 3
author **auteur/femme auteur** *m., f.* 15
autumn **automne** *m.* 5
 in autumn **en automne** 5
available *(free)* **libre** *adj.* 7
avenue **avenue** *f.* 12
avoid **éviter de** *v.* 10

B

back **dos** *m.* 10
backpack **sac à dos** *m.* 1
bad **mauvais(e)** *adj.* 3

to be in a bad mood **être de mauvaise humeur** 8
to be in bad health **être en mauvaise santé** 10
badly **mal** *adv.* 7
I am doing badly. **Je vais mal.** 1
to be doing badly **se porter mal** *v.* 10
baguette **baguette** *f.* 4
bakery **boulangerie** *f.* 9
balcony **balcon** *m.* 8
banana **banane** *f.* 9
bank **banque** *f.* 12
to have a bank account **avoir un compte bancaire** *v.* 12
banker **banquier/banquière** *m., f.* 13
banking **bancaire** *adj.* 12
baseball **baseball** *m.* 5
baseball cap **casquette** *f.* 6
basement **sous-sol** *m.*; **cave** *f.* 8
basketball **basket(-ball)** *m.* 5
bath **bain** *m.* 6
bathing suit **maillot de bain** *m.* 6
bathroom **salle de bains** *f.* 8
bathtub **baignoire** *f.* 8
be **être** *v.* 1
sois (être) *imp. v.* 7;
soyez (être) *imp. v.* 7
beach **plage** *f.* 7
beans **haricots** *m., pl.* 9
green beans **haricots verts** *m., pl.* 9
bearings: to get one's bearings **s'orienter** *v.* 12
beautiful **beau (belle)** *adj.* 3
beauty salon **salon** *m.* **de beauté** 12
because **parce que** *conj.* 2
become **devenir** *v.* 9
bed **lit** *m.* 7
to go to bed **se coucher** *v.* 10
bedroom **chambre** *f.* 8
beef **bœuf** *m.* 9
been **été (être)** *p.p.* 6
beer **bière** *f.* 6
before **avant (de/que)** *adv.* 7
before (*o'clock*) **moins** *adv.* 2
begin (*to do something*) **commencer (à)** *v.* 2;
se mettre à *v.* 10
beginning **début** *m.* 15
behind **derrière** *prep.* 3
Belgian **belge** *adj.* 7
Belgium **Belgique** *f.* 7
believe (that) **croire (que)** *v.* 12
believed **cru (croire)** *p.p.* 12
belt **ceinture** *f.* 6
to buckle one's seatbelt **attacher sa ceinture de sécurité** *v.* 11
bench **banc** *m.* 12
best: the best **le mieux** *super. adv.* 9; **le/la meilleur(e)** *super. adj.* 9
better **meilleur(e)** *comp. adj.*; **mieux** *comp. adv.* 9
It is better that… **Il vaut mieux que/qu'…** 14
to be doing better **se porter mieux** *v.* 10
to get better (*from illness*) **guérir** *v.* 10
between **entre** *prep.* 3
beverage (carbonated) **boisson** *f.* **(gazeuse)** 4
bicycle **vélo** *m.* 5
to go bike riding **faire du vélo** *v.* 5
big **grand(e)** *adj.* 3; (*clothing*) **large** *adj.* 6
bill (*in a restaurant*) **addition** *f.* 4
bills (*money*) **billets** *m., pl.* 12
biology **biologie** *f.* 2
bird **oiseau** *m.* 3
birth **naissance** *f.* 6
birthday **anniversaire** *m.* 5
bit (of) **morceau (de)** *m.* 4
black **noir(e)** *adj.* 3
blackboard **tableau** *m.* 1
blanket **couverture** *f.* 8
blonde **blond(e)** *adj.* 3
blouse **chemisier** *m.* 6
blue **bleu(e)** *adj.* 3
blush **rougir** *v.* 4
boat **bateau** *m.* 7
body **corps** *m.* 10
book **livre** *m.* 1
bookstore **librairie** *f.* 1
bored: to get bored **s'ennuyer** *v.* 10
boring **ennuyeux/ennuyeuse** *adj.* 3
born: to be born **naître** *v.* 7;
né (naître) *p.p., adj.* 7
borrow **emprunter** *v.* 12
bottle (of) **bouteille (de)** *f.* 4
boulevard **boulevard** *m.* 12
boutique **boutique** *f.* 12
bowl **bol** *m.* 9
box **boîte** *f.* 9
boy **garçon** *m.* 1
boyfriend **petit ami** *m.* 1
brake **freiner** *v.* 11
brakes **freins** *m., pl.* 11
brave **courageux/courageuse** *adj.* 3
Brazil **Brésil** *m.* 7
Brazilian **brésilien(ne)** *adj.* 7
bread **pain** *m.* 4
country-style bread **pain** *m.* **de campagne** 4
bread shop **boulangerie** *f.* 9
break **se casser** *v.* 10
breakdown **panne** *f.* 11
break down **tomber en panne** *v.* 11
break up (*to leave one another*) **se quitter** *v.* 11
breakfast **petit-déjeuner** *m.* 9
bridge **pont** *m.* 12
bright **brillant(e)** *adj.* 1
bring (*a person*) **amener** *v.* 5; (*a thing*) **apporter** *v.* 4
broom **balai** *m.* 8
brother **frère** *m.* 3
brother-in-law **beau-frère** *m.* 3
brown **marron** *adj., inv.* 3
brown (*hair*) **châtain** *adj.* 3
brush (hair/tooth) **brosse** *f.* **(à cheveux/à dents)** 10
to brush one's hair/teeth **se brosser les cheveux/ les dents** *v.* 9
buckle: to buckle one's seatbelt **attacher sa ceinture de sécurité** *v.* 11
build **construire** *v.* 6
building **bâtiment** *m.* 12; **immeuble** *m.* 8
bumper **pare-chocs** *m.* 11
burn (CD/DVD) **graver** *v.* 11
bus **autobus** *m.* 7
bus stop **arrêt d'autobus (de bus)** *m.* 7
bus terminal **gare** *f.* **routière** 7
business (*profession*) **affaires** *f., pl.* 3; (*company*) **entreprise** *f.* 13
business administration **gestion** *f.* 2
businessman **homme d'affaires** *m.* 3
businesswoman **femme d'affaires** *f.* 3
busy **occupé(e)** *adj.* 1
but **mais** *conj.* 1
butcher's shop **boucherie** *f.* 9
butter **beurre** *m.* 4
buy **acheter** *v.* 5
by **par** *prep.* 3
Bye! **Salut!** *fam.* 1

C

cabinet **placard** *m.* 8
café **café** *m.* 1; **brasserie** *f.* 12
café terrace **terrasse** *f.* **de café** 4
cybercafé **cybercafé** *m.* 12
cafeteria (school) **cantine** *f.* 9
cake **gâteau** *m.* 6
calculator **calculatrice** *f.* 1
call **appeler** *v.* 13
calm **calme** *adj.* 1; **calme** *m.* 1
camcorder **caméra vidéo** *f.* 11; **caméscope** *m.* 11
camera **appareil photo** *m.* 11

digital camera **appareil photo** *m.* **numérique** 11
camping **camping** *m.* 5
to go camping **faire du camping** *v.* 5
can (of food) **boîte (de conserve)** *f.* 9
Canada **Canada** *m.* 7
Canadian **canadien(ne)** *adj.* 1
cancel (a reservation) **annuler (une réservation)** *v.* 7
candidate **candidat(e)** *m., f.* 13
candy **bonbon** *m.* 6
cap: baseball cap **casquette** *f.* 6
capital **capitale** *f.* 7
car **voiture** *f.* 11
to ride in a car **rouler en voiture** *v.* 7
card *(letter)* **carte postale** *f.* 12;
credit card **carte** *f.* **de crédit** 12
to pay with a credit card **payer avec une carte de crédit** *v.* 12
cards *(playing)* **cartes** *f.* 5
carbonated drink/beverage **boisson** *f.* **gazeuse** 4
career **carrière** *f.* 13
carpooling **covoiturage** *m.* 14
carrot **carotte** *f.* 9
carry **apporter** *v.* 4
cartoon **dessin animé** *m.* 15
case: in any case **en tout cas** 6
cash **liquide** *m.* 12
to pay in cash **payer en liquide** *v.* 12
cat **chat** *m.* 3
catastrophe **catastrophe** *f.* 14
catch sight of **apercevoir** *v.* 12
CD(s) **CD** *m.* 11
CD/DVD player **lecteur de CD/DVD** *m.* 11
CD-ROM(s) **CD-ROM, cédérom(s)** *m.* 11
celebrate **célébrer** *v.* 5; **fêter** *v.* 6
celebration **fête** *f.* 6
cellar **cave** *f.* 8
cell(ular) phone **portable** *m.* 11
center: city/town center **centre-ville** *m.* 4
certain **certain(e)** *adj.* 9; **sûr(e)** *adj.* 15
It is certain that... **Il est certain que...** 15
It is uncertain that... **Il n'est pas certain que...** 15
chair **chaise** *f.* 1
champagne **champagne** *m.* 6
change *(coins)* **(pièces** *f. pl.* **de) monnaie** 12
channel (television) **chaîne** *f.* **(de télévision)** 11
character **personnage** *m.* 15
main character **personnage principal** *m.* 15
charming **charmant(e)** *adj.* 1
chat **bavarder** *v.* 4
check **chèque** *m.* 12; *(bill)* **addition** *f.* 4
to pay by check **payer par chèque** *v.* 12;
to check (the oil/the air pressure) **vérifier (l'huile/la pression des pneus)** *v.* 11
checking account **compte** *m.* **de chèques** 12
cheek **joue** *f.* 10
cheese **fromage** *m.* 4
chemistry **chimie** *f.* 2
chess **échecs** *m., pl.* 5
chest **poitrine** *f.* 10
chest of drawers **commode** *f.* 8
chic **chic** *adj.* 4
chicken **poulet** *m.* 9
child **enfant** *m., f.* 3
childhood **enfance** *f.* 6
China **Chine** *f.* 7
Chinese **chinois(e)** *adj.* 7
choir **chœur** *m.* 15
choose **choisir** *v.* 4
chorus **chœur** *m.* 15
chrysanthemums **chrysanthèmes** *m., pl.* 9
church **église** *f.* 4
city **ville** *f.* 4
city hall **mairie** *f.* 12
city/town center **centre-ville** *m.* 4
class *(group of students)* **classe** *f.* 1; *(course)* **cours** *m.* 2
classmate **camarade de classe** *m., f.* 1
classroom **salle** *f.* **de classe** 1
clean **nettoyer** *v.* 5; **propre** *adj.* 8
clear **clair(e)** *adj.* 15
It is clear that... **Il est clair que...** 15
to clear the table **débarrasser la table** 8
client **client(e)** *m., f.* 7
cliff **falaise** *f.* 14
clock **horloge** *f.* 1
alarm clock **réveil** *m.* 10
close (to) **près (de)** *prep.* 3
very close (to) **tout près (de)** 12
close **fermer** *v.* 11
closed **fermé(e)** *adj.* 12
closet **placard** *m.* 8
clothes dryer **sèche-linge** *m.* 8
clothing **vêtements** *m., pl.* 6
cloudy **nuageux/nuageuse** *adj.* 5
It is cloudy. **Le temps est nuageux.** 5
clutch **embrayage** *m.* 11
coast **côte** *f.* 14
coat **manteau** *m.* 6
coffee **café** *m.* 1
coffeemaker **cafetière** *f.* 8
coins **pièces** *f. pl.* **de monnaie** 12
cold **froid** *m.* 2
to be cold **avoir froid** *v.* 2
(weather) It is cold. **Il fait froid.** 5
cold **rhume** *m.* 10
color **couleur** *f.* 6
What color is... ? **De quelle couleur est... ?** 6
comb **peigne** *m.* 10
come **venir** *v.* 7
come back **revenir** *v.* 9
Come on. **Allez.** 2
comedy **comédie** *f.* 15
comic strip **bande dessinée (B.D.)** *f.* 5
compact disc **compact disque** *m.* 11
company *(troop)* **troupe** *f.* 15
completely **tout à fait** *adv.* 6
composer **compositeur** *m.* 15
computer **ordinateur** *m.* 1
computer science **informatique** *f.* 2
concert **concert** *m.* 15
congratulations **félicitations** 15
consider **considérer** *v.* 5
constantly **constamment** *adv.* 7
construct **construire** *v.* 6
consultant **conseiller/conseillère** *m., f.* 13
continue *(doing something)* **continuer (à)** *v.* 12
cook **cuisiner** *v.* 9; **faire la cuisine** *v.* 5; **cuisinier/cuisinière** *m., f.* 13
cookie **biscuit** *m.* 6
cooking **cuisine** *f.* 5
cool: *(weather)* It is cool. **Il fait frais.** 5
corner **angle** *m.* 12; **coin** *m.* 12
cost **coûter** *v.* 4
cotton **coton** *m.* 6
couch **canapé** *m.* 8
cough **tousser** *v.* 10
count (on someone) **compter (sur quelqu'un)** *v.* 8
country **pays** *m.* 7
country(side) **campagne** *f.* 7
country-style **de campagne** *adj.* 4
couple **couple** *m.* 6
courage **courage** 13
courageous **courageux/courageuse** *adj.* 3
course **cours** *m.* 2
cousin **cousin(e)** *m., f.* 3
cover **couvrir** *v.* 11
covered **couvert (couvrir)** *p.p.* 11
cow **vache** *f.* 14
crazy **fou/folle** *adj.* 3
cream **crème** *f.* 9
credit card **carte** *f.* **de crédit** 12

to pay with a credit card **payer avec une carte de crédit** *v.* 12
crêpe **crêpe** *f.* 5
crime film **film policier** *m.* 15
croissant **croissant** *m.* 4
cross **traverser** *v.* 12
cruel **cruel/cruelle** *adj.* 3
cry **pleurer** *v.*
cup (of) **tasse (de)** *f.* 4
cupboard **placard** *m.* 8
curious **curieux/curieuse** *adj.* 3
curly **frisé(e)** *adj.* 3
currency **monnaie** *f.* 12
curtain **rideau** *m.* 8
customs **douane** *f.* 7
cybercafé **cybercafé** *m.* 12

D

dance **danse** *f.* 15
to dance **danser** *v.* 4
danger **danger** *m.* 14
dangerous **dangereux/dangereuse** *adj.* 11
dark *(hair)* **brun(e)** *adj.* 3
darling **chéri(e)** *adj.* 2
darn **zut** 11
dash *(punctuation mark)* **tiret** *m.* 11
date *(day, month, year)* **date** *f.* 5; *(meeting)* **rendez-vous** *m.* 6
to make a date **prendre (un) rendez-vous** *v.* 13
daughter **fille** *f.* 1
day **jour** *m.* 2; **journée** *f.* 2
day after tomorrow **après-demain** *adv.* 2
day before yesterday **avant-hier** *adv.* 7
day off **congé** *m.*, **jour de congé** 7
dear **cher/chère** *adj.* 2
death **mort** *f.* 6
December **décembre** *m.* 5
decide *(to do something)* **décider (de)** *v.* 11
deforestation **déboisement** *m.* 14
degree **diplôme** *m.* 2
degrees *(temperature)* **degrés** *m., pl.* 5
It is... degrees. **Il fait... degrés.** 5
delicatessen **charcuterie** *f.* 9
delicious **délicieux/délicieuse** *adj.* 4
Delighted. **Enchanté(e).** *p.p., adj.* 1
demand (that) **exiger (que)** *v.* 14
demanding **exigeant(e)** *adj.* 13
demanding profession **profession** *f.* **exigeante** 13
dentist **dentiste** *m., f.* 3
department store **grand magasin** *m.* 4
departure **départ** *m.* 7
deposit: to deposit money **déposer de l'argent** *v.* 12
depressed **déprimé(e)** *adj.* 10
describe **décrire** *v.* 7
described **décrit (décrire)** *p.p., adj.* 7
desert **désert** *m.* 14
design (fashion) **stylisme (de mode)** *m.* 2
desire **envie** *f.* 2
desk **bureau** *m.* 1
dessert **dessert** *m.* 6
destroy **détruire** *v.* 6
destroyed **détruit (détruire)** *p.p., adj.* 6
detective film **film policier** *m.* 15
detest **détester** *v.* 2
I hate... **Je déteste...** 2
develop **développer** *v.* 14
dial (a number) **composer (un numéro)** *v.* 11
dictionary **dictionnaire** *m.* 1
die **mourir** *v.* 7
died **mort (mourir)** *p.p., adj.* 7
diet **régime** *m.* 10
to be on a diet **être au régime** 9
difference **différence** *f.* 1
different **différent(e)** *adj.* 1
differently **différemment** *adv.* 7
difficult **difficile** *adj.* 1
digital camera **appareil photo** *m.* **numérique** 11
dining room **salle à manger** *f.* 8
dinner **dîner** *m.* 9
to have dinner **dîner** *v.* 2
diploma **diplôme** *m.* 2
directions **indications** *f.* 12
director *(movie)* **réalisateur/réalisatrice** *m., f.*; *(play/show)* **metteur en scène** *m.* 15
dirty **sale** *adj.* 8
discover **découvrir** *v.* 11
discovered **découvert (découvrir)** *p.p.* 11
discreet **discret/discrète** *adj.* 3
discuss **discuter** *v.* 11
dish *(food)* **plat** *m.* 9
to do the dishes **faire la vaisselle** *v.* 8
dishwasher **lave-vaisselle** *m.* 8
dismiss **renvoyer** *v.* 13
distinction **mention** *f.* 13
divorce **divorce** *m.* 6
to divorce **divorcer** *v.* 3
divorced **divorcé(e)** *p.p., adj.* 3
do *(make)* **faire** *v.* 5
to do odd jobs **bricoler** *v.* 5
doctor **médecin** *m.* 3
documentary **documentaire** *m.* 15
dog **chien** *m.* 3
done **fait (faire)** *p.p., adj.* 6
door *(building)* **porte** *f.* 1; *(automobile)* **portière** *f.* 11
dorm **résidence** *f.* **universitaire** 8
doubt (that)... **douter (que)...** *v.* 15
doubtful **douteux/douteuse** *adj.* 15
It is doubtful that... **Il est douteux que...** 15
download **télécharger** *v.* 11
downtown **centre-ville** *m.* 4
drag **barbant** *adj.* 3; **barbe** *f.* 3
drape **rideau** *m.* 8
draw **dessiner** *v.* 2
drawer **tiroir** *m.* 8
dreadful **épouvantable** *adj.* 5
dream (about) **rêver (de)** *v.* 11
dress **robe** *f.* 6
to dress **s'habiller** *v.* 10
dresser **commode** *f.* 8
drink (carbonated) **boisson** *f.* **(gazeuse)** 4
to drink **boire** *v.* 4
drive **conduire** *v.* 6
to go for a drive **faire un tour en voiture** 5
driven **conduit (conduire)** *p.p.* 6
driver (taxi/truck) **chauffeur (de taxi/de camion)** *m.* 13
driver's license **permis** *m.* **de conduire** 11
drums **batterie** *f.* 15
drunk **bu (boire)** *p.p.* 6
dryer *(clothes)* **sèche-linge** *m.* 8
dry oneself **se sécher** *v.* 10
due **dû(e) (devoir)** *adj.* 9
during **pendant** *prep.* 7
dust **enlever/faire la poussière** *v.* 8

E

each **chaque** *adj.* 6
ear **oreille** *f.* 10
early **en avance** *adv.* 2; **tôt** *adv.* 2
earn **gagner** *v.* 13
Earth **Terre** *f.* 14
easily **facilement** *adv.* 7
east **est** *m.* 12
easy **facile** *adj.* 2
eat **manger** *v.* 2
to eat lunch **déjeuner** *v.* 4
éclair **éclair** *m.* 4
ecological **écologique** *adj.* 14
ecology **écologie** *f.* 14
economics **économie** *f.* 2
ecotourism **écotourisme** *m.* 14

education **formation** *f.* 13
effect: in effect **en effet** 14
egg **œuf** *m.* 9
eight **huit** *m.* 1
eighteen **dix-huit** *m.* 1
eighth **huitième** *adj.* 7
eighty **quatre-vingts** *m.* 3
eighty-one **quatre-vingt-un** *m.* 3
elder **aîné(e)** *adj.* 3
electric **électrique** *adj.* 8
electrical appliance **appareil** *m.* **électrique** 8
electrician **électricien/électricienne** *m., f.* 13
elegant **élégant(e)** *adj.* 1
elevator **ascenseur** *m.* 7
eleven **onze** *m.* 1
eleventh **onzième** *adj.* 7
e-mail **e-mail** *m.* 11
emergency room **urgences** *f., pl.* 10
to go to the emergency room **aller aux urgences** *v.* 10
employ **employer** *v.* 5
end **fin** *f.* 15
endangered **menacé(e)** *adj.* 14
endangered species **espèce** *f.* **menacée** 14
engaged **fiancé(e)** *adj.* 3
engine **moteur** *m.* 11
engineer **ingénieur** *m.* 3
England **Angleterre** *f.* 7
English **anglais(e)** *adj.* 1
enormous **énorme** *adj.* 2
enough (of) **assez (de)** *adv.* 4
not enough (of) **pas assez (de)** 4
enter **entrer** *v.* 7
envelope **enveloppe** *f.* 12
environment **environnement** *m.* 14
equal **égaler** *v.* 3
erase **effacer** *v.* 11
errand **course** *f.* 9
escargot **escargot** *m.* 9
especially **surtout** *adv.* 2
essay **dissertation** *f.* 11
essential **essentiel(le)** *adj.* 14
It is essential that... **Il est essentiel/indispensable que...** 14
even **même** *adv.* 5
evening **soir** *m.*; **soirée** *f.* 2
... (o'clock) in the evening **... heures du soir** 2
every day **tous les jours** *adv.* 7
everyone **tout le monde** *m.* 9
evident **évident(e)** *adj.* 15
It is evident that... **Il est évident que...** 15
evidently **évidemment** *adv.* 7
exactly **exactement** *adv.* 9
exam **examen** *m.* 1
Excuse me. **Excuse-moi.** *fam.* 1; **Excusez-moi.** *form.* 1
executive **cadre/femme cadre** *m., f.* 13
exercise **exercice** *m.* 10
to exercise **faire de l'exercice** *v.* 10
exhibit **exposition** *f.* 15
exit **sortie** *f.* 7
expenditure **dépense** *f.* 12
expensive **cher/chère** *adj.* 6
explain **expliquer** *v.* 2
explore **explorer** *v.* 4
extinction **extinction** *f.* 14
eye (eyes) **œil (yeux)** *m.* 10

F

face **visage** *m.* 10
facing **en face (de)** *prep.* 3
fact: in fact **en fait** 7
factory **usine** *f.* 14
fail **échouer** *v.* 2
fall **automne** *m.* 5
in the fall **en automne** 5
to fall **tomber** *v.* 7
to fall in love **tomber amoureux/amoureuse** *v.* 6
to fall asleep **s'endormir** *v.* 10
family **famille** *f.* 3
famous **célèbre** *adj.* 15; **connu (connaître)** *p.p., adj.* 8
far (from) **loin (de)** *prep.* 3
farewell **adieu** *m.* 14
farmer **agriculteur/agricultrice** *m., f.* 13
fashion **mode** *f.* 2
fashion design **stylisme de mode** *m.* 2
fast **rapide** *adj.* 3; **vite** *adv.* 7
fat **gros(se)** *adj.* 3
father **père** *m.* 3
father-in-law **beau-père** *m.* 3
favorite **favori/favorite** *adj.* 3; **préféré(e)** *adj.* 2
fax machine **fax** *m.* 11
fear **peur** *f.* 2
to fear that **avoir peur que** *v.* 14
February **février** *m.* 5
fed up: to be fed up **en avoir marre** *v.* 3
feel *(to sense)* **sentir** *v.* 5; *(state of being)* **se sentir** *v.* 10
to feel like *(doing something)* **avoir envie (de)** 2
to feel nauseated **avoir mal au cœur** 10
festival (festivals) **festival (festivals)** *m.* 15
fever **fièvre** *f.* 10
to have fever **avoir de la fièvre** *v.* 10
fiancé **fiancé(e)** *m., f.* 6
field *(terrain)* **champ** *m.* 14; *(of study)* **domaine** *m.* 13
fifteen **quinze** *m.* 1
fifth **cinquième** *adj.* 7
fifty **cinquante** *m.* 1
figure *(physique)* **ligne** *f.* 10
file **fichier** *m.* 11
fill: to fill out a form **remplir un formulaire** *v.* 12
to fill the tank **faire le plein** *v.* 11
film **film** *m.* 15
adventure/crime film **film** *m.* **d'aventures/policier** 15
finally **enfin** *adv.* 7; **finalement** *adv.* 7; **dernièrement** *adv.* 7
find (a job) **trouver (un/du travail)** *v.* 13
to find again **retrouver** *v.* 2
fine **amende** *f.* 11
fine arts **beaux-arts** *m., pl.* 15
finger **doigt** *m.* 10
finish *(doing something)* **finir (de)** *v.* 4, 11
fire **incendie** *m.* 14
firefighter **pompier/femme pompier** *m., f.* 13
firm *(business)* **entreprise** *f.* 13;
first **d'abord** *adv.* 7; **premier/première** *adj.* 2; **premier** *m.* 5
It is October first. **C'est le 1er (premier) octobre.** 5
fish **poisson** *m.* 3
fishing **pêche** *f.* 5
to go fishing **aller à la pêche** *v.* 5
fish shop **poissonnerie** *f.* 9
five **cinq** *m.* 1
flat tire **pneu** *m.* **crevé** 11
flight *(air travel)* **vol** *m.* 7
floor **étage** *m.* 7
flower **fleur** *f.* 8
flu **grippe** *f.* 10
fluently **couramment** *adv.* 7
follow (a path/a street/a boulevard) **suivre (un chemin/une rue/un boulevard)** *v.* 12
food (item) **aliment** *m.* 9; **nourriture** *f.* 9
foot **pied** *m.* 10
football **football américain** *m.* 5
for **pour** *prep.* 5; **pendant** *prep.* 9
For whom? **Pour qui?** 4
forbid **interdire** *v.* 14
foreign **étranger/étrangère** *adj.* 2
foreign languages **langues** *f., pl.* **étrangères** 2
forest **forêt** *f.* 14

tropical forest **forêt tropicale** *f.* 14
forget *(to do something)* **oublier (de)** *v.* 2
fork **fourchette** *f.* 9
form **formulaire** *m.* 12
former *(placed before noun)* **ancien(ne)** *adj.* 15
fortunately **heureusement** *adv.* 7
forty **quarante** *m.* 1
fountain **fontaine** *f.* 12
four **quatre** *m.* 1
fourteen **quatorze** *m.* 1
fourth **quatrième** *adj.* 7
France **France** *f.* 7
frankly **franchement** *adv.* 7
free *(at no cost)* **gratuit(e)** *adj.* 15
free time **temps libre** *m.* 5
freezer **congélateur** *m.* 8
French **français(e)** *adj.* 1
French fries **frites** *f., pl.* 4
frequent *(to visit regularly)* **fréquenter** *v.* 4
fresh **frais/fraîche** *adj.* 5
Friday **vendredi** *m.* 2
friend **ami(e)** *m., f.* 1; **copain/copine** *m., f.* 1
friendship **amitié** *f.* 6
from **de/d'** *prep.* 1
from time to time **de temps en temps** *adv.* 7
front: in front of **devant** *prep.* 3
fruit **fruit** *m.* 9
full *(no vacancies)* **complet (complète)** *adj.* 7
full-time job **emploi** *m.* **à plein temps** 13
fun **amusant(e)** *adj.* 1
to have fun *(doing something)* **s'amuser (à)** *v.* 11
funeral **funérailles** *f., pl.* 9
funny **drôle** *adj.* 3
furious **furieux/furieuse** *adj.* 14
to be furious that… **être furieux/furieuse que…** *v.* 14

G

gain: gain weight **grossir** *v.* 4
game *(amusement)* **jeu** *m.* 5; *(sports)* **match** *m.* 5
game show **jeu télévisé** *m.* 15
garage **garage** *m.* 8
garbage **ordures** *f., pl.* 14
garbage collection **ramassage** *m.* **des ordures** 14
garden **jardin** *m.* 8
garlic **ail** *m.* 9
gas **essence** *f.* 11
gas tank **réservoir d'essence** *m.* 11
gas warning light **voyant** *m.* **d'essence** 11
generally **en général** *adv.* 7
generous **généreux/généreuse** *adj.* 3
genre **genre** *m.* 15
gentle **doux/douce** *adj.* 3
geography **géographie** *f.* 2
German **allemand(e)** *adj.* 1
Germany **Allemagne** *f.* 7
get *(to obtain)* **obtenir** *v.* 13
get along well (with) **s'entendre bien (avec)** *v.* 10
get off **descendre (de)** *v.* 6
get up **se lever** *v.* 10
get up again **se relever** *v.* 10
gift **cadeau** *m.* 6
wrapped gift **paquet cadeau** *m.* 6
gifted **doué(e)** *adj.* 15
girl **fille** *f.* 1
girlfriend **petite amie** *f.* 1
give *(to someone)* **donner (à)** *v.* 2
to give a shot **faire une piqûre** *v.* 10
to give a tour **faire visiter** *v.* 8
to give back **rendre (à)** *v.* 6
to give one another **se donner** *v.* 11
glass (of) **verre (de)** *m.* 4
glasses **lunettes** *f., pl.* 6
sunglasses **lunettes de soleil** *f., pl.* 6
global warming **réchauffement** *m.* **de la Terre** 14
glove **gant** *m.* 6
go **aller** *v.* 4
Let's go! **Allons-y!** 4; **On y va!** 10
I'm going. **J'y vais.** 8
to go back **repartir** *v.* 15
to go downstairs **descendre** *v.* 6
to go out **sortir** *v.* 7
to go over **dépasser** *v.* 11
to go up **monter** *v.* 7
to go with **aller avec** *v.* 6
golf **golf** *m.* 5
good **bon(ne)** *adj.* 3
Good evening. **Bonsoir.** 1
Good morning. **Bonjour.** 1
to be good for nothing **ne servir à rien** *v.* 9
to be in a good mood **être de bonne humeur** *v.* 8
to be in good health **être en bonne santé** *v.* 10
to be in good shape **être en pleine forme** *v.* 10
to be up to something interesting **faire quelque chose de beau** *v.* 12
Good-bye. **Au revoir.** 1
government **gouvernement** *m.* 14
grade *(academics)* **note** *f.* 2
grandchildren **petits-enfants** *m., pl.* 3
granddaughter **petite-fille** *f.* 3
grandfather **grand-père** *m.* 3
grandmother **grand-mère** *f.* 3
grandparents **grands-parents** *m., pl.* 3
grandson **petit-fils** *m.* 3
grant **bourse** *f.* 2
grass **herbe** *f.* 14
gratin **gratin** *m.* 9
gray **gris(e)** *adj.* 6
great **formidable** *adj.* 7; **génial(e)** *adj.* 3
green **vert(e)** *adj.* 3
green beans **haricots verts** *m., pl.* 9
greenhouse **serre** *f.* 14
greenhouse effect **effet de serre** *m.* 14
grocery store **épicerie** *f.* 4
groom: to groom oneself *(in the morning)* **faire sa toilette** *v.* 10
ground floor **rez-de-chaussée** *m.* 7
growing population **population** *f.* **croissante** 14
grow old **vieillir** *v.* 4
grow up **grandir** *v.* 4
guaranteed **garanti(e)** *p.p., adj.* 5
guest **invité(e)** *m., f.* 6; **client(e)** *m., f.* 7
guitar **guitare** *f.* 15
guy **mec** *m.* 10
gym **gymnase** *m.* 4

H

habitat **habitat** *m.* 14
habitat preservation **sauvetage des habitats** *m.* 14
had **eu (avoir)** *p.p.* 6
had to **dû (devoir)** *p.p.* 9
hair **cheveux** *m., pl.* 9
to brush one's hair **se brosser les cheveux** *v.* 9
to do one's hair **se coiffer** *v.* 10
hairbrush **brosse** *f.* **à cheveux** 10
hairdresser **coiffeur/coiffeuse** *m., f.* 3
half **demie** *f.* 2
half past ... (o'clock) **... et demie** 2
half-brother **demi-frère** *m.* 3
half-sister **demi-sœur** *f.* 3
half-time job **emploi** *m.* **à mi-temps** 13
hallway **couloir** *m.* 8
ham **jambon** *m.* 4
hand **main** *f.* 5
handbag **sac à main** *m.* 6
handsome **beau** *adj.* 3
hang up **raccrocher** *v.* 13
happiness **bonheur** *m.* 6

happy **heureux/heureuse** *adj.*; **content(e)** 13
to be happy that... **être content(e) que...** *v.* 14; **être heureux/heureuse que...** *v.* 14
hard drive **disque (dur)** *m.* 11
hard-working **travailleur/travailleuse** *adj.* 3
hat **chapeau** *m.* 6
hate **détester** *v.* 2
I hate... **Je déteste...** 2
have **avoir** *v.* 2; **aie (avoir)** *imp., v.* 7; **ayez (avoir)** *imp. v.* 7; **prendre** *v.* 4
to have an ache **avoir mal** *v.* 10
to have to *(must)* **devoir** *v.* 9
he **il** *sub. pron.* 1
head *(body part)* **tête** *f.* 10; *(of a company)* **chef** *m.* **d'entreprise** 13
headache: to have a headache **avoir mal à la tête** *v.* 10
headlights **phares** *m., pl.* 11
health **santé** *f.* 10
to be in good health **être en bonne santé** *v.* 10
health insurance **assurance** *f.* **maladie** 13
healthy **sain(e)** *adj.* 10
hear **entendre** *v.* 6
heart **cœur** *m.* 10
heat **chaud** *m.* 2
hello *(on the phone)* **allô** 1; *(in the evening)* **Bonsoir.** 1; *(in the morning or afternoon)* **Bonjour.** 1
help **au secours** 11
to help *(to do something)* **aider (à)** *v.* 5
to help one another **s'aider** *v.* 11
her **la/l'** *d.o. pron.* 7; **lui** *i.o. pron.* 6; *(attached to an imperative)* **-lui** *i.o. pron.* 9
her **sa** *poss. adj., f., sing.* 3; **ses** *poss. adj., m., f., pl.* 3; **son** *poss. adj., m., sing.* 3; **la/les sienne(s)** *poss. pron.* 15
Here! **Tenez!** *form., imp. v.* 9; **Tiens!** *fam., imp., v.* 9
here **ici** *adv.* 1; *(used with demonstrative adjective* **ce** *and noun or with demonstrative pronoun* **celui***);* **-ci** 6;
Here is.... **Voici...** 1
heritage: I am of... heritage. **Je suis d'origine...** 1
herself *(used with reflexive verb)* **se/s'** *pron.* 10
hesitate *(to do something)* **hésiter (à)** *v.* 11
Hey! **Eh!** *interj.* 2
Hi! **Salut!** *fam.* 1
high **élevé(e)** *adj.* 13
high school **lycée** *m.* 1
high school student **lycéen(ne)** *m., f.* 2
higher education **études supérieures** *f., pl.* 2
highway **autoroute** *f.* 11
hike **randonnée** *f.* 5
to go for a hike **faire une randonnée** *v.* 5
him **lui** *i.o. pron.* 6; **le/l'** *d.o. pron.* 7; *(attached to imperative)* **-lui** *i.o. pron.* 9
himself *(used with reflexive verb)* **se/s'** *pron.* 10
hire **embaucher** *v.* 13
his **sa** *poss. adj., f., sing.* 3; **ses** *poss. adj., m., f., pl.* 3; **son** *poss. adj., m., sing.* 3; **le(s) sien(s)** *poss. pron.* 15
history **histoire** *f.* 2
hit **rentrer (dans)** *v.* 11
hold **tenir** *v.* 9
to be on hold **patienter** *v.* 13
hole in the ozone layer **trou dans la couche d'ozone** *m.* 14
holiday **jour férié** *m.* 6; **férié(e)** *adj.* 6
home *(house)* **maison** *f.* 4
at (someone's) home **chez...** *prep.* 4
home page **page d'accueil** *f.* 11
homework **devoir** *m.* 2
honest **honnête** *adj.* 15
honestly **franchement** *adv.* 7
hood **capot** *m.* 11
hope **espérer** *v.* 5
hors d'œuvre **hors-d'œuvre** *m.* 9
horse **cheval** *m.* 5
to go horseback riding **faire du cheval** *v.* 5
hospital **hôpital** *m.* 4
host **hôte/hôtesse** *m., f.* 6
hot **chaud** *m.* 2
It is hot (weather). **Il fait chaud.** 5
to be hot **avoir chaud** *v.* 2
hot chocolate **chocolat chaud** *m.* 4
hotel **hôtel** *m.* 7
(single) hotel room **chambre** *f.* **(individuelle)** 7
hotel keeper **hôtelier/hôtelière** *m., f.* 7
hour **heure** *f.* 2
house **maison** *f.* 4
at (someone's) house **chez...** *prep.* 2
to leave the house **quitter la maison** *v.* 4
to stop by someone's house **passer chez quelqu'un** *v.* 4
household **ménager/ménagère** *adj.* 8
household appliance **appareil** *m.* **ménager** 8
household chore **tâche ménagère** *f.* 8
housewife **femme au foyer** *f.* 13
housework: to do the housework **faire le ménage** *v.* 8
housing **logement** *m.* 8
how **comme** *adv.* 2; **comment?** *interr. adv.* 4
How are you? **Comment allez-vous?** *form.* 1; **Comment vas-tu?** *fam.* 1
How many/How much (of)? **Combien (de)?** 1
How much is... ? **Combien coûte... ?** 4
huge **énorme** *adj.* 2
Huh? **Hein?** *interj.* 3
humanities **lettres** *f., pl.* 2
hundred: one hundred **cent** *m.* 5
five hundred **cinq cents** *m.* 5
one hundred one **cent un** *m.* 5
one hundred thousand **cent mille** *m.* 5
hundredth **centième** *adj.* 7
hunger **faim** *f.* 4
hungry: to be hungry **avoir faim** *v.* 4
hunt **chasse** *f.* 14
to hunt **chasser** *v.* 14
hurried **pressé(e)** *adj.* 9
hurry **se dépêcher** *v.* 10
hurt **faire mal** *v.* 10
to hurt oneself **se blesser** *v.* 10
husband **mari** *m.*; **époux** *m.* 3
hyphen *(punctuation mark)* **tiret** *m.* 11

I

I **je** *sub. pron.* 1; **moi** *disj. pron., sing.* 3
ice cream **glace** *f.* 6
ice cube **glaçon** *m.* 6
idea **idée** *f.* 3
if **si** *conj.* 13
ill: to become ill **tomber malade** *v.* 10
illness **maladie** *f.* 13
immediately **tout de suite** *adv.* 4
impatient **impatient(e)** *adj.* 1
important **important(e)** *adj.* 1
It is important that... **Il est important que...** 14
impossible **impossible** *adj.* 15
It is impossible that... **Il est impossible que...** 15

improve **améliorer** *v.* 13
in **dans** *prep.* 3; **en** *prep.* 3; **à** *prep.* 4
included **compris (comprendre)** *p.p., adj.* 6
incredible **incroyable** *adj.* 11
independent **indépendant(e)** *adj.* 1
independently **indépendamment** *adv.* 7
indicate **indiquer** *v.* 5
indispensable **indispensable** *adj.* 14
inexpensive **bon marché** *adj.* 6
injection **piqûre** *f.* 10
  to give an injection **faire une piqûre** *v.* 10
injury **blessure** *f.* 10
instrument **instrument** *m.* 1
insurance (health/life) **assurance** *f.* **(maladie/vie)** 13
intellectual **intellectuel(le)** *adj.* 3
intelligent **intelligent(e)** *adj.* 1
interested: to be interested (in) **s'intéresser (à)** *v.* 10
interesting **intéressant(e)** *adj.* 1
intermission **entracte** *m.* 15
internship **stage** *m.* 13
intersection **carrefour** *m.* 12
interview: to have an interview **passer un entretien** 13
introduce **présenter** *v.* 1
  I would like to introduce (*name*) to you. **Je te présente…** , *fam.* 1
  I would like to introduce (*name*) to you. **Je vous présente…** , *form.* 1
invite **inviter** *v.* 4
Ireland **Irlande** *f.* 7
Irish **irlandais(e)** *adj.* 7
iron **fer à repasser** *m.* 8
  to iron (the laundry) **repasser (le linge)** *v.* 8
isn't it? *(tag question)* **n'est-ce pas?** 2
island **île** *f.* 14
Italian **italien(ne)** *adj.* 1
Italy **Italie** *f.* 7
it: It depends. **Ça dépend.** 4
  It is… **C'est…** 1
itself *(used with reflexive verb)* **se/s'** *pron.* 10

J

jacket **blouson** *m.* 6
jam **confiture** *f.* 9
January **janvier** *m.* 5
Japan **Japon** *m.* 7
Japanese **japonais(e)** *adj.* 1
jealous **jaloux/jalouse** *adj.* 3
jeans **jean** *m. sing.* 6
jewelry store **bijouterie** *f.* 12
jogging **jogging** *m.* 5
  to go jogging **faire du jogging** *v.* 5
joke **blague** *f.* 2
journalist **journaliste** *m., f.* 3
juice (orange/apple) **jus** *m.* **(d'orange/de pomme)** 4
July **juillet** *m.* 5
June **juin** *m.* 5
jungle **jungle** *f.* 14
just *(barely)* **juste** *adv.* 3

K

keep **retenir** *v.* 9
key **clé** *f.* 7
keyboard **clavier** *m.* 11
kilo(gram) **kilo(gramme)** *m.* 9
kind **bon(ne)** *adj.* 3
kiosk **kiosque** *m.* 4
kiss one another **s'embrasser** *v.* 11
kitchen **cuisine** *f.* 8
knee **genou** *m.* 10
knife **couteau** *m.* 9
know *(as a fact)* **savoir** *v.* 8; *(to be familiar with)* **connaître** *v.* 8
  to know one another **se connaître** *v.* 11
  I don't know anything about it. **Je n'en sais rien.** 14
  to know that… **savoir que…** 15
known *(as a fact)* **su (savoir)** *p.p.* 8; *(famous)* **connu (connaître)** *p.p., adj.* 8

L

laborer **ouvrier/ouvrière** *m., f.* 13
lake **lac** *m.* 14
lamp **lampe** *f.* 8
landlord **propriétaire** *m.* 3
landslide **glissement de terrain** *m.* 14
language **langue** *f.* 2
  foreign languages **langues** *f., pl.* **étrangères** 2
last **dernier/dernière** *adj.* 2
lastly **dernièrement** *adv.* 7
late *(when something happens late)* **en retard** *adv.* 2; *(in the evening, etc.)* **tard** *adv.* 2
laugh **rire** *v.* 6
laughed **ri (rire)** *p.p.* 6
laundromat **laverie** *f.* 12
laundry: to do the laundry **faire la lessive** *v.* 8
law *(academic discipline)* **droit** *m.* 2; *(ordinance or rule)* **loi** *f.* 14
lawyer **avocat(e)** *m., f.* 3
lay off *(let go)* **renvoyer** *v.* 13
lazy **paresseux/paresseuse** *adj.* 3
learned **appris (apprendre)** *p.p.* 6
least **moins** 9
  the least… *(used with adjective)* **le/la moins…** *super. adv.* 9
  the least… , *(used with noun to express quantity)* **le moins de…** 14
  the least… *(used with verb or adverb)* **le moins…** *super. adv.* 9
leather **cuir** *m.* 6
leave **partir** *v.* 5; **quitter** *v.* 4
  to leave alone **laisser tranquille** *v.* 10
  to leave one another **se quitter** *v.* 11
  I'm leaving. **Je m'en vais.** 8
left: to the left (of) **à gauche (de)** *prep.* 3
leg **jambe** *f.* 10
leisure activity **loisir** *m.* 5
lemon soda **limonade** *f.* 4
lend *(to someone)* **prêter (à)** *v.* 6
less **moins** *adv.* 4
  less of… *(used with noun to express quantity)* **moins de…** 4
  less … than *(used with noun to compare quantities)* **moins de… que** 14
  less… than *(used with adjective to compare qualities)* **moins… que** 9
let **laisser** *v.* 11
  to let go *(to fire or lay off)* **renvoyer** *v.* 13
  Let's go! **Allons-y!** 4; **On y va!** 10
letter **lettre** *f.* 12
  letter of application **lettre** *f.* **de motivation** 13
  letter of recommendation/reference **lettre** *f.* **de recommandation** 13
lettuce **laitue** *f.* 9
level **niveau** *m.* 13
library **bibliothèque** *f.* 1
license: driver's license **permis** *m.* **de conduire** 11
life **vie** *f.* 6
life insurance **assurance** *f.* **vie** 13
light: warning light *(automobile)* **voyant** *m.* 11
  oil/gas warning light **voyant** *m.* **d'huile/d'essence** 11
  to light up **s'allumer** *v.* 11
like *(as)* **comme** *adv.* 6; to like **aimer** *v.* 2
  I don't like … very much. **Je n'aime pas tellement…** 2

I really like... **J'aime bien...** 2
to like one another **s'aimer bien** *v.* 11
to like that... **aimer que...** *v.* 14
line **queue** *f.* 12
to wait in line **faire la queue** *v.* 12
listen (to) **écouter** *v.* 2
literary **littéraire** *adj.* 15
literature **littérature** *f.* 1
little *(not much)* (of) **peu (de)** *adv.* 4
live (in) **habiter (à)** *v.* 2
living room *(informal room)* **salle de séjour** *f.* 8; *(formal room)* **salon** *m.* 8
located: to be located **se trouver** *v.* 10
long **long(ue)** *adj.* 3
a long time **longtemps** *adv.* 5
look *(at one another)* **se regarder** *v.* 11; *(at oneself)* **se regarder** *v.* 10
look for **chercher** *v.* 2
to look for work **chercher du/un travail** 12
loose *(clothing)* **large** *adj.* 6
lose: to lose (time) **perdre (son temps)** *v.* 6
to lose weight **maigrir** *v.* 4
lost: to be lost **être perdu(e)** *v.* 12
lot: a lot of **beaucoup de** *adv.* 4
love **amour** *m.* 6
to love **adorer** *v.* 2
I love... **J'adore...** 2
to love one another **s'aimer** *v.* 11
to be in love **être amoureux/amoureuse** *v.* 6
luck **chance** *f.* 2
to be lucky **avoir de la chance** *v.* 2
lunch **déjeuner** *m.* 9
to eat lunch **déjeuner** *v.* 4

M

ma'am **Madame.** *f.* 1
machine: answering machine **répondeur** *m.* 11
mad: to get mad **s'énerver** *v.* 10
made **fait (faire)** *p.p., adj.* 6
magazine **magazine** *m.* 15
mail **courrier** *m.* 12
mailbox **boîte** *f.* **aux lettres** 12
mailman **facteur** *m.* 12
main character **personnage principal** *m.* 15
main dish **plat (principal)** *m.* 9
maintain **maintenir** *v.* 9
make **faire** *v.* 5
makeup **maquillage** *m.* 10
to put on makeup **se maquiller** *v.* 10
make up **se réconcilier** *v.* 15
malfunction **panne** *f.* 11
man **homme** *m.* 1
manage *(in business)* **diriger** *v.* 13; *(to do something)* **arriver à** *v.* 2
manager **gérant(e)** *m., f.* 13
many (of) **beaucoup (de)** *adv.* 4
How many (of)? **Combien (de)?** 1
map *(of a city)* **plan** *m.* 7; *(of the world)* **carte** *f.* 1
March **mars** *m.* 5
marital status **état civil** *m.* 6
market **marché** *m.* 4
marriage **mariage** *m.* 6
married **marié(e)** *adj.* 3
married couple **mariés** *m., pl.* 6
marry **épouser** *v.* 3
Martinique: from Martinique **martiniquais(e)** *adj.* 1
masterpiece **chef-d'œuvre** *m.* 15
mathematics **mathématiques (maths)** *f., pl.* 2
May **mai** *m.* 5
maybe **peut-être** *adv.* 2
mayonnaise **mayonnaise** *f.* 9
mayor's office **mairie** *f.* 12
me **moi** *disj. pron., sing.* 3; *(attached to imperative)* **-moi** *pron.* 9; **me/m'** *i.o. pron.* 6; **me/m'** *d.o. pron.* 7
Me too. **Moi aussi.** 1
Me neither. **Moi non plus.** 2
meal **repas** *m.* 9
mean **méchant(e)** *adj.* 3
to mean (*with* **dire**) **vouloir** *v.* 9
means: that means **ça veut dire** *v.* 9
meat **viande** *f.* 9
mechanic **mécanicien/mécanicienne** *m., f.* 11
medication (against/for) **médicament (contre/pour)** *m., f.* 10
meet *(to encounter, to run into)* **rencontrer** *v.* 2; *(to make the acquaintance of)* **faire la connaissance de** *v.* 5, **se rencontrer** *v.* 11; *(planned encounter)* **se retrouver** *v.* 11
meeting **réunion** *f.* 13; **rendez-vous** *m.* 6
member **membre** *m.* 15
menu **menu** *m.* 9; **carte** *f.* 9
message **message** *m.* 13
to leave a message **laisser un message** *v.* 13
Mexican **mexicain(e)** *adj.* 1
Mexico **Mexique** *m.* 7
microwave oven **four à micro-ondes** *m.* 8
midnight **minuit** *m.* 2
milk **lait** *m.* 4
mine **le(s) mien(s), la/les mienne(s)** *poss. pron.* 15
mineral water **eau** *f.* **minérale** 4
mirror **miroir** *m.* 8
Miss **Mademoiselle** *f.* 1
mistaken: to be mistaken *(about something)* **se tromper (de)** *v.* 10
modest **modeste** *adj.* 13
moment **moment** *m.* 1
Monday **lundi** *m.* 2
money **argent** *m.* 12; *(currency)* **monnaie** *f.* 12
to deposit money **déposer de l'argent** *v.* 12
monitor **moniteur** *m.* 11
month **mois** *m.* 2
this month **ce mois-ci** 2
moon **Lune** *f.* 14
more **plus** *adv.* 4
more of **plus de** 4
more ... than *(used with noun to compare quantities)* **plus de... que** 14
more ... than *(used with adjective to compare qualities)* **plus... que** 9
morning **matin** *m.* 2; **matinée** *f.* 2
this morning **ce matin** 2
Moroccan **marocain(e)** *adj.* 1
most **plus** 9
the most... *(used with adjective)* **le/la plus...** *super. adv.* 9
the most... *(used with noun to express quantity)* **le plus de...** 14
the most... *(used with verb or adverb)* **le plus...** *super. adv.* 9
mother **mère** *f.* 3
mother-in-law **belle-mère** *f.* 3
mountain **montagne** *f.* 4
mouse **souris** *f.* 11
mouth **bouche** *f.* 10
move *(to get around)* **se déplacer** *v.* 12
to move in **emménager** *v.* 8
to move out **déménager** *v.* 8
movie **film** *m.* 15
adventure/horror/science-fiction/crime movie **film** *m.* **d'aventures/d'horreur/de science-fiction/policier** 15
movie theater **cinéma (ciné)** *m.* 4
much (as much ... as) *(used with noun to express quantity)* **autant de ... que** *adv.* 14
How much *(of something)*? **Combien (de)?** 1
How much is... ? **Combien coûte... ?** 4

museum **musée** *m.* 4
to go to museums **faire les musées** *v.* 15
mushroom **champignon** *m.* 9
music: to play music **faire de la musique** 15
musical **comédie** *f.* **musicale** 15; **musical(e)** *adj.* 15
musician **musicien(ne)** m., f. 3
must *(to have to)* **devoir** *v.* 9
One must **Il faut...** 5
mustard **moutarde** *f.* 9
my **ma** *poss. adj., f., sing.* 3; **mes** *poss. adj., m., f., pl.* 3; **mon** *poss. adj., m., sing.* 3
myself **me/m'** *pron., sing.* 10; *(attached to an imperative)* **-moi** *pron.* 9

N

naïve **naïf (naïve)** *adj.* 3
name: My name is... **Je m'appelle...** 1
named: to be named **s'appeler** *v.* 10
napkin **serviette** *f.* 9
nationality **nationalité** *f.*
I am of ... nationality. **Je suis de nationalité...** 1
natural **naturel(le)** *adj.* 14
natural resource **ressource naturelle** *f.* 14
nature **nature** *f.* 14
nauseated: to feel nauseated **avoir mal au cœur** *v.* 10
near (to) **près (de)** *prep.* 3
very near (to) **tout près (de)** 12
necessary **nécessaire** *adj.* 14
It was necessary... *(followed by infinitive or subjunctive)* **Il a fallu...** 6
It is necessary.... *(followed by infinitive or subjunctive)* **Il faut que...** 5
It is necessary that... *(followed by subjunctive)* **Il est nécessaire que/qu'...** 14
neck **cou** *m.* 10
need **besoin** *m.* 2
to need **avoir besoin (de)** *v.* 2
neighbor **voisin(e)** *m., f.* 3
neighborhood **quartier** *m.* 8
neither... nor **ne... ni... ni...** *conj.* 12
nephew **neveu** *m.* 3
nervous **nerveux/nerveuse** *adj.* 3
nervously **nerveusement** *adv.* 7
never **jamais** *adv.* 5; **ne... jamais** *adv.* 12
new **nouveau/nouvelle** *adj.* 3
newlyweds **jeunes mariés** *m., pl.* 6
news **informations (infos)** *f., pl.* 15; **nouvelles** *f., pl.* 15
newspaper **journal** *m.* 7
newsstand **marchand de journaux** *m.* 12
next **ensuite** *adv.* 7; **prochain(e)** *adj.* 2
next to **à côté de** *prep.* 3
nice **gentil/gentille** *adj.* 3; **sympa(thique)** *adj.* 1
nicely **gentiment** *adv.* 7
niece **nièce** *f.* 3
night **nuit** *f.* 2
nightclub **boîte (de nuit)** *f.* 4
nine **neuf** *m.* 1
nine hundred **neuf cents** *m.* 5
nineteen **dix-neuf** *m.* 1
ninety **quatre-vingt-dix** *m.* 3
ninth **neuvième** *adj.* 7
no *(at beginning of statement to indicate disagreement)* **(mais) non** 2; **aucun(e)** *adj.* 10
no more **ne... plus** 12
no problem **pas de problème** 12
no reason **pour rien** 4
no, none **pas (de)** 12
nobody **ne... personne** 12
none (not any) **ne... aucun(e)** 12
noon **midi** *m.* 2
no one **personne** *pron.* 12
north **nord** *m.* 12
nose **nez** *m.* 10
not **nez ne... pas** 2
not at all **pas du tout** *adv.* 2
Not badly. **Pas mal.** 1
to not believe that **ne pas croire que** *v.* 15
to not think that **ne pas penser que** *v.* 15
not yet **pas encore** *adv.* 7
notebook **cahier** *m.* 1
notes **billets** *m., pl.* 11
nothing **rien** *indef. pron.* 12
It's nothing. **Il n'y a pas de quoi.** 1
notice **s'apercevoir** *v.* 12
novel **roman** *m.* 15
November **novembre** *m.* 5
now **maintenant** *adv.* 5
nuclear **nucléaire** *adj.* 14
nuclear energy **énergie nucléaire** *f.* 14
nuclear plant **centrale nucléaire** *f.* 14
nurse **infirmier/infirmière** *m., f.* 10

O

obey **obéir (à)** *v.* 4
object **objet** *m.* 1
obtain **obtenir** *v.* 13
obvious **évident(e)** *adj.* 15
It is obvious that... **Il est évident que...** 15
obviously **évidemment** *adv.* 7
o'clock: It's... (o'clock). **Il est... heure(s).** 2
at ... (o'clock) **à ... heure(s)** 4
October **octobre** *m.* 5
of **de/d'** *prep.* 3
of medium height **de taille moyenne** *adj.* 3
of the **des (de + les)** 3
of the **du (de + le)** 3
of which, of whom **dont** *rel. pron.* 13
of course **bien sûr** *adv.*; **évidemment** *adv.* 2
of course not *(at beginning of statement to indicate disagreement)* **(mais) non** 2
offer **offrir** *v.* 11
offered **offert (offrir)** *p.p.* 11
office **bureau** *m.* 4
at the doctor's office **chez le médecin** *prep.* 2
often **souvent** *adv.* 5
oil **huile** *f.* 9
automobile oil **huile** *f.* 11
oil warning light **voyant** *m.* **d'huile** 11
olive oil **huile** *f.* **d'olive** 9
to check the oil **vérifier l'huile** *v.* 11
okay **d'accord** 2
old **vieux/vieille** *adj.*; *(placed after noun)* **ancien(ne)** *adj.* 3
old age **vieillesse** *f.* 6
olive **olive** *f.* 9
olive oil **huile** *f.* **d'olive** 9
omelette **omelette** *f.* 5
on **sur** *prep.* 3
On behalf of whom? **C'est de la part de qui?** 13
on the condition that... **à condition que** 15
on television **à la télé(vision)** 15
on the contrary **au contraire** 15
on the radio **à la radio** 15
on the subject of **au sujet de** 14
on vacation **en vacances** 7
once **une fois** *adv.* 7
one **un** *m.* 1
one **on** *sub. pron., sing.* 1
one another **l'un(e) à l'autre** 11

one another **l'un(e) l'autre** 11
one had to... **il fallait...** 8
One must... **Il faut que/ qu'...** 14
One must... **Il faut...** *(followed by infinitive or subjunctive)* 5
one million **un million** *m.* 5
one million *(things)* **un million de...** 5
onion **oignon** *m.* 9
online **en ligne** *11*
to be online **être en ligne** *v.* 11
to be online (with someone) **être connecté(e) (avec quelqu'un)** *v.* 7, 11
only **ne... que** 12; **seulement** *adv.* 7
open **ouvrir** *v.* 11; **ouvert(e)** *adj.* 11
opened **ouvert (ouvrir)** *p.p.* 11
opera **opéra** *m.* 15
optimistic **optimiste** *adj.* 1
or **ou** 3
orange **orange** *f.* 9; **orange** *inv. adj.* 6
orchestra **orchestre** *m.* 15
order **commander** *v.* 9
organize (a party) **organiser (une fête)** *v.* 6
orient oneself **s'orienter** *v.* 12
others **d'autres** 4
our **nos** *poss. adj., m., f., pl.* 3; **notre** *poss. adj., m., f., sing.* 3; **le(s) nôtre(s), la/les nôtre(s)** *poss. pron.* 15
outdoor *(open-air)* **plein air** 14
over **fini** *adj., p.p.* 7
overpopulation **surpopulation** *f.* 14
overseas **à l'étranger** *adv.* 7
over there **là-bas** *adv.* 1
owed **dû (devoir)** *p.p., adj.* 9
own **posséder** *v.* 5
owner **propriétaire** *m., f.* 3
ozone **ozone** *m.* 14
hole in the ozone layer **trou dans la couche d'ozone** *m.* 14

P

pack: to pack one's bags **faire les valises** 7
package **colis** *m.* 12
paid **payé (payer)** *p.p., adj.* 13
to be well/badly paid **être bien/ mal payé(e)** 13
pain **douleur** *f.* 10
paint **faire de la peinture** *v.* 15
painter **peintre/femme peintre** *m., f.* 15
painting **peinture** *f.* 15; **tableau** *m.* 15
Palm Pilot **palm** *m.* 1
pants **pantalon** *m., sing.* 6
paper **papier** *m.* 1
Pardon (me). **Pardon.** 1
parents **parents** *m., pl.* 3
park **parc** *m.* 4
to park **se garer** *v.* 11
parka **anorak** *m.* 6
parking lot **parking** *m.* 11
part-time job **emploi** *m.* **à mi-temps/à temps partiel** *m.* 13
party **fête** *f.* 6
to party **faire la fête** *v.* 6
pass **dépasser** *v.* 11; **passer** *v.* 7
to pass an exam **être reçu(e) à un examen** *v.* 2
passenger **passager/passagère** *m., f.* 7
passport **passeport** *m.* 7
password **mot de passe** *m.* 11
past: in the past **autrefois** *adv.* 7
pasta **pâtes** *f., pl.* 9
pastime **passe-temps** *m.* 5
pastry **pâtisserie** *f.* 9
pastry shop **pâtisserie** *f.* 9
pâté **pâté (de campagne)** *m.* 9
path **sentier** *m.* 14; **chemin** *m.* 12
patient **patient(e)** *adj.* 1
patiently **patiemment** *adv.* 7
pay **payer** *v.* 5
to pay by check **payer par chèque** *v.* 12
to pay in cash **payer en liquide** *v.* 12
to pay with a credit card **payer avec une carte de crédit** *v.* 12
to pay attention (to) **faire attention (à)** *v.* 5
peach **pêche** *f.* 9
pear **poire** *f.* 9
peas **petits pois** *m., pl.* 9
pen **stylo** *m.* 1
pencil **crayon** *m.* 1
people **gens** *m., pl.* 7
pepper *(spice)* **poivre** *m.* 9; *(vegetable)* **poivron** *m.* 9
per day/week/month/year **par jour/semaine/mois/an** 5
perfect **parfait(e)** *adj.* 2
perhaps **peut-être** *adv.* 2
period *(punctuation mark)* **point** *m.* 11
permit **permis** *m.* 11
permitted **permis (permettre)** *p.p., adj.* 6
person **personne** *f.* 1
personal CD player **baladeur CD** *m.* 11
pessimistic **pessimiste** *adj.* 1
pharmacist **pharmacien(ne)** *m., f.* 10
pharmacy **pharmacie** *f.* 10
philosophy **philosophie** *f.* 2
phone booth **cabine téléphonique** *f.* 12
phone card **télécarte** *f.* 13
phone one another **se téléphoner** *v.* 11
photo(graph) **photo(graphie)** *f.* 3
physical education **éducation physique** *f.* 2
physics **physique** *f.* 2
piano **piano** *m.* 15
pick up **décrocher** *v.* 13
picnic **pique-nique** *m.* 14
picture **tableau** *m.* 1
pie **tarte** *f.* 9
piece (of) **morceau (de)** *m.* 4
piece of furniture **meuble** *m.* 8
pill **pilule** *f.* 10
pillow **oreiller** *m.* 8
pink **rose** *adj.* 6
pitcher (of water) **carafe (d'eau)** *f.* 9
place **endroit** *m.* 4; **lieu** *m.* 4
planet **planète** *f.* 14
plans: to make plans **faire des projets** *v.* 13
plant **plante** *f.* 14
plastic **plastique** *m.* 14
plastic wrapping **emballage en plastique** *m.* 14
plate **assiette** *f.* 9
play **pièce de théâtre** *f.* 15
play **s'amuser** *v.* 10; *(a sport/a musical instrument)* **jouer (à/de)** *v.* 5
to play regularly **pratiquer** *v.* 5
to play sports **faire du sport** *v.* 5
to play a role **jouer un rôle** *v.* 15
player **joueur/joueuse** *m., f.* 5
playwright **dramaturge** *m.* 15
pleasant **agréable** *adj.* 1
please: to please someone **faire plaisir à quelqu'un** *v.* 13
Please. **S'il te plaît.** *fam.* 1
Please. **S'il vous plaît.** *form.* 1
Please. **Je vous en prie.** *form.* 1
Please hold. **Ne quittez pas.** 13
plumber **plombier** *m.* 13
poem **poème** *m.* 15
poet **poète/poétesse** *m., f.* 15
police **police** *f.* 11; **policier** *adj.* 15
police officer **agent de police** *m.* 11; **policier** *m.* 11; **policière** *f.* 11
police station **commissariat de police** *m.* 12
polite **poli(e)** *adj.* 1
politely **poliment** *adv.* 7

political science **sciences politiques (sciences po)** *f., pl.* 2
politician **homme/femme politique** *m., f.* 13
pollute **polluer** *v.* 14
pollution **pollution** *f.* 14
pollution cloud **nuage de pollution** *m.* 14
pool **piscine** *f.* 4
poor **pauvre** *adj.* 3
popular music **variétés** *f., pl.* 15
population **population** *f.* 14
growing population **population** *f.* **croissante** 14
pork **porc** *m.* 9
portrait **portrait** *m.* 5
position (*job*) **poste** *m.* 13
possess (*to own*) **posséder** *v.* 5
possible **possible** *adj.* 15
It is possible that… **Il est possible que…** 14
post **afficher** *v.* 13
post office **bureau de poste** *m.* 12
postal service **poste** *f.* 12
postcard **carte postale** *f.* 12
poster **affiche** *f.* 8
potato **pomme de terre** *f.* 9
practice **pratiquer** *v.* 5
prefer **aimer mieux** *v.* 2; **préférer (que)** *v.* 5
pregnant **enceinte** *adj.* 10
prepare (for) **préparer** *v.* 2
to prepare (*to do something*) **se préparer (à)** *v.* 10
prescription **ordonnance** *f.* 10
present **présenter** *v.* 15
preservation: habitat preservation **sauvetage des habitats** *m.* 14
preserve **préserver** *v.* 14
pressure **pression** *f.* 11
to check the tire pressure **vérifier la pression des pneus** *v.* 11
pretty **joli(e)** *adj.* 3; *(before an adjective or adverb)* **assez** *adv.* 7
prevent: to prevent a fire **prévenir l'incendie** *v.* 14
price **prix** *m.* 4
principal **principal(e)** *adj.* 12
print **imprimer** *v.* 11
printer **imprimante** *f.* 11
problem **problème** *m.* 1
produce **produire** *v.* 6
produced **produit (produire)** *p.p., adj.* 6
product **produit** *m.* 14
profession **métier** *m.* 13; **profession** *f.* 13
demanding profession **profession** *f.* **exigeante** 13
professional **professionnel(le)** *adj.* 13
professional experience **expérience professionnelle** *f.* 13
program **programme** *m.* 15; (*software*) **logiciel** *m.* 11; (*television*) **émission** *f.* **de télévision** 15
prohibit **interdire** *v.* 14
project **projet** *m.* 13
promise **promettre** *v.* 6
promised **promis (promettre)** *p.p., adj.* 6
promotion **promotion** *f.* 13
propose that… **proposer que…** *v.* 14
to propose a solution **proposer une solution** *v.* 14
protect **protéger** *v.* 5
protection **préservation** *f.* 14; **protection** *f.* 14
proud **fier/fière** *adj.* 3
psychological **psychologique** *adj.* 15
psychological drama **drame psychologique** *m.* 15
psychology **psychologie** *f.* 2
psychologist **psychologue** *m., f.* 13
publish **publier** *v.* 15
pure **pur(e)** *adj.* 14
purple **violet(te)** *adj.* 6
purse **sac à main** *m.* 6
put **mettre** *v.* 6
to put (on) (yourself) **se mettre** *v.* 10
to put away **ranger** *v.* 8
to put on makeup **se maquiller** *v.* 10
put **mis (mettre)** *p.p.* 6

Q

quarter **quart** *m.* 2
a quarter after … (o'clock) **… et quart** 2
Quebec: from Quebec **québécois(e)** *adj.* 1
question **question** *f.* 6
to ask (*someone*) a question **poser une question (à)** *v.* 6
quick **vite** *adv.* 4
quickly **vite** *adv.* 1
quite *(before an adjective or adverb)* **assez** *adv.* 7

R

rabbit **lapin** *m.* 14
rain **pleuvoir** *v.* 5
acid rain **pluie** *f.* **acide** 14
It is raining. **Il pleut.** 5
It was raining. **Il pleuvait.** 8
rain forest **forêt tropicale** *f.* 14
rain jacket **imperméable** *m.* 5
rained **plu (pleuvoir)** *p.p.* 6
raise (in salary) **augmentation (de salaire)** *f.* 13
rapidly **rapidement** *adv.* 7
rarely **rarement** *adv.* 5
rather **plutôt** *adv.* 1
ravishing **ravissant(e)** *adj.* 13
razor **rasoir** *m.* 10
react **réagir** *v.* 4
read **lire** *v.* 7
read **lu (lire)** *p.p., adj.* 7
ready **prêt(e)** *adj.* 3
real *(true)* **vrai(e)** *adj.*; **véritable** *adj.* 3
real estate agent **agent immobilier** *m., f.* 13
realize **se rendre compte** *v.* 10
really **vraiment** *adv.* 5; *(before adjective or adverb)* **tout(e)** *adv.* 3; *(before adjective or adverb)* **très** *adv.* 7
really close by **tout près** 3
rear-view mirror **rétroviseur** *m.* 11
reason **raison** *f.* 2
receive **recevoir** *v.* 12
received **reçu (recevoir)** *p.p., adj.* 12
receiver **combiné** *m.* 13
recent **récent(e)** *adj.* 15
reception desk **réception** *f.* 7
recognize **reconnaître** *v.* 8
recognized **reconnu (reconnaître)** *p.p., adj.* 8
recommend that… **recommander que…** *v.* 14
recommendation **recommandation** *f.* 13
record **enregistrer** *v.* 11
(*CD, DVD*) **graver** *v.* 11
recycle **recycler** *v.* 14
recycling **recyclage** *m.* 14
red **rouge** *adj.* 6
redial **recomposer (un numéro)** *v.* 11
reduce **réduire** *v.* 6
reduced **réduit (réduire)** *p.p., adj.* 6
reference **référence** *f.* 13
reflect (on) **réfléchir (à)** *v.* 4
refrigerator **frigo** *m.* 8
refuse (*to do something*) **refuser (de)** *v.* 11
region **région** *f.* 14
regret that… **regretter que…** 14
relax **se détendre** *v.* 10
remember **se souvenir (de)** *v.* 10
remote control **télécommande** *f.* 11
rent **loyer** *m.* 8
to rent **louer** *v.* 8
repair **réparer** *v.* 11
repeat **répéter** *v.* 5
research **rechercher** *v.* 13

researcher **chercheur/chercheuse** *m., f.* 13
reservation **réservation** *f.* 7
  to cancel a reservation **annuler une réservation** 7
reserve **réserver** *v.* 7
reserved **réservé(e)** *adj.* 1
resign **démissionner** *v.* 13
resort (ski) **station** *f.* **(de ski)** 7
respond **répondre (à)** *v.* 6
rest **se reposer** *v.* 10
restart **redémarrer** *v.* 11
restaurant **restaurant** *m.* 4
restroom(s) **toilettes** *f., pl.* 8; **W.-C.** *m., pl.*
result **résultat** *m.* 2
résumé **curriculum vitæ (C.V.)** *m.* 13
retake **repasser** *v.* 15
retire **prendre sa retraite** *v.* 6
retired person **retraité(e)** *m., f.* 13
retirement **retraite** *f.* 6
return **retourner** *v.* 7
  to return (home) **rentrer (à la maison)** *v.* 2
review (*criticism*) **critique** *f.* 15
rice **riz** *m.* 9
ride: to go horseback riding **faire du cheval** *v.* 5
  to ride in a car **rouler en voiture** *v.* 7
right **juste** *adv.* 3
  to the right (of) **à droite (de)** *prep.* 3
  to be right **avoir raison** 2
  right away **tout de suite** 7
  right next door **juste à côté** 3
ring **sonner** *v.* 11
river **fleuve** *m.* 14; **rivière** *f.* 14
riverboat **bateau-mouche** *m.* 7
role **rôle** *m.* 14
room **pièce** *f.* 8; **salle** *f.* 8
  bedroom **chambre** *f.* 7
  classroom **salle** *f.* **de classe** 1
  dining room **salle** *f.* **à manger** 8
  single hotel room **chambre** *f.* **individuelle** 7
roommate **camarade de chambre** *m., f.* 1
  (*in an apartment*) **colocataire** *m., f.* 1
round-trip **aller-retour** *adj.* 7
  round-trip ticket **billet** *m.* **aller-retour** 7
rug **tapis** *m.* 8
run **courir** *v.* 5; **couru (courir)** *p.p., adj.* 6
  to run into someone **tomber sur quelqu'un** *v.* 7

S

sad **triste** *adj.* 3
  to be sad that… **être triste que…** *v.* 14
safety **sécurité** *f.* 11
said **dit (dire)** *p.p., adj.* 7
salad **salade** *f.* 9
salary (a high, low) **salaire (élevé, modeste)** *m.* 13
sales **soldes** *f., pl.* 6
salon: beauty salon **salon** *m.* **de beauté** 12
salt **sel** *m.* 9
sandwich **sandwich** *m.* 4
sat (down) **assis (s'asseoir)** *p.p.* 10
Saturday **samedi** *m.* 2
sausage **saucisse** *f.* 9
save **sauvegarder** *v.* 11
  save the planet **sauver la planète** *v.* 14
savings **épargne** *f.* 12
savings account **compte d'épargne** *m.* 12
say **dire** *v.* 7
scarf **écharpe** *f.* 6
scholarship **bourse** *f.* 2
school **école** *f.* 2
science **sciences** *f., pl.* 2
  political science **sciences politiques (sciences po)** *f., pl.* 2
screen **écran** *m.* 11
screening **séance** *f.* 15
sculpture **sculpture** *f.* 15
sculptor **sculpteur/femme sculpteur** *m., f.* 15
sea **mer** *f.* 7
seafood **fruits de mer** *m., pl.* 9
search for **chercher** *v.* 2
  to search for work **chercher du travail** *v.* 12
season **saison** *f.* 5
seat **place** *f.* 15
seatbelt **ceinture de sécurité** *f.* 11
  to buckle one's seatbelt **attacher sa ceinture de sécurité** *v.* 11
seated **assis(e)** *p.p., adj.* 10
second **deuxième** *adj.* 7
security **sécurité** *f.* 11
see **voir** *v.* 12; (*catch sight of*) **apercevoir** *v.* 12
  to see again **revoir** *v.* 12
  See you later. **À plus tard.** 1
  See you later. **À tout à l'heure.** 1
  See you soon. **À bientôt.** 1
  See you tomorrow. **À demain.** 1
seen **aperçu (apercevoir)** *p.p.* 12; **vu (voir)** *p.p.* 12
  seen again **revu (revoir)** *p.p.* 12
self/-selves **même(s)** *pron.* 6
selfish **égoïste** *adj.* 1
sell **vendre** *v.* 6
seller **vendeur/vendeuse** *m., f.* 6
send **envoyer** *v.* 5
  to send (*to someone*) **envoyer (à)** *v.* 6
  to send a letter **poster une lettre** 12
Senegalese **sénégalais(e)** *adj.* 1
sense **sentir** *v.* 5
separated **séparé(e)** *adj.* 3
September **septembre** *m.* 5
serious **grave** *adj.* 10; **sérieux/sérieuse** *adj.* 3
serve **servir** *v.* 5
server **serveur/serveuse** *m., f.* 4
service station **station-service** *f.* 11
set the table **mettre la table** *v.* 8
seven **sept** *m.* 1
seven hundred **sept cents** *m.* 5
seventeen **dix-sept** *m.* 1
seventh **septième** *adj.* 7
seventy **soixante-dix** *m.* 3
several **plusieurs** *adj.* 4
shame **honte** *f.* 2
  It's a shame that… **Il est dommage que…** 14
shampoo **shampooing** *m.* 10
shape (*state of health*) **forme** *f.* 10
share **partager** *v.* 2
shave (oneself) **se raser** *v.* 10
shaving cream **crème à raser** *f.* 10
she **elle** *pron.* 1
sheet of paper **feuille de papier** *f.* 1
sheets **draps** *m., pl.* 8
shelf **étagère** *f.* 8
shh **chut** 15
shirt (short-/long-sleeved) **chemise (à manches courtes/longues)** *f.* 6
shoe **chaussure** *f.* 6
shopkeeper **commerçant(e)** *m., f.* 9
shopping **shopping** *m.* 7
  to go shopping **faire du shopping** *v.* 7
  to go (grocery) shopping **faire les courses** *v.* 9
shopping center **centre commercial** *m.* 4
short **court(e)** *adj.* 3; (*stature*) **petit(e)** 3
shorts **short** *m.* 6
shot (*injection*) **piqûre** *f.* 10
  to give a shot **faire une piqûre** *v.* 10
show **spectacle** *m.* 5; (*movie or theater*) **séance** *f.* 15

to show (*to someone*) **montrer (à)** *v.* 6
shower **douche** *f.* 8
shut off **fermer** *v.* 11
shy **timide** *adj.* 1
sick: to get/be sick **tomber/être malade** *v.* 10
sign **signer** *v.* 12
silk **soie** 6
since **depuis** *adv.* 9
sincere **sincère** *adj.* 1
sing **chanter** *v.* 5
singer **chanteur/chanteuse** *m., f.* 1
single *(marital status)* **célibataire** *adj.* 3
single hotel room **chambre** *f.* **individuelle** 7
sink **évier** *m.* 8; (*bathroom*) **lavabo** *m.* 8
sir **Monsieur** *m.* 1
sister **sœur** *f.* 3
sister-in-law **belle-sœur** *f.* 3
sit down **s'asseoir** *v.* 10
sitting **assis(e)** *adj.* 10
six **six** *m.* 1
six hundred **six cents** *m.* 5
sixteen **seize** *m.* 1
sixth **sixième** *adj.* 7
sixty **soixante** *m.* 1
size **taille** *f.* 6
skate **patiner** *v.* 4
ski **skier** *v.* 5; **faire du ski** 5
skiing **ski** *m.* 5
ski jacket **anorak** *m.* 6
ski resort **station** *f.* **de ski** 7
skin **peau** *f.* 10
skirt **jupe** *f.* 6
sky **ciel** *m.* 14
sleep **sommeil** *m.* 2
to sleep **dormir** *v.* 5
to be sleepy **avoir sommeil** *v.* 2
sleeve **manche** *f.* 6
slice **tranche** *f.* 9
slipper **pantoufle** *f.* 10
slow **lent(e)** *adj.* 3
small **petit(e)** *adj.* 3
smell **sentir** *v.* 5
smile **sourire** *m.* 6
to smile **sourire** *v.* 6
smoke **fumer** *v.* 10
snack (afternoon) **goûter** *m.* 9
snake **serpent** *m.* 14
sneeze **éternuer** *v.* 10
snow **neiger** *v.* 5
It is snowing. **Il neige.** 5
It was snowing… **Il neigeait…** 8
so **si** 11; **alors** *adv.* 1
so that **pour que** 15
soap **savon** *m.* 10
soap opera **feuilleton** *m.* 15
soccer **foot(ball)** *m.* 5
sociable **sociable** *adj.* 1
sociology **sociologie** *f.* 1
sock **chaussette** *f.* 6
software **logiciel** *m.* 11
soil (*to make dirty*) **salir** *v.* 8
solar **solaire** *adj.* 14
solar energy **énergie solaire** *f.* 14
solution **solution** *f.* 14
some **de l'** *part. art., m., f., sing.* 4
some **de la** *part. art., f., sing.* 4
some **des** *part. art., m., f., pl.* 4
some **du** *part. art., m., sing.* 4
some **quelques** *adj.* 4
some (of it/them) **en** *pron.* 10
someone **quelqu'un** *pron.* 12
something **quelque chose** *m.* 4
Something's not right. **Quelque chose ne va pas.** 5
sometimes **parfois** *adv.* 5; **quelquefois** *adv.* 7
son **fils** *m.* 3
song **chanson** *f.* 15
sorry **désolé(e)** 11
to be sorry that… **être désolé(e) que…** *v.* 14
sort **sorte** *f.* 15
So-so. **Comme ci, comme ça.** 1
soup **soupe** *f.* 4
soup spoon **cuillère à soupe** *f.* 9
south **sud** *m.* 12
space **espace** *m.* 14
Spain **Espagne** *f.* 7
Spanish **espagnol(e)** *adj.* 1
speak (on the phone) **parler (au téléphone)** *v.* 2
to speak (to) **parler (à)** *v.* 6
to speak to one another **se parler** *v.* 11
specialist **spécialiste** *m., f.* 13
species **espèce** *f.* 14
endangered species **espèce** *f.* **menacée** 14
spectator **spectateur/spectatrice** *m., f.* 15
speed **vitesse** *f.* 11
speed limit **limitation de vitesse** *f.* 11
spend **dépenser** *v.* 4
to spend money **dépenser de l'argent** 4
to spend time **passer** *v.* 7
to spend time (*somewhere*) **faire un séjour** 7
spoon **cuillère** *f.* 9
sport(s) **sport** *m.* 5
to play sports **faire du sport** *v.* 5
sporty **sportif/sportive** *adj.* 3
sprain one's ankle **se fouler la cheville** 10
spring **printemps** *m.* 5
in the spring **au printemps** 5
square (*place*) **place** *f.* 4
squirrel **écureuil** *m.* 14
stadium **stade** *m.* 5
stage (*phase*) **étape** *f.* 6
stage fright **trac** 13
staircase **escalier** *m.* 8
stamp **timbre** *m.* 12
star **étoile** *f.* 14
starter **entrée** *f.* 9
start up **démarrer** *v.* 11
station **station** *f.* 7
subway station **station** *f.* **de métro** 7
train station **gare** *f.* 7
stationery store **papeterie** *f.* 12
statue **statue** *f.* 12
stay **séjour** *m.* 7; **rester** *v.* 7
to stay slim **garder la ligne** *v.* 10
steak **steak** *m.* 9
steering wheel **volant** *m.* 11
stepbrother **demi-frère** *m.* 3
stepfather **beau-père** *m.* 3
stepmother **belle-mère** *f.* 3
stepsister **demi-sœur** *f.* 3
stereo system **chaîne stéréo** *f.* 11
still **encore** *adv.* 3
stomach **ventre** *m.* 10
to have a stomach ache **avoir mal au ventre** *v.* 10
stone **pierre** *f.* 14
stop (doing something) **arrêter (de faire quelque chose)** *v.*; (*to stop oneself*) **s'arrêter** *v.* 10
to stop by someone's house **passer chez quelqu'un** *v.* 4
bus stop **arrêt d'autobus (de bus)** *m.* 7
store **magasin** *m.*; **boutique** *f.* 12
grocery store **épicerie** *f.* 4
stormy **orageux/orageuse** *adj.* 5
It is stormy. **Le temps est orageux.** 5
story **histoire** *f.* 2
stove **cuisinière** *f.* 8
straight **raide** *adj.* 3
straight ahead **tout droit** *adv.* 12
strangle **étrangler** *v.* 13
strawberry **fraise** *f.* 9
street **rue** *f.* 11
to follow a street **suivre une rue** *v.* 12
strong **fort(e)** *adj.* 3
student **étudiant(e)** *m., f.* 1; **élève** *m., f.* 1
high school student **lycéen(ne)** *m., f.* 2
studies **études** *f.* 2
studio (*apartment*) **studio** *m.* 8
study **étudier** *v.* 2

suburbs **banlieue** *f.* 4
subway **métro** *m.* 7
subway station **station** *f.* **de métro** 7
succeed (*in doing something*) **réussir (à)** *v.* 4
success **réussite** *f.* 13
suddenly **soudain** *adv.* 7; **tout à coup** *adv.* 7.; **tout d'un coup** *adv.* 7
suffer **souffrir** *v.* 11
suffered **souffert (souffrir)** *p.p.* 11
sugar **sucre** *m.* 4
suggest (that) **suggérer (que)** *v.* 14
suit (*man's*) **costume** *m.* 6; (*woman's*) **tailleur** *m.* 6
suitcase **valise** *f.* 7
summer **été** *m.* 5
in the summer **en été** 5
sun **soleil** *m.* 5
It is sunny. **Il fait (du) soleil.** 5
Sunday **dimanche** *m.* 2
sunglasses **lunettes de soleil** *f., pl.* 6
supermarket **supermarché** *m.* 9
sure **sûr(e)** 9
It is sure that... **Il est sûr que...** 15
It is unsure that... **Il n'est pas sûr que...** 15
surf on the Internet **surfer sur Internet** 11
surprise (someone) **faire une surprise (à quelqu'un)** *v.* 6
surprised **surpris (surprendre)** *p.p., adj.* 6
to be surprised that... **être surpris(e) que...** *v.* 14
sweater **pull** *m.* 6
sweep **balayer** *v.* 8
swell **enfler** *v.* 10
swim **nager** *v.* 4
swimsuit **maillot de bain** *m.* 6
Swiss **suisse** *adj.* 1
Switzerland **Suisse** *f.* 7
symptom **symptôme** *m.* 10

T

table **table** *f.* 1
to clear the table **débarrasser la table** *v.* 8
tablecloth **nappe** *f.* 9
take **prendre** *v.* 4
to take a shower **prendre une douche** 10
to take a train (plane, taxi, bus, boat) **prendre un train (un avion, un taxi, un autobus, un bateau)** *v.* 7
to take a walk **se promener** *v.* 10
to take advantage of **profiter de** *v.* 15
to take an exam **passer un examen** *v.* 2
to take care (of something) **s'occuper (de)** *v.* 10
to take out the trash **sortir la/les poubelle(s)** *v.* 8
to take time off **prendre un congé** *v.* 13
to take (*someone*) **emmener** *v.* 5
taken **pris (prendre)** *p.p., adj.* 6
tale **conte** *m.* 15
talented (*gifted*) **doué(e)** *adj.* 15
tan **bronzer** *v.* 6
tape recorder **magnétophone** *m.* 11
tart **tarte** *f.* 9
taste **goûter** *v.* 9
taxi **taxi** *m.* 7
tea **thé** *m.* 4
teach **enseigner** *v.* 2
to teach (*to do something*) **apprendre (à)** *v.* 4
teacher **professeur** *m.* 1
team **équipe** *f.* 5
teaspoon **cuillére à café** *f.* 9
tee shirt **tee-shirt** *m.* 6
teeth **dents** *f., pl.* 9
to brush one's teeth **se brosser les dents** *v.* 9
telephone (*receiver*) **appareil** *m.* 13
to telephone (*someone*) **téléphoner (à)** *v.* 2
It's Mr./Mrs./Miss ... (on the phone.) **C'est M./Mme/Mlle ... (à l'appareil.)** 13
television **télévision** *f.* 1
television channel **chaîne** *f.* **de télévision** 11
television program **émission** *f.* **de télévision** 15
television set **poste de télévision** *m.* 11
tell one another **se dire** *v.* 11
temperature **température** *f.* 5
ten **dix** *m.* 1
tennis **tennis** *m.* 5
tennis shoes **baskets** *f., pl.* 6
tenth **dixième** *adj.* 7
terminal (bus) **gare** *f.* **routière** 7
terrace (café) **terrasse** *f.* **de café** 4
test **examen** *m.* 1
than **que/qu'** *conj.* 9, 14
thank: Thank you (very much). **Merci (beaucoup).** 1
that **ce/c', ça** 1; **que** *rel. pron.* 13
Is that... ? **Est-ce... ?** 2
That's enough. **Ça suffit.** 5
That has nothing to do with us. That is none of our business. **Ça ne nous regarde pas.** 14
that is... **c'est...** 1
that is to say **ça veut dire** 10
theater **théâtre** *m.* 15
their **leur(s)** *poss. adj., m., f.* 3
theirs **le(s) leur(s), la/les leur(s)** *poss. pron.* 15
them **les** *d.o. pron.* 7, **leur** *i.o. pron., m., f., pl.* 6
then **ensuite** *adv.* 7, **puis** *adv.* 7, **puis** 4; **alors** *adv.* 7
there **là** 1; **y** *pron.* 10
Is there... ? **Y a-t-il... ?** 2
over there **là-bas** *adv.* 1
(over) there (*used with demonstrative adjective* **ce** *and noun or with demonstrative pronoun* **celui**) **-là** 6
There is/There are... **Il y a...** 1
There is/There are.... **Voilà...** 1
There was... **Il y a eu...** 6; **Il y avait...** 8
therefore **donc** *conj.* 7
these/those **ces** *dem. adj., m., f., pl.* 6
these/those **celles** *pron., f., pl.* 14
these/those **ceux** *pron., m., pl.* 14
they **ils** *sub. pron., m.* 1; **elles** *sub.* and *disj. pron., f.* 1; **eux** *disj. pron., pl.* 3
thing **chose** *f.* 1, **truc** 7
think (about) **réfléchir (à)** *v.* 4
to think (that) **penser (que)** *v.* 2
third **troisième** *adj.* 7
thirst **soif** *f.* 4
to be thirsty **avoir soif** *v.* 4
thirteen **treize** *m.* 1
thirty **trente** *m.* 1
thirty-first **trente et unième** *adj.* 7
this/that **ce** *dem. adj., m., sing.* 6; **cet** *dem. adj., m., sing.* 6; **cette** *dem. adj., f., sing.* 6
this afternoon **cet après-midi** 2
this evening **ce soir** 2
this one/that one **celle** *pron., f., sing.* 14; **celui** *pron., m., sing.* 14
this week **cette semaine** 2
this weekend **ce week-end** 2
this year **cette année** 2
those are... **ce sont...** 1
thousand: one thousand **mille** *m.* 5
one hundred thousand **cent mille** *m.* 5
threat **danger** *m.* 14
three **trois** *m.* 1
three hundred **trois cents** *m.* 5
throat **gorge** *f.* 10
throw away **jeter** *v.* 14
Thursday **jeudi** *m.* 2

ticket **billet** *m.* 7
round-trip ticket **billet** *m.* **aller-retour** 7
bus/subway ticket **ticket de bus/de métro** *m.* 7
tie **cravate** *f.* 6
tight **serré(e)** *adj.* 6
time *(occurence)* **fois** *f.*; *(general sense)* **temps** *m., sing.* 5
a long time **longtemps** *adv.* 5
free time **temps libre** *m.* 5
from time to time **de temps en temps** *adv.* 7
to lose time **perdre son temps** *v.* 6
tinker **bricoler** *v.* 5
tip **pourboire** *m.* 4
to leave a tip **laisser un pourboire** *v.* 4
tire **pneu** *m.* 11
flat tire **pneu** *m.* **crevé** 11
(emergency) tire **roue (de secours)** *f.* 11
to check the tire pressure **vérifier la pression des pneus** *v.* 11
tired **fatigué(e)** *adj.* 3
tiresome **pénible** *adj.* 3
to **à** *prep.* 4; **au (à + le)** 4; **aux (à + les)** 4
toaster **grille-pain** *m.* 8
today **aujourd'hui** *adv.* 2
toe **orteil** *m.* 10; **doigt de pied** *m.* 10
together **ensemble** *adv.* 6
tomato **tomate** *f.* 9
tomorrow (morning, afternoon, evening) **demain (matin, après-midi, soir)** *adv.* 2
day after tomorrow **après-demain** *adv.* 2
too **aussi** *adv.* 1
too many/much (of) **trop (de)** 4
tooth **dent** *f.* 9
to brush one's teeth **se brosser les dents** *v.* 9
toothbrush **brosse** *f.* **à dents** 10
toothpaste **dentifrice** *m.* 10
tour **tour** *m.* 5
tourism **tourisme** *m.* 12
tourist office **office du tourisme** *m.* 12
towel (bath) **serviette (de bain)** *f.* 10
town **ville** *f.* 4
town hall **mairie** *f.* 12
toxic **toxique** *adj.* 14
toxic waste **déchets toxiques** *m., pl.* 14
traffic **circulation** *f.* 11
traffic light **feu de signalisation** *m.* 12
tragedy **tragédie** *f.* 15
train **train** *m.* 7
train station **gare** *f.* 7; **station** *f.* **de train** 7
training **formation** *f.* 13
translate **traduire** *v.* 6
translated **traduit (traduire)** *p.p., adj.* 6
trash **ordures** *f., pl.* 14
travel **voyager** *v.* 2
travel agency **agence de voyages** *f.* 7
travel agent **agent de voyages** *m.* 7
tree **arbre** *m.* 14
trip **voyage** *m.* 7
troop *(company)* **troupe** *f.* 15
tropical **tropical(e)** *adj.* 14
tropical forest **forêt tropicale** *f.* 14
true **vrai(e)** *adj.* 3; **véritable** *adj.* 6
It is true that... **Il est vrai que...** 15
It is untrue that... **Il n'est pas vrai que...** 15
trunk **coffre** *m.* 11
try **essayer** *v.* 5
Tuesday **mardi** *m.* 2
tuna **thon** *m.* 9
turn **tourner** *v.* 12
to turn off **éteindre** *v.* 11
to turn on **allumer** *v.* 11
to turn (oneself) around **se tourner** *v.* 10
twelve **douze** *m.* 1
twentieth **vingtième** *adj.* 7
twenty **vingt** *m.* 1
twenty-first **vingt et unième** *adj.* 7
twenty-second **vingt-deuxième** *adj.* 7
twice **deux fois** *adv.* 7
twist one's ankle **se fouler la cheville** *v.* 10
two **deux** *m.* 1
two hundred **deux cents** *m.* 5
two million **deux millions** *m.* 5
type **genre** *m.* 15

U

ugly **laid(e)** *adj.* 3
umbrella **parapluie** *m.* 5
uncle **oncle** *m.* 3
under **sous** *prep.* 3
understand **comprendre** *v.* 4
understood **compris (comprendre)** *p.p., adj.* 6
underwear **sous-vêtement** *m.* 6
undress **se déshabiller** *v.* 10
unemployed person **chômeur/chômeuse** *m., f.* 13
to be unemployed **être au chômage** *v.* 13
unemployment **chômage** *m.* 13
unfortunately **malheureusement** *adv.* 2
unhappy **malheureux/malheureuse** *adj.* 3
union **syndicat** *m.* 13
United States **États-Unis** *m., pl.* 7
university **faculté** *f.* 1; **université** *f.* 1
university cafeteria **restaurant universitaire (resto U)** *m.* 2
unless **à moins que** *conj.* 15
unpleasant **antipathique** *adj.* 3; **désagréable** *adj.* 1
until **jusqu'à** *prep.* 12; **jusqu'à ce que** *conj.* 15
upset: to become upset **s'énerver** *v.* 10
us **nous** *i.o. pron.* 6; **nous** *d.o. pron.* 7
use **employer** *v.* 5
to use a map **utiliser un plan** *v.* 7
useful **utile** *adj.* 2
useless **inutile** *adj.* 2; **nul(le)** *adj.* 2
usually **d'habitude** *adv.* 7

V

vacation **vacances** *f., pl.* 7
vacation day **jour de congé** *m.* 7
vacuum **aspirateur** *m.* 8
to vacuum **passer l'aspirateur** *v.* 8
valley **vallée** *f.* 14
vegetable **légume** *m.* 9
velvet **velours** 6
very *(before adjective)* **tout(e)** *adv.* 3; *(before adverb)* **très** *adv.* 7
Very well. **Très bien.** 1
veterinarian **vétérinaire** *m., f.* 13
videocassette recorder (VCR) **magnétoscope** *m.* 11
video game(s) **jeu vidéo (des jeux vidéo)** *m.* 11
videotape **cassette vidéo** *f.* 11
Vietnamese **vietnamien(ne)** *adj.* 1
violet **violet(te)** *adj.* 6
violin **violon** *m.* 15
visit **visite** *f.* 6
to visit *(a place)* **visiter** *v.* 2; *(a person or people)* **rendre visite (à)** *v.* 6; *(to visit regularly)* **fréquenter** *v.* 4
voicemail **messagerie** *f.* 13
volcano **volcan** *m.* 14
volleyball **volley(-ball)** *m.* 5

W

waist **taille** *f.* 6
wait **attendre** *v.* 6
to wait (*on the phone*) **patienter** *v.* 13
to wait in line **faire la queue** *v.* 12
wake up **se réveiller** *v.* 10
walk **promenade** *f.* 5; **marcher** *v.* 5
to go for a walk **faire une promenade** 5; **faire un tour** 5
wall **mur** *m.* 8
want **désirer** *v.* 5; **vouloir** *v.* 9
wardrobe **armoire** *f.* 8
warming: global warming **réchauffement de la Terre** *m.* 14
warning light (gas/oil) **voyant** *m.* **(d'essence/d'huile)** 11
wash **laver** *v.* 8
to wash oneself (one's hands) **se laver (les mains)** *v.* 10
to wash up (in the morning) **faire sa toilette** *v.* 10
washing machine **lave-linge** *m.* 8
waste **gaspillage** *m.* 14; **gaspiller** *v.* 14
wastebasket **corbeille (à papier)** *f.* 1
waste time **perdre son temps** *v.* 6
watch **montre** *f.* 1; **regarder** *v.* 2
water **eau** *f.* 4
mineral water **eau** *f.* **minérale** 4
way (*by the way*) **au fait** 3; (*path*) **chemin** 12
we **nous** *pron.* 1
weak **faible** *adj.* 3
wear **porter** *v.* 6
weather **temps** *m., sing.* 5; **météo** *f.* 15
The weather is bad. **Il fait mauvais.** 5
The weather is dreadful. **Il fait un temps épouvantable.** 5
The weather is good/warm. **Il fait bon.** 5
The weather is nice. **Il fait beau.** 5
web site **site Internet/web** *m.* 11
wedding **mariage** *m.* 6
Wednesday **mercredi** *m.* 2
weekend **week-end** *m.* 2
this weekend **ce week-end** *m.* 2
welcome **bienvenu(e)** *adj.* 1
You're welcome. **Il n'y a pas de quoi.** 1
well **bien** *adv.* 7
I am doing well/badly. **Je vais bien/mal.** 1
west **ouest** *m.* 12
What? **Comment?** *adv.* 4; **Pardon?** 4; **Quoi?** 1 *interr. pron.* 4
What day is it? **Quel jour sommes-nous?** 2
What is it? **Qu'est-ce que c'est?** *prep.* 1
What is the date? **Quelle est la date?** 5
What is the temperature? **Quelle température fait-il?** 5
What is the weather like? **Quel temps fait-il?** 5
What is your name? **Comment t'appelles-tu?** *fam.* 1
What is your name? **Comment vous appelez-vous?** *form.* 1
What is your nationality? **Quelle est ta nationalité?** *sing., fam.* 1
What is your nationality? **Quelle est votre nationalité?** *sing., pl., fam., form.* 1
What time do you have? **Quelle heure avez-vous?** *form.* 2
What time is it? **Quelle heure est-il?** 2
What time? **À quelle heure?** 2
What do you think about that? **Qu'en penses-tu?** 14
What's up? **Ça va?** 1
whatever it may be **quoi que ce soit** 13
What's wrong? **Qu'est-ce qu'il y a?** 1
when **quand** *adv.* 4
When is ...'s birthday? **C'est quand l'anniversaire de ...?** 5
When is your birthday? **C'est quand ton/votre anniversaire?** 5
where **où** *adv., rel. pron.* 4, 13
which? **quel(le)(s)?** *adj.* 4
which one **à laquelle** *pron., f., sing.* 13
which one **auquel (à + lequel)** *pron., m., sing.* 13
which one **de laquelle** *pron., f., sing.* 13
which one **duquel (de + lequel)** *pron., m., sing.* 13
which one **laquelle** *pron., f., sing.* 13
which one **lequel** *pron., m., sing.* 13
which ones **auxquelles (à + lesquelles)** *pron., f., pl.* 13
which ones **auxquels (à + lesquels)** *pron., m., pl.* 13
which ones **desquelles (de + lesquelles)** *pron., f., pl.* 13
which ones **desquels (de + lesquels)** *pron., m., pl.* 13
which ones **lesquelles** *pron., f., pl.* 13
which ones **lesquels** *pron., m., pl.* 13
while **pendant que** *prep.* 7
white **blanc(he)** *adj.* 6
who? **qui?** *interr. pron.* 4; **qui** *rel. pron.* 13
Who is it? **Qui est-ce?** 1
Who's calling, please? **Qui est à l'appareil?** 13
whom? **qui?** *interr.* 4
For whom? **Pour qui?** 4
To whom? **À qui?** 4
why? **pourquoi?** *adv.* 2, 4
widowed **veuf/veuve** *adj.* 3
wife **femme** *f.* 1; **épouse** *f.* 3
willingly **volontiers** *adv.* 10
win **gagner** *v.* 5
wind **vent** *m.* 5
It is windy. **Il fait du vent.** 5
window **fenêtre** *f.* 1
windshield **pare-brise** *m.* 11
windshield wiper(s) **essuie-glace (essuie-glaces** *pl.*) *m.* 11
windsurfing **planche à voile** *v.* 5
to go windsurfing **faire de la planche à voile** *v.* 5
wine **vin** *m.* 6
winter **hiver** *m.* 5
in the winter **en hiver** 5
wipe (the dishes/the table) **essuyer (la vaisselle/la table)** *v.* 8
wish that... **souhaiter que...** *v.* 14
with **avec** *prep.* 1
with whom? **avec qui?** 4
withdraw money **retirer de l'argent** *v.* 12
without **sans** *prep.* 8; **sans que** *conj.* 5
woman **femme** *f.* 1
wood **bois** *m.* 14
wool **laine** *f.* 6
work **travail** *m.* 12
to work **travailler** *v.* 2; **marcher** *v.* 11; **fonctionner** *v.* 11
work out **faire de la gym** *v.* 5
worker **ouvrier/ouvrière** *m., f.* 13
world **monde** *m.* 7
worried **inquiet/inquiète** *adj.* 3
worry **s'inquiéter** *v.* 10
worse **pire** *comp. adj.* 9; **plus mal** *comp. adv.* 9; **plus mauvais(e)** *comp. adj.* 9
worst: the worst **le plus mal** *super. adv.* 9; **le/la pire** *super. adj.* 9; **le/la plus mauvais(e)** *super. adj.* 9

wound **blessure** *f.* 10
wounded: to get wounded **se blesser** *v.* 10
write **écrire** *v.* 7
to write one another **s'écrire** *v.* 11
writer **écrivain/femme écrivain** *m., f.* 15
written **écrit (écrire)** *p.p., adj.* 7
wrong **tort** *m.* 2
to be wrong **avoir tort** *v.* 2

Y

yeah **ouais** 2
year **an** *m.* 2; **année** *f.* 2
yellow **jaune** *adj.* 6
yes **oui** 2; *(when making a contradiction)* **si** 2
yesterday (morning/afternoon evening) **hier (matin/après-midi/soir)** *adv.* 7
day before yesterday **avant-hier** *adv.* 7
yogurt **yaourt** *m.* 9
you **toi** *disj. pron., sing., fam.* 3; **tu** *sub. pron., sing., fam.* 1; **vous** *pron., sing., pl., fam., form.* 1
you neither **toi non plus** 2
You're welcome. **De rien.** 1
young **jeune** *adj.* 3
younger **cadet(te)** *adj.* 3
your **ta** *poss. adj., f., sing.* 3; **tes** *poss. adj., m., f., pl.* 3; **ton** *poss. adj., m., sing.* 3; **vos** *poss. adj., m., f., pl.* 3; **votre** *poss. adj., m., f., sing.* 3;
yours **le(s) tien(s), la/les tienne(s), le(s) vôtre(s), la/les vôtre(s)** *poss. pron.* 15
yourself **te/t'** *refl. pron., sing., fam.* 10; **toi** *refl. pron., sing., fam.* 10; **vous** *refl. pron., form.* 10
youth **jeunesse** *f.* 6
youth hostel **auberge de jeunesse** *f.* 7
Yum! **Miam!** *interj.* 5

Z

zero **zéro** *m.* 1

About the Authors

Cherie Mitschke received her Ph.D. in Foreign Language Education with specializations in French and English as a Second Language from the University of Texas at Austin in 1996. She has taught French at Southwest Texas State University, Austin Community College, and was Assistant Professor of French at Southwestern University in Georgetown, Texas. Dr. Mitschke is also an experienced writer and editor of French educational materials who has worked with several major educational publishing houses.

Cheryl Tano received her M.A. in Spanish and French from Boston College and has also completed all course work toward a Ph.D. in Applied Linguistics with a concentration in Second Language Acquisition at Boston University. She is currently teaching French at Emmanuel College and Spanish at Tufts University.

Text Credits

241 © Reprinted by permission of Comité du tourisme des îles de Guadeloupe; ad produced by Comité du tourisme des îles de Guadeloupe in 2005 **373** © Reprinted by permission of BlackBerry® **392–393** © Reprinted by permission of Renée Lévy; www.reneelevy.com **407** © Reprinted by permission of Relais du Silence Silencehotel **445** © Reprinted by permission of BNP Paribas **459** © Reprinted by permission of Groupe Vedior France **502–503** © Excerpt from LE PETIT PRINCE by Antoine de Saint-Exupéry, copyright 1943 by Harcourt, Inc. and renewed 1971 by Consuelo de Saint-Exupéry, reprinted by permission of the publisher **540–541** © Reprinted by permission of Mariama Mbengue Ndoye.

Photography Credits

All images ©Vista Higher Learning unless otherwise noted.

Special thanks to: Martin Bernetti, Sophie Casson, John DeCarli, Tom Delano, Rachel Destier, Janet Dracksdorf, Daniel Finkbeiner, Beth Kramer, Rossy Llano, Anne Loubet, Hermann Mejía, Pascal Pernix, and Pere Virgili.

Front Matter: Cover (t) @ Skynesher I Dreamstime.com; Cover (cr) © Martin Child /Getty Images; Cover (bl) O Larry Wittiams/Corbis; Cover (br) © Getty Photodisc; Cover (cl) © Getty Photodisc; © HIRB (s/b "© photolibrary. All rights reserved."; **v** (tr) © Tahiti Tourisme; **v** (tcr) © iStockphoto.com/mddphoto; **v** (bcr) "© Vista Higher Learning; Special thanks to: Daniel Finkbeiner"; **v** (br) © David Osborne/Alamy; **vii** (tr) © iStockphoto.com/Dianne Maire; **vii** (tcr) © iStockphoto.com/Philip Lange; **vii** (bcr) © iStockphoto.com/Andreas Karelias; **vii** (br) © Chromacome/Stockbyte/Getty Images; **ix** (tcr) © iStockphoto.com/Denis Jr. Tangney; **ix** (bcr) © Christie's Images/Corbis; **xi** (tr) © Stephen Lloyd Morocco/Alamy; **xi** (cr) © Leanne Logan/Lonely Planet Images; **xi** (br) © Melba Photo Agency/Alamy.

Unit One: 9 (t) © Ian Dagnall/Alamy; **11** (t) © iStockphoto.com/Luca di Filippo; **11** (ml)/#2 © 1996-98 AccuSoft Inc. All Rights Reserved; **11** (bl)/#3 © Image Ideas/Jupiterimages; **11** (tr)/#4 © iStockphoto.com/Dmitry Kutlayev; **11** (mr)/#5 © 1996-98 AccuSoft Inc. All Rights Reserved; **23** (t) © LOB/Gotlib/Alexis/Fluide Glacial; **24** (right panel: tl)/#1 © Rune Hellestad/Corbis; **24** (right panel: bl)/#3 © 1996-98 AccuSoft Inc.; All rights reserved; **24** (right panel: tr)/#4 © iStockphoto.com; **25** (left panel: t) © Reuters/Corbis; **25** (left panel: tl)/#1 © Frank Trapper/Corbis; **25** (left panel: mr)/#5 © Reuters/Lucy Nicholson/Corbis; **25** (left panel: br)/#6 © iStockphoto.com/Rasmus Rasmussen; **28** (tml) © Robert Lerich/Fotolia; **30** (left panel: t) © Hulton-Deutsch Collection/Corbis; **30** (left panel: tm) © Caroline Penn/Corbis; **30** (left panel: bm) © Jean-Pierre Amet/BelOmbra/Corbis; **30** (left panel: b) © Eddy Lemaistre/For Picture/Corbis; **30** (right panel: t) © Tahiti Tourisme; **30** (right panel: mr) © Ariadne Van Zandbergen/Lonely Planet Images/Getty Images; **30** (right panel: b) © Eddy Lemaistre/For Picture/Corbis; **31** (tr) © Antoine Gyori/Corbis Sygma; **31** (bl) © Owen Franken/Corbis; **31** (br) Published with the kind authorization of the Service de communication pour la Francophonie..

Unit Two: 38 © Tom Stewart/Corbis; **45** (t) © Megapress/Alamy; **54** (r) © 2009 Jupiterimages Corporation; **66** (left panel: t) © Christie's Images/Corbis; **66** (left panel: m) © Bettmann/Corbis; **66** (left panel: b) © Gyori Antoine/Corbis Sygma; **66** (right panel: ml) © Martine Coquilleau/Fotolia; **66** (right panel: mr) © iStockphoto.com/mddphoto; **67** (tl) © David Gregs/Alamy; **67** (br) © iStockphoto.com/Caroline Beecham; **68–69** top © Art Kowalsky/Alamy.

Unit Three: 81 (t) © ELISE AMENDOLA/2009 The Associated Press; **81** (m) © NBAE/Getty Images; **81** (b) © Tony Barson/WireImage/Getty Images; **82** (left panel: r) © FogStock LLC/photolibrary. All rights reserved.; **82** (right panel) © Hemera Technologies/AbleStock.com/Jupiterimages; **84** (tl)/#1 © iStockphoto.com/Dmitry Kutlayev; **85** (bl) © Dynamic Graphics/Dynamic Graphics Group/Jupiterimages; **90** (ml)/#1 © 2009 Jupiterimages Corporation; **90** (mr)/#4 © Vstock; LLC/photolibrary. All rights reserved.; **95** (tl) © Henri Tuillio/Corbis; **95** (tr) © Patrick Roncen/Corbis; **95** (m) © Pascalito/Sygma/Corbis; **102** (left panel: t) © Stapleton Collection/Corbis; **102** (left panel: bl) © Kurt Krieger/Corbis; **102** (left panel: br) © Popperfoto/Alamy; **102** (right panel: b) © Benjamin Herzoq/Fotolia; **103** (bl) © Keren Su/Corbis.

Unit Four: 117 (t) © Inge Yspeert/Corbis; **117** (m) © Philippe Cabaret/Sygma/Corbis; **117** (b) © Imgram Publishing/Purestock/Jupiterimages; **131** (t) © Yadid Levy/Alamy; **131** (m) © Kevin Foy/Alamy; **131** (b) © Garcia/photocuisine/Corbis; **138** (left panel: t) © Chris Hellier/Corbis; **138** (left panel: b) © Hulton-Deutsch Collection/Corbis; **138** (right panel: tr) © Christophe Boisvieux/Corbis; **138** (right panel: ml) © David Osborne/Alamy; **138** (right panel: mr) © iStockphoto.com/Dan Moore; **138** (right panel: b) © iStockphoto.com/Daniel Brechwoldt; **139** (tl) "© Vista Higher Learning; Special thanks to: Janet Dracksdorf"; **139** (bl) © Brian Harris/Alamy.

Unit Five: 152 (l) © 2009 The Associated Press; **152** (r) © Neil Marchand/Liewig Media Sports/Corbis; **153** (t) © Victor Fraile/Reuters/Corbis; **153** (m) © Arko Datta/Reuters/Corbis; **153** (b) © FogStock LLC/photolibrary. All rights reserved.; **160** © IS4078RF-00014472-001/photolibrary. All rights reserved.; **167** (m) © Reuters/Stefano Rellandini/Corbis; **167** (b) © Universal/TempSport/Corbis; **174** (left panel: t) © Bettmann/Corbis; **174** (left panel: b) © Hulton-Deutsch Collection/Corbis; **174** (right panel: tr) © Dean Conger/Corbis; **174** (right panel: ml) © Reuters/Daniel Joubert/Corbis; **174** (right panel: mr) © iStockphoto.com/Dianne Maire; **174** (right panel: b) © iStockphoto.com/Edyta Pawlowska; **175** (tl) © iStockphoto.com/Demid Borodin; **175** (tr) © graphisme: Lola Duval/photo: Dietmar Busse (Courtesy of Clamp Art; New York City); **175** (bl) © Daniel Joubert/Reuters/Corbis; **175** (br) © iStockphoto.com/James Warren; **179** (l) © Martine Coquilleau/Fotolia.

Unit Six: 188 (l) © Eric Gaillard/Reuters/Corbis; **188** (r) © Earl & Nazima Kowell/Corbis; **189** (t) © Reuters/Mal Langsdon/Corbis; **189** (m) © Trevor Pearson/Alamy; **197** (t) © Ben Blankenburg/Corbis; **197** (ml) © Hemera Technologies/Jupiterimages Corporation/Getty Images; **197** (mr) © Purestock/Jupiterimages Corporation; **197** (b) ©Ablestock/Getty Images/Jupiterimages Corporation; **202** (l) © Philippe Wojazer/Reuters/Corbis; **203** (t) © Hulton-Deutsch Collection/Corbis; **203** (m) © Corbis Sygma/Corbis; **203** (b) © Corbis Sygma/Corbis; **210** (left panel: t) © Bettmann/Corbis; **210** (left panel: b) © Bettmann/Corbis; **210** (right panel: t) © Frédérik Astier/Sygma/Corbis; **210** (right panel: ml) © iStockphoto.com/Peter Leyden; **210** (right panel: mr) © Mikhail Lavrenov/123RF; **210** (right panel: b) © Bettmann/Corbis; **211** (tl) © foodfolio/Alamy; **211** (tr) © iStockphoto.com/Philip Lange; **211** (bl) © Owen Franken/Corbis; **211** (br) © Historical Picture Archive/Corbis; **212** (tr) © THE CANADIAN PRESS/Trois-Rivieres Le Nouvelliste-Sylvain Mayer; **214** (tr) © Jeff Greenberg / Alamy; **215** ©Karl Prouse/Catwalking/Contributor/Getty Images.

Unit Seven: 224 (t) © Tahiti Tourisme; **224** (b) © Tahiti Tourisme; **225** (t) © Vista Higher Learning; **225** (m) © The Art Archive/Corbis; **225** (b) © Comstock/Getty Images/2009 Jupiterimages Corporation; **229** (t) © Tahiti Tourisme; **233** (b) © photolibrary/age fotostock; **234** © Vista Higher Learning; **238** (l) © Hubert Stadler/Corbis; **239** (t) © Johner Images/Alamy; **239** (b) © photolibrary. All rights reserved; **243** (l) Alantide Phototravel/Corbis; **246** (left panel: t) © Patric Forestier (Special)/Corbis; **246** (left panel: bl) © Bettmann/Corbis; **246** (left panel: br) © Stefano Bianchetti/Corbis; **246** (right panel: t) © Beyond Fotomedia GmbH / Alamy; **246** (right panel: ml) © Ferdericb/Dreamstime; **246** (right panel: mr) © Larry Dale Gordon/zefa/Corbis; **246** (right panel: b) © Tom Brakefield/Corbis; **247** (tl) © Pitchal Frederic/Corbis SYGMA; **247** (tr) © John Schults/Reuters/Corbis; **247** (br) © iStockphoto.com/Andreas Karelias; **248–249** (background) ©Ladislav Janicek/Corbis; **249** (l) © L. Janicek/Zefa/Corbis; **251** (br) © FAN travelstock / Alamy.

Unit Eight: 260 (tr) © Michele Molinari/Alamy; **268** © Directphoto.org/Alamy; **275** (t) © Ace Stock Limited/Alamy; **275** (m) © Robert Holmes/Corbis; **278** (right panel: ml)/#1 © Corbis; **282** (left panel: t) © Bettmann/Corbis; **282** (left panel: b) © Stephane Cardinale/Corbis; **282** (right panel: t) © iStockphoto.com/Katarzyna Mazurowska; **282** (right panel: ml) © iStockphoto.com/Bogdan Lazar; **282** (right panel: mr) © iStockphoto.com/Katarzyna Mazurowska; **282** (right panel: b) © iStockphoto.com/Andreas Kaspar; **283** (tl) © Chromacome/Stockbyte/Getty Images; **283** (tr) © Gianni Dagli Orti/Corbis; **283** (bl) © Thierry Tronnel/Corbis; **283** (br) © Annie Griffiths Belt/Corbis; **284** (t) © Adam Woolfitt/Corbis; **284** (b) © Jan Butchofsky-Houser/Corbis; **285** (m) © Adam Woolfitt/Corbis; **287** (m) ©iStockphoto.com/Terry J Alcorn.

Unit Nine: 299 (l) © Jupiterimages; **311** t © Sergio Pitamitz/Corbis; **311** m © FoodCollection/photolibrary. All rights reserved.; **311** b © Ablestock/Getty Images/2009 Jupiterimages Corporation; **313** (t) © photolibrary. All rights reserved.; **313** (ml)/#1 © FogStock LLC/photolibrary. All rights reserved.; **313** (bl)/#2 © Design Pics Inc./Alamy; **315** (left panel: tr) © Bold Stock/Unlisted Images; Inc.; **315** (left panel: bl) © photolibrary. All rights reserved.; **315** (right panel: t) © Comstock/2009 Jupiterimages Corporation; **318** (left panel: t) © Bettmann/Corbis; **318** (left panel: m) © Bettmann/Corbis; **318** (left panel: b) © Sygma/Corbis; **318** (right panel: t) © Robert Paul Van Beets/Fotolia; **318** (right panel: ml) © Adam Woolfitt/Corbis; **318** (right panel: mr) © Hansok/Dreamstime.com; **319** (br) © The Gallery Collection/Corbis.

Unit Ten: 332 (tr) © Max Alexander/Getty Images; **333** (b) © iStockphoto.com/Viorika Prikhodko; **340** (t) © www.imagesource.com; **346** (r) © Gilles Fonlupt/Corbis; **347** (b) © JupiterImages/Photos.com/Jupiterimages; **349** (right panel: l) © Dynamic Graphics/2009 Jupiterimages Corporation; **349** (right panel: r) © photolibrary. All rights reserved; **352** (l) © Pere Virgili/Vista Higher Learning; **354** (left panel: t) © Bettmann/Corbis; **354** (left panel: b) © Pierre Vauthey/Corbis Sygma; **354** (right panel: t) © iStockphoto.com/Tatiana Egorova; **354** (right panel: ml) © Createsima/Dreamstime; **354** (right panel: mr) © iStockphoto.com/Denis Jr. Tangney; **354** (right panel: b) © Carl & Ann Purcell/Corbis; **355** (tr) © The Art Archive/Corbis; **355** (bl) © Goodshoot Royalty Free Photograph/Fotosearch; **355** (br) © David Hughes/Fotolia; **356** (t) © Pete Saloutos/Corbis; **358** (t) © Ebby May/Getty Images; **359** (m) © Commercial Eye/Getty Images.

Unit Eleven: 362 (left panel: b) © Hermann Mejia/Vista Higher Learning; **362** (right panel: t) © David Sanger Photography/Alamy; **362** (right panel: bl)/#2 © Danita Delimont/Alamy; **362** (right panel: mr)/#3 © Ray Roberts/Alamy; **362** (right panel: br)/#4 © Richard Klune/Corbis; **368** (l) © Goodshot/Jupiterimages Corporation; **369** (t) © Alain Nogues/Corbis Sygma; **369** (b) © Philippe Eranian/Corbis; **371** (r) © Thomas Mueller/Photographers Direct; **383** (t) © Bettmann/Corbis; **383** (b) © iStockphot.com/Mark Evans; **385** (left panel) © Bernard Annebicque/Corbis/RF; **385** (right panel) © Royalty-Free/Corbis; **388** © Philippe Eranian/Corbis; **390** (left panel: t) © Corbis KIPA; **390** (left panel: bl) © Robert Galbraith/Corbis; **390** (left panel: br) © Stephane Cardinale/Corbis; **390** (right panel: t) © Paul Springett B/Alamy; **390** (right panel: ml) © Paul Springett 09/Alamy; **390** (right panel: mr) © Melba Photo Agency/Alamy; **390** (right panel: b) © A. J. Cassaigne/Photononstop; **391** (tl) © iStockphoto.com/Franky DeMeyer; **391** (tr) © Danita Delimont/Alamy; **391** (bl) © Dave Bartruff/Corbis; **391** (br) © Christie's Images/Corbis.

Unit Twelve: 405 (t) © Reuters/Matt Dunham/Corbis; **419** (b) © iStockphoto.com/Peter Garbet; **421** (left panel: bl) © Getty Images/Ablestock/Jupiter Images; **421** (right panel: t) © MedioImages/Corbis; **421** (right panel: b) © Richard T. Nowitz/Corbis; **424** (left panel) © iStockphoto.com/Andre Nantel; **425** (right panel: l) © Pere Virgili/Vista Higher Learning; **425** (right panel: r) © Pere Virgili/Vista Higher Learning; **426** (left panel: t) © Bassouls Sophie/Corbis Sygma; **426** (left panel: m) © Stephane Cardinale/People Avenue/Corbis; **426** (left panel: b) © Reuters/Jason Cohn/Corbis; **426** (right panel: t) © Carlos Sanchez Pereyra/123RF; **426** (right panel: tm) © Stephen Saks Photography/Alamy; **426** (right panel: b) © Richard T. Nowitz/Corbis; **427** (tl) © Reuters/Mike Blake/Corbis; **427** (bl) © Rubens Abboud/Alamy; **428** (left panel) © Stapleton Collection/Corbis; **428–429** (left panel) © Thinkstock/Getty Images; **431** (t) ©PhotoAlto/Alamy.

Unit Thirteen: 441 (t) © Anna Clopet/Corbis; **441** (b) © Reuters/PhilippeWojazer/Corbis; **446** (left panel: b) ©Bill Lai/Index Stock Imagery; **446** (right panel: t) © Bill Lai/Index Stock Imagery; **456** (m) © Owen Franken/Corbis; **456** (t) © Peter Turnley/Corbis; **464** (left panel: b) © Mike King/Corbis; **464** (right panel: t) © Idealink Photography/Alamy; **464** (right panel: ml) © A.Anwar Sacca/Fotolia; **464** (right panel: mr) © Nik Wheeler/Corbis; **464** (right panel: b) © Frans Lemmens/zefa/Corbis; © Library and Archives Canada; **465** (tl) © Stephen Lloyd Morocco/Alamy; **465** (tr) © Sophie Bassouls/Sygma/Corbis; **465** (bl) © Paul Springett B/Alamy; **465** (br) © Jonny Le Fortune/zefa/Corbis; **466** (left panel) © Annebicque/Corbis Sygma.

Unit Fourteen: 478 (tr) © iStockphoto.com/Raphael Daniaud; **478** (l) © Bernard Bisson/Sygma/Corbis; **479** (t) © Yann Arthus-Bertrand/Corbis; **479** (m) © Bernard Bisson/Sygma/Corbis; **479** (b) © Manfred Vollmer/Corbis; **481** (r) © Vista Higher Learning; **483** (l) © Mark Karrass/Corbis; **484** (left panel: tl)/#1 © photolibrary. All rights reserved.; **484** (left panel: bl)/#2 © iStockphoto.com; **484** (left panel: tr)/#3 © FogStock LLC/photolibrary. All rights reserved.; **484** (left panel: br)/#4 © Hemera Technologies/2009 Jupiterimages Corporation; **484** (right panel: bl)/#2 © 2009 Jupiterimages Corporation; **484** (right panel: tr)/#3 © Ablestock.com/2009 Jupiterimages Corporation; **487** (cr) © Paul A. Souders/Corbis; **488** (l) © iStockphoto.com/Jonathan Heger; **488** (r) © iStockphoto.com/William Wang; **492** (tr) © iStockphoto.com/Christophe Fouquin; **492** (l) © Vincent Lowe/Alamy; **493** (t) © iStockphoto.com/Gail A. Johnson; **493** (m) © Thomas Pozzo Di Borgo/123RF; **493** (b) © Russeil Christophe/Corbis KIPA; **495** (b) © 2009 Jupiterimages Corporation; **498** (left panel: bl)/#2 © iStockphoto.com; **498** (left panel: tr)/#3 © Anastasiya Maksimenko/123RF; **498** (left panel: br)/#4 © Keith Levit Photography/photolibrary. All rights reserved.; **498** (right panel: b) © Nick Greaves/Alamy; **499** (tr) © Reuters/Daniel Joubert; **500** (left panel: t) © Reuters/Shaun Best/Corbis; **500** (left panel: b) © Kai Pfaffenbach/Reuters/Corbis; **500** (right panel: t) © brianafrica/Alamy; **500** (right panel: ml) © Authors Image/Alamy; **500** (right panel: mr) © Leanne Logan/Lonely Planet Images; **500** (right panel: b) © iStockphoto.com/Guenter Guni; **501** (tl) © Sophie Bassouls/Sygma/Corbis; **501** (tr) © Eric Fougere/VIP Images/Corbis; **501** (bl) © Kevin Schafer/Alamy; **501** (br) FESPCO 2007 Poster; with the kind authorization of the Festival Panafricain du Cinema et de la television de Ouagadougou (FASPCO).; **502** (bl) © Bettmann/Corbis; **504** (tr) © Kevin Fleming/Corbis.

Unit Fifteen: 506 (tl) © Eric Robert/Corbis; **514** (ml) © Tom Stewart/Corbis; **515** (t) © Lebrecht Music & Arts/Alamy; **515** (b) © Jacques Morell/Corbis; **514** (right panel: t) © David Sanger/Alamy; **514** (right panel: bl)/#2 © AnitaDelimont.com/Alamy; **514** (right panel: tr)/#3 © Ray Roberts/Alamy; **514** (right panel: br)/#4 © Richard Klune/Alamy; **519** © Swim Ink 2; LLC/Corbis; **520** (tl) © www.imagesource.com; **526** (l) © Jeff Morgan/Alamy; **526** (r) © Vista Higher Learning; **530** (l) © DanitaDelimont.com/Alamy; **530** (tr) © DanitaDelimont.com/Alamy; **530** (br) © Kelly/Mooney Photography/Corbis; **531** (t) © Robbie Jack/Corbis; **531** (m) © Rune Hellestad/Corbis; **531** (b) © Kin Cheung/Corbis; **536** (right panel: b) © Dallas & John Heaton/Alamy; **536** (right panel) © Sophie Casson/Vista Higher Learning; **533** (r) © Archivo Iconografico/Corbis; **538** (left panel: t) © Bassouls Sophie/Corbis Sygma; **538** (left panel: b) © Lori Conn/ZUMA/Corbis; **538** (right panel: t) © MedioImages/Corbis; **538** (right panel: m) © Melba Photo Agency/Alamy; **538** (right panel: b) © David Sanger Photography/Alamy; **539** (tl) © Bettmann/Corbis; **539** (tr) © Frederic/Fotolia; **539** (bl) "© Tahiti Tourisme; Special thanks to: Tahiti Tourisme"; **539** (br) © Philippe Giraud/Sygma/Corbis.

Video Credits

Production Company: Klic Video Productions, Inc.
Lead Photographer: Pascal Pernix
Photographer, Assistant Director: Barbara Ryan Malcolm
Photography Assistant: Pierre Halart

Film Credits

303 *Le far breton* © Office du Tourisme de Rennes
411 *Rennes* © Office du Tourisme de Rennes
447 *Mi-temps* © Premium Films
521 *La tartine* © Superlux

Le zapping Credits

15 *La Triplette de Moulinex* © Groupe SEB
51 © Clairefontaine
87 © Pages d'Or
123 © Swiss Airlines International
159 © SwissLife
195 *La Poste belge* © La Poste
231 *Le TER* © SNCF
267 © Century 21 with the kind authorization of Pierre Palmade
339 © Diadermine
375 *KellyMobile* © NRJ
485 © BMCE Bank